THE OXFORD HANDBOOK OF

INTERNATIONAL ADJUDICATION

THE OXFORD HANDBOOK OF INTERNATIONAL ADJUDICATION

Editors

CESARE PR ROMANO

Professor of Law, Loyola Law School Los Angeles

KAREN J ALTER

Professor of Political Science and Law, Northwestern University

YUVAL SHANY

Professor of Law, Faculty of Law, Hebrew University

OXFORD
UNIVERSITY PRESS

OXFORD
UNIVERSITY PRESS

Great Clarendon Street, Oxford, OX2 6DP,
United Kingdom

Oxford University Press is a department of the University of Oxford.
It furthers the University's objective of excellence in research, scholarship,
and education by publishing worldwide. Oxford is a registered trade mark of
Oxford University Press in the UK and in certain other countries

First published 2014
First published in paperback 2015

Published in the United States of America by Oxford University Press
198 Madison Avenue, New York, NY 10016, United States of America

British Library Cataloguing in Publication Data
Data available

Library of Congress Cataloging in Publication Data
Data available

ISBN 978–0–19–966068–1 (Hbk.)
ISBN 978–0–19–874828–1 (Pbk.)

Printed and bound by CPI Group (UK) Ltd, Croydon, CR0 4YY

To Shepard Forman, without whom this handbook would have never come into being.

Editors' Preface

The Oxford Handbook series brings together top researchers to explain the state-of-the-art knowledge in a given field of study. The Oxford Handbook on International Adjudication shares this purpose, but it is also more ambitious. We seek to significantly advance a new field of study: the interdisciplinary investigation of international adjudication.

In 1997, the Project on International Courts and Tribunals (PICT) was jointly established by the Center on International Cooperation (CIC), at New York University, and the Foundation for International Environmental Law and Development (FIELD), at the School of Oriental and African Studies, University of London. Cesare Romano and Shepard Forman, in New York, and Ruth Mackenzie and Philippe Sands, in London, spearheaded the early days of PICT's work. Since those days, PICT has evolved into a network of researchers and practitioners sharing an interest in the study of international courts and tribunals, and the implications of their operation for the broader field of international law. Nowadays, PICT is directed by five academics: Philippe Sands (University College London), Thordis Ingadottir (Reykjavik University), Ruth Mackenzie (University of Westminster), Cesare Romano (Loyola Law School Los Angeles) and Yuval Shany (Hebrew University). Members of the network regularly cooperate with one another, in various combinations and with other interested individuals (such as Karen Alter, as in the case of this handbook) and institutions (for instance, the Amsterdam Centre for International Law), to generate innovative research activities and to further knowledge about international adjudicative bodies.

PICT's main contribution to the field has been to look at specific international adjudicative bodies as the pieces of a larger whole—an emerging international judiciary, with much in common and much to learn from each other—rather than as separate institutions, as had been done hitherto. PICT's website (<http://www.pict-pcti.org>) provided the first portal through which newcomers could learn about each and every international judicial body, providing scholars data to start making comparisons across the board.

Others soon joined the effort. The Brandeis Institute for International Judges picked up the task of helping the actors directly involved in international adjudication—international judges—learn from one another so as to address judicial, ethical, and management questions and improve international adjudication.

The Brandeis Institute's reports and periodic email updates help scholars stay abreast of developments across international adjudicative bodies. In 2002, the London "home" of PICT moved to University College London, where the Centre for International Courts and Tribunals was established. Philippe Sands and Ruth Mackenzie continued their pioneering work from their new base, addressing key questions of ethics and independence of international judges and practitioners.

Thus, thanks to the hard work of a small group of dedicated scholars and funding from several foundations sponsoring them—including the Ford, MacArthur, Hewlett, and JEHT foundations, the European Union and many others—knowledge about international adjudicative bodies has blossomed.

The first generation of scholarship, pre-PICT, focused primarily on legal documents and single-institution studies, with a few basic comparisons made across like institutions. Most studies remained tied to a single discipline, and there was very little interdisciplinary cross-fertilization. Had this handbook been written 15 years ago, when the first-generation scholarship was the accepted standard, it would have included theorizing based on one or maybe two international adjudicative institutions; empirical analysis of a small handful of international legal systems; and side-by-side descriptions of like systems.[1] It would have had, for example, a chapter focusing on the history of the World Trade Organization's adjudicative system, another on the law and procedure of WTO dispute adjudication, and a third on empirical aspects of WTO dispute settlement. A first-generation handbook would have put the International Court of Justice at the forefront. It would have approached international adjudication mostly as a dispute settlement means. It would have focused primarily on adjudicative institutions based in Europe. It would have included chapters that described in formal terms how new adjudicative bodies were supposed to operate—but not their actual workings, and least of all the actual workings of those located in the developing world. In other words, it would have looked very different from this handbook.

We believe now it is time for a somewhat different approach. Perhaps thanks to those early pioneering projects, and surely thanks to a much larger set of institutions to study, scholars and practitioners now collectively seem ready to engage in more ambitious research. This handbook epitomizes what the second generation of scholarship on international adjudication embodies. It introduces a new understanding of international adjudication that is broader than a focus on a few well-known permanent courts. Whereas before each international adjudicative body seemed *sui generis*, unique and isolated, now we can explore how different institutional designs, political contexts, and compositions shape judicial decision-making and the ability of international adjudicative institutions to affect political outcomes. For legal scholars, comparatively studying international adjudicative mechanisms

[1] See e.g., R Mackenzie, C Romano, P Sands, and Y Shany (eds.), *Manual on International Courts and Tribunals* (Oxford University Press 2009).

can illuminate how different institutions facilitate the resolution of different types of disputes—and perhaps how to improve the design of international adjudicative mechanisms. For social scientists, the possibility of comparing like institutions provides theoretical leverage to develop and test hypotheses. By comparing international legal regimes with and without associated international adjudicative bodies, we can also gain insight into how establishing international adjudicative bodies influences state decision-making, domestic politics, and international relations more generally.

Our approach in this handbook departs from old-school scholarship in a number of ways. We decided to focus on "international adjudication" rather than the narrower field of international judicial bodies because we recognize that non-permanent international adjudicative bodies are part of the broader trends toward international legalization and the judicialization of international relations. In fact, as André Nollkaemper does in this volume, it is increasingly plausible to consider national courts, whenever applying international law, as part of this broad universe of international adjudicative procedures.

Since most scholars are still specialized in a single institution, we asked our contributing authors to do their best to think across international adjudicative systems. For example, we asked William Schabas to write on criminal courts, not just the International Criminal Court. We also organized the chapters to facilitate comparisons. We asked the authors of parts IV, V, and VI to write comparatively about different approaches to a number of critical issues, including electing and selecting judges, involving third parties in adjudication, deciding on remedies, fact finding, and managing financing.

Admittedly, broadening the focus can wreak havoc on efforts to create firm categories and lists of adjudicative bodies. We decided to add visual representations of current international adjudicative bodies, but careful readers will immediately recognize that our visual images do not fully correspond to the categories and lists of adjudicative bodies discussed in this volume. The problem is in part scholarly disagreement on categories, but the source of the disagreement is the changing world around us. International adjudicative bodies now span well-established categories. Sean Murphy's focus on international judicial bodies analyzes their core features and the role they continue to play in an increasingly complex world of dispute settlers. David Caron questions how one can even ascertain if a court is permanent given that certain "temporary" claims and compensation bodies, as well as certain international criminal tribunals, can operate for indefinite periods of time. William Schabas discusses the difficulty in demarcating international criminal enforcement from nationally based adjudicative bodies created with international input that apply international criminal law and include judges and prosecutors from outside the region. Solomon Ebobrah points out that there are many courts of regional integration agreements that exercise jurisdiction over human rights legal instruments. A recent article by Alexandra Huneeus in the *American Journal of International Law* examines the Inter-American Court of Human Rights as an international criminal court.[2] Still, taxonomies and categories, however changing and imperfect, provide useful roadmaps. They make it possible to immediately grasp the scope of the field and the essential traits of the classified body.

We put together a volume that is theoretically informed and interdisciplinary, even though doing so caused some overlap across chapters. For example, the selection of international judges chapter is a lawyer's approach to how international judges are or should be selected, but we also needed a separate chapter on "who becomes a judge" to answer the more sociological question of who actually makes it through the international judicial selection labyrinth. We then needed an additional chapter focused on "international judicial behavior" to connect the questions of how international judges are selected, who international judges actually are and how this information influences international judicial behavior.

Much scholarly conversation, and indeed the vast majority of the scholarship on international adjudication, is still written from within a single paradigm. Part III of this book includes chapters on specific theoretical approaches to studying international adjudication, including chapters on transnational legal process theories, political science theories, and philosophical and sociological approaches. Mark Pollack asked us if we really needed a separate chapter on political science approaches, as he saw the paradigms invoked in political science scholarship already present in the transnational politics and sociological chapters—and in chapters on empirical questions, such as the effectiveness of international adjudicators and international judicial behavior. However, we asked Professor Pollack to write a political science chapter because political science is one of the few places where scholars increasingly speak across paradigms. His hesitation is itself a positive development in the study of international adjudication. It suggests that we are beginning to transcend long-defended disciplinary confines.

The third generation of scholarship on international adjudication will be undertaken by a new kind of scholar. Nearly all of those contributing to this volume were traditionally trained. We earned our law, sociology, and political science degrees within disciplinary silos, and then largely self-trained to be able to study the phenomenon of international adjudication across institutions. Some of us took to co-authoring to ensure that empirical work would be legally accurate and theoretically informed. Yet, the next generation of scholars has opportunities we did not. For one thing, now, in the age of the internet, data and information are much easier to find. Moreover, there are now joint doctoral programs where scholars can gain both law and social science degrees. There are now special programs that teach experts in one discipline about scholarly approaches in other disciplines.

[2] A Huneeus, "International Criminal Law by Other Means: The Quasi-Criminal Jurisdiction of the Human Rights Courts" (2013) 107 AJIL 1.

For example, lawyers and legal scholars can be trained to do statistical work, qualitative investigations, fieldwork, experimental studies, and ethnographic studies, thus bringing methodological strengths from one discipline to questions of study in related fields. The combination of much wider access to information, much deeper comparative knowledge about international adjudicative systems, and scholars trained to reach outside academic silos will transform the study of international adjudication. And all of this, in turn, will probably transform international adjudication itself, as the opening of scholarship in the field will engage adjudicative institutions in a richer dialogue with members of their academic, political, and social environments.

This handbook showcases the latest scholarship from the disciplines of law, political science, history, legal philosophy, sociology, and even graphic design. We organized the handbook to be accessible to those who know little, yet interesting and helpful for those who are already part of this burgeoning field of international adjudication. Parts I and II provide an updated mapping of the international adjudicative system and begin to explain how we got to this system as it exists today. Part III provides a window into some of the major theoretical approaches and debates applied to the study of international adjudication. Part IV showcases some of the most salient issues in contemporary international adjudication, revealing how empirical and middle-range theorizing can be used to study international adjudication in action. Part V defines the key actors in international adjudication—those who make the process of international adjudication what it is today. Finally, Part VI considers some key legal and procedural factors essential to understanding how international adjudication actually works in practice.

This book is meant to be used alongside a number of useful internet resources. The PICT website,[3] and its sister website focused on African international judicial bodies,[4] remain useful first-stop resources for scholars who want to learn about individual international legal systems. A new Danish Center of Excellence—iCourts, sponsored by the Danish National Research Foundation—is the latest addition to the field. It aims to become a repository for empirical investigations and scholarly contributions to the study of international courts and tribunals.[5] It has updated links to data sources and shares data sets compiled by authors (including taking over the maintenance of Erik Voeten's personal website[6] on quantitative empirical research). Another new Norwegian center of excellence, PluriCourts, focuses

[3] Project on International Courts and Tribunals <http://www.pict-pcti.org/> accessed April 25, 2013.

[4] PICT, "African International Courts and Tribunals" <http://www.aict-ctia.org/> accessed April 25, 2013.

[5] The Danish National Research Foundation, "iCourts, the Centre of Excellence for International Courts" <http://jura.ku.dk/icourts/> accessed April 25, 2013.

[6] E Voeten, "International Courts Data" <http://www9.georgetown.edu/faculty/ev42/ICdata.htm> accessed April 25, 2013.

on legitimacy-related questions given the plurality of adjudicators assessing state respect for international norms.[7]

There are many questions about international adjudication that we did not ask because we cannot answer them yet. But we asked contributors to flag these questions so as to plant the seeds for future scholarship. The larger project of studying international adjudication has already spread around the globe. A number of universities are organizing conferences and publishing books on different aspects of international adjudication, such as how international adjudicative bodies develop and maintain political legitimacy, how they can be more effective, and what relationship should exist between national and international institutions. Asking these pertinent questions—and applying new methods of analysis—is the task we turn over to our colleagues and readers, and also continue to pursue ourselves.

Finally, we would like to thank all those whose support, work, and patience made this handbook possible: At Oxford University Press, Merel Alstein and John Louth for encouraging us to pursue this project at a time when each of us had more than a full plate, and Anthony Hinton for helping us with the many chores that publishing a book entails. Our heartfelt thank you goes to our authors for agreeing to work with us on this long project, for their excellent contributions and for redoubling their efforts when asked. A special thank you goes to Francesco Sebregondi of the Forensics Architecture Project at Goldsmiths, University of London, who generated, under very tight time constraints, the creative tables and charts that provide a visual approach to the topic of international adjudication. Finally, we are grateful to Loyola Law School Los Angeles for awarding Cesare Romano the W Joseph Ford Fellowship, allowing him to dedicate the time and effort it took to see this project to completion, and for making it possible to recruit the small team of research assistants who facilitated completion of this project: Sarah Frost, Negar Tehrani, Janna Brancolini, and Emerald Law (students of Cesare Romano's course on International Jurisprudence), and Amber Bissell.

CR/KJA/YS
Santa Monica, CA/Evanston, IL/Reut, Israel
June 2013

[7] Faculty of Law, University of Oslo, "PluriCourts: The Legitimate Roles of the Judiciary in the Global Order" <http://www.pluricourts.net/> accessed April 25, 2013.

Contents

PART II ORDERS AND FAMILIES OF INTERNATIONAL ADJUDICATIVE BODIES

PART III THEORETICAL APPROACHES TO STUDYING INTERNATIONAL ADJUDICATION

PART IV CONTEMPORARY ISSUES IN INTERNATIONAL ADJUDICATION

PART V KEY ACTORS

PART VI SELECTED LEGAL AND PROCEDURAL ISSUES OF INTERNATIONAL ADJUDICATION

Table of Cases

International Adjudicative Bodies

INTERNATIONAL JUDICIAL BODIES

African Commission on Human and Peoples' Rights

Caribbean Court of Justice

Central American Court of Justice

Council of Europe Appeals Board

Court of Eurasian Economic Community

Court of Justice of the Economic Union of West African States

East African Court of Justice

Economic Community of West African States Court of Justice

Eritrea-Ethiopia Claims Commission

European Court of Human Rights

European Court of Justice

European Free Trade Association Court

GATT

ICSID

Inter-American Court of Human Rights

International Court of Justice

International Criminal Court

International Criminal Tribunal for Former Yugoslavia

International Criminal Tribunal for Rwanda

International Labour Organization Administrative Tribunal

International Tribunal for the Law of the Sea

Iran-US Claims Tribunal

League of Nations Tribunal

London Court of International Arbitration

MERCOSUR

NAFTA

NATO Appeals Board

OECD Appeals Board

Organization of American States Administrative Tribunal

Organization for European Economic Cooperation Appeals Board

Permanent Court of Arbitration

Permanent Court of International Justice

Southern Africa Development Community Tribunal

Special Court for Sierra Leone

Special Tribunal for Lebanon

UN Administrative Tribunal

UN Human Rights Committee

World Bank Administrative Tribunal

WTO

AD HOC INTERNATIONAL ARBITRATIONS

NATIONAL COURTS

Argentina

Australia

Barbados

Botswana

Brazil

Bulgaria

Canada

Colombia

Croatia

Cyprus

Dominican Republic

Germany

Ireland

Italy

Nepal

Netherlands

New Zealand

Peru

Portugal

Russian Federation

Singapore

South Africa

Sri Lanka

Uganda

United Kingdom

United States

Venezuela

Table of Instruments

List of Abbreviations

AB	Appellate Body (World Trade Organization)
ACABQ	Advisory Committee on Administrative and Budgetary Questions (United Nations)
ACHR	American Convention on Human Rights
ACIL	Amsterdam Center for International Law
ACJ	Arab Court of Justice
ACtHPR	African Court on Human and Peoples' Rights
ADAD	Association des Avocats de la Défense
ADB	Asian Development Bank
ADBAT	ADB Administrative Tribunal
ADC-ICTY	Association of Defence Counsel practicing before the International Criminal Tribunal for the Former Yugoslavia
AEC CJ	Court of Justice of the African Economic Community
AIC	Arab Investment Court
AJIL	American Journal of International Law
AMU	Arab Maghreb Union
AMU CJ	Court of Justice of the Arab Maghreb Union
APS	American Peace Society
ARSP	Archiv für Rechts- und Sozialphilosophie
ASEAN	Association of Southeast Asian Nations
ASEAN AB	ASEAN Appellate Body
ASIL	American Society of International Law
ASP	Assembly of States Parties
AT	Administrative Tribunal
ATJ	Andean Tribunal of Justice (Tribunal de Justicia de la Comunidad Andina)
AU	African Union
B&H WCC	Court of Bosnia & Herzegovina (Section I—War Crimes Chamber)
BCJ	Benelux Economic Union Court of Justice
BerkeleyJIntlL	Berkeley Journal of International Law
BIT	Bilateral Investment Treaty

BRICS	Brazil, Russia, India, China and South Africa
Burgh House Principles	The Burgh House Principles on the Independence of the International Judiciary
BVerfGE	Entscheidungen des Bundesverfassungsgerichts
BYIL	British Yearbook of International Law
CACJ (Cartago)	Central American Court of Justice (Corte de Justicia Centroamericana)
CACJ (Managua)	Central American Court of Justice (Corte Centroamericana de Justicia) (Managua)
CAFTA-DR	Dominican Republic–Central America–United States Free Trade Agreement
Caricom	Caribbean Community
CAS	Court of Arbitration for Sports
CCBE	Council of Bars and Law Societies of Europe
CCJ	Caribbean Court of Justice
CCJELR	Community Court of Justice, Economic Community of West African States (ECOWAS) Law Report
CEEAC CJ	Court of Justice of the Economic Community of Central African States
CEEC	Court of the Eurasian Economic Community
CEMAC	CJ Court of Justice of the Central African Monetary Community
CIC	Center on International Cooperation (New York University)
CIETAC	China International Economic & Trade Arbitration Commission
CIS	Commonwealth of Independent States
CJAU	Court of Justice of the African Union
CJEU	Court of Justice of the European Union (see ECJ—European Court of Justice)
CoE	Council of Europe
CoEAB	Council of Europe Appeals Board
CoEAT	Council of Europe Administrative Tribunal
ColumLRev	Columbia Law Review
COMESA	Common Market for Eastern and Southern Africa
COMESA CJ	Court of Justice of the Common Market for Eastern and Southern Africa
Cornell ILJ	Cornell International Law Journal
CRT-1	Claims Resolution Tribunal for Dormant Accounts in Switzerland (First)
CSME	CARICOM Single Market and Economy
DIRC	Deeply Integrating Regional Court
DRC	Democratic Republic of Congo
DSB	Dispute Settlement Body (World Trade Organization)

DSU	Dispute Settlement Understanding (aka Marrakesh Agreement Establishing the World Trade Organization, Understanding on Rules and Procedures Governing the Settlement of Disputes (World Trade Organization))
EACJ	East African Court of Justice
EBRD	European Bank for Reconstruction and Development
ECCAS CJ	Court of Justice of the Economic Community of Central African States
ECCC	Extraordinary Chambers in the Courts of Cambodia
ECCIS	Economic Court of the Commonwealth of Independent States
ECCJ	European Coalition for Corporate Justice
ECHR	European Convention on Human Rights and Fundamental Freedoms
ECJ	European Court of Justice (see also CJEU—Court of Justice of the European Union)
ECmHR	European Commission of Human Rights
ECOWAS	Economic Community of West African States
ECOWAS CJ	Court of Justice of the Economic Community of West African States
ECR	European Court Reports
ECSC	European Coal and Steel Community
ECT	Energy Charter Treaty
ECtHR	European Court of Human Rights
EEA	European Economic Area
EECC	Eritrea–Ethiopia Claims Commission
EEZ	Exclusive Economic Zone
EFTA	European Free Trade Association
EFTA C	EFTA Court
EGC	European Union General Court
EGP	Ethics and Global Politics
EJIL	European Journal of International Law
EJIR	European Journal of International Relations
EL Rev	European Law Review
ENET	European Nuclear Energy Tribunal
ESA	EFTA Surveillance Authority
ESAAB	Appeals Board of the European Space Agency
ETSI	European Tribunal on State Immunity
EU	European Union
FIDE	Fédération internationale pour le droit européen
FIELD	Foundation for International Environmental Law and Development
FTA	Free trade agreement
GAL	Global Administrative Law

GATT	General Agreement on Tariffs and Trade
GC	General Court
GerLJ	German Law Journal
HarvIntlLJ	Harvard International Law Journal
HJRL	Hague Journal on the Rule of Law
HLR	Harvard Law Review
IACIJ	Inter-American Court of International Justice
IACmHR	Inter-American Commission on Human Rights
IACtHR	Inter-American Court of Human Rights
IAT	International Administrative Tribunal
IBA	International Bar Association
IC	International court
ICAT	International Central American Tribunal
ICC	International Criminal Court
ICCPR	International Covenant on Civil and Political Rights
ICDAA	International Criminal Defence Attorneys Association
ICJ	International Court of Justice
ICLQ	International and Comparative Law Quarterly
ICSID	International Centre for Settlement of Investment Disputes
ICTR	International Criminal Tribunal for Rwanda
ICTY	International Criminal Tribunal for Former Yugoslavia
IDA	International Development Association
IDB	Inter-American Development Bank
IDBAT	IDB Administrative Tribunal
IDI	Institut de Droit International
IDR	International Dispute Resolution
IFAD	International Fund for Agricultural Development
IFC	International Finance Corporation
IGO	Intergovernmental organization
IHRCs	International Human Rights Courts
IICJ	International Islamic Court of Justice
IL	International law
ILA	International Law Association
ILC	International Law Commission
ILDC	International Law in Domestic Courts
ILM	International Legal Materials
ILO	International Labour Organization

ILOAT	ILO Administrative Tribunal
ILR	International Law Reports
IMF	International Monetary Fund
IMFAT	International Monetary Fund Administrative Tribunal
IMT	International Military Tribunal at Nuremberg
IMTFE	International Military Tribunal for the Far East
INTAL	Institute for the Integration of Latin America and the Caribbean
IOLR	International Organization Law Review
IPC	International Prize Court
IR	International relations
ITLOS	International Tribunal for the Law of the Sea
IUSCT	Iran–United States Claims Tribunal
JB OAPEC	Judicial Board of the Organization of Arab Petroleum Exporting Countries
JDI	Journal du droit international (Clunet)
JIDS	Journal of International Dispute Settlement
JIEL	Journal of International Economic Law
JUNAT	Judgments of the UNAT
LCIA	London Court of International Arbitration
LJIL	Leiden Journal of International Law
LLM	Master of Laws
LN	League of Nations
LNT	League of Nations Tribunal
LoyLAIntl& CompLRev	Loyola of Los Angeles International & Comparative Law Review
LPICT	Law and Practice of International Courts and Tribunals
McGeorgeLRev	McGeorge Law Review
Mercosur	Southern Common Market (Mercado Común del Sur)
MFN	Most favoured nation
MICT	Mechanism for International Criminal Tribunals (United Nations)
MJIL	Michigan Journal of International Law
MPTR	Mercosur Permanent Tribunal of Review
N.Y.U. J. Int'l L. & Pol.	New York University Journal of International Law and Politics
NAAEC	North American Agreement on Environmental Conservation
NACEC	North American Commission on Environmental Conservation
NAFTA	North American Free Trade Agreement
NATO	North Atlantic Treaty Organization

NGO	Non-Governmental Organization
NYU	New York University
OAPEC	Organization of Arab Petroleum Exporting Countries
OAS	Organization of American States
OASAT	Organization of American States Administrative Tribunal
OAU	Organization of African Unity
ODECA	Organization of Central American States
OECD	Organization for Economic Cooperation and Development
OEEC	Organization for European Economic Cooperation
OHADA CCJ	Common Court of Justice and Arbitration of the Organization for the Harmonization of Business Law in Africa
OPEC	Organization of Petroleum Exporting Countries
OSCE	Organization for Security and Cooperation in Europe
OTP	Office of the Prosecutor
PacMcGeorge GlBus&DevLJ	Pacific McGeorge Global Business & Development Law Journal
PCA	Permanent Court of Arbitration
PCIJ	Permanent Court of International Justice
PICT	Project on International Courts and Tribunals
PPU	Urgent Preliminary Reference or procédure préliminaire d'urgence
PRIME	Panel of Recognized International Market Experts in Finance
R64	Regulation 64 Panels
RBUS CJ	Court of the Union State between the Russian Federation and the Republic of Belarus
RCADI	Recueil des cours de l'Académie de droit international
RGDIP	Revue générale de droit international public
RLS	Registries and Legal Secretariats
RoP	Rules of Procedure
RPE	Rules of Procedure and Evidence
RPF	Rwandan Patriotic Front
SADC	Southern African Development Community
SADC T	Southern Africa Development Community Tribunal
SCA	Agreement between the European Free Trade Agreement States on the Establishment of a Surveillance Authority and a Court of Justice
SCSL	Special Court for Sierra Leone
SFDI	Société française pour le droit international
SICA	Central American Integration System

SPLOS	States Parties to the United Nations Convention on the Law of the Sea
SPSC	Special Panels for Serious Crimes (East Timor)
StanJIntlL	Stanford Journal of International Law
StanLRev	Stanford Law Review
STL	Special Tribunal for Lebanon
TATJ	Treaty Creating the Andean Tribunal of Justice
TEU	Treaty on European Union
Texas Int'l L. J.	Texas International Law Journal
TFEU	Treaty on the Functioning of the European Union
TRIPS	Trade-Related Aspects of Intellectual Property
UEMOA CJ	Court of Justice of the West African Economic and Monetary Union
UK	United Kingdom
UN	United Nations
UNAT	United Nations Administrative Tribunal
UNC	United Nations Charter
UNCC	United Nations Compensation Commission
UNCITRAL	United Nations Commission on International Trade Law
UNCLOS	United Nations Convention on the Law of the Sea
UNDT	United Nations Disputes Tribunal
UNESCO	United Nations Educational, Scientific and Cultural Organization
UNGA	United Nations General Assembly
UNHRC	United Nations Human Rights Committee
UNMIK	United Nations Interim Administration Mission in Kosovo
UNRWA	United Nations Relief and Works Agency
UNSC	United Nations Security Council
UNSG	United Nations Secretary-General
UNTS	United Nations Treaty Series
US	United States
USA	United States of America
VCCR	Vienna Convention on Consular Relations
VCLT	Vienna Convention on the Law of Treaties
WAEMU CJ	Court of Justice of the West African Economic and Monetary Union
WBAT	World Bank Administrative Tribunal
WEUT	Western European Union Tribunal
WHC	World Heritage Committee
WHO	World Health Organization

WTO	World Trade Organization
WTO AB	World Trade Organization Appellate Body
WTO DSS	World Trade Organization Dispute Settlement System
ZAORV	Zeitschrift für Ausländisches Öffentliches Recht und Völkerrecht
ZSR	Zeitschrift für Schweizerisches Recht

Notes on the Contributors

EDITORS

Karen J Alter is Professor of Political Science and Law at Northwestern University, and a permanent visiting professor at the iCourts Center for Excellence, University of Copenhagen Faculty of Law. Alter is author of *The European Court's Political Power* (Oxford University Press 2009), *Establishing the Supremacy of European Law* (Oxford University Press 2001), and *The New Terrain of International Law: Courts, Politics, Rights* (Princeton University Press 2014).

Cesare PR Romano is Professor of Law and W Joseph Ford Fellow at Loyola Law School Los Angeles. He has degrees in political science (Università degli Studi di Milano: Laurea, 1992; Istituto per gli Studi di Politica Internazionale, Diploma, 1993); international relations (Graduate Institute of International and Development Studies: Diplôme d'Études Supérieures, 1995, and Ph.D., 1999); and law (New York University: LL.M., 1997). His expertise is in international law, but he also has substantial background in diplomatic history and economics. In 1997, he co-founded the Project on International Courts and Tribunals, which he continues to co-direct. In 2012, he became Senior Fellow of Pluricourts, the center of excellence for the study of international courts of the Faculty of Law of the University of Oslo, and of iCourts, the Danish National Research Foundation's center of excellence for international courts.

Yuval Shany is the Hersch Lauterpacht Chair in International Law and Dean of the Law Faculty of the Hebrew University of Jerusalem. He also serves currently as a member of the UN Human Rights Committee, a senior fellow at the Israel Democracy Institute, and a co-director in the Project on International Courts and Tribunals (PICT). Shany has degrees in law from the Hebrew University (LL.B., 1995 cum laude), New York University (LL.M., 1997) and the University of London (Ph.D., 2001). He has published a large number of books and articles on international courts and arbitration tribunals, international human rights law, international humanitarian law, and international criminal law. He is the recipient of the 2004 American Society of International Law book award (creative legal scholarship) and a 2008 recipient of a European Research Council grant awarded to pioneering research leaders. Shany has taught in a number of law schools in and outside Israel, and has been in recent years a research fellow at Harvard and Amsterdam Universities and the Max Planck Institute in Heidelberg.

CONTRIBUTORS

José E Alvarez is the Herbert and Rose Rubin Professor of International Law at New York University Law School where he directs the graduate program in International Legal Studies. Previously he was the Hamilton Fish Professor of International Law and Diplomacy and the executive director of the Center on Global Legal Problems at Columbia Law School. He has also taught at the law schools at the University of Michigan and George Washington University. He is a past president of the American Society of International Law (ASIL) and served as an advisor to the first prosecutor of the International Criminal Court. He is co-editor in chief of the American Journal of International Law.

Chittharanjan F Amerasinghe, B.A., LL.B., Ph.D. (Public International Law), LL.D. (Public International Law, Constitutional Law, Roman-Dutch Private Law)—Cambridge, UK; LL.M. (Public International Law)—Harvard, USA; Ph.D. (Roman-Dutch Private Law)—University of Ceylon; Member, Institut de droit international. Formerly, Judge, UN Administrative Tribunal; Judge, Commonwealth Secretariat Tribunal; Registrar, World Bank Administrative Tribunal; Full Professor of Law, University of Ceylon; Adjunct Professor of International Law, American University School of Law, USA; Fellow, Trinity Hall, Cambridge University (UK). Certificate of Merit, American Society of International Law (1988/9), Yorke Prize (1964), Cambridge University, UK. He has published extensively books, articles, and essays on, inter alia, public international law and international administrative law, and has had a consulting practice in those fields.

Carl Baudenbacher has been President of the EFTA Court since 2003, and Judge since 1995. Former Member of the Supreme Court of the Principality of Liechtenstein. Full Professor of Private, Commercial and Economic Law at the University of St. Gallen HSG, Former Permanent Visiting Professor at the University of Texas School of Law.

Samantha Besson is Professor of Public International Law and European Law at the University of Fribourg (Switzerland) and Co-Director of the European Law Institute of the Universities of Bern, Fribourg and Neuchâtel (Switzerland). Her publications and research interests lie in European law and public international law, legal and political philosophy, and in particular in human rights law and theory.

Armin von Bogdandy is the Director of the Max Planck Institute for Comparative Public Law and International Law at Heidelberg University, and Professor at the Goethe-Universität in Frankfurt. He is President of the OECD Nuclear Energy Tribunal and a member of the Scientific Committee of the European Union Agency for Fundamental Rights (2008–2013).

Chester Brown is Professor of International Law and International Arbitration at the Faculty of Law, University of Sydney; a barrister at 7 Selborne Chambers, Sydney, and a door tenant at Essex Court Chambers, London. He is the author of *A Common Law of International Adjudication* (Oxford University Press 2007).

David D Caron is Dean of The Dickson Poon School of Law, King's College, London. He served as a Commissioner with the United Nations Compensation Commission, and worked with or appeared before the Marshall Island Nuclear Claims Tribunal, the Eritrea–Ethiopia Claims Commission, and the Iran–United States Claims Tribunal. He also served as a member of the PCA Steering Committee on International Mass Claims.

Stéphanie Cartier is a Legal Officer with the UN Office of Legal Affairs (OLA). Prior to joining OLA, she taught at Fordham University and collaborated with the Brandeis Institute for International Judges and the Project on International Courts and Tribunals. She also worked with human rights NGOs, the ILO, and the WTO Appellate Body. Stephanie earned a B.C.L. and LL.B. from McGill, a Master's from the GIIDS, Geneva, and a Ph.D. from Maastricht University.

Michael-James Clifton is Legal Secretary in the President's Chambers of the EFTA Court. He obtained his LL.B. (EU) from the University of Leicester and graduated *cum laude* and Valedictorian in European Business Law from Leiden University. Called to the Bar in 2009. Formerly, Associate at VVGB in Brussels and *stagiaire* to ECJ Advocate-General Eleanor Sharpston.

Pierre-Marie Dupuy is Emeritus Professor at the University of Paris (Panthéon-Assas) and at The Graduate Institute of International and Development Studies, Geneva. He also held the Chair of General International Law at the European University Institute, Florence (2000–2008). Professor Dupuy has wide experience in international legal practice, in particular as counsel for governments in numerous cases before the ICJ as well as an international arbitrator. He is a member of the Institut de Droit International.

Solomon T Ebobrah, LL.B. (Rivers State University); LL.M., LL.D. (University of Pretoria) is a Senior Lecturer at the Faculty of Law, Niger Delta University, Nigeria and an Extra-Ordinary Lecturer with the Centre for Human Rights, University of Pretoria. He is an editor of the African Human Rights Law Journal.

Kate Gibson is the Lead Counsel of Justin Mugenzi at the ICTR, and Co-Counsel of Charles Taylor at the SCSL. She has previously worked in the ICTY Appeals Chamber, as a victims' lawyer at the ECCC, and on defense teams at the ICC and ICTR. She is admitted to practice in the Supreme Court of Queensland, Australia, and holds an LL.M. from Cambridge University.

Tom Ginsburg is the Leo Spitz Professor of International Law at the University of Chicago, where he also holds an appointment in the Political Science Department. He is a member of the American Academy of Arts and Sciences. He holds B.A., J.D., and

Ph.D. degrees from the University of California at Berkeley. He currently co-directs the Comparative Constitutions Project, a National Science Foundation-funded data set cataloging the world's constitutions since 1789. His recent co-authored book, *The Endurance of National Constitutions* (2009), won the best book award from the Comparative Democratization Section of the American Political Science Association. His other books include *Judicial Review in New Democracies* (2003), *Administrative Law and Governance in Asia* (2008), *Rule By Law: The Politics of Courts in Authoritarian Regimes* (with Tamir Moustafa, 2008), and *Comparative Constitutional Law* (with Rosalind Dixon, 2011). Before teaching law, he served as a legal advisor at the Iran–US Claims Tribunal in The Hague, Netherlands, and he has consulted with numerous international development agencies and governments on legal and constitutional reform.

Christine Gray is Professor of International Law at the University of Cambridge and a Fellow of St John's College, Cambridge. Her first major publication was *Judicial Remedies in International Law* (Oxford University Press 1987), and she has maintained an interest in this area. Her recent work has mainly focused on the use of force.

Laurence R Helfer is the Harry R Chadwick, Sr. Professor of Law at Duke University School of Law, where he co-directs the Center for International and Comparative Law. He has authored more than 60 publications on his diverse research interests, which include human rights, international adjudication, and interdisciplinary analysis of international institutions.

Kevin Jon Heller is Associate Professor and Reader at Melbourne Law School. His book *The Nuremberg Military Tribunals and the Origins of International Criminal Law* was published by Oxford University Press in 2011. He holds a Ph.D. in Law from Leiden University and a J.D. from Stanford Law School.

Cristina Hoss is a Legal Officer with the ICJ and Visiting Lecturer at Leiden University. Before joining the ICJ staff in 2005, Cristina was a Research Fellow at the Max-Planck Institute for Comparative Public Law and Public International Law in Heidelberg. Cristina earned her Masters and Ph.D. in law from the University of Paris II.

Alexandra Huneeus is an Assistant Professor of Law at the University of Wisconsin. Her current research examines the evolution of regional human rights systems, with a focus on the Inter-American Court. Her article "International Criminal Law by Other Means: the Quasi-Criminal Jurisdiction of the Human Rights Courts" will appear in the American Journal of International Law (2013).

Thordis Ingadottir is Associate Professor at Reykjavik University. She has law degrees from the University of Iceland and New York University School of Law. She is a Co-Director of the Project on International Courts and Tribunals (PICT) and the Director of the Project on the Impact of International Proceedings on National Proceedings in Mass Atrocity Situations (DOMAC).

Natalie Klein is the Dean of Macquarie Law School, Macquarie University, Australia, where her teaching and research focus on the law of the sea and international dispute settlement. Prior to joining Macquarie, she worked in international arbitration and litigation at Debevoise & Plimpton LLP, served as counsel to Eritrea, and was a consultant at the UN.

Ruth Mackenzie is Senior Lecturer in International Law at the University of Westminster. She was previously Principal Research Fellow and Deputy Director at the Centre for International Courts and Tribunals at University College London. Ruth has been associated with the Project on International Courts and Tribunals since its inception in 1997. She was a member of the Steering Committee of the DOMAC research project on the Impact of International Courts on Domestic Criminal Procedures in Mass Atrocity Cases. Ruth has also worked extensively in the field of international environmental law.

Mikael Rask Madsen is Professor of Law at the University of Copenhagen and Director of iCourts—The Danish National Research Foundation's Centre of Excellence for International Courts. Trained as both a lawyer and a sociologist, his work concerns the interface of international courts, transnational elites, and the structuring of global society.

Sean D Murphy is the Patricia Roberts Harris Research Professor of Law at George Washington University and a Member of the UN International Law Commission. He has served on the Board of Editors of the American Journal of International Law and in the US Department of State Legal Adviser's Office.

Yael Naggan (LL.B. and B.A. in International Relations, Hebrew University of Jerusalem 2013) is a Teaching Assistant at the Hebrew University of Jerusalem, Israel.

André Nollkaemper is Professor of Public International Law and Vice-Dean for Research at the Faculty of Law of the University of Amsterdam. He is also (external) Advisor to the Minister of Foreign Affairs of the Netherlands, Vice-President of the Board of the European Society of International Law and Member of the Royal Academy of Sciences of the Netherlands. He is Editor-in-Chief of International Law in Domestic Courts (Oxford University Press).

Mary Ellen O'Connell holds the Robert and Marion Short Chair in Law and is Research Professor of International Dispute Resolution at the Kroc Institute for International Peace Studies, University of Notre Dame. She has also taught at The Ohio State University; the George C. Marshall European Center for Security Studies at Garmisch, Germany; the Johns Hopkins University Nitze School of Advanced

International Studies, Bologna, Italy; and Indiana University, Bloomington. She practiced law with the Washington, D.C. law firm of Covington & Burling. Her research interests are in general international law, international legal theory, international law on the use of force, and international dispute resolution. She has published widely on these subjects, including a casebook, *International Dispute Resolution, Cases and Materials* (2nd edn, Carolina 2012).

Mark A Pollack is Professor of Political Science and Jean Monnet Chair *ad personam* at Temple University. His most recent book is *Interdisciplinary Perspectives on International Law and International Relations: The State of the Art*, co-edited with Jeffrey L. Dunoff (Cambridge University Press 2013).

Anna Riddell is Publications Editor at the British Institute of International and Comparative Law in London, and currently finishing her Ph.D. at the European University Institute in Florence. Her thesis is on the connection between international environmental protection and human rights under the supervision of Professor Francesco Francioni. Prior to commencing the Ph.D., she was a Research Fellow in Public International Law at the British Institute of International and Comparative Law, and Director of the Institute's Project on Evidence in International Courts and Tribunals. In 2009 she co-authored the study "Evidence Before the International Court of Justice," published by the Institute, which was cited with approval in the International Court of Justice by Judges Al-Khasawneh and Simma in their Dissenting Opinion in the *Case Concerning Pulp Mills on the River Uruguay (Argentina v. Uruguay)* (20 April 2010). She has also published articles on the subject of evidence in international litigation in several referred journals. She holds LL.M.s from the European University Institute and the University of Exeter (European Law), an M.A. from Brasenose College, Oxford, and was called to the Bar of England and Wales by Lincoln's Inn in 2005.

Yaël Ronen (Ph.D., Cambridge 2006) is Senior Lecturer at Sha'arei Mishpat College in Hod Hasharon, Israel. Her publications include, with Shabtai Rosenne, *Law and Practice of the International Court* (Brill 2006), as well as books and articles on human rights, international humanitarian law, and territorial status.

William A Schabas is Professor of International Law at Middlesex University in London. He is also professor of international criminal law and human rights at Leiden University, emeritus professor of human rights law at the National University of Ireland Galway and honorary chairman of the Irish Centre for Human Rights.

Christoph Schreuer is a graduate of the Universities of Vienna, Cambridge and Yale. He is a former Professor at Johns Hopkins University and University of Vienna, member of the Permanent Court of Arbitration and ICSID Panel of Arbitrators, arbitrator in ICSID and UNCITRAL cases.

Francesco Sebregondi is an architect, a designer, and a researcher within the European Research Council-funded project *Forensic Architecture,* based at Goldsmiths, University of London. His research explores the agency of architecture as media, with a focus on the representation of contemporary spatial problems and phenomena.

Anja Seibert-Fohr is Professor of International Law at Goettingen University Law School in Germany, and a member of the UN Human Rights Committee. Between 2008 and 2013, she directed the Minerva Research Group on Judicial Independence at the Max-Planck-Institute for Comparative Public Law and International Law in Heidelberg.

Maya Steinitz is Associate Professor of Law at the University of Iowa College of Law. Professor Steinitz teaches, researches, and practices widely in public and business international law and dispute resolution. Prior to joining the University of Iowa she taught at Columbia Law School. She served as a litigator at Latham & Watkins and clerked for Israeli Supreme Court Justice Esther Hayut. She currently serves as an arbitrator and arbitration expert.

Eran Sthoeger is a member of several legal teams in interstate disputes, past and present, and a Research Analyst at Security Council Report, New York. He holds an LL.M. from New York University in International Legal Studies and an LL.B. in law, history, and Jewish history from the Hebrew University of Jerusalem.

Leigh Swigart is Director of programs in international justice and society at the International Center for Ethics, Justice, and Public Life at Brandeis University. She oversees the Brandeis Institute for International Judges and is the author (with Cesare P.R. Romano and Daniel Terris) of *The International Judge: An Introduction to the Men and Women Who Decide the World's Cases* (Brandeis University Press/Oxford University Press 2007).

Daniel Terris is Director of the International Center for Ethics, Justice, and Public Life at Brandeis University. He is the founder of the Brandeis Institute for International Judges and the author (with Cesare P.R. Romano and Leigh Swigart) of *The International Judge: An Introduction to the Men and Women Who Decide the World's Cases* (Brandeis University Press/Oxford University Press 2007).

Lenore VanderZee is a Ph.D. Candidate in Political Science and Peace Studies at the University of Notre Dame. She also holds a J.D. and LL.M. from Notre Dame Law School. While she is completing her dissertation, she is serving as the President's Chief of Staff at SUNY Canton and teaches in its Social Sciences department.

Antoine Vauchez is a Research Professor at the Centre européen de sociologie et science politique (Université Paris 1-Sorbonne and CNRS). He has recently published *L'Union par le droit. L'invention d'un programme institutionnel pour l'Europe* (Presses de Sciences Po 2013) and an edited volume with Bruno de Witte: *Lawyering Europe. European Law as a Transnational Social Field* (Hart Publishing 2013).

Ingo Venzke is a Senior Research Fellow and Lecturer at the University of Amsterdam. He was previously a Hauser Research Scholar at New York University and a Research Fellow at the Max-Planck-Institute in Heidelberg. He is the author of *How Interpretation Makes International Law: On Semantic Change and Normative Twists* (Oxford University Press 2012).

Jorge E Viñuales is Harold Samuel Professor of Law and Environmental Policy at the University of Cambridge, United Kingdom. He formerly held the Pictet Chair in International Environmental Law at The Graduate Institute, in Geneva, where he also directed the Program on Environmental Governance. Professor Viñuales has substantial experience as a practitioner, particularly in the areas of public international law, investment law, and environmental law.

Erik Voeten is the Peter F Krogh Associate Professor of Geopolitics and Justice in World Affairs at Georgetown University's School of Foreign Service and Department of Government. He received his Ph.D. in politics from Princeton. His main area of research is international law and institutions.

Michael Wood is a member of the International Law Commission. He is a barrister at 20 Essex Street, London, where he practices in the field of public international law—including before international courts and tribunals. He was a lawyer at the UK Foreign and Commonwealth Office between 1970 and 2006.

PART I

MAPPING INTERNATIONAL ADJUDICATIVE BODIES

CHAPTER 1

MAPPING INTERNATIONAL ADJUDICATIVE BODIES, THE ISSUES, AND PLAYERS

CESARE PR ROMANO, KAREN J ALTER, AND YUVAL SHANY

THE editors' preface to this volume explained how the study of international adjudication has changed over time, and how this handbook takes a new approach to the topic of international adjudication. Our primary goal for this introductory chapter is to document the institutional, legal, and empirical terrain that is the focus of this handbook, thereby saving individual contributors the task of engaging in mapping exercises for their specific issue area. We also want to put forward a quick digest for the rest of the volume. However, rather than trying to summarize the contributions of the 40-plus authors, we aim here to elucidate how the individual chapters connect and relate to aspects of international adjudication.

We begin our mapping exercise by establishing definitional criteria and explaining key concepts, particularly what differentiates adjudicative bodies from diplomatic means and other non-binding procedures; judicial bodies from arbitral bodies; and international adjudicative mechanisms from their domestic counterparts. We then arrange the dozens of international adjudicative bodies currently existing into two large groups: judicial bodies and arbitral bodies, and then divide these two groups into several sub-groups, according to similarities in structure or function.

A classification might help legal scholars who are interested in bodies applying similar subject matter law and need to consider litigation options. It might guide social scientists who want to know about institutions that share design elements. But, for us, it is mostly a tool to organize this handbook. Yet, as any tool, it comes with some operating instructions and must be used with a great amount of care and flexibility. Categories are often arbitrary and rarely watertight and can, to a degree, overlap.[1] Indeed, since international adjudicative bodies—and most certainly international judicial bodies—are expensive to create and maintain, states often try to economize by giving multiple roles to individual institutions.

After laying down some key concepts and terms (Section 1), we propose a basic classification (Section 2). Then we present the greatest challenges faced by contemporary international adjudication (Section 3), the actors who participate in international adjudication and the main stakeholders (Section 4), and, finally, we overview the main theoretical models applied to the study of international adjudication (Section 5).

1 Some Key Definitions and Concepts

The term adjudication, from Latin *adjudicare* (*ad* = to/toward + *judicare* = to judge), indicates a particular law-based way of reaching a final decision in a contention.

[1] For examples of possible classifications of international adjudicative bodies, see C Romano, "The Proliferation of International Judicial Bodies: The Pieces of the Puzzle" (1999) 31 N.Y.U.J. Int'l L. & Pol. 709; C Romano, "A Taxonomy of International Rule of Law Institutions" (2011) 2(1) JIDS 241; KJ Alter, *The New Terrain of International Law: Courts, Politics, Rights* (Princeton University Press 2014); B Kingsbury, "International Courts: Uneven Judicialization in Global Order" in J Crawford and M Koskenniemi (eds), *Cambridge Companion to International Law* (Cambridge University Press 2012) 203–27.

Often referred to as "litigation," adjudication involves one or more individuals (i.e., the adjudicators), making a binding decision after an adversarial procedure during which the parties benefit, to varying degrees, from an equality of rights. The law-based nature of adjudicative decision-making distinguishes adjudication from other processes, such as political decision-making and mediation. Also key is that adjudication leads to a binding outcome that has the force of law. The legally binding nature of outcomes distinguishes adjudication from mediation, conciliation, good offices, and the like, known as "alternative dispute resolution" nationally and "diplomatic means" internationally.

In essence, there are two distinct modes of adjudication: by way of judicial bodies and by way of arbitration. Judicial bodies (also generically referred to as "courts" or "tribunals") *pre-exist* the question that is to be decided. The adjudicators are selected, elected, or nominated through a mechanism that does not depend on the will of the litigating parties. They sit on the body's bench and decide a series of cases. The judge's authority derives from a public mandate and the outcome is, in essence, a "public good."[2] Conversely, in arbitration, the adjudicators are selected by the parties *after* the dispute arises, with the aim of deciding a particular case. The arbitral tribunal or panel is dismissed after issuing the decision (known as the "award"). Since the parties select the members of arbitral bodies, the mandate of arbitrators is circumscribed to administering "private justice." These important differences notwithstanding, both judicial decision-making and arbitration are law-based processes that render legally binding decisions. Furthermore, since international judicial bodies have developed from institutionalized forms of arbitration, both processes share some common attributes (such as the ability of parties to some judicial and arbitral procedures to influence the composition of the bench, and the establishment of both procedures pursuant to an international law instrument). These fundamental similarities are why these two distinct processes are often treated together, as is often the case in this handbook.

These concepts and the two distinct modes of adjudication are universal, valid across time and space.[3] Yet there are some key differences between how adjudication is framed nationally and internationally. At the national level, adjudication is often compulsory, meaning that it does not depend on litigating parties explicitly accepting the jurisdiction of the adjudicating body. Generally, litigation is initiated by one party suing or indicting the other; enforcement of the decision is ensured by the national public authorities. Internationally, adjudication has traditionally depended on some form of consent of the parties, either through an explicit endorsement of the adjudicator's compulsory jurisdiction or consent to adjudicate a particular case. The ruling of the adjudicative body is legally binding at both national and international levels, but at the latter level there is no centralized authority to

[2] C Romano, "The Price of International Justice" (2005) 4 LPICT 281.

[3] See M Shapiro, *Courts: A Comparative and Political Analysis* (University of Chicago Press 1981) 1–17.

enforce the ruling. While these are important differences between domestic and international adjudication, this handbook shows that international adjudication has evolved in some fields and regions to the point that adjudication is often compulsory. Moreover, as William Schabas (Ch. 10) and André Nollkaemper (Ch. 24) explain in their contributions to this volume, increasingly national or supra-national authorities ensure enforcement of decisions of international adjudicative bodies or these rulings are given the force of law within national systems.

While international dispute settlement mechanisms are the common ancestor of the current array of international adjudicative bodies, starting from the middle of the twentieth century, international adjudication has evolved and diversified (to some extent in concert with national judicial evolutions). As José Alvarez explains in his essay in this handbook (Ch. 8), settling disputes has become just one of the several functions that international adjudication fulfills; one that nowadays is at the core of the mandate of just a minority of the current range of adjudicative bodies.[4] These developments mean that the traditional distinction between "international adjudication" and "diplomatic means" makes sense only in the context of dispute settlement, a largely surpassed theoretical framework that this handbook deliberately eschews.

What are the essential features of international adjudicative bodies? What distinguishes them from "diplomatic means" and even political decision-making and quasi-judicial bodies, such as United Nations agencies and expert committees? In the scholarly literature, there seems to be consensus that international adjudicative bodies are:[5]

1. international governmental organizations, or bodies and procedures of international governmental organizations, that…
2. hear cases where one of the parties is, or could be, a state or an international organization, and that…
3. are composed of independent adjudicators, who…
4. decide the question(s) brought before them on the basis of international law…
5. following pre-determined rules of procedure, and…
6. issue binding decisions.

[4] For instance, Karen Alter has classified the four main functions of contemporary international judicial bodies as: "dispute settlement"; "constitutional review"; "administrative review"; and "enforcement." Alter, note 1. The chapters by Samantha Besson (Ch. 19), and by Armin von Bogdandy and Ingo Venzke (Ch. 23) identify additional functions adjudicative bodies serve.

[5] Compare C Tomuschat, "International Courts and Tribunals with Regionally Restricted and/or Specialized Jurisdiction" in *Judicial Settlement of International Disputes: International Court of Justice, Other Courts and Tribunals, Arbitration and Conciliation: An International Symposium* (Springer 1987) 285–416, at 290–312 (defining "international courts and tribunals"); Romano, note 1, at 711 (defining "International Judicial Body"); C Tomuschat, "International Courts and Tribunals" in *Max Planck Encyclopedia of Public International Law* (3rd edn, Oxford University Press 2011) para. 1 (defining "international courts and tribunals"); Alter, note 1, at 70 (defining "international courts and tribunals"); JE Alvarez, *International Organizations as Law-Makers* (Oxford University Press 2005) (defining "international courts and tribunals").

The first two criteria are needed to distinguish international adjudicative bodies from national or transnational dispute settlement bodies. Thus, the International Chamber of Commerce, the London Chamber of Commerce, or the Stockholm Chamber of Commerce are essentially private organizations incorporated in the national legal system of some states (i.e., France, the UK, and Sweden, respectively) that offer arbitral services for interested parties. By contrast, the European Court of Human Rights (ECtHR) was created by the European Convention on Human Rights—a treaty—and the International Criminal Tribunal for Rwanda was created by a resolution of the UN Security Council—a binding decision of an international organization. Because international adjudicative institutions have a public international origin, their legal personality does not depend on the national law of any given state.

The second defining criterion is that states, or international organizations, or their organs, are usually the parties to the cases that international adjudicative bodies decide. This criterion must be understood correctly and applied with a modicum of flexibility. For example, in international criminal courts the parties are the public "Office of the Prosecutor," which is an organ of an international institution, and an indicted individual. Sometimes, international adjudicative bodies might hear cases where neither party is a state or an international organization. For instance, the Court of Appeals of the Organization of Harmonization of Business Law in Africa (OHADA) hears appeals of national courts' decisions in cases that involve two private actors. The Court of Justice of the European Union and the Andean Tribunal of Justice can issue preliminary rulings, at the request of national judges, in cases between private parties. Still, both also have jurisdiction over states or international organizations and their organs, which other kinds of transnational and national adjudicative bodies typically do not have. For some issues and cases, these bodies may even have exclusive jurisdiction.

The third defining trait is that international adjudicative bodies are composed of individuals who serve independently in their own professional capacity and do not represent any state. These individuals—called "judges" in the case of international judicial bodies, and "arbitrators" in the case of arbitration, or sometimes just plainly "members"—are required to possess certain minimum qualifications, such as having high moral character, expertise in a legal subject matter, language qualifications, or judicial experience (some adjudicators have also held the highest judicial office in their own countries before being appointed to an international court). To say that adjudicators are independent does not mean that the parties do not have significant influence and sometimes even control over who serves in these bodies. Members of adjudicative bodies are generally nominated by governments. They can be even handpicked by the litigating parties, as often happens in arbitration. This volume includes a chapter on the appointment process and who becomes a judge (Mackenzie, Ch. 34), the background of judges (Swigart and Terris, Ch. 28), international judicial behavior (Voeten, Ch. 25), and judicial ethics (Seibert-Fohr, Ch. 35), to better understand the behavior, background, and actions of adjudicators. But a key point is that, regardless of how adjudicators are selected and appointed, in the end, they do not represent a country or a party to the dispute and they are required to act independently.

The fourth defining criterion—international adjudicative bodies decide cases on the basis of legal standards and apply pre-determined rules of procedure—signifies that adjudicators act "under the shadow of the law"[6] and specifically under the shadow of international law.[7] This too is an important distinctive feature. The International Court of Justice (ICJ), the UN Security Council, the Organization for Security and Cooperation in Europe (OSCE), and the Assembly of the African Union all engage in international dispute settlement. But in contrast to the political bodies, the ICJ justifies its decisions solely on legal considerations.[8]

The fifth defining trait—international adjudicative bodies act on the basis of publicly articulated rules of procedure that are abstract, being set before the arising of any case or situation—is important because it means that the litigating parties do not control the terms of decision-making once the adjudicative process has begun. Adjudicative bodies often draft their own rules of procedure, and as Yuval Shany's chapter on jurisdiction and admissibility (Ch. 36) and Chester Brown's chapter on inherent powers (Ch. 38) demonstrate, key procedural elements can end up being defined through practice. But the fundamental point is that unlike arbitration, where the parties can choose the procedural law,[9] international adjudicative bodies rely on their own rules of procedure when adjudicating disputes.

The sixth and final defining criterion—that decisions of international adjudicative bodies are legally binding—means that governments and private actors are obligated to follow the ruling. Whether an international legal decision will be or might be enforced or complied with is a separate and rather intricate issue, discussed by Alexandra Huneeus (Ch. 20). The reality that respect for international legal rulings can be improved does not detract from the essential binding nature of the legal ruling. It should be noted that some international adjudicative bodies can also render decisions that are advisory in nature, and thus not legally binding. Advisory opinions are often influential and even authoritative, but as a matter of

[6] JE Alvarez, "The New Dispute Settlers: (Half) Truths and Consequences" (2003) 38 Texas Int'l L. J. 405; Alvarez, note 5.

[7] Be that as it may, it should be noted that sometimes some international adjudicative bodies might apply, besides international law, other bodies of law. For example, hybrid international criminal courts, like the Special Court for Sierra Leone, can apply, in addition to international law, the criminal laws of the country in which they have been set up. Arbitral tribunals might be asked to apply the law of this or that state, together with or instead of international law, to decide an international dispute.

[8] Yet, sometimes, if the parties so wish, an international adjudicative body might be able to set aside the law and reach a decision purely on considerations of fairness and equity (the so-called decision *ex aequo et bono*).

[9] In arbitration, the parties often choose off-the-shelf sets of rules of procedure, like those of the United Nations Commission on International Trade Law (UNCITRAL), or delegate the task of drafting

law they are not considered legally binding. The key point is that what differentiates adjudicative bodies from expert and sundry quasi-judicial bodies is the ability to issue binding rulings.

2 Mapping International Adjudicative Bodies

One of the most remarkable features of contemporary international relations is the large and growing array of international adjudicative bodies. In little over a century, the world went from one adjudicative institution—the Permanent Court of Arbitration—to dozens. Mary Ellen O'Connell and Lenore VanderZee chronicle the early days of international adjudication (Ch. 3), while Karen Alter identifies factors driving this more recent multiplication of judicial bodies (Ch. 4). Yet, far from being unstoppable, the march of international adjudication has been full of obstacles and dead-ends, as Cesare Romano explains (Ch. 6). The result is a very large array of bodies, operative or idle, that have been mapped in the pull-out chart included at the beginning of this volume.[10]

Admittedly, sheer numbers aside, ordering this disparate collection of rather heterogeneous bodies and procedures is a methodological more than visual challenge, for any ordering is to some extent arbitrary and ultimately depends only on what criteria one adopts. Several caveats are in order. First, the galaxy of adjudicative bodies still does not form a coherent judicial system. As Cesare Romano explains in his other chapter on the shadow zones of international judicialization (Ch. 5), inconsistencies and loopholes still abound. Ordering risks giving the illusion of order and structures when in reality there are none. Second, all maps are arbitrary. Often they contain arbitrary distinctions or emphasize features that may not be very salient (e.g., waterways of historical rather than contemporary relevance, or notional borders in a desert), while omitting factors that may sometimes be very important. Indeed, a number of chapters in this volume question our categories. William Schabas (Ch. 10) asks whether a criminal court set up by a multilateral treaty is all that different from a body set up by a single country or the parties to the military conflict, especially since the laws of the two bodies and the personnel of the court can be the same and since nationally focused bodies can apply international law and include international jurists. Solomon Ebobrah (Ch. 11) asks whether

and adopting them to the arbitrators. Rarely, if ever, do the parties themselves draft ad hoc their applicable rules of procedure.

[10] For an explanation of the illustrations see, in this handbook, Romano, Alter, and Sebregondi, Ch. 2.

it makes sense to label as "human rights courts" bodies associated with specific binding international human rights instruments when there are also regional courts that apply the same instruments, review human rights practices, and grant similar types of remedies. David Caron (Ch. 13) asks whether it makes sense to distinguish between permanent bodies and bodies that are not permanent but still operate for an indefinite period of time. Sean Murphy's treatment of adjudicative bodies for state-to-state disputes (Ch. 9) raises a related concern and blurs distinctions as he considers adjudication by permanent courts and ad hoc mechanisms, both of which render binding rulings for disputes between states. Laurence Helfer (Ch. 21) adds weight to these critiques when he notes that the legal effect of a ruling can spill beyond the case, the country litigating, and even the adjudicative body.

All in all, while there are reasonable and important critiques to consider, we think that even imperfect maps are helpful in orienting a person entering a new terrain. Our purpose in this chapter and in the pull-out charts is merely to provide a basic guide and a touchstone for discussion.

We have already mentioned one fundamental distinction between "judicial bodies" (also referred to as "international courts and tribunals") and "arbitral bodies." Judicial bodies pre-exist the dispute and have judges that are selected, elected, or nominated through a mechanism that does not depend, by and large, on the will on the parties to a given dispute. In contrast, arbitral panels are selected and nominated by the parties to the dispute, after the dispute arises, with the aim of settling it and disbanded after the award is rendered. This is the first branching out in the classification of international adjudicative bodies, separating judicial settlement from arbitration.

Even with this fundamental distinction we see some classificatory blurring in practice. Sometimes one can find arbitration intermingled with judicial settlement. For example, the World Trade Organization (WTO), Southern Common Market (Mercosur), South African Development Community, and OHADA all allow for disputes to be adjudicated by ad hoc arbitral panels composed of experts chosen by the parties, with decisions subject to appeal before permanent appellate judicial bodies.

Of course, both international judicial bodies and arbitral bodies and procedures can be further divided into sub-categories.

2.1 Arbitral bodies

One way to classify arbitral bodies and procedures is to distinguish between ad hoc arbitration—a purely isolated, one-time exercise—and arbitration taking place within *institutionalized frameworks*. Most of the international arbitration that took place during the nineteenth century was of the former kind. For instance, in 1893, the United States and Great Britain appointed seven arbitrators (two each by the

United States and Great Britain and the remaining three appointed by the President of France, the King of Italy, and the King of Norway) to settle a dispute over the management of fur seals in the Bering Sea.[11] However, as Mary Ellen O'Connell and Lenore VanderZee explain (Ch. 3), the creation of the Permanent Court of Arbitration (PCA), in 1899, led to the beginning of the institutionalization of arbitration, a first step towards the current universe of international adjudication. With the PCA, states had a ready-made list of trusted experts from which they could pick their arbitrators, a venue where proceedings could take place (at the Peace Palace in The Hague), specialized secretarial support, and a ready-made set of procedural rules to follow.

Nowadays, most international arbitration takes place within institutional frameworks, such as the PCA, but also the International Center for Investment Disputes (ICSID), which is discussed in this handbook by Christoph Schreuer (Ch. 14). These institutional frameworks can be permanent, existing independently from the vicissitudes of a single case or historical event, or temporary. ICSID and PCA are a good example of permanent arbitral institutions, while international claims and compensation bodies, discussed by David Caron (Ch. 13), such as the Iran–US Claims Tribunal, or the United Nations Compensation Commission, are temporary. These are institutions created in the aftermath of a major catastrophe or conflict to decide appropriate compensation for international claims. Almost 90 mixed arbitral tribunals and claims commissions were created in the nineteenth and twentieth centuries in the wake of armed conflicts and revolutions.

Nowadays, purely ad hoc inter-state arbitration, of the kind practiced in the early days of the history of international adjudication is relatively rare. Even when arbitration does not take place within an institutional framework, there might be a legal framework that threads together the otherwise independent and separate arbitral panels. For instance, states that are party to the United Nations Convention on the Law of the Sea have a number of options to settle their disputes, including the ICJ, the International Tribunal for the Law of the Sea (ITLOS) and two kinds of arbitrations (one generic—the so-called Annex VII, and one by way of scientific experts—the so-called Annex VIII). While each arbitral panel convened to settle a dispute under the Law of the Sea Convention is a one-time temporary, arbitral tribunal, the legal framework of the convention ensures a certain degree of continuity and coherence between the various panels. The same happens, for instance, in the case of bilateral investment treaties, another source of much arbitral activity these days. Each dispute generates its own arbitral panel, which is dismissed after the award is rendered, but the investment treaty provides the unifying legal framework for the

[11] *Fur Seal Arbitration: Proceedings of the Tribunal of Arbitration, Convened at Paris Under the Treaty Between the United States of America and Great Britain, Concluded at Washington February 29, 1892 for the Determination of Questions Between the Two Governments Concerning the Jurisdictional Rights of the United States in the Waters of Bering Sea* (Government Printing Office 1895).

activities of each arbitral body. Both Murphy and Schreuer (Chs 9 and 14) address these issues.

2.2 International judicial bodies

There are at least five distinct types of international judicial bodies, if one groups them by their fundamental institutional and jurisdictional attributes.

2.2.1 *Courts for disputes between states*

As Mary Ellen O'Connell and Lenore VanderZee describe in their chapter (Ch. 3), at the outset, contemporary international adjudication was mostly, if not solely, aimed at peacefully settling disputes between states. The first international courts were of this kind.[12] These days, there are only three courts with jurisdiction mostly, if not exclusively, over disputes arising between sovereign states: the ICJ, the ITLOS and the World Trade Organization Appellate Body (WTO AB). Of the three, the ICJ has the broadest potential jurisdiction. It can hear any dispute between any states on any matter of international law (provided that the two states consent to the court's jurisdiction). The other two have a narrower, specialized jurisdiction, in a specific area of international law (i.e., law of the sea and WTO law). Disputes between states are also often settled through international arbitration, ad hoc, or under the aegis of some arbitral organization. Sean Murphy tackles international adjudication of disputes between states (in Ch. 9).

2.2.2 *Human rights courts*

Human rights courts hear cases concerning violations of an individual's human rights. Cases are brought to these courts directly by the victims, or indirectly through specially designated human rights commissions that vet individual and state complaints.[13] Although human rights courts can also hear cases raised by one state against another state, such litigation is rare. Currently there are three courts whose jurisdiction is solely focused on human rights: the ECtHR, the Inter-American Court of Human Rights (IACtHR), and the African Court on Human and Peoples' Rights (ACtHPR). Human rights courts are discussed by Solomon Ebobrah (Ch. 11). As Ebobrah notes, however, there are also bodies that have not been conferred jurisdiction to adjudicate human rights violations as such, but because of the nature of the cases they decide, from time to time they carry out functions very much similar to those of courts specialized in human rights. For instance, the Court of Justice

[12] Karen Alter uses the label "old style" international court to capture this category. See Alter, note 1.

[13] The African Union system allows governments to raise cases on behalf of their citizens, but it still requires that governments first consent to let individuals bring cases to the commission.

of the Economic Community of West African States has jurisdiction to adjudicate human rights complaints raised by individuals. This court's docket is dominated by human rights cases and it has issued some landmark judgments where it has concluded that certain international human rights standards have been violated.[14] The Caribbean Court of Justice serves as an appellate body for some national legal systems, hearing cases that often involve human rights issues.[15] Since 2010, with the entry into force of the Charter of Fundamental Rights of the European Union, the Court of Justice of the European Union (CJEU) has a specific mandate to adjudicate complaints that EU law violates human rights.

2.2.3 *Courts of regional economic and/or political integration agreements*

These are courts embedded in regional arrangements for economic cooperation and integration. They comprise the largest family of international judicial bodies, numerically speaking. In this handbook, Carl Baudenbacher and Michael-James Clifton (Ch. 12) identify 12 courts for regional economic and political integration agreements, but if one counts formally negotiated legal instruments establishing regional courts, the number would be closer to 20, as the pull-out chart in this handbook illustrates.

Of all international courts, courts of regional integration agreements have the most diverse and complex subject matter jurisdiction and the greatest variation in the types of adjudication and the range of actors that can be legal parties in adjudication. For example, in regional courts of economic and political integration agreements, states can often bring noncompliance suits against other states; directly affected parties can challenge community rules and/or state application of these rules; and institutional actors can challenge rules adopted using improper procedures or in violation of provisions of the regional agreement. Some regional courts also serve as international administrative tribunals, hearing employment disputes between the organization and its employees and contract disputes involving third parties. Others, as we have just noted, cross over to human rights courts. Most regional courts allow national judges to refer questions of interpretation to the community court and receive a "preliminary ruling" that they then apply to the case at hand.[16]

As Karen Alter (Ch. 4) explains, many regional courts mimic the model of the CJEU (formerly known as the European Court of Justice). Yet, a number of regional bodies also follow the template of the WTO dispute settlement system. For example, the North American Free Trade Agreement dispute settlement system does not rely on

[14] For more, see KJ Alter, L Helfer and J McAllister, "A New International Human Rights Court for West Africa: The Court of Justice for the Economic Community of West African States" (2013) 107 AJIL (4).

[15] See e.g., *DaCosta Cadogan v. The Queen* [2006] CCJ 4 (AJ) (Caribbean Ct. J. Dec. 4, 2006).

[16] The name is somewhat of a misnomer in that "preliminary rulings" are not subject to a final determination of the matters in question, but are in fact final determinations of certain legal questions.

permanent courts but rather on a series of ad hoc arbitral panels. Then again, a number of regional courts mix and match, incorporating design features of both the European Union and the WTO. For example, the Andean Tribunal of Justice largely replicates the European Court of Justice, but it allows for retaliatory sanctions against countries that have violated community rules, as is done at the WTO. The Mercosur system copies primarily the WTO's system of ad hoc dispute resolution, but national supreme courts can also seek preliminary ruling references from the Permanent Review Body.

2.2.4 *International criminal courts and tribunals*

These international courts and tribunals exercise just one kind of jurisdiction—criminal jurisdiction—but it is a jurisdiction that is not exercised by any other international judicial body.[17] Defendants in international criminal cases are always individuals, particularly high-level political and military leaders, and the Office of the Prosecutor shoulders the burden of the prosecution; thus an organ of an international institution (generally the UN) initiates prosecution. International criminal courts and tribunals form a very heterogeneous family, one that could be further divided into sub-classes. For instance, one could distinguish between permanent and temporary institutions, or between international and hybrid—international/national—criminal courts, or between bodies focused only on a given region or state and bodies with potentially global jurisdiction (see pull-out charts). William Schabas provides an overview of this family (Ch. 10). Kevin Jon Heller explains the role of the international prosecutor (Ch. 31) and Kate Gibson the role of defense counsels (Ch. 32) in the international criminal process.

2.2.5 *International administrative tribunals*

Last but not least, there are International administrative tribunals. International administrative tribunals, boards, and commissions are bodies of a judicial character attached to an international organization, whose main function is adjudicating disputes between international organization and their staff members. These bodies do apply international law (primarily the internal regulations of international organizations), but they are more similar to domestic labor courts than to international courts. International administrative tribunals meet all criteria to be classified as international judicial bodies, but because of their limited mandate and because they do not apply general international law or issue rulings that bind states, but only the international organization in question and its employee, legal scholars and

[17] Criminal courts are the only bodies that hold individuals accountable. David Caron (Ch. 13) observes that claims and compensation bodies generate state liabilities for legal violations in war, and Alexandra Huneeus notes that the IACtHR acts as a criminal court when it identifies violations and orders remedies, including the prosecution of individuals responsible for human rights atrocities. A Huneeus, "International Criminal Law by Other Means: The Quasi-Criminal Jurisdiction of Human Rights Courts" (2013) 107 AJIL 1.

political scientists usually ignore this category. Chittharanjan Amerasinghe's essay (Ch. 15) aims to fill this gap.

3 Common Challenges

The growth in number of international adjudication bodies, the expansion of their jurisdictional mandate, and their increased diversification has transformed international courts and tribunals into important tools of international governance.[18] Beyond their traditional dispute-settling role, international courts and tribunals increasingly find themselves in the business of law interpretation, law application, administrative review, and even constitutional review. These functions often involve a degree of law creation, and almost always the prioritization and advancement of policy goals inscribed in the DNA of the judicial institution (or its overarching international organization), for example promoting trade liberalization, protecting human rights, and prosecuting mass atrocities. The growing visibility of international adjudication bodies renders their shortcomings more apparent, and the increased influence of international courts and tribunals invites criticism by those discontented with their operation or rulings. The more powerful these institutions become, the louder and more urgent the calls for reforms to address known problems.

This section considers challenges international adjudicative bodies face. The previous sections grouped international courts and tribunals into like families. Each family has its own distinct challenges, some of which are discussed in the individual contributions in Part II of this handbook. But it is also the case that certain challenges are common to all, or at least most, international courts and tribunals. Pierre-Marie Dupuy and Jorge Viñuales have contributed a chapter (Ch. 7) discussing the challenge created by the proliferation of international courts. Here, we discuss problems in their most common and general form.

Four groups of challenges have been repeatedly raised: legitimacy concerns, effectiveness challenges, quality control, and systemic problems. Some of these concerns are legal, while others are more politically charged. Several raise practical issues, yet others are more conceptual in nature. Although the four types of concern overlap with one another to some extent, they represent different issues common to

[18] See e.g., Y Shany, "No Longer a Weak Department of Power? Reflections on the Emergence of a New International Judiciary" (2009) 20 EJIL 73, 79–83.

international judicial structures and procedures, and the outcomes these adjudicative bodies generate.

3.1 Legitimacy challenges

One set of challenges directed against virtually all international courts and tribunals involves the questioning of their legitimacy, understood here as a justified claim to authority informed by notions of fairness, justice, and legality.[19] Like most other international governance organs, international adjudicative bodies suffer from a democratic deficit.[20] Of course courts by their very nature are not democratic institutions. (While some states in the United States allow for the election of judges, in most of the world it is considered inappropriate to elect judges or to subject judges to popular review.) Nationally, a court's legitimacy rests on the government's legitimacy. But the more international courts are able to rule on the validity of policies created by accountable democratic governments, the more problematic it becomes that unelected international adjudicators far removed from the communities affected by their decisions can sit in judgment of the actions of accountable political actors.[21] The difficulty of changing international rules should governments disagree with judicial interpretations only underscores the extent to which international adjudicators are by and large non-accountable to local communities or to the governments that created them.[22]

Another set of legitimacy concerns involves the relationship between international governance and international justice. To the extent that international adjudication supports legal norms and political institutions that are associated in the eyes of important constituencies with controversial political and ideological projects such as imperialism, colonialism, capitalism, and other -isms, their legitimacy is likely to be challenged. For instance, during the past few years some Latin American countries have withdrawn from ICSID, alleging that the investment

[19] See e.g., WC Gay, "The Violence of Domination and the Power of Non-violence" in LF Bove and LD Kaplan (eds), *Philosophical Perspectives on Power and Domination: Theories and Practices* (Amsterdam: Rodopi 1997) 15, 24.

[20] See e.g., C Romano "Deciphering the Grammar of the International Jurisprudential Dialogue" (2009) 41(4) N.Y.U.J. Int'l L. & Pol. 755, 780.

[21] For example, the CJEU decides upon controversial social issues, such as the enlistment of female soldiers or limiting industrial activities near nature reserves. See *Kreil v. Bundesrepublik Deutschland*, Case C-285/98, 2000 E.C.R. I-69; *Commission v Spain (Marimas De Santona)*, Case C 355/90, 1993 E.C.R. I-4221. In the past, such issues were addressed by elected domestic institutions or by domestic courts monitored to some extent by elected institutions. (See also, in this handbook, Besson, Ch. 19).

[22] See e.g., D Terris, C Romano, and L Swigart, *The International Judge: An Introduction to the Men and Women Who Decide the World's Cases* (Brandeis University Press/Oxford University Press 2007) 150; BZ Tamanaha, *On the Rule of Law: History, Politics, Theory* (Cambridge University Press 2004) 135.

regime is pro-investors and neo-colonial.[23] The heads of the African Union have complained that the International Criminal Court (ICC) focuses exclusively on African disputes while ignoring mass atrocities by powerful Western countries and their allies.[24] These critiques can be explained in part by reference to broader North–South tensions that underlie the specific operations of these international adjudicative bodies.

Concerns about the legitimacy and accountability of adjudicators are not unique to international courts. Parallel concerns are often raised with respect to domestic legal systems and international institutions in general. Still, international adjudication is often more contested. One reason international courts are critiqued is that they operate in a more volatile political environment than their domestic counterparts. Domestic courts are able to establish their reputation for sound decision-making through their handling of many mundane cases. By contrast, many international courts focus primarily on high politics cases. International criminal tribunals target political leaders "who bear the greatest responsibility,"[25] yet, precisely in these cases, it is often difficult to establish a link between a political decision and the perpetration of an atrocity. The most straightforward cases of trade barriers tend to be resolved out of court, with the result that the WTO's dispute settlement mechanism ends up dealing with the most difficult and contentious cases.[26]

The fact that international courts are relatively new bodies, without a tradition of acceptance of their authority, further contributes to the questioning of their legitimacy, as does the different nature of international judicial procedure compared to domestic procedure.[27] Also, as is the case with most adjudicatory processes, no full equality of arms exists. Before domestic courts, certain litigants are more advantaged than others since they might have easier access to lawyers with greater experience and expertise.[28] In the international realm, this difference means that rich countries sometimes out-lawyer less well-off countries. All of these differences

[23] See C Schreuer, "Denunciation of the ICSID Convention and Consent to Arbitration" in M Waibel et al. (eds), *The Backlash Against Investment Arbitration: Perceptions and Reality* (Alphen aan den Rijn: Wolters Kluwer 2010) 353–354; see, in this handbook, Romano, Ch. 5.

[24] See D Akande, "The African Union takes on the ICC Again: Are African States Really Turning from the ICC?" (June 26, 2012) <http://www.ejiltalk.org/the-african-union-takes-on-the-icc-again> accessed May 12, 2013.

[25] See e.g., Statute of the Special Court of Sierra Leone, 16 January 2002, Art. 1(1).

[26] See e.g., ML Busch and E Reinhardt. "Bargaining in the Shadow of the Law: Early Settlement in GATT/WTO Disputes" (2000) 24 Fordham Int'l L.J. 148; C Davis, *Why Adjudicate: Enforcing Trade Rules in the WTO* (Princeton University Press 2012) 246.

[27] See e.g., R Mackenzie and P Sands, "International Courts and Tribunals and the Independence of the International Judge" (2003) 44 Harv. Int'l L.J. 271, 275; Terris, Romano, and Swigart, note 22, at 147 ff.

[28] M Galanter, "Why the 'Haves' Come Out Ahead: Speculations on the Limits of Legal Change" (1974) 9 Law & Society Rev. 95.

make observers question the fairness of international court procedures, and as a result, the legitimacy of some international adjudicative processes.[29]

A number of handbook chapters address directly legitimacy challenges facing international adjudication. Cesare Romano (Ch. 5), Leigh Swigart and Daniel Terris (Ch. 28), and Natalie Klein (Ch. 26) document the dominance of certain countries in supplying international judges and litigants, implicitly challenging the claim that international adjudication is indeed a global phenomenon. Samantha Besson (Ch. 19) argues that a number of philosophical questions need to be addressed before we proceed further with judging international law. Tom Ginsburg (Ch. 22) discusses the political constraints under which international courts and tribunals operate (a question that reflects, inter alia, on the perceived legitimacy of international adjudication). Other chapters, for example, Armin von Bogdandy and Ingo Venzke's chapter on judicial law-making (Ch. 23), Ruth Mackenzie's chapter on Judicial Election and Selection (Ch. 34), and Anja Seibert-Fohr's chapter on Ethics of International Adjudication (Ch. 35), present key factors which may affect the evaluation of any particular court or tribunal's legitimacy.

3.2 Effectiveness concerns

Another set of common challenges facing international adjudicative bodies concerns their effectiveness—understood narrowly as their ability to engender respect for their legal rulings and the rules they help enforce,[30] or more broadly as their ability to promote the attainment of a set of policy goals assigned by the political organs that create them.[31] Adjudication has been thought to be a cost-effective method for settling disputes (or solving problems), supporting legal norms and international institutions, and conferring a degree of accountability on international governance projects.[32] The more resources devoted to international adjudication and the more powerful international courts become, the more observers expect adjudication to resolve disputes and promote the policy goals of the organization. With expectations high and growing, international adjudicative bodies may be destined to disappoint some of their core constituencies.

Twenty years after the end of the Cold War, the record of accomplishment of many international courts and tribunals remains uneven at best. While some have

[29] See generally, N Grossman, "Legitimacy and International Adjudicative Bodies" (2009) 41 Geo. Wash. Int'l L. Rev. 107, 128–9; D Bodansky, "Legitimacy in International Law and International Relations" in J Dunoff and M Pollack (eds), *Interdisciplinary Perspectives on International Law and International Relations: The State of the Art* (Cambridge University Press 2013) 321–41.

[30] See, in this handbook, Helfer, Ch. 21.

[31] Y Shany, "Assessing the Effectiveness of International Courts: A Goal-Based Approach" (2012) 106 AJIL 225, 230.

[32] Shany, note 31, at 244–7.

clearly made an impact on the policy areas on which they adjudicate (human rights, trade, investment), the normative direction that they have pursued has sometimes met with criticism by important stakeholders.[33] At the same time, the impact of some newer adjudicative bodies, especially international criminal courts, on state actor performance and norm-internalization by such actors is often rather limited.[34]

More specifically, concerns have been raised with respect to the negative correlation that some commentators have identified between the increased ambition of certain adjudicative bodies and the level of compliance with their decisions. It sometimes seems that the more ambitious and far-reaching judicial decisions, the greater the resistance displayed by losing parties.[35] International adjudication bodies may even face a trade-off between immediate compliance with their rulings, and with it the perceived effectiveness of the institution in the short run, and building legal doctrines that might contribute to long-term changes but which produce short-term non-compliance. For example, compliance with decisions of the IACtHR is lower than those of the ECtHR. This is in part because the Inter-American Court requests a number of restorative remedies other than compensation that are often difficult for the targeted state to implement, leading to just partial compliance with any given ruling.[36] Recent statistics on reduced levels of compliance with general measures issued by the ECtHR,[37] and the suspension of the Tribunal of the Southern African Development Community, in response to its perceived judicial activism,[38] may also illustrate the trade-off between ambition and effectiveness.

In a world where resources assigned to international adjudication may get scarcer, and international judicial bodies find themselves in competition with other important international governance projects, one may expect increased demands being made on international courts and tribunals to provide good value for money. Indeed, the completion strategy for both the International Criminal Tribunal for Former Yugoslavia (ICTY) and the International Criminal Tribunal for Rwanda

[33] See e.g., A Lang, *World Trade Law after Neoliberalism: Re-imagining the Global Legal Order* (Oxford University Press 2011) 150–1; G Conway, *The Limits of Legal Reasoning and the European Court of Justice* (Cambridge University Press 2012) 77–8.

[34] See e.g., D McGoldrick, "The Legal and Political Significance of a Permanent International Criminal Court" in D McGoldrick et al. (eds), *The Permanent International Criminal Court: Legal and Policy Issues* (Oxford: Hart Publishing 2004) 453, 458; A Huneeus. "Courts Resisting Courts: Lessons from the Inter-American Court's Struggle to Enforce Human Rights" (2011) 44 Cornell Int'l L.J. 493, 507–511.

[35] See generally, Y Shany, "Compliance with Decisions of International Courts as Indicative of Their Effectiveness: A Goal-based Analysis" (2010) 3 Select Proceedings of the Eur. Soc'y Int'l L. 229; D Hawkins and W Jacoby, "Partial Compliance: A Comparison of the European and Inter-American Courts for Human Rights" (2010) 6 J. Int'l L. & Int'l Rel. 35.

[36] Hawkins and Jacoby, note 35, at 35.

[37] See Council of Europe, Supervision of the execution of judgments and decisions of the European Court of Human Rights (2012) 11.

[38] E de Wet, "The Rise and Fall of the Tribunal of the Southern African Development Community: Implications for Dispute Settlement in Southern Africa," ICSID Review (2013) 1–19.

(ICTR),[39] and the move to consolidate the as yet non-existing African Court of Justice with the ACtHPR[40] may suggest that the long-term existence of international adjudication bodies should not be taken for granted. International judges increasingly need to worry that institutional design, court procedures, and even judicial outputs will be subject to review by stakeholders who are concerned with both their effectiveness and cost-effectiveness.

A number of handbook chapters are concerned with the effectiveness of international adjudication. Laurence Helfer's chapter discusses different ways of assessing the effectiveness of international adjudicative bodies (Ch. 21). Other chapters address interesting components of any effectiveness and cost-effectiveness evaluation. Alexandra Huneeus focuses on the question of compliance with decisions of international courts (Ch. 20), and André Nollkaemper investigates the interaction between international and national courts more generally—an issue that comprises an important area of judicial impact (Ch. 24). Christine Gray discusses the various remedies international adjudicative bodies issue, identifying a range of legal outputs that one might put on a continuum of the degree in which remedial objectives can be attained (Ch. 40). Finally, Thordis Ingadottir's chapter on financing (Ch. 27) considers the cost of international adjudication.

3.3 Quality control

Both the legitimacy and effectiveness of international adjudicative bodies are tied to the quality of the work generated by international courts—objective and subjective (i.e., as perceived by external and internal observers). Several commentators monitoring different international courts and tribunals have expressed concerns about the qualification of certain judges, their independence and impartiality, the paucity of the administrative support they receive, and the inadequacy of certain court procedures.[41] More generally, the machinery of international justice has been viewed at times as over-worked and under-funded, and, at other times, under-utilized and even facing the risk of irrelevance.[42]

[39] See e.g., D Raab, "Evaluating the ICTY and its Completion Strategy," (2005) 3 J. Int'l Crim. Just. 82, 84.

[40] See e.g., R Mackenzie et al., *Manual on International Courts and Tribunals* (Oxford University Press 2009) 389–90.

[41] See e.g., R Falk, *Reviving the World Court* (University Press of Virginia 1986); SW Tiefenbrun, "The Role of the World Court in Settling International Disputes: A Recent Assessment" (1997) 20 Loy. L.A. Int'l & Comp. L.J. 1, 2; M Bohlander, "Pride and Prejudice or Sense and Sensibility? A Pragmatic Proposal for the Recruitment of Judges at the ICC and Other International Criminal Courts" (2009) 12 New Crim. L. R. 529, 530; C Romano, "The Americanization of International Litigation" (2003) 19 Ohio St. J. on Disp. Resolution 89, 95–104.

[42] See e.g., JM Czarnetzky and RJ Rychlak "An Empire of Law?: Legalism and the International Criminal Court" (2003) 79 Notre Dame L. Rev. 55, 59; LA Dickinson, "Transitional Justice in

Problems associated with deficient court structures and procedures may translate to weak decisions that misconstrue the law, fail to establish the relevant facts, and serve as poor legal precedents. Capacity problems, exacerbated by limited funding prospects, further reduce the possibility of maintaining high professional quality standards. There can be considerable turnover in the staff of international courts, and the newness of many international courts and their judges generates high-profile growing pains. For example, the first group of judges of the Court of Justice of the Economic Community of West African States (ECOWAS CJ) was appointed in 2001 when the court lacked any human rights jurisdiction. Since these judges were not selected because of their human rights expertise, it should not come as a surprise that the court lacked sufficient human rights expertise when member states gave the court a human rights jurisdiction in 2005.[43]

Several handbook authors address the question of the capacity and qualification of international adjudicators. Ruth Mackenzie writes about the process of electing and selecting international judges (Ch. 34). Several chapters discuss the role of the publicly-funded international prosecutors (Kevin Jon Heller, Ch. 31), defense counsels (Kate Gibson, Ch. 32), and registries and legal secretariats (Cristina Hoss and Stephanie Cartier, Ch. 33). Leigh Swigart and Daniel Terris analyze the attributes of judges who make it through the selection process (Ch. 28). Other relevant chapters that deal with the quality of judicial structures, procedures, and outcomes include the aforementioned chapters on judicial law-making (von Bogdandy and Venzke, Ch. 23), the financing of international adjudication (Ingadottir, Ch. 27), as well as the chapters on evidence and fact-finding by Anna Riddell (Ch. 39) and inherent powers by Chester Brown (Ch. 38).

3.4 Systemic problems

A final set of challenges for international adjudication involves the effects that the empowerment of international courts and tribunals has on the unity of the international legal system. According to a number of scholars and practitioners, the rise of specialized courts contributes to "tunnel vision" types of decision, meaning rulings that consider complex problems from one perspective only or that apply one particular treaty or branch of international law without considering other relevant parts of international law. The concern is that such decisions can accelerate the fragmentation of international law, leading to different outcomes depending on the

Afghanistan: The Promise of Mixed Tribunals" (2002) 31 Denv. J. Int'l L. & Pol'y 23, 33; Terris, Romano, and Swigart, note 22, at 160–4; M Parish, *Mirages of International Justice: The Elusive Pursuit of a Transnational Legal Order* (Cheltenham: Edward Elgar Publishing 2011) 73–81.

[43] Alter et al., note 14.

venue in which a case is adjudicated and the law applied there.[44] The creation of specialized legal bodies with compulsory jurisdiction that treat a set of cases in a relatively isolated manner may render some parts of international governance more effective and legitimate compared to other areas. Still, excessive specialization might come at the expense of the broader project of international governance, which may itself become less manageable as different adjudicative bodies pull law in different directions.[45]

The concern about coherence raises the ontological and sociological question of whether there is, or ever can be, a single international legal system that international courts belong to. Can or do international courts speak on behalf of the broad objective of an international rule of law? Is there an international community of legal adjudicators, or rather are these adjudicators constituent elements of specific separate regimes (e.g., trade regimes, human rights regimes)? In practice, the jury is out on these questions. Whereas decisions such as *Kadi v. Council*[46] and *Brazil—Retreaded Tyres*[47] suggest an interest in sustaining self-contained regimes and rejecting calls to coordinate different branches of law, decisions such as *Bosphorus v. Ireland*[48] and *Continental Casualty v. Argentina*[49] may be reflective of a greater interest by some judicial bodies in harmonization across different legal regimes.

The existence of numerous adjudication bodies, often exercising parallel, comparable and even overlapping jurisdictional powers, raises numerous practical concerns such as: what should be the proper division of labor between the different courts? Should the adjudication processes be synchronized? Should, for example, the WTO reject cases that were heard first in regional adjudicative systems or that could be heard in such bodies? Should actors in one set of proceedings be prevented from litigating further in other forums by the outcomes of other proceedings?

[44] See e.g., J Pauwelyn, "Fragmentation of International Law" in *Max Planck Encyclopedia of International Law* (Oxford University Press 2006); Report of the Study Group of the International Law Commission, *Fragmentation of International Law: Difficulties Arising from the Diversification and Expansion of International Law (Analytical Study)* (UN Doc A/CN.4/L.682, 2006); see, in this handbook, Dupuy and Viñuales, Ch. 7.

[45] See G Abi-Saab, "Fragmentation or Unification: Some Concluding Remarks" (1999) 31 N.Y.U.J. Int'l L. & Pol. 919, 925 ("The further the division of labor and specialization, the greater the need for the preservation of the unity of the whole that makes specialization possible and meaningful, but which becomes harder to maintain because of the centrifugal effects of specialization").

[46] Joined Cases C-402/05 P and C-415/05 P, *Kadi v. Council* [2008] ECR I-6351 (rejecting a Security Council Resolution adopted in a manner that violated EU human rights standards).

[47] Case WT/DS332/AB/R *Brazil—Measures Affecting Imports of Retreaded Tyres*, WTO Doc. 07-2682 (AB Report, 2007) (rejecting a defense claim for a WTO infringement based on a Mercosur norm).

[48] *Bosphorus v. Ireland* 2005-VI ECtHR Reports 107.

[49] *Continental Casualty v. Argentine Republic*, ICSID Case no. ARB/03/9, Award (Sept. 5, 2008), at para. 192 (harmonizing necessity under the Bilateral Investment Treaty (BIT) with necessity under the General Agreement on Tariffs and Trade (GATT)). The award was upheld by an ad hoc annulment committee on September 16, 2011.

The systemic attributes of the universe of international adjudication are discussed in a number of handbook chapters. These include Cesare Romano's chapter on the shadow zones of international adjudication (Ch. 5), Karen Alter's chapter on the multiplication of international courts in the post-Cold War period (Ch. 4), and Pierre-Marie Dupuy and Jorge Viñuales's chapter on the challenge of proliferation (Ch. 7).

4 The Actors Involved

The different challenges presented above reveal certain tensions between the expectations from international adjudication and actual court performance. International courts and tribunals are expected to promote legitimate, effective, high quality, and comprehensive international governance, yet are perceived by some to fall short of these expectations. In actuality, however, some of the frustrated expectations are a reflection of the divergent constituency of international adjudication. International courts and tribunals serve a variety of parties—states, intergovernmental organizations (IGOs), and private litigants (e.g., corporations and individuals). Furthermore, their decisions impact a variety of third parties—non-participating states, other IGOs and, more generally, civil society. Some may be able to participate in proceedings, but some may not have had a voice during the process of adjudication.[50] Since international judicial rulings apply to countries with significant geographical, economic, and political diversity, and differing legal cultures and traditions, it is not surprising that judges fail to find solutions that please all and that there is a broad range of conflicting expectations applied to international adjudication.

One example of this tension is the well-known peace versus justice conundrum that confronts international criminal courts. One set of actors prioritizes peace-restoring measures, such as amnesties, and this objective may be in conflict with the objective of pursuing justice, which may disappoint a different set of actors. Yet a third group of actors may be focused on the long-term development of international criminal law. It may well be impossible to satisfy all of these audiences, and the effort to do so might make every audience unhappy. Another example concerns disappointment in the administration of trade law by international judicial bodies. Judges applying trade law, or adjudicating investor disputes, may generate outcomes that are at odds with values that are not fully covered by

[50] See e.g., in this handbook, Ronen and Naggan, Ch. 37.

the regime in question, such as the promotion of environmental concerns.[51] Tom Ginsburg's chapter on political constraints on adjudication (Ch. 22) deals with some of these issues.

But a diversity of actors exists not only outside the judicial institution, but also inside it. An international court is a complex organization, manned by groups of individuals with distinct career paths and institutional roles and structural incentives. While, traditionally, the focus in the literature has been on judges—the "men and women who decide the world's cases"[52]—and on their selection process, ethical commitment, different judicial roles, and the judicial strategy they employ (see e.g., Swigart and Terris, Ch. 28; Madsen, Ch. 18; and Seibert-Fohr, Ch. 35), there is increased appreciation of the function of other actors involved in the operation of the international justice machinery, such as prosecutors, counsel, and registrars (see e.g., Sthoeger and Wood, Ch. 29; Heller, Ch. 31; Gibson, Ch. 32; and Hoss and Cartier, Ch. 33).

The litigants and their legal representatives initially motivate the court to act and provide it with cases, that is, they offer it opportunities to make judicial impact. During the litigation they may open up or constrain the legal options available to the adjudicators, as litigators choose which legal arguments to pursue, populate the factual dockets and delineate the space available for judicial resolution (e.g., by agreeing or disagreeing across the aisle on law and fact). Natalie Klein (Ch. 26) examines which countries invoke international litigation; Antoine Vauchez (Ch. 30) deals with communities of international litigators, and Eran Sthoeger and Michael Wood (Ch. 29) discuss the international bar and their role in international adjudication. In some areas, the work of the legal representatives is so essential to the proper functioning of an international court and its legitimacy, so as to justify their integration into the court's structure. Thus, in the field of international criminal law, the office of the prosecutor operates as a branch of the court; and, increasingly, international criminal courts also integrate the office of defense (or public counsel) into their organizational frameworks. Kevin Jon Heller (Ch. 31) and Kate Gibson (Ch. 32) address, respectively, the role of prosecutors (from a sociological and legal perspective) and defense counsels.

The court's secretariat and registry, addressed in the handbook by Cristina Hoss and Stéphanie Cartier (Ch. 33), is another important locus of judicial-supporting activity. Not only does it provide the court with a range of legal and administrative services; the registry often serves as the court's *de facto* "foreign ministry," responsible for many of the interactions between the court and the outer world of national and international government institutions. In busy courts, such as

[51] See e.g., E Brown Weiss and J Jackson, "The Framework for Environment and Trade Disputes" in E Brown Weiss, JH Jackson, and N Bernasconi-Osterwalder (eds), *Reconciling Environment and Trade* (2nd edn, Leiden: Martinus Nijhoff 2008) 16–20.

[52] See Terris, Romano, and Swigart, note 22.

the ECtHR and the WTO dispute settlement system, the registry (or secretariat) offers adjudicators significant assistance in formulating decisions. This service is particularly important where judges serve on the bench for a short time only, and have little, if any, institutional memory of the court.

5 Theoretical Models

One final perspective to the study of international adjudication offered in the handbook is a theoretical one. There is already a considerable body of literature which places international adjudication under tools of academic investigation developed in a variety of intellectual disciplines, including political science, political philosophy, international relations, sociology, economics, behavioral studies, and inter-disciplinary critical studies. Such disciplines provide us with rich perspectives and important insights about international adjudication. Part III of the handbook comprises chapters surveying the state of the art in applying a multiplicity of disciplines to international adjudication

Other chapters too contain important theoretical insights about international adjudication, merging legal theory and other academic disciplines. Such insights may ultimately lead to the emergence of distinct inter-disciplinary theoretical frameworks for the study of international adjudication. For example, one strand of the theoretical literature views international courts and tribunals as a particular sub-set of international organizations. Under this approach, discussed for instance in Yuval Shany's chapter on jurisdiction and admissibility (Ch. 36), delegation and consent are key determinates in understanding the legal powers and authority of international adjudication bodies. Furthermore, as discussed in José Alvarez's chapter on the functions of international adjudication (Ch. 8) international judicial functions are intertwined with those of the international regimes in which they are institutionally embedded. Thus, the study of international courts cannot be divorced from the study of international organizations—their history, legal competences, and manner of operation, as made clear by Mary-Ellen O'Connell and Lenore VanderZee's chapter on the history of international adjudication (Ch. 3), Karen Alter's analysis of the decision to add international courts to existing multilateral agreements (Ch. 4), and also Cesare Romano's chapter (Ch. 6) on the dead-ends of international adjudication.

Second, an increasingly rich body of academic literature applies theories and analytical tools developed with a view to studying the operation of domestic courts in respect of the study of international courts. These "theoretical transplants" include the study of judicial behavior (Erik Voeten, Ch. 25) and legal sociology observations concerning the influence of the personal backgrounds of legal actors and social and political environments on the outcomes of adjudication processes (Mikael Madsen, Ch. 18).

Finally, a strand of the rational choice literature applies some distinct approaches to the relations between international courts and tribunals as well as the states and IGOs that created them. According to the principal–agent model, courts are tools in the hand of states and/or other entities that create and continue to control them in order to advance thereby their joint policy preferences; yet, under a competing trusteeship model, courts are understood as delegates no longer subject to direct state control. Such trustees are invested with considerable autonomy to decide legal issues pursuant to objective criteria, even if such decisions run contrary to the wishes of the litigating parties or the author's original intent. Law serves under both models as a central point of reference, controlling the mutual obligations and expectations of all of the relevant actors. These different ideas are discussed by José Alvarez (Ch. 8).

To some extent, all of these theoretical directions deal with the same core questions: what renders international courts legitimate and whom do they represent? What is their role in the promotion of international governance? Are they effective? Do they attain their goals? Do they advance the cause of justice? And are they fair? All handbook chapters provide us with important information and insights that may help us in confronting these problems and developing a better understanding of the promise and limits of international adjudication.

CHAPTER 2

ILLUSTRATIONS: A READER'S GUIDE

CESARE PR ROMANO,* KAREN J ALTER,** AND FRANCESCO SEBREGONDI***

THIS handbook contains a fold-out chart with several illustrations. They were prepared by Francesco Sebregondi of the Forensic Architecture Project at Goldsmiths, University of London, relying on data collected by Karen Alter and Cesare Romano. Our aim is to provide the reader with a quick overview of the rapidly expanding world of international adjudicative bodies.

Data visualization is not new, and in recent years it has benefited greatly from advances in software and computer graphics. Widely employed in science, data visualization allows readers to access and process large amounts of data in ways that would not otherwise be possible. A good visualization tool unlocks access to

* Professor of Law and W. Joseph Ford Fellow, Loyola Law School Los Angeles; Co-Director Project on International Courts and Tribunals.

** Professor of Political Science and Law at Northwestern University, and Permanent Visiting Professor at the iCourts Center for Excellence, University of Copenhagen Faculty of Law.

*** Researcher, Forensic Architecture Project, Goldsmiths, University of London.

knowledge, and does so quickly, efficiently, and effectively.[1] Yet legal scholarship is still largely devoid of visual representations, despite scholars' increasing reliance on large data sets and analyses of multiple institutions.[2] Given the considerably large and growing number of international adjudicative bodies, we believe these illustrations will help readers grasp with much greater ease some of the key points we try to express in words.

This guide explains what is included in and excluded from the illustrations. Excel documents with the raw data is available upon request.[3] The coding is also summarized in Annexes 1 and 2 at the end of this handbook. The abbreviations used are explained in the Abbreviations section of this handbook.

1 International Judicial Bodies: A Taxonomic Timeline

The timeline provides the reader with the following information, which is explained in greater detail in this guide:

1) Type of international judicial body: a list of the international judicial bodies organized by type.
2) Status: whether the body is functionally operational or inoperative.
3) Year: the year the body became functionally operational. For inactive bodies, we include the year the legal instrument became binding, or, if the instrument never entered into force, the year the instrument was adopted.
4) Number of states subject to the judicial body's compulsory jurisdiction.
5) Average rulings on the merits per year (2006–2011): a gauge of the body's level of activity.
6) Decade: decade during which the various judicial bodies became operational.

[1] See generally, E Tufte, *Envisioning Information* (Cheshire, CT: Graphics Press 1990); M Lima, *Visual Complexity: Mapping Patterns of Information* (New York: Princeton Architectural Press 2011).

[2] For an early attempt to visualize information on international adjudicative bodies, see C Romano, Research Matrix (*Project on International Courts and Tribunals*, 1999) <http://www.pict-pcti.org/matrix/matrixintro.html> accessed May 1, 2013. For a more recent attempt to utilize visual images to map international courts (criminal international courts), see <http://www.leitnercenter.org/files/News/International%20Criminal%20Tribunals.pdf> accessed June 1, 2013.

[3] Contact Cesare Romano at cesare.romano@lls.edu.

1.1 Type of international judicial body

As Chapter 1 explains, every classification requires making choices about what to include and exclude. Chapter 1 identifies two basic modes of international adjudication: through judicial bodies and through arbitration. The typology adopted for these illustrations follows the one used in Part II of this handbook, with the following exceptions:

First, to keep the timeline manageable, we focused on international judicial bodies, excluding arbitral bodies and international claims and compensation bodies. Because of their rather limited functions and jurisdiction, we also excluded international administrative tribunals, even though they are international judicial bodies.

Second, we divided the judicial bodies into four major types:

a) Inter-State Judicial Bodies
b) Human Rights Courts
c) Judicial Bodies of Regional Integration Agreements
d) International Criminal Courts

We further divided them into sub-types, depending on the fundamental institutional and jurisdictional attributes they shared.

Inter-State Judicial Bodies: This group includes judicial bodies that are accessible mostly, if not exclusively, by states. We say mostly because there are exceptions. For instance, the early Central American Court of Justice (Corte de Justicia Centroamericana), also known as the Court of Cartago, has been listed in this group even though it could—and did—hear cases brought by individuals.[4] Also, while theoretically all existing human rights courts can hear disputes brought by states against other states for violations of human rights, in practice that very rarely occurs. For that reason they have not been listed in this group but in a category of their own. Judicial bodies could be further divided into those whose jurisdiction is not limited to any area of the world (*global*), and those whose jurisdiction can only be accepted by states in a particular region (*regional*). Again, for the sake of simplicity, we omitted this from the timeline.

Human Rights Courts: Following Solomon Ebobrah's discussion, under this heading we listed the three regional courts currently in existence: European Court of Human Rights; Inter-American Court of Human Rights; and the African Commission on Human and Peoples' Rights, whose raison d'être is adjudicating cases brought by individuals alleging violation of certain human rights treaties.[5] As we discuss in the next paragraph, the images also reflect the fact that some regional economic courts have delegated jurisdiction over human rights issues.

[4] For more on the Court of Cartago, see, in this handbook, Romano, Ch. 6, at section 2.4.

[5] See, in this handbook, Ebobrah, Ch. 11.

Judicial Bodies of Regional Integration Agreements: This group includes a wide range of different judicial bodies. Their commonality is that they are organs of regional organizations aiming to integrate their member states, either economically and/or politically. Some of these regional courts focus solely on resolving trade disputes and were designed based on the template provided by the World Trade Organization (WTO) dispute settlement system (e.g. the Association of Southeast Asian Nations, or ASEAN, Appellate Body, and the Permanent Review Tribunal of the Mercosur). Others follow the model of the Court of Justice of the European Union (CJEU) (e.g. the Court of Justice of the African Union, the Andean Tribunal of Justice, and the Court of the European Free Trade Association).[6] Some blend functions of international courts with those of national courts (e.g. the Caribbean Court of Justice, or CCJ). Others have very narrow subject matter focus (e.g. the European Nuclear Energy Tribunal and the Judicial Board of the Organization of Arab Petroleum Exporting Countries). Again, for the sake of simplicity, we omitted further subdivision of this group.

It should be noted that, in recent years, a number of Courts of Regional Integration Agreements have been explicitly endowed with jurisdiction over human rights legal instruments (e.g. the CJEU and the Court of Justice of the Economic Community of Western African States, or the ECOWAS Court of Justice). We decided to list these bodies as belonging both to the Courts of Regional Integration Agreements and the Human Rights Courts groups. The Southern Africa Development Community Tribunal (SADC T) has recently been stripped of its jurisdiction to consider cases brought by individuals, including human rights cases.[7] We did not list it twice.

A number of other bodies have assumed, by way of jurisprudential reasoning, jurisdiction over human rights legal instruments (e.g. the East African Court of Justice).[8] Because this is not the result of a direct delegation by states but rather the voluntary, sometimes one-off, assumption of jurisdiction by these bodies, we decided not to double-list those in the Human Rights Courts group.

International Criminal Courts: We broke down these bodies into three sub-types: permanent courts, ad hoc tribunals, and military and hybrid tribunals. Although these categories are well established in literature, as the contribution from William Schabas explains, classifying international criminal courts is somewhat difficult.[9] Our definition follows more traditional categorizations.[10]

[6] See, in this handbook, Alter, Ch. 4.

[7] See, in this handbook, Romano, Ch. 6 and Ginsburg, Ch. 22.

[8] See, in this handbook, Ebobrah, Ch. 11.

[9] See, in this handbook, Schabas, Ch. 10.

[10] See C Romano, "A Taxonomy of International Rule of Law Institutions" (2011) 2 JIDS 241; C Romano, "Mixed Criminal Tribunals," in *Max Planck Encyclopedia of Public International Law* (3rd rev. edn, Oxford University Press 2012) 312–24.

1.2 Status

The judicial bodies we list are further distinguished by whether they are functionally operational or inoperative at the time this handbook is being finalized. We considered bodies operational when their constituting legal instrument entered into force; judges had been appointed; and the court had received cases (or, in the case of international criminal courts, investigations had been started). Annex 1 to this handbook includes the raw data that we used to divide inoperative bodies into three sub-types.

- "Forsaken" bodies are those whose constitutive legal instruments have not entered into force (e.g. the International Prize Court).
- "Dormant" bodies are those whose constitutive legal instruments have entered into force, but judges have not yet been selected or cases have not yet been filed (e.g. the ASEAN dispute settlement system). It also includes bodies that have been active in the past but have not received a case for the past three years (2009–2012) (e.g. the Judicial Board of the Organization of Arab Petroleum Exporting Countries).
- "Terminated" bodies are those that have ceased operations or have been replaced by other courts (e.g. the Permanent Court of International Justice).

We could have limited our illustration to currently operational bodies, but we felt that including inoperative courts helps to capture the fluidity of the international adjudicative domain over time. These images help to underscore the point made by Cesare Romano that not every effort to establish international adjudicative bodies succeeds.[11]

1.3 Year

It can be very hard to ascertain the year a judicial body is created. Does one use the date states decided to establish a judicial body? The year its founding legal instrument entered into force? The year when its judges were appointed? Or the year the judicial body formally opened its doors to litigants? These different founding benchmarks can be spread out over a decade. Usually, legal scholars date judicial bodies from the year their constituting legal instruments enter into force. However, this practice can be misleading, since it suggests the judicial body has remained idle for a number of years. Since this handbook is interested in practice and activity, we specify the year in which the judicial body became operational, meaning judges were appointed and the court stood ready to receive cases. For inoperative bodies

[11] See, in general, in this handbook, Romano, Ch. 6.

(e.g. dormant courts such as the Court of Justice of the Arab Maghreb Union), we list the year the legal instrument became binding. If the instrument never entered into force, we use the year the constituting legal instrument was adopted (e.g. for forsaken courts such as the International Prize Court). The last column to the right groups into decades the years in which the various judicial bodies became active.

1.4 Number of states consenting to the judicial body's compulsory jurisdiction

Since compulsory jurisdiction makes it hard for states to avoid litigation,[12] we decided to count how many states are subject to any given judicial body's compulsory jurisdiction. In the timeline, the thickness of the line is proportional to the number of states. There are three levels of thickness: less than 5 states, 6 to 30 states, and more than 30 states. The levels are somewhat arbitrary, of course. In Annex 1, we provide detailed data, accurate as of 1 July 2013, on which states are subject to the compulsory jurisdiction of which judicial bodies.[13]

Nowadays, most international judicial bodies enjoy *compulsory jurisdiction*. Their power to adjudicate a case does not derive from a direct, explicit, or an ad hoc act of consent (*consensual jurisdiction*), but derives from an act of consent removed in time from the act of adjudication. In some cases, consent to jurisdiction is required for membership in an international organization. For example, a state cannot be a member of the Council of Europe without accepting jurisdiction of the European Court of Human Rights (ECtHR). Joining the WTO requires accepting its compulsory dispute settlement process. Membership does not mean that the state in question will actually litigate. Some never do. But the member state is exposed to the possibility of litigation should an individual (as in the ECtHR) or another member state (as in the ECtHR and WTO) decide to initiate judicial proceedings.

For the other judicial bodies, a second act of consent is required, often in the form of ratification of an additional protocol or the filing of an optional declaration giving the judicial body compulsory jurisdiction. For example, the Inter-American Court of Human Rights (IACtHR) has compulsory jurisdiction over members of the Organization of American States (OAS) that have both ratified the American Convention of Human Rights (ACHR) and also made an optional declaration accepting the court's jurisdiction.

For judicial bodies with jurisdiction over all members and judicial bodies where a second act of consent is required, counting how many states are subject to any

[12] C Romano, "The Shift from the Consensual to the Compulsory Paradigm in International Adjudication: Elements for a Theory of Consent" (2007) 39 N.Y.U. J. Int'l L. & Pol. 791; K Alter, *The New Terrain of International Law: Courts, Politics, Rights* (Princeton University Press 2014) Chapter 1.

[13] This updates Alter's data from note 12, which ends in 2011 or 2012.

judicial body's jurisdiction is a straightforward task. There are several judicial bodies, however, for which assessing jurisdictional reach is fraught with difficulties. The first example is the Caribbean Court of Justice (CCJ). Like the CJEU, it is an international judicial body. It settles disputes between the state members of the Caribbean Community (currently 12) and/or the community institutions. It is also, however, a sort of national court of appeal, acting as the last instance of jurisdiction for Caribbean states that have accepted its appellate jurisdiction (currently only three). We could therefore count within its jurisdiction 12 states or only three. We decided to count 12 states, even though 80 percent of cases decided to date have been brought under the court's appellate jurisdiction and not its original jurisdiction.

Global courts also present significant challenges. For international criminal bodies, states that ratify the Rome Statute of the International Criminal Court (ICC) accept the court's compulsory jurisdiction. However, states that have not ratified the Rome Statute can still be subject to the ICC jurisdiction via a UN Security Council resolution.[14] Our illustration included only states party to the Rome Statute (a total of 122).

For ad hoc criminal tribunals, the question becomes how one counts the legal obligations of UN members. Only the perpetrators of crimes in the designated geographical space and time fall under the compulsory jurisdiction of ad hoc and hybrid criminal courts. Since Yugoslavia fragmented into a puzzle of states, one might list six, or even seven (counting Kosovo), states that fall under the jurisdiction of the International Criminal Tribunal for Former Yugoslavia (ICTY). Yet one could say that all UN members (currently 193) are subject to the jurisdiction of those two ad hoc criminal tribunals because they were created by the UN Security Council exercising its power under Chapter VII of the UN Charter, meaning all members must comply with the tribunal's orders. The same could be said about the International Criminal Tribunal for Rwanda (ICTR). In the end, we decided to count seven states for the ICTY and one for the ICTR as falling under each court's compulsory jurisdiction. The same challenge exists for some hybrid courts (e.g. those in East Timor or Kosovo) that have been created by fiat of the UN. Other hybrid criminal courts have been created by a treaty between a state and the UN (e.g. those in Cambodia, Sierra Leone, and Lebanon). For courts created by such treaties, one could count one state, or one state and one international organization, or one state and all members of the international organization in question, as being subject to that judicial body. We counted only one state as subject to the jurisdiction of each. The same counting method was used for the two international military tribunals (Nuremberg and Tokyo).

A different sort of challenge is presented by the International Court of Justice (ICJ) and International Tribunal for the Law of the Sea (ITLOS). A state can accept

[14] Sudan and Libya are two examples of states that have been referred to the ICC by resolution of the Security Council, notwithstanding their failure to ratify the court's Statute.

the compulsory jurisdiction of the ICJ in four distinct ways, making it difficult, if not impossible, to tell with certainty how many states are subject to the ICJ's compulsory jurisdiction at any given time. Cases can be heard by the ICJ if both states have agreed, ad hoc, to refer the matter; if there is a clause in a treaty conferring jurisdiction to the court for that specific treaty; if both states have made a unilateral optional declaration conferring jurisdiction to the court; or if the state decides to accept jurisdiction and appear before the court subsequent to the time the case was filed (*forum prorogatum*).[15] Here we decided to count only the 69 states that currently have on file an optional declaration of acceptance of the court's jurisdiction.[16]

ITLOS is even more complicated. The United Nations Convention on the Law of the Sea specifies four methods of dispute adjudication. States are largely free to choose between ITLOS, the ICJ, or one of two different types of special arbitration (called Annex VII and Annex VIII arbitration). The mechanism that will be used in any given dispute is the one that both parties accept. Should the parties not accept the same mechanism, and the dispute is subject to compulsory adjudication, the default mechanism is not ITLOS but rather ad hoc arbitration under Annex VII of the Convention.

While choice exists for most inter-state disputes, ITLOS has exclusive jurisdiction on a few limited issues, such as orders to promptly release detained vessels. Also, for disputes involving the mining of the deep seabed, the ITLOS Seabed Chamber has mandatory and exclusive jurisdiction. As explained in this handbook, ratification of the Law of the Sea Convention, although necessary, is not sufficient to establish compulsory jurisdiction of its various dispute settlement bodies and procedures.[17] Although the Convention provides in general for compulsory adjudication,[18] there are numerous and significant exceptions.[19] For example, neither disputes concerning overlapping territorial claims of coastal states nor disputes regarding coastal states' sovereign rights with respect to the living resources in their exclusive economic zones, are subject to compulsory adjudication.[20] Moreover, states can opt out of compulsory dispute-settlement procedures in disputes concerning sea boundary delimitations, historic bays or titles, military and law enforcement activities, and issues related to maintaining peace and security that are being dealt with by the UN Security Council.[21] So far, at least 35 states have opted out of compulsory

[15] See, in this handbook, Romano, Ch. 5.

[16] See International Court of Justice, "Jurisdiction" <http://www.icj-cij.org/jurisdiction/index.php?p1=5&p2=1&p3=3> accessed April 1, 2013.

[17] See, in this handbook, Romano, Ch. 5.

[18] United Nations Convention on the Law of the Sea (adopted 10 December 1982, entered into force November 16, 1994) 1833 U.N.T.S. 397, Article 286.

[19] United Nations Convention on the Law of the Sea, note 18, Art. 287.

[20] United Nations Convention on the Law of the Sea, note 18, Arts 297–8.

[21] United Nations Convention on the Law of the Sea, note 18, Art. 298.

adjudication for one or more of the allowed issues.[22] Thus, while all 165 states (plus the EU) that to date have ratified the Law of the Sea Convention are subject to compulsory jurisdiction of one or more of its adjudicative bodies for certain matters, because of the opt-out provisions and exceptions, adjudication may in fact not be compulsory, or the ITLOS may not have exclusive jurisdiction.

In the end we decided to list 33 states party to the Law of the Sea Convention that have made a declaration indicating ITLOS as a chosen means of dispute settlement—either exclusively or in concurrence with others.[23]

1.5 Average rulings on the merits per year (2006–2011)

To give a sense of the level of activity of international judicial bodies, we decided to provide the reader with the yearly average number of cases decided from 2006 to 2011.We chose a five-year span instead of the total number of cases decided by each judicial body because different courts have had considerably different life spans.[24] Raw data is included in Annex 1 at the end of this handbook.

We adopted some of Karen Alter's conservative counting methods from *The New Terrain of International Law: Courts, Politics, and Rights.*[25] By "cases decided" we mean cases that have been concluded, either because they have been decided on the merits, or because the court declared it lacked jurisdiction. For criminal courts, we counted cases in which the prosecution had begun.[26] But in general we did not take into consideration interim decisions, such as provisional measures, orders, and decisions on motions. Often, these represent the majority of the work of courts, with the final decision being only the tip of a much larger iceberg. We excluded appeals, too, as not all judicial bodies allow for appeals, and we did not want to double count individual cases. Whereas Alter included WTO panel rulings, this handbook classifies panels as ad hoc arbitral bodies so we include only WTO Appellate Body rulings. Alter excluded advisory opinions, which are not binding, but we have chosen to include them. We continue to exclude employee disputes, as only some of

[22] See United Nations Division for Ocean Affairs and the Law of the Sea "Settlement of Dispute Mechanisms" <http://www.un.org/Depts/los/settlement_of_disputes/choice_procedure.htm> accessed February 1, 2013.

[23] <http://www.un.org/Depts/los/settlement_of_disputes/choice_procedure.htm> accessed September 26, 2013.

[24] All data has been collected from international judicial bodies that post reports rulings on the internet, or that responded to Karen Alter's enquiries, counting the number of final and binding rulings in contentious cases issued in any given year.

[25] Alter, note 12.

[26] In certain criminal courts, such as the Special Court for Sierra Leone or the Extraordinary Chambers in the Courts of Cambodia, one case means one trial. Within the same trial, there might be multiple defendants.

the judicial bodies in this chart can adjudicate labor disputes brought by employees of international organizations.

This counting method significantly undercounts the activity of most courts. For example, of more than 80 decisions of the ECOWAS court through 2011—which include rulings on procedural and jurisdictional questions and staff cases—we counted only 51 as binding rulings. More than 150 cases have entered the ICJ's general list since its founding, but Alter counted only 77 binding rulings in contentious cases.[27] The WTO lists 427 cases formally filed in its dispute settlement system between 1994 and 2011.[28] Many of these were settled in the shadow of the law. Only 176 of the cases filed have resulted in binding panel rulings, and we drew from the smaller category of 114 in appellate body rulings.

Alter adopted a conservative counting method because she focused on rulings that bind states and international organizations. However, excluding interim and advisory opinions has warping effects, too. For instance, the ICC might look inactive because it has not concluded a case during the period of study. But during the same period, there have been several ongoing trials and many interim rulings. Thus, we included ICC cases that were initiated in our time period as long as the indicted individual was present in The Hague.

We indicated N/A (not available) where we were unable to find reliable data (e.g. for the Court of Justice of the Central African Monetary Community and the Court of Justice of the Common Market for Eastern and Southern Africa). We marked "—" for those judicial bodies that ceased to operate before our chosen time frame, even though they might have decided dozens of cases. Additionally, our data from the West African Economic and Monetary Union (WAEMU) ended in 2008.

Another caveat is that this data lags in time. Cases were counted in the year the case was concluded, not the year the case began. Especially for the ICTY and ICTR, where years may pass between the initiation of a formal investigation and the issuing of a legal verdict, the lag time and counting method surely understate the influence and activity of the international tribunals at any given moment.

Counting cases is a crude measurement to be sure. We did not control for the number of states falling under the judicial body's jurisdiction for two reasons. First, because, as we said, it can be difficult to determine how many to count. Second, a court might have few member states but many binding legal provisions and subject-matter violations, or many member states but few binding legal rules and

[27] Alter's count excludes ICJ advisory opinions (24), cases that are settled or dropped before the ICJ issues a ruling related to the merits of the case (31), and cases in which a party asked the ICJ to reconsider or clarify aspects of previous rulings. It includes 26 ICJ rulings in which the cases ended with the court declaring the case inadmissible or finding that it lacked jurisdiction to proceed. Alter, note 12, at 78.

[28] See WTO, "Disputes Status" <http://www.wto.org/english/tratop_e/dispu_e/dispu_status_e.htm> accessed February 1, 2013.

few violations. For criminal courts and human rights, a dearth of litigation might signal a dearth of serious legal violations, or it could represent highly limited access rules. For regional courts, there may be few binding legal texts that are applicable, and thus few rules to violate. For all of these reasons, we do not think that controlling by number of states is especially meaningful.

Finally, we need to stress that we decided to measure levels of activity, but not because we equate litigation with political salience or effectiveness. Levels of activity are largely determined by the scope of the given judicial body's jurisdiction and the extent of legal violations. The ICJ, which can decide only disputes between sovereign states, of which there are nearly 200 at present, cannot be expected to have the same level of activity as the ECtHR, which can, in theory, be accessed by 800 million individuals in 47 states. The jurisdiction of all international criminal courts has been tailored so that only a handful of, or at most a few dozen, indictees will be prosecuted and tried by each body. Still, we believe that levels of activity tell us something. Litigation is a sign of perceived value. Arguably judicial bodies are resorted to when the parties believe the judges will be independent legal interpreters, and that a ruling in one's favor will have a legal and political value.

2 International Judicial Bodies—Compulsory Jurisdiction Across the Globe

This illustration provides more fine-grained information on which states are subject to the compulsory jurisdiction of each international judicial body.

The image at the top maps acceptance of the compulsory jurisdiction of the three international judicial bodies with global reach: ICJ, ITLOS, and the WTO AB. The legend to the left provides the key for interpreting the colors:

- ICJ: Red
- ITLOS: Blue
- WTO AB: Green
- States subject to the jurisdiction of the ICJ and ITLOS but not the WTO: Purple
- States subject to the jurisdiction of the WTO AB and ITLOS but not the ICJ: Light blue
- States subject to the jurisdiction of the ICJ and WTO AB, but not ITLOS: Yellow
- States which have accepted the compulsory jurisdiction of all three courts: White
- States accepting the jurisdiction of none: Black

The second image is dedicated to the ICC. It maps ratification of the Rome Statute of the ICC; the states that have concluded bilateral agreements with the United States agreeing not to surrender US citizens to the ICC (so-called Article 98 agreements); and the states for which the ICC Prosecutor has initiated a formal investigation and/or prosecution.[29]

The third image focuses on judicial bodies of regional agreements of economic or political integration, again tracking which states are subject to the jurisdiction of each body. These Euler diagrams have been borrowed from Alter's book, *The New Terrain of International Law*, with a few modifications.[30] We omitted international criminal bodies. We listed only currently operative judicial bodies, and left out inoperative bodies even if they are just dormant.[31] The only exception is the ASEAN Appellate Body, which, to date, has not entered into operation, but which we believe will be activated soon and therefore was included. The data in these charts is accurate as of July 1, 2013, with a few exceptions.[32]

We list states that are not currently subject to the jurisdiction of a regional integration court or a human rights court. A number of these are subject to the jurisdiction of some judicial body, but those bodies are either inoperative (e.g. the Judicial Body of the Organization of the Arab Petroleum Exporting Countries—OAPEC) or are not strictly speaking judicial bodies. For instance, Canada and the United States are subject to compulsory adjudication under the North American Free Trade Agreement (NAFTA), but under NAFTA disputes are subject to arbitration, not judicial settlement, the focus of these illustrations.

[29] To date, the ICC has opened formal investigations into eight situations: the Democratic Republic of the Congo; Uganda; the Central African Republic; Darfur (Sudan); the Republic of Kenya; the Libyan Arab Jamahiriya; the Republic of Côte d'Ivoire; and Mali. Of these eight, four were referred to the court by the concerned state parties themselves (Uganda, Democratic Republic of the Congo, Central African Republic, and Mali), two were referred by the UN Security Council (Darfur and Libya) and two were begun *proprio motu* by the prosecutor (Kenya and Côte d'Ivoire). In addition to the eight situations where the prosecutor has opened formal investigations, several other situations are currently under "preliminary examination" including Afghanistan, Colombia, Guinea, Georgia, Honduras, Korea, Nigeria, and Palestine. We did not include these in our visual representation, as they might not lead to prosecution. For instance, earlier preliminary examinations regarding Iraq and Venezuela were closed when the prosecutor concluded that no investigation would be initiated because the necessary requirements had not been met. <http://www.icc-cpi.int/en_menus/icc/situations%20and%20cases/Pages/situations%20and%20cases.aspx> accessed June 1, 2013.

[30] Alter, note 12. [31] See section 1.2.

[32] We listed Bolivia as being a member of Mercosur, and thus subject to the jurisdiction of its Permanent Tribunal of Revision, even though Bolivia's accession to Mercosur had not been completed as of July 1, 2013. Also, we listed only four states as being subject to the jurisdiction of the Central American Court of Justice, even though in a recent case the court has said that by virtue of having ratified the Protocol of Tegucigalpa and becoming a member of the Central American Integration System (SICA), Costa Rica is *ipso facto* subject to the jurisdiction of the court, with no need for separate ratification of the court's Statute. Central American Court of Justice, Judgment No. 12-06-12-2011, June 21, 2012 <http://vianica.com/downloads/docs/1.pdf> accessed February 1, 2013. See in this handbook, Romano, Ch. 6, at section 2.4.

Finally, the last image shows the locations of the seats of the various operational judicial bodies. Most international judicial bodies carry out their functions exclusively at their seat, but a few are able to move their locations temporarily. For instance, since the early 2000s the IACtHR has started holding some of its sessions in various cities across the Americas. The ECOWAS Court of Justice hears one or two cases a year in a different locale. Although the seat of the Special Court for Sierra Leone is in Freetown, Sierra Leone, in recent years the Special Court has held most of its hearings in The Hague.

Suggested Reading

Alter, K, *The New Terrain of International Law: Courts, Politics, Rights* (Princeton University Press 2014).

Lima, M, *Visual Complexity: Mapping Patterns of Information* (New York: Princeton Architectural Press 2011).

Mackenzie, R, Romano, C, Sands, P, Shany, Y (eds), *The Manual on International Courts and Tribunals* (2nd edn, Oxford University Press 2010).

Romano, C, *Research Matrix* (*Project on International Courts and Tribunals*, 1999) <http://www.pict-pcti.org/matrix/matrixintro.html> accessed May 1, 2013.

Romano, C, "A Taxonomy of International Rule of Law Institutions" (2011) 2 JIDS 241.

Tufte, E, *Envisioning Information* (Cheshire, CT: Graphics Press 1990).

CHAPTER 3

THE HISTORY OF INTERNATIONAL ADJUDICATION

MARY ELLEN O'CONNELL* AND LENORE VANDERZEE**

For decades, international law scholars have cited with approval HLA Hart's inclusion of international law in the general category of "law" in his classic work,

* Robert and Marion Short Chair in Law and Research Professor of International Dispute Resolution—Kroc Institute, University of Notre Dame.

** J.D., LL.M.; Ph.D. Candidate, Political Science and Peace Studies, University of Notre Dame; Chief of Staff and Adjunct Instructor of Political Science, SUNY Canton. I wish to express my appreciation and gratitude to my co-author, constant mentor and friend.

The Concept of Law (Oxford: Clarendon Press 1961). Hart was the renowned Oxford scholar of jurisprudence who critiqued his nineteenth-century predecessor, John Austin, for, among other errors, dismissing international law as nothing more than "positive morality."[1] Hart's defense of international law was, however, hardly robust. While he acknowledged that international law qualified as law, he also found it to be only a kind of "primitive" law. One of the reasons Hart gave for international law's lower status included the lack of a judicial system in which the courts have compulsory jurisdiction. Hart raised this point for the first time in Chapter 10. In the nine preceding chapters he never mentioned the necessity for sophisticated legal systems to have courts with compulsory jurisdiction. Only when he reached international law did he focus on this particular condition of advanced legal systems.

The international legal system has courts and other means of adjudication and has always had such means. What the system lacks are courts with general, compulsory jurisdiction over states. Not only does international law lack such courts, international law scholars ceased advocating for general compulsory jurisdiction more than 30 years ago. For around a century, from the 1880s to the 1980s, scholars emphasized the need for international courts with compulsory jurisdiction. These scholars, together with peace activists, strove to convince governments to create international courts. Then the effort ended.

This chapter on the history of international adjudication will show that courts and tribunals have been part of international law since the emergence of modern international law with the rise of the state system in the mid-seventeenth century. Courts and their role within international law have also been a persistent part of the theoretical debates about the nature of international law. From an early emphasis on arbitration, support grew for the creation of courts with general compulsory jurisdiction. By the late twentieth century, the theoretical trend shifted toward interest in courts with special subject matter jurisdiction, including human rights, trade, law of the sea, and international crime. Interestingly, the rise or "proliferation" of specialized courts has resulted in quite wide-reaching compulsory jurisdiction in specialized areas, as Karen Alter discusses in the next chapter. At the same time, the shift away from a focus on a strong hierarchical judicial system to a more horizontal one may also be leading to fragmentation in the law and a weakening of international law's identity as a unified legal system.

[1] J Austin, *The Province of Jurisprudence Determined* (first published 1954, London: Weidenfeld and Nicolson 1998) 127, 140–2.

1 Early History of International Adjudication

Formal processes of inter-group dispute resolution long pre-date the rise of modern international law in 1648. David Bederman describes the practice of arbitration among the Greek city states and communities within the Roman Empire: "The institution of settling disputes by the decision of a third party was begun, reputedly, by the Olympian gods."[2] In analyzing this ancient practice, he does not inquire into why it arose but does consider why it functioned. He indicates that it was the "reasoned character" of awards that "was essential for their legitimacy and enforcement."[3] He also acknowledges the link between religious faith and arbitration but concludes that the production of reasoned opinions gets the credit for the success of inter-group dispute resolution.[4] The facts indicate, however, that both faith and reason were in play.

Both faith and reason plainly influenced the architects of international law who advocated arbitration as an alternative to war. Several of the Spanish Scholastics, Dominican priests writing in the fifteenth and sixteenth centuries during the decline of papal authority over secular politics, urged that arbitration substitute for decision-making by the Pope on such issues as whether resorting to war complied with the Just War Doctrine.[5] Hugo Grotius, whose 1625 treatise, *On the Law of War and Peace*, is the founding text of modern international law, was a devout Christian, indeed a Protestant theologian. Grotius offered arbitration as an alternative to war that could provide for peaceful settlement of disputes among rulers who no longer recognized a common political or religious leader.

Grotius made his case for arbitration in part by citing Christ's teaching respecting peace, but also by citing the teachings of other traditions.[6] He cited the Greek historian Thucydides for the proposition that "[i]t is not lawful to proceed against

[2] D Bederman, *International Law in Antiquity* (Cambridge University Press 2001) 82. Loosely analogous developments can also be seen in early periods of Middle Eastern history, in the Far East, and in the rise of Islam. A Giustini, "Compulsory Adjudication in International Law: The Past, the Present, and Prospects for the Future" (1985) 9 Fordham Int'l L. J. 213, 217. For a discussion of continuity in the history of international dispute resolution, see CG Roelofsen, "International Arbitration and Courts" in B Fassbender and A Peters (eds), *The Oxford Handbook of The History of International Law* (Oxford University Press 2012) 145–69.

[3] Bederman, note 2, at 84. [4] Bederman, note 2, at 85.

[5] ME O'Connell, "Arbitration and the Avoidance of War: The Nineteenth-Century American Vision" in C Romano (ed.), *The United States and International Courts and Tribunals* (Cambridge University Press 2009), at 24–5.

[6] H Grotius, *De Jure Belli ac Pacis Libri Tres* (1646, FW Kelsey, tr., Oxford University Press 1925, reprinted 1995) bk II, ch xxiii, sec. 8 and bk III, ch. xx, sec. xlvi–xlviii.

one who offers arbitration just as against a wrongdoer."[7] Grotius also supplied precedents to bolster his argument, such as the 12th century treaty concluded by the Kings of Castile and Navarre in which they agreed to submit their differences for resolution to Henry II of England, the King of Castile's father-in-law, and the King of Navarre's nephew.[8] In the thirteenth century, the German cities of Hamburg and Lübeck agreed to settle their disputes by arbitration, and in 1291, the cantons of Uri, Schwyz, and Nidwald, in what would later become Switzerland, also agreed to resolve disputes peacefully through arbitration.[9]

Grotius's ideas are reflected in the treaties known as the Peace of Westphalia that formally ended the Thirty Years War in Europe. After three years of negotiation, more than 300 parties adopted two treaties that committed the warring parties to principles of non-intervention, religious tolerance, and the peaceful settlement of disputes through "amicable settlement or legal discussion."[10] Should the disputing parties prove unable to agree after three years, all other parties to the treaties were to "take up arms with all council and might in order to subdue the offender."[11] The Peace of Westphalia essentially established the modern system of sovereign, co-equal states and with that, the modern system of international law.

After Grotius, Emmerich de Vattel is considered the most important writer on international law. Vattel was a practicing diplomat and brought to his book, *The Law of Nations* (1758), a practical appreciation of how the world works and, therefore, how international law could be made to work in the real world. Vattel also promoted arbitration as a practical, rational and ethical means of resolving interstate disputes. He described the methods available to ensure that the outcome of arbitrations would be honored. One method involved weak states arranging with stronger ones to act as guarantors, meaning the guarantor would go to war on behalf of the weak state if the weak state won the arbitration but the stronger state failed to comply.[12] Vattel also suggested having parties pay a performance bond to a neutral party or exchange hostages to be held until the arbitration ended and the dispute was settled.[13]

[7] Grotius, note 6, at 562.

[8] Grotius, note 6, at 562; see, Giustini, note 2, at 217 (citing G Schwartzenberger, *A Manual of International Law* (5th edn, London: London Institute of World Affairs 1967) 242).

[9] J Allain, *A Century of International Adjudication: The Rule of Law and its Limits* (The Hague, Netherlands: T.M.C. Asser Press 2000) 14.

[10] O'Connell, note 5, at 31 (citing the Peace of Westphalia, 1648).

[11] O'Connell, note 5, at 31.

[12] E de Vattel, *The Law of Nations or the Principles of Natural Law, Applied to the Conduct and the Affairs of Nations and of Sovereigns* (1758 edn, CG Fenwick, tr., Washington D.C.: Carnegie Institute of Washington 1916) 193–4.

[13] De Vattel, note 12, at 189–92.

2 The Golden Age of Arbitration

Vattel's practical advice proved useful to the founders of the United States. The Americans managed through war to create an independent sovereign state but realized that to maintain their independence, they would need international law and peaceful processes. In the Jay Treaty of 1794, the United States and Great Britain agreed to use arbitration to settle the disputes remaining from the War of Independence. The Jay Treaty provided for the creation of three mixed commissions, composed equally of nationals of the two countries, to settle matters that were left outstanding after a process of negotiation.[14] Between 1794 and 1804, 536 arbitral awards were made under the Jay Treaty, beginning with the St. Croix River Arbitration of 1798, which delineated much of the Canada–United States boundary.[15] The use of arbitration among states grew steadily thereafter so that the nineteenth century can been seen as a kind of golden age of arbitration.

The Jay Treaty's provision for arbitration was a result of practical necessity and familiarity with the writing of Grotius and Vattel by America's founding fathers. The use of arbitration, especially to settle a boundary, was also an inspiration to the developing global peace movement. The peace movement had begun through the efforts of pacifist religious communities—Quakers, Mennonites, Anabaptists—and Christian anti-war leaders. International law and processes such as arbitration gave the peace movement secular and practical alternatives to war. While less prominent today, the peace movement continues and may be counted as the most sustained effort by non-state actors to influence public policy in the global sphere.[16]

The movement's early efforts to promote alternatives to war consisted of speaking tours and essay competitions, but these led to direct pressure on governments by petitions, letter-writing campaigns, and meetings with governmental officials.[17] Following the creation of peace societies in several US states, Britons formed the British Society for the Promotion of Permanent and Universal Peace. Similar societies followed in France and Switzerland. The various US organizations consolidated into the American Peace Society (APS) in 1828 under the leadership of William Ladd. In 1838, the APS secured a resolution from the Legislature of the

[14] International Court of Justice, "History" at <http://www.icj-cij.org/court/index/php?p1=1&p2=1> accessed July 7, 2012.

[15] O'Connell, note 5, at 32. Roelofsen seems to underplay the importance of the Jay Treaty by, for example, not citing the sheer number of awards. Roelofsen, note 2, at 160.

[16] See e.g., LS Wittner, *Rebels Against the War: The American Peace Movement* (Philadelphia, PA: Temple University Press 1984); D Cortright, *Peace: A History of Movements and Ideas* (Cambridge University Press 2008).

[17] Allain, note 9, at 13–14.

Commonwealth of Massachusetts that was forwarded to the US president, calling on him to lead in forming an international congress to codify international law and to establish a court for the settlement of international disputes.[18]

While the APS fragmented over the issue of abolishing slavery, there were efforts to consolidate the movement internationally. The first international peace conference met in London in 1843. The delegates agreed to advocate for compulsory arbitration clauses in bilateral and multilateral treaties to settle disputes over treaty interpretation and application.[19] As the international movement grew in numbers and strength, more of its proponents became elected officials, both in the US and Europe. This allowed the movement to "assail governments from within" and gain more direct—and perhaps more effective—influence.[20]

The international peace movement may even claim some credit for the establishment of the landmark *Alabama* Claims arbitration of 1872, which addressed US charges that Britain violated its neutral duties by failing to prevent the building and outfitting of ships for the Confederacy during the US Civil War. Arbitrators from Brazil, Italy, Switzerland, Great Britain, and the United States sitting in Geneva awarded the United States $15.5 million in damages, which Great Britain paid in full just one year later. This award—and, indeed, the arbitral process itself—energized the peace movement and motivated states to engage in arbitration to settle more disputes.[21] The single most important fact about the *Alabama* Claims was the example of a great power voluntarily entering into arbitration with a weaker state over an important issue and abiding by the result. Following the award, the US House of Representatives unanimously passed a motion requesting that the president ensure that arbitration clauses be included in future treaties.[22]

In 1873, the Russian Tsar acted as sole arbitrator in a dispute between Peru and Japan, the *Maria Luz case*, which Japan won. The decision helped demonstrate the universality of international law and the rise of internationally protected human rights.[23] In 1874, the Italian Chamber of Deputies passed a resolution promoting arbitration as:

> an acceptable and frequent mode of solving, according to the dictates of equity, such international questions as may admit of that mode of arrangements, as well as to introduce

[18] Allain, note 9, at 11. [19] Allain, note 9, at 13. [20] Allain, note 9, at 20.

[21] Cortright, note 16, at 49. According to Grewe, there were varying numbers depending on the classification criteria. Conciliation and arbitration can frequently look quite similar. It is safe to say, however, that arbitral awards were copious and the number grew throughout the 1800s. See O'Connell, note 5, at 37 (citing W Grewe, *The Epochs of International Law* (M Byers tr. & ed., Berlin: De Gruyter 2000) 519).

[22] O'Connell, note 5, at 37.

[23] AAM Stuyt, *Survey of International Arbitrations* no. 104 (Dordrecht: Martinus Nijhoff 1990), 107; see also Roelofson, note 2, at 163–4.

opportunely into any treaty with those Powers a clause to the effect that any difference of opinion respecting the interpretation and execution of those treaties is to be referred to arbitration.[24]

In 1889, the Universal Peace Congress was organized again, almost 50 years since the previous congress. Significantly, the discussion clearly shifted from arbitration to international courts. The Congress occurred at a time when the "peace through law" movement was gaining political and intellectual support. Adherents of this movement believed that international judicial bodies were effective alternatives to war, and permanent courts were predicted to be a particularly effective mechanism to settle international disputes.[25] The American peace movement was particularly enthusiastic about courts, inspired by the US Supreme Court's effectiveness in settling disputes between the semi-sovereign states of the Union.[26] With this model in mind, permanent courts were viewed as more effective than arbitral tribunals because they could "respond quickly to international crises, generate accumulated jurisprudence that would somewhat reduce the uncertainties attendant on adjudication, and attract, by virtue of their accumulated prestige, a good level of compliance."[27] The possibility of developing international law was a common theme among those who advocated for international courts in preference to arbitral tribunals. The Russian legal scholar Kamarowsky, for example, in *Le Tribunal International* (1887) proposed a voluntary court of international justice, which would not only settle international disputes between states but also aid in the codification and promulgation of international law.[28]

US President and Chief Justice of the Supreme Court William Howard Taft raised another advantage of courts over arbitration, again illustrated by the US Supreme Court. At the core of the court is the centrality of the law rather than the desire to achieve some agreed-upon solution acceptable to both sides: "[A court] has the authority to decide questions according to right and justice, and it does."[29] This was, in Taft's view, the primary shortcoming of international arbitration and the best argument for a world court. The campaign for a permanent international court with compulsory jurisdiction thus grew out of both positive experiences with arbitration but also its limitations.

[24] Allain, note 9, at 14 (citing L Levi, *War and Its Consequences: Economical, Commercial, Financial, and Moral; With a Proposal for the Establishment of a Court of International Reference and Arbitration* (1882) 74–5).

[25] Y Shany, "No Longer a Weak Department of Power? Reflections on the Emergence of a New International Judiciary" (2009) 20 EJIL 73.

[26] DD Caron, "War and International Adjudication: Reflections on the 1899 Peace Conference" (2000) 94 AJIL 4, 10.

[27] Allain, note 9, at 77.

[28] JH Ralston, *International Arbitration, from Athens to Locarno* (Palo Alto, CA: Stanford University Press 1929) 125–6.

[29] Ralston, note 28, at 102–3.

Of course there were setbacks on the road to establishing international courts. US President William McKinley had been a strong proponent of arbitration and other means for the peaceful settlement of international disputes. When Spain offered to settle the United States' claims respecting Cuba, however, McKinley declined. Instead, the United States went to war with Spain in 1898, and subsequently acquired its first colonies.[30] Anger within the peace movement and beyond over the Spanish-American War did re-energize the movement, but victory in the war was another sign of the United States' growing military power, a fact that brought with it the belief that the United States did not need arbitration—it could impose its will on other states by force or the threat of force.

Russia, by contrast, was a declining military power, as Tsar Nicholas II well knew. Concerned about the proliferation of new military technologies and knowing that Russia was unable to keep pace, the Tsar called for a conference in The Hague in 1899 on arms limitations. Twenty-six states attended, including Austria-Hungary, Germany, France, Great Britain, Italy, and the United States. The peace movement succeeded in having arbitration and peaceful settlement of disputes added to the agenda.[31]

3 From Arbitration to Courts

Working from the writing of William Ladd earlier in the nineteenth century,[32] Ivan Bloch produced a multi-volume treatise calling for a permanent international court; all six volumes were published in full in 1898.[33] The work was so influential that Tsar Nicholas, who initiated the 1899 Conference, was said to have read it in its entirety and even had several conversations with Bloch.[34] Bloch did not think simply that international adjudication *could* be an alternative to war. He argued that the technologies of war rendered armed conflict so horrifying and destructive, the leaders of nations needed to be persuaded that international adjudication *must* be used to avoid war.[35]

Informed by the peace-through-law movement, including Bloch and his associates, many of the proposals by various national delegations at the First Hague Peace Conference included plans for an international court. Elihu Root, who would found

[30] O'Connell, note 5, at 39. [31] O'Connell, note 5, at 21 n. 60.

[32] W Ladd, *Essay on a Congress of Nations for the Adjustment of International Disputes Without Resort to Arms* (first published 1840, Oxford University Press 1916).

[33] Caron, note 26, at 11. [34] Caron, note 26, at 11. [35] Caron, note 26, at 12.

the American Society of International Law in 1906, was US Secretary of War in 1899. He did not attend the Hague Conference but sent instructions with the US delegation to propose the establishment of a permanent international court.[36] Root had been a successful lawyer in New York City before taking up government service. He was a pragmatist and appreciated the ability of courts to settle disputes efficiently and effectively. He admired the way the US Supreme Court settled disputes among the states of the Union and believed an international court could perform in the same manner respecting sovereign state disputes. Root did not see arbitration as capable of producing the type of results that the Supreme Court produced—a court was needed for that.[37]

Perhaps due to the lack of a supreme court in Britain at this period, prominent British legal scholars approached the international court idea more cautiously than Root. Sir Henry Maine, a prominent British international law professor at Cambridge, was not entirely convinced that a permanent court would be the panacea the peace movement claimed. He well understood the limitations of arbitration, particularly ad hoc tribunals that were slow to be established and lacked reliable means for enforcing awards. Maine also believed, however, that a permanent international court would have similar challenges: "[T]he want of coercive power is, in fact, the one important drawback which attends all attempts to improve International Law by contrivances imitated from the internal economy of states... like the administration of law by organized tribunals."[38] Yet in the end, Maine supported the creation of a permanent court, because even with its limitations, it would be better than reliance on ad hoc arbitration.[39]

Indeed, the British were the first at the Hague Conference to present a proposal for international dispute resolution. It included a permanent international arbitral tribunal—a proposal supported by the Americans and the French, although the French wanted only consensual jurisdiction with arbitrators chosen by the states.[40] The Russians wanted compulsory arbitration with respect to certain pre-designated disputes. These four delegations worked together to come up with a compromise proposal that could be widely accepted. The British proposal for a permanent international court was dropped, as was the less ambitious goal of a permanent arbitral

[36] RP Anand, *Studies in International Adjudication* (Dobbs Ferry, NY: Oceana Publications 1969) 2 (citing E Root, *Instructions to the American Delegates to the Hague Peace Conferences*, J Brown Scott (ed.) (Oxford University Press 1916) 79–80).

[37] Root saw arbitration as focused too much on diplomacy rather than law. He saw the need at the Second Peace Conference for a more judge-based, permanent tribunal. See E Root, "The Hague Peace Conferences, Address in Opening the National Arbitration and Peace Congress" in R Bacon and J Brown Scott (eds), *Addresses on International Subjects* (Cambridge, MA: Harvard University Press 1916) 142.

[38] Caron, note 26, at 12 (quoting HS Maine, *International Law: The Whewell Lectures* (London: J. Murray 1888) 213).

[39] Caron, note 26, at 12. [40] Caron, note 26, at 15.

tribunal. Even in its diminished form, the Germans remained steadfastly opposed to the proposal for arbitration. For them, arbitration was a delaying tactic that gave rivals time to prepare for war.[41] Yet the Germans, in the end, agreed to an arbitral tribunal, under the condition that it would be tested before being established on a permanent basis. Some delegates credited the peace movement for helping to soften Germany's position.[42]

While no permanent court was established, to the disappointment of the peace movement, the delegates to the 1899 Peace Conference agreed in the Hague Convention on the Pacific Settlement of International Disputes (I) to establish the Permanent Court of Arbitration (PCA), consisting of a registry, a Permanent Administrative Council made up of diplomatic representatives from state parties, and a list of arbitrators from which states could select should they voluntarily submit a dispute to arbitration. James Brown Scott famously wrote that the PCA "is not permanent, because it is not composed of permanent judges; it is not accessible because it has to be formed for each individual case; and finally is not a court, because it is not composed of judges."[43] However, despite its modest goal of encouraging states to submit disputes to international arbitration, it did signify progress toward a permanent judicial body with compulsory jurisdiction.[44] As the first permanent arbitral body with jurisdiction to hear any type of inter-state legal dispute, it was hailed as a major accomplishment.[45] After the establishment of the PCA in 1903, Britain and France concluded a general arbitration treaty that served as a model for similar instruments among other states, using the PCA as the third-party dispute settlement mechanism.[46]

More importantly, the various dispute resolution mechanisms established in 1899 and later at the Second Hague Peace Conference in 1907 did have some success. Proponents of peaceful settlement have long cited two cases in particular as successes under the Pacific Settlement Conventions. The 1909 *Deserters of Casablanca* arbitration settled a dispute between France and Germany in which France tried to prevent Germany's consul in Morocco from taking French Foreign Legion deserters out of the country by ship.[47] In the 1906 *Dogger Bank* case, a commission of inquiry found that the Russian Navy's attack on British fishing vessels could not be defended under a claim of mistake. The Russians argued that they believed the British vessels were Japanese torpedo boats. The claim could not be sustained in light of the facts,

[41] Caron, note 26, at 16. [42] Caron, note 26, at 16.

[43] J Brown Scott, *The Hague Court Reports* (Oxford University Press 1916) xiii.

[44] See EA Posner and JC Yoo, "A Theory of International Adjudication" (Boalt Working Papers on Public Law, March 3, 2004) 7 at <http://escholarship.org/uc/item/0h7602tx> accessed July 7, 2012.

[45] WE Butler, "The Hague Permanent Court of Arbitration" in MW Janis (ed.), *International Courts for the Twenty-First Century* (Dordrecht: Martinus Nijhoff 1992) 44.

[46] Allain, note 9, at 31.

[47] *Deserters of Casablanca* (France v. Germany), at <www.pca-cpa.org/showfile.asp?fil_id=188> accessed July 18, 2012.

and Russia agreed to pay significant compensatory damages. This inquiry probably averted a retaliatory attack and even an armed conflict between the parties.[48]

The 1899 Conference also had the result of moving the issue of peaceful settlement of disputes fully onto government agendas. Instead of the creative and committed members of the peace movement advocating for more robust means of peaceful settlement of disputes, politicians and civil servants took up the issue. This shift may well account for why courts with universal compulsory jurisdiction were never finally established.[49] After the 1899 Conference, the peace movement had lost some of its momentum. Still, several developments stimulated interest in expanding the results of the 1899 Conference, including US President Theodore Roosevelt's successful mediation of the Russo-Japanese War and the Dogger Bank inquiry. Activists began lobbying for another peace conference.[50]

In 1907, states gathered for the Second Hague Peace Conference. Again the British and American delegations brought plans for a world court. Elihu Root joined the American delegation this time,[51] and arrived in The Hague with the goal of bringing "about in the Second Conference a development of the Hague tribunal into a permanent tribunal... The court should be of such dignity, consideration, and rank that the best and blest jurists will accept appointment to it, and the whole world will have absolute confidence in its judgments."[52] The proposal had wide support among the delegations but floundered on the issue of the selection of judges. The small powers wanted equal authority to appoint judges as the great powers; the great powers, however, would not accept this proposal.[53]

There was also a move to revive compulsory jurisdiction for the PCA. Elihu Root said in his instructions to the 1907 delegates that while states might be reluctant to bring cases before arbitrators, "subject to all the considerations and influences which affect diplomatic agents," they may be more inclined to resort to courts, whose judges decide "questions of fact and law upon the record before them under a sense of judicial responsibility."[54] Once again, Germany blocked the proposal, arguing that commitments to arbitrate should be created through bilateral treaties, not a multilateral one.[55] The most that advocates of compulsory jurisdiction could manage

[48] MW Janis, "The International Court" in MW Janis (ed.), *International Courts for the Twenty-First Century* (Dordrecht: Martinus Nijhoff Publishers 1992) 16.

[49] Butler, note 45, at 24.

[50] See RN Lebow, "Accidents and Crises: The Dogger Bank Affair" (1978) 31 Nav. War. Col. Rev. 66.

[51] M Pomerance, *The United States and the World Court as a Supreme Court of the Nations* (Dordrecht: Martinus Nijhoff 1996) 54–5.

[52] Anand, note 36, at 3 (citing E Root, *Instructions to the American Delegates to the Hague Peace Conferences*, J Brown Scott (ed.) (New York 1916), at 8–9).

[53] Anand, note 36, at 4.

[54] E Root, "Instructions to the U.S. Delegation to the Second Hague Conference 1907" (1907) U.S. Foreign Relations 1135.

[55] Butler, note 45, at 26.

was a sort of default jurisdiction for the PCA in disputes over contract debts where the parties had agreed to arbitrate, but had not specified an alternative to the PCA.[56]

This default clause as well as the Convention of 1907 Respecting the Limitation of the Employment of Force for the Recovery of Contract Debts[57] was prompted by the British, German, and Italian blockade of Venezuelan ports when Venezuela suspended payment on debts. The European creditor nations had won an award in the PCA, the *Venezuelan Preferential* case,[58] and so apparently had the right to impose the blockade. The delegates to the 1907 Conference agreed, however, that the Drago Doctrine holding the resort to armed force inappropriate to collect a public debt would be the rule going forward.[59] The rule has been in effect for over 105 years and constitutes a clear example of effective legal restraint against resort to force and the impact of law on state behavior.

Regarding the goal of transforming the PCA into a real court, however, the Hague Conference delegates had less to show for their efforts. They did agree to the formation of one actual court in a specialized area of international law. They agreed to form a permanent prize court, but then never actually created it.[60] Very likely the prize court was not established for the same reason that the delegates had managed to agree to its formation in the first place. By 1907, the taking of prizes was coming to an end. The beginning of the end had occurred as far back as 1856, when parties to the Paris Declaration on Maritime Law had agreed to end the practice of commissioning private persons to carry out actions on the high seas such as combating pirates. By World War I, most naval powers had ended the practice of sharing revenues from the sale of captured ships even with their own officers. National admiralty courts could handle the few prize cases that arose.

Root was understandably disappointed with the modest results of the 1907 Conference. He turned his efforts to the Americas and helped Central American states establish the Central American Court of Justice (CACJ) in 1908.[61] The Central American Court was the first permanent court for the settlement of inter-state disputes.[62] The hope of its founders was that, as a dispute settlement body of last resort, the very presence of the court would prevent the escalation of disputes. Indeed,

[56] Hague Convention for the Pacific Settlement of International Disputes of 1907 (I), Art. 53.2.

[57] Hague Convention Respecting the Limitation of the Employment of Force for the Recovery of Contract Debts, October 18, 1907, 36 Stat. 2241.

[58] *Venezuelan Preferential Case* (Germ, GB, and Italy v. Venezuela) (1904) Scott Hague Court Rep 123–8.

[59] Allain, note 9, at 29.

[60] O'Connell, note 5, at 40.

[61] FL Grieves, *Supranational and International Adjudication* (Champaign, IL: University of Illinois Press 1969) 22; see also PC Jessup, 2 *Elihu Root* 50 (1937); see also E Root—Biographical (*Nobel Prize*) <www.nobel.se/peace/laureates/1912/root-bio.html> accessed July 7, 2012.

[62] HM Hill, "Central American Court of Justice" in *Max Planck Encyclopedia of Public International Law* (Rudolf Bernhardt (ed.), vol. 1, Oxford University Press 1992) 41–4.

according to William I. Buchanan, High Commissioner of the Court, who represented the United States at the court's inauguration, "[a]n entire absence of business for the court would be the highest justification for its creation."[63] The CACJ had broad jurisdiction that included a right of individuals to bring cases against states, including states of which they were not nationals. Of the ten cases heard by the CACJ, individuals brought five.

The CACJ statute stipulated that the court would remain in existence for only ten years unless the state parties agreed to renew it. For the first several years, renewal seemed likely, but in 1916, the United States ended its support for implementation of the CACJ's decisions. This change of policy proved to be the court's undoing.[64] Root's influence in Washington had waned, with the election of the new president, Woodrow Wilson. Wilson had been a professor of government at Princeton University and proved himself to be far more interested in governance institutions than courts. Wilson defied the peace movement and entered World War I on the side of Britain. After the war, the US delegation to the Paris Peace Conference contained no prominent advocates for international courts.

Britain's Lord Phillimore also turned away from international courts at the Peace Conference. He presented a draft in Paris for a new organization without any plan for a court, despite the UK's vigorous support of a world court at the Hague Conferences. The French plan did include a court and specified that it should have broad jurisdiction.[65] Many in the United States continued to support a court and Wilson's adviser, Colonel House, included a world court in his draft plan. The court would have "jurisdiction to determine any difference between nations which has not been settled by diplomacy, arbitration or otherwise."[66] President Wilson, however, remained indifferent—if not hostile—to the idea of a world court. Wilson did not like lawyers and did not share the passion of other prominent Americans to extend the concept of a superior court modeled on the US Supreme Court to the international community. Wilson's own subsequent drafts of a post-war plan, although based on that of House, omitted any reference whatsoever to an international court. An Anglo-American synthesis, the Hurst-Miller Draft of February 2, 1919, included an international court, but "[g]reat care was taken not only to avoid creating an international court with supranational power, but also to avoid creating even a very strong international court."[67]

In the end, the Treaty of Versailles, which formally ended World War I and provided for the post-war order, did include a reference to a court. The plan's

[63] Report of William I Buchanan, High Commissioner, Representing the President of the United States to Attend the Inauguration of the Court of Justice for Central America, U.S. Foreign Relations 1908, at 247.
[64] Allain, note 9, at 92. [65] Grieves, note 61, at 49. [66] Grieves, note 61, at 49.
[67] Grieves, note 61, at 51.

principal institution, however, was the League of Nations. Among the League's many tasks spelled out in the treaty was the establishment of a Permanent Court of International Justice (PCIJ). The only other decision on the contentious issues that had surrounded discussions of courts in the past was the provision that the court "be competent to hear and determine any dispute of an international character which the parties thereto submit to it."[68] In February 1920, the Council of the League organized a commission of ten prominent jurists, including Lord Phillimore and Elihu Root, to draft the statute of the new court. The draft was adopted in December 1920 and entered into force in 1921. The court began work on its first cases in 1922.[69]

4 Toward Compulsory Jurisdiction

The two most difficult issues in drafting the PCIJ Statute for the Committee of Jurists were the selection of judges—the issue that had prevented agreement to a court in 1907—and the issue of compulsory jurisdiction. The US Supreme Court has compulsory jurisdiction in disputes between states. Indeed, courts of last resort within states generally have compulsory jurisdiction in the matters over which they have jurisdiction. In 1920, a number of states took the position that the new world court should also have compulsory jurisdiction over the subjects of international law in their legal disputes.

From the first serious discussions of a world court in the 1870s, there seemed to be a growing trend in favor of compulsory jurisdiction.[70] By the time of the drafting of the PCIJ statute, Lord Phillimore appeared to have come around to the idea of a permanent court with broad and compulsory jurisdiction. Phillimore stated that the PCIJ should be a "Court of Justice in the true sense of the word, a court before which it should be possible to call States having broken the law of Nations, without having to obtain their consent in advance."[71] The Dutch jurist Bernard C. J. Loder

[68] Covenant of the League of Nations, Art. 14. The Article continues with a reference to advisory opinions: "The Court may also give an advisory opinion upon any dispute or question referred to it by the Council or by the Assembly."

[69] See Publications of the Permanent Court of International Justice <http://www.icj-cij.org/pcij/index.php?p1=9> accessed July 18, 2013.

[70] See CW Jenks, *The Prospects of International Adjudication* (London: Stevens & Sons 1964) 13.

[71] Permanent Court of International Justice, Advisory Committee of Jurists, Procès-Verbaux of the Proceedings of the Committee June 16 to July 24, 1920 (first published Van Langenhuysen Brothers 1920, Clark, NJ: The Lawbook Exchange 2005) 104.

echoed this sentiment, arguing that compulsory jurisdiction was a crucial step forward from arbitral jurisdiction.[72]

Other members of the committee were not certain that the time was yet right for compulsory jurisdiction or were opposed to it altogether. Elihu Root argued that while most states would submit to compulsory jurisdiction, this was not the same thing as "accepting it in advance for all cases without exception, even those entailing principles which were differently interpreted in the different countries."[73] The more suitable venue for such cases would be an arbitral tribunal. Mineichiro Adatci of Japan, while not objecting to compulsory jurisdiction theoretically, considered that the premature adoption of such a clause at the outset of the League of Nations experiment could be risky for the future of dispute settlement.[74] Eventually the jurists reached a compromise, known as the Root-Phillimore plan. The plan provided for a court with compulsory jurisdiction by means of inter-state agreements on specific categories of disputes. Articles 33 and 34 of the final version of the PCIJ statute, as accepted by the state parties, "modified" these articles:[75] states could elect to be bound by the compulsory jurisdiction of the court, either through compromissory clauses in treaties or by accepting the "optional clause." Twenty-nine states accepted the optional compulsory jurisdiction of the PCIJ, among them many of the world's great powers at the time.[76]

The drafting committee also discussed providing jurisdiction for the new court to try individuals for international crimes.[77] Baron Descamps of Belgium, the President of the Committee of Jurists, recommended that the PCIJ's jurisdiction should include criminal offenses "recognized by the civilized nations but also by the demands of public conscience [and] the dictates of the legal conscience of civilized nations."[78] The International Law Association adopted a statute for an international criminal court as a division of the PCIJ. The idea was understandable given that the drafting of the PCIJ Statute followed the attempt to prosecute the Kaiser through a provision in the Treaty of Versailles. However, the Netherlands gave asylum to the Kaiser, so he never faced prosecution despite the treaty provision.

Leila Sadat believes the proposals for international criminal jurisdiction did not go very far at this time because international law was not sufficiently developed to allow for a criminal division of the PCIJ or a distinct criminal court.[79] International

[72] PCIJ Procès-Verbaux, note 71, at 224.

[73] PCIJ Procès-Verbaux, note 71, at 308.

[74] PCIJ Procès-Verbaux, note 71, at 651–2.

[75] See L Lloyd, "'A Springboard for the Future': A Historical Examination of Britain's Role in Shaping the Optional Clause of the Permanent Court of International Justice" (1985) 79 AJIL 28.

[76] Allain, note 9, at 13.

[77] PCIJ Procès-Verbaux, note 71, at 503.

[78] WA Schabas, *An Introduction to the International Criminal Court* (4th edn, Cambridge University Press 2011) 5.

[79] LN Sadat, *The International Criminal Court and the Transformation of International Law: Justice for the New Millennium* 24 (Ardsley, NY: Transnational Publishers 2001) (citing Commission on the Responsibility of the Authors of the War and on Enforcement of Penalties: Report Presented to the Preliminary Peace Conference (1920) 14 AJIL 95, 123).

law was still principally conceived as concerning inter-state relations. Perhaps more importantly, the peace movement was the driving force behind international courts. Its members wanted courts for war prevention. Scholars and activists had no understanding that an international criminal court could actually help prevent war.[80] On the contrary, some opponents of trials for individuals argued that an international criminal court would harm the cause of world peace. They hypothesized that when the fighting ended and soldiers were ready to lay down their arms and live in peace, the court would stir up accusations and counter-accusations, punishments and recriminations.[81]

Even without a criminal court or trial of the Kaiser, there were plenty of recriminations following World War I. By the 1920s, the League was already faltering. The US refusal to join the League is often cited among the reasons for the League's eventual failure. The US refusal can also be associated with slowing down the effort toward general compulsory judicial jurisdiction in international law. Ironically, it was Elihu Root as a member of the United States Senate who convinced other Republicans to reject President Wilson's plan for a world organization. Root opposed the League Council's authority to order member states to participate in armed conflict. This power conflicted too directly with both the US tradition of avoiding "entangling alliances" and the US's own growing military strength. Root did work for the rest of his life to convince the Senate to join the PCIJ, but the PCIJ was not viewed independently from the League and the Senate never gave its consent to join.

As these events were unfolding, Guieu describes a split among international law scholars with implications for the project of general compulsory jurisdiction. Rather than continuing to support a universal organization, some turned to regional institutions as Root had done after 1907. Alvarez, for example, vigorously promoted the Pan-American Union, and Georges Scelle advocated a European organization.[82] This diversion of energy and intellect away from universalism gained pace, of course, after World War II.

Other developments, however, supported universalism, including the perception that the PCIJ had been a success. Over the course of its brief existence, from 1922 to 1940, the PCIJ decided 66 cases—39 contentious cases and 27 advisory opinions.[83] Eight of the contentious cases were referrals by unilateral application under the

[80] See Sadat, note 79, at 25.

[81] Statement of Sir Graham Bower to the 1926 meeting of the International Law Association, quoted in Leila Sadat Wexler, "The Proposed Permanent International Criminal Court: An Appraisal" (1996) 29 Cornell J. Int'l L. 665, 672.

[82] J-M Guieu, "The Debate about a European Institutional Order among International Legal Scholars in the 1920s and its Legacy" (2012) 21 Contemporary European History 319, 319–37.

[83] General Statistics, Permanent Court of International Justice, World Courts Database, <www.worldcourts.com/pcij/eng/statistics.htm> accessed July 7, 2012.

optional clause; twelve were brought by application to the court based on jurisdiction under binding compromissory clauses.[84] In addition to resolving particular disputes, the PCIJ developed a respected body of jurisprudence. Many of its decisions are still cited by its successor, the International Court of Justice (ICJ), and other courts.[85] The decision to include an American judge, despite the failure of the United States to join the court, helped keep the PCIJ present in the United States. One of those judges, Manley O Hudson, also reported regularly on the work of the court in the pages of the *American Journal of International Law*, which no doubt helped to sustain the long-held American interest in international courts.

The PCIJ formally came to an end along with the League as a result of World War II. Blame for the war fell on the League, however, not the court. As a result, when the League was refashioned into the United Nations, the court itself was left relatively unchanged. A major effort was made to avoid the failings of the League but no effort was made to create a better world court. As early as 1938, US President Roosevelt had begun the work on creating a new international organization under a new charter that would work more effectively than the League. The court was renamed the International Court of Justice (ICJ), and, more importantly, its relationship with the world body changed. Indeed, the major change respecting the court from the League to the UN was the modification of the League Council's obligation to assist in the enforcing of PCIJ judgments and arbitral awards. The UN Security Council has discretion to assist the ICJ and no express role respecting arbitral awards.[86]

The most dramatic change, however, concerned the United States. Not only did it join the international court, it accepted the ICJ's optional compulsory jurisdiction. True, the US Senate would only give its consent following the addition of extensive reservations. That should have been a sign of the need to strengthen the commitment to compulsory jurisdiction in the post-war period. In addition, the United States was gaining even greater status as a military power after the war, becoming a super-power along with the Soviet Union. This development, too, should have signaled concern and the need for continuing advocacy for acceptance of international adjudication.

Despite the signs of trouble, the international legal community had reached a moment of consensus respecting compulsory jurisdiction. For perhaps a decade after World War II, international law literature reflected wide adherence to the importance of general compulsory jurisdiction consistent with the views of Hans Kelsen, who produced important and persuasive scholarship on why a world court was critical to the future of international law. From the inter-war period until the 1960s, Kelsen was widely regarded as the leading scholar of jurisprudence in the West. His early work focused on constitutional law, but by the 1930s he was known for his work on international law as well. Kelsen had been a critic of the League of

[84] Allain, note 9, at pp. 44–5. [85] See, in this handbook, von Bogdandy and Venzke, Ch. 23.

[86] United Nations Charter, Art. 94.

Nations because he believed the PCIJ, not the League Council or League Assembly, should have been at the heart of the organization:

One of the most important, if not the decisive, causes [of the demise of the League of Nations] is a fatal fault of its construction, the fact that the authors of the Covenant placed at the center of this international organization not the Permanent Court of International Justice, but a kind of international administration, the Council of the League of Nations. The Assembly of the League—its other organ—placed beside the Council, gives the impression of an international legislature... It might have been foreseen from the very beginning that a world government would not succeed if its decisions had to be taken unanimously, binding no member against his will, and if there is no centralized power to execute them.[87]

Kelsen believed that a world organization needed to begin with a competent court empowered with compulsory jurisdiction and featuring expert and impartial judges. With this centralized and essential core in place, a council would be obliged to carry out the decisions of the court. A legislative body could be established later for the purpose of creating new laws to be applied by the court and enforced by the council. Kelsen expected that the development of these institutions would take time but that such a slow, evolutionary process was required for the creation of a successful world organization.[88]

Kelsen also argued that the most important aspect of the judicial system at the heart of a successful world organization is compulsory jurisdiction. Without it, the world court would be unable to function to the extent needed to prevent the escalation of conflicts between nations. A judicial system needed to be devised that would guarantee as far as possible that all disputes among states would be subject to the future court's compulsory jurisdiction.[89] Kelsen was well aware of the opposition to compulsory jurisdiction. Some scholars again raised concerns about whether international law was adequate to answer the range of issues arising in inter-state disputes. Kelsen foresaw that the future world court would be just as capable as national courts in finding legal answers to the unlimited questions that confronted them.[90]

Despite his support for courts, Kelsen was a strong critic of the post-World War II criminal tribunals. His principal critique was that only nationals of the vanquished states were held accountable, despite clear and dramatic violations of the laws of war and human rights by nationals of the victors. The prospect of American leaders being tried before an international court became and remains a chief obstacle to US support of international criminal courts.

[87] H Kelsen, *Law and Peace in International Relations* (first published 1942, Buffalo, NY: William S. Hein & Co., Inc. 1997) 151–2. For more on Kelsen's view on international law and tribunals, see H Kelsen, *Peace Through Law* (Chapel Hill, NC: University of North Carolina Press 1944); H Kelsen, *General Theory of Law and State* (A Wedberg tr., Cambridge, MA: Harvard University Press 1945).

[88] See J von Bernstorff, *The Public International Law Theory of Hans Kelsen: Believing in Universal Law* (Cambridge University Press 2010) 201.

[89] Von Bernstorff, note 88, at 159. [90] Von Bernstorff, note 88, at 164.

As for the sort of court Kelsen did advocate, as discussed above, some of the interest in universal institutions had already shifted to regions by the 1920s. The real challenge to Kelsen's advocacy, however, came from political science. The British academic, E.H. Carr, in his book, *The Twenty Years' Crisis 1919–1939*, argued directly against Kelsen's vision of world order. For Carr, "the view of international law as a legal system that was institutionally completed by compulsory jurisdiction was another 'distinguished international lawyer's dream of an international community whose center of gravity is in the administration of international justice.'"[91] For Carr, the legal process is fundamentally different from the political process because it blocks out the importance of power in international relations. The idea that nations are equal before the law, regardless of the asymmetries of material power, was a "fiction [which] contradicted the inherent logic of international politics, where the strength of the individual states had to be considered a crucial factor in the solution of conflicts of interest."[92] This critique of Kelsen's theory gained adherents in the United States as it amassed its own material power. The interest of US leaders in international law and institutions became eclipsed by the prominence of the political science realists.

One of the most influential realists was Hans Morgenthau, a former scholar of international law who, starting in 1948, launched an attack on international law and his one-time mentor, Hans Kelsen.[93] Morgenthau had no problem with minor treaties such as trade agreements or diplomatic exchanges. It was the UN Charter and the rules against the use of force that drew his opprobrium. In his mind, humanity's lust for material power means the only path to security is possessing more physical strength than one's opponents. A national leader has a duty to build military strength regardless of international law.

5 From General to Specialized Compulsory Jurisdiction

The shifting intellectual trends from universal law and institutions to realist material power and regionalism came just as the new UN and ICJ could have used continuing US support and leadership. The United States did little or nothing to encourage

[91] Von Bernstorff, note 88, at 220 (citing EH Carr, *The Twenty Years' Crisis 1919–1939* (London: Macmillan & Co. 1939) 186).

[92] Von Bernstorff, note 88, at 221 (citing Carr, note 91, at 188).

[93] Astonishingly, Morgenthau's book that was first published in 1948 continues to be read by nearly every student of political science in the United States today. H Morgenthau, *Politics Among Nations: The Struggle for Power and Peace* (New York: Knopf 1948). There may be no other work that is so dominant in any other field or in political science in any other country.

other states to join the ICJ's optional compulsory jurisdiction. The United States never invoked its own acceptance of the optional clause to bring a complaint against any other state. In 1980, France withdrew from the optional clause following a case brought by two close US allies, Australia and New Zealand. Then, in 1984, Nicaragua brought a case against the United States for American use of military force against it. Nicaragua based the IJC's jurisdiction on the optional clause.

In a series of embarrassing legal maneuvers, the United States tried to keep the ICJ from taking jurisdiction.[94] The court's main decision in the case confirmed and reinforced international law's general prohibition on the use of force. The court handed a victory to the small nation, Nicaragua, against the superpower. US officials argued that the court, like other organs and agencies of the United Nations, had become biased against the United States. Their primary evidence of this was the fact the court had taken jurisdiction in the case. Contrary to the claims made by the United States in the media, the judges could not reasonably have rejected the entire case. Fifteen of sixteen judges voted to find jurisdiction on some basis. Only the US judge found no basis for jurisdiction. Nevertheless, US officials characterized the jurisdiction decision as unfair. The United States then withdrew from the court's optional compulsory jurisdiction. In the accompanying statement, it said the ICJ had been used as a political tool by Nicaragua.[95]

Well before the United States withdrew from the ICJ's compulsory jurisdiction, American interest in general compulsory jurisdiction had waned. The United States has continued to be party to more cases before the ICJ than any other state owing to the number of compromissory clauses in treaties that provide for ICJ jurisdiction.[96] Yet a return to the optional clause is never discussed. The American interest in courts as essential to law has continued, but in new directions. Just prior to the filing of the *Nicaragua* case, the United States had been a leader in the negotiation for a new, comprehensive treaty on the law of the sea. The UN Convention on the Law of the Sea (UNCLOS) III has a court with compulsory jurisdiction in certain matters. And the United States is principally responsible for the compulsory system of dispute resolution developed for the World Trade Organization (WTO) in 1994.[97] The WTO's Dispute Settlement Body hears more inter-state disputes under international law than any other court.

[94] US officials learned that Nicaragua planned to file a case and just a few days before it did so, the United States tried to "amend" its optional jurisdiction acceptance by excluding cases relating to Central America. See e.g., A Chayes, "Nicaragua, the United States, and the World Court" (1985) 85 Colum. L. Rev. 1445.

[95] "US Withdrawal Another Blow to 'World Court'" *Financial Times* (London, October 15, 1985) 10.

[96] In 1987, it invoked one of these treaties to take Italy to the court to settle a claim by US nationals of unlawful expropriation, Elettronica Sicula S.p.A. (ELSI) 1887 ICJ (*US v. Italy*). The case was heard by a chamber of the court composed of five judges selected by the parties. Iran, Germany, and Mexico have all taken the United States to court since the *Nicaragua* decision.

[97] RZ Lawrence, "The United States and the WTO Dispute Settlement System," Council on Foreign Relations CSR No. 25, March 2007, <www.cfr.org/content/publications/attachments/WTO_CSR25.pdf> accessed July 7, 2012.

In Europe, the European Court of Human Rights and the European Court of Justice have compulsory jurisdiction, as do other specialized and regional international courts. The United States has generally avoided commitment to human rights courts that might look into US conduct, but has been a driving force behind the international criminal court phenomenon for international trials of non-Americans. Today, the greater interest and enthusiasm in the world of international adjudication is around international criminal courts. These courts have grown up in the wake of the human rights revolution after World War II and the acceptance in international law of greater rights and duties for individuals. As discussed earlier, however, these courts have their roots in steps leading to the post-World War I call for a trial of the Kaiser and other Germans, as well as the post-World War II criminal courts.

6 Conclusions

What explains the departure from the long struggle for a court of general, compulsory jurisdiction? And what are the implications for international law practically and theoretically? Of utmost concern is that without some supranational court or means of recourse, decisions of the various international courts could be inconsistent with and even contradict one another. International law, like all law, is built in part on precedent. Without a superior court, conflicting decisions can harm the continued development of international law, and its perception as authoritative in international affairs.[98]

Yet, it may be that given the opposition of powerful states to strong central institutions of international law, the only path forward has been an indirect one leading to the same result. And there is, of course, the ICJ, which has helped to resolve competing legal concepts. Scholars have argued that the non-hierarchical proliferation of international courts and tribunals is the only way—and perhaps a good way—to increase third-party legal settlement of international disputes. It may be the case that many courts can work consistently and cooperatively to build jurisprudence and respect for international law.[99]

One may wonder how HLA. Hart would assess international law in the second decade of the twenty-first century. He could point to the fact international law still

[98] See e.g., G Hafner, "Risks Ensuing from the Fragmentation of International Law," Official Records of the General Assembly, 55th Session, Supplement No. 10, 321 (UNDoc A/55/0).

[99] B Kingsbury, "Forward: Is the Proliferation of International Courts and Tribunals a Systemic Problem?" (1999) 31 J. Int'l L. & Pol. 679, 686. Moreover, former ICJ Judge Thomas Buergenthal submits

lacks a general system of compulsory adjudication or to the impressive variety of regional and subject matter specific courts. These courts often have some compulsory jurisdiction, providing a patchwork of obligations to go to court that could eventually become comprehensive, especially if state obligations attendant to countermeasures ripen into an obligation to go to binding dispute resolution.[100]

Still, an essential purpose of international law and of its courts is the control of violence and especially prevention of war. Since the adoption of the United Nations Charter, there have been more than 300 armed conflicts. At the time of writing, armed conflicts are either under way or could break out in Afghanistan, Azerbaijan, Congo, Mali, Palestine, the Philippines, Somalia, Sudan, Syria, and Yemen. The state of the world cries out for a reinvigorated peace movement, one that renews the campaign for international law and institutions—perhaps even for a world court with general compulsory jurisdiction.

Research Questions

1. Is it detrimental to a legal system to lack a superior court with general compulsory jurisdiction? If so, is it merely a theoretical problem for international law given the growing areas of special subject matter compulsory jurisdiction? Or is the very fact of robust specialized courts a point of concern for the coherence of international law?
2. Are there indications that as the United States declines relative to other military powers, its traditional interest in general, compulsory jurisdiction will re-awaken? Are there other loci of support emerging for general compulsory jurisdiction?
3. What explains the decline in interest in compulsory jurisdiction in the world today? Is it the decline of the peace movement; the shift of interest among scholars to regional and specialized courts; the general view that the ICJ is successful without general compulsory jurisdiction; the view that the ICJ is not successful; the view that the ICJ is not worthy of general compulsory jurisdiction, or some other reason or reasons?

Suggested Reading

Briggs, HW, "Reservations to the Acceptance of Compulsory Jurisdiction of the International Court of Justice" Collected Courses 93, I (The Hague: Hague Academy of International Law 1958).

Cortright, D, *Peace: A History of Movements and Ideas* (Cambridge University Press 2008).

that this proliferation actually has a socializing effect on states, leading to ever-growing acceptance of the jurisdiction of international courts and tribunals.

[100] ME O'Connell, "Controlling Countermeasures" in M Ragazzi (ed.), *International Responsibility Today: Essays in Memory of Oscar Schachter* (Dordrecht: Martinus Nijhoff 2005) 49.

Eyffinger, A, *The International Court of Justice 1946–1996* (Alphen an den Rhijn, Netherlands: Kluwer Law International 1995).

Fassbender, B and Peters, A (eds), *The Oxford Handbook of The History of International Law* (Oxford University Press 2012).

Grewe, W, *The Epochs of International Law* (Michael Byers tr. & ed., Berlin: Walter de Gruyter 2000).

Janis, MW (ed.), *International Courts for the Twenty-First Century* (Dordrecht: Martinus Nijhoff Publishers 1992).

Jenks, CW, *The Prospects of International Adjudication* (London: Stevens & Sons 1964).

O'Connell, ME, "The Nicaragua Case, Preserving World Peace and the World Court" in John Noyes et al. (eds), *International Law Stories* (New York: Foundation Press 2007) 339.

O'Connell, ME, "Arbitration and the Avoidance of War: The Nineteenth-Century American Vision" in Cesare Romano (ed.), *The United States and International Courts and Tribunals* (Cambridge University Press 2009).

Pomerance, M, *The United States and the World Court as a Supreme Court of the Nations* (Dordrecht: Martinus Nijhoff 1996) 54–5.

CHAPTER 4

THE MULTIPLICATION OF INTERNATIONAL COURTS AND TRIBUNALS AFTER THE END OF THE COLD WAR

KAREN J ALTER*

* Professor of Political Science and Law at Northwestern University, and permanent visiting professor at the iCourts Center for Excellence, University of Copenhagen Faculty of Law. Thanks to Cesare Romano and Yuval Shany for comments on this chapter, to Cesare, Larry Helfer, and Erik Voeten for numerous iterations of feedback on the pieces that gave rise to this chapter, and to Tanja Borzel and Thomas Risse for making me think more systematically about my observation of the spread of the European model abroad.

When the Cold War ended in 1989, there were six permanent international courts plus the non-compulsory dispute settlement system of the General Agreement on Tariffs and Trade (GATT). The European Court of Justice (ECJ) offered the model of an active and effective international court. The other six international legal mechanisms did not inspire much enthusiasm or attention from litigants or observers. Today, however, there are at least two dozen permanent international courts (ICs) that have collectively issued over 37,000 binding legal judgments, more than 90 percent of which were issued since the fall of the Berlin Wall. Contemporary ICs attract much more attention from litigants, journalists, activists, governments, scholars, and critics. Irrelevant institutions are mostly ignored. So, although it might seem counter-intuitive to say, the calls for greater action coupled with the complaints about how ICs are infringing on national political autonomy are actually signs that today's international courts are of growing political importance.

The greater influence of ICs today is not simply a matter of numbers. Today's ICs are fundamentally different from their historical predecessors. Mary Ellen O'Connell and Lenore VanderZee's contribution to this handbook explains how the first ICs were primarily voluntary dispute settlement bodies, institutions litigants could use if they wanted a legal resolution to a disagreement. The big shift was towards ICs with compulsory jurisdiction, a change that started during the Cold War and has since accelerated. Today's ICs, what I call "new-style ICs," have compulsory jurisdiction and they allow non-state actors to initiate litigation. ICs' compulsory jurisdiction makes it harder for defendant governments to block inconvenient cases from proceeding. Access for non-state actors to initiate litigation increases the likelihood that issues people care about can be adjudicated by an international court. Today's ICs have also been delegated a broader range of judicial roles. ICs have been constituted to serve as dispute settlers, administrative review bodies, enforcers, and constitutional review bodies.[1] Today, the lion's share of all international legal rulings are issued in cases initiated by supranational commissions and prosecutors or private litigants with the plaintiff seeking to have state or international organization actions reviewed and international legal rules enforced.

Section 1 of this chapter provides an empirical overview of the multiplication of international courts since the fall of the Berlin Wall, and explains how most ICs today emulate the European model of new-style ICs and embedded law enforcement, raising a question of why regions are embracing European-style ICs. Section 2 summarizes the external and internal forces promoting the multiplication of international courts and examines three case studies that help us see how external and

[1] KJ Alter, "The Multiple Roles of International Courts and Tribunals: Enforcement, Dispute Settlement, Constitutional and Administrative Review" in J Dunoff and M Pollack (eds), *International Law and International Relations: Synthesizing Insights from Interdisciplinary Scholarship* (Cambridge University Press 2012).

internal forces contribute to the multiplication of ICs and the copying of European design models. Section 3 concludes.

1 The Multiplication of International Courts Since the Fall of the Berlin Wall

By the end of 2011, there were nearly two dozen operational permanent international courts—courts with appointed or elected judges that were being invoked by litigants to render binding legal rulings in cases where states or international institutions were the defendants. Four of these legal bodies were global in reach—the International Court of Justice (ICJ), International Tribunal for the Law of the Sea (ITLOS), the Appellate Body of the World Trade Organization (WTO AB), and the International Criminal Court (ICC). The rest were regional bodies located in Africa (9), Europe (6), and Latin America (5). Asia had a proposed dispute settlement system that includes a permanent appellate body. These bodies have jurisdiction to hear cases involving economic disputes (17), human rights issues (4), and war crimes (3 + hybrid courts). A number of these bodies also have a general jurisdiction that allows them to adjudicate any case state litigants choose to bring. Figure 4.1 shows the proliferation of operational courts considered in this analysis, including in parentheses the year the courts were created. The creation of three of the most active and important international courts in the world today and what became an informal dispute settlement system of the General Agreement on Tariffs and Trade are linked to the aftermath of World War II. Three more permanent ICs were created during the Cold War. The remaining ICs were created following the end of the Cold War.

A number of the above-mentioned legal bodies were also reformed in the post-Cold War period. Most of these reforms were intended to increase the reach and effectiveness of international courts by removing the requirement that states consent to litigation, by widening access to initiate adjudication, and by extending subject matter jurisdiction. Both pre-existing and new international legal bodies were also more active in the post-Cold War period. [2] Whereas ICs had collectively

[2] The European Court of Justice, European Court of Human Rights, GATT/WTO system, Inter-American Court of Human Rights, Andean, Mercosur, ECOWAS, EAC, SADC, and ASEAN legal systems all experienced meaningful reforms in the post-Cold War era. See KJ Alter, *The New Terrain of International Law: Courts, Politics, Rights* (Princeton University Press 2014), figure 3.3.

Figure 4.1: International courts, by subject matter and year IC became operational

	Economic Bodies	Human Rights Bodies	Mass Atrocities	Other
Post WWII ICs	*General Agreement on Tariffs and Trade (1948)* European Court of Justice (1952)	European Court of Human Rights (1958)		International Court of Justice (1945)
Cold War ICs	Benelux court (1974) Andean Tribunal of Justice (1984)	Inter-American Court of Human Rights (1979)		
Post Cold War ICs	Economic Court of the Commonwealth of Independent States (1993) European Free Trade Area Court (1992) Central American Court of Justice (1992) World Trade Organization Appellate Body (1994) West African Economic and Monetary Union (1995) Organization for the Harmonization of Corporate Law in Africa (1997) Court of Justice for the Common Market of Eastern and Southern Africa (1998) Common Court of Justice for the Central African Monetary Community (2000)	African Court on Human and Peoples' Rights (2006) Economic Community of West African States Court of Justice* (2005)	International Criminal Tribunal for the Former Yugoslavia (1993) International Criminal Tribunal for Rwanda (1994) International Criminal Court (2002) Special Court for Sierra Leone (2002)	International Tribunal for the Law of the Sea (1996)

	Court of Justice of the East African Community (2001) Caribbean Court of Justice (2001) Economic Community of West African States Court of Justice* (2001) Southern Common Market (2004) Dispute resolution system of the Association of Southeast Asian Nations (2004) Southern African Development Community Tribunal (2005)		Extraordinary Chambers in the Courts of Cambodia (2004) + Hybrid and special courts for Kosovo, East Timor, Lebanon & Bosnia	
Number ICs	17	4	3 + hybrids	2

* Section 3 explains that the Economic Community of West African States Court of Justice was created in 2001 and gained a human rights jurisdiction in 2005.

This figure is based on Alter, note 2, figure 3.1.

issued not quite 3,300 binding rulings from their founding through to 1989, the expanding number and greater activity of ICs has led to nearly 34,000 binding international judicial rulings between 1990 and 2011. Quasi-legal bodies—such as investor dispute systems and human rights treaty bodies—and domestic legal bodies have also experienced a rise in adjudication of international law related cases in the post-Cold War period.

1.1 Multiplication through emulation

We might consider it plagiarism or a violation of intellectual property if individuals assiduously copied the ideas of others, but in the legal realm the name for the phenomenon is "legal transplants." As lawyers well know, there are tremendous similarities in national constitutions and bodies of law, and in fact most national legal systems are based on a European model, and then referred to as "legal families."[3] It should thus come as no surprise that the multiplication of ICs involves copying pre-existing models. Given that Europe's ICs are known for being activist and sovereignty compromising, the extent to which European models have also influenced international judicial design is, however, surprising.

International economic courts tend to follow one of two basic models. The GATT/WTO model has compulsory jurisdiction and only states can initiate non-compliance suits. This design ensures that only the disputes governments care about are adjudicated. Regional systems that adopt the GATT/WTO model often also adopt its panel system of dispute settlement, which allows governments to first use consultation and then try a more arbitral style of dispute adjudication, before any appeal to a more legalized appellate body. The other basic template is the ECJ model, which has a supranational commission that monitors state compliance and brings non-compliance cases to the supranational court; a preliminary ruling mechanism that allows private litigants to raise cases in national courts, which can then be referred to the supranational court; and systems of administrative and constitutional review that allow states, community institutions, and private litigants to challenge community acts in front of the supranational court.[4] Figure 4.2 classifies ICs by which model they copy. I have also included NAFTA and ICSID, even though these are ad hoc systems that lack permanent appellate bodies. Elsewhere, I explore meaningful variations in these basic designs.[5]

[3] D Berkowitz, K Pistor and J-F Richard, "The Transplant Effect" (2003) 51 Am. J. Comp. L. 163; T Ginsburg, *Comparative Constitutional Design* (Cambridge University Press 2012); A Watson, *Legal Transplants: An Approach to Comparative Law* (University of Georgia Press 1993).

[4] States can also bring disputes against other states, although they seldom do, preferring to let the commission pursue violations instead.

[5] See KJ Alter, "The Global Spread of European Style International Courts" (2012) 35 West Eur. Pol. 135; KJ Alter et al., *Comparative Dispute Settlement Systems* (manuscript under review).

International criminal tribunals build on the basic design of the Nuremburg trials. Criminal tribunals have compulsory jurisdiction, and an international prosecutor selects which cases to pursue. Modern international criminal tribunals improve on the Nuremburg model in that all parties to the conflict can, in theory, be prosecuted; the international prosecutorial office and tribunals include a broader representation of states and there is an appeals mechanism.

ICs with human rights jurisdictions follow one of two models, both of which are associated with the European Court of Human Rights (ECtHR). The original ECtHR relied on states to consent to the court's compulsory jurisdiction and to allow private actors to bring complaints to the commission. Governments could consent to the court's jurisdiction for short periods of time (e.g., three to five years), and withdraw their consent if they were unhappy with court rulings. The original ECtHR also had a supranational commission that vetted human rights complaints and served as a gatekeeper to the court. This is the model copied by the African Court on Human and Peoples' Rights (ACtHPR), and it has contributed to the dearth of cases reaching that court. It is also the model copied by the Inter-American Court of Human Rights (IACtHR), albeit with certain important differences.[6] The post-Protocol 11 ECtHR has compulsory jurisdiction and direct private access. This revised model has been copied by the Court of Justice of the ECOWAS. Figure 4.3 shows the different design templates used for international human rights and criminal tribunals.

There are of course important differences across human rights, mass atrocities and economic courts: human rights courts adjudicate state violations affecting private individuals; mass atrocities bodies hold individuals accountable for crimes they have committed; and international economic bodies adjudicate state and international institutional violations of international law. Notwithstanding these critical differences, ICs that borrow from European models share essential features. All European-style adjudicative systems have international rules embedded into national systems. These "international" legal rules are more than statutes that ratify treaties, yet can be overridden by subsequent national legislation. Domestically embedded international criminal, human rights, and regulatory law are part of the fabric of the domestic legal order; it is domestic law that, although perhaps formally distinct, is intrinsically connected to international legal obligations. Also, all of these systems include institutional mechanisms (e.g., appellate review, preliminary ruling mechanisms, complementarity principles) that facilitate dialogue between national and supranational legal interpreters, so that interpretation and enforcement of international legal rules becomes an interactive, if not collaborative, enterprise undertaken by domestic and international judges applying what are basically

[6] The Inter-American Court has made it hard for states to withdraw consent once given, and private actors have always been able to raise complaints in front of the Inter-American Human Rights Commission. See C Romano, "The Shift from the Consensual to the Compulsory Paradigm in International Adjudication: Elements for a Theory of Consent" (2007) 39 N.Y.U. J. Int'l L. & Pol. 791.

Figure 4.2: Economic ICs following the WTO and ECJ Models (year IC created, organized chronologically)

International Court (N=	Compulsory jurisdiction	Arbitral process for first stage of trade dispute	Permanent Court (first and or last instance)	States may initiate litigation against other states	Supranational Commission can raise non-compliance suits	Private litigants can initiate litigation	Preliminary ruling system of national court referrals
WTO Model							
World Trade Organization (1994)	X	X	X	X			
International Centre for the Settlement of Disputes (1966)	Set by treaties	X		X		X	
Economic Court of the Commonwealth of Independent States (1993)	X		X	X			
Southern Common Market (2004)	X	X	X	X			X
North American Free Trade Agreement (2004)	X	X		X		Chapter 19 disputes (anti-dumping, countervailing duties)	
Association of Southeast Asian States (2004)	X	X	X	X			
ECJ Model							
European Court of Justice (1952)	X		X	X	X	X	X

Benelux court (BCJ) (1974)	X		X	X		In national courts only	X
Andean Tribunal of Justice (1984)	X		X	X	X	X	X
Central American Court of Justice (1992)	X		X	X		X	X
European Free Trade Area Court (1994)	X		X	X	X	X	Advisory opinions Only
West African Economic and Monetary Union (1995)	X		X	X	X	Via national courts only	X
Common Market for East African States (COMESA) (1998)	X		X	X	X	X	X
Central African Monetary Community Court (1999)	X		X	X	X	X	X
East African Community Court (2001)	X	X (Trade Protocol)	X	X	X	X	X
Caribbean Court of Justice (2004)	X		X	X	Currently under discussion	X	X
Court of Justice of the Economic Community of West African States (2002)	X		X	X	X	X (Human rights cases only)	
Southern African Development Community (2007)	X	X (Trade Protocol)	X	X		X	X
Total ICs with this feature	17 (+ many BITS)	7	16	18	8	13 + NAFTA	12

This figure is based on Alter, note 1, figure 3.5.

Figure 4.3: **Design templates for international human rights and criminal tribunals (year IC first operational)**

International Court	Compulsory or Optional Jurisdiction	Int'l Actor initiate litigation	Private litigant initiate litigation
Human rights courts templates (ECtHR model)			
European Court of Human Rights (1958)	Optional (1958–1997) Compulsory (1998)	Commission (1958–1997)	X (1998)
Inter-American Court of Human Rights (1979)	Optional	Commission	
Caribbean Court of Justice (2004)	Optional		Appellate review for certain countries
Economic Community of West African States Court of Justice (2005 for human rights jurisdiction)	Compulsory		X (2005)
African Court on Human and Peoples' Rights (2006)	Optional	Commission	
Criminal tribunal templates (building on Nuremburg model)			
International Criminal Tribunal for the Former Yugoslavia (1993)		Prosecutor	
International Criminal Tribunal for Rwanda (1994)		Prosecutor	
International Criminal Court (2002)	Optional (except for Security Council references)	Prosecutor	

Previously published in Alter, note 2, as figure 3.6.

the same set of legal rules. These basic features are present in systems of regional integration that emulate the European Community, in regional human rights systems and in today's war crimes systems, and aspects of this model are present in the Law of the Sea and with respect to contemporary international security law articulated via the United Nations Security Council.[7]

[7] The Law of the Sea allows the Enterprise to regulate deep-sea mining and the Seabed Chamber to adjudicate disagreements with the Enterprise. Law of Sea regulatory rulings are binding on states and firms. Security related decisions of the UN Security Council lead to binding domestic legislation. For more on the links between national and international security regulations, see K Scheppele,

This dominance of the European model is somewhat ironic. European governments did not set out to create the supranational judicial institutions that they have today. By all accounts, legal practice, rather than state intention, led to the European legal model that is so widely copied.[8] Moreover, it is fair to say that European political elites remain ambivalent about the encroachments of European law and supranational legal authority in the domestic realm. Despite Europe's ambivalence about its model, the European model diffuses (and one might note that this continued voiced ambivalence is belied by repeated decisions to improve the functioning of Europe's legal institutions.)

There is little evidence that European leaders pressure others to accept their model. Instead, European legal models have drawn their own adherents. In the 1960s, a number of regions copied Europe's approach to regional economic integration, omitting, however, the Economic Community's legal mechanisms. Most of these regional integration efforts were seen as failures. While observers did not attribute the failure to a lack of a supranational legal structures, participants in these endeavors could not help but notice that the European Economic Community's supranational court—the ECJ—was proving useful in addressing legal issues associated with regional integration. When regional integration returned as a policy objective in the 1980s and 1990s, integration architects paid greater attention to the legal problems presented by regional integration. Legal advocates drew lessons, proposing international legal systems that borrowed from Europe. It took a while to convince governments to embrace international judicial oversight, but eventually the European approach to international law spread.

2 External Forces Contributing to the Multiplication of International Courts

Institutions get built by people—political entrepreneurs who recognize and seize political opportunities for change, individuals who draft statutes, advocacy movements that put pressure on governments, and governmental actors that decide on the possibilities

The International State of Emergency: Constitutional Exceptions and the Globalization of Security Law after 9/11 (Cambridge, MA: Harvard University Press 2013).

[8] For more information on how the European Community's legal institutions varied from what member states expected, see A Boerger-De Smedt, "La Court de Justice dans les négociationis du traité de Paris instituant la CECA" (2008) 14 J. Eur. Hist. 7; A Boerger-De Smedt, "Negotiating the Foundations of European Law, 1950–1957: The Legal History of the Treaties of Paris and Rome" (2012) 21 Contemp. Eur. Hist. 339; KJ Alter, "Who are the Masters of the Treaty?: European Governments and the European Court of Justice" (1998) 52 Int'l Org. 125.

advocates put in front of them. A full account of the multiplication of international courts would, of course, consider who these actors are and how European ideas diffused. With a few exceptions, however, we lack negotiating histories that can tell us why local actors looked to European models.[9] I focus instead on how external forces generated the opportunities that local advocates seized upon as they pushed for adding international courts. My argument is that these external forces created a permissive environment which proponents could seize upon to advocate the creation of an IC, borrowing European models.

Undoubtedly, a large systemic force indirectly at play was the end of the Cold War. In Europe, the end of the Cold War meant that political bargains designed to keep Communist parties out of power could be reassessed. Political coalitions shifted, and judges and other societal groups felt freer to question the old status quo. The end of the Cold War led to the expansion of the North Atlantic Treaty Organization (NATO), and the enlarging of the European Union and the Council of Europe to include former Soviet bloc states. This pending enlargement, and the creation of a common currency in Europe, became an impetus to reform Europe's existing legal infrastructure before enlargement, when negotiating change would be relatively easier. The conclusion of the Cold War also led to war in the Balkans, which brought the issue of international adjudication of war crimes back to the fore. Outside Europe, the Cold War's close had a different effect. With the conclusion of the Cold War came the discrediting of Marxism and Socialism, the cessation of Soviet economic subsidies and the ascendance of neoliberal economic thought in international institutions and the American and European foreign policy elite. Henceforth, any state that wanted help from foreign investors, the International Monetary Fund, or the World Bank needed to show that they were undertaking economic and political reform. The 1990s were the high point of what was known as the "Washington Consensus."[10] American and European leaders were convinced that the superior capitalist economic model had defeated communism. Enamored by the compelling social science finding that democracies do not fight wars,[11] international institutions became conveyer belts of liberal economic policies, human rights, and democratization.[12]

The worldwide conjunctural moment of the end of the Cold War created the opportunity for advocates to press for adding ICs. European models became benchmarks that offered potential solutions and lessons. If the problem was that

[9] Exceptions include KJ Alter, L Helfer and O Saldias, "Transplanting the European Court of Justice: The Experience of the Andean Tribunal of Justice" (2012) 60 Am. J. Comp. L. 709; T Lenz, "Spurred Emulation: The EU and Regional Integration in Mercosur and SADC" (2011) 31 (1) West Eur. Pol. 155.

[10] See J Williamson, "What Washington Means by Policy Reform" in J Williamson (ed.), *Latin American Adjustment: How Much Has Happened* (Peterson Institute for International Economics 1990).

[11] B Russett, *Grasping the Democratic Peace* (Princeton University Press 1993).

[12] Y Dezalay and BG Garth, *Global Prescriptions: The Production, Exportation, and Importation of a New Legal Orthodoxy* (University of Michigan Press 2002).

people distrusted governments' empty promises of the past, then the solution was to self-bind to independent external institutions that were more likely to be trusted. If the problem was that regional economic rules were not implemented or they were ignored, then advocates suggested a solution of making community regulations directly applicable and supreme to national laws, and empowering private litigants to bring violations of the rules to court. If the problem was that war criminals escaped prosecution and created an environment of local intimidation, then the solution was to create international adjudicative mechanisms that could provide assurance that adjudication might be fair and effective. Advocates might need to adapt European models to address concerns of member governments, but they could then wait for another permissive moment when governments might want the system to work better. When new opportunities arose, advocates could once again borrow from Europe and suggest reforms that would bring the legal system closer to the European model.

The critical juncture of the end of the Cold War, and with it the search for resources and solutions, created a permissive environment and perhaps even an impetus for change. But the reason governments were more open to agreeing to sovereignty-compromising international judicial solutions was that the world had changed, and so had their options. Three systemic changes—all arguably affected by the end of the Cold War—fundamentally changed the choices governments faced. The following overly brief discussions are expanded elsewhere.[13]

The first major change was the expansion of the WTO from just over 100 countries when the Cold War ended to 157 members as of this writing. During the Cold War, governments had to pick sides in the conflict. Members of GATT enjoyed preferential access to American and European markets and a seat at the negotiating table. But to join GATT signaled that a government was picking the Western capitalist side, a decision that brought with it the distrust and displeasure of major communist powers and perhaps even a loss of economic, political, and military support. The collapse of the Soviet Union, followed by the embrace of market reforms by China, basically eliminated the political costs of joining GATT. As it became clear that many states would want to join GATT, the goal of the Uruguay round of negotiations shifted to undertaking major reform in advance of enlargement. American and European governments put together a "single undertaking" that would be the price of admission to the WTO's "most favored nation" market access status. The new WTO would be a member association, with all members agreeing to abide by a package of WTO free trade rules. To be a member meant that neither Europe nor the United States could revoke your "most favored nation" market access privilege.

States joined GATT and the WTO to gain preferential access to major economic markets and to show their commitment to neoliberal economic ideas, and thereby

[13] KJ Alter, *New Terrain of International Law*, note 2, at Chapter 4.

attract investment and foreign aid from Western powers and multilateral institutions. The WTO's legal rules and dispute adjudication system changed state preferences about international courts in a number of ways. First, the WTO system created a free trade floor of rules. There was no point in states within regional organizations having less favorable trade rules among each other than they had under the WTO. Moreover, since the WTO allows for regional economic communities to grant preferential market access to members, regional economic integration became more attractive in its own right. Second, WTO member states were already committed to compulsory adjudication of economic disputes. By 1994, WTO members faced the choice of suing each other in the WTO system or creating regional compulsory enforcement mechanisms as a complement to the WTO system. Regional ICs offered the advantage of judges from the region applying rules adapted by the region's member states.

The second major change involved the expansion of extraterritorial enforcement of human rights and international humanitarian law. With war crimes on the rise in the 1990s and pictures of mass atrocities telecast around the world, national courts in Belgium and the United Kingdom became more willing to invoke universal jurisdiction and to limit claims of foreign sovereignty immunity. The prospect of adjudicating human rights violations in Europe, America, and elsewhere meant that the choice facing governments changed. Governments could create their own review bodies to adjudicate major human rights violations, or they could let foreign bodies adjudicate the cases. According to Kathryn Sikkink, this choice led Latin American courts to reverse grants of amnesty so as to prosecute human rights violations themselves.[14] Foreign trials also shored up the position of those who advocated improving national and regional mechanisms to deal with human rights violations. Creating local remedies at the national and regional level could decrease assertions of extraterritorial jurisdiction by creating a viable alternative to foreign trials.

The third global force for change was the United Nations response to war in Yugoslavia. Evidence of mass atrocities in Yugoslavia had led the UN Security Council to use its Chapter VII powers to create an international tribunal to prosecute war crimes committed in Yugoslavian wars and the crime of genocide and crimes against humanity committed in Rwanda. Inspired by these political advances, human rights activists advocated for a global model. Surely, a global international criminal court made more sense than multiple ad hoc international tribunals. Political mobilization from the General Assembly and a group of "like-minded" states led to the new International Criminal Court (the ICC, which started operating in 2002 after 60 countries had ratified the Rome Statute), and a host of ad hoc hybrid systems to deal with crimes that were committed before and outside the framework of the new ICC (e.g., abuses in Sierra Leone, East Timor, Bosnia & Herzegovina, Kosovo,

[14] See K Sikkink, *The Justice Cascade: How Human Rights Prosecutions Are Changing World Politics* (New York: Norton 2011).

Cambodia, and Lebanon).[15] This reality has changed the situation of governments. Leaders who are accused of mass atrocities might hope that pressure by powerful allies will keep the Security Council from referring the case to the ICC, but ratification of the Rome Statute has led many countries to enact domestic legislation that authorizes the prosecution of war crimes. Activists can continually pressure governments to bring leaders to court. Maybe the ICC will end up hearing the case, but perhaps equally as likely is that courts in other countries or in other regional systems will one day end up prosecuting the case—as is currently happening with Chad's former leader Hissene Habré.[16]

As a result of these systemic changes, governments around the world faced the very real prospect that absent local international adjudicative mechanisms, international and national institutions dominated by Americans and Europeans would fill in. WTO membership changed the default choice of governments, making regional courts attractive because regional courts are closer to home and staffed by representatives of the regional organizations' member states. Local adjudication is preferable to human rights and mass atrocities trials in national or international institutions dominated by Western powers. This changing reality has made regional adjudicative solutions newly attractive.

2.1 External pressures combine with internal forces: three decisions to add international courts

External forces provide a backdrop and contributed to changing the calculation of governments. They do not on their own explain the decision to create an IC. Rather, local actors embrace local ICs to address local problems. There are doubtless many stories one could tell about how the Nuremburg trials shaped today's ICCs, and how the Council of Europe's human rights system shaped the Inter-American and African human rights systems. But I am going to focus on economic systems because legal architects had a choice of two models: the WTO model and the European Community model. In what follows, I discuss how the European model shaped decision-making in the Andean, OHADA, and ECOWAS legal systems.[17]

The 1990s led to the reinvigoration of regionalism, which in practice often meant re-launching integration movements around the world.[18] Regional integration

[15] For more on these changes see, in this handbook, Schabas, Ch. 10.

[16] "ICJ Hissène Habré" Questions relating to the Obligation to Prosecute or Extradite (Belgium *v.* Senegal) ICJ Judgment of July 20, 2012 <http://www.icj-cij.org/docket/index.php?p1=3&p2=3&case=144&code=bs&p3=4> accessed July 25, 2012.

[17] This discussion draws from Alter, Helfer and Saldias, note 9; Alter, "The Global Spread of European Style International Courts," note 5.

[18] PJ Katzenstein, *A World of Regions: Asia and Europe in the American Imperium* (Ithaca, NY: Cornell University Press 2005); E Mansfield and E Reinhardt, "Multilateral Determinants of

systems adopted new policies and policy-making procedures intended to enhance economic and political cooperative endeavors. The question inevitably arose of how to ensure that these new rules would be implemented and what to do should there be disputes about the rules. The re-launching of regional integration systems became moments to discuss creating or enhancing existing dispute settlement provisions.

2.1.1 *Creating the Andean Tribunal of Justice*

From the Andean Pact's inception, governments believed that they possessed the authority to implement the Cartagena Agreement—the Andean Pact's founding charter—and Andean secondary legislation (*Decisiones*) via presidential decrees. This legislative route had the advantage of avoiding national parliaments, in which fractious political parties might attempt to block or revise implementing legislation. But the approach also engendered opposition from business elites who disliked the Andean Pact's import-substitution policies. Opponents raised legal suits in national courts invoking the failure to submit the treaty to national parliaments as they challenged the legal validity of the presidential decrees. National legal challenges to Andean rules in the 1960s and early 1970s ultimately failed. But the manner in which domestic actors responded to these challenges, especially in Colombia, suggested that Andean *Decisiones* would not be given domestic effect. The creation of an Andean Tribunal of Justice, and with it the declaration of the direct effect and supremacy of Andean rules, provided a way to avoid national judicial invalidation of Andean rules.

When Andean officials discussed the creation of a supranational court, several potential models were available for their consideration. The officials could have emulated an early regional tribunal, the Central American Court of Justice, which heard ten cases between 1907 and 1917 before its founding treaty expired. Or they could have embraced the GATT dispute settlement system, although emulating GATT would not have established the direct effect of Andean *Decisions* nor created a mechanism for supranational judicial review of Andean institutions and their decisions. Without such review, national courts might challenge the authority of community law or interpret Andean rules in inconsistent ways. A third alternative—the ECJ model—was the most obvious fit given the preexisting similarities between other Andean and European institutions. The selection of the ECJ model was virtually guaranteed when the *Junta* asked the Institute for the Integration of Latin America and the Caribbean (INTAL) to evaluate the best model for the Andean Pact.[19]

Regionalism: The Effects of GATT/WTO on the Formation of Preferential Trading Arrangements" (2003) 57 Int'l Org. 829.

[19] INTAL is a research center established by the Inter-American Development Bank in 1965 with the mission of promoting and consolidating regional integration. Its network of consultants—many of whom are part-time scholars—provides technical assistance to implement and enforce integration policies.

The INTAL network recommended bundling the creation of an ECJ-style tribunal with foundational ECJ doctrines establishing the direct effect and supremacy of community law in national legal orders. These suggestions came in a meeting in June 1972, leading to draft statute that member states discussed in November, and a formal proposal that went to the legislative body of member states in December of that year. The proposal focused on two key requirements: the doctrines of supremacy and direct effect, and a supranational mechanism to review the legality of community acts. Copying the ECJ's preliminary reference procedure achieved both of these goals. The meeting endorsed the creation of an Andean judicial body to review Andean rules and to ensure their uniform interpretation by national judges, and to "reduce unnecessary and sometimes disproportionate political tensions" with those judges—an implicit reference to Colombian Supreme Court rulings that had raised questions about the legal effect of Andean secondary legislation in Colombia.

This proposal then languished for a number of years. The Andean Pact's difficulties in the 1970s underscored that something fundamental needed to change if the member states were to move the integration process forward. Yet even during this troubled period, the EC continued to serve as a model for Andean integration. Europe, too, faced significant challenges to integration in the 1970s. In response, it adopted several institutional innovations. In 1970, the EC launched the European Political Cooperation initiative to coordinate member states' foreign policies, and, in 1974, it formalized the system of Councils of Heads of States to adopt major decisions related to integration. In 1979, the EC replaced a regional legislative body comprised of national parliamentarians with a system of direct elections to a new European Parliament.

When integration advocates later revived the Andean integration project, they tracked these developments. The re-launch of the Andean integration project provided the impetus for creating the Andean Tribunal of Justice (ATJ). In 1979, the member states agreed to create an Andean Parliament and a Council of Foreign Ministers. And, in the same year, they finally adopted the Treaty Establishing the Tribunal of Justice of the Cartagena Agreement, accepting nearly *in toto* the text drafted by INTAL in 1972, which the *Junta* had incorporated into its 1975 recommendation.[20]

By 1979, member states had adopted the required texts and, by 1984, the ATJ began operation. The ATJ was modeled on the ECJ, but with certain adjustments designed to protect national sovereignty. Private actors could raise cases in national courts, but the Andean Secretariat only considered noncompliance complaints

INTAL served as a conveyer belt for the transmission of European ideas into conversations about integration in Latin America. See O Saldias, "Networks, Courts and Regional Integration: Explaining the Establishment of the Andean Court of Justice" (2010) Working Paper of the KFG The Transformative Power of Europe <http://papers.ssrn.com/sol3/papers.cfm?abstract_id=1708040> accessed July 1, 2013.

[20] Alter, Helfer and Saldias, note 9, at 725.

raised by member states. Since Andean governments wanted to avoid legal suits, the system sat empty for a number of years. The first case to arise, in 1987, involved a private litigant trying to get his challenge to a Colombian tariff adjudicated by the ATJ. The court refused the case, since private actors lacked standing to raise noncompliance suits; the judges instead instructed the litigant to pursue the issue in the national court. References from national courts trickled in thereafter, but the system remained barely used in its first decade of operation.[21]

The Andean legal system became activated when Andean member states overhauled their existing intellectual property rules in anticipation of member countries joining the WTO. The changes adopted made Andean rules compatible with the agreement on Trade-Related Aspects of Intellectual Property (TRIPS), and these changes in turn unleashed demand for local trademarks and patents. Regional intellectual property law became the governing rules. As applications for patents and trademarks increased, so too did national court references for preliminary ruling decisions.[22] This litigation has made the ATJ the third most active IC, with over 2,000 rulings to date. But as we explain elsewhere, active does not mean activist. The ATJ's law-making style differs from its transplanted parent in important ways.[23]

2.1.2 *Creating a legal system for the Organization for the Harmonization of Business Laws in Africa (OHADA)*

The Organization for the Harmonization of Business Law in Africa (OHADA), formed in 1993, creates unified business codes for African countries. Its members are predominately francophone African countries, all of which had anachronistic business rules left over from French colonialism and adapted in a hodgepodge fashion so that few lawyers or judges even knew what governing law applied. The result, everyone seemed to agree, was legal uncertainty that was worrisome to potential investors.[24] The solution that ended up being adopted borrowed heavily from Europe, although the OHADA court is not a direct transplant. Rather, member states borrowed the idea of having directly applicable supranational rules, the interpretation of which would be overseen by a regional court.

The impetus to create OHADA came both internally and externally. Foreign investment in the region fell in the 1980s due to political instability and the reorientation of financial supports in the post-Cold War era. Political leaders wanted more foreign investment, and they became convinced that legal and juridical insecurity

[21] Alter, Helfer and Saldias, note 9, at 725.

[22] See L Helfer, K Alter and MF Guerzovich, "Islands of Effective International Adjudication: Constructing an Intellectual Property Rule of Law in the Andean Community" (2009) 103 AJIL 1.

[23] K Alter and L Helfer, "Nature or Nurture: Judicial Lawmaking in the European Court of Justice and the Andean Tribunal of Justice" (2010) 64 Int'l Org. 563.

[24] A Mouloul, *Understanding the Organization for the Harmonization of Business Laws in Africa (O.H.A.D.A.)* (2009), 10–11. Pamphlet on file with the author.

made investing in their markets less desirable. Adopting a common commercial code offered many advantages.[25] By having the same set of rules across countries, foreign investors could save on the legal expertise needed for each national system. OHADA Uniform Acts were also adapted specifically for the needs of developing countries, so that they became more attractive than competing rules—existing French, American, or EU business law.[26] Member states may not amend the Uniform Acts, and the Acts are widely available on the internet and in source books, providing legal stability and certainty. The promulgation of ten detailed multilaterally-crafted Uniform Acts has activated the OHADA system. OHADA's legal system was also one of OHADA's chief attractions. Foreign lawyers have little faith in Africa's national legal systems, where judges are perceived to be ill-informed and often corrupt. International dispute resolution is an alternative, but it is expensive because cases are litigated outside the region. OHADA created its own arbitration system that is managed by the Common Court of Justice and Arbitration (CCJA). This arbitration system is yet to take root, in part because most contract agreements do not yet specify OHADA as the arbitral venue. But the CCJA has become activated as a body that provides an international review of national judicial rulings involving OHADA law.

Externally, the OHADA system was strongly supported by the French government with the encouragement of the *Conseil Français des Investisseurs en Afrique*. The French government was interested in any solution that might help stabilize the Franc zone, because regional instability could generate currency pressures felt in France. A 1991 meeting of African finance ministers from African Franc countries, held in France, led to the commissioning of a study on the feasibility of creating regional business law.[27] The French Foreign Ministry reached out to Kéba Mbaye, a former Senegalese Supreme Court judge and President of the ICJ, who, in the 1960s, had advocated legal harmonization among newly independent states. The French Foreign Ministry underwrote and provided technical support for Mbaye's efforts, which led to the founding of OHADA.[28] France, other EU and non-EU countries, and other international institutions provided financial support to pay for OHADA. While member states now also provide support for the system, it is safe to say that foreign support has been instrumental to the functioning of OHADA. Also the French Foreign Ministry, to this day, has at least one attaché at the OHADA secretariat.

When it appeared that the soon-to-be-implemented OHADA Uniform Acts had been largely forgotten, French patrons, with the support of funding from various

[25] See Mouloul, note 24, at 10–11.

[26] Mouloul, note 24, at 10–11; CM Dickerson, "Harmonizing Business Laws in Africa: OHADA Calls the Tune" (2005) 44 Colum. J. Transnat'l L. 18, 25.

[27] P Tiger, *Le droit des affaires en Afrique* (3rd edn, Presses Universitaires de France 2001) 23.

[28] F Katendi and J-B Placca, "Savoir accepter la pauvreté: Interview de Kéba MBAYE" (OHADA.com) <www.afrology.com/eco/pdf/kebam.pdf> accessed November 19, 2012.

international institutions, created a non-governmental organization to promote awareness of OHADA and its laws. The Association for the Unification of African Law plays an analogous role to Eurolaw associations, which in Europe helped to promote European Community law within national systems in the 1960s.[29] The Association helps with training sessions and maintains a website—OHADA.com—that makes available OHADA Uniform Acts and CCJA and national court rulings applying OHADA law. The French journal *Juriscope*, with the support of *Coopération Français*, publish commentary and compendiums of Uniform Acts and community case law, which they help to distribute throughout the region. This is important because in many African countries journals publishing laws and legal rulings are irregularly maintained and hard to access. Members of the Association's network regularly visit national courts to collect rulings that pertain to OHADA. The rulings are transcribed and published online. While the collection of national legal rulings on OHADA.com is surely incomplete, the website supplies what may be the only publicly available searchable source for case law in OHADA member states.[30] I know of no conversation where participants actively discussed borrowing from Europe, although such a conversation may well have occurred. But France was funding and participating in the conversations, and it may well have seemed natural that aspects of Europe's supranational system could help address the challenges OHADA countries faced. There was also probably no conversation about following the jurist advocacy strategy that took place in Europe. Indeed, the European strategy was itself barely a strategy—it was mostly an adaptation of the traditional role of legal advocates coming together to discuss important developing legal issues.[31]

The combination of the Uniform Acts and international review of national court rulings makes the OHADA system a "European style" IC. Why not create, however, a supranational court modeled on the ECJ with commission enforcement and a preliminary ruling mechanism? One reason perhaps is that OHADA is intentionally different from a common market. If OHADA had a larger political objective, like establishing a monetary union or good governance norms, it would be in direct competition with the West and Central African Economic and Monetary Unions, which promote economic integration among former French colonies.[32] Moreover, OHADA aspires to provide a set of business laws that any country can adopt.

[29] KJ Alter, "Jurist Advocacy Movements in Europe: The Role of Euro-Law Associations in European Integration (1953–1975)" in KJ Alter (ed.), *The European Court's Political Power* (Oxford University Press 2009).

[30] Based on interviews with members of Association for the Unification of African Law (Paris, France, March 22, 2007).

[31] A Vauchez, "The Transnational Politics of Judicialization: Van Gend en Loos and the Making of EU Polity" (2010) 16 Eur. L.J. 1.

[32] Benin, Burkina Faso, Ivory Coast, Guinea, Mali, Niger, Nigeria, and Senegal are members of OHADA, the West African Economic and Monetary Community and the Economic Community of West African States. Cameroon, the Central African Republic, Chad, the Republic of Congo, Equatorial Guinea, and Gabon are members of both OHADA and the Central African Monetary Community.

OHADA is also primarily designed for business contracts, thus it does not need to replicate the inter-state dispute resolution mechanisms of the WTO or the supranational enforcement mechanism of the EU. The 2008 Québec reforms have brought OHADA institutions closer in form to the EU,[33] but the format for creating Uniform Acts in OHADA remains multilateral more than supranational. There is thus no reason to create administrative and constitutional review roles as checks on supranational authority.

The existence of detailed OHADA law and mobilized litigants who wanted OHADA rules respected explain why the OHADA court has become the fourth most active permanent IC today, with 569 rulings by the end of 2011. But while OHADA law is formally speaking the supreme business law of the land, and CCJA decisions the highest legal authority on the meaning of OHADA law, the OHADA system works quite differently than its transplanted originator. Much of the OHADA state economies remain informal and thus outside the sphere of OHADA law. Within the sphere of business adjudication, litigants may choose arbitration, and sometimes litigants choose to remain in the national system instead of appealing to the CCJA. Also hindering OHADA is that national supreme courts remain wary about working with the CCJA and many national judges are ignorant of the workings of OHADA. In Europe, it is clear that the EU sets the business law tune, in coordination with member states. But for the above-mentioned reasons there is a real question whether Africa's business affairs are truly governed by OHADA rules.[34]

2.1.3 *The Economic Community of West African States (ECOWAS)*

The Court of Justice of the ECOWAS (ECOWAS CJ) did not start out as an ECJ-style IC. The original treaty for the ECOWAS, adopted in 1975, expected that the governing authority would adopt—and member states would then implement—a series of legally binding protocols to promote economic integration. The treaty included a provision that contemplated the establishment of a Community Court, but no court was ever created. In the late 1980s, member states began discussing a new charter for ECOWAS, creating an "Eminent Persons Group" to make recommendations. In the meantime, states adopted a Protocol on the Community Court of Justice (the 1991 protocol)[35] that authorized the ECOWAS CJ to hear disputes between member states and suits brought by states on behalf of their citizens. The protocol gave

[33] The reforms created a Council of Ministers, which can adopt and amend Uniform Acts and oversee the operation of the OHADA Secretariat and Court. The Permanent Secretariat manages the legal affairs and accounting, and it works with the Council of Ministers to propose new areas of business law harmonization and to draft new laws.

[34] CM Dickerson, "The Cameroonian Experience under OHADA: Business Organizations in a Developing Economy" (2007) 112 Bus. & Soc'y Rev. 191.

[35] Protocol on the Community Court of Justice A/P.1/7/91 adopted in Abuja, Nigeria on July 6, 1991.

the Secretariat no role in monitoring or helping to enforce community rules, and neither national judges nor private actors were authorized to refer cases to the community court. According to Kufuor, the Eminent Persons Group expressed dissatisfaction with the 1991 protocol, recommending that a revised ECOWAS charter should allow private actors to invoke certain ECOWAS legal rights directly before the ECOWAS CJ. These recommendations were not heeded.[36] Implementing this protocol in 2000, member states made what, in retrospect, was a portentous decision; in their expectation of a major re-launching of regional integration, the protocol made the new court a permanent body.[37]

It took until 1996 for the requisite number of states to ratify the court protocol, and until 2001 for the first group of judges to be appointed. Then the fully staffed ECOWAS CJ sat unused because states never brought any cases. The ECOWAS Secretariat grew frustrated that ECOWAS CJ judges consumed significant community expenses without actually contributing to the goals of the community. The problem was the court's extremely limited access rules. Member states had borrowed from Europe, but they had added in adaptations to protect national sovereignty. Private litigants could ask their attorney general to bring a case against another member state on their behalf, but one obvious flaw in the original design was that private actors had no means of filing complaints against their own country. A second limitation was that few national justice ministries or attorney generals knew about the ECOWAS legal system and mobilizing them to raise a case on behalf of private actors was as difficult as it was unlikely.

In 2003, a case finally reached the ECOWAS court. A Nigerian goods trader challenged Nigeria's closing of its border with Benin in clear violation of ECOWAS law. The plaintiff asked the ECOWAS CJ to purposively interpret its jurisdiction and access rules to overcome the "absurdity" that expects a state to be both a plaintiff and a defendant when it violates community rules. The ECOWAS CJ refused the invitation, sticking to the plain wording of its mandate that only allowed "disputes instituted by member states on behalf of its nationals against another Member State." The court recognized that the ECJ had interpreted its mandate expansively "in the interest of justice." But it also expressed concerns that, because some ECJ decisions had attracted criticism, they did not "want to tow on the same line."[38]

The ECOWAS CJ then used the dismissal of the suit to lobby for an expansion of its jurisdiction. Judges asked for changes that included bringing the ECOWAS CJ

[36] KO Kufuor, *The Institutional Transformation of the Economic Community of West African States* (Farnham: Ashgate 2006).

[37] KJ Alter, L Helfer, and J McAllister, "A New International Human Rights Court for West Africa: The Court of Justice for the Economic Community of West African States" (2013) 107 AJIL (4).

[38] *Olajide Afolabi v. Federal Republic of Nigeria* (2004) ECW/CCJ/APP/01/03, para. 56.

closer in design to the ECJ model by adding a preliminary ruling procedure similar to what exists in the West African Economic and Monetary Union (WAEMU). The future role of the court was discussed at a 2004 "Consultative Forum on Protecting the Rights of ECOWAS citizens through the ECOWAS Court of Justice." A number of human rights groups participated in this forum, which produced a declaration calling on the ECOWAS legal secretariat to draft a supplementary protocol to revise the ECOWAS CJ's jurisdiction.[39] The reforms brought the ECOWAS court closer to the European model, but differences still remain. The 2005 Supplementary Protocol allows national courts to refer cases involving community law to the ECOWAS CJ, but it does not copy the WAEMU provision that requires national courts of last instance to refer such cases. The protocol also authorizes the Executive Secretariat to initiate noncompliance suits. But by far the most important revision—borrowed from Europe's human rights system—was the decision to grant the ECOWAS CJ jurisdiction to review complaints from individuals alleging human rights violations.

Why add a human rights jurisdiction, especially if the problem was the under-enforcement of ECOWAS economic rules? We explore this question at length elsewhere.[40] Relevant for this discussion is the desire of political leaders to adopt policies that might give real meaning to the catchphrase of the time—an "ECOWAS of the people." Human rights activists were frustrated with the highly politicized and slow-moving African Union human rights system. They sought a quicker and more meaningful mechanism to pursue human rights claims. Governments acceded to their request in part to show progress towards addressing some of the concerns and the needs of the people.

I lack space to explain the switch from copying the ECJ to borrowing from the ECtHR.[41] But in many other ways, ECOWAS continues to borrow from Europe. It has transformed its Secretariat into a body more like the European Commission that can propose legislation and hear noncompliance complaints from states and private actors. It has adopted the legislative instruments of Europe including directly applicable community regulations and directives that still require national implementing legislation. But the failure to provide direct private access to challenge violations of economic rules coupled with the decision to allow direct access for violations of human rights rules has made the ECOWAS court more similar in practice to the ECtHR than it is to the ECJ.

My claim is not that governments wanted to import activist and encroaching international judicial models, and I have not really explained the diffusion of the

[39] N Nwogu, "Regional Integration as an Instrument of Human Rights: Reconceptualizing ECOWAS" (2007) 6 J. Hum. Rts. 345, 352.

[40] Alter, Helfer and McAllister, note 37.

[41] See, however, Alter, Helfer and McAllister, note 37.

European model. Rather, my goal is to explain multiplication of ICs in the post-Cold War Period and to suggest why multiplication involves emulating existing models. My basic argument is that opportunities presented themselves, governments became more open to regionally-based supranational courts and advocates pushed governments to borrow from Europe as they generated regional courts. European supranational institutions served as models because they are associated with success. Pro-integration advocates recommended European models but local governments often preferred to adapt European models for their own specific needs and so as to protect national sovereignty. Two of the three cases involved subsequent reforms during which changes were made that brought the IC even closer to the European model. By embracing and later reforming courts, governments could show their commitment to the integration project and the rule of law. In the Andean context, the European model helped to address a concern that national judges might reject Andean decisions. In OHADA, creating regional business law made investing in the region easier for foreigners, and the fact that governments could not change these rules helped to generate legal certainty and arguably diminish incentives for corruption. Allowing domestic judicial decisions to be appealed to a supranational court increased the credibility of promises that national courts would enforce the common business law. In ECOWAS, the ECJ model served as an inspiration to the Eminent Persons Group charged with making recommendations for a new ECOWAS charter; it shaped the arguments and ECOWAS CJ decision-making in the *Afolabi* case;[42] and it shaped the WAEMU preliminary ruling system that ECOWAS judges wanted to replicate.

These three examples all borrowed from Europe. Meanwhile both Mercosur and ASEAN made a different choice. According to people I spoke with, Brazil became concerned when NAFTA was created that the American-dominated system would spread south. Changing the dysfunctional Mercosur dispute settlement system became a priority, but, despite suggestions by smaller powers, Brazil preferred a WTO system. After all, adopting the European model would allow three countries that comprise less than 30 percent of the population and market to outvote the economically dominant regional hegemon.[43] I am not aware of the history of the ASEAN decision, but given Asian countries' aversion to international courts, their adoption of the WTO model is not very surprising.

[42] *Olajide Afolabi v. Federal Republic of Nigeria*, note 38.

[43] Larry Helfer and I have not yet written up this research, but this argument is based on fieldwork in Argentina in 2011. It cuts against the argument of Lenz, note 9, who is more optimistic that suggestions

3 Implications for the Study of Today's International Courts

For social scientists, the multiplication of international courts generates both a puzzle and an opportunity. The puzzle is why sovereignty-jealous governments suddenly became more willing to submit to compulsory international judicial oversight, and what does this change actually mean in practice? This chapter argued that the end of the Cold War created a conjunctural moment where old international political arrangements were disrupted and governments around the world needed to search for new strategies. Americans and Europeans were looking for evidence of economic, democratic, and human rights reforms, and their preferences shaped the policies and strategies of the World Bank, the International Monetary Fund, and the United Nations. This changing context combined with growing extraterritorial assertions of jurisdiction—by the United States enacting punishments for "unfair trade" and by American and European courts applying global human rights and mass atrocities law—made committing to international judicial oversight for free trade and human rights agreements newly attractive. Local advocates took advantage of governments' new openness, advocating international judicial models that they associated with success.

The end of the Cold War and the evolution of extraterritorial law enforcement explain both the timing and the fact that most ICs today borrow from European models. While global forces contribute to change, local issues determine how copied models are adapted. Each institution has its own unique history, but one constant is the new reality countries faced in the 1990s. In 1945, governments faced a choice between proposed international courts or no international judicial review of their policies and choices. Today a WTO-violating barrier to trade could well give rise to WTO adjudication regardless of whether there is or is not a functioning regional adjudive system. The African Union's human rights system may well be subject to political delays, but any government official who commits human rights violations and then moves abroad may well face prosecution in a foreign court. Omar Al-Bashir may win promises not to be arrested or extradited to The Hague, and Bashar Al-Assad may not as of this writing been indicted by the ICC but both these political leaders need to be very selective when it comes to international travel, and they should make sure that they retain political and financial resources to ensure their protection. In other words, ineffective local

of an ECJ-style court might be embraced. Johannes Rühl of the Graduate Institute of International and Development Studies Geneva is working on diffusion of models and Mercosur.

adjudive mechanisms may well give rise to foreign legal enforcement. The more extraterritorial enforcement exists, the more attractive local adjudicative strategies become. This reality explains why the African Union and the East African Community are today discussing adding a criminal chamber to its regional legal system.

The reality of European-style ICs spreading around the world is a boon for social scientists because there are now laboratories of experimentation. We can now investigate how context intersects with the design of international judicial institutions to shape international legal and judicial politics. We can study how international courts become authoritative political and legal actors, and why some international courts remain perennially irrelevant. We can study when international judges become activist, and when they remain conservative legal formalists. And we can study the factors that generate opposition to international legal enforcement. Of course, we want to know more about how and why international courts have multiplied in number and replicated in form. But ultimately, we want to know what becomes of these many international judicial transplants.

Research questions

1) How does compulsory jurisdiction affect the law and politics of international courts? How does the ability of private actors and/or supranational prosecutors to initiate litigation change the content of international litigation and the legal outputs of international judges?
2) Why do local leaders choose to adapt existing international models, and how are these adaptations important?
3) How does the context shape the operation of similarly designed international judicial institutions? Do variations in legal rules and adjudicative mechanisms across regional systems contribute to changing law and outcomes?
4) Clearly the dynamics of human rights and mass atrocities litigation will be different from enforcing international economic agreements. But how does the content of the law and the nature of the defendant influence adjudication politics? Do advocates have different litigation strategies for different countries and different issues?

Suggested Reading

Alter, KJ, *The New Terrain of International Law: Courts, Politics, Rights* (Princeton University Press 2014).

Alter, KJ and Helfer, L, *Supranational Legal Transplants: The Law and Politics of the Andean Tribunal of Justice* (Oxford University Press, forthcoming).

Dezalay, Y and Garth, BG, *Global prescriptions: the production, exportation, and importation of a new legal orthodoxy* (Ann Arbor: University of Michigan Press 2002).

Dezalay, Y and Garth, BG, *The internationalization of palace wars: lawyers, economists, and the contest to transform Latin American states* (University of Chicago Press 2002).

Reus-Smit, C, "The Constitutional Structure of International Society and the Nature of Fundamental Institutions" (1997) 51 Int'l Org. 555.

Romano, C, "The Proliferation of International Judicial Bodies: The Pieces of the Puzzle" (1999) 31 N.Y.U. J. Int'l Law & Pol. 709.

Sassen, S, *Territory, authority, rights: from medieval to global assemblages* (Princeton University Press 2006).

Scheppele, K, *The International State of Emergency: Constitutional Exceptions and the Globalization of Security Law after 9/11* (Cambridge, MA: Harvard University Press 2013).

CHAPTER 5

THE SHADOW ZONES OF INTERNATIONAL JUDICIALIZATION

CESARE PR ROMANO*

DESPITE the plethora of international adjudicative bodies created over time and across regions, international judicialization is still remarkably uneven. First, while some regions of the globe contain multiple, overlapping, international adjudicative bodies, others have none. Second, patterns of utilization are inconsistent. Even where international adjudicative bodies exist, certain actors use them more frequently than others. Third, certain areas of international relations have been judicialized significantly more than others. This chapter describes the current state of judicialization along these three main dimensions, highlighting the areas and issues

* Professor of Law and W. Joseph Ford Fellow, Loyola Law School Los Angeles; Co-Director Project on International Courts and Tribunals. I would like to acknowledge the assistance, at Loyola, of Mark Oknyansy, and the helpful feedback of the co-editors of this handbook.

where judicialization has not arrived, and advances some possible explanations for this puzzle.

1 Uneven Geographic Distribution

One can distinguish between two types of international adjudicative bodies: global ones, whose jurisdiction could be accepted by any state, and regional ones, whose jurisdiction extends only to states within a certain region of the world.

1.1 Global

Only four global judicial bodies are currently active: the International Court of Justice (ICJ); the World Trade Organization (WTO) dispute settlement system; the International Tribunal for the Law of the Sea (ITLOS); and the International Criminal Court (ICC). There are also a number of global international arbitral bodies, the two most important of which are the Permanent Court of Arbitration (PCA) and the International Center for the Settlement of Investment Disputes (ICSID).

All of these, however, are only global in theory because none has jurisdiction that actually extends to all states.[1] That is either because the organization to which the judicial body is attached does not have universal membership (i.e. the WTO); the treaty creating the court has not attracted universal ratification (i.e. the ICC); or because while the organization does have universal—or virtually universal—membership (e.g. the U.N.), the judicial bodies attached to it, such as the ICJ or ITLOS, have jurisdiction only insofar as states have expressly accepted it.[2]

Currently, the WTO has 159 members, including a few entities that are not sovereign states, such as the European Union, Hong Kong and Macao, and Taiwan, whose sovereignty is contested. Since Russia joined in 2012, all of the world's major economies are members. The most significant outliers of this system are found in

[1] For an overview at a glance of the reach of global judicial bodies, see, in this handbook, Fold-out Chart 1, International Judicial Bodies: Compulsory Jurisdiction Across the Globe (Inter-State Judicial Bodies) and Ch. 2.

[2] There is a clear trend toward locking in states' consent to jurisdiction and making it less dependent on ad hoc expressions of consent. See generally, C Romano, "The Shift from the Consensual to the Compulsory Paradigm in International Adjudication: Elements for a Theory of Consent" (2009) 39 NYU J Intl L & Pol 791; K Alter, *The New Terrain of International Law: Courts, Politics, Rights* (Princeton University Press 2014).

North Africa, the Middle East, and Central Asia, while a few others reside in East Africa, the Balkans, and the Caribbean.[3] All are troubled states and second- or third-rate economies. Many, for various reasons, have been pariahs of the international community at some point since the birth of the WTO. Yet, considering the gravitational effect that the WTO has gained by now, boasting among its membership all of the world's significant economies, one day the WTO might reach global membership, thus turning its dispute settlement system into the first and only truly global jurisdiction.

Like the WTO dispute settlement system, in theory, the Rome Statute of the ICC could be ratified by any state, thus making it potentially a truly universal court. However, so far its statute has been ratified by just under two-thirds of the world's states (122).[4] What is more, ratification is quite uneven across the globe. Forty-two European states are party to the Rome Statute of the ICC, including all members of the European Union. Numerically, Europe is the most represented region in the Assembly of States Parties. However, as one moves east, commitment to the ICC decreases. Turkey, Russia, Ukraine, and Belarus are not parties and, for their own political and strategic reasons, unlikely to join anytime soon. Thirty-three African states (out of 55) have ratified the Rome Statute, making it the second largest group in the ICC. Notably absent are most of North Africa (but Tunisia is party) and Eastern Africa (Kenya and Djibouti are party), and a good swath of Southern Africa (although Angola, Zimbabwe, and Mozambique are party). Africa is also the site of all ongoing prosecutions, which, for practical purposes and for the time being, makes the ICC an African international criminal court of sorts. Twenty-eight out of 35 states of the Americas are party, including Canada, but not the United States, El Salvador, Nicaragua, Cuba or a number of other small Caribbean states. Finally, only 17 Asian and Pacific region states are ICC members. China, India, Pakistan, Iran, Iraq, and Indonesia are not. The only parties in the Arab world are Jordan and Tunisia. Each of these states has joined either because it is a western-style, liberal democracy (e.g. Japan, South Korea, Australia, New Zealand, and a handful of Pacific Island nations), or because it fears internal conflict or external aggression, and hopes the ICC might deter those threats (e.g. Mongolia, Afghanistan, Bangladesh, and Cambodia). The paltry acceptance of the ICC in Asia probably correlates with the absence of regional courts of any sort—human rights, economic integration, or otherwise—in this part of the world.

One day the ICC might reach universal acceptance, but that seems unlikely at least in this generation. Then again, the fact that a state has not ratified the Rome

[3] For a complete list, see in this handbook, Annex 2, States Subject to Compulsory Jurisdiction (as at July 1, 2013).

[4] For an overview at a glance of the reach of the ICC, see, in this handbook, Fold-out Chart 1, International Judicial Bodies: Compulsory Jurisdiction Across the Globe (International Criminal Court.)

Statute does not mean that it is beyond the ICC's reach. ICC jurisdiction can be extended by fiat of the Security Council to any state, which has happened in the cases of Sudan and Libya. This shields the five permanent members of the Security Council and their closest allies, but not always and not each ally. A state can also refer itself, as Mali recently did in order to grapple with a nasty Al Qaeda-inspired insurgence in the north.

Mapping the reach of the ICJ and ITLOS is a considerably more challenging exercise, for ratification of the legal instruments that created them—the UN Charter and the UN Convention on the Law of the Sea, respectively—does not guarantee acceptance of jurisdiction.[5]

To date, the Law of the Sea Convention has received 163 ratifications, including that of the European Union. Most prominent among the outliers is the United States. Notably, one of the reasons the United States has adduced for failing to ratify this global treaty, despite overwhelming evidence that it would be in its national interest to do so, is the fact that the treaty has a compulsory dispute settlement procedure for certain kinds of disputes.[6] Yet the United States is not alone in its rejection of the Law of the Sea Convention. It is joined by other significant states that are otherwise familiar with international adjudication, such as Turkey, Peru, Colombia, and Venezuela. Each of these has failed to ratify the Law of the Sea Convention for its own legal and political reasons. Finally, in the list of states that are not party to the Convention, we also find several of the usual outliers of international adjudication, such as Syria, most central Asian former Soviet Union Republics, Ethiopia, Eritrea, Iran, and Libya.

As previously explained, ratification of the Law of the Sea Convention, although necessary, is not sufficient to establish jurisdiction of its dispute settlement bodies and procedures.[7] Although under the Convention the default is compulsory adjudication of disputes—that is to say, dispute settlement procedures can be triggered unilaterally—disputes arising out of the exploration and exploitation of the seabed, and disputes concerning coastal states' sovereign rights with respect to the living resources in their exclusive economic zones, are not subject to compulsory adjudication.[8] Moreover, states can opt out of compulsory dispute-settlement procedures in disputes concerning sea boundary delimitations, historic bays or titles, military and law enforcement activities, and issues related to maintaining peace and security

[5] For a complete list, see in this handbook, Annex 2, States Subject to Compulsory Jurisdiction (as at July 1, 2013). See also Ch. 2.

[6] See J Alvarez, "Judicialization and Its Discontents" (American Society of International Law, President's Column, January 31, 2008). <http://www.asil.org/ilpost/president/pres080131.html> accessed February 1, 2013.

[7] UN Convention on the Law of the Sea (adopted December 10, 1982, entered into force November 16, 1994) 1833 UNTS 397.

[8] See generally N Klein, *Dispute Settlement in the UN Convention on the Law of the Sea* (Cambridge University Press 2005).

that are being dealt with by the UN Security Council.[9] At least 35 states have indeed opted out of compulsory adjudication for one of these issues.[10]

Further, the Convention does not provide for a single dispute settlement procedure, but rather offers four alternatives: the ITLOS, the ICJ, and two different types of special arbitration, called Annex VII and Annex VIII arbitration, respectively. The mechanism that will be used is the one that both parties accept. Should the parties not accept the same mechanism, and the dispute is of a type subject to compulsory adjudication, the default mechanism is not ITLOS but rather ad hoc arbitration under Annex VII of the Convention.

All of this creates an intricate and ever-changing matrix that makes it impossible to neatly and precisely map which states are subject to the jurisdiction of what procedures or bodies for a given kind of dispute.[11] To date, 33 states party to the Law of the Sea Convention have made a declaration indicating ITLOS as a chosen means of dispute settlement—either exclusively or in concurrence with others.[12]

Likewise, it is difficult to tell which states are subject to the jurisdiction of the ICJ at any given time. Cases can be heard by the ICJ if both states have agreed, ad hoc, to refer the matter; if there is a clause in the treaty at dispute conferring jurisdiction to the court; if both states have made a unilateral optional declaration conferring jurisdiction to the court; or if the state has not accepted jurisdiction at the time the case had been filed, but subsequently decides to nonetheless accept jurisdiction and appear before the court (*forum prorogatum*). There are hundreds of bilateral and multilateral treaties that give the ICJ jurisdiction to hear disputes at the request of any party. To date, 69 states have filed optional declarations of acceptance of the court's jurisdiction. Most of these are states that usually participate in international adjudication and are subject to the jurisdiction of other international courts. Often, however, their declarations to the ICJ are replete with exceptions. There are endless opportunities for states to agree to refer disputes ad hoc or to accept the court's jurisdiction after the beginning of proceedings.

The United States' history with the court perfectly illustrates the difficulty of mapping the ICJ's reach. While it is often said that the United States is reluctant to submit itself to compulsory international adjudication and, in particular, shuns the ICJ, in reality it is the state that has most often appeared before the court, both as applicant and respondent. Just by number of cases litigated—or attempted to

[9] UN Convention on the Law of the Sea, note 7, Art. 298.

[10] See United Nations Division for Ocean Affairs and the Law of the Sea, "Settlement of Dispute Mechanisms" <http://www.un.org/Depts/los/settlement_of_disputes/choice_procedure.htm> accessed February 1, 2013.

[11] For up-to-date data on choice of dispute settlement procedures, see "Settlement of Dispute Mechanisms," note 10.

[12] "Settlement of Dispute Mechanisms," note 10.

litigate—the United States should be considered the ICJ's most ardent supporter. But the story is much more complicated than that.[13]

At the global level, the two main bodies arbitrating disputes involving states are the PCA and ICSID. Again, participation in these two arbitration mechanisms is not complete. To date, 158 states have ratified the ICSID Convention,[14] a number comparable to the membership of another international regime that fosters international trade and investment: the WTO. However, there are significant discrepancies between the memberships of the two. Notable ICSID absences are: Canada; EU member Poland; several economic superpowers-to-be, including India, Brazil, Mexico, South Africa, and Russia; a populist trio of Latin American states comprised of Venezuela, Bolivia, and Ecuador, all of which withdrew recently; and some of the usual outliers of international adjudication, such as Libya, Iran, Iraq, Ethiopia, Myanmar, and Cuba. It should be stressed that states that are members of ICSID are not *ipso facto* exposed to litigation. Whether arbitral tribunals convened under the aegis of ICSID have compulsory jurisdiction depends on the given investment treaty. Moreover, disputes can still be arbitrated within the ICSID framework even if the investor state against which the case is brought is not party to the Convention. This is done under an additional set of rules, called the Additional Facility, but is a relatively rare event.

As for the PCA, 115 states have acceded to one or both of the regime's founding conventions: the 1899 and 1907 Hague Conventions.[15] All major developed states are members of the PCA. Again, the absences are concentrated in Africa, Central Asia, the Caribbean, the Pacific Islands, and parts of Southeast Asia. As in the case of the ICSID, PCA members are not exposed *ipso facto* to litigation. Whether a PCA arbitral tribunal has jurisdiction and whether that is compulsory depends on the language of the given treaty. In the end, being a member of the PCA just means having a stake in its functioning—including paying for its expenses and having a say in its management—but it does not signal acceptance of international adjudication per se.

1.2 Regional

As Karen Alter illustrated, most international adjudicative bodies are not found at the global level, but at the regional one.[16] There are several dozen of them if one

[13] See S Murphy, "The United States and the International Court of Justice: Coping with Antinomies" in C Romano (ed.), *The Sword and the Scales: The United States and International Courts and Tribunals* (Cambridge University Press 2009) 46.

[14] For information on ICSID, see, in this handbook, Schreuer, Ch. 14.

[15] For information on the PCA, see, in this handbook, Murphy, Ch. 9.

[16] See, in this handbook, Alter, Ch. 4, at section 1. See also Fold-out Chart 1, International Judicial Bodies: Compulsory Jurisdiction Across the Globe (Judicial Bodies of Regional Integration Agreements and Human Rights Courts: Overlapping Jurisdictions).

includes those that are barely active or dormant.[17] A complete review is beyond the scope of this chapter, but we will examine the major ones.

1.2.1 *Europe*

Europe is arguably the most judicialized continent, although one probably needs to distinguish between Western and Eastern Europe. Indeed, judicialization is high in the west but less so in the east. After the devastations suffered during World War II, Europeans seem to have had a "Kantian epiphany,"[18] launching a continent-wide quest for peace, security, and prosperity hinged on democracy and the rule of law, first in the West and then, after the end of the Cold War, extending to the East. The construction of Europe essentially rested on two main judicial pillars: the European Court of Justice (ECJ), now called the Court of Justice of the European Union (CJEU), and the European Court of Human Rights (ECtHR). Of the two, only the ECtHR has continent-wide reach.

Forty-seven European states, all members of the Council of Europe, are subject to the jurisdiction of the ECtHR, the only notable exception being Belarus. However, only the 28 members of the European Union are subject to the jurisdiction of the CJEU. Unlike the Council of Europe, the European Union does not have continent-wide reach. Its reach into the North, Balkans, Alps, and East is somewhat limited, spurring alternative projects of judicialization. Thus, Norway, Iceland, and Lichtenstein are subject to the European Free Trade Association (EFTA) Court, an appendix of the EU project.[19] At the eastern end of the continent, Russia has led a judicialization project that serves as an alternative to that of the EU and CJEU. Together with other former Soviet republics it has created two regional courts: the Economic Court of the Commonwealth of Independent States, which has been striving to make its voice heard and respected in a region of the world where the rule of law still struggles mightily,[20] and, more recently, the Court of the Eurasian Economic Community, an organ of the five-member Eurasian Economic Community, Customs Union and Common Economic Space.[21]

In the European landscape, one intriguing peculiarity is the Holy See. Although it has a tradition of welcoming international adjudication as a peaceful alternative

[17] See, in this handbook, Romano, Ch. 6, at section 1 and Ch. 1, at section 2, and Fold out Chart 1, International Judicial Bodies: Taxonomic Timeline.

[18] J Alvarez, "The New Dispute Settlers: (Half) Truths and Consequences" (2003) 38.3 Tex. Int'l L.J. 405–44, 429 and ff.

[19] See, in this handbook, Baudenbacher and Clifton, Ch. 12, at section 2.2.

[20] See Z Kembayev, *Legal Aspects of the Regional Integration Processes in the Post-Soviet Area* (Berlin: Springer 2009) 60 ("... As of the present, the Court consists of merely five judges representing only five CIS countries: Belarus, Kazakhstan, Kyrgyzstan, Russia and Tajikistan, which fully reflects a rather insignificant volume of workload of this judicial body and consequently the corresponding degree of unwillingness on the part of the CIS states to solve their disputes through the Court.").

[21] See <http://sudevrazes.org/en/main.aspx> accessed June 1, 2013.

to power and violence—and has supported, in words, the creation of many international courts and tribunals—it is the only state in Europe not to have accepted the compulsory jurisdiction of any judicial body. This can probably be explained by the idiosyncratic nature of that state and its politics. A study of the Holy See's attitude towards international adjudication is still missing.

1.2.2 *Americas*

The Western Hemisphere has been primarily shaped by Spanish colonization and decolonization, the rise of the United States and, during the second half of the twentieth century, resistance to communism. Bound together by their common Spanish heritage and the Bolivarian myth, states in Central and South America have tried since the nineteenth century to bring about economic and political integration. Remarkably, Central America started moving toward judicialization a half-century before Europe.[22]

After the end of World War II, a desire to keep communism outside the western hemisphere led to the creation of the Organization of American States (OAS), which, in turn, gave rise to the only pan-continental judicial body: the Inter-American Court of Human Rights (IACtHR). Yet unlike the ECtHR, whose jurisdiction is obligatory for all Council of Europe member states, the jurisdiction of the IACtHR is only optional for member states of the OAS. Currently, only 21 out of a total of 35 OAS members have accepted its jurisdiction. Canada and the United States in North America, Cuba and Jamaica in the Caribbean, and, recently, Venezuela in South America are the most glaring absences. The other outliers are mostly small Caribbean island states. The hostility of "Chavista" Venezuela toward international adjudication has manifested itself also in its withdrawal from the ICSID, and the like-minded governments of Ecuador and Bolivia have followed suit.[23]

The long tradition of integration between states in the region has given rise to several more regional adjudicative bodies promoting regional economic integration. However, it should be noted that, with the exception of Bolivia, soon to be member of both the Andean Community and Mercosur, regional bodies in the Americas so far do not overlap.[24] They interlock like a puzzle. States are subject to the jurisdiction of one regional court and, possibly, the IACtHR. The only OAS members not subject to any adjudicative system are the Bahamas and Cuba, plus a handful of micro-states such as Antigua and the Turks and Caicos Islands, which are not members of the OAS. While the United States and Canada are not subject to the jurisdiction of any regional adjudicative bodies, they are party to the North

[22] See, in this handbook, Romano, Ch. 6, at section 2.4. [23] Romano, Ch. 6, at section 2.3.

[24] See in this handbook, Fold-out Chart 1, International Judicial Bodies: Compulsory Jurisdiction Across the Globe (Judicial Bodies of Regional Integration Agreements and Human Rights Courts: Overlapping Jurisdictions).

American Free Trade Agreement, which provides for compulsory dispute settlement and arbitration on a limited number of issues.[25]

1.2.3 *Sub-Saharan Africa*

Sub-Saharan Africa is home to the largest number of international adjudicative bodies.[26] To date, the only two states in this continent not subject to any international court are São Tomé and Príncipe and Somalia.[27] Much of Africa's international judicial landscape has been shaped by the forces of the Cold War and rejection of European colonialism. The continent's fight for self-determination culminated in the early 1960s with the birth of 32 new sovereign states. In 1963, these states created the Organization of African Unity (OAU), a precursor to today's African Union. The goal of the OAU was to promote African solidarity and cooperation, and to help African countries overcome the legacy of colonialism. For nearly 20 years the OAU focused on decolonization and fighting the apartheid systems of South Africa and Rhodesia—two objectives that the various African governments could all endorse.

The OAU (or African Union since 2002) is the linchpin of the only pan-African adjudicative body: the African Court on Human and Peoples' Rights (ACtHPR). The institution emerged slowly, starting in 1979 with the drafting of the Banjul Charter of Human and Peoples' Rights, then the African Commission, then the Court, and maybe someday the African Court of Justice and Human Rights. Still, most of the AU members have not yet accepted the ACtHPR's jurisdiction. To date, only 23 states have done so. Those that have not include the whole of the Horn of Africa, half of Northern Africa (although Algeria, Tunisia, and Libya have ratified), and most of Southern Africa.

From Africa's big bang in 1960 through to the end of the 1980s, African countries began a number of initiatives aimed at intra-Africa integration. They generally failed. Recently emerged from colonization, new African leaders gave priority to crafting specific national identities, an exercise that ran counter to economic and political integration. Moreover, most African states traded very little with each other. Privileged economic relationships with former colonial powers (and now with the EU) diminished the importance of inter-African integration. Finally, support for authoritarian leaders during the Cold War and the funding of proxy wars kept African governments divided.

The end of the Cold War left free trade and market-based economies the only viable paradigm for development. It also opened the way for democracy and accountability of national leaderships, creating space for the rise of regional economic courts and criminal courts. Thus, in the struggle to achieve a certain degree of stability and

[25] See, in this handbook, Baudenbacher and Clifton, Ch. 12.

[26] For an overview of African international courts and tribunals, see, *African International Courts and Tribunals*, <http://www.aict-ctia.org/> accessed February 1, 2013.

[27] However, São Tomé and Príncipe is a member of ICSID.

prosperity, Africa has given birth to a large number of international judicial institutions—although the overwhelming majority has only sub-regional scope.[28] As we saw, the only potentially pan-African court is the ACtHPR. Yet many of these courts have either been nonstarters, have floundered after a few years, or are languishing with a paltry docket.[29] All in all, given that most of these institutions are very new, it is hard to know what they will become. This, however, could also suggest that commitment to independent third-party adjudication and international rule of law might be, at least for the ruling elites of many African states, only skin-deep.

1.2.4 *Arab World*

The contemporary history of the Arab world is similar to that of Africa: colonialism gave way to self-determination, and during the intoxicating nationalist days that followed independence it seemed that waning colonial influence would bring with it democracy, respect for human rights, and greater economic justice. However, as in Africa, Cold War tensions stymied calls for democracy and human rights and instead gave birth to and nurtured dictatorial political leaderships. Still, there are a few crucial differences between Africa and the Arab world. First, several Arab states have significant oil and gas deposits. The West's thirst for these resources kept oil-rich Arab leaders close to the West and away from the USSR. Also, oil and gas revenue meant that these states were not dependent on outside powers or international institutions for financial and economic support. Second, Arab politics have long been monopolized by the Israeli question, with some states taking a hard line and others accepting co-existence. Third, the 1979 Iranian revolution and the Soviet invasion of Afghanistan—along with the decade-long jihad to liberate it—exacerbated tensions in the Islamic world, creating a divide between secularly minded and theocratic and fundamentalist actors.

To these political and historical factors, one might add some general cultural ones, particularly relating to Islam and the Arab milieu from which it sprang. These cultural preferences typically disfavor layering judicial remedies, the absence of hierarchy in religious—and, consequently, legal—authority, and hesitation to admit into the adjudicative process sources of law other than Sharia.[30] But one has to be extremely wary of cultural stereotypes and generalization. A satisfactory treatment of the attitudes and behaviors of the Islamic world, or at least the Arabic world, toward international adjudication has yet to be written.

[28] See K Alter, *The New Terrain of International Law: Courts, Politics, Rights* (Princeton University Press 2014) 98–9 and 151–2. See in this handbook, Fold-out Chart 1, International Judicial Bodies: Compulsory Jurisdiction Across the Globe (Judicial Bodies of Regional Integration Agreements and Human Rights Courts: Overlapping Jurisdictions).

[29] See, in this Handbook, Romano, Ch. 6.

[30] M Shapiro, *Courts: A Comparative and Political Analysis* (University of Chicago Press 1981) 194–222.

Be that as it may, these are some factors that might explain why, in stark contrast to Africa, the Arab world is one of the least judicialized areas of the world despite somewhat similar political evolutions. But it was not destined to be so. The main international organization in this region is the Arab League, which comprises 22 states, including Somalia, stretching from the Atlantic Ocean in the west to the Arabian Sea in the east, and from the Mediterranean Sea in the north to the Horn of Africa and the Indian Ocean in the southeast. Although the Arab League should have been endowed from the outset with an Arab Court of Justice, the project did not take off.[31] In the early 1980s, the League successfully gave birth to a judicial body with very limited jurisdiction, the Arab Investment Court (AIC). Yet, the AIC started operating only in 2003 and, to date, has issued only nine rulings.[32] In the larger Islamic World other attempts at judicialization have also been made, mostly to ensure a prominent role of Islamic Sharia in judicial decision-making, but with no success.

As to international criminal law, again, attitudes are lukewarm if not outright hostile in this part of the globe. The only states in the region that have ratified the Rome Statute are Tunisia and Jordan. Palestine might be next, should its statehood finally be accepted. There is also a hybrid international criminal court, the Special Tribunal for Lebanon, but the Byzantine process that led to its creation—and the fact that, for reasons of security, it is not based in Lebanon but in a suburb of The Hague—is telling of the generally hostile attitude toward international adjudication that prevails in the region.

Judicialization can hardly take root in a region where the rule of law is not firmly accepted and entrenched domestically. But if politics change in the Arab region, the fortunes of international judicialization might do so as well. Starting with the end of the Cold War and Iraq's invasion of Kuwait, the whole Arab world has entered a turbulent phase of its history that has not yet ended. The "Arab Spring," which begun in 2011 and swept away many of the historical leaders in the region, is just its latest chapter. In March 2013, at the Arab League Summit in Doha, Qatar, a proposal presented by Bahrain to create an Arab Court of Human Rights was approved.[33] A high-level committee of legal experts was charged with drafting the statute of the court, and asked to submit its conclusions to the Ministerial Council of the League at its next session.[34] Yet, the fact that, to date, the Arab Charter of Human Rights has been ratified by only 11—including embattled Syria—out of 22 members of the Arab League,[35] and that the proposal was presented by the Kingdom of Bahrain, a state

[31] See, in this handbook, Romano, Ch. 6, at section 1.2.

[32] See WB Hamida, "The First Arab Investment Court Decision" (2009) 7.5 Journal of World Investment & Trade 699–721.

[33] <http://www.mofa.gov.bh/egovservices/achr/InfoEn.aspx> accessed April 1, 2013.

[34] Final Statement of the Doha Meeting, held on March 26, 2013, Order 573 (p. 6) (translated from Arabic), available at <www.lasportal.org/> accessed April 1, 2013.

[35] Arab Charter on Human Rights, concluded on May 22, 2004, reprinted in 12 Int'l Hum. Rts. Rep. 893 (2005), entered into force March 15, 2008.

that has responded to Arab Spring uprisings in its territory with a ham fist, makes one question the actual aims of this project.

1.2.5 *Asia-Pacific*

Finally, as is the case of the Arab World, there are few adjudicative bodies in the vast Asia-Pacific region, stretching from Iran to the west, to the Pacific shores in the east. So far, the only active regional courts with jurisdiction extending into the Asian continent—which for that matter only cover former Soviet Republics—are actually European courts: the ECtHR, the Economic Court of the Commonwealth of Independent States, and the Court of the Eurasian Economic Community.[36]

The shortage of adjudicative bodies in a vast region—home to two-thirds of the world population—is a puzzle to scholars and a mortgage on the future of the international judicialization project. History, power, philosophical and religious traditions, and geography could all provide some explanations. However, the vastness and sheer diversity of the region make it impossible to articulate plausible pan-Asian accounts.

Emphasis on social harmony—a distinctive trait of Confucianism, Daoism, and Buddhism—and the corresponding rejection of the typical Western system of adversarial legalism (in favor of mediation as dispute-settlement tool of choice) might explain diffidence towards international adjudication in Eastern Asia.[37] But those factors do not explain the growing share of litigation of East Asian nations in the international trade and commercial sector before international and transnational adjudicative bodies. Further, these cultural factors do not explain the attitude of India, or of the many predominantly Islamic states of Central, Southern, and Western Asia.

The larger historical forces that sparked judicialization in other regions did not have the same effects here. Decolonization did not give rise to any pan-Asian integration movement, as it did in Africa. Throughout the Cold War and beyond, communist China remained domestically and regionally powerful, able to support friendly local leaders and challenge the United States. The robust presence of a socialist/communist alternative in the region reduced demands for liberal reform. The absence of a common external threat provided few incentives for Asian states to cooperate, whereas opposition to communism unified many states in the Americas and Western Europe. After the end of the Cold War, while the market-economy paradigm spread—and was embraced even by China—democracy and guarantees of human rights did not follow suit. Again, China, which historically has shunned

[36] One should add to these the OSCE Court of Conciliation and Arbitration, which is not active. See, in this handbook, Romano, Ch. 6, at section 1.3.

[37] See generally, R Peerenboom (ed.), *Asian Discourses of Rule of Law: Theories and Implementation of Rule of Law in Twelve Asian Countries, France and the US* (London: Routledge 2003); Shapiro, note 30, 157–93.

international adjudication (with a partial and very recent exception of the WTO), provides a convincing alternative to paradigms of judicialization, be them of the EU–ECJ or the NAFTA–WTO kind.

Power distribution and imbalances might be another explanation. The area is the scene of bitter rivalries between many major powers: India/Pakistan; India/China; Iran/Iraq; China/Japan; Japan/South Korea; or Thailand/Cambodia. In other parts of the globe, judicialization has often happened because there has been one or more hegemonic power that has taken the lead toward first integration and then judicialization. Here, none of these—each for its own cultural, political, and historical reasons—has taken on a similar role. The lack of catalysts and the lack of near-neighbors willing to submit to robust regional or global judicial oversight have reduced peer pressure to submit to international judicial oversight.

Judicialization on a continent-wide scale in Asia is probably not attainable as it happened in Europe. Regional courts could emerge, but only away from the shadow of major regional hegemons. In this regard, Southeast Asia seems to have all the necessary ingredients. The Association of Southeast Asian Nations (ASEAN) was created in 1967 in the heat of the Vietnam War by Indonesia, Malaysia, the Philippines, Singapore, and Thailand. The five founding members were brought together by the common fear of communism, a reduced faith in or mistrust of external powers, and a desire for economic development. From the outset the mantras of the organization have been sovereignty, non-interference, minimal institutionalization, and non-confrontation. Judicialization was definitively not on the cards. Indeed, the "ASEAN Way" has been described as a process of "regional interactions and cooperation based on discreteness, informality, consensus building and non-confrontational bargaining styles" that contrasts with "the adversarial posturing, majority vote and other legalistic decision-making procedures in Western multilateral organizations."[38]

Over the years, ASEAN membership expanded to ten and included former communist states, such as Vietnam and Laos, and troubled countries, such as Myanmar and Cambodia. Yet this did not prevent ASEAN from evolving—and probably caused it to change. Since the beginning of the 2000s there has been a shift in attitudes within ASEAN, calling into question the "ASEAN Way" and moving toward greater institutionalization, legalization, and possibly judicialization. First, in November 2004, the bare-bones ASEAN dispute settlement system was enhanced via adoption of a WTO-style process—ad hoc panels for the first stage and then an ASEAN Appellate Body, called the Enhanced Dispute Settlement Mechanism.[39] As in the case of Mercosur (Southern Common Market, an association of Latin American States),

[38] A Acharya, *Constructing a Security Community in South East Asia: ASEAN and the Problem of Regional Order* (London: Routledge 2001) 63.

[39] W Woon, "The ASEAN Charter Dispute Settlement Mechanisms" in T Koh, R Manalo and W Woon (eds), *The Making of the ASEAN Charter* (Singapore: World Scientific Publishing 2008).

ASEAN member states can choose to adjudicate cases in the WTO system instead of the ASEAN system, and thus far member states seem to prefer the WTO system. This probably explains why the ASEAN mechanism remains unused. Second, the adoption of the ASEAN Charter in 2007 turned ASEAN into a formal international organization that aims to create a single free-trade area, EU-style, for the region.[40] Among the fundamental principles inspiring the new ASEAN are: adherence to the rule of law, good governance, the principles of democracy and constitutional government, respect for fundamental freedoms, and promotion and protection of human rights—all precursors of judicialization. The Charter also led to the creation of the ASEAN Intergovernmental Commission on Human Rights in 2009,[41] which in turn led to adoption of the ASEAN Human Rights Declaration in 2012.[42] Should ASEAN follow the same trajectory followed by the OAS and the Council of Europe, there might one day be an ASEAN Charter of Human Rights whose implementation might be supervised by a quasi-judicial and/or a judicial body.

Finally, only 17 out of about 40 states in the Asian Pacific are ICC members—and most of these are Pacific Islands, including Australia and New Zealand. The overall scarcity of judicialization in the Asian-Pacific region probably explains the generally cold attitude toward international criminal adjudication. Yet again, in relative terms, Southeast Asia seems to be more positively inclined toward international adjudication than most of the continent. The three states in this sub-region that have ratified the ICC statute are Cambodia, the Philippines, and Timor-Leste. The same sub-region is home to two Asian hybrid criminal courts: the Serious Crimes Unit/Panel in East Timor (now discontinued) and the troubled Extraordinary Chambers in the Courts of Cambodia.

2 Uneven Usage

Existence of an international adjudicative body and acceptance of its jurisdiction create only a *potential* for litigation. Whether the body is going to be activated in any given situation depends on a cost–benefit analysis done by the applicant (the plaintiff or, in the case of international criminal courts, the Prosecutor), or both

[40] Association of South East Asian Nations Charter, adopted November 20, 2007, entered into force December 15, 2008, <http://www.asean.org/asean/asean-charter/asean-charter> accessed February 25, 2012.

[41] ASEAN Intergovernmental Commission on Human Rights <http://aichr.org/> accessed February 1, 2013.

[42] ASEAN Human Rights Declaration, adopted November 18, 2012, <http://www.asean.org/news/asean-statement-communiques/item/asean-human-rights-declaration> accessed February 1, 2013.

parties (if litigation is consensual). However, even when jurisdiction has been accepted and is compulsory, cases often fail to be litigated for a number of factors, including issues of admissibility or jurisdiction, or because the issue is addressed through alternative dispute resolution means.[43]

Thus, actual use by all kinds of parties is a much more precise indicator of the attitudes toward international adjudication than availability. In this handbook, Natalie Klein's chapter analyzes patterns of utilization of several bodies.[44] She has also published recently a collection of scholarly essays that map for what themes and by which states which international adjudicative bodies are resorted to.[45] It is not the place here to summarize that extensive research. However, the main takeaway is that patterns of utilization are considerably uneven. While a significant number of actors (states or non-governmental entities) at some point have participated in the odd international litigation, a large share of all cases in any given international adjudicative forum has been litigated by a small number of repeat users. As international litigation has the effect of reasserting and reinforcing the institutions of international law where cases are being litigated, thus strengthening the international legal system as such, arguably those actors that do not participate in international litigation are free riding, reaping the benefits of the existence of an adjudicative system, paying neither the price of its financing, nor sharing the risks inherent in litigation.[46] Normatively, one can wonder whether action should and could be taken to ensure that as wide a range of actors as possible participates in the system.

3 Uneven Thematic Coverage

The areas of international law and relations where judicialization has been so far the most salient are largely those close to the classical liberal interests: trade liberalization, intellectual property, property rights—including territorial delimitation, investors' rights, protection of basic human rights (including those of corporations and associations), and retrospective trials of perpetrators of certain kinds of carefully delimited atrocities.[47]

[43] On jurisdiction and admissibility, see generally, in this handbook, Shany, Ch. 36.

[44] See, in this handbook, Klein, Ch. 26.

[45] N Klein (ed.), *Litigating International Law Disputes: Weighing the Options* (Cambridge University Press 2014).

[46] C Romano, "Litigating international Disputes: Whereto?" in Klein, note 45.

[47] B Kingsbury, "International Courts: Uneven Judicialization in Global Order" in J Crawford and M Koskenniemi (eds), *Cambridge Companion to International Law* (Cambridge University Press 2012) 203–27.

Yet, while extensive, judicialization has not reached many aspects of international law and relations. Many issues, while sometimes largely legalized,[48] are not judicialized. The list is long. These include most military and intelligence activities, including collective defense, arms control, disarmament, nuclear weapons, nuclear energy governance, and counter-terrorism; global and regional financial governance; cyberspace policing and data-sharing; most religious issues; migrations and most refugees' rights; most issues of taxation, education, social welfare, labor, and local government; urban policy; corruption; social violence; land, water, and atmosphere—including climate—management, as well as management of global commons and natural resources; hazardous waste management and disposal; decision-making processes in international bodies; forms of pressure (e.g. sanctions) or encouragement (e.g. aid) by global bodies toward specific governments and their policies; humanitarian assistance and disaster response; and most forms of inequality and distributive justice.[49]

Granted, occasionally issues in some of these broad areas do reach an international court. For instance, the ICJ has ruled on some security-related issues, such as the legality of nuclear weapons or the wall in Palestine.[50] Environmental disputes have been litigated before a wide variety of adjudicative bodies—global and regional, judicial and arbitral—and there is definitively potential for more, especially under the Law of the Sea Convention.[51] But what these areas are lacking are specialized and dedicated bodies, which are to be found in the more judicialized fields. There is not yet an international court for the environment,[52] an international bankruptcy court,[53] or an international loans tribunal,[54] a cyberspace and Internet international court,[55] or a NATO court. The relative scarcity of judicialization of these subject areas, or dedicated adjudicative bodies, is explicable.[56] In many cases it

[48] K Abbot et al., "The Concept of Legalization" (2000) 54.3 Int'l Org. 401–19.

[49] Kingsbury, note 47, at 212.

[50] *Legality of the Threat or Use of Nuclear Weapons, Advisory Opinion*, I.C.J. Reports 1996, 226; *Advisory Opinion Concerning Legal Consequences of the Construction of a Wall in the Occupied Palestinian Territory*, I.C.J. Reports 2004, 136.

[51] For examples of international environmental disputes litigated before international adjudicative bodies, see generally, C Romano, *The Peaceful Settlement of International Environmental Disputes: A Pragmatic Approach* (The Hague: Kluwer 2000).

[52] Romano, note 51, at 125–9.

[53] C Seavey, "The Anomalous Lack of an International Bankruptcy Court" (2006) 24 Berkeley J. Int'l L. 499–520.

[54] M Hudson, *International Tribunals: Past and Future* (Washington D.C.:Carnegie Endowment for International Peace and Brookings Institution 1944) 204.

[55] However, the Arbitration and Mediation Center of the World Intellectual Property Organization adjudicates disputes over Internet domain names. See WIPO ADR Arbitration and Mediation Center, "Domain Name Dispute Resolution" <http://www.wipo.int/amc/en/domains/> accessed February 1, 2013.

[56] See e.g., A Mondré et al., "Uneven Judicialization: Comparing International Dispute Settlement in Security, Trade, and the Environment" (2010) 4.1 New Global Studies 1–32; Seavey, note 53; Kingsbury, note 47; Romano, *Environmental Disputes*, note 51.

may even be welcome, given the severe limits of what adjudication per se can manage or achieve.

Even in those areas where judicialization has taken place, it might be rather thin. For instance, while human rights in general are fairly judicialized, not all aspects of human rights are. The jurisdiction of most human rights judicial and quasi-judicial bodies is limited to civil and political rights. The judicialization of economic, social, and cultural rights is limited. Also, so far, the ICJ is the only adjudicative body with jurisdiction over "... any question of international law."[57] The subject-matter jurisdiction of all other international courts, global or regional, is limited to a specific area of international law. Almost all new adjudicative bodies have been created to serve and enhance specialized regimes, rather than as courts of general jurisdiction that might reach too far beyond what the creating states wish to see investigated and adjudicated. Moreover, many of these specialized bodies do not have mandates to adjudicate issues concerning the conduct of institutions of which they are part. For instance, the WTO Appellate Body does not rule on major actions or inactions of the WTO, only on what member states do. In NAFTA and the WTO, the contracting states retain the power to re-interpret a treaty if they disagree with a tribunal's interpretation, without needing to formally amend the treaty.[58]

One day these areas of international law and relations might become more judicialized. The global financial crisis that started in 2007 has led many to wonder whether new international judicial institutions would be needed to unravel the complex issues of who owes what to whom when markets melt down. In 2012, a new arbitral institution called the Panel of Recognized International Market Experts in Finance (PRIME) was launched in The Hague with the aim of providing a settlement mechanism for disputes over complex financial products such as derivatives.[59] PRIME offers mediation and arbitration services to settle disputes between private entities such as banks, insurance firms, and pension funds; institutions such as clearinghouses, exchanges, and regulators; and possibly even customers. This is a private endeavor, not unlike a law firm, that is not supported by states. As such, it does not qualify as an international adjudicative body,[60] but its creation might signal a significant trend.

Since the early 1990s, many multilateral environmental regimes have been equipped with so-called "non-compliance procedures."[61] These serve two main

[57] Statute of the International Court of Justice, 33 U.N.T.S. 993, Art. 36.2.b, adopted on June 26, 1945, entered into force on October 24, 1945.

[58] The NAFTA Free Trade Commission used this power in 2001 in response to the first *Pope & Talbot Inc. v. Canada* arbitral award. See NAFTA Claims, "Pope & Talbot Inc. and Canada" <http://www.naftaclaims.com/disputes_canada_pope.htm> accessed February 1, 2013.

[59] See P.R.I.M.E. Finance, "Finance Experts" <http://www.primefinancedisputes.org/index.php/expert-list/financial-experts.html> accessed February 1, 2013.

[60] See in this handbook, Romano, Alter, and Shany, Ch. 1, at section 1.

[61] At the last count (2011), there were 18 of them. See C Romano, "A Taxonomy of International Rule of Law Institutions" (2011) 2.1 JIDS 259–61.

functions: the review of periodic reports by states about the measures they have taken to implement obligations contained in the relevant treaties, and consideration of cases of alleged non-compliance. Typically, non-compliance procedures are "non-confrontational, non-judicial and consultative in nature."[62] In most cases, they are made of representatives of states, even though sometimes they might be bound to "serve objectively and in the best interest of the Convention."[63] However, in a few significant cases, such as the Kyoto Protocol to the United Nations Framework Convention on Climate Change, they are comprised of independent experts serving in their personal capacity, as international judicial bodies do. Some of these procedures might one day acquire more judicial features.

4 Conclusions

International judicialization is inevitably uneven.[64] As long as the world is divided into sovereign states, judicialization that is truly universal, complete and homogeneous across regions and subjects will never happen. The international judicial system will remain incomplete and fragmented, reflecting the wide and uneven international distribution of power. Indeed, if there is any lesson to draw from the history of the creation of national judicial systems, it is that where power is not centralized and consolidated, a true judicial system, with comprehensive coverage, will not emerge.

If incomplete judicialization is thus an inevitable, if not outright desirable, fact, what should be made of it? We tried to tease out historical, political, and cultural reasons for variations in judicialization between the regions of the globe. We showed how participation in litigation before international judicial bodies is increasing, involving a large number of states and non-state actors, but also how only a handful of states have become repeat users and been strongly socialized to the practice of international litigation. We showed how starting from issues close to the classical

[62] Convention on Access to Information, Public Participation in Decision-Making and Access to Justice in Environmental Matters (Aarhus Convention), 2161 UNTS 447, Art. 15 (adopted on June 25, 1998, entered into force on October 30, 2001).

[63] Basel Convention on the Control of Transboundary Movements of Hazardous Wastes and Their Disposal, 1673 UNTS 126 (adopted on March 22, 1989, entered into force on May 5, 1992); Decision VI/12 on Establishment of a Mechanism for Promoting Implementation and Compliance (February 10, 2003), UNEP/CHW.6/40, Annex, para. 5.

[64] C Romano, "Progress in International Adjudication: Revisiting Hudson's Assessment of the Future of International Courts" in R Miller and R Bratspies (eds), *Progress in International Law* (Leiden: Nijhoff 2008) 433–50, at 449.

liberal interests, international courts have gradually addressed a longer list of concerns, but that several salient aspects of international law and relations still show little sign of judicialization. The aim was not to put forward an exhaustive treatment of the shadow zones of international adjudication, but rather to highlight how little we still know about why and where international adjudicative bodies are not created; when states decide not to subject themselves to international jurisdiction and why; why certain issues seem to be off-limits for international courts; and why certain states or other actors still do not litigate, or litigate less than they would be expected to do.

It is just as important to understand the conditions under which international judicialization does not happen as it is to understand the conditions under which it does. Knowing the limits of international judicialization helps us to trace its future trajectory with greater confidence. As Benedict Kingsbury observed, at the beginning of the twenty-first century, perceptible changes in the global distribution of power among major states—and shifts in dominant approaches to the international legal order—put into question both the prospects of governance through major new comprehensive global legal regimes, and the creation of new courts under such treaties.[65] No new adjudicative bodies with global scope are in sight, and a World Court of Human Rights is a necessity that remains a hardly attainable dream.[66] Yet the global level has traditionally been difficult terrain for judicialization. If new international courts are going to emerge, it will be at the regional level.

If the establishment of more is unlikely, at least at the breakneck pace of the past two decades, the increase in caseload and judicial output of existing adjudicative bodies is likely to continue. With few exceptions, most bodies have excess capacity that has not yet been tapped and potential users are still climbing the learning curve. Yet beyond these incremental advances, shifts in the tectonic plates of international politics raise serious questions over the long term.

Adjudication is a product of liberal and legalist juridical orders that are particularly associated with democracy, rule of law, open markets and information flows, basic liberal property and political rights setting limits on state powers, and some hierarchical governance structures dominated by liberal polities and their corporate and civil society groupings.[67] A multi-polar global political order, especially one where the relative power of the United States and Europe is decreasing, is already bringing about ideas about what global governance is and how law and legal

[65] Kingsbury, note 47, at 223–4.

[66] M Nowak, "It's Time for a World Court of Human Rights" in C Bassiouni and W Schabas (eds), *New Challenges for the UN Human Rights Machinery: What Future for the UN Treaty Body System and the Human Rights Council Procedures?* (Cambridge: Intersentia 2011); J Kozma, *A World Court of Human Rights, Consolidated Statute and Commentary* (Vienna: Neuer Wissenschaftlicher Verlag 2010); C Romano, "Can You Hear Me Now? Making the Case for Extending the International Judicial Network" (2009) 9 Chi. J. Int'l L., 233, 267–8.

[67] Kingsbury, note 47, at 223–4.

institutions can and should function that are quite different from those embodied by contemporary international adjudicative bodies. In this regard, the marginal role played so far in the judicialization project by the vast Asia-Pacific region and the Arab World should be a concern, and not just an academic curiosity.

Research Questions

1. What are the historical, cultural and political factors explaining differences in judicialization between regions? What factors explain the different attitudes and practices of the rising major players of the twenty-first century (e.g. China, India, South Korea, Japan, Brazil, Russia, South Africa, Nigeria)? How do they compare with those of the major members of the European Union (e.g. Germany, France, the United Kingdom, or Italy) and/or the United States?
2. Does participation in international adjudication make states more willing to participate in the future? In other words, does international litigation socialize states to international adjudication? Does participation in one judicial forum increase chances a state will also participate in litigation in another? What does empirical evidence tell us?
3. What are the patterns of utilization of international adjudicative bodies by non-state actors, and what are the factors explaining utilization or neglect?
4. How is it possible to reconcile uneven judicialization of human rights across the globe with their postulated universality and the right of everyone to an effective judicial remedy?

Suggested Reading

Abbot, K et al., "The Concept of Legalization" (2000) 54.3 Int'l Org. 401–19.

Alter, K, *The New Terrain of International Law: Courts, Politics, Rights* (Princeton University Press 2014).

Alvarez, J, "The New Dispute Settlers: (Half) Truths and Consequences" (2003) 38.3 Tex. Int'l L. J., 405–44.

Kingsbury, B, "International Courts: Uneven Judicialization in Global Order" in J Crawford and M Koskenniemi (eds), *Cambridge Companion to International Law* (Cambridge University Press 2012) 203–27.

Klein, N (ed.), *Litigating International Law Disputes: Weighing the Options* (Cambridge University Press 2014).

Mackenzie, R, Romano, C, and Shany, Y (eds), *The Manual on International Courts and Tribunals* (2nd edn, Oxford University Press 2010).

Mondré, A et al., "Uneven Judicialization: Comparing International Dispute Settlement in Security, Trade, and the Environment" (2010) 4.1 New Global Studies 1.

Romano, C, "Progress in International Adjudication: Revisiting Hudson's Assessment of the Future of International Courts" in R. Miller and R. Bratspies (eds), *Progress in International Law* (Leiden: Nijhoff 2008) 433–50.

Romano, C, "Can You Hear Me Now? Making the Case for Extending the International Judicial Network" (2009) 9 Chi. J. Int'l L. 233.
Romano, C (ed.), *The Sword and the Scales: The United States and International Courts and Tribunals* (Cambridge University Press 2009).
Shapiro, M, *Courts: A Comparative and Political Analysis* (University of Chicago Press 1981).

CHAPTER 6

TRIAL AND ERROR IN INTERNATIONAL JUDICIALIZATION

CESARE PR ROMANO*

"I didn't fail 9,999 times. I just found 9,999 ways that do not work."[1]

THERE is a lamentable tendency amongst scholars of our field to acclaim each flourishing adjudicative institution as a foreordained achievement, to think of them as permanent features of the landscape with indefinite lasting power and to study only what exists and is easy to research. International judicialization—that is to say the increasing creation and use of international judicial bodies—is generally depicted as moving slowly, steadily, and almost inexorably. In this handbook, Mary Ellen

* Professor of Law and W. Joseph Ford Fellow, Loyola Law School Los Angeles; Co-Director Project on International Courts and Tribunals. I would like to acknowledge the assistance, at Loyola, of Mark Oknyansky, and the helpful feedback of the co-editors of this handbook.

[1] Attributed to Thomas Alva Edison, allegedly answering a question regarding his many failed attempts at finding a long-lasting and practical light bulb.

O'Connell and Lenore VanderZee as well as Karen Alter told the story of international judicialization from inception to present day. They tell what could be dubbed the "standard narrative of international judicialization," a largely linear story of successes from nineteenth-century arbitration to the current constellation of adjudicative bodies.

The stars of the standard narrative are the International Court of Justice (ICJ), the dispute settlement system of the World Trade Organization (WTO), the European Court of Justice (ECJ) and the European Court of Human Rights (ECtHR), the International Criminal Tribunal for the Former Yugoslavia (ICTY) and the International Criminal Court (ICC). These are the protagonists of most of scholarly literature on international adjudication. However, there are other possible narratives, equally true and instructive. One could tell, for instance, the story of the many international courts that never opened their doors and exist only on paper. Or, one could tell the story of the lesser known and less successful siblings of the heroes of the standard narrative of international judicialization.

The addition of this alternative narrative yields a more credible and precise picture of the rise of international courts and its dynamics. Indeed, if one considers that for every contemporary thriving body, there are at least twice as many that failed to set sail, or got caught in the doldrums, or even sunk after launch, the most plausible account of the rise of international adjudication is one of progress through trial and error.

"Trial and error" is a heuristic, and rather primitive, method for problem solving. No theory or plan guides progress, there are no hypotheses and experiments, but rather repeated attempts and progressive fine-tuning based on inferences drawn from failures. Much of the development of international adjudication has taken place without the support of sophisticated theories. It is only recently that theorizing has been brought to bear on this field.[2] For at least the past 200 years, since the age of enlightenment, the building of national judiciaries has often been a centrally planned endeavor that benefits from vast and sophisticated scholarship from a wide range of social sciences. Conversely, the growth of the constellation of international adjudicative bodies, which has taken place between the end of the twentieth and the beginning of the twenty-first century, has been organic, unplanned, and uncoordinated. To the extent precedents have inspired new courts it is only the success stories of the stars of the standard narrative that have been taken into account.[3] As Karen Alter wrote, "[I]rrelevant institutions are mostly ignored."[4]

This chapter presents just a sample of the less-known, but hard-won, lessons of international adjudication. An exhaustive treatment is more suitable for a

[2] See in this handbook, Pollack, Ch. 17, at section 3. See also D Caron, "Towards a Political Theory of International Courts and Tribunals" (2006) 24(2) Berkeley J. Int'l L. 401.

[3] See in this handbook, Alter, Ch. 4, at section 1.1. See also K Alter, "The Global Spread of European Style International Courts" (2012) 35(1) West Eur. Pol. 135.

[4] See in this handbook, Alter, Ch. 4.

monograph. First, we will tell the stories of some of the courts that failed to come into existence or that were never activated. Second, we will look at the difficulties experienced by some contemporary international adjudicative bodies. Yet, in no case should inclusion in this chapter be read as a death certificate. In the long run, courts that were never activated could all of a sudden be marshaled into action at historical critical junctures and beleaguered courts might find a firm footing.

1 Nipped in the Bud

It is remarkable how many international adjudicative bodies never started operating, or decided a couple of cases and then fell into disuse. An incomplete list might include:[5]

1. Arbitral Tribunal of the Inter-governmental Organization for International Carriage by Rail (1890)
2. Central American Arbitration Tribunal (1902)
3. International Prize Court (1907)
4. Central American Tribunal (1923)
5. Inter-American Court of International Justice (1938)
6. Arab Court of Justice (1945)
7. European Nuclear Energy Tribunal of the Organization for Economic Cooperation and Development (1957)
8. Arbitral College of the Benelux Economic Union (1958)
9. Court of Arbitration of the French Community (1959)
10. Arbitration Tribunal of the Central American Common Market (1960)
11. European Tribunal on State Immunity (1972)
12. Judicial Board of the Organization of Arab Petroleum Exporting Countries (1980)
13. Court of Justice of the Economic Community of Central African States (1983)
14. International Islamic Court of Justice (1987)
15. Court of Justice of the Arab Maghreb Union (1989)
16. Court of Justice of the African Economic Community (1991)
17. Court of Conciliation and Arbitration of the Organization for Security and Cooperation in Europe (1994)

[5] The date of adoption of the legal instrument that created them or provided for their creation is provided in parentheses.

18. Court of the Union State between the Russian Federation and the Republic of Belarus (1999)
19. Court of Justice of the Central African Economic and Monetary Community (2000)
20. Court of Justice of the African Union (2003)

Some of these bodies have been condemned. Others can be said to be simply dormant. Indeed, as we said, the fact that a judicial body never started operating does not necessarily mean that it will never be called into action. Yet, all these bodies have been inactive for at least a decade and, for this reason, it is prudent to group them together in this list.

Of course, there is a story behind each that explains why, after spending significant negotiating time, states failed to ratify their constitutive instruments, or why, after the judicial body was officially open for business, cases failed to be brought. Literature on many of these is scant, with some offering no more than a few footnotes. Given the numbers, comprehensive treatment is beyond the scope of this chapter. However, a few will suffice to shed light on the most common problems that kill international adjudicative institutions in the crib, so to speak.

1.1 International Prize Court

The International Prize Court (IPC) was one of the first international adjudicative bodies ever. In 1907, the Second Hague Peace Conference convened and agreed on rules regulating conduct during wartime by belligerents, with a particular focus on naval warfare. Amongst the many legal documents adopted by the conference, there was the statute for an international court to adjudicate disputes over prize.[6]

"Prize money" is the reward paid out to the crew of a ship for capturing an enemy vessel, or a vessel of a neutral trying to run a blockade. The practice of paying prize money to captains and crews to reward and encourage their fighting zeal at no cost to their government had been widespread amongst European navies since the sixteenth century. Lawfulness of the confiscation was decided in court. The captain of the vessel executing the capture would choose a port—in a third, neutral state or the state of nationality of the captor—where the prize would be ordered; a "prize court" (a national court with specialized knowledge of maritime law and international law but sometimes even just a single individual, such as a consul or an ambassador) in that port would adjudicate on the matter. Typically, the flag state or the ship-owner could challenge the judgments of prize courts, and in several instances these legal

[6] Convention (XII) Relative to the Creation of an International Prize Court, concluded at The Hague, October 18, 1907, 3 Martens (3rd) 388, reprinted in (1908) 2 AJIL 174.

challenges led to international arbitrations,[7] but national courts were suspected of being highly partial and the practice of prize money was frequently abused for obvious reasons.[8]

The IPC was the supposed remedy to the need for an impartial forum. National prize court decisions were to be appealable before the IPC. Although the adoption of the IPC Statute by the Second Hague Conference was hailed at the time as a "first step toward the establishment of an international judicial system,"[9] it turned out to be a false first step. The IPC was dead in the water before it was launched. To begin with, there were grave divergences between the major maritime powers, especially Great Britain and Germany, with regard to the rules of prize law in question.[10] Second, there was a rift between the major maritime powers and the smaller ones on the composition of the court. The major powers were going to have eight permanent judges and the minor powers had seven rotating judges. Numerous states made reservations to the proposed rotation. In the end, agreement on a method of electing judges could not be reached. Finally, the United States harbored major reservations to the creation of a court that could hear appeals against decisions of the US Supreme Court, which had final jurisdiction upon appeal over prize cases.[11] At the insistence of the United States, a special protocol was adopted to permit a signatory to the convention to restrict the right of appeal.[12]

For these reasons, the treaty establishing the IPC failed to attract any ratification and never entered into force. It is likely, however, that the IPC was obsolete even before it was designed. First, for centuries states had given an incentive to crews to seize vessels by giving them a share of the value of the confiscated ship and cargo, but by the beginning of the twentieth century, it was believed that sailors could be trusted to do their duty without personal gain incentives. The United States had already abolished the practice of prize money in 1899.[13] Second, the rise of submarine warfare meant that navies were going to try to sink enemy and neutral shipping rather than capturing it, a complicated and perilous maneuver.[14]

[7] Claims in a dozen or more prize cases which had been decided by the US Supreme Court during or after the American Civil War in the United States, were later submitted to an American–British arbitral tribunal.

[8] On prize taking in the age of sails and prize courts, see, in general, D Petrie, *The Prize Game* (Annapolis, MD: Naval Institute Press 1999).

[9] M Hudson, *International Tribunals: Past and Future* (Washington D.C.: Carnegie Endowment for International Peace and Brookings Institution 1944) 165.

[10] A restricted conference with only ten maritime powers that was convened in London soon after the end of the Hague Conference adopted a declaration on that that failed to attract any ratification. Additional Protocol to the Convention Relative to the Creation of an International Prize Court, adopted at the Hague, September 19, 1910, reprinted in (1911) 5 AJIL Supplement 95.

[11] On prize cases decided by the US Supreme Court, see J Scott Brown, *Prize Cases Decided in the US Supreme Court (1789–1918)* (Oxford University Press 1923).

[12] Declaration Concerning the Laws of Naval War, 208 Consol. T.S. 338 (1909).

[13] 30 Statutes at Large 1007 (1899).

[14] The practice of prize money has been suspected of prolonging the practice of boarding and hand-to-hand fighting long after naval cannons developed the ability to sink the enemy from afar.

Still, the IPC and the Second Hague Conference were not quite complete dead-ends of international judicialization. It was the testing ground for some then still-novel concepts. For instance, the IPC Statute provided for judges ad hoc, an idea later adopted in the World Court and a number of other courts.[15] Moreover, it is little known that the Second Hague Conference of 1907 also considered the adoption of the statue of an International Court of Arbitral Justice, which is effectively the missing link in the evolutionary chain between the Permanent Court of Arbitration (PCA) and the Permanent Court of International Justice (PCIJ).[16]

1.2 Arab and Islamic courts

Another noteworthy non-starter is the Arab Court of Justice (ACJ). This adjudicative body is provided for in the constitutive act of the Arab League: the Pact of the League of Arab States, adopted in March 1945 by six Arab states (Egypt, Iraq, Transjordan (renamed Jordan in 1949), Lebanon, Saudi Arabia, and Syria), to expand eventually to the current 22-state membership. Article 19 provides for procedures to amend the Pact ". . . in particular for the purpose of . . . creating an Arab Court of Justice."[17] Over the years, several draft statutes were prepared, but the required majority to adopt the amendment and bring the ACJ into existence could never be reached.[18]

Several factors have probably contributed to nip it in the bud. First, the Arab League has always been a very weak regional organization. It has never aspired to economic integration of its members, unlike many regional organizations that have successfully judicialized. It has worked mostly as a forum where Arab leaders could meet and discuss common concerns—and mostly to form a common front against Israel—rather than to coordinate and integrate. Member states have been careful not to cede any aspect of sovereignty to the Arab League; ruling elites prefer to maintain their power and independence in decision-making both from other Arab nations and their population, paying only lip service to Pan-Arab nationalism and the rule of law. Moreover, several feuds, if not outright wars, among Arab rulers and the influence of external powers that fear Arab unity, have been impassable obstacles to deeper integration.

What makes the ACJ worthy of notice is that it should have been able to apply, besides international law (customary and treaty-based), also the Shari'ah, the religious law of Islam.[19] Interestingly, the need for a dedicated international adjudicative

[15] Convention (XII) Relative to the Creation of an International Prize Court, note 6, Art. 16.

[16] On the International Court of Arbitral Justice, see Hudson, note 9, at 8.

[17] Pact of the League of Arab States, adopted in Cairo, March 22, 1945, UNTS Vol. 70 (1950), p. 247.

[18] AAF Thani, "The Projected Arab Court of Justice: A Study to Its Draft Statute and Rules, with Specific Reference to the International Court of Justice and Principles of Islamic Shariah." Ph.D. thesis, University of Glasgow (1999).

[19] Draft Statute of the Arab Court of Justice, Art. 23.1.b, reproduced in Thani, note 18, at 335.

body, one that not only takes Shari'ah into full account, but gives it preeminence over international law, has inspired another project. In 1987, the Organization of the Islamic Conference, a 57-state organization, gathering all states where Islam prevails, from Suriname to Indonesia, adopted the statute of the International Islamic Court of Justice (IICJ).[20] This court, which also never came into existence, was to apply mainly Shari'ah law to settle international disputes.

Besides these two projects, the only three adjudicative bodies ever created in the Arab world are the Judicial Body of the Organization of Arab Petroleum Exporting Countries (OAPEC),[21] the Tribunal of the Arab Maghreb Union (AMU),[22] and the Arab Investment Court (AIC).[23] The first two barely ever functioned and have long been inactive. The third one was inactive for 20 years after its creation and has issued in the past decade just nine rulings.

In 1989, five North African states (Libya, Tunisia, Algeria, Morocco, and Mauritania) created the AMU, a political and economic integration organization. From the outset, the organization was endowed with a judicial body, to be based in Nouakchott, Mauritania, to settle disputes between member states or between the Council of the Heads of State and member states. The AMU Tribunal never issued any rulings. It was the victim of rivalries between members (between Morocco and Algeria over Western Sahara, and between Libya and Mauritania), which to this date paralyze the organization. Moreover, until the recent Arab Spring, none of the AMU members was seriously committed to democracy and the rule of law, the liberal values that are the lifeblood of international courts.

OAPEC was created in 1968 by three then-politically conservative oil producing States—Saudi Arabia, Libya, and Kuwait—as an exclusive club that would insulate oil from street pressures by excluding more radical and less oil-rich member states, namely Egypt and Algeria, who wanted to pool it as a weapon of the people of Arab nations. It was also an alternative, more easily controllable, club to the more prominent Organization of Petroleum Exporting Countries (OPEC). In the 1970s, nationalist objectives led a number of Arab countries to seize control of their oil industries. OAPEC also succumbed to political pressure following the 1973 Yom Kippur war, expanding membership, to include presently ten states, and becoming a coordinating organization for Arab responses to the conflict with Israel. In 1978,

[20] M Lombardini, "The International Islamic Court of Justice: Towards an International Islamic Legal System?" (2001) 14(3) LJIL 665.

[21] (الهيئة القضائية لمنظمة الأقطار العربية المصدرة للبترول—Al-Hay'ah al-Ga-dha-'Yyah Le-mona-ddha-mat al-ag-Tar al-'Arabiya al-Mo-sad-De-rah Le-al-Pet-rool) <http://oapecorg.org/> accessed February 1, 2013.

[22] (الأمانة العامة لاتحاد المغرب العربي—Al-amanah Al-'Ammah Le-Ittihad Al-Maghrib Al-'Arabi—Instance Judiciaire de l'Union du Maghreb Arabe) <http://www.maghrebarabe.org/> accessed February 1, 2013.

[23] See in this handbook, Romano, Ch. 5, at section 1.2.4.

OAPEC was endowed with the Judicial Body of the OAPEC, based in Kuwait City.[24] The body has rarely been utilized, with just two cases to its record,[25] and four vacancies on its bench have been unfilled for years. As the AMU, OAPEC has been hampered by bitter rivalries between its members and a weak culture of the rule of law, which is a necessary precondition to accept binding rulings by independent judges.

All in all, the Arab world has proven to be impervious terrain for judicialization. Should the Arab Spring bring about robust democracies in the region, however, this might change. The Arab Spring might inspire, for example, the creation of an Arab Court of Human Rights, or to some quasi-judicial body.[26]

1.3 ICJ and PCA rivals: The Court of Conciliation and Arbitration of the Organization for Security and Cooperation in Europe

The need for courts of general jurisdiction, like the ICJ, but headquartered closer to its users and able to take into account regional preferences, priorities, and traditions, has inspired other projects, particular in Latin America. For instance, the PCA had barely been established when, at the Second Conference of American States, Mexico proposed the creation of an American Permanent Court of Arbitration, on the blueprint of the PCA, to be based in Quito, Ecuador.[27] At the Fifth Conference of American States, in 1923, Costa Rica proposed the creation of an American Court of Justice, to provide for a regional alternative to the Europe-centered PCIJ.[28] The Eighth Conference, in 1938, led to the adoption of a draft by a Committee of Experts on the Codification of International Law of the statute of an Inter-American Court of International Justice (IACIJ).[29] All these projects met strong opposition from the United States and Brazil, which believed that a regional court of general jurisdiction would undermine the PCIJ, and because the troubled relations between many Latin-American states would make it impossible to devise an effective mechanism to select its judges.[30]

Many of these regional attempts have ultimately failed to take off for fear of fragmenting international law by allowing regional interpretation of its norms. Also,

[24] Protocol establishing the Judicial Tribunal of the Organization of the Arab Petroleum-Exporting Countries (OAPEC), concluded in Kuwait, May 9, 1978.

[25] The first judgment was rendered in Kuwait in 1989 and the second was rendered in Cairo in 1994. The first one was dismissed by the tribunal because of its political character (*Iraq v. Syria*). The second case was between Algeria and the Arab Transportation Company.

[26] See in this handbook, Romano, Ch. 5, at section 1.2.4.

[27] Hudson, note 9, at 175.

[28] Hudson, note 9, at 175.

[29] Hudson, note 9, at 169–79.

[30] Hudson, note 9, at 175–6.

the lives of many more adjudicative bodies have been cut short due to an unwillingness to create competition for the Hague-based World Court (first the PCIJ and then the ICJ), believed to be the ultimate custodian of the unity of international law, and the PCA.

One such body is the Court of Conciliation and Arbitration of the Organization for Security and Cooperation in Europe (OSCE).[31] This court was the result of a long process of negotiations, which was started by Switzerland in 1978 and lasted throughout the end of the Cold War. It finally came to light in 1992 with the adoption of the Convention on Conciliation and Arbitration within the Conference on Security and Cooperation in Europe.[32] Its mission is to settle disputes between states: first, by conciliation, which can be triggered unilaterally by any party to the statute, and, should that fail, by arbitration, but only if both parties have agreed to it. Like the PCA, this court in itself is not permanent. It has a small secretariat, based in Geneva, and a list of conciliators and arbitrators. To date, it has not yet been activated.

To begin with, it enjoys limited support. Only 33 out of 57 OSCE members have ratified its statute.[33] Those states that have declined to ratify are a mixed bag, including the United States, United Kingdom, Canada, Spain, Netherlands, Ireland, Iceland, Russia, Kazakhstan, Turkmenistan, Georgia, Estonia, Turkey, and the Holy See. Each has its own reasons to disregard it. For instance, the Netherlands does not want to endorse an institution that duplicates the ICJ and PCA, two courts based in The Hague. The United States has an ambivalent attitude toward state-to-state litigation. It begrudgingly accepts to litigate before the ICJ, but not without reservations. Moreover, it enjoys a prominent role as mediator of European disputes; a role that it would not want to delegate to this or any other court.[34] The other major power in the OSCE, Russia, is even colder toward international litigation. Second, this court does not have compulsory jurisdiction, since arbitration can take place only if both states have agreed to it. Although states can file a declaration accepting compulsory arbitration, along the lines of the optional declaration used at the ICJ, to date only six have done so.[35]

In the end, what hinders the OSCE Court is competition from already-established international adjudicative bodies. The ICJ needs every case it can get to buttress its

[31] On the history and politics behind the creation of this adjudicative body, see P Schneider and TJA Müller-Wolf, "The Court of Conciliation and Arbitration within the OSCE: Working Methods, Procedures and Composition," Centre for OESC Research (CORE), Working Paper 16 (2007) <http://www.isn.ethz.ch/isn/Digital-Library/Publications/> accessed February 1, 2013.

[32] Convention on Conciliation and Arbitration within the Conference on Security and Cooperation in Europe, adopted in Stockholm on December 15, 1992, Annex II <http://www.osce.org/mc/40342> accessed February 1, 2013.

[33] <http://www.osce.org/cca/40119> accessed February 1, 2013.

[34] L Caflisch, "Cent ans de règlement pacifique des différents Interétatiques" (2002) 288 Recueil des Cours de l'Académie de Droit International 245, 362.

[35] <http://www.osce.org/cca/40119> accessed February 1, 2013.

legitimacy. When it comes to arbitration, the PCA offers a valid alternative, and the PCA, too, needs every state-to-state case it can get. Of course, the OSCE Court cannot compete with the institutions of the European Union, including the Court of Justice of the European Union (ECJ), in the settlement of intra-EU disputes, nor can it tackle trade disputes over which the WTO has a monopoly. Most disputes within the European Energy Charter are settled under the aegis of the International Center for the Settlement of Investment Disputes (ICSID), a judicial body with greater expertise over financial and investment matters. Finally, since individuals do not have access to it, it cannot be an alternative to the ECtHR, which could very well delegate a few cases, for instance on matters of treatment of minorities. For the OSCE Court to have a chance, it needs a major re-design and mission reconfiguration, but few states other than Switzerland seem to be willing to dedicate the necessary negotiating time that this would require. For the time being, it will remain a sleeping beauty.

1.4 Yet, sometimes they come back: The Permanent Court of Arbitration

The fact that an adjudicative body has never been activated does not mean that it could not be activated at some point in the future, or that it could not be re-designed to address some of the issues that keep it slumbering. Indeed, sometimes, sleeping beauties do wake up. The PCA is a fitting example. Accounts of the history of international adjudication usually start with the creation of the PCA in 1899 in The Hague. Then, the success of the PCA led to the creation of a universal and permanent jurisdiction, the Permanent Court of International Justice (PCIJ), which morphed into a very similar court after the end of World War II: the ICJ. What is not usually told is what happened to the PCA once the PCIJ entered the scene.

Over the 15 years between the birth of the PCA and the outbreak of World War I, 17 state-to-state arbitrations and three inquiries were conducted under the auspices of the PCA, a remarkable figure not only for the time, but even for some contemporary adjudicative institutions. In the 20 years between the two world wars, however, the number of arbitrations administered by the PCA dropped to seven, of which only five were actually decided before the outbreak of World War II, and it handled one inquiry. Clearly, the PCA thrived while it had no rivals. The arrival of the PCIJ marked the beginning of its end. Both were competing for the same pool of cases: disputes between sovereign states. As the PCA, the PCIJ offered states the possibility of having their disputes bindingly decided, but as an organ of the League of Nations, it had the extra advantage of being able to count on the support of that organization to ensure compliance with its decisions. When given a choice, states decided to bring their dispute to the PCIJ. The Peace Palace, which had been built to host the PCA, was taken over by the new World Court. Like Sleeping Beauty sidelined by the arrival of the step-mother, the International Bureau, the PCA secretariat, was rapidly confined to a few rooms of the palace and staffed with skeleton personnel to oversee a few minor cases.

After the end of World War II, as the ICJ replaced the PCIJ and regional and specialized international adjudicative bodies started spreading, the caseload of the PCA further dwindled and then completely dried up. Between the end of World War II and the end of the Cold War (1946–1989), the only arbitration conducted was between a private company and Sudan over the interpretation of a construction contract.[36] By the end of the Cold War, the PCA was a relic of the past. The only function the list of arbitrators of the PCA continued serving was to provide a pool of qualified jurists to states looking for fitting candidates for the ICJ bench.

However, the end of the Cold War proved to be a critical juncture that, besides leading to the multiplication of international courts, led also to the resurgence of the PCA. In the mid-1990s, Sleeping Beauty began stirring. A combination of factors led to its resurgence. First, the PCA had reinvented itself, adopting new rules of procedure for various kinds of disputes, and expanding its jurisdiction to disputes between private entities and states, or between private entities.[37] Second, it started providing services and support to states and international organizations wanting an arbitration option regarding disputes falling under various legal regimes. It facilitated, for instance, disputes arising under the compulsory dispute settlement clauses of the United Nations Convention on the Law of the Sea, or other regional treaties. Since the beginning of the 2000s, the PCA has facilitated dozens of arbitrations.[38] Granted, by diversifying, the PCA entered into competition with other adjudicative regimes, such as the ICSID and the North American Free Trade Agreement (NAFTA), but by the beginning of the 2000s, the number of international commercial investment disputes being litigated had expanded so much that there was still plenty to go around for multiple players. While not active at levels comparable to those of major international courts, these days the PCA docket compares quite well with that of the ICJ, which still occupies most of the Peace Palace.

[36] *Turriff Construction (Sudan) Limited v. Sudan,* Award of April 23, 1970, <http://www.pca-cpa.org/> accessed February 1, 2013.

[37] Permanent Court of Arbitration <http://www.pca-cpa.org/>, (Rules of Procedure), accessed February 1, 2013.

[38] Permanent Court of Arbitration <http://www.pca-cpa.org/>, (Cases), accessed February 1, 2013.

2 Growing Pains

The story of many international adjudicative bodies is far from linear. Many, during their early years, face significant challenges, and it is not uncommon for adjudicative bodies to experience prolonged periods of low levels of activity or downright irrelevance before they can entrench themselves and become significant players in their legal regime. Some survive this phase, while others remain crippled for a long time or succumb.

There is a growing body of literature on the criteria that could be used to gauge an adjudicative body's degree of effectiveness. Much of the debate has been well summarized by Helfer in this handbook.[39] We will not test here those criteria, and we deliberately refrain from passing a final judgment on the relative degree of effectiveness or ineffectiveness of this or that institution. This would be a task that could not be satisfactorily undertaken within the confines of a chapter of this handbook. Besides, many others have shied away from this challenge. Indeed, if a criticism can be leveled to existing literature, it is that it has resulted yet again in the survey of the well-known and largely effective adjudicative bodies, but has largely ignored the less-known and more problematic ones.[40]

All we aim to do is to put forward a few examples out of the many possible to illustrate the insight that walking the less-known paths of the story of international adjudication can yield. For instance, Africa and Latin America, two regions which have given birth to the largest number of international judicial bodies, provide several illuminating anecdotes. At this time in history, in each region there are a number of adjudicative bodies facing significant difficulties.

2.1 Southern African Development Community

The Southern African Development Community (SADC) is a regional organization grouping all states in Africa south of Congo (15 in total). As many other regional economic integration organizations, it is equipped with an adjudicative body—the SADC Tribunal—to ensure compliance with the community laws and which can hear cases brought by member states, community organs, and individuals to that

[39] For a discussion of the various dimensions along which the "effectiveness" of an international adjudicative body can be measured, see in this handbook, Helfer, Ch. 21.

[40] Two notable exceptions are L Helfer, K Alter, and F Guerzovich, "Islands of Effective International Adjudication: Constructing an Intellectual Property Rule of Law in the Andean Community" (2009) 103(1) AJIL 1; KJ Alter, L Helfer, and J McAllister, "A New International Human Rights Court for West Africa: The Court of Justice for the Economic Community of West African States" (2013) 107 AJIL (4).

effect. Yet, the SADC Tribunal's life has been star-crossed from the very beginning.[41] Although established on paper in 1992, the judges were only appointed in late 2005. The court's building in Windhoek, Namibia, burned down before the court heard its first case. After restoration, it started operating, but soon ran into the super-charged question of human rights, racial politics, and the transition from apartheid, locking horns with Robert Mugabe, an influential and despotic regional player, charismatic leader of the 1960s and 1970s liberation movement against the white-minority apartheid rule, and turned dictator of Zimbabwe in the 1990s.

In 2000, Mugabe started expropriating land from white farmers for redistribution to black ones, mostly his cronies, in an attempt to right historical wrongs. It was a populist move welcomed by the black majority of Zimbabwe's population and the governments of many SADC member states, largely black. Yet, it was an economically disastrous measure, plunging Zimbabwe into economic collapse and hyperinflation and, eventually, international sanctions. Besides, legal justification was lacking. The legality and constitutionality of the expropriation process was regularly challenged in the Zimbabwean High and Supreme courts, but with little result, as the Mugabe dictatorship could not tolerate an independent judiciary. Eventually, in a desperate attempt to obtain recognition of their property rights, some white farmers turned to the SADC Tribunal, which ruled in their favor.[42] When the Zimbabwean government proceeded with evictions, the tribunal declared Zimbabwe in contempt. After the ruling, Mugabe's government immediately denounced the Tribunal and then moved to kill it. First, it filibustered and blocked the nomination of new judges, paralyzing it. Then, it put on the agenda of the SADC Summit of Heads of State and Government the review of its jurisdiction and functioning. Relying on the large network of old-fighters' friendships and alliances, and the unwillingness of South Africa, the largest and most influential state in the region, to oppose Mugabe, Zimbabwe eventually managed to convince the SADC summit of 2012 to turn the tribunal into an ICJ-like adjudicative body, narrowing its jurisdiction to state-to-state disputes only. This move not only shielded Zimbabwe from legal suit by farmers, but also by any member of the opposition to Mugabe's government. Crucially, it also protected many illiberal governments in central and southern Africa, too.

Civil society tried to fight back. In November 2012, two African NGOs requested the African Court on Human and Peoples' Rights (ACtHPR) an advisory opinion

[41] See in this handbook, Ginsburg, Ch. 22, at section 3.2.2. For a detailed review of the troubles affecting the SADC Tribunal, see E de Wet, "The Rise and Fall of the Tribunal of the Southern African Development Community: Implications for Dispute Settlement in Southern Africa" (2013) 28 ICSID Review, 1.

[42] *Mike Campbell (Pvt) Ltd and Others v. Republic of Zimbabwe* (2/2007) [2008] SADCT 2 (November 28, 2008), <http://www.saflii.org/sa/cases/SADCT/2008/2.html> accessed February 1, 2013. On the Campbell case, see P Ndlovu, "Campbell v Republic of Zimbabwe: A Moment of Truth for the SADC Tribunal" (2011) 1 SADC L.J. 63.

on whether the actions of the SADC leaders to curtail the tribunal amounted to violations of the African Charter of Human and Peoples' Rights provisions on judicial independence, access to justice, the right to effective remedies, and the rule of law.[43] It remains to be seen what effect this move will have. First, the ACtHPR might find a way not to answer the question and wisely avoid being engulfed in a fight that has already consumed another international tribunal. Besides, while international courts have regularly reviewed national governments' decisions to change the structure of their judiciary, an international tribunal reviewing the decision of a separate and independent international organization to change the jurisdiction of its own judicial body would be unprecedented. This is yet another reason for the ACtHPR to tread lightly. Second, even if it does issue an opinion, it is not binding and it is unclear how this might compel SADC leaders to undo the 2012 decision. Finally, the referral of the matter directly to the court as an advisory opinion and not to the African Commission on Human Rights as a case sounds like a vote of no-confidence in the commission, undermining its tenuous credibility in the eyes of African civil society.

As Erika de Wet wrote, the rise and fall of the SADC Tribunal can be attributed first to the member states' lack of understanding of the legal implications of the SADC Treaty regime.[44] States in the region tend to enter into ambitious, western-modeled regimes for economic and political integration, without sufficiently reflecting on the legal implications resulting from a comprehensive and consistent application of the rules embodied in the treaty regime in question.[45] Second, many SADC states lack a rule-of-law culture. Most have a poor domestic track record in relation to human rights protection and judicial independence.[46] With these considerations in mind and with hindsight "one may question the wisdom of bringing the Zimbabwean land cases to a fledgling tribunal, which hardly had any opportunity to foster a culture of acceptance amongst member States. Had the Tribunal instead been allowed to deal with less controversial cases for a number of years, its credibility—and therefore its chances of survival—might have improved by the time it took on controversial human rights disputes."[47] While in West Africa the Court of Justice of the Economic Community of Western African States (ECOWAS) has successfully managed, so far, to expand its role and carry out functions of human rights courts, in Southern Africa the SADC Tribunal's troubles are a cautionary tale.[48]

[43] Open Society Initiative for Southern Africa (Johannesburg), "Southern Africa: Court Asked to Rule on SADC Tribunal" (November 26, 2012) <http://allafrica.com/stories/201211270066.html> accessed February 1, 2013.

[44] De Wet, note 41, at 18. [45] De Wet, note 41, at 18. [46] De Wet, note 41, at 18.

[47] De Wet, note 41, at 18.

[48] On human rights courts in Africa, see in this handbook, Ebobrah, Chapter 11.

2.2 The Court of Justice of the West African Economic and Monetary Union and the Court of Justice of the Common Market of Eastern and Southern Africa

In Africa there are two further troubled courts: The Court of Justice of the West African Economic and Monetary Union (WAEMU) and the Court of Justice of the Common Market of Eastern and Southern Africa (COMESA). The WAEMU Court was created in 1994, started operating in 1995 and, to date, has issued about 50 rulings. The COMESA Court was created in 1993, started operating in 1998 and, to date, has decided about as many cases. Neither of the two has managed to assert itself in a region crowded with international adjudicative bodies and shaken by periodic conflicts. All eight members of the WAEMU are also members of ECOWAS, which is endowed with a thriving regional court.[49] Moreover, six out of eight are also members of the Organization for the Harmonization of Business Law in Africa (Organisation pour l'Harmonisation en Afrique du Droit des Affaires—OHADA), which is also endowed with a successful regional court.[50] While the WAEMU Court, the COMESA Court and the OHADA Common Court of Justice and Arbitration exercise different kinds of jurisdiction, it is doubtful whether this region of the world is economically and democratically developed enough to sustain three international courts.

A large number of states are members of COMESA (to date 20), including Libya and Egypt in the north and Zambia in the south. Probably, the court has a membership too large for its own good. Over the years, it has lost five members, for various reasons, and the fact that much of central Africa, and in particular in and around Congo, has been engulfed in protracted conflicts for almost two decades now does not help the organization to achieve its ambitious goals of economic integration. The decision to move the court from Lusaka, Zambia, to Khartoum, Sudan, only to suspend the move when Sudan started becoming an international pariah, has surely not helped the court entrench itself.

It remains to be seen whether the WAEMU and the COMESA courts will be able to establish themselves in this judicially crowded region. Their fate is ultimately tied to the success of the organizations to which they are attached, and the stabilization of the Central African region.

2.3 The Mercosur Permanent Review Tribunal

In the Americas there are two currently beleaguered regional adjudicative bodies: the Mercosur Permanent Review Tribunal and the Central American Court

[49] See, in this handbook, Ebobrah, Chapter 11, at section 2.2.2, Alter, Chapter 4, at section 2.1.3 and Alter et al., note 40.

[50] On OHADA, see in this handbook Alter, Chapter 4, at section 2.1.2.

of Justice. Mercosur, short for *Mercado Común del Sur*, or Common Market of the South, is a regional economic integration organization established in 1991. Originally, it had four members: the two southern America giants, Argentina and Brazil, and two small states pinned between them, Uruguay and Paraguay. Since inception, Mercosur has gone through several mutations, including of its dispute settlement procedure. Recently, its membership has expanded to include Venezuela (in 2012) and Bolivia (in 2013).

The organization is endowed with a dispute settlement body, but unlike many which mimic the structure and function of the ECJ, the Mercosur dispute settlement system, in its current incarnation, resembles the WTO and NAFTA systems: a two-stage process where disputes are adjudicated first by an arbitral panel and then awards can be appealed before a standing appellate body, in this case the Permanent Review Tribunal.[51]

The tribunal started operating in 2004 but never quite took off, hamstrung by two factors. The first one is of jurisdictional nature: the Mercosur system cannot consider cases that have been brought before the WTO dispute settlement system.[52] The WTO system, being a much larger, stronger, and well-established system, naturally siphons off much of the potential caseload of the Mercosur system, which explains the paltry docket of its tribunal. The second problem is much more severe and has to do with political rifts between Mercosur members. In 2008, Fernando Lugo, a Catholic bishop and liberation theologian, won Paraguay's presidential election and broke the 61-year chokehold on power of the right-wing Colorado Party. Shortly after his inauguration, the Liberal party, whose support had propelled Lugo to the presidency, repudiated him. In June 2012, after he was accused of mishandling a clash between police and landless peasants, Congress summarily impeached him and removed him from office, installing a temporary president until political elections could be held. In the eyes of the leftist leaders of Argentina, Brazil, and Uruguay the lightning-fast impeachment was a coup. They suspended the country from Mercosur for the violation of the "democratic clause" contained in the Protocol of Ushuaia. At the same time, they admitted Hugo Chavez's Venezuela into Mercosur—a hardly democratic country in itself and whose application for membership had been blocked by Paraguay since 2006—and, later in the year, Bolivia, currently headed by another populist and leftist leader, Evo Morales.

[51] See A Perotti, *Tribunal permanente de revisión y estado de derecho en el Mercosur (Permanent Tribunal of Review and rule of law in Mercosur)* (Madrid: Pons 2009). The original Mercosur dispute settlement system was provided for in the Protocol of Brasilia, concluded on December 17, 1991, 36 ILM 3 (1997). The system was reconfigured to add the Permanent Review Tribunal by the Protocol of Olivos, concluded on February 18, 2002, 42 ILM 2 (2003).

[52] Protocol of Olivos, Art. 1.

Paraguay dragged the Permanent Review Tribunal, which is headquartered in Asunción, Paraguay, into the dispute. In July 2012, it filed a request for provisional measures challenging the legality of its suspension and the accession of Venezuela. Within a few days the tribunal rejected the request because its power to issue provisional measures is limited only to order the release of confiscated perishable goods, or goods necessary in times of crisis in the importing state.[53] It is anyone's guess what the tribunal's future will be. General elections were held in Paraguay in April 2013, returning government back to the right-wing Colorado party. To date, Paraguay has not yet been readmitted to Mercosur.

Paraguayan crisis notwithstanding, the longer-term prognosis is uncertain. The accession of Venezuela and Bolivia has permanently altered the politics of the Mercosur. Enlargement might dilute the sway of the two super-powers of the region—Argentina and, mostly, Brazil—and create more breathing room for the Mercosur tribunal by enlarging its potential support basis. However, the accession to Mercosur of Bolivia accelerated the process of integration between Mercosur and the Andean Community, the other South American trading block, which is already endowed with a well-established and somewhat effective adjudicative body: the Andean Tribunal of Justice.[54] Finally, neither Bolivia, under Evo Morales, nor Venezuela, both under Hugo Chavez and under the Chavistas who succeeded him, has shown any inclination to accept decisions of independent international adjudicators.[55]

2.4 Central American courts

Central America has a long history of attempts to unite politically, which, at times, have also led to the creation of regional adjudicative bodies. It is the first region of the world to move towards judicialization. In 1902, with the Treaty of Corinto, Nicaragua, Honduras, Costa Rica, and El Salvador established the Central American Arbitration Tribunal.[56] It was an attempt to create a PCA-like regional forum of international adjudication. The Central American Arbitration Tribunal never became operative, but it is worth remembering for a few features. First, the

[53] Procedimiento Excepcional de Urgencia solicitado por la República del Paraguay en relación con la suspensión de su participación en los Órganos del Mercado Común del Sur (MERCOSUR) y la incorporación de Venezuela como Miembro Pleno (Extraordinary Urgent Proceedings Instituted at the Request of the Republic of Paraguay on its Suspension from the Organs of the Southern Common Market and the Admission of the Republic of Venezuela as Full Member), Judgment N° 01/2012 <http://www.tprmercosur.org/es/docum/laudos/Laudo_01_2012_es.pdf> accessed February 1, 2013.

[54] On the Andean Tribunal, see Helfer, Alter, and Guerzovich, note 40.

[55] See in this handbook, Romano, Ch. 5, at section 1.2.2.

[56] *Treaty Between Central American States Providing for the Arbitration of Differences*, 1902 Papers Relating to Foreign Rel. U.S. 881 (1903).

Treaty of Corinto provided for compulsory adjudication of any kind of dispute between members,[57] a feature that was ahead of its time and not to be found again in international adjudication until the rise of regional courts in Europe. Second, the tribunal was composed of an arbitrator and an alternate arbitrator for each of the four member states. Singularly, in case of dispute between two parties, the arbitrators of their nationality would sit out and the dispute would have been resolved by the arbitrators of the other members.[58] In case of a deadlock preventing adoption of the award, an arbitrator selected by lottery amongst the alternate arbitrators of the states not involved in the dispute was to cast the decisive vote.[59]

The United States played a prominent role in regional politics throughout the twentieth century. Protection of American companies' interests (particularly those growing crops such as bananas) and the project to build a canal across the isthmus led to numerous interventions, political and military, in the region to buttress this or that dictator. The first years of the 1900s were tumultuous with constant armed interventions and counter-interventions between Guatemala, Honduras, Nicaragua, and El Salvador. To stabilize the region, in 1907 the United States called for and hosted a Central American Peace Conference in Washington D.C. where the five republics of Central America (Guatemala, El Salvador, Honduras, Nicaragua, and Costa Rica) adopted the statute of a Central American Court of Justice (Corte de Justicia Centroamericana), a permanent judicial institution, as opposed to the arbitral body of 1902, to be based in Cartago, Costa Rica.[60]

The "Court of Cartago" was permanent in the sense that it had a seat and judges ready to hear any cases submitted to it, but like the ICTY and ICTR in modern times it was not to last indefinitely. When its status expired after ten years, few, and especially the United States, had little interest in keeping it alive.[61] Among the many ailments that killed it are some judicial ones (such as scarce independence of its judges, who were paid directly by their national states; probably too broad jurisdiction; and poorly written rules of procedure) and political ones (such as the court was no longer viewed as a neutral environment; and perceived over-influence of the United States in its functioning). But what sank the court for good was a politically supercharged case involving the Bryan-Chamorro Treaty between the United States and Nicaragua.[62] The treaty gave the United States rights to any canal built in Nicaragua in perpetuity (thus making sure no canal could be build to rival the

[57] *Treaty Between Central American States*, note 56, Art. II. However, territorial disputes could be submitted for resolution to a single arbitrator of US nationality: Art. X.

[58] *Treaty Between Central American States*, note 56, Art. IV.

[59] *Treaty Between Central American States*, note 56, Art. V.

[60] *Convention for the Establishment of a Central American Court of Justice*, 1907 Papers Relating to Foreign Rel. U.S. 697, 697 (1910).

[61] The ten-year life of the court was agreed upon in the treaty, but could have been modified through Article 27 of the Convention.

[62] Convention between the United States and Nicaragua ceding rights for construction of ship canal by Nicaraguan route, etc., concluded in Washington D.C., August 5, 1914, 39 Stat. 1661 (1916).

US-controlled Panama Canal), a renewable 99-year option to establish a naval base in the Gulf of Fonseca, and a renewable 99-year lease to the Great and Little Corn Islands (Islas del Maíz) in the Caribbean.[63] Both Costa Rica and El Salvador brought cases before the court challenging the validity of that treaty, particularly the provisions giving the United States rights to the Corn Islands.[64] When the court found in favor of Costa Rica and El Salvador, it lost support of both the United States and Nicaragua, sealing its fate.

Yet, this was not the end of attempts to set up an adjudicative body in that tormented region. After a failed attempt to create a Federation of Central America (El Salvador, Guatemala, Honduras) between 1912 and 1922, the five Central American states tried judicialization again in 1923, always under the tutelage of the United States, concluding in Washington D.C. a treaty to establish the International Central American Tribunal (Tribunal Internacional Centroamericano).[65] Like the 1902 Central American Arbitration Tribunal, this was an arbitral tribunal, PCA-style. The tribunal foundered when Guatemala and Honduras failed to agree to refer to it a territorial dispute. While Guatemala—and the United States—insisted that the tribunal had competence to hear the case and the dispute should be decided under its authority, Honduras resisted. The question was eventually referred to an ad hoc arbitral tribunal, presided by Charles Evans Hughes, Chief Justice of the US Supreme Court.[66]

After World War II, the same five states tried for the fourth time. In 1951, they adopted the Charter of the Organization of Central American States (Organización de Estados Centroamericanos—ODECA). The charter was modified in 1962 by adding to the organization a new Central American Court of Justice (Corte Centroamericana de Justicia), this time based in Managua, Nicaragua. Yet, the new court remained idle for the next three decades. It was only in 1991 that the Protocol of Tegucigalpa injected new life into the ODECA by creating the Central American Integration System (Sistema de Integración Centroamericana—SICA). The Central American Court of Justice was accordingly reconfigured, taking stock of the lessons learned with the Court of Cartago, and started functioning again in 1994.[67]

The Court of Managua suffers from multiple problems. For example, it has limited support amongst SICA members and it is prone to jurisdictional overreach. For the first ten years, the only three states to have ratified its statute were Nicaragua,

[63] Both the Gulf of Fonseca and the Corn Islands have been subject to several arbitrations and decisions of the ICJ.

[64] See SM Jordison, "The Central American Court of Justice: Yesterday, Today and Tomorrow?" (2009) 183 Connecticut J. Int'l L. 201–2.

[65] CE Hughes et al., "Protocol Between the United States and the Central American States, Signed at Washington, February 7th, 1923", 1923 Papers Relating to Foreign Rel. Vol. I 327 (1938).

[66] Honduras borders (Guatemala, Honduras), January 23, 1933, Reports of International Arbitral Awards, Volume II 1307–66.

[67] Jordison, note 64, at 220.

Honduras, and El Salvador. In 2004 Honduras suspended its participation in the court, refusing to appoint its judges, leaving only Nicaragua and El Salvador to support it. Eventually, Honduras rejoined in 2007 and Guatemala followed suit, joining in 2008. Yet, to date the other four SICA members (Costa Rica, Panama, Dominican Republic, and Belize) have not yet ratified the statute. Recently, the question of whether all state members of SICA are subject to the jurisdiction of the court or only those that have ratified its statute has become the focus of a heated dispute.

In 2011, two Nicaraguan environmental NGOs filed a case before the court against Costa Rica, claiming that the construction of a freeway near the border with Nicaragua is in violation of a number of SICA legal instruments as well as several regional environmental treaties.[68] The court argued that by virtue of having ratified the Protocol of Tegucigalpa and becoming member of SICA, Costa Rica is *ipso facto* subject to the jurisdiction of the court, with no need for separate ratification of the court's statute.[69] Costa Rica refused to participate in proceedings and rejected the decision. The governments of Panama, Belize, and the Dominican Republic cried foul as well.

Further, its functions are probably too extensive, particularly for a relatively young court in a turbulent region. They encompass the whole spectrum of possible international judicial powers, including contentious, advisory, preliminary, arbitral, appellate, constitutional, and administrative functions. On the whole, the court can hear cases brought before it by member states of SICA; states which are not members of SICA that have a dispute with member states and agree to the court's jurisdiction; organs of SICA; Supreme Courts of the members of SICA; national courts; and natural and legal persons.[70] It can issue advisory opinions when requested by SICA members on any international treaty, including on the compatibility of those treaties with domestic laws of member states,[71] and can issue advisory opinions on the laws of the SICA legal system, which become binding for all SICA member states.[72] That notwithstanding, requests for advisory opinions are almost 40 percent of its caseload.[73] The only thing that is excluded from the court's jurisdiction is human right cases, which, the court's statute says,

[68] The case was filed on December 6, 2011. On December 22, 2012, Nicaragua filed a case before the ICJ on the same issue: *Construction of a Road in Costa Rica along the San Juan River* (*Nicaragua v. Costa Rica*). The case is currently pending.

[69] Central American Court of Justice, Judgment No. 12-06-12-2011, June 21, 2012 <http://vianica.com/downloads/docs/1.pdf> accessed February 1, 2013.

[70] Estatuto de la Corte Centroamericana de Justicia [Convention on the Statute of the Central American Court of Justice], Dec. 10, 1992, 1821 U.N.T.S. 280, Art. 22.

[71] Convention on the Statute of the Central American Court of Justice, note 70, Art. 23.

[72] Convention on the Statute of the Central American Court of Justice, note 70, Art. 24.

[73] Between 1994 and 2011, the Court received 69 cases and 41 requests for advisory opinions. <http://portal.ccj.org.ni/ccj2/Historia/tabid/57/Default.aspx> (Casos) accessed February 1, 2013.

are only for the IACtHR to decide.[74] Yet, even a statutory prohibition has not prevented the court, from time to time, to hear cases touching on human rights issues.

Third, unlike many international adjudicative bodies, the court also has strong supra-national features. It acts as a permanent consultative organ for supreme courts of the region and, under Article 22(f) of its statute, can even hear disputes between constitutional organs of member states. This latter aspect of its jurisdiction accounts for much of the troubles affecting the Court of Managua.

In 2005, the President of Nicaragua filed a case before the court against the Nicaraguan National Assembly, the national legislature, claiming violation of a number of regional and UN treaties as well as several articles of the Nicaraguan Constitution.[75] The constitutional dispute was triggered by the adoption by the National Assembly of a legal reform that would make any appointment made by the president subject to the approval of the National Assembly. Not only did the court take the case, but it also issued provisional measures, issuing an injunction to the National Assembly.[76] Throughout proceedings, the National Assembly refused to send an agent to appear before the court or to argue its case. Eventually, the court found in favor of the President and declared the National Assembly in violation of Nicaraguan law.[77] It also added that its decision should be treated as if it were a decision of a Nicaraguan court. Yet, at the same time, the matter had also been reviewed by the Nicaraguan Supreme Court, which not only disagreed with the court, but also declared Article 22(f) of the court's statute unconstitutional because it was in conflict with the Nicaraguan Constitution.[78] The dispute caused a major crisis in Nicaragua, the state on whose territory the court has its seat, at a time in which, with Honduras in auto-suspension, the only two SICA states supporting the court were Nicaragua itself and El Salvador. It also caused a major debate in the press, public, and at governmental level throughout the SICA region, with many accusing the court of grossly overreaching.

The powers given to the court under Article 22(f) have been controversial since the outset. In 1997 the XIX Summit of the Presidents of Central America issued a declaration (Panamá II) aimed at reforming the Central American parliament and the court. In the case of the court, one of the reforms they agreed to was abolishing the controversial provision.[79] The reform, however, was never implemented because

[74] Statute of the Central American Court of Justice, note 70, Art. 25.

[75] Corte Centroamericana de Justicia, *La Gaceta [L.G.] Oficial Corte Centroamericana de Justicia No. 19*, at 1, (May 24, 2005) <http://portal.ccj.org.ni/ccj2/CeDoc/GacetasOficiales/tabid/82/ItemId/48/Default.aspx > accessed February 1, 2013.

[76] Corte Centroamericana de Justicia, Anexo a Memoria Período 2004–2005, <http://portal.ccj.org.ni/CCJ2/LinkClick.aspx?fileticket=DvcCfypBidI%3D&tabid=70> accessed February 1, 2013.

[77] Corte Centroamericana de Justicia, note 76.

[78] Corte Centroamericana de Justicia, note 76.

[79] XIX Cumbre de Presidentes Centroamericanos, Declaración de Panamá II (XIX Summit of Central American Presidents, Declaration of Panama II), "Sobre la Corte Centroamericana de Justicia"

the SICA states could not subsequently agree to take the formal legal step to implement the reform. When Honduras suspended its participation in the court, one of the reasons it cited for the step was that all attempts to modify the court's statute, in particular Article 22(f), had not produced results and a general lack of compliance with the court's decisions.[80] Finally, one of the reasons Costa Rica adduces for refusing to accept the jurisdiction of the court is exactly the powers the court has, and uses, under Article 22(f).[81]

3 Conclusions

The building of an international judiciary has been a largely unscientific, trial-and-error process. Some bodies, like the IPC, have been on clear dead-end roads. They were either ahead of their time, made moot before they could start operating or sapped by design flaws. Yet, some might still wake up from their slumber. After all, most international courts have been created since the end of the Cold War. It took the ECtHR and the ECJ three decades before their dockets took off, states accepted them, key actors figured out how to use them, and their overall effectiveness increased.

Although one has to be cautious in drawing too-firm conclusions in such a large field, populated with considerably different institutions, there are a few lessons that can be drawn even from a quick survey such as this. To begin with, international courts appear to be fragile institutions—probably more fragile than most international institutions—that need to be carefully designed, groomed, and tended to, especially in their early days. Overly ambitious constitutive legal instruments can cripple them from the outset, as the Central American stories tell us. International courts can also be suffocated by too much competition. Excessive enthusiasm for the promise of adjudication or impatience can lead states to create duplicates or alternative courts, crowding the field. The case of the OSCE Court and courts in Sub-Saharan Africa are illustrative of this problem. Regional clones of the ICJ or the

(on the Central American Court of Justice), 12/7/1997, para. B, available at <http://www.sica.int/> accessed February 1, 2013.

80 Jordison, note 64, at 233.

81 People Daily, "Costa Rica propondrá suprimir Corte Centroamericana de Justicia (Costa Rica Will Propose Abolishing the Central American Court of Justice)" (May 7, 2012) <http://spanish.peopledaily.com.cn/31617/7866767.html> accessed February 1, 2013.

PCA, that is to say judicial bodies with function to settle disputes between states, have not taken root in part because there is a tacit, or deliberate, desire to keep The Hague at the center of that kind of international adjudication. It is very telling that most of the courts that have populated the field since the end of the Cold War are not ICJ- or PCA-like.

Once established, the early taking on of cases that are too big or too difficult can make testy governments pull the plug or head for the exit, as happened to the SADC Tribunal or the Central American Court of Justice. On the other hand, while civil society often has great expectations about what international adjudication could do, it rarely has the necessary patience to wait for international courts to root themselves. International adjudicative bodies can be prone to yield to the pressure to take on marquee cases to show their relevance. Yet, this strategy can backfire. A slow and low-aim approach can pay off. For example, it took almost three decades for the ECtHR and the ECJ to take off. The IACtHR took at least a decade and dozens of cases before it started taking on truly controversial issues that could irk major regional players.

All in all, for international judicialization to take roots there must be a fair degree of peace and stability. Leaving aside the somewhat special case of international criminal courts, which are expected to play a part in becalming and healing, international judicial bodies cannot function when members are deeply polarized or outright fighting, as the examples of the Mercosur, Central America, Arab League and COMESA illustrate. The rise of the European courts—the ECJ and ECtHR—has largely been possible due to the fact that both had a chance to grow over a few decades within a peaceful political space: Western Europe. Many clones of those two courts are struggling to achieve comparable results because they have to grow in significantly more polarized environments.

All of this is largely unexplored terrain for all scholars from various disciplines. Granted, one of the biggest challenges is finding information as often failed courts have left little trace behind them, while ailing courts do not have the resources to let the world know about their existence. Yet, this is a gap that can be filled by entrepreneurial scholars willing to hit the road to shed light on some relatively obscure corners of the international judicial landscape.[82] The future of international adjudication depends on learning and internalizing what are the factors that stymie international judicialization.

[82] For examples of entrepreneurial scholars, see note 40.

Research Questions

1. If the growth of the international judiciary was not a trial and error affair, but a planned endeavor sustained by the application of theoretical inquiry, what would the international judicial landscape look like?
2. If one was to apply existing literature on the criteria to determine the relative effectiveness/ineffectiveness of international adjudicative bodies to the less known and research bodies, what insight would be gained?
3. Why do states spend considerable negotiating time and energies creating new international adjudicative bodies but then fail to follow through by ratifying the constitutive instrument, or accepting the body's jurisdiction, or using it?
4. What lessons can be drawn from the long history of largely failed judicialization in Central America?

Suggested Reading

Allain, J, *A Century of International Adjudication: The Rule of Law and its Limits* (The Hague: T.M.C. Asser Press 2000).

Alter, K, *The New Terrain of International Law: Courts, Politics, Rights* (Princeton University Press 2014).

Caflisch, L, "Cent ans de règlement pacifique des différents interétatiques (A Century of Peaceful Settlement of Disputes between States)" (2001) 288 Recueil des Cours de l'Académie de Droit International 245.

Eyffinger, A, *The International Court of Justice: 1946–1996* (The Hague: Kluwer 1996).

Fernández-Liesa, C (ed.), *Tribunales internacionales y espacio iberoamericano (International Tribunals and the Spanish-American Space)* (Madrid: Thompson Reuters 2009).

Hudson, M, *International Tribunals: Past and Future* (Washington D.C.: Carnegie Endowment for International Peace and Brookings Institution 1944).

Jordison, SM, "The Central American Court of Justice: Yesterday, Today and Tomorrow?" (2009) 25 Conneticut J. Int'l L. 183.

Lombardini, M, "The International Islamic Court of Justice: Towards an International Islamic Legal System?" (2001) 14(3) LJIL 665–80.

Perotti, A, *Tribunal permanente de revisión y estado de derecho en el Mercosur (Permanent Tribunal of Review and Rule of Law in Mercosur)* (Madrid: Pons 2009).

Shany, Y, "Assessing the Effectiveness of International Courts: A Goal-Based Approach" (2012) 106 AJIL 225.

Thani, AAF, "The Projected Arab Court of Justice: A Study to its Draft Statute and Rules, with Specific Reference to the International Court of Justice and Principles of Islamic Shariah" (University of Glasgow 1999).

CHAPTER 7

THE CHALLENGE OF "PROLIFERATION": AN ANATOMY OF THE DEBATE

PIERRE-MARIE DUPUY* AND
JORGE E VIÑUALES**

* Emeritus Professor at the University of Paris (Panthéon-Assas) and at The Graduate Institute, Geneva.

** Harold Samuel Professor of Law and Environmental Policy at the University of Cambridge, United Kingdom.

1 Introduction

In domestic legal systems, disputes are settled by permanent courts with compulsory jurisdiction to hear certain matters. Thus, claims against an individual, a corporation, or even an institution (e.g. a state agency or the state itself) may be brought before a court with the power to make a binding decision on the basis of law. This basic feature of domestic systems is deeply foreign to the realm of international law. For most of the history of international law, compulsory jurisdiction was indeed a taboo. No permanent adjudication mechanism existed prior to the creation in the 1920s of the Permanent Court of International Justice (PCIJ)[1] and, even then, the PCIJ's jurisdiction was subject to state consent.[2] In addition, even when states did consent to submit their dispute to a judicial body, it was mostly to ephemeral arbitration tribunals, often of a quasi-judicial nature.[3] With this background in mind, it is easy to understand why many international lawyers have seen the so-called "proliferation" of international courts and tribunals in the last few decades as a fundamental turn.[4] If international disputes are increasingly settled through judicial means, is this not likely to change the nature of international law from a horizontal system of sovereign states to a vertical one where states (and other subjects) can be brought to justice?

The term "proliferation," in this context, can be defined by reference to two main elements. The first is *factual*: (i) the development, in the second half of the twentieth century, of an increasingly complex web of international judicial and quasi-judicial mechanisms; (ii) the expansion of the jurisdictional powers of some international courts; (iii) the increasingly frequent resort to international judicial and quasi-judicial mechanisms; (iv) the increasing application

[1] The only exception to this was the short-lived Central American Court of Justice established in 1907. See J Eyma, *La Cour de justice Centre-Américaine* (Paris: E. Sagot & Cie 1928).

[2] See CJ Loder, "The Permanent Court of International Justice and Compulsory Jurisdiction" (1921) 2 BYIL 6.

[3] See JI Charney, "Is International Law Threatened by Multiple International Tribunals?" (1998) 271 RCADI 101, 117.

[4] See e.g., "Implications of the Proliferation of International Adjudicatory Bodies for Dispute Resolution" (1995) ASIL Bulletin 9; Symposium: "The Proliferation of International Tribunals: Piecing Together the Puzzle" (1999) 31(4) N.Y.U. J. Int'l L. & Pol.; SFDI, "La multiplication des juridictions internationales: Un système anarchique?" (Paris: Pedone 2003); Symposium: "Diversity or Cacophony: New Sources of Norms in International Law" (2004) 25(4) MJIL; Symposium: "The Normalizing of Adjudication in Complex International Governance Regimes" (2009) 41(4) N.Y.U. J. Int'l L. & Pol.

of international law by domestic courts.[5] The second element is of a *perceptual* nature. The very term "proliferation" conveys the somewhat negative light under which the above factual developments were perceived—at least initially—by many scholars. At the root of this bias was the fear that the operation of a growing number of unconnected judicial bodies may lead to undesired outcomes, including judicial interference with diplomacy, conflicts of norms and jurisdiction, forum shopping, and, more generally, to the purported "fragmentation" of international law.

This chapter provides an anatomy of the "proliferation" debate. The impact of "proliferation" on the international legal order is analyzed through the prism of three core questions: legalization; coherence; and openness. The question of "legalization" refers to the increasing availability and reach of international adjudication to address questions hitherto covered by considerations of sovereignty, non-intervention, and political opportunity. In this context, the term "legalization" is therefore a shortcut for the advancement of the judicial rule of law in international affairs. The question of "coherence" encompasses issues such as forum competition and forum shopping, conflicting decisions, the role of precedent, the development and use of coordination techniques and/or of control systems. The question of "openness" looks at the integration of values and interests, protected by certain branches of international law, into other branches. Openness is also important because the very existence and availability of international adjudication may shift the level at which certain decisions are made and, therefore, raise issues of transparency and participation in international proceedings. In conclusion, we offer some observations on a question where the three debates above intersect, namely the legitimacy of international adjudication.

Given the nature of the present volume, we devote limited attention to the technical legal questions raised by "proliferation"[6] and focus on its broader implications. Also, our focus is on "debates," rather than on "debaters." The chapter is not intended to provide a literature review[7] but the authors' own analysis of the fundamental questions raised by "proliferation."

[5] Y Shany, "No Longer a Weak Department of Power? Reflections on the Emergence of a New International Judiciary" (2009) 20 EJIL 73, 75–6; C Romano, "The Proliferation of International Judicial Bodies: The Pieces of the Puzzle" (1998–1999) 31 N.Y.U. J. Int'l L. & Pol. 709. See in this handbook, the Introduction and Alter, Ch. 4, at section 1.

[6] See A Gattini, "Un regard procédural sur la fragmentation du droit international" (2006) RGDIP 303; Y Shany, *The Competing Jurisdictions of International Courts and Tribunals* (Oxford University Press 2003).

[7] But see note 4.

2 Legalization: A Tribunal to Subject Leviathan to the International Rule of Law?

The starting point of any discussion of the "proliferation" debate is the institutional situation that an international judiciary was expected to change. The topic is vast and would require an analysis of the role of law in international politics, which exceeds the bounds of this chapter. But the debate in the late nineteenth and the early twentieth centuries on the creation of a permanent international court offers a good proxy.[8]

The need for a permanent international court was cherished by both liberal ("peace through law") and positivistic circles.[9] Law was seen as the only alternative to war and conflict and, for a genuine law of nations to develop, a permanent court was deemed necessary. After World War I, the preamble of the Treaty of Versailles had called for "the firm establishment of the understandings of international law as the actual rule of conduct among governments." In this context, the creation of a permanent court was expected to clarify and apply these rules.[10]

In hindsight, it is difficult to fully grasp how challenging this idea was at the time. International adjudication would indeed collide with three fundamental ideas of classical international law: sovereignty, non-intervention, and political opportunity. A brief discussion of how each of them has evolved in a context characterized by "proliferation" is therefore important to understand the foundations of the debate.

2.1 "Proliferation" and sovereignty

In classical international law, sovereign states were by far the most important subjects of the system and their relations were organized according to a strictly horizontal logic. This was the result of the political reality of the time, which international law in part reflected and in part sought to tame. This configuration can be read in the voluntary nature of the PCIJ's jurisdiction[11] and the "contractual" nature of the

[8] See H Wehberg, *Das Problem eines internationalen Staatengerichtshofes* (Berlin: Duncker & Humblot 1912); H Lauterpacht, *The Development of International Law by the International Court* (London: Stevens & Sons 1958). A historical analysis of these and other materials is provided in O Spiermann, *International Legal Argument in the Permanent Court of International Justice* (Cambridge University Press 2005).

[9] See JN Shklar, *Legalism* (Cambridge, MA: Harvard University Press 1964) 128.

[10] Lauterpacht, note 8, at 5. See also Spiermann, note 8, at 8–9.

[11] See Loder, note 2.

rules it was meant to apply. Contemporary international law reflects a very different reality—characterized by a wide variety of subjects of growing importance—and its regulatory function has much advanced, largely as a result of "proliferation."

Although the rule, as regards jurisdiction, is still the need for state consent, a number of important exceptions has arisen over time in different areas of international law, including a variety of opt-in or opt-out systems, and even compulsory jurisdiction as a pre-condition to becoming a party to a treaty. For example, part XV of the United Nations Convention on the Law of the Sea sets out a compulsory system of dispute settlement.[12] Similarly, membership of the WTO is conditional upon acceptance of its compulsory dispute settlement mechanism.[13] In these cases, the principle of prior state consent is not challenged, but the consent is given once and for all by the state as a pre-condition for its participation in the conventionally established legal regime.

With respect to the nature of the applicable rules, "proliferation" has also changed the picture considerably, most notably by giving certain international norms an "objective" nature that escapes the will of individual states. An example is the role asserted by certain bodies with respect to the illegality of reservations contrary to the object and purpose of human rights treaties.[14] Another illustration is the recognition that certain norms, because of their very nature, cannot be set aside by the will of states.[15] The ability of these norms to deploy such effects is heavily dependent on the existence of a judicial or quasi-judicial body to apply them. Still another illustration is the judicial "conquest" of the prerogative to determine the limits of what falls under the "domaine réservé" of states at any given time.[16] From a systemic perspective, this development could be compared to the assertion by domestic courts of the prerogative to review the constitutionality of executive and legislative action.[17]

These assertions of judicial authority on matters of state policy provide a first assessment of how "proliferation" is influencing the international legal order.

[12] United Nations Convention on the Law of the Sea (December 10, 1982) 1833 UNTS 397, Part XV, particularly Arts 286 and 287. See MH Nordquist (ed.), *United Nations Convention on the Law of the Sea 1982. A Commentary*, vol. V (Leiden: Martinus Nijhoff 1989) 37.

[13] Agreement establishing the World Trade Organization, April 15, 1994, 1867 UNTS 154, Art. XVI: 5 and Annex 2 (Understanding on rules and procedures governing the settlement of disputes, Art. 1.1.). See P van den Bossche, *The Law and Policy of the World Trade Organization* (Cambridge University Press 2008) 178.

[14] See e.g., *Belilos v. Switzerland* [1988] ECHR Series A no. 132 [§ 50–60]; *Loizidou v. Turkey* (preliminary objections) [1995] ECHR Series A no. 310 [§ 65–89]; UN Human Rights Committee, "General Comment 24," (1994) UN Doc CCPR/C/21/Rev.1/Add.6; See R Goodman, "Human Rights Treaties, Invalid Reservations, and State Consent" (2002) 96 AJIL 531.

[15] See A Verdross, "*Jus dispositivum* and *jus cogens* in International Law" (1966) 60 AJIL 55; A Orakhelashvili, *Peremptory Norms in International* Law (Oxford University Press 2006).

[16] See *Nationality Decrees issued in Tunis and Morocco*, Advisory Opinion, PCIJ Series B No 4, 24.

[17] See P-M Dupuy, "The Danger of Fragmentation or Unification of the International Legal System and the International Court of Justice" (1998–1999) 31 N.Y.U. J. Int'l L. & Pol. 791, 796.

2.2 "Proliferation" and non-intervention

Another related assessment can be conducted in connection with non-intervention. Sovereignty and non-intervention are closely related. However, by zooming in on non-intervention, one can highlight how certain judicial prerogatives "conquered" over sovereignty is still felt in some political circles as an unacceptable intervention in domestic affairs.

A prominent illustration is the debate over who should try the heir of Muammar Gaddafi, his son Saif al-islam. The International Criminal Court (ICC) issued an arrest warrant against him in June 2011, a few months before he was captured in Libya, where he is currently held.[18] Thereafter, a debate ensued over whether he should be tried by the ICC or by a court in Libya. The Libyan authorities have so far resisted attempts by the ICC to obtain information and even interfered with the ICC defense team sent to Libya. Leaving aside the legal details raised by this case, the fundamental question is clearly the extent to which an international court can assert jurisdiction over a situation that the concerned state sees as eminently domestic. The resistance displayed by Libya, as well as by other states in analogous situations,[19] to submit to the action of an international court provides a good illustration of the potential clash between "proliferation" and non-intervention. Resistance can take many forms, ranging from *de facto* uncooperative behavior to the development of a sophisticated web of treaties creating an exception with respect to the nationals of certain states.[20]

Examples of resistance can also be found beyond international criminal law. In international environmental law, the action of certain quasi-judicial committees has also been resisted in the name of sovereignty and non-intervention. For example, the World Heritage Committee (WHC) has faced nationalist hostility in several cases where it sent delegations to investigate the effects of mining projects on protected sites, such as Yellowstone National Park in the United States or Kakadu National Park in Australia. One manifestation, among many others, of the nationalist reaction against such action is the statement by a member of the United States House of Representatives calling for the "protection of the rights of people in the democratic process of a sovereign nation [Australia] from interference by

[18] The situation is particularly controversial because Libya has not ratified the ICC Statute. An additional question is, therefore, whether the ICC can legally extend its jurisdiction when the matter has been referred to it by the Security Council, as in the Libyan case. See L Condorelli and S Villalpando, "Can the Security Council extend the ICC's jurisdiction?," in A Cassese, P Gaeta, J Jones (eds), *The Rome Statute of the International Criminal Court: A Commentary* (Oxford University Press 2002) 571–82; S Williams and W Schabas, "Article 13. Exercise of Jurisdiction," in O Triffterer (ed.), *Commentary on the Rome Statute of the International Criminal Court* (Berlin/Oxford: Beck/Hart/Nomos 2008) 563, 569.

[19] See A Cassese, *International Criminal Law* (Oxford University Press 2003) 355.

[20] See JP Cerone, "Dynamic Equilibrium: The Evolution of US Attitudes toward International Criminal Courts and Tribunals" (2007) 18 EJIL 277.

international bureaucrats with no accountability whatsoever."[21] Despite the legality of the WHC's intervention in the two cases, the hostility of some domestic constituencies to what is perceived as inadmissible external intervention is most striking. Such hostility can seek grounding in several arguments, including unaccountability but also the "foreign" nature of the intervention or the inadequacy of the relevant international institution to deal with certain political questions.

2.3 "Proliferation" and political questions

One fundamental issue raised by "proliferation" is the adequacy of judicial and quasi-judicial institutions to address political questions. The limited role played by international adjudication in classical international law can largely be explained by the perceived inadequacy of this approach to deal with deeply political questions. The decisions of states were not seen as subject to any sort of review, which would at best impose a legal straitjacket on the subtle and patient work of diplomacy. Legally, this perception was translated into the distinction between disputes capable of "judicial" settlement and those which were not.[22] Whereas in contemporary international law the distinction as such is of limited use,[23] its rationale can still be found at the roots of some legal doctrines[24] or mechanisms.[25] There is no need to open this vast debate here. Two main observations will suffice to capture its main implications.

The first observation concerns the perceived advantage of having judges decide questions hitherto managed through diplomacy or even the threat or the use of force. An important illustration is the remarkable development of investment arbitration proceedings in an area historically characterized by foreign political intervention. In the 1960s, the conclusion of the Convention on the International Center for the Settlement of Investment Disputes (ICSID Convention) was indeed seen by many as a way to remove investment disputes from the realm of politics.[26] In

[21] See Hon. Helen Chenoweth, of Idaho, Thursday July 1, 1999, "World Heritage Committee Meddling in the Internal Affairs of Sovereign Nations—Yet Again," <http://www.bock.com.au/jabiluka/debate.pdf> accessed on July 14, 2012.

[22] See H Lauterpacht, "La théorie des différends non justiciables en droit international" (1930) 34 RCADI 493–654.

[23] See, however, C Schreuer et al., *The ICSID Convention: A Commentary* (Cambridge University Press 2009) 98.

[24] See e.g., the "Act of State doctrine" according to which US Courts decline to review decisions of foreign sovereigns.

[25] See ICJ Statute, Art. 65, and J Frowein and K Oellers-Frahm, "Article 65," in A Zimmermann, C Tomuschat and K Oellers-Frahm (eds), *The Statute of the International Court of Justice. A Commentary* (Oxford University Press 2006) 1411.

[26] See Schreuer et al., note 23, at 419.

retrospect, this objective was successfully achieved. It is now widely acknowledged that resort to home state diplomatic protection is the exception rather than the rule when it comes to foreign investment.[27] Thus, in some respects at least, investment tribunals have lived up to the expectations placed on them by the architects of the ICSID Convention.

The second observation relates to the perceived disadvantages of having international judges meddling with political questions. A prominent illustration is the debate over the issuance of arrest warrants during a peace negotiation.[28] There are several examples of this occurrence, such as the arrest warrant issued in 1995 against Radovan Karadžić shortly before the peace talks in Dayton,[29] or those against the Sudanese president Al Bashir[30] during the Darfur crisis, or against Muammar Gaddafi and others[31] during the Libyan crisis. These and other occurrences came under severe criticism as examples of judicial intrusion in an already delicate peace process.[32] The conception underlying this criticism is that some political questions are best tackled by political means or, in other words, that the "policy of justice," to use the expression of Judith Shklar, is not always adapted to the management of certain questions.

Many other examples could be provided, either in connection with political questions or with clashes between the legalistic logic and sovereignty or non-intervention. The overall trend in the debate is, however, clear. "Proliferation" seems to strengthen the impact of international law on the conduct of international relations. In other words, the new layer of judicial institutions has made international law less horizontal, despite the continued importance of sovereignty and its corollaries. But, unlike domestic systems, this institutional layer lacks structure. Neither a clear hierarchy nor an explicit coordination system among the different bodies has emerged. This situation has raised another important question: is "proliferation" leading to inconsistency and fragmentation?

[27] *Ahmadou Sadio Diallo* (*Republic of Guinea v. Democratic Republic of the Congo*) (Preliminary Objections) [2007] ICJ Rep 582, para. 88.

[28] See P Gaeta and L Calder, "The Impact of Arrest Warrants Issued by International Criminal Courts on Peace Negotiations," in L Boisson de Chazournes, M Kohen and JE Viñuales (eds), *Diplomatic and Judicial Means of Dispute Settlement* (Leiden: Martinus Nijhoff 2012).

[29] *Prosecutor v. Karadžić and Mladić* (Indictment) (1995) ICTY-95-5-I.

[30] *Prosecutor v. Al Bashir* (Arrest Warrant) [2009] ICC-02/05-01/09.

[31] *Prosecutor v. Muammar Mohammed Abu Minyar Gaddafi, Saif Al-Islam Gaddafi and Abdullah Al-Senussi* (Arrest Warrant) [2011] ICC-01/11-01/11.

[32] See P Hazan, *Justice in a Time of War* (Texas University Press 2004) 64–89; R Falk, "The International Criminal Court Plays Politics? The Qaddafi Arrest Warrants" (Wordpress 2011) <http://richardfalk.wordpress.com> accessed July 15, 2012, referred to in Gaeta and Calder, note 28.

3 Coherence: Is "Proliferation" Leading to "Fragmentation"?

The mainstream debate on "proliferation" focuses on the question of coherence or, viewed from a different angle, on the "fragmentation" of both international *fora* and international law. The starting point of the debate is the absence of a vertically or horizontally integrated judiciary at the international level. Unlike domestic judicial systems, the international legal order has no "supreme" or even "coordinating" judicial authority (e.g. a *tribunal des conflits*). For many commentators, this fragmentation of *fora* would lead to the fragmentation of international law itself.

However, despite their correlation, for the link between institutional and substantive fragmentation to be established, some additional elements are needed. The first element concerns the definition of jurisdictional scopes. If each and every institution had a neatly distinct jurisdictional scope, frictions between them would be rare. In practice, of course, there is considerable overlap between the jurisdictional scopes of different courts and tribunals, some of which have general (e.g. the ICJ) or at least broad (e.g. ITLOS) jurisdiction, whereas others have narrow but in practice expanding jurisdiction (e.g. the WTO dispute settlement body or the Court of Justice of the European Union—CJEU).

The second element is the absence of conflict techniques capable of compensating for the lack of structural coordination among the different judicial institutions.

The third element is factual, namely the idiosyncrasies of each tribunal. Some tribunals seem more willing to make a comprehensive harmonization effort (i.e. to look beyond their own fields) than others.[33]

Thus, although related, the questions raised by the debate on the fragmentation of *fora* are distinct from those concerning the fragmentation of law. This difference justifies their separate treatment.

3.1 "Proliferation" and the Fragmentation of International *Fora*

Domestic judicial systems are usually organized in a pyramidal structure at the top of which there is a higher tribunal that has the last word whenever there are inconsistencies in the positions taken by subordinate tribunals. This picture is made more complex by divisions according to territorial, personal, and subject-matter jurisdiction or to the type of question (e.g. competing jurisdiction or different views on the

[33] See section 4.1 of this chapter.

constitutionality of a given act), but all the institutions composing the judiciary are integrated in a coherent structure.

The situation in the international legal order is in part similar and in part different to that of domestic systems. Like domestic systems, the areas and issues covered by international law have become increasingly diverse and complex. Yet, no explicit coordination has been developed between the institutions established to implement this growing body of obligations. Thus, what can be called the "expansion of the international legal order"[34] has led to the emergence of a disorganized array of (mainly) specialized judicial and quasi-judicial bodies.[35] This, in turn, has raised a number of problems, including: the assertion of competing jurisdictions and parallel proceedings;[36] forum shopping;[37] or conflicting decisions with respect to fundamentally similar facts[38] or on a given legal concept or principle.[39] Here, we focus on two main approaches that can be envisaged to tackle this problem:[40] 1) create a formal system of coordination; or 2) manage coordination on an ad hoc basis.

The first approach involves reforming the layer of international judicial and quasi-judicial institutions to introduce, at a global or a partial level, a hierarchical structure. There are different options in this regard. One would be to create a global (or partial[41]) appellate body or review mechanism. Another would be to allocate this function to an existing body. The discussion in this regard has mostly focused on the potential role of the ICJ. In an ideal model of vertical organic integration, the ICJ would statutorily occupy the top of an effective international judicial system. The court would impose its authority on the other international courts and tribunals, at least when it comes to the interpretation of the general rules of international law that might be applied by all. Several proposals have been made to achieve this result, whether, as was suggested by C Pinto and F Orrego Vicuña, by formally

[34] Dupuy, note 17, at 795.

[35] For a broader conceptualization of international regime complexity from a political science perspective see KJ Alter and S Meunier, "The Politics of International Regime Complexity" (2009) 7 Perspectives on Politics 13.

[36] See Shany, note 6; N Lavranos, *Jurisdictional Competition: Selected Cases in International Law and European Law* (Groningen: Europa Law Publishing 2009). A prominent illustration is the *MOX Plant* cases. See S Maljean-Dubois and J-C Martin, "L'affaire de l'*Usine Mox* devant les tribunaux internationaux" (2007) 134 JDI 437.

[37] See e.g., J Pauwelyn and LE Salles, "Forum Shopping Before International Tribunals: (Real) Concerns, (Im)Possible Solutions" (2009) 42 Cornell ILJ 77, referring to WTO, *Mexico—Tax Measures on Soft Drinks and Other Beverages* (2002) WT/DS308/AB/R.

[38] See e.g. JE Viñuales and F Spoorenberg, "Conflicting Decisions in International Arbitration" (2009) 8 LPICT 91.

[39] See section 3.2 of this chapter.

[40] See generally C Romano, "Deciphering the Grammar of the International Jurisprudential Dialogue" (2009) 41 N.Y.U. J. Int'l L. & Pol. 755.

[41] See e.g., N Gal-Or, "The Concept of Appeal in International Dispute Settlement" (2008) 19 EJIL 43.

recognizing the ICJ as the supreme court of the international legal order,[42] by granting prejudicial competence to the court,[43] by extending the field of its consultative role, or by accepting that the court may act as an international *tribunal des conflits* (e.g. to settle a jurisdictional dispute between courts from different treaty systems). All these proposals should be taken seriously, as they may influence, in the future, the elaboration of a structured international judiciary. This said, one must not underestimate the important technical and, of course, the political challenges that the shaping of an international judiciary would have to overcome.[44]

It is precisely because of such challenges that it appears more realistic to resort to a variety of ad hoc coordination techniques, such as (i) the exceptions of *electio fori*, *lis pendens*, and *res judicata* or private international law techniques, (ii) an informal rule of "precedent," or (iii) a wider use of comity between tribunals. The first technique may be useful in some cases, but it has significant limitations. Private international law techniques are indeed designed to govern the relations between different legal systems and not among purported "special regimes" (e.g. environmental law, trade law, etc.), which have no legal existence in international law,[45] or even among treaty regimes or norms, which belong to the same legal order (international law).[46] As for procedural exceptions, they were developed to operate in organically integrated systems, which international law is not. The practice of the ICJ helps illustrate this point.[47] Whereas the Court may decline jurisdiction if it appears that a previous agreement between the states gives jurisdiction to another judicial body,[48] it sees no reason to do so when non-judicial means, such as mediation and perhaps also some quasi-judicial mechanisms, have stepped in.[49] With respect to *lis pendens* and *res judicata*, their exacting requirements (identity of subjects, cause and object)

[42] See F Orrego Vicuña and C Pinto, *The Peaceful Settlement of Disputes: Prospects for the Twenty-First Century, Preliminary Report prepared for the 1999 Centennial of the First International Peace Conference*, C. E. Doc. CAHDI (98) 15.

[43] See G Guillaume, "The Future of International Judicial Institutions" (1995) 44 ICLQ 848, 862; T Treves, "Advisory Opinions of the International Court of Justice on Questions Raised by Other International Tribunals" (2000) 4 Max Planck UN Ybk 215.

[44] See Dupuy, note 17, at 800.

[45] See JE Viñuales, "Cartographies imaginaires: Observations sur la portée juridique du concept de « régime spécial » en droit international" JDI, forthcoming.

[46] See P-M Dupuy, "Competition among International Tribunals and the Authority of the International Court of Justice," in U Fastenrath et al. (eds), *Essays in Honour of Bruno Simma* (Oxford University Press 2011) 863–76.

[47] See Gattini, note 6.

[48] *Mavrommatis Concessions in Palestine* (*Greece v. UK*) PCIJ Rep Series A No 2, p. 31.

[49] See *Aegean Sea Continental Shelf Case* (*Greece v. Turkey*) (Jurisdiction) [1978] ICJ Reps 3, p. 12, at para. 29; *Free Zones of Upper Savoy and the District of Gex* (France/Switzerland) [1932] PCIJ Rep Series A No 22 [13]; *Passage through the Great Belt* (*Finland v. Denmark*) (Request for the Indication of Provisional Measures: Order) [1991] ICJ Rep 12 [20].

are rarely met in international disputes.[50] This is why less formalistic techniques could play a major role in practice.

One such technique is the generalization of an informal rule of precedent. Although there is no rule of precedent in international law, some consideration for the decisions of other tribunals could help avoid conflicting decisions and provide a higher degree of legal certainty. Such deference could be explicit (e.g. open endorsement of a previous holding) or implicit (e.g. harmonizing two prior decisions without disavowing any of them or avoiding a pronouncement on legal points decided by another tribunal). Much has been written on this question.[51] Examples of deference abound both among international tribunals and between these and domestic courts. For example, one can hardly conceive that a national judge may ignore not only the content of the European Convention on Human Rights (ECHR), but also its evolving interpretation by the European Court of Human Rights (ECtHR). In fact, cases of open confrontation such as the *Nicaragua/Tadić/Genocide* "saga" are rather exceptional.[52] What seems more challenging is the determination of the conditions under which such deference "is" and "should" be given. Both questions would require further research particularly as regards the set of criteria, which could help determine the priority among competing international adjudicative bodies.[53]

Another—closely related—pragmatic technique would be a wider use of comity in international adjudication.[54] Indeed, the coordinated articulation of competing jurisdictions does not seem possible in the absence of an empirical alliance between flexibility and authority.[55] Flexibility calls for each judge to pragmatically evaluate what should be the answer given in a specific context to the following questions: Should she assert or decline jurisdiction? Should she stay her decision? Should she defer to the views of another court on a given point? Here, the *Solange* doctrine developed by the German *Bundesverfassungsgericht* could be of great help.[56] This method—by which a tribunal accepts to limit its own jurisdiction to

[50] See Gattini, note 6, at 326. See e.g. Svea Court of Appeals *Czech Republic v. CME Czech Republic BV* [2003] 42 ILM 919.

[51] See e.g., G Guillaume, "Le précédent dans la justice et l'arbitrage international" (2010) 137 JDI 685.

[52] See section 3.2 of this chapter. In investment arbitration several questions (e.g. the scope of umbrella clauses, the MFN clause, the availability of the necessity defence, or the definition of investment) have led to awards disavowing prior awards. In the trade context, see London Court of International Arbitration, *United States of America v. Canada* (award) no. 81010 (2011) [323] § 127.

[53] An important question is how the capacity of each of these bodies is defined by its own statute as well as the legal and material scope covered in each case by such jurisdiction. See Maljean-Dubois and Martin, note 36.

[54] On this concept see T Schultz and D Holloway, "Retour sur la *comity* (Première partie)" (2011) 138 JDI 863.

[55] See R Higgins, "Respecting Sovereign States and Running a Tight Courtroom" (2001) 50 ICLQ 121, 122.

[56] See *Internationale Handelsgesellschaft mbH v. Einfuhr—und Vorratsstelle für Getreide und Futtermittel* (Solange I), BVerfGE 37, 271; *Wünsche Handelsgesellschaft* (Solange II) case (1986), BVerfGE 73, 339.

respect that of another tribunal—was used by the ECtHR in the *Bosphorus* case[57] for the benefit of the now CJEU. Yet, the *Bosphorus* case also shows the limits of this doctrine. The assessment of the scope and conditions of applying the jurisdiction of one court by another tribunal remains subject to errors and approximations.[58] A similar approach could be used to stay the proceedings in one court until another court legally characterizes facts relevant for both proceedings.[59] However, this raises the question of the extent to which a case can be divided into separate questions, each capable of being decided separately by a different body.

The limits of formal and ad hoc coordination among different international courts and tribunals would suggest that there is a real risk of fragmentation of international law. However, as discussed next, aside from some rare examples, such a risk has yet to materialize.

3.2 "Proliferation" and the fragmentation of international law

The link between "proliferation" and the fragmentation of substantive international law is often portrayed by reference to the *Nicaragua/Tadić/Genocide* "saga," where the views of the ICJ and the International Criminal Tribunal for Former Yugoslavia (ICTY) came into frontal collision. In *Tadić*, the ICTY used a test of "overall control" to conclude that the acts of the Bosnian Serb armed forces were attributable to the Federal Republic of Yugoslavia.[60] In doing so, it distanced itself from the more demanding test of "effective control" developed by the ICJ in the *Nicaragua* case.[61] A decade later, in the *Genocide* case,[62] the ICJ took issue with this interpretation of general international law and, in a sharp statement that seems to be a call to order from a superior to a subordinate, concluded that the "overall control" test is unsuitable, for it stretches too far the connection which must exist between the conduct of a state's organs and its international responsibility.[63]

[57] *Bosphorus v. Ireland* [GC], no. 45036/98 [2005-VI] ECHR.

[58] See A Ciampi, "L'Union Européenne et le respect des droits de l'homme dans la mise en oeuvre des sanctions devant la Cour européenne des droits de l'homme" (2006) 110 RGDIP 85.

[59] Gattini (note 6) refers to the case *Prosecutor v. Kvocka et al* (Decision on the Interlocutory Appeal by the accused Zoran Zigic against the decision of Trial Chamber I [2000] ICTY-98-30/1) [2001].

[60] The Appeals Chamber of the ICTY noted that: "in international law, every tribunal is a self-contained system (unless otherwise provided)," *Prosecutor v. Tadić* (Decision on the Defence Motion for Interlocutory Appeal on Jurisdiction) [1995] ICTY-94-1 [para. 11]. In a subsequent case, the same tribunal also stated that "there is no hierarchical relationship" between the tribunal and the ICJ, *Prosecutor v. Mucić* et al (Judgment) [2011] ICTY-96-21-A [para. 24].

[61] *Military and Paramilitary Activities in and against Nicaragua (Nicaragua v. United States of America)* (Merits) [1986] ICJ Rep 14 [paras. 105–115].

[62] *Application of the Convention on the Prevention and Punishment of the Crime of Genocide (Bosnia and Herzegovina v. Serbia and Montenegro)* (Merits) [2007] ICJ Rep 43.

[63] *Bosnia and Herzegovina v. Serbia and Montenegro*, note 62, at para. 406.

This saga epitomizes the danger of fragmentation of substantive international law for a number of reasons. First, the debate touched upon a rule of general international law (i.e. the rule governing the attribution of the acts of *de facto* organs to a state) and not on a rule arising from a specialized branch of international law. The ICJ noted that the ICTY was, in fact, analyzing attribution for the purpose of establishing the nature of the conflict (i.e. a question of humanitarian and criminal law) and not in the context of general international law. But this is not how the *Tadić* tribunal had understood its own reasoning. In fact, as noted by Antonio Cassese, it is likely that the ICJ added that note "as a gracious concession to the ICTY."[64] Second, the saga opposed two judicial bodies, which, although separate, are clearly related in their capacity as organs of the United Nations Organization (the ICJ is a principal organ of the UN, whereas the ICTY is a subsidiary organ of the Security Council). Third, the confrontation was explicit, particularly in the *Genocide* case, and not just implicit as is often the case. Fourth, the factual situation addressed by the two tribunals was fundamentally similar. Finally, this saga is one of the rare cases of open confrontation between tribunals, which also explains the recurring references to it in the apocalyptic literature on fragmentation.

There are, of course, some other examples of interpretive friction between tribunals,[65] but that is a normal feature of any developed legal system. The problems encountered by the international legal order are, in fact, more a sign of its increasing maturity than of an endemic crisis.[66] The main challenge in this regard is not one of fragmentation but one of "integration." An example will help illustrate this point. The role of "precaution" in international law has been debated since the 1980s: whether it is a "principle" or an "approach"; whether it is grounded in general international law or only in treaty-law; and whether it is merely an interpretative tool or a primary rule requiring (or at least authorizing) states to take action in the absence of conclusive scientific evidence. Different tribunals

[64] A Cassese, "The *Nicaragua* and *Tadić* Tests Revisited in Light of the ICJ Judgment on Genocide in Bosnia" (2007) 18 EJIL 649, 651.

[65] See e.g., the Hissène Habré "saga," in particular the conflicting decisions of the Court of Justice of the Economic Community of Western African States (which concluded that Senegal could not prosecute Habré under a statute enacted after the conducts were incriminated) and the ICJ (which concluded that Senegal had a duty to prosecute Habré or extradite him). See *Hissène Habré v. Senegal*, Court of Justice of the Economic Union of West African States, Decision No ECW/CCJ/JUD/06/10 (2010); *Questions relating to the Obligation to Prosecute or Extradite* (*Belgium v. Senegal*) General List No 144 [2012] ICJ 1. We can also refer to the stance taken by the CJEU with respect to the legality of treaties that create an international court likely to affect the homogeneity of European law. Although this is not, as such, a conflict between two judicial stances, it is a clear assertion of hierarchy by the CJEU with respect to any potential interpretation of European law by another international court. See M Parish, "International Courts and the European Legal Order" (2012) 23 EJIL 141.

[66] See B Simma, "Fragmentation in a Positive Light" (2004) 25 MJIL 847.

have taken different stances on these questions, with the ICJ[67] and the WTO dispute settlement body[68] adopting a skeptical stance, while, on the other side of the spectrum, the ECtHR[69] and, to some extent, the ITLOS[70] being more receptive. But this is less a display of fragmentation than one of limited openness for the following reasons.

First, precaution as a legal concept stems from a "court-less" area of international law (i.e. environmental law), so no tribunal would be entitled to claim substantive priority in its interpretation. Second, the analysis of the relevant case law shows that tribunals do look at what other tribunals say to inform their own views. Third, and more fundamentally, the tribunals reach their own conclusions without openly disavowing the stance taken by other tribunals. Fourth, some measure of disagreement is inherent to the judicial development of any body of law because judicial decisions are taken in different factual and legal contexts, which, in turn, influence the interpretation of legal concepts. Over time, differences are progressively harmonized by the development of principles capable of "integrating" different solutions into a common framework.[71] The spelling out of this judicial "dialectics" is useful because it adds a time dimension to the question of fragmentation. Whereas the views of different tribunals may partially conflict at some point in time, they are often harmonized by subsequent tribunals (irrespective of the lack of a hierarchical or coordinated structure) as they seek to distill a coherent jurisprudential line from a variety of prior decisions. This underlines the importance of states appointing generalists (as opposed to narrow field-specific technicians) to some key international judicial offices, as no effort at integration can succeed if judges themselves are unwilling or simply unable to keep the "big picture" of international law in mind. Only if the interpretive tension turns into open confrontation, which is a highly exceptional occurrence, will fragmentation become a genuine problem. More problematic is how to facilitate a proper circulation and recognition of different legal concepts among judicial bodies.

67 *Pulp Mills on the River Uruguay* (*Argentina v. Uruguay*) [2010] ICJ Rep 14 [164].

68 *European Communities—Measures Affecting the Approval and Marketing of Biotech Products—Panel Report* (WT/DS291/R, WT/DS292/R, WT/DS293/R 2006) (EC—Biotech) paras 7.88–7.89.

69 *Tătar v. Romania*, no. 67021/01 [2009] ECHR [§ 120].

70 *Southern Bluefin Tuna Cases* (*New Zealand v. Japan*; *Australia v. Japan*) (Order) [1999] ITLOS cases Nos 3 and 4 [para. 77] (the French text speaks of "prudence et précaution"); *MOX Plant case*, (Order) [2001] ITLOS case No 10 [para. 84] (the French text speaks of "prudence et précaution").

71 See Viñuales and Spoorenberg, note 38, at 104.

4 Openness: Expressing Different Values and Views

An important question arising from "proliferation" is how permeable a judicial or quasi-judicial body may be to the values protected by other areas of international law.

As noted above, legal systems evolve over time and they must integrate new values. In a context characterized by the "proliferation" of specialized judicial and quasi-judicial bodies, the integration of such values may pose significant challenges, as these bodies may try to preserve the orthodoxy of their treaty regime or specialty area. The constraints on the integration of new values are not only of a legal nature (e.g. jurisdictional scope and applicable law), but also of a sociological one, as adjudicators may have their own idiosyncrasies shaped by their education, context, and position ("where you stand depends on where you sit").

In addition, the very influence of courts on the evolution of different values makes their role deeply political, calling in turn for another type of "openness," i.e. transparency and participation.

4.1 "Proliferation" and the integration of values

An ideal setting to explore the dynamics of the circulation of values in a judicialized international legal order is the uneven integration of a "court-less" field such as international environmental law into other areas with highly sophisticated judicial systems, such as human rights, trade, and investment law. One may contrast in this regard the broad integration of environmental law in the case law of human rights courts with the limited (albeit expanding) role given to it by trade or investment tribunals.

One of the main reasons why the "human-rights approach" to environmental protection[72] has been so influential lies in the stronger enforcement mechanisms—including three regional courts and several quasi-judicial bodies—available in the human rights arena. Although there are some limitations in the extent to which environmental protection can be furthered through human rights claims (mostly the need for a link between environmental degradation and a substantial impact on the enjoyment of a protected human right[73]), human rights bodies such as the

[72] See A Boyle and MR Anderson (eds), *Human Rights Approaches to Environmental Protection* (Oxford: Clarendon Press 1998); D Shelton and DK Anton, *Environmental Protection and Human Rights* (Cambridge University Press 2011).

[73] See F Francioni, "International Human Rights in an Environmental Horizon" (2010) 21 EJIL 41.

ECtHR,[74] the IACtHR,[75] the African Commission of Human and Peoples' Rights (ACtHPR),[76] or the Human Rights Committee[77] have widely integrated environmental protection in their decisions.

This situation contrasts with the rather reluctant attitude adopted by trade and investment tribunals until quite recently. Examples of this attitude include the decision of the WTO panel in *EC-Biotech* with respect to the relevance of the Convention on Biological Diversity and the Cartagena Protocol,[78] or the utter disregard of environmental treaties by the tribunal in *CDSE v. Costa Rica*.[79] Although the role of environmental considerations is now becoming increasingly important in the trade[80] and investment contexts,[81] from a theoretical perspective, one may inquire into the reasons explaining the differing pace and extent of integration of environmental values by different bodies.

In this connection, an important consideration is the legal framework governing a court's jurisdiction and the law it may apply. Whereas independent environmental claims (i.e. claims exclusively based on the breach of an environmental treaty or customary norm) will normally fall outside the jurisdictional scope of these tribunals,[82] reference to environmental law for interpretation purposes is explicitly authorized (and arguably encouraged) by the law of treaties.[83] Perhaps the best evidence of the latter is that the expanding role of environmental considerations in the trade and investment arenas has been prompted by a change in interpretation and not by a change of law. Thus, one must look beyond the law to explain different levels of openness. Adjudicators are subject to a variety of constraints in the

[74] The seminal case is *Lopez Ostra v. Spain* (merits) [1994] ECHR Series A no. 303-C. For an overview of the case law of the ECHR see Council of Europe, *Manual on Human Rights and the Environment* (Strasbourg: Council of Europe, 2006).

[75] See e.g., IACtHR *Mayagna (Sumo) Awas Tingni Community v. Nicaragua* (merits) [2001] Series C No 79 [para. 149].

[76] See *Social and Economic Rights Action Center and the Center for Economic and Social Rights v. Nigeria* [2001] African Commission on Human and Peoples' Rights, Communication No 155/96 [para. 52].

[77] The seminal case is Human Rights Committee, *Bernard Ominayak and the Lubicon Band v. Canada*, [1990] Communication No 167/1984. See S Joseph, J Schultz, and M Castan, *The International Covenant on Civil and Political Rights: Cases, Materials and Commentary* (Oxford University Press 2000) 572.

[78] See *EC—Biotech*, note 68, at paras 7.74–7.75.

[79] See *Compañía del Desarrollo de Santa Fe SA v. Costa Rica* (Award) [2000] ICSID Case No ARB/96/1 [para. 71].

[80] See S Charnovitz, "The WTO Environmental Progress" (2007) 10 JIEL 685, and, more recently, the decision of the WTO Appellate Body, *United States—Measures Concerning the Importation, Marketing and Sale of Tuna and Tuna Products* [2012] WT/DS381/AB/R (US—Tuna/dolphin 2012) [paras 311–333].

[81] See JE Viñuales, *Foreign Investment and the Environment in International Law* (Cambridge University Press 2012) chs 12–15.

[82] See e.g. *Fadeyeva v. Russia*, no. 55723/00, [2005-IV] ECHR [§68]; Viñuales, note 81, at 90.

[83] See R Pavoni, "Mutual Supportiveness as a Principle of Interpretation and Law-Making: A Watershed for the 'WTO-and-Competing Regimes' Debate?" (2010) 21 EJIL 649; Viñuales, note 81, at 148.

performance of their function.[84] Moreover, as individuals with a personal history, training, and preferences, as well as commitment to social groups, adjudicators may have different levels of receptiveness to (certain) new values or simply to jurisprudential innovation.[85]

These questions are only starting to be elucidated in the literature, and they would benefit from more empirical research on ways to manage potentially dysfunctional idiosyncratic behavior. This is even more necessary in areas such as investment arbitration or trade adjudication where ad hoc tribunals are given the power to make far-reaching decisions without necessarily grasping the full social context of the dispute.[86] The very delegation of such decisions to these tribunals has, understandably, raised issues of transparency and participation.

4.2 "Proliferation" and the integration of views

As a growing number of high-impact decisions are taken by international judicial and quasi-judicial bodies, transparency and participation have become increasingly important issues. At the same time, "proliferation" is a vector of transparency and participation, as some *fora* are now available to enforce international obligations of transparency and participation. The comparison between human rights courts and international economic adjudication mentioned in the previous section is also useful to illustrate the two dimensions of the link between "proliferation" and transparency/participation.

One important aspect of "proliferation" is the re-allocation of certain decisions to international courts and away from the domestic political process. The shift of decision-making powers from (domestic) representative institutions to (international) judicial institutions has been perceived in some circles as introducing a democratic deficit.[87] The debate has been particularly intense in the areas of trade and investment adjudication where, in the view of many, decisions are sometimes made on the basis of purely economic considerations without fully taking into account the broader socio-political context.[88] A prominent example is provided by the case

[84] See D Kennedy, "Freedom and Constraint in Adjudication: A Critical Phenomenology" (1986) 36 Journal of Legal Education 518.

[85] On the need for a sociology of international law see M Hirsch, "The Sociology of International Law: Invitation to Study International Rules in their Social Context" (2005) 55 The University of Toronto Law Journal 891.

[86] See G van Harten, *Investment Arbitration and Public Law* (Oxford University Press 2007).

[87] See D Shelton, "The Participation of Nongovernmental Organizations in International Judicial Proceedings" (1994) 88 AJIL 611; H Ruiz Fabri and J-M Sorel (eds), *Le tiers à l'instance devant les juridictions internationals* (Paris: Pedone 2005).

[88] See B Stern, "Civil Society's Voice in the Settlement of International Economic Disputes" (2007) 22 ICSID Review 280; F Grisel and JE Viñuales, "L'*amicus curiae* dans l'arbitrage d'investissement" (2007) 22 ICSID Review 380; P-M Dupuy, F Francioni, and E-U Petersmann (eds), *Human Rights in International Investment Law and Arbitration* (Oxford University Press 2009).

Foresti v. South Africa.[89] The dispute arose from a mining investment made by Italian nationals, who claimed inter alia that their mining rights had been expropriated by South Africa as a result of measures adopted in the context of Black Economic Empowerment (BEE) policies to eliminate the consequences of the apartheid regime. The tribunal wisely anticipated that several civil society groups would likely seek to intervene and, in agreement with the parties, prepared a short summary of the dispute as well as rules governing *amicus curiae* intervention.[90] Although the claim was eventually withdrawn, the fundamental issue is clear: to what extent can an ephemeral investment tribunal take a stance on an economic dispute with such profound socio-political ramifications? Or, alternatively, under what conditions of transparency and participation (of "procedural justice") could such a decision be made? In this specific case, the tribunal took pains to give civil society groups the opportunity to express their views, and even took the unusual step of requesting feedback from those groups on the adequacy of the intervention framework.[91] But this openness is not necessarily the rule, as suggested by a more recent decision in which an investment tribunal denied the petition of a human rights group to intervene as *amicus curiae*.[92] There may be good reasons for admitting or denying a petition, but the very fact that each tribunal is allowed to take such a decision in isolation from a settled body of case law or without appeal raises important questions of legitimacy.

This said, "proliferation" may also strengthen transparency and participation, either by incorporating the views of civil society in the selection of adjudicators or by helping enforce transparency and participation obligations. Two examples illustrate this point. One important synergy between human rights and environmental protection has been the increasing recognition of the three pillars of "environmental democracy" (access to information, participation in decision-making, and access to justice)[93] by human rights courts. The ECtHR has referred to the Aarhus Convention to strengthen the informational and participatory components of the rights protected by the ECHR, even when the respondent state is not a party to the Aarhus Convention.[94] The second illustration is the Compliance Committee established

[89] *Piero Foresti, Laura de Carli and others v. Republic of South Africa* (Award) [2010] ICSID Case No ARB(AF)/07/1.

[90] See *Foresti v. South Africa*, "Agreed text for potential non-disputing parties," <http://www.investmenttreatynews.org> accessed July 15, 2012.

[91] See "Letter of 5 October 2009 from the Secretary of the Tribunal" <http://www.investmentreatynews.org> accessed July 15, 2012.

[92] See *Bernhard von Pezold v. Republic of Zimbabwe*, [2012] ICSID Case No ARB/10/15; *Border Timbers Limited v. Republic of Zimbabwe*, ICSID Case No ARB/10/25 (Joint Order).

[93] See Report of the United Nations Conference on Environment and Development (Rio de Janeiro, Annex I, Rio Declaration on Environment and Development, A/CONF.151/26, Vol. I, 1992) Principle 10; Convention on Access to Information, Public Participation in Decision-making and Access to Justice in Environmental Matters, (1998) 2161 UNTS 447 (Aarhus Convention).

[94] See e.g., *Taskin and others v. Turkey*, no. 46117/99, [2004-X] ECHR [§ 99–100]; *Okyay and Others v. Turkey*, no. 36220/97, [2005-VII] ECHR [§ 51-2]; *Demir and Baykara v. Turkey* [GC], no. 34503/97, [2008] ECHR [§ 83]. Turkey is not a party to the Aarhus Convention.

under the Aarhus Convention to supervise the effective implementation of the three pillars. Unlike most international adjudicative or quasi-adjudicative bodies, there is an express provision calling for the intervention of civil society in the nomination of candidates for this committee.[95] In addition, the number of complaints brought to this committee has grown steadily since it started operations in 2004, with now some sixty cases decided or pending. Moreover, national implementation reports suggest that the committee's recommendations play a significant practical role in the implementation of participatory rights.[96]

These examples suggest that the impact of "proliferation" on participation and transparency is not necessarily negative. As discussed next, underlying this assessment is the broader question of the legitimacy of international courts and tribunals, either with respect to their composition or with respect to their effects.

5 Pulling the Threads Together: Some Concluding Observations on the Legitimacy of International Adjudication

The question of legitimacy cuts across the three debates discussed so far. Although it is covered in other chapters of this volume, an "anatomy" of the debate on international adjudication cannot be complete without a reference to it. From an analytical perspective, this question has two core components.

First, one can inquire into the "legitimacy of principle" of a given body, i.e. all the legitimacy issues that arise from how it has been constituted (e.g. victor's justice,[97] ad hoc tribunals, representativeness[98]) or from its structural position (e.g. *a priori* legitimacy to interfere with politics,[99] role as agents or trustees[100]). Although law and political science can provide important insights into these questions, the answers called for by

[95] "Review of Compliance," Decision I/7 (UN Doc. ECE/MP.PP/2/Add.8, 2004) Addendum, p.1, annex paras 2 and 4.

[96] National Implementation Report <www.unece.org> accessed July 15, 2012.

[97] See G Bass, *Stay the Hands of Vengeance: The Politics of War Crimes Tribunals* (Princeton University Press 2000).

[98] On these two issues see section 4.2 of this chapter.

[99] See section 2 of this chapter.

[100] See e.g. K Alter, "Agents or Trustees? International Courts in their Political Context" (2008) 14 EJIR 33.

this first component lie beyond the province of empirical sciences and must be sought in (legal and political) philosophical inquiry. The role of empirical sciences seems more important for the second component of the debate, namely "legitimacy based on effects." The fundamental question here is to what extent international adjudication is desirable when one considers its aggregate effects with respect to the pursuit of different goals.[101] Of course, the selection of these goals would require a "normative" or philosophical inquiry in the first place, although such a selection (as most normative inquiries) is more often a retrospective rather than a prospective exercise. Yet, it is clear that the two components are closely intertwined. This connection has, in turn, important analytical implications.

To understand these implications, it seems useful to introduce a parallel with the American debate on the legitimacy of judicial review. Judicial review was initially challenged on the basis of the unelected and unaccountable character of judges[102] or, in other words, on questions concerning the judiciary's legitimacy of principle to perform this function. Such criticism was answered by several scholars by reference to different arguments, touching on both principle and effects. Thus, it was argued that representation can take different forms (including unelected judicial functions), particularly in connection with the defense of long-term values enshrined in the constitution.[103] Alternatively, it was also argued that judicial review was necessary for the American system to function properly.[104] The main counter-arguments leveled against judicial review moved then to challenge the latter—empirical—claim, stressing that the overall impact of judicial review on the performance of a democratic system is not necessarily positive.[105]

In a similar vein, the "proliferation" debate is gradually moving from the questions of principle mentioned above to questions of effects. In other words, as the factual component of "proliferation" develops—thus providing a body of practice that can be studied—its perceptual component is increasingly assessed in the light of empirical ("effects") considerations and less from a normative

[101] See Y Shany, "Assessing the Effectiveness of International Courts: A Goal-Based Approach" (2012) 106 AJIL 225.

[102] See e.g., H Steele Commager, "Judicial Review and Democracy" (1943) 19 Virginia Quarterly Review 417, 418.

[103] This was the initial thesis of A Hamilton in *The Federalist*, No. 78. See A Hamilton, J Madison, and J Jay, *The Federalist* (Chicago, IL: William Benton 1970) 231. See also E Rostow, "The Democratic Character of Judicial Review" (1952) 66 HLR 193; A Bickel, *The Least Dangerous Branch* (Binghamton, NY: Bobbs-Merrill 1962).

[104] See JH Ely, *Democracy and Distrust: A Theory of Judicial Review* (Cambridge, MA: Harvard University Press 1980) 7–8. See also H Wechsler, "Toward Neutral Principles of Constitutional Law" (1959) 73 HLR 1; M Perry, *The Constitution, the Courts and Human Rights* (New Haven, CT: Yale University Press 1982).

[105] See M Tushnet, *Taking the Constitution Away from the Courts* (Princeton University Press 1999) 141, 152–3.

("principled") perspective. At the same time, the results of empirical analyses are changing the perception of "proliferation" as a fact of international life. This is sometimes referred to as "normalization," although the dynamics of the debate is seldom spelled out. In this regard, the debate on legitimacy can be seen as the backbone of the "anatomy" we have outlined in this chapter. By looking more closely at how normative and empirical studies provide answers to the two components of the legitimacy debate, we will be in a better position to understand the evolution of the two components (factual and perceptual) of "proliferation" and, thereby, of the current (empirical) and proper (normative) place of adjudication in international affairs.

Research Questions

1. Is the fragmentation of international law a problem in practice? If so, under what conditions?
2. Under what conditions may (or should) a tribunal exercise comity or defer to another tribunal?
3. What are the main variables explaining the degree of "openness" of different tribunals as regards legal concepts arising either from general international law or from a specialized branch thereof, other than the tribunal's?
4. If proliferation entails a shift in the level at which certain decisions are made from domestic political processes to international adjudicative processes, what "design" features (appointment, transparency, participation, etc.) could make such a shift legitimate?

Suggested Reading

American Society of International Law, "Implications of the Proliferation of International Adjudicatory Bodies for Dispute Resolution" (1995) *American Society of International Law Bulletin* 9.

Boisson de Chazournes, L, Kohen, M, and Viñuales, JE (eds), *Diplomatic and Judicial Means of Dispute Settlement* (Leiden: Martinus Nijhoff 2012).

Charney, JI, "Is International Law Threatened by Multiple International Tribunals?" in *Recueil des cours de l'Académie de droit international*, vol. 271 (1998), 101–382.

Dupuy, P-M, "L'unité de l'ordre juridique international: Cours général de droit international public 2000" in *Recueil des cours de l'Académie de droit international*, vol. 297 (2002), 9–489.

Gattini, G, "Un regard procédural sur la fragmentation du droit international" (2006) Revue générale de droit international public 303.

Koskenniemi, M and Leino, P, "Fragmentation of International Law? Postmodern Anxieties" (2002) 15 LJIL 553.

Romano, C, "Can You Hear Me Now? The Case for Extending the International Judicial Network" (2009) 10 Chicago Journal of International Law 233.

Shany, Y, *The Competing Jurisdictions of International Courts and Tribunals* (Oxford University Press 2003).

Société française pour le droit international, *La Multiplication des Juridictions Internationales: Un Système Anarchique?* Colloque de Lille (Paris: Pedone 2003).

Symposium: The Proliferation of International Tribunals: Piecing Together the Puzzle (1999) 31(4) N.Y.U. J. Int'l L. & Pol. (including articles by B Kingsbury, J Charney, C Romano, E-U Petersmann, P-M Dupuy, T Treves, J Jackson, M Pinto, E Benvenisti, B Brown, G Danilenko, and G Abi-Saab).

Symposium: Diversity or Cacophony? (2004) 25(4) MJIL (including articles by B Simma, G Hafner, A Tahvanainen, J Jackson, C Koch, J Pauwelyn, J Meltzer, P S Rao, W Burke-White, D Philpott, A Fischer-Lescano and G Teubner, A Paulus, S Krasner, J Kurtz, D Sarooshi, S Sassen, K Wellens, F Francioni et al.).

Symposium: The Normalizing of Adjudication in Complex International Governance Regimes (2009) 41(4) N.Y.U. J. Int'l L. & Pol. (including articles by C Romano, A Schneider, A-C Martineau, S Vasciannie, L Helfer and K Alter, E Benvenisti and G Downs, R Teitel and R Howse, J Alvarez and G Abi-Saab).

CHAPTER 8

WHAT ARE INTERNATIONAL JUDGES FOR? THE MAIN FUNCTIONS OF INTERNATIONAL ADJUDICATION

JOSÉ E ALVAREZ*

* Herbert and Rose Rubin Professor of International Law, New York University School of Law. The author gratefully acknowledges the assistance of the Filomen D'Agostino and Max E. Greenberg Research Fund.

1 Introduction

International judges and arbitrators are commonly portrayed in simple terms: they are interstate dispute settlers engaged in avoiding or deterring threats to peace. This is suggested by the United Nations Charter,[1] other treaties,[2] and scholarship across time.[3] The intertwined functions of settling disputes and maintaining peace, self-evident to those at the turn of the nineteenth century, continue to explain the function of today's diverse courts and tribunals. Those functions are clearly engaged when International Court of Justice (ICJ) judges settle territorial disputes or those involving the use of force, when the UN Security Council establishes the International Criminal Tribunals for the Former Yugoslavia (ICTY) and International Criminal Tribunal for Rwanda (ICTR) pursuant to its Chapter VII powers, or when the International Criminal Court (ICC) is established on the premise that without criminal accountability there can be no lasting peace in societies victimized by mass atrocities. Trade and investment lawyers also rely on the "conflict resolution" rationale. Trade lawyers describe the function of the World Trade Organization's (WTO's) dispute settlement system as resolving disputes that historically have led to wider interstate frictions while defenders of the International Centre for Settlement of Investment Disputes (ICSID) argue that investor-state arbitrations are necessary alternatives to "gunboat diplomacy." Of course, the "dispute settlement" function also has been affirmed by innumerable international judges and arbitrators, most often in the course of disclaiming that they have any role other than applying pre-existing law to settle the narrow dispute before them.[4]

The dispute settlement function explains much of what international adjudicators do, but as many contributors to this volume indicate, it is insufficient. To the extent that

[1] See UN Charter Art. 1(1) (affirming as one of the purposes of the UN the "adjustment or settlement of international disputes or situations which might lead to a breach of the peace"); Art. 33 (listing "judicial settlement" as one of the "peaceful means" through which interstate disputes ought to be settled); Statute of the Court, Art. 38 (the function of the Court is "to decide... disputes as are submitted to it").

[2] See, e.g., Marrakesh Agreement Establishing the World Trade Organization, Understanding on Rules and Procedures Governing the Settlement of Disputes (DSU), Art. 3.7 ("The aim of the dispute settlement mechanism is to secure a positive solution to a dispute").

[3] See, e.g., H Lauterpacht, *The Function of Law in the International Community* (first published 1933, Oxford University Press 2011) (defining "international judicial settlement" including arbitration to be "a method of settling disputes between States by a binding decision based upon rules of law") and JH Jackson, *Legal Problems of International Economic Relations* (3rd edn, St. Paul, MN.: West Pub. Co. 1995), 327 (describing the evolution of the WTO DSU as a turn away from resolving interstate disputes through "power politics" or "diplomacy"). See also, in this handbook, Besson, Ch. 19, at sections 1, 2, and 3.1; Ebobrah, Ch. 11, at section 3; Murphy, Ch. 9, at section 1; and Ginsburg, Ch. 22, at section 1.

[4] See, e.g. in this handbook, von Bogdandy and Venzke, Ch. 23, at section 2 (noting how judges resort to "timorous fictions" to mediate between the positivisitic myth that judges do not make law and the "systemic effects of precedent").

a theory of adjudication aspires to explain the "functions" of judges or arbitrators, as Besson suggests in her contribution,[5] we might focus, alternatively, on what those who establish courts and tribunals seek to achieve directly in the course of adjudication,[6] on the broader societal goals that such legal proceedings are believed to secure,[7] or adopting a more internal perspective, on what the adjudicators themselves see as their function.[8] In addition, a functional analysis might address only the most generalizable functions shared by all or most of these bodies at the expense of considering the more specialized roles that only some of these courts take on.[9] To add to the terminological confusion, those who address the "systemic" functions of adjudication, at the most general of levels, rarely agree on the descriptive labels they use. In this volume, Besson, for example, distinguishes the "law-identifying" from the "lawmaking" function, indicating that both occur in the course of settling disputes (which she describes as the "law-enforcement" function).[10] She also identifies a distinct "review" function consisting of judicial control over executive action.[11] Elsewhere, von Bogdandy and Venzke have described the functions of courts as settling disputes, stabilizing normative expectations, making law, and controlling and legitimating public authority.[12] At the risk of inspiring more confusion, this chapter seeks to describe the complex and sometimes contradictory systemic aspects of "dispute settlement" as an objective matter, taking into account both the goals of stakeholders as well as the adjudicators themselves. It pays particular attention to the ICJ, international criminal courts and the respective mechanisms used to resolve trade and investment disputes.

[5] See, in this Handbook, Besson, Ch. 19, at sections 1 and 3.1.

[6] As do, for example, Ginsburg, Ch. 22, at sections 3.1 and 3.2 in this handbook. Both Murphy and Ginsburg examine the systemic functions of inter-state courts from the perspective of the states that establish them. See also, in this handbook, Baudenbacher and Clifton, Ch. 12 (examining the political integrative aspirations of those who establish certain regional courts).

[7] See, e.g., in this handbook, Ebobrah, Ch. 11, at section 3 (discussing, in addition to the goals of the stakeholders of human rights tribunals, the broader aspirational functions of those courts both for the national and international rule of law).

[8] See, e.g., in this handbook, von Bogdandy and Venzke, Ch. 23, at section 2 (providing a more internal account of judges' "communicative practices" in terms of their needs to explain their decisions to litigants and others).

[9] Thus, many roles that Ebobrah attributes to human rights courts (such as to prevent relapse by subsequent governments) to show the world that a nation has nothing to hide, or to satisfy the victims' need for justice by apportioning responsibility for reparation, are distinctive to such bodies, while others, such as to signal respect for international obligations, to resolve disputes, and to avoid situations that deteriorate into violations of the peace, are more generalizable.

[10] See, in this handbook, Besson, Ch. 19, at section 3.

[11] Besson, Ch. 19, at section 2.

[12] See, e.g., A von Bogdandy and I Venzke, "On the Functions of International Courts: An Appraisal in Light of Their Burgeoning Public Authority," Amsterdam Law School Legal Studies Research Paper No. 2012-69. Compare B Kingsbury, "International courts: uneven judicialization in global order" in J Crawford and M Koskenniemi (eds), *The Cambridge Companion to International Law* (Cambridge University Press 2012), 203 (describing the same as settling disputes, making commitments credible, governance, and producing legal knowledge).

2 The Complex Dispute Settlement Function

The dispute settlement function follows from the standard "rational actor" explanation for why states establish international courts and tribunals: these exist in response to states' functionalist needs. Since states sometimes need to settle disputes between themselves, they establish systems to adjudicate such disputes when this is in their interests. Under one version of this functionalist or "rational choice" account, binding dispute settlement emerges only when states' needs to secure compliance with a regime outweigh the reputational or other costs associated with breach.[13]

The simplest version of the dispute settlement function views international courts and tribunals simply as vehicles for securing the goals of the state disputants before them. This approach treats international adjudicators as "agents" for state principals.[14] As a Weberian "ideal type," this principal/agent account of dispute settlement has distinct implications. As state agents, international adjudicators owe their delegated powers to their principals. They owe no duties to non-litigating states or others, including the ephemeral "international community." Since the function of these agents is to amicably settle interstate disputes where the results have to be voluntarily accepted by the losers, adjudicators should avoid exacerbating them. Accordingly, the wise international dispute settler should not exceed the basis of the jurisdictional consent given by the parties and should exercise the "passive virtues"—they should deploy concepts of admissibility, standing, and mootness to narrow the dispute before them and increase the likelihood of successful settlement or compliance.[15] Adjudicators should not take on legal or factual issues not raised by the disputants and should resist third party interventions or court-initiated processes for fact-finding. Adjudicator-agents should avoid accusations of "judicial

[13] See, e.g., A Guzman, "The Cost of Credibility: Explaining Resistance to Interstate Dispute Settlement Mechanisms" (2002) 31 J. Leg. Stud. 303 (arguing that dispute resolution clauses in treaties are most likely when rates of compliance with the treaty are already expected to be high, when the stakes are small, and when the adjudicator is interpreting norms that both parties are equally likely to violate).

[14] See, e.g., EA Posner and JC Yoo, "Judicial Independence in International Tribunals" (2005) 93 Calif. L. Rev. 1 (arguing that the only effective international tribunals are those that are "dependent," that is, ad hoc tribunals whose adjudicators are closely controlled by governments). See generally DL Nielson and MJ Tierney, "Delegation to International Organizations: Agency Theory and World Bank Environmental Reform" (2003) 57 Int'l Org. 241 (applying principal/agency theory to international organizations).

[15] See, e.g., A Perez, "The Passive Virtues and the World Court: Pro-Dialogic Abstention by the International Court of Justice" (1997) 18 MJIL 399. See also in this handbook, Ginsburg, Ch. 22, at section 3.1.

lawmaking" by rendering opinions containing only as much reasoning as necessary, by applying deferential canons of interpretation and by adhering to codes of judicial behavior consistent with the formal "rule of law." A faithful agent of the litigating parties should, for example, adhere strictly to the "plain meaning" rule in the interpretation of treaties; find customary law only in express state practice paired with explicit *opinio juris*; and avoid filling gaps in the existing law in ways that would be seen as exceeding the narrow delegation of power given in the tribunal's choice of law clause.[16] According to this "ideal type," tribunals within discrete regimes, such as those concerned with international criminal law, trade, or investment, should consider only the regime-specific law that they are licensed to apply and leave consideration of general public international law to courts authorized to examine it (like the ICJ). Adjudicators, in short, should avoid rulings that would make state principals reluctant to comply with them.[17]

Posner and Yoo, among others, have argued that the principal/agent theory best explains the institutional features of effective international courts and tribunals.[18] States' efforts to protect themselves against "agency slippage" explain their efforts to screen potential adjudicators, to limit and monitor their decisions, to punish and reward faithful agents, and to build "checks and balances" requiring continued coordination between adjudicators and their state principals.[19] In this fashion, principal/agent theorists explain other common institutional features, including why the enforcement of international adjudications remains subject to state control, why state-appointed ad hoc adjudicators continue to be encouraged (even in the ICJ) or why even widely touted "independent" international criminal courts remain tethered to state principals in some respects.[20] The principal/agent theory also explains what adjudicators do even when they are given more extensive powers. It explains why, for instance, the ICJ seems reluctant to exercise its powers to appoint its own fact-finders or to permit third party interventions or *amicus*; why WTO panels have generally adhered to the principle of judicial economy; or why most ICSID

[16] Compare, for example, the Statute of the ICJ, Art. 38, to the WTO's DSU, Art. 3.2 ("Recommendations and rulings of the DSB [dispute settlement body] cannot add to or diminish the rights and obligations provided in the covered agreements").

[17] The dispute settlement function is therefore viewed as consistent with efforts to encourage the disputing parties to settle their dispute through less formal methods such as negotiation, mediation, or conciliation. See, e.g., UN Charter, Art. 33 and the WTO's DSU, Arts 3.3–3.7, 4, and 5, as well as provisions requiring negotiation or other methods of peaceful dispute settlement prior to resorting to arbitration in a number of treaties.

[18] Posner and Yoo, note 14.

[19] See generally, in this handbook, Ginsburg, Ch. 22, at section 3.

[20] See, e.g., JE Alvarez, "The Proposed Independent Oversight Mechanism for the International Criminal Court" UCLA Human Rights & International Criminal Law Online Forum, May–September 2011 <http://iccforum.com/oversight> accessed April 17, 2013 (enumerates the ways the ICC's Assembly of State Parties continues to exert its influence over that court through financing, enforcement, and supervisory mechanisms).

arbitrators resist factual assertions or legal arguments not presented by the disputants.[21] It also may explain why, as noted, all or most international adjudicators routinely deny, consistent with the Weberian "ideal type," that they are engaging in "lawmaking."[22] Finally, it may explain a number of prominent ICSID annulments deferring to the interests of sovereigns,[23] shifts in ICJ jurisprudence over time,[24] as well as European courts' resort to judicially-created innovations, like the margin of appreciation or proportionality.[25]

But many of those who would defend the centrality of the dispute settlement function would resist the simplistic principal/agent explanation for how it works or the resulting "ideal type" prescriptions for how it should work.[26] Few see adjudicators as mere puppets subject only to the pull of states. Most international lawyers, judges, and arbitrators, contend, on the contrary, that successful dispute settlement requires autonomous impartial adjudicators who are *and are seen as* independent of the states that consent to litigate before them.

Consider, for example, the complex views of what it means to be a "dispute settler" propounded by Hersch Lauterpacht in 1933, when the only sitting permanent international court in existence was the Permanent Court of International Justice (PCIJ).[27] While Lauterpacht saw international courts as solvers of disputes that could threaten the peace, he would have recoiled at the suggestion that international adjudicators were the mere "agents" of the disputing parties.[28] His classic book on *The Function of Law in the International Community* sought to prove that there was no such thing as a "political" dispute not subject to legal scrutiny, notwithstanding

[21] See, e.g., United States, *Measure Affecting Imports of Woven Wool Shirts and Blouses from India* (WT/DS33/AB/R, April 25, 1997) (applying the principle of judicial economy); ICJ, *Military and Paramilitary Activities in and Against Nicaragua* (*Nicaragua v. United States*) (Declaration of Intervention, ICJ Rep. 215, 1984) (denying El Salvador's attempt to intervene); *Glamis Gold, Ltd. v. United States*, ICSID Award (June 8, 2009) (adopting the narrow views of what constitutes custom urged by the United States as respondent). On the ICJ's refusal to engage in its own fact-finding, see note 49.

[22] See, e.g., von Bogdandy and Venzke, note 4.

[23] See, e.g., JE Alvarez, "The Return of the State" (2011) 20 MJIL 223 (enumerating the ways that states are reasserting their voice and power in the international investment regime, including the impact of recent ICSID annulment committees).

[24] See, e.g., E Gordon, "The ICJ: On Its Own" in A Nanda and A Mundt (eds), *Perspectives on International Law in an Era of Change* (University of Denver, Sturm College of Law 2012) 74.

[25] See, e.g., R StJ Macdonald, "The Margin of Appreciation" in R St J Macdonald et al. (eds), *The European System for the Protection of Human Rights* (Boston, MA: M. Nijhoff 1993) 83.

[26] See LR Helfer and AM Slaughter, "Why States Create International Tribunals: A Response to Professors Posner and Yoo" (2005) 93 Calif. L. Rev. 899 (providing an alternative to the principal/agent rationale for the institutional constraints faced by international adjudicators).

[27] Lauterpacht, note 3. Of course, the views of Lauterpacht, who went on to serve on the ICJ himself, are relevant precisely because they are representative of a generation of international lawyers who went on to establish the ICJ and other contemporary courts and tribunals, to serve as lawyers to litigants before these tribunals or to serve as adjudicators themselves.

[28] As Martti Koskenniemi points out in his introduction to the new edition to Lauterpacht's text, for Lauterpacht, international adjudicators were comparable to Ronald Dworkin's "Herculean" judge.

the efforts of some states to restrict the jurisdiction of international courts from considering states' "essential interests."[29] Such "self-judging" clauses reflected, in his view, a disreputable refusal to be bound by the rule of law, which should not be countenanced. Lauterpacht argued that international judges were not the agents of political elites; they were servants of the rule of law beholden to much wider stakeholder considerations. For Lauterpacht, as for others present at the creation of modern systems for institutionalized international adjudication, states resort to legalized international dispute resolution *because* it is an alternative to politicized dispute resolution by diplomats.[30] They turn to legalistic dispute resolution because it is based on the application of recognized legal rules. Lauterpacht enumerated the many ways that international judges were entitled (indeed duty-bound) to engage in innovative lawmaking (including teleological treaty interpretations) to avoid the degeneration of disputes into threats to peace. Since he argued that international judges were enjoined from invoking *non liquet*, Lauterpacht suggested ways for them to "find" law where no formal law on a point exists, including through the use of creative analogies based on general rules, ready recourse to general principles, applications of private law concepts, and forms of judicial "reconciliation" to balance competing principles—all deployed under a canon of "effectiveness" that would embrace the "larger needs of the international community."[31] Lauterpacht's prescient descriptions of the dispute settlement function explain the myriad departures from the "ideal type" exhibited by contemporary courts of general jurisdiction or those operating within human rights, international criminal law, trade, or investment.[32]

Martin Shapiro's account of the "triadic" dispute settlement function insightfully distinguishes adjudicators from mere state agents. Shapiro argues that the root concept involved in all adjudication is a triad: two persons coming into conflict that they cannot themselves resolve who call upon a third party, a stranger to both and therefore impartial, for resolving it.[33] Shapiro focuses on how the third party in dispute settlement overcomes the basic instability of the triad, that is, how the

Their impartiality is what enables legalized dispute settlement to succeed and why states turn to it in the first place. As Koskenniemi points out, in this conception there is no need for additional principal/agent constraints on the discretion of adjudicators since the legal rules that they apply are, themselves, sensitive to principles of proportionality, reasonableness, and other modes of "realist" adjustment. M Koskenniemi, "The Function of Law in the International Community: Introduction" in Lauterpacht, note 3, at xli–xliii.

[29] Lauterpacht, note 3.

[30] For more on the distinctions between forms of political dispute settlement and more legalized methods, see generally, RO Keohane et al., "Legalized Dispute Settlement: Interstate and Transnational" (2000) 54 Int'l Org. 457.

[31] Lauterpacht, note 3, at 118–19. See also von Bogdandy and Venzke, note 12, at 19 (enumerating examples of courts acting as "organs of a value-based international community").

[32] See generally, in this handbook, von Bogdandy and Venzke, Ch. 23, Baudenbacher and Clifton, Ch. 12, Schreuer, Ch. 14, and Murphy, Ch. 9.

[33] M Shapiro, *Courts: A Comparative and Political Analysis* (University Of Chicago Press 1981) 1.

adjudicator avoids the delegitimizing perception that he or she has ruled in favor of one of the disputants by simply rendering a decision that is "two against one."[34] Like Lauterpacht, Shapiro accepts that triadic conflict resolution, even when based on pre-existing rules of law, inevitably involves "judicial lawmaking."[35] But unlike Lauterpacht who urges that judicial lawmaking be done explicitly and publically, Shapiro argues that the need for successful conflict resolution requires the third party, the adjudicator, to "lie" about whether they are making law in their rulings, that is, to pretend to engage in the mere application of law.[36] This account of triadic dispute settlement is consistent with but does not require the deployment of the passive virtues. It accepts that third-party adjudicators may deploy diverse legitimizing strategies that vary with the institutional context.

Like Shapiro and Lauterpacht, Karen Alter argues that international courts and tribunals are typically established to exercise relative autonomy (or what others call "bounded discretion") from the states that establish them or the litigants before them.[37] This explains why those who establish such entities take pains to emphasize their independence, as through rules precluding conflicts of interest for adjudicators and barring *ex parte* contacts, provisions enumerating professional qualifications for office and lengthy terms for those serving on permanent courts. Alter argues that international adjudicators are more appropriately seen as "trustees" rather than mere agents. The trustee account explains not only many of the characteristic institutional features of these tribunals but also why, contrary to the "ideal type," we expect international adjudicators to give reasoned opinions that have expansive potential—the better to guide the behavior of regime participants and to prevent future disputes. It also explains why international adjudicators of all stripes—from the ICJ to the WTO—respect and produce regime-specific precedent even without explicit authority from their principals.[38] If judges are in effect trustees this would also explain why some of them adopt expansive notions of admissibility, standing,

[34] Shapiro, note 33, at 1; see also J Alvarez, *International Organizations as Law-makers* (Oxford University Press 2005) at 528–9.

[35] Shapiro, note 33, at 29 ("Because no human society has ever sought to set down an absolutely complete and particularized body of preexisting law designed exactly to meet every potential conflict, judicial "discovery" must often of necessity be judicial law making"). See also, in this handbook, von Bogdandy and Venzke, Ch. 23, at section 4.

[36] M Shapiro, "Judges as Liars" (1994) 17 Harv. J. Law and Public Policy 155; See, in this handbook, von Bogdandy and Venzke, Ch. 23, at section 3.

[37] K Alter, "Agents or Trustees? International Courts in Their Political Context" (2008) 14 EJIR 33; T Ginsburg, "Bounded Discretion in International Judicial Lawmaking" (2005) 45 Virg. J. Int'l L. 1. See also KW Abbott and D Snidal, "Why States Act Through Formal International Organizations" (1998) 42 J. Conflict Res. 3 (arguing that states turn to international institutions, including courts, because they need tools for both centralization and independence); T-H Cheng, *When International Law Works* (Oxford University Press 2012), at 124–5 (discussing the value of "legalism" in justifying judicial action).

[38] For an explanation of the appeal of precedent to international adjudicators that is consistent with triadic dispute settlement, see in this handbook, von Bogdandy and Venzke, Ch. 23, at section 3.

and mootness when these are seen (within particular regimes such as trade) as appropriate legitimizing strategies,[39] or why some adjudicators favor greater transparency or accept views beyond those of the litigants (as through *amicus* briefs in ICSID or efforts toward victim participation in the ICC).[40]

3 The Fact-Finding Function

Closely related to the dispute settlement function—and as widely accepted if rarely labeled as such—is the proposition that all or most international adjudicators, like their national counterparts, make conclusive factual determinations of what actually occurred as a necessary concomitant to resolving disputes. Finding facts is as essential as identifying the law.[41] It is assumed that all adjudicators need to establish "the truth" and not merely determine the law. Depending on the nature of the dispute and the regime, some international dispute settlement mechanisms pay closer attention to the fact-finding function than others. Some contain specific rules for engaging in fact-finding, include authorizations to appoint special masters or permit the tribunal to change its location to better accommodate the evidence or witnesses. Some, like the WTO, may reserve the fact-finding function to a "lower" chamber (i.e. WTO panels).[42] On the other hand, the dominance of facts in some cases, as in international criminal courts or disputes involving claims over territory, may make fact-finding the most important function of some adjudications.[43]

The fact-finding function has generated a number of controversies that need not be addressed here, including whether the fact or law distinction itself is viable.[44] The relevant literature also enumerates the ways that international adjudicators, whether

[39] See generally, JHB Pauwelyn, "The Role of Public International Law in the WTO: How Far Can We Go?" (2001) 95 AJIL 535.

[40] Efforts to promote greater transparency and accountability within ICSID appear to be motivated by legitimacy concerns. See, e.g., B Kingsbury and S Schill, "Investor-State Arbitration as Governance: Fair and Equitable Treatment, Proportionality and the Emerging Global Administrative Law" in *El Nuevo derecho administrativo global en América Latina* (Buenos Aires: Rap 2009) at 221.

[41] Compare, in this handbook, Besson, Ch. 19, at section 2.

[42] See D Palmeter, "The WTO Appellate Body Needs Remand Authority" (1998) 32 J. World Trade 41.

[43] Note that the dominance of facts in international criminal tribunals relates not only to determinations of the defendant's guilt. Fact-finding is also vital to producing the definitive history of atrocity in a region or country that is sometimes sought. See José E. Alvarez, "Rush to Closure: Lessons of the Tadić Judgment" (1998) 96 Mich. L. Rev. 2031 (discussing the tensions between such goals and the need to focus attention only on the factual allegations made against the defendant).

[44] See, e.g. RE Bilder, "The Fact/Law distinction in International Adjudication" in RB Lillich (ed.), *Fact-Finding Before International Tribunals* (Ardsley-on-Hudson, NY: Transnational 1992) 95.

or not operating under a set of specific rules, have developed the law relating to the production, admission, and evaluation of evidence.[45] By engaging in fact-finding, international adjudicators develop law, including rules on the burden and standards of proof, the propriety of drawing adverse inferences from a party's failure to produce evidence or the weight to be given admissions against interest by a party.[46] Indeed, for tribunals that do not operate under a set of detailed rules of procedure and evidence, such as the ICJ, the legal rules applicable to the fact-finding function are almost entirely judicially created.[47] These rules, like other judge-made law produced by the ICJ, exert a powerful influence on other tribunals, which also resolve comparable questions.[48]

A considerable portion of the relevant literature has been critical of how international adjudicators engage in fact-finding. While there is agreement that, absent institutional rules to the contrary, judges and arbitrators are necessarily charged with making those factual findings needed to apply the law, there is widespread disparagement of whether international courts and tribunals have done a good job in finding facts and no shortage of suggestions for institutional (and attitudinal) reform. Some have contrasted the fact-finding that occurs in national courts or arbitrations with that evident in ICJ opinions, for example. It is said that unlike ICSID arbitrations, for instance, the ICJ too often relies on fact-finding undertaken by others, rarely deviates from written pleadings, fails to cross-examine witnesses and does not encourage *amicus* or conduct on-site hearings.[49] For these reasons, the ICJ is often accused of being insufficiently pro-active in deploying its own powers to find facts (including by appointing experts as needed). Some suggest, more generally, that international adjudicators fear or avoid certain forms of facts, such as "scientific" facts requiring technical expertise or probabilistic judgments.[50]

The fact-finding difficulties faced by international adjudicators have been explained or rationalized on a number of grounds. International adjudicators face special problems in undertaking the fact-finding function, after all, including the need to operate at a considerable geographic, cultural, and linguistic remove from

[45] See, e.g., DV Sandifer, "Evidence Before International Tribunals (1975)" in Lillich, note 44.

[46] This is an example of adjudicative lawmaking that results from the adjudicative process itself. See section 4 of this chapter.

[47] See, e.g., K Highet, "Evidence, The Chamber and the ELSI Case" in Lillich, note 44, at 33; K Highet, "Evidence, the Court, and the Nicaragua Case" (1987) 81 AJIL 1.

[48] They are part of the "common rules of international procedure" on which some international courts and tribunals rely.

[49] See, e.g., TM Franck, "Fact-Finding in the ICJ" in Lillich, note 44, at 21 (criticizing the ICJ's avoidance of the facts and reliance on a paper trial in Temple of Preach Vihear, the Nicaragua Case, and its Advisory Opinion in Western Sahara). See also JE Alvarez, "Are International Judges Afraid of Science? A Comment on Mbengue" (2011) 34 Loy. L.A. Int'l & Comp. L. Rev. 81, 83.

[50] Compare MM Mbengue, "International Courts and Tribunals as Fact-Finders: The Case of Scientific Fact-finding in International Adjudication" (2011) 34 Loy. L.A. Int'l & Comp. L. Rev. 53 (making this claim) with Alvarez, note 49 (questioning Mbengue's premises and conclusions).

the place giving rise to the dispute and the absence of enforcement or subpoena powers to compel the production of evidence or secure witnesses. Some international adjudicators, particularly those who lack trial-level experience, may also lack the expertise to decide complex factual issues.[51] Others contend that we tolerate a high level of fact-finding errors by international criminal courts, for example, because its judges can take refuge in the fact that even if these defendants did not commit some of the acts alleged, they are likely to have committed equally heinous offenses.[52] This highlights a more important point: the extent and quality of judicial fact-finding is heavily dependent on structural factors such as the tribunal's budgetary constraints, the availability of other institutional support (such as that provided by the WTO's legal secretariat or by judicial clerks), or the possibility of higher court review of the facts as well as the law (as is the case with the ad hoc war crimes tribunals and the ICC but not the ICJ, the trade regime, or ICSID).[53]

4 The Lawmaking Function

The foregoing functions are incomplete to the extent that a discrete function is to produce law—and not merely as an adjunct to settling a particular dispute or to legitimize efforts to resolve conflict. As a number of contributions to this volume suggest, in many cases, the main function of an international adjudication is to render an authoritative judgment on a disputed point of law and not merely to fill those "interstitial" legal gaps needed to resolve a concrete dispute.[54]

The lawmaking account of what judges and arbitrators generally do begins by acknowledging that today's courts and arbitrators do not just settle *interstate* disputes. "Interstate dispute settlement" does not really describe, for example, the functions

[51] See, e.g., Bilder, note 44, at 98 (but also suggesting that in some cases their fact-finding difficulties are self-imposed insofar as they see decision-making based on analysis of legal principle as more prestigious or "weighty"); NA Combs, *Fact-Finding Without Facts* (Cambridge University Press 2010) 350–9.

[52] Combs, note 51 (discussing the many subjective and probabilistic assessments made by criminal judges, including the degree of certainty needed to make a determination that someone is guilty "beyond a reasonable doubt").

[53] See generally, Helfer and Slaughter, note 26 (surveying the impact of diverse institutional constraints). Of course, the fact-finding approach of even established tribunals may change over time in response to internal or external pressures. See generally, M Langer, "Managerial Judging Goes International, But Its Promise Remains Unfulfilled: An Empirical Assessment of the ICTY Reforms" (2011) 36 Yale J. Int'l L. 241.

[54] See generally, in this handbook, von Bogdandy and Venzke, Ch. 23; and Besson, Ch. 19.

of international criminal courts (which pits a prosecutor, who might be seen as a representative of the international community, against an individual), regional human rights courts (which consider whether states have abused individual rights), or ICSID arbitrations (which consider whether a state has abused the rights of a foreign investor). International adjudication, as much else in international law, no longer involves states as the only litigants. Rather than modes of interstate conflict resolution, these adjudications, whose rulings are triggered by non-state actors (namely an independent prosecutor, a human rights claimant, or a foreign investor), might be more accurately described as applying and necessarily making, respectively, international criminal law, human rights law, and international investment law.[55]

In other instances, international adjudication, even when involving states or state entities such as international organizations, are not seen by the litigants as involving actual "disputes." ICJ Advisory Opinions, whether dealing with the effects of UN sanctions against Namibia, the extent to which "legal personality" can be attributed to the UN, the extent to which the UN General Assembly can exercise its power of the purse, the legality of nuclear weapons or the Israeli Wall, or the effects of a declaration of independence by Kosovo authorities, are not characterized as concrete "disputes," at least not by the entity requesting the opinion nor by the majority of members of that Court. Indeed, for some ICJ judges, if a request for an advisory opinion is in reality a disguised form of a dispute between states that is not otherwise subject to the contentious jurisdiction of the court, that is a reason why that case should not be heard.[56] Moreover, even those ICJ advisory opinions that might plausibly be cast as involving a (disguised) dispute between states, are at least equally directed at providing authoritative (if not formally binding) interpretations of organizational charters or providing guidance to international civil servants seeking the same.[57] Indeed, these opinions seem most effective when they render authoritative interpretations of the law (including the UN Charter) helpful to bureaucrats and least successful when they attempt to resolve an underlying interstate dispute. To view efforts to seek the ICJ's advice on the law as principally or solely occasions for "dispute settlement" seems disingenuous. But it seems equally disingenuous to describe other instances—from the Avena/La Grande line of contentious ICJ judgments to any of a

[55] See, e.g., in this handbook, Murphy, Ch. 9, Ebobrah, Ch. 11, and Schreuer Ch. 14; see more generally, P Stephan, "Privatizing International Law" (2011) 97 Virg. L. Rev. 1573 (seeing such non-state involvement as part of a larger trend toward "private" law-makers and enforcers).

[56] But see the dissenting opinion of Judge Oda, *Legality of the Use by a State of Nuclear Weapons in Armed Conflict* (Request for Advisory Opinion by the World Health Organization) (ICJ Rep., 1996) (WHO Opinion) (suggesting that the advisory jurisdiction of the court should be used only in case of conflict or dispute).

[57] This is implicit in the pre-conditions for permissible advisory opinions suggested by the court, e.g. WHO Opinion, note 56 (finding that the advisory jurisdiction of the court is triggered when the agency requesting the opinion is duly authorized under the UN Charter to request such an opinion, where the opinion requested is a legal question, and where the question is one arising within the scope of the activities of the requesting agency).

number of WTO panel and Appellate Body decisions—as principally or solely about dispute settlement when those bringing such cases appear to be seeking a thoroughly reasoned (and therefore authoritative) legal ruling—and not merely a quiet way to resolve a discrete dispute.[58]

At the same time, as the chapters by von Bogdandy and Venzke as well as Besson address in detail, those who contend that international adjudicators have a "lawmaking" function face special jurisprudential burdens. As those authors suggest, judicial gap-filling seems an inescapable by-product of the application of any kind of law (no matter how precise) to fact. It also seems an inevitable by-product of adjudication because of the communicative practices of this particular interpretative community, most of whom are under, as von Bogdandy and Venzke contend, the "spell of precedents."

Notably, von Bogdandy and Venzke's explanations for judicial lawmaking do not rely on a rational agent model. Those who establish international courts and tribunals often do not anticipate that they have delegated the power to make law or the extent to which they have done so. Like all actors who engage in contracting, states sometimes fail to anticipate the legal gaps or uncertainties in their agreements or the extent to which their adjudicators will need to fill them and are surprised when their judges or arbitrators make law.[59] At the same time, as Murphy's chapter indicates, there is no scarcity of functionalist explanations for the lawmaking function.[60]

5 The Governance Function

Adjudicators, including national judges, are sometimes expected to give meaning to, or endorse, public values. This view of the task of judging, most often propounded by US scholars such as Owen Fiss (describing the function of decisions by the US Supreme Court such as *Brown v. Board of Education*)[61] or Harold Koh

[58] See, in this handbook, Besson, Ch. 19, at section 2 (describing the "review" function), Baudenbacher and Clifton, Ch. 12, at section 2.2.1 (describing how regional courts establish *sui generis* regimes) and Murphy, Ch. 9, at section 4.3.2 (describing the gap-filling function of ICJ advisory opinions). See more generally, AT Guzman, *How International Law Works: A Rational Choice Theory* (Oxford University Press 2008) 49–54 (discussing the general value of judicially determined "focal points" to guide the behavior of states).

[59] Compare Art. 3.2 of the WTO's DSU (barring rulings by the DSB that "add to or diminish" rights in the covered agreements).

[60] See, in this handbook, Murphy, Ch. 9, at section 4.3. See also J Trachtman, "The Domain of WTO Dispute Resolution" (1999) 40 Harv. Int'l L. J. 333 (discussing how the negotiators of the WTO delegated to WTO adjudicators the task of completing their treaty contracts, thereby avoiding the costs of time-consuming *ex ante* treaty negotiations).

[61] OM Fiss, "Foreword: The Forms of Justice" (1979) 93(1) Harv. L. Rev. 18.

(describing the function of decisions in, for example, *Filartiga v. Peña-Irala*),[62] challenges the principal/agent account as well as "triadic" dispute settlement more generally. It goes beyond the fact-finding and lawmaking/law-ascertainment functions insofar as it accepts that judges and arbitrators, or some of them, can and do engage in autonomous normative action while still adhering to the rule of law.[63] Since it assumes that adjudicators are entitled (and may even be under a duty) to consider the policy implications of their rulings, it goes beyond the assumptions of those who defend interstitial lawmaking.[64]

The governance function anticipates that judges and arbitrators, at the national and international level, must generally (or at least sometimes) consider the impact of their rulings on states, persons, or entities not directly represented in the case before them. This function sees adjudication as a polycentric, not merely triadic, enterprise.[65] Particularly for those who see a trend towards the "constitutionalization" of international law, the function of international adjudications is not merely to "complete" the contracts of states or make vague standards more precise. Judges are supposed to act as super-legislators engaged in resolving those difficult conflicts between community values that other international actors and sources of law dare not touch. The contention that judges should function as supreme guardians of public virtue or general policy-makers, and not passive positivistic umpires calling legal "balls and strikes" between litigants, is controversial, even among US Supreme Court judges.[66] But while controversial, there is evidence that the governance function is not a figment of the academic imagination.

The governance function's polycentricity might help to explain, for example, the many instances of adjudicators who, while operating within a specific regime, have attempted to "de-fragment" international law by using, for example, Art. 31.3.c of the Vienna Convention on the Law of Treaties (VCLT) as a tool of systemic integration.[67] While some of these efforts might be explained as routine interpretations

[62] HH Koh, "Why do Nations Obey International Law" (1997) 106 Yale L.J. 2599.

[63] The governance function does not assume that judges or arbitrators can ignore legal constraints on their choice of law or jurisdiction, but it assumes that in applying those legal constraints adjudicators consider the policy or governance implications of distinct interpretations of the law. See, e.g., Cheng, note 37, at 124–31 (arguing that this is demanded by "specific morality" and suggesting that judges may need to suggest changes to unjust laws).

[64] While this conception of the task of judging is most often propounded with respect to national judges operating within a constitutional scheme, Lauterpacht hinted at the governance function back in 1933, when he urged judges to respond to the needs of the "international community" and not merely the parties before them. See note 3.

[65] See Alvarez, note 34, at 535–6.

[66] Compare J Roberts, Opening Statement, Senate Judiciary Committee (2005) (suggesting that his job as Chief Justice of the US Supreme Court would be to "call balls and strikes and not to pitch or bat") <http://articles.cnn.com/2005-09-12/politics/roberts.statement_1_judicial-role-judges-judicial-oath?_s=PM:POLITICS> accessed April 17, 2013.

[67] See, e.g., V Gowlland-Debbas, "Issues Arising from the Interplay Between Different Areas of International Law" (2010) 63 Current Legal Problems 597.

of the relevant law consistent with the dispute settlement function as traditionally construed,[68] efforts to go beyond the confines of a specific regime may be motivated by Lauterpacht's injunction to respect the goals of the "international community," by desires to promote certain normative values (such as human rights), by felt needs to propound harmonious law grounded in respect for the adjudicative rulings made by others, or by "socialization" pressures prompted by ever-rising contacts among national and international adjudicators.[69] This normative urge to merge, while inconsistently applied, has surfaced across diverse courts and tribunals. These departures from the "ideal type" described in section 2 lead some to conclude that there is no such thing as a "self-contained" international regime.[70]

Like the fact-finding and lawmaking functions, the governance function is sometimes anticipated by those who establish international courts and tribunals, especially (but not only) by those who establish courts to advance political integration.[71] Consider the numerous functions that have been attributed to international criminal courts, from the ICTY to the ICC. Those present at the creation of such courts have argued that these bodies are necessary, not only to convict the guilty and absolve the innocent (including the collective), but also to: (1) threaten those in positions of power to deter further violence; (2) make atonement possible for perpetrators; (3) honor the dead; (4) serve the victims of mass atrocity by providing psychological relief, compensation, identifying remains, and restoring lost property; (5) re-channel the thirst for revenge at the national level where the atrocities occurred; (6) assist in restoring the rule of law at the national level; (7) affirm the Nuremberg Principles and the international rule of law; (8) tell the truth of what occurred by providing an accurate historical record; and (9) restore lost civilities in torn societies to achieve national reconciliation.[72] These are grandiose goals for proceedings that might be seen, more simply, as merely efforts to provide fair trials for those charged with very serious crimes. While we can dismiss all or most of these "functions" as rhetorical or suggest that they would be better allocated to

[68] See D Regan, "International Adjudication: A response to Paulus—Courts, Custom, Treaties, Regimes, and the WTO" in S Besson and J Tasioulas, *The Philosophy of International Law* (Oxford University Press 2010) (suggesting that the relevant WTO agreements themselves enable such cross-references).

[69] For examples, see, in this handbook, Ebobrah, Ch. 11, at section 4.4 and Baudenbacher and Clifton, Ch. 12, at section 2.2.2. See, more generally, Gowlland-Debbas, note 67; A Paulus, "International Adjudication" in Besson and Tasioulas, note 68; RG Teitel, *Humanity's Law* (Oxford University Press 2011).

[70] See, e.g., B Simma and D Pulkowski, "Of Planets and the Universe: Self-Contained Regimes in International Law" (2006) EJIL 17. But see Regan, note 68, at 232 (defending self-contained regimes).

[71] See, in this handbook, Baudenbacher and Clifton, Ch. 12, at section 2.

[72] Alvarez, note 43, at 2031–2. Many of these goals suggest an "expressive theory of trials" in which these are used to defend the rule of law over politics, particularly in pursuit of achieving "transitional justice." See, e.g., D Luban, "Fairness to Rightness: Jurisdiction, Legality, and the Legitimacy of International Criminal Law" in Besson and Tasioulas, note 68, at 574–777.

non-judicial actors such as truth commissions, it would be a mistake to assume that these policy goals have not influenced judges on these courts or the expectations of influential stakeholders who react to their rulings.

There is considerable evidence that those who serve on these tribunals, including its judges, see themselves as Lauterpacht would have described them as agents of the "international community" bent on the pursuit of "justice" broadly understood. Some of the institutional features of these bodies suggest the same. The Rome Statute for the ICC, as is well-known, contains numerous provisions for "victim-centered" justice, as the ICC's prosecutor has advocated a model of "positive complementarity" designed to promote the national rule of law, and the judicial opinions of these tribunals are routinely scrutinized to see whether they advance or retard the attainment of all of these goals.[73] There is no reason to think that international criminal judges have been unresponsive to these goals in their day-to-day decisions regarding the affirmation of charges to be brought, in determining how to conduct procedures and accept evidence, their treatment of witnesses and victims, or in their ultimate rulings and sentencing decisions. On the contrary, there is considerable evidence that despite the *nullum crimen* principle, judges on the ICTY and ICTR have engaged in "judicial legislation" (as with respect to innovative gender crimes) that respond to these "expressive" goals and particularly to the need to satisfy the needs of victims.[74] There is also evidence that the ICTY has attempted, at least in its early days when less constrained by completion pressures, to serve a wider "truth-telling" function than was strictly necessary to try the particular defendants before it.[75] While it is true that international criminal judges rarely invoke these broad policy goals in their decisions explicitly, adjudicative silence—as Shapiro would be the first to remind us[76] —does not disprove the existence of a function.

The governance function can be particularized in at least two ways: adjudicative governance as directed at specific institutions and as directed at states. As Murphy's chapter indicates, many of the Advisory Opinions issued by the ICJ can be appreciated as occasions where that court exercised a governance function over the UN. But the ICJ's governance function over the UN has not been limited to its advisory opinions. That court's interim decisions in the Lockerbie case, for example, while deferential to the Security Council, contained subtle forms of *de facto* judicial review.[77] Other bodies, such as the ICTY in its jurisdictional decision in *Tadić*, as well as the European Court of Justice in *Kadi*, have engaged in indirect forms of

[73] See, e.g., TM Antkowiak, "An Emerging Mandate for International Courts: Victim-Centered Remedies and Restorative Justice" (2011) 47 Stan. J. Int'l L. 279.

[74] See generally, T Meron, "The Humanization of Humanitarian Law" (2000) 94 AJIL 239; Teitel, note 69, at 73–104.

[75] See, e.g., Alvarez, note 43, at 2044–6.

[76] See Shapiro, note 36.

[77] See, e.g. T Franck, "The 'Powers of Appreciation': Who Is the Ultimate Guardian of UN Legality?" (1992) 86 AJIL 519; JE Alvarez, "Judging the Security Council" 90 AJIL 1.

review over the Council.[78] These decisions suggest that judicial contributions to regime governance need not be restricted to a regime's own courts or tribunals.

Other examples of regime-specific governance decisions include WTO panel or Appellate Body decisions, from those that opined on the legality of the US Trade Act to those concerning the timing of implementation measures in the protracted *Bananas* dispute.[79] These decisions have been important steps in constructing WTO governance.

International criminal tribunals supply a number of examples of the governance function as applied to states. As noted, it is widely accepted that one of the key functions of international criminal courts is deterrence. Since many international crimes involve the actions of states, it is widely assumed that one of the functions of these courts is to deter governments from committing international crimes as well as to encourage them to take action (at least within their territory) to prevent non-state actors from committing such crimes. The deterrence function is not just about deterring individuals. It is about convincing government actors to take affirmative measures—such as making international crimes domestic ones, removing amnesty provisions or taking necessary executive action to make the conviction of these "political" crimes more likely.[80] The deterrence function of international criminal tribunals also includes deterring states from violating the obligations contained in the Torture Convention, the Genocide Convention, and the Geneva Conventions. The shadow of international criminal accountability encourages states to modify their government manuals and disciplinary procedures over local police or national militaries. When an international criminal court renders a judgment that involves a government actor or a crime that could have been prevented by state action, that ruling, as von Bogdandy and Venzke contend, is an effort to "control and legitimate public authority."[81]

Deterring WTO members from engaging in violations of their trade agreements, to cite another example, is often stated to be a function, perhaps the principal one, of the WTO and its Dispute Settlement Understanding (DSU). For trade lawyers, that dispute settlement system is most successful when it prevents trade disputes from arising, or, in the words of Andrew Guzman, when the information provided by dispute settlers deters members from cheating or engaging in comparable trade practices.[82] Indeed, most regard the actual issuance of authorization of trade

[78] See, e.g., von Bogdandy and Venzke, note 12, (discussing these as weak systems of "horizontal" control and legitimation of authority).

[79] United States, Trade Act of 1974, Sections 301–10; United States, Import Measures on Certain Products from the European Communities, WT/DS165/AB/R (2000).

[80] On this view, one of the functions of the ICC is to promote or encourage parties to the Rome Statute to reform their laws and procedures to enable them to exercise the duties suggested by the complementarity regime.

[81] von Bogdandy and Venzke, note 12.

[82] Guzman, note 58, at 52–4. A complementary perspective on how trade "governance" works is provided by those who focus on its effects within states. On this view, the shadow of WTO dispute

countermeasures by WTO dispute settlers as a regrettable failure in a system designed to avoid such tit-for-tat responses. From this perspective, the WTO regime, especially its adjudicative centerpiece, is all about exercising trade "governance."[83] It is also why some describe that regime as "constitutional."[84]

Human rights courts are also seen as instruments for regulating states, that is, for deterring states from engaging in human rights abuses. Indeed, this may explain why only some of these bodies can be described as "victim-centered" courts principally designed to order compensation to recompense the victims of abuse.[85] As Ebobrah's contribution to this volume indicates, the principal goals of the Inter-American and European systems for human rights have been to render factual and legal conclusions that clarify the human rights obligations of their respective state parties.[86] Although these regional human rights systems now may be becoming more sensitive to the plight of victims, one of their principal functions continues to be to prevent future human rights abuses by "mobilizing shame" against states.[87]

The Global Administrative Law (GAL) project provides a more thorough account of the governance function exercised by these and other international adjudicative bodies. An extensive GAL literature catalogues and critiques various contemporary modes of regulating states (not only in the relations between states but within them). While GAL considers the efforts of transnational networks of government regulators, formal international organizations, and hybrid public/private bodies, it also includes as part of the governance function the adjudicators involved.[88] To GAL scholars, investor-state arbitrators tasked with settling disputes under investment protection treaties and providing compensation to foreign investors, are, for example, as engaged in the "public" regulation of states as are WTO dispute settlement bodies and human rights courts.[89] GAL's view of adjudications as polycentric tools of governance is dramatically at odds with the principal/agent or triadic dispute settlement accounts of dispute settlement. Their prescriptions

settlement enables government elites to blame the WTO—or its dispute settlers—for their inability to legislate the trade protectionist measures that may be sought by certain interest groups within the state. See ML Movsesian, "The WTO Constitution" (2000) 114 Harv. L. Rev. 511.

[83] See generally, R Stewart and MR Sanchez-Badin, "The World Trade Organization and Global Administrative Law" in C Joerges and EU Petersmann, *Constitutionalism, Multilevel Trade Governance and International Economic Law* (Oxford University Press 2011), at 457, 467 (discussing how the WTO dispute settlement system has assumed a "regulatory and even an incipient administrative character").

[84] Movsesian, note 82.

[85] See, in this handbook, Ebobrah, Ch. 11, at section 3. See also, Antkowiak, note 73.

[86] See, in this handbook, Ebobrah, Ch. 11, at section 3.

[87] See also von Bogdandy and Venzke, note 12 (discussing the "vertical" governance function of both human rights courts and WTO dispute settlement bodies).

[88] See, e.g., Stewart and Sanchez-Badin, note 83; Kingsbury and Schill, note 40.

[89] See SW Schill, "Enhancing International Investment Law's Legitimacy: Conceptual and Methodological Foundations of a New Public Law Approach" (2011) 52 Virg. J. Int'l L. 57.

for how adjudicators should behave are, accordingly, vastly different from those suggested by the "ideal type" described in section 2 of this chapter.[90]

6 Conclusions

The question posed in the title of this chapter can be answered in different ways. The determination by a chamber of the ICC that defendants retain certain rights even when presented by evidence produced by intermediaries,[91] for example, might be categorized (1) as settling an interpretative dispute between the prosecutor and the defense; (2) as assisting in furthering the truth of what actually occurred in a particular case; (3) as providing an authoritative interpretation of that tribunal's rules; or (4) as purporting to guide how future prosecutors need to behave. That decision can, in short, be explained in terms of the dispute settlement, fact-finding, lawmaking, or governance functions described in this chapter.

Indeed, when viewed from a sufficient distance, all the functions of adjudicators can be reduced to one: to provide useful independent information to rational state actors. Consistent with this rational choice account, Andrew Guzman explains that adjudicative findings of law or fact are essentially disinterested "focal points" that serve to guide state behavior and enable common understandings of what occurred.[92] Whether or not adjudicators resort to normative policy judgments, their clarifications of law and fact serve a governance function by reducing uncertainty within distinct regimes as well as within states.[93] On this view, all the functions of international adjudication point in a single direction. Adjudicative fact-finding and lawmaking serve to promote the settlement of a dispute, increase the costs of a discrete violation of the law, and, by clarifying the law for other WTO parties (and/or the GATT secretariat), assists in the governance of the trade regime as well as the regulation of states that are presumptively deterred from taking certain measures or actions. More simply and concisely, we might see what international adjudicators do as efforts to "stabilize the normative expectations" of relevant actors.[94]

But categorizing the functions of international adjudicators is more than an exercise in semantics. For those engaged in the day-to-day business of judging, it matters

[90] Thus, Kingsbury and Schill argue that investor-state arbitrators must themselves respect the norms of transparency, participation, and thorough reason-giving that rule of law states require of any other regulator of public action. Kingsbury and Schill, note 40, at 276–89.

[91] Situation in the Democratic Republic of the Congo, Redacted Decision on Intermediaries, Trial Chamber I, ICC-01/04-01/06, 31 May 2010.

[92] Guzman, note 58, at 51. [93] Guzman, note 58, at 51–2.

[94] Von Bogdandy and Venzke, note 12.

how they see what they do. Adjudicators who see themselves as either state agents, third parties in a triad or as trustees may follow different scripts in settling disputes. They may or may not apply the "passive virtues," expand or narrow the factual or legal issues raised, engage in more or less creative interpretations of the relevant sources of law; or consider or ignore broad policy considerations. Adjudicators also may act differently depending on whether they value (either generally or in a particular instance) one function over another. The main functions of adjudication, when applied, often conflict. The fact-finding function, for example, may be at odds with the dispute settlement function—as where a decision based on impugning a state's factual assertions may prove more offensive than a ruling based on the law[95] or where a ruling based on a finding of scientific fact is undermined, after an adjudicative opinion is rendered, by new scientific information.[96] Adjudicators who insist on telling "the truth" about what occurred when that is inconsistent with what a state party says or who act as trustees in an institutional setting where they are expected to act as agents may issue rulings that fail to resolve disputes because they are ignored. Those who prioritize the needs of "transitional justice," historic truth telling, or the needs of victims in judging international crimes may short-change defendants' needs for fair trials.[97] A failure to exercise the fact-finding function with sufficient rigor may foster overly expansive law generation, and so on.[98] International adjudicators cannot always pursue or expect to achieve all the functions expected of them. They have considerable discretion on whether and how to exercise them.

At the same time, "considerable discretion" is not carte blanche. As Ginsberg's chapter indicates, adjudicators operate against a backdrop of extensive *and distinct* constraints, which change over time along with the goals of the particular adjudicative scheme.[99] The extent to which judges and arbitrators can pursue the main functions of adjudication varies with the *ex ante* and *ex post* institutional constraints within each court or arbitral institution.[100] These constraints, as well as their own views of their function, determine how judges and arbitrators exercise their often-considerable discretion.[101]

[95] See, e.g., Bilder, note 44, at 98.

[96] Alvarez, note 49, at 94–5 (discussing why, in the Methanex ICSID ruling, it was important for that tribunal to answer a legal and not a purely factual question).

[97] See, e.g., RB Birn, "Fifty Years After: A Critical Look at the Eichman Trial" (2011) 44 Case Western Reserve J. Int'l L. 443; C Van den Wyngaet, "Victims Before International Criminal Courts: Some Views and Concerns of an ICC Trial Judge" (2011) 44 Case Western Reserve J. In't L. 475, 487–8.

[98] See, e.g., Franck, note 49, at 31.

[99] See, e.g., Y Shany, "Assessing the Effectiveness of International Courts: A Goal-Based Approach" (2012) 106 AJIL 225.

[100] See, in this handbook, Ginsburg, Ch. 22, at section 3. See also Helfer and Slaughter, note 26.

[101] See, e.g., Helfer and Slaughter, note 26, at 955 (concluding that judges and arbitrators are not "lone rangers" untouched by structural, political, and discursive constraints).

Research Questions

1. Are there adjudicative functions not encompassed by dispute settlement, fact-finding, lawmaking, and governance that ought to be considered?
2. Are there hierarchies of value or systems of prioritization that would suggest when one of the main functions should give way to another?
3. How do we measure whether a particular court or tribunal is succeeding in achieving its functions? How do we measure the effectiveness of international adjudicators?
4. When are analogies between the functions of international adjudicators and national courts appropriate? Are international adjudicators expected to perform some functions that national judges are not?

Suggested Reading

Alter, K, "Agents or Trustees? International Courts in Their Political Context" (2008) 14 EJIR 33.

von Bogdandy, A, and Venzke, I, "On the Functions of International Courts: An Appraisal in Light of Their Burgeoning Public Authority" Amsterdam Law School Legal Studies Research Paper No. 2012–69.

Helfer, LR, and Slaughter, A-M, "Why States Create International Tribunals: A Response to Professors Posner and Yoo" (2005) 93 Calif. L. Rev. 899.

Lauterpacht, H, *The Function of Law in the International Community* (first published 1933, Oxford University Press 2011).

Lillich, R, *Fact-Finding Before International Tribunals* (Ardsley-on-Hudson, NY: Transnational 1992).

Shapiro, M, *Courts: A Comparative and Political Analysis* (University Of Chicago Press 1981).

Trachtman, J, "The Domain of WTO Dispute Resolution" (1999) 40 Harv. Int'l L. J. 333.

PART II

ORDERS AND FAMILIES OF INTERNATIONAL ADJUDICATIVE BODIES

CHAPTER 9

INTERNATIONAL JUDICIAL BODIES FOR RESOLVING DISPUTES BETWEEN STATES

SEAN D MURPHY*

* Patricia Roberts Harris Research Professor of Law, George Washington University; Member, UN International Law Commission.

1 Introduction

This chapter assesses those international judicial bodies that are established principally to resolve disputes between states, notably the International Court of Justice (ICJ), the International Tribunal for the Law of the Sea (ITLOS) and the World Trade Organization (WTO) Appellate Body. Unlike courts oriented toward regional economic integration or regional human rights, such as the European Court of Justice or the Inter-American Court of Human Rights, these courts and tribunals primarily focus on resolving disputes between states. Contentious cases before these bodies, for the most part, do not involve institutional organs or other non-state actors as litigants. Unlike international criminal courts, these courts focus exclusively on issues of state responsibility, generally finding that international law has or has not been violated; if a violation is found, the matter is usually negotiated to a resolution by the states concerned. Although reparation in the form of restitution, compensation, or satisfaction is possible, criminal sanctions are not. Unlike ad hoc arbitral tribunals formed to address matters of investment or commerce, such as under the auspices of the International Centre for the Settlement of Investment Disputes (ICSID) or the International Chamber of Commerce, these judicial bodies are permanent institutions; they are designed to operate for decades, with adjudicators who serve for years on a range of cases, not for just a single claim or group of claims. Unlike processes for mediation or conciliation, these courts or tribunals issue decisions that are legally binding on the parties appearing before them.

Such international judicial bodies have a prominent place in the pantheon of international adjudication; indeed, the ICJ is often viewed—symbolically—as at the pinnacle of international adjudication. Yet with the rise of numerous other dispute resolution bodies, including those before which non-state actors may appear and that may hear hundreds of cases per year, questions have arisen as to whether such "old school" fora still play a dominant or even important role for international law, especially given the relative paucity of their caseloads.

2 Key Elements Common To These International Judicial Bodies

The various chapters in this volume demonstrate the great variety existing in the world of international adjudication. Such variety makes it difficult to regard any international dispute settlement system as purely a "state-only" system, for even the ICJ allows non-state actors to appear before it in advisory opinion proceedings.[1] Nevertheless, the family of judicial bodies at issue in this chapter are generally oriented toward the resolution of disputes between states and may be regarded as sharing certain common elements,[2] which will be briefly discussed in this section by reference to the ICJ, the ITLOS, and the WTO Appellate Body.

2.1 Establishment by international agreement/governed by international law

The first key element common to these international judicial bodies is that they are established by means of a multilateral treaty adopted by states. The ICJ was created in 1945 pursuant to the UN Charter[3] and the ICJ Statute.[4] It was preceded by the League of Nations' Permanent Court of International Justice (PCIJ), with which it has considerable continuity. The ITLOS was created by the 1982 UN Convention on the Law of the Sea (UNCLOS).[5] The WTO Appellate Body was created by the 1994 Uruguay Round Understanding on Rules and Procedures Governing the Settlement of Disputes,[6] though it was preceded by a dispute resolution process that existed for decades under the General Agreement on Tariffs and Trade (GATT).

Such judicial bodies are governed by, and apply in their decision-making, international law. The ICJ famously applies four classic sources of international law: treaties, custom, general principles, and, on a subsidiary basis, judicial decisions and the writing of publicists.[7] The ITLOS applies the rules set forth in the UN Convention

[1] See CPR Romano, "The Proliferation of International Judicial Bodies: The Pieces of the Puzzle" (1999) 31 N.Y.U. J. Int'l L. & Pol. 709, 739.

[2] Regional judicial bodies share some of these elements, including the Caribbean Court of Justice, the Central American Court of Justice, the Court of Justice for the Common Market of Eastern and Southern Africa and the European Court of Justice. Yet such courts typically have inter-state dispute resolution as just one component of their jurisdiction, with further possibilities for jurisdiction over disputes with non-state actors or appeals of decisions reached in national court systems. Even so, the analysis set forth in this chapter is relevant for understanding the use of such other courts and tribunals in respect of their jurisdiction to address disputes between states. Non-judicial bodies, such as some of the committees established under human rights treaties, can also hear disputes between states, though to date such disputes have not been brought before those committees.

[3] Charter of the United Nations (adopted 26 June 1945, entered into force October 24, 1945) Arts 7.1, 92–6, 1 UNTS XVI (UN Charter).

[4] Statute of the International Court of Justice (adopted 26 June 1945, entered into force October 24, 1945) 59 Stat. 1055, 33 UNTS 933 (ICJ Statute).

[5] UN Convention on the Law of the Sea (UNCLOS), Annex VI (ITLOS Statute) (adopted 10 December 1982, entered into force November 16, 1994) 1833 UNTS 3.

[6] Marrakesh Agreement Establishing the World Trade Organization, Annex 2, Understanding on Rules and Procedures Governing the Settlement of Disputes 1994 (signed April 15, 1994, entered into force January 1, 1995) Art. 17, 1869 UNTS 401 (DSU).

[7] ICJ Statute, Art. 38.1.

on the Law of the Sea and other rules of international law not incompatible with that Convention.[8] The WTO Appellate Body addresses "issues of law" and "legal interpretations" covered in WTO panel reports,[9] which address the interpretation and application of certain WTO agreements[10] against the backdrop of other rules of international law.[11] In the course of such decision-making, it is possible that the court or tribunal will take account of rules expressed in national law if necessary when applying international law.

2.2 Permanent institution and quasi-permanent (repeat) adjudicators

These judicial bodies are permanent institutions, housed in buildings in The Hague (ICJ), Hamburg (ITLOS), or Geneva (WTO Appellate Body), where they are supported by a permanent registry or secretariat. As such, there is a strong sense of institutional continuity, with formal and informal traditions passed along through persons who spend much, if not all, of their careers at the institution.

Each institution establishes its own rules of procedure which, although capable of being modified over time, create a relatively permanent framework of detailed rules for how cases are to be decided, often supplemented by further instruments setting forth practical guidelines. The Rules of the Court of the ICJ, which were drafted by and are periodically revised by the ICJ's judges, were thoroughly revised in 1978, although some further amendments have been made since that time.[12] The ITLOS Rules of the Tribunal were drafted and revised by its judges, with the most recent version adopted in 2009.[13] The WTO Appellate Body's Working Procedures for Appellate Review have been adopted and revised by the Appellate Body, in consultation with the WTO Director-General and the Chair of the Dispute Settlement Body, most recently in 2010.[14] While such rules can be modified over time to take account of changed circumstances, they are largely stable, allowing for well-settled practice to develop. Indeed, many of the ICJ's current rules can be traced back to the PCIJ rules first adopted in the 1920s.

[8] UNCLOS, Art. 293; ITLOS Statute, Art. 23; see JE Noyes, "The International Tribunal for the Law of the Sea" (1998) 32 Cornell Int'l L.J., 109, 123–5; G Eiriksson, *The International Tribunal for the Law of the Sea* (The Hague: Martinus Nijhoff 2000).

[9] DSU, Annex 2, Art. 17.6. [10] DSU, Annex 2, Arts 3.2, 7.

[11] See D Palmeter and PC Mavroidis, "The WTO Legal System: Sources of Law" (1998) 92 AJIL 398, 399 (viewing DSU Art. 7 "as the WTO substitute, *mutatis mutandis*, for Article 38" of the ICJ Statute).

[12] International Court of Justice, "Rules of Court" (April 14, 1978) <http://www.icj-cij.org/documents/index.php?p1=4&p2=3&p3=0> accessed August 23, 2013.

[13] International Tribunal for the Law of the Sea, "Rules of the Tribunal" (2009) Doc. ITLOS/8 <http://www.itlos.org/fileadmin/itlos/documents/basic_texts/Itlos_8_E_17_03_09.pdf> accessed August 23, 2013.

[14] WTO Appellate Body Working Procedures for Appellate Review (2010) Doc. WT/AB/WP/6.

The judges or members who sit on these judicial bodies are not permanent, but they are elected or appointed for relatively long terms, during which they participate in a large number of cases, again reinforcing a culture of continuity as well as reliance on past decision-making.[15] The ICJ consists of 15 respected jurists from across the globe, elected for nine-year terms by the UN General Assembly and UN Security Council.[16] Five judges of the ICJ are elected every three years,[17] allowing continuity of membership even amidst change, with no term limits. In fact, several judges have served more than 20 years. The court may sit in chambers if requested by the parties appearing before it. The ITLOS consists of 21 judges elected by secret ballot of the states parties to UNCLOS, also for renewable, nine-year terms. Like the ICJ, the ITLOS terms are staggered so that one-third of the judges' terms expire every three years, and the judges may sit in chambers.[18] Disputes between states as to the interpretation or application of the UNCLOS Part XI (on activities in the seabed "Area") may be submitted to either[19] a special chamber of the ITLOS[20] or to the ITLOS Seabed Disputes Chamber. The latter consists of 11 of the ITLOS judges selected by majority vote but, when hearing a dispute among states, it is to form an ad hoc chamber composed of three of its members.[21] The WTO Appellate Body consists of seven members, who are appointed for four-year terms by the WTO Dispute Settlement Body and may be reappointed once.[22]

For all three institutions, the persons are elected or appointed based on their independence, character, and expertise. These individuals are paid international civil servants; they receive no pay and take no instructions from governments, and they cannot be recalled or dismissed by the governments of their nationalities. While judges or members are precluded from sitting in a case in which they were previously involved as counsel, they are not prevented from sitting in a case simply because it involves a state of the judge's or member's nationality. Even so, the issue of nationality is not ignored. Two persons of the same nationality would not be elected or appointed to serve on the judicial body simultaneously and the selection processes are designed to ensure broad geographic representation. Moreover, if a state has no judge of its nationality on the ICJ or the ITLOS, then it may appoint a judge ad hoc for the purposes of its case.

2.3 General dominance of states and exclusion of non-state actors

States generally dominate these inter-state judicial bodies, but there are some important exceptions to that dominance. The UN Charter provides that the ICJ shall be the "principal judicial organ" of the United Nations and that all UN member states are *ipso facto* parties to the ICJ Statute.[23] As such, all 193 member states

[15] See E Voeten, "The Politics of International Judicial Appointments" (2009) 9 Chi. J. Int'l L. 387.
[16] ICJ Statute, Arts 3–4, 13. [17] ICJ Statute, Art. 13. [18] Noyes, note 8, at 126–8.
[19] UNCLOS, Art. 188.1. [20] ITLOS Statute, Arts 15, 17. [21] ITLOS Statute, Art. 36.
[22] DSU, Art. 17.2. [23] UN Charter, Arts 92, 93.1.

of the United Nations are parties to the ICJ Statute and thus capable of appearing before the court in either contentious cases or advisory proceedings.[24]

Only states may participate in contentious cases before the ICJ;[25] this precludes contentious cases brought by or against international organizations, non-governmental organizations, transnational corporations, or individuals. By contrast, written and oral pleadings have been submitted to the court in advisory opinion proceedings by the UN Secretariat, by representatives from other international organizations, and by "quasi-state" entities not yet universally recognized as states and not admitted as such to the United Nations (such as representatives from Palestine[26] or Kosovo[27]). While such proceedings are "advisory" under the terms of the UN Charter and the ICJ Statute, sometimes the proceedings have a contentious case quality to them, such as Palestine versus Israel in the *Wall* case or Serbia versus Kosovo in the *Kosovo* case. Moreover, certain treaty instruments, such as the headquarters agreement of an international organization, in essence can transform the advisory opinion into a "decision" that is binding on the entities appearing before the court (such as the international organization and the host state). When this happens, the phenomenon is referred to as "binding advisory opinions."[28]

States also dominate in the proceedings before the WTO Appellate Body but, here too, the practice is not uniform. A regional organization that has been accorded exclusive competence by states over matters covered by the relevant WTO agreements can appear before the Appellate Body, as has occurred on many occasions with respect to the European Community/Union, as both claimant and respondent. Moreover, certain non-state entities such as Hong Kong, Macau, and Taiwan can be parties to cases before the WTO Appellate Body.

The UNCLOS Part XV only allows for UNCLOS states parties to appear before the ITLOS to resolve their disputes. Yet the UNCLOS defines states parties as including some actors not normally considered states.[29] Thus, the European Union has appeared as a party.[30] Further, natural or juridical persons may appear before ITLOS to seek the prompt release of a vessel and its crew when detained by a coastal state, though they only do so "on behalf of" the flag state of the detained vessel

[24] States that are not UN members are able to adhere to the court's statute if they so choose. ICJ Statute, Art. 35.2.

[25] ICJ Statute, Art. 34.1.

[26] *Legal Consequences of the Construction of a Wall in the Occupied Palestinian Territory* (Advisory Opinion) [2004] ICJ Rep 136.

[27] *Accordance with International Law of the Unilateral Declaration of Independence in Respect of Kosovo* (Advisory Opinion) [2010] ICJ Rep 403.

[28] See R Ago, "'Binding' Advisory Opinions of the International Court of Justice" (1991) 85 AJIL 439.

[29] UNCLOS, Art. 1.2.2 (including in the definition self-governing associated states and territories entitled to participate in the UNCLOS under Art. 305 and international organizations entitled to participate in the UNCLOS under Annex IX).

[30] See *Conservation and Sustainable Exploitation of Swordfish Stocks in the South-Eastern Pacific Ocean (Chile/European Union)*, ITLOS Case No. 7 <http://www.itlos.org/index.php?id=99> accessed August 23, 2013.

(and therefore must first receive authorization from that state).[31] Moreover, not only may UNCLOS states parties and state enterprises appear before the ITLOS Seabed Disputes Chamber to resolve disputes relating to Part XI of the Convention, but so may two entities created by the Convention—the International Seabed Authority and the Enterprise[32]—as well as, in certain circumstances, natural or juridical persons and prospective contractors who have been sponsored by a state.[33] The ITLOS' jurisdiction under agreements other than the UNCLOS may extend beyond a dispute between two states; its jurisdiction appears capable of allowing disputes brought consensually under other agreements by non-state actors, though no such dispute has yet been filed.[34] Finally, non-state actors may appear as *amicus curiae* in advisory opinion proceedings, as recently occurred before the Seabed Disputes Chamber.[35]

2.4 Broad and yet limited jurisdiction

When the ICJ has jurisdiction in a contentious case, it may apply the classic sources of law identified in Article 38.1 of the ICJ Statute: treaties; customary international law; general principles of law; and judicial decisions and the teachings of the "most highly qualified publicists of the various nations."[36] Further, any state that is a party to the statute may consent to appear before the court in a contentious case. As such, the potential range of the court's decisions is quite broad, covering all aspects of international law and all members of the United Nations and other states that have joined the statute. Yet a state's consent to the court's jurisdiction does not exist simply by virtue of the state being a party to the ICJ Statute; instead, the state must expressly consent to such jurisdiction.

There are three means by which a state can express consent to the jurisdiction of the court. States can accept the court's jurisdiction on an ad hoc basis for the adjudication of a dispute that has arisen.[37] Alternatively, states can conclude a bilateral or multilateral treaty that provides for future ICJ jurisdiction over certain issues in the event that a dispute arises.[38] Finally, jurisdiction may arise under the "optional

[31] UNCLOS, Art. 292.2.

[32] The International Seabed Authority administers the resources of the deep seabed area. The Enterprise will serve as the Authority's mining operator, but as of 2013 has not yet been established.

[33] UNCLOS, Art. 187.

[34] ITLOS Statute, Arts 20–21; UNCLOS, Arts 291.2, 308; see AE Boyle, "Dispute Settlement and the Law of the Sea Convention: Problems of Fragmentation and Jurisdiction" (1997) 46 Int'l & Comp. L.Q. 37, 47–54.

[35] *Responsibilities and Obligations of States Sponsoring Persons and Entities with Respect to Activities in the Area*, ITLOS Case No. 17 (Advisory Opinion) [2011] 50 ILM 458, para. 14.

[36] ICJ Statute, Art. 38.1. [37] ICJ Statute, Art. 36.1.

[38] ICJ Statute, Art. 36.1. Treaties pre-dating the existence of the ICJ that provide for jurisdiction of the PCIJ are also regarded, under the ICJ Statute, as triggering ICJ jurisdiction. ICJ Statute, Art. 37.

clause" or "compulsory jurisdiction" of the court, if the two disputing states have made unilateral declarations that "they recognize as compulsory *ipso facto* and without special agreement, in relation to any other state accepting the same obligation, the jurisdiction of the Court in all legal disputes..." involving issues of law or fact governed by rules of international law.[39] Of the 193 UN Members, 70 have accepted the court's compulsory jurisdiction as of mid-2013.[40]

In all three instances, the court's jurisdiction will be limited by the terms as set forth in the consent granted. Thus, the treaties providing for the court's jurisdiction are limited to the terms set forth in those treaties, while many of the declarations accepting the court's compulsory jurisdiction contain conditions, limitations, or reservations significantly limiting the state's consent. States have formulated their exceptions to the court's jurisdiction in many ways, including carve-outs with respect to matters relating to national security, delimitation of territory, or internal affairs.

Dispute settlement before the ITLOS is also potentially broad, covering most disputes on the interpretation or application of the UNCLOS and related treaties,[41] with the potential application of broader international law.[42] Part XV of the UNCLOS provides that states parties must select one of four options for compulsory dispute resolution when they ratify or accede to the convention.[43] One option is dispute settlement at the ITLOS under UNCLOS Annex VII (to date selected by about 30 states); a second option is dispute settlement at the ICJ (selected by about 25 states); and two further options are general arbitration under UNCLOS Annex VII (selected by about nine states) or specialized arbitration under UNCLOS Annex VIII (selected by about nine states).[44] If a state party fails to select a forum (which is the case for most states), it is deemed to have selected Annex VII arbitration.

When a dispute arises concerning the interpretation or application of the convention, if two parties to the dispute have both selected the same forum, then that forum is used to resolve the dispute, unless the parties agree otherwise.[45] If two states cannot agree on a forum, then the dispute is submitted to Annex VII arbitration.[46] Thus, the ITLOS or the ICJ is only used when the two disputing states have both selected either the ITLOS or the ICJ, or decide ad hoc to avail themselves of those fora; otherwise, the most likely scenario is for the matter to default to

[39] ICJ Statute, Art. 36.2; see JG Merrills, "The Optional Clause Revisited" (1993) 64 Brit. Y.B. Int'l L. 197.

[40] For the list, see, International Court of Justice, "Jurisdiction" <http://www.icj-cij.org/jurisdiction/index.php?p1=5&p2=1&p3=3> accessed August 23, 2013.

[41] ITLOS Statute, Art. 21; ICJ Statute, Art. 36.1.

[42] See, e.g., Michael Wood, "The International Tribunal for the Law of the Sea and General International Law" (2007) 22 Int'l J. Marine & Coastal L. 351.

[43] For the UNCLOS dispute settlement options selected (or not selected) by the states parties, see UN Oceans & Law of the Sea, "Settlement of Disputes Mechanism" <http://www.un.org/Depts/los/settlement_of_disputes/choice_procedure> accessed August 23, 2013.

[44] UNCLOS, Art. 287.1. [45] UNCLOS, Art. 287.4. [46] UNCLOS, Art. 287.5.

arbitration. Whichever forum receives the dispute, the matter is decided through application of the UNCLOS and other rules of international law.[47] Further, as noted above, for certain disputes with respect to activities in the deep seabed under Part XI of the convention, jurisdiction rests with the ITLOS Seabed Disputes Chamber, though two states may alternatively agree to submit their Part XI dispute to a special chamber of ITLOS or submit their contract dispute relating to Part XI to binding arbitration.[48]

Part XV envisages compulsory dispute settlement for most aspects of the convention, but it excludes some important types of disputes. For example, Part XV excludes any claim that the coastal state is denying other states the freedoms and rights to which they are entitled in the coastal state's exclusive economic zone (EEZ),[49] or a claim regarding the coastal state's power to determine for that zone the allowable catch of fish, the coastal state's harvesting capacity, and its allocation of any surplus to other states.[50] Further, states are allowed to exclude certain additional disputes relating to the convention, including disputes concerning maritime delimitation, military activities, and disputes in respect of which the Security Council is exercising its functions.[51] Though such matters fall outside the UNCLOS compulsory dispute settlement, the ITLOS and the ICJ remain available for consensual referral of any disputes concerning the UNCLOS or related agreements, or arising under customary international law.[52]

The provisions on settlement of disputes set forth in Part XV apply, *mutatis mutandis*, to disputes arising under agreements "related to the purposes of the Convention," in accordance with the terms of that agreement.[53] As such, the ICJ and the ITLOS potentially have jurisdiction over disputes arising under several other conventions whether or not those agreements expressly provide for dispute resolution, including the 1993 FAO Compliance Agreement,[54] the 1995 UN Convention on Straddling and Highly Migratory Fish Stocks (FSA),[55] or the 2001 Convention on the Protection of the Underwater Cultural Heritage.[56] Further, the FSA has a cascading effect by providing in its Article 30.2 that UNCLOS Part XV applies *mutatis mutandis* to any dispute concerning the interpretation or application of a regional

[47] UNCLOS, Art. 293. [48] UNCLOS, Art. 188. [49] UNCLOS, Art. 297.1.a.

[50] UNCLOS, Art. 297.3.a. [51] UNCLOS, Art. 298. [52] ITLOS Statute, Art. 21.

[53] UNCLOS, Art. 288.2; see T Treves, "A System for Law of the Sea Dispute Settlement" in D Freestone, R Barnes and DM Ong (eds), *The Law of the Sea* (Oxford University Press 2006) 417.

[54] Agreement to Promote Compliance with International Conservation and Management Measures by Fishing Vessels on the High Seas (adopted November 24, 1993, entered into force April 24, 2003) 33 ILM 968 (FAO Compliance Agreement).

[55] Agreement for the Implementation of the Provisions of the United Nations Convention on the Law of the Sea of December 10, 1982 Relating to the Conservation and Management of Straddling Fish Stocks and Highly Migratory Fish Stocks (adopted August 4, 1995, entered into force December 11, 2001) Art. 30.2, 2167 UNTS 88, 34 ILM 1542.

[56] Convention on the Protection of the Underwater Cultural Heritage (adopted November 2, 2001, entered into force January 2, 2009) 41 ILM 40.

or global agreement relating to straddling or highly migratory stocks, such as the 2000 Convention on the Conservation and Management of Highly Migratory Fish Stocks in the Western and Central Pacific Ocean.[57] That effect only exists, however, if the parties to the dispute are parties to both the FSA and the relevant regional or global fisheries agreement.[58] Parties concluding new treaties on maritime matters also may expressly provide for referral of disputes to the ITLOS or the ICJ, as may be seen in the 1993 FAO Compliance Agreement.[59] Finally, Article 22 of the ITLOS Statute allows parties to earlier treaties concerning the UNCLOS, such as MARPOL 1973/78,[60] to submit their disputes arising under those treaties to the ITLOS.

The WTO Appellate Body has considerable breadth in its jurisdiction over any disputes arising under the GATT and its annexes, to which more than 150 states are parties.[61] Four annexes contain agreements addressing trade in goods, services, and intellectual property rights, as well as "plurilateral agreements" addressing certain sectors and government procurement. Disputes concerning these "covered agreements" are addressed in the first instance through arbitral dispute panels; their decisions, called "reports," can be appealed to the Appellate Body.

2.5 Final and binding decisions

These inter-state judicial bodies render decisions that are regarded as final (except as noted below) and as legally binding.

Judgments issued by the ICJ in contentious cases are final, without further appeal and binding on the parties, including those rendered pursuant to the UNCLOS. ITLOS decisions are also final and binding on the parties.[62] Decisions of the WTO Appellate Body are binding on the parties, but they technically are not final; they must be adopted by the Dispute Settlement Body (DSB), a WTO organ that is essentially the WTO's plenary General Council operating under a different name and in accordance with special rules. Though not final, when an arbitral panel or the Appellate Body's report is placed before the DSB, the report *will* be adopted and become binding, unless there is a consensus of the DSB *not* to do so (the process

[57] Convention on the Conservation and Management of Highly Migratory Fish Stocks in the Western and Central Pacific Ocean (adopted September 5, 2000, entered into force June 19, 2004) 40 ILM 278.

[58] T McDorman, "An Overview of International Fisheries Disputes and the International Tribunal for the Law of the Sea" (2002) 40 Canadian Ybk Intl L. 119. Even so, as noted above, important EEZ activities may be excluded from compulsory dispute settlement.

[59] FAO Compliance Agreement, Art. 9.

[60] International Convention for the Prevention of Pollution from Ships and Protocol (adopted November 2, 1973 and February 17, 1978, entered into force October 2, 1983) 1340 UNTS 184, 12 ILM 1319, as amended.

[61] DSU, Art. 1.

[62] UNCLOS, Art. 296; ITLOS Statute, Art. 33.

is known as "reverse consensus").[63] Since normally the party that prevailed before the Appellate Body will block any such consensus, the likelihood of the Appellate Body's decision not being adopted is extremely low and to date has not happened.

As of mid-2013, more than 150 cases had been filed with the ICJ, leading to the issuance of 113 binding judgments and 27 advisory opinions. From 1996 to mid-2013, 21 cases were submitted to the ITLOS, leading to the issuance of several orders on the provisional release of vessels and crew, one judgment on maritime delimitation and one advisory opinion. Hundreds of "consultations" have been pursued as a first step in WTO dispute settlement and, as of mid-2013, 463 disputes have been filed, leading to the adoption of 187 panel decisions and 119 Appellate Body decisions.[64] Determining whether the decisions reached in those cases have resulted in compliance can be complicated, but in many instances compliance is forthcoming.[65]

If compliance is not forthcoming, the relevant treaties for the ICJ, ITLOS, and WTO Appellate Body generally do not provide that their decisions are enforceable in national courts, although such enforcement may occur under national law. With respect to the ICJ, each UN member state "undertakes to comply with the decision of the International Court of Justice in any case to which it is a Party."[66] If that does not happen, the recourse envisaged by the UN Charter is for the victorious party to appeal non-compliance to the UN Security Council, "which may, if it deems necessary, make recommendations or decide upon measures to be taken to give effect to the judgment."[67]

The UNCLOS does not compel enforcement in national courts of ITLOS decisions as among states, except with respect to disputes relating to the deep seabed. For those disputes, any UNCLOS dispute settlement body decision concerning "the rights and obligations of the Authority and of the contractor shall be enforceable in the territory of each State Party"[68] and decisions of the Seabed Disputes Chamber are "enforceable in the territories of the States Parties in the same manner as judgments or orders of the highest court of the State Party in whose territory the enforcement is sought."[69]

Similarly, the Uruguay Round agreements do not oblige states to allow litigation in national courts for enforcement of the agreements, including enforcement

[63] DSU, Arts 6.1, 16.4, 17.14, 22.6.

[64] For up-to-date information on the case-law, see the relevant Internet sites: ICJ <http://www.icj-cij.org/homepage/>; ITLOS <http://www.itlos.org>; WTO Appellate Body <http://www.wto.org> all accessed August 23, 2013.

[65] See, e.g., C Schulte, *Compliance with Decisions of the International Court of Justice* (Oxford University Press 2004) (finding that most ICJ decisions result in compliance); B Wilson, "The WTO Dispute Settlement System and Its Operation: A Brief Overview of the First Ten Years" in R Yerxa and B Wilson (eds), *Key Issues in WTO Dispute Settlement: The First Ten Years* (Cambridge University Press 2005) 24 (finding that WTO members have "showed great respect for the decisions emanating from the panels and the Appellate Body, even where they strongly disagreed with those decisions").

[66] UN Charter, Art. 94.1.

[67] UN Charter, Art. 94.2.

[68] UNCLOS, Annex III, Art. 21.2.

[69] ITLOS Statute, Art. 39.

of Panel or Appellate Body reports.[70] Indeed, although the reports find a violation of international law, they only "recommend that the member concerned bring the measure into conformity with that agreement."[71] The remedies contemplated are that the state will terminate its wrongful action within a reasonable period of time or, failing that, will pay compensation for the harm it continues to cause by that action. In the absence of doing so, the other state's remedy is to seek authorization from the Panel to suspend its own concessions to the violating state—in essence, authorized retaliation.[72]

3 Shifting Terrain

Chapter 3 of this volume discusses in some depth the history of international adjudication. For present purposes, a shift in emphasis since the 1980s is discernible with respect to judicial bodies for resolving disputes between states. When establishing the PCIJ in 1920 and the ICJ in 1945, the model of "international court" was selected, with an almost exclusive focus on litigation by states. More recent structures, such as dispute settlement under the 1982 UNCLOS and at the WTO, have sought to accommodate more complex forms of adjudication, allowing or requiring states to use arbitration. The drafters of the UNCLOS neither selected an existing inter-state court (ICJ) nor created a new inter-state tribunal (ITLOS) as the sole venue for compulsory dispute settlement. Instead, they opted for a menu of potential options, with the default being inter-state arbitration. For the WTO, the initial proceedings are arbitral in nature; only after issuance of the Panel's decision can the matter be appealed to the WTO Appellate Body. These developments are no doubt influenced by the burgeoning use of arbitration in commercial, trade, and investment disputes against states.

Moreover, more recent inter-state processes evince some greater sensitivity to the accommodation of non-state actors in the dispute settlement process. As previously discussed, the ITLOS Seabed Disputes Chamber is capable of hearing disputes involving natural or juridical persons—there is no need for the government of those persons to bring a claim on their behalf—and non-governmental organizations

[70] See, e.g., 19 U.S.C. § 3512.c.1 (2006). [71] DSU, Art. 19.1.

[72] See J Jackson, "International Law Status of WTO Dispute Settlement Reports: Obligation to Comply or Option to 'Buy Out'?" (2004) 98 AJIL 109.

may appear as *amicus curiae* in ITLOS advisory opinion proceedings. Although non-state parties do not appear before the WTO Appellate Body, opportunities exist for the filing of *amicus* briefs by such actors.[73] Even the ICJ in recent years has allowed parties to appear before it (Palestine, Kosovo) that do not fit the mold of the typical state party. Even so, the traditional approach of "only states" remains largely intact. When Yugoslavia brought suit at the ICJ against NATO states concerning the 1999 aerial bombing campaign relating to Kosovo, Yugoslavia had to file ten cases against individual NATO members, as there was no means of suing NATO directly. Similarly, when NATO allowed Greece to block Macedonia's accession to NATO in 2008, Macedonia was only able to file its case against Greece. Although Macedonia successfully proved that Greece wrongfully blocked Macedonia's accession to NATO, the court's decision had no direct effect on NATO. Even as of the mid-1990s, former ICJ President Sir Robert Jennings viewed the court's narrow jurisdiction in this regard as an unfortunate and anomalous artifact, largely out-of-step with contemporary needs.[74]

The difficulty for these courts and tribunals to accommodate the rise of non-state actors as important players in the creation, interpretation, and enforcement of international law raises an important question: are these bodies relics of the past, incapable of keeping up with the complex and ever-changing domain of international law? Observers note that these judicial bodies have relatively modest caseloads, with the ICJ averaging about ten cases on its docket at any given time and the ITLOS only a few. Even when taking account of the limited number of states (as of mid-2013, there are 193 UN member states) among whom disputes might be litigated, and taking into consideration that a tribunal such as the ITLOS is only one of several options for dispute settlement, critics still maintain that such judicial bodies are significantly under-utilized. While there are reasons to regard inter-state courts and tribunals as having a much less dominant role in the realm of contemporary international adjudication than they used to enjoy,[75] they still serve important and indispensable systemic functions, as discussed below.

[73] See V Donaldson, "The Appellate Body: Institutional and Procedural Aspects" in PFJ Macrory, AE Appleton, and MG Plummer (eds), *I The World Trade Organization: Legal, Economic and Political Analysis* (New York: Springer 2005) 1332–3.

[74] RY Jennings, "The United Nations at Fifty: The International Court of Justice after Fifty Years" (1995) 89 AJIL 493.

[75] See K Alter, "Private Litigants and the New International Courts" (2006) 39 Comp. Pol. Stud. 22.

4 Systemic Functions Served By These Judicial Bodies

4.1 Promoting the conclusion of major sectoral agreements

An initial reason why inter-state judicial bodies remain an important component of the international system is that they continue to be viewed as such by states. Despite the rise of other mechanisms for international adjudication, inter-state courts or tribunals continue to be a valuable option when concluding important multilateral agreements.

Thus, when bringing to conclusion the principal treaty on the law of the sea in 1982, states regarded it as important to establish the ITLOS (composed of persons with recognized competence in the field of the law of the sea) and to use the ICJ as potential options for compulsory dispute settlement. Inter-state arbitration was included in the mix, but such a dispute settlement mechanism was not regarded by all states as sufficient; some states wanted a more formal, judicial option.[76] Though not limited to inter-state courts or tribunals, the overall system of UNCLOS dispute settlement—including the establishment of the ITLOS—was viewed throughout the negotiations of the UNCLOS as a critical component for moving beyond unilateral exercises of power over maritime areas. As key US negotiators asserted early in the process: "In the broadest sense, the purpose of the law of the sea negotiations is to put an end to the direct relationship that such a system entails between the enjoyment of a right and the application of power. A system of compulsory, impartial, third-party adjudication is thus an essential element of the overall structure."[77] Likewise, Alan Boyle notes that the "main object of the LOS Convention's scheme for compulsory jurisdiction is to guarantee the integrity of the Convention and to act as a restraint or moderating influence on the excessive claims and tensions likely to arise over time."[78] John Noyes argues that "States likely perceive that the threat of adjudication will constrain unreasonable unilateral interpretations of substantive Convention provisions."[79]

[76] See JE Noyes, "Compulsory Third Party Adjudication and the 1982 United Nations Convention on the Law of the Sea" (1989) 4 Conn. J. Int'l L. 675, 685 ("the politics of the negotiations were such that insistence on only one or two forums would have meant a lack of consensus on including provisions for binding adjudication in the text of the Convention").

[77] JR Stevenson and BH Oxman, "The Preparations for the Law of the Sea Conference" (1974) 68 AJIL 1, 31.

[78] A Boyle, "Problems of Compulsory Jurisdiction and the Settlement of Disputes Relating to Straddling Fish Stocks" (1999) 14 Int'l J. Marine & Coastal L. 1, 6.

[79] Noyes, note 76, at 683.

Further, most states apparently regarded the availability of compulsory dispute settlement as critical to the successful completion of negotiations because ambiguities in the text not resolved through negotiation would require resolution by an authoritative third-party. The first President of the negotiating conference, Hamilton Shirley Amerasinghe, observed in 1976 that: "the provision of effective dispute settlement procedures is essential for stabilizing and maintaining the compromises necessary for the attainment of agreement on a convention. [Without such procedures,] the compromise will disintegrate rapidly and permanently."[80]

Likewise, when negotiating the principal treaties to establish the WTO, states regarded it as important to create an inter-state tribunal—the WTO Appellate Body—charged with promoting unified interpretations of the relevant agreements. As John Jackson has observed, "the GATT contracting parties resolved at the 1986 launching meeting of the Uruguay Round (at Punta del Este) to deal with some of the defects and problems of existing dispute settlement rules."[81] The negotiators ultimately concluded that the "negotiation-oriented" approach to dispute resolution characteristic of the GATT was no longer tenable; less powerful states were unwilling to participate in an ambitious new system of trade rules if dispute resolution could be dominated by the negotiating strength of powerful states. Consequently, the turn was made to a more "judicialized" and "rules-oriented" approach to dispute resolution.[82] In setting up that system, arbitration was fine for the initial round of dispute resolution, but only if the arbitral decisions could be appealed to a more permanent, court-like body capable of maintaining uniformity in interpretation and application of the law. In short, establishing a dispute settlement system capped by an inter-state tribunal helped bring to a conclusion the Uruguay Round negotiations.

Despite the rise of other possibilities, the ICJ also remains a desirable forum to select for inter-state dispute resolution when concluding contemporary multilateral treaties, such as the 1999 International Convention for the Suppression of the Financing of Terrorism,[83] the 2001 Convention on Persistent Organic Pollutants,[84]

[80] Quoted in Noyes, note 76, at 682.

[81] J Jackson, *The Jurisprudence of GATT and the WTO* (Cambridge University Press 2000) 134; see generally "Dispute Settlement Mechanisms" in TP Stewart (ed.), *The GATT Uruguay Round: A Negotiating History (1986–1992)* (The Hague: Kluwer Law and Taxation 1993) 2663.

[82] JH Jackson, *The World Trading System: Law and Policy of International Economic Relations* (Cambridge, MA: MIT Press 1997) 107–37; see PL Chang, "The Evolution and Utilization of the GATT/WTO Dispute Settlement Mechanism" in JC Hartigan (ed.), *Trade Disputes and the Dispute Settlement Understanding of the WTO: An Interdisciplinary Assessment* (Bingley, UK: Emerald Group 2009) 92 ("Although not immune from the influence of power politics, the WTO procedure, given its more automatic and rule-based structure, leaves less room for power play. The procedure has established itself as the norm for resolving trade conflicts in the international community.").

[83] International Convention for the Suppression of the Financing of Terrorism (adopted December 9, 1999, entered into force April 10, 2002) Art. 24.1, 2178 UNTS 197.

[84] Stockholm Convention on Persistent Organic Pollutants (adopted May 22, 2001, entered into force May 17, 2004) Art. 16.2, 2256 UNTS 119.

or the 2003 UN Convention against Corruption.[85] If negotiators wish to include binding dispute resolution as one element of a major multilateral treaty, the ICJ is one obvious, respected, and impartial forum to select.

In short, notwithstanding whatever flaws that may exist with inter-state courts and tribunals, such fora are viewed as an important component when concluding major multilateral agreements. Though other venues have emerged for the resolution of certain kinds of disputes, inter-state courts and tribunals retain certain comparative advantages when considering where an interpretive dispute under the agreement might be brought, including broad subject matter jurisdiction, global membership, and an attractiveness to states precisely because non-state actors are largely not present. Though habitual resort to these courts or tribunals to vindicate rights under the multilateral agreement is not apparent, the actual *use* of the forum may be secondary to its *availability* for use.

4.2 Promoting negotiated resolution of disputes

The availability of inter-state courts and tribunals, especially for compulsory adjudication, also provides a useful "shadow" when a dispute arises between states, encouraging them to negotiate an out-of-court resolution. For this reason, a metric by which one assesses the utility of inter-state judicial bodies solely based on the number of cases before those courts misses the effect that their existence has in conditioning state behavior *ab initio* when the dispute arises. Anytime a state embarks on a major policy initiative, one question for that state will be whether the action violates the state's obligations under international law and, if so, whether other states will react in an adverse manner. If such reactions include the possibility of a highly visible resort to dispute resolution, such as at the ICJ, the ITLOS, or the WTO Appellate Body, then it serves as a disincentive for the state to pursue its policy initiative and an incentive to pursue other legally available options.

Empirically establishing and measuring this deterrence factor is difficult, since it involves proving that a state did *not* act in a certain way due to the presence of potential litigation at an inter-state court or tribunal. Nevertheless, it appears to be the case that most disputes arising under agreements for which inter-state courts or tribunals are available, such as the law of the sea, are resolved through negotiation[86] and, further, "it is conceivable that in some cases the parties have settled a

[85] UN Convention Against Corruption (adopted October 31, 2003, entered into force December 14, 2005) Art. 66.2, 2349 UNTS 41.

[86] T McDorman, "Global Ocean Governance and International Adjudicative Dispute Resolution" (2000) 43 Ocean & Coastal Management 255, 257.

dispute consensually because of a desire to avoid compulsory settlement" under the convention.[87]

An example of the phenomenon may be seen in the *Swordfish Stocks* case, which arose after Chile imposed a port ban on Spanish vessels that were fishing swordfish near Chile's EEZ. The European Community initiated dispute resolution before the WTO, after which Chile initiated proceedings at the ITLOS. The dispute was then resolved by negotiation before hearings went forward in either venue. In filing their cases, both sides signaled the seriousness with which they took the dispute and raised the prospect of an inter-state court or tribunal resolving the matter, which entailed uncertainty in the outcome. In light of that, the two sides instead chose to resolve the matter as between themselves, negotiating and compromising in the shadow of potential third-party inter-state court or tribunal dispute resolution.[88]

4.3 Promoting and protecting a coherent legal system

Inter-state judicial bodies provide a unique service by acting as the promoter and guardian of the system of international law in which they operate, capable of providing authoritative action that speaks to the broader functioning and stability of the international legal system than is the case for arbitral or other fora. This role may be seen in three discrete functions.

4.3.1 *Promoting stability and predictability in inter-state relations*

A paradox in the operation of inter-state courts and tribunals is that, while it is generally accepted that their decisions only bind the two parties that appear before them in any given case, it is also generally accepted that the decision reached has ramifications that extend well beyond those two parties. Thus, when the ICJ decides that particular conduct by state X violates, for example, the Vienna Convention on Consular Relations, the decision speaks not just to state X but also to state Y if the latter were to engage in essentially the same conduct. Moreover, while there is little doubt that if state Y were brought before the ICJ, it would receive a comparable finding, it also appears that a comparable finding would be issued if state Y were brought before any other international dispute forum. As Shabtai Rosenne has observed:

> While there is no formal hierarchy of international courts and tribunals, the pre-eminence of the Permanent Court and the present International Court is today generally accepted. Any other international adjudicative body which ignored relevant dicta and decisions of

[87] R Churchill, "Some Reflections on the Operation of the Dispute Settlement System of the UN Convention on the Law of the Sea During its First Decade" in Freestone, Barnes and Ong, note 53, at 388, 390, 414.

[88] MA Orellana, "The Swordfish Dispute Between the EU and Chile at the ITLOS and the WTO" (2002) 71 Nordic J. Int'l L. 55, 65.

the International Court would jeopardize its credibility. The constant accretion of judicial precedents is creating what is now a substantial body of international case-law.[89]

As such, even if state Y could not itself be brought before the ICJ, the decision rendered by the ICJ against state X makes it easier for other states to argue authoritatively that state Y may not engage in such action. That same observation is equally applicable to decisions rendered by other inter-state courts and tribunals, such as ITLOS and the WTO Appellate Body, but it is not true of the decisions rendered by ad hoc arbitral panels, which often disagree as among themselves when addressing comparable issues of international law.[90]

A broader ramification with respect to the ICJ's decision is that it adds a further building block to the development of a coherent system of law, with its decisions often influencing the development of new treaty regimes and then refining those treaty regimes through subsequent interpretations. An example of this phenomenon may be seen with respect to the law of the sea. Over the past century, there can be little doubt that the decisions of the PCIJ and ICJ concerning fishing, transit, and maritime boundaries have had an enormous effect on the formation of a comprehensive and organized law of the sea, beginning with the 1958 treaties and continuing up through the emergence of the UNCLOS and related treaties.[91] This influence appears set to continue with decisions by the ICJ and the ITLOS, supplemented by UNCLOS arbitral panels, in interpreting the meaning of these regimes. As Alan Boyle asserts, "the principal purposes of the Convention's provisions on dispute settlement are to provide authoritative mechanisms for determining questions relating to 'interpretation or application' of the treaty, to guarantee the integrity of the text and to control its implementation and development by states parties."[92]

Yet there is a further ramification as well. The basic reasoning employed by the international court or tribunal—what matters and what does not matter in pursuing an authoritative decision—has a broad conditioning effect on the way states themselves engage in legal reasoning, thereby promoting greater harmony and predictability in inter-state legal reasoning. Petros Mavroidis explains the phenomenon in his discussion of the WTO Appellate Body (AB), but the explanation is equally applicable to the ICJ or the ITLOS:

The AB is there not only to solve a particular dispute but also to make the adjudication of similar future transactions (more) predictable. It is not that the outcome (winner/loser) does

[89] S Rosenne, *The Law and Practice of the International Court, 1920–1996* (The Hague: Martinus Nijhoff 1997) 1609.

[90] See, e.g., JA Maupin, "MFN-based Jurisdiction in Investor–State Arbitration: Is There Any Hope for a Consistent Approach?" (2011) 14 J. Int'l Econ. L. 157.

[91] See S Oda, "The International Court of Justice Viewed from the Bench (1976–1993)" (1993) 244 Recueil des Cours 9, 127–55.

[92] Boyle, note 34, at 38–9.

not matter, it does. But... [so does]... the thought pattern that the AB will employ in order to respond to the questions submitted to it. The process, in other words, is as important as, if not more important, than the outcome.[93]

Inter-state courts and tribunals have been instrumental in helping solidify the fabric of international law, carefully and judiciously explaining broad but core matters such as: the rules on sources of international law; the background or "secondary" rules of state responsibility; the nature of states, international organizations, and other actors in the international system; and how to reconcile conflicts between different areas of law, on both the international plane and between the international and national planes. No other dispute resolution forum is comparably situated to perform this function.

4.3.2 *Advisory opinions on "constitutional" issues*

Inter-state judicial bodies can also serve an important function by rendering advisory opinions that can help structure core areas of the law within their domain, serving almost as "constitutional" courts for the whole international legal system. Thus, separate from the ICJ's jurisdiction over contentious cases between two states, the court also has jurisdiction to issue advisory opinions on legal questions, which can address rudimentary issues about the actors and processes of international law. This advisory jurisdiction of the ICJ may only be invoked by UN organs and by the specialized agencies of the United Nations that have been authorized to do so. The ITLOS also has advisory jurisdiction, though it is more narrowly focused on certain aspects of the UNCLOS and related agreements. Specifically, the Seabed Disputes Chamber of ITLOS may give advisory opinions at the request of the Assembly or the Council of the International Seabed Authority, while the ITLOS may advise on any legal question where an international agreement related to the convention specifically provides for such an opinion.[94] The WTO Appellate Body has no advisory jurisdiction.

Although advisory opinions are not legally binding—they are, after all, "advisory"—they invariably project juridical authority by legitimating certain conduct of states and organizations and by filling gaps in a system where judicial precedents are relatively scarce.[95] To name just a few: the ICJ's 1949 advisory opinion on *Reparations for Injuries* helped secure the status of international organizations as "subjects" of international law;[96] its 1951 advisory opinion on *Reservations to*

[93] P Mavroidis, "Licence to Adjudicate: A Critical Evaluation of the Work of the WTO Appellate Body So Far" in Hartigan, note 82, at 81.

[94] ITLOS Rules, Art. 138.

[95] See MM Aljaghoub, *The Advisory Function of the International Court of Justice 1946–2005* (New York: Springer 2006); G Oduntan, *The Law and Practice of The International Court of Justice (1945–1996): A Critique of the Contentious and Advisory Jurisdictions* (Enugu, Nigeria: Fourth Dimension 1999).

[96] *Reparation for Injuries Suffered in the Service of the United Nations* (Advisory Opinion) [1949] ICJ Rep 174.

the Genocide Convention served as an important forerunner to contemporary law on treaty reservations;[97] and its 1962 *Certain Expenses* advisory opinion was instrumental in clarifying the power of the UN General Assembly to deploy peacekeeping missions, the legal obligation of states to support them, and the role of the Assembly vis-à-vis the Security Council in matters of peace and security.[98] In 2011, the Seabed Disputes Chamber of ITLOS issued its first advisory opinion, which importantly clarified that a state that sponsors contractors who engage in exploratory activities on the deep seabed is responsible for supervising them and, in doing so, must engage in a precautionary approach, must use best environmental practices, and must conduct environmental impact assessments.[99]

4.3.3 *Interim measures of protection*

A third way that inter-state judicial bodies serve as a guardian of the system in which they operate is by issuing interim measures of protection in situations where immediate action is needed to prevent irreparable harm on a matter relevant to the filed case. Although judicial proceedings generally are time-consuming, the procedures for interim measures of protection are expedited, measured in days, not weeks or months. Moreover, greater leeway typically is given to the court or tribunal to issue such provisional measures, even if the court or tribunal is later found to have no jurisdiction over the merits of the case. Of course such measures may also be permitted to arbitral tribunals, but the permanent existence of international courts and tribunals provides them a comparative advantage, for it allows immediate action without any delay caused by the appointment and convening of adjudicators.

The ICJ has received about 40 requests for interim measures of protection. As a general matter, the court is willing to issue such measures so long as a *prima facie* showing of jurisdiction exists, the requested measure is linked to the underlying case before the court, and irreparable harm is likely in the absence of the issuance of the requested measure.[100] In recent cases, the court also has stated that it "may exercise this power only if it is satisfied that the rights asserted by a party are at least plausible."[101] Further, the court has found that an order on provisional measures is binding upon the states to whom it is directed.[102]

[97] *Reservations to the Convention on the Prevention and Punishment of Genocide* (Advisory Opinion) [1951] ICJ Rep 15.

[98] *Certain Expenses of the United Nations (Article 17, Paragraph 2, of the Charter)* (Advisory Opinion) [1962] ICJ Rep 151.

[99] *Responsibilities and Obligations of States Sponsoring Persons and Entities with Respect to Activities in the Area*, note 35, at paras 121–50, 242.

[100] See ICJ Statute, Art. 41; see generally, S Oda, "Provisional Measures: The Practice of the International Court of Justice" in V Lowe and M Fitzmaurice, *Fifty Years of the International Court of Justice* (Cambridge University Press 1996) 541.

[101] See, e.g., *Request for Interpretation of the Judgment of June 15, 1962 in the Case Concerning the Temple of Preah Vihear (Cambodia v. Thailand)* (Provisional Measures) [2011] ICJ Gen. List 151, para. 33.

[102] *LaGrand Case (Germany v. United States)* (Jurisdiction) [2001] ICJ Rep 466.

The ITLOS may also issue binding provisional measures of protection, if "appropriate under the circumstances to preserve the respective rights of the parties to the dispute or to prevent serious harm to the marine environment, pending the final decision."[103] Moreover, ITLOS may receive applications for the prompt release of a detained vessel or its crew where the authorities of a state have detained a vessel or crew flying the flag of another state and it is alleged that the detaining state did not act in compliance with the UNCLOS.[104] Such applications may only be made by or on behalf of the vessel's flag state.[105] While the relevant states can choose to take the provisional measures or a prompt release proceeding before some other UNCLOS dispute resolution forum, ITLOS remains the "default" tribunal. In other words, it matters not whether the responding state selected the ITLOS for binding dispute resolution when it joined the UNCLOS; unless the parties select some other fora for provisional measure proceedings, the responding state may be brought before the ITLOS.

The WTO Appellate Body does not have the power to issue interim measures of protection, nor do WTO arbitral panels, largely because of the nature of the violations at issue (denial of trade benefits) and the relatively speedy process at the WTO for resolving the dispute on the merits.

4.4 Authoritative resolution of important disputes

Sometimes lost in the discussion of inter-state courts and tribunals is that, while their dockets are not extensive, they often include extremely important disputes for those states involved. For example, Nicaragua's case against the United States in the mid-1980s before the ICJ was a critical component of its foreign policy, as was Macedonia's case against Greece in this century. An inter-state court or tribunal can provide a well-known and respected forum for addressing major grievances; while resort to that forum may be rare, when it occurs the stakes can be high. While the numerous land and boundary delimitation cases before the ICJ do not attract much global notice, they typically concern important bilateral disputes that, left to fester, might well lead to armed conflict.

Likewise, the jurisprudence of the WTO Appellate Body is incrementally solidifying the meaning of key global trade agreements as they apply in bilateral trade relations, which in turn is influencing national decision-making and national laws.[106] Resort to WTO dispute settlement is a highly public affair, taken

[103] UNCLOS, Art. 290.

[104] UNCLOS, Art. 292. The relevant provisions of the UNCLOS call for the prompt release of the vessel or its crew upon the posting of a reasonable bond or other financial security.

[105] See S Rosenne, *Provisional Measures in International Law: The International Court of Justice and the International Tribunal for the Law of the Sea* (Oxford University Press 2005).

[106] WJ Davey, "The WTO Dispute Settlement System: The First Ten Years" (2005) 8 J. Int'l Econ. L. 17.

by a government for the purpose of protecting key sectors of a state's economy from allegedly unfair and unlawful trade practices, involving goods, services, intellectual property, government procurement, and a range of other matters. Even in the early years of the WTO, John Jackson noted that the "addition of the right to appeal to an Appellate Body made up of a permanent cadre... in conjunction with the automatic approval of panel reports, has already had a very profound impact on the world trading system as embodied in the GATT and WTO."[107]

The ITLOS, the youngest of the three inter-state courts discussed here, has attracted the least use, in part because it competes with other dispute settlement fora. Nevertheless, it too has addressed important disputes, most recently the maritime boundary delimitation between Bangladesh and Myanmar, the first judgment of an international court or tribunal to delimit the continental shelf beyond 200 nautical miles from the coast.[108]

5 Decline and Fall?

In considering whether inter-state judicial bodies are becoming relics, it is worth considering whether their role has really changed in recent years. Such courts and tribunals were never a dominant feature of international dispute settlement in terms of caseload or exposure of states to compulsory jurisdiction; there was never a "golden era" of habitual resort to these courts or tribunals for all disputes arising amongst states. If anything, the number of cases before these courts or tribunals has significantly *increased* as measured against 50 or even 25 years ago. Concomitantly, there has been a very significant increase in the establishment and use of other forms of transnational dispute settlement before institutions such as the ICSID, but that burgeoning practice has not collaterally diminished the resort to inter-state courts or tribunals.

Arguably the "rising tide" of resort to international adjudication is raising all of the dispute settlement "boats," including those consisting of inter-state courts and tribunals. At the same time, the emergence of "blended" models when creating new

[107] Jackson, note 81, at 180.

[108] *Delimitation of the Maritime Boundary in the Bay of Bengal (Bangladesh/Myanmar)* (Judgment) 2012 ITLOS Case No. 16. <http://www.itlos.org/fileadmin/itlos/documents/cases/case_no_16/C16_Judgment_14_03_2012_rev.pdf> accessed August 23, 2013.

courts and tribunals—in which there exists an option for resort to a court or an arbitral body (e.g. under the UNCLOS) or an arbitral body from which appeal may be made to a court or tribunal (e.g. the WTO)—may reflect an effort to respond creatively to new challenges facing states in a changing world. What have not changed are the functions of inter-state judicial bodies, functions that cannot readily be supplanted by other forms of adjudication.

Research Questions

1. For the major multilateral treaties adopted in recent years, how many have incorporated compulsory or optional dispute settlement? Of those that do, how many use an inter-state court or tribunal? In reviewing the *travaux préparatoires* of treaties that incorporate dispute settlement, what are the principal explanations for the use (or lack of use) of inter-state courts or tribunals when concluding a major multilateral treaty?
2. To what extent are a state's policy-makers influenced by the presence of compulsory dispute settlement when pursuing a policy initiative that likely violates the state's obligations under international law? If the influence exists, is it stronger in the presence of dispute settlement before inter-state courts or tribunals than before other forms of dispute settlement?
3. Dispute settlement at the WTO represents a "blended" model, in that disputes are first addressed by ad hoc arbitration but then can be appealed to a more "judicialized" tribunal. Has this model succeeded in accomplishing the goals set by the Uruguay Round negotiators, such that a similar arbitration/court structure might be replicated in other areas of international law, where arbitration is used but has resulted in unresolved conflicts among disparate arbitral panels?
4. Dispute settlement under the UNCLOS represents a different "blended" model, in which an inter-state court or tribunal is just one option for dispute settlement. Most states joining the UNCLOS have not opted for the use of an inter-state court or tribunal, but have either opted for arbitration or have declined to select a forum, which then results by default in arbitration. What are the explanations given by those states (internally and externally) in declining to opt for an inter-state court or tribunal? Do these explanations suggest a declining desire by states for such courts and tribunals?

Suggested Reading

Chandrasekhara Rao, P and Khan, R (eds), *The International Tribunal for the Law of the Sea: Law and Practice* (The Hague: Kluwer 2001).

Jackson, J, *The Jurisprudence of GATT and the WTO* (Cambridge University Press 2000).

Karaman, IV, *Dispute Resolution in the Law of the Sea* (Leiden: Martinus Nijhoff 2012).

Klein, N, *Dispute Settlement in the UN Convention on the Law of the Sea* (Cambridge University Press 2005).

Lowe, V and Fitzmaurice, M, *Fifty Years of the International Court of Justice* (Cambridge University Press 1996).

Sacerdoti, G, Yanovich, A, and Bohanes, J (eds), *The WTO at Ten: The Contribution of the Dispute Settlement System* (Cambridge University Press 2006).

Shaffer, GC and Melendez-Ortiz, R (eds), *Dispute Settlement at the WTO: The Developing Country Experience* (Cambridge University Press 2010).

Tomuschat, C, "International Courts and Tribunals" in Rüdiger Wolfrum (ed.), *Max Planck Encyclopedia of Public International Law* (Oxford University Press, online edition, last updated Feb. 2011), <http://www.mpepil.com> accessed August 23, 2013.

Zimmermann, A, Tomuschat, C, and Oellers-Frahm, K (eds), *The Statute of the International Court of Justice: A Commentary* (2nd edn, Oxford University Press 2012).

CHAPTER 10

INTERNATIONAL CRIMINAL COURTS

WILLIAM A SCHABAS*

1 Introduction: What Makes a Criminal Court "International"?

The title of this chapter, international criminal courts, requires some explanation because there is no simple way to identify the subject. Great diversity characterizes the modes of establishment, the powers, and the jurisdictional framework

* Professor of international law, Middlesex University, London; professor of international criminal law and human rights, Leiden University; *emeritus* professor of human rights law, National University of Ireland Galway. Officer of the Order of Canada (OC) and Member of the Royal Irish Academy (MRIA).

of international criminal courts and tribunals. The second of the two adjectives, "criminal" does not pose much of a problem. A court is "criminal" if its trials involve the prosecution, conviction, and punishment of individuals, including corporate entities. At the international level, many courts are concerned with international criminal law, such as the International Court of Justice (ICJ) and the European Court of Human Rights (ECtHR). But they address this body of law in the context of litigation about state responsibility, rather than in cases involving individual defendants who are accused of crimes.

The first adjective, "international," is more problematic. Describing a criminal court as "international" is more than a convenient label for the purposes of classification, because legal consequences are attached to this determination. In a celebrated decision, the ICJ referred to "certain international criminal tribunals" and provided three examples—the International Criminal Court (ICC) and the ad hoc tribunals for the former Yugoslavia and Rwanda—but without indicating the basis on which it made its determination. It held that a head of state or similar official would be deprived of the immunity offered under customary international law before "certain international criminal courts, where they have jurisdiction."[1] The implication was that, to the extent an institution could be considered to belong to this category, the rules concerning immunity would not be the same as before other courts.

At the center of the small universe of international criminal courts is the eponymous ICC. Established by treaty, its subject-matter jurisdiction is confined to well-accepted international crimes, namely genocide, crimes against humanity, war crimes, and the crime of aggression, although the court may also prosecute the ordinary crimes of perjury and contempt when perpetrated in association with its proceedings. Its judges, prosecutor, registrar, and other officials are elected by the States Parties. Though widely ratified, the Rome Statute of the ICC is still very far from universal in scope. Three of the five permanent members of the Security Council are not parties to the statute, nor are some of the world's most populous countries, including India, Indonesia, Pakistan, and Bangladesh. One region of the world, the Middle East, is barely represented.

Four other criminal courts have also been established by treaty, something that gives them a good claim to be of the same international genus as the ICC. They are the International Military Tribunal (IMT), the Special Court for Sierra Leone, the Residual Special Court for Sierra Leone,[2] and the Special Tribunal for Lebanon. The first of these, known colloquially as the Nuremberg Tribunal, is the product of a four-power agreement that was subsequently ratified by 19 other states.[3] The

[1] *Arrest Warrant of April 11, 2000 (Democratic Republic of the Congo v. Belgium)* (Judgment) [2002] ICJ Rep 3, para. 61.

[2] "Agreement between the United Nations and the Government of Sierra Leone on the Establishment of a Residual Special Court for Sierra Leone" (August 2010).

[3] International Military Tribunal (1948), 22 IMT 411.

word "international" appeared in its name, although the judgment explained that the Charter of the IMT constituted "the exercise of the sovereign legislative power by the countries to which the German Reich unconditionally surrendered; and the undoubted right of these countries to legislate for the occupied territories has been recognized by the civilised world." They did "together what any one of them might have done singly; for it is not to be doubted that any nation has the right thus to set up special courts to administer law." At the same time, it was "the expression of international law existing at the time of its creation; and to that extent is itself a contribution to international law."[4]

The other post-World War II court, the International Military Tribunal for the Far East (known as the "Tokyo Tribunal"), was created by proclamation of the Supreme Commander Allied Powers, United States General Douglas Macarthur. This was not a unilateral act, however, because it resulted from consultation with the United Kingdom, the Soviet Union, and China, and received direction from the Far Eastern Commission, which was even more broadly composed.[5]

Three international criminal courts have been established by resolution of the United Nations Security Council acting pursuant to Chapter VII of the Charter of the United Nations. They are the International Criminal Tribunal for the former Yugoslavia (ICTY), the International Criminal Tribunal for Rwanda (ICTR) and the International Residual Mechanism for Criminal Tribunals.[6] It may be contended that the Special Tribunal for Lebanon was also established by the Security Council because its statute, negotiated between the government of Lebanon and the United Nations, was never ratified and was decreed to be in force by Security Council resolution.[7]

Finally, there are the mixed model or hybrid tribunals. The Extraordinary Chambers of the Courts of Cambodia are the product of Cambodian legislation. However, the legislation was adopted to give effect to an international agreement between Cambodia and the United Nations. It requires a decisive level of international participation, with some judges and one of two prosecutors appointed by the Secretary-General of the United Nations. The War Crimes Chamber of the Court of Bosnia and Herzegovina is also the indirect product of an international agreement, although, like the Cambodian institution, it operates pursuant to national law. Two such tribunals have been created by the United Nations itself, acting alone, as the provisional administration of East Timor and Kosovo: the Serious Crimes Panels in the District Court of Dili, East Timor and the Panels in the Courts of Kosovo.

[4] International Military Tribunal, note 3, at 461.

[5] N Boister and R Cryer, *The Tokyo International Military Tribunal, A Reappraisal* (Oxford University Press 2008) 23–5.

[6] UN Res 1966 (2010) UN Doc. S/RES/1966.

[7] UN Res 1757 (2007) UN Doc. S/RES/1757; *Prosecutor v. Ayyash et al.* [2012] STL-11-OIIPT/AC/AR90.1, Decision on the Defense Appeals Against the Trial Chamber's "Decision on the Defense Challenges to the Jurisdiction and Legality of the Tribunal."

It is extremely difficult to pigeonhole any of these institutions. The mode of creation varies considerably, as does the applicable law, and there are lingering debates about the entitlement of the ancestor of them all, the Nuremberg Tribunal, to claim that it is international. With the exception of the Special Tribunal for Lebanon, they all exercise jurisdiction over international crimes. However, that is not really a good criterion in identifying an international court because many national courts are also empowered to punish international crimes, whether they occur within their traditional jurisdictional frames or as an exercise of universal jurisdiction. Some domestic courts have mixed panels, with judges drawn from both the national judiciary and from international sources, suggesting that they are international or internationalized. But that too may be a misleading criterion, because many countries allow judges from other national judiciaries to sit in their own courts. Although it never functioned properly, the Supreme Constitutional Court and the High Court of Justice of Cyprus established by the 1960 Constitution required that the presidents of both tribunals be a "neutral judge" who was not a subject or citizen of Greece, Turkey, the United Kingdom, or its colonies.[8] That did not make it an international tribunal.

Academic writers speak of "internationalized" courts or of courts with an "international dimension." But ultimately it seems quite impossible to provide a succinct definition or to offer a formula for identifying an "international criminal court." The literature provides little enlightenment with respect to defining the scope of the term "international court."[9] Perhaps a negative approach furnishes the most clarity, or at least a predictable test for distinguishing an international court: it is a criminal court that is not one established by national law to prosecute so-called ordinary (as opposed to international) crimes. Typically, international courts can be identified by one or more of the following features: establishment by treaty or by resolution of an international organization, subject-matter jurisdiction over international crimes, and significant international representation among the judiciary and other judicial officers.

2 The History of International Courts

National courts have exercised jurisdiction over the prosecution of international crimes for more than a century. For example, after the American Civil War a military tribunal prosecuted Henry Wirz, commander of the Andersonville prison camp, for what the judge advocate said was a violation of "the code international," described

[8] Constitution of Cyprus 1960, Arts 133.3, 153.3.

[9] For an attempt, see R Woetzel, *The Nuremberg Trials in International Law* (London: Stevens and Sons 1962) 42–57.

as "a higher law, a law paramount to any rule of action" that was "sanctioned by the great tribunal of nations."[10] The first serious manifestation of an attempt to prosecute such international crimes before an international body came at the conclusion of World War I. The Commission on Responsibilities set up at the Paris Peace Conference noted that every belligerent possessed, "according to international law, the power and authority to try [alleged perpetrators of international crimes] if such persons have been taken prisoners or have otherwise fallen into its power."[11] It recommended the establishment of a "High Tribunal" comprised of judges from 12 allied countries. Its jurisdiction was to consist of "the principles of the law of nations as they result from the usages established among civilised peoples, from the laws of humanity and from the dictates of the public conscience," a formulation drawn from the so-called Martens Clause in the preamble of the 1907 Hague Convention.[12] The two American members submitted a memorandum of reservations objecting to "the unprecedented proposal of creating an international criminal tribunal."[13] The objection was about the law to be applied, including prosecution for violations of the "laws of humanity," and waiver of head of state immunity, and not about the concept of an international tribunal as such. A modified version of the proposal from the Commission was contained in Art. 227 of the Treaty of Versailles:

> A special tribunal will be constituted to try the accused, thereby assuring him the guarantees essential to the right of defence. It will be composed of five judges, one appointed by each of the following Powers: namely, the United States of America, Great Britain, France, Italy and Japan. In its decision the tribunal will be guided by the highest motives of international policy, with a view to vindicating the solemn obligations of international undertakings and the validity of international morality. It will be its duty to fix the punishment which it considers should be imposed.

It was to try a single accused individual, the former German Emperor. Because he successfully obtained asylum in the Netherlands, the tribunal was never established.

In 1920, the League of Nations appointed an Advisory Committee of Jurists to make proposals for the establishment of an international court of justice. At the initiative of one of its members, Baron Descamps of Belgium, the committee recommended the creation of a "High Court of International Justice" with jurisdiction to try crimes "against international public order and the universal law of nations."[14] The Advisory Committee eventually concluded

> that it would be useless to establish side by side with the Court of International Justice another Criminal Court, and that it is best to entrust criminal cases to the ordinary tribunals as is at present the custom in international procedure. If crimes of this kind should in future be brought

[10] SS Gregory, "Criminal Responsibility of Sovereigns for Wilful Violations of the Laws of War" 1920 6 Virginia Law Review 400, 404–5.

[11] *Violations of the Laws and Customs of War, Reports of Majority and Dissenting Reports of America and Japanese Members of the Commission of Responsibilities* (Conference of Paris 1919) 23.

[12] *Violations of the Laws and Customs of War*, note 11, at 24–5.

[13] *Violations of the Laws and Customs of War*, note 11, at 60.

[14] "Historical Survey of the Question of International Criminal Jurisdiction" (1949) UN Doc A/CN.4/7, 10.

within the scope of international penal law, a criminal department might be set up in the Court of International Justice. In any case, consideration of this problem is, at the moment, premature.[15]

During the next decade, the international criminal court project was addressed by several professional organizations, notably by the International Law Association.[16] A resolution adopted at its 1922 Conference, held in Buenos Aires, stated: "In the opinion of this Conference the creation of an International Criminal Court is essential in the interests of justice, and the Conference is of the opinion that the matter is one of urgency."[17] At the initiative of Vespasian V. Pella, the Inter-Parliamentary Union adopted a resolution recommending that the Permanent Court of International Justice (PCIJ) be given jurisdiction over international offenses and international crimes.[18] A draft statute for an international criminal court prepared by Pella was adopted by the International Association of Penal Law in 1928.[19] In 1937, the League of Nations adopted the *Convention for the Prevention and Punishment of Terrorism*. A second treaty adopted at the same time provided for the creation of an international criminal tribunal. The *Convention* was signed by 13 states, but India was the only state to ratifiy and the instrument never entered into force.[20]

The post-World War II period saw the first operational international criminal tribunals: the IMT and the International Military Tribunal for the Far East. Each held a single trial with multiple defendants. More trials were foreseen, especially in the European theater, but rather than hold a second full-blown international trial the major powers decided that each occupation zone would be responsible for its own proceedings pursuant to Control Council Law No. 10. The Americans used the Nuremberg courtroom, which was within their zone, for a series of thematic "subsequent proceedings." Reporting on this to the Secretary of the Army, Telford Taylor spoke of them as "international trials."[21] Although they applied essentially the same international law used by the IMT, institutionally these were United States Military Tribunals and the judges were all drawn from the American judiciary.[22]

15 "Historical Survey," note 14, at 12.

16 "Report of the Permanent International Criminal Court Committee," International Law Association, (Report of the Thirty-fourth Conference, Vienna 1926) 109. See also, e.g., JL Brierly, "Do We Need an International Criminal Court?" (1923) 8 British Ybk of Intl L 86.

17 "Historical Survey," note 14, at 12.

18 VV Pella, "La criminalité de la guerre d'agression et l'organisation d'une répression internationale," (report presented to the Twenty-third Conference of the Inter-Parliamentary Union) (Compte rendu de la XXIIIe Conférence 1926) 205.

19 VV Pella, *La Guerre-Crime et les Criminels de Guerre* (Éditions de la Baconnière 1964) 129; See also "Historical Survey," note 14, 75–88.

20 League of Nations, *Convention for the Creation of an International Criminal Court* (1936) OJ Spec. Supp. No. 156, LN Doc. C.547(I).M.384(I).1937. V (1938). See "The Convention for the Creation of an International Criminal Court" (1938) 19 BYIL 216.

21 T Taylor, *Final Report to the Secretary of the Army on the Nuremberg War Crimes Trials Under Control Council Law No. 10* (Washington D.C. 1949) 137.

22 See "Were the NMT's International Tribunals?" in KJ Heller, *The Nuremberg Military Tribunals and the Origins and International Criminal Law* (Oxford University Press 2011) 112.

The Convention on the Prevention and Punishment of the Crime of Genocide, adopted by the United Nations General Assembly (UNGA) on December 9, 1948, pointed the way toward a permanent international criminal court. Article 6 of the convention states: "Persons charged with genocide or any of the other acts enumerated in article 3 shall be tried by a competent tribunal of the State in the territory of which the act was committed, or by such international penal tribunal as may have jurisdiction with respect to those Contracting Parties which shall have accepted its jurisdiction." In a companion resolution, the Assembly mandated the International Law Commission (ILC) to begin work on the draft statute of an international criminal court.[23]

The ILC appointed two special rapporteurs on the subject, one of whom, Ricardo Alfaro, was very keen while the other, Emil Sandström, was decidedly unenthusiastic.[24] The General Assembly set up its own commission to deal with the question. Known as the Committee on International Criminal Jurisdiction, it issued two reports.[25] The General Assembly voted to defer consideration of the reports, first in 1954[26] and again in 1957,[27] and yet again in 1968,[28] because it felt the question of an international criminal jurisdiction was closely linked to agreement on a definition of aggression, something that was only reached in 1974.[29] The previous year, the General Assembly had adopted the Apartheid Convention which contained a provision similar to Art. 6 of the Genocide Convention.[30] But only in 1989 did the General Assembly authorize the ILC, after the latter's incessant prodding, to resume the work on the draft statute of an international criminal court that it had suspended in the early 1950s.[31]

Suddenly, there was enormous momentum for international criminal justice. Two factors seem to have contributed to this new environment: the end of the Cold War;[32] and the dynamic international human rights movement, which was increasingly focused on promoting accountability and challenging impunity. Working at an unprecedented pace, in 1994 the ILC submitted a draft statute for the proposed international court.[33] Meanwhile, a proposal for an ad hoc tribunal to prosecute

[23] UNGA "Study by the International Law Commission of the Question of an International Criminal Jurisdiction" (1948) UNGA Res 216 B(III).

[24] "Report by Ricardo J. Alfaro, Spécial Rapporteur" (1950) UN Doc A/CN.4/15; "Report by Emil Sandström, Spécial Rapporteur" (1950) UN Doc. A/CN.4/20.

[25] "Report of the Committee on International Criminal Jurisdiction" (1952) UN Doc A/2136; "Report of the Committee on International Criminal Jurisdiction" (1954) UN Doc A/2645.

[26] UNGA Res 898 (IX). [27] UNGA Res 1187 (XII).

[28] This "24-year aggression struggle" is described in detail in O Solera, *Defining the Crime of Aggression* (Cameron May 2007) 109–203.

[29] UNGA Res 3314 (XXIX).

[30] International Convention on the Suppression and Punishment of the Crime of Apartheid 1976, 1015 UNTS 243, Art. 5.

[31] UNGA Res 44/39.

[32] On this point, see, in this handbook, Alter, Ch. 4, at section 1.

[33] Report of the International Law Commission on the work of its forty-sixth session (May 2–July 22, 1994) UN Doc A/49/10, para. 90.

those responsible for Iraq's invasion of Kuwait was mooted by the United States and the United Kingdom, and later by the European Union.[34] In early 1993, the Security Council decided to establish the ICTY, the first international criminal court since the 1940s.[35] The following year, the Security Council established a second ad hoc tribunal for Rwanda.[36]

The General Assembly reacted positively to the report of the ILC, first setting up an ad hoc Committee[37] and then a Preparatory Committee[38] before convening a plenipotentiary conference in Rome at which the Statute of the ICC was adopted. The 60 ratifications or accessions required by Art. 125 of the statute were obtained by April 2002 and the statute entered into force on July 1, 2002.[39] By the following year, judges and the prosecutor had been elected, making the court fully operational. Its first arrest warrants were issued in 2005.

The ad hoc tribunals for the former Yugoslavia and Rwanda flourished, and eventually managed to prosecute most of the major suspects. The institutions took on huge proportions, consuming a considerable part of the United Nations budget. Violence returned to Kosovo in the late 1990s. Although the ICTY had jurisdiction, and did indeed prosecute some cases related to that conflict, the United Nations Interim Administration Mission in Kosovo (UNMIK) set up so-called "Regulation 64 Panels" courts where international judges sat alongside domestic judges in existing domestic courts. A similar approach was followed in East Timor in March 2000 when the United Nations Transitional Authority for East Timor created the Serious Crimes Panel of the Dili District Court charged with prosecuting atrocity crimes perpetrated during 1999. The most elaborate of such mixed tribunals was the Extraordinary Chambers of the Courts of Cambodia, created in 2004 by domestic legislation but pursuant to an agreement with the United Nations.[40]

Although the Security Council rejected calls to establish additional courts in places like Burundi, it responded favourably in 2000 to an initiative directed at Sierra Leone. This time, rather than proceed by resolution pursuant to Chapter VII of the Charter of the United Nations, the Security Council directed the Secretary-General to negotiate a bilateral agreement with the Government of Sierra Leone.[41] The Special Court for Sierra Leone was established in 2002.[42] Unlike the two earlier

[34] US Department of State Dispatch (October 22, 1990) Vol. I (8), 205; US Department of State Dispatch (November 12, 1990) Vol. I (11), 260.

[35] UN Res 808 (1993) UN Doc S/RES/808; UN Res 827 (1993) UN Doc S/RES/827.

[36] UN Res 955 (1994) UN Doc S/RES/955. [37] UNGA Res 49/53 (1994).

[38] UNGA Res 50/46 (1995). The mandate given by the General Assembly was reaffirmed in UNGA Res 51/207, adopted on the basis of a report from the Sixth Committee: Establishment of an International Criminal Court, Report of the Sixth Committee (1996) UN Doc A/51/627.

[39] Rome Statute of the ICC 2002, 2187 UNTS 90.

[40] Khmer Rouge trials (2002) UN Doc A/RES/57/228.

[41] UN Res 1315 (2000) UN Doc S/RES/1315.

[42] Agreement between the United Nations and the Government of Sierra Leone on the Establishment of a Special Court for Sierra Leone (2002) 2178 UNTS 138.

ad hoc tribunals, it was funded by voluntary contributions from interested states rather than out of the general budget of the United Nations.

By then, attention had turned to winding down the activities of the Yugoslavia and Rwanda tribunals. In Bosnia and Herzegovina, which was under a degree of international supervision as a result of the Dayton Peace Agreement, an internationalized War Crimes Chamber of the national courts was set up by agreement with the High Representative designated by the Organization for Security and Cooperation in Europe. In addition, recognizing that even when the ad hoc tribunals had finished the trials that were under way, some sort of judicial body would always be needed to deal with issues concerning convicted persons in detention, as well as the remote possibility that a few of the indicted suspects who had never been apprehended might eventually appear for trial. Therefore, a single residual tribunal was created for the ad hoc tribunals for the former Yugoslavia and Rwanda.[43] A second such institution was also established for the Special Court for Sierra Leone.[44] Technically, these residual mechanisms are distinct, autonomous tribunals, and they are constructed in such a way as to be in a position to conduct a full trial. In practice, it is unlikely that this will occur, and the institutions will mainly address detention-related issues.

The Security Council decided to establish a fourth international criminal court to deal with terrorist bombings in Lebanon that occurred in 2005. Although 2005 is within the temporal jurisdiction of the ICC, terrorism is not a crime punishable by the court. As it had done with Sierra Leone, the Security Council instructed the Secretary-General to negotiate an agreement with Lebanon. However, when Lebanon's ratification was not forthcoming, the Security Council decreed the establishment of a tribunal.[45] Judicial activities began in earnest in 2009. By 2012, proceedings were under way for an *in absentia* trial of four persons charged with the murder of Rafik Hariri and several other persons.

There is now very little interest in establishing additional international criminal tribunals to deal with crimes perpetrated in the distant past. As for contemporary crises involving territories that do not fall under the jurisdiction of the ICC, because the state in question is not a party to the statute, there have been isolated calls for the creation of new bodies. For example, in early 2005, the United States proposed that a new tribunal be established to deal with Darfur. It later reached agreement on a resolution of the Security Council establishing jurisdiction for the ICC.[46] This seems now to be the preferred option. In February 2011, the Security Council conferred jurisdiction on the ICC with respect to the situation in Libya.[47] Dissatisfied with aspects of the court's activity in the region, the African Union considered

[43] UN Res 1966 (2010) UN Doc S/RES/1966.

[44] Agreement on the Establishment of a Residual Special Court for Sierra Leone, note 42.

[45] UN Res 1757 (2007) UN Doc S/RES/1757.

[46] UN Res 1593 (2005) UN Doc S/RES/1593.

[47] UN Res 1970 (2011) UN Doc S/RES/1970.

the creation of a specialized criminal chamber of the African Court of Justice and Human Rights which could prosecute the crimes listed in the Rome Statute, as well as such offenses as piracy, terrorism, corruption, and money laundering.[48]

3 Jurisdiction of International Criminal Courts

International criminal courts and tribunals are principally concerned with the exercise of a repressive jurisdiction over individuals and organizations rather than states themselves, as is the case with most international courts and tribunals. Indeed, all international criminal courts and tribunals have the authority to try natural persons. In some cases this is stated explicitly,[49] while in others a general reference to "persons" opens the possibility that corporations and similar entities may also be prosecuted.[50] The most extensive discussion of this issue took place during the drafting of the Rome Statute, when it was decided that jurisdiction should not be exercised over corporate bodies. At Nuremberg, the IMT exercised jurisdiction over natural persons, but it was also empowered to make a declaration that a group or organization to which an individual accused belonged was a "criminal organization."[51] In some cases, the constitutive instruments of tribunals have excluded the prosecution of persons for crimes committed under a certain age.[52] For most institutions, however, an age limit is not specified; there appear to be no decisions where an international court or tribunal has had to rule on whether such a limit on criminal responsibility of juvenile offenders is implied where the text is silent. Although unusual, in some circumstances certain categories of individuals, such as international peacekeeping troops, have been explicitly excluded from the jurisdiction of an international court or tribunal.[53]

[48] Draft Protocol on Amendments to the Protocol on the Statute of the African Court of Justice and Human Rights (2012) Exp/Min/IV/Rev.7; Decision on the Protocol on Amendments to the Protocol on the Statute of the African Court on Human and Peoples' Rights (2012) Doc EX.CL/731(XXI) a; Decision on the Protocol on Amendments to the Protocol on the Statute of the African Court on Human and Peoples' Rights (2012) AU Doc Assembly/AU/13(XIX) a.

[49] Rome Statute of the ICC, Art. 25.1; Statute of the ICTY, Art. 6; Statute of the ICTR, Art. 5.

[50] Statute of the Special Court for Sierra Leone, Art. 7.1.

[51] Charter of the IMT, Art. 9.

[52] Rome Statute of the ICC, Art. 26 (18 years); Statute of the Special Court for Sierra Leone, Art. 7 (15 years).

[53] Statute of the Special Court for Sierra Leone, Art. 1.2 and 1.3; UN Res 1593 (2005) UN Doc S/RES/1593, OP 6; UN Res 1970 (2011) UN Doc S/RES/1970, OP 6.

The IMT's jurisdiction was confined to persons "acting in the interests of the European Axis countries"[54] while the International Military Tribunal for the Far East was empowered to prosecute "Far Eastern war criminals."[55] Most international criminal courts and tribunals have had their jurisdiction defined with respect to territory. For example, the ICTY was empowered to prosecute offenses committed "in the territory of the former Yugoslavia since 1991." On this basis, it seems possible to prosecute persons who were not in fact physically present but whose conduct abroad had effects on the territory in question.[56] The ICTR has perhaps the most complex formula, applying both to the territory of Rwanda and, with respect to Rwandan citizens, to "neighbouring States."[57]

By analogy with jurisdictional issues at the national level, it is sometimes said that international courts and tribunals may exercise so-called universal jurisdiction. During negotiations on the establishment of the ICC, there were keenly supported proposals to confer jurisdiction of this nature. In effect this would have enabled the court to prosecute crimes committed on any territory regardless of the nationality of the offender. Many people insisted that without such jurisdiction the court would be unable to operate effectively. Ultimately, however, agreement could only be reached upon a court with jurisdiction to prosecute crimes perpetrated on the territory of a state party to the Rome Statute or by nationals of a state party.[58] A non-party state may also make a declaration conferring jurisdiction over its nationals and its territory.[59] In the case of the crime of aggression, jurisdiction may only be exercised over nationals of states parties.[60] Exceptionally, the ICC may exercise a broader jurisdiction when so authorized by Security Council resolution. It appears that the Security Council may confer jurisdiction on the ICC with respect to the territory of a non-party state and even to a portion of the territory within such a state.[61]

Although no temporal jurisdiction was defined at Nuremberg or Tokyo, in the modern-day tribunals this is invariably specified. Most of the tribunals provide for a date when the jurisdiction starts but do not make provision for an end date. The ICTR is the exception; its jurisdiction *ratione temporis* was limited to the calendar year 1994. Because of the multi-lateral nature of the Rome Statute of the ICC, jurisdiction may not be exercised with respect to any particular state party prior to the entry into force of the statute for that state party.

Although not strictly speaking a matter of jurisdiction, the authority of the ICC to proceed in a given case is also circumscribed by what is colloquially referred to as the "triggering" of jurisdiction. An investigation and prosecution may not proceed until the exercise of jurisdiction has been authorized. This may be accomplished in a

54 Charter of the IMT, Art. 6.
55 Charter of the International Military Tribunal of the Far East, Art. 5.
56 *Prosecutor v. Taylor* (Judgment) [2012] SCSL-03-1-T.
57 Statute of the ICTR, Art. 1.
58 Rome Statute of the ICC, Art. 12.2.
59 Rome Statute of the ICC, Art. 12.3.
60 Rome Statute of the ICC, Art. 15*bis*5.
61 UN Res 1593 (2005) UN Doc S/RES/1593.

declaration by a state party or by a ruling of the Pre-Trial Chamber following a request from the Prosecutor, as well as in a resolution of the Security Council. As a general rule, the authorization to exercise jurisdiction will specify the territory and a start date. To date, no end-limit has been placed on such declarations; a legitimate question arises as to whether they automatically expire at some point through change of circumstances.

The subject matter jurisdiction of international criminal courts and tribunals, with some exceptions, is confined to certain types of international crime associated with serious violations of human rights, the laws of armed conflict and international peace and security. Although the concept of international crime also extends to a range of offenses including piracy and trafficking in drugs, persons, and pornography, as well as damaging undersea telecommunications cables, these matters do not fall within the jurisdiction of international courts and tribunals. The same is true with respect to torture and enforced disappearance, to the extent that the crimes are isolated and do not fulfil the criteria of crimes against humanity. The international dimension of these offenses has several significant legal consequences, but, in principle, they are prosecuted at the national level.

Genocide is sometimes described as "the crime of crimes." Although the word has existed since 1944, it was not used in the Charter of the IMT, where the attempted destruction of the Jews of Europe was addressed as the crime against humanity of extermination. A widely accepted definition of genocide appears in Art. 2 of the 1948 Convention. This text is incorporated, without any significant modification, into the Rome Statute and the statutes of the international criminal tribunals for the former Yugoslavia and Rwanda. The Elements of Crimes, which is a supplementary document to be used to assist the ICC in interpreting and applying the definitions of crimes in the Rome Statute, spells out a "contextual element" that is relevant to the scope of the crime genocide. There is debate as to whether the Elements of Crimes is consistent with or actually narrows the definition in the 1948 Convention.[62]

Crimes against humanity consist of a range of atrocity crimes perpetrated as part of a widespread or systematic attack on a civilian population. The list of punishable acts is informed by international human rights law. It includes torture and enforced disappearance, for instance. Crimes against humanity have been punished by the international military tribunals at Nuremberg and Tokyo, the ad hoc tribunals for the former Yugoslavia, Rwanda and Sierra Leone, and the ICC. The text defining crimes against humanity is somewhat different for each one of these tribunals. At Nuremberg and Tokyo, a *nexus* was required, linking crimes against humanity to the armed conflict, and no convictions were registered for acts perpetrated before the outbreak of the war. Subsequent case law declared the requirement of a connection with armed conflict to have disappeared,[63] a jurisprudential development

[62] *Prosecutor v. Bashir* (Decision on the Prosecution's Application for a Warrant of Arrest against Omar Hassan Ahmad Al Bashir) [2009] ICC-02/05-01/09-3, paras 117–33.

[63] *Prosecutor v. Tadić* (Decision on the Defence Motion for Interlocutory Appeal on Jurisdiction) [1995] IT-94-1-AR72, paras 78, 140–1.

later codified in the Rome Statute in 1998. Although the Rome Statute eliminates the *nexus* requirement, it makes explicit another contextual element by which crimes against humanity be perpetrated "in furtherance of a State or organizational policy."[64] As with the case of the crime of genocide, it is not settled as to whether this is consistent with customary law and therefore implied in definitions of crimes against humanity where the policy element is not made explicit.[65]

All of the international tribunals (with the exception of the Special Tribunal for Lebanon) have also had jurisdiction over war crimes, albeit with varying definitions. The texts used at Nuremberg and Tokyo were inspired by the 1907 Hague Convention, although the enumeration of specific acts was left open-ended. Definitions of war crimes in the more modern tribunals have drawn upon post-World War II codifications, including both the grave breaches and other provisions of the 1949 Geneva Conventions. They also distinguish between war crimes depending upon whether they are perpetrated in international or non-international armed conflict, although there is much overlap in terms of the punishable acts.

Crimes against peace, which is to say the waging of an aggressive war, were at the heart of the work of the post-World War II international military tribunals. However, this category of international crime was not included in the ad hoc tribunals set up by the UN Security Council. The Rome Conference was unable to agree upon how the crime of aggression should be defined and under what conditions the court would be empowered to initiate a prosecution, essentially due to the insistence by permanent members of the Security Council that their consent would be necessary. At the 2010 Kampala Review Conference, amendments to the Rome Statute were adopted that included a definition of the crime as well as elaborate provisions for its prosecution that did not require preliminary endorsement by the Security Council.

4 Structure of International Criminal Courts

That criminal courts, be they national or international, manifest both independence and impartiality is a feature that should be beyond debate. Should a text be necessary, Art. 10 of the Universal Declaration of Human Rights suffices: "Everyone is entitled in full equality to a fair and public hearing by an independent and impartial

[64] Rome Statute of the ICC, Art. 7.2.a.

[65] *Prosecutor v. Kunarac et al.* (Judgment) [2002] IT-96-23/1-A, para. 98, n. 114; *Situation in Kenya* (Dissenting Opinion of Judge Hans-Peter Kaul) [2010] ICC-01/09-19, paras 54–70.

tribunal, in the determination of his rights and obligations and of any criminal charge against him." At the national level, well-established practice that has matured over centuries provides the formal structure by which courts are insulated from improper interference in their work. The rule of law, ensured by constitutional provisions and the availability of judicial review, as well as international norms and their enforcement through treaty bodies and international human rights courts, are present in order to copper-fasten the integrity of the judiciary.

But at the international level, the mechanisms for ensuring independence and impartiality of criminal courts and tribunals do not operate as clearly. In part, this is an inevitable consequence of the temporary nature of such institutions, where judges and prosecutors are elected or appointed, often following a rather opaque process, to relatively short terms of office. The Rome Statute of the ICC satisfactorily addresses many of the difficulties of the temporary courts and tribunals, providing for nine-year mandates that are non-renewable, and partially clarifying such important issues as the grounds and procedure for suspension or removal from office.

At Nuremberg and Tokyo, there was no appeal to a higher court. This changed with the establishment of the ICTY in 1993, it being acknowledged that appeal from conviction was an imperative dictated by international human rights standards. Most other international courts and tribunals confine themselves to a single tier, the notable exception being the ECtHR which allows for a *de novo* recourse to its seventeen-judge Grand Chamber following a ruling of a seven-judge Chamber. The existence of permanent appeals chambers in the modern international criminal tribunals has probably encouraged a very generous approach to interlocutory appeal of various evidentiary and procedural matters, something that is generally frowned upon by national justice systems. Also, in contrast with the national models, the judges themselves exercise a high level of control over their own governance. For example, the president and the composition of the appeals chamber are often determined by the judges sitting in plenary session, whereas at the national level such decisions are usually the preserve of the executive branch of government.[66]

International criminal courts have provided a battleground for proponents of different national models of judicial organization. In adversarial-type systems, the pre-trial preparation is generally governed by the parties, defense and prosecution. Inquisitorial models allow for more robust judicial intervention at an earlier stage in the proceedings. There is no doubt that Nuremberg and Tokyo, as well as the early ad hoc tribunals for the former Yugoslavia and Rwanda, followed an essentially adversarial model by which judicial oversight and involvement was absent until preparations for trial were ripe. The Rome Statute, however, tilted toward a more inquisitorial approach by the establishment of pre-trial chambers

[66] See, in this handbook, A Seibert-Fohr, Ch. 35, at section 1, on international judicial ethics.

and the requirement that the Prosecutor "investigate incriminating and exonerating circumstances equally" so as "to establish the truth."[67] The Special Tribunal for Lebanon and the Extraordinary Chambers of the Courts of Cambodia go even further in their adoption of inquisitorial approaches. Because both institutions operate in regions once under French influence and control, they are inevitably more receptive to continental criminal procedure. In contrast, the Special Court for Sierra Leone, operating in a former colony of the British Empire, is probably the most rigorously adversarial of the international criminal courts.

All of the international criminal tribunals host two main organs, the judiciary and the prosecution. These must be kept separate and distinct, although in practice, because of the size of international criminal justice institutions, they are often housed within the same building. The administrative functions of international courts are usually the responsibility of a "registry." Defense counsel tend to operate outside the formal structure of international courts or tribunals, although there may be a small office charged with assisting unrepresented defendants such as the Principal Defender at the Special Court for Sierra Leone and the Office of Public Counsel for the Defence at the ICC. A degree of supervision of the defense bar may be exercised by the registry, especially to the extent that the defense lawyers are remunerated by the court's own legal aid system. Nothing prevents an accused from employing his or her own private counsel, although defendants who do not benefit from legal aid are very much the exception. With the proliferation of international criminal courts, there is a growing body of highly competent and experienced defense lawyers, some of whom honed their skills working initially for the prosecution.[68]

International criminal courts and tribunals lack many of the features of a fully-developed criminal justice system at the national level. The most significant absence is a prison or penitentiary regime. Although the tribunals have their own detention facilities or lease them from national authorities, these are temporary in nature and are meant to house accused persons during the trial procedure. Upon conviction, the criminal is sent to a national prison. Practice varies as to the amount of supervision of the detention regime exercised by the national authorities, for example in matters of conditional release, and the ongoing involvement of the tribunal itself in such matters.

The international justice mechanisms are extraordinarily expensive. At one point, it was estimated that the two ad hoc tribunals established by the United Nations were costing the institution about 10 percent of its total budget. In reaction to the huge expense of these institutions, which was almost certainly not anticipated when they were created, the United Nations opted for other models whereby the financial

[67] Rome Statute of the ICC, Art. 54.1.a.

[68] See, in this handbook, Gibson, Ch. 32, at section 3 on the subject of defense counsel in international criminal trials.

burden was borne by voluntary contributions, generally coming from so-called "interested states." The inevitable result was to focus international justice upon crises that were strategically important to wealthy states, that is, those who would bankroll the work. Another undesirable consequence of funding by voluntary contribution was instability because the institutions often found themselves with empty bank accounts, uncertain as to whether their judicial work could continue. Nor was such a situation ideal in terms of judicial independence and impartiality. Precisely to avoid such defects, the ICC is premised on assessed contributions from its members following a scale developed within the United Nations. Voluntary contributions, although not explicitly excluded, are tightly controlled and in practice frowned upon. When the Security Council refers work to the court, the Rome Statute requires that this be funded by the United Nations.[69] Despite the Security Council's refusal to provide financial support when situations have been referred,[70] the court has proceeded without significant objection and paid for the prosecutions from its general funds.

5 Relationship with other Courts and Tribunals

There is no hierarchical relationship amongst the international criminal courts and tribunals. Most would insist that they are not subject to a strict rule of *stare decisis*, even within the institution itself, although decisions of other chambers at the same level and even of appeals chambers are treated with deference and have a persuasive if not a binding effect. The same applies at the inter-institutional level, where principles and interpretations adopted by one body resonate through the jurisprudence of the other. There has been a certain amount of movement by judges from one tribunal to another, a factor that has contributed to this phenomenon.

Nevertheless, significant differences in approach have manifested themselves in the case law even where the applicable legal provisions are identical or similar, or where there is no relevant text to provide direction to judges. Some of this divergence, as it relates to genocide and crimes against humanity, has already been discussed. It also presents itself at the procedural level. For example, judges at the ad

[69] Rome Statute of the ICC, Art. 115.b.

[70] UN Res 1593 (2005) UN Doc S/RES/1593, OP 7; UN Res 1970 (2011) UN Doc S/RES/1970, OP 7.

hoc tribunals, perhaps inspired by common law adversarial traditions but nevertheless on benches exhibiting a large degree of judicial pluralism, have been rather tolerant of so-called "witness proofing."[71] This is a process by which counsel prepare their witnesses for testimony, including cross-examination. By comparison, at the ICC the extent of witness-proofing has been sharply curtailed.[72]

The international criminal courts and tribunals proudly proclaim their commitment to international human rights standards. Judicial decisions frequently make reference to the case law of the ECtHR and the United Nations Human Rights Committee with respect to due process and rule of law issues. Nevertheless, they have managed to resist any meaningful oversight by the international human rights bodies. In effect, by participating in an international criminal court, a state may deprive accused persons subject to their jurisdiction of a final remedy to an international human rights body. Or, this may be the consequence of a Security Council referral. The precedent for such a firewall between international criminal courts and international human rights institutions goes back to the aftermath of Nuremberg. Rudolf Hess, who was sentenced to life imprisonment by the IMT, unsuccessfully petitioned the European Commission of Human Rights on various matters. The commission held that it was without jurisdiction to review the work of an international body such as the four-power committee responsible for the detention of Hess.[73] Similar questions have arisen more recently, given the presence, on European soil, of activities and detainees (with the exception of the Special Tribunal for Lebanon, at least for the time being) of all of the international criminal courts.[74]

In February 2007, the ICJ issued a final ruling in a case that had been filed 14 years earlier and that concerned the conflict in Bosnia and Herzegovina during the early 1990s. While its proceedings had plodded along, the ICTY had issued several important rulings on the nature of the conflict, and more particularly on whether a range of atrocities perpetrated by Serb forces should be labelled genocide. For the most part, the Yugoslavia Tribunal had rejected the genocide charge, but with one exception: the July massacre of thousands of men in the Srebrenica enclave. Lawyers for Bosnia and Herzegovina urged the ICJ to go much further than the ad hoc Tribunal, noting in particular that the burden of proof was not as

[71] *Prosecutor v. Limaj et al.* (Decision on Defense Motion on Prosecution Practice of "Proofing Witnesses") [2004] IT-03-66-T; *Prosecutor v. Karemera et al.* (Decision on Interlocutory Appeal Regarding Witness Proofing) [2006] ICTR-98-44-AR73.8.

[72] *Prosecutor v. Lubanga* (Decision Regarding the Practices Used to Prepare and Familiarize Witnesses for Giving Testimony at Trial) [2007] ICC- 01/04-01/06.

[73] *Hess v. United Kingdom* (1975) App. 6231/73, 2 D&R 72.

[74] E.g., *Milošević v. Netherlands* (2002) App. No. 77631/01 [rec.]; *Naletilić v. Croatia* (2000) App. No. 51891/99 [rec.]; *Blagojević v. Netherlands* (2009) App. No. 49032/07 [rec.]; *Galić v. Netherlands* (2009) App. No. 22617/07 [rec.].

high in matters of state responsibility. In its ruling, the ICJ consistently endorsed and adopted the findings of the Yugoslavia Tribunal. On the matter of the burden of proof, it recalled that "charges of exceptional gravity must be proved by evidence that is fully conclusive."[75] Accordingly, the court showed great deference for the factual findings of the specialized criminal tribunal,[76] as well as for its conclusions on matters of international criminal law.

There was one exception: the controversial conclusion of the ICTY that Serbia had exercised "overall control" over the Bosnian Serbs. This had been a sore point since 1999, when the Appeals Chamber of the Yugoslavia Tribunal explicitly departed from a precedent set by the ICJ more than a decade earlier.[77] Ruling against the United States of America in a case filed by Nicaragua, the ICJ had required that "direct control" be shown in establishing the liability of a state for paramilitaries operating outside its own borders.[78] The court reaffirmed the point in its 2007 judgment, declaring that the "overall control" test "is unsuitable, for it stretches too far, almost to breaking point, the connection which must exist between the conduct of a state's organs and its international responsibility."[79] The court behaved much like an apex court in a national system acknowledging the expertise of a lower, specialized tribunal, but insisting that it remains the final arbiter when questions of general law are concerned.

6 Concluding Remarks

The enormous productivity of the international criminal courts and tribunals in the two decades beginning in 1993 has built an impressive body of case law. Some of it is quite specific to the peculiarities of the legal framework of its source, but most is germane to other institutions and even transposable in some circumstances to the domestic legal environment. Alongside the rich judicial activity is an equally

[75] *Application of the Convention on the Prevention and Punishment of the Crime of Genocide (Bosnia and Herzegovina v. Yugoslavia [Serbia and Montenegro])* [2007] ICJ Reports, 43, para. 209.

[76] *Application of the Convention on the Prevention and Punishment of the Crime of Genocide*, note 75, para. 223.

[77] *Prosecutor v. Tadić* (Judgment) [1999] App. 6231/73, para. 146.

[78] *Military and Paramilitary Activities in and against Nicaragua (Nicaragua v. U.S.)* (Merits) [1986] ICJ Rep 14, para. 115.

[79] *Application of the Convention on the Prevention and Punishment of the Crime of Genocide*, note 75, at para. 406.

dynamic academic literature. In 1993, even the largest university libraries had a small shelf at best with relevant monographs, most of them written or edited by Cherif Bassiouni and Benjamin Ferencz. There were no specialized journals in the discipline. Twenty years later, there are at least three academic journals as well as an immense catalogue of single-authored books and collections of essays. Most of this is legal scholarship, with a certain amount in the discipline of international relations. What is largely missing is serious research in the criminology of international crime. This is a gap to be filled.

Historically, international criminal courts and tribunals have followed cycles of activity. An initial burst, following the end of World War I, effectively launched the idea but generated little in the way of concrete accomplishments. Within a few years, the idea had faltered. It was really only kept alive during the inter-war years as a result of efforts by academic and professional bodies. The second phase began during World War II. It lasted about a decade. The period was enormously fecund for international criminal law, producing not only successful tribunals and enduring case law, but also in generating positive legal provisions including those of the 1948 Genocide Convention and the 1949 Geneva Conventions. But again, everything went into hibernation for a period of decades. Interest in international criminal justice only began to revive again in the 1980s through the work of the ILC on the Code of Crimes, a process that was surely nourished by the growing human rights movement. The first of many international criminal courts and tribunals was established in 1993.

Most of the institutions of the modern period were meant to be temporary in nature. Indeed, several of the most important have virtually completed their work and are preparing to transfer any future functions to residual mechanisms. It had long been assumed that the ICC would fill the gap, replacing a complex mixture of ad hoc institutions with a coherent and consistent permanent body. Yet, in so many respects the ICC had underperformed by comparison with the temporary institutions. In its first decade of operation, it managed to complete a single trial of a mid-level warlord. An indication of the relative gravity of the matter is the sentence of 14 years' imprisonment imposed by the Trial Chamber. The curious result is that after two decades of constant growth and activity within the sector, it now seems likely to undergo very considerable shrinkage. Is it possible that a third cycle of decline is taking place? Despite the lacklustre performance of the ICC, enthusiasm for the institution remains very high. There is a strong commitment within civil society for criminal prosecution as one of the principal ways of addressing large-scale human rights abuses. But as Mark Twain is reported to have said, nothing is more difficult to predict than the future.

Research Questions

1. The discipline of criminology is relatively sophisticated with respect to so-called ordinary crimes, but largely absent at the international level. Can criminology make a useful contribution to international criminal justice?
2. Does the hybridization of international criminal law at the procedural level, where elements of quite different procedural regimes are mixed, inadvertently contribute to unfairness?
3. Is the aim of depoliticizing international criminal justice realistic? Are the international courts in fact inherently political in nature, and to that extent quite different and distinct from national criminal courts that address ordinary crimes?
4. Should we expect a merging of the national and the international in favor of a globalized criminal justice that deals with all forms of criminal behavior and not just what are called international crimes?

Suggested Reading

Bernaz, N and Schabas, W (eds), *Routledge Handbook of International Criminal Law* (London and New York: Routledge 2010).

Boister, N and Cryer, R, *The Tokyo International Military Tribunal* (Oxford University Press 2008).

Fernandez J and Pacreau X (eds), *Commentaire article par article du Statut de Rome de la Cour pénale internationale* (Paris: Pedone 2012).

Hankel, G, *Die Leipziger Prozesse, Deutsche Kriegsverbrechen und ihre strafrechtliche Verfolgung nach dem Ersten Weltkrieg* (Hamburg: Hamburger Edition 2003).

Schabas, W, *The UN International Criminal Tribunals: the former Yugoslavia, Rwanda and Sierra Leone* (Cambridge University Press 2006).

Schabas, W, *The International Criminal Court: A Commentary on the Rome Statute* (Oxford University Press 2010).

Schabas, W, *Introduction to the International Criminal Court*, (4th edn, Cambridge University Press 2011).

Stahn, C and Sluiter, G (eds), *The Emerging Practice of the International Criminal Court* (Leiden: Brill 2009).

Stahn C and El Zeidy, MM (eds), *The International Criminal Court and Complementarity* (Cambridge University Press 2011).

Taylor, T, *The Anatomy of the Nuremberg Trials: A Personal Memoir* (New York: Knopf 1992).

Triffterer, O (ed.), *Commentary on the Rome Statute of the International Criminal Court, Observers' Notes, Article by Article* (2nd edn, Munich: C.H. Beck, Hart Publishing, Nomos Verlagsgesellschaft mbH 2008).

CHAPTER 11

INTERNATIONAL HUMAN RIGHTS COURTS

SOLOMON T EBOBRAH*

1 Introduction

International human rights contribute significantly to the increased legalization and judicialization of international relations and politics, both in terms of number of international adjudicative bodies and their increased usage. The traditional

* Extra-Ordinary Lecturer, University of Pretoria and Senior Lecturer, Niger Delta University, Nigeria.

landscape of international adjudication, dominated by states and state-related concepts, has been considerably altered by the emergence of international human rights law and practice. Thus, any attempt to understand international adjudication must address international human rights courts (IHRCs).

What is an "international human rights court"? In its strictest meaning, an international human rights court is an international court whose *ratione materiae* jurisdiction is attached to a binding international human rights instrument.[1] Generally, dedicated IHRCs are created specifically to supervise the implementation of their respective human rights treaties. As such, those courts function solely to decide on human rights violations on the basis of specific human rights treaties. Currently, there are three such courts (in order of appearance): the African Court on Human and Peoples' Rights (ACtHPR), the Inter-American Court of Human Rights (IACtHR), and the European Court of Human Rights (ECtHR).

However, if one were to employ a less strict definition of IHRCs, focusing more on the effects than structure, then there is a second, less obvious kind of IHRC, which we could loosely call "non-dedicated human rights courts." These are international courts created for purposes other than the supervision of international human rights treaties. Often, these are courts created primarily to supervise regional economic integration or political integration treaties. The courts in this category exercise human rights jurisdiction that has been acquired and legitimated either through years of practice and sustained engagement with other actors in their system, or by express conferral by states, or by a combination of both.

There exists a third category of IHRCs, which can also be included in the class of "non-dedicated human rights courts." These are courts which, like the courts in the second category, were created for purposes other than the supervision of human rights treaties. The courts in this third category commonly hear and decide human rights and rights-related cases on the basis of other branches of international law[2] or on the basis of municipal constitutional or statutory law.[3] Generally, the human rights jurisdiction exercised by the courts in this third category is still evolving and

[1] F Viljoen, *International Human Rights in Africa* (2nd edn, Oxford University Press 2010) 436, 437. Viljoen confronted a similar challenge in a bid to determine treaties that fall under the substantive jurisdiction of the African Human Rights Court. First, he tackled the question whether treaties with some human rights content qualify as "human rights treaties" to fall under the substantive jurisdiction of the court. He preferred a liberal interpretation that accommodates any treaty with human rights content rather than just classical human rights treaties.

[2] For instance, the international criminal courts and tribunals hear cases involving issues relevant to human rights, but the body of law that such tribunals apply is, strictly speaking, not international human rights law.

[3] Certain international courts such as the Caribbean Court of Justice hear and determine appeals from national courts that address human rights issues. However, the applicable law in such cases is usually the domestic laws of the originating state. The European Court of Justice also started off applying fundamental rights as contained in the constitutional laws of the state parties to the European Union Treaty, but it combined this with reference and subsequently reliance on the European Convention on Human Rights.

acquiring increasing legitimacy. The list of non-dedicated IHRCs could be long, and it would cut across all other families of adjudicative bodies identified in this handbook. Because of space constraints, in this chapter we will address only three of them: the Court of Justice of the European Union (CJEU), the Court of Justice of the Economic Community of West African States (ECOWAS CJ), and the Caribbean Court of Justice (CCJ). The CJEU and the ECOWAS CJ are in the second category while the CCJ is in the third category of non-dedicated IHRCs.

This chapter examines certain attributes of IHRCs in order to determine whether they form a distinct judicial system within the budding international legal system. Section 2 describes contemporary "dedicated" and "non-dedicated" international human rights courts. Section 3 discusses the rationale for international human rights adjudication. Section 4 examines fundamental institutional design features and operational concepts common to international human rights courts, while section 5 peeks at the effectiveness of international human rights courts. Section 6 presents a brief conclusion.

2 Profile of Contemporary Human Rights Courts

2.1 Dedicated international human rights courts

"Dedicated" IHRCs currently exist in Africa, the Americas, and Europe.[4] Each of these regions hosts a regional human rights system complete with norms and institutions dedicated to the protection of human rights. The IHRCs in all three regions share certain common attributes, yet each retains distinctive features that are either the outcome of deliberate institutional design at inception or the product of contextual practice over time. An important question is whether the similarities sufficiently forge these courts into a distinct international human rights judicial system.

2.1.1 *The African Court on Human and Peoples' Rights (ACtHPR)*

The ACtHPR was not included in the institutional supervisory framework of the African Charter when the Charter was adopted in 1981.[5] Following sustained civil

[4] As at March 2013, approval had been given by the Arab League for the establishment of an Arab Court of Human Rights which is expected to be a dedicated IHRC.

[5] Viljoen, note 1, at 411, discusses the background to the establishment of the African Human Rights Court.

society pressure, the Protocol to the African Charter on Human and Peoples' Rights on the Establishment of the African Court on Human and Peoples' Rights (African Court Protocol) was adopted on June 9, 1998 by the now defunct Organization of African Unity (OAU).[6] The court consists of eleven judges elected for a once-renewable term of six years. The judges are required to be nationals of any of the member states of the OAU (since 2001 the African Union (AU)). However, only state parties to the court's protocol are allowed to nominate three candidates each for election, out of which two must be nationals of the nominating state.[7] While only state parties may nominate candidates, all AU member states are entitled to participate in electing the judges.[8] The judges are elected in an individual capacity from a pool of jurists of high moral character and recognized practical, judicial, or academic competence and experience in the field of human and peoples' rights.[9] A judge cannot be part of a panel hearing a case involving the state of which he is a national.[10]

The ACtHPR has both contentious and advisory jurisdictions. The contentious jurisdiction extends to cases involving the interpretation and application of the African Charter on Human and Peoples' Rights (African Charter), the African Court Protocol and any other relevant human rights instrument ratified by the states concerned. Once a state ratifies the court's protocol, it accepts the contentious jurisdiction of the court over cases brought by other states, as well such cases initiated by the African Commission on behalf of individuals. Similarly, jurisdiction is accepted over matters initiated by other African intergovernmental organizations. However, jurisdiction over cases brought by non-state actors requires further consent by the state party in the form of a declaration.[11]

The advisory jurisdiction of the ACtHPR is open to the AU, its organs, its member states, and any African organization recognized by the AU, provided the request does not touch on any matter pending before the African Commission. There is some ambiguity regarding the phrase "African organization recognized by the AU," since nothing limits that jurisdiction to intergovernmental organizations. However, there appears to be no justification for non-governmental organizations to be given the opportunity to request an advisory opinion from the court when an option for adversarial proceedings exists.

The ACtHPR can only hear matters that meet certain admissibility requirements, including the exhaustion of local remedies. The court is empowered to receive oral evidence and is required to deliver judgment within 90 days of completing its deliberations. The court's rulings on provisional measures and final judgments are

[6] The African Court Protocol entered into force on January 25, 2004 but the court only became operational in July 2006.

[7] African Court Protocol 1998, Art. 12. [8] Viljoen, note 1, at 420, 421.

[9] African Court Protocol, Arts 11–14. [10] African Court Protocol, Art. 22.

[11] As of September 30, 2013, only seven states (Burkina Faso, Cote d'Ivoire, Ghana, Malawi, Mali, Rwanda, and Tanzania) had made this declaration.

binding, since states commit to compliance under supervision of implementation by the AU Council of Ministers.[12] Although the court started operating in 2006, not many cases have been submitted to the court.[13]

2.1.2 *The Inter-American Court of Human Rights (IACtHR)*

The IACtHR was created in 1969 as a supervisory organ of the American Convention of Human Rights (American Convention). The court started operating in 1979, after the convention entered into force. The IACtHR is an autonomous judicial body composed of seven judges who are required to be nationals of member states of the Organization of American States (OAS) but not necessarily parties to the American Convention. Judges of the IACtHR are elected in their individual capacity from among jurists of the highest moral authority and of recognized competence in the field of human rights. They possess the qualifications required for the exercise of the highest judicial functions in the state of which they are nationals or of the state that proposes them as candidates. Each state party is entitled to nominate three judges, at least one of which should be a national of a state other than the nominating state. Judges are elected by secret ballot for a once-renewable term of six years.

The IACtHR exercises both contentious and advisory jurisdictions. Its contentious jurisdiction extends to all matters regarding the interpretation and application of the American Convention and is only open to the Inter-American Commission of Human Rights and state parties. The advisory jurisdiction covers a wider *ratione materiae*, as it relates to interpretation of the American Convention and "other treaties concerning the protection of human rights in the Americas."[14] Only state parties to the convention and OAS organs—insofar as they keep within their sphere of competence—can access the IACtHR's advisory jurisdiction. Originally, individuals and NGOs played absolutely no part in the processes before the IACtHR. However, in 2010, the Rules of Procedure of the court were amended to give alleged victims of violations a greater role in the actual proceedings in contentious cases brought to the IACtHR by the Inter-American Commission.[15] An important feature of the court's process is that a judge retains the right to sit on the panel of a case brought against a state party of which he or she is a national. An ad hoc judge may be appointed to represent a state involved in proceedings where that state does not have its nationals on the bench.

[12] Generally, see the African Court Protocol, Arts 26–30.

[13] As at December 31, 2012, only about 13 cases had been concluded by the ACtHPR, of which 12 were concluded between 2011 and 2012.

[14] American Convention, Art. 64.

[15] See 2011 Annual Report of the IACtHR, p. 7, which notes that alleged victims or their representatives have to submit written arguments after witnesses have presented their evidence, whereas the Inter-American Commission can only submit a written address if it deems it necessary.

In addition to the requirement that petitions can only be submitted against a state that has made a declaration accepting the jurisdiction of the court, petitions must meet admissibility conditions, which include the exhaustion of local remedies. By Art. 63 of the American Convention, the IACtHR is empowered to issue remedial orders as well as orders for payment of fair compensation where it finds that there has been a violation of convention rights. The IACtHR is also empowered to issue orders of provisional measures. Decisions of the court are final and binding as states undertake to comply with such judgments. Orders for compensatory damages are enforceable according to domestic procedure for execution of judgments against the affected state.

After the IACtHR delivers its judgment in a given matter, it notifies the parties and transmits the judgment to all other states of the convention. The transmission serves as a shaming device to pressure the affected state to comply, just as it conveys the current state and scope of convention rights to all parties. The IACtHR is required to also submit reports of its activities to the OAS General Assembly, highlighting cases of non-compliance and setting out recommendations for action. While this looks like a mandate on the OAS General Assembly to supervise compliance with judgments of the court, it is the IACtHR itself that monitors compliance with its own judgments. The IACtHR claims the monitoring authority from a so-called inherent jurisdiction.

2.1.3 *The European Court of Human Rights (ECtHR)*

In November 1950, the European Convention for the Protection of Human Rights and Fundamental Freedoms (European Convention) was adopted. From inception through to 1998, supervision of the convention was a two-stage process involving the European Commission of Human Rights (ECmHR) first, and the ECtHR eventually, and the Council of Ministers of the Council of Europe (CoE) supervising and supporting both.

At inception, the ECtHR was only endowed with a contentious jurisdiction over cases involving interpretation and application of the European Convention and Protocols.[16] Cases reached the court after they have been considered by the ECmHR and only if the ECmHR decided to transmit them to the court. Originally, where a state had accepted the compulsory jurisdiction of the ECtHR, only the ECmHR or a state party could trigger the court's jurisdiction, three months after the submission of a report on status to the Committee of Ministers.[17] Petitions on behalf of individuals could only be submitted against a state party that had additionally recognized and accepted the competence of the ECtHR to receive individual complaints.

[16] The ECtHR's advisory opinion was added by Protocol No. 2 (adopted 1963), and is only available to the Committee of Ministers for interpretation of the convention. It is rarely used.

[17] European Convention 1950, Art. 44.

From a poor record of three out of ten original state parties accepting the court's competence to receive individual petitions, over time the ECtHR gradually gained acceptance by all members of the CoE. By 1994, with the adoption of Protocol No. 9, the filter of the ECmHR was removed and individuals were given direct access to the court. With the adoption of Protocol No. 11 in 1998, not only was direct access for private non-state actors entrenched, but the contentious jurisdiction of the ECtHR became compulsory with respect to petitions from state parties and private non-state actors alike.

The ECtHR is composed of such number of judges equal to the number of state parties to the convention. Each state party nominates three candidates out of which the Parliamentary Assembly elects one in respect of the given state. The European Convention also sets out admissibility criteria, the most important of which is the requirement to exhaust local remedies.[18] Proceedings before the court are public; witnesses can be called, although the court adopts a largely written procedure, mainly because it has a docket of several thousand cases. Article 41 of the European Convention empowers the ECtHR to order just satisfaction where it finds a violation but the internal laws of the state only allow for partial reparation. Judgments of the ECtHR are final and binding on the parties to the given case, and the Committee of Ministers is responsible for monitoring execution of such judgments. Hence, unlike the IACtHR, the ECtHR does not concern itself with supervising the implementation of its judgments. An important feature of the current procedure of the court is that if a matter is not finalized summarily by a three-judge committee, the presence of the national judge representing a state party is a requirement for continuation. In the event that the national judge is unable to be part of a Chamber panel, the presiding judge will appoint an ad hoc judge for the state.

All three dedicated IHRCs enjoy jurisdiction over human rights treaties of their respective regional human rights system. This creates separate regimes for each of the courts, thus excluding jurisdictional overlap and reducing the risk of jurisprudential conflict. However, the ACtHPR is given competence over treaties adopted on platforms other than the AU, insofar as such have been ratified by the relevant African states. From the perspective of legitimacy and authoritativeness, the competence of the judges of the ACtHPR over non-AU human rights documents is debatable. Further, at least at inception, all three courts operated two-tier structures, allowing states to progressively attune to the idea of supranational adjudication without the hazard of facing a full-scale international court.[19] Judicialization of international human rights has therefore been evolutionary rather than revolutionary. Additionally, the common requirement that prospective judges have a human

[18] European Convention, Art. 35.

[19] Although the African human rights system began operation with only the African Commission as its treaty monitoring body, when the idea of a court was introduced, similar to the other two regional systems, a two-tiered structure was created.

rights qualification sets IHRCs apart from other international tribunals and arguably justifies the authoritative value of their judgments before national courts. This also means that, in judicial dialogues, IHRCs export more than they import, at least within the sphere of human rights.

As far as their contentious jurisdictions are concerned, the nature of access that non-state actors enjoy before IHRCs differs significantly. Under the African Court Protocol, indirect access, via the commission, against a state by non-state actors is guaranteed once the state accepts the jurisdiction of the ACtHPR by ratifying the court's Treaty. However, direct access requires a further expression of consent. Under the ACtHPR regime, the state under scrutiny does not have the benefit of having its representative on the panel and therefore, theoretically, has very little if any direct influence on the decision-making process of that court. By contrast, both the IACtHR and the ECtHR regimes permit (and indeed insist on) the right of a respondent state to have its representative on the panel. Despite this assurance of state party representation, the IACtHR does not allow non-state actors direct access. The ECtHR has progressed from prohibition of direct access for non-state actors to a regime of compulsory direct access for that category of prospective litigants. Despite the absence of direct non-state actor access in the IACtHR regime, that regime follows the ECtHR in terms of volume of usage and challenges the wisdom that greater direct access potentially improves usage of IHRCs.

2.2 "Non-dedicated" International Human Rights Courts

Other than the so-called "dedicated" IHRCs, a number of other international courts, with differing frequency, decide cases that require the application of international human rights instruments or (in one case) domestic laws that clone international human rights instruments. These can be termed "non-dedicated human rights courts." Three examples are the CJEU, the ECOWAS CJ, and the CCJ. The CJEU has been discussed in this handbook in Chapter 5. Basic information on the structure and jurisdiction of the ECOWAS CJ and the CCJ can be found elsewhere.[20] We will thus only make mention of their work as human rights courts.

2.2.1 *Court of Justice of the European Union (CJEU)*

At inception, the CJEU had no jurisdiction in the field of human rights. By the late 1960s, challenges from the municipal courts of certain member states forced the CJEU to claim jurisdiction in the field of human rights on the basis that it formed

[20] R Mackenzie et al. (eds), *The Manual on International Courts and Tribunals* (2nd edn, Oxford University Press 2010) at 253 and 278.

part of the general principles of law which the court was empowered to apply.[21] The CJEU asserted further that "international treaties for the protection of human rights... can supply guidelines which should be followed within the framework of Community law."[22] Increasingly, the CJEU narrowed its competence in international human rights law to application of the European Convention on Human Rights and Fundamental Freedoms (ECHR), moving from its use as a source of inspiration to invoking it as a source of rights in litigation before the CJEU.[23] By 1987, when the Single European Act Amending the European Economic Community (EEC) Treaty was adopted, the ECHR had become expressly mentioned as a source of fundamental rights in the European Communities. With the adoption of the EU's Lisbon Treaty in 2009, the ECHR and the European Charter of Fundamental Rights have become the two most important international human rights treaties that the CJEU applies within the framework of its human rights jurisdiction.

A basic feature of human rights adjudication before the CJEU is that the court's jurisdiction is only operative within the context of EU Community law and its application or derogation by an EU member state or institution. By Arts 226 and 227 of the Amsterdam Treaty, access to the CJEU is open to the European Commission and member states of the EU for action against failure of a state to perform obligations under the Treaty. Natural and legal persons enjoy access against certain EU organs and institutions for the purpose of seeking review of the legality of acts addressed to such persons. However, non-state actor access to the CJEU against EU member states is mostly indirect, as it involves the participation of the municipal courts of the states through the preliminary ruling procedure contained in Art. 234 of the Amsterdam Treaty. With the CJEU's adherence to the principles of subsidiarity, the preliminary ruling procedure has been the most common and effective means by which international human rights adjudication occurs in the CJEU framework.

2.2.2 *Court of Justice of the Economic Community of West African States (ECOWAS)*

Originally characterized as the "Tribunal" of the ECOWAS Community under the 1975 founding ECOWAS Treaty, the Court of Justice of the ECOWAS (ECOWAS CJ) was formally established by Protocol in 1991. Its main function was to "ensure the observance of law and of the principles of equity in the interpretation and application of the... Treaty." Under its original protocol, access to both the ECOWAS CJ's contentious and advisory jurisdiction was only

[21] See *Stauder v. City of Ulm* [1969] Case 29/69, ECR 419.
[22] *Nold KG v. Commission of the European Communities* [1974] Case 4/73, ECR 491.
[23] *Rutili v. Minister for the Interior* [1975] Case 36/75, ECR 1219.

open to member states and organs or institutions of ECOWAS. The adoption of the 2005 Supplementary Protocol on the ECOWAS CJ radically changed both the jurisdiction of and access to the court. Significantly, the Supplementary Protocol granted access to individuals in human rights cases, and to corporate bodies for acts or omissions of a community official which violate the rights of the corporate body. Cases submitted by non-state actors are admissible insofar as they are not pending before another international court, but there is no requirement that litigants exhaust local remedies before bringing such cases. Notably, the human rights jurisdiction of the ECOWAS CJ is not tied to any specific human rights instrument since there are no ECOWAS human rights treaties. Accordingly, the ECOWAS CJ has adopted the African Charter as its treaty of reference since certain provisions of the 1993 revised ECOWAS Treaty make reference to that charter. However, the ECOWAS CJ's adoption and application of the African Charter is not exclusive, as other international human rights instruments are invoked in claims before the court.

2.2.3 *The Caribbean Court of Justice (CCJ)*

The Agreement Establishing the Caribbean Court of Justice was adopted in 2001 but the CCJ was only inaugurated in April 2005. The CCJ is a *sui generis* in the family of international courts, as it is both a municipal court and an international court. In its capacity as an international court, the CCJ enjoys original contentious and advisory jurisdiction on matters involving the interpretation and application of the Treaty of the Caribbean Community and applies rules of international law. In relation to this international court character, the human rights jurisdiction of the CCJ is still prospective and relates to treaty provisions that prohibit discrimination and guarantee the right to free movement of workers on the one hand, and the right to establishment of self-employed people on the other.[24]

The CCJ's credentials as a human rights court are more robust in relation to the court's character as a municipal court. As the highest appeal court for certain states in the Caribbean region,[25] the CCJ hears and determines appeals from lower municipal courts on civil and criminal matters. A number of these cases touch on human rights issues. The CCJ's relevance in a discussion of IHRCs partly arises from the fact that it facilitates access to the enjoyment of rights protected in international instruments as well as processes of international human rights law. In both situations, the CCJ directly or indirectly applies international law.

[24] See N Bernaz, "Delivering Justice in the Caribbean: A Human Rights Assessment of the CCJ" (2012) Public Law 703.

[25] Guyana, Barbados, and Belize are currently parties to the CCJ's appellate jurisdiction.

3 The Rationale for International Human Rights Adjudication

Right from the onset of the internationalization of human rights, it was recognized by stakeholders that the protection of human rights is more effective, and therefore preferably should take place, closest to the beneficiaries of human rights guarantees. This presupposes the protection of rights at the municipal level. Added to the fact that international adjudication of rights necessarily limits the sovereignty of states, it is essential to identify the motivation for and the justification of international human rights adjudication. Apparently, different actors have different motivations or justifications for participating in international human rights adjudication.

Although the evolution of international human rights hinges on the collective resolve to put domestic practices under scrutiny in order to avoid deterioration of the kind that led to World War II, there are different theories to explain why states subscribe to international human rights treaties. While states in different regions might have different motivations for subjecting themselves to international adjudication, some of those theories also explain why states accept international human rights adjudication.[26]

States might "self-bind," i.e. accept the jurisdiction of IHRCs, to lock in commitment to human rights treaties and ensure that changes in administration do not jeopardize such commitment. This motivation is linked to the reputational concerns of states and their desire to demonstrate that a commitment to respect international obligations will be adhered to for as long as the state remains a member of the given treaty regime. Similar to Elster's argument in his discussion on addiction and precommitment, states that have undergone some level of democratization, but dread relapse into undemocratic governance, may commit themselves and succeeding municipal regimes to international treaties.[27] Such a commitment is sustained when membership of the treaty regime is fortified by signing up to an accompanying international adjudicative system.[28] Helfer captures this in his argument that states benefit from enhanced credibility when they delegate powers to international adjudicative bodies.[29] In such cases, a justification for international human rights

[26] Generally, see A Moravcsik, "The Origins of Human Rights Regimes; Democratic Delegation in Postwar Europe" (2000) 54 International Organization 211.

[27] J Elster, *Ulysses Unbound: Studies in Rationality, Precommitment, and Constraints* (Cambridge University Press 2000) 64–5.

[28] Peru's failed attempt to avoid treaty obligations under the Inter-American System as a result of the refusal of the IACtHR to recognize the attempt at withdrawal is one example of this point. The Peru example can be contrasted with the Greek pull-out from the European system after military takeover in the 1960s.

[29] L Helfer, "Why States Create International Tribunals: A Theory of Constrained Independence" in Stefan Voigt et al (eds), *International Conflict Resolution* (Mohr Siebeck 2006) 255–76.

adjudication is that it sustains pressure on democratic states to remain democratic while at the same assisting undemocratic, as well as democratizing states, to strengthen municipal human rights regimes.

Occasionally, governments might be motivated by a desire to show the world that they have nothing to hide. They might be convinced their own municipal system for human rights protection is so effective that it shields them from international adjudication. In other cases, governments might have no illusion of the effectiveness of their municipal human rights system, but they might be convinced that their citizens would be too impoverished, too timid, too ignorant, or too frightened to take advantage of the potentials of international adjudication. The choice to submit to the jurisdiction of IHRCs can also be justified on the grounds that it provides opportunity for authoritative interpretation of international human rights treaties, which are notoriously vague. In the event of disputes as to the correct interpretation of such vague treaty provisions, political actors may prefer "disinterested international judges, rather than actors in powerful Western countries or lawyers appointed jointly with private firms" to resolve such disputes.[30]

From the perspective of the individual, international human rights adjudication is justifiable because it provides a realistic alternative to ineffective or non-existent municipal judicial mechanisms for human rights protection. This applies to states in which political repression undermines the efficacy of municipal courts. In those states, national judges, either out of self-interest or lack of will, might try to avoid offending regime officials who deny citizens the opportunity to enjoy internationally guaranteed rights. In other cases, sections of a state may lack sufficient political clout to secure their interests domestically.[31] In these and in similar situations, international rights adjudication replaces rather than complements municipal judicial proceedings for the protection of rights.

A further justification for international human rights adjudication is that it adds the judicial character of unbiased, apolitical, and relatively certain decision-making, to international human rights supervision. The establishment of IHRCs in regional human rights systems arguably triggers a perception that regional systems, especially the ECtHR, are more effective for the protection of rights than the UN human rights system which continues to operate with quasi-judicial institutions. Although quasi-judicial institutions have contributed significantly to international protection of rights, they have their shortcomings, hence the need for IHRCs.

International quasi-judicial human rights bodies are commonly criticized by some scholars for being mostly composed of state officials with a duty to protect

[30] K Alter, "The Multiple Roles of International Courts and Tribunals: Enforcement, Dispute Settlement, Constitutional and Administrative Review" in J Dunoff and M Pollack (eds), *International Law and International Relations: Synthesizing Insights from Interdisciplinary Scholarship* (Cambridge University Press 2012).

[31] E Benvenisti, "Margin of Appreciation, Consensus and Universal Standards" (1998–1999) 31 International Law and Politics, 484.

state interests. By contrast, international judges are expected to be more independent and less susceptible to political influence. The independence of international judges guarantees that a state need not have a representative on a panel to protect any state interest, since cases ought to be decided apolitically. Thus, it serves the interest of all parties to have very little (if any) political consideration leading up to the final decision.

Another shortcoming of international quasi-judicial proceedings is that they are usually confidential.[32] This confidentiality stands in contrast with the acclaimed transparency of modern, democratic justice systems. Conversely, international courts operate under public scrutiny. In this regard, at least theoretically, IHRCs are considered to be more transparent and less susceptible to negative political influence, and thus better guarantors of international human rights than quasi-judicial bodies.

A further reason why IHRCs are preferable to quasi-judicial bodies is that court decisions are binding in international law, notwithstanding their status in the municipal system of participating states.[33] By contrast, the decisions of the quasi-judicial bodies are, strictly speaking, non-binding "recommendations" or "views." In the African system, recommendations of the Commission are not even final, as they are required to be submitted to the AU Assembly of Heads of State and Government for approval before they become final and ready for publication. However, increasingly, bodies such as the UN Human Rights Committee have made compelling arguments that decisions of quasi-judicial bodies are binding on states to the extent that such decisions constitute authoritative interpretations of the relevant treaties.[34] Considering the character of international law, it is debatable whether there is any practical significance in classifying one set of decisions as binding and another set as "non-binding," since in either case failure by a state to comply would ordinarily not be sanctioned by any central authority exercising coercive power.

Notwithstanding the similarity of enforcement impotence, at least in the context of the Inter-American system, states do not generally comply with decisions of the Inter-American Commission, yet are willing to comply with the judgments of the Inter-American Court.[35] Generally, enforcement of decisions of the courts is a duty of political organs of the parent international organization, which may account for the supposed higher rate of effectiveness of the courts. In reality, political organs

[32] See Viljoen, note 1, at 16 on the confidential nature of the African Commission's work; and M Nowak, "The European Convention on Human Rights and its Control System" (1989) 1 NQHR 100 in relation to the ECHR system.

[33] The status of international law generally and international decisions specifically are functions of the respective municipal legal systems.

[34] UNCHR GAOR, *Bradslaw v. Barbados*, No. 489/1992, Supp No 40, Annex X, at 305, 307 (1994) UN Doc A/49/40.

[35] C Cerna, "The Inter-American Human Rights System" (2001) 95 American Society of International Law Proceedings 75, 77.

rarely use any enforcement powers they might have.[36] For their part, quasi-judicial bodies often have to invent creative "sanctions" such as the reporting obligation to pressure states into compliance.[37] A possible explanation for the higher rate of compliance with IHRCs' decisions relative to decisions of quasi-judicial bodies is that state functionaries might equate the international obligation to comply with the judgment of IHRCs with the obligation to comply with the decisions of their municipal courts.

The evidence-gathering powers of IHRCs may be another justification for international human rights adjudication. For instance, the UN HRC cannot undertake independent fact-finding nor can it hear oral evidence and arguments from parties to its proceedings.[38] Consequently, in situations of divergence in facts, unlike the courts, the UN HRC is unable to employ the crucial judicial tool of firsthand assessment of witness credibility.[39] Thus, the procedure before the UN HRC lacks the adversarial character essential for an alleged victim to confront the agents of the offending state. However, the quasi-judicial organs of the regional human rights systems are not very dissimilar to IHRCs in this regard, as they commonly conduct oral hearings, which occasionally involve calling witnesses.[40]

Though in no way exhaustive, these justifications for international human rights adjudication offer a glimpse of the comparative advantage of IHRCs. However, some writers contend that adjudication through the individual petition procedure cannot address widespread, massive, and gross violations. In those cases, tools other than adversarial adjudication, which are at the disposal of the quasi-judicial bodies, are better suited to meet the challenges.[41] Nevertheless, the individual case procedures of the courts are very useful mechanisms to "avoid regression into an authoritative structure" and also for "expanding rights" in a manner that "performs a preventive role and serves as an early-warning function."[42] The right of petition has the additional value of "satisfying the feelings of justice" of those already used to the sophisticated municipal Western-type judicial remedies.[43] Overall, adjudication

[36] The threat of enforcement may pressure some states to comply but enforcement by coercion in international human rights adjudication is rare.

[37] The experiences of the Inter-American and African systems are good examples. In the case of the UN HRC, a Special Rapporteur for Follow-Up was appointed to ensure a greater degree of compliance. See L Hefferman, "A Comparative View of Individual Petition Procedures under the European Convention on Human Rights and the International Covenant on Civil and Political Rights" (1997) 19 Hum. Rts. Q 78, 103.

[38] L Helfer and AM Slaughter, "Towards a Theory of Effective Supranational Adjudication" (1997) 107 Yale Law Journal 273 at 343.

[39] Hefferman, note 37, at 108.

[40] The Inter-American Commission engages in limited public hearings that involve taking evidence from witnesses. Viljoen, note 1, at 322 also notes that the African Commission accommodates oral hearings by the parties.

[41] C Grossman, "Strengthening the Inter-American Human Rights System: The Current Debate" (1998) 92 Am. Soc'y Int'l L. Proc. 186, 188.

[42] Grossman, note 41.

[43] Nowak, note 32, at 101.

before IHRCs provides the benefit of authoritative interpretation of treaty obligations and "definite resolution of... intractable disputes,"[44] while at the same time apportioning responsibility for violations of treaty obligations and reparation for damages resulting from such violations.[45]

4 The Nature and Workings of International Human Rights Courts

Over the years, IHRCs have developed certain common fundamental institutional design features and operational concepts. Although relatively minor institutional differences exist, the operational concepts employed by the courts differ, at least, in degree of usage. This raises the question whether specific design structures and concepts are necessary preconditions for the effective operation of international human rights courts. It also opens the debate whether there are sufficient similarities to suggest that IHRCs form a distinct judicial system in international law.

4.1 From optional to compulsory jurisdiction?

Historically, because of the traditional consent based nature of international law, international adjudication required explicit state consent. In its 1923 advisory opinion on the *Status of Eastern Carelia*,[46] the Permanent Court of International Justice affirmed that a state could only appear before an international court if that state had consented to take part in those proceedings.[47] IHRCs, at least initially, followed the "optional paradigm." Over time, the jurisdictions of IHRCs have become compulsory.

Between 1953 when the original European Convention entered into force and 1994 when major convention reforms were carried out, the jurisdiction of the ECtHR was optional and dependent on state consent. Although by the 1980s all members

[44] C Romano, "The Shift From the Consensual to the Compulsory Paradigm in International Adjudication: Elements for a Theory of Consent"(2007) 39 International Law and Politics 799.

[45] See also M Schienin, "Towards a world court of human rights?" (2009) 16 Agenda for Human Rights 1, who argues that "human rights courts are mechanisms of accountability for attributing the action to a state or other entity for the assessment whether it is to be held responsible for a human rights violation."

[46] *Status of Eastern Carelia* (Advisory Opinion) [1923] PCIJ (ser. B) No 5.

[47] Normally this applies to inter-state proceedings.

of the CoE had submitted to the jurisdiction of the ECtHR, the 1994 reforms still made the court's jurisdiction compulsory. Thus, of all the existing dedicated IHRCs, the ECtHR stands out as the one whose jurisdiction is entrenched in the operative treaty and is not dependent on a further explicit acceptance.[48]

In contrast to the ECtHR, the designers of the two other dedicated IHRCs impose other consent-barriers on their exercise of jurisdiction.[49] First, states must either explicitly accept the court's jurisdiction by a special declaration or a special agreement on the one hand,[50] or ratify or accede to a separate treaty establishing the given court.[51] In some cases, a second barrier is the requirement that states make an additional declaration of consent to allow non-state actors to submit petitions.[52] Absent such a declaration, non-state actor access can usually take place only indirectly, via an inter-governmental quasi-judicial body. In the case of the IACtHR and the CJEU, there is absolutely no provision for direct access for non-state actors. Accordingly, non-state actors' access is either through reference from national courts[53] or through a commission after the given state has consented to the jurisdiction of the court.[54]

Overall, consent to international human rights adjudication remains relevant in all but a few Europe-based courts. This creates difficulties for any claim that compulsory jurisdiction is now a distinct feature of IHRCs. It also leaves open the question whether there is a link between compulsory jurisdiction and effectiveness of IHRCs. Two-stage consent requirements in the treaties establishing some IHRCs might be explained by the often contentious nature of human rights and, by extension, possibly the need to placate states for the partial sacrifice of sovereignty. Existing literature makes the claim that the Europe-based courts are currently by far the most effective IHRCs. Whether this higher level of effectiveness has anything to do with compulsory jurisdiction is still open to empirical proof.

4.2 Subsidiarity of international human rights adjudication

Subsidiarity is a principle generally associated with international human rights law. It is a complex yet often employed principle (at least in the European context) that

[48] The ECtHR and the CJEU do not require separate declarations recognizing a right of non-state actor access.

[49] With regards to the IACtHR, there is a prior consent requirement for a state to ratify the American Convention even before the declaration recognizing the court's jurisdiction is made.

[50] As is the case of the IACtHR by the requirement in Art. 62.4 of the American Convention.

[51] See Art. 34.4 of the African Court Protocol 1998 as well as Art. 34 of the ECOWAS Protocol A/P.1/7/91 on the Community Court of Justice 1991. It should be noted that the said Art. 34 allows for this latter instrument to enter into force provisionally upon signature and definitely upon the receipt of a number of ratification instruments.

[52] African Court Protocol, Art. 36.4.

[53] As is the case with the CJEU.

[54] As is the case with the IACtHR.

is understood differently by different people. According to Carozza, the principle of subsidiarity entails the requirement that "each social and political group should help smaller or more local ones accomplish their respective ends without... arrogating those tasks to itself."[55] Carter argues that subsidiarity means "... standards are best implemented at the lowest level of government that can effectuate those standards."[56]

A common usage of "subsidiarity" in international human rights adjudication is to define "the relationship between international human rights treaties and domestic law."[57] In one of its earliest judgments, the ECtHR noted that the convention's protection mechanism "is subsidiary to the national systems safeguarding human rights."[58] Accordingly, the ECtHR expressed the opinion that international mechanisms could only make their contribution after "all domestic remedies have been exhausted."[59] Effectively, this dictum considers the exhaustion of local remedies a practical manifestation of the principle of subsidiarity.

The requirement to exhaust domestic remedies is present in all dedicated international human rights regimes, but not necessarily in the non-dedicated regimes. By the indirect nature of international human rights proceedings before the CJEU and the nature of the CCJ jurisdiction, the absence of a requirement to exhaust domestic remedies is understandable. This is not the case with the ECOWAS CJ, which allows for direct, non-state actor access. Although one state[60] has challenged the exclusion of the requirement to exhaust domestic remedies in the ECOWAS CJ regime, other states parties to the ECOWAS CJ have actively cooperated and participated in the court's processes despite the omission of that requirement. However, the risks of jurisdiction competition with national systems and the challenge of fact reception and evaluation before an international court present themselves significantly in the ECOWAS CJ practice.[61] Nevertheless, there is currently no significant evidence to support a claim that exhaustion of local remedies is essential for effective international human rights adjudication. More importantly, exhaustion of local remedies is not exclusive to IHRCs, since other international courts share this feature.

[55] PG Carozza, "Subsidiarity as a Structural Principle of International Human Rights Law" (2003) 97 AJIL 38.

[56] WM Carter, "Rethinking Subsidiarity in International Human Rights Adjudication" (2008–2009) 30 Hamline Journal of Public Law and Policy 319–34.

[57] Carozza, note 55, at 39.

[58] ECtHR *Handyside v. United Kingdom* (1979) App. No. 5493/72, 24 ECtHR (ser. A), para. 48.

[59] *Handyside v. United Kingdom*, note 58.

[60] The Gambia in a number of cases.

[61] The case of *Koroua v. Niger* (2004–2009) CCJELR 217 is an example of these complications.

4.3 Regionalization in international human rights adjudication

Although norm creation in the field of human rights began as a global affair, judicial supervision of implementation and international human rights adjudication has always been a regional affair. The creation of a world court of human rights, albeit an old idea often resurrected, has never gained much traction.[62] As some argue, regional courts have been "established... to move forward with the effective enforcement of human rights in line with regional needs, experiences and legal traditions."[63] The link between regionalism and effectiveness of enforcement comes in the argument that "a self-enforcing and renegotiation-proof international treaty will... consist of only a small subset of countries."[64] Regionalism in international human rights adjudication has specific characteristics and prompts certain consequences that differentiate existing IHRCs.

Regionalism entails proximity in territory, usually resulting in some similarity of purpose and practices that "tends towards homogeneity."[65] IHRCs have been created on the platform of organizations founded by states located within the same region. Consequently, at a general level, it is possible to speak of shared socio-political, economic, and legal cultures within the territorial jurisdiction of each court. States parties to treaties creating these courts also belong to the same human rights treaty regime so that the legitimacy of the applicable basic document is hardly challenged. Further, based on the similarities, commentators find the existence of some level of agreement in the perception of the substance of rights guaranteed[66] and in domestic attitude to the categorization and enforcement of rights.[67] Equally important is the observation that the pattern of rights violations differs from region to region in the same way that "political climate on the ground" and general willingness to comply with the court's orders differ.[68] These regional characteristics in some ways influence the practices and processes of international human rights adjudication in each

[62] K McCall-Smith, "The European Voice in International Human Rights" (2010) 1 Edinburgh Student L Rev 31, 36, records Churchill's call for a world court early in the history of the UN. The main selling point of a world court for human rights seems to be that it would judicialize and unify the supervision of UN-based human rights treaties. However, getting states to buy in to such an idea has always been difficult. Generally, see S Trechsel, "A World Court for Human Rights?"(2004) 1 NW UJ Int'l Hum Rts 3.

[63] G Oberleitner, "Towards an International Court of Human Rights" in Baderin and Ssenyonjo (eds), *International Human Rights Law: Six Decades after the UDHR and Beyond* (Farnham: Ashgate 2010) 359, 363.

[64] E Neumayer, "Do international Human Rights Treaties Improve Respect for *Human Rights*?" (2005) 49 Journal of Conflict Resolution 928.

[65] B Weston et al., "Regional Human Rights Regimes: A Comparison and Appraisal" (1987) 20 Vanderbilt J. Transnatl L. 585, 589.

[66] B Weston et al., note 65. [67] Hefferman, note 37, at 85.

[68] J Cavallaro and S Brewer, "Re-evaluating Regional Human Rights Litigation in the Twenty-First Century: The Case of the Inter-American Court" (2008) 102 AJIL 768.

region. An important point to note is that in the context of international adjudication, regionalism is peculiar to IHRCs. The question is, thus, whether regionalism results in fundamental regional differences in the scope and content of international human rights law.

Although IHRCs all address rights violations, the regionalization of international human rights adjudication affects the nature of cases that are typically brought before each court, the approach to judicial decision-making, the nature of remedies available, and the response to the orders of the courts. For instance, from its inception up until the end of the Cold War, the ECtHR was mostly confronted with cases alleging violation of due process guarantees and similar relatively minor violations. By contrast, the IACtHR has had to deal with cases that concerned violations affecting the physical integrity of the human person. The ECOWAS CJ, for its part, has dealt with cases as diverse as violation of protection from slavery and violation of the right to democratic participation.

It would appear that the prevailing socio-political environment in states within a region cumulatively shape both the volume and the character of adjudication that occur before the courts. In regions where there is a well-developed domestic culture of litigation, people are more willing and able to approach IHRCs. Hence, despite the relative similarity in institutional designs, the courts in Europe are far busier than those in Africa, even though European states are not necessarily worse violators of human rights. Further, as some commentators correctly observe, the difference in the nature of alleged violations that the courts confront also impacts the relative effectiveness of the courts.[69] Thus, notwithstanding the possibility of attributing the high rate of compliance enjoyed by the ECtHR to the potential role of the Committee of Ministers, the IACtHR without an equivalent political organ enjoys encouraging rates of compliance when its orders do not negatively affect powerful interests at the domestic level.[70]

Regional influence may also have a bearing on the attitude of the courts to the principle of subsidiarity, as can be gleaned from the type of cases that courts are willing to declare admissible. IHRCs located in Europe, where independent municipal court systems are well developed, have a tendency to reject repeat cases based on the expectation that similar cases would be adjudicated by municipal courts following earlier jurisprudence of the international court on the same subject matter. The pilot judgment procedure of the ECtHR is representative of this attitude. By contrast, repetition is a feature of the IACtHR system[71] and cannot be ruled out in

[69] Helfer and Slaughter, note 38, at 329.

[70] Generally, see Helfer and Slaughter, note 38; D Hawkins and W Jacoby, "Partial compliance: A comparison of the European and Inter-American Courts of Human Rights" (2010) 6 Journal of Intl Law and Intl Relations 35.

[71] Cerna, note 35, at 78.

the regimes of the Africa-based courts if the experience of the African Commission is anything to go by.

Even more fundamental is the impact of regionalization on the character of orders and remedies granted by the respective IHRCs. Observers of the IACtHR identify four cardinal objectives of remedies in that court's regime. They include reparation through compensation and restitution of rights, prevention of future violations through the training of officials and reform of laws and institutions, investigation and punishment of violators, and protection of victims and witnesses.[72] As "dispensers of corrective justice"[73] all IHRCs award damages upon a finding of violation. However, the willingness to fix a quantum and the actual quantum fixed differ according to region. The more obvious differences, however, can be found in the areas of prevention of future violations, the investigation and punishment of violators, and the protection of victims and witnesses. Whereas the IACtHR habitually makes orders in those areas, until the recent enlargement of the CoE to admit former Communist states, ECtHR's orders very rarely required training of officials or reform of institutions. Although the ACtHPR is yet to be approached for such far-reaching orders, the ECOWAS CJ has demonstrated more eagerness to order reparations than make orders requiring structural changes at the domestic level.[74] Generally, although a few other international courts make orders of reparation, all IHRCs boast of competence to make reparative orders.

The cautious approach of the ECOWAS CJ to judgments that could alter domestic arrangements on the basis of alleged rights violation may be characteristic of its original functions, rather than regional influence, since the CJEU is reputed to be even less eager to require invalidation of state action on the grounds of alleged rights violation. It is also important to note the link between the nature of remedies ordered and the relative frequency of compliance with judgments that the respective courts enjoy.[75] European states with relatively better economies have demonstrated a higher tendency for compliance with judgments than states in the Americas and Africa, even though there have been reports of compliance in those regions.[76] This makes international human rights adjudication more profitable for litigants in some regions than in others.

[72] F Basch et al., "The Effectiveness of the Inter-American System of Human Rights Protection: A Quantitative Approach to its Functioning and Compliance With its Decisions" (2010) 12 SUR Intl J on HR 9, 10.

[73] See C Romano, "Can you Hear me now? The Case for Extending the International Judicial Network" (2009) 9 Chicago Journal of Intl Law 245.

[74] For instance, see the *SERAP v. Nigeria* case (2010) Unreported Suit No ECW/CCJ/APP/12/07.

[75] See Hawkins and Jacoby, note 70.

[76] Hawkins and Jacoby, note 70, concede monetary awards in the ECtHR and IACtHR regimes are more frequently implemented but also suggest that other factors contribute to the high percentage of compliance in the ECtHR regime. They argue further that partial compliance is a zone of reality in the measurement of compliance with decisions of IHRCs.

4.4 Jurisprudential dialogue in international human rights adjudication

Universality of human rights presupposes that people in different regions should enjoy comparable quality of protection of rights. Accordingly, notwithstanding in what region a matter is adjudicated, expectations of results should be comparable. This raises issues of fragmentation, but especially the danger of conflicting jurisprudence, and amplifies the need for coherence, cooperation, and judicial dialogue at the intra-regional and inter-regional levels.[77] At the intra-regional level, there is insufficient material to generate analysis as between the ACtHPR and the ECOWAS CJ. However, as between the CJEU and the ECtHR, there is evidence of jurisprudential dialogue and cross-referencing. Helfer and Slaughter assert that both courts "enhance each other's authority by referring to one another's decisions."[78] Jacobs adds that the CJEU has cited and followed the ECtHR for years.[79] The ECtHR also carefully observes "the case-law of the CJEU and follows it when necessary."[80] Although dialogue and cross-referencing between the CJEU and the ECtHR occur infrequently and are sometimes indirect, it is unavoidable since both courts apply the same instrument—the ECHR. Despite this sort of jurisprudential interaction, occasional conflicting interpretations remain.[81] With the adoption of the EU's Lisbon Treaty and the possibility of EU accession to the ECHR, it remains to be seen what kind of relationship would exist between the two Europe-based courts. There is too little data to sustain analysis of the dialogue between the IACtHR and the CCJ.

Inter-regional dialogue and cross-referencing is not inevitable, since courts apply region-specific instruments. There is even a claim that generally international courts will "sparingly, selectively and reluctantly" cite other courts.[82] However, Romano concedes that some international judges are more likely to cite others.[83] IHRCs are some of those known to cite or acknowledge decisions of their peers. The IACtHR sometimes cites the jurisprudence of the ECtHR to either justify or explain its own position.[84] At other times, the IACtHR avoids comparative

[77] Generally, see Y Shany, *The Competing Jurisdictions of International Courts and Tribunals* (Oxford University Press 2003).

[78] Helfer and Slaughter, note 38, at 323.

[79] F Jacobs, "Judicial Dialogue and the Cross-Fertilization of Legal Systems: The European Court of Justice" (2003) 38 Texas Int'l LJ 547.

[80] JP Costa, "The European Court of Human Rights and its Recent Case Law" (2003) 38 Texas Int'l LJ 455.

[81] Jacobs, note 79.

[82] C Romano, "Deciphering the Grammar of the International Jurisprudential Dialogue"(2009) 41 N.Y.U. J. Int'l L. & Pol. 755, 758.

[83] Romano, note 82.

[84] McCall-Smith, note 62, at 43; Case of *Ximenes-Lopes v. Brazil* (2006) IACtHR; para. 102.

jurisprudence in order to give itself space to widen the scope of protection that it can accord to litigants.[85] The ECtHR occasionally refers only to the jurisprudence of the IACtHR, perhaps because other IHRCs have not generated relevant jurisprudence.[86] The ECOWAS CJ also makes occasional reference to the jurisprudence of the ECtHR but not so much reference to the IACtHR. Considering that dedicated IHRCs are supposed to be masters of their respective human rights treaties, it should have been the case that only non-dedicated IHRCs cite or borrow the wisdom in the case-law of other courts. Hence, reference to the jurisprudence of another regional IHRC may well be acknowledgement of the expertise or experience of the court that is cited, but it could also be as a result of resort to those judgments by counsel appearing in subsequent cases. In fact, Romano's assertion that international judicial dialogue occurs more than is obvious since it can take the form of acculturation aptly captures the experience of IHRCs.[87] The actual volume of dialogue that occurs between IHRCs is perhaps one of the most distinguishing factors that sets them apart from other courts in the international law family. Even in the absence of a formal *stare decisis* rule, IHRCs more commonly engage in active and latent jurisprudential dialogue.

5 Assessing the Effectiveness of International Human Rights Courts

In one sense, effectiveness entails the enjoyment by a court, of direct or indirect compliance with its decision in a manner that protects the rights in the treaty supervised by that court.[88] However, in this handbook, Helfer outlines four distinct ways by which the effectiveness of international courts can be measured.[89] They apply to IHRCs and partly form the basis for the following analysis to assess the individual and collective effectiveness of IHRCs.

[85] See e.g., *Moinawa Village v. Suriname* (2005) IACtHR, which ignored the ECtHR case of *Moldavan and Rostas v. Romania*. Romano, note 82, at 766, also notes this practice and argues that judges omit to cite contradictory decisions in order to minimize conflicts.

[86] The ECtHR's own research records 24 cases in which IACtHR case law has been cited.

[87] Romano, note 82, at 771, 772.

[88] Generally, see Helfer and Slaughter, note 38, at 278; Also see Hawkins and Jacoby, note 70, for a distinction between compliance and effectiveness.

[89] See, in this handbook, Helfer, Ch. 21.

In relation to case-specific effectiveness, IHRCs trigger similar responses. The rate of compliance with monetary reparations is relatively high in all regimes whereas states only partially or hardly ever comply with orders requiring other forms of corrective action.[90] Further, apart from the IACtHR, IHRCs rarely issue detailed "checklist" orders requiring concrete action by states, therefore eliciting lower resistance from states.[91] In all regimes, states comply faster and more thoroughly when orders are not complicated and compliance costs are relatively low.[92] With regards to what Helfer brands "*erga omnes*" effectiveness, in contrast to general international law expectations, IHRCs commonly expect their state parties to adjust behavioral patterns on the basis of existing case law even when states have not been parties to the specific case. The pilot judgment practice of the ECtHR and the IACtHR's practice of alerting all state parties to new judgments are indicative of this trend. IHRCs also generally provoke domestic resistance or at least reaction to rights violation on the basis of international jurisprudence.[93] Finally, the increasing rate of jurisprudential dialogue is an indication of the effectiveness of the ECtHR and IACtHR in norm development.

In comparative terms, the ECtHR is generally considered to be the most effective court as a result of the reportedly high rate of compliance with its decisions.[94] However, the relatively higher compliance in the ECtHR regime can partly be explained by the nature of cases handled by that court and the political stability enjoyed by its state parties. The IACtHR also enjoys some respectable rate of compliance though lower than the ECtHR. There is relatively little material to support any meaningful analysis of compliance of human rights courts in Africa. Yet, the case of the ECOWAS CJ suggests that despite the acclaimed resistance of African states to external control, they are willing to comply with the decisions of African international courts. Finally, the nature of judgments of the CJEU does not create much difficulty for compliance since the CJEU acts more like the review court that it is than as a caricature of an appellate court. Hence, the CJEU also enjoys almost a universal rate of compliance even though this can partly be explained by its relatively strong enforcement and sanction regime.

90 Hawkins and Jacoby, note 70, at 37; Basch et al., note 72, at 18.

91 Hawkins and Jacoby, note 70, compare the IACtHR and ECtHR systems, but other IHRCs also avoid detailed orders requiring state action.

92 Hawkins and Jacoby, note 70.

93 See Costa, note 80, at 458 on the domestic reaction to ECtHR judgments. The International Law in Domestic Courts (ILDC) project has recorded a number of such domestic reactions from all regions of the globe.

94 Hawkins and Jacoby, note 70.

6 Conclusion

Recent trends in the literature allude to the existence of an "emerging system of international law," "community of courts," "international judicial network," and so on.[95] Some view these terms or at least "community of courts" as applying to courts, such that when "mechanisms are overlapping, mutually supportive and mutually dependent... jurisdictions intersect. They apply a similar body of law. They draw on each other's jurisprudence."[96] This chapter has evaluated the nature and workings of IHRCs to establish whether they form a distinct judicial system within the international legal system. There may not be enough to support a claim that IHRCs constitute such a distinct system, but to the extent that IHRCs have mutually supportive and interdependent mechanisms that apply a comparative system of laws, they form a "community of courts."

Research Questions

1. Is there any real link between compulsory jurisdiction and the overall effectiveness of international human rights courts? What impact will compulsory jurisdiction have on the effectiveness of an international human rights court where socio-economic factors are not at their best?
2. Apart from requiring exhaustion of local remedies and granting a margin of appreciation to states, are there other possible manifestations of subsidiarity in international human rights adjudication that can enhance positive state response to international human rights courts?
3. Is *stare decisis* emerging as a "customary" rule in international human rights adjudication? If so, (or if not), is this a desirable state of affairs? What should be the scope and limits of *stare decisis* in international human rights adjudication?
4. What is the exact nature of the relationship between the existing international human rights courts? Is there a global network of international human rights courts or are there merely regional or sub-regional networks of international human rights courts? What factors trigger the perception of a network among judges and court users?

[95] E.g., W Burke-White, "A Community of Courts: Toward a System of International Law Enforcement" (2003) 24 MJIL 1; Romano, note 73.

[96] Burke-White, note 95.

Suggested Reading

Basch, F et al., "The Effectiveness of the Inter-American System of Human Rights Protection: A Quantitative Approach to its Functioning and Compliance with its Decisions" (2010) 12 SUR International Journal on Human Rights 9.

Bernaz, N, "Delivering Justice in the Caribbean: A Human Rights Assessment of the Caribbean Court of Justice" (2012) October, Public Law 703.

ChavaLaudau, E, "A New Regime of Human Rights in the EU?" (2008) 10 European Journal of Law Reform 557.

Dothan, S, "Judicial Tactics in the European Court of Human Rights" 2011, Public Law and Legal Theory Working Paper Series. Available at <http://www.law.uchicago.edu/academics/publiclaw/index.html> accessed July 23, 2013.

Grossman, C, "The Inter-American Human Rights System: Challenges for the Future" (2008) 83 Indiana Law Journal 1267.

Hawkins, D and Jacoby, W, "Partial compliance: A comparison of the European and Inter-American Courts of Human Rights" (2010) 6 Journal of International Law and International Relations 35.

Keller, H, and Stone Sweet, A (eds), *A Europe of Rights: The Impact of the ECHR in National Legal Systems* (Oxford University Press 2008).

Mackenzie, R et al. (eds), *The Manual on International Courts and Tribunals* (2nd edn, Oxford University Press 2010).

Shelton, D, *Remedies in International Human Rights Law* (2nd edn, Oxford University Press 2006).

Steiner, HJ, Alston, P, and Goodman, R, *International Human Rights in Context* (3rd edn, Oxford University Press 2007).

Trechsel, S, "A World Court for Human Rights?" (2004) 1 NW University Journal of International Human Rights 3.

Viljoen, F, *International Human Rights in Africa* (2nd edn, Oxford University Press 2010).

Weston, BH et al., "Regional Human Rights Regimes: A Comparison and Appraisal" (1987) 20 Vanderbilt Journal Transnational Law 585.

CHAPTER 12

COURTS OF REGIONAL ECONOMIC AND POLITICAL INTEGRATION AGREEMENTS

CARL BAUDENBACHER* AND MICHAEL-JAMES CLIFTON**

* Dr. jur., Dr. rer. pol. h.c., President of the EFTA Court, Full Professor of Private, Commercial and Economic Law and Director of the Institute of European and International Economic Law at the University of St. Gallen.

** LL.B. (EU), LL.M. Adv., Barrister, Legal Secretary in the Chambers of President Carl Baudenbacher of the EFTA Court.

1 Introduction

Regional economic and political organizations, of whatever level of integration, often have their own adjudicative body. These entities can be divided into three main groups: permanent courts, ad-hoc arbitral tribunals, and hybrid mechanisms. There are approximately 55 active dispute settlement bodies worldwide,[1] of which 12 are courts of regional economic and political integration agreements.[2] To better understand their functioning, it may be helpful to break them down by genera to determine their similarities, differences, and idiosyncrasies as well as to compare them with other families of international tribunals.

An example of a regional political integration agreement is the "Union State of Russia and Belarus." Article 4.1 of the Treaty on the Establishment of a Union State of 8 December 1999,[3] which entered into force on 26 January 2000, provides that a "Court of the Union State" shall be established. However, this court is yet to be founded. While this Treaty has had little obvious impact due to divergent views as to the model the Union State should take (whether federation, confederation, or European Union (EU)-style union),[4] it has formed the basis for the current plans to create a Eurasian Union by 2015—a proposed economic and political union of Belarus, Kazakhstan, Kyrgyzstan, the Russian Federation, and potentially Tajikistan.[5]

The stillborn Court of the Union State is a clear example of a judicial body of a regional political integration agreement. However, some other courts are less easy to pin down. Certainly the Court of Justice of the European Union (ECJ) may be considered such a court. Regional human rights courts, such as the European Court of Human Rights (ECtHR), could be labeled as part of a

[1] For an overview, see C Romano, "A Taxonomy of International Rule of Law Institutions" (2011) 2(1) JIDS 241–77.

[2] The 12 are: Court of Justice of the European Union (ECJ), EFTA Court, Benelux Economic Union Court of Justice, Economic Court of the Commonwealth of Independent States (CIS), Court of the Eurasian Economic Community, Permanent Review Tribunal of the Mercado Común del Sur (Mercosur), Caribbean Court of Justice (CCJ), Andean Tribunal of Justice (ATJ), Common Court of Justice and Arbitration of the Organization for the Harmonization of Business Law in Africa (OHADA Court), The African Court of Justice and Human Rights, ECOWAS Court of Justice and East African Court of Justice. The North American Free Trade Agreement (NAFTA) and Association of Southeast Asian Nations (ASEAN) use ad hoc arbitration. Mercosur uses both ad hoc arbitration and a court (in a similar way to the WTO).

[3] Treaties and international agreements registered or filed and recorded with the Secretariat of the United Nations [2003] Volume 2121, 1-36929.

[4] A Žulys, "Towards a Union State of Russia and Belarus," Lithuanian Foreign Policy Review, 1516/2005, 148–69, at 157, 160.

[5] See e.g. Channel RT TV, "Eurasian Union: Greater than EU, but not new USSR," edited November 20, 2011 <http://www.rt.com/news/eurasian-union-eu-better-667> accessed July 24, 2012.

political integration agreement. Indeed, it has been argued that "although integration through human rights is an incomplete process, the European courts' trans-organizational co-operation has decisively contributed to effectively setting up a new normative basis for further political integration,"[6] and that "[i]ntegration through human rights is a phenomenon that is increasingly shaping the emergence of a political Europe."[7] Nevertheless, this remains dependent upon how one defines "political integration."

In the following, the three basic genera of regional economic courts or tribunals will be addressed: (1) the ECJ and those courts with an ECJ-esque set-up; (2) bodies following an arbitration model; and (3) hybrid bodies.

2 Deeply Integrating Regional Courts (DIRCs)

The ECJ, the EFTA Court, and the Andean Tribunal of Justice (Tribunal de Justicia de la Comunidad Andina—ATJ) may be characterized as DIRCs. These three courts form part of integration agreement structures which do not only contain free trade rules, but which also regulate economic activity in a more general sense including, for example, competition policy, investment law, product standards, labor law, public procurement law, and intellectual property law.[8] Likewise, these agreements give individuals and business operators far-reaching rights. The EFTA Court and the ATJ were modeled after the ECJ—which was an entirely novel experiment at its inception—and so are best considered slightly apart from the ECJ, as ECJ-esque.

2.1 ECJ

2.1.1 *History, competences, composition, and role*

The ECJ, initially designed to implement the legal framework of the European Coal and Steel Community (ECSC), began operating in Luxembourg in 1952. It was

[6] L Scheeck, "The Relationship between the European Courts and Integration through Human Rights" (2005) 65 Zaör 837–85, 883.

[7] Scheeck, note 6, at 837.

[8] S Claar and A Nölke, "Deep Integration" (2010) 3 E+Z (Development and Cooperation) 114–17.

created in the "classical, continental European, Montesquieu'an third power terms" between the High Contracting Parties and ECSC.[9] Article 8 of the ECSC placed the High Authority (the forerunner of the European Commission) at the apex of the ECSC's institutional hierarchy with the court languishing at the bottom.[10] It was by Art. 164 of the 1957 Treaty of Rome, now Art. 19 of the Treaty on European Union (TEU) that the ECJ was entrusted with ensuring "that in the interpretation and application of the Treaties the law is observed."

The European Union is a supranational economic and political partnership between, at present, 27 countries with common organs. Its economic core is the single market. The ECJ is tasked, in particular, to rule on infringement actions brought by the European Commission or a member state against a member state, to render preliminary rulings upon questions posed by national courts or tribunals on the interpretation of EU law or the validity of acts adopted by the institutions, to decide on actions brought by a member state or a natural or legal person against an institution and to rule in other cases provided for in the treaties.[11] Courts of last resort are, under Art. 267.3 of the Treaty on the Functioning of the European Union (TFEU), obliged to make a reference to the ECJ if a question of EU law is not clear.[12]

The ECJ shall include the "Court of Justice, the General Court and specialized courts."[13] At present, there is only one specialized court: the European Civil Service Tribunal, which consists of seven judges and began operating in 2005. The Court of Justice consists of one judge from each EU member state appointed by common accord of the member states' governments.[14] It is assisted by eight advocates-general who are full members of the court, but not judges. They present an impartial and independent legal opinion in important cases.[15] To be eligible to serve as a judge or an advocate-general, a candidate must be a person whose independence is beyond doubt and who possesses the qualifications required for appointment to the highest judicial offices in his or her country or who is a jurisconsult of recognized competence.[16] The Lisbon Treaty brought about a momentous innovation to the appointment process: the Art. 255 TFEU[17] panel, which gives an opinion on candidates' suitability before the appointments are made.[18]

[9] H Rasmussen, *On Law and Policy in the European Court of Justice: A Comparative Study in Judicial Policymaking* (Dordrecht: Martinus Nijhoff Publishers 1986) 201–2.

[10] Rasmussen, note 9, at 207.

[11] Treaty on European Union (TEU) (Consolidated version 2012), Art. 19.3.

[12] *CILFIT v. Italian Ministry of Health* [1982] Case C-283/81, ECR 3415, 3430.

[13] TEU, Art. 19.1. [14] Treaty on the Functioning of the European Union (TFEU) (Consolidated version 2012), Art. 253.

[15] TFEU, Art. 252. [16] TFEU, Art. 253.

[17] Implemented by Council Decisions of February 25, 2010 (2010/125/EU) and (2010/124/EU).

[18] TFEU, Art. 255. See generally, Lord Mance's speech, "The Composition of the European Court of Justice" (October 19, 2011) <http://www.supremecourt.gov.uk/docs/speech_111019.pdf> accessed July 26, 2012.

The judicial term of office is a renewable period of six years,[19] although the bench is partially renewed every three years.[20] The judges elect a President and Vice-President of the court from among themselves by secret ballot for a renewable term of three years.[21]

The court may sit as a full court, in a Grand Chamber of 15 judges or in chambers of three or five judges, depending upon the importance of the case.[22] The court's deliberations and the judges' vote are secret.[23] Minority judges do not have the right to dissent.

All 23 languages of the EU are used to varying degrees at the ECJ. In direct actions the "language of the case" is that of the application, while for references for preliminary ruling it is that of the referring national court.[24] Hearings are simultaneously interpreted, as required, into those official EU languages relevant in the case at hand. The "working language" of the court remains French. Deliberations are held and judgments first prepared in French before being translated into the language of the case (if not French) and the other official languages. Advocates-General, meanwhile, are free to prepare their opinions in their own EU language.[25]

The ECJ might well be considered as the mother of all the judicial bodies of regional economic frameworks.[26] It may even serve as a role model for global courts.

2.1.2 *General Court*

The General Court (GC)[27] is made up of at least one judge per member state. The appointment procedure is the same as at the Court of Justice, as are the terms of office.[28] GC judges must have the ability required "for appointment to high judicial office"[29] as opposed to "the highest judicial offices" at the Court of Justice. The judges elect their President, for a period of three years, from among themselves by secret ballot.[30] Unlike the Court of Justice, the GC does not have permanent advocates-general. However, that task may be carried out by a judge, although that has not occurred for many years.[31]

19 TFEU, Art. 253.

20 TFEU, Art. 253; Statute of the Court of Justice of the European Union (ECJ Statute) 2012, Art. 9.

21 TFEU, Art. 253; ECJ Rules of Procedure (RoP) 2012, Art. 8.

22 ECJ RoP, Arts 25, 60.

23 ECJ Statute, Art. 35. The procedure for the deliberations may be seen at ECJ RoP, Art. 32.

24 ECJ RoP, Art. 36.3. Also applicable to the General Court.

25 ECJ RoP, Art. 38.8.

26 R Mackenzie et al., *The Manual on International Courts and Tribunals* (2nd edn, Oxford University Press 2010) 250.

27 Founded in 1989 as the Court of First Instance.

28 ECJ Statute, Art. 47.

29 TFEU, Art. 254.

30 TFEU, Art. 254; GC RoP, 7. Heikki Kanninen was elected as the first Vice-President of the General Court on 17 September 2013 although the new GC RoP have yet to be adopted: see Regulation (EU, EURATOM) No 741/2012.

31 ECJ Statute, Art. 49. To give an example, President Vesterdorf later participated in *Rhône-Poulenc v. Commission* [1991] Case T-1/89, ECR II-867.

The GC sits in chambers of five or three[32] judges or, in some cases, as a single judge.[33] It may also sit as a Grand Chamber of 13 judges or as a full court when this is justified by the legal complexity or importance of the case.[34]

2.1.3 *Caseload*

In 2012, the Court of Justice had 632 new cases and completed 595 cases.[35] Of 886 pending cases, 537 were references for a preliminary ruling, 134 were direct actions, and 205 were appeals.[36] The duration of those cases completed in 2012 was, on average, 15.7 months for a preliminary reference, 1.9 months for an urgent preliminary reference (PPU), 19.7 months in direct action cases, and 15.3 months in cases on appeal.[37]

The GC in 2012 received 617 new cases, completed 688 cases and had 1237 cases pending.[38] Of the new cases, 257 were actions for annulment, 238 were intellectual property cases, and 78 concerned special forms of procedure.[39] The average duration of those cases completed in 2011 was 31.5 months for State aid cases, 48.4 months for competition cases, 20.3 months for intellectual property cases, 22.2 months for other direct actions, and 16.8 months for cases on appeal.[40]

From a global comparative perspective, the sheer scale of the EU's judicial set-up is readily apparent. However, such statistics do question the extent to which the ECJ is suffering from "institutional overload" and the consequences in the near future if, as is probable, its human rights jurisdiction substantially increases its caseload.

The ECJ has developed its own rules of interpretation of EU law. It has defined, and in many ways directed, the course of EU integration. This was done by formulating many new concepts and principles including, inter alia, direct effect, primacy, conformity, State liability, proportionality, and other general principles.[41] Its interpretation of the treaties has given decisive impetus to achieving the goal of "an ever closer union among the peoples of Europe."[42]

The reasoning of ECJ judgments remains relatively short, or even laconic, although it has substantially increased in length since the court's foundation[43] (albeit with some exceptions[44]).

[32] In over 80 percent of cases it sits in a formation of three judges, Presentation of the General Court <http:/curia.europa.eu/jcms/jcms/J02_7033/> accessed on July 26, 2012.

[33] GC RoP, Art. 11. [34] GC RoP, Arts 14, 51, 106, 118, 124, 127, 129.

[35] ECJ Annual Report—Provisional Version (2012), 89. [36] ECJ Annual Report, note 35, at 105.

[37] ECJ Annual Report, note 35, at 104. [38] ECJ Annual Report, note 35, at 183.

[39] ECJ Annual Report, note 35, at 185. [40] ECJ Annual Report, note 35, at 191.

[41] For a good introduction see generally, D Chalmers et al., *European Union Law, Texts and Materials* (Oxford University Press 2009).

[42] First Recital to the Preamble of the TFEU.

[43] For example, in *F.E.R.A.M. v. High Authority* [1959] Case 23/59, ECR 501, contains 16 paragraphs of reasoning, while *EMS-Bulgaria Transport OOD v. Direktor na Direktsia "Obzhalvane i upravlenie na izpalnenieto" Plovdiv* (Judgment) [July 12, 2012] Case C-284/11, contains 35 paragraphs of reasoning.

[44] For example the reasoning in Grand Chamber's judgment in the important case *Ruiz Zambrano v. Office National de l'Emploi (ONEm)* (Judgment) [March 8, 2011] Case C-34/09, amounted to 10 paragraphs.

2.2 EFTA Court

2.2.1 *History, competences, composition, and role*

The Agreement on the European Economic Area (EEA), "an international treaty *sui generis* which contains a distinct legal order of its own,"[45] aims at extending the EU single market law to the EEA/EFTA States[46] with the exception of certain common policies such as agriculture, fisheries, taxation, or foreign trade. It is made up of two pillars: one from the EU and another from EFTA. EU and EEA law, which apply in the EU and EFTA pillars of the EEA respectively, form two separate legal orders, but are largely identical in substance.

The EFTA Court is a single instance court. The most important procedures before it are the infringement procedure, whereby the EFTA Surveillance Authority (ESA) or an EEA/EFTA state brings an action against an EEA/EFTA state; the preliminary reference procedure; and actions brought by an EEA/EFTA state or a natural or legal person against ESA. Although rulings rendered in the preliminary reference procedure are called advisory opinions in Art. 34 of the Agreement between the EFTA States on the Establishment of a Surveillance Authority and a Court of Justice (SCA), they are of equivalent authority to an ECJ preliminary ruling.[47] Article 34 SCA does not oblige national courts of last resort to make a preliminary reference if a question of EEA law is not clear.[48] However, the EFTA Court held that an obligation to refer may follow from the duty of loyalty laid down in Art. 3 of the EEA, which mirrors Art. 4.3 of the TEU, and from the principle of reciprocity which is underlying the EEA Agreement as a whole.[49]

The EFTA Court, while certainly a DIRC, is also clearly ECJ-esque. Originally, the EEA contracting parties planned to create an EEA Court consisting of ECJ and EFTA State judges. In its (in)famous Opinion 1/91, the ECJ rejected this idea.[50] Originally intended to comprise seven judges, one from each EFTA State, the EFTA Court lost its prospective member from Switzerland following a negative referendum in December 1992. Once up and running, the judges from Austria, Finland, and Sweden were forced to resign on account of their countries' accession to the EU. The Court has subsequently

[45] *Erla María Sveinbjörnsdóttir v. Iceland* [1998] Case E-9/97, EFTA Ct. Rep, p.5, para. 59; see also *Opel Austria GmbH v. Council of the European Union* [1997] Case T-115/94, ECR, II-39, para. 107.

[46] Norway, Iceland, and Liechtenstein.

[47] S Magnússon, "On the Authority of Advisory Opinions: Reflections on the Functions and the Normativity of Advisory Opinions of the EFTA Court" (2010) 3 Europarättslig Tidskrift 528.

[48] *CILFIT* [1982] Case 283/81, ECR, 3415.

[49] *Irish Bank Resolution Corporation Ltd v. Kaupthing Bank* [2012] Case E-18/11, EFTA Ct. Rep. 592, paras 57–8; even clearer *Jonsson* (Judgment) [March 20, 2013] Case E-3/12, not yet reported, para. 60 (duty to refer "if the legal situation lacks clarity").

[50] Opinion 1/91 [1991] ECR I-6079; B Brandtner, "The 'Drama' of the EEA: Comments on Opinions 1/91 and 1/92" (1992) 3 EJIL 300–28; S Norberg, "Justice in the European Economic Area—The Role of the EFTA Court" in EFTA Court (ed.), *Judicial Protection in the European Economic Area* (Stuttgart: German Law Publishers 2012) 29, 40.

consisted of three judges and six ad hoc judges sitting in a single three-judge formation. The fact that with Norway, Iceland, and Liechtenstein as member states the EFTA pillar resembles a pond with one big and two small fish has in no way affected the Court's functioning. But it has led to certain imbalances in other respects. For example, with one very short interruption, the ESA President—who is appointed by the EEA/EFTA State governments—has always been a Norwegian civil servant. With one exception, all of them returned to government service after their term at ESA.

The criteria for eligibility for and terms of appointment to the EFTA Court bench are identical to those for the ECJ bench.[51] In recent times, Norway and Iceland have had vacancies on the EFTA Court. In Iceland, for the first time, an ad hoc committee of three experts was established to evaluate candidates that reported to the Minister for Foreign Affairs. Meanwhile in Norway, the Foreign Minister decided without the assistance of independent experts.[52] In light of this, the EFTA Court has proposed to the EFTA governments the "establishment of an Evaluation Panel…in line with Article 255 TFEU."[53]

EFTA Court judges are obliged to preserve the secrecy of their deliberations.[54] This is understood to encompass the vote. Therefore the judgments contain no dissenting opinions. The working language of the EFTA Court is English. In direct actions, English must be used by all. In principle, this also applies to any documents submitted to the court. The judgment or order shall only be given in English.[55] Preliminary references may be submitted in the language of the national court.[56] Documents may be handed in by the national court and the parties to the main proceedings in their own language. The latter are also entitled to address the court in their own language during the oral procedure.[57] The ruling is rendered in English and in the language of the national court. Both language versions are authentic, although the non-English version is a simple translation.[58]

On account of, inter alia, the size of the EFTA pillar, the number of cases dealt with by the EFTA Court is limited. The court has, however, decided on the most important issues of EEA law, such as the scope of the homogeneity principle,

[51] Agreement between the EFTA States on the Establishment of a Surveillance Authority and a Court of Justice (SCA) 1992, Art. 30.1 and TFEU, Art. 253.

[52] C Baudenbacher, "Some Thoughts on the EFTA Court's Phases of Life" in EFTA Court (ed.), *Judicial Protection in the European Economic Area* (Stuttgart: German Law Publishers 2012) 23.

[53] SCA, proposed new Art. 30a.2—"The panel shall comprise of five persons: one chosen from among former members of the Court who shall also be Chairman, and one from among the former members of the Court of Justice of the European Union. The other members of the panel, each coming from a separate EFTA State, shall be chosen from among present or former members of the highest judicial offices of the EFTA States or be lawyers of recognised competence. The EFTA States shall adopt a decision establishing the panel's operating rules and a decision appointing its members as well as their remuneration. It shall act on the initiative of the President of the Court."

[54] EFTA Court Statute, Art. 2.

[55] EFTA RoP, Art. 25; EFTA Court, *Legal Framework and Case Law* (3rd edn, Art. 25) 11.

[56] Note for Guidance on Requests by National Courts for Advisory Opinions [1999] Notice 1/99.

[57] EFTA RoP, Art. 27.

[58] *Irish Bank*, note 49, para. 84.

reciprocity, effect, primacy and state liability, and the relevance of fundamental rights, as well as on many important substantive issues. It has been recognized that the EFTA Court has developed its own distinct culture determined by openness, service-mindedness, rapidity, a liberal approach with regard to the admission of interveners,[59] and a judicial style that is less oriented towards decreeing than explaining.[60] Recently the EFTA Court has begun to cite relevant academic literature in order to take up the dialogue with scholars, but also for reasons of transparency and intellectual honesty.[61]

In 2012, the EFTA Court received 15 new cases, had 12 cases pending and completed 16 cases. At present both direct action and advisory opinion proceedings take on average 8 months from lodging to handing down.[62]

2.2.2 *Practice and principles*

The EEA single market can only function in an undistorted way if there is a regulatory level playing field for citizens and business operators. This is achieved through special homogeneity rules. The EFTA Court is bound to follow relevant pre-EEA Agreement ECJ case law,[63] and is required to "pay due account" to relevant ECJ case law postdating the signature of the Agreement where those rules in the EU pillar are "identical in substance" to the ones in the EFTA pillar.[64] For a number of reasons, the EFTA Court is, however, in the majority of its cases faced with novel legal questions ("going-first constellation"). The written homogeneity rules have therefore to a large extent been replaced by judicial dialogue.[65]

The EFTA Court uses essentially the same interpretive toolkit as the ECJ.[66] It has developed three branches of the homogeneity principle: substantive, effect-related, and procedural homogeneity. Homogeneity is realized to its greatest extent in substantive law. With regard to effect, there is an obligation of result for the EFTA pillar. EFTA and EU citizens and business operators must enjoy, as a result, the same

[59] See S Magnússon, "Procedural Homogeneity v. Inconsistency in European Courts, Comments on an Order by EFTA Court President of 15 June 2012" (Social Science Research Network, September 1, 2012) <papers.ssrn.com/sol3/papers.cfm?abstract_id=2140717> accessed April 29, 2013.

[60] J Temple Lang, "Judicial Review of Competition Decisions under the European Convention on Human Rights and the Importance of the EFTA Court: The *Norway Post* Judgment" (2012) 4 EL Rev 464.

[61] *ESA v. Iceland* (Judgment) [January 28, 2013] Case E-16/11, not yet reported, para. 167; *Norway v. Stig Arne Jonsson* (Judgment) [March 20, 2013] Case E-3/12, not yet reported, para. 56.

[62] According to internal EFTA Court statistics. [63] (EEA), Art. 6 and SCA, Art. 3.1.

[64] SCA, Art. 3.2.

[65] See Posner, note 194 at 201, and Opinion of Advocate-General Trstenjak, (Opinion) [July 5, 2012] Case C 300/10, not yet reported, *Vítor Hugo Marques Almeida v. Companhia de Seguros Fidelidade-Mundial SA*, fn. 24.

[66] C Baudenbacher, "Lecture 4" in *The EFTA Court in Action: Five Lectures* (Stuttgart: German Law Publishers 2010) 47–68; see with regard to dynamic interpretation *Pedicel AS v. Sosial- og helsedirektoratet* [2005] Case E-4/04, EFTA Ct. Rep 1, para. 28, with regard to the principle of effectiveness *Arnulf Clauder* [2001] Case E-4/11, EFTA Ct. Rep 216, paras 34, 46, 48.

rights in the EFTA pillar when it comes to relying on EEA law as their counterparts in the EU pillar.[67] The full ambit of the concept of procedural homogeneity is yet to be discovered.[68]

The General Court held in its landmark judgment *Opel Austria* that provisions of EEA law are capable of having direct effect in the EU pillar.[69] In the EFTA pillar, the EFTA Court has recognized quasi-direct effect (citizens and businesses may invoke in national courts provisions of EEA law which have been implemented into the national legal orders) and quasi-primacy (directly effective provisions take precedence over conflicting national law).[70] National courts are furthermore obliged to construe national law as far as possible in compliance with EEA law.[71] In its landmark ruling *Sveinbjörnsdóttir*, the EFTA Court held that State liability is part of EEA law.[72] The ECJ endorsed this finding in *Rechberger*.[73] It may be concluded from the EFTA Court in *Kolbeinsson* that EEA state liability also applies to judicial wrongdoing.[74] All these principles follow from EEA law and not from the domestic legal orders of the EEA/EFTA States.

According to settled EFTA Court case law, the provisions of the EEA Agreement are to be interpreted in the light of fundamental rights. The European Convention on Human Rights (ECHR) and the judgments of the ECtHR are important sources for determining the scope of those rights.[75] Unlike the ECJ, the EFTA Court has not refrained from basing itself on ECtHR case law in competition law matters.[76]

[67] *Irish Bank*, note 49, at para. 122.

[68] *DB Schenker v. ESA*, [2012] Case E-14/11 EFTA Ct. Rep, 1178, paras 77, 78; and case law cited.

[69] *Opel Austria GmbH v. Council of the European Union* [1997] Case T-115/94, ECR, II-39, para. 102.

[70] *Restamark* [1994–1995] Cases E-1/94, EFTA Ct. Rep, 15; *Einarsson* [2002] E-1/01, EFTA Ct. Rep, 1; See H Graver, "The Effects of EFTA Court Jurisprudence on the Legal Orders of the EEA/EFTA States" in C Baudenbacher, P Tresselt, and T Örlygsson (eds), *The EFTA Court Ten Years On* (Oxford and Portland, OR: Hart Publishing 2005) fn 273, 79, 96 *et seq.*; Supranationality and National Legal Autonomy in the EEA-Agreement, ARENA Working Papers (2000) WP 00/23 <http://www.sv.uio.no/arena/english/research/publications/arena-publications/workingpapers/working-papers2000/wp00_23.htm> accessed June 12, 2012, 3; EU Petersmann, "De-Fragmentation of International Economic Law Through Constitutional Interpretation and Adjudication with Due Respect for Reasonable Disagreement" (2008) 6 Loy U Chi Intl L Rev 209, 226.

[71] *Karlsson* [2002] Cases E-4/01, EFTA Ct. Rep, 240; *Criminal proceedings against A* [2007]; E-1/07, EFTA Ct. Rep, 246.

[72] *Erla María Sveinbjörnsdóttir v. Iceland* [1998] Case E-9/97, EFTA Ct. Rep, 95, para. 44, *et seq.* 60.

[73] *Rechberger* [1999] ECR, Case C-140/97, I-3499, para. 39; concerning EEA state liability for judicial wrongdoing in particular *Þór Kolbeinsson v. the Icelandic State* [2009–2010] E-2/10, EFTA Ct. Rep, 234, para. 77.

[74] *Kolbeinsson*, note 73, at 234, para. 77.

[75] *Ásgeirsson* [2003] Cases E-2/03, EFTA Ct. Rep, 185, para. 23; *Clauder* [2011] E-4/11, EFTA Ct. Rep, 216, para. 49; *Posten Norge AS v. EFTA Surveillance Authority* (Judgment) [2012] Case E-15/10, EFTA Ct. Rep, 246, para. 85; *Irish Bank*, note 49, at para. 63 *et seq.*

[76] *Posten Norge AS v. ESA*, note 75, at para. 85 *et seq.*; Case E-14/11 *DB Schenker*, note 68, at para. 166; with regard to the ECJ's approach see K Lenaerts, "Due process in competition cases" *NZKart*, Vol. 1, No. 5, May 2013, 175–83.

Indeed, it has been said that the court did not "shy away from directly confronting the issue" when considering the weight of the criminal charge in a competition law case.[77] The EFTA Court has also recognized other general principles of EEA law.

Until recently, it was commonly assumed that ESA (like the Commission in the EU pillar) is essentially free to decide whether and when to bring an infringement action. The first President of ESA, Knut Almestad, has, however, aptly observed that EEA/EFTA States seem "to engage ESA in a protracted dialogue, often by promising solutions once lengthy studies and legislative processes covering broader issues have been completed, but which in the end turn out to be inadequate."[78] In *ESA v. Norway*, the EFTA Court held that where ESA, whether upon a complaint or on its own motion, considers that an EEA/EFTA State has failed to fulfill an obligation under the EEA Agreement, it must, in the interest of the proper functioning of the Agreement, proceed within an appropriate time in assessing whether to bring a contracting party before the court.[79]

2.3 Court of Justice of the Andean Community

2.3.1 *History, composition, competences, and role*

The ATJ was founded in 1979 as the "Court of Justice of the Cartagena Agreement" and began operating on 2 January 1984 in Quito, Ecuador. It was renamed by the Cochabamba Protocol in 1996 to Court of Justice of the Andean Community. The ATJ's structure and competences are largely modeled on the ECJ.[80] The Andean Community is a sub-regional economic and social integration bloc, presently composed of four member states—Bolivia, Colombia, Ecuador, and Peru, with Chile and the Mercosur states as associate members.

The ATJ is a single instance court comprising four judges—one from each member state[81]—with exclusive jurisdiction[82] over the Andean Community

[77] E Barbier de la Serre, "A lesson on judicial review from the other European Court in Luxembourg" (Kluwer Competition Law Blog, April 27, 2012) <http://kluwercompetitionlawblog.com/2012/04/27/a-lesson-on-judicial-review-from-the-other-european-court-in-luxembourg/> accessed August 6, 2012; see also Advocate-General Kokott *Schindler* (Opinion) [April 18, 2013], nyr, paras 18 and 20;

[78] K Almestad, "Reflections on the Postal Services Directive and the EEA Review" in EFTA Court (ed.), *Judicial Protection in the European Economic Area* (Stuttgart 2012) 77, 82.

[79] *ESA v. Norway* [2012] Case E-9/11 EFTA Ct. Rep. 442, para. 68.

[80] ATJ Statute, Art. 4. See generally, W Kuehn, *Die Andengemeinschaft—Juristische Aspekte der internationalen Bezeihungen zwischen der Europaeischen Union und latenamerikaneischen Integrationssystemen im Zeitalter des Neuen Regionalismus* (Aachen: Shaker Verlag 2003).

[81] Treaty Creating the Andean Tribunal of Justice (TATJ), Art. 7 provides for five judges but by Andean Council of Foreign Ministers Decision 633 of June 12, 2006 this was modified by providing that the number of judges be equal to the number of member states (thus, following Venezuela's withdrawal the total is four).

[82] TATJ, Art. 42.

treaties and decisions of the Council of Foreign Ministers, Commission as well as Resolutions of the Secretariat General.[83] Each member state presents a list of three candidates and the judges are selected from those lists by unanimous decision of the member states. Candidates must possess a "good moral reputation" and be competent to exercise the highest judicial roles in their respective countries or be highly competent jurists.[84] The judges are appointed for a six-year term, which is renewable once.[85] Unlike the ECJ or the EFTA Court, however, the function of the president rotates annually.[86] Provision is made for the creation of an advocate-general.[87]

The ATJ is competent to hear actions for: failure to fulfil obligations, annulment, failure to act, preliminary rulings, voluntary arbitration and has an administrative jurisdiction over the employees of the community's institutions.[88] Once published in the Official Gazette of the Cartagena Agreement, all decisions of the court are binding and final.[89]

There are two forms of preliminary rulings: optional references from lower courts and mandatory references from courts of last instance.[90] Unlike preliminary references to the ECJ or the EFTA Court, which automatically suspend national proceedings, this suspensory effect only applies if the reference to the ATJ is from a court of last instance. Pursuant to an optional reference ("consulta facultativa"), if the ATJ does not render its preliminary ruling before the national court's decision is due, the national court may rule without waiting for the ATJ to issue its ruling.[91] This set-up certainly ensures that the ATJ's docket is not overwhelmed by preliminary references from perhaps more "curious" lower courts. However, despite avoiding unduly long proceedings, it may perhaps be self-defeating, as it delays the ATJ from addressing difficult issues.

The ATJ works in Spanish.[92] The languages and dialects of ethnic groups may be used before the court, provided that they are submitted with a Spanish translation; an official translation may be requested by a party or the court *ex officio*.[93] Decisions are taken by a majority of three judges out of four,[94] which may make deliberations particularly lengthy. No dissenting votes or opinions may be expressed.[95]

[83] TATJ, Art. 17, and ATJ Statute, Arts 101–6. [84] TATJ, Art. 6. [85] TATJ, Arts 14, 15.

[86] ATJ Statute, Art. 14. [87] TATJ, Art. 6 and ATJ Statute, Art. 142.

[88] For some detail of the procedures see R Mackenzie et al., *The Manual on International Courts and Tribunals* (2nd edn, Oxford University Press 2010) 294–7.

[89] TATJ, Art. 41 and ATJ Statute, Art. 91. [90] ATJ Statute, Arts 122, 123.

[91] TATJ, Art. 33 and ATJ Statute, Art. 122. [92] ATJ Statute, Art. 34.

[93] ATJ Statute, Art. 34. [94] ATJ Statute, Art. 32. [95] ATJ Statute, Art. 90.

2.3.2 *Practice and principles*

There are several readily recognizable general principles in the law of the Andean Community: "supremacy or pre-eminence,"[96] "direct application,"[97] and "direct or immediate effect."[98] As with similar principles in EEA law, it would be unwise to presume that they will correspond identically to those in EU law. There will, of course, be nuances in the interpretation of such maxims to suit the nature of each regional arrangement. Indeed, it has been contended that "blind mimicry [...] is likely to generate a 'transplant effect' in which local actors resist transplanted ideas and institutions. In contrast, the existence of local adaptations may indicate that importers are considering local needs and making adjustments that increase the likelihood of the transplant's success."

There has been perhaps a failure to adapt what clearly works for the EU to the circumstances of the Andean Community. Despite its evident caseload,[99] the implementation of this judicial mechanism within the Andean region has been characterized as being "far from successful. On the one hand, there is no consensus on the efficacy of Andean Community law, and on the other hand, [32] years after its foundation, the Andean Community has not been able to achieve its main goal of establishing a common market. Indeed, what exists today is an imperfect customs union."[100] Consequently, if the "success of European integration through law was the goal for the Andean Community, importing its polity design and its legal doctrines [has] proved unsuccessful."[101]

[96] Supremacy or pre-eminence is based on TATJ, Arts 2, 3 "[...] the legal system of the Andean integration prevails in its application to internal and national standards, being an essential feature of Community law, as a basic requirement for building integration," Case 3-AI-96.

[97] This derives from the concept of supremacy. Community rules do not require national implementing provisions to fully apply. See E Álvarez, "Derecho de la Integración y Derecho Comunitario" (Scribd) <http://www.scribd.com/doc/34476705/DERECHO-DE-LA-INTEGRACION-Y-DERECHO-COMUNITARIO> accessed August 9, 2012.

[98] The Andean legal rules must be applied uniformly in the territory of the member states. They are also a ready source of rights and obligations for member states, individuals, bodies and institutions of the Andean Integration System, see Álvarez, note 97.

[99] The ATJ had received 1819 preliminary references and given 2197 rulings by 2011, Tribunal de Justicia de la Comunidad Andina, "Presentación" <http://www.tribunalandino.org.ec/sitetjca/index.php?option=com_content&view=article&id=1&Itemid=2> accessed August 9, 2012.

[100] O Saldías, "Supranational Courts as Engines of Disintegration: The Case of the Andean Community," Berlin Working Paper on European Integration No. 5, (October 2007) 9 <http://www.polsoz.fu-berlin.de/polwiss/forschung/international/europa/arbeitspapiere/2007-5_Saldias.pdf> accessed August 9, 2012.

[101] Saldías, note 100, at 29.

3 Arbitral Model

At the other end of the regional economic dispute spectrum from DIRCs lies the arbitration system of the North American Free Trade Agreement (NAFTA).[102]

3.1 NAFTA Dispute Settlement System

NAFTA removes barriers to trade and investment in both goods and services between Canada, Mexico, and the United States. The NAFTA set-up also contains two supplemental agreements concerning the environment[103] and labor.[104] Unlike the EU, EEA, and Andean Community, NAFTA does not aim at any form of deep integration, but remains an almost classical free trade agreement (FTA).

Perhaps intertwined and inherent in the notion of a regional FTA is the undesirability of having a regional judicial body. NAFTA relies essentially on ad hoc arbitration and is thus less judicialized[105] and much more fragmented than other regional agreements. And yet, "NAFTA has been beneficial to businesses and investors in all three countries and has helped promote the competitiveness of North America, much like the European Union has helped promote the competitiveness of Europe."[106]

Dispute resolution is carried out by bi-national arbitration tribunals. There are three relevant NAFTA Chapters: Chapter 11 on Foreign Investment, Chapter 19 on Anti-Dumping and Countervailing Duties, and Chapter 20 on General Dispute Settlement. Chapter 20 general dispute settlement procedure borrows heavily from the US–Canada Free Trade Agreement. The respective rules apply to any dispute between the state parties concerning the interpretation or application of NAFTA, or allegations that the application of an actual or proposed measure taken by a party is inconsistent with its NAFTA obligations or would cause the impairment or nullification of certain benefits that the complainants expect to attain under NAFTA.[107]

[102] Although not discussed here, the NAFTA set-up has been copied in the Dominican Republic–Central America–United States Free Trade Agreement (CAFTA-DR)—made up of Costa Rica, El Salvador, Guatemala, Honduras, Nicaragua, Dominican Republic, and the United States signed on August 5, 2004. On August 9, 2011, the United States requested the establishment of an arbitral panel under Art. 20.6 of the CAFTA-DR alleging that Guatemala had failed to effectively enforce its labor laws.

[103] The North American Agreement on Environmental Cooperation 1993.

[104] The North American Agreement on Labor Cooperation 1993.

[105] P Hansen, "Judicialization and Globalization in the North American Free Trade Agreement" (2003) 38 Tex Intl LJ 489 *et seq.*

[106] L Glick, *Understanding the North American Free Trade Agreement, Legal and Business Consequences of NAFTA* (3rd edn, Alphen aan den Rijn: Kluwer Law International 2010) 2.

[107] NAFTA, Art. 2004.

Once a dispute arises, the state parties must first enter into consultations.[108] If no solution is found during a fixed period, the complaining party may request the convening of the Free Trade Commission—formed of the parties' cabinet level trade ministers or their designees—and its good offices, conciliation, mediation, and expert advice to facilitate settlement.[109] If no agreement is reached within a fixed period, any party may request the commission to establish an ad hoc arbitration panel.[110] Interestingly, if a dispute arises within both the jurisdictions of NAFTA and the World Trade Organization (WTO), the complaining party chooses the forum.[111] However, if one party objects to the WTO, the dispute must be heard pursuant to NAFTA.[112] Additionally, if one of the parties to a dispute involving the environment, health, sanitary, or phytosanitary matters so requests, the dispute must be resolved pursuant to NAFTA.[113] The forum chosen or required will be the exclusive forum for the resolution of the dispute.[114]

Private operators have access to the NAFTA dispute settlement process under Chapter 11. According to Arts 1116 and 1117 NAFTA, an investor of a party or a juridical person that an investor owns or controls directly or indirectly may submit to arbitration that another party has breached its obligations.

A panel is composed of five independent experts.[115] Each party selects two persons who are citizens of the other party to the dispute. The chairperson is jointly selected by the parties. The arbitrators are chosen from a roster of legal, trade, and other experts, including those from non-parties.[116] Any party may exercise a pre-emptory challenge against the appointment of an arbitrator not on the roster.[117]

Ninety days after the panel has been selected, or such other period set by the Model Rules of Procedure, or by the agreement of the parties, the panel issues its confidential initial report.[118] The parties then have 14 days to comment.[119] The final report is forwarded to the Free Trade Commission for publication 15 days later, unless the panel decides otherwise.[120] Importantly, and as with many sets of arbitration rules, the report does not state which panelists decided with the majority or minority.[121]

Once the final report has been issued, the parties are again to negotiate without resorting to compensation.[122] If the final resolution of the dispute involves a finding that a measure is inconsistent with NAFTA obligations, or causes a nullification or impairment of a NAFTA benefit, the emphasis is placed on amending or removing the offending domestic law.[123] Compensation is only a last resort and may only be

[108] NAFTA, Art. 2006. [109] NAFTA, Art. 2007. [110] NAFTA, Art. 2008.
[111] NAFTA, Art. 2005. [112] NAFTA, Art. 2005. [113] NAFTA, Art. 2005.
[114] NAFTA, Art. 2005. [115] NAFTA, Art. 2011. [116] NAFTA, Arts 2009, 2010.
[117] NAFTA, Art. 2011. [118] NAFTA, Art. 2016. [119] NAFTA, Art. 2016.
[120] NAFTA, Art. 2017. [121] NAFTA, Art. 2017.

[122] NAFTA, Art. 2018. For the Decisions and Reports, see NAFTA Secretariat <http://www.nafta-sec-alena.org/en/DecisionsAndReports.aspx?x=312> accessed on December 20, 2012.

[123] NAFTA, Art. 2018.

granted in limited circumstances.[124] The injured party may suspend benefits, i.e. impose trade sanctions against the offending party in the same sector(s).[125]

4 Hybrids

Between pure arbitration systems, such as NAFTA and DIRCs, lies a range of hybrid judicial or quasi-judicial bodies. These include the Mercosur dispute resolution system and the more integrationist judicial bodies of the CCJ and the Economic Court of the Commonwealth of Independent States (CIS). However, the level of integration and the choice between an arbitration-based or court-based system are not the only factors that may distinguish a hybrid, as the appellate jurisdiction of the CCJ brings into sharp relief.

4.1 Mercosur dispute settlement system

4.1.1 *General*

Mercosur is composed of Argentina, Brazil, (Paraguay),[126] Uruguay, and (Venezuela).[127] Currently in turmoil,[128] it was established by the Treaty of Asunción in 1991 and seeks to establish a common market. The Treaty of Asunción set up a basic dispute settlement system merely providing for negotiations followed by mediation by the Common Market Group (Mercosur's executive body coordinated by the foreign ministries of the state parties).

[124] NAFTA, Art. 2019. [125] NAFTA, Art. 2019.

[126] Paraguay was formally suspended from Mercosur on June 29, 2012 for the "democratic rupture," which according to Argentina, Brazil, and Uruguay took place with the removal of Fernando Lugo as President a week earlier after impeachment by the Paraguayan Senate.

[127] The Paraguayan government disputes Venezuela's accession of 1 August 2012, stating that "until the Republic of Paraguay, as founding member of Mercosur, does not deposit the pertinent ratification of Venezuela's incorporation done without complying with this requisite, the whole action is null and void." MercoPress, "Venezuela's Mercosur membership 'null and void' says Paraguayan government," (August 1, 2012) <http://en.mercopress.com/2012/08/01/venezuela-s-mercosur-membership-null-and-void-says-paraguayan-government> accessed on April 29, 2013.

[128] George Lyon MEP has called for trade talks between the EU and Mercosur to be suspended until the South American countries resolve Venezuela's accession and the suspension of Paraguay. A Arbuckle, "Call for end to EU's negotiations with South American bloc," Business.scotsman.com, August 16, 2012, <http://www.scotsman.com/business/call-for-end-to-eu-s-negotiations-with-south-american-bloc-1-2469601> accessed August 17, 2012.

The dispute settlement procedures were changed by the Olivos Protocol 2002, which entered into force on 1 January 2004. This protocol provides for different mechanisms to settle disputes between the state parties related to the interpretation, application, and breach of the Treaty of Asunción.

Disputes falling within the scope of the Mercosur dispute settlement system, which can also be settled according to the WTO Dispute Settlement Body (DSU), may be submitted to either forum at the complainant's discretion—as under NAFTA. However, the parties may choose the forum by mutual agreement. Once a dispute settlement procedure has commenced, neither party may have recourse to other forums in the same case.[129]

There are three dispute settlement organs: the Common Market Group,[130] Ad Hoc Arbitration Tribunals,[131] and the Permanent Review Tribunal.[132] The Common Market Group is an executive body, which among its other functions ensures compliance with the Treaty of Asunción. Its decisions are binding upon state parties.[133] However, when requested to take part in the settlement of a dispute it issues recommendations (the binding nature of which is not expressly stated in the protocol[134]). The ad hoc arbitration tribunals consist of three members: one chosen by each party and the third chosen by mutual agreement. The arbitrators are selected from lists deposited by each state party with the Mercosur Administrative Secretariat. The member states may appeal to the Permanent Review Tribunal against the decision of the Ad Hoc Arbitration Tribunal, which may only review the decision in terms of points of law. Decisions of the Ad Hoc Arbitration Tribunals are binding on the parties and are *res judicata* once the period for appealing to the Permanent Review Tribunal has expired.

The Olivos Protocol refers to the members of the Permanent Review Tribunal as "arbitrators."[135] From a functional point of view, however, they undoubtedly are international judges. The Permanent Review Tribunal is formed of five members, with each contracting state designating a judge and a substitute for a period of two years. The fifth judge is elected unanimously for three years. Oddly, given its name, the Permanent Review Tribunal does not sit permanently but may be convened at any time. It is supported by a Technical Secretariat. Decisions of the Permanent Review Tribunal are final and take precedence over those of the ad hoc arbitration tribunals. They are binding on the parties and have the force of *res judicata*.

If the dispute involves two state parties, the Permanent Review Tribunal is made up of three judges—two being nationals of the parties to the dispute and

[129] Olivos Protocol, Art. 1. [130] Olivos Protocol, Chapter V.

[131] Olivos Protocol, Chapter VI.

[132] Olivos Protocol, Art. 18; see, with regard to the Permanent Review Tribunal, R Vinuesa, "Enforcement of MERCOSUR Arbitration Awards Within the Domestic Legal Orders of Member States" (2005) 40 Tex Intl LJ 425, 438 *et seq.*

[133] Ouro Preto Protocol 1994, Art. 15. [134] Olivos Protocol, Art. 7.

[135] Olivos Protocol, Art. 10.

the presiding member designated by lot drawn by the Director of the Mercosur Administrative Secretariat from among the remaining members not being nationals of the state parties to the dispute. If the dispute involves more than two state parties, the Permanent Review Tribunal is made up of all five judges.[136]

A dispute may be initiated by any state party, on the Common Market Group's own initiative or following a claim submitted by a citizen. The first phase of dispute settlement is direct negotiations. If the dispute is settled only in part or not at all during direct negotiations, either party may bring proceedings before the Ad Hoc Arbitration Tribunal. However, the state parties to the dispute may, by mutual agreement, submit it for consideration by the Common Market Group for its recommendations.

Should the state parties to the dispute not wish to engage in either of the optional phases, they may submit the dispute to the Ad Hoc Arbitration Tribunal or by mutual agreement initiate the proceedings directly before the Permanent Review Tribunal—where it sits as a panel of five. This *per saltum* action distinguishes the Mercosur dispute settlement system from the WTO model, which otherwise has obviously inspired the Mercosur system.

The Ad Hoc Arbitration Tribunal announces its decision within 60 days (which may be extended by 30 days).[137] The decision is binding on the state parties to the dispute once notification has been given; in relation to the parties it is *res judicata* after the 15-day appeal period has expired.[138]

Either party may appeal the dispute to the Permanent Review Tribunal with the appeal being restricted to the matters of law and the judicial interpretations contained in the tribunal's decision. However, decisions of the Ad Hoc Arbitration Tribunals made *ex aequo et bono* are not subject to appeal.[139] The Permanent Review Tribunal announces its decision within 30 days of the date of the appeal. The Permanent Review Tribunal may confirm, modify, or vacate the legal basis of the Ad Hoc Arbitration Tribunal's decision.[140] This enables the Permanent Review Tribunal to enforce discipline with its own previous arbitral decisions.[141]

An additional hybrid characteristic of the Permanent Review Tribunal is its ability to give advisory opinions on any legal issue covered by Mercosur law upon request of the state parties acting jointly, the Mercosur decision-making bodies, or the higher courts of the state parties. Unlike a true DIRC, however, these opinions have no binding or obligatory force.

4.1.2 *Practice and principles*

The Permanent Review Tribunal has developed distinctive case law aimed at securing the autonomy of the Mercosur juridical order based on the principle of

[136] Olivos Protocol, Art. 20. [137] Olivos Protocol, Art. 16.
[138] Olivos Protocol, Art. 26. [139] Olivos Protocol, Art. 15. [140] Olivos Protocol, Art. 15.
[141] T O'Keefe, "Dispute Resolution in MERCOSUR" (2002) 3 J World Investment 507.

integration.[142] Autonomy has been emphasized in Orders 1/07 and 1/08 where, in a long-running dispute between Argentina and Uruguay over remolded tires, Argentina relied heavily on WTO and GATT authorities to interpret its obligations.[143] However, the Permanent Review Tribunal summarily rejected Argentina's reliance on WTO case law on the basis of the language of integration in Art. 1 of the Treaties of Asunción and Montevideo, highlighting the different objectives of Mercosur and the WTO. It considered that the role of the WTO is to facilitate trade among its members, whereas Mercosur's role is to establish a community of interests based on much more diverse criteria.[144]

4.2 Caribbean Court of Justice (CCJ)

The CCJ is the judicial body for the Caribbean Community but also a shared "national" court of last instance for several Caribbean countries. There are at present 12 signatories to the CCJ Agreement: Antigua and Barbuda, Barbados, Belize, Grenada, Guyana, Jamaica, St. Kitts and Nevis, St. Lucia, Suriname, Trinidad and Tobago, Dominica, and St. Vincent and The Grenadines.[145]

The CCJ was established on 14 February 2001[146] and inaugurated on 16 April 2005.[147] Currently based in the Port of Spain in Trinidad and Tobago, it is an itinerant court and may travel and operate in any contracting party. The court is composed of the President and no more than nine judges.[148] At present there are seven on the bench, including the President. At least three judges, other than the President, must possess expertise in international law, including international trade law.[149] In combination with the "standard" requirements in Art. IV of the CCJ Agreement, the candidate must have "intellectual and analytical ability" and an "understanding of people and society." These additional criteria do not have an overly narrowing effect on the pool of candidates, as selection is open to any judge of a court of unlimited jurisdiction or teacher of law for 15 years or more of a contracting party, some part of the Commonwealth or a state exercising civil law common to the contracting parties.[150] Indeed, nationality is not an active consideration.[151] The selection from

[142] Mercosur [2005] Order 1/05, para. 9.

[143] Argentina argued for the use of WTO authorities under the principles of Arts 31–4 of the Vienna Convention on the Law of Treaties. (See Laudo [2007] 1/07 paras 3.1.9–3.1.14.)

[144] Permanent Review Tribunal [2007] Order 1/07, para. 7.2.

[145] The Caribbean Court of Justice, "The CCJ: From Concept to Reality" <http://www.caribbeancourtofjustice.org/about-the-ccj/ccj-concept-to-reality> accessed August 19, 2012.

[146] By the Agreement Establishing the Caribbean Court of Justice.

[147] Agreement Establishing the Caribbean Court of Justice.

[148] CCJ Agreement, Art. IV. [149] CCJ Agreement, Art. IV. [150] CCJ Agreement, Art. IV.

[151] In 2010, the bench included two judges from Trinidad and Tobago (The Rt. Hon. Mr. Justice de la Bastide and the Hon. Mr. Justice Nelson) and two from Guyana (the Hon. Mr. Justice Pollard

this wide pool of candidates is made, not by the contracting parties, but by a majority vote of the Regional Judicial and Legal Services Commission.[152] The President alone is appointed by a 75 percent super-majority of the contracting parties on the recommendation of the commission.[153] Once appointed, the judges have life tenure with mandatory retirement at 72, which is extendable to 75 at the discretion of the commission.[154] This balances the need to impartially select the best candidates—like the Art. 255 TFEU panel—but also ensures political neutrality in the selection, given that not all the contracting parties are represented on the bench.[155]

The CCJ has two jurisdictions: original[156] and appellate.[157] Mandatory original jurisdiction encompasses the Revised Treaty of Chaguaramas (Revised Treaty) and the CARICOM Single Market and Economy (CSME). In this regard, the CCJ operates as a fledgling DIRC.[158] Indeed, the Hon. Mr. Justice Anderson characterized the Revised Treaty as "the Constitution of the Caribbean Community" and stated that "[A]n appropriate analogy for the Revised Treaty is probably the 1957 Treaty of Rome creating the European Community."[159]

The CCJ settles disputes involving the contracting parties, community, individuals, or community institutions on the implementation of CSME law.[160] The standing of natural and legal persons is limited and is granted only with special leave of the court if a right has been conferred for the benefit of the person directly and if that person establishes that he has been prejudiced in respect of the enjoyment of the benefit. In addition, the contracting party of the person concerned must have either omitted or declined to espouse the claim or have expressly permitted the person to

and the Hon. Mrs. Justice Bernard); see T Dannenbaum, "Nationality and the international judge: the nationalist presumption governing the international judiciary and why it must be reversed" (2012) 45(77) Cornell Intl LJ 25.

152 Established by CCJ Agreement, Art. V. 153 CCJ Agreement, Art. V.

154 CCJ Agreement, Art. IX and Art. II Protocol to the Agreement Establishing the Caribbean Court of Justice Relating to the Tenure of Office of Judges of the Court, 2007.

155 At present there is a British and a Dutch judge on the CCJ bench: the Hon. Mr. Justice Hayton and the Hon. Mr. Justice Wit.

156 In its original jurisdiction the CCJ has to date handed down 12 judgments. The Caribbean Court of Justice, "Original Jurisdiction Judgments" <http://www.caribbeancourtofjustice.org/judgments-proceedings/original-jurisdiction-judgments> accessed August 20, 2012.

157 In its appellate jurisdiction the CCJ has to date handed down 58 judgments. The Caribbean Court of Justice, "Appellate Jurisdiction Judgments" <http://www.caribbeancourtofjustice.org/judgments-proceedings/appellate-jurisdiction-judgments> accessed August 20, 2012.

158 Article 214 of the Revised Treaty contains the CARICOM referral obligation. Article 239 of the Revised Treaty, however, lists five areas critical to the CSME but on which agreement is yet to be reached: electronic commerce, government procurement, treatment of goods produced in free zones, free circulation of goods, and contingent rights, see Hon. Mr. Justice Anderson, "Is Joining the Appellate jurisdiction of the CCJ an Option for Suriname?" (January 2011) 13 <chooseavirb.com/ccj/wp-content/uploads/2011/papers_addresses/4IsJoiningtheCCJ4Suriname2010%20_2_.pdf> accessed August 20, 2012. It is with no disrespect that the word "fledgling" is used: the Hon. Mr. Justice Anderson himself characterizes the Caribbean Community as "fledgling" and "fledging," at 14.

159 Anderson, note 158, at 7. 160 Revised Treaty, Art. 211.

bring the claim. Finally, the court must find that it is in the interest of justice that the person be allowed to espouse the claim.[161] The substantive law is international law.[162] Nevertheless, the court may also employ other principles of law or equity where necessary.[163] Indeed, echoes of ECJ jurisprudence have been seen which, although noted by the CCJ, illustrate that it is determined to carve its own path.[164]

The CCJ also has exclusive jurisdiction to deliver advisory opinions concerning the interpretation and application of the Revised Treaty at the request of contracting parties or the community.[165]

The optional appellate jurisdiction is the most distinctive aspect of the CCJ. The CCJ replaces the Judicial Committee of the Privy Council in acting as the final Court of Appeal for, at present, Barbados, Guyana, and Belize. Consequently, the CCJ must be seen as a DIRC with an entirely different and separate appellate jurisdiction designed to break the historical links with London and to complete the political independence of those Commonwealth Caribbean member states.[166]

Judgments under the appellate jurisdiction may contain dissenting opinions. However, by contrast, in its original jurisdiction, CCJ rulings or advisory opinions are published as a single judgment of the court with no other opinion or judgment permitted.[167] This emphasizes that the drafters of regional integration agreements perhaps consider it necessary to protect the future bench from political pressure namely as at the ECJ and EFTA Court, even if such a perspective is outdated[168].

The applicable substantive law in the CCJ's appellate jurisdiction is the municipal law of the referring court—typically derived from English common law.[169] Nevertheless,

[161] CCJ Agreement, Art. XXIV, might be characterized as a common law style variant of TFEU, Art. 263.

[162] CCJ Agreement, Art. XVII.

[163] Revised Treaty, Art. 217.

[164] D Berry, "*Trinidad Cement Ltd. v. Caribbean Community*; *Doreen Johnson v. CARICAD*" (2009) 103 AJIL 561–7.

[165] CCJ Agreement, Art. VIII. The Court has not yet been requested to give an Advisory Opinion.

[166] Anderson, note 158, at 1. It is interesting to note that the Privy Council's role may not be waning. Honduras, not a Commonwealth country, has sought to make special economic zones subject to Mauritian law and hence to the final jurisdiction of the Privy Council: see O. Bowcott and M. Wolfe-Robinson, "Honduras may appeal to London courts: Cases originating in Honduras could end up before privy council in Westminster under complex constitutional agreement," Guardian.co.uk, July 22, 2012 <http://www.guardian.co.uk/law/2012/jul/22/honduras-london-courts> accessed May 2, 2013; and P. Spiro, "Postnational Justice: Honduras Looks to Outsource Appeals to Mauritius (and London)," Opinio Juris, July 24, 2012 <http://opiniojuris.org/2012/07/24/postnational-justice-honduras-looks-to-outsource-appeals-to-mauritius-and-london/> accessed May 2, 2013.

[167] CCJ (Original Jurisdiction) Rules 2006, Rule 3.4.4.

[168] V Perju, "Reason and Authority in the European Court of Justice" (2009) 49 Va J Intl L 307; and Baudenbacher, note 66, Lecture 1, at 7.

[169] Haiti has a French-based and Suriname a Dutch-based legal system. The other contracting parties' laws are based on English law. The CCJ has been largely modeled on the English common law—this is particularly evident from the Court's rules of procedure both in its appellate and original jurisdictions. While ECJ-esque, the original jurisdiction procedural rules have been drafted in the manner of the common law.

it has been suggested that Suriname should join the appellate jurisdiction of the CCJ or perhaps initially "consider making appeals to the Court in relation to human rights cases only."[170] While there is precedence for a supreme court to have jurisdiction over common and civil law in the form of the Supreme Court of Canada, it is the advancement of a human rights jurisdiction that is of greatest interest and innovation. Indeed, "[W]hether spurred by a regional treaty or not, the harmonious interpretation of human rights provisions in [the member states'] constitutions by the CCJ would seem to make for good sense in the process of community building. It could even lessen the existing dependence on international human rights adjudication."[171]

The present situation implies that there is a judicial body above the CCJ (in the form of the Inter-American Commission on Human Rights and the IACtHR).[172] This variable geometric judicial architecture is comparable with that in the EU and EEA/EFTA States with regard to the ECtHR. The redistribution of jurisdiction envisaged by the proposal would take the CCJ well beyond the current understanding of a DIRC and would potentially metamorphose it into a federative supreme court.

5 Protagonists of our Age

The three genera of regional dispute settlement addressed encompass various degrees of economic and political integration. There is a cross-pollination of structures, ideas, and concepts between DIRCs through their institutional set-up and judicial dialogue. The secrecy of the vote and the denial of dissenting opinions thus appear in all three DIRCs. These features derive from the civil law tradition. It may be noted at this point that ECtHR judges have the right to dissent,[173] inspired by the ICJ's own provisions.[174]

The DIRC model is clearly popular. Yet it must be considered why they have been regarded as successful as well as why and how they differ from other families of judicial bodies. If parameters can be set, it may be possible to objectively determine relative levels of success and, more usefully, to create some sort of guide for judicial architects.

Certain factors such as the respect for the binding nature of judgments must be taken as a given. There is little to be gained from discussing judicial bodies which may have an impeccable treaty base, statute, and rules of procedure, but whose

170 Anderson, note 158, at 15. 171 Anderson, note 158, at 15. 172 Anderson, note 158, at 15.

173 Convention for the Protection of Human Rights and Fundamental Freedoms, Arts 45.2, 49.2.

174 ICJ Rules, Art. 95, para. 2 (*ex* Art. 74, para. 2).

rulings are "[M]ore honour'd in the breach than the observance."[175] A list of relevant factors might include those discussed below.

5.1 Ambitions

The three DIRCs have different political ambitions. The ECJ is arguably the most politically ambitious of all. Following the economic self-interest of the ECSC, the noble mantle was put on to deny future armed conflict through European integration and thus denying the repetition of the earlier ghastly horrors. This has colored the ECJ's actions almost to the present.[176] However, gradually the motivation for integration has shifted in favor of individual and later fundamental rights. In fact, the ECJ's "unique achievement is to have fashioned a judicially enforceable constitution out of international treaty law, transforming the European polity in the process."[177] The ECJ also benefits, in terms of its level of impact within its regional setting and outside, from a substantial "first-mover" advantage. In a way, the ECJ sees itself as the European counterpart of the US Supreme Court. The ATJ too has been politically active—yet it has really only established a "rule of law island" for intellectual property, while "[i]n the vast seas surrounding this island, however, Andean rules remain riddled with exceptions, under enforced, and often circumvented by domestic actors."[178] The ambition of the EFTA Court is to ensure that the EEA remains a homogenous and dynamic economic area. Homogeneity is thereby understood as a two-way street.

These "political" ambitions at the ECJ and ATJ certainly find echoes at the CCJ. This perhaps is unsurprising given the English-speaking Caribbean's previous attempt to unify as the Federation of the West Indies.[179] Political goals are also apparent, although less in the present structure than might be anticipated, in Mercosur. The other end of the scale is represented by NAFTA. It is worth mentioning at this juncture the seemingly "hollow" national political will behind the Economic Court of the CIS and its new partial replacement: the Court of the Eurasian Economic Community. Elsewhere, of course, there are politically ambitious regional and international courts. Certainly the ECtHR and the International Criminal Court may be considered as at least the ECJ's equal in this regard. An alternative, but no less significant, form of "political" ambition is demonstrated by the Organization for the Harmonization of Business Law in Africa (OHADA) Court in supporting

[175] W Shakespeare, *Hamlet* Act I, Scene IV. [176] As well as those of the ECtHR.

[177] A Sweet, *Governing with Judges: Constitutional Politics in Europe* (Oxford University Press 2000) 153.

[178] L Helfer, K Alter, and F Guerzovich, "Islands of Effective International Adjudication: Constructing an Intellectual Property Rule of Law in the Andean Community" (2009) 109 AJIL 1, 2.

[179] Certainly the inclusion of Suriname and Haiti in CARICOM changes the perspective but does not deny the underlying ambition.

its contracting parties' economic development by enforcing the modern regional business code of West Africa.[180] Nevertheless, the increasing judicialization of international affairs since the late 1950s must be seen as a general trend covering both new areas of the law and delving deeper into the internal workings of states than earlier-established international courts have sought.[181]

5.2 Selection of judges

There is an increasing tendency for both DIRCs and hybrids to better regulate the selection of judges. In the EU, the Art. 255 TFEU panel has certainly left its mark on the appointment process. In the short time of its existence, it has rejected nominees from Italy, Romania, Greece, Malta, and Sweden.[182] As mentioned, the EFTA Court has proposed that the EEA/EFTA States to set up a similar committee, and the CCJ's "cosmopolitan"[183] system could almost be described as autonomous.

These three methods each respect very similar judicial selection criteria, whose original formulation may be found at the ICJ. Nevertheless, they mark almost a watershed moment in denying through regulation the merely politically determined access to the bench. These states are starting to be more concerned by judicial impartiality, as well as the DIRC's reputation, than by having "control" over their person on the bench, as is often the case in arbitration[184] (something which the NAFTA arbitrator selection rules are intentionally designed to counter).

5.3 Access to justice

Locus standi before the regional courts varies quite significantly. Even in the DIRCs the rights of individuals and economic operators to challenge pieces of legislation is significantly restricted. Nation states are not, historically, that comfortable with individuals challenging the legislature or the executive through judicial review. This, therefore, should come as less of a surprise even if it is unwelcome. Nevertheless, in the EU and the EEA individuals and businesses have become additional "guardians" of the various treaties through court-fashioned principles. These principles ensure that the treaties' observance by the EU and EEA/EFTA States is monitored in a way

[180] See generally, C Dickerson, "Harmonizing Business Laws in Africa: OHADA calls the tune" (2005) 44 Columbia Journal of Transnational Law 17.

[181] R Mackenzie and P Sands, "International Courts and Tribunals and the Independence of the International Judge" (2003) 44 Harv. Int'l L.J. 271, 272–3.

[182] See, with regard to the last case, S Johansson, "Stefan Strömberg anses ej lämplig som EU-domare," Realtid, August 3, 2012 <http://www.realtid.se/ArticlePages/201208/03/20120803151050_Realtid881/20120803151050_Realtid881.dbp.asp> accessed August 22, 2012.

[183] Anderson, note 158, at 25.

[184] T Dannenbaum analyses this issue in depth: see note 151.

in which the European Commission and ESA, with their limited resources, could never hope to achieve on their own.[185] Indeed, Burley and Mattli have explained in neo-functionalist terms that the doctrine of direct effect "created a pro-Community constituency of private individuals by giving them a direct stake in the promulgation and implementation of Community law."[186] Yet, such a structure has been departed from at the CCJ, as in the Hon. Mr. Justice Hayton's view "as a result of the *compulsory* and *exclusive* nature of the jurisdiction conferred upon the CCJ by Article 211 [of the Revised Treaty], there is simply no possibility of national courts being allowed to give domestic effect to the [Revised Treaty]."[187]

5.4 Breadth of jurisdiction

The breadth of jurisdiction is important insofar as judicial bodies obtain cases across their competencies. This necessarily interrelates with the level of activism of the court and the perception it gains. As may be seen particularly at the CCJ, the breadth of its two jurisdictions has not, at present, had a cross-competence impact. While it has been very active in its appellate jurisdiction, it has had less than one original jurisdiction case per year. The paucity of original jurisdiction cases can be perhaps explained by a local preference to resolve "disputes with the government of a member state at ministerial level rather than resort to legal proceedings."[188] By contrast, one may see in the future a form of judicial "mission creep" at the ECJ, with the EU Charter of Fundamental Rights and Freedoms potentially limiting a litigant's desire to bring a case before the ECtHR.

5.5 Time factor

The maxim "justice delayed is justice denied" applies to all courts. The duration of proceedings at the ECJ and the backlog at the ECtHR[189] certainly push this maxim to its limit. Indeed, dealing with such backlogs raises concerns of the potential

[185] S Douglas-Scott, *Constitutional Law of the European Union* (Harlow: Pearson Longman 2002) 291.

[186] AM Burley and W Mattli, "Europe before the Court: A Political Theory of Legal Integration" (1993) 47 Winter 1 Int'l Org. 41–76.

[187] D O'Brien and S Morano-Foadi, "The Caribbean Court of Justice and Legal Integration within CARICOM: Some Lessons from the European Community" (2009) 8 The Law and Practice of International Courts and Tribunals 399, 415.

[188] O'Brien and S Morano-Foadi, note 187, at 427.

[189] At present approximately 150,000 cases (Sir Nicholas Bratza and E Fribergh, "House of Lords, House of Commons: Oral evidence taken before the Joint Committee on Human Rights: Human Rights Judgments" (March 13, 2012) Uncorrected Transcript of Oral Evidence, 8. To be published as HC 873-iii <http://www.parliament.uk/documents/joint-committees/human-rights/JCHR_Transcript_13_March_2012_UNCORRECTED.pdf> accessed August 21, 2012.).

reduction in the quality of judicial output. Such a level of "institutional overload" is not shared elsewhere. Indeed, it is rather the exception. Certainly, one blessing of a fully or partly arbitration-based model, such as NAFTA or the Permanent Review Tribunal, is the speed with which decisions are rendered. Despite this, Alter has shown that in the first two decades from the start-up of a regional economic court structure, the number of binding decisions handed down annually typically rises very substantially.[190] Surprisingly, the opposite trend is apparent in arbitration-style set-ups.[191] Alter considers that an ECJ-style set-up "is neither necessary nor sufficient for [a regional economic court] to be active because the extent of secondary legislation may be more important in shaping both trade and litigation rates."[192] Additional factors could include institutional entrenchment at regional economic courts with the impermanent nature of arbitration panels causing institutional inertia.

5.6 Overall success

The level of respect for a regional judicial body and its impact within the regional setting and beyond are crucial for its success. Posner and Yoo have observed that the ECJ and ECtHR "are more like domestic courts than international courts."[193] They are successful because they are specialized,[194] independent, and consequently "are more likely to deliver impartial judgments, to be used by states, and to enjoy a high rate of compliance with their judgments."[195] They argue, however, that their effectiveness is a consequence of the political community in Europe, which does not exist elsewhere. Consequently, the two courts cannot be models for international tribunals.[196] The same would seem to apply to the EFTA Court.

Certainly, Posner and Yoo's perspective relies upon two bases—the independence of the court and the requirement of a political community in order for such a court to flourish. Considering the ATJ, it has certainly developed a significant body of case law concerning intellectual property, yet this is an "island of law" in the Andean Community.[197] Likewise, at the CCJ, the overwhelming proportion of the case law is in its appellate jurisdiction. However, there is, given its historical background, a decent chance that the CCJ may prove Posner and Yoo's thesis to be flawed given the

[190] K Alter, "The Global Spread of European Style International Courts" Buffett Center for International and Comparative Studies Working Paper Series 11/003, Social Science Research Network, June 17, 2011, 13 <http://ssrn.com/abstract=1866787> accessed August 22, 2012.

[191] Alter, note 190, at 13. [192] Alter, note 190, at 14.

[193] E Posner and J Yoo, "Judicial Independence in International Tribunals" (2005) 93(1) Cal L Rev 55.

[194] E Posner, "Diplomacy, Arbitration, and International Courts" in C Baudenbacher and E Busek (eds), *The Role of International Courts* (Stuttgart: German Law Publishers 2008) at 59.

[195] E Posner and J Yoo, "Reply to Helfer and Slaughter" (2005) 93(1) Cal L Rev 957.

[196] Posner and Yoo, note 195, at 966. [197] Helfer, Alter, and Guerzovich, note 178, at 1.

passage of time. Nevertheless, the ECJ, EFTA Court, ATJ, and CCJ remain the "most active and consequential" courts of regional economic integration.[198]

Elsewhere, the Court of the Eurasian Economic Community founded on 1 January 2012, which, at least at the moment, appears to have solid political backing from the Kremlin, has had its first case. In the press release on Case 1-7/1-2012 the court notes that there are several regional economic groups worldwide, each with its own form of dispute resolution and wonders whether it will be as successful.[199] If Posner and Yoo are correct, its likelihood of success would be low. Yet this does not mean that alternatives to the European models may be as successful or even more so elsewhere. Indeed, it may be that arbitration-style models are better suited to the present political ambitions of regional bodies outside Europe. The WTO Dispute Settlement Mechanism is successful as is NAFTA's (even if not uniformly so). Mercosur, whose dispute settlement procedure can only be described as having a modest record at present, may, with the rise of Brazil, Russia, India, China, and South Africa (BRICS), be reinvigorated. Consequently, this is an ongoing subject ripe for research as countries seek to develop and refine regional dispute settlement systems for the benefit of themselves, individuals, and economic operators on the global stage.

All in all, the courts of regional integration agreements take a lot of inspiration from the ECJ. This holds true for the EFTA Court, the ATJ, the CCJ (to a certain extent), and the Permanent Review Tribunal. That the latter orients itself towards the ECJ is particularly interesting, since it is not modeled on the ECJ but the WTO Appellate Body.[200] In the case of the ATJ and the Permanent Review Tribunal, this is one-way.[201] The EFTA Court seems to be the only regional court that has an influence on the case law of the ECJ. This is illustrated by numerous references to EFTA Court jurisprudence by the ECJ, its Advocates General, and the General Court. ECJ President Skouris has summarized the ECJ's attitude in this respect saying that "ignoring EFTA Court precedents would simply be incompatible with the overriding objective of the EEA agreement which is homogeneity."[202]

[198] D Terris, C Romano and L Swigart, *The International Judge: An Introduction to the Men and Women Who Decide the World's Cases* (Lebanon, NH: Brandeis University Press 2007) 5.

[199] Court of Eurasian Economic Community, press release on Case No 1-7/1-2012, June 26, 2012 <http://sudevrazes.org/en/main.aspx?guid=14211> accessed August 22, 2012.

[200] L Biukovic, "Dispute Resolution Mechanisms and Regional Trade Agreements: South American and Caribbean Modalities" (2008) 14 UC Davis J Intl L & Poly 255, 271.

[201] Biukovic, note 200, at 255 *et seq.*

[202] V Skouris, "The ECJ and the EFTA Court under the EEA Agreement: A Paradigm for International Cooperation between Judicial Institutions" in C Baudenbacher, P Tresselt, T Örlygsson (eds), note 70, at 123, 125; see, with regard to the judicial dialogue between the EFTA Court and the EU judiciary in general C Baudenbacher, "The EFTA Court, the ECJ, and the Latter's Advocates General—a Tale of Judicial Dialogue" in A Arnull, P Eckhout and T Tridimas (eds), *Continuity and Change in EU Law, Essays in Honour of Sir Francis Jacobs* (Oxford University Press 2008) 90; Allan Rosas, "Methods of Interpretation—Judicial Dialogue" in Baudenbacher/Busek, note 194, 185 *et seq.*; see, with regard to the "unique nature" of this dialogue most recently Opinion of Advocate-General Verica Trstenjak, *Vitor Hugo Marques Almeida v. Companhia de Seguros Fidelidade-Mundial SA* [July 5, 2012] Case C-300/10.

Research Questions

1. Would the creation of an advocate-general position benefit the CCJ as a hybrid with a common law heritage?
2. In light of the CCJ's funding structure, it is evidently a structural concern to deny the potential political control of a court by its member states. To what extent is such a concern justified?
3. How can regional agreements best tailor their dispute settlement bodies to the benefit of individuals and economic operators without denying elements of national sovereignty?
4. To what extent do regional courts in the Americas enter a judicial dialogue with regional courts in Europe?

Suggested Reading

Alter, K, Helfer, L, and Saldias, O, "Transplanting the European Court of Justice: The Experience of the Andean Tribunal of Justice" (2012) 60(3) American Journal of Comparative Law 629.

Baudenbacher, C, *The EFTA Court in Action: Five Lectures* (Stuttgart: German Law Publishers 2010).

Burley, A-M and Mattli, W, "Europe before the Court: A Political Theory of Legal Integration" (1993) 47(1) Int'l Org. 41–76.

Del Vecchio, A, *Giurisdizione Internationale e Globalizzazione, I Tribunali Internazionali tra Globalizzazione e Frammentazione* (Milan: Giuffrè Editore 2003).

EFTA Court (ed.), *Judicial Protection in the European Economic Area* (Stuttgart: German Law Publishers 2012).

Glick, LA, *Understanding the North American Free Trade Agreement, Legal and Business Consequences of NAFTA* (3rd edn, Alphen aan den Rijn: Kluwer Law International 2010).

Mackenzie, R et al., *The Manual on International Courts and Tribunals* (2nd edn, Oxford University Press 2010).

Magnússon, S, "On the Authority of Advisory Opinions: Reflections on the Functions and the Normativity of Advisory Opinions of the EFTA Court" (2010) 3 Europarättslig Tidskrift NR.

O'Brien, D and Morano-Foadi, S, "The Caribbean Court of Justice and Legal Integration within CARICOM: Some Lessons from the European Community" (2009) 8 The Law and Practice of International Courts and Tribunals 399.

Oppong, RF, *Legal Aspects of Economic Integration in Africa* (Cambridge University Press 2011).

Temple Lang, J, "Judicial Review of Competition Decisions under the European Convention on Human Rights and the Importance of the EFTA Court: The *Norway Post* Judgment" (2012) EL Rev 4.

CHAPTER 13

INTERNATIONAL CLAIMS AND COMPENSATION BODIES

DAVID D CARON*

* Dean, The Dickson Poon School of Law, King's College London.

1 Introduction

International claims and compensation bodies[1] are a recurring and politically significant form of international adjudication. Sitting at the space between a terrible upheaval that shreds lives and relations and an unknown future, they recur because these spaces are regrettably common. They are politically significant because states often seek ways to settle the complaints resulting from such upheavals in order for their relations to renew, to go forward.

Most often these compensation commissions follow armed conflicts and revolutions, but they should be seen more broadly as a means to address situations where many individuals, either natural or corporate, have been harmed by major upheaval, whatever its particular form. These commissions are concerned with compensation, not with the criminal responsibility of individuals that may arise out of the same events, although such responsibility may be another aspect of finding a way forward. Compensation commissions are often thought of as being concerned with compensation of the victor state and its nationals, but this is too narrow a view of the range of upheavals giving rise to these commissions. And, even after armed conflict, these bodies may be a means for both sides to settle outstanding differences and move forward on the basis of a new relationship.

Despite the great significance of these bodies for both international relations and the compensation of those harmed by the upheaval, the scholarly literature examining them is limited. Moreover, while international courts at large have attracted the attention of scholars outside the legal field, as this handbook illustrates, literature on these commissions is still overwhelmingly legal, being mostly concerned with jurisprudence rather than institutional design. As a consequence, many fundamental questions await further investigation. Why are compensation commissions created

[1] The categorical name given to particular international claims and compensation bodies varies. Through the period up to World War II, the panels often included representatives of both parties and were referred to as "mixed arbitral tribunals." An example is the German-American Mixed Arbitral Tribunal created after WW I. W Kiesselbach, *Problems of the German-American Claims Commission* (Washington D.C.: Carnegie Endowment 1930). Today it is more common to see such bodies referred to as "compensation commissions" or "claims tribunals." The former term emphasizes the task of providing compensation, while the latter emphasizes the legal aspect of claims resolution. On occasion, the term "mixed international arbitration" continues to be used; however, it tends not to refer to compensation commissions in particular but rather to arbitration between states and private parties. See S Toope, *Mixed International Arbitration* (Cambridge: Grotius 1990). For the sake of brevity, the entire class of bodies hereinafter will be referred to as "compensation commissions."

in some instances and not others? Why are compensation commissions, rather than lump sum settlements, chosen? What factors drive the variations seen in the structures of such commissions, and what factors influence their effectiveness and operations? This chapter addresses this gap in literature.

This chapter introduces claims commissions by discussing (1) their functions and (2) the ways in which they differ both from international arbitration and international courts. The chapter then proceeds to consider (3) the factors that appear to affect the particular structures and claims processes of such commissions and (4) their future trajectories.

About 90 claims commissions were created in the nineteenth and twentieth centuries, primarily after armed conflicts and revolutions.[2] This chapter references some of these, but primarily utilizes the most recent bodies as touchstones: the Iran–United States Claims Tribunal (IUSCT) addressing claims arising out of, or left unresolved by, the 1979 Iranian Revolution;[3] the United Nations Compensation Commission (UNCC) addressing claims arising out of the 1990 Gulf War;[4] and the Eritrea–Ethiopia Claims Commission (EECC) addressing claims arising out of the 1998–2000 war between these two nations.[5]

[2] As to the figure of 90 such commissions, see C Romano, "A Taxonomy of International Rule of Law Institutions" (2011) 2 J. Intl Disp. Settlement 264. In addition, there are several excellent surveys of the claims commissions of the nineteenth century, see e.g., AM Stuyt, *Survey of International Arbitrations 1794–1970* (Leiden: Sijthoff 1976). Likewise, there are in-depth studies of numerous specific commissions. See e.g., AH Feller, *The Mexican Claims Commissions 1923–1934: A Study in the Law and Procedure of International Tribunals* (New York: MacMillan 1935). For a valuable synoptic study of ten contemporary claims commissions, see H Holtzmann and E Kristjandottir (eds), *International Mass Claims Procedures: Legal and Practical Procedures* (Oxford University Press 2007) (prepared under the auspices of the Permanent Court of Arbitration Steering Committee on International Mass Claims Procedures).

[3] See D Caron and J Crook (eds), *The Iran-United States Claims Tribunal and the Process of International Claims* (Ardsley, NY: Transnational 2000).

[4] See V Heiskanen, "The United Nations Compensation Commission" (2003) 296 Recueil des Cours 393; R Lillich (ed.), *The United Nations Compensation Commission* (Ardsley, NY: Transnational 1995) 367. See also M di Rattalma, *Nazioni Unite e danni derivanti dalla guerra del Golfo* (Milan: A Giuffrè 1995); A Kolliopoulos, *La Commission d'indeminisation des Nations Unies et le droit de la Responsabilité International* (Paris: LGDJ 2001).

[5] The EECC was created by an Agreement Between Eritrea and Ethiopia dated December 12, 2000 that with reference to other agreements provides for an end to hostilities (Art. 1), a resolution of the border dispute (Art. 4), and a claims commission (Art. 5).

2 Why Compensation Commissions: Motives and Functions

To appreciate the function or functions of an international adjudicative body requires an understanding of why it came into being. Such an examination for compensation commissions suggests at least three different motivating forces. In approaching these forces, it is important to appreciate the difference between a commission's direct function and a less obvious indirect function: the motivation behind creating the commission at all. Compensation commissions exist to achieve their direct function—compensating legitimate claimants—but they may have been created to further other functions as well.[6] These other functions are important because they can shape how a commission carries out its work. If a commission views its work primarily as rectifying the harms suffered by meritorious claimants and not as helping manage a transition to peace, then like a Human Rights body it may find itself leaning toward compensation rather than, for example, toward speedy closure of an incident.

In the following sections, I suggest that there are at least three such functions at play in claims commissions. Simultaneously, regardless of the impulse behind the commission, it must be asked why a compensation commission rather than a lump sum settlement agreement is chosen.

2.1 The direct function of providing compensation

The obvious and most likely stated function of compensation commissions is to provide compensation to a defined set of individuals who have suffered harm as the result of a defined event, usually some major social upheaval spawning numerous claims. The fact that an international, rather than national process, is chosen likely reflects something about the national options. National options may not be trusted to be fair to foreigners. Or, they may not be respected at home as able to resist foreigners. Feller argues that this was a motivation behind the several Mexican Claim Commissions.[7]

[6] This distinction is discussed in D Caron, "International Courts and Tribunals: Their Roles Amidst a World of Courts" (2011) 26 ICSID Foreign Investment LJ 1.

[7] Feller, note 2, writes: "The military inferiority of Mexico and the subserviency to foreign interests of some transitory government occasionally led to the acknowledgment of fraudulent or inflated claims. Such acquiescence would embitter Mexican public opinion and lead to further antagonism to aliens. The chronic difficulties of the Mexican treasury would make it difficult to liquidate the claims, and the net result would be an increase of ill-feeling between the two countries. In such circumstances, the submission of claims to an international tribunal offered a way out."

The direct function of compensating individuals is often stated explicitly in a commission's mandate, but this may not be the primary motivation behind its creation. Other motivations may be in play.

2.2 The indirect function of limiting compensable losses and the scope of claims

By defining what is compensable, claims commissions may put limits on, and ultimately an end to, the liability of the various state parties involved. This extends beyond merely ensuring that there is no double recovery by claimants through actions in multiple fora.[8] Claims stemming from revolution or war likely have few, if any, national fora available for their pursuit. Often they are simply never addressed or are waived as part of a peace agreement.[9]

Ending litigation and limiting liability as an indirect function of claims commissions may be a legal or may be simply a practical consequence. Thus, for example, a "general principle" of the Algiers Accords was "to bring about the settlement and termination of all such claims."[10] But this was not to be accomplished solely through the IUSCT. The Algiers Accords also require that the United States "bar and preclude the prosecution against Iran of any pending or future claim of the United States or a United States national arising out of events occurring before the date of this Declaration related to (A) the seizure of the 52 United States nationals on November 4, 1979, (B) their subsequent detention, (C) injury to the United States property...within the United States Embassy...and (D) injury to United States nationals... as a result of the popular movements in the course of the Islamic Revolution in Iran which were not an act of the Government of Iran."[11] The IUSCT provided compensation to many individuals injured by acts of the Government of Iran, but it did not consider these other claims.[12] In short, the instruments creating

[8] For example, the Claims Resolution Tribunal for Dormant Accounts in Switzerland (CRT-1) addressed the issue of double recovery in part by requiring claimants to sign an agreement to arbitrate under Swiss arbitration law, therefore extending the recognition possibilities available under the 1958 New York Convention on Foreign Arbitral Awards to CRT-1 decisions on claims.

[9] See e.g., Art. 14.b, Treaty of Peace with Japan [1952] 3 U.S.T. 3169, TIAS No. 2490 (1951).

[10] The Declaration of the Government of the Democratic and Popular Republic of Algeria (1981) General Principle B.

[11] The Declaration of the Government, note 10, at para. 11.

[12] Article II.1 of the Claims Settlement Declaration specifically excludes from the jurisdiction of the Iran–United States Claims Tribunal those claims "described in Paragraph 11 of the Declaration of the Government of Algeria of January 19, 1981." Whether individuals' claims can be terminated presents questions both of international human rights law and of the internal law of the terminating state. As to the claims of the 52 US hostages, see B Budros, "The Former American Hostages' Human Rights Claims Against Iran: Can They be Waived?" (1981) 4 Houston J Intl L 101, 101–31; and J Tichy, "Hostage Compensation: United States Liability for Injuries Suffered by Nationals Held in Iran—President's Commission on Hostage Compensation" (1982) 23 Harv Intl L J 131, 131–8.

the IUSCT provided a forum for deciding some claims arising out of the Iranian revolution, barred other fora from considering these claims (thereby channeling them to the IUSCT) and placed other claims outside both US and IUSCT jurisdiction, thereby effectively denying their viability.

In the case of the UNCC, excluded claims were not barred from prosecution elsewhere, so the liability of Iraq was not limited as a legal matter. But as a practical matter the exclusion of certain claims from the UNCC process meant they were no longer pursued given the sovereign immunity that would be granted Iraq in most fora.

2.3 The creation or operation of a compensation commission as an indirect means to other ends

Although a compensation commission's formal mandate likely speaks of its function as providing compensation to a defined set of claimants and disputes, the commission may potentially have accomplished other functions simply by being created.

2.3.1 *The compensation commission as a part of a larger negotiation*

For example, the central driving consideration for the United States when negotiating the Algiers Accords with Iran was the prompt release of Americans held hostages in Iran. Indeed, the establishment of the IUSCT arguably can be seen primarily as a means to meet Iranian demands that the United States terminate litigation against Iran in US courts, rather than the end of providing compensation to injured parties.

2.3.2 *The compensation commission as part of a strategy for peace*

A compensation commission may be part of a broader mix of measures aimed at securing political objectives. The possibility of a UNCC was first introduced in a UN Security Council resolution as part of a package of sanctions and condemnations intended to induce President Saddam Hussein to withdraw from Kuwait. Similarly, the December 12, 2000 Agreement Between Eritrea and Ethiopia provides for not only the EECC but also the Eritrean–Ethiopian Boundary Commission and a variety of others measures. In the Agreement's Preamble, the state parties welcome "the commitment . . . of the international community to mobilize resources for the resettlement of displaced persons, as well as rehabilitation and peace building in both countries." The Preamble makes no mention of claims as the agreement's primary object. Rather, claims resolution is one of several means to pursue rehabilitation and peace building.[13]

2.4 Why not a lump-sum settlement agreement?

In asking why a compensation commission is created, we should ask both what functions it furthers and why another means to pursue those same ends, a lump sum settlement agreement in particular, was not used instead.[14] Why is a compensation commission, which decides upon submitted claims, preferred over a lump sum settlement, in which funds are transferred to a domestic process for the allocation among claimants of that nationality?[15]

Indeed, lump sum settlement agreements were common in the decades after World War II with claims commissions virtually absent until they were resurrected with the establishment in 1981 of the IUSCT.[16] This 35-year absence might suggest that negotiators doubted the relative efficiency (or perhaps even competence) of international claims commissions compared to domestic ones. It might also indicate that negotiators had simply grown unfamiliar with such bodies and employed that which they knew.

A further explanation may be that lump sum settlements are possible when there is time to agree on the amount of a lump sum or when the amount is not significant to one or both of the parties. In the specific case of the Iran–US negotiations, however, reaching agreement on the amount of a lump sum was likely impossible because time was too limited. A driving force behind the Algiers Accords was the prompt release of the US diplomatic personnel held hostage in Tehran. Further, negotiation of a lump sum settlement requires a certain amount of information on the aggregate amount and strength of the relevant claims. But, Iran and the United States wildly disagreed on such figures. Finally, lump sum settlement negotiations require a minimum amount of goodwill between the state parties, goodwill that

[13] Indeed, it has been speculated that the creation of the EECC and the Boundary Commission had the salutary effect of focusing the attention of the two nations on those two processes for several years, thereby reinforcing the cessation of violence called for in Art. 1 of the 2000 Agreement.

[14] Similarly, it could be asked why the claims were not simply waived by both parties.

[15] The practice of particular lump sum settlements and the domestic claims commissions that ultimately distributed those settlements have been studied extensively. In the case of the United States, see e.g., R Lillich, *International Claims: Their Adjudication by National Claims Commissions* (Syracuse University Press 1962). As one would anticipate, there are many similarities between international and domestic claims commissions with domestic claims commissions often charged with applying the same applicable law.

[16] Several observers have written that the success of the Iran–US Tribunal placed claims commissions back into the diplomatic tool bag. See e.g., C Brower and J Brueschke, *The Iran-United States Claims Tribunal* (The Hague: Martinus Nijhoff 1998) 669; and Caron and Crook, note 3, at 363.

may be lacking, as with Iran and the United States, if the negotiation follows immediately on the heels of a conflict or crisis.[17]

Creating an international claims commission can sidestep such barriers to negotiation of a lump sum. It is easier to agree to create a commission that will decide on disputed amounts years down the line, rather than agreeing here and now on the whole. Politically, this move may finesse domestic opposition, but it may also shift the underlying political tensions to the commission.

It is important to bear these various functions in mind in the case of a particular commission because its success in terms of one function does not necessarily require or ensure success in terms of others.

3 How Compensation Commissions are Distinct from International Courts and Tribunals

Compensation commissions are one of three types in Romano's taxonomy of international adjudicative bodies. For him, they sit between international arbitral tribunals and international courts because they possess some characteristics of both, but not all the characteristics of either.[18]

According to Romano, both international arbitral tribunals and compensation commissions differ from international courts in that they do not have what he calls "permanency." In my opinion, this choice of words does not capture the quality I believe intended; what Romano really means is an institution with an "indefinite existence." Both international arbitral tribunals and compensation commissions typically address a particular dispute or a defined category of disputes. They may be given jurisdiction over future disputes that are derivative of the past claims, but such forward-looking jurisdiction is rare.[19] Romano also distinguishes international arbitral tribunals and compensation commissions from international courts because

[17] See e.g., J Greenberg, "*Algerian Intervention in the Iranian Hostage Crisis*" (1984) 20 Stan J Intl L 259, 250–89 (discussing the necessary intermediary role played by Algeria given the inability of the United States and Iran to communicate).

[18] C Romano, "A Taxonomy of International Rule of Law Institutions" (2011) 2 JIDS 241, 261–4 (providing at page 246 a taxonomic chart of international adjudicative bodies).

[19] For example, the IUSCT possessed jurisdiction both over the claims of nationals arising out of, or left unaddressed by, the Iranian Revolution, and over interpretative disputes regarding the Algiers Accords.

the parties to tribunals and commissions tend to have a greater involvement in the selection of the adjudicators.

Romano's observations are generally accurate. They are generally accurate in that these adjudicative institutions generally conform to a pattern and Romano describes the range well, but it is crucial to emphasize that any particular institution need not fit this pattern. Indeed, there are few legal limitations, if any, to the design of these institutions. It is more valuable in this sense to ask what factors or circumstances time after time lead the designers of such institutions to create bodies that follow the pattern. I would suggest three factors: (1) the fact that the claims to be addressed already exist, (2) the number of claims requiring resolution, and (3) the identity of the actors working to create the body.

3.1 The claims already exist

Claims commissions are similar to international arbitral tribunals in that the designers of both create them to address an existing claim or claims. They are ad hoc and retrospective exercises in justice. This characteristic corresponds with the direct function of resolving claims arising out of a major societal upheaval that by definition has already occurred. The commission's function is not to uphold the objectives of a legal regime, for example relating to trade, by resolving future disputes. Rather it looks to a past event and aims to resolve the trail of claims reaching from the past into the present. The precise number of claims a commission will need to resolve may not be known at the outset, but it is known that the number is limited. It may not be known when the commission will complete its work, but it is known that at some point its work will be declared complete. It is in this sense that arbitral tribunals and claims commissions do not possess an indefinite existence, while an international court with jurisdiction encompassing claims yet to arise has such existence.

3.2 The number of claims requiring resolution

Although the designers of international arbitral tribunals and claims commissions are confronted with resolving disputes that already exist, these institutions face different challenges. An arbitral tribunal most often addresses a single dispute, just as international courts typically deal with disputes that arise and are decided one at a time. On the other hand, a compensation commission may address thousands, even millions, of claims.

Indeed, if we focus only on the forms of international arbitral tribunals and claims commissions, it is evident that the number of claims drives the differences in design. A single claim requires a single ad hoc arbitration tribunal. Two claims might be handled by two separate ad hoc tribunals, or if they are sufficiently similar they might be addressed by the same tribunal. But once designers are confronted with hundreds, thousands, or millions of claims, the claims are placed before a single ad hoc institution that we call a compensation commission or a claims tribunal.

The tendency to place the claims before a single ad hoc institution is almost irresistible for three reasons. First, there is the obvious pull of efficiency, with the single institution gaining expertise and advantages of scale. Second, this approach does much to resolve questions of coordination between the state parties involved and the many claims themselves. Third, and perhaps most subtly, the single institution enhances legitimacy of the entire process by promoting consistency in the handling and outcome of the various claims.

3.3 The identity of the actors working to create the body

Similarly, it is not always the case as Romano suggests that the parties have a greater voice in selecting the adjudicators in claims commissions than in international courts. It is correct that the composition of both the IUSCT and the EECC were greatly influenced by the state parties involved. This is, however, not an inherent characteristic of claims commissions, but rather a consequence of the fact that those two commissions were created by the state parties involved. The result is quite different if a larger community creates the commission. Thus, the UNCC, created by the UN Security Council, is a case in which adjudicators were selected through a much different process in which Iraq played very little role. While claimant states had some role in that process, it was heavily shaped by the UNCC Secretariat and by the presence of non-claimant states on the Governing Council in Geneva, which mirrored the states on the Security Council.

These circumstances suggest several observations on the distinctions between compensation commissions, international arbitral tribunals, and international courts. First, recent compensation commissions frequently stem from agreements by the particular state parties involved, and in this sense have certain characteristics in common with international arbitral tribunals—such as greater influence of the two states in selecting adjudicators and a jurisdiction that addresses existing rather than future disputes. Second, because of the large number of claims involved, compensation commissions can have a longer life span and a standing institutional structure that more resembles an international court than an international arbitration tribunal.

4 How International Compensation Commissions are Distinct from National Compensation Commissions

The definition of an international compensation commission is not as sharp as it once might have been. At one time the definition could rest on formal grounds, such as whether the international claims commission originated in an international instrument such as a treaty, possessed the immunities and privileges of an international organization, and, to a lesser degree, applied international law. These more formal distinctions remain relevant but are less and less a definitive basis for definition. The IUSCT, the UNCC, and the EECC all had their origins in international instruments, and all three institutions possessed a degree of international personality. The law they applied was often international law. More problematic, however, is the example of the first Claims Resolution Tribunal for Dormant Accounts in Switzerland (CRT-1), the origin of which can be traced to an Independent Committee of Eminent Persons formed in 1996 by a Memorandum of Understanding between the Swiss Bankers Association, the World Jewish Restitution Organization, and the World Jewish Congress. The CRT-1 was established in October 1997 as an independent arbitral tribunal under Swiss law. Claimants were required to sign an agreement to arbitrate placing the CRT-1 process for their claim under the Swiss arbitration law. Although a formal lens would indicate that the CRT-1 is not an international compensation commission, the circumstances—based on the Holocaust—that underlie its creation have a strong international political aspect. The fact that the CRT-1 received 9,918 claims from 27 countries further underlines its international scope.

Such broadening of the types of claims and situations addressed by international compensation commissions corresponds to the broadening of international law itself. The upheaval addressed need no longer be one involving several states but can be totally internal, as where a commission addresses the human rights of citizens harmed by a repressive government.[20] Similarly, the broadening range of international actors suggests, as in the case of the CRT-1, that international commissions may originate in actors other than states, although placing a commission within the framework of a national system, as with the CRT-1, may raise questions as to, for example, its openness, or limit

[20] A Carrillo and J Palmer, "Transnational Mass Claim Type Procedures (TMCPs) in International Law and Practice" (2010) 28 Berkeley J Intl L 343.

the commission's approach to claims resolution because of national conceptions of due process. Thus, while definitional boundaries remain, they are becoming increasingly blurred.

5 Understanding the Structure of, and Claims Process Utilized in, Modern Compensation Commissions

The previous sections outline why states and other actors create compensation commissions and argue that the challenge of a large number of claims arising out of a major upheaval likely leads to one institution rather than a set of separate arbitral tribunals. Beyond that basic choice of structure, there can be wide variations in institutional structure and claims process. The following section offers six propositions concerning these variations.

5.1 Compensation commissions often have two organs

Commissions normally possess two organs, while an ad hoc tribunal addressing a single claim has but one. In commissions, adjudicators have the core function of deciding claims, but a substantial secretariat typically assists the adjudicators by running an institution that facilitates and supports their work.[21] In practice, the strength and role of these two organs can vary. An example of strong adjudicators with a constrained secretariat is the IUSCT, where the members of the tribunal took up full time residence in The Hague and exercised great day-to-day control over the tribunal's operations, reducing the secretariat's role to administrative functions. By contrast, with the UNCC, the secretariat first came to reside full-time in Geneva and played a central role in the commission's operations. The secretariat designed a structure that reduced the Commissioners' role to that of non-resident adjudicators who arrived perhaps once a month for five days to decide a group of claims assembled and briefed by secretariat teams. The adjudicators decided the tranches of claims assembled for them, but it was not their function to decide, for example, on the strategy behind the organization of the tranches.

[21] On the role played by registries and legal secretariats in international adjudication, see, in this handbook, Hoss and Cartier, Ch. 33.

5.2 The influence of large numbers: individualized adjudication vs mass claim techniques

A major social upheaval can produce thousands or millions of claims. They can all be small or large in amount or vary tremendously. They can all be of one type (e.g., forced deportation) or involve many types of injury. These differences have an effect on how commissions approach their work. A difference in the order of magnitude of the number of claims in particular yields commissions with very different approaches.

When a commission faces numerous claims that vary in type and may involve substantial amounts, the typical tendency is to utilize some form of individualized adjudication. Due process normally leads to an individualized sense of justice and the common domestic impulse toward individualized adjudication as central to due process tends to pervade thinking in commissions. Simultaneously, the variety in claim amounts and types makes efficiencies in grouping issues less apparent and attainable. The IUSCT is an example of a commission that for the most part approached each claim through individualized adjudication, although it also attempted to decide some important issues (for example, involving recurring jurisdictional issues) through test cases.

The increase from hundreds to thousands to millions of claims creates an impulse toward two other variations in design. First, as the number of claims grows, the number of decision-makers may increase. Thus, for example, the Claims Settlement Declaration for the IUSCT provided that the "Tribunal shall consist of nine members or such larger multiple of three as Iran and the United States may agree as necessary to conduct its business expeditiously,"[22] although this authority was never used.

Second, as the number of claims grows, particularly as they reach into the thousands, the method of decision may change. Individualized adjudication maximizes accuracy and due process in the case of a single claim. As the number of claims increases, however, the time required to simply work through them becomes of greater and greater importance; claimants themselves may press for quicker resolution. This tendency toward valuing practical justice, as opposed to perfect justice, can lead to the adoption of various mass claims processing techniques.[23] The UNCC is the primary contemporary example of the use of mass claims techniques involving multiple claims categories, fixed damage amounts for some categories, and varying evidentiary burdens reflecting the type of claim and amount of compensation sought.

[22] Claims Settlement Declaration, Art. III.1.

[23] See D Caron, *The UNCC and the Search for Practical Justice, in The United Nations Compensation Commission* (ed. by R Lillich, Ardsley, NY: Transnational 1995) 367.

5.3 The consequences of a closed docket—whether large or small

The fact that there is a finite number of claims before a claims commission makes its decision-making process quite different from an international court that will operate indefinitely to address an as yet unknown number of future claims. For claims commissions, the closed universe of claimants can lead to a deep concern with equity and consistency between claimants. An international court is pulled not only by what it has done already, but also by future claimants unrepresented in its current proceedings. The claims commission, however, in seeking consistency is pulled by its first decisions.[24] These can be critically important for the pattern of the commission's entire work.

5.4 The relationship between budgetary resources and structure

A compensation commission's budget profoundly impacts the complexity of its structure and processes, particularly the extent of secretariat support and the extent to which a secretariat can utilize technology or the services of experts in adopting mass claims techniques.[25] These techniques utilize categorical decisions, thereby tolerating some loss of individualized justice, but allow consideration of greatly increased numbers of claims. Thus, for example, the UNCC established a category of claims for forced departure from Kuwait during the Iraq War. These provided modest fixed amounts of compensation where specified types of evidence established a claimant's departure in the relevant time period. The UNCC received over 900,000 such departure claims, so expert studies and computer assistance were important to understanding the patterns of departure and damage, as well as in seeking to avoid double recovery. A compensation commission can operate without such studies and assistance, but the result will be necessarily less nuanced. The five-member EECC, in contrast to the UNCC and the IUSCT, operated on a small budget with very limited secretariat assistance.

5.5 The potentially lasting influence of the negotiating context in which the commission is created

If the commission is created by two states whose relationship remains strained, as in the cases of the IUSCT and EECC, both parties are likely to insist they are present in the commission's structure, notably in terms of adjudicator selection.

[24] On this point, see also P Karrer, "Mass Claims Proceedings in Practice: A Few Lessons Learned" (2005) 23 Berkeley J Intl L 463, 471–2.

[25] On the cost and financing of international adjudication, see, in this handbook, Ingadottir, Ch. 27.

To the degree that the party-appointed members consciously or unconsciously carry within themselves the tension between the two nations, the situation will test the commission's capacity to decide according to the law.[26] Conversely, if the institution is created by a larger community with the most politically involved states not necessarily represented, their absence, as with the significant absence of Iraq in most UNCC proceedings, may give rise to assertions of illegitimacy in the process as a whole.

5.6 The significance of the availability of monies to satisfy claims

Lastly, it is important to recognize the vital need for sufficient monies to fund a commission's operations and satisfy its awards of compensation. In the case of the IUSCT, the Algiers Accords provided for a US$1 billion security account to satisfy awards against Iran. In the case of the UNCC, the commission could tap a fund made up of a portion of Iraq's oil sale revenues to cover its substantial operating expenses and awards of compensation. Certainly, the availability of monies to fund operations and awards that are, to a degree, independent of interested states strengthens a commission's judicial independence and in a sense renders the commission autonomous. Conversely, significant uncertainty that funds will ever be available to satisfy awards, as was the case with the EECC, may lead the members of the commission to focus not only on the direct (albeit unlikely) function of compensation but also the indirect functions of that particular commission, for example, contributing to peace and security in the region.

6 Conclusions and Trends in Compensation Commissions and Claims Tribunals

In closing, I would note three trends in the use and structure of compensation commissions.

First, since the 1980s there has been a diplomatic rejuvenation in the use of claims commissions. What that increase indicates and what factors give rise to it

[26] For an insightful discussion of the relationship of the IUSCT's origin and the later presence of politics within it, see C Brower and J Brueschke, *The Iran-United States Claims Tribunal* (Dordrecht: Kluwer 1998) 660–4.

are not entirely clear. The increased use may reflect in part an increased demand for compensation paralleling the growth of human rights law. Injuries to individuals perhaps can no longer be simply overlooked in many cases. But the commissions that have been successful in actually delivering compensation often have succeeded because of circumstances that do not necessarily repeat. The IUSCT's security account and the UNCC's access to Iraq's oil revenues were both the result of highly unusual circumstances. Will such circumstances repeat? Or will commissions without funds to pay awards, such as the EECC, be the more usual situation? The present resort to commissions, however, appears to reflect a conclusion within the international community that they work and are worth the substantial effort involved.

Second, there is an incomplete trend from state espousal of claims in such commissions to the filing of the claims of defined individuals. This trend reflects a move from an image of claims where the state is the principal to one where the state is an agent of its nationals and environment.[27] In the case of the UNCC, the state was not the claimant asserting the harm to its national as its own; the state instead served as a sort of agent for forwarding claims and distributing payments for persons within its territory. However, the transition away from state espousal is not necessarily easy. The EECC included in its rules rudimentary optional procedures allowing the parties to file mass claims on behalf of large numbers of identified individual claimants should they wish, but the commission did not have the resources to implement those procedures had they been used. In any event, the parties could not prepare thousands of individual claims given their limited resources and the short one-year mandatory time limit for filing claims.

Third, there is discussion occasionally, particularly within the skilled secretariats of commissions, that a standing institution housing mass claims expertise and computer capability would be a valuable and important innovation. Like domestic claims commissions such as the US Foreign Claims Settlement Commission, the size of this organization could range from a permanent, small core of expert advisers to a larger institution that could be adapted and sized appropriately to administer claims programs for particular situations. It is unclear to this author whether this suggestion is desirable. On the one hand, it would be valuable to preserve the expertise that develops with each new commission. On the other hand, experience has shown that the circumstances shaping each commission require a flexibility in approach that might be stifled in a standing institution.

[27] For a discussion of this principal-agent distinction, see D Caron, "The Profound Significance of the UNCC for the Environment" in C Payne and P Sand (eds), *Gulf War Reparations and the UN Compensation Commission* (Oxford University Press 2011) 265.

In closing, it is important to emphasize that despite the crucial roles played in international affairs and justice by the IUSCT, the UNCC, and the EECC, the scholarly attention placed on claims commissions is quite limited compared to that placed on international arbitral tribunals and international courts. Four questions for further scholarly reflection follow below.

Research Questions

1. Why are compensation commissions created in some instances but not in others?
2. Why is the form of a compensation commission preferred over that of a lump sum settlement?
3. What factors drive the variations seen in the structures of such commissions?
4. What factors influence the effectiveness and operations of such commissions?

Suggested Reading

Brower, CN and Brueschke, J, *The Iran-United States Claims Tribunal* (Dordrecht: Kluwer 1998).

Caron, DD and Crook, JR (eds), *The Iran-United States Claims Tribunal and the Process of International Claims* (Ardsley, NY: Transnational 2000).

Carrillo, AJ and Palmer, JS, "Transnational Mass Claim Type Procedures (TMCPs) in International Law and Practice" (2010) 28 Berkeley J. Int'l L. 343.

Feller, AH, *The Mexican Claims Commissions 1923–1934: A Study in Law and Procedure of International Tribunals* (New York: MacMillan 1935).

Heiskanen, V, "The United Nations Compensation Commission" (2003) 296 Recueil des Cours 393.

Holtzmann, HM and Kristjandottir, E (eds), *International Mass Claims Procedures: Legal and Practical Procedures* (Oxford University Press 2007).

International Bureau of the PCA (ed.), *Institutional and Procedural Aspects of Mass Claims Settlements Systems* (Dordrecht: Kluwer 2000).

Kiesselbach, W, *Problems of the German-American Claims Commission* (Washington D.C.: Carnegie Endowment 1930).

Lillich, RB (ed.), *The United Nations Compensation Commission* (Ardsley, NY: Transnational 1995).

Nielsen, FK, *American and British Claims Arbitration Under the Special Agreement Concluded Between the United States and Great Britain, August 18, 1910* (Washington Government Printing Office 1926).

Payne, CR and Sand, PH (eds), *Gulf War Reparations and the UN Compensation Commission* (Oxford University Press 2011).

Ralston, JH, *International Arbitration From Athens to Locarno* (Stanford University Press 1929).

Simpson, JL and Fox, H, *International Arbitration* (London: Stevens 1959).

CHAPTER 14

INVESTMENT ARBITRATION

CHRISTOPH SCHREUER*

* Professor emeritus, University of Vienna.

1 The Function of Investment Arbitration in International Dispute Settlement

Arbitration is the preferred method for the settlement of investment disputes between states and foreign investors. In its absence, investors would have to turn to domestic courts to seek a remedy against adverse action by the host state. From the investor's perspective, the host state's courts are not an attractive solution for several reasons. In many countries an independent judiciary cannot be taken for granted. Executive interventions in court proceedings or a sense of judicial loyalty to the forum state are likely to influence the outcome of proceedings. This is particularly so in cases involving large amounts of money. In addition, legislation is often the cause of complaints by investors. Domestic courts are typically bound to apply the local law even if it is at odds with international standards for the protection of investors. In fact, in some countries the relevant treaties containing these standards are not part of the domestic legal order. At times, domestic courts may be the perpetrators of the alleged violation of investor rights.

The courts of the investor's home country and of third states are usually not a viable alternative either. In most cases, they lack territorial jurisdiction over investments taking place in another state. An additional obstacle to the use of these courts is state immunity.

Under the traditional system of diplomatic protection the investor's state espouses the claim of its national and pursues it in its own name on the international plane against the host state. This system carries serious disadvantages for the protected investor. Diplomatic protection is discretionary: the investor has no right to it. The investor's state of nationality may refuse to pursue the claim or may abandon it at any stage. In addition, diplomatic protection requires the exhaustion of local remedies in the host state.

Diplomatic protection on behalf of investors also carries important disadvantages for the states concerned. It can constitute a serious strain on their relations. Developing countries, in particular, resent pressure from capital exporting countries, whether it is exercised bilaterally or in multilateral fora.

Arbitration provides a depoliticized international forum that is independent of the host state's judicial system. It may be initiated by the investor regardless of any decision of its home state. Investment arbitration carries advantages for both the investor and the host state. The advantage for the investor is obvious: it gains access to an effective international remedy. The advantage to the host state is twofold: by offering an international procedure for dispute settlement it improves its investment climate and is likely to attract more foreign investment. Also, by consenting to international arbitration the host state shields itself against other processes, notably diplomatic protection.

Investment arbitration uses a mechanism originally developed for the settlement of commercial disputes between private parties. But it has developed into an important branch of international adjudication. Investment arbitration involves two diverse parties, a sovereign state and a private investor. In the vast majority of cases the state is in the role of respondent and the investor is in the role of claimant.

The primary function of investment arbitration is an examination of the legality of state action vis-à-vis foreign investors. This may involve the scrutiny of the activity of all branches of the government: executive, judiciary, and legislature. In the exercise of this function, investment tribunals apply a variety of international law rules stemming from all fields of international law. Apart from specific treaties, the rules on treaty interpretation and questions of state responsibility are particularly prominent.

A distinctive feature of investment arbitration is its ad hoc nature: each tribunal is specifically constituted for the particular dispute. The parties to the dispute play a major role in the composition of tribunals. This goes considerably beyond the appointment of an ad hoc judge. A typical investment tribunal is composed of two party appointees and a president who is appointed by agreement of the parties. Alternatively, the president may be appointed by the two party appointed arbitrators or by an appointing authority. This method of appointment is designed to strengthen the confidence of the parties in the arbitral process. But the ad hoc nature of tribunals also has a serious effect on the coherence of the system and the consistency of decisions.[1]

Investment arbitration has developed into a particularly active form of international adjudication. Hundreds of cases are pending and there is a constant stream of decisions by investment tribunals. These decisions play an important role in the practice of international law.

2 Arbitration Institutions, Rules, and Regimes

Arbitration between a host state and a foreign investor may take place in the framework of a variety of institutions or rules. Exceptionally, arbitration may take place unsupported by a particular arbitration institution.

[1] On coherence and consistency, see section 14.1 of this chapter.

2.1 International Centre for Settlement of Investment Disputes (ICSID)

Nowadays the majority of investment arbitrations take place under the Convention on the Settlement of Investment Disputes between States and Nationals of Other States.[2] The convention was drafted in the framework of the World Bank in Washington and entered into force on October 14, 1966. It created the International Centre for Settlement of Investment Disputes (ICSID, the Centre). This is why the convention is commonly referred to as the ICSID Convention or the Washington Convention. By mid-2012 the convention had 147 parties.[3]

ICSID provides a system of dispute settlement for investor–state disputes. It offers standard clauses for the use of the parties, detailed rules of procedure, and institutional support.[4] The ICSID Convention offers a procedural framework for arbitration. It does not contain substantive rules on the protection of foreign investments. The Centre has its headquarters in Washington, D.C. It is a permanent administrative body but not a court. Arbitral tribunals are constituted separately for each case. The seat of a tribunal is to be fixed by agreement between the parties and the tribunal after consultation with the Secretary-General of ICSID.

The jurisdiction of ICSID requires an investment dispute of a legal nature between a state party to the convention and a national of another state party to the convention. In addition, both parties to the dispute (the host state and the investor) must have consented to ICSID's jurisdiction.[5] Proceedings under the ICSID Convention are independent of the intervention of any outside bodies. In particular, domestic courts do not have the power to stay, to compel, or to otherwise influence ICSID proceedings. Also, domestic courts do not have the power to set aside or otherwise review ICSID awards.

ICSID had a slow start. The first case was not registered before 1972. The 1970s and 1980s saw steady but only intermittent action: one or two cases per year were typical for that period. Since the mid-1990s there has been a dramatic increase in activity. In 1995 there were four ICSID arbitrations pending. At the beginning of 2013 there were 166 cases pending. During 2012 the Secretary-General registered 40 new cases.

[2] 575 UNTS 159; 4 ILM 524 (1965). For detailed information, see <https://icsid.worldbank.org/ICSID/Index.jsp> accessed May 16, 2013.

[3] Three states have terminated their participation by denouncing the ICSID Convention in accordance with its Art. 71: Bolivia on May 2, 2007, Ecuador on July 6, 2009, Venezuela on January 24, 2012.

[4] For a concise overview see L Reed, J Paulsson, and N Blackaby, *Guide to ICSID Arbitration* (2nd edn, The Hague, London, New York: Kluwer 2011). For more detail see C Schreuer et al., *The ICSID Convention: A Commentary* (2nd edn, Cambridge University Press 2009).

[5] ICSID Convention, Art. 25. For a more detailed treatment of consent to arbitration see section 5 of this chapter.

2.2 ICSID Additional Facility

In 1978 the Administrative Council of ICSID created the Additional Facility. It is open to parties that submit to its jurisdiction in certain cases that are outside ICSID's jurisdiction. The most important situation involves cases where either the host state or the investor's home state is not a party to the ICSID Convention. This has become especially important in the context of the North American Free Trade Agreement (NAFTA) since only the United States has ratified the ICSID Convention but Canada and Mexico have not.

Additional Facility proceedings receive institutional support from ICSID in a similar way as proceedings under the ICSID Convention. Arbitration under the Additional Facility is not governed by the ICSID Convention but by separate Additional Facility Rules. This means, in particular, that the ICSID Convention's provisions on the recognition and enforcement of awards are not applicable to awards rendered under the Additional Facility.

2.3 Other arbitration institutions

Institutions that deal primarily with commercial arbitration between private parties are also available, in principle, for investor–state arbitration. These include the International Chamber of Commerce; the London Court of International Arbitration (LCIA); the Arbitration Institute of the Stockholm Chamber of Commerce; Regional Arbitration Centres in Frankfurt, Vienna, Cairo, Kuala Lumpur, and Hong Kong; or the China International Economic and Trade Arbitration Commission (CIETAC). In current practice such arbitrations are often conducted under the UNCITRAL Arbitration Rules of 1976 (revised in 2010) and under the International Chamber of Commerce's Arbitration Rules of 1998 (revised in 2011). In addition, the Permanent Court of Arbitration (PCA) administers investment arbitrations.[6]

3 The Subject Matter of Investment Disputes

Under the ICSID Convention, jurisdiction is limited to legal disputes arising directly out of an investment. But the convention does not define the notion of investment. This has led to much debate and controversy. Most treaties providing

[6] At the beginning of 2013 there were about 50 investment arbitrations pending in proceedings administered by the PCA.

for investment arbitration contain broad definitions of "investment." These definitions include tangible and intangible property, participation in companies, claims to money, claims to performance, and intellectual property, as well as rights conferred by law or contract.

Tribunals have identified a number of typical elements for the concept of investment for purposes of the ICSID Convention. These include a substantial commitment, certain duration, risk, and, less clearly, a contribution to the host state's development. The significance of these definitional elements is disputed among tribunals.[7]

Tribunals have emphasized the unity of the overall investment operation. What matters is not so much ownership of specific assets but rather the combination of rights that is necessary for the economic activity that constitutes the investment. An investment is typically a complex operation composed of a number of elements each of which on its own may not qualify as an investment.[8]

The classical issue in investment disputes is expropriation and the resulting duty to pay compensation. More recently, additional standards of treatment have gained in importance. These are mostly contained in treaties, especially in bilateral investment treaties (BITs) and some multilateral treaties such as the NAFTA and the Energy Charter Treaty (ECT). These standards include fair and equitable treatment, full protection and security, protection against arbitrary and discriminatory treatment, national treatment, and most favoured nation (MFN) treatment.

4 The Parties to the Investment Arbitration

Investment arbitration involves a sovereign state (the host state) on one side and a private, foreign investor on the other. In many cases, it is not the state as such that deals with a foreign investor but a territorial subdivision such as a province or

[7] *Salini v. Morocco* (Decision on Jurisdiction) [July 23, 2001] para. 56; *Malaysian Historical Salvors v. Malaysia* (Decision on Annulment) [April 16, 2009] paras 56–81; *Pantechniki v. Albania* (Award) [July 30, 2009] paras 42–4; *Inmaris. v Ukraine* (Decision on Jurisdiction) [March 8, 2010] paras 126–34; *Fakes v. Turkey* (Award) [July 14, 2010] paras 99–113; *Alpha v. Ukraine* (Award) [November 8, 2010] paras 310–32; *Abaclat v. Argentina* (Decision on Jurisdiction) [August 4, 2011] paras 362–71; *Quiborax v. Bolivia* (Decision on Jurisdiction) [September 27, 2012] paras 218–37.

[8] *CSOB v. Slovakia* (Decision on Jurisdiction) [May 24, 1999] para. 72; *Enron v. Argentina* [January 14, 2004] para. 70; *Joy Mining v. Egypt* (Award) [August 6, 2004] para. 54; *Mitchell v. Congo* (Decision on Annulment) [November 1, 2006] para. 38; *Duke Energy v. Peru* (Decision on Jurisdiction) [February 1, 2006] para. 92; *Saipem v. Bangladesh* (Decision on Jurisdiction) [March 21, 2007] paras 110, 114.

municipality or a state entity. Under the rules of state responsibility, acts of territorial subdivisions will be attributed to the state. Where the state acts through a separate entity, attribution will depend on whether the entity exercises governmental authority or is directed or controlled by the state.[9]

In principle, only the state itself has party status in investment arbitration. But under Art. 25 of the ICSID Convention a state's constituent subdivision or agency may become a party to proceedings if so authorized by the state.[10]

Investment arbitration is designed for the protection of private investors. This would indicate that the investor must be a private individual or corporation. But state-owned corporations and state entities may be accepted as investors if they act in a private commercial capacity.[11]

It has always been beyond doubt that arbitral proceedings are open to more than one claimant in one and the same case. The practice under the ICSID Convention shows numerous proceedings with more than one party on the claimants' side. More recently, this has led to mass claims involving thousands of claimants in connection with defaults under government bonds.[12]

The investor's nationality is relevant for several purposes. In order to gain access to dispute settlement under the ICSID Convention, the investor must not be a national of the host state but must be a national of another state party to the ICSID Convention.[13] To rely on a clause in a treaty that offers consent to arbitration the investor must have the nationality of one of the states parties to that treaty.

An individual's nationality is determined by the law of the state whose nationality is claimed. An investment tribunal need not unquestioningly accept a passport or certificate of nationality as proof of nationality.[14]

For juridical persons the decisive criterion to determine nationality is the place of incorporation or registration.[15] The place of the *siège social* (corporation's seat) may also be relevant to determine its nationality. Control of the company, for instance

[9] See Arts 4, 5, 8 of the International Law Commission's Articles on State Responsibility.

[10] The Convention requires that the constituent subdivision or agency be designated to ICSID. ICSID maintains a public register of designated subdivisions and agencies of states, but relatively few countries have made designations under this provision. Constituent subdivisions or agencies have played a limited role in ICSID practice. See *Cable Television v. St Kitts and Nevis* (Award) [January 13, 1997]; *Tanzania Electric v. Independent Power Tanzania* (Award) [July 12, 2001] para. 13; *Repsol v. Petroecuador* (Decision on Annulment) [January 8, 2007]; *Noble Energy v. Ecuador* (Decision on Jurisdiction) [March 5, 2008] para. 6.

[11] *CSOB v. Slovakia* (Decision on Jurisdiction) [May 24, 1999] paras 15–27; *Telenor v. Hungary* (Award) [September 13, 2006] para. 16; *Rumeli Telekom v. Kazakhstan* (Award) [July 29, 2008] paras 325–8.

[12] *Abaclat et al v. Argentina* (Decision on Jurisdiction) [August 4, 2011] paras 216, 294–8, 480–92, 506–51.

[13] Exceptionally, under Art. 25.2.b of the ICSID Convention a corporation registered in the host state may be treated as a foreign company for the purposes of the ICSID Convention if, because of its foreign control, the parties to the dispute have so agreed.

[14] *Soufraki v. United Arab Emirates* (Award) [July 7, 2004].

[15] *Tokios Tokelės v. Ukraine* (Decision on Jurisdiction) [April 29, 2004] paras 21–71; *Saluka v. Czech Republic* (Partial Award) [March 17, 2006] paras 1, 73, 183–6, 197, 240, 241.

through majority ownership, is relevant only in exceptional circumstances. This would be the case if the relevant treaty requires effective control over the corporation by nationals of the state whose nationality is claimed or a genuine economic activity in that state.[16]

Nationality planning through the establishment of a corporation in a state that has favourable treaty relations with the host state is possible and accepted, in principle.[17] But it will work only if it is undertaken before the outbreak of a dispute with the host state.[18] Some states counteract practices of this kind through so-called denial of benefits clauses such as Art. 17.1 of the Energy Charter Treaty. Under such a clause, the states reserve the right to deny the benefits of the treaty to a company that does not have an economic connection to the state whose nationality it claims.[19]

The nationality of corporate investors has somewhat lost importance through the generous granting of standing to shareholders. Most investment treaties include shareholding or participation in companies in their definitions of investment. In this way, it is not the company that is seen as the investor but the shareholder whose participation in the company becomes the investment. The foreign shareholder may then pursue claims for unlawful action by the host state that affects the company's value and profitability. This practice is particularly relevant where the company is incorporated in the host state.[20]

5 Consent to Arbitration

5.1 Different forms of consent: contracts, legislation, and treaties

Arbitration is always based on an agreement between the disputing parties. In practice, consent to investment arbitration is given in one of three ways: (i) a consent clause may be included in a direct agreement between the investor and the host

[16] *Champion Trading v. Egypt* (Decision on Jurisdiction) [October 21, 2003] sec 3.4.2.

[17] *Aguas del Tunari v. Bolivia* (Decision on Jurisdiction) [October 21, 2005] paras 330–2.

[18] *Mobil v. Venezuela* (Decision on Jurisdiction) [June 10, 2010] paras 200, 201.

[19] *Plama v. Bulgaria* (Award) [August 27, 2008] paras 77–95; *Petrobart v. Kyrgyz Republic* (Award) [March 29, 2005], (2005) 3 Stockholm Intl Arb Rev 45, 64; *AMTO v. Ukraine* (Award) [March 26, 2008] paras 59–69; *Libananco v. Turkey* (Award) [September 2, 2011] paras 549–56.

[20] See e.g.,: *Genin v. Estonia* (Award) [June 25, 2001] para. 324; *CMS v. Argentina* (Decision on Jurisdiction) [July 17, 2003] paras 36–48; *LG&E Energy v. Argentina* (Decision on Jurisdiction) [April 30, 2004] paras 50–63; *GAMI v. Mexico* (Award) [November 15, 2004] paras 33–5; *Sempra Energy v. Argentina* (Decision on Jurisdiction) [May 11, 2005] paras 92–4; *El Paso Energy v. Argentina* (Decision

state; (ii) a provision in the host state's national legislation may offer arbitration to foreign investors in general terms; (iii) a treaty between the host state and the investor's state of nationality may offer arbitration to the nationals of the respective states.

An agreement between the parties recording consent to arbitration may be achieved through a compromissory clause in an investment agreement between the host state and the investor submitting future disputes arising from the investment operation to arbitration. Consent may be given with respect to existing or future disputes.[21]

The host state may offer consent to arbitration to foreign investors in its legislation in general terms. Not every reference to investment arbitration in national legislation, however, amounts to consent to jurisdiction. Some provisions are unclear and have led to disputes as to whether the host state had given its consent.[22]

A legislative provision containing consent to arbitration is merely an offer by the state to investors. In order to perfect an arbitration agreement that offer must be accepted by the investor. The investor may accept the offer simply by instituting arbitration.[23] The host state may repeal its offer at any time before it is accepted.[24]

By far the largest number of investment arbitrations is based on clauses in BITs offering arbitration. Through these clauses the states parties to the BIT offer consent to arbitration to investors who are nationals of the other contracting party. The arbitration agreement is perfected through the acceptance of that offer by an eligible investor. Most investor–state dispute settlement clauses in BITs offer unequivocal consent to arbitration.[25] But some clauses in BITs referring to arbitration merely hold out a promise or a prospect of future consent.

A number of regional multilateral treaties also offer consent to investment arbitration. These offers are also subject to an acceptance on the part of the investor. Article 1122 of the NAFTA contains such an offer. Article 1120 of the NAFTA specifies that an investor may submit a claim to arbitration under the ICSID Convention, under the ICSID Additional Facility Rules, or under the UNCITRAL Arbitration Rules. Of the three NAFTA States, only the United States has ratified the ICSID Convention while Canada and Mexico have not. Therefore, at present ICSID arbitration under the NAFTA is impossible.

on Jurisdiction) [April 27, 2006] para. 138; *Phoenix v. Czech Republic* (Award) [April 15, 2009] paras 121–3; *Hochtief v. Argentina* (Decision on Jurisdiction) [October 24, 2011] paras 112–19.

[21] Agreements to submit existing disputes to arbitration are rare. But see *MINE v. Guinea* (Award) [January 6, 1988] 4 ICSID Rep 61, 67; *Compania del Desarrollo de Santa Elena SA v. Costa Rica* (Award) [February 17, 2000] para. 26.

[22] *Mobil v. Venezuela* (Decision on Jurisdiction) [June 10, 2010] paras 67–140; *CEMEX v. Venezuela* (Decision on Jurisdiction) [December 30, 2010] paras 63–139; *Brandes v. Venezuela* (Award) [August 2, 2011] paras 79–118.

[23] *Tradex v. Albania* (Decision on Jurisdiction) [December 24, 1996] 5 ICSID Rep 47, 63; *Zhinvali v. Georgia* (Award) [January 24, 2003] para. 342.

[24] *SPP v. Egypt* (Decision on Jurisdiction) (I) [November 27, 1985] para. 40.

[25] *RosInvest v. Russia* (Award on Jurisdiction) [October 1, 2007] paras 56–75.

Similarly, the ECT in Art. 26 provides consent to investment arbitration. Under the ECT the investor may submit the dispute to arbitration under the ICSID Convention, the ICSID Additional Facility Rules, the UNCITRAL Arbitration Rules, or under the Arbitration Institute of the Stockholm Chamber of Commerce.

A provision of consent to arbitration in a treaty is merely an offer by the respective states that requires acceptance by the other party. That offer may be accepted by a national of the other state party to the BIT. An investor may accept an offer of consent contained in a treaty simply by instituting ICSID proceedings.[26]

In the case of arbitration clauses contained in treaties, a withdrawal of an offer of consent before its acceptance would be more difficult than in the case of national legislation. Once the arbitration agreement is perfected through the acceptance of the offer contained in the treaty, it remains in existence even if the states parties to the BIT agree to amend or terminate the treaty.

5.2 The scope of consent

The scope of consent to arbitration offered in treaties varies. Many BITs refer to "disputes concerning investments" or "any legal dispute concerning an investment." These provisions do not restrict a tribunal's jurisdiction to claims arising from the BIT's substantive standards. By their own terms, these consent clauses encompass disputes that go beyond the interpretation and application of the BIT itself and would include disputes that arise from a contract in connection with the investment.[27]

Other BITs contain a more limited offer of consent to arbitration covering only violations of the BIT's substantive standards. Similarly, under Art. 1116 of the NAFTA, the scope of the consent to arbitration is limited to claims arising from alleged breaches of the NAFTA itself. Also, under Art. 26.1 of the ECT the scope of the consent is limited to claims arising from alleged breaches of the ECT.[28]

Some expressions of consent to arbitration are narrowly confined as to their subject matter. Typical examples for narrow clauses of this kind are expressions of consent that are limited to disputes relating to expropriations or to the amount of compensation for expropriations.[29]

[26] *Toto v. Lebanon* (Decision on Jurisdiction) [September 11, 2009] para. 94; *Generation Ukraine v. Ukraine* (Award) [September 16, 2003] paras 12.2, 12.3.

[27] *Salini v. Morocco* (Decision on Jurisdiction) [July 23, 2001] para. 61; *Compañía de Aguas del Aconquija, SA & Vivendi Universal v. Argentina* (Decision on Annulment) [July 3, 2002] para. 55; *SGS v. Philippines* (Decision on Jurisdiction) [January 29, 2004] paras 131–5; *Chevron & Texaco v. Ecuador* (Interim Award) [December 1, 2008] paras 203, 209–211; *SGS v. Paraguay* (Decision on Jurisdiction) [February 12, 2010] paras 129, 183; *Alpha v. Ukraine* (Award) [November 8, 2010] para. 243.

[28] *Kardassopoulos v. Georgia* (Decision on Jurisdiction) [July 6, 2007] paras 249–51.

[29] *Telenor v. Hungary* (Award) [September 13, 2006] paras 18.2, 25, 57, 81–3; *ADC v. Hungary* (Award) [October 2, 2006] paras 12, 445; *Tza Yap Shum v. Peru* (Decision on Jurisdiction) [June 19, 2009] paras 129–88; *Saipem v. Bangladesh* (Award) [June 30, 2009] paras 120–32.

6 Procedural Requirements for the Institution of Proceedings

6.1 Attempt at amicable settlement

A common condition in treaties providing for investor–state arbitration is a prior attempt at amicable settlement through negotiations within a certain period of time. A typical waiting period under BITs would be six months. The NAFTA (Arts 1118 to 1120) also prescribes a waiting period of six months since the events giving rise to the claim. Article 26.2 of the ECT offers consent to arbitration if the dispute cannot be settled within three months from the date on which either party requested amicable settlement.

The reaction of tribunals to non-compliance with these waiting periods has varied. In some cases the tribunals found that non-compliance with the waiting periods did not affect their jurisdiction.[30] Other tribunals have found the claims inadmissible under these circumstances.[31] A compromise solution is to suspend proceedings to allow additional time for negotiations if these appear promising.

6.2 Requirement to resort to domestic courts

Where consent has been given to investor–state arbitration, there is generally no need to exhaust local remedies.[32] One of the purposes of investor–state arbitration is to avoid the vagaries of proceedings in the host state's courts. Article 26 of the ICSID Convention specifically excludes the requirement to exhaust remedies "unless otherwise stated."

Some BITs provide that before an investor may bring a dispute before an international tribunal he or she must seek its resolution before the host state's domestic courts for a certain period of time, often 18 months. In practice, investors are often able to avoid the application of such a rule by invoking an MFN clause in the BIT.

[30] *Ethyl Corp v. Canada* (Decision on Jurisdiction) [June 24, 1998] paras 76–88; *Lauder v. Czech Republic* (Final Award) [September 3, 2001] para. 187; *SGS v. Pakistan* (Decision on Jurisdiction) [August 6, 2003] para. 184; *Bayindir v. Pakistan* (Decision on Jurisdiction) [November 14, 2005] paras 88–103; *Biwater Gauff v. Tanzania*, (Award) [July 24, 2008] paras 338–50.

[31] *Goetz v. Burundi* (Award) [February 10, 1999] paras 90–3; *Enron v. Argentina* (Decision on Jurisdiction) [January 14, 2004] para. 88; *Wintershall v. Argentina* (Award) [December 8, 2008] paras 133–57; *Burlington Resources v. Ecuador* (Decision on Jurisdiction) [June 2, 2010] paras 312–18, 332–40; *Murphy v. Ecuador* (Award) [December 15, 2010] paras 90–157.

[32] *Amco v. Indonesia* (Decision on Annulment) [May 16, 1986] para. 63; *Lanco v. Argentina* (Decision on Jurisdiction) [December 8, 1998] para. 39; *IBM v. Ecuador* (Decision on Jurisdiction) [December 22, 2003] paras 77–84; *AES v. Argentina* (Decision on Jurisdiction) [April 26, 2005] paras 69, 70; *Saipem v. Bangladesh* (Award) [June 30, 2009] paras 174–84.

This allows them to rely on other BITs of the host state that do not contain that requirement.[33] In some cases tribunals have discarded the treaty requirement to first go to domestic courts because such an attempt would have been evidently futile.[34]

6.3 Fork in the road

Fork in the road clauses provide that the investor must choose between the litigation of its claims in the host state's domestic courts or through international arbitration and that the choice, once made, is final.

Not every appearance before a court or tribunal of the host state will constitute a choice under a fork in the road provision. Tribunals have held that the loss of access to international arbitration under a fork in the road clause applies only if the same dispute involving the same cause of action between the same parties has been submitted to the domestic courts of the host state.[35]

7 The Applicability of MFN Clauses to Dispute Settlement

Most BITs and some other treaties for the protection of investment, including the NAFTA and the ECT, contain MFN clauses. An MFN clause contained in a treaty will extend the better treatment granted to a third state or its nationals to a

[33] *Maffezini v. Spain* (Decision on Jurisdiction) [January 25, 2000] paras 54–64; *Siemens v. Argentina* (Decision on Jurisdiction) [August 3, 2004] paras 32–110; *Gas Natural SDG, SA v. Argentina* (Decision on Jurisdiction) [June 17, 2005] paras 24–49; *Suez, Sociedad General de Aguas de Barcelona SA, and InterAguas Servicios Integrales del Agua SA v. Argentina* (Decision on Jurisdiction) [May 16, 2006] paras 52–66; *National Grid plc v. Argentina* (Decision on Jurisdiction) [June 20, 2006] paras 80–93; *Suez, Sociedad General de Aguas de Barcelona SA, and Vivendi Universal SA v. Argentina and AWG Group Ltd* v *Argentina* (Decision on Jurisdiction) [August 3, 2006] paras 52–68; *Impregilo v. Argentina* (Award) [June 21, 2011] paras 51–109; *Hochtief v. Argentina* (Decision on Jurisdiction) [October 24, 2011]; *Teinver v. Argentina* (Decision on Jurisdiction) [December 21, 2012] paras 137–86. But see *Wintershall v. Argentina* (Award) [December 8, 2008] paras 158–97; *ICS Inspection v. Argentina* (Award) [February 10, 2012] paras 243–327; *Daimler v. Argentina* (Award) [August 22, 2012] paras 160–281.

[34] *Abaclat v. Argentina* (Decision on Jurisdiction and Admissibility) [August 4, 2011] paras 585–90; *Urbaser v. Argentina* (Decision on Jurisdiction) [December 19, 2012] paras 196–200; *Ambiente Ufficio v. Argentina* (Decision on Jurisdiction and Admissibility) [February 8, 2013] paras 589–628.

[35] *CMS v. Argentina*, note 20 at paras 77–82; *LG&E v. Argentina*, note 20, at paras 75, 76; *Champion Trading v. Egypt*, note 16, at sec. 3.4.3; *Pan American v. Argentina* (Decision on Preliminary Objections) [July 27, 2006] paras 155–7; *Toto v. Lebanon* (Decision on Jurisdiction) [September 11, 2009] paras

beneficiary of the treaty. This has led to the question whether the effect of a generally worded MFN clause extends to the arbitration clauses in these treaties.

This issue has led to much controversy and to conflicting decisions. One school of thought regards dispute settlement as an essential aspect of the treatment that is covered by an MFN clause. A different approach distinguishes between substantive and procedural questions restricting the effect of MFN treatment to substance.

Most of the cases in which the tribunals have accepted the applicability of the MFN clauses to dispute settlement concerned procedural obstacles, such as the requirement first to resort to the domestic courts for 18 months.[36] Most of the cases in which the effect of the MFN clauses was denied concerned attempts to extend the scope of jurisdiction substantively to issues not covered by the arbitration clauses in the basic treaties.[37] Nevertheless, there is substantial contradiction in the reasoning of the tribunals. In particular, both groups of tribunals made broad statements as to the applicability, or otherwise, of MFN clauses to dispute settlement that are impossible to reconcile.

8 Selection of Domestic Courts in Contracts

Contracts between host states and foreign investors often contain forum selection clauses referring disputes arising from the application of these contracts to the host states' domestic courts. When disputes in connection with the investments arose, investors would invoke the provisions of treaties, usually BITs, granting them access to international arbitration. In turn, the host states would rely on the forum selection clauses in the contracts, arguing that the investors had waived their right to international arbitration.

The tribunals have adopted a distinction between contract claims, which are subject to contractual forum selection clauses, and treaty claims, which are unaffected

203–17; *Victor Pey Casado v. Chile* (Award) [May 8, 2008] paras 467–98; *Total v. Argentina* (Decision on Liability) [December 27, 2010] paras 442–3.

[36] See note 33.

[37] *Salini v. Jordan* (Decision on Jurisdiction) [November 29, 2004] para. 119; *Plama v. Bulgaria* (Decision on Jurisdiction) [February 8, 2005] paras 183–227; *Berschader v. Russia* (Award) [April 21, 2006] paras 159–208; *Telenor v. Hungary* (Award) [September 13, 2006] paras 83–100; *Tza Yap Shum v. Peru* (Decision on Jurisdiction) [June 19, 2009] paras 189–220; *Austrian Airlines v. Slovakia* (Final Award) [October 9, 2009] paras 109–40. But see *RosInvest v. Russia* (Award on Jurisdiction) [October 2007] paras 124–39.

by such clauses. Under this consistent practice the treaty-based jurisdiction of international arbitral tribunals to decide on violations of these treaties is not affected by domestic forum selection clauses in contracts. The contractual selection of domestic courts is restricted to violations of the respective contracts.[38]

A particular course of action by the host state may well constitute a breach of contract and a violation of international law. The two categories are not mutually exclusive. Rather, two different standards must be applied to determine whether one or the other or both have been violated.

The situation is made even more complex by the fact that some treaties offer jurisdiction for investment disputes in general terms, which includes contract claims. Therefore the jurisdiction of treaty-based tribunals is not necessarily restricted to violations of the treaty's substantive provisions.

The separate treatment of contract claims and treaty claims leads to situations where the claimant may be compelled to pursue part of its claim through national and another part through international procedures. This has undesirable consequences. The need to dissect cases into contract claims and treaty claims to be dealt with by separate fora requires claim-splitting and has the potential of leading to parallel proceedings. This is uneconomical and contrary to the goal of reaching final and comprehensive resolutions of disputes.

9 Applicable Law

Investments typically are complex operations involving numerous transactions under the host state's local law. These transactions will have their closest connection to the host state's legal system. At the same time, there is a considerable body of substantive international law protecting foreign investors. It consists of treaty law, contained mostly in BITs, but also in multilateral treaties such as the NAFTA and the ECT. In addition, other treaties and customary international law remains

[38] *Compañia de Aguas del Aconquija, SA & Vivendi Universal v. Argentina*, note 27, at paras 60, 72, 76, 95, 96, 101, 103; *National Grid plc v. Argentina* (Decision on Jurisdiction) [June 20, 2006] paras 167–70; *Inceysa v. El Salvador* (Award) [August 2, 2006] paras 43, 212–17; *Total v. Argentina* (Decision on Jurisdiction) [August 25, 2006] paras 82–5; *Fraport v. Philippines* (Award) [August 16, 2007] paras 388–91; *Vivendi v. Argentina* (Resubmitted Case: Award) [August 20, 2007] paras 7.3.–7.3.11; *Helnan v. Egypt* (Award) [July 3, 2008] paras 102–3; *TSA Spectrum v. Argentina* (Award) [December 19, 2008] paras 42–66; *Enron v. Argentina* (Decision on Annulment) [July 30, 2010] paras 128–50; *Impregilo v. Argentina* (Award) [June 21, 2011] paras 141–89; *SGS v. Paraguay* (Award) [February 10, 2012] paras 75, 96–109.

relevant to various questions, including state responsibility, nationality, or the international minimum standard.

Some treaties providing for investment arbitration refer to the parties' agreement on choice of law. Some of the relevant treaties contain their own choice of law clauses in case there is no agreement on applicable law between the parties. For instance, Art. 42 of the ICSID Convention refers primarily to any agreement on choice of law that the parties may have reached. In the absence of such an agreement, it provides for the application of the host state's law and international law.[39]

In non-ICSID arbitration between investors and host states, tribunals also apply a combination of international law and host state law. The UNCITRAL Arbitration Rules refer the tribunal to the law designated by the parties. In the absence of a choice of law, the tribunal is to apply the law that it determines to be appropriate.[40]

Many of the treaties that offer investor–state arbitration, such as the NAFTA, the ECT, and some BITs, also contain provisions on applicable law. Some of these provisions, including Art. 1131 of the NAFTA and Art. 26 of the ECT, refer exclusively to international law. Some BIT provisions dealing with applicable law, combine the host state's domestic law with international law.[41] Where jurisdiction is based on a BIT that does not contain a provision on governing law, tribunals have sometimes construed such a choice from the parties' reliance on the BIT.[42]

In most cases the applicable substantive law in investment arbitration combines international law and host state law. This is so whether or not the parties have made a choice of law that combines international law with host state law. In the majority of cases tribunals have, in fact, applied both systems of law.[43] Host state law is particularly important to determine the existence and the legality of investments. Where there was a contradiction between the two, international law had to prevail.[44] It is

[39] See also Art. 54 of the ICSID Additional Facility Rules.

[40] UNCITRAL Arbitration Rules 2010, Art. 35.1.

[41] *Antoine Goetz v. Burundi* (Award) [February 10, 1999] paras 95–133; *Maffezini v. Spain* (Award) [November 13, 2000] paras 47–50, 52, 57, 67–69, 71, 77, 83, 89–93; *Occidental v. Ecuador* (Final Award) [July 1, 2004] para. 93; *Eastern Sugar v. Czech Republic* (Partial Award) [March 27, 2007] paras 191–7. *BG Group v. Argentina* (Final Award) [December 24, 2007] paras 89–103; *National Grid v. Argentina* (Award) [November 3, 2008] paras 81–90.

[42] *AAPL v Sri Lanka* (Award) [June 27, 1990] paras 18–24; *Wena Hotels v. Egypt* (Award) [December 8, 2000] paras 78, 79; *ADC v. Hungary* (Award) [October 2, 2006] paras 288–91; *LG&E v. Argentina* (Decision on Liability) [October 3, 2006] paras 85, 97–8; *Saipem v. Bangladesh* (Award) [June 30, 2009] para. 99; *Bayindir v. Pakistan* (Award) [August 27, 2009] paras 109, 110.

[43] *CMS v. Argentina* (Award) [May 12, 2005] para. 117. See also, *Wena v. Egypt* (Decision on Annulment) [February 5, 2002] paras 37–40; *Azurix v. Argentina* (Award) [July 14, 2006] para. 67; *LG&E v. Argentina*, note 42, at paras 82–99; *Enron v. Argentina* (Award) [May 22, 2007] paras 203–9; *Tokios Tokelės v. Ukraine* (Award) [July 26, 2007] paras 138–45; *Sempra v. Argentina* (Award) [September 28, 2007] paras 231–40.

[44] *LG&E v. Argentina*, note 42, at para. 94; *CDSE v. Costa Rica* (Award) [February 17, 2000] paras 64, 65; *Duke Energy v. Peru* (Decision on Jurisdiction) [February 1, 2006] para. 162.

left to the tribunals to classify the various issues before them as to which international law or host state law is to apply.

10 Remedies

Under the international law of state responsibility, reparation for a wrongful act takes the form of restitution, compensation, and satisfaction.[45] In investment arbitration the remedy nearly always consists of monetary compensation. Restitution in kind or specific performance is ordered infrequently.[46] Satisfaction also plays a subordinate role in investment arbitration.[47]

If an illegal act has been committed the guiding principle is that reparation must, as far as possible, restore the situation that would have existed had the illegal act not been committed. Under this principle, damages for a violation of international law have to reflect the damage actually suffered by the victim. Therefore, punitive or moral damages will not usually be granted.[48] Lost profits will be awarded only if they are not speculative, that is, in cases where the investment has a record of profitability or there are other clear indicators of future profits.

The calculation of compensation for a lawful expropriation follows different standards. Many of the treaties dealing with compensation for expropriation refer to the expropriated investment's fair market value immediately before the expropriation became publicly known.

An award of damages or compensation normally includes interest. Interest is due from the date at which the principal amount was due. In the case of damages, this is normally the date of the wrongful act. In the case of compensation, interest is due normally from the date of the expropriation. The rate of interest is usually

[45] Art. 34 of the International Law Commission's Articles on State Responsibility.

[46] *Texaco v. Libya* (Award on the Merits) [January 19, 1977] 53 ILR 389, 497–511; *Goetz v. Burundi* (Award) [September 2, 1998 and February 10, 1999] paras 132–3; *Semos v. Mali* (Award) [February 25, 2003]; *Enron v. Argentina* (Decision on Jurisdiction) [January 14, 2004] paras 76–9; *ADC v. Hungary* (Award) [October 2, 2006] para. 523; *Siemens v. Argentina* (Award) [February 6, 2007] para. 403.5; *Micula v. Romania* (Decision on Jurisdiction and Admissibility) [September 24, 2008] paras 158–68; *ATA v. Jordan* (Award) [May 18, 2010] paras 129–32.

[47] *Biwater Gauff v. Tanzania* (Award) [July 24, 2008] paras 465–67, 807; *Europe Cement v. Turkey* (Award) [August 13, 2009] paras 146–8, 176, 181; *Quiborax v. Bolivia* (Decision on Jurisdiction) [September 27, 2012] paras 37, 299–308.

[48] *Siag v. Egypt* (Award) [June 1, 2009] paras 544–8; *Europe Cement v. Turkey*, note 47, at paras 177–81; *Cementownia v. Turkey* (Award) [September 17, 2009] paras 164–72; *Lemire v. Ukraine* (Decision on Jurisdiction and Liability) [January 14, 2010] paras 426–86. But see *Desert Line v. Yemen* (Award) [February 6, 2008] paras 284–91.

calculated on the basis of the legal interest rate in an applicable legal system or some inter-bank rate such as the London Interbank Offered Rate (LIBOR). The practice of tribunals shows a trend toward compounding interest.

11 Costs

The costs of major investment arbitrations can be considerable and may run into millions of US dollars for complex cases. The costs consist of three elements: the charges for the use of the facilities and expenses of ICSID or any other arbitration institution, the fees and expenses of the arbitrators, and the expenses incurred by the parties in connection with the proceedings. Of these three categories, the third, consisting mainly of the costs for legal representation, is typically by far the largest.

The ICSID Convention leaves it to the tribunal's discretion as to who will pay these costs, unless the parties agree otherwise.[49] The UNCITRAL Arbitration Rules state that, in principle, the unsuccessful party shall bear the costs of the arbitration.[50] But in a particular case, both parties may be partly successful. This is the case if the claimant wins on jurisdiction but the respondent state wins on the merits, or if only part of the claims and arguments of one party is accepted.

In many cases tribunals have found that the fees and expenses of ICSID and of the arbitrators were to be shared equally and that each party had to bear its own expenses. In some cases the tribunals awarded costs as a sanction for improper conduct of one of the parties. More recently, tribunals have shown a growing tendency to adopt the principle that costs follow the event. An award of costs against the losing party may be total or, more frequently, may cover a certain proportion of the overall costs.

12 Challenge and Review of Decisions

Awards are final and not subject to any appeals procedures.[51] It is only under very limited circumstances that a review of awards is possible. In non-ICSID arbitration, including arbitration under the Additional Facility, the normal way to

[49] Art. 61.2. [50] Art. 42.1. [51] ICSID Convention, Art. 53.

challenge an award is through national courts. This is done in the courts of the country in which the tribunal had its seat or by the courts charged with the task of enforcing the award. In many countries, this process is subject to the New York Convention on the Recognition and Enforcement of Foreign Arbitral Awards of 1958.[52]

ICSID awards are not subject to annulment or any other form of scrutiny by domestic courts. Rather, the ICSID Convention offers its own self-contained system for review. Under this procedure, an ad hoc committee appointed by ICSID may annul the award upon the request of a party on the basis of five narrowly defined grounds.[53] Annulment is concerned only with the legitimacy of the process of decision but not with its substantive correctness. An annulment merely removes the original decision without replacing it. Therefore, an ad hoc committee acting under the ICSID Convention does not have the power to render its own decision on the merits. After an annulment, the dispute may be resubmitted to a new tribunal.

13 Enforcement of Awards

Arbitral awards are binding upon the parties and carry an obligation to comply. Non-compliance with an award by a state would be a breach of the ICSID Convention and would lead to a revival of the right to diplomatic protection by the investor's state of nationality.

The enforcement of non-ICSID awards, including Additional Facility awards, is subject to the national law of the place of enforcement and to the New York Convention on the Recognition and Enforcement of Foreign Arbitral Awards.

ICSID awards are to be recognized as binding, and their pecuniary obligations are to be enforced like final domestic judgments in all states parties to the convention. The obligation to enforce the pecuniary obligations arising from ICSID awards is limited by any immunity from execution of states.[54]

[52] 330 UNTS 38 (1959). [53] ICSID Convention, Art. 52.
[54] ICSID Convention, Arts 54, 55.

14 Problems and Challenges

14.1 Coherence and consistency

Tribunals frequently refer to and rely on earlier decisions. Despite that practice, the lack of consistency of case law has become a matter of concern. A system that operates with a large number of differently composed tribunals is more vulnerable to discrepancies than courts with a permanent composition and courts embedded in a hierarchical judicial system.

A permanent court for investment disputes is not a realistic goal in the foreseeable future. The idea of appeals procedures has been widely discussed and has found entry into some US BITs. If applied separately for each treaty, appeals procedures are unlikely to lead to more coherence. Also, Art. 53 of the ICSID Convention explicitly states that awards "shall not be subject to any appeal." A possible alternative would be the creation of a central facility that gives preliminary rulings in pending proceedings.

14.2 Transparency

Confidentiality is traditionally considered one of the major advantages of arbitration. But in investment arbitration the presence of issues of public interest has increasingly led to demands for more openness and transparency. Two issues are typically discussed under the heading of transparency: access to information and third party participation.

Awards are not published automatically. ICSID publishes awards only with the consent of both parties.[55] Since 2006 the Centre has been under an obligation to publish excerpts of the legal reasoning of each award.[56] The parties are free to release awards and other decisions for publication unless it is otherwise agreed. Most ICSID awards have been published in one way or another, but there are some awards and other decisions that have remained unpublished. Non-ICSID awards are published sporadically.

Most hearings are closed to the public. Under a rule introduced in 2006, ICSID tribunals may, under certain circumstances, allow other persons to attend all or part of the hearings.[57] Some investment treaties provide that investor–state arbitration hearings shall be open to the public.

[55] ICSID Convention, Art. 48.5. [56] ICSID, Arbitration Rule 48.4.
[57] ICSID, Arbitration Rule 32.

In some cases ICSID tribunals have permitted the submission of *amicus curiae* briefs by non-disputing parties. Under a procedure introduced in 2006, the tribunal may, after consulting the parties, allow an entity that is not a party to file a written submission regarding a matter within the scope of the dispute.[58]

Non-ICSID tribunals operating in the framework of NAFTA under the UNCITRAL Rules have allowed third parties to make written submissions. In October 2003 the NAFTA Free Trade Commission issued a statement regarding the participation of non-disputing parties.[59]

14.3 Regulatory chill

Concerns about the impact of investment arbitration on the states' ability to exercise their regulatory functions have been voiced for some time. These concerns appear to be mostly theoretical. An examination of tribunal practice shows a high degree of sensitivity towards public order concerns. This is particularly manifest in cases involving environmental issues. Tribunals have generally respected *bona fide* environmental measures and other measures serving a genuine public interest taken by host states.

14.4 Pro-investor bias

Accusations of pro-investor bias in investment tribunals are highly subjective and difficult to verify. Statistics do not support these concerns. A large proportion of cases are dismissed as early as the jurisdictional stage. Of the remaining cases, roughly half are dismissed on the merits. Even in cases in which the investor prevails, typically only a fraction of the relief demanded is awarded.

Tribunals react rigorously when they find illegal or improper action by investors. This concerns corruption, misleading information, illegality under host state law, and abuse of process. Practices of this kind lead to the dismissal of claims.

Research Questions

1. How do tribunals deal with evidence and proof of facts, including production of documents, witnesses and experts, standard of proof, and burden of proof, in international investment arbitration?

[58] ICSID, Arbitration Rule 37.2.

[59] NAFTA Free Trade Commission Statement on Non-Disputing Party Participation (October 7, 2003) 44 ILM 796 (2005).

2. What is the role of provisional measures in international investment arbitration? How do tribunals deal with issues of urgency and necessity, the legal nature and the circumstances requiring provisional measures?
3. Is there room for non-pecuniary remedies in international investment arbitration? Are Arts 34–37 of the ILC Articles on state responsibility, dealing with restitution, satisfaction, and declaratory relief applicable?
4. To what extent do third parties, i.e. non-participating states and *amici curiae*, have access to investment arbitration?

Suggested Reading

Binder, C et al. (eds), *International Investment Law for the 21st Century* (Oxford University Press 2009).

Bishop, D R, Crawford, J, and Reisman, WM (eds), *Foreign Investment Disputes: Cases, Materials and Commentary* (The Hague: Kluwer 2005).

Dolzer, R and Schreuer, C, *Principles of International Investment Law* (2nd edn, Oxford University Press 2012).

Douglas, Z, *The International Law of Investment Claims* (Cambridge University Press 2010).

McLachlan, C, Shore, L, and Weiniger, M, *International Investment Arbitration Substantive Principles* (Oxford University Press 2007).

Muchlinski, P, Ortino, F, and Schreuer, C (eds), *The Oxford Handbook of International Investment Law* (Oxford University Press 2008).

Newcombe, A and Paradell, L, *Law and Practice of Investment Treaties* (Alphen aan den Rijn: Wolters Kluwer 2009).

Salacuse, JW, *The Law of Investment Treaties* (Oxford University Press 2010).

Schill, S, *International Investment Law and Comparative Public Law* (Oxford University Press 2010).

Schreuer, C et al., *The ICSID Convention: A Commentary* (2nd edn, Cambridge University Press 2009).

Rigo Sureda, A, *Investment Treaty Arbitration: Judging Under Uncertainty* (Cambridge University Press 2012).

Yannaca-Small, K (ed.), *Arbitration under International Investment Agreements* (Oxford University Press 2010).

CHAPTER 15

INTERNATIONAL ADMINISTRATIVE TRIBUNALS

CHITTHARANJAN F AMERASINGHE*

* Member, Institut de droit international; former Judge, UNAT; Registrar, WBAT; Professor of Law, University of Ceylon.

1 Introduction

With the growth and development of international society during the twentieth century there came into existence the League of Nations, the United Nations (UN), and a host of other international agencies such as the World Bank, the International Labour Organization (ILO), and the World Health Organization (WHO). They all have one important feature in common: they are all organized as corporate bodies which have international personality.[1] They have been, in general, accorded a limited liability from the jurisdiction of member states.[2] These organizations employ staff of one kind or another to carry out their objectives. In the League of Nations there were no more than a few hundred employees; in the UN there are thousands.

Thus, there is generally a need both for the total employment relationship to be subject to some system of legal regulation and control and for a forum before which disputes arising from the employment relationship may be litigated.

1.1 The internal law

It has come to be generally accepted now that it is the *internal* law of the organization that governs the employment relationship of international civil servants with the international organization for which they work. Regardless of whether there are courts to decide disputes relating to the employment relationship in the organization, it is a real system of law. In its very first case, the League of Nations Tribunal (LNT) conceded that it was "bound to apply the *internal law* of the League of Nations."[3]

There is evidence that there may be certain general principles of law applicable within internal legal systems of international organizations pertaining to the employment relationship which extend beyond the limits of the internal system of any one organization. In addition, all things considered, the internal legal system of international organizations relating to employment relations would qualify as a binding system of law in a sense similar to that in which public international law may be considered a binding system of law.

[1] See the *Advisory Opinion on Reparation for Injuries Suffered in the Service of the United Nations* [1949] ICJ Rep 174, at 185, 187; CF Amerasinghe, *Principles of the Institutional Law of International Organizations* (Cambridge University Press 2005) 66.

[2] Article 105 of the UN Charter states that: "The Organizations shall enjoy in the territories of each of its Members such privileges and immunities as are necessary for the fulfillment of its purposes."

[3] *Di Palma Castiglione* (LNT Judgment) [1929] 3.

This internal law of international organizations is sometimes generically referred to as international administrative law.[4]

1.2 International Administrative Tribunals (IATs)

IATs are judicial bodies that are generally established by international organizations and have the authority to settle disputes between international organizations and employees on employment matters. Administrative tribunals settling the internal disputes of international organizations relating to employment have been referred to by high authority as "international" tribunals, thus confirming that they exist in the realm of the public international law system. In the *Judgments of the I.L.O Administrative Tribunal* Case, the ICJ stated categorically: "The Court does not deny that the Administrative Tribunal is an international tribunal."[5] IATs are international tribunals in the sense that they operate in the international legal system. They have no connection with national courts. They stand on their own, though one or two of them have a relationship with other international courts.

2 The Need for IATs

A practical reason for having administrative tribunals is that it is always desirable to have judicial machinery available for the settlement of legal disputes. Recourse to national courts is possible, but it would appear that most national legal systems recognize that international organizations are immune from their jurisdiction

[4] This administrative law system is different from the administrative law system about which there has been much discussion in the context of global governance, particularly in order to establish whether such an administrative system has global reach. The latter system, if indeed there is one, relates to the legal effects within national legal systems in the field of administrative law. It does not deal with the internal law of international organizations concerned with employment relations: see, especially the collection of articles in "Symposium: Global Governance and Global Administrative Law in the International Legal" (2006) 17 Eur. J. Int'l L. 1. See also Kingsbury, "The Administrative Law Frontier in Global Governance" in *Proceedings of the ASIL* (Washington D.C.: ASIL 2005) 143; articles in (2005) 68(3) Law & Contemp. Problems 15; S Cassese, "Administrative Law Without the State: The Challenge of Global Regulation" (2005) 37(4) N.Y.U. J. Int'l L. & Pol. 663; RB Stewart, "The Global Regulatory Challenge to U.S. Administrative Law" (2005) 37(4) N.Y.U. J. Int'l L. & Pol. 695; BS Chimni, "Co-Option and Resistance: Two Faces of Global Administrative Law" (2005) 37(4) N.Y.U. J. Int'l L. & Pol. 799. The other articles in volume 37(4) of the N.Y.U. Journal of International Law and Politics are also instructive.

[5] *Judgments of the I.L.O. Administrative Tribunal* [1956] ICJ Reports 77, 97.

in regard to employment matters or that employment matters of organizations are outside their subject matter jurisdiction. Conversely, if staff members are not afforded due process because there are no means of impartial and independent judicial settlement available to them, bolder national courts may be inclined and encouraged to ignore claims of immunity and exercise jurisdiction in employment cases. International organizations would, in general, be averse to being subjected to the jurisdiction of national courts in internal disputes relating to employment matters. Thus, either way, because settlement by national courts is not possible or not acceptable to organizations, their chosen option is to accept the jurisdiction of international administrative courts specially created for the settlement of internal employment disputes.

A cogent reason for international organizations submitting to the jurisdiction of specially created administrative courts, it now has come to be realized, is related to respect for human rights. In 1980, when the World Bank Administrative Tribunal (WBAT) was being established, one of the reasons given by the President of the World Bank for establishing a tribunal was one of principle.[6] It was a principle accepted in many national legal systems and reaffirmed in the Universal Declaration of Human Rights. This principle required that where administrative power was exercised, there should be available machinery, in the event of disputes, to accord a fair hearing and due process to the aggrieved party. Hence, there was a need for an independent *judicial* body to decide complaints relating to the exercise of administrative power.[7]

Also to be respected is the argument that provision of a judicial organ to decide employment disputes will make for better and smoother employment relations within the international organization.

3 Authority to Establish Administrative Tribunals

Many international organizations have either their own internal administrative tribunals or use the administrative tribunals of other organizations to settle employment disputes judicially. A question that arises is whether they have the power to establish these tribunals.

[6] Memorandum to the Executive Directors (January 14, 1980), from the President of the World Bank, Doc R80-8, IDA/R80-8, and IFC/R80-6, 1-2.

[7] See also Art. 6 of the European Convention on Human Rights.

In the view of the International Court of Justice (ICJ) the UN General Assembly (UNGA) did have an implied power to establish an IAT. In the *Effect of Awards* Case the court explained the reasons for its conclusion:

When the Secretariat was organized, a situation arose in which the relations between the staff members and the Organization were governed by a complex code of law... It was inevitable that there would be disputes between the Organization and staff members as to their rights and duties. The Charter contains no provision which authorizes any of the principal organs of the United Nations to adjudicate upon these disputes and Article 105 secures for the United Nations jurisdictional immunities in national courts. It would, in the opinion of the Court, hardly be consistent with the expressed aim of the Charter to promote freedom and justice for individuals and with the constant preoccupation of the United Nations Organization to promote this aim that it should afford no judicial or arbitral remedy to its own staff for the settlement of any disputes which may arise between it and them.[8]

Moreover, the IAT set up by the UN was not a subordinate organ of the UNGA exercising delegated powers and without power to bind the UNGA by its judgments.[9]

The absence of express provisions dealing with the staff and personnel relations in the constituent instrument of an organization does not detract from such an implied power, because it is within the accepted purpose and function of all international organizations to employ staff and conduct smooth and effective personnel relations.

Since the creation in 1929 of the first true international administrative tribunal—the League of Nations Administrative Tribunal—which ceased to exist when the League died, several more IATs have come into existence. The most important of these are the International Labour Organization Administrative Tribunal (ILOAT);[10] the United Nations Administrative Tribunal (UNAT); the Council of Europe Appeals Board (CoEAB), which has now become the Council of Europe Administrative Tribunal (CoEAT); the Court of Justice of the European Communities (CJEC), which has now become the European Court of Justice (ECJ); the Appeals Board of the European Space Agency (ESAAB); the Administrative Tribunal of the Organization of American States (OASAT); the World Bank Administrative Tribunal (WBAT); the Inter-American Development Bank Administrative Tribunal (IDBAT); the International Monetary Fund Administrative Tribunal (IMFAT); the Asian Development Bank Administrative Tribunal (ADBAT); the African Development Bank Administrative Tribunal; the UN Dispute Tribunal (UNDT) (and the UN Appeals Tribunal), which replaced the UNAT. More recently in 2005, the European Civil Service Tribunal was established by the EU to exercise

[8] *Effect of Awards Case* [1954] ICJ Reports, 57. [9] *Effect of Awards Case*, note 8, at 61.

[10] The International Labour Organization Administrative Tribunal acts also as administrative tribunal for a number of other international organizations, including specialized agencies of the UN.

jurisdiction in employment-related cases against the EU, replacing a jurisdiction which had been exercised by the CJEC and ECJ.

4 Independence of IATs

The WBAT, which was created in 1980, has had a special impact on the development of the administrative judicial systems of international organizations.[11] Article 1 of the WBAT Statute provides explicitly that the WBAT is a judicial body which functions independently of the management of the World Bank Group and that the independence of the tribunal shall be guaranteed and respected by the Bank Group at all times. Apart from this provision there are some features of the WBAT that are particularly important.

First, unlike the Statute of the ILOAT which is open, Article IV.1 of the WBAT Statute states that the judges "shall be persons of high moral character and must possess the qualifications required for appointment to high judicial office or be jurisconsults of recognized competence," and is modeled on Art. 2 of the ICJ Statute. The same article explicitly provides that current or former staff members of the World Bank Group are not eligible for appointment and that judges may not be employed by the Bank Group after their service on the tribunal,[12] effectively depoliticizing the appointment of judges to the WBAT.

The second characteristic is the recognition in the statute of the independence of the Secretariat of the WBAT.[13] The statute clearly provides that the Executive Secretary (Registrar) shall be responsible in the performance of his duties only to the tribunal. The statutes of the IATs of some European organizations[14] have similar provisions. Since the WBAT Statute was enacted other IATs have had similar provisions incorporated into their statutes. In the World Bank itself the Secretariat and its director (Executive Secretary) are regarded as an independent department, which is

[11] The Inter-American Development Bank (IDB), the Asian Development Bank (ADB), the Commonwealth Secretariat and the IMF have all created administrative courts modeled on the WBAT. The Bank for International Settlements, the ADB, the African Development Bank, and the European Bank for Reconstruction and Development (EBRD) have, in effect, looked to the WBAT Statute in the process of deciding how to establish grievance procedures. The distinction between global and regional organizations is irrelevant in this connection.

[12] On at least one occasion in the past, the UNAT had on its bench a former staff member of the UN, which does not say much for the UN's past appointment process.

[13] WBAT Statute (2010), Art. VI.2.

[14] See e.g., Council of Europe (CoE) Administrative Tribunal Statute, Art. 14, para. 2; European Space Agency Appeals Board Statute, Reg. 40.

part of the IAT and outside the regular institutional structure. Special institutional rules also apply to it. It is noteworthy that the Secretariat has its own budget, pursuant to the statute of the WBAT.[15]

Some 25 years or more after the establishment of the WBAT the UN took a hard look at its internal judicial system and implemented some important changes. There is a provision now for the UN Dispute Tribunal (UNDT), which is an administrative court of first instance. Internal remedies through an Appeals Board have been abolished. There is also now established a UN Appeals Tribunal which hears appeals by either party from the UNDT on certain grounds (Art. 2.1 of its statute). The reforms are far-reaching and supportive of independence, efficiency, and impartiality of the tribunals and cover, inter alia, qualifications of judges and the process of appointment. Article 4 of the UNDT Statute provides that judges shall be appointed by the UNGA on the recommendation of the Internal Justice Council. The Internal Justice Council referred to is a new body and makes for independent tribunals. It consists of five members—two appointed by the UN Secretariat, two appointed by the staff of the UN, and the fifth a neutral. Also, judges shall be of high moral character and possess at least ten years of judicial experience in the field of administrative law, or the equivalent, within one or more national jurisdictions. Judges are to be appointed for one non-renewable term of seven years and shall not be eligible for any appointment within the UN, except another judicial post, for a period of five years following their term of office. Judges are to serve in their personal capacity and enjoy full independence. Article 3 of the Statute of the UN Appeals Tribunal has similar provisions with some appropriate minor changes.

In the case of some IATs there may be an added element, which increases the danger of partisanship, where judges are appointed for terms that can be renewed.[16] In some cases, it is true that there are limits to renewal.[17] The question is whether the existence of the possibility of renewal by the organization could induce judges to favor the organization in their judgments in order to ensure or make more likely their reappointment. It is noted with distinct approval that the statutes of the two UN tribunals generally provide for no renewals of appointments.

Another matter requiring satisfactory attention is remuneration for judicial services provided by judges. If the quality and independence of judges of IATs is to be preserved, respectable compensation must be provided for work done. In the past, for example, the judges of the old UNAT were paid an *honorarium*, which was hardly proportionate to the amount of time and work expended. It is noted with approval that the UN has now changed its system. Judges of both UN Tribunals

[15] Moreover, beginning with the current Executive Secretary it has been made a condition of appointment that he does not seek employment with the World Bank Group after his terms expire. He has been appointed for a five-year term with the possibility of renewal only for another five-year term.

[16] See WBAT Statute, Art. IV.3.

[17] WBAT Statute, Art. IV.3; OASAT Statute, Art. III.3.

are paid appointees—the judges of the UNDT being paid the salary of D-II staff members of the UN and the judges of the Appeals Tribunal being paid at the rate underlying the salaries of D-II staff members of the UN.[18]

5 Sources of the Law

In seeking the sources of employment law (international administrative law) the statutes of the IATs are not very helpful, as they are generally silent on the subject.[19] The UNAT[20] and the ILOAT[21] have also accepted the fact that the contract of appointment is a source of law. Where appointments are statutory the instrument of appointment would be a relevant source of law, particularly as regards salary, grade, and the nature of the appointment. Reference has also been made in several cases to the specific circumstances of each contract as a source of law.[22] The terms of employment may be expressed or implied and may be gathered from correspondence and surrounding facts and circumstances.[23]

IATs have readily and generally conceded that the constituent instrument of an international organization is a source of law in employment relations.[24] It is the highest written law governing employment.[25]

The decisions of the main legislative organs of international organizations are also a source of law.[26] In the case of the UN, the Charter gives the UNGA the power to establish the regulations governing the staff.[27] Staff rules or their equivalent may be

[18] Judges of the WBAT are paid approximately at the rate of $250 per hour ($1,500 for a six-hour working day) for work done, which is comparable to legal fees in the US legal sector. The ADB and Inter-American Development Bank (IDB), among other organizations, also have provision for respectable judges' remuneration.

[19] The Commonwealth Secretariat Tribunal Statute refers to international administrative law as the source of law for the tribunal.

[20] *Kaplan*, UNAT (Judgment) No. 19 [1953] 73. See also, *Mortished*, UNAT (Judgment) No. 273 [1981].

[21] *Lindsey*, ILOAT (Judgment) No. 61 [1962] 6. For other tribunals see, e.g. *de Merode*, (Decision) No. 1 [1981] WBAT Rep 9; *Steivenart*, NATO Appeals Board (Decision) No. 24 [1971]; and *Uehling*, OASAT (Decision) No. 9 [1974] 10.

[22] *de Merode*, note 21, at 12; see also, *de Merode*, at 14, 54, 56, for an explanation of what this means.

[23] See, e.g., *Sikand*, UNAT (Judgment) No. 95 [1968] 79; and *Belchamber*, UNAT (Judgment) No. 236 [1978] 16.

[24] *Howrani*, UNAT (Judgment) No. 4 [1951] 21. See also *Mortished*, note 20, at 8; *Mullan*, UNAT (Judgment) No. 162 [1972]; *Duberg*, ILOAT (Judgment) No. 17 [1955]; *Aicher*, OECD Appeals Board (Decision) No. 37 [1964]; *von Lachmüller*, CJEC Cases Nos. 43, 45, 48/59 [1960] ECR 463.

[25] See *de Merode*, note 21, at 9–11.

[26] *de Merode*, note 21, at 11.

[27] Article 101.1 of the Charter. See also the *Application for Review of Judgment No. 273 of the United Nations Administrative Tribunal Case*, 1982 ICJ Rep 362; *Howrani*, note 24; *Smith*, UNAT (Judgment)

established by the administration of an organization.[28] They must not conflict with staff regulations.[29] Manuals, circulars, and other statements issued by the administration also have a law-creating character.[30]

General principles of law are a source of international administrative law, too.[31] Most of the general principles of law applied over a wide range of subject matter are those of administrative or civil service law found mainly in civil law systems.

Another source of law is the practice of the organization.[32] Of course these practices must be followed out of the conviction that they are mandatory.[33]

International law is another possible source of law for international administrative tribunals, though a remote one. Insofar as international law embodies general principles of law, there is no problem.[34] Further, international law may have to be applied by tribunals because it is incorporated implicitly in the written law of an organization.[35] Similarly, international law may be applied by reference in interpreting the written law of an organization.[36] Apart from the above situations where international law *per se* may be applied, tribunals have not expressly recognized international law as a common source of law.[37]

National law may in certain circumstances be a source of law for IATs but generally not per se.[38] The commonest situation where national law becomes relevant is where it is specifically incorporated in the written law of the organization.[39] Clearly national law could also give rise to general principles of law.[40] While the general

No. 249 [1979]; *Lanner*, OEEC Appeals Board (Decision) No. 31 [1960]; *Pagani*, Council of Europe Appeals Board (Decision) No. 76/1981 [1982]; *Bonneman*, NATO Appeals Board (Decision) No. 8 [1968].

28 See *de Merode*, note 21, at 11.

29 See *Wallach*, UNAT (Judgment) No. 53 [1954]; *Poulain d'Andecy*, ILOAT (Judgment) No. 51 [1960]. See also OEEC Appeals Board (Decisions) Nos. 24–6 [1957].

30 See, e.g., *Robinson*, UNAT (Judgment) No. 15 [1952]; *Harris*, UNAT (Judgment) No. 67 [1956]. For other tribunals see, e.g., *Duberg*, note 24; *Fisher*, ILOAT (Judgment) No. 48 [1960]; *Huber*, CJEC Case No. 27/63 [1964]; *Garcia*, OASAT (Decision) No. 56 [1980] 6.

31 *Di Palma Castiglione* [1929], LNT (Judgment) No. 1. For other tribunals see *de Merode*, note 21, at 12; *Vassiliou*, UNAT (Judgment) No. 275 [1981]; *Gubin and Nemo*, ILOAT (Judgment) 429 [1980]; *Pagani*, Council of Europe Appeals Board (Decision) No. 76/1981 [1982]; *Warren*, NATO Appeals Board (Decision) No. 57 [1974]; *Alaniz*, OASAT (Decision) No. 12 [1975]; *Angelopoulos*, OECD Appeals Board (Decision) No. 57 [1976]; *Algera*, CJEC Case No. 7/56 [1957].

32 *De Merode*, note 21, at 11–12. The ICJ expressed the view that practice could alter the written law: *Effect of Awards Case* [1954] ICJ Rep 91.

33 *De Merode*, note 21, at 11–12; *Vanhove*, UNAT (Judgment) No. 14 [1952]; *Garcin*, ILOAT (Judgment) No. 32 [1958].

34 *Artzet*, CoEAB (Appeal) No. 8 [1972] 88.

35 *Jurado*, ILOAT (Judgment) No. 70 [1964].

36 *Stepczynski*, UNAT (Judgment) No. 64 [1956].

37 *Champoury*, UNAT (Judgment) No. 76 [1959]. See also, *Lindsey*, ILOAT (Judgment) No. 61 [1962].

38 See, e.g., *Zihler*, ILOAT (Judgment) No. 435 [1980]; *Breukmann (No. 2)*, ILOAT (Judgment) No. 322 [1977]; and *Gallianos*, UNAT (Judgment) No. 126 [1969].

39 See, e.g., M Morgenstern, "The Law Applicable to International Officials" (1969) 18 ICLQ 739.

40 E.g., see *Wakley*, ILOAT (Judgment) No. 53 [1961].

principle is that the written law of the organization is the main source of the internal law governing employment relations, it is with regard to general principles of law and practice that problems may arise. General principles of law may conflict with the written law. In a few cases the view taken has apparently been that the written law per se takes precedence over general principles of law.[41] There is, however, some authority for the view that general principles of law can override the written law of an international organization. First, there are some general principles of law, such as the rule against an amendment, which violate acquired or essential rights that are in fact applied even in the face of written rules to the contrary.[42] Secondly, the ILOAT said in *Ferrechia* that the rule that a staff member must be given the right to be heard before a disciplinary sanction is imposed on him, deriving as it does from a general principle of law, must be respected "even where contrary provisions exist."[43] Thirdly, it is clear from the jurisprudence of tribunals that they do try to interpret the written law so as to conform to general principles of law and to establish that the written law does not violate general principles of law.[44]

Considerable importance is attached to general principles of law in the hierarchy of sources of law, even if there are statements to the contrary. The reasonable conclusion seems to be that, as regards the general principles of law of a *fundamental* nature, they are superior hierarchically to any written law in particular and could, indeed, be the supreme source of law. The rule against discrimination or equality of treatment and the principle that a staff member has a right to be heard before a disciplinary sanction is imposed on him are examples of general principles of a fundamental nature.

As for practice, in certain instances tribunals have held that a practice could not as such modify the written law, as opposed to interpret it.[45] On the other hand, both the ICJ[46] and the ILOAT[47] have recognized the contrary. No serious doubt has been raised about the proposition that practice cannot override the constituent treaty of the organization.[48] However, in regard to staff regulations and staff rules or their equivalent (the contracts of employment or other written sources),

[41] In *di Palma Castiglione*, LNT (Judgment) No. 1 [1929] 3, the LNT stated that it was only in the absence of rules of positive law that the application of general principles of law could be considered. See also, e.g., *Vukmanovic*, ILOAT (Judgment) No. 896 [1988]; *Mullan*, UNAT (Judgment) No. 162 [1972], JUNAT Nos. 114–66, 387.

[42] See, in particular, *de Merode*, note 21, and the discussion below.

[43] *Ferrechia*, ILOAT (Judgment) No. 203 [1973].

[44] E.g. NATO Appeals Board (Decision) No. 203(a) [1985]; *Beydoun*, CJEC Cases 75 and 117/82 [1984] ECR 1,530; *Callewaert-Haezebrouck* (No. 2), ILOAT (Judgment) No. 344 [1978]; and *Artzet*, CoEaB (Appeal) No. 8 [1973], Case Law Digest (1985) 42.

[45] *Broemser* (Decision) [1985] WBAT Rep No. 27.

[46] *Judgments of the ILO Administrative Tribunal Case* [1956] ICJ Rep 91.

[47] *Duberg*, note 24. See also, e.g., *Redfern*, ILOAT (Judgment) No. 679 [1985] 6–7; *Rosetti*, ILOAT (Judgment) No. 910 [1988] 6–7.

[48] Advocate-General Roemer in *von Lachmüller*, CJEC Cases 54, 45 and 48/59 [1960] ECR 484.

the cases referred to above reveal conflicting views. It is reasonable that practices that are to the disadvantage of staff in that they take away rights given by the written law, cannot override the written law because staff rights should be given adequate protection. As for practices that benefit the staff, the ICJ and ILOAT have taken the view that in regard to the renewal of fixed-term contracts, practice can override the written law. Although in *Léger*, the ILOAT thought that a practice which contradicted the written law on the determination of residence could not override the written law.[49] While accepting in general the view of the ICJ and ILOAT, one may leave open the possibility that in exceptional situations the view taken in *Léger* will be adopted.[50]

6 Jurisdiction

IATs are international courts of limited jurisdiction (*juridiction d'attribution*). As such, they enjoy the jurisdiction given by their statutes by which, being creatures specifically of international organizations, they are established.

Admissibility has created no problems. It is determined by provisions in statutes and concerns such matters as time limits for filing of applications and exhaustion of internal remedies. The interpretation and application of these provisions by IATs have been reasonable. On the other hand, with jurisdiction there are two problems that arise. First, there is the question of how far statutes should place restrictions on jurisdiction. Clearly, IATs should by their very nature exercise jurisdiction only in employment disputes between organizations and their staff. In some instances IATs have been given jurisdiction *ratione materiae* over a wide range of disputes.[51] The real issue, however, is whether statutes should expressly limit jurisdiction within the area of employment disputes so as to exclude jurisdiction over certain kinds of disputes. Some of the more recently adopted statutes do just this by excluding jurisdiction over certain kinds of disputes arising from the application of resolutions of the highest legislative bodies of the organization, as in the case of the Statute of the IMF Administrative Tribunal (IMFAT).[52] This is unfortunate. The highest legislative body of an organization may well adopt resolutions that violate a fundamental

[49] *Léger*, ILOAT (Judgment) No. 486 [1982].

[50] On changes of practice see *Cachelin*, ILOAT (Judgment) No. 767 [1986] 7. On misapplication of practice see *Novak*, ILOAT (Judgment) No. 975 [1989] 6–7.

[51] See Art. II, particularly para. 4 of the ILOAT Statute. See also the Statute of the Arbitral Tribunal of the Commonwealth Secretariat.

[52] See Arts II and III of the IMFAT Statute, which limit the court's jurisdiction.

norm (*jus cogens*) of international administrative law, such as that prohibiting discrimination or that requiring due process.

Second, there may be some inclination in some IATs to *interpret* their jurisdiction narrowly. While *Mullan*,[53] decided by the UNAT, is not an easy case to explain, as has been indicated elsewhere,[54] early on the case revealed signs of caution, if not fear, on the part of the UNAT. The case suggests hesitancy on the part of the tribunal to assume jurisdiction to decide the legality of acts of the UNGA, the highest general legislative body of the UN. In contrast, the WBAT has on more than one occasion[55] examined the acts of what is the effective legislative body of the World Bank in order to determine whether they were legal. This is the better approach.

International administrative law normally requires an administrative decision to be questioned for jurisdiction to be exercised by an IAT. In general, IATs will not exercise jurisdiction in a case without such a decision being put in issue. However, can employees seize IATs when the administration fails to act in fulfillment of a direct substantive obligation (as opposed to abusing a discretion)? An answer in the affirmative may be, in the interests of justice, too formalistic an approach for an IAT to take in all cases. One possibility is for IATs to develop a theory of "implied decision," where appropriate, in such cases. This would avoid dismantling the formal acquisition of an administrative decision, which is intrinsic to administrative law as it is known at present.

7 Matters of Substance

Obviously, IATs that have published their decisions have contributed to most of the development of international administrative law. Nowadays, there is a very mature body of this law, which has benefited especially from the experience of the French administrative courts for over a century and a half. The substantive law applied by IATs, however, has a unique character as international administrative law and is not a clone of any particular national law.

With the interpretation of rules and regulations of organizations relating to staff IATs have had no problem. They implicitly, if not expressly, apply general principles

[53] *Mullan* (Judgment) No. 162 [1972].

[54] See, the discussion in CF Amerasinghe (1994) 1 Law of the International Civil Service 140.

[55] See the discussion particularly in *von Stauffenberg* et al., (Decision) No. 38 [1987] WBAT Rep Part I.

of interpretation to be found in both public international law and national legal systems. The developments that have taken place are through the elaboration of principles especially in the areas of substantive irregularity, procedural irregularity, and discrimination and inequality of treatment, relating to discretionary decisions, and through a very singular and intricate treatment of the law relating to unilateral amendment of the written law by organizations.

In the area of substantive irregularity, the well-established categories of abuse of discretion, such as error of law, error of fact, and mistaken conclusions, will continue to be refined and given application. A residual concept, described generally as "arbitrariness," was recognized by the WBAT, initially in *Durrant-Bell*.[56] This covers any abuse of discretion that cannot conveniently be fitted into the conventional categories. The failure of the respondent to provide transparency was characterized as a fault, which, while not capable of rendering the decision of the administration null and void, was nevertheless a violation of the applicant's rights that needed to be compensated.

In the field of procedural irregularities the law has been refined by a general elaboration of a broad concept of due process. Courts have not felt themselves limited by the traditional categories, such as the right of defense and the requirements of warnings and notice, which they do indeed recognize, but have formulated a residual idea of fair treatment in regard to procedures for administrative decision-making.

In regard to unilateral amendment of the written law by organizations, it is well known that there are several approaches to the protection of staff members from what could have been an unfettered discretion. In general, IATs have been particularly appreciative of the need to protect certain rights of staff members, whether they have considered them based on acquired rights, essential conditions of employment, or some other such concept; what is important is that IATs have with no uncertain emphasis concluded that there are certain rights enjoyed by staff members which cannot unilaterally be abrogated by the organization.

Some IATs have been bolder and have sought ways and means of recognizing a body of such fundamental law (*ius cogens*).[57] In *de Merode*,[58] for instance, the WBAT recognized clearly that the principle of non-retroactivity was such a fundamental norm that the organization could not violate. There may be certain aspects of due process that are inviolable, while the principle of non-discrimination may be a fundamental norm which cannot be violated.[59]

Discretionary powers are numerous, and include the power to transfer, promote, classify, and dismiss. Disciplinary powers are a special example of discretionary

[56] Decision No. 24 [1985] WBAT Rep. For "arbitrariness" see also, e.g., *Apkarian*, (Decision) No. 58 [1983] WBAT Rep Part I; *Chakra* (Decision) No. 70 [1988] WBAT Rep Part II.

[57] See, e.g., *Artzet*, CoEAB (Appeal) No. 8 [1973].

[58] (Decision) No. 1 [1981] WBAT Rep.

[59] On *ius cogens*, see *De los Cobos and Wenger*, ILOAT (Judgment) No. 39 [1980] (ILO).

powers and need particular attention. The reason for this is that in disciplining, staff administrations exercise a *quasi-judicial* power. The quasi-judicial nature of the power was adverted to and emphasized for the first time by the UNAT in a series of cases beginning in 1998.[60] In earlier cases, this tribunal took the approach that "in disciplinary matters the Secretary-General has a broad power of discretion."[61] But, in fact, strict control of the discretion to discipline was exercised, as was demonstrated by what the tribunal actually did in the cases. The consequence is that the control exercised by the tribunal to prevent what may generically be called "abuse of discretion" in disciplinary cases is somewhat strict in many respects, though it may fall short of a substitution of judgment. The WBAT followed this approach, starting with the decision in *Singh*.[62] The ILOAT's approach has been similar.[63]

Briefly, the particular strictures are especially in the areas of the establishment of facts incriminating the staff member, the legality of the characterization of offences, and the nature of the penalty imposed. It is appropriate to cite from *Kiwanuka* (UNAT) the statement of general principle relating to the control of disciplinary powers:

> The jurisprudence…has been developing and definitions have been refined. In reviewing this kind of quasi-judicial decision and in keeping with the relevant general principles of law, in the disciplinary cases the Tribunal generally examines (i) whether the facts on which the disciplinary measures were based have been established; (ii) whether the established facts legally amount to misconduct or serious misconduct; (iii) whether there has been any substantive irregularity (e.g., omission of facts or consideration of irrelevant facts); (iv) whether there has been any procedural irregularity; (v) whether there was an improper motive or abuse of purpose; (vi) whether the sanction is legal; (vii) whether the sanction imposed was disproportionate to the offence; (viii) and, as in the case of discretionary powers in general, where there has been arbitrariness…. Most recently in Judgment No. 898, *Uggla*, paragraph II (1998), the Tribunal made a similar general statement.
>
> Clearly the Tribunal takes the view that the imposition of disciplinary sanctions involves the exercise of a discretionary power by the Administration. It further recognizes that, unlike other discretionary powers, such as transferring and terminating services, it is also a special exercise of *quasi-judicial* power. For these reasons the process of review exercised by the Tribunal is of a particular nature. The Administration's interest in maintaining high standards of conduct and thus protecting itself must be reconciled with the interest of staff in being assured that they are not penalized unfairly or arbitrarily.[64]

[60] See e.g., *Augustine*, UNAT (Decision) No. 890 [1998]; *Jhuthi*, UNAT (Decision) No. 939 [1999]; *Kiwanuka*, UNAT (Decision) No. 941 [1999].

[61] See e.g., *Djimbaye*, UNAT (Decision) No. 583 [1992] para VI; *Shahrour*, UNAT (Decision) No. 939 [1999] para IX.

[62] *Singh*, WBAT Decision No. 105 [1991]. See also *King*, WBAT (Decision) No. 131 [1993]; *Carew*, WBAT (Decision) No. 142 [1995]; and *Planthara*, WBAT (Decision) No. 143 [1995].

[63] E.g. *Connolly-Battisti (No. 2)*, ILOAT (Decision) No. 274 [1976].

[64] UNAT (Decision) No. 941 [1999] 11. The three judges included the present author.

What is of interest is the reference particularly to the areas of establishment of facts, characterization of the offense and proportionality of sanctions.[65]

It would seem that tribunals have been careful, and rightly so, to protect staff members from prejudice in this area because injustice could result in serious damage to their careers—even more so apparently than in the case of dismissal, e.g., for unsatisfactory service. While the interest of the administration to maintain high standards of conduct is acknowledged and respected and cannot be ignored, tribunals are most concerned to protect the interests of staff members in not being punished improperly for disciplinary violations.

8 A Matter of Procedure

IATs have developed through their rules and other means a sophisticated procedure regulating proceedings before them. The fairness of these has not, in general, been questioned. The rules provide for elaborate written proceedings, which form the basis of the procedure before the IATs, for interventions as parties, for participation as *amici curiae*, for oral hearings, and for other matters. An aspect that may raise problems is oral hearings.

The rules of all the more important IATs provide for oral hearings.[66] These are at the discretion of the tribunal rather than a right of the parties. Some tribunals, such as the administrative tribunals of the Organization of American States (OAS) and IDB, have oral hearings as a matter of routine; many, such as the UNAT (UNDT now) and ILOAT, have them often, while the WBAT in particular has had them very rarely. It may be asked why there are such differences in this regard. The recourse to oral hearings is a function of the culture of an IAT. Clearly, the OAS Administrative Tribunal and IDB Administrative Tribunal and most of the administrative courts of European organizations have a tradition of relying heavily on oral hearings in order to gather information and evidence necessary to decide cases, while the UNAT (UNDT now), the ILOAT, and, more especially, the WBAT do not in their practice place an absolute value on such hearings. It would be inaccurate to postulate that oral hearings are always necessary or that they are always unnecessary. Indeed, the quality and fairness of judgments resulting from either procedure have never been

[65] The WBAT has taken a similar approach: see, e.g., *Carew*, WBAT (Decision) No. 142 [1995]; *Planthara*, WBAT (Decision) No. 143 [1995]; *Mustafa*, WBAT (Decision) No. 207 [1999]; *AJ*, WBAT (Decision) No. 389 [2009].

[66] See e.g., R. 15 of the WBAT Rules; Art. 12 of the ILOAT Rules of Court.

questioned in general. In reality, there are no grounds for concluding that obligatory oral hearings result in fairer and better judgments. The practice of leaving the incidence of oral hearings to the discretion of the court is perhaps the best solution from many points of view.

9 Remedies

The efficacy of a legal system depends to a large extent on the nature of the remedies available to its courts. The remedies that IATs can prescribe are generally referred to in their statutes.[67] Some statutes appear to specify only certain kinds of remedies. Thus, the Statute of the Administrative Tribunal of the Council of Europe (CoEAT) refers to annulment of the administrative decision as apparently the only remedy that may be ordered. There are consequently two questions that arise. The first concerns the extent of the limitations that seem to be imposed on the prescription of remedies. The second question relates to the attitude that IATs have taken to limitations that may be delineated in their statutes.

In regard to the first question, it might be counterproductive to explicitly limit available remedies to a narrow range. Thus, in the case of the CoEAT, the explicit reference to annulment as apparently the only remedy has led the tribunal only to annul administrative decisions or to declare them legally valid. The resort to one of these two alternatives could result in a miscarriage of justice, as where a defect in an administrative decision is, in reality, not sufficiently serious to render the decision a nullity. Either the applicant is not compensated at all or the administration's decision is declared a nullity when it should not be, with the result that the applicant is overcompensated.

Many IATs have been commendably courageous in their approach to the problem of limitations in general, which is the answer to the second question. Practically all statutes of the more important and better known IATs contain provisions which deal with available remedies in no uncertain terms. The intention is purportedly to place limitations on the available remedies. The manner in which limitations are formulated and their extent vary. Limitations relating to the amount of monetary compensation that may be awarded have been scrupulously respected. When these limitations are two-tiered and permit circumvention in exceptional circumstances

[67] See e.g. Art. VIII of the ILOAT Statute; Art. XVII of the WBAT Statute.

there is, in effect, no limitation, although a justification must be given for exceeding the specified limit. Where statutes on their face have limited available remedies in other ways, most IATs have resorted to what may be described as "inherent powers" in order to prescribe remedies in a manner or to an extent not envisaged in the statutes. Thus, though compensation—other than as an alternative to reinstatement—may not be referred to in their statutes as a possible remedy, IATs have in general arrogated to themselves the power to award compensation per se, without ordering annulment or reinstatement, as the case may be. This practice respects the maxim: there cannot be a wrong without a remedy.

10 Enforcement

There is an absence in international administrative law of machinery to enforce judgments of IATs against organizations. Attempts effectively to enforce judgments through national courts would be met with claims of immunity, while there is no mechanism within international law to enforce such judgments against organizations. There are many questions that arise consequently, such as: is international administrative law effective? Can international administrative law be characterized as law in the absence of enforcement mechanisms? Why should organizations carry out judgments of IATs?

Organizations do carry out judgments of IATs. Practically speaking, judgments have never been disrespected by them. The reason for this is a psychological one, relating to the need to promote morale and confidence among staff and respect for the good faith of the organizations themselves in international society.

As for the characterization of international administrative law as law, this is a jurisprudential question for legal theory. It is my opinion that the element of enforcement is not an *essential* requirement of law defined as such.[68] Suffice it to say here that, unlike international law in general, international administrative law has never seriously been denied the quality of law.

[68] CF Amerasinghe, "Theory with Practical Effects: Is International Law Neither Fish nor Fowl?" (1999) 37 Archiv des Völkerrechts (1999) 1.

11 Review by Another Judicial Body

The statute of the former UNAT provided for review by another international court, the ICJ, of its judgments in limited situations. The statute of that tribunal permitted reference to the ICJ on the ground that the tribunal had exceeded its jurisdiction or competence; or failed to exercise jurisdiction vested in it; erred on a question of law relating to the provisions of the UN charter; or committed a fundamental error in procedure which had caused a failure of justice. The case had to be referred to the ICJ for an advisory opinion by a committee that examined written applications received from a member state of the UN, the Secretary-General, or the person in respect of whom a judgment had been rendered. The committee was appointed by the General Assembly of the UN. The review by the ICJ was done through an Advisory Opinion, which was binding on the UN.[69]

Review had unsuccessfully been requested in relation to three judgments rendered by the UNAT.[70] Currently, before the creation of the UNDT and the UN Appeals Tribunal, the ICJ's review of UNAT judgments was abolished by the UNGA through an amendment to the UNAT Statute. Now appeals from UNDT judgments may be taken to the Appeals Tribunal by either party on grounds similar to those contained in the former Art. 11 of the statute of the former UNAT.

The statute of the ILOAT still permits reference of a judgment to the ICJ for an advisory opinion where the relevant organization or the Administrative Branch of the Pension Fund challenges a judgment confirming the jurisdiction of the ILOAT or considers that the judgment is vitiated by a fundamental fault in the procedure followed.[71] There have been two advisory opinions given by the ICJ in cases referred to it and decided by the ILOAT.[72]

[69] See Art. 11 of the UNAT Statute.

[70] For these judgments, see CF Amerasinghe, note 54, at 253.

[71] Article XII of the ILOAT Statute. Arrangements have been made for other organizations which have subscribed to the Statute of the ILOAT to seek review of ILOAT judgments concerning them from the ICJ.

[72] *Judgments of the ILO Administrative Tribunal Case* [1956] ICJ Rep 77; *Judgment No. 2867 of the ILO Administrative Tribunal Case* [2010] <www.icj-cij.org> accessed June 1, 2013.

An appeal from the judgments of the European Civil Service Tribunal to the ECJ is available.

12 Concluding Observations

The international administrative legal system and the law it embodies are really the backbone of international organizations and their successful functioning. It is unlikely and practically impossible that the system of administrative justice, as it now exists in international organizations, will ever be displaced. Even innovations, such as the creation of a unified administrative tribunal, just serving the UN system or part of it, are unlikely, because the system seems today to function without the independence of IATs being affected in practice, and the integrity of judges and of the system appears by and large not to be in question.

In the areas of jurisdiction there are some improvements that could be useful. The substantive law has, in general, been developed accurately and adequately. The approach to available remedies in most statutes is somewhat limiting, but the practice of interpreting provisions so as to permit the grant of a variety of remedies on the basis of inherent power, apparently, is welcome. The question of oral hearings in the procedure before courts requires a more balanced and less peremptory answer than has thus far generally been given.

Research Questions

1. Is the protection given to staff in their relations with international organizations through international administrative tribunals adequate? Is there a need to improve it?
2. Do the mechanisms for the appointment of judges to international administrative tribunals need improvement?
3. Do the procedures currently employed by IATs in deciding cases before them need to be improved?
4. Should limitations on the remedies which may be granted by IATs be removed, or are they unavoidable because of the nature of international organizations?

Suggested Reading

Akehurst, M, "Renewal of Fixed-Term Contracts of Employment in International Organizations" (1965) 32 Revue international des sciences administrative 83.

Akehurst, M, *The Law Governing Employment in International Organizations* (Cambridge University Press 1967).

Amerasinghe, CF, "The Implications of the *de Merode Case* for International Administrative Law" (1983) 43 ZAORV 1.

Amerasinghe, CF, "Sources of International Administrative Law" in *International Law at the Time of its Codification, Essays in Honour of Roberto Ago* (Milan: A. Giuffrè 1987) 67.

Amerasinghe, CF, *Law of the International Civil Service* (2nd edn, Oxford: Clarendon Press 1994).

Amerasinghe, CF, "The Future of International Administrative Law" (1996) 45 Int'l & Comp. L.Q. 273.

Amerasinghe, CF, "Theory with Practical Effects: Is International Law Neither Fish nor Fowl" (1999) 37 *Archiv des Völkerrechts* 1ff.

Amerasinghe, CF, *Principles of the Institutional Law of International Organizations* (Cambridge University Press 2005).

Amerasinghe, CF, "Reflections on the Internal Judicial Systems of International Organizations" in O. Elias (ed.), *The Development and Effectiveness of International Administrative Law* (Leiden: Nijhoff 2012) 33.

Bedjaoui, M, "Application de la loi locale aux fonctionnaires internationaux" (1956) 86 JDI 216.

Carlston, KS, "International Administrative Law, A Venture in Legal Theory"(1959) 8 J. Public L. 329.

Dhinakaran, R, "Law of the International Civil Service: A Venture into Legal Theory" (2011) 8 IOLR 137.

Morgenstern, M, "The Law Applicable to International Officials" (1969) 18 Int'l & Comp. L.Q. 739.

Plantey, A, *The International Civil Service: Law and Management* (New York: Masson 1981).

Richardson, R, "The Legal Relations between an International Organization and its Personnel" (1956) 2 Wayne L. Rev. 75.

PART III

THEORETICAL APPROACHES TO STUDYING INTERNATIONAL ADJUDICATION

CHAPTER 16

TRANSNATIONAL LEGAL PROCESS THEORIES

MAYA STEINITZ*

* Maya Steinitz is an Associate Professor of Law at the University of Iowa College of Law. A special thanks to Nathan Miller for his comments and to Henri Nkuepo for his research assistance. Some disclosures: the author admits a common law and English language bias, though literature in French was also reviewed in authoring this chapter. Further, given the space limitation, the chapter seeks to be illustrative rather than exhaustive with respect to the literature discussed.

1 Introduction

This chapter is devoted to transnational legal process theories. In 1955, Philip Jessup, in his Storrs Lectures at Yale, famously coined the term "transnational law" as he searched for a concept that would capture the legal regulation of actions or events that transcend national boundaries and that can accommodate both public and private international law. Further, while the traditional concept of "international law" referred to the law regulating relationships between states, the new term encompassed legal relationships of and amongst individuals, corporations, and organizations as well as states.[1]

In other words, as early as the 1950s, and thereafter with increased urgency, scholars have been pointing out that the concept of the inter-national, including international law, no longer suffices to explain the reality they were observing: a reality of increasing interrelatedness of various types of social actors interacting in the international sphere. "International law" no longer contained the multitude of legal relations and of legal disputes, including disputes that were in fact being resolved, such as cross-border business disputes between individuals and/or corporations that were being resolved in international commercial arbitration. Different scholars have, over time, given somewhat different names to the new reality. For example, they have used "transnational" or "cross-border" to connote the traversing of national boundaries; "supranational" to emphasize new regional arrangements such as the European Union; "global" to invoke the processes, predominantly economic and technological, collectively known as "globalization." Irrespective of the specific terminology selected, scholars and practitioners have been experiencing and explaining the breakdown of old dichotomies and categories—the paradigm shift in international affairs that characterized the twentieth century.

The chapter opens with both negative and affirmative definitions of the idea of "transnational legal process(es)" and with a brief note on the origin and history of this concept. In order to provide a representative sample of the field, the main section presents some of the leading theories, grouped based upon the underlying perspective of the theorists: the lawyers and legal theorists, the political science and international relations theorists, and the sociologists and socio-legal theorists.[2] In addition to describing these dominant approaches, the chapter highlights competing methodologies and key themes, including the internationalization of the rule of law and its discontents and the intended and unintended consequences of the

[1] See generally, Philip C. Jessup, *Transnational Law* (New Haven, CT: Yale University Press 1956); see also, Peer Zumbansen, "Transnational Law, Evolving" (2011) Osgoode CLPE Research Paper no. 27/2011 <http://ssrn.com/abstract=1975403> accessed March 4, 2013 (describing the evolution of the idea of transnational law).

[2] The labels "lawyers," "political scientists," and so forth describe the perspective rather than the formal training of the individuals whose scholarship is discussed.

transplantation of institutional models from one realm to another. The chapter concludes with the observation that the nascent field of transnational legal theory suffers from a lack of conceptual clarity that stems, in part, from its attempts to cover disparate phenomena that pull in different directions.

It is helpful to note at the outset that certain, important theories inform and partly overlap with theories of the transnational legal process, but are not themselves directly and properly understood theories of that process. These include theories of international law and international governance; theories that subsume the transnational legal process in the domestic process; purely doctrinal or comparative scholarship of transnational litigation; and theories of non-adjudicative international dispute resolution mechanisms, such as diplomacy.[3] These are hereby acknowledged but excluded from the discussion.

Similarly, certain important discussions on issues such as the finance of international courts, the desirability of proliferation and fragmentation of international judicial bodies versus harmonization and international access to justice, are perhaps better characterized as in the realm of policy rather than theory and thus, are also excluded from the current discussion.[4]

2 The Origin and History of Theorizing on Transnational Legal Processes

Harold Koh was the first to introduce the notion of "transnational legal process" as a predicate of "transnational law." In his telling of the evolution of twentieth century international legal theory, he wedded the concept of the "international legal

[3] Examples of scholarship in these areas include P Zumbansen, "Transnational Law" (2008) CPLE Research Paper 09/2008, <http://ssrn.com/abstract=1105576> accessed March 3, 2013 (global governance); G Born, *International Civil Litigation in United States Courts: Commentary and Materials* (1st edn, Deventer: Springer 1994) (a doctrinal focus on transnational litigation in US courts); E Posner, "Transnational Legal Process and the Supreme Court's 2003–2004 Term: Some Skeptical Observations" (2004–2005) 12 Tulsa J. Comp. & Int'l L. 23 (advocating that American courts resist enforcing international and foreign norms unless such norms have first been domesticated by Congress); G Born, *International Commercial Arbitration: Commentary and Materials* (2nd edn, The Hague: Hotei Publishing 2001); and S McCaffrey and T Main, *Transnational Litigation in Comparative Perspective: Theory & Application* (Oxford University Press 2009) (respectively, doctrinal and comparative scholarship of the transnational legal process).

[4] The Project on International Courts and Tribunals (PiCT), for example, is dedicated to the study and development of such policy issues and provides a wealth of analysis and resources. See Project on International Courts and Tribunals <http://www.pict-pcti.org> accessed July 1, 2012.

process" (emphasis on "process"), or the study of law's role in the process of policy decisions in the international realm, and the idea of "transnational legal problems," which mixes the public and the private, the domestic and the international, law and policy. By positioning transnational legal process within the larger Legal Process Movement, Koh emphasized that legal issues mainly arise not before courts, but rather in the process of making policy decisions, with lawyers playing a more important role than judges, and with consent playing a more important role than command.

Despite the commitment to out-of-court processes of the Legal Process Movement, however, Koh himself applied the theory to litigation and, in fact, was informed in part by his work in public law litigation.[5] Indeed, once defined as a trans-substantive process whereby states and other transnational actors come to internalize legal norms other than domestic law,[6] it is hard to resist employing the theory to describe litigation. In fact, around the same time, others in private practice were reaching similar conclusions. In 1989, Gary Born and David Westin published *International Civil Litigation in United States Courts*, a book often credited as the first to identify the interrelationships among different aspects of transnational litigation in domestic courts and the need to analyze, study, and teach these different aspects as one cohesive field of practice. "In dealing with the unique problems raised by foreign litigants and transactions, U.S. courts have begun to develop a distinct, cohesive body of law," they wrote.[7] They identified issues such as jurisdiction over foreign defendants, service of process abroad, forum selection and parallel litigation, sovereign immunity and the act of state doctrine and the enforcement of foreign judgments as interrelated stages in a certain type—in the Weberian sense of the word—of litigation. In addition, they identified a set of themes that often come up in such litigation. These themes include the need to balance domestic and foreign interests, the role of foreign relations and of governmental division of powers, the effects of and on federalism, the interplay of domestic commercial litigation and public international law, and international comity.[8]

Of course, the primary alternative to transnational litigation, understood as involving a party litigating in the courts of a foreign nation, is international commercial arbitration. These are the two paths open to resolve commercial disputes that cross national boundaries. Given that transnational litigation and international arbitration are alternatives, and given that international arbitration is supported by recourse to domestic courts at certain steps of the process (such as jurisdictional

[5] HH Koh, "Transnational Public Law Litigation" (1991) 100 Yale L.J. 2347, 2347–72 (a form of litigation which he characterized as "brought in United States courts by individual and governmental litigants challenging violations of international law").

[6] See HH Koh, "Why Transnational Law Matters" (2006) 24 Penn State Int'l L. Rev. 745, 746; HH Koh, "Transnational Legal Process" (1996) 75 Neb. L. Rev. 181, 181–207.

[7] See Born, *International Civil Litigation*, note 3, at 1.

[8] G Born, note 3, at 1–10.

challenges, interim measures, and enforcement) or, otherwise stated, that an aspect of international arbitration is transnational litigation, both areas share topics, doctrine, and theory. Indeed some of the most interesting debates that partly overlap or inform the theory of the transnational legal process have developed in relation to international commercial arbitration and the body of law associated with it—*lex mercatoria*.[9] This development is not surprising given that international commercial arbitration is one of the oldest and the most effective transnational dispute mechanisms.

A multitude of theories seeking to portray and explain the various mechanisms of binding, non-domestic dispute resolution, to catalogue the challenges they face or to critique their advent, continue to occupy a significant space in contemporary international legal theory. The next section is devoted to these theories.

3 Transnational Legal Process Theories

3.1 The lawyers and legal theorists

As noted and illustrated above, transnational legal process theories have emerged to a large extent through lawyers—practitioners and scholars of international dispute resolution—observing a changing legal environment. Since dispute resolution is a core function of any legal system, transnational dispute resolution, namely litigation and arbitration, received much of the attention of those theorizing about the new global legal order. As students of law *qua* law, they grapple with key aspects of litigation. First and foremost are the twin challenges of jurisdiction and enforcement. Other components that call for theorizing include the challenges of *forum non conveniens*, parallel proceedings, and international choice of law. In asking what the proper doctrinal solutions are to such problems as choice of law or territorial jurisdiction, scholars are also asking the questions of efficacy and coordination, of sovereignty and legitimacy, of judicial independence and the rule of law.

[9] See e.g., T Schultz, "The Concept of Law in Transnational Arbitral Legal Orders and Some of its Consequences" (2011) 2 J. Int'l Disp. Settlement 59; R Michaels, "A Fuller Concept of Law Beyond the State? Thoughts on Lon Fuller's Contributions to the Jurisprudence of Transnational Dispute Resolution—A Reply to Thomas Schultz" (2011) 2 J. Int'l Disp. Settlement 417; and P Zumbansen, "Debating Autonomy and Procedural Justice: The Lex Mercatoria in the Context of Global Governance Debates—A Reply to Thomas Schultz" (2011) 2 JIDS 427.

Two themes in particular emerge in reviewing this literature. First, the model of international commercial arbitration, one of the oldest and most successful forms of modern dispute resolution, looms large in either the foreground or in the background of much of this scholarship. A second, related theme is that many insights emerge from grappling, more generally, with what happens when we adopt, adapt, and stretch one form of adjudication to fit a new, different, transnational context, which the said system was never meant to accommodate. What happens, for example, when we model international tribunals on domestic courts? What happens when we model international public law adjudication on contract-based international arbitration? What happens when we model arbitration against a sovereign on commercial arbitration between private parties? The following paragraphs illustrate this strand of transnational legal process theorizing by examining the scholarship of Harold Koh, Yuval Shany, Jens Dammann and Henry Hansmann, and Gas Van Harten.

Koh's work, introduced above, seeks to explain the critical issue of compliance with international law generally.[10] Like Jessup, his starting point is to broaden the focus beyond states and some of his conclusions are similar. In enumerating what he sees as the four distinctive features of transnational legal processes, he first lists the "break down [of] two traditional dichotomies that have historically dominated the study of international law: between domestic and international, public and private" and then notes its non-statist nature: "the actors in this process are not just, or even primarily, nation-states, but include non-state actors as well."[11] To those he adds that the transnational legal process is dynamic, not static: "Transnational law transforms, mutates, and percolates up and down, from the public to the private, from the domestic to the international level and back down again."[12] Finally, for Koh, the transnational legal process is normative in that it is a process of interactions from which new rules of law emerge. These new rules are internalized, enforced, interpreted, and reinterpreted, thus beginning the process all over again. So the focus is "not simply upon how international interaction among transnational actors shapes law, but also on how law shapes and guides future interactions: in short, how law influences why nations obey."[13]

[10] Koh, note 6, at 183–4. It is therefore also equally part of the significant body of literature on compliance, a literature that overlaps with the transnational legal process theory of dispute resolution. See e.g., K Alter, *The New Terrain of International Law: Courts, Politics, Rights* (Princeton University Press 2014).

[11] Koh, note 6, at 203–4.

[12] Koh, note 6, at 203–4.

[13] Koh, note 6, at 203–4. Gregory Shaffer, Terence Halliday, and several other scholars have developed an empirical, socio-legal framework to answer precisely that question: a framework that illuminates the kinds of changes transnational legal processes can effect on states, as well as the specific factors that influence the extent and limits of those changes. GC Shaffer (ed.), *Cambridge Studies in Law and Society: Transnational Legal Ordering and State Change* (Cambridge University Press 2013).

Indeed, the main thrust of Koh's theory of the transnational legal process, focused as it is on enforcement and compliance, is internalization through interaction. State and non-state actors obey international law as a result of repeated interaction with other state and non-state actors in the international sphere. (One might add including in, and in the shadow of international courts and tribunals.) The "process" in "transnational legal process" is an *iterative* process of interaction and internalization "through which international law acquires its 'stickiness,' that nation-states acquire their identity, and that nations define promoting the rule of international law as part of their national self-interest."[14]

Yuval Shany examines the equally central issue of jurisdiction and asks how to regulate jurisdictional relationships between national and international fora. He explains that looming in the background of jurisdictional competitions are some of the larger, traditional questions in international legal theory. These are the old questions of monism versus dualism in international legal theory (namely, the view that national and international courts are part of a single normative system versus the view that they are two, sharply delineated systems); of the proper structure (unified or isolated) and hierarchy within the global judiciary; and of the proper role of judges as purely law-applying versus problem solvers who actively promote coordination and harmonization.[15]

Dammann and Hansmann also focus on jurisdiction but as an entry point for reform of global rule of law through institutional competition in the service of

Shaffer directly acknowledges the influence of Koh, particularly the latter's schematization of the vertical and horizontal flow of transnational norms. See Koh, note 6, 745–6. Their work draws on empirical studies of money laundering law in Brazil and Argentina; bankruptcy law in China, Korea, and Indonesia; education law in several dozen low-income countries; patent law in South Africa; and regulation of water services in Chile, Bolivia, and Argentina. Respectively, M Machado, "Similar in Their Differences: Transnational Legal Processes Addressing Money Laundering in Brazil and Argentina" and TR Halliday, "Architects of the State: International Organizations and the Reconstruction of States in East Asia," M Kim and E Boyle, "Neoliberalism, Transnational Education Norms, and Education Spending in the Developing World, 1983–2004," H Klug, "Access to Medicines and the Transformation of the South African State," B Morgan, "The Limits of Transnational Transformations of the State: Comparative Regulatory Regimes in the Delivery of Urban Water Services," all in GC Shaffer (ed.), *Cambridge Studies in Law and Society: Transnational Legal Ordering and State Change* (Cambridge University Press 2013). See also TR Halliday and GC Shaffer (eds), *Transnational Legal Orders* (Cambridge University Press, forthcoming) (shifting the study of transnational legal orders from a dualist framework to an integrative framework that focuses on dynamic, cross-border social processes).

[14] Koh, note 6, at 204. For an account applying social psychology to explain the process of internalization of international legal norms and of the formation of Self through face-to-face interactions patterned by international courts, see generally, M Steinitz, "The Milošević Trial-Live!' An Iconical Analysis of International Law's Claim of Legitimate Authority" (2005) 3 J. Int'l Crim. Justice 103; and M Steinitz, "The International Criminal Tribunal for Rwanda as Theater: The Social Negotiation of the Moral Authority of International Law" (2006) 5 U. Penn. J. Int'l L. & Pol. 1.

[15] Y Shany, *Regulating Jurisdictional Relations between National and International Courts* (Oxford University Press 2009) 3–4, 198–201.

global economic development. They use as their starting point the fact that the quality of national judicial systems varies widely from country to country. Such differences affect not only a particular litigant, but also nations as a whole given the key role that effective courts, and effective resolution of civil disputes, play in economic development (the same premise that underlies the theory and practice of international commercial arbitration). Since judicial reform is difficult and slow to achieve, and since international arbitration is insufficient to remedy this structural feature of the global economy, Dammann and Hansmann envision a global system of "extraterritorial litigation" in which litigants from jurisdictions characterized by dysfunctional court systems may opt to have their domestic and commercial disputes adjudicated in more highly functioning foreign courts for an appropriate fee that compensates the taxpayers of the jurisdiction that the foreign litigants select.[16]

Straddling the line of public and commercial international affairs and international law is the world of international investment law with its unique dispute resolution mechanism at the International Centre for the Settlement of Investment Disputes (ICSID) under the auspices of the World Bank. This unique transnational legal process serves as a laboratory that allows for testing what happens when the lines between the public and the private and between the domestic and the international blur—that celebrated feature of the transnational legal process as defined by the field's forefathers. Gus Van Harten's critique of the ICSID regime locates the origins of many of the problems plaguing the field in the transplantation of the modality and rules of international commercial arbitration, i.e. arbitration between two private parties, into a system of public international arbitration against sovereigns, which in his account undermines some of the core precepts of the rule of law.[17]

In the investment arbitration system, the structure of international commercial arbitration has been adopted for public, regulatory disputes instead of a conventional court model, explains Van Harten. These arbitrations are structurally similar to commercial arbitration even though their contents are that of public law. This means that private arbitrators have the power to resolve regulatory disputes between individuals and multinational corporations (foreign investors), on the one hand, and a state, on the other (but not vice versa) and to ultimately discipline states.[18] Such private arbitration is used in the regulatory sphere to arbitrate disputes between individuals and states without due regard to judicial independence and accountability, basic tenets of the rule of law, and with almost no court

[16] JC Dammann and HB Hansmann, "Globalizing Commercial Litigation" (2008) 94 Cornell L. Rev. 1 (drawing on economic concepts of information asymmetries and negative externalities but engaging largely in normative argumentation).

[17] See generally, G Van Harten, *Investment Treaty Arbitration and Public Law* (Oxford University Press 2007).

[18] Van Harten, note 17, at 3.

supervision—all of which are arguably unnecessary in contract-based international commercial arbitration. In setting up this system:

> states have enabled privately contracted adjudicators to determine the legality of sovereign acts and to award public funds to businesses that sustain loss as a result of government regulation. This undermines basic hallmarks of judicial accountability, openness and independence. Above all, the lack of security of tenure of arbitrators in a one-sided system of state liability... makes the adjudicator dependent on prospective claims and thus biased... against respondent governments [...] because they receive appointments only if investors bring claims.[19]

To remedy the undermining of the rule of law caused by a system in which public law matters are arbitrated in a manner that developed in the context of privatized justice designed by private parties through their contracts, in the context of international commercial arbitration, he suggested that a public law adjudication system must be designed to uphold the principles of accountability, openness, coherence, and independence. Implicitly, however, one can read this analysis as calling into question more generally whether we should, in all circumstances, celebrate the blurring of the lines of public and private and distinctions between states versus non-state actors as parties in transnational litigations.

The next section provides examples of scholarship that question the normative desirability of breaking down the states-focused Westphalian world order and the debate surrounding both the breakdown and its discontents.

3.2 The political scientists and international relations theorists

Since political science and international relations are the sciences of domestic and international government(s), bureaucracies and administration scholars in this category study how the mechanisms and outcomes of transnational dispute resolution are both produced by and, in turn, produce power-sharing and governance and the particular characteristics of dispute resolution mechanisms that double as administrations and bureaucracies. The following section illustrates how these two disciplines come to bear on the analysis of transnational legal processes by looking at the scholarship of Anne-Marie Slaughter, Robert Keohane, and Andrew Moravcsik and the debates between them, on the one hand, and Eric Posner and John Yoo, on the other. In this debate, politically liberal or conservative underpinnings of theories of transnational legal processes are openly discussed.

As a starting point, there is a shared understanding that transnational legal processes are a form of governance that mimics or, more precisely, functionally replaces

[19] Van Harten, note 17, at 5.

(albeit only partially) the three branches of government, which do not exist in the international sphere in the forms recognizable at the national level. As such, transnational legal processes of binding dispute resolution are recast in terms of an international judicial branch of governance but, importantly, not of government.

Slaughter, Keohane, and Moravcsik identify and celebrate two new forms of international judicial functions. One is "transjudicial communication": a new judicial mechanism that facilitates, at the national judicial level, transnational litigation through new forms of cooperation by international and national courts. The other is "supranantional adjudication": non-statist adjudication (more on that below).

In a book by that name, Anne-Marie Slaughter describes in detail a New World Order, comprised of so-called disaggregated states, in which global governance occurs through networked interactions by non-state actors, such as private individuals and groups, across national polities and within international institutions, with the result of a higher degree of *de facto* regulation of global affairs.[20] For example, in today's interconnected world, judges in different countries, especially on supreme courts, formally and informally interact with each other. In particular, judicial cooperation in the context of transnational litigation is visibly increased, enabled by "transjudicial communication"—communication among courts, whether national or supranational, across borders. Such communications take the form, for example, of citing with agreement or disagreement one another's cases or of face-to-face meetings in international conferences and at international judges' training programs.[21] Judges are evaluating the quality of fellow judges and are, in turn, being evaluated by peers in other nations; as members of an epistemic community that is as important, psychologically, as the nation. Judges are negotiating with one another, importantly, to facilitate transnational litigation, redefining judicial comity to enable the new, global economy.[22]

In addition, Slaughter and her co-authors also introduce the concept of supranational adjudication to describe and theorize international dispute resolution that is distinguishable from traditional, state-to-state international adjudication. In contrast with the latter, supranational adjudication is characterized by a high degree of independence from states, increased access of parties other than states and by "embeddedness"—the ability to implement outcomes directly without government's mediation. Conversely, interstate adjudication is characterized by a low level of all three.[23] Supranational adjudication, thus defined, increases the ability of

[20] See generally, A-M Slaughter, *A New World Order* (Princeton University Press 2004).

[21] See generally, A-M Slaughter, "Human Rights International Law Symposium: Article: A Typology of Transjudicial Communication" (1994) 29 U. Rich. L. Rev. 99.

[22] Slaughter, note 20, at 86.

[23] RO Keohane, A Moravcsik, and A-M Slaughter, "Legalized Dispute Resolution: Interstate and Transnational" (2000) 54 Int'l Org. 457, 458.

supranational tribunals to serve as checks-and-balances on national governments as compared with interstate tribunals. Therefore, it empowers domestic players other than the state. And it facilitates a higher degree of development of the law and the assertion of new legal norms.[24] Last but not least, it allows for a greater degree of effectiveness.[25]

Normatively, the emergence and expansion of supranational adjudication and the development of transjudicial communication, egged on by high technology and increasing economic interdependence, are viewed as a positive development by Slaughter and fellow theorists of the transnational legal process writing in the liberal tradition of international relations and international law. This is because the judicialization of international law in the form of more international bodies that are more court-like enhances the effectiveness of international law, advances the rule of law and increases the legitimacy of international law according to this view.

But not everyone is either convinced that effectiveness is in fact thus enhanced nor enthralled with the prospect that it might be. Conservative legal scholars, such as Eric Posner and John Yoo, enter the transnational legal process discourse to sound the alarm over the loss of sovereignty and the debatable legitimacy of the transnational legal process as it relates to international courts and tribunals. They recast the call for more, not only better, international adjudicative bodies as a liberal agenda and a liberal call to arms. This strand of scholarship is properly positioned in the tradition of international relations Realism and in a dualist understanding of international law. It critiques the rise of transnational legal processes that function as governance, especially those that do so though adjudication.[26]

Posner and Yoo, specifically, question the value of judicial independence—long a mainstay of the rule of law—where such tribunals are concerned. Arguing against a liberal consensus that the use of independent international tribunals enhances their effectiveness and the spread of the rule of law, these authors argue that it is political unification that makes independent tribunals possible and effective in the spreading of the rule of law whereas in the international realm, where no unification exists, international tribunals cannot be both independent and effective.[27] They offer empirical evidence that the most successful (i.e., effective) international tribunals are dependent tribunals, namely ad hoc tribunals staffed by judges who are controlled by governments. Conversely, independent tribunals are undesirable according to this view because they are likely to allow their own (liberal) normative

[24] See generally, Keohane, Moravcsik, and Slaughter, note 23.

[25] Keohane, Moravcsik, and Slaughter, note 23; A-M Slaughter and LR Helfer, "Toward a Theory of Effective Supranational Adjudication" (1997) 107 Yale L.J. 273.

[26] J Yoo and E Posner, "Judicial Independence in International Tribunals" (2005) 93 Cal. L. Rev. 1 (also introducing a game-theoretical perspective in suggesting that international tribunals' usefulness is in allowing states to overcome certain cooperative problems).

[27] Yoo and Posner, note 26.

ideals, ideological imperatives, and the interests of third parties to influence their decisions.[28]

A different perspective on power and its distribution, which eschews the clear liberal/conservative divide, is a focus of sociological and socio-legal theories of transnational legal process. These are presented in the next sub-section.

3.3 The sociologists and socio-legal theorists

Taking individuals as the constitutive elements of the international order and conceiving of them as socially constructed agents of change or of preservation of the status quo, this strand of scholarship views institutions, such as international courts and tribunals, as emergent of individuals' patterned interactions. The patterns are contingent on variables such as culture and history. Following the trail of power, this tradition asks *qui bono* from transnational dispute resolution thus constituted. The following paragraphs illustrate this scholarship of transnational legal processes by looking at the scholarship of Dezaley and Garth as well as of Terris, Romano, and Swigart.

Following in the footsteps of the anthropologist and social philosopher Pierre Bourdieu and firmly rooted in the critique-of-capitalism tradition, Yves Dezaley and Bryant Garth employ qualitative empirical methodologies to explore the secretive world of international commercial arbitration. International commercial arbitration is first conceived of as a "field"—a setting in which agents and their social positions are located. Conceptualizing international commercial dispute resolution as a field means understanding it as a "symbolic terrain with its own networks, hierarchical relationships, and expertise and more generally its own rules of the game…[W]ithin a field, agents and institutions constantly struggle, according to the regularities and rules constitutive of this space of play."[29] A field is the social space in which institutions, such as the International Chamber of Commerce International Court of Arbitration, the leading international arbitration body, are "created, rendered obsolete, or reinvented."[30]

Within this framework, they describe the international arbitration community as a tightly-knit group with "[m]embers of the inner circle and outsiders often

[28] See LR Helfer and AM Slaughter, "Why States Create International Tribunals: A Response to Professors Posner and Yoo" (2005) 93 Cal. L. R. at 899–900. Helfer and Slaughter provide a strident critique both of the soundness of Posner and Yoo's empirical work and the validity of its normative underpinnings. Posner and Yoo then provide a counter-reply in "Reply to Helfer and Slaughter" (2005) 93 Cal. L. R. 957.

[29] Y Dezaley and BG Garth, *Dealing in Virtue: International Commercial Arbitration and the Construction of a Transnational Legal Order* (University of Chicago Press 1996) 16 (internal quotation marks omitted).

[30] Dezaley and Garth, note 29, at 16.

referring to this group as a 'mafia' or a 'club.'"[31] They chronicle how an elite cadre of Western transnational lawyers constructed an autonomous legal field, rarified and exclusive, that has given them a central role in the global marketplace and allowed them to charge premium rates for their services. They portray how, in the last four decades, the field has been shaped by struggles for dominance between "Grand Old Men"—European grand professors who come into international arbitration as the spoils of a long and distinguished academic career, and younger "arbitration technocrats," mostly partners in US multinational law firms who practice international arbitration full time (or aspire to do so). The symbolic capital of the former is comprised mostly of scholarly achievements; the latter of their position in powerful multinational firms representing the global business elite. In both cases, the symbolic capital is then converted into cash in the form of arbitral fees.

In the process, this mostly intra-Western competition for appointments, based on rules of the game shaped by and for Western imperialist agendas, has transformed domestic methods of dispute resolution and of an informal, settlement-oriented system into a formalized and litigious one, in the image of Anglo-, and even more so American, litigation. Non-Western lawyers who attempt to gain entry into the "club" must acquire and traffic in the same symbolic capital. Acquiring such capital, for example through studies in the elite universities of the West, involves a process of cooption. These non-Western lawyers thus become moral entrepreneurs who construct international justice out of the competition for transnational business disputes.

In addition, in the development of new frontiers, which take the form of the establishments of regional arbitral institutions and affiliates of international ones, local legal elites:

> follow their own interests [in becoming insiders and obtaining lucrative engagements and appointments and] at the same time they serve the interests of their protectors... Thus, while being agents of symbolic colonialism, these institutional importers also set the stage for third worldism—often becoming, however, its first victims when the movements became radicalized and demanded to exercise power themselves.[32]

These takeovers happen when large, US-based or UK-based law firms transform the field's periphery attacking local, fragmented justice and in its stead promoting a universal business justice in which they are more proficient, and more competitive, and which therefore is more profitable for them.

In this telling, international commercial arbitration is understood as privatized justice *cum* symbolic colonialism rather than a neutral mechanism for the impartial resolution of cross-border commercial disputes. Critically, the transnational in this

[31] Dezaley and Garth, note 29, at 11.

[32] Dezaley and Garth, note 29, at 13, 284–5.

view does not refer only to activity that takes place at the transnational level. Rather, the transnational level is:

> best understood as a virtual space that provides strategic opportunities for competitive struggles engaged in by *national* actors—struggles, for example, about whether international commercial arbitration should resemble litigation in court, and if so, whose courts, or how much it should reflect a perspective of the third-world... the transnational opportunities and struggles [] tend to disrupt the established national categories and, as a result, are significant for their impacts on the national landscapes of business disputing as they are in the creation of an international private justice.[33]

All this is arrived at by mapping, as a point of entry, the kind of *individuals* who are named most often as international arbitrators, thus arriving from the particular to the general: to an understanding of the social (as opposed to purely legal) functions of the international commercial arbitration system. Here too, the larger inquiry is into the international rule of law.[34]

Interesting similarities and differences in methodology, outlook, and choice of research object is evident in the work of the historian Daniel Terris, the jurist Cesare Romano, and the anthropologist Leigh Swigart on the international judge.[35] Working from the premise that "the work of international judges has changed the character of the world we inhabit,"[36] they too select as their focal point the individuals who comprise the studied phenomenon, namely international judges. They, too, have embarked on an extensive campaign of not-for-attribution interviews. However, unlike the Dezaly and Garth's external critique, Terris, Romano, and Swigart aim to bring the voices of the judges themselves, as such, into the discourse about international adjudication. Their goal is to better explain and more fully portray the human complexities involved in the work on the international bench and to stimulate other social scientists to engage in the study of global legal institutions.[37]

Using this methodology, they hit on some of the major flash points in the popular and academic debates about international adjudication: the tension between the international mandate and the local impact, the realities and perception of both

[33] Dezaley and Garth, note 29, at 3–4 (noting, importantly for a discussion of the present state and future directions of transnational legal process theories, that practitioners are accustomed to thinking in terms of strategies and positions in the legal field but that legal academics tend to resist thinking in terms of the internal politics of the field or acknowledging their role in such politics. Emphasis supplied).

[34] Dezaley and Garth, note 29, at 3.

[35] See generally, D Terris, C Romano, and L Swigart, *The International Judge: An Introduction to the Men and Women Who Decide the World's Cases* (Oxford University Press 2007).

[36] Terris, Romano, and Swigart, note 35, at xii.

[37] Terris, Romano, and Swigart, note 35, at xvi (they also include a call to arms for the United States to more fully engage with the international judiciary and with international law generally). Such calls for more engagement are a theme in the American scholarship on international law alluded to above, in notes 25–6 accompanying text, in the discussion of the Posner/Yoo–Helfer/Slaughter debate.

public and state pressures and of conflicting loyalties, the legitimacy of law-making by the judiciary and the role of material resources in the operation of international courts. Their methodology also enables them to document the familiar problem of a lack of diversity in the international judiciary—a phenomenon traditionally referred to more generally in the words of Oscar Schachter as "the invisible college of international law." Men are more than four times more likely to be international judges than women and the international judiciary is characterized by a certain homogeneity of biographies, such as common patterns of education.[38]

Their analysis concludes with some somber predictions on the future of international adjudication. Some signs they identify point toward a slowdown in the growth in the numbers of new courts and tribunals. The resistance to the authority and legitimacy of international courts by some of the world's leading powers may lead to a marginalization of existing courts. And, activist law-making by judges in international courts may create a backlash even as courts remain dependent on nation states and governments for resources, legitimacy, and enforcement.[39]

4 Conclusion

Borrowing HLA Hart's metaphor of a core and a penumbra of legal concepts, one can identify the core issues that occupy the theory of adjudication as a transnational legal process. Core procedural issues are clearly the issues of jurisdiction (power) and enforcement (the effect of the power). A paradigmatic transnational legal process is that of international commercial arbitration. Core themes are those of sovereignty, international rule of law, independence, and the role of individuals in shaping transnational

[38] Terris, Romano, and Swigart, note 35, at xviii, 223 (concluding that "[t]here once was a time when the 'invisible college' of international judges consisted of a small band of men, principally Europeans, clustered tightly in The Hague. Today's more extensive network has much more diversity in terms of geography, race, and gender, but the common bonds across space and time... [and t]raining in a relatively small number of key universities ensure significant commonalities in the legal mindset of international judges."). In international arbitration, only 5 percent of arbitrators are women. See G Van Harten, "The (lack of) women arbitrators in investment treaty arbitration" (2012) 59 Columbia FDI Perspectives <http://www.vcc.columbia.edu/content/lack-women-arbitrators-investment-treaty-arbitration> accessed March 3, 2013 (finding that only 4 percent of arbitrators appointed to international investment arbitration are women that "Th[is] story is also almost entirely that of two women, Gabrielle Kaufmann-Kohler and Brigitte Stern, who together captured 75% of appointments of women.").

[39] Van Harten, note 38, at 222.

litigation and international adjudication.[40] Owing to the fact, however, that the processes in question are tremendously diverse, and given that the intention underlying the project of transnational legal process theorizing has been, very deliberately and from the outset, to craft a concept that *blurs* lines, rather than sharpens distinctions, the penumbra is much larger than the core. It encompasses issues as diverse as the monist/dualist debate, symbolic colonialism in the developing world, and the governmental division of power under American constitutional law.

In a strand of scholarship that can perhaps be described as a scholarship of self-doubt, some scholars of the very same transnational legal processes detail why they believe, in the words of Gertrude Stein, that "there is no there there." Scholars writing in this vein are skeptical as to whether, indeed, there is a field distinct from international legal theory and comparative law on the one hand and domestic civil procedure on the other. In her rendition of the development of the field of "transnational litigation," or at least of a perception that a distinct field is arising, Linda Silberman observed that transnational litigation has become a field because the discrete pieces of such litigation can only be understood in relation to each other and to the whole and because lawyers who handle transnational cases see themselves as operating in a distinct field.[41] But ultimately, in her view, transnational litigation as a field derives much of its content "from the domestic law of civil procedure, conflict of laws, international sales, economic and trade law, and public international law."[42]

The concepts in use by transnational legal process theorists, starting with the concept of a transnational legal process itself, are far from clear. Different scholars brand different transnational dispute resolution processes using a multiplicity of partly overlapping concepts such as supranational adjudication, transnational litigation, extraterritorial litigation, transnational dispute resolution and more. These can be inelegantly grouped under the umbrella of "non-national binding dispute resolution," to encompass arbitration and litigation in non-domestic courts but to

[40] HLA Hart, *The Concept of Law* (Oxford University Press 1961) at 134 ("indeed even key terms used in the [English theory of precedent] '*ratio decidendi*,' 'material facts,' 'interpretations,' have their own penumbra of uncertainty.").

[41] L Silberman, "Transnational Litigation: Is There A 'Field'? A Tribute to Hal Maier" (2006) 39 Vand. J. Transnat'l L. 1427, 1430–1 (lawyers who understand themselves as transnational litigators "understand how a case will be shaped in any one of a number of fora and consider strategic steps available to them to ensure that litigation proceeds in the forum of their choice…Before litigation is even commenced, they consider where the defendant's assets are or might be in the future in order to assess whether foreign enforcement of the judgment is likely to be required and, if so, how a particular country will treat a foreign judgment. These questions are all interrelated pieces of a large litigation puzzle which is the field of transnational litigation"); see also PR Dubinsky, "Is Transnational Litigation A Distinct Field? The Persistence of Exceptionalism in American Procedural Law" (2008) 44 Stan. J. Int'l L. 301; JH Carter, "Transnational Law: What Is It? How Does It Differ from International Law and Comparative Law" (2004) 23 Penn St. Int'l L. Rev. 795.

[42] Silberman, note 41, at 1429.

exclude non-dispute related legal processes, that is, other features of global governance. Either way, the upshot is that there is little by way of a shared discourse (let alone a unifying theory or a set of competing unifying theories), unlike many other fields of study, say, free speech theory or theory of tort remedies, in which individuals understand themselves as engaged in a shared discourse and the object of study is relatively well-defined.

An overarching recommendation, then, for further research is to incorporate analytic legal philosophy, currently almost entirely absent from the debate, to help crisply define a concept of non-national binding dispute resolution. Such an enterprise would aim to define the necessary (though possibly insufficient) attributes of such a process. In addition, legal philosophy is key in developing normative argumentation for and against the legitimacy of any given form of transnational legal process.[43] The field would equally benefit from bringing under its big tent other absentee theories, particularly critical studies and law and economics. Transnational legal process theories have made great strides in the second half of the twentieth century but much more is left to be done. Examples of what such inquiries might look like are provided below.

Research Questions

1. What can critical race theory—which developed in the United States to explain racism in the context of race relations between black and white Americans—both teach us and learn from African-on-African racial relations as portrayed and constructed in international criminal courts?
2. What can feminist and queer theories—which are adept at studying the de- and re-construction of fundamental social institutions such as "family"—teach us about de- and re-constructing the idea of "court" to fit a global society?
3. What can behavioral law and economics teach us about how to fairly price legal claims so as to fairly settle disputes in investment arbitration, where foreign investors are seeking compensation from taxpayers in sometimes devastated economies?
4. What can neo-classical law and economics teach us about whether or not the level of international litigation is optimal?

[43] As the debate revolving Schultz's work, note 9, does in respect to international arbitration. International law, more generally, has long been a child of a lesser god as far as analytic jurisprudence is concerned. "Where legal philosophy has addressed internationalization and globalization, it has predominantly remained in the realm of public international law." Michaels, note 9, at 418.

Suggested Reading

Born, G, *International Civil Litigation in United States Courts: Commentary and Materials* (1st edn, Deventer: Springer 1994).

Dammann, JC and Hansman, HB, "Globalizing Commercial Litigation" (2008) 94 Cornell L. Rev. 1.

Dezaley, Y and Garth, BG, *Dealing in Virtue: International Commercial Arbitration and the Construction of a Transnational Legal Order* (University of Chicago Press 1996).

Halliday, TR and Shaffer, GC (eds), *Transnational Legal Orders* (Cambridge University Press, forthcoming).

Jessup, PC, *Transnational Law* (New Haven, CT: Yale University Press 1956).

Koh, HH, "Transnational Legal Process" (1996) 75 Neb. L. Rev. 181.

Schultz, T, "The Concept of Law in Transnational Arbitral Legal Orders and Some of its Consequences" (2011) 2 J. of Int'l Dispute Settlement 59.

Shaffer, GC (ed.), *Transnational Legal Ordering and State Change* (Cambridge Studies in Law and Society January 2013).

Shany, Y, *Regulating Jurisdictional Relations between National and International Courts* (Oxford University Press 2009).

Slaughter, A-M, *A New World Order* (Princeton University Press 2004).

Steinitz, M, "'The Milošević Trial-Live!' An Iconical Analysis of International Law's Claim of Legitimate Authority" (2005) 3 J. of Int'l Crim. Justice 103.

Terris, D, Romano, C, and Swigart, L, *The International Judge: An Introduction to the Men and Women Who Decide the World's Cases* (Oxford University Press 2007).

Zumbansen, P, "Transnational Law, Evolving" (2011) Osgoode CLPE Research Paper no. 27/2011.

CHAPTER 17

POLITICAL SCIENCE AND INTERNATIONAL ADJUDICATION

MARK A POLLACK*

* Professor of Political Science and Law and Jean Monnet Chair, Temple University. This chapter draws extensively upon joint research that I have conducted with Jeffrey L Dunoff, and I am indebted to Dunoff for many of the ideas expressed here. See Jeffrey L Dunoff and Mark A Pollack (eds), *Interdisciplinary Perspectives on International Law and International Relations: The State of the Art* (CUP 2013); and Jeffrey L Dunoff and Mark A Pollack, "What Can International Relations Learn from International Law?" paper presented at the Woodrow Wilson School, Princeton University, February 25, 2013. I am also grateful to Karen Alter, Cesare Romano, and Yuval Shany for excellent comments on an earlier draft of this chapter. Responsibility for any errors or omissions remains strictly my own.

1 Introduction

For many years, the workings and the jurisprudence of international adjudication bodies, such as courts and arbitral tribunals, have been the bread and butter of international legal scholarship. By comparison, political scientists historically have paid little attention to international courts and tribunals, which were seen through the prevailing realist lens as being of little or no importance in global politics. In recent decades, however, political scientists writing in the international law and international relations (IL/IR) tradition have taken up the study of international adjudication, driven both by the diversification of available IR theories and by the empirical proliferation of international courts in the post-Cold War era. In the process, political scientists have made a substantial contribution, applying a distinctive set of theoretical lenses and epistemological and methodological tools to questions about the design, behavior, and independence of these bodies.

The aim of this chapter is to examine the essential features of political science theories and methods as applied to international adjudication, and to identify the value-added insights as well as the gaps or lacunae of this research. The chapter proceeds in five parts. Following this introduction, the second part of the chapter considers a fundamental epistemological distinction between law and political science as disciplines, with the former taking a largely—but not exclusively—doctrinal and "internalist" approach to international law, while the latter generally adopts a positivist and "externalist" approach. Next, in the third section, I briefly explore the range of political science theories about international politics, and the ways in which these theories have been adapted to the study of international adjudication. Building on this epistemological and theoretical basis, part four identifies five substantive contributions of political science to the study of international adjudication, which I organize under the rubrics of institutional design, judicial behavior, the behavior of litigants, judgment compliance, and the dynamic evolution of international adjudication systems over time. The fifth and final section identifies weaknesses, lacunae, and blind spots of the extant political science literature, which I argue has drawn too heavily on off-the-shelf IR approaches and not enough on the insights of international legal scholarship. The chapter concludes with a call for a more truly interdisciplinary law-and-politics approach to the study of international adjudication.

2 Political Science Epistemology and Methodology

One of the most fundamental distinctions between law and political science is epistemological, relating to the aims of scholarship and the means whereby scholars establish the validity of their theories and learn about the empirical world.[1] Within political science, it has become common to argue that the modal epistemological approach is *positivist*, in the scientific rather than the legal sense of that term.[2] As Hollis and Smith summarize, the use of positivism in IR places an emphasis on "experience (on observation and testing) as the only way to justify claims to knowledge of the world, and hence on methods of verification as the key to the meaning of scientific statements."[3] To be sure, political science is not monolithic in its commitment to positivism, and a substantial group of non-positivist or post-positivist scholars have made contributions to the study of IR.[4] Nevertheless, recent surveys of the field demonstrate a widespread epistemological consensus on scientific positivism, particularly among IR scholars and journals based in the United States.[5]

By contrast with political science, legal scholarship appears both more diverse and less systematically self-aware on the question of epistemology. In a provocative essay, legal scholar Geoffrey Samuel asks, "Should social scientists take law, as it has been constructed by history, seriously as a modern intellectual discipline?"[6] Samuel argues that we should *not* do so, largely on epistemological grounds. Legal scholarship, he argues, generally adopts an "authority" paradigm, in which the legal text is taken as authoritative, and the study of law is explicitly "internal" to these legal sources. More precisely, doctrinal, formalist, or "black-letter" legal approaches determine the validity of legal claims internally, with respect to the law itself.[7]

[1] C Wight, "Philosophy of Social Science and International Relations" in W Carlsnaes, T Risse, and BA Simmons (eds), *Handbook of International Relations* (London: Sage Publications 2002) 35.

[2] This scientific or epistemological positivism should not be confused with legal positivism, which holds that "international law is no more or less than the rules to which states have agreed through treaties, custom, and perhaps other forms of consent." SR Ratner and A-M Slaughter, "Appraising the Methods of International Law: A Prospectus for Readers" (1999) 93(2) AJIL 291, 293. Unless otherwise indicated, in the rest of this chapter, when I refer to positivism, I refer to its scientific variant.

[3] M Hollis and S Smith, *Explaining and Understanding International Relations* (Oxford University Press 1990) 12.

[4] Hollis and Smith, note 3, at 12 ; Wight, note 1, at 26.

[5] D Maliniak et al., "International Relations in the US Academy" (2011) 55(2) Int'l Stud. Q. 1.

[6] G Samuel, "Interdisciplinarity and the Authority Paradigm: Should Law Be Taken Seriously by Scientists and Social Scientists?" (2009) 36(4) J. Law & Soc'y 431, 432.

[7] Samuel, note 6, at 435.

By contrast, Samuel continues, social scientists generally pursue a broadly positivist "enquiry paradigm," which judges the validity of scientific claims against "external" sources of evidence. In such an "externalist" approach, mastery of doctrine is not sufficient for the study of international law and courts, because hypotheses about the causes and effects of international law must be tested with respect to variables—such as state power and interest—external to the law itself. With respect to the study of international courts in particular, if we follow legal realists in arguing that legal doctrine is indeterminate, then international judicial decisions inevitably reflect *extra-legal* factors including judges' personal ideologies, partisan allegiances, and pressures from political actors and public opinion.[8]

These epistemological differences between law and political science have given rise to a sometimes virulent debate about the appropriateness of each approach and about the adequacy of international legal and political science scholarship, respectively. Some scholars, like Lee Epstein and Gary King, criticize empirical legal scholarship as "deeply flawed" in terms of its research design and methodology.[9] Legal scholars have responded, not only by defending the quality of empirical legal research, but also by arguing that much legal scholarship pursues fundamentally different doctrinal, interpretive, and normative aims.[10] Hence, for example, international legal scholars Jack Goldsmith and Adrian Vermeule criticize Epstein and King's "resolutely externalist approach to legal scholarship" for its "inability to participate in and identify empathetically with the practice of legal discourse."[11]

In contemporary scholarship, the epistemological battle lines between internalist, doctrinal scholarship and externalist, positivist scholarship no longer correspond with the boundaries of the legal and political science professions, if indeed they ever did. Within the legal academy we find a vibrant community of empirical legal studies scholars conducting ever more rigorous positivist scholarship,[12] and within political science we find some scholars taking a post-positivist critical approach. Nevertheless, the epistemological debate sketched out above has influenced the study of international law by political science and legal scholars, respectively. Among political science scholars, a positivist and externalist approach does indeed dominate, and one can argue that much of this scholarship fails to appreciate the specifically *legal* aspects of international adjudication.[13] Among international

[8] On legal realism and its influences on international law scholarship, see V Nourse and G Shaffer, "Varieties of New Legal Realism: Can a New World Order Prompt a New Legal Theory?" (2009) 95(1) Cornell L. Rev. 61; on extra-legal influences on international judges, see, in this handbook, Voeten, Ch. 25.

[9] L Epstein and G King, "The Rules of Inference" (2002) 69 U. Chicago L. Rev. 1, 6.

[10] J Goldsmith and A Vermeule, "Empirical Methodology and Legal Scholarship" (2002) 69(1) U. Chicago L. Rev. 153, 153–4.

[11] Goldsmith and Vermeule, note 10, at 158.

[12] T Ginsburg and GC Shaffer, "The Empirical Turn in International Legal Scholarship" (2012) 106(1) AJIL 1.

[13] JL Dunoff and MA Pollack, "What Can International Relations Learn from International Law?" paper presented at the Woodrow Wilson School, Princeton University, February 25, 2013.

legal scholars, by contrast, we sometimes see a rejection of externalist social-science epistemology that is seen as reducing international judges and litigants to rational utility maximizers, ignoring the internal logic of legal discourse and adopting a relentlessly instrumentalist view of law that ignores its essential normativity.[14] In fairness to political science scholars, however, assumptions such as these are not inherent to political science, but depend on the specific theoretical perspective of the scholars in question. It is to that subject that we now turn.

3 Political Science Theories and International Adjudication

Much of the distinctive contribution of political science to the study of international adjudication arises from the application of IR theories, which generate theoretical concepts, questions, and hypotheses that are largely ignored in international legal scholarship. In the immediate post-war era, realist theory largely dominated the IR literature, yet contemporary IR scholarship is theoretically pluralist, with major strains of realist, institutionalist, liberal, and constructivist theories co-existing in the discipline, and each of these strains has approached the subject of international law in distinctive ways. A complete review of these theories is beyond the scope of this chapter,[15] but a brief discussion of these four theories and their application to international courts will illustrate the diversity of, and insights from, IR theories for the study of international adjudication.

3.1 Realism

Among political science theories, realism is widely, and accurately, seen to be particularly hostile to the idea that international law can meaningfully constrain states'

[14] Dunoff and Pollack, note 13; J Klabbers, "The Bridge Crack'd: A Critical Look at Interdisciplinary Relations" (2009) 23(1) Int'l Rel. 119; see also JL Dunoff and MA Pollack, "Introduction: International Law and International Relations—Taking Stock" in Dunoff and Pollack (eds), *Interdisciplinary Perspectives on International Law and International Relations: The State of the Art* (Cambridge University Press 2013) 17.

[15] But see e.g., B Koremenos, "Institutionalism and International Law" on institutionalism, A Moravcsik, "Liberal Theories of International Law" on liberalism, J Brunnée and SJ Toope, "Constructivism and International Law" on constructivism, and RH Steinberg, "Wanted: Dead or Alive—Realist Approaches to International Law" on realism, all in Dunoff and Pollack, note 14.

pursuit of their individual self-interest.[16] In the realist approach, the international system is characterized by anarchy, self-help, and the necessary pursuit of power, and the key players are states, with other actors—including international adjudicators—playing at best a secondary role. In such a world, statesmen driven by a relentless concern for the national interest and national security would be unwise to place their hopes in what Hans Morgenthau called the "legalism-moralism" that had dominated IR scholarship during the interwar period.[17] Perhaps for this reason, postwar realists largely ignored international law, which was seen as "epiphenomenal," reflecting the interests of the great powers and exerting no causal force independent of those powers.[18]

For this reason, realist theory is often seen as irrelevant to the study of international law and adjudication, and vice-versa. Nevertheless, as Richard Steinberg argues, realism does offer a coherent account of international law, emphasizing state interests and state power as the context for all international law-making, interpretation, and application.[19] With respect to international courts in particular, realists do not dispute that such courts are sometimes established by states, that they engage in a process of legal interpretation, or that they sometimes rule against powerful states in individual cases. In a realist view, however, any international court is ultimately embedded in an international system characterized by unequal distribution of power, and powerful states retain the right to sanction or ignore any international court that rules against its vital interests. Hence, in the long run, "interpretation replicates power."[20]

3.2 Institutionalism

Growing out of realism, but departing from it in several key assumptions, is the "modified structural realist" theory known in contemporary scholarship as neoliberal or rational-choice institutionalism, sometimes referred to simply as "institutionalism."[21] Like realists, institutionalists posit an anarchic world of unitary, self-interested states. By contrast with realists, however, institutionalists argue that international institutions can help states cooperate under anarchy, by reducing the

[16] A-M Slaughter Burley, "International Law and International Relations Theory: A Dual Agenda" (1993) 87(2) AJIL 205.

[17] H Morgenthau, *Politics Among Nations: The Struggle for Power and Peace* (New York: Knopf 1948).

[18] KN Waltz, *Theory of International Politics* (New York: McGraw-Hill 1979).

[19] Steinberg, note 15, at 150.

[20] Steinberg, note 15, at 163–4; JL Goldsmith and EA Posner, *The Limits of International Law* (Oxford University Press 2005). Goldsmith and Posner reject the label of realism, but their influential account of the limits of international law is guided by many of the same assumptions as classical realist theory.

[21] RO Keohane (ed.), *Neorealism and Its Critics* (Columbia University Press 1985); Koremenos, note 15.

transaction costs of negotiating cooperative agreements, by interpreting and settling disputes about those agreements and by monitoring state compliance.[22]

Although early institutionalist work on international cooperation overlapped heavily with the study of international law, institutionalist scholars of the 1980s and 1990s deliberately deemphasized the legal nature of the norms and rules they studied. By the 1990s, however, a number of legal scholars had begun to identify the promise of institutionalist theory for those seeking to understand the workings of international law,[23] and a collective project on the legalization of world affairs established an influential framework and opened the floodgates for political science scholarship on international law. This "legalization" project sought, more precisely, to provide a framework for studying the causes and effects of international law, which the project leaders defined in terms of three fundamental properties: obligation (whether a norm or rule is considered binding on states), precision (the clarity of states' responsibilities) and delegation (particularly of dispute-settlement powers to a third-party adjudicator).[24] All else being equal, international agreements with high values for obligation, precision, and delegation were considered to be "hard law," which could be costly to conclude but had significant advantages in terms of enhancing credible commitments and compliance, while those with lower values fell toward the "soft" end of the spectrum, being easier to negotiate and more flexible in response to change.[25] The legalization framework proved controversial, with constructivist scholars arguing that such an instrumental approach to law missed its essential normative features,[26] but the revived focus on legalization has led to a renaissance of political science scholarship on international law.

With respect to the making of international law, the dominant approach has been the so-called rational-design tradition, which has focused on identifying the conditions under which states adopt specific types of legal understandings, including treaties and customary international law,[27] exit clauses,[28] safeguard clauses,[29] state

[22] RO Keohane, *After Hegemony: Cooperation and Discord in World Political Economy* (Princeton University Press 1984); RO Keohane, "Neoliberal Institutionalism: A Perspective on World Politics" in RO Keohane (ed.), *International Institutions and State Power* (Boulder, CO: Westview Press 1989).

[23] KW Abbott, "Modern International Relations Theory: A Prospectus for International Lawyers" (1989) 14(2) Yale J. Int'l L.335; Slaughter Burley, note 16.

[24] KW Abbott et al., "The Concept of Legalization" (2000) 54(3) Int'l Org. 401.

[25] KW Abbott and D Snidal, "Hard and Soft Law in International Governance" (2000) 54(3) Int'l Org. 421.

[26] Abbott and Snidal, note 25, at 421; C Reus-Smit (ed.), *The Politics of International Law* (Cambridge University Press 2004).

[27] AT Guzman, *How International Law Works: A Rational Choice Theory* (Oxford University Press 2008).

[28] LR Helfer, "Exiting Treaties" (2005) 91 Virginia L. Rev. 1579–1648; LR Helfer, "Flexibility in International Agreements" in Dunoff and Pollack, note 14.

[29] BP Rosendorff and HV Milner, "The Optimal Design of International Trade Institutions: Uncertainty and Escape" (2001) 55(4) Int'l Org. 829; Helfer, "Flexibility," note 28.

reservations to treaties,[30] and—of particular importance for our purposes here—third-party dispute settlement.[31]

With respect to the application and adjudication of international law, the rational-choice tradition has fostered an explosion of work, considered below, on the autonomy and independence of international secretariats and courts, which is seen to vary considerably across different types of international executive and judicial "agents" as a function of their institutional statutes or frameworks as well as the preferences of their state "principals."[32]

3.3 Liberalism

Rational-choice institutionalism has created a promising and highly influential theoretical framework for the study of international law, yet it has done so on the basis of a debatable assumption, of states as unitary rational actors. Since the 1990s, however, we have witnessed the revival of a liberal tradition that rejected this assumption and sought instead to ground the study of international relations in a theory of state-society relations that seeks to explain the domestic origins of, and variation in, national preferences as a necessary prelude to studying the interactions among those states.

In its most influential formulation by Andrew Moravcsik, liberalism can be said to rest on three broad assumptions: (1) the primacy of societal actors, who place policy demands on governments; (2) the importance of representative institutions, which act as a "transmission belt" aggregating societal interests with greater or lesser fidelity or bias; and (3) the resulting configuration of interdependent state

[30] ET Swaine, "Reserving" (2006) 31(2) Yale J. Int'l L. 307; E Neumayer, "Qualified Ratification: Explaining Reservations to International Human Rights Treaties" (2007) 36(2) J. Legal Stud. 397.

[31] RO Keohane, A Moravcsik, and A-M Slaughter, "Legalized Dispute Resolution: Interstate and Transnational" (2000) 54(3) Int'l Org. 457; BP Rosendorff, "Stability and Rigidity: Politics and Design of the WTO's Dispute Settlement Procedure" (2005) 99(3) Am. Pol. Sci. Rev. 389; B Koremenos, "If Only Half of International Agreements Have Dispute Resolution Provisions, Which Half Needs Explaining?" (2007) 36(1) J. Legal Stud. 189; B Koremenos and T Betz, "The Design of Dispute Settlement Procedures in International Agreements" in Dunoff and Pollack, note 14.

[32] See e.g., KJ Alter, "Agents or Trustees? International Courts in their Political Context" (2008) 14(1) Eur. J. Int'l Rel. 33; MA Pollack, "Principal-Agent Analysis and International Delegation: Red Herrings, Theoretical Clarifications and Empirical Disputes" College of Europe, Bruges Political Research Papers, No. 2/February 2007, <http://www.coleurope.eu/content/studyprogrammes/pol/docs/wp2_Pollack.pdf> accessed July 25, 2013; and the debate between CJ Carrubba, M Gabel, and C Hankla, "Judicial Behavior under Political Constraints: Evidence from the European Court of Justice" (2008) 102(4) Am. Pol. Sci. Rev. 435; CJ Carrubba, M Gabel, and CR Hankla, "Understanding the Role of the ECJ in European Integration" (2012) 106(1) Am. Pol. Sci. Rev. 214; and A Stone Sweet and T Brunell, "Trustee Courts and the Judicialization of International Regimes: The Politics of Majoritarian Activism in the ECtHR, the EU, and the WTO" (2013) 1(1) J. Law & Courts 61.

preferences, which determine the nature of the "game" being played by states at the international level. Put simply, liberalism is a two-stage, "bottom-up" approach that focuses on societal interests and their aggregation through institutions into a putative "national interest" in the first stage, and subsequently examines the interactions among states in the second stage.[33]

Stated in such broad terms, liberalism is a loose framework for analysis, or what Wendt has called a second-order theory,[34] but several efforts have been made to specify substantive first-order theories of international cooperation based on liberal assumptions. Three of the most influential in political science have been Robert Putnam's "two-level games" model,[35] Moravcsik's "liberal intergovernmentalist" theory of European integration,[36] and David Lake's "Open Economy Politics" approach to international political economy.[37] The implications of the liberal approach for international law are also important, and were first explored systematically by Anne-Marie Slaughter, who derived specific, testable hypotheses from liberal IR theory for the study of international law, focusing in particular on the systematic differences in legal commitment and compliance between liberal, democratic states on the one hand, and illiberal, authoritarian regimes on the other.[38]

Liberal scholarship in the two decades since Slaughter's classic article has established that the making of, interpretation of, and compliance with international law are all influenced substantially by domestic institutions and state-society relations. With respect to international adjudication in particular, liberal scholars have focused largely on the interaction of international adjudicators with domestic actors inside of states, including individual litigants and domestic courts. In this, they have taken inspiration largely from the legal system of the European Union (EU), in which individual litigants can bring cases under EU law in their domestic courts, without national-government gatekeeping, and in which national courts can request a "preliminary ruling" from the European Court of Justice (ECJ) on the reading of EU law, which is then applied and enforced within national legal systems. Systematizing these features, Slaughter and Helfer,[39] and later Keohane et al.,[40] offered theoretical frameworks for analyzing the relations between international courts on the one hand, and domestic legal and political actors on the other.

[33] Stone Sweet and Brunell, note 32.

[34] A Wendt, *Social Theory of International Politics* (Cambridge University Press 1999).

[35] RD Putnam, "Diplomacy and Domestic Politics: The Logic of Two-Level Games" (1988) 42 Int'l Org. 427.

[36] Moravcsik, note 15.

[37] DA Lake, "International Political Economy" in BR Weingast and D Wittman (eds), *The Oxford Handbook of Political Economy* (Oxford University Press 2008).

[38] Ratner and Slaughter, note 2.

[39] LR Helfer and A-M Slaughter, "Toward a Theory of Effective Supranational Adjudication" (1997) 107(2) Yale L.J. 273.

[40] Keohane et al., note 31.

In the influential Keohane et al. framework, international courts can be characterized along three dimensions: access (limited to governments or granted to individual litigants), independence (of the international adjudicator from its member-state principals) and embeddedness (the extent to which international rulings are accepted and enforced by national courts within the domestic legal order). Courts that score low on each of these three dimensions are referred to as "interstate courts," such as the International Court of Justice (ICJ), where national governments serve as gatekeepers with considerable control over the docket of the court and compliance with its rulings. By contrast, courts that score high on these three dimensions are considered "transnational courts," in which individuals can bring cases (including cases that are inconvenient for governments) to independent international adjudicators, and in which countries seeking to defy international rulings would have to defy not only those adjudicators, but their own domestic courts.[41] To the extent that international courts approximate this transnational ideal—and we shall see below that a growing number of international courts do so—their behavior and effects can *only* be studied in the context of a liberal framework that disaggregates and looks inside individual states.

Even with respect to interstate courts, however, liberals have looked to domestic state-society relations to understand the conditions under which states commit to accept the jurisdiction of an international court. Moravcsik, for example, has influentially suggested that certain types of states, and particularly transitional democracies, are particularly likely to accept the jurisdiction of human rights courts to "lock in" democratic reforms,[42] and Sarah McLaughlin Mitchell and Emilia Justyna Powell have more recently offered an innovative argument that links varying state acceptance of international court jurisdiction to the nature of states' domestic legal (common, civil, or Islamic law) tradition.[43]

Finally, liberal theorists argue that a state's propensity to comply with international law is likely to vary as a function of domestic interests, including "compliance constituencies" that favor obedience to international rules as well as those that favor defiance, and the representative institutions that shape the influence of these constituencies.[44] Furthermore, in the liberal view, "enforcement" of international law can take the form of "horizontal" or interstate arrangements, such as state retaliation or loss of international reputation for noncompliance, or they can take a "vertical" form as states "internalize" the commitments of international law, in a given state's legal, political, or social system.[45] To the extent that such vertical enforcement

[41] Keohane et al., note 31.

[42] A Moravcsik, "The Origins of Human Rights Regimes: Democratic Delegation in Postwar Europe" (2000) 54(2) Int'l Org. 217.

[43] S McLaughlin Mitchell and EJ Powell, *Domestic Law Goes Global: Legal Traditions and International Courts* (Cambridge University Press 2011).

[44] M Kahler, "Conclusion: The Causes and Consequences of Legalization" (2000) 54(3) Int'l Org. 661; Moravcsik, note 15, at 92.

[45] HH Koh, "Bringing International Law Home" (1998) 35(3) Houston L. Rev. 623; RO Keohane, "When Does International Law Come Home?" (1998) 35(3) Houston L. Rev. 699; BA Simmons,

and internationalization take place, we are forced once again to disaggregate and look inside the state, an area of strength for liberal IR theory.

3.4 Constructivism

Despite their substantial differences, realism, institutionalism, and liberalism have evolved as essentially rationalist theories, which assume that actors have fixed, exogenously given preferences, and that each of these actors attempts to maximize their utility subject to the constraints of the domestic and international order. Constructivist theorists, by contrast, proceed from profoundly different core assumptions, arguing that human beings and their preferences "do not exist independently from the social environment and its collectively shared systems of meanings ('culture' in a broad sense)." Instead, "[t]he social environment in which we find ourselves, 'constitutes' who we are, our identities as social beings."[46] For constructivist IR theorists, the international environment is not simply material but also normative, and international ideas, norms, and rules are expected to "constitute" actors, i.e., to shape their identities and their preferences.

Taking this argument to its logical conclusion, constructivists generally reject the rationalist conception of actors as utility-maximizers operating according to a "logic of consequentiality," in favor of March and Olsen's conception of a "logic of appropriateness." In this view, actors confronting a given situation do not consult a fixed set of preferences and calculate their actions in order to maximize their expected utility, but look to socially constructed roles and institutional rules and ask what sort of behavior is appropriate in that situation.[47]

In more recent work, Thomas Risse has identified a third potential logic of social action, which he calls the "logic of arguing," or deliberation.[48] In a logic of arguing, political actors do not simply bargain based on fixed preferences and relative power, they may also "argue," questioning their own beliefs and interests and being open to persuasion and the power of a better argument.[49] Risse concedes, however, that genuine argumentative rationality is likely only under a fairly restrictive set of preconditions, including the existence of a "common lifeworld" among the participants,

Mobilizing for Human Rights: International Law in Domestic Politics (Cambridge University Press 2009); Moravcsik, note 15, at 96–100.

[46] T Risse, "Social Constructivism and European Integration" in A Wiener and T Diez (eds), *European Integration Theory* (Oxford University Press 2004) 161; see also Wendt, note 34; I Hurd, "Constructivism" in C Reus-Smit and D Snidal (eds), *The Oxford Handbook of International Relations* (Oxford University Press 2008).

[47] JG March and JP Olsen, *Rediscovering Institutions: The Organizational Basis of Politics* (New York: Free Press 1989) 160–2.

[48] T Risse, "'Let's Argue!': Communicative Action in International Relations" (2000) 54(1) Int'l Org. 1.

[49] Risse, note 48, at 7.

the presence of uncertainty or imperfect information, and international institutions enabling dense interactions in informal, network-like settings.[50]

Although IR constructivists have only recently turned their attention to the study and specific features of international *legal* norms as such,[51] the focus on norms and their power to define appropriate behaviour and constitute actors makes constructivism an appealing theory for many international legal theorists. Given the emphasis of constructivist theory on the constitutive power of international norms, it should not be surprising that much of the constructivist literature has been given over to the "non-instrumental" mechanisms whereby international law may influence states, including Franck's concept of "compliance pull" of legitimate legal norms;[52] Brunnée and Toope's related conception of "interactional international law" arising out of ongoing practices that generate "fidelity to the rule of law" in international affairs[53]; Harold Koh's transnational legal process theory of domestic social, political, and legal internalization and obedience[54]; and Goodman and Jinks's concept of national "acculturation" to international norms and rules.[55]

By contrast with this rich literature on the effects of international laws and norms, constructivists have devoted far less attention to international adjudication as such. Constructivists have, however, demonstrated a greater sensitivity to the nature of law as a distinctive realm "characterized by an institutionally autonomous, distinctive discourse that draws on a pre-existing set of norms and practices of justification, and which delegitimizes the raw pursuit of power and self-interest."[56] Ian Johnstone has similarly put forward a constructivist account of international legal deliberation, in which legal discourse emerges as a "distinctively powerful form of argumentation," which requires states to engage in "justificatory discourse" before an "interpretive community" of both state and non-state actors that distinguish good arguments from unpersuasive claims.[57] These accounts of international law as a distinctive, and partially autonomous, form of reasoning, discourse, and argumentation are of obvious relevance to the study of international adjudication. Yet it is striking that constructivist scholars have thus far focused primarily on the emergence and effects of such discourse in inter-state settings, with less attention to the workings of international courts or arbitrators, which represents an obvious next step in the constructivist research program.

[50] Risse, note 48, at 19–20.

[51] M Finnemore, "Are Legal Norms Distinctive?" (2000) 32(3) N.Y.U. J. Int'l L. & Pol. 699.

[52] TM Franck, *The Power of Legitimacy Among Nations* (Oxford University Press 1990).

[53] J Brunnée and SJ Toope, *Legitimacy and Legality in International Law: An Interactional Account* (Cambridge University Press 2010).

[54] HH Koh, "Why Do Nations Obey International Law?" (1997) 106(8) Yale L.J. 2599; Koh, note 45.

[55] R Goodman and D Jinks, "How to Influence States: Socialization and International Human Rights Law" (2004) 54(3) Duke L.J. 621.

[56] Brunnée and Toope, note 15, at 127; summarizing Reus-Smit, note 26, 37–8; see also FV Kratochwil, *Rules, Norms, and Decisions: On the Conditions of Practical and Legal Reasoning in International Relations and Domestic Affairs* (Cambridge University Press 1989).

[57] Brunnée and Toope, note 15, at 132, summarizing Ian Johnstone, *The Power of Deliberation: International Law, Politics and Organization* (Oxford University Press 2011).

In sum, the four leading theories of international relations each ask a particular set of questions about international law and adjudication, and each theory directs our attention to specific causal mechanisms: distributive conflict and power for realists; information and institutions for institutionalists; domestic state-society relations and institutions for liberals; and norms and ideas for constructivists. Each of these theories is therefore potentially useful, and the competition among these research programs promises to sharpen our understanding of international law and adjudication. It is, nevertheless, worth highlighting two potential dangers of using IR theories as guides to the study of international adjudication.

First, as David Lake has recently argued, the existence of discrete IR theories and research programs runs the risk of producing an "isms" war, in which the proponents of competing theories engage in gladiatorial combat designed more to shore up their respective theories than to understand and explain specific outcomes in international relations. While this is certainly a danger, a growing number of IR scholars today advocate pragmatic, theoretically eclectic approaches to the *problem-driven empirical research* that increasingly dominates IL/IR scholarship,[58] and much of the best political science scholarship adopts precisely a "tool kit" approach to competing theories, drawing from each theory concepts and hypotheses suitable for testing with respect to the author's specific research question.

A second danger of the tendency for political science scholars to draw from existing IR theories is that these "off-the-shelf" theories, designed in most cases for the study of international security, political economy, or international organizations, may be poorly suited to study the specifically *legal* features of international adjudication. I shall return to this point below.

4 The Substantive Contributions of Political Science Scholarship

Political science, I have argued, promises to contribute to the study of international law both through its epistemological and methodological approaches and through its distinctive theories. Yet, as we have also seen, the subject of international

[58] See e.g., J Fearon and A Wendt, "Rationalism v. Constructivism: A Skeptical View" in W Carlsnaes, T Risse, and BA. Simmons (eds), *Handbook of International Relations* (London: Sage Publications 2002); P Katzenstein and R Sil, "Eclectic Theorizing in the Study and Practice of International Relations" in Reus-Smit and Snidal, note 46; JL Dunoff and MA Pollack, "Conclusions: Reviewing Two Decades of IL/IR Scholarship: What We've Learned, What's Next" in Dunoff and Pollack, note 14.

adjudication was largely ignored by political scientists for most of the twentieth century.

With the rise of an IL/IR approach and the proliferation of international courts since the end of the Cold War, however, the long neglect by IR scholars of international adjudication has come to an end, and recent scholarship has illuminated—albeit selectively—at least five significant questions or themes: (1) the *design of international adjudication bodies*; (2) *judicial behavior*, with an emphasis on judicial independence; (3) the behavior of *litigants*, which can be either states or non-state actors; (4) variations in *state compliance* within international judicial rulings; and (5) the *dynamic evolution* of dispute settlement systems over time.[59] Political science approaches are not without their weaknesses, to which I will turn in section 5, but let us first consider these five distinctive contributions.

4.1 Design of international adjudication bodies

First, in keeping with the increasing focus on rational design, a handful of scholars have sought systematically to understand and explain the delegation to and design of international adjudication bodies. With respect to delegation, "Some issue areas—such as arms control and the environment—are bereft of courts, while others—most notably criminal law and human rights—are populated by a multiplicity of judicial bodies."[60] Even within a single issue-area, moreover, delegation of adjudicative authority varies dramatically, such that, for example, some human rights agreements (such as the European Convention on Human Rights, ECHR) have strong courts with individual access, while others (including all of the United Nations (UN) human rights treaties) lack any court at all. Furthermore, even among regimes that provide for standing courts, we find a dizzying array of design features, including provisions for the nomination and appointment of judges, their terms of office, the question of open or closed deliberation and dissent, the question of access or standing for non-state actors, the presence or absence of an appellate procedure, the nature of remedies in cases of non-compliance, and many others. Each of these dimensions represents a collective state choice, calling out for explanation.

This is not, of course, an entirely new subject, as legal scholars had long devoted significant attention to the charters and other design features of individual courts. In general, however, IL/IR scholarship has sought not only to analyze and critique the design of individual courts and tribunals, but also to classify and explain broad *patterns* in the design of international adjudication bodies. For example, the "legalization" volume of *International Organization* provided an influential analytical framework which classified various international dispute settlement mechanisms

[59] This section draws extensively on Dunoff and Pollack, note 58.

[60] LR Helfer, Chapter 21 of this handbook.

along three dimensions—access, independence, and embeddedness—characterizing courts that were low in all three dimensions as "interstate" courts and those that were high as "transnational" courts. Such differences in design, Keohane, Moravcsik, and Slaughter argued, largely determine how frequently and by whom courts are used, whether those courts provide for the credible and neutral adjudication of disputes, and whether the resulting decisions have immediate effects in the legal orders of their member states.[61] Karen Alter makes a related distinction in her book, *The New Terrain of International Law*, where she distinguishes between traditional international courts and what she calls "new-style" courts, which combine two key elements: compulsory jurisdiction, and the ability of non-state actors (international commissions, prosecutors, institutional actors, and private litigants) to initiate litigation. These new-style courts, she argues, can provide external support to compliance constituencies within states, and thus promote the rule of law.[62]

Beyond classifying international adjudication systems, political science scholarship has begun to generate and test hypotheses about the *conditions* under which states design particular types of dispute settlement bodies. In the most extensive such study, Koremenos, and Koremenos and Betz, adapt the rational design research project to the study of dispute settlement systems, demonstrating that international dispute settlement systems vary dramatically across regions and across issue-areas. Koremenos and Betz hypothesize that states systematically adopt dispute settlement mechanisms (informal vs. formal, arbitration vs. adjudication, etc.) in response to particular types of cooperation problems, including enforcement problems, commitment problems, and various kinds of uncertainty, and they find considerable support for these hypotheses in their empirical analysis.[63]

Rational choice scholars do not, of course, exercise a monopoly on the study of the design of international courts. Nicole Deitelhoff, for example, has argued that the design of the International Criminal Court (ICC) represents the outcome of a discursive process in which weaker powers were able to persuade more powerful actors and secure the creation of a powerful new criminal court.[64] Works such as these have taken an important first step, yet the social-scientific study of the design of international adjudication is nevertheless in its infancy, seeking thus far to explain only very broad patterns of variation in design. By contrast, political scientists have so far paid less attention to the more fine-grained design choices that states make

[61] Keohane et al., note 31.

[62] KJ Alter, *The New Terrain of International Law: Courts, Politics, Rights* (Princeton University Press 2014).

[63] Koremenos, note 31; Koremenos and Betz, note 31.

[64] N Deitelhoff, "The Discursive Process of Legalization: Charting Islands of Persuasion in the ICC Case" (2009) 63(1) Int'l Org. 33; but see also BA Simmons and A Danner, "Credible Commitments and the International Criminal Court" (2010) 64(2) Int'l Org. 225, who offer a rationalist, credible-commitments explanation for the establishment of the ICC and for the decision of states to become parties to the Rome Treaty.

about the nomination and appointment of international arbitrators and judges[65]; the terms of office served by judges;[66] access to the court by non-state actors; and the nature of the remedies available to complainants in the event of non-compliance,[67] which constitute the frontier for rational design scholarship.

4.2 International judicial behavior and independence

A large and well-developed second strand of political science scholarship has focused on explaining *international judicial behavior*, with an emphasis on the related question of *judicial independence*. The focus in this literature has been on characterizing and explaining the voting behavior of international judges, often with an eye to establishing the extent and the determinants of their independence from the states that appoint them to their positions.[68] While a few legal studies had previously examined the independence of specific international courts,[69] political science scholarship over the past two decades has systematized such analysis, providing comprehensive theoretical frameworks identifying a wide range of potential control mechanisms available to states,[70] as well as other legal and political sources of influence[71] over international judicial behavior. Just as significantly, this research agenda has given rise to a spate of qualitative and quantitative empirical work seeking to establish, despite considerable methodological challenges, the nature and sources of judicial independence in the ECJ,[72] the ECtHR,[73] the ICJ,[74] and WTO panels and the Appellate Body,[75] among others.

[65] E Voeten, "The Politics of International Judicial Appointments" (2009) 9(2) Chicago J. Int'l L. 387; M Elsig and MA Pollack, "Agents, Trustees, and International Courts: The Politics of Judicial Appointment at the World Trade Organization" (forthcoming) Eur. J. Int'l Rel.

[66] Voeten, note 65. [67] Dunoff and Pollack, note 13.

[68] E Voeten, "International Judicial Independence" in Dunoff and Pollack, note 14.

[69] EB Weiss, "Judicial Independence and Impartiality: A Preliminary Inquiry" in L Damrosch (ed.), *The International Court of Justice at a Crossroads* (Dobbs Ferry, NY: Transnational Publishers 1987).

[70] Helfer, "Flexibility," note 28; Voeten, note 68.

[71] LR Helfer, "Why States Create International Tribunals: A Theory of Constrained Independence" in S Voight, M Albert and D Schmidtchen (eds), *International Conflict Resolution* (Tubingen: Mohr Siebeck 2006) 253–76; and see, in this handbook, Voeten, Ch. 25.

[72] The political science literature on the ECJ is voluminous. See the excellent review of the literature in A Stone Sweet, "The European Court of Justice and the Judicialization of EU Governance" (2010) 5(2) Living Reviews in European Governance, <http://www.livingreviews.org/lreg-2010-2> accessed July 25, 2013.

[73] E Voeten, "The Impartiality of International Judges: Evidence from the European Court of Human Rights" (2008) 102(4) Am. Pol. Sci. Rev. 417.

[74] EA Posner and MF de Figueiredo, "Is the International Court of Justice Biased?" (2005) 34(2) J. Legal Stud. 599.

[75] On judicial behavior at the WTO, see e.g., ML Busch, "Overlapping Institutions, Forum Shopping, and Dispute Settlement in International Trade" (2007) 61(4) Int'l Org. 735; ML Busch and E Reinhardt, "Three's a Crowd: Third Parties and WTO Dispute Settlement" (2006) 58(3) World Politics 446; ML

Controversies remain within this literature, but the focus of analysis has increasingly moved from broad questions of whether international courts are entirely dependent or epiphenomenal at one extreme or entirely independent trustees at the other extreme, to more fine-grained analysis of the effectiveness of specific control mechanisms such as judicial appointment and reappointment practices,[76] legislative overruling, and the prospect of state noncompliance.[77] In addition to these principal-agent features, recent research points to the significance of domestic factors, suggesting that, at least with respect to transnational courts, "international judges are likely to become expansionist law-makers when they are supported by sub-state interlocutors and compliance constituencies, including government officials, advocacy networks, national judges and administrative agencies."[78]

Interestingly, Voeten suggests that, in addition to studying judicial independence as a dependent variable, scholars increasingly ask whether judicial independence as an independent variable may help to explain other phenomena, including the effectiveness of international courts.[79] This research in turn raises the intriguing concept of *optimal judicialization*. In an influential paper, Helfer asks whether international human rights law has become "overlegalized," prompting a backlash against such treaties by some states,[80] and similar concerns have been raised by scholars of the international trade regime.[81] Identifying optimal levels of judicialization thus represents another frontier subject for IL/IR research.[82]

Busch and KJ Pelc, "The Politics of Judicial Economy at the World Trade Organization" (2010) 64(2) Int'l Org. 257; and CL Davis, *Why Adjudicate? Enforcing Trade Rules in the WTO* (Princeton University Press 2012).

[76] Voeten, note 65; and Elsig and Pollack, note 65.

[77] See e.g. the vigorous methodological debate between Carrubba, Gabel and Hankla, "Judicial Behavior under Political Constraints," note 32; Carrubba, Gabel and Hankla, "Understanding the Role of the ECJ," note 32; and A Stone Sweet and T Brunell, "The European Court of Justice, State Noncompliance, and the Politics of Override" (2012) 106(1) Am. Pol. Sci. Rev. 204.

[78] KJ Alter and LR Helfer, "Nature or Nurture? Judicial Lawmaking in the European Court of Justice and the Andean Tribunal of Justice" (2010) 64(4) Int'l Org. 563.

[79] Voeten, note 68; compare LR Helfer and A-M Slaughter, "Why States Create International Tribunals: A Response to Professors Posner and Yoo" (2005) 93(3) Cal. L. Rev. 889; EA Posner and JC Yoo, "Judicial Independence in International Tribunals" (2005) 93(1) Cal. L. Rev. 1; and the extended discussion of effectiveness in this handbook, Helfer, Ch. 21.

[80] LR Helfer, "Overlegalizing Human Rights: International Relations Theory and the Commonwealth Caribbean Backlash against Human Rights Regimes" (2002) 102(7) Columbia L. Rev. 1832.

[81] J Goldstein and LL Martin, "Legalization, Trade Liberalization, and Domestic Constituents: A Cautionary Note" (2000) 54(3) Int'l Org. 603; J Pauwelyn, "The Transformation of World Trade" (2005) 104(1) Michigan L. Rev. 1.

[82] Voeten, note 68.

4.3 Litigant behavior

A third major contribution of political science scholarship has been to problematize, theorize, and study empirically the behavior of *litigants* in international adjudication. Simplifying a rich literature, this work can be divided into two major categories, the first focusing on the behavior of states as litigants before interstate courts, and the second examining the behavior of non-state litigants before the growing number of transnational courts.

With respect to the behavior of state litigants, political science scholars have only recently turned their attention to understanding the behavior of states in initiating (or opting not to initiate) litigation. As Todd Allee notes, however, the "decision to sue" is an important and under-studied question, of interest not only for its own sake but also because the cases that actually reach international courts constitute a small, and potentially biased, subset of the universe of international legal disputes.[83]

Fortunately, recent political science scholarship has begun to address this question systematically, across a number of issue-areas. In one study of international territorial disputes, for example, Allee and Huth hypothesize that states are most likely to refer international disputes to judicial settlement when the domestic audience costs of making significant political concessions are high. In such settings, they argue, international judicial rulings can provide "political cover" for domestically unpopular decisions, and their analysis of nearly 1,500 territorial disputes provides support for the claim that "state leaders opt for legal dispute resolution when they are highly accountable to domestic political opposition, as well as when the dispute is highly salient to domestic audiences."[84] This study supports the liberal view that state behavior with respect to international litigation is driven in large part by domestic political considerations.

Christina Davis, in a recent study of interstate litigation in the WTO trade regime, offers a similar argument, suggesting that international litigation is particularly useful for democratically accountable governments as a means of responding to domestic pressure and signaling to domestic industries that the government supports their demands:

> Engaging in political theater by initiating legal action against a foreign government proves to be an effective strategy not only for dealing with foreign governments but also for managing domestic pressure. Willingness to bear the costs of going to court signals that the government gives priority to enforcement. As a result, incentives to use courts arise from their usefulness as a political tool and not only from their role to interpret the law and allocate punishment.[85]

[83] TL Allee, "Legal Incentives and Domestic Rewards: The Selection of Trade Disputes for GATT/WTO Dispute Resolution" (2004) (unpublished paper). See also Davis, note 75, at 1–3.

[84] TL Allee and PK Huth, "Legitimizing Dispute Settlement: International Adjudication as Domestic Political Cover" (2006) 100(2) Am. Pol. Sci. Rev. 219.

[85] Davis, note 75, at 2.

Other work on state behavior in WTO dispute settlement points to additional influences on state litigation choices, including state power,[86] estimates of the probability of winning,[87] concerns about setting useful precedents in various legal fora,[88] and previous litigation experience.[89] Still other work has explored the conditions under which states join WTO litigation as third parties,[90] and agree to settle disputes prior to a judicial ruling.[91]

Given the rise of transnational or new-style courts, no account of litigant behavior is complete without a discussion of the behavior of individual, non-state litigants. Traditionally, individuals and other non-state actors enjoyed no direct access to international adjudication systems, and relied on their own national governments to espouse (or, more frequently, not to espouse) their claims under international law. Today, however, non-state actors enjoy the opportunity to initiate litigation through a variety of avenues:

- Individuals may initiate complaints before international adjudicators against their own states for human rights violations, as in the European Court of Human Rights (ECtHR), the Inter-American Court of Human Rights, and the committees established to hear petitions under the various UN human rights treaties.[92]
- Individuals in some international regimes can initiate litigation in national courts, which then consult international courts under a "preliminary reference" mechanism, most notably in the EU but also in other legal settings such as the Andean Community.[93]
- Investors may also initiate binding arbitration proceedings against states in investor–state arbitration disputes, as under the North American Free-Trade Agreement as well as the growing number of bilateral investment treaties (BITs).[94]

In addition to these various legal avenues through which they can initiate litigation, non-state actors in some interstate adjudication systems enjoy the limited right to

[86] T Sattler and T Bernauer, "Gravitation or Discrimination? Determinants of Litigation in the World Trade Organisation" (2011) 50(2) Eur. J. Pol. Research 143; see also, in this handbook, Klein, Ch. 26.

[87] Allee, note 83. [88] Busch, note 75.

[89] CL Davis and S Blodgett Bermeo, "Who Files? Developing Country Participation in GATT/WTO Adjudication" (2009) 71(3) J. Politics 1033.

[90] Busch and Reinhardt, note 75.

[91] ML Busch and E Reinhardt, "Bargaining in the Shadow of the Law: Early Settlement in GATT/WTO Disputes" (2000/2001) 24 Fordham Int'l 58; A Guzman and BA Simmons, "To Settle or Empanel? An Empirical Analysis of Litigation and Settlement at the WTO" (2002) 31(1) J. Legal Stud. S205.

[92] See, in this handbook, Klein, Ch. 26.

[93] KJ Alter, *Establishing the Supremacy of European Law: The Making of an International Rule of Law in Europe* (Oxford University Press 2001); Alter and Helfer, note 78.

[94] BA Simmons, "The International Investment Regime: Sovereignty, Investor Security, and Dispute Settlement Since the 1980s" (2010) Straus Institute Working Paper 04/10, N.Y.U. School of Law, <http://nyustraus.org/pubs/0910/docs/Simmons.pdf> accessed July 25, 2013.

bring *amicus curiae* briefs before courts.[95] Finally, with the increase in international criminal tribunals, individual actors may also find themselves as defendants in international criminal proceedings.[96]

Political scientists have waded selectively into this question of non-state litigant behavior, focusing nearly all of their attention on patterns of litigation in the EU's preliminary reference procedure, where they have problematized both the behavior of litigants in bringing cases to their national courts, as well as the relationship between national courts and the ECJ. With respect to individual litigants, both political scientists and lawyers have examined systematic differences in the behavior of "one-shot" and "repeat players" in EU litigation,[97] and in particular the importance of well-financed corporate litigants,[98] as well as state-subsidized groups such as women claiming gender discrimination.[99] Stone Sweet and Brunell find that individual litigants under the preliminary reference procedure are most likely to target regulations adopted by states representing substantial economic markets, which they interpret as evidence in favor of a neo-functionalist account of European integration.[100]

Just as important as individuals claiming their rights under EU law, however, is the question of whether, when, and why national courts submit questions for preliminary rulings to the ECJ, and also whether and why those national courts accept the direct effect and supremacy of those decisions. Within the political science literature, responses to this question fall into three broad camps.[101] In the first, neo-functionalist, view, the willingness of national courts to accept ECJ jurisdiction and jurisprudence can be explained in terms of the extent to which ECJ rulings "empowered" national courts within their own domestic political and legal systems.[102] In the second, "inter-court competition" model, Karen Alter demonstrates that the preliminary reference procedure was accepted most readily and used most ambitiously by lower courts, whose judges stood to gain in various ways

[95] See, in this handbook, Klein, Ch. 26.

[96] G Bass, *Stay the Hand of Vengeance: The Politics of War Crimes Tribunals* (Princeton University Press 2001).

[97] L Conant, *Justice Contained: Law and Politics in the European Union* (Ithaca, NY: Cornell University Press 2002).

[98] R Rawlings, "The Eurolaw Game: Some Deductions from a Saga" (1993) 20 J. Law & Soc'y 309.

[99] KJ Alter and J Vargas, "Explaining Variation in the Use of European Litigation Strategies: European Community Law and British Gender Equality Policy" (2000) 33 Comp. Pol. Stud. 452; JA Caporaso and J Jupille, "The Europeanization of Gender Equality Policy and Domestic Structural Change" in M Green Cowles, JA Caporaso, and T Risse (eds), *Transforming Europe: Europeanization and Domestic Change* (Ithaca, NY: Cornell University Press 2001).

[100] A Stone Sweet and T Brunell, "Constructing a Supranational Constitution: Dispute Resolution and Governance in the European Community" (1998) 92(1) Am. Pol. Sci. Rev. 63.

[101] MA Pollack, "The New EU Legal History: What's New, What's Missing?" Am. U. Int'l L. Rev. (forthcoming), Temple University Legal Studies Research Paper No. 2013-09 <http://papers.ssrn.com/sol3/papers.cfm?abstract_id=2207170> accessed August 24, 2013.

[102] A-M Burley and W Mattli, "Europe Before the Court: A Political Theory of Legal Integration" (1993) 47(1) Int'l Org. 41.

from a direct relationship with the ECJ, and far more slowly and reluctantly by national high courts.[103] Over the past decade, a third, "sustained resistance" view has emerged in the political science literature, in which national courts in various member states persistently resist either sending preliminary references to Luxembourg, or else attempt to "contain" the effects of ECJ decisions in the domestic legal order.[104]

Despite these advances in the study of EU litigation, the systematic political science study of individual litigation before other international adjudicative bodies remains in its infancy. By contrast with the large EU literature, we know relatively little about the determinants of litigation in other interstate courts such as the ECtHR and the Andean Tribunal, and political science scholars have also largely ignored the admittedly low levels of individual activity before UN human rights committees.[105]

4.4 Judgment compliance

The twin questions of compliance with, and effectiveness of, international law, are among the core themes of political science scholarship, which has gone to great pains to problematize the question whether, and under what conditions, states comply with their international legal commitments, making both methodological and theoretical contributions. In methodological terms, political scientists have joined empirically oriented legal scholars in an effort to measure, systematically and usually quantitatively, state compliance with various international legal agreements. In theoretical terms, political scientists have identified various *causal mechanisms* whereby international law may induce compliance, including instrumentalist mechanisms such as retaliation, reciprocity, and reputation, and normative mechanisms whereby international law may be internalized by actors.[106]

By and large, the majority of this compliance literature is focused on what Jana von Stein calls "first-order" compliance with substantive international legal rules, rather than on "second-order" compliance with the rulings of international adjudicative bodies.[107] As Alexandra Huneeus shows in her excellent chapter in this volume, the study of "judgment compliance" is very much in its infancy, challenged both by the familiar methodological problems of measuring compliance empirically, and by the fact that

[103] Alter, note 93.

[104] See e.g., Conant, note 97; J Golub, "The Politics of Judicial Discretion: Rethinking the Interaction between National Courts and the European Court of Justice" (1996) 19(2) West Eur. Pol. 360; and M Wind, D S Martinsen, and GP Rotger, "The Uneven Legal Push for Europe: Questioning Variation When National Courts Go to Europe" (2009) 10(1) Eur. Union Pol. 63.

[105] See, in this handbook, Klein, Ch. 26, for an excellent discussion of these questions.

[106] J Von Stein, "The Engines of Compliance" in Dunoff and Pollack, note 14.

[107] J Von Stein, note 106, at 478; see, in this handbook, Huneeus, Ch. 20 (using the term "primary-norm compliance" as a synonym for von Stein's first-order compliance, and "judgment compliance" for second-order compliance).

hypotheses about the determinants of compliance have thus far outpaced rigorous empirical studies to test those hypotheses. Nevertheless, she demonstrates, some preliminary findings have begun to emerge from the work of both political scientists and legal scholars, who point to various features of international adjudicators, target states, and the nature of disputes that might influence state compliance with rulings. With respect to international adjudicators, for example, Huneeus finds evidence that the vagueness or specificity of a ruling, the type of order (provisional measures vs. final judgments), and the nature of the remedy (monetary vs. legislative or constitutional change) may influence state compliance with court rulings; by contrast, existing studies provide too little data to establish whether the independence or legitimacy of a court influences state compliance with that court's rulings.[108] Moving from the adjudicator to the target state, Huneeus finds some evidence that factors emphasized by liberal scholars, such as the nature of the domestic legal system and the number of veto players in the domestic political system, make a difference; by contrast, she suggests, the independence of the domestic judiciary appears to cut both ways, allowing powerful domestic courts to either accept, or defy, rulings of international courts.[109] Finally, with respect to the nature of the dispute, extant studies provide some evidence that subject matter (e.g., territorial disputes, the use of force, etc.) as well as power disparities among the parties may influence state compliance.[110] These preliminary findings are highly suggestive, but they rest on only a handful of studies, and more work on all of these questions is clearly needed.

4.5 Dynamic evolution of international adjudication

Finally, and most tentatively, IL/IR scholars have begun to develop and test hypotheses about the conditions under which, and the ways in which, international adjudication systems develop dynamically over time. IL/IR scholars have suggested that transnational dispute settlement systems, characterized by high levels of access, independence, and embeddedness, should show greater dynamism over time, as individuals (not subject to governmental gatekeeping) bring cases that are likely to be decided independently and then enforced through domestic legal systems, creating a feedback loop of ever more developed law and ever-growing caseloads.[111]

The two most striking examples of vibrant, dynamic transnational courts in the literature are the ECJ and the ECtHR, both of which have seized upon an initial trickle of claims from individual litigants to create legally enforceable rights under international law, which have in turn provided incentives for further litigation in a virtuous

[108] See, in this handbook, Huneeus, Ch. 20. [109] Huneeus, Ch. 20.

[110] Huneeus, Ch. 20.

[111] Keohane, Moravcsik, and Slaughter, note 31; see also Helfer and Slaughter, note 39; Stone Sweet and Brunell, note 100; Alter, note 62.

circle.[112] Indeed, Moravcsik suggests that the explanation of dynamic development of dispute settlement regimes is one of the signature contributions of liberal theory to the study of international law.[113] In this view, the development of international adjudication systems depends not only on the design of international courts, but also on domestic civil society and rule-of-law institutions inside the court's constituent member states. In this vein, Alter and Helfer have documented the very different ways in which similar preliminary reference systems have played out in the different domestic societies under the jurisdictions of the ECJ and the Andean Tribunal of Justice, respectively.[114] If this is correct, then the development of a dynamic international court or tribunal is something of a hothouse flower, requiring just the right combination of domestic as well as international conditions to flourish.

At the other extreme of interstate courts, Eric Posner and Miguel de Figueiredo have argued that the ICJ, which scores low in terms of access, embeddedness, and arguably independence, has stagnated over its nearly seven decades of existence; indeed, despite being the only international court of general jurisdiction in the world, the ICJ has enjoyed only a trickle of cases each year, as well as a decreasing number of countries that accept the Court's compulsory jurisdiction.[115] Interstate courts are not, however, doomed to stagnation and decline, as demonstrated by the rapid growth and development of the WTO Dispute Settlement Body, which has adjudicated a steady stream of hundreds of cases and dozens of appellate decisions, developing a substantial body of law since its creation in 1995.[116] The dynamic development of both interstate and transnational courts, as well as arbitration schemes, represents another challenging frontier in the social-scientific study of international adjudication.

5 Weaknesses in Political Science Scholarship, and the Way Ahead

Despite these substantial contributions, political science scholarship on international adjudication has suffered from a systematic bias in favor of certain research questions and empirical subjects, while ignoring others that have been studied far more extensively by international legal scholars. Indeed, as Jeffrey Dunoff and I have

[112] Helfer and Slaughter, note 39; Stone Sweet and Brunell, note 100; and Alter, note 62.

[113] Moravcsik, note 15. [114] Alter and Helfer, note 78.

[115] Posner and de Figueiredo, note 74.

[116] KJ Pelc, "Shaping Precedent in International Trade Law: A Social Network Application," paper presented at the Conference on Judicial Institutions: Courts in Domestic & International Affairs, Princeton University, October 19–20, 2012.

argued elsewhere, political science scholars have generally ignored the theoretical, methodological, and substantive insights of international legal scholarship, drawing instead on off-the-shelf IR theories and methods that may be poorly suited to the study of international adjudication. Such an approach not only does an injustice to international legal scholarship, which is theoretically and epistemologically more diverse than most political scientists understand or allow; it also closes off promising avenues of inquiry and useful theoretical frameworks that might otherwise contribute to the social-scientific study of international law and courts.[117]

In this concluding section, therefore, I briefly identify three questions on which political science scholarship on international adjudication is currently incomplete or lacking, and where careful consideration of IL scholarship could enrich future work. First, I suggest that IR scholars' treatment of judicial independence, while progressive in the sense of putting forward testable hypotheses about the determinants of judicial independence and member-state control, has adapted off-the-shelf principal-agent theories designed for non-judicial bodies without adequately adapting them to the specifically legal features of international adjudicative bodies. Second, I suggest that the IR literature, while examining international judicial behavior, has neglected almost entirely the question of legal interpretation, and I identify some recent work that approaches questions of interpretation in ways that take account of doctrinal concerns while also asking social-scientific questions about patterns and causation. Third and finally, I argue that, after ignoring international adjudication for many decades, IR scholarship of the past two decades now suffers from an overemphasis on international courts, as opposed to other actors engaged in the interpretation of international law.

5.1 Judicial independence

The study of judicial independence has been one of the strongest features of political science scholarship, and a growing number of studies have employed the language of principal-agent analysis to predict and explain variations in the independence of international courts.[118] Such principal-agent approaches have not been without their critics, however, and Alter has argued that international courts and tribunals should not be construed as agents of their member states, because the control mechanisms ("recontracting tools") emphasized by principal-agent analysts are likely to be unavailable or ineffective as a means to influence the international judiciary, who should be considered not as agents but as "trustees" of the international community.[119] Efforts by member-state principals to influence international courts, she suggests, will be channeled away from traditional control mechanisms and toward either "rhetorical politics," in which actors attempt to persuade judicial

[117] Dunoff and Pollack, note 13. [118] Voeten, note 68. [119] Alter, note 32, at 33.

actors in the language of the law, or "legitimacy politics," in which actors attempt to influence the public perception of the legitimacy of a court's decision, or of the court itself.[120] I have argued elsewhere that the distinction between agents and trustees should not be overdrawn, and that the availability or unavailability of various judicial control mechanisms is an empirical rather than a theoretical question.[121] Yet Alter is surely correct that principal-agent analysis is drawn primarily from the study of non-adjudicative bodies, and that it may therefore systematically direct our attention away from other, primarily legal, factors that might influence the independence and the behavior of international adjudicators.

Helfer, for example, suggests that any theory of an international tribunal's "constrained independence" or "strategic space" should incorporate *both* the full array of specific control mechanisms anticipated by principal-agent analysis *and* what Helfer calls the "global community of law," which he defines as "discursive constraints (e.g., procedural rules, interpretive methodologies, and substantive norms) generated by interactions among participants in the global community of law and internalized by tribunal members."[122] In so doing, Helfer holds out the promise of a genuinely interdisciplinary and synthetic account of international judicial independence, which takes into account both the panoply of principal-agent control mechanisms available to states, as well as the resources and constraints imposed by the more diffuse global community of law.

In another recent study, Alec Stone Sweet and Thomas Brunell provide an alternative conception of international courts as trustees, making clear that only certain courts meet what they identify as the three necessary features of any trustee court: (a) the court is the authoritative interpreter of a given regime's law, and possesses the authority to review the legality of acts taken by any contracting state; (b) the court's jurisdiction is compulsory; and (c) it is difficult, or impossible as a practical matter, for the contracting states to reverse the court's important rulings on treaty law. Certain international courts, such as the ECJ, ECtHR, and WTO Appellate Body, meet these criteria, while others, such as the ICJ, fall short. Trustee courts, they argue, are in a particularly strong position vis-à-vis their member states, and are essentially free to rule without fear of legislative punishment or override. Stone Sweet and Brunell go further, however, arguing that trustee courts engage in what they call "majoritarian activism," tending to rule against states whose positions are out of synch with a majority of other state-parties. In so doing, *trustee courts act in effect as agents of the majority*, allowing them to achieve outcomes that would otherwise be impossible under consensus-based decision-making rules.[123] Stone Sweet and Brunell's claims, tested in their paper with respect to the ECJ, ECtHR, and WTO, represent a promising synthesis of legal and political science insights,

[120] Alter, note 32, at 44. [121] Pollack, note 32. [122] Helfer, note 71, at 266.
[123] Stone Sweet and Brunell, note 32.

operationalizing the legal concepts of trusteeship and majoritarian activism in ways that facilitate social-scientific testing and falsification.

5.2 International judicial *interpretation*

A second limit of existing IL/IR scholarship in this area is its almost exclusive emphasis on judicial *behavior* and its relative neglect of *legal interpretation*.[124] With its increasingly extensive use of quantitative methods to detect patterns of international judicial decision-making as well as correlations between judicial rulings and other factors, much of the existing literature reduces judicial rulings to a single dimension, namely whether a court ruled for or against any given state on a particular issue. The results of these studies have been valuable, demonstrating the ability of at least certain courts to rule against the interests of powerful states as well as identifying some important predictors of judicial behavior.[125] Yet in so doing most of the IL/IR literature ignores other aspects of judicial interpretation, including questions about the principles used to guide interpretation, the formal or informal use of precedent, the nature of legal arguments, etc. A notable exception to this trend is Pauwelyn and Elsig's groundbreaking interdisciplinary effort to conceptualize the dependent variable of international judicial interpretation along five dimensions, *and* to explain judges' interpretive choices with a simple model of judicial constraints and incentives.[126]

Pauwelyn and Elsig suggest that existing international tribunals make highly varied choices, not only in terms of the winners and losers of individual decisions, but also in the interpretive strategies they employ to reach those decisions. For the sake of tractability, they reduce these strategies to choices along five dimensions. First, they identify a "dominant hermeneutic" guiding judicial interpretation, which can focus alternately on the plain meaning of legal texts (text), the intent of the original drafters of the text (intent), or the underlying objectives of the treaty (object). Judges in different courts have historically made different interpretive choices, with, for example, ICJ judges generally reading international treaties with respect to the ordinary meaning of the words contained therein, while other judicial bodies (e.g., early GATT panels) have looked at the intent of the framers, and others still (most notably the ECJ) have taken a teleological approach, seeking to advance the broad objectives of a treaty or organization. Along a second dimension of "timing," judges can interpret the terms of an agreement in line with their meanings at the time of

[124] This section draws from a more extended discussion of legal interpretation in Dunoff and Pollack, note 13.

[125] See the excellent review in Voeten, note 68.

[126] J Pauwelyn and M Elsig, "The Politics of Treaty Interpretation: Variations and Explanations Across International Tribunals" in Dunoff and Pollack, note 14.

drafting, an "originalist" approach, or they can take an "evolutionary" approach that interprets terms in line with their contemporary meaning. Third, courts can vary in their degree of "activism," taking either a "work to rule" approach that interprets legal texts narrowly, or a "gap-filling" approach in which courts feel free to fill the gaps in what are often vague and outdated international agreements. Fourth, while international law contains no formal rule of *stare decisis*, international courts can vary in their treatment of precedent, either ignoring precedents and addressing each case afresh on its own merits, or alternatively drawing and building on legal precedents when deciding new cases. Fifth, courts vary in what the authors call "linkage" to other international legal regimes, in some cases interpreting legal texts in a particular regime in "splendid isolation" from the rest of the legal order, while in other cases being more outward-looking, interpreting their constitutive treaties with respect to general international law and to treaties in related issue-areas. For Pauwelyn and Elsig, interpretive choices such as these are not only doctrinal or normative decisions to be critiqued, but also and especially choices to be explained in social-scientific terms.

Pauwelyn and Elsig's explanatory framework is complex, and a full explication of it is beyond the scope of this chapter, but put simply the authors hypothesize that "*interpretation choice* is a result of the interaction of two key variables: (a) the demand-side *interpretation space* that is made available to a tribunal and (b) the supply-side *interpretation incentives*, defined as intrinsic motivations of a tribunal's members when operating within this space."[127] Pauwelyn and Elsig emphasize that their approach is exploratory, but it brings together the lawyer's attention to doctrine, discourse, and process with the political scientist's effort to explain broad patterns of and variations in behavior, and it opens up a major new research agenda for political science scholars to study doctrinal questions systematically using the tools of social science.

To some extent, we can already point to emerging examples of "best practice" in the study of precedent before international courts and tribunals. In one recent study, for example, Yonatan Lupu and Erik Voeten examine the use of precedent by judges of the ECtHR, arguing that international judges employ citations to precedent strategically in an effort to persuade domestic courts, and demonstrating that citation to precedent is highest in cases that raise politically sensitive issues.[128] In another innovative study, Krzysztof Pelc examines the behavior of state-litigants in the WTO, which he characterizes as a legal system with a *de facto* rule of precedent. Drawing, like Lupu and Voeten, on social-network analysis, Pelc demonstrates that states pursue deliberate and systematic efforts to establish precedents in WTO trade law, raising novel legal arguments in low-stakes disputes, and subsequently

[127] Pauwelyn and M Elsig, note 126, at 459.

[128] Y Lupu and E Voeten, "Precedent in International Courts: A Network Analysis of Case Citations by the European Court of Human Rights" (2012) 42 Brit. J. Pol. Sci. 413, 438.

invoking these precedents in later, high-stakes litigation.[129] To some extent, these ground-breaking studies represent the ascendance of a particular methodology, namely social-network analysis, which is unlikely to illuminate other aspects of international judicial interpretation. Yet they demonstrate the possibilities of political science studies that are attentive to interpretive strategies and not merely to final outcomes of litigation.

5.3 Interpretation by *non-judicial* actors

Finally, political science scholars have thus far focused their analyses of international legal interpretation almost exclusively on courts and judges, effectively ignoring the large number of other quasi-judicial or non-judicial actors who interpret international law on a regular basis. Cesare Romano, a legal scholar, has recently catalogued the full range of international legal interpretation bodies, noting that in many areas, the law is interpreted not by international courts (which may be absent or lack compulsory jurisdiction) but by other international bodies including arbitration systems, intergovernmental and expert human rights commissions, environmental compliance systems, and trade and regulatory committees, as well as national governments and national courts.[130] Strikingly, this broader canvas reveals that much of the work of legal interpretation is carried out not by judicial but by *political* bodies, the analysis of which might be seen as a comparative advantage for political science scholars; up to now, however, the work of these bodies has been examined almost exclusively by legal scholars.

Political scientists have, for example, largely ignored the workings of international arbitration schemes, although a spate of recent scholarship on investor–state arbitration demonstrates the promise of interdisciplinary scholarship in understanding the decisions by states to accept arbitration, the subsequent behavior of arbitrators, and the apparent backlash against arbitral decisions by some states.[131] Similarly, political scientists have focused growing attention on the powerful European Court of Human Rights, but have devoted little or no study to the various UN human rights bodies, which have issued many controversial interpretations of international human rights law.[132] And while a large number of scholars

[129] Pelc, note 116.

[130] CPR Romano, "A Taxonomy of International Rule of Law Institutions" (2011) 2(1) J. Int'l Disp. Settlement 241.

[131] Simmons, note 94.

[132] K Mechlem, "Treaty Bodies and the Interpretation of Human Rights" (2009) 42 Vanderbilt J. Transnat'l L. 905; Y Shany, "The Effectiveness of the Human Rights Committee and the Treaty Body Reform" (February 24, 2013), Hebrew University of Jerusalem Research Paper No. 02-13, <http://papers.ssrn.com/sol3/papers.cfm?abstract_id=2223298> accessed August 24, 2013.

study patterns of litigation in the WTO dispute settlement system, far fewer have examined the resolution of disputes in WTO intergovernmental bodies such as the Sanitary and Phytosanitary Committee, or how the North American Free Trade Agreement (NAFTA) parties can issue authoritative interpretations of NAFTA treaty provisions.[133] These non-judicial bodies would seem a natural object of study for IR scholars, but they have thus far been studied primarily by international legal scholars.

5.4 Toward an international law-and-politics scholarship

Given these weaknesses and lacunae in the existing political science scholarship on international law, Dunoff and I have called for a truly interdisciplinary IL/IR scholarship, one that retains the explanatory epistemology and methods of political science but draws more effectively on legal scholarship and pays greater attention to the specifically *legal* features of international adjudication.[134] Put differently, we suggest that IR scholars follow in the footsteps of their domestic law-and-politics colleagues, who have pursued a resolutely positivist, largely theory-driven, and quantitative research program that, however, takes into account the specifically legal features of domestic courts and judicial behavior, such as the use of precedent and dissent, to produce a more fine-grained understanding of law and courts.[135] Indeed, if we accept the recent arguments of Staton and Moore, the differences between international and domestic courts have been exaggerated.[136] Hence political science scholars of international courts should look *both* to international lawyers *and* to their domestic law-and-politics colleagues for insights into the behavior of international judges *as judges* and of international courts *as courts*.

[133] JL Dunoff, "Lotus Eaters: Reflections on the Varietals Dispute, the SPS Agreement and WTO Dispute Resolution" in GA Bermann and P Mavroidis (eds), *Trade and Human Health and Safety* (Cambridge University Press 2006); A Lang and J Scott, "The Hidden World of WTO Governance" (2009) 20(3) Eur. J. Int'l L. 575.

[134] Dunoff and Pollack, note 13.

[135] See e.g., the essays in the excellent collection by KE Whittington, RD Kelemen, and GA Caldeira (eds), *The Oxford Handbook of Law and Politics* (Oxford University Press 2008).

[136] JK Staton and WH Moore, "Judicial Power in Domestic and International Politics" (2011) 65(3) Int'l Org. 553.

Research Questions

1. How can we explain decisions by states to select specific design features of international adjudication bodies, such as the appointment and terms of judges, rules of procedure, and remedies for noncompliance?
2. Is there an optimal level of legalization and judicialization of international politics—and if so, what factors determine that level?
3. What explains the decisions by different international adjudicative bodies to adopt different interpretive strategies and rules of procedure?
4. What systematic knowledge can we glean about the behavior, independence, and interpretive strategies of international arbitrators and treaty review bodies, who have thus far been neglected by political science scholars in favor of standing courts and tribunals?

Suggested Reading

Abbott, KW, "Modern International Relations Theory: A Prospectus for International Lawyers" (1989) 14(2) Yale J. Int'l L. 335.

Alter, KJ, *The New Terrain of International Law: Courts, Politics, Rights* (Princeton University Press 2014).

Slaughter Burley, A-M, "International Law and International Relations Theory: A Dual Agenda" (1993) 87(2) AJIL 205.

Dunoff, JL and Pollack, MA (eds), *Interdisciplinary Perspectives on International Law and International Relations: The State of the Art* (Cambridge University Press 2013).

Goldsmith, JL and Posner, EA, *The Limits of International Law* (Oxford University Press 2005).

Goldstein, JL et al. (eds), "Legalization and World Politics" (2000) 54(3) Int'l Org. (special issue).

Guzman, AT, *How International Law Works: A Rational Choice Theory* (New York: Oxford University Press 2008).

Hafner-Burton, EM, Victor, D, and Lupu, Y, "Political Science Research on International Law: The State of the Field" (2012) 106(1) AJIL 47.

Helfer, LR, "Why States Create International Tribunals: A Theory of Constrained Independence" in S Voight, M Albert and D Schmidtchen (eds), *International Conflict Resolution* (Tübingen: Mohn Siebeck 2006) 255–76.

Helfer, LR and Slaughter, AM, "Toward a Theory of Effective Supranational Adjudication" (1997) 107(2) Yale L.J. 273.

Koremenos, A, Lipson, C, and Snidal, D, "The Rational Design of International Institutions" (2001) 55(4) Int'l Org. 761.

Stone Sweet, A and Brunell, T, "Constructing a Supranational Constitution: Dispute Resolution and Governance in the European Community" (1998) 92(1) Am. Pol. Sci. Rev. 63.

Voeten, E, "The Impartiality of International Judges: Evidence from the European Court of Human Rights" (2008) 102(4) Am. Pol. Sci. Rev. 417.

CHAPTER 18

SOCIOLOGICAL APPROACHES TO INTERNATIONAL COURTS

MIKAEL RASK MADSEN*

I am almost compelled to begin a chapter on sociological approaches to international courts (ICs) by mentioning that one of the first major international judges, Second President of the Permanent Court of International Justice (PCIJ) Max Huber (1874–1960), pioneered the use of sociology in studies of international law in his work as a professor of law at the University of Zurich before being appointed to the international

* Mikael Rask Madsen is professor of law at the University of Copenhagen and Director of iCourts—The Danish National Research Foundation's Centre of Excellence for International Courts. Mail to: mikael.madsen@jur.ku.dk. This research is funded by the Danish National Research Foundation Grant no. DNRF105.

bench.[1] Huber wrote his seminal work at the precise moment that the founding fathers of sociology were providing a set of radical new tools for understanding law and legal institutions in society. Yet, while early sociologists shared an interest in the place of law in the formation of modern society, international law, and particularly international courts (ICs) had little relevance to them as objects of study. With the rare exception of the work of Huber and a few others,[2] many of the insights of the pioneers of sociology have been lost to students of ICs. The subsequent development of both general sociology and the Law and Society Movement, an important sub-section of sociology directly involved in research on law, provided a way to bring sociological insights into the study of ICs. But, as I will argue below, Law and Society took somewhat of an anti-institutional turn in the 1970s, whilst mainstream sociology long avoided engaging in research on international phenomena. The result has been a dearth, although not a disappearance, of sociological perspectives in the study of many international issues. The sociological voice has been most noticeably absent in the field of human rights studies,[3] but it is also surprisingly little heard in debates about ICs.

Since sociology as a discipline more or less took itself out of the study of global institutions until quite recently, it is unsurprising that legal and political scientific analysis has come to dominate studies of ICs.[4] A plethora of advanced theories, particularly about the law and politics of European regional ICs, has been developed by political scientists and lawyers, but the "social," as in sociology, has generally evaporated from the understanding of international law and courts over the last 50 years. However, as I will draw attention to below, explicit references may be missing, but contemporary law and political science approaches to ICs implicitly draw on sociological insights about the role of law and courts in society. Moreover, since the early 2000s, substantial sociological studies of ICs and global governance structures have been carried out, more openly acknowledging the insight of some of the giants of sociology who early on developed advanced ways of understanding the role of law and legal institutions in society. In this chapter, I will reintroduce both classical and contemporary sociology into debates about international adjudication, highlighting important differences among the various fields of social science.

[1] Huber's original study, "Beiträge zur Kenntnis der soziologischen Grundlagen des Völkerrechts und der Staatengesellschaft" was published in 1910 in *Jahrbuch des öffentlichen Rechts der Gegenwart*.

[2] Martti Koskenniemi argues that French public international law scholarship in the period 1871–1950 had a distinct sociological dimension. M Koskenniemi, *The Gentle Civilizer of Nations: The Rise and Fall of International Law 1870–1960* (Cambridge University Press 2001).

[3] MR Madsen and G Verschraegen, "Making Human Rights Intelligible: An Introduction to Sociology of Human Rights" in MR Madsen and G Verschraegen (eds), *Making Human Rights Intelligible: Towards a Sociology of Human Rights* (Oxford: Hart 2013).

[4] This is also more generally true for the sociological analysis of international law. See M Hirsch, "The Sociology of International Law: Invitation to Study International Rules in Their Social Context" (2005) 55 U. Toronto L.J. 891. See on the corresponding developments in anthropology, SE Merry, "Anthropology and International Law" (2006) 35 Ann. Rev. Anthrop. 99.

The chapter is divided into three parts. In the first section, I outline how classical sociology can contribute to the study of ICs. My goal is to revitalize the rich heritage of the works of particularly Max Weber and Emile Durkheim and thereby frame a more macro-sociological perspective about the role of international adjudication in the contemporary world. Next I discuss first the ambiguity of law and society scholarship with regard to institutions, particularly legal institutions, so as to explain the paradox of both its relative scholarly absence in the field of ICs and its important insights into law and courts in the modern political sphere. Against this background I will demonstrate how the insights of both law and society and mainstream sociology of the period, in combination with work of the pioneers of sociology, were in the last decade turned into a set of innovative approaches to studying ICs as institutions embedded in society. Against this analysis and outline of theories, section three identifies a set of sociologically salient questions with respect to understanding ICs using both classical and contemporary sociology. It first looks into the question of institutions from a sociological perspective, then the place of agency in studies of ICs, and, finally, the notion of legitimacy as it is found in both classical and contemporary sociology and its implications for studying ICs.

1 Classical Sociological Perspectives on Law and Courts

Sociologists have long studied law and legal institutions in society. This is true for both the classics such as Weber and Durkheim and leading contemporary sociologists, for example Jürgen Habermas,[5] Pierre Bourdieu,[6] Niklas Luhmann,[7] and Bruno Latour.[8] Sociologists, however, study law and courts using a distinct starting-point. If law has as its overarching object of inquiry the normative order of legal norms, and political science's key object is politics and associated institutions and actors, sociology is above all concerned with society: either in the Durkheimian sense, as a pre-existing but evolving social structure within which action takes place, or in the revitalized Tardeian sense, as suggested by contemporary sociologists such as Bruno Latour,

[5] J Habermas, *Faktizität und Geltung: Beiträge zur Diskurstheorie des Rechts und des demokratischen Rechtsstaats* (Frankfurt am Main: Suhrkamp Verlag 1992).

[6] P Bourdieu, "The Force of Law: Toward a Sociology of the Juridical Field" (1987) 38 Hastings L. J. 805.

[7] N Luhmann, *Das Recht der Gesellschaft* (Frankfurt am Main: Suhrkamp 1993).

[8] B Latour, *La fabrique du droit: Une ethnographie du Conseil d'État* (Paris: La Découverte 2002).

as the outcome of networks of actors (and actants).[9] Between these two extremes, one finds a great diversity in approaches that differ most profoundly in their view on structures, agency, and materials. With regard to studying ICs more specifically, sociology typically construes institutions in a broader sense than is found in both law and political science: either as assemblages of practices within larger social fields or more generally as devices for ordering society. Both perspectives will be introduced in the following subsections in which I focus on what classic sociological theories can contribute to our understanding of law and courts. Classic sociology generally has twin objectives, namely to establish a new discipline and to conduct actual empirical studies of modern society. In other words, early sociologists wanted to explain modern society both by theory and empirical study, as well as develop the necessary tools for these undertakings. For the same reasons, the theories presented in the following tend to involve both macro-level theorizing of more general societal logics and middle-range empirical exploration of law and courts in society.

1.1 Interpretive sociology

Max Weber's analysis of the evolution of law in terms of a set of different ideal-typical forms of rationality is probably the most cited among the classics. It is also the one that comes closest to contemporary mainstream social science studies of ICs. Generally, Weber provides a set of typologies for describing the rise of modern Western law as an evolution from "formally irrational" and "substantively irrational" to law becoming "formally rational" and "substantively rational."[10] According to Weber, these rationalities generally correspond to different forms of domination: from charismatic to traditional to legal. Importantly, at no point does Weber claim a complete conversion from one domination or rationality to another. Rather, he maintains that elements of each of these ideal-typical representations of law are present in contemporary society, but to varying degrees. They are indeed ideal-typical representations in the sense that they are abstracted models devised to help identify society in a clearer and more systematic way in order to allow for comparison. When grounded in empirical studies, they provide a conceptual apparatus for the inevitable task of any social science, namely to make a selection and abstraction from the infinite multitude of social reality. With respect to examining ICs, they basically help turn ICs into tangible empirical objects of research.

As demonstrated in a recent study of the European Court of Human Rights (ECtHR), Weber provides a set of reflexive tools for understanding ICs as evolutionary institutions that develop specific institutional and legal rationalities, which are reflective of institutions' embedded rationality—or situated cognition—in their

[9] B Latour, *Reassembling the Social: An Introduction to Actor-Network Theory* (Oxford University Press 2005).

[10] M Weber, *Wirtschaft und Gesellschaft. Grundriss der verstehenden Soziologie* (Tübingen: Mohr 1980).

decision-making processes.[11] Most law and political science scholarship tends to view ICs in predetermined categories, for example, as transplanted institutions that resemble their national counterparts or other ICs, or on the basis of an abstracted hypothesis of institutional behavior or institutional design. A Weberian approach has instead its focal point in the historically founded different rationalities of the institution in question, and how these are reflective of both society at large and the very agents of the institution.[12] This particular way of approaching ICs also provides a sociologically-informed alternative for understanding questions related to the legitimacy of ICs; that is, legitimacy in this approach is neither tied up to a legalist notion of legitimacy via legality, nor as an abstracted political philosophical notion. Max Weber seeks instead to explain how legitimacy is contingent on different forms of domination—from traditional to charismatic to legally rational—and thereby embedded in society.[13]

According to Weber, at the end of the day what makes a certain practice of power legitimate is the process through which authority justifies its exercise of power and gains social acceptance. Applied to ICs, it follows that their legitimacy does not stem from them being *representative* of society; it stems from them being *reflective* of society.[14] For example, the US Supreme Court is not demographically or politically representative of American society, but it might very well reflect society and, thereby, justify its practices. In other words, the legitimacy of a given IC cannot simply be statistically deduced from the judges' representativeness of society and politics at large. This also means that even the best and most carefully thought-out procedures of elections of judges, in the most extreme cases seeking to make courts representative as a sort of quasi-democratic political institution, might ultimately fail if the court's practices are not reflective of society. On the other hand, the profiles of a specific set of judges might very well help them gain legitimacy in specific environments, ranging from law to politics and civil society.[15] Using this framework, it could be argued with respect to the cited example of the genesis of the ECtHR that its institutionalization in a way followed what Weber termed the "routinization of charisma": the initial institutionalization process was a legitimization process around the specific individuals and their practices. Ultimately, the authority of the ECtHR was largely derived from the high status of the bench and the way

[11] MR Madsen, "Legal Diplomacy—Law, Politics and the Genesis of Postwar European Human Rights" in SL Hoffmann (ed.), *Human Rights in the Twentieth Century: A Critical History* (Cambridge University Press 2011).

[12] Madsen, note 11. [13] Weber, note 10.

[14] The argument is further developed in MR Madsen, "Explaining the Power of International Courts in Their Context: From Legitimacy to Legitimization" RSCAS Policy Paper (Courts, Social Change and Judicial Independence) (2012) 7, 23.

[15] See also D Terris, CPR Romano, and L Swigart, *The International Judge: An Introduction to the Men and Women Who Decide the World's Cases* (Oxford University Press 2007). See also, in this handbook, Swigart and Terris, Ch. 28 and Romano, Ch. 5.

these judges developed a set of politically fine-tuned legal practices that reflected the social and political conditions under which it operated.[16]

From this brief introduction to Weber, the difference between contemporary law and political science explorations of ICs and the particular empirical and conceptual sensitivity of sociology generally speaking becomes clear. While mainstream political scientific examinations of ICs typically test rationalized hypotheses against different sets of data, the goal of a Weberian approach is different: it seeks to make law and courts intelligible as societal institutions.[17] The aim of this so-called "interpretive sociology" [*Verstehende Soziologie*] is precisely to link habits and motives to action, that is, to make action intelligible by corresponding action to the agents in terms of a specific form of "methodological individualism."[18] The prime example of this approach is Weber's famous analysis of the role of the Protestant spirit in the making of capitalism. Here the "spirit" of the agents—notably internalized norms of duty and correctness—is the backdrop for explaining the rapid growth of a capitalist economy in Germany. But as just shown, the same could be done on a smaller scale with regard to ICs, either by a study of the judges or the normative schemes in society, which drive the push for ICs.

Although Weberian sociology might appear as yet another grand attempt at deducing universal socio-logics, it should be stressed that its actual goal is not to devise a universal theory, but to explain society by creating a framework of inquiry that facilitates an exploration of micro- and macro-levels of society. First of all, Weber is not seeking to get rid of the usual units of middle-range social scientific analysis such as groups, collectives, and institutions, but is instead pointing to the basic observation that only individuals can have intentions. Consequently, individuals provide a key unit of analysis, even if the goal is not to understand individuals' motivations as such but societal development as driven by groups of individuals or, for example, institutions. As demonstrated in the above-cited study on the ECtHR, this is directly applicable to analyses of ICs. Yet, different from both the traditional legal realist take on legal actors and many of the subsequent legal realist-inspired studies of judicial behaviour, the focal point of such a Weberian study of ICs is not the individuals as such, but the societal and institutional developments, which can be made intelligible by exploring the individuals' motivations, and their impact on the rationalization of the institutions.[19] Thus, Weber provides above all

[16] MR Madsen, "The Protracted Institutionalisation of the Strasbourg Court: From Legal Diplomacy to Integrationist Jurisprudence" in MR Madsen and J Christoffersen (eds), *The European Court of Human Rights between Law and Politics* (Oxford University Press 2011).

[17] An exception to this trend is some historical institutionalist scholarship. See e.g., K Alter, *Establishing the Supremacy of European Law: The Making of an International Rule of Law in Europe* (Oxford University Press 2001).

[18] For an overview of the notion, see S Hewa, "The Genesis of Max Weber's 'Verstehende Soziologie'" (1988) 31 Acta Sociologica 143.

[19] Cf. Madsen, note 16.

a historical-sociological approach to law with a focus on the transformation of the institutions of society of which courts are but one. Similarly, ICs are institutions of global society and can be studied as such using Weber.

1.2 Structural functionalism and systems theory

Weberian insights have also inspired subsequent notions of rational choice, which are central to much current scholarship on ICs. Drawing on Weber's notion of "purposive" or "goal rationality" [*Zweckrationalität*],[20] it was Talcott Parsons, a Weber follower himself, who set the scene for some of this later influential scholarship in his seminal book *The Structure of Social Action* (1937) in which he introduced the notion of the "action frame of reference."[21] I will not, however, pursue this connection further, but instead outline the other key inspiration to Parsons's work, namely Emile Durkheim, another of the classical sociologists, who made an early contribution to the understanding of law in society. As I will argue, Durkheim has had a monumental impact on studies of international law and courts, even if it is rarely acknowledged.

According to Durkheim, law is an index of social solidarity—it represents the evolution of social integration. This is explained in Durkheim's famous evolutionary model, outlining the transformation from primitive to modern society and with that, a change in forms of solidarity from mechanical to organic, following a thesis of societal differentiation.[22] Just like Weber, he basically links law and its institutions to the emergence of modern society. Durkheim has, however, less to offer with regard to understanding courts specifically. He views them as mainly "deliberating on behalf of society in a manner somewhat similar to that of the legislature."[23] His main interest is instead law as a means of stabilizing and integrating society. According to Durkheim, primitive (or traditional) societies are generally kept together by kinship and tribal justice. In modern societies interdependences between different specialized areas of work secure the integration of society. In this regard, law has an important function as an instrument of integrating these differentiated social spheres. This is precisely what he means by arguing that courts "deliberate" on behalf of society at large—and with the goal of securing society's coherence against its increased differentiation and specialization.

[20] Corresponding to the overall framework, Weber operated with more forms of action rationalities. In addition to the instrumental character of "purposive rationality," his notion of "value-rationality" [*Wertrationalität*] should be mentioned here.

[21] T Parsons, *The Structure of Social Action* (New York: McGraw Hill 1937) 43–51.

[22] É Durkheim, *De la division du travail social: étude sur l'organisation des sociétés supérieures* (Paris: Alcan 1893).

[23] R Cotterrell, *Emile Durkheim: Law in a Moral Domain* (Stanford University Press 1999) 172.

Durkheim's approach is directly applicable to understanding the role of ICs in contemporary global society. In modern social scientific terms, the question is what function ICs perform with respect to integrating regional or global society, rather than, as is most often the case in the current literature, the more specific and limited functional aims of individual ICs. The heuristic take-away of posing the question in the broader sociological way, which is proposed by Durkheimian sociology, is that it avoids trapping the research in the functional purposes of specific institutions which have tended to dominate debates on ICs. Instead it is concerned with a set of broader questions, which involves states, international courts, and organizations as providers of specialized labor of a crucial kind in contemporary society. The overall aim is to understand society at large—both its specialized components and what ensures coherence notwithstanding specialization. Such a macro-level analysis of ICs and global society is yet to be conducted using post-Durkheimian sociology, but the basic social scientific tools are clearly available.[24]

The most direct and pervasive influence of Durkheimian sociology is clearly the focus on functions, as well as what later becomes the notion of systems in structural-functionalism and systems theory which both draw on the Durkheimian differentiation thesis. In fact, considering the vast body of functionalist literature, particularly in political science and law, the impact of this way of perceiving and constructing the social world can hardly be overstated. To illustrate, Armin von Bogdandy and Ingo Venzke even describe functionalism as virtually the orthodoxy of legal research.[25] Another example is the often-cited thesis of the fragmentation of international law, which is also based on such a functionalist reading of public international law.[26] In both cases, they build on a very long tradition in international law of perceiving public international law in functionalist terms. Hersch Lauterpacht's *The Function of Law in the International Community* (1933) is an important reference to legal scholarship as well as to the application of the Durkheimian idea of precisely linking international law and international community.[27] In political science, one will come across similar claims to those of lawyers with respect to understanding ICs and international law in terms of functions and functionalities. Although the bigger societal picture is often missing in the analysis of both lawyers and political

[24] Although not focused on ICs, the most explicit attempt at understanding the international legal ordering of society is probably found in G Teubner, *Constitutional Fragments: Societal Constitutionalism and Globalization* (Oxford University Press 2012). As concerns the European level, see particularly C Thornhill, "The Formation of a European Constitution: An Approach from Historical-Political Sociology" (2012) 8 Int'l J.L. in Context 354. See also R Münch, "Constructing a European Society by Jurisdiction" (2008) 14 Eur. L.J. 519.

[25] A von Bogdandy and I Venzke, "On the Functions of International Courts: An Appraisal in Light of Their Burgeoning Public Authority" (2013) 26 Leiden J. Int'l L. 49.

[26] M Koskenniemi et al., "Fragmentation of International Law? Postmodern Anxieties" (2002) 15 Leiden J. Int'l L. 553; see also, in this handbook, Dupuy and Viñuales, Ch. 7.

[27] H Lauterpacht, *The Function of Law in the International Community* (Oxford University Press 1933).

scientists, this is nevertheless an important point of convergence between classic sociology and contemporary law and political science explorations of ICs.

Drawing on socio-legal studies of (national) courts and society, von Bogdandy and Venzke offer a good summary of how functionalism is also helpful for more specifically theorizing the functions of ICs in international society. These are: 1) *settling disputes*, 2) *stabilizing normative expectations*, 3) *making Law*, and 4) *controlling and legitimating public authority*.[28] Although they do not cite Durkheim, these functions clearly echo a Durkheimian way of thinking of courts in society. Similar functionalist claims can be found in a host of sociologies of courts in society in the tradition of structural functionalism and systems theory, starting with Parsons, who argues that a court's main function is to integrate society's different sub-systems by "mitigat[ing] potential elements of conflicts and to oil the machinery of social intercourse."[29] Building on the combined insights of structural functionalism and notions of differentiation and integration, key students of Parsons have provided even more detailed explorations of particularly the "integrative functions" of courts in society as in the case of Harry C Bredemaier[30] and the specific role of law and courts to "stabilize normative expectations" as developed by Niklas Luhmann.[31]

What functionalism basically offers is a general sociological theory of law and courts in society based on a specific rational reading of courts as being functional to a differentiated society. While it is hard to disagree with the overriding claims of these theories, partly because of the level of abstraction they operate on, it is plain to see that they also tend, to a considerable extent, to reproduce the very claims of formalist legal scholarship and even law itself. This criticism can also be directed at much political science literature using functionalism in a narrow way, establishing a direct causality link between an identified problem and its solution via ICs.[32] This critique is also precisely the starting-point for what can be labeled "critical studies of international law and courts," which as a common thread seek to go beyond the self-descriptions of institutions and agents with the goal of providing what they believe is a more realistic understanding of law and society. In fact, they seek to study what one well-known sociological functionalist, Robert K Merton, famously termed the "dysfunctions of courts" whereby he himself approached critical studies as well as fundamentally challenged functionalism as a viable sociological paradigm.[33]

[28] Compare this to the goals defined in Y Shany, "Assessing the Effectiveness of International Courts: A Goal-Based Approach" (2012) 106 AJIL 225, 243–7.

[29] T Parsons, "The Law and Social Control" in WM Evan (ed.), *Law and Sociology: Exploratory Essays* (New York: Free Press 1962).

[30] HC Bredemaier, "Law as an Integrative Mechanism" in WM Evan, note 29.

[31] Luhmann, note 7.

[32] E.g., B Koremenos, C Lipson, and D Snidal, "The Rational Design of International Institutions" (2001) 55 Int'l Org.761.

[33] RK Merton, *Social Theory and Social Structure* (New York: Simon & Schuster 1949).

1.3 Marxism and critical theory

As regards sociology, critical studies can at a general level be said to have their origins in Marxism, traditionally described as the third branch of classic sociology. While it shares with the Durkheimian school an interest in social structures, the underlying assumption of coherence of functionalism is explicitly rejected in the Marxist scholarship, for which the overriding driver of societal evolution is conflict and domination.[34] Classic Marxism has mainly an interest in courts and justice as expressions and tools of social domination as exercised by existing dominant classes. Judges are likewise viewed as agents of a suppressive superstructure mainly put in place to ensure the status quo and, thus, the interests of the ruling elite. Put simply, if functionalism takes its starting-point in a thesis of differentiation, classic Marxism takes it in stratification. There are, however, very important differences between classic (and orthodox) Marxism and its main focus on industrial relations in terms of property owners and laborers, and modern critical studies and their ambition to critique modern society more generally with the goal of liberating the individual from the forms of domination characterizing it.[35]

I will not dwell here on the myriad of schools of critical studies and their differences and convergences, but simply underscore that some important elements of Marxist and critical thinking have made significant impact on contemporary sociological studies of ICs—and often in combination with Weberian readings of institutions and professions. These include, for example, the emphasis on elites as key agents of law, the conceptualization of international law and courts as adversarial social spaces and the focus on the power of law—both as symbolic power, following the Bourdieusian tradition,[36] and as a structural phenomenon with regard to, for example, notions of empire. Whereas functionalist sociology, as argued above, has significantly influenced both legal and political scientific analysis of ICs, starting in the late 1960s it overall tended to lose much of its appeal as a sociological paradigm.[37] The actual fate of functionalism is of course debatable, but what is certain is that the combined issues of elites, power, and conflict of the critical camp have much more come to define contemporary sociological scholarship on ICs. In the following section, emphasis will therefore be put on this branch of sociology with the goal of accentuating distinct sociological contributions to understanding ICs.

[34] An attempt at devising an explicit Marxist agenda for the study of international law is found in B. S. Chimni, "Marxism and International Law: A Contemporary Analysis" (1999) 34 Econ. & Pol. Wkly. 337.

[35] The term critical theory is largely contested and covers in practice a whole range of approaches, ranging from the Frankfurter School to many contemporary post-structural sociologies.

[36] P Bourdieu, *Language and Symbolic Power* (Cambridge, MA: Harvard University Press 1991).

[37] Notable exceptions to this overall trend is the work of Niklas Luhmann and some contemporary organization theory as explained below.

2 From Law and Society to International Courts in Context

I have so far sought to demonstrate how classical sociological theories have provided a series of general studies of law and courts in society with considerable relevance for understanding ICs and society. Sociology has obviously evolved considerably since Weber, Marx, and Durkheim. The more recent specialization of sociology into sub-disciplines such as sociology of law and, in the US context, the Law and Society movement, have further made for some more specific yet ambiguous research paths in this regard.[38] Generally, the sociology of law has maintained an overall interest in (national) courts[39] —an interest that in recent years has been intensified in the debates on judicialization and the growing role of constitutional courts.[40] However, in what might be termed the anti-institutional turn of much law and society research, beginning in the 1970s, many scholars started shying away from research on international law and institutions. As an observable consequence, in the United States, contemporary judicial studies have been increasingly dominated by political scientists and not sociologists. In the following, I first explore the original law and society stance on legal institutions. I then outline a recent scholarship, which draws on law and society and contemporary sociology for explaining ICs and their linkage to global society.

2.1 The ambiguity of institutions in law and society scholarship

From its very beginnings in the mid-1960s, law and society has been a heterogeneous field of research. Nevertheless, what has kept it together is a collective interest in a critique of both formal law and legal formalism. In some ways, law and society has developed as an outgrowth of earlier legal realism, particularly American legal realism with which it also shared its original geographical focus. With respect to the subject of this chapter, however, the anti-formalism and anti-institutionalism of much law and society scholarship has in one important aspect made it take a very different turn than American legal realism, which was largely court-centered. On the contrary, and inspired by the *Zeitgeist* of the late 1960s and 1970s, law and society scholarship has developed a distinct focus on the alternatives to courts in terms

[38] A third related path which shall not, however, be examined here is of course Critical Legal Studies.

[39] For an overview of this literature, see Ch. 7 in R Cotterrell, *The Sociology of Law: An Introduction* (London: Butterworths 1992).

[40] For a good overview of this literature, see Thornhill, note 24, at 354–5.

of alternative dispute resolution and even alternatives to law in terms of informal law.[41] This, combined with its original US focus, has become somewhat of an obstacle to studying international law and institutions.[42] Or, as I will argue below, it has required a "detour" via less formalized international law and institutions to eventually find a converging interest in particularly international criminal law over the last decade.

Similar patterns of relative disinterest with regard to law and legal institutions can also be found in mainstream sociology during the same period.[43] The area of human rights, perhaps one of the most salient societal evolutions of the post-World War II era and thus seemingly of interest to both sociology and law and society, is highly illustrative in this respect. Law and society research, due to its precise object of inquiry, took an interest in international human rights fairly early on, but mainly as part of the overall critical agenda, and thus opted for studying NGOs in international law and other ways of addressing international law from below. Sociology at large was in fact far more reluctant to address human rights and its corresponding architecture of international law and courts. Human rights, to put it simply, were not considered a genuine sociological object of study.[44] Sociologists generally saw it as marred by debates which, as concerns law, were either highly normative or formalist or, in the case of political science, dominated by rationalist theoretical notions essentially foreign to the core of sociology, or entirely driven by statistical demonstration based on positivist assumptions. Further alienating sociologists from this specific field has been, on the one hand, the normative philosophical explorations of the idea and ideal of universal human rights, and, on the other hand, the parallel debates in anthropology on universalism and relativism of human rights. Many sociologists simply perceived this as an ideological abstraction.[45]

The eventual emergence of what now is undoubtedly a growing sociological scholarship on international law and ICs was in part driven by studies interested in the globalization and transnationalization of law and legal professionals. Since at least the early 1980s, a number of sociologists of law started investigating what

[41] Compare BG Garth, "Tilting the Justice System: From ADR as Idealistic Movement to a Segmented Market in Dispute Resolution" (2002) 18 Georgia State U. L. Rev. 927.

[42] An exception to the US focus was the so-called Law and Development Movement, which was led by Law and Society scholars such as Bill Felstiner, Marc Galanter, and David Trubek.

[43] It should perhaps be pointed out that during the same period in IR, as well as political science more generally, studies of ICs was predominantly the domain of a small specialized group of researchers. The proliferation of studies of ICs has in practice gone hand in hand with the proliferation of ICs themselves in recent years.

[44] Madsen and Verschraegen, note 3.

[45] There is in a way nothing particularly new about this as Durkheim, Weber, and Marx were all highly skeptical about the possibility of and indeed need for a universalistic and normative basis for human rights. In fact, until recently the sociology of citizenship has in many ways come to function as a kind of substitute for a sociology of human rights. See e.g., BS Turner, *Vulnerability and Human Rights* (Pennsylvania University Press 2006).

was increasingly termed "transnational legal phenomena."[46] A seminal book in this regard, as well as with respect to subsequent sociological scholarship on international institutions and courts, is the analysis of international commercial arbitration conducted by Yves Dezalay and Bryant Garth in *Dealing in Virtue*.[47] Using both legal and sociological insights, they demonstrated how the battle over the form and the law of international commercial arbitration could be explained as a battle between not only different forms of expertise (European academic law vs. American-style Wall Street law), but also as a clash between different global elites. The work is based on two different research traditions which are brought together via a set of broader conceptual frameworks provided by the sociologist Pierre Bourdieu: first, a sociology of professions with a view to analyzing how professions increasingly compete with one another in the construction of new transnational markets and arenas;[48] secondly, a sociology of elites with the aim of exploring how a set of distinct social groups of (legal) agents hold the power to define new areas of legal practice, with consequences not only for the profession at large, but also for international politics and society.[49] Drawing on Pierre Bourdieu, they frame these battles as social *fields*, that is, as spaces of contestation over defining the law in which different agents occupy positions relative to the portfolio of capitals they can muster and which are "capitalized" according to the logic of the specific field in question.[50]

Dezalay and Garth's work has also a methodological feature, which has turned out to be of special interest to understanding ICs. Although legal institutions are clearly important to their studies, they are not taking center stage in the original study on international commercial arbitration and even less so in their subsequent studies of the role of professional battles in the transformation of states in Latin America[51] and Asia.[52] What they instead provide is a sociological alternative to the assumption of many studies in both law and political science that institutions in themselves can explain the emergence of new transnational legal fields. Much closer to neo-institutionalist scholarship on organizational fields,[53] yet different,

[46] E.g., Boaventura de Sousa Santos, *Toward a New Common Sense: Law, Science and Politics in the Paradigmatic Transition* (London: Routledge 1995). See also, in this handbook, Steinitz, Ch. 16.

[47] Y Dezalay and BG Garth, *Dealing in Virtue. International Commercial Arbitration and the Construction of a Transnational Legal Order* (Chicago: University of Chicago Press 1996).

[48] Y Dezalay and D Sugerman (eds), *Professional Competition and Professional Power: Lawyers, Accountants and the Social Construction of Markets* (London: Routledge 1995).

[49] Y Dezalay, "Les courtiers de l'international: Héritiers cosmopolites, mercenaires de l'impérialisme et missionnaires de l'universel" (2004) 151–2 Actes de la recherche en sciences sociales 5.

[50] Bourdieu, note 6; see also Y Dezalay and MR Madsen, "The Force of Law and Lawyers: Pierre Bourdieu and the Reflexive Sociology of Law" (2012) 8 Ann. Rev. L. & Soc. Sci. 433.

[51] Y Dezalay and BG Garth, *The Internationalization of Palace Wars: Lawyers, Economists, and the Contest to Transform Latin American States* (University of Chicago Press 2002).

[52] Y Dezalay and BG Garth, *Asian Legal Revivals: Lawyers in the Shadow of Empire* (University of Chicago Press 2010).

[53] E.g., PJ DiMaggio and WW Powell, "The Iron Cage Revisited: Institutional Isomorphism and Collective Rationality in Organizational Fields" (1983) 48 Am. Sociological Rev. 147.

they claim that individual agents, and particularly the agents' personal and professional trajectories into the fields and institutions in question, provide unique data for understanding how institutions come about and transform. Using a methodology, which they term "collective biographies," a form of prosopography, they map out the social characteristics of the social spaces of institutions in terms of the combined and accumulated trajectories of the main agents.[54] This is also where they deploy Bourdieusian notions of capitals—social, educational, political, legal, etc.—to explore the specific legal elite formations of these socio-legal spaces. Dezalay and Garth's identification of legal elites as an entrance to studying transnational legal fields has had considerable impact on a series of in-depth empirical studies of ICs, ranging from the areas of international criminal law to European law, which emerged at about the same time in the beginning of the 2000s.

2.2 The new sociology of international courts

The International Criminal Tribunal for the Former Yugoslavia (ICTY) was analyzed in the influential book *Justice in the Balkans* by John Hagan.[55] Coming from criminology and law and society studies, Hagan very openly states that his inspiration came from the insights of Dezalay and Garth on the role of legal agency as particularly developed in *Dealing in Virtue*.[56] His goal is, however, more institutional than that found in Dezalay and Garth, yet he uses precisely the described methodology of examining the trajectories of the main agents in order to map the institution in question and its transformation. Hagan more concretely scrutinizes the interplay between investigators, prosecutors, and witnesses, as well as specific powerful individuals employed by the tribunal (emblematically Richard Goldstone, Louise Arbour, and Carla Del Ponte), in a complex analysis of the making of humanitarian and international criminal law, and how it eventually gains a force of law with a reference to the Bourdieusian conception of the legal field.[57] What is meant by the latter is that to understand the power of law, one has to study the social conditions making that power possible. And that is precisely what John Hagan's study does through its in-depth examination of the various players and emerging institutions producing international justice with a legal force in the Balkans.

[54] Compare this to the more institutionalist version of Bourdieusian sociology of organizations presented in M Emirbayer and V Johnson, "Bourdieu and organizational analysis" (2008) 37 Theory & Soc'y 1.

[55] J Hagan, *Justice in the Balkans. Prosecuting War Crimes in the Hague Tribunal* (University of Chicago Press 2003).

[56] Hagan explains the precise usage in Ch. 22 of S Halliday and P Schmidt, *Conducting Law and Society Research: Reflections on methods and Practices* (Cambridge University Press 2009).

[57] See J Hagan and R Levi, "Crimes of War and the Force of Law" (2005) 83 Soc. Forces 1499.

From Hagan's original study one can trace a more general sociological interest in international criminal law and its new set of associated institutions.[58] Interestingly, this scholarship manages very well to combine insights from earlier law and society studies on the informal sides of law with the analysis of the less institutionalized practices of international law and institutions. An example is the role of mediation and alternative conflict resolution in the area of international criminal law and war crimes.[59] Similarly, they combine contemporary criminology with new questions derived from the movement towards criminalizing war crimes and its international institutionalization and judicialization. Generally, by defining their object of inquiry in less institutional and legal terms than the mainstream law and political science scholarship in the area, they open up for an analysis of the various social spaces in which the possible—and sometimes failed—push for institutionalization and judicialization are played out.[60] A common thread in this literature is the focus on the agency of international law and institutions, yet its actual place is clearly disputed among the scholars in question.

The other branch of sociology of ICs that has found an inspiration in both the work of Bourdieu and that of Dezalay and Garth is a set of projects related to exploring the emergence of a field of European law with a particular focus on the two European inter- and supranational courts: the ECtHR and the Court of Justice of the EU (formerly the ECJ). Using these approaches has enabled these authors to examine the interplay between the agency of European supranational courts and the simultaneous transformation of the social structures in which they evolve.[61] Moreover, this novel approach to the double-structuring of European law by the interplay of agency and structural transformation has allowed them to revise the taken-for-granted story of the emergence of European law and the role played by supra- and international courts in this process.[62] By using a distinct

[58] A number of these scholars have contributed to two of the special issues (nos 173 and 174) in 2008 of *Actes de la recherche en sciences sociales*.

[59] E.g., SK Ivkovich and J Hagan, "La politique de punition et le siège de Sarajevo: Vers une application de la théorie du conflit à la perception d'une (in)justice internationale"(2008) 3 Actes de la recherche en sciences sociales 62.

[60] An example is Julien Serrousi, "The Cause of Universal Jurisdiction: The Rise and Fall of an International Mobilisation" in Y Dezalay and BG Garth (eds), *Lawyers and the Construction of Transnational Justice* (London: Routledge 2012); see also P-Y Condé, *Des juges à La Haye. Formation d'une judiciabilité universaliste, des amis de la paix à la lutte contre l'impunité* (Paris: École Normale Supérieure de Cachan 2012).

[61] Most explicitly in Madsen, note 16.

[62] See e.g., A Vauchez, "The transnational politics of judicialization. *Van Gend en Loos* and the making of EU polity" (2010) 16 Eur. L.J. 1; see also A Cohen, "Constitutionalism Without Constitution: Transnational Elites Between Political Mobilization and Legal Expertise in the Making of a Constitution for Europe (1940s–1960s)" (2007) 32 Law & Social Inquiry 109. On human rights, see MR Madsen, *La genèse de l'Europe des droits de l'homme: Enjeux juridiques et stratégies d'Etat (France, Grande-Bretagne et pays scandinaves, 1945–1970)* (Presses universitaires de Strasbourg 2010).

power-perspective on the making of international (European) law and its relative force, they have highlighted how larger societal and geopolitical currents have had an enduring impact on the evolution of European law and institutions, as well as European integration more generally.[63] Not unlike many of the studies cited above, these inquiries into the deeper socio-logics of European ICs combine insights from theories of professions and professionals with critical approaches to law and its power in society, which highlights how law is mobilized, in specific cases or as part of broader legal movements.[64] It is exactly because of these combined interests that their analysis tends to find their overriding frameworks in sociological theories in the tradition of, on the one hand, Max Weber and the power and evolution of professions, and, on the other hand, theories of social configurations such as those of Norbert Elias, Michel Foucault, and Pierre Bourdieu.

Contemporary sociology-based studies of ICs are not, however, confined to the cited studies, even if they right now stand out as the perhaps most distinct sociological contributions to the understanding of ICs.[65] Within the broader camps of sociological institutionalism and, to a slightly lesser extent, historical institutionalism, one finds numerous studies, which could be assigned the label sociological. However, as already suggested above in the section on classical sociology, some currents of sociology are by definition more focused on institutions than others and, thus, more inclined to be interested in ICs as such. Functionalism in this respect has a rather large group of followers in both law and political science. In sociology its role has been used in either more organizational analysis of ICs or to depict the global structures of society. The latter is either in a Luhmannian tradition of global society,[66] in terms of world system theory of Immanuel Wallerstein[67] or, in more constructivist terms, as "global culture."[68] While organizational studies are focused on deeper institutional logics, neither of the approaches in the second camp is interested in ICs per se, but rather—following broadly speaking the

[63] A Cohen and MR Madsen, "Cold War Law: Legal Entrepreneurs and the Emergence of a European Legal Field (1945–1965)" in V Gessner and D Nelken (eds), *European Ways of Law: Towards a European Sociology of Law* (Oxford: Hart Publishing 2007); MR Madsen, "The Geopolitics of European Law: The ECtHR, the ECJ and the Foundation of the European Legal Field (1950–1980)" (Law and Society Annual Conference 2011).

[64] E.g., Vauchez, note 62; see also Ch. 4 on jurist advocacy networks in K Alter, *The European Court's Political Power. Selected Essays* (Oxford University Press 2009).

[65] These sociological insights have also been widely used by historians interested in European law and integration, E.g., M Rasmussen, "The Origins of a Legal Revolution: The Early History of the European Court of Justice" (2008) 14:2 J. Eur. Integration Hist. 77.

[66] E.g., R Stichweh, *Die Weltgesellschaft: Soziologische Analysen* (Frankfurt am Main: Suhrkamp 2000); see also note 24.

[67] E.g., I Wallerstein, *The Modern World-System I: Capitalist Agriculture and and the Origins of the European World-Economy in the Sixteenth Century* (New York: Academic Press 1974).

[68] FJ Lechner and J Boli, *World Culture. Origins and Consequences* (Oxford: Blackwell 2005).

Durkheimian tradition—of how ICs to varying degrees are important institutions in the transformation of the deeper structures of society under contemporary globalization.[69]

It is self-evidently in the field of sociology of organizations that one comes across studies that more specifically address questions directly relevant to understanding the institutional dynamics and problems of ICs. Yet, while organizational sociologists have offered sophisticated frameworks and theories for such analysis, it has been predominantly lawyers and political scientists who have done the actual empirical work, importing insights from the sociology of organizations for solving puzzles in existing research on ICs. The work of law professor Yuval Shany on the effectiveness of ICs is illuminating in this regard.[70] With regard to the second camp of research, a particularly interesting branch of sociology is the "world culture" literature, which in many ways builds on the earlier Stanford school of "world polity" theory.[71] Frank J. Lechner and John Boli's analysis of the making of the International Criminal Court (ICC) provides in this regard a highly illustrative case of the sociological "world culture" research paradigm.[72] Being precisely interested in the production of world culture by a host of different globalizing practices, they emphasize the ways in which the idea of the ICC and its legal codification triggered the mobilization of more than a hundred states and some 800 NGOs.[73] This mass mobilization around the ICC they perceive as "world culture in action" and, thus, as a distinct indicator of the very existence of a global societal layer in certain fields of practice.[74] Characteristic of this scholarship on the evolving structures of world society, a single court, even one as emblematic as the ICC, is seen as no more than a specific attempt at instituting global culture. It is clearly an important attempt with a long history of fighting war by international law dating back at least a century, but the actual research interest is broader and when it includes ICs they are seen as particular ways, among many others, of instituting and articulating global society.

[69] A somewhat similar view, although based on a more historical sociological account of globalization is found in S Sassen, *Territory, Authority, Rights: From Medieval to Global Assemblages* (Princeton University Press 2006).

[70] Shany, note 28.

[71] E.g., JW Meyer, "World Society, Institutional Theories, and the Actor" (2010) 36 Ann. Rev. Sociology 1.

[72] Lechner and Boli, note 68, at Ch. 10.

[73] Lechner and Boli, note 68, at 221. For a further analysis of the role of NGOs in world culture see J Boli and GM Thomas, "World Culture in the World Polity: A Century of International Non-Governmental Organization" (1997) 62 Am. Sociological Rev. 171.

[74] Lechner and Boli, note 68, at 230.

3 Key Questions of Sociology and International Courts

In the following sections I will summarize the presented classical and contemporary sociological studies in terms of some overriding sociological questions with respect to understanding ICs. I first recapitulate what sociologists generally understand as institutions and the implications for defining ICs as objects of inquiry. I then address the place of agency (and structure) in the sociological analysis of ICs, and finally analyze questions of ICs' legitimacy from a sociological perspective. In each of the sections, I highlight what non-sociologists can gain from adding a dose of sociology to their work on ICs.

3.1 Institutions and courts—a sociological view

With few exceptions, across the range of sociological literature presented in this chapter, sociological approaches to ICs connect, unsurprisingly, the study of ICs to society, national or international. They do so, however, in considerably different ways. A telling example is the cited study by John Hagan on the ICTY. This study is generally illustrative of an unambiguously sociological take on institutions, indeed a distinct form of sociological institutionalism of ICs, which is to an extent driven by Bourdieusian insights, yet goes well beyond this original inspiration in its final analysis. Although Hagan is not seeking to enter the long-standing debate on sociological institutionalism, his study can be read as a sophisticated application of sociological institutionalism to the study of ICs. Generally, sociological institutionalism is understood as a form of neo-institutionalism that conceives institutions in a broader sense—often in terms of processes or fields—broader than both historical and rational choice institutionalism. Moreover, it generally emphasizes the interplay of the formal and the informal sides to institutions by highlighting, for example, relationships, routines, and other "frames of meaning."[75] This is also precisely the reason that earlier law and society scholarship on the informal processes of law now connects increasingly well with contemporary sociological inquiries into international law and institutions as argued above.

This apparent broadening of the field of inquiry of ICs also underlines more generally the aim of many sociologists in their encounter with ICs. Above all, they seek to find ways to break with the formalism of both law and political science in the

[75] For a good comparative introduction, see PA Hall and RCR Taylor, "Political Science and the Three New Institutionalisms" (1996) XLIV Pol. Stud. 936.

understanding of ICs. They attempt this by, at one and the same time, paying more attention to both agency and social structures, and to how these combined levels of social life have an impact on the formation of legal knowledge, its practice and eventual institutionalization and juridification. With the exception of some forms of functionalism that has its focal point in the interplay of complex systems in a more stabilized order, a common focus in most of the cited literature is precisely processes of change and how this impacts on institutional evolution. The overriding question of many sociological studies of ICs is therefore how to explain change at the level of ICs and at the level of global society. The response is anything but unified and involves practically all the outlined approaches from Weber and Marx to contemporary sociologies such as those developed by Bourdieu and Latour with their opposing views of the notion of social structures.

Accordingly, an important contribution of sociological studies of ICs is in many ways at the level of methodology—and even epistemology. Instead of taking for granted the notion of institutions as merely a legal-political phenomenon which more or less delineates itself, sociologists are in search of ways of exploring legal institutions as social institutions. They are thus in search of finding tangible empirical objects for making institutions intelligible as a sociological phenomenon, but without leaving out law and politics. In simple terms, if the dominant nexus for understanding ICs has been law and politics, most of the cited sociological studies are highly evocative of how ICs can be studied using a different nexus consisting of law, politics, *and* society. And it is precisely by this turn to what can be referred to as "political sociology of ICs" that they at times provide a radically different reading of ICs where agents and their collective rituals—for example *Festschrifte*[76] or the semi-scholarly behavior of judges in terms of *Professorenrecht*—might be decisive micro-institutional practices for the successful development of an IC when analyzed with respect to macro-evolution of a given social sphere. This has real implications for the study of ICs, as the very fundamental category at stake—courts—are subject to scrutiny. In other words, rather than uncritically taking a starting-point in the pre-existing legal circumscriptions of ICs, sociologists suggest instead that a critical stage in the analysis of ICs is to find that the actual social spaces in different ICs exist as a set of specific social practices.

3.2 Agency, structures and international courts

Closely linked to these observations on the broader sociological notion of institutions is the question of the agency of ICs; that is, who besides judges constitute the agency of ICs. With the exception of systems theory and its variations, the cited

[76] A Vauchez, "Keeping the dream alive: the European Court of Justice and the transnational fabric of integrationist jurisprudence" (2012) 4 Eur. Pol. Sci. Rev. 51.

literature seems to quite consequentially combine analysis of social movements and transnational elites with an examination of the usual suspects of ICs, such as international judges and agents of state politics and strategies. A distinction can, however, be drawn between studies that analyze NGOs and legal networks in terms of transnational "norm entrepreneurs" following the work of Margaret E Keck and Kathryn Sikkink,[77] *and* a post-structuralist approaches that seek to understand the overlapping and interdependent practices of a larger set of mobilizations toward a given IC or field of law. It is typically in the latter that one finds a more complex set of agents.

With regard to the "norm entrepreneur" literature, the distinction between sociology and political science is in practice razor-thin. While sociology largely provided the original impetus to "social movements" studies, political scientists have undoubtedly been better at capturing new transnational movements around, for example, human rights or the International Criminal Court. Nevertheless, in the most studied area of judicialized international law, EU law, the vast majority of studies pay little attention—and most often none—to these levels of agency.[78] An exception is the more recent work of Karen Alter. Here she makes the claim that to explain the supranational revolution of the ECJ in the 1960s, one needs to carefully examine the role of transnational jurist advocacy networks in Europe during the same period, and, in particular, the different law associations established, often with the help of the European institutions themselves, to precisely promote European law, i.e., EC law.[79] Studying the same period, the political sociologist, Antoine Vauchez, concurs that what Alter terms the "kitchen cabinet" of European law is crucial for explaining the eventual success of the ECJ's landslide decisions of the early 1960s. As Vauchez provocatively but convincingly argues, these decisions were not initially perceived as landslide decisions. Establishing them as landslide decisions was largely the outcome of a systematic lobbying by jurist networks and associations seeking to promote EC law and using these early decisions as their case in point.[80] These findings might come across as extreme constructivism, but they are empirically well-grounded as well as evocative of a sociological explanation of the creation of case law as a symbolic form and force.

The clearest difference between political science approaches to networks and sociological studies of this level of agency is, however, the way in which networks are understood with regard to larger social structures.[81] While political scientists

[77] ME Keck and K Sikkink, *Activists Beyond Borders: Advocacy Networks in International Politics* (Ithaca, NY: Cornell University Press 1998).

[78] The exception being H Schepel and R Wesseling, "The Legal Community: Judges, Lawyers, Officials and Clerks in the Writing of Europe" (1997) 3 Eur. L.J. 165.

[79] Alter, note 64. [80] Vauchez, note 62.

[81] For a sociological critique of the dominant transnational advocacy network theory, see MR Madsen, "Reflexivity and the Construction of the International Object: The Case of Human Rights" (2011) 5 Int'l Pol. Sociology 259, 265–7.

engaged in this branch of research tend to couple ICs, civil society, and global governance in a more abstract analysis,[82] sociologists on their part tend to link specific mobilizations around international law to larger structural social changes. An example is the cited "world culture" literature where these mobilizations, as outlined, are used as empirical evidence of the emergence of large-scale societal structures at the global level. In a more empirically detailed way, political sociologist Antonin Cohen has explored the emergence of what he has termed the European field of power with the goal of examining the particular role and power of law and legal institutions (in particular the ECJ) in the making of European integration.[83] A central claim is that Europe is constructed in a competition between different transnational elites over defining this new area of practice. The actual European institutional set-up, including the ECJ, is a causal consequence of the successes of specific legal and economic elites in these battles. Using an even larger framework of inquiry, I have studied the emergence and transformation of the ECtHR by tracking the genesis and transformation of human rights as new and powerful legal, political, and social forces in Europe since World War II.[84] In this study transnational legal entrepreneurs take center stage, yet in an ever-changing encounter with other experts, including diplomats, statesmen, and activists. It is the interface of "transnational power elites,"[85] and the social structures and legal and political institutions they help produce, that form the core of the explanation of the rise of the ECtHR in this study. Using these broader approaches, sociologists provide a very different take on how law is produced. They launch a significant critique of the widespread assumption that law exists as a normative structure by instead exploring law in terms of knowledge and symbolic power and how it in some cases produces norms, including legal norms.

3.3 Legitimacy and legitimization

These examples of the structural and institutional effects of the permanent mêlées between competing transnational elites offer yet another illustration of the different way sociologists define the object of inquiry when they embark on studying ICs. While many find their preferred theoretical tool for both conceptualizing and empirically exploring these social configurations in, for example, the work of Pierre Bourdieu, notably his notion of social fields, at the more institutional level, they link

[82] As is done extremely well in HN Haddad, "Judicial Institution Builders: NGOs and International Human Rights Courts" (2012) 11 J. Hum. Rts. 126; see also R Cichowski, *The European Court and Civil Society* (Cambridge University Press 2007).

[83] Most recently A Cohen, "The Genesis of Europe: Competing Elites and the Emergence of a European Field of Power" in N Kauppi and MR Madsen (eds), *Transnational Power Elites: The New Professionals of Governance, Law and Security* (London: Routledge 2013).

[84] Madsen, note 62.

[85] As the notion is developed in Kauppi and Madsen, note 83.

up with Weberian ideas on both professionals and institutionalization and rationalization. Generally, they share with historical institutionalism an interest in the genesis of institutions, yet they tend to go for more Weberian models for explaining the institutionalization of certain forms of legal knowledge and its legitimacy in society. More generally, as a result of the growing power of ICs in recent years, the question of legitimacy has become a focal point for understanding the practices—and even existence—of ICs. The dominant debates have either played out in more normative terms as part of discussions of the alleged democratic deficits of ICs[86] or in more pragmatic terms with respect to the effectiveness of ICs.[87] Sociology, and particularly classical sociology in the tradition of Max Weber, offers a third position, which has inspired—directly or indirectly—many of the sociological studies cited in this chapter.

As outlined above, the Weberian perspective on legitimacy relates directly to his analysis of power. In his classic essay on authority, he argues that the legitimacy of any given institution can be derived from a number of different practices aiming at different environments. Although often overlooked in studies of ICs, which have mostly explored their interface with government practices in the law and politics tradition, this is perhaps particularly true for ICs. As a matter of fact, the interaction of ICs with governments in a more politicized manner is the exception rather than the norm. ICs interact instead most often and most directly with highly differentiated legal fields where their practices are legitimized in shared epistemologies of professional legal knowledge. For the most part, this comes across as unproblematic and part of an everyday legal practice, not all that different from what happens at the level of national courts. In the words of Niklas Luhmann, it is "Legitimation durch Verfahren," or in English: "legitimacy via common approaches and processes."[88] But it is precisely this ongoing, and in recent years expanding, juridification and judicialization of international law[89] that is the backdrop of the growing normative critique of an international "juristocracy" by reference to the alleged lack of democratic legitimacy of transnational legal elite networks. According to this critique, international judges have basically become a sort of global superclass that, to borrow from Huntington's analysis, denationalizes and basically acts as the judicial variant of the "Davos men."[90]

What the critics tend to overlook, however, is that ICs might all the same still be legitimate. Transnational power elites such as international judges are not by definition illegitimate, at least not as long as they can justify their exercise of power and

[86] See e.g., A Follesdal, "The Legitimacy of International Human Rights Review: The Case of the European Court of Human Rights" (2009) 40 J. Soc. Phil. 595.

[87] See the discussion in Shany, note 28.

[88] N Luhmann, *Legitimation durch Verfahren* (6 edn, Frankfurt am Main: Suhrkamp 2001).

[89] CPR Romano, "The Proliferation of International Tribunals: Piecing together the Puzzle" (1999) 31 NYU J. Int'l L. & Pol. 709.

[90] SP Huntington, *Who are We?: America's Great Debate* (New York: Free Press 2005).

gain social acceptance as suggested by Weber. This way of conceiving legitimacy is potentially enriching for studies of ICs. Above all, it provides a way out of the rather limited law and politics focus of most existing literature by introducing a third dimension to the equation: society. However, as shown by Erik Voeten, the latter is hard to capture if it is simply understood as public opinion in a traditional sense.[91] Paradoxically, one way of studying the broader societal legitimization of ICs is to examine legal and political elites as they to a large extent form public opinion on highly technical issues such as international courts and law.[92] Of course, elites and masses do not fully converge. There are likely to be noticeable differences in this regard depending on the subject matter with which the IC in question is dealing with, in the sense that human rights, the law of the sea, or trade tend to mobilize very different segments of society. The point is, however, that neither do transnational elites converge when it comes to ICs. This is unsurprising considering that society at large is deeply divided over precisely the major questions dealt with by ICs—trade, crime, and human rights. In this view, many of the normative critics of ICs are creating a false dichotomy between an international and a national level of agency. They are basically promoting political cleavages, which largely pre-exist in society at large, to a supposedly disconnected international level.

This brings us back to the starting point of the place of (international) society in the legitimacy of ICs. As suggested by, for example, Cohen and Madsen, contemporary international society cannot be understood simply as a diplomatic interface of states and international organizations but instead as a space of contestation between different transnational elites, including states, international organizations, and NGOs. In other words, international society is not simply residual to national society and providing functional responses to the new needs for states in the area of globalization; international society is also political in and of itself, meaning that there is a real politics of ICs—not just merely problems of legitimacy. This underlying societal dimension to the question of the legitimization of ICs is key if one is to understand the very debate on the legitimacy—or lack thereof—of ICs in terms of a broader social process of legal and political restructuring with respect to globalization. Indeed, connecting the question of legitimacy of ICs to the sociological globalization literature provides important insights into how globalization at large is creating new divisions in society between, for example, those who are inside the new global networks and those who are literally "off-line."[93] If globalization is as pervasive as most scholars of

[91] See the attempt made in E Voeten, "Public Opinion and the Legitimacy of International Courts" in *Theoretical Inquiries in Law* (forthcoming).

[92] B Cali, "The Social Legitimacy of Human Rights Courts: A Grounded Interpretivist Theory of the Legitimacy of the European Court of Human Rights" Hum. Rts. Q. (forthcoming).

[93] As suggested by M Castells, *The Rise of the Network Society* (Oxford: Blackwell 2000).

ICs tend to claim, it seems hard to maintain that questions of the legitimacy of ICs can be answered with a singular focus on the law and politics of ICs. The real question seems increasingly to be what kind of global society is being produced by ICs, among others, and the social and political responses and cleavages that these developments entail.

4 Conclusion

Providing an outline of sociological approaches to ICs, this chapter has focused on the particularities of sociological views and imaginations of ICs and the differences in the construction of research objects they entail. As argued, the actual sociological work on ICs is still limited and this chapter generally reflects that. Sociology, following the (unofficially) declared death of structural functionalism, has seen the development of a plethora of approaches ranging from post-structuralism to sociological pragmatism, but sociological studies of ICs have yet to fully benefit from this broader sociological tool box. But even with the more limited sets of sociological tools presented here, there is arguably still a lot to be gained, theoretically, methodologically, and ultimately empirically, by using sociological perspective either as an add-on to existing research or as a new paradigm for understanding ICs. As highlighted in the last three sub-sections, adding sociology to the study of ICs provides some fresh analytical points of departure for understanding ICs. While the mainstream literature on ICs is predominantly based on middle-range theorizing and testing, using sociology implies mobilizing theories of society. One thing is certain—in sociology, society and its institutions cannot be taken for granted, and this has consequences for the study of ICs. As argued, basic notions of institutions and agency are defined differently in sociology, and this has an impact on the very questions asked about ICs, including the central question of legitimacy. This is not to claim, however, that sociological perspectives are superior, but rather to underline that they give rise to different kinds of inquiries, which, in some cases, challenges widespread assumption of what ICs are in the first place. At the end of the day, the success of sociological approaches for our understanding of ICs will depend as much on lawyers and political scientists and their wish to engage in different ways of understanding ICs as it will depend on sociologists' own ability to engage in dialogue with existing research strands in law and political science. It seems, however, that both camps have something to gain from engaging in this intellectual cross-fertilization.

Research Questions

1. What kind of connection is there between international courts and the formation of global society?
2. How are international courts and particularly the judges of international courts embedded in national as well as international society?
3. Besides international judges, what kinds of actor are relevant to study for understanding international courts?
4. How does societal evolution impact on international courts' adjudication?

Suggested Reading

Bourdieu, P, "The Force of Law: Toward a Sociology of the Juridical Field" (1987) 38 Hastings L.J. 805, 805–53.

Cohen, A and Rask Madsen, M, "Cold War Law: Legal Entrepreneurs and the Emergence of a European Legal Field (1945–1965)" in V Gessner and D Nelken (eds), *European Ways of Law: Towards a European Sociology of Law* (Oxford: Hart Publishing 2007) 175–202.

Cotterrell, R, *Emile Durkheim: Law in a Moral Domain* (Stanford University Press 1999).

Dezalay, Y and Garth, BG, *Dealing in Virtue: International Commercial Arbitration and the Construction of a Transnational Legal Order* (University of Chicago Press 1996).

Hagan, J, *Justice in the Balkans: Prosecuting War Crimes in the Hague Tribunal* (University of Chicago Press 2003).

Latour, B, *La Fabrique Du Droit: Une Ethnographie Du Conseil D'état* (Paris: La Découverte 2002).

Lechner, FJ and Boli, J, *World Culture: Origins and Consequences* (Oxford: Blackwell 2005).

Madsen, MR, "The Protracted Institutionalisation of the Strasbourg Court: From Legal Diplomacy to Integrationist Jurisprudence" in M Rask Madsen and J Christoffersen (eds), *The European Court of Human Rights between Law and Politics* (Oxford University Press 2011) 43–60.

Thornhill, C, "The Formation of a European Constitution: An Approach from Historical-Political Sociology" (2012) 8:3 Int'l J.L. in Context 354, 354–93.

Vauchez, A, "The Transnational Politics of Judicialization: Van Gend En Loos and the Making of Eu Polity" (2010) 16:1 Eur. L.J. 1–28.

Weber, M, *Wirtschaft Und Gesellschaft: Grundriss Der Verstehenden Soziologie* (Tübingen: Mohr 1980).

CHAPTER 19

LEGAL PHILOSOPHICAL ISSUES OF INTERNATIONAL ADJUDICATION

GETTING OVER THE *AMOUR IMPOSSIBLE* BETWEEN INTERNATIONAL LAW AND ADJUDICATION

SAMANTHA BESSON*

* Professor of Public International Law and European Law, University of Fribourg. Many thanks to my research assistant Alexandre Biedermann for his help with the formal lay-out of the chapter, and to Karen Alter and the editors of this handbook for their feedback on previous versions of the chapter.

1 Introduction

Adjudication, i.e., the function, role, or task of courts to state and apply the law in the specific disputes brought before them, is among the most classical topics in jurisprudence or legal philosophy. The existence of a system of courts with general and compulsory jurisdiction is often regarded as a key feature of a legal system.[1] As a result, even though the theory of adjudication does not exhaust the field of legal theory, to the extent that it cannot tell us what the law is and that one needs a theory of law to identify the law before it can guide judges,[2] a theory of adjudication is part and parcel of any good theory of law. More specifically, a theory of adjudication does two things: first, it explains the role of courts and how judges decide, or should decide, cases brought to them about the content of the law and, second, it guides and justifies their activities.[3]

The question raised in this chapter is whether the same applies to international adjudication and theorizing international adjudication. Like other facets of international law, international adjudication is now beginning to catch the eye of legal philosophers, and particularly philosophers of international law.[4] Although

[1] See e.g., R Dworkin, *Law's Empire* (London: Fontana Press 1986); J Raz, *The Authority of Law* (Oxford University Press 1979); J Raz, "On the Nature of Law" (1996) 82 ARSP 1; HLA Hart, *The Concept of Law* (2nd edn, Oxford: Clarendon Press 1994) 213–16.

[2] See e.g., J Dickson, "Interpretation and Coherence in Legal Reasoning" [2010] The Stanford Encyclopedia of Philosophy <http://plato.stanford.edu/archives/spr2010/entries/legal-reas-interpret/> accessed September 3, 2012; Raz, *Authority*, note 1; Raz, *Nature of Law*, note 1; Hart, note 1; *contra*: Dworkin, note 1.

[3] See e.g., Dickson, note 2.

[4] See e.g., E Jouannet, "La notion de jurisprudence internationale en question" in SFDI (ed.), *La juridictionnalisation du droit international* (Paris: Pedone 2003); H Ascensio, "La notion de juridiction internationale en question" in SFDI (ed.), *La juridictionnalisation du droit international* (Paris: Pedone 2003); J Allard and A Garapon, *Les juges dans la mondialisation* (Paris: Le Seuil 2005); A Paulus, "International Adjudication" in S Besson and J Tasioulas (eds), *The Philosophy of International Law* (Oxford University Press 2010); DH Regan, "International Adjudication: A Response to Paulus—Courts, Custom, Treaties, Regimes and the WTO" in Besson and Tasioulas (eds), *The Philosophy of International Law*; B Kingsbury, "International Courts: Uneven Judicialization in Global Order" in

international adjudication was long absent from international law, since 1945, and most definitely since the 1990s, it has become a largely accepted and central feature in the practice of contemporary international law—though it has turned out to be quite an uneven process and is not necessarily states' first choice among international dispute settlement mechanisms.[5] As a result, current international law can no longer be understood without its judicial dimension. It does not come as a surprise, therefore, that important research has been conducted in recent years on the various institutional and legal dimensions of international adjudication.[6] Curiously, the philosophical and especially the normative questions international adjudication generates have only started to be raised, as if the concepts of "judge," "court," "jurisdiction," "adjudication," "judicial reasoning," "jurisprudence," "judgement," "case-law" and "precedent" were self-evident in international law. We know very well, however, that, even domestically, those notions are fraught with complexity and have been debated at great length.

A first explanation for the neglect of the topic may be found in the close connection recognized by most international lawyers between international adjudication and the questionable legality of international law. In Benedict Kingsbury's words, the general approach to international judicialization among scholars is one of accomplishment, and no longer one of program and even less of critique. This is a way, he claims, of assuaging "Diceyan doubts about the law in international law" and may be traced back to the connection made since the nineteenth century between the existence of law or a legal system, on the one hand, and a system of courts with general and compulsory jurisdiction, on the other.[7] Placating concerns about the applicability of the rule of law to international law may constitute yet another explanation for the philosophical neglect of international adjudication. After all, given the importance of the judicial review function of courts for the respect of the rule of law in domestic jurisprudence, questioning the existence and legitimacy of international adjudication may threaten the credentials of one of the few dimensions of the rule of law that scholars have been able to identify in international legal practice and hence arguably a key feature of its legality.[8]

J Crawford and M Koskenniemi (eds), *The Cambridge Companion to International Law* (Cambridge University Press 2012).

[5] See, e.g., in this handbook, Romano, Ch. 5; Kingsbury, note 4; A Pellet, "Judicial Settlement of International Disputes" in R Wolfrum (ed.), *Max Planck Encyclopedia of Public International Law* (Oxford University Press 2012).

[6] See e.g., A Boyle and C Chinkin, "Law-Making by International Courts and Tribunals" in A Boyle and C Chinkin (eds), *The Making of International Law* (Oxford University Press 2007) 263–312; C Brown, *A Common Law of International Adjudication* (Oxford University Press 2007).

[7] See Kingsbury, note 4, Conclusion; see also Jouannet, note 4, at 344–5.

[8] See A Nollkaemper, "The Internationalized Rule of Law" (2009) 1 HJRL 74; see also J Waldron, "Are Sovereigns Entitled to the Benefit of the International Rule of Law?" (2011) 22:2 EJIL 315; and a response by S Besson, "Sovereignty, International Law and Democracy" (2011) 22:2 EJIL 373.

The difficulty, however, is that the concept of international adjudication, like that of adjudication itself, is neither self-evident nor understandable, except by reference to the specificities of international legality, which in turn requires discussing international adjudication. In fact, international adjudication raises even more complex philosophical difficulties than its domestic counterpart. It is time, therefore, to disambiguate the notion of international adjudication and to look more closely into what Hervé Ascensio has referred to as the "*amour impossible*" between international adjudication and international law.[9] The risk otherwise is not only a serious loss of perspective on what international judges ought to be doing, but also turning a blind eye on the crisis of legitimacy looming large in international adjudication.[10]

Of course, this is not to say that international adjudication has been completely neglected by legal philosophers. Yet, on the rare occasions in which the philosophical issues pertaining to international adjudication have been discussed, it has mostly been done either in the context of critical legal theory and outside analytical legal theory,[11] or in the context of a natural law paradigm and outside legal positivism.[12] Another difficulty looming large in recent theoretical accounts of international adjudication is the tendency to reinvent the wheel; classical issues raised by (domestic) adjudication and their perennial discussions in (domestic) jurisprudence are often ignored or at most eluded to. While it is true that international adjudication raises many of the same questions as domestic adjudication, the largely indeterminate role of international adjudication and the specificities of the international legal order itself magnify some of them, while also giving rise to new questions of their own.[13] This chapter will discuss and refer to the former as issues in the general jurisprudence or legal philosophy of adjudication, and to the latter as issues in the special jurisprudence of international adjudication. My argument will be three-pronged. It will first clarify what adjudication is and whether international adjudication in one or all of its various forms may actually be regarded as adjudication; second, re-examine classical questions of general jurisprudence of adjudication in the context of international law; and, finally, broach the new questions that constitute the core of the special jurisprudence of international adjudication.

[9] See Ascensio, note 4, at 202. [10] See Paulus, note 4, at 223; Kingsbury, note 4, Conclusion.

[11] See e.g., M Koskenniemi, "The Ideology of International Adjudication and the 1907 Hague Conference" in Y Daudet (ed.), *Topicality of the 1907 Hague Conference, The Second Peace Conference* (Leiden: Brill Academic Publishers 2008).

[12] See e.g., G Letsas, "Strasbourg's Interpretive Ethic: Lessons for the International Lawyer" (2010) 21 EJIL 1.

[13] On this diagnosis, see Regan, note 4, at 226 ff.

2 The Concept of International Adjudication

Adjudication may be defined as (i) the function, role, or task (ii) belonging to permanent and independent judges (as a court) (iii) to state and apply the law (iv) in order to settle the specific disputes brought before them (v) by issuing legally binding decisions (vi) according to a pre-determined set of rules of procedure.[14] Of course, adjudication also refers sometimes to a *process* that has that function, i.e., the process of adjudicating. Adjudication *qua* function or *qua* process is intricately tied (i) to an institution, i.e., a court; (ii) to a competence or power, i.e., jurisdiction; and (iii) to an outcome, i.e., judicial decisions and judgments. When courts exercise their jurisdiction and issue judgments, they adjudicate and the process is referred to as adjudication.

Interestingly, adjudication is best regarded as a normative concept, like the concept of law, to the extent that it encapsulates a value, i.e., applying the law to a given dispute, and its correct application implies some evaluative assessment. As such, it cannot merely be described and reduced to criteria whose existence could then simply be verified or not in practice. It cannot, however, because it is also an institution-related concept, be applied correctly, and in particular help criticize and guide judicial practice, independently from a reference to its institutional reality. The relationship between the ideal-type of adjudication and its institutional practice is therefore one of mutuality.[15]

International adjudication differs from domestic adjudication to the extent that (i) international courts are not centralized and not in a hierarchical relationship to one another; (ii) their jurisdiction is not necessarily compulsory (e.g., Art. 36.2 of the ICJ Statute), although there are exceptions among specialist and regional courts;[16] and (iii) their judicial decisions are legally binding, albeit not necessarily institutionally enforceable internationally (so-called *imperium*),[17] although there are exceptions among specialist and regional courts.

In this respect, a ready objection to international adjudication is whether it is "adjudication" in the sense developed in domestic jurisprudence. This objection resembles another one that takes issue with the legality of international law *qua* law in the domestic jurisprudential sense, and hence with the applicability of traditional

[14] See also Kingsbury, note 4; Regan, note 4, at 227; C Tomuschat, "International Courts and Tribunals" in R Wolfrum (ed.), *Max Planck Encyclopedia of Public International Law* (Oxford University Press 2012).

[15] See Kingsbury, note 4; Ascensio, note 4.

[16] See Pellet, note 5, para. 11 ff.

[17] See also Ascensio, note 4, at 177 ff.

legal philosophy to international law. Looking at adjudication in practice, whether domestically or internationally, it is apparent that international adjudication now comes very close to domestic adjudication, at least in its minimal law-enforcement function in a given dispute.[18] Of course, international jurisdiction may not always be compulsory, general, and centralized, but this only affects the other functions vested on international adjudication in the international legal order as a whole. Hence, perhaps the legality of international law or its systemic quality may be affected, but not the adjudicative function itself. Furthermore, the institutional embedding of international law in domestic legal orders means that domestic adjudication can no longer be conceived of independently from international adjudication. As a result, the concept of adjudication has to be shared by both domestic and international law alike, and thus discussed by domestic and international jurisprudence together.

The next question actually pertains to the exact contours of the internationality of international adjudication, and, conversely, the domesticity of domestic adjudication. Indeed, domestic courts may be applying international law and therefore contributing to the enforcement of international law. In certain cases, they may also participate in the review function of international courts, especially when exercising judicial control over international executive activity. As a result, some authors regard them as practicing international adjudication.[19] In a nutshell, and by reference to the three elements identified before, adjudication may be deemed *international* when the court, its jurisdiction, and its procedure are created and regulated by international law.[20] Strictly speaking, then, domestic courts *qua* institutions are not international courts in terms of their constitutive law, jurisdiction, and procedures. They cannot, as a result, be said to contribute to international judicial law-making[21] —except perhaps through the indirect consolidation of transnational interpretations and then of general principles of international law recognized by international judges (see e.g., Art. 38.1.c and d of the ICJ Statute), as is the case in the human rights context.[22]

Of course, a recurrent issue in this volume pertains to the sheer diversity of international courts, and hence of the institutional entities exercising international adjudication in practice. The question is then how that diversity should be reflected in the various doctrinal and theoretical efforts at analyzing and systematizing the

[18] See also Regan, note 4, at 227; Tomuschat, note 14, at 35.

[19] See A Tzanakopoulos, "Domestic Courts in International Law: the International Judicial Function of National Courts" (2011) 34 Loy. L.A. Int'l & Comp. L. Rev. 101.

[20] See Ascensio, note 4, at 163, 167 ff.

[21] See also Jouannet, note 4, at 391–3; A Pellet, "Article 38" in A Zimmermann, C Tomuschat and K Oellers-Frahm (eds), *The Statute of the International Court of Justice: A Commentary* (Oxford University Press 2006) 312.

[22] See S Besson, "General Principles in International Law—Whose Principles?" in S Besson et al. (eds), *Les principes en droit européen—Principles in European Law* (Zurich: Schulthess 2011).

phenomenon of international adjudication.[23] The present chapter, because it is normative, and not descriptive, and general in scope, and not specific, aims at identifying and discussing a basic and common concept of international adjudication underlying a diverse institutional practice. The fact that international jurisdiction may not always be compulsory, general, and centralized merely affects the various functions of international adjudication that may be attributed in the international legal order as a whole, and not the adjudicative function itself. The function of stating the law in a given dispute remains largely the same across different international courts.[24] True, adjudication is an institutional function and, as a result, there is a relationship between the single ideal-type of adjudication discussed and its polymorphous institutional practice.[25] This is why normative abstraction and generalization should not lead to minimizing the importance of international adjudication's multifaceted institutional reality. Accordingly, the chapter's main emphasis is on the International Court of Justice (ICJ) *qua* sole "international" court and "judicial organ of international law"[26] to date, due to its general and universal jurisdiction (ICJ Statute, Art. 36.1), though appropriate reference is sometimes made to other international courts with distinct jurisdiction and different issues, and especially the European Court of Human Rights (ECtHR) as an example of a specialist and regional court.

3 The General Jurisprudence of International Adjudication

There are two famous puzzles pertaining to adjudication in legal philosophy: the first is the question of judicial law-making and its contrast with mere law-enforcement,[27] and hence the opposition between (judicial) law and (democratic) politics; and

[23] See also Jouannet, note 4, at 364 ff; Regan, note 4, at 230 ff, on why judicial proliferation is a problem neither for international law nor for international jurisprudence; Pellet, note 5; Boyle and Chinkin, note 6, at 266; J Charney, "Is International Law Threatened by Multiple International Tribunals?" (1998) 271 Recueil des cours 101, at 373.

[24] Since I have defined the concept of adjudication as the function of stating the law to settle a dispute, the chapter does not address further functions attributed to adjudication (by various international actors, or by reference to their respective legal regimes). For functionalist discussions of the practice of international adjudication, see e.g., in this handbook, Alvarez, Ch. 8; A von Bogdandy and I Venzke, "Beyond Dispute: International Judicial Institutions as Lawmakers" (2011) 12 German L.J. 979.

[25] See Kingsbury, note 4; Ascensio, note 4, at 164–6.

[26] See also *Corfu Channel Case* (Merits) [1948] ICJ Rep 1949, para. 35.

[27] Law enforcement is used interchangeably with law application in this chapter. It should not, however, be conflated with the distinct question of the practical enforcement of legal or even judicial decisions and the latter's enforceability as a result. See also S Besson, "International Judges' Function(s)

the second is the related question of judicial discretion and its contrast with mere legal cognition, and hence the opposition between (judicial) law and morality. Obviously, those two difficulties are even greater in international adjudication where there is not only less determinate and less unified law and fewer politics in the absence of a centralized international legislator, but also less common morality in the absence of a single international political community or polity with shared values.

3.1 International judicial law-making

In contrast to non-judicial dispute settlement mechanisms, adjudication and judicial decisions are based on law: they settle particular legal disputes between the parties of a concrete case by applying the law to specific circumstances. To the extent that they settle a dispute between parties, their legal pronouncements specify the law in the specific context of the case and have *decisional authority* for those parties. At the same time, however, judicial decisions often reach beyond the case at hand and influence the court's future interpretation and application of the law. This is what one may refer to as the *interpretive authority* of judicial decisions. When that interpretive authority applies to the court itself, one usually also speaks of a *precedent*.[28]

Because the application or enforcement of the law implies identifying and interpreting it in a specific case, and because law-enforcing judicial decisions may have interpretive authority beyond the specific case, adjudication may also be referred to as the creation and development of legal norms through judicial practice. This is why one speaks of judicial law-identifying and judicial law-making. Of course, judicial interpretation is not necessary in all cases of law enforcement, and the law's meaning may sometimes be clear. Most of the time, however, interpretation is central to adjudication because the authority of law is communicative; it stems from a communication from those in authority to those to whom it applies and who have to be able to understand it.[29]

Judicial law-making, and especially the judicial identification of legal principles, bring up the legal philosophical question of the applicability of the "sources thesis" to international adjudication and hence to international law-making itself. The

between Dispute-Settlement and Law-Enforcement—From International Law without Courts to International Courts without Law. A Reply to Anna Spain" (2012) 34 Loy. L.A. Int'l & Comp. L. Rev. 101.

[28] See S Besson, "The Erga Omnes Effect of the European Court of Human Rights Judgments" in S Besson (ed), *La Cour européenne des droits de l'homme après le Protocole 14—Premier bilan et perspectives/The European Court of Human Rights after Protocol 14—First assessment and perspectives* (Zurich: Schulthess 2011); see also Boyle and Chinkin, note 6, at 293–320; R Jennings, "The Judiciary, International and National, and the Development of International Law" (1996) 45 ICLQ 1.

[29] See Raz, *Authority*, note 1; Raz, *Nature of Law*, note 1.

sources thesis is a key element to any legal positivist account of law. According to that view, law is source-based if its existence and content can be identified by reference to social facts alone, without resort to any evaluative argument. Its applicability to adjudication has been challenged by theorists who understand judicial law as the only or main source of law or, at least, conceive of its validity as independent from being posited and identifiable as a social fact alone.[30]

Various replies to this challenge are available.[31] To start with, judicial law-making is a slow process, but it is definitely based on a rule of recognition. As a result, there is nothing worrying in the legalization of moral values or principles in adjudication. Legal principles are identified through legal and judicial interpretation and become part of law *qua* judicial law, i.e., some kind of judicial customary law. The analogy between judicial law and customary law as sources of law stems from their sharing the same accretion process: the repetition of practices for customary law and of precedents for judicial law. Another reply one may make to the challenge pertains to the existence of gaps in the law. Even if general principles were deemed moral and not legal norms once they have become part of judicial law, their legal import may be explained as a way to fill in gaps in the law. Gaps in the law need to be filled by judges by reference to extra-legal materials.

The main difficulty with judicial law-making lies further down the road, however, in the distinction between judicial law and legislative or ordinary law, and hence between judicial law and democratic politics. It would be wrong, indeed, to see judicial law-making as the epitome of law-making. Nor should judicial law-making be conflated with ordinary law-making. First of all, adjudication implies that law pre-exists judicial enforcement or else it could not be identified, applied, and interpreted in the specific case. In practice, of course, the identification of pre-existing law and its development or modification by judges is often straddled.[32] Secondly, the law-making function of judges is either relative to the parties in the case of their decisional authority, or general albeit limited and partial in nature in the case of their interpretive authority.[33] The primary law-making function remains vested in the legislative power as a result. As a matter of fact, the judicial law-making function is defined by reference to that primarily legislative function (and vice versa); the function of judicial law-making is only tenable in combination and in response to legislative or political authority. This may be verified institutionally, since judges work within the constraints of coherence with existing law and of other institutional limitations. This explains, for instance, why

[30] See Dworkin, note 1. In international law, see e.g., Letsas, note 12; Paulus, note 4.

[31] See R Guastini, "Les principes de droit en tant que source de perplexité théorique" in S Caudal (ed.), *Les principes en droit* (Paris: Economica 2008).

[32] See Dickson, note 2; Raz, *Authority*, note 1; Raz, *Nature of Law*, note 1; *contra*: Dworkin, note 1.

[33] See Dickson, note 2; Jouannet, note 4, at 386.

judges have to defer to the democratic legislature and its authoritative directives. Further evidence may be found in the fact that there are so few legal principles identified by judges in practice.[34]

Transposed to international law, the question is whether international adjudication *qua* judicial law enforcement also amounts to judicial law-making. Clearly, because the specificity of international dispute settlement through adjudication is law enforcement, and because the enforcement of international law implies identifying and interpreting international law, international adjudication cannot but include law-making, albeit of a judicial kind.[35]

True, international judges are not, strictly speaking, law-makers,[36] and their decisions cannot be counted among the formal sources of international law (see e.g., ICJ Statute, Art. 38.1.d). They cannot, however, avoid identifying and interpreting the law before applying it.[37] This is what one should understand from the reference in Art. 38.1.d of the ICJ Statute to "judicial decisions" as "subsidiary means for the determination of rules of law," themselves created by formal sources of international law. Legal interpretations made by judges have consequences for their own future legal reasoning (so-called precedents or *stare decisis*), but also the general understanding of the law beyond the specific court (so-called interpretive authority or *erga omnes* effect of international judicial decisions). While some authors see an exclusion of the interpretive authority (*res interpretata)* of international decisions and especially ICJ decisions in Art. 59 of the ICJ Statute and Art. 94.1 of the UNC,[38] those provisions are best understood as a reminder of the relative scope of those decisions' decisional authority (*res judicata*), and not as an exclusion of their interpretive authority.[39] Nor should they be understood to exclude the existence of precedents and coherence with previous decisions in the ICJ's case law itself, as confirmed in the Court's own decisions.[40]

[34] See P Brunet, "Les principes généraux du droit et la hiérarchie des normes" in D de Béchillon et al. (eds), *L'architecture du droit. Mélanges en l'honneur de Michel Troper* (Paris: Economica 2006).

[35] See also von Bogdandy and Venzke, note 24, at 984–9; M Jacob, "Precedents: Lawmaking Through International Adjudication" (2011) 12:5 German L.J. 1005; Boyle and Chinkin, note 6, at 266, 272; Besson, note 27.

[36] See e.g., *Legality of the Threat or Use of Nuclear Weapons* (Advisory Opinion) [1996] ICJ Rep 1996, at 226, 237, para. 18; see also *Legality of the Threat or Use of Nuclear Weapons* (Advisory Opinion) [1996] ICJ Rep 1996, at 592 para. 40 (dissenting opinion of Judge Higgins).

[37] See e.g., *Legality of the Threat or Use of Nuclear Weapons,* note 36, at 226, 237, para. 18; see also Boyle and Chinkin, note 6, at 272.

[38] See e.g., R. Bernhardt, "Article 59" in Zimmermann, Tomuschat, and Oellers-Frahm, note 21, at 1233, 1244.

[39] See e.g., Pellet, note 5; Jouannet, note 4, at 359.

[40] See e.g., *Land and Maritime Boundary between Cameroon and Nigeria* (Preliminary Objections) [1998] ICJ Rep 1998, pp. 275, 292, para. 28; see also Boyle and Chinkin, note 6, at 293 ff; Pellet, note 21, at 305 ff.

In fact, the law-identifying and law-making functions of international judges are even more important in international legal practice than in the domestic context.[41] This has to do, first, with the limited number of sources of international law: there are more gaps in international law than in domestic law.[42] By virtue of the application of *non-liquet* in international law,[43] international judges are called to identify and interpret applicable law to a greater extent than domestic judges. This is particularly true in relatively new fields of international law, such as international criminal law or international environmental law. Secondly, due to the indeterminate nature of certain sources of international law, and in particular of customary international law and general principles,[44] the judge plays a key law-identifying role. Unlike treaties, the latter sources require a judge for the validation of their legal norms: ascertaining the existence of a given practice and *opinio juris*, on the one hand, and of a principle in domestic traditions and its transposability to international relations, on the other.

A third reason for the importance of the judicial law-making function of international adjudication pertains to international legal pluralism and the absence of hierarchy among norms, regimes, and sources of international law. When their jurisdiction allows it, international judges are called to identify all the norms, regimes, and sources that bear in a given case (see e.g., the Vienna Convention on the Law of Treaties, Art. 31.2 and 3),[45] and then interpret them coherently.[46] Fourthly, the norms in certain regimes of international law, like international human rights law, are necessarily abstract, calling for the specification of the corresponding duties in context and hence for their constantly renewed identification and interpretation through judicial decisions. This explains why many understand human rights treaties as "living instruments."[47] Judicial law-making is actually even more central to international human rights law than it is to other regimes of international law in that the minimal protection of human rights requires a mutual validation by both domestic and international judges.[48]

Of course, international judicial law-making cannot exhaust international law-making and something has to prevent judicial law-making from being identified with international law-making itself. This jurisprudential objection is harder

[41] See e.g., R Higgins, *Problems and Process: International Law and How We Use It* (Oxford University Press 1993) 202; H Lauterpacht, *The Development of International Law by the International Court* (first published 1958, Cambridge University Press 1982) 5.

[42] See Boyle and Chinkin, note 6, at 289–90.

[43] See PCIJ, Advisory Committee of Jurists, *Procès verbaux* of the Proceedings of the Committee, 16 June–24 July, The Hague 1920, at 312.

[44] See Boyle and Chinkin, note 6, at 278–85 ff.

[45] See Boyle and Chinkin, note 6, at 273–5.

[46] Boyle and Chinkin, note 6, at 273–5; Regan, note 4, at 230 ff; Pellet, note 5.

[47] See *Tyrer v. United Kingdom* (1978) Series A no 26, paras 15–16.

[48] See S Besson, "Human Rights and Democracy in a Global Context—Decoupling and Recoupling" (2011) 4:1 EGP 19.

to fight back in international law in the absence of a centralized international legislature, however. The primary international law-making power remains vested in states, even though it is sometimes delegated to international organizations and associates other subjects of international law more directly than through their states as officials.

The question that arises, then, is how international courts may institutionally be organized so as to make their law-making function responsive to the primary law-making function of states. The latter are indeed both subjects of international law, and hence of international adjudication, and its authors. Moreover, *qua* authors of international law, states usually make international law without institutional mediation. And it is difficult, as a result, to identify that institutional respondent to judges that delineates judicial law-making from law-making. Within international organizations, the question has been solved by reference to the division of powers and their mediation among legislative, executive, and judicial institutions distinct from the states. The same may be said by reference to international treaty-making conferences. Outside international organizations, however, and in the absence of a centralized and universalized legislature, the distinctiveness of international judicial law-making from ordinary law-making remains to be established.

In any case, in practice many states resist both the idea of international judicial law-making and of internationally institutionalized law-making mechanisms themselves. The idea that individual judges called on to settle a dispute between states can also contribute to interpreting international law and hence substitute themselves for its authors and primary law-makers and law-interpreters, i.e., states, contradicts the consensualist approach to the validity of international law.[49] A subjective understanding of the validity of international law is matched therefore by a subjective notion of international adjudication: according to that approach, states remain the only validators, interpreters, and enforcers of the law to which they have consented.

Those difficulties explain the persistence of a tension and uneasy separation in practice between the dispute resolution function of international courts, and the law-enforcing, and hence law-identifying and law-making roles that come with the judicial function itself. Evidence of this resistance to international judicial law-making may be found in the kind of jurisdiction exercised by international courts. As we saw before, indeed, international jurisdiction has remained largely non-compulsory and non-exclusive. On the one hand, international adjudication remains one of many international dispute resolution (IDR) mechanisms. As a result, judicial interpretation is not even necessary to resolve legal issues that may be resolved through other IDR mechanisms that do not use the law to do so. International courts themselves may sometimes resort to other IDR mechanisms to settle a dispute without fully enforcing the law. In general, they regard themselves

[49] See E Lauterpacht, *Aspects of the Administration of International Justice* (Cambridge University Press 1991) 23–6.

as competing with other IDR mechanisms, and often give priority to settling the dispute between the parties over developing international law. Interestingly, this may also explain the reluctance of the ICJ to use its advisory function to identify new principles of international law in indeterminate areas of international law and outside any actual dispute. Even when they apply and interpret international law to resolve a dispute, international courts do not have a sufficiently important and regular flow of cases to interpret it authoritatively. On the other hand, the international judge is not necessarily called to interpret the law in an exclusive and authoritative fashion for all international law subjects. Contrary to domestic law, international law may currently be interpreted differently by different courts and there can be as many judicial interpretations as there are courts. As long as it remains non-compulsory and non-exclusive, international adjudication cannot fulfill its usual functions of law enforcement the way it would in the domestic legal order.

This in turn explains why the relations between the dispute settlement dimension of international adjudication and international law-making are particularly problematic in areas where non-consent-based objective and general international law has developed, but where adjudication remains mainly subjective or consent-based and non-exclusive. One may think, for instance, of cases in which the ICJ applies international human rights law. As long as the legitimate authority of international law was deemed equivalent to that of a contract between private parties, consent-based adjudication fitted very well: the scope of judges' legitimate authority matched that of the applicable law. This explains, for instance, why third party interventions are allowed or even compulsory in some cases: to fill the gap between a bilateral dispute resolution mechanism and multilateral law-making consequences.[50] Of course, the disconnect between objective international law and subjective international adjudication is not present everywhere in the international legal order. Regional and specialized courts that are both compulsory and exclusive, such as the ECtHR or the Court of Justice of the European Union, have long combined dispute settlement and law-making functions. And the reason again lies in the institutional framework in which those courts are embedded, i.e., institutions that mediate international law-making for states and to which those international courts are accountable to, such as European Union institutions for the CJEU and domestic institutions and human rights courts for the ECtHR.

Whereas international law has long developed as "law without courts" to coin the famous dictum,[51] it is now no longer the case. Not only is there a multitude of international courts applying it, but international law itself has caught up with that reality and often needs the kind of interpretation and implementation that only international courts can provide. For the time being, however, not only is international law often left to function without proper courts, but the problem is actually

[50] See Boyle and Chinkin, note 6, at 295.

[51] See Kingsbury, note 4, referring to Grotius on this.

best approached from the other side: courts themselves are requested to function without international law and a distinct law-maker that can turn them into full judges and let them be. I will come back to the question of the legitimacy of international courts in adjudicating and of those in whose name international judges are deciding in the last section of this chapter.

3.2 International judicial discretion

It follows from the previous section's considerations that the law is not completely determinate and that adjudication is not merely about legal cognition but also implies judicial discretion. Judicial discretion, however, does not only raise institutional and legitimacy questions about the procedure of law-making and the relationship between (judicial) law and politics, but also substantive concerns about the content of law-making and the relationship between (judicial) law and morality. This second challenge is that judge-made law implies incorporating morality into the law, and the question again is whether this may be explained in a legal positivist framework and without endorsing a natural law approach.

Various responses to this challenge are available.[52] Before considering them, it is important to stress that the distinction at stake here between law and morality is a conceptual one and not a factual one; no one denies any longer that there is a factual relationship between law and morality.[53] First of all, law cannot, strictly speaking, incorporate morality since law is already part of morality, and morality applies anyway to us and to our legal institutions, legal reasoning being a special kind of moral reasoning. In those circumstances, law can only modulate or exclude morality. Judicial law acts precisely as modulator of morality into the legal order: it transposes and specifies moral principles or moral values in an institutional context by making normative choices. Furthermore, and this is a second objection to the challenge, even in cases in which legal principles and other judge-made legal standards are regarded as mere reflections of moral principles, they do not turn morality into law but simply give legal effects to morality within the legal order. This is done in the same way a legal order gives foreign law legal effects without turning it into domestic law.

Transposed to international adjudication, the question of judicial discretion is even more problematic and the natural lawyers' challenge to judicial discretion greater in international law than domestically.[54] There is indeed less determinate law to be directly ascertained due to the few sources of international law, their diversity, and their fragmentation, as I explained in the previous section. Moreover, the moral

[52] See e.g., Guastini, note 31.

[53] Guastini, note 31; see e.g., J Raz, "Incorporation by Law" (2004) 10 Legal Theory 1.

[54] See e.g., Letsas, note 12; Paulus, note 4.

values and interests protected through many norms and regimes of international law are readily considered as universal and, as a result, the moral origins of those norms and the moral justification for their authority are often held as more self-evident than those of domestic law.[55] A confirmation may be found in the value-discourse that often predominates in discussions of international adjudication.[56] As a matter of fact, moral values are regarded by some international judges and scholars as a "judicial lodestar"[57] in deciding international cases.

Of course, the same objections to the challenge may be made internationally as domestically.[58] Moreover, there is, as a matter of fact, less common or shared morality available to international judges than one would think *prima facie*. This is due to the absence of an international community with clearly ascertained common values. As a result, identifying and implementing global values may not be that self-evident for international judges.[59]

There are at least two difficulties with the suggested role of morality within international adjudication. The first one has to do with the existence of a global morality beyond the state. Scope precludes providing a full argument here. Although it is feasible, it is important not to underestimate the need not only to rebut state-of-nature-type arguments about international relations, i.e., relations between states outside the boundaries of a political community, but also to explain how global justice principles and duties come close to domestic ones. A second issue has to do with the higher degree of pluralism that affects global morality. Moral conflicts make orderings of values necessarily parochial, thus raising difficult legitimacy questions about decision-making procedures that identify them and consequently about judicial orderings of those values. It suffices to say in this respect that considerations about social epistemology and institutional design may help conceive of inclusive and deliberative institutions and procedures to adjudicate those conflicts and hence to constrain international judicial discretion. Certain institutional mechanisms, like the margin of appreciation of domestic courts or the European consensus in the ECtHR's toolbox, are examples of restrictions on supranational judicial discretion in the human rights context. Another example is the domestic judicial filter and the resulting deference to the domestic judge in the ICJ's practice, especially when recognizing general principles of international law stemming from domestic judicial decisions.[60] However, all those institutional mechanisms confirm

[55] See S Besson, "The Authority of International Law—Lifting the State Veil" (2009) 31:3 Sydney L. Rev. 343, Introduction.

[56] See e.g., Paulus, note 4; A von Bogdandy and I Venzke, "On the Functions of International Courts: An Appraisal in Light of their Burgeoning Public Authority" (ACIL Research Paper October 2012) < http://papers.ssrn.com/sol3/papers.cfm?abstract_id=2084079> accessed December 19, 2012.

[57] See *Legality of the Threat or Use of Nuclear Weapons*, Dissenting Opinion of Judge Higgins, note 36, at 370, para. 41.

[58] See also *South West Africa Cases*, (Second phase) [1966] ICJ Rep 1966, at 34, paras 49–51.

[59] See Regan, note 4, at 230 ff, in response to Paulus, note 4.

[60] See Besson, note 22.

one thing: judicial law and morality are clearly distinct. I will come back to the question of the legitimacy of international courts in adjudicating on those difficult moral issues in the last section of the chapter.

4 The Special Jurisprudence of International Adjudication

Besides sharing the same difficulties, albeit magnified, as domestic adjudication, international adjudication also presents jurisprudential difficulties of its own. The first set of difficulties has to do with the sources of applicable international law and the second set with the legitimacy of international law.

4.1 International adjudication and the sources of international law

The place of international judicial law-making among the sources of international law raises distinct questions relating to the specificity of the international legal order and its sources. International judges are called to do much more than interpret and apply the law. They also have to identify international law, especially general international law when it stems from non-written sources such as customary international law or general principles.

The international judge's role in the identification of international law goes beyond the scope of ordinary identification of any given rule of law in domestic judicial law-making; it comes very close to validating international law and hence to supplementing the formal sources of international law. This occurs either through transforming an emergent rule into an existent one by stating its crystallization, or through focusing on an emergent rule for validation at a later stage.[61] Without judicial validation of those international legal norms, there could be no legal validity through formal sources of general international law in the current state of the international legal order: there are no universal institutions available outside international courts to universally validate the practice of all states as customary international law or general principles. One possible alternative would be the UN General

[61] See Boyle and Chinkin, note 6, at 283; A Cassese and JH Weiler (eds), *Change and Stability in International Law-Making* (Berlin: W. De Gruyter 1988) 3.

Assembly, but the lack of external binding force of its recommendations and decisions is an obstacle. This is even more important as those sources of general international law constitute an important bulk of the international legal order.

The law-identifying role of international judges raises difficult jurisprudential questions that go beyond reconciling judicial law-making with the sources thesis and, as explained in the previous section, identifying some kind of rule of recognition behind judicial law itself. In the present constellation, indeed, judicial law is made instrumental to other sources of general international law. Here, the fact that all states are subjects to the legal norms stemming from those sources, but without ultimately having to consent to them as a prior condition, turns adjudication into a validating mechanism. Judicial law becomes an intermediary source of customary international law[62] and general principles as a result.[63] This intermediary role of adjudication among the sources of international law is actually confirmed by Art. 38.1.d of the ICJ Statute, which refers to judicial decisions as "subsidiary means for the determination of rules of law."

The jurisprudential difficulty is both practical and theoretical. First of all, vesting international judges with such a validating function is not only problematic from the perspective of the judicial function, but also from that of the organization of the international legal order itself. International judges are usually elected by states and their jurisdiction is mostly subjective as a result. The gap between subjective jurisdiction and objective international law-making discussed before becomes salient again; it is the way the function of the international judge is currently institutionalized that prevents judges from properly exercising the law-validating function vested on them. Secondly, the law-validating function of international judges begs the question of what the basis is for judicial law's validity in a legal positivist framework. Indeed, drawing a difference between judicial law *qua* form of customary international law, as I argued before, and judicial law *qua* subsidiary source of customary international law becomes difficult. Whatever one thinks of the analogy between judicial law and customary law made earlier in the chapter and how close they really are, the validating function of international judges threatens the possibility of applying the sources thesis to international judicial law-making itself. Alternative sources of international law listed in Art. 38 ICJ Statute cannot be used to account for the validity of judicial law-making. The implicit rule of recognition applicable to judicial law-making is to be found elsewhere in the international legal order. The problem is that international courts, and especially the ICJ, contribute to developing the theory of sources of international law and the international rule of recognition itself, by stating how international law sources work. For instance, the ICJ has clarified the constitutive elements of customary international law, the

[62] On the sources of general principles of international law and judicial law, see e.g., Besson, note 22; Boyle and Chinkin, note 6, at 285 ff.

[63] On customary international law and judicial law, see e.g., Boyle and Chinkin, note 62, at 278 ff.

relationship between international customary and conventional law, the role of soft law in international law, the value of the International Law Commission's codifications of general international law, and the conditions for the development of *jus cogens* norms. This confirms the meta-role of international adjudication in the international legal order, and the fact that that function has not been endorsed or corroborated by other subjects of international law so far.

A solution to both those practical and theoretical difficulties could lie in the institutionalization of international law-making processes, so as to provide for multilateral institutional fora for objective international law-making alongside international adjudication.[64] This would gradually emancipate the making of general international law from international adjudication, and contribute to solving the puzzle of the applicability of the sources thesis to international judicial law. An important benefit of the proposed institutionalization also lies elsewhere: it would enhance the legitimacy of international judicial law-making itself.

4.2 International adjudication and the legitimacy of international law

The role of international judicial law-making in the justification of the authority of international law raises distinct questions that have to do with the specificity of the international legal order. International judges are called to identify and interpret international law, and hence to validate and make it, thus raising difficulties pertaining to the justification of the authority of the international law they contribute to validating and making. Further, international judges are called to exercise discretion on disputed issues of global justice and morality, without being embedded in an institutional framework that makes them responsive and accountable, either directly or indirectly, to the individual subjects of those global legal norms.

In a nutshell, legitimacy is used here in an objective way to refer to justified authority, or the right to rule and to generate obligations, the latter being understood as exclusionary reasons for action. This explains why legitimacy and justification are sometimes used interchangeably. Legitimacy can be used by reference to an institution, such as a court, or to the law, such as judicial law. Both are usually related, to the extent that the legitimacy of law is tributary of the legitimacy of law-making institutions and vice versa. This objective meaning of legitimacy ought to be carefully distinguished from another understanding of legitimacy that is widespread, albeit unreflectively, in the literature: subjective legitimacy, i.e., legitimacy *qua* acceptance. In practice, however, subjective legitimacy often goes hand in hand

[64] See already *Legality of the Threat or Use of Nuclear Weapons* (Advisory Opinion), note 36, at 43, para. 103.

with objective legitimacy, as it is difficult to have sustainable objective legitimacy without some subjective legitimacy along the way and vice versa.[65] In what follows, the focus is on objective legitimacy only. It is important to emphasize, however, that most chapters in this volume broach various aspects of subjective legitimacy through, for instance, the impartiality and independence of courts and the fairness of judicial procedures.

The legitimacy of international law, and hence of international institutions like international courts and their decisions, is a complex topic; it pertains to the reasons for action given by those in authority to those subject to international law, i.e., in most cases, by states to states. A way out of that complexity, as I have argued elsewhere,[66] is to lift the state veil and to understand the reason-givers as states *qua* officials for their constituency of individuals and the reason-takers as states *qua* proxies for their constituency of individuals. When international organizations act as law-makers, they mediate the reason-giving and allow to see more clearly the difference between states as officials and states as proxy-subjects. International courts as well may be seen as officials and proxies of individuals through their constituent states. They could be seen as adjudicating in the states' and their people's name, as a result.

When one considers different justifications for the authority of international adjudication, it is important to start by putting consent aside. Consent reinforces the legitimate authority of international law by strengthening the salience of a coordinating solution, for instance, and it may explain respect for international law in practice. Alone, however, it is not a sufficient justification for legal authority.[67] Various other justifications for the legitimacy of international adjudication may be provided, however, and its legitimacy is likely to be piecemeal like that of international law as a whole and not holistic.[68]

As explained above, there is one justification of authority that matters more than others in the context of adjudication, however, and that is democratic legitimacy. If judges make law, their authority to do so has to be justified in democratic terms as well. Hence the question of those whose law is being interpreted and applied by judges, in short, those in whose name judges decide, persists.

Transposed to international law and adjudication, the democratic legitimacy of adjudication raises not only magnified issues by reference to domestic adjudication, especially when it is contrasted with universal values being considered as a lodestar of the international judge by certain authors and judges, but also issues of its own that have to do with the inherent limitations of international institutionalization and hence of its democratization.

[65] On the legitimacy of international law, see Besson, note 55; J Tasioulas, "The Legitimacy of International Law" in Besson and Tasioulas, note 4; A Buchanan, "The Legitimacy of International Law" in Besson and Tasioulas, note 4.

[66] See Besson, note 55. [67] Besson, note 55. [68] See Tasioulas, note 65.

One important reason for the reluctance of democratic states toward international judicial law-making, and especially judicial discretion on morally disputed issues, is the lack of institutional and democratic maturity of international law and hence of international adjudication. In the absence of other institutions and especially of a legislature to interact with, and, more generally, of a political community to represent, the judiciary cannot play its interpretive and judicial law-making role. It is neither checked by nor accountable to any institution or community. Nor is it really checking on any institution. Judicial law-making as a reasoning and discursive exercise requires the pre-existence of law, and judges cannot be asked to interpret and develop international law without that law being clearly identified for them. In general international law, not only are those legal rules and principles not clearly identified for courts, but courts are asked to identify them themselves.

It is important, as a result, to explore ways of developing an international institutional order besides courts. One could work, for instance, on ways of enhancing the institutional nature of international decision-making in order to provide judges with an institutional opponent with legitimate authority to which judges may in turn account and respond with the corresponding legitimate authority. It is not possible, in the absence of a separation of powers within international institutions whose law is to be interpreted by international judges, and in the absence of an international legislature representing the international community, to envisage (democratic or other) constraints on judicial discretion and ways of making sure international judges feel responsible. As explained before, this lack of institutional framework of international adjudication may explain why some international courts' jurisdiction remains optional (see e.g., ICJ), while others' is already compulsory (see e.g., ECtHR, CJEU).

This, however, implies more than democratic reforms in the judicial process and in the election of international judges.[69] It requires building a set of institutions outside courts but also around and including them, whether at the same level of governance or across levels of governance in connection with domestic courts and institutions. Of course, in the meantime, international judicial review of multilateral law-making may also acquire another democratic justification of its own, especially in circumstances in which those multilateral law-making processes still suffer from an important democratic deficit.[70] It suffices here to think of the democratizing function of the CJEU in the EU, and of the various decisions through which it reinforced the legislative power of the European Parliament.

[69] See A von Bogdandy and I Venzke, "In Whose Name? An Investigation of International Courts Public Authority and its Democratic Justification" (2012) 23:1 EJIL 7.

[70] See Boyle and Chinkin, note 6, at 310.

5 Conclusions

In his 2010 seminal piece on international adjudication, Donald H. Regan concluded rightly that "many writers move too easily from the premise that we need a lot more effective international law than we currently have [. . .] to the problematic conclusion that since no other institution is currently able to give it to us, judges should step in to supply our need."[71]

The idea that international adjudication can be a cure to all ills is actually quite widespread. For various reasons, many scholars think we need a stronger international community and legal order, and turn to judges to give it to us. This approach, however, puts the cart before the horse. This chapter shows that judges should not be asked to step in without previous clarification of important theoretical issues about the sources of international law itself and its legitimacy. This implies in particular making sure that processes of general international law-making are institutionalized so as to warrant the respect of the sources thesis and the democratic accountability of international judges. International adjudication scholars have moved too quickly from a programmatic take on international adjudication to one of accomplishment and contentment. It is time to revert to a more critical stance. It is only at this price that the problem that was long described as the *amour impossible* between international law and its judges can be faced openly, but also eventually overcome.

Research Questions

1. The law-making function of international courts and legal positivism: is the sources thesis applicable to international judicial law?
2. The judicial discretion of international courts: is there a way to distinguish international judicial law from morality?
3. The law-validating function of international courts: what does it mean for the legality of international law itself?
4. The legitimacy of international courts: how does it relate to that of international law and how can one enhance the democratic legitimacy of international adjudication?

[71] See Regan, note 4, at 241.

Suggested Reading

Allard, J and Garapon, A, *Les juges dans la mondialisation* (Paris: Le Seuil 2005).

Ascensio, H, "La notion de juridiction internationale en question" in SFDI (ed.), *La juridictionnalisation du droit international* (Paris: Pedone 2003).

von Bogdandy, A and Venzke, I, "Beyond Dispute: International Judicial Institutions as Lawmakers" (2011) 12 German L.J. 979.

von Bogdandy, A and Venzke, I, "In Whose Name? An Investigation of International Courts Public Authority and its Democratic Justification" (2012) 23:1 EJIL 7.

Boyle, A and Chinkin, C, "Law-Making by International Courts and Tribunals" in A Boyle and C Chinkin (eds), *The Making of International Law* (Oxford University Press 2007).

Jouannet, E, "La notion de jurisprudence internationale en question" in SFDI (ed.), *La juridictionnalisation du droit international* (Paris: Pedone 2003).

Kingsbury, B, "International Courts: Uneven Judicialization in Global Order" in J Crawford and M Koskenniemi (eds), *The Cambridge Companion to International Law* (Cambridge University Press 2012).

Koskenniemi, M, "The Ideology of International Adjudication and the 1907 Hague Conference" in Y Daudet (ed.), *Topicality of the 1907 Hague Conference, The Second Peace Conference* (Leiden: Brill Academic Publishers 2008).

Lauterpacht, H, *The Development of International Law by the International Court* (first published 1958, Cambridge University Press 1982).

Pellet, A, "Article 38" in A Zimmermann, C Tomuschat, and K Oellers-Frahm (eds), *The Statute of the International Court of Justice: A Commentary* (Oxford University Press 2006).

Regan, D H, "International Adjudication: A Response to Paulus—Courts, Custom, Treaties, Regimes and the WTO" in S Besson and J Tasioulas (eds), *The Philosophy of International Law* (Oxford University Press 2010).

Tzanakopoulos, A, "Domestic Courts in International Law: the International Judicial Function of National Courts" (2011) 34 Loy. L.A. Int'l & Comp. L. Rev. 101.

PART IV

CONTEMPORARY ISSUES IN INTERNATIONAL ADJUDICATION

CHAPTER 20

COMPLIANCE WITH JUDGMENTS AND DECISIONS

ALEXANDRA HUNEEUS*

OFTEN we speak as if international courts were a form of enforcement: we assume that once a legal regime acquires a court, it has teeth. Both within national and international legal systems, however, implementation of adjudicated decisions is itself an enforcement problem. Compliance is not always a straightforward or likely outcome. It is the product of an uncertain and, at times, lengthy process shaped by political and social dynamics. For scholars of the international realm—wherein courts still lack purse and sword and yet are more loosely linked to the state actors on whom they depend to implement court orders—compliance has become a focal point. This chapter explores when and how the rulings of international adjudicative bodies receive compliance. What do recent studies in social science and law reveal

* Assistant Professor, University of Wisconsin Law School.

about when and how international courts achieve compliance, and what impact, in turn, does compliance—or its absence—have on international courts?

The discussion unfolds in three parts. It begins at the conceptual level, analyzing what compliance means and why it matters, and raising the thorny question of how we measure compliance. Second, it reviews the literature on judgment compliance, with an emphasis on competing explanations of what factors influence compliance. It closes with suggestions for future inquiry.

1 Definition, Significance, and Measurement

Compliance occupies a central place in both the international relations and legal literature on international legal institutions in general, and on courts in particular. Yet there is a persistent ambivalence about its precise contours, and, more deeply, whether it is useful in revealing the impact of legal institutions on politics and society. Indeed, it seems *de rigueur* for articles that analyze the impact of international legal institutions to include a section disavowing compliance as a useful indicator—although it often manages to sneak back into the study.[1]

We begin with definitions. All agree that "legal compliance" describes correspondence between what the law requires, on the one hand, and the behavior of its subjects, on the other. But scholars disagree about whether compliance refers to mere correspondence, or whether that correspondence must be the product of a causal relation, with the subject yielding to the law. Kal Raustiala and Anne-Marie Slaughter declare themselves "agnostic on causality,"[2] whereas Yuval Shany defined judgment compliance as "a causal relationship between the contents of judicial decisions and state practice, leading to a convergence of the two."[3] Insistence on something more than mere correspondence seems to be the majority view. As Diana Kapiszewski and Mathew Taylor write, "A practical—and operationalizable—definition of

[1] L Martin, "Against Compliance," in JL Dunoff and M Pollack (eds), *International Law and International Relations: Synthesizing Insights from Interdisciplinary Scholarship* (Cambridge University Press 2012).

[2] K Raustiala and A-M Slaughter, "International Law, International Relations and Compliance" in W Carlnaes, T Risse and B Simmons (eds), *The Handbook Of International Relations* (London: Walter Sage Publications Ltd 2002) 539.

[3] Y Shany, "Assessing the Effectiveness of International Courts: A Goal-based Approach" (2012) 2 Am. J. of Int'l L. 225, 261.

compliance must reference some change in behavior."[4] Similarly, Abraham and Antonia Chayes define compliance as when "nations alter their behavior, their relationships, and their expectations of one another over time in accordance with" the terms of a treaty commitment.[5] In the end, however, perhaps the definition depends on the theoretical commitments of the writer. Benedict Kingsbury writes that compliance is not a "free-standing" concept that different scholars can share, but one that they must imbue with meaning "by reference to a theory... of international law."[6]

1.1 The case against compliance

These differences over definition reflect a wider debate about the utility of compliance as an indicator of law's effectiveness. The debate is often described as starting with two seminal articles. In 1993, Abram and Antonia Chayes argued that states comply with treaties at a high rate. What little non-compliance did exist was not deliberate, but was due to ambiguity in treaty law, lack of state capacity, and time lag. George Downs, David Rocke, and Peter Barsoom countered that high compliance rates were symptomatic of treaties having shallow depth of cooperation, defined as "the extent to which [the treaty] requires states to depart from what they would have done in its absence."[7] Treaties requiring deeper cooperation would be met with a higher level of deliberate non-compliance. Downs et al. attacked the Chayes' assumption that high compliance rates provided useful information. What matters to political scientists, they argued, is not mere correspondence between the requirements of a legal rule and a state's behavior, but rather whether treaties impact state behavior, in this case by helping states achieve the collective benefits of cooperation. The concept of compliance was thus too broad: it encompassed behavior that conformed to law for reasons not having to do with the law, and, specifically, behavior that conformed to law because the law reflected only shallow commitments.

At the same time, the concept of compliance is too narrow. No matter which definition you choose, compliance cannot tell us the full extent of law's impact because it excludes other important effects that law may have.[8] A state may fail to comply with the particular demands of a court ruling, for example, but there may be ways

[4] D Kapiszewski and M Taylor, "Compliance: Measuring and Explaining Adherence to Judicial Rulings" Law and Social Inquiry (forthcoming).

[5] A Chayes and AH Chayes, "On Compliance" (1993) 2 Int'l. Org. 175, 176.

[6] B Kingsbury "The Concept of Compliance as a Function of Competing Conceptions of International Law" (1998) 19 MJIL. 345, 368.

[7] GW Downs, DM Rocke, and PN Barsoom, "Is the Good News about Compliance Good News about Cooperation?" (1996) 50 Int'l. Org. 379, at 383.

[8] R Howse and R Teitel, "Beyond Compliance: Rethinking Why International Law Really Matters" (2010) 2 Global Policy 127.

in which that ruling nonetheless alters its behavior. Rulings can also have significant effects on non-party states and non-state actors. One of the contributions of Law and Society scholars has been to reveal the myriad and sometimes contradictory effects of a court ruling after it comes down, beyond the courtroom and beyond the litigants.[9] Even if we conceive of actors as rational and law as an instrument to alter incentive structures, its impact occurs through many different channels. Compliance to court rulings is but one.

Especially critical of compliance studies are those who emphasize law's role not as an instrument with which to effect change, but rather as constitutive—as constructing cognitive categories and shaping identities. Under constitutive views, laws are not linked causally to discrete acts. They *do* have effects—they may guide, inspire, rationalize, or justify behavior[10]—it is just that these effects are not perceived by measuring the correspondence between law's requirements and a given subject's behavior. The focus on compliance with international law tends to "ignore the centrality of interpretation to the generation of legal meaning."[11] Rulings enunciate and clarify rules; they give civil society groups discursive tools with which to pursue their goals; they may influence how other judges and political actors frame an issue; and they may influence bargaining among actors "in the shadow of the law"—all regardless of compliance.

The focus on compliance is rooted in the history of international relations, long dominated in the United States by realists who argued that states obeyed law only when it was in their self-interest.[12] It persists in part because compliance data is readily available, whereas measuring impact is a costly and uncertain undertaking.[13] So problematic has it been, Lisa Martin argues, that social scientists would do better to jettison the concept: "relying on compliance measures as an indicator of institutional effects has unfortunately caused the field to veer off in less-than-productive directions."[14]

1.2 Why judgment compliance still matters

Compliance nonetheless matters, particularly in the study of adjudication. It is, after all, the essence of legality. The rule of law derives its core legitimacy from the uniform application of rules to all. "Public authorities' compliance with judicial

[9] For an insightful discussion of law's effects in society, see MW McCann, "Reform Litigation on Trial" (1992) 17 Law & Social Inquiry 715; GN Rosenberg, "Hollow Hopes and Other Aspirations: A Reply to Feeley and McCann" (1992) 17 Law & Social Inquiry 761.

[10] Howse and Teitel, note 8; JG Ruggie, "Epistemology, ontology, and the study of international regimes" in JG Ruggie (ed.) *Constructing the World Polity: Essays on International Institutionalization* (New York: Routledge 1998).

[11] Howse and Teitel, note 8, at 3. [12] Howse and Teitel, note 8, at 3. [13] Martin, note 1.

[14] Martin, note 1

dictates is central to legality and constitutionality,"[15] Kapiszewski and Taylor write. This is a normative commitment, and helps explain why legal actors are keen to measure compliance. Judges care about whether their strictures receive compliance, regardless of other effects they may have, because it conforms to their understanding of who they are and what law is. This is true even if, at times, they forego compliance for other judicial goals. In other words, perhaps it is true that both effective and ineffective international courts (ICs) can show high compliance rates.[16] But even effective courts would be alarmed if they had a genuinely low compliance level, and their remedial orders were simply ignored. Compliance with remedial orders assures that the adverse effects of a legal violation are attenuated and individual justice is done. Compliance with interim orders assures that something of value is safeguarded from immediate jeopardy while a dispute is resolved. Compliance with orders to assist with a criminal investigation allows prosecutions to move forward. Those who design courts structure them in ways that foster compliance; those who choose them as the venue through which to resolve a dispute want to know orders will be obeyed. For these legal actors—and therefore for social scientists interested in understanding legal phenomena—the dynamics surrounding compliance matter quite apart from general assessments of efficacy.

The problem with assuming—as opposed to proving—that a legal instrument has a causal relation to compliance is often less acute in the study of judgment compliance than in the study of primary-norm compliance (or state compliance to treaty law).[17] When a state complies with a court judgment, there is a detectable change in behavior: the state's behavior before the judgment differs from its behavior after. Something in its calculus changed. In this scenario, it is less fraught to assume that the behavior constituting compliance is an outcome of the decision, and that it goes against a fairly strong reason for non-compliance (strong enough to justify the risk of a negative international ruling). Similarly, when a court orders a state to pay a specific amount of compensation to a victim of a human rights violation, for example, and the state pays precisely the amount in question, causality is less fraught. The answer to the counterfactual—"Would the state have done the same without the order?"—seems self-evident. A focus on compliance is still too narrow in that it excludes important effects the ruling may have, for example on actors not bound by the ruling. But it acts as a more reliable measure of this one kind of effect that a ruling may have.

Finally, compliance is of interest as both an independent and an intervening variable. The conclusion that it is not a reliable indicator of a regime's effectiveness opens

[15] Kapiszewski and Taylor, note 4, at 2.

[16] Y Shany, "Compliance with Decisions of International Courts as Indicative of their Effectiveness: A Goal-Based Analysis" (2010) Proc. Eur. Soc'y Int'l L. 229.

[17] D Hawkins and W Jacoby, "Partial Compliance: A Comparison of the European and Inter-American Courts for Human Rights" (2010) 6 J. Int'l. L. & Int'l. Rel. 35, 40.

up an important research question: under what conditions does compliance to court rulings engender greater effectiveness, however that may be defined? Does judgment compliance lead to greater IC legitimacy?[18] How does it affect judicial behavior? Compliance can "have powerful feedback effects on judicial decision-making, independence, and power."[19] Non-compliance, for example, can erode a court's legitimacy, or alter the way a court makes subsequent rulings.[20] Further, compliance can be viewed as a tool that courts and their subjects strategically wield in their pursuit of other goals.[21] These themes have been under-studied both in the field of national judicial politics, where compliance has been assumed,[22] and in the field of international law, where the focus has been on compliance as a dependent variable.

1.3 Defining judgment compliance

Judgment compliance occurs when a state or other actor subject to a court carries out the actions required by a ruling of the court or refrains from carrying out actions prohibited by said ruling. *Sensu stricto*, it does not include actions taken by actors not subject to the ruling, nor does it include actions taken in response to the ruling but not required by the ruling.

There are two distinct types of judgment compliance. The first, more specific type refers to compliance to court orders that request a concrete action from a particular party. Compliance with remedial orders clearly qualifies, as does compliance with interim orders meant to grant relief prior to a substantive ruling. This category also includes compliance with orders issued by the international criminal courts that solicit states' help in conducting investigations (when those states are legally bound to do so). Assessing specific compliance requires that one examine the behavior of the parties burdened by a specific order. The domestic process that leads to specific compliance is often referred to as "implementation."

But judgments also include authoritative interpretations of underlying laws, and at times claim to exert a diffuse *erga omnes* (as opposed to *inter partes*) authority.[23] For example, US Supreme Court judgments create binding precedent, and must be

[18] JL Gibson and GA Caldeira, "The Legitimacy of Transnational Legal Institutions: Compliance, Support, and the European Court of Justice" (1995) 39 American Journal of Political Science 459.

[19] Kapiszewski and Taylor, note 4, at 1.

[20] CJ Carrubba, M Gabel, and C Hankla, "Judicial Behavior under Political Constraints: Evidence from the European Court of Justice" (2008) 4 American Political Science Review 435; L Helfer and A-M Slaughter, "Why States Create International Tribunals: A Response to Professors Posner and Yoo" (2005) 93 Calif. L. Rev. 899.

[21] Carrubba, Gabel, and Hankla, note 20; Y Shany, note 16; JK Staton and G Vanberg, "The Value of Vagueness: Delegation, Defiance and Judicial Opinions" (2008) 3 Am. J. Pol. Sci. 504.

[22] Kapiszewski and Taylor, note 4.

[23] The term *erga omnes* is used here, as it is in national law, to refer to a judgment that binds not only the parties to the case, but also others under the court's authority. See LR Helfer and E Voeten, "International Courts as Agents of Legal Change: Evidence from LGBT Rights in Europe" (2014) 68(2) International Organizations.

followed not only by the parties to the case, but by all federal judges adjudicating similar cases. This *stare decisis* system—in which the rulings of the adjudicative body are unmoored from the dispute in which a rule is enunciated and become primary norms—creates a more diffuse form of legal compliance. To measure it, one must look beyond the losing party to all the actors subject to the court, and measure their subsequent behavior against the rule enunciated by the particular ruling. International judgments, however, do not claim to create binding precedent. And while the role precedent plays in institutionalized legal systems such as the EU is virtually indistinguishable from the role it plays in Anglo-American common law systems,[24] it does not carry the formal title of law. For this reason, most studies in international law, including this chapter, focus only on the first, more specific sense of judgment compliance. But the second, broader category of diffuse compliance may grow in importance if ICs are able to convince subjects that their rulings, like those of the US Supreme Court, provide interpretations of primary norms that are themselves binding.[25]

1.4 Measuring judgment compliance

The concept of compliance is relational.[26] It refers to the correspondence of two things: the ruling's demands and the behavior of parties subject to the ruling. Measuring judgment compliance requires at least three separate steps: an interpretation of what behavior the ruling demands and of whom; an assessment of the subject parties' behavior; and a comparison of the two.[27] Each step presents measurement challenges.

The first problem is figuring out what, exactly, a ruling demands. As the constructivists complain, compliance studies tend to "begin with the notion that there is a stable and agreed meaning to a rule, and we need merely to observe whether it is obeyed."[28] But the meanings of rules are subject to different interpretations and can change over time. Remedial orders can be clearly delineated; they usually come at the end of a decision and can even be set apart in their own section. They can be quite specific, as when a court gives a dollar amount by which the losing party must compensate the winner. But they can also lead to interpretive difficulty and, indeed, are at times deliberately vague.[29] Further, remedy compliance might not be the same as compliance with the judgment in its entirety. Thus, a human rights court might

[24] B Hofstötter, *Non-Compliance of National Courts: Remedies in European Community Law and Beyond* (The Hague: TMC Asser Press 2006) 42.

[25] For an argument that the Inter-American Court is moving in this direction, see A Dulitzk, "El impacto del control de convencionalidad: ¿Un cambio de paradigma en el sistema interamericano de derechos humanos?" in S Elias et al. (eds), *Tratado de los Derechos Constitucionales* (forthcoming).

[26] Kapiszewski and Taylor, note 4.

[27] Kapiszewski and Taylor, note 4.

[28] Howse and Teitel, note 8, at 127.

[29] Staton and Vanberg, note 21.

find that a state violated the right to access to justice and then order compensation to the victim as the remedy. But if the state, having compensated the victim, does not fix its justice system, has it complied with the ruling?

The second step requires ascertaining what the burdened actor has done in response. This can be a difficult empirical inquiry. Even where it is clear what actions the actor must take, it can be difficult to obtain data to assess whether it has taken those actions. Some international court systems monitor compliance and issue supervisory reports, but they usually rely on the state to volunteer information about their implementation of the ruling, and the reports can be incomplete.

The third step, determining if the acts comprise compliance, is again a matter of interpretation; it requires applying the rule or the order to the messy facts on the ground. Often there is no actor that has the power to authoritatively decide whether there is compliance. Where an official actor is charged with monitoring and deciding on compliance, such as the Committee of Ministers in the European Council System, there arises the question of whether to adopt the official judgment on compliance, which carries legal weight, or whether an independent assessment must be made, which may differ from that of the official body.

Further, there is the question of how much compliance is enough. At first glance compliance looks like a dichotomous variable; the burdened actor's behavior either does or does not qualify. However, there is growing interest in conceptualizing and measuring partial compliance—the broad spectrum of behavior that seems better described as falling in-between the two extremes.[30] Partial compliance refers to behavior that moves toward, but doesn't achieve, full implementation of a particular ruling. Or, in a ruling that encompasses various orders, it can refer to compliance/non-compliance to some orders and not others. By coding certain types of non-compliance as partial compliance, several recent studies of the regional rights systems have been able to reveal interesting patterns in compliance behavior.[31]

The passage of time also poses an analytical challenge. The definition of judgment compliance given above is atemporal. But it clearly matters *when* the burdened party acts. An act of compliance that takes place six months after the ruling seems qualitatively different from one that take place ten years later. Time

[30] Hawkins and Jacoby, note 17; C Hillebrecht, "Rethinking Compliance: The Challenges and Prospects of Measuring Compliance with International Human Rights" (2009) 1 Journal of Human Rights Practice 362; Kapiszewski and Taylor, note 4.

[31] See, for example, Hawkins and Jacoby, note 17; C Hillebrecht, "Implementing International Human Rights Law at Home: Domestic Politics and the European Court of Human Rights" (2012) 13 Human Rights Review 279; A Huneeus, "Courts Resisting Courts: The Inter-American Court's Struggle to Enforce Human Rights" (2011) 44 Cornell Int'l L. J. 493; F Basch et al., "The Effectiveness Of The Inter-American System Of Human Rights Protection: A Quantitative Approach To Its Functioning And Compliance With Its Decisions" (2010) 7 Sur—International Journal on Human Rights 9.

must therefore be incorporated into any assessment of compliance.[32] Indeed, some courts already do this by giving states deadlines. The European Committee, for example, has begun recording the percentage of payments states make on time.[33] At the very least, if we define compliance as behavior *caused* by a judgment, "our confidence in labeling behavior in line with a judicial ruling as 'compliance' should probably decrease as time between the ruling and the 'response' increases."[34]

Despite the challenges outlined above, there are rich empirical studies on individual ICs. Scholars have developed methods to study compliance with judgments of the International Court of Justice (ICJ),[35] World Trade Organization (WTO),[36] European Court of Justice (ECJ)[37] and Andean Court of Justice,[38] as well as the regional human rights courts.[39] One lacuna, however, is comparison across courts, especially across different types of international adjudicative bodies. Factors such as styles of remedial design and different record-keeping practices make it challenging to derive meaningful comparisons. At the most extreme, some comparisons should be avoided: it seems unlikely that the compliance behavior of states can be fruitfully compared to that of other types of international-court subjects, such as international organizations, corporations, or individual defendants on the international criminal dockets. Recent scholarship has begun deriving systematic measures with an eye to comparison across courts and across legal systems.[40] But systematic applications of such methods are still lacking.

[32] Hillebrecht, note 30; Kapiszewski and Taylor, note 4.

[33] Hillebrecht, note 30, at 376.

[34] Kapiszewski and Taylor, note 4, at 22.

[35] See C Schulte, *Compliance with Decisions of the International Court of Justice* (Oxford University Press 2005); C Paulson, "Compliance with Final Judgments of the International Court of Justice Since 1987" (2004) 98 AJIL 434.

[36] See K Leitner and S Lester, "WTO Dispute Settlement from 1995 to 2005: A Statistical Analysis" (2006) 9 JIEL 219; WJ Davey, "Evaluating WTO Dispute Settlement: What Results Have Been Achieved Through Consultations and Implementation of Panel Reports?" in Y Taniguchi, A Yanovich, and J Bohanes (eds), *The WTO in the 21st Century: Dispute Settlement, Negotiations, and Regionalism* (Cambridge University Press 2007).

[37] See M Blauberger, "With Luxembourg in mind... the remaking of national policies in the face of ECJ jurisprudence" (2012) 19 Journal of European Public Policy 109, 122; TA Börzel, T Hofmann and D Panke, "Caving in or sitting it out? Longitudinal patterns of non-compliance in the European Union" (2012) 19 Journal of European Public Policy 454, 467.

[38] See K Alter, L Helfer, and MF Guerzovich, "Islands of Effective International Adjudication: Constructing an Intellectual Property Rule of Law in the Andean Community" (2009) 109 AJIL 1.

[39] See Hawkins and Jacoby, note 17.

[40] J Etienne, "Compliance Theory: A Goal Framing Approach" (2011) 3 Law and Policy 305; Kapiszewski and Taylor, note 4; Hillebrecht, note 30.

2 Understanding IC Judgment Compliance

Although most compliance studies have focused on a particular court without looking comparatively, a review of the literature allows us to derive shared themes across courts. This section divides into four parts. It begins by examining studies that explain judgment compliance by focusing on features of the court, or of the structure of the legal regime of which the court is part. Second, it turns to studies highlighting factors relating to the state, including its legal and political features. The third part addresses studies that highlight features of the dispute itself, such as subject matter and the type of problem it seeks to solve. Finally, the section turns the equation around, and examines studies that view compliance not as a dependent but as an independent or intervening variable. The entire section draws especially on studies of the transnational human rights courts, the international criminal courts, and the ECJ and the ICJ.

Throughout, the emphasis is on studies that treat judgment compliance as distinct from primary norm compliance. This is not because general compliance studies are not relevant. They are. However, theories that seek to explain primary norm compliance cannot, without more, claim to explain judgment compliance. In arguing against concern with reputation as an explanation for judgment compliance, Ginsburg and McAdams write: "If reputation were strong enough to compel compliance with adjudication, one wonders why it was not also strong enough to resolve the dispute *without* adjudication. Why is reputation too weak to induce compliance before a third party pronounces a nation's legal obligations, but still strong enough to induce compliance after such a pronouncement."[41] Their question raises a challenge to any general compliance theory that does not specifically account for the dynamics of adjudication.

2.1 Judgment compliance and features of the IC regime

2.1.1 *Consent structure*

Several studies query whether the manner in which states consent to court jurisdiction matters to judgment compliance. The jurisdiction of the ICJ can be accepted in four ways, each reflecting a different level of commitment by the litigating parties. Scholars have long assumed that, "Defiance is less likely where states have given their

[41] T Ginsburg and RH McAdams, "Adjudicating in Anarchy: An Expressive Theory of International Dispute Resolution" (2004) 25 Wm. & Mary L. Rev. 1229, 1240.

specific consent to proceedings before the Court,"[42] particularly through special agreement. Cases of compulsory jurisdiction (through optimal clause declaration or compromissory clause) "present a far greater challenge for the Court's authority."[43] In 2004, however, Colter Paulsen published an article concluding that there is "no link between submission by special agreement and compliance."[44] Llamzon took up the question in a later study examining cases subsequent to *Nicaragua v. U.S.*, and concluded: "The mode by which the ICJ was seised of jurisdiction thus appears to be a rather poor predictor of subsequent compliance."[45] Llamzon and Paulsen's findings can be understood as showing not that consent does not matter, but rather that, as Schulte himself emphasizes, the ICJ jurisdictional structures are not a reliable proxy for consent. Several states have been reluctantly dragged into litigation through special agreement jurisdiction.

The consent argument has also been explored in the setting of the International Criminal Court (ICC). There are three ways in which cases can come before the ICC: through a UN Security Council referral of a non-state party;[46] through the prosecutor's referral of a state party;[47] and through self-referral.[48] Some argue that the ICC will be more successful in obtaining state compliance to its orders to apprehend subjects in cases of self-referrals than in cases imposed on an unwilling non-party state by the United Nations Security Council (UNSC), such as the investigations in Sudan and Libya, or by the prosecutor acting *propiu motu*.[49] Again, however, a state's self-referral might not indicate its true level of commitment to prosecutions; the Democratic Republic of Congo, for example, only referred its case when a referral by the prosecutor was imminent.[50] Even where a state willingly refers its case, this consent may be a weak predictor of state commitment to the process over time: investigations

[42] Schulte, note 35, at 406. See also JI Charney, "Disputes Implicating the Institutional Credibility of the Court: Problems of Non-Appearance, Non-Participation, and Non-Performance" in LF Damrosch (ed.), *The International Court of Justice at a Crossroads* (Dobbs Ferry, NY: Transnational 1987); S Oda, "The Compulsory Jurisdiction of the International Court of Justice: A Myth?" (2000) 49 Int'l & Comp LQ 251, 264.

[43] Schulte, note 35, at 411. [44] Paulson, note 35, at 457.

[45] AP Llamzon, "Jurisdiction and Compliance in Recent Decisions of the International Court of Justice" (2007) 5 Eur. J. Int'l L. 815, 852.

[46] The situations in Darfur, Sudan, and in Libya were referred by the UNSC.

[47] The situations in Kenya and Ivory Coast were referred by the Office of the Prosecutor.

[48] The situations in Congo, Central African Republic, Uganda, and Mali are self-referrals. Under the Rome Statute, state parties can also refer fellow state parties, but this has yet to take place.

[49] SD Roper and LA Barria, "State Cooperation and International Criminal Court Bargaining Influence in the Arrest and the Surrender of Suspects" (2008) 21 Leiden Journal of International Law 457, 464. See also V Peskin, "Caution and Confrontation in the International Criminal Court's Pursuit of Accountability in Uganda and Sudan" (2009) 31 Human Rights Quarterly 655. Note that state parties have a duty to comply with ICC requests even if the crimes being investigated did not take place on their territories and the suspects are not their nationals. Coaxing compliance from third states poses a different set of challenges for the ICC; suspects sometimes flee to non-party states, which do not have this duty of cooperation.

[50] Roper and Barria, note 49, at 469–70.

take years, and political will can shift quickly. Uganda, one of the states that referred itself to the ICC, suffered buyer's remorse when it realized the ICC was hampering its ability to broker a peace deal with the Lord's Resistance Army.[51]

2.1.2 *Remedy design*

Scholars concur that the rate of remedial compliance tends to reflect the cost the particular order imposed on the burdened state. The record of the human rights tribunals, for example, shows that orders requiring monetary compensation are more likely to receive compliance than those requiring equitable relief.[52] It is easier for states to pay out money than it is to undertake actions, such as bureaucratic reform, as a form of compensation. Among the Inter-American Court's creative array of equitable relief orders, those requiring more challenging actions, such as an order to investigate and punish a crime, receive lower compliance.[53] An alternative hypothesis is that the equitable orders that require action by multiple players within the state, and are thus more susceptible to veto, are less likely to be fulfilled. Thus, remedial orders requiring action by distinct government branches or institutions are less likely to spur compliance than those that can be carried out by a single institutional actor.[54]

Another remedy design feature that seems to matter is the degree of vagueness of the order. Jeffrey Staton and Georg Vanberg write that an "established line of research demonstrates that vague judicial opinions are less likely to be implemented than clear opinions."[55] Greater specificity means greater transparency and accountability, which raises the cost of non-compliance. Studies also show that courts strategically use vague language when they fear non-compliance, as a way to mask their inability to command compliance.[56]

2.1.3 *Provisional measures and order type*

International courts issue many different kinds of orders, including provisional measures, remedial orders, and orders to assist with a criminal investigation. While there is no study that compares compliance rates across order type, some studies of provisional measures suggest that they have features that would make the dynamics of compliance different than for final judgments. First, it has not always been clear whether provisional measures are binding in the same way as final judgments.

[51] HA Moy, "International Criminal Court's Arrest Warrants and Uganda's Lord's Resistance Army: Renewing the Debate over Amnesty and Complementarity" (2006) 19 Harv. Hum Rts. J. 267.

[52] Hawkins and Jacoby, note 17. [53] Hawkins and Jacoby, note 17.

[54] Huneeus, note 31.

[55] Staton and Vanberg, note 21, at 504; JK Staton and A Romero "Clarity and Compliance in the Inter-American Human Rights System" (IPSA-ECPR Joint Conference, February 16 to 19, 2011, Sao Paulo, Brazil) <http://saopaulo2011.ipsa.org/sites/saopaulo2011.ipsa.org/files/papers/paper-883.pdf> accessed September 24, 2013.

[56] Staton and Vanberg, note 21.

Compliance with ICJ provisional measures, for example, has improved since the court clearly stated in the *LaGrand* judgment that they had binding force.[57] Second, courts issue provisional measures before they have reached a final decision on whether they have jurisdiction over the merits of the case. In the eyes of the burdened state, the exercise may therefore lack legitimacy.[58] Further, Schulte argued that final judgments create clarity, whereas provisional measures limit states' "freedom of action pending the proceedings without creating clarity."[59] States therefore get little benefit from complying.

In the Inter-American system, provisional measures are often used to ensure the security of individuals immediately at risk. Burbano Herrera argued that the court has had a high compliance rate with such measures. Non-compliance of these provisional measures most commonly occurred in areas over which the state had less control, either because the state did not protect beneficiaries from *third* parties (as opposed to directly violating the right to life or physical integrity); because the beneficiaries did not trust the state; or because the measures backfired and further imperiled the beneficiary.[60]

2.1.4 *Enforcement mechanisms*

National courts rely on the executive to enforce judgments. International courts often do as well. But as ICs' judgments are often directed against the very state that would be charged with execution of the order, they find themselves on weaker ground (although public law litigation leaves national courts in a similar place). To overcome resistance to self-enforcement, some founding treaties create mechanisms by which enforcement problems can be referred to a separate political, as opposed to judicial, body. In cases of non-compliance to an ICJ ruling, the UN Charter provides that the aggrieved state can refer the case to the Security Council, "which may, if it deems necessary, make recommendations or decide upon measures to be taken to give effect to the judgment."[61] Similarly, the Statute for the International Criminal Tribunal for the Former Yugoslavia (ICTY) allows the court to report states' non-compliance with orders to assist with the investigation to the Security Council;[62] the American Convention on Human Rights allows the Inter-American

[57] Schulte, note 35, at 428–9.

[58] S Rosenne, *Provisional Measures in International Law* (Oxford University Press 2005) 189. Of course, one might also argue that states benefit from compliance with such measures because they maintain the court's good will and prevent the dispute from deteriorating. Both scenarios are possible. (I owe this point to Yuval Shany.)

[59] Schulte, note 35, at 418.

[60] CB Herrera, *Provisional Measures in the Case Law of the Inter-American Court of Human Rights* (Antwerp/Oxford: Intersentia 2010).

[61] UN Charter, Art. 94. 2.g.

[62] See International Criminal Tribunal for the former Yugoslavia, S.C. Res. 827, U.N. SCOR, 48th Sess., 3217th mtg. at 29, U.N. Doc. S/827/1993 (1993).

Court to refer non-compliance to the Organization of American States (OAS) General Assembly; and the Council of Europe (CoE) allows the Council to suspend membership for failure to implement ECtHR judgments.

These enforcement mechanisms, however, have not proved effective. Few ICJ cases have been referred to the Security Council, in part because "cases of defiance regularly involved a permanent member either on the applicant or the respondent side, reinforcing the institution's Cold War stasis."[63] The ICTY soon learned that the Security Council was unwilling to enforce states' duties to assist tribunal investigations. However, the referrals had the virtue of putting outside pressure on recalcitrant states.[64] The Inter-American Court similarly learned that the OAS General Assembly lacks political will to pressure states to comply with its judgments; indeed, as one judge observed, there exists no mechanism for the OAS General Assembly to regularly discuss the court's compliance reports.[65] Neither has the CoE ever suspended a noncompliant member: As Courtney Hillebrecht notes, "[it] is not politically viable for the CoE to expel Western European states on whom their operating budget depends, nor is it necessarily expedient to expel states from Central and Eastern Europe if one of the core objectives . . . is their socialization into democratic and European institutions."[66] The one time it seemed the CoE would suspend a member, the state preempted the action by withdrawing.[67]

Traditional forms of international law enforcement do play a role in IC regimes. The WTO regime, for example, relies on self-help. Aggrieved states can enforce judgments by retaliating against non-compliant states, taking trade measures that would otherwise be in breach of the underlying treaties.[68] The threat of retaliation makes non-compliance costly to the burdened state—and thus less likely[69]—and creates incentives for exporters to lobby their governments to comply.[70] One problem, however, is that compliance incentives are different for different states. As one study noted, "It is one thing for the E.U. to be excluded from the Ecuadorian market,

[63] Schulte, note 35, at 417.

[64] CK Lamont, *International Criminal Justice and the Politics of Compliance* (Farnham: Ashgate Publishing Ltd. 2010) 171.

[65] *Caesar Case* (Dissenting Opinion Judge Manuel E. Ventura Robles) Inter-American Court of Human Rights Serie C No. 123 (March 11, 2005), para. 26.

[66] Hillebrecht, note 31, at 5.

[67] The state was Greece, during its military dictatorship. See MT Kamminga, "Is the European Convention on Human Rights Sufficiently Equipped to Cope with Gross and Systematic Violations?" (1994) 12 Neth. Q. Hum. Rts. 153, 155.

[68] However, different views exist on exactly what sorts of obligation follow from a WTO Dispute Resolution Mechanism decision. See JH Jackson, "Editorial Comment: the WTO dispute settlement understanding—misunderstandings on the nature of legal obligation" (1997) 91 AJIL 60. For a contrary view, see JH Bellow, "The WTO DSU: Less is More" (1996) 90 AJIL 416.

[69] AT Guzman, *How International Law Works: A Rational Choice Theory* (Oxford University Press 2008).

[70] ML Movsesian, "Enforcement of WTO Rulings: An Interest Group Analysis" (2003) 32 Hofstra Law Review 1.

and yet quite another for Ecuador to be excluded from the E.U. market."[71] Some IC treaties also impose upon member states a specific duty to enforce judgments. UN member states have a duty to enforce ICJ judgments when they are party to the case, whereas all members of the International Centre for Settlement of Investment Disputes (ICSID) have a duty to enforce its judgments, regardless of whether they were a party. ICSID judgments are therefore enforceable as if they were domestic court decisions.[72]

2.1.5 *Monitoring mechanisms*

IC regimes have developed supervision mechanisms as a way to pressure for implementation of decisions. The European Committee of Ministers, for example, supervises implementation of ECtHR rulings and issues reports on compliance. The Inter-American Court has interpreted its mandate to allow it to remain seized of a case until it deems there is compliance and to demand states to report on their efforts toward compliance. More recently, the court has begun ordering states to participate in closed compliance hearings that include representatives of the Inter-American Commission, representatives of the victims, and judge, who in this context act as mediators. Supervision mechanisms are not, strictly speaking, forms of enforcement; they could be just as easily eluded by states as the ruling itself. Rather, they resemble non-compliance procedures—procedures built into treaty regimes to foster primary-norm compliance.[73] While Cesare Romano found non-compliance procedures to be effective alternatives to adjudication in environmental treaty regimes, there is no systematic study that shows whether these procedures increase compliance once they are incorporated by ICs into the post-adjudication phase. Perhaps one is due. Nonetheless, it seems clear these procedures provide compliance incentives by publicizing non-compliance and by giving discursive tools to civil society and other states interested in pressuring for compliance.

2.1.6 *Legalization*

Scholars debate how the level of legalization of an international law regime affects primary-norm and judgment compliance. The concept of legalization refers to the degree to which the IC regime conforms to each of three dimensions: level of formal state obligation to comply, level of precision of rules, and level of delegation

[71] PC Mavroidis, "On Compliance in the WTO: Enforcement amongst Unequal Disputants" [2012] 4 Briefing Paper Cuts International, <http://www.cuts-citee.org/pdf/Briefing_Paper12-On_Compliance_in_the_WTO_Enforcement_Amongst_Unequal_Disputants.pdf> accessed July 27, 2012, at 3.

[72] LF Damrosch, "A Comparative Look at Domestic Enforcement of International Tribunal Judgments" (2009) 103 Proceedings of the Annual Meeting (American Society of International Law) 39.

[73] CPR Romano, *The Peaceful Settlement of International Environmental Disputes: A Pragmatic Approach* (The Hague: Kluwer Law 2000).

of the power to decide to the IC.[74] Of course, once we are talking about a regime that includes binding adjudication, we are already at a high level of legalization; the opposite extreme would be soft law or norms without binding force. But there is variation even within IC regimes. We could consider compulsory jurisdiction, precise remedies, and greater monitoring to be signs of greater legalization. Scholars have not always found a direct link between legalization on the one hand, and greater primary norm or judgment compliance on the other.[75] Looking to the WTO dispute settlement procedure, for example, scholars have debated what level of legalization is optimal, thereby yielding the greatest level of compliance.[76] One concern is that over-legalization leads to backlash and non-compliance.[77] The move by the Inter-American Court to incorporate compliance hearings in which judges act as mediators would seem to be an acknowledgement that sometimes less formal adjudication and more informal negotiation is better.

2.1.7 *IC soft power and compliance constituencies*

A court's ability to use its soft power to publicize instances of non-compliance and garner third-party support may foster compliance. Victor Peskin argued that the degree to which the ICTY and ICTR were able to get favorable press coverage and convince third states to support their orders proved key to their relative success. Peskin noted that the ICTY "has wielded more soft power than the ICTR."[78] Relations with civil society actors can also have an impact on compliance. The ICC has been strategic in building alliances with civil society as a way to legitimate itself, but also as a way of pressuring states to comply with its orders to assist. The ICC has arguably made many political missteps as well. Some argue that it has alienated African states by focusing its investigations on African nations, undermining its efficacy in the region.[79] Implicit in such critiques is the notion that by proactively mobilizing third states and civil society, courts are able to exert influence and enhance compliance. More comparative work is needed, however, to understand when courts play a hand in successfully mobilizing such alliances, and when they fail to do so.

[74] KW Abbott et al., "The Concept of Legalization" (2000) 54 Int'l. Org. 401.

[75] Raustiala and Slaughter, note 2.

[76] See RE Hudec, "The New WTO Dispute Settlement Procedure: An Overview of the First Three years" (1999) 8 Minnesota Journal of Global Trade 1.

[77] L Helfer, "Overlegalizing Human Rights: International Relations Theory and the Commonwealth Caribbean Backlash Against Human Rights Regimes" (2002) 102 Colum. L. Rev. 1832.

[78] V Peskin, *International Justice in Rwanda and the Balkans: Virtual Trials and the Struggle for State Cooperation* (Cambridge University Press 2008) 7.

[79] See M Du Plessis, *The International Criminal Court that Africa wants* (Institute for Security Studies, Pretoria 2010); K Mills, "Bashir is Dividing Us: Africa and the International Criminal Court" (2012) 34 Human Rights Quarterly 404; CC Jalloh, "Universal Jurisdiction, Universal Prescription? A Preliminary Assessment of the African Union Perspective on Universal Jurisdiction" (2010) 21 Crim. L. Forum 15.

2.1.8 *IC legitimacy and independence*

Thomas Franck defined legitimacy as "a property of a rule or rule-making institution which itself exerts a pull toward compliance on those addressed normatively because those addressed believe that the rule or institution has come into being and operates in accordance with generally accepted principles of right process."[80] It can be identified by a relevant audience's "willingness to continue to support the continued function of the institution despite disagreement with its outputs."[81] There is a long sociological tradition that links legitimate authority and obedience to law, and it is often assumed that a court's legitimacy enhances compliance to its rulings. But the relationship has received little direct scholarly inquiry.[82] One study did find that the ECJ had low legitimacy among individual EU citizens, negatively affecting their acceptance of rulings with which they disagreed, and, most likely, compliance.[83] But more direct research on legitimacy is needed, both as leading to compliance, and, in turn, as its product.

Counter-intuitively, there seems to be no positive correlation between IC independence and compliance. John Yoo and Eric Posner noted that dependent courts will be more deferential to states, and thus may actually enjoy high compliance rates.[84] Conversely, Laurence Helfer and Anne-Marie Slaughter's constrained courts, with compulsory jurisdiction and tenured judges, issue rulings that are at times distasteful to the losing parties, and encounter greater compliance problems.[85] No direct generalization can be drawn from their model about a link between judicial independence and judgment compliance, however, since many other factors weighed into their equation.

2.2 Judgment compliance and features of the state

In recent years a surge of studies has examined the role of diverse sub-national actors and institutions to explain why states obey international law. This trend has also been influential in the study of compliance. Increasingly, scholars argue that "implementation is inherently a domestic issue."[86] Within the domestic sphere, some studies emphasize legal institutions and actors, while others emphasize the impact of political factors, such as regime type, on judgment compliance.

[80] TM Franck, *The Power of Legitimacy among Nations* (Oxford University Press 1990) 16.

[81] Gibson and Caldeira, note 18, at 460.

[82] N Grossman, "Legitimacy and International Adjudicative Bodies" (2010) 41 Geo. Wash. Int'l. L. Rev. 107; Franck, note 80.

[83] Gibson and Caldeira, note 18.

[84] EA Posner and JC Yoo, "Judicial Independence in International Tribunals" (2005) 93. Calif. L. Rev. 1.

[85] Helfer and Slaughter, note 20. [86] Hillebrecht, note 31.

2.2.1 *Domestic legal factors*

Legal scholars point to formal features of the legal system. For example, some suggest that whether a national system treats an IC judgment as self-executing matters to compliance. The US Supreme Court ruled in 2007 that the ICJ's remedial order in *Avena* was not self-executing, and thus could not be enforced unless Congress passed enacting legislation. Several high courts in Latin America, by contrast, have in recent years decided that the Inter-American Court's orders are automatically binding and justiciable in the domestic sphere. It can also matter what rank an international court ruling holds within the domestic hierarchy of laws: is it akin to constitutional law, or does it come in at the level of legislation? If the latter, subsequent legislation trumps the ruling in many, although not all, legal systems.

Those concerned with the implementation of rulings also emphasize the role of domestic mechanisms of implementation. One reason why Inter-American Court orders receive higher compliance when they demand compensation rather than injunctive remedies is that, in many nations, monetary award judgments can be directly enforced in national courts.[87] For implementation of complex injunctive relief orders, by contrast, there may be no clear mechanism. Even where the executive is committed to implementation, difficult orders can require complex decision-making and coordination between different state institutions, for which an established method of proceeding would fare better. US courts appoint special masters to implement complex structural reform orders, but there is no analog to the special master in international legal regimes.

Domestic judicial politics are another factor that influences implementation at the national level. Studies of primary-norm compliance suggest that independent courts are more willing to rule against the interests of powerful actors, such as the executive, and enforce treaty obligations.[88] Scholars of the ECJ have pointed to national judicial power as fostering compliance to the ECJ's interpretations of the underlying treaty obligations. Courts use international instruments such as judicial rulings to enhance their own standing or preferences, which, in turn, heighten the impact of international law judgments.[89] However, independent courts can also resist judgment compliance.[90] Shany has pointed out that US courts have a poor

[87] V Krsticevic, *Implementación de las Decisiones del Sistema Interamericano de Derechos Humanos: Aportes para los Procesos Legislativos* [Implementation of the Decisions of the Inter-American System for Human Rights: Suggestions for Legislative Processes] (Buenos Aires: Center for Justice and Int'l L. 2009).

[88] BA Simmons, "Compliance with International Agreements" (1998) 1 Annual Review of Political Science 75.

[89] K Alter, *Establishing the Supremacy of European Law: The Making of an International Rule of Law in Europe* (Oxford University Press 2001).

[90] K Alter, "The European Union's Legal System and Domestic Policy: Spillover or Backlash?" in JL Goldstein et al. (eds), *Legalization and World Politics.* (Cambridge, MA: MIT Press 2001).

record on compliance to ICJ rulings, with the Supreme Court declaring in 2007 that ICJ judgments were not justiciable within the United States.[91] In the Inter-American setting, two studies suggest that judicial independence does not necessarily predict remedy compliance.[92] One possibility is that when ICs issue orders that require specific action by national courts, and particularly high courts, compliance is lower. In this scenario, the IC casts the domestic courts not as partners in monitoring state compliance, but as subjects that must obey orders.[93]

Related to judicial independence is the concept of compliance partnerships between transnational and national courts. Starting in the 1990s, scholars sought to explain how the ECJ had "gradually secured compliance with its judgments and created a far more powerful role for itself than the founders of the Community had ever envisaged."[94] One school of thought emphasized the links the ECJ established with sub-national actors while shielding itself from political interference.[95] In particular, these theorists highlighted the role of national courts as partners that bolstered the ECJ by enforcing its rulings domestically. The crux of the debate was not about compliance per se, but political impact—did the ECJ push states to accept rulings they would not have otherwise preferred? Geoffrey Garret and Barry Weingast countered that state actors had expected and foreseen the path taken by the court; ECJ judgments reflected state interest,[96] and thus national courts were only enforcing state preferences. Nonetheless, the debate revealed how national courts and other subnational actors could play a pivotal role in enhancing compliance, and how domestic and international political and legal factors would make such compliance partnerships more likely.

Finally, legal culture—either generally held norms about legality and the rule of rule of law or more specific commitments to specific norms—may also influence state compliance. Comparing Serbia's and Croatia's compliance to orders from the ICTY, David Lamont argued that Croatia's general commitment to legality helped explain why it had a better compliance record than Serbia.[97] Kathryn Sikkink and Ellen Lutz pointed to a norm cascade to explain Latin American states' move toward

[91] Y Shany, note 16; see also, *Medellín v. Texas* [2008] 552 U.S. 491.

[92] Huneeus, note 31; Staton and Romero, note 55.

[93] See Huneeus, note 31.

[94] Raustiala and Slaughter, note 2, at 541.

[95] K Alter, "Who are the Masters of the Treaty? European Governments and the European Court of Justice" (1998) 52 Int'l. Org. 121; W Mattli and A-M Slaughter, "Law and Politics in the European Union: A Reply to Garrett" (1995) 1 Int'l. Org. 183; A Stone Sweet, "Judicialization and the Construction of Governance" (1999) 32 Comparative Political Studies 147; JHH Weiler, "A Quiet Revolution: The European Court of Justice and Its Interlocutors" (1994) 26 Comparative Political Studies 510.

[96] G Garret and BR Weingast, "Ideas, Interests and Institutions: Constructing the European Community's Internal Market" in J Goldstein and RO Keohane (eds), *Ideas in Foreign Policy: Beliefs, Institutions and Political Change* (Ithaca, NY: Cornell University Press 1993); G Garrett, "The Politics of Legal Integration in the European Union" (1995) 49 Int'l. Org. 171.

[97] Lamont, note 64.

striking down amnesties and prosecuting dictatorship-era crimes.[98] Prosecution of these crimes is mandated by the Inter-American Court in dozens of rulings.

2.2.2 *Domestic political factors*

International relations scholars have emphasized that "domestic regime-type, in general, and liberal democracy, in particular, are important factors for explaining compliance with international commitments."[99] Fewer studies, however, have taken these insights into the realm of judgment compliance. An exception is an article that focuses on the European Court of Human Rights. Courtney Hillebrecht tracked how different sub-state actors used the rulings of the ECtHR to advance their own political agendas.[100] More studies of this type are needed. Potential factors that impact judgment compliance are regime-type—that is, whether we are speaking of a democracy or autocracy—and also whether the state is a transitional country keen on signaling its participation in the international arena, or whether it is an established international player. Also, it may matter if the state has an active civil society.[101] Finally, state capacity is an important issue when remedies require structural change; executives may have the political will to comply, but simply cannot. In examining compliance to pilot judgments of the European Court of Human Rights, in which the court mandates structural reform of state bureaucracies, Philip Leach, Helen Hardman, and Svetlana Stephenson found that one cause of non-compliance was simply lack of capacity.[102] This likely also holds true for cases of non-compliance to orders to prosecute in the Inter-American System. Some states subject to complex orders have weak and corrupt legal systems; for them, compliance will not come quickly.

2.2.3 *Non-state subjects of IC orders*

States are not the only subjects of international court orders. The international criminal courts, in particular, hold trials in which witnesses, defense counsel, and individual defendants are subject to the tribunal's authority as individuals. In managing trials, the criminal courts are uniquely able to enforce their orders—they can hold individuals in contempt, and can even have them detained. Trials have not always gone smoothly. Defendants such as Slobodan Milošević have been keen to

[98] E Lutz and K Sikkink, "The Justice Cascade: The Evolution and Impact of Foreign Human Rights Trials in Latin America" (2001) 2 Chi. J. Int'l. L. 1.

[99] Helfer and Slaughter, note 20. [100] Hillebrecht, note 31.

[101] LJ Conant, *Justice Contained: Law and Politics in the European Union* (Ithaca, NY: Cornell University Press 2002); RA Cichowski, *The European Court and Civil Society* (Cambridge University Press 2007).

[102] P Leach, H Hardman, and S Stephenson, *Responding to Systemic Human Rights Violations—An Analysis Of Pilot Judgments of the European Court of Human Rights and Their Impact at National Level* (Antwerp: Intersentia 2010).

disrupt trials with non-compliant courtroom behavior; corrupt defense lawyers have split fees with clients; staffers have leaked confidential information; and witnesses frequently bear false testimony.[103] This is an area deserving of more study, but the insights it reveals might not be applicable beyond the criminal realm.

A closer analog to state compliance is the compliance of international organizations. Again, the ICTY proves illustrative. The ICTY faced the challenge of issuing orders to assist with investigations in Kosovo, where sovereignty was unclear and shifting. In 1999, the UN created the United Nations Interim Administration Mission in Kosovo (UNMIK), which took on most administrative responsibilities. David Lamont reported that the court had less success in garnering compliance from UNMIK than it did from the nation states, in part because of UNMIK's uncertain status before a Security Council court.[104] Arguably, compliance dynamics will be different between a court and an intergovernmental organization to which the court is linked institutionally, versus a situation in which the intergovernmental organization is more loosely linked to the court (as in the ICTY/UNMIK scenario). The ECJ, for example, reviews state legislation, but it also subjects EU secondary legislation such as directives to judicial review.[105] The ICJ, through its advisory jurisdiction, also reviews legal and factual determinations of other UN bodies.[106]

2.3 Judgment compliance and features of the dispute

Features of the dispute itself can be viewed separately from factors relating to the IC treaty regime or the state. Those studying compliance with ICJ judgments, for example, have focused on whether the disputes have to do with competing interstate claims over territory and bodies of water, and are therefore more intractable.[107] Colter Paulson found that such disputes "received the lowest levels of compliance."[108] Constanze Schulte argued that ICJ judgments in cases of a "highly political character of the underlying dispute, which often involved the use of force," are more likely to be defied.[109] The level of maturity of the relevant body of law also mattered, with the ICJ being considered "particularly ill equipped for situations where the law is very much in development."[110]

[103] N Combs, *Fact-Finding without Facts: The Uncertain Evidentiary Foundations of International Criminal Convictions* (Cambridge University Press 2010).

[104] Lamont, note 64.

[105] A famous case in this respect was the *Kadi* case. See G de Búrca, "The European Court of Justice and the International Legal Order after Kadi" (2010) 51 Harv. Int'l. L. J. 1.

[106] See M Angehr, "The International Court of Justice's Advisory Jurisdiction and the Review of Security Council, and General Assembly Resolutions" (2009) 103(2) Nw. U. L. Rev. 1007.

[107] S McLaughlin Mitchell and PR Hensel, "International Institutions and Compliance with Agreements" (2007) 51. Am. J. Pol. Sci. 721.

[108] Paulson, note 35, at 457. [109] Schulte, note 35, at 413. [110] Schulte, note 35, at 414.

Subject matter might also be significant in that some disputes attract the interest of third parties, raising the stakes on non-compliance. In the realm of international criminal law, for example, third states have played a key role in pressuring states to comply with the tribunals' orders. The African Union had to move its 2012 summit when Malawi, the state originally designated to host, capitulated to threatened aid cuts from third countries, and refused to allow Sudanese President Al Bashir to attend. The concern was that the ICC had issued an arrest warrant for Bashir. Of course, third-country pressure can cut both ways. The African Union has encouraged states to thwart ICC arrest warrants, undermining the court's efficacy in the region.

A more structural feature of the dispute is whether the underlying problem can be described as a "coordination game," in which "parties have fully or partially common interests that can be achieved only if they coordinate their strategies among multiple possible equilibria."[111] Ginsburg and McAdams argued that most international disputes fell into this category. The reason there is, generally speaking, high compliance to IC rulings is that ICs provide states with important information that helps them better coordinate to achieve shared interests. In a nutshell, "Adjudication works in part by clarifying ambiguity in the underlying conventions players observe, thereby facilitating coordination between the players."[112] Compliance, therefore, is a symptom of improved coordination.

The relative power of the parties to the dispute might also matter to judgment compliance, as realists predict and WTO studies suggest. Developing states are less successful in enforcing the WTO's dispute settlement procedure judgments against larger states.[113]

2.4 The effects of judgment compliance and non-compliance

So far the focus in this chapter, as in most of the compliance scholarship, has been on factors that predict compliance, with compliance cast as the dependent variable. But the effects of compliance deserve more attention. Once we separate compliance from its role as an indicator for effectiveness, for example, the question arises: Does compliance ever correlate with effectiveness? If so, under what circumstances? Further, if judgment compliance and primary-norm compliance are distinct phenomena, what is their relationship? When does judgment compliance foster compliance with the underlying treaty obligation? James Gibson and Gregory Caldeira argued that legitimacy promotes compliance;[114] does compliance, in turn, engender

[111] Ginsburg and McAdams, note 41, at 1235.
[112] Ginsburg and McAdams, note 41, at 1235.
[113] Mavroidis, note 71.
[114] Gibson and Caldeira, note 18.

legitimacy? Such questions have received little systematic inquiry as they pertain to ICs.

A key insight of judicial politics scholars is that courts strategically design remedies to attain particular goals, including compliance.[115] Thus, Shai Dothan argues that the ECtHR consistently issues "the costliest judgment that it expects the state to actually comply with."[116] Over time, if the court gets it right, "its reputation is likely to increase, which in turn will enable it to issue increasingly costly judgments that states are able to comply with."[117]

Non-compliance has also received attention. Several studies highlight how political actors use non-compliance as a tool to constrain courts and temper their rulings.[118] The ECJ, Clifford Carubba et al. argued, shapes its rulings to conform to state preferences in response to threats (as opposed to actual acts) of non-compliance and override. Further, "[t]hreats of noncompliance are more influential on judicial rulings than threats of override."[119] This argument is another approach to the question of whether the ECJ independently influences the direction of the EU, or merely reflects state preferences. The first group aimed at explaining compliance to ECJ rulings; this group seeks to explore the effects of threats of non-compliance on ECJ rulings. Sweet and Brunquell rejected Carubba et al.'s findings, arguing that the effect of non-compliance is only to create more litigation, pressuring governments to comply.[120]

3 Further Study

It is true, as compliance skeptics suggest, that many of the aforementioned factors that lead to higher compliance rates also reflect shallow cooperation. Thus, states comply more when the order is less costly; compliance is greater when states agree to litigation of the particular dispute; and enforcement mechanisms do not work against the stronger states. Even these studies, however, are useful: they reveal specific sources and mechanisms of non-compliance, and thus allow legal actors to work toward overcoming those obstacles. The good news on compliance may be

[115] Carrubba, Gabel, and Hankla, note 20; Helfer and Slaughter, note 20; S Dothan, "Judicial Tactics in the European Court of Human Rights" (2011) 12 Chi. J. Int'l. L. 115; Y Shany, note 16; Staton and Vanberg, note 21.

[116] Dothan, note 115, at 3. [117] Dothan, note 115, at 3.

[118] Carrubba, Gabel, and Hankla, note 20; Helfer and Slaughter, note 20.

[119] Carrubba, Gabel, and Hankla, note 20, at 449.

[120] A Stone Sweet and T Brunquell, "The European Court of Justice, State Noncompliance, and the Politics of Override" (2012) 1 Am. Pol. Sci. Rev. 204.

bad news on cooperation, but it is nonetheless important information for those interested in improving compliance within particular regimes.

Some studies, however, point to a different dynamic. They reveal that courts are not epiphenomenal, with their judgments merely reflecting pre-existing levels of cooperation. Rather, they exert independent influence on states. These studies highlight the role of ICs as political actors able to alter compliance dynamics, with litigation in some ways altering the stakes from what they would have been without adjudication. Thus, it is argued that the ICTY effectively used soft power to pressure states to comply with its judgments; that the ECJ forged compliance partnerships with national courts that pushed states in directions they had not foreseen; that the ECtHR strategically uses remedial compliance to construct its legitimacy; and that the Inter-American Court effectively shames states into greater compliance by publishing compliance reports.

While there has been a flourishing of compliance studies in recent years, there are still areas that could use more systematic exploration. Below are four suggestions for deepening the study of judgment compliance.

3.1 Compare across treaty regimes and IC types

One objective of the editors of this handbook is to provoke dialogue among those who study adjudication within different treaty regimes, and to foster more comparative study of ICs. However, if measuring compliance to a single IC is tricky, as argued above, the problem is compounded when we try to compare across ICs. Scholars have begun conceptualizing ways of measuring compliance so as to facilitate comparison.[121] More such work is needed. In particular, it is important to take into account the effects of differing remedy designs and of different areas of law.

3.2 Deepen dialogue with scholars of national courts

Since the 1990s, comparative judicial politics has emerged as a rich and productive field of study. These studies, focused on national legal systems, have arguably understated the incidence and importance of non-compliance with court rulings.[122] However, there is an emergent interest in implementation and compliance, and these studies provide insight into the roles that courts, national executive branches, and civil society play in the enforcement of rulings. As Jeffrey Staton and Will Moore explained, "Scholars writing about judicial power at the domestic and international

[121] Hillebrecht, note 30; Kapiszewski and Taylor, note 4. [122] Kapiszewski and Taylor, note 4.

levels are, and should be, writing in one coherent literature."[123] These scholars would benefit from greater dialogue. Some have already begun crossing these boundaries in their own work, particularly those focusing on Europe.[124] But there is room for more. For example, many comparative public law scholars have focused on public law litigation of economic and social rights.[125] They should include in their inquiries into implementation of complex injunctive relief the experiences of the transnational human rights tribunals. Uncovering differences between the national and transnational court settings would shed light on implementation of complex injunctive orders generally.

3.3 Research the effects of compliance

Several new studies take a different tack, and cast compliance as the independent variable, seeking to understand the effects of non-compliance, and of the threat of non-compliance, on the court's subsequent decisions. More such studies are needed. We also need research that seeks empirical support for causal relations that are often presumed, but may not hold up under scrutiny: For example, does judgment compliance lead to greater primary-norm compliance? Does it lead to greater legitimacy? Under what conditions does it contribute to IC effectiveness?

3.4 Focus on implementation as a domestic political process

Remedy compliance is an outcome; implementation is the process—shaped by political and social dynamics—that leads to it. Much of the interest in compliance is actually an interest in understanding the political and social dynamics of implementation and reception of international judgments. This is especially the case as ICs move further into the realm of injunctive relief, as opposed to monetary compensation. What domestic implementation mechanisms work, and how? How do national actors use court orders to advance their own agendas in the political arena? What constellations of different actors yield state compliance? By shifting the focus from compliance to implementation, we shift the focus to domestic social

[123] JK Staton and WH Moore, "Judicial Power in Domestic and International Politics" (2011) 65 Int'l. Org. 553.

[124] For example, Clifford Carubba, Martin Shapiro, Jeffrey Staton, and Alec Stone Sweet all do work on both international and national courts' judicial politics.

[125] See e.g., M Tushnet, *Weak Courts, Strong Rights: Judicial Review and Social Welfare Rights in Comparative Constitutional Law* (Princeton University Press 2008).

and political processes. For many studies, particularly for those that seek to improve compliance, this may be a better fit.

Research Questions

1. How can we fruitfully compare judgment compliance across different types of international adjudicative bodies?
2. How can we fruitfully compare national to international adjudication, and, specifically, what can the two fields learn from each other on the topic of judgment compliance?
3. What impact does judgment compliance have on effectiveness, legitimacy, and judicial power?
4. What domestic political processes foment implementation and reception of international judgments?

Suggested Reading

Alter, K, *Establishing the Supremacy of European Law: The Making of an International Rule of Law in Europe* (New York: Oxford University Press 2001).

Carrubba, CJ, Gabel, M, and Hankla, C, "Judicial Behavior under Political Constraints: Evidence from the European Court of Justice" (2008) 102 Am. Political Science Review 43.

Downs, GW, Rocke, DM, and Barsoom, PN, "Is the Good News about Compliance Good News about Cooperation?" (1996) 50 Int'l. Org. 379.

Etienne, J, "Compliance Theory: A Goal Framing Approach" (2011) 33 Law and Policy 305.

Hawkins, D and Jacoby, W, "Partial Compliance: A Comparison of the European and Inter-American Courts for Human Rights" (2010) 6 J. Int'l. L. & Int'l. Rel. 35.

Hillebrecht, C, "Rethinking Compliance: The Challenges and Prospects of Measuring Compliance with International Human Rights" (2009) 3 Journal of Human Rights Practice 362.

Kapiszweski, D and Taylor, M, "Compliance: Measuring and Explaining Adherence to Judicial Rulings" Law and Social Inquiry (forthcoming).

Lamont, CK, *International Criminal Justice and the Politics of Compliance* (Farnham: Ashgate Publishing Ltd. 2010).

Martin, L, "Against Compliance" in JL Dunoff and M Pollack (eds), *International Law and International Relations: Synthesizing Insights from Interdisciplinary Scholarship* (New York: Cambridge University Press 2012) 591–610.

Raustiala, K and Slaughter, A-M, "International Law, International Relations and Compliance" in W Carlnaes, T Risse and B Simmons (eds), *The Handbook Of International Relations* (London: Sage Publications Ltd. 2002) 538–58.

Rosenne, S, *Provisional Measures in International Law: The International Court of Justice and the International Tribunal for the Law of the Sea* (Oxford University Press 2005).

Schulte, C, *Compliance with Decisions of the International Court of Justice* (Oxford University Press 2005).

Shany, Y, "Compliance with Decisions of International Courts as Indicative of their Effectiveness: A Goal-Based Analysis" (2012) 2010 Proc. Eur. Soc'y Int'l L. 251.

CHAPTER 21

THE EFFECTIVENESS OF INTERNATIONAL ADJUDICATORS

LAURENCE R HELFER*

1 Introduction

The conditions under which international courts (ICs) and tribunals can be considered effective is an issue of increasing interest to judges, government officials, attorneys, and scholars. The fresh attention devoted to IC effectiveness is the inevitable consequence

* Harry R. Chadwick, Sr. Professor of Law, Duke University, Durham, NC, USA. Thanks to Suzanne Katzenstein, Yonatan Lupu, and Yuval Shany for comments on earlier drafts, and to James Waters for excellent research assistance.

of a more active international judiciary.[1] As litigants ask courts to adjudicate an expanding and diverse array of controversies, judges must inevitably clarify the meaning of ambiguous treaty provisions and customary rules, and apply them to new and unforeseen contexts. Yet the rising number of IC rulings bears no necessary relationship to whether those rulings influence state behavior. Nor does it answer the more fundamental question of "effective for what purpose?"—an inquiry that depends on a prior conception of the functions that ICs perform and the goals they are expected to achieve.[2]

Traditionally, the principal function of ICs was to provide a judicial forum to assist nation states in settling their disputes. As the number and variety of ICs has increased, however, international judges have been given or have assumed a broad range of other tasks. These include exercising constitutional, enforcement, and administrative review;[3] stabilizing normative expectations and legitimating the exercise of public authority;[4] improving state compliance with primary legal norms;[5] engaging in judicial lawmaking to clarify or expand substantive obligations;[6] and enhancing the legitimacy of international norms and institutions, including of ICs themselves.[7]

Recent scholarship on IC effectiveness analyzes these functions from a range of vantage points. Some studies focus on developing typologies to categorize the multiple roles that ICs perform. Others assess empirically whether a particular IC, or the international judicial system in general, is successful in achieving one or more identified objectives. Yet another group of studies makes normative claims about which goals international judges ought to prioritize, regardless of the tasks that they in fact perform.

The literature exploring these issues includes works by legal scholars, political scientists, and interdisciplinary research teams. It would be impossible in this short chapter to do justice to this burgeoning literature.[8] The chapter focuses instead on

[1] For recent statistics, see K Alter, *The New Terrain of International Law* (Princeton University Press 2014), ch. 3.

[2] Y Shany, "Assessing the Effectiveness of International Courts: A Goal-Based Approach" (2012) 106 AJIL 225; D Shelton, "Form, Function, and the Powers of International Courts" (2009) 9 Chi. J. Int'l L. 537.

[3] Alter, note 1, at chs 5–8.

[4] A von Bogdandy and I Vetzke, "Beyond Dispute: International Judicial Institutions as Lawmakers" (2011) 12 German L.J. 979, 989–96.

[5] A Guzman, "International Tribunals: A Rational Choice Analysis" (2008) 157 U. Pa. L. Rev. 171, 188; Shany, note 2, at 244–5.

[6] K Alter and LR Helfer, "Nature or Nurture? Judicial Law-Making in the European Court of Justice and the Andean Tribunal of Justice" (2010) 64 Int'l Org. 563, 566; von Bogdandy and Vetzke, note 4, at 986–9.

[7] N Grossman, "Legitimacy and International Adjudicative Bodies" (2009) 41 Geo. Wash. Int'l L. Rev. 107, 110; Shany, note 2, at 246–7.

[8] For references to other scholarship on IC effectiveness, see Shany, note 2; G Shaffer and T Ginsburg, "The Empirical Turn in International Legal Scholarship" (2012) 106(1) AJIL 16–19.

four dimensions of IC effectiveness that, in this author's view, are important either because they have engendered debates among scholars, or, conversely, because they relate to core IC functions but have received insufficient scrutiny.

The first dimension, *case-specific effectiveness* (Section 2), evaluates whether the litigants to a specific dispute follow the orders and provide the remedies that a court awards—an issue closely linked to compliance with IC judgments.[9] The second variant, erga omnes *effectiveness* (Section 3), assesses whether IC rulings have systemic precedential effects that influence the behavior of all states subject to a tribunal's jurisdiction. The third dimension, *embeddedness effectiveness* (Section 4), evaluates the extent to which ICs anchor their judgments in domestic legal orders, enabling national actors to remedy potential treaty violations at home and avoid the need for international litigation. The fourth type, *effectiveness in developing international law* or *norm-development effectiveness* (Section 5), considers how IC decisions contribute to building a body of international jurisprudence—a topic relevant to the decentralized nature of the international legal system and debates over the fragmentation of international law. A brief conclusion (Section 6) follows.

For each dimension of IC effectiveness, the chapter reviews recent studies, identifies contested or under-analyzed issues and suggests avenues for future research. It does not, however, defend the substantive merits of the four effectiveness measures, nor does it evaluate their consequences for other values or objectives. For example, an IC that is adroit at developing international legal norms or embedding its judgments in domestic law may, as a result, narrow the discretion of government policymakers or diminish state sovereignty. Whether these or other consequences of IC effectiveness are normatively desirable or problematic is beyond the scope of this chapter.

2 Case-Specific Effectiveness

Among the four dimensions of effectiveness, scholars have focused most heavily on whether the parties to a particular dispute obey an IC's judgment. This section reviews the theoretical literature on case-specific effectiveness and analyzes debates among scholars over its relationship to the distinct concept of state compliance with IC rulings. The section concludes by suggesting how future studies might help to resolve these debates and gain greater traction on the causal impact of IC rulings.

Early studies of case-specific effectiveness focused on whether a state found in breach of international law changed its behavior following an IC judgment. Laurence

[9] See, in this handbook, Huneeus, Ch. 20.

Helfer and Anne-Marie Slaughter, for example, defined effectiveness in terms of an IC's "ability to compel compliance with its judgments by convincing domestic government institutions, directly and through pressure from private litigants, to use their power on its behalf."[10] This definition recognized that most ICs cannot count on international enforcement mechanisms and must instead build support from domestic actors who in turn induce governments to respect IC rulings. The definition also expressly equated the concepts of case-specific effectiveness and compliance.

Subsequent theoretical contributions, however, emphasized the distinction between compliance and effectiveness. In an influential article, Kal Raustiala defined compliance as conformity between behavior and a specified legal rule, and effectiveness as "observable, desired changes in behavior" attributable to that rule.[11] In applying these definitions, Raustiala disaggregated the two concepts. High levels of compliance can occur "for reasons entirely exogenous to the legal process," such as where states draft treaties to mirror their preexisting behavior.[12] Conversely, international rules "can be effective even if compliance with them is low. If a legal standard is quite demanding, even widespread failure to meet it may still correlate with observable, desired changes in behavior."[13]

The basic insight is that international rules with high compliance rates may be entirely ineffective, whereas those with low compliance rates may be quite effective if they engender some modification of state behavior. The dangers of conflating the two concepts have led some scholars boldly to assert that compliance is "unusually ill-suited to [a] central social-scientific pursuit: the identification and measurement of causal effects," and to argue in favor of "dropping compliance as a central concept in the study of institutional effects."[14]

Scholars of ICs also stress the need to disentangle compliance and effectiveness. Karen Alter argues that "the real effectiveness test... is not compliance but the counterfactual of what the outcome would have been absent the IC. Those concerned with effectiveness should ask whether the IC contributed to moving a state in a more law-complying direction."[15] Shany makes a similar claim regarding judicial remedies: "[A] low-aiming court, issuing minimalist remedies, may generate a high level of compliance but have little impact on the state of the world."[16] Andrew Guzman

[10] LR Helfer and A-M Slaughter, "Toward a Theory of Effective Supranational Adjudication" (1997) 107 Yale L.J. 273, 290.

[11] K Raustiala, "Compliance and Effectiveness in International Regulatory Cooperation" (2000) 32 Case W. Res. J. Int'l L. 387, 391, 394.

[12] Raustiala, note 11, at 393. [13] Raustiala, note 11, at 394.

[14] L Martin, "Against Compliance" in J Dunoff and MA Pollack (eds), *Interdisciplinary Perspectives on International Law and International Relations: The State of the Art* (Cambridge University Press 2012) 591–2. For further analysis, see E Hafner-Burton, D Victor and Y Lupu, "Political Science Research on International Law: The State of the Field" (2012) 106 AJIL 47, 89.

[15] K Alter, "Agents or Trustees? International Courts in their Political Context" (2008) 14 Eur. J. Int'l Rel. 33, 52.

[16] Shany, note 2, at 227 (emphasis omitted).

emphasizes the converse point, stating that "even when a state fails to comply with a tribunal's ruling, the tribunal may be effective at promoting compliance if it imposes sufficient costs on the state to discourage future violations of the underlying legal rule."[17]

These studies suggest that the conflation of compliance and effectiveness is as problematic when applied to the study of ICs as it is for the analysis of international law in general. Yet other scholars have argued, to the contrary, that compliance *is* an appropriate—and even a superior—measure of IC effectiveness in at least one important instance: when a court rules that a state has violated international law. As Darren Hawkins and Wade Jacoby explain:

> When a country persists in behaviour long enough for an international court to rule against that country's practices, and the country subsequently changes its practices, we assume that the court's ruling helped trigger the change in behaviour, even if other factors may also have been important.... Compliance in these circumstances is very unlikely to be the result of chance: most international litigation takes years and costs states significant money to defend; it is therefore reasonable to assume that the state prefers to persist in the behaviour being challenged in court. *Hence, any resulting behavioural changes after an adverse court ruling can suggest court effectiveness. This creates a class of cases where instances of compliance will be coextensive with those of effectiveness and where effectiveness can therefore be objectively measured through the proxy of state compliance.*[18]

Alexandra Huneeus expands upon this insight. She recognizes the risks of conflating compliance and effectiveness, but asserts that those risks are "arguably less acute" for compliance with court orders than for compliance with treaty commitments more generally. If an IC "orders compensation of the victim by a certain amount, and the state compensates by that amount, drawing a causal inference is not particularly fraught. The answer to the counterfactual—would the state have done the same without the order—seems self-evident."[19]

What accounts for this sharp division in the literature? One possible explanation is different scholars are analyzing distinct phenomena. Studies that equate compliance and effectiveness focus on whether states that litigate and lose a case carry out the IC judgments against them, whereas studies that disaggregate the two concepts measure an IC's ability to encourage compliance with underlying legal obligations.[20] Scholars in the first group implicitly assume that IC rulings impose meaningful

[17] Guzman, note 5, at 187.

[18] D Hawkins and W Jacoby, "Partial Compliance: A Comparison of the European and Inter-American Courts of Human Rights" (2010) 6 J. Int'l L. & Int'l Rel. 35, 40 (emphasis added). Measuring compliance is preferable, Hawkins and Jacoby argue, because accurately identifying the subset of "cases of efficacy from the wider sample of compliance" puts "enormous data demands on researchers," at 39.

[19] A Huneeus, "Courts Resisting Courts: Lessons from the Inter-American Court's Struggle to Enforce Human Rights" (2011) 44 Cornell Int'l L.J. 493, 505 n.61.

[20] Guzman, note 5, at 188. See also Shany, note 2, at 227, 244 (labeling these concepts, respectively, as "judgment-compliance" and "primary norm compliance").

constraints on state sovereignty and freedom of action—and thus can be effective even if compliance is slow, partial, or incomplete.[21] Scholars in the second group suspect that many IC rulings mirror preexisting state behavior—and thus lead to high levels of compliance but low levels of effectiveness.[22]

As abstract propositions, both views are equally plausible—and equally non-falsifiable. Future studies should expose the assumptions underlying the two approaches and test them empirically. The claim that IC judgments mirror the outcomes that states would have obtained through negotiation or politics may be a reasonable assumption in some issue areas or contexts, but not in others.[23] An example of the first category are cases in which two nations submit a dispute over a territorial or maritime boundary to the International Court of Justice (ICJ) or International Tribunal for the Law of the Sea (ITLOS) on an ad hoc basis. The tribunals' jurisprudence in such cases tends toward compromise and acknowledges the merits of both parties' claims.[24] An illustration of the second category are human rights complaints filed by private litigants. Such suits often target domestic laws and practices that reflect deeply held national values. IC judgments challenging those values are sometimes met with skepticism or overt resistance.[25]

More careful attention to counterfactuals will also narrow the gap between the two approaches and assist in making plausible causal inferences about case-specific effectiveness. Recall Hawkins and Jacoby's assertion, quoted above, that when a state changes its behavior following a judgment against that state, it is reasonable to assume that the judgment materially influenced the behavioral change "even if other factors may also have been important."[26] Identifying the causal contribution of those "other factors" is critical to evaluating the case-specific effectiveness of ICs.

Consider the March 2011 provisional measures issued by the African Court on Human and Peoples' Rights (ACtHPR) during the civil war in Libya. The court ordered the state, then headed by Muammar Gaddafi, to "immediately refrain from any action that would result in loss of life or violation of physical integrity of persons."[27]

[21] Hawkins and Jacoby, note 18, at 83–5. [22] Guzman, note 5, at 187.

[23] LR Helfer and A-M Slaughter, "Why States Create International Tribunals: A Response to Professors Posner and Yoo" (2005) 93 Calif. L. Rev. 899, 941 (explaining that, in bilateral interstate disputes, ICs "may operate as an extension of nonlegal, diplomatic methods of…compliance inducement").

[24] See e.g., S Ratner, "Land Feuds and their Solutions: Finding International Law Beyond the Tribunal Chamber" (2006) 100 AJIL 808, 815–16.

[25] See e.g., LR Helfer, "The Benefits and Burdens of Brighton" (2012) ESIL Reflections, Vol. 1, Issue 1 <http://esil-sedi.eu/node/138> accessed December 30, 2012 (describing backlash to ECtHR judgments by government officials and voters in the United Kingdom); LR Helfer, "Overlegalizing Human Rights: International Relations Theory and the Commonwealth Caribbean Backlash Against Human Rights Regimes" (2002) 102 Colum. L. Rev. 1832 (analyzing strident opposition of Caribbean governments to human rights litigation aimed at curtailing or abolishing capital punishment).

[26] Hawkins and Jacoby, note 18, at 40.

[27] African Court of Human and Peoples' Rights, "Order for Provisional Measures" (March 30, 2011), at para. 25.1, <http://www.african-court.org/en/index.php/judgments/orders> accessed December 30, 2012.

The violence markedly diminished a few weeks later, but only after the UN Security Council authorized NATO to use military force to protect civilians. An acontextual analysis of state behavior in this instance might erroneously attribute compliance to the court's ruling, rather than to the humanitarian intervention by NATO.

Other, less obvious examples cast doubt on the presumption that compliance in the wake of an adverse ruling is indicative of effectiveness. Newly elected democratic governments sometimes implement IC judgments against their predecessors as a signal to foreign and domestic audiences of their commitment to abjuring the repressive policies of the past.[28] In established democracies, IC litigation may be only one component of a multifaceted civil society campaign that includes domestic mobilization, national court challenges, and transnational naming and shaming strategies.[29] In these and similar situations, it is plausible to attribute compliance, at least in part, to broader political or geostrategic factors rather than to an IC ruling.

A final consideration relates to time horizons.[30] All other things being equal, a court whose decisions are implemented quickly is more effective than one whose judgments are complied with after delays. This assumption is appropriate as a preliminary baseline, but it must be adjusted to account for a range of other factors. It would be reasonable, for example, to expect compliance with broad or costly remedies to require more time than compliance with more modest judicial orders.[31] The compliance delays associated with a "high-aiming court," to paraphrase Yuval Shany, should be discounted when evaluating that court's case-specific effectiveness. Conversely, even immediate adherence should be given little or no weight in assessing case-specific effectiveness if, as in the Libya example above, circumstances indicate that the court's decision had little to do with the change in state behavior.

3 *Erga Omnes* Effectiveness

The numerous studies of case-specific effectiveness reflect a basic feature of international adjudication: IC judgments are legally binding only *inter partes* and do not bind other states or the court in future cases.[32] Nevertheless, many IC rulings

[28] See e.g., D Cassel, "Does International Human Rights Law Make a Difference?" (2001) 2 Chi. J. Int'l L. 121, 128–34 (describing Peru's implementation of IACtHR judgments following the ousting of President Alberto Fujimori).

[29] See e.g., SL Cummings, "The Internationalization of Public Interest Law" (2008) 57 Duke L.J. 891, 994–5 (discussing the coordinated campaign to abolish the juvenile death penalty in the United States, which included international litigation as one of several complementary strategies).

[30] Shany, note 2, at 134.

[31] Huneeus, note 19, at 509–10.

[32] See e.g., ICJ Statute [1945] Art. 59 ("The decision of the Court has no binding force except between the parties and in respect of that particular case").

have—or at least purport to have—*erga omnes* effects that extend to all treaty parties.[33] This section first compares the *inter partes* rule to the *erga omnes* effect. It then reviews the literature that examines whether IC decisions are effective in influencing the behavior of actors beyond the litigants to a particular dispute.

The limited binding effect of IC rulings is an artifact of sovereignty. By recognizing an IC's compulsory jurisdiction, a state undertakes a legal obligation to comply with judgments against it. The state does not, however, consent to be bound by rulings in which it did not participate, nor does it waive the right to argue that a new case should be distinguished from similar suits involving other nations.[34] This limitation on international judicial authority sometimes results in repetitive litigation in which the only material difference is the identity of the countries involved in the proceedings. The trilogy of ICJ cases against the United States for violating the consular rights of foreign criminal defendants is one prominent example.[35]

If the *inter partes* rule were rigidly followed, international adjudication would be highly inefficient. In practice, however, ICs view their prior decisions as persuasive, especially when they have coalesced into a *jurisprudence constant*. The weight given to precedent means that "absent cogent reasons, an adjudicative body will resolve the same legal question in the same way in a subsequent case."[36] Some ICs have been bolder, characterizing their decisions as authoritative for all actors in a legal system. For example, the European Court of Human Rights (ECtHR) has asserted that it "determin[es] issues on public-policy grounds in the common interest, thereby... extending human rights jurisprudence throughout the community of Convention States,"[37] and the World Trade Organization Appellate Body stated that "the legal interpretation embodied in adopted panel and Appellate Body reports becomes part and parcel of the *acquis* of the WTO dispute settlement system."[38]

An IC's assertion that its decisions have an *erga omnes* effect may, however, engender resistance by some countries. The United States, for example, has argued that the "concept of *erga omnes* is squarely at odds with the fundamentally bilateral nature of WTO and GATT dispute settlement."[39] Further, many European countries

[33] The Latin phrase *erga omnes* means "flowing to all."

[34] These statements have even greater force for ICs whose jurisdiction states recognize on an ad hoc basis.

[35] See e.g., R Graebne, "Dialogue and Divergence: The Vienna Convention on Consular Relations in German, American, and International Courts" (2011) 42 Geo. J. Int'l L. 605, 607–11.

[36] *United States—Final Anti-Dumping Measures on Stainless Steel from Mexico* [2008] WT/DS344/AB/R [160] (Anti-Dumping Measures).

[37] *Karner v. Austria* [2003] App. No. 40016/98, 2003-IX Eur. Ct. H.R. [26].

[38] Anti-Dumping Measures, note 36, at para. 160.

[39] US Statement at the DSB Meeting of May 7, 2003, Item 2, US—Tax Treatment for Foreign Sales Corporations, WT/DSB/M/149 (July 8, 2003), para. 20.

do not consider the *erga omnes* effect of ECtHR rulings to be a legal requirement.[40] Yet there are also counter-examples. Canada abandoned its "zeroing" policy on dumping with explicit reference to prior WTO rulings against the EU and United States.[41] High courts in Argentina and Colombia struck down amnesty laws based on judgments of the Inter-American Court of Human Rights (IACtHR) invalidating amnesties in Peru.[42] And a 2010 Council of Europe report identifies countries whose parliaments have revised statutes following ECtHR judgments condemning similar laws adopted by other states.[43]

The politically contested and empirically unsettled nature of the *erga omnes* effect is reflected in the wide range of studies that consider whether ICs are effective in influencing the behavior of all actors subject to their authority.[44] One strand of scholarship has an overtly normative bent. Works in this vein seek to clarify the divergent meanings of *erga omnes* in judicial decisions and legal discourse, assess the desirability of strong or weak versions of the effect and suggest proposals to enhance the systemic impact of IC rulings. Two recent noteworthy examples are Samantha Besson's study of the ECtHR and Karin Oellers-Frahm's analysis of ICJ advisory opinions.[45]

A related literature considers whether states should redesign ICs to bolster the *erga omnes* effect. Attention has focused primarily on the ECtHR, due to its massive backlog of pending applications. The court's docket crisis has generated political declarations, such as the 2010 Interlaken Action Plan, which urges governments to consider "the conclusions to be drawn from a judgment finding a violation of the [European] Convention by another State, where the same problem of principle exists within their own legal system."[46] The crisis has also engendered arguments from scholars and judges that the ECtHR should focus on novel legal issues and articulate general principles applicable to all states parties.[47] Studies advocating

[40] S Besson, "The Erga Omnes Effect of Judgments of the European Court of Human Rights—What's in a Name?" in S Besson (ed.) *The European Court of Human Rights After Protocol 14* (Geneva: Schulthess 2011) at 125, 141.

[41] J Kanargelidis, "New Anti-Dumping Rules Applied by Canada: The Zeroing Debate" (September 7, 2005) Mondaq Business Briefing.

[42] C Binder, "The Prohibition of Amnesties by the Inter-American Court of Human Rights" (2011) 12 German L.J. 1203, 1222–3.

[43] Committee on Legal Affairs and Human Rights, "Strengthening Subsidiarity—Integrating the Court's Case-Law into National Law and Judicial Practice" (Oct. 1–2, 2010), <http://assembly.coe.int/CommitteeDocs/2010/20101125_skopje.pdf> accessed December 31, 2012.

[44] The issue is closely linked to whether ICs are effective in promoting what Shany refers to as "primary norm compliance" by states. Shany, note 2, at 245.

[45] Besson, note 40; K Oellers-Frahm, "Lawmaking Through Advisory Opinions?" (2011) 12 German L.J. 1033.

[46] "High Level Conference on the Future of the ECtHR," Interlaken Declaration, February 19, 2010, Action Plan, sec. 4.c.

[47] See e.g., S Greer, *The European Convention on Human Rights: Achievements, Problems and Prospects* (Cambridge University Press 2006); L Wildhaber, "A Constitutional Future for the European Court of Human Rights" (2002) 23 Hum. Rts. L.J. 161.

a more permissive approach to third-party interventions and *amicus* briefs often reflect similar concerns.[48] The more that IC decisions depart from the *inter partes* rule, the greater the need for all potentially affected actors to have a meaningful opportunity to influence those decisions.

A third cluster of research uses quantitative empirical methods to analyze the behavior of governments, both as policymakers and as prospective litigants. A recent paper by Helfer and Erik Voeten considers the first issue. It finds that ECtHR judgments on LGBT rights increase the likelihood that other countries in Europe—in particular states in which public acceptance of homosexuality is low—will adopt pro-LGBT policies. To measure the *erga omnes* effect, the authors code national LGBT policies by country and year adopted, control for confounding variables that could explain policy reforms and isolate the extent to which ECtHR judges respond to preexisting legal and social trends.[49] Quantitative analyses of dispute settlement patterns in the WTO analyze the behavior of states as litigants.[50] These studies, including articles by Guzman and Beth Simmons, as well as by Marc Busch and Eric Reinhardt, do not address the *erga omnes* effect directly. They do, however, implicitly assume that prior panel and Appellate Body decisions cast a shadow that influences whether other nations litigate or settle a dispute over alleged violations of free trade rules.

Future research on *erga omnes* effectiveness should focus on identifying the specific conditions under which IC decisions are more or less likely to influence the behavior of non-parties. For example, qualitative process tracing and case studies can document variations in behavior among different branches of government in countries subject to an IC's jurisdiction. Quantitative studies can compare the strength of the *erga omnes* effect across tribunals and issue areas. Both types of studies face similar challenges: determining whether behavioral changes are attributable to IC rulings as opposed to other factors, and identifying the specific mechanisms of IC influence. As discussed in the previous section, developing credible counterfactuals and considering plausible alternative explanations for rule-consistent conduct will be critical to overcoming these challenges.

48 See e.g., A von Bogdandy, "In Whose Name? An Investigation of International Courts' Public Authority and its Democratic Justification" (2012) 23 EJIL 7, 27–30.

49 LR Helfer and E Voeten, "International Courts as Agents of Legal Change: Evidence from LGBT Rights in Europe" (forthcoming 2014) 67 Int'l Org.

50 See e.g., A Guzman and B Simmons, "To Settle or Empanel? An Empirical Analysis of Litigation and Settlement at the WTO" (2002) 31 J. Leg. Stud. 205; M Busch and E Reinhardt, "Bargaining in the Shadow of the Law: Early Settlement in GATT/WTO Disputes" (2000) 24 Fordham Int'l L. J. 158. See also M Gilligan et al., "Strengthening International Courts and the Early Settlement of Disputes" (2010) 54 J. Conflict Res. 5.

4 Embeddedness Effectiveness

A third dimension of effectiveness considers whether ICs enhance the ability of domestic actors to prevent or remedy violations of international rules "at home," thus avoiding the need for international litigation. This section reviews studies that evaluate whether ICs are effective in embedding international law and international judicial rulings in national legal orders.

Embeddedness effectiveness received little attention when the primary task of ICs was to settle interstate disputes. The issue became far more salient when ICs were given authority to review challenges to domestic laws and policies in response to complaints filed by private actors. Yet ICs have neither the competence nor the resources to review all such challenges. This raises the critical question of whether national judges, legislators, and administrators can be incentivized to serve as the first-line defenders of international law, adopting measures that promote rule compliance and provide remedies for any violations that do occur.

Studies of whether ICs are effective in inducing domestic actors to carry out these functions focus on institutional design features, most notably jurisdiction and access rules. For example, tribunals that require complainants to exhaust domestic remedies must inevitably assess whether national judicial and administrative procedures offer viable opportunities for litigants to obtain redress for colorable violations of international law. Scholarship on regional human rights courts—such as Helfer's study of the ECtHR,[51] and analyses of the IACtHR by James Cavallaro and Stephanie Brewer, and by Huneeus[52]—identify how these courts construct their interpretative methods and remedial orders to incentivize compliance by national decision-makers. Prominent among these strategies is giving greater deference to decision-makers who treat IC decisions as persuasive when reviewing complaints alleging violations of individual rights.

Different embeddedness issues emerge when international judges can forge direct links to their national counterparts. Scholars have widely attributed the success of the European Court of Justice (ECJ) in promoting regional integration to the court's preliminary reference procedure, which enables domestic judges to seek guidance on the meaning of European Union law.[53] Spurred by requests from private litigants who benefited from favorable European rules, national courts became the ECJ's

[51] LR Helfer, "Redesigning the European Court of Human Rights: Embeddedness as a Deep Structural Principle of the European Human Rights Regime" (2008) 19 EJIL 125, 144–6, 152–5.

[52] J Cavallaro and SE Brewer, "Reevaluating Regional Human Rights Litigation in the Twenty-First Century: The Case of the Inter-American Court" (2008) 102 AJIL 768, 816–22; Huneeus, note 19, at 526–9.

[53] See e.g., GF Mancini, "The Making of a Constitution for Europe" (1989) 26 Common Mkt. L. Rev. 595.

primary interlocutors and compliance partners. Over time, judges referred a growing number of cases and became habituated to following the ECJ's rulings.[54] When EC rules and the supranational cases interpreting them had been firmly entrenched in national judicial mindsets, the ECJ announced the doctrine of *acte clair*, which directed national judges to refrain from referring cases that raised settled legal issues, including cases in which courts were expected to—and did—invalidate the offending domestic law or policy.[55]

Preliminary reference mechanisms also enable ICs to forge alliances with domestic actors other than courts. Alter and Helfer's work on the Andean legal system demonstrates that more than 90 percent of Andean Tribunal of Justice (ATJ) rulings emanate from administrative agencies that apply Andean intellectual property rules when reviewing applications to register trademarks and patents. A litigant dissatisfied with an agency's decision can appeal to national courts, which refer questions of Andean law to the ATJ and then apply the tribunal's legal interpretation to resolve the case. In practice, however, national judges have been mostly passive intermediaries in a mutually constitutive relationship between Andean judges and domestic administrators. The agencies encouraged references and participated in litigation before the tribunal, and the ATJ issued decisions that responded to the agencies' concerns. ATJ rulings improved the agencies' decision-making procedures, clarified ambiguities in Andean rules, helped to insulate officials from political pressure and bolstered administrators' fidelity to the rule of law. The agencies, in turn, acted as compliance constituencies for Andean judges, scrupulously following Andean law as interpreted by the ATJ even in the face of conflicting national decrees.[56]

Other studies have analyzed embeddedness issues in international criminal law. The founders of the International Criminal Court (ICC) recognized that domestic trials of genocide, war crimes, and crimes against humanity would sometimes be preferable to international prosecutions. They thus directed the ICC to declare inadmissible, inter alia, cases being investigated or prosecuted domestically, "unless the State is unwilling or unable genuinely to carry out the investigation or prosecution."[57] This complementarity principle requires the ICC to make fine-grained evaluations of the intent and capacity of government officials[58]—assessments that are facilitated by domestic trust

[54] K Alter, *The European Court's Political Power: Selected Essays* (Oxford University Press 2009) chs 4, 5.

[55] See e.g., H Rasmussen, "The European Court's Acte Clair Strategy in C.I.L.F.I.T. or Acte Clair, of Course! But what does it Mean?" (1984) 9 Eur. L. Rev. 242.

[56] LR Helfer and K Alter, "The Andean Tribunal of Justice and its Interlocutors: Understanding the Preliminary Ruling Reference Patterns in the Andean Community" (2009) 42 N.Y.U. J. Int'l & Pol. 871, 912–20; LR Helfer, K Alter, and MF Guerzovich, "Islands of Effective International Adjudication: Constructing an Intellectual Property Rule of Law in the Andean Community" (2009) 103 AJIL 1, 21–6.

[57] Rome Statute of the International Criminal Court 1998, 2187 U.N.T.S. 90, Art. 17.1.

[58] Rome Statute of the International Criminal Court 1998, note 57, Arts 17.2 and 17.3. See also L Yang, "On the Principle of Complementarity in the Rome Statute of the International Criminal Court" (2005) 4 Chinese J. Int'l L. 121.

in international proceedings. Unfortunately, the ICC's emphasis on atrocities in Africa has stirred controversy and precipitated a public rebuke by African leaders. Behind the scenes, however, scholars have highlighted how the ICC's Office of the Prosecutor is building relationships with national decision-makers and encouraging them to develop trial and accountability mechanisms that satisfy the complementary standard.[59] These efforts will determine the extent to which the ICC is effective in anchoring its vision of international criminal justice in national legal orders.

Future research on embeddedness effectiveness should address several under-studied issues. First, a few ICs with human rights jurisdiction, including the Court of Justice of the ECOWAS Court of Justice (ECOWAS CJ) and the East African Court of Justice (EACJ), do not require exhaustion of local remedies. African NGOs have praised the omission of exhaustion as enabling litigants to bypass overburdened and unresponsive domestic courts and file complaints directly with these ICs. But direct international review of complaints can create frictions with national judges, making it harder to forge the judicial partnerships on which effective embeddedness often depends.[60] A second issue concerns ICs that must occasionally act as first-instance courts. The ECtHR, for example, has assumed this function when reviewing "hot spots" of civil unrest in Turkey and Chechnya.[61] A key challenge, however, is how a tribunal steps back from this front-line position when domestic conditions improve. A third underexplored topic concerns courts that exercise jurisdiction over countries in which governments are unstable, the rule of law is weak, or judges are only partially independent. An IC's ability to embed its rulings in such countries may require cultivating the support of sub-state institutions that "forge a relationship with a supranational tribunal as an ally in a domestic political battle against corruption or oppression."[62]

5 Effectiveness in Developing International Law

The previous three types of effectiveness evaluate the extent to which IC rulings alter the behavior of litigants, states, and government actors. A fourth dimension of effectiveness analyzes the norm-generating functions of ICs. The literature on this

[59] See e.g., W Burke-White, "Proactive Complementarity: The International Criminal Court and National Courts in the Rome System of International Justice" (2008) 49 Harv. Int'l L.J. 53.

[60] AO Enabulele, "Sailing against the Tide: Exhaustion of Domestic Remedies and the ECOWAS Community Court of Justice" (2012) 56 J. Afr. L. 268.

[61] Helfer, note 51, at 142–4.

[62] Helfer and Slaughter, note 10, at 335.

topic is vast and includes studies of treaty interpretation,[63] judicial lawmaking,[64] judicial activism,[65] transjudicial communication,[66] and the fragmentation of international law.[67] This section reviews a subset of this literature—studies of how the disaggregated nature of the international legal system and the quality of a tribunal's reasoning influence whether ICs are effective in developing international law.

Most ICs are specialized bodies that interpret and apply only the treaty that establishes them, or a family of closely related treaties within a single legal regime.[68] The ECtHR, for example, can review complaints alleging violations of the European Convention on Human Rights and its Protocols—not other human rights agreements. An IC's norm-development effectiveness is thus most often assessed by reference to how its judges interpret and apply the particular treaty or area of international law that falls within its purview.

Within these specialized domains, courts often develop a reputation for particular doctrinal innovations. The IACtHR, for example, is a pioneer in fashioning creative and far-reaching remedies for human rights abuses.[69] The ECtHR is famous for using the margin of appreciation doctrine to temper global human rights standards to local particularities.[70] The WTO jurists are well known for consulting dictionaries to deduce the ordinary meaning of trade treaties.[71] The ATJ has made its mark by balancing intellectual property rights against consumer protection and public health goals.[72] Even the ICJ—a court of general jurisdiction—has developed a niche market in territorial and maritime boundary disputes.[73]

[63] See e.g. I Venzke, "The Role of International Courts as Interpreters and Developers of the Law: Working Out the Jurisgenerative Practice of Interpretation" (2011) 34 Loy. L.A. Int'l & Comp. L. Rev. 99.

[64] See e.g., T Ginsburg, "Bounded Discretion in International Judicial Lawmaking" (2005) 43 Va. J. Int'l L. 631; R Steinberg, "Judicial Lawmaking at the WTO: Discursive, Constitutional, and Political Constraints" (2004) 98 AJIL 247.

[65] See e.g., F Zarbiyev, "Judicial Activism in International Law—A Conceptual Framework for Analysis" (2012) 3 J. Int'l Disp. Settlement 247.

[66] See e.g., A-M Slaughter, "A Typology of Transjudicial Communication" (1994) 29 U. Rich. L. Rev. 99; M Waters, "Mediating Norms and Identity: The Role of Transnational Judicial Dialogue in Creating and Enforcing International Law" (2005) 93 Geo. L.J. 487.

[67] See e.g., OK Fauchald and A Nollkaemper (eds), *The Practice of International and National Courts and the (De)Fragmentation of International Law* (Oxford: Hart 2012).

[68] The ICJ is an obvious exception, although the court's ability to interpret international law in general is constrained by the limited number of nations that have accepted its compulsory jurisdiction, the broad reservations that often accompany such acceptances, and the paucity of disputes referred to the court on an ad hoc basis.

[69] See e.g., T Antkowiak, "Remedial Approaches to Human Rights Violations: The Inter-American Court of Human Rights and Beyond" (2008) 46 Colum. J. Transnat'l L. 351.

[70] See e.g., Y Arai-Takahashi, *The Margin of Appreciation Doctrine and the Principle of Proportionality in the Jurisprudence of the ECHR* (Antwerp: Intersentia 2002).

[71] C Lo, "Good Faith Use of Dictionary in the Search of Ordinary Meaning under the WTO Dispute Settlement Understanding" (2010) 1 J. Int'l Disp. Settlement 431.

[72] Helfer, Alter and Guerzovich, note 56, at 21–36.

[73] See e.g., A Alvarez-Jimenez, "Boundary Agreements in the International Court of Justice's Case Law, 2000–2010" (2012) 23 EJIL 495.

The more closely that an IC is associated with regime-specific innovations, the greater the likelihood that observers will evaluate its norm-development effectiveness by reference to its performance in that specialized area, such as whether its decisions clarify ambiguities, fill lacunae, and promote the underlying objectives of the legal obligations that the court supervises.

As the number of IC rulings has increased, however, scholars have begun to focus on "the systematic fashion in which some [ICs] are developing a body of law of general relevance."[74] The Appellate Body's statement that WTO agreements are "not to be read in clinical isolation from public international law"[75] is often cited as evidence of this trend. The extent to which ICs are effective in elucidating broader legal principles may depend on whether their decisions are emulated elsewhere. For example, the jurisprudence of the ECtHR—the oldest and most active IC—has long inspired other human rights tribunals, a phenomenon documented in case studies of transjudicial dialogue and more systematic analysis of citations to IC precedents.[76] More recently, the decisions of newer human rights courts have influenced ECtHR judges searching for doctrinal responses to systemic human rights abuses that plague some corners of Europe.[77]

A related issue concerns cases that straddle the border between legal domains. Such suits arise less frequently than cases within the heartland of an IC's jurisdiction. But how judges resolve these "boundary disputes" often receives disproportionate attention in assessments of a court's effectiveness in developing international law. Examples include the Appellate Body's accommodation of multilateral efforts to protect the environment and public health when adjudicating free trade disputes,[78] and the IACtHR's interpretation of human rights in light of international humanitarian law.[79] The heightened salience of these cases is a consequence of the uneven distribution of ICs across the international legal system. Because ICs do not exist in some areas of international law (such as the environment and arms control),

[74] Von Bogdandy and Vetzke, note 4, at 980. See also Shaffer and Ginsburg, note 8, at 18 (arguing that a "central question regarding international tribunals…is whether [and the conditions under which] they affect the production, consolidation, and application of international law").

[75] United States—Standard for Reformulated and Conventional Gasoline [1996] WT/DS2/AB/R, sec. III.B.

[76] See e.g., Y Lupu and E Voeten, "Precedent in International Courts: A Network Analysis of Case Citations by the European Court of Human Rights" (2012) 42 Brit. J. Pol. Sci. 413; A-M Slaughter, "A Global Community of Courts" (2003) 44 Harv. Int'l L.J. 191.

[77] G Neuman, "Import, Export, and Regional Consent in the Inter-American Court of Human Rights" (2008) 19 EJIL 101, 116–18.

[78] See e.g., *Appellate Body Report, United States—Import Prohibition of Certain Shrimp and Shrimp Products* [1998] WT/DS58/AB/R. Scholars disagree over the extent to which WTO jurists can apply non-WTO law. Compare J Pauwelyn, "The Role of Public International Law in the WTO: How Far Can We Go?" (2001) 95 AJIL 535, with JP Trachtman, "The Domain of WTO Dispute Resolution" (1999) 40 Harv. Int'l L.J. 333.

[79] L Burgorgue-Larse et al., *The Inter-American Court of Human Rights: Case-Law and Commentary* (Oxford University Press 2011) 69–71.

litigants often ask courts in other regimes (human rights and trade, for example) to apply legal rules beyond their primary areas of competence.

A more fine-grained dimension of norm-development effectiveness concerns the quality of an IC's legal reasoning. Studies of supranational adjudication in Europe, for example, attribute the success of the ECJ and ECtHR to the courts' adept use of "the language of reasoned interpretation, logical deduction, systemic and temporal coherence."[80] These attributes created a "compliance pull"[81] for judicial rulings that influenced all actors within the EC and the European Convention legal systems, in particular national judges.[82]

Scholarly assessments of legal reasoning generally focus on several issues. The first relates to the structure of IC opinions and the extent to which they faithfully recount the litigants' arguments before the court provides its own analysis. Such an approach offers tangible proof that the judges have at least understood the parties' claims. Litigants who believe that their arguments have been heard are more likely to participate in a future case.[83] A second issue concerns adherence to precedent. ICs are not bound by their own prior judgments. Yet most recognize that treating previous rulings as authoritative furthers the "interests of legal certainty, foreseeability and equality before the law,"[84] and encourages doctrinal consistency over time.[85] A third metric for evaluating legal reasoning emphasizes decisions that overturn or revise existing jurisprudence. International judges acknowledge that such rulings require a heavy burden of justification.[86] The weighty reasons they cite often involve the application of evolutive methods of treaty interpretation to ensure that existing case law does not become outmoded.[87]

[80] JHH Weiler, "A Quiet Revolution: The European Court of Justice and its Interlocutors" (1994) 26 Comp. Pol. Stud. 510, 521. See also Helfer and Slaughter, note 10, at 318–23 (identifying the "quality of legal reasoning" as an attribute of effective supranational adjudication).

[81] TM Franck, *The Power of Legitimacy Among Nations* (Oxford University Press 1990) 24.

[82] See e.g., A-M Burley and W Mattli, "Europe Before the Court: A Political Theory of Legal Integration" (1993) 47 Int'l Org. 41; H Keller and A Stone Sweet, *A Europe of Rights: The Impact of the ECHR on National Legal Systems* (Oxford University Press 2008); P Popelier, et al., *Human Rights Protection in the European Legal Order: The Interaction Between the European and the National Courts* (Antwerp: Intersentia 2011).

[83] See e.g., H Lauterpacht, *The Development of International Law by the International Court* (Cambridge University Press 1958) 39 ("governments as a rule reconcile themselves to the fact that their case has not been successful—provided the defeat is accompanied by the conviction that their argument was considered in all its relevant aspects").

[84] *Chapman v. United Kingdom*, App. No. 27238/95, 2001-I (ECHR, Grand Chamber, 2001), at para. 70.

[85] See e.g., B Simma, "Universality of International Law from the Perspective of a Practitioner" (2009) 20 EJIL 265.

[86] See e.g., A Mowbray, "An Examination of the European Court of Human Rights' Approach to Overruling its Previous Case Law" (2009) 9 Hum. Rts. L. Rev. 179.

[87] See e.g., J Arato, "Subsequent Practice and Evolutive Interpretation: Techniques of Treaty Interpretation over Time and Their Diverse Consequences" (2010) 9 L. & Prac. Int'l Cts. & Trib. 443; K Dzehtsiarou, "European Consensus and the Evolutive Interpretation of the European Convention on Human Rights" (2011) 12 German L.J. 1730.

Future scholarship on IC effectiveness in developing international law will likely proceed along a number of tracks. As the number of international judicial rulings continues to increase, legal scholars and practicing lawyers will continue to analyze the jurisprudence of individual ICs. These court-specific studies provide indispensable guides to case law that is becoming too voluminous for non-specialists to digest without assistance. The studies also expose the doctrinal innovations of lesser-known sub-regional or specialized ICs to a wider audience of practitioners, scholars, and civil society advocates, who can then assess whether a particular court is effective in developing the legal norms within its purview.[88] The growing scrutiny of IC jurisprudence may generate feedback loops as judges review and potentially reassess the persuasiveness of their legal reasoning in light of these external evaluations.

The collective contributions of ICs to developing legal norms will be aided by the growing scholarly interest in the comparative dimensions of international adjudication.[89] The Oxford University Press book series on ICs includes several volumes that contrast the doctrines and practices of multiple tribunals. Specialized journals, such as the *Law and Practice of International Courts and Tribunals* and the *Journal of International Dispute Settlement*, have published many similar studies. Several universities have also established interdisciplinary centers devoted to ICs.[90] The output of these scholarly venues will provide a rich body of evidence to evaluate the ways in which ICs, both individually and collectively, are effective in developing international law.

6 Conclusion

This chapter has reviewed four dimensions of IC effectiveness. These dimensions are conceptually distinct. For example, an IC judgment may be ignored by the respondent state but trigger policy reforms in other nations subject to the tribunal's jurisdiction.

[88] Solomon Ebobrah's pioneering work on three sub-regional community courts in Africa is a noteworthy example. See e.g., S Ebobrah, "Litigating Human Rights Before Sub-Regional Courts in Africa: Prospects and Challenges" (2009) 17 Afr. J. Int'l & Comp. L. 79.

[89] See e.g., C Brown. *A Common Law of International Adjudication* (Oxford University Press 2007); J Martinez, "Towards an International Judicial System" (2003) 56 Stan. L. Rev. 429.

[90] See e.g., "iCourts: The Danish National Research Foundation's Centre of Excellence for International Courts" <http://jura.ku.dk/icourts/> accessed December 31, 2012; "ERC Project on Effective International Adjudication" <http://www.effective-intl-adjudication.org/> accessed December 31, 2012; UiO Faculty of Law, "MultiRights: The Legitimacy of Multi-Level Human Rights Judiciary" <http://www.jus.uio.no/english/research/projects/multirights/> accessed December 31, 2012; "PluriCourts: The Legitimate Roles of the Judiciary in the Global Order" <http://www.follesdal.net/ pluricourts/> accessed December 31, 2012.

Such a ruling would have low case-specific effectiveness but high *erga omnes* effectiveness. There is, however, a degree of overlap between the four dimensions at the margins, such as where an IC persuades national judges to remedy international law violations "at home" (increasing embeddedness effectiveness) and also influences the jurisprudence of other ICs (enhancing norm-development effectiveness). Careful attention to the multiple functions that international judges perform will help determine whether a court is effective in one or more of the four categories.

Future research might also consider the relationships among different types of effectiveness. ICs vary in their ability to influence state behavior, anchor their judgments in domestic law, and develop international norms. Scholars might investigate the causes of these variations and their consequences for issues such as the legitimacy of international institutions. A related line of inquiry would consider when different efficacy objectives are mutually reinforcing or in tension with each other. For example, an IC that is effectively embedded in national legal orders might generate fewer international complaints and, as a result, have fewer opportunities to articulate *erga omnes* norms applicable to all states. Similarly, a court that encourages litigants to settle their disputes may receive high marks for case-specific effectiveness but be less effective in developing international law.

Research Questions

1. Under what conditions can a change in a state's behavior following an international court judgment against that state be attributed to the judgment as opposed to other factors?
2. Under what circumstances do international court decisions influence the behavior of actors other than the parties to a particular dispute?
3. What strategies do international judges use to incentivize compliance by national decision-makers, thereby avoiding the need for international litigation?
4. How does the disaggregated nature of the international legal system affect whether international courts are effective in developing international legal norms?

Suggested Reading

Alter, KJ, *The New Terrain of International Law* (Princeton University Press 2014).

Besson, S, "The Erga Omnes Effect of Judgments of the European Court of Human Rights—What's in a Name?" in S Besson (ed.), *The European Court of Human Rights After Protocol 14* (Geneva: Schulthess 2011).

Cavallaro, JL and Brewer, SE, "Reevaluating Regional Human Rights Litigation in the Twenty-First Century: The Case of the Inter-American Court" (2008) 102 AJIL 768.

Ebobrah, ST, "Litigating Human Rights Before Sub-Regional Courts in Africa: Prospects and Challenges" (2009) 17 Afr. J. Int'l & Comp. L. 79.

Guzman, AT, "International Tribunals: A Rational Choice Analysis" (2008) 157 U. Pa. L. Rev. 171.

Hafner-Burton, EM, Victor, DG, and Lupu, Y, "Political Science Research on International Law: The State of the Field" (2012) 106 AJIL 47.

Hawkins, D and Jacoby, W, "Partial Compliance: A Comparison of the European and Inter-American Courts of Human Rights" (2010) 6 J. Int'l L. & Int'l Rel. 35.

Helfer, LR, "Redesigning the European Court of Human Rights: Embeddedness as a Deep Structural Principle of the European Human Rights Regime" (2008) 19 EJIL 125.

Helfer, LR and Slaughter, A-M, "Why States Create International Tribunals: A Response to Professors Posner and Yoo" (2005) 93 Calif. L. Rev. 899.

Helfer, LR, Alter, KJ, and Guerzovich, MF, "Islands of Effective International Adjudication: Constructing an Intellectual Property Rule of Law in the Andean Community" (2009) 103 AJIL 1.

Huneeus, A, "Courts Resisting Courts: Lessons from the Inter-American Court's Struggle to Enforce Human Rights" (2011) 44 Cornell Int'l L.J. 493.

Shany, Y, "Assessing the Effectiveness of International Courts: A Goal-Based Approach" (2012) 106 AJIL 225.

CHAPTER 22

POLITICAL CONSTRAINTS ON INTERNATIONAL COURTS

TOM GINSBURG*

* Leo Spitz Professor of International Law, Ludwig and Hilde Wolf Research Scholar, and Professor of Political Science at the University of Chicago Law School; Research Professor at the American Bar Foundation. Thanks to the Russell Baker Scholars Fund for support and to Nathan Bishop for helpful research assistance.

1 Introduction: The Problem of Political Constraints

The complicated relationship between politics and law has long been a central concern among international lawyers. The project of international law has, for more than a century, sought to construct a zone for autonomous legal decision-making, immune from political considerations, to resolve international disputes. Yet the context of international adjudication is, almost by definition, an intensely political one, and the efficacy of international law requires some consideration of that context. International disputes frequently involve high stakes, and so the dream of autonomous law providing technically correct solutions to resolve problems has always confronted the hard realities of international politics.

At the same time, the very success of international adjudication suggests that some courts and tribunals have been able to effectively navigate this tension. We know that courts operate under political constraints, but this is not something to be ignored or wished away. Indeed, the specifications of those constraints help us understand both the possibilities and limits of international adjudication. Political constraints are a central issue in the study of international law and politics.

The increased institutionalization of international law in the post-Cold War era has provoked a renewed debate about international adjudication, and the normative and positive questions about its relationship to politics. Some see in the rise of international law a new set of threats to traditional concerns of sovereignty, and as such fear the increasing power of judges. Political constraints, according to this view, are necessary to ensure accountability. Others see a risk of "politicization" that threatens the viability of beneficial international solutions to problems of governance. The debate has been useful but has not resolved all the issues. This chapter surveys some of the main arguments, providing a synthetic positive theory of political constraints on courts. It also provides illustrative examples from the practice of selected international courts. In doing so, it notes the important contributions made by scholars of domestic courts, who have developed a set of important tools that also help elucidate political constraints in the international sphere.

2 Between Lauterpacht and Morgenthau: The Evolving Literature

Contrary to the caricatures of some later scholars, international lawyers have long had some sensitivity to the real world context in which international law must operate.[1] The high-minded rhetoric of the Hague Peace Conferences of 1899 and 1906, which articulated the dream that international disputes could be resolved through peaceful means as a substitute for war, gave rise to significant efforts to institutionalize international dispute resolution. These culminated in the creation of the Permanent Court of Arbitration and the Permanent Court of International Justice. In examining these bodies, international legal scholars recognized that the international context limited the ability of courts to deliver on their promise in a purely legal way. The theory of the League of Nations architecture was not that all disputes were inherently capable of legal resolution. Rather, it was that *some* disputes were of this character. For other disputes, the League's political institutions would play a more central role.

Legal scholars debated whether political or legal considerations ultimately dominated.[2] Hans Morgenthau, who later founded the realist school of international relations in the United States, argued in his doctoral dissertation that the distinction lay with matters of state interest. Where vital interests were concerned, the state could not be subjected to external constraint by courts, and so these disputes were inherently incapable of resolution through adjudication.[3] Because it was ultimately up to the state to determine, as a political matter, whether to comply with judicial decisions, Morgenthau thought that politics overwhelmed law. Hersch Lauterpacht's important work, *The Function of Law in the International Community*, attacked both this view and the broader claim that some disputes, by their nature, are not capable of adjudication.[4] International judges, as judges, were obligated to find solutions to questions properly posed, and there was no dispute, in principle, that was not capable of judicial resolution, according to Lauterpacht.

The two schools took hold in different disciplines. In international relations the Morgenthau view was dominant, leading to realists such as John Mearsheimer to argue that international law was "epiphenomenal."[5] On the other hand, international

[1] Compare J Goldsmith and E Posner, *The Limits of International Law* (Oxford University Press 2005).

[2] See, in this handbook, O'Connell and VanderZee, Ch. 3.

[3] H Morgenthau, *Die internationale Rechtspflege, ihr Wesen und ihre Grenzen* (Leipzig: Universitätsverlag Noske 1929), as discussed in M Koskaniemmi, "C Schmitt, Hans Morgenthau and the Image of Law in International Relations" in M Byers (ed), *The Role of Law in International Politics* (Oxford University Press 2000) at 17.

[4] H Lauterpacht, *The Functions of Law in the International Community* (Oxford University Press 1933).

[5] JJ Mearsheimer, "The False Promise of International Institutions" (1994–1995) 19 International Security 5.

lawyers tended to assume the efficacy of legal solutions and to bemoan evidence to the contrary. The former view raised the question of what exactly international tribunals were doing, while the latter failed to provide any theories on the observed limitations on the scope of international adjudication.

The post-Cold War era saw a boom in international courts and, with it, some progress on the theory and rationale behind their creation and functioning.[6] However, there was a revival at this time of views that the courts were purely political. Eric Posner and John Yoo, for example, launched a major attack on international tribunals, arguing that they are least effective when they are "independent."[7] Conflating independence with institutionalization, Posner and Yoo defined independent courts as those that are permanent, staffed by judges with fixed terms, and possessed of compulsory jurisdiction over certain kinds of disputes. Posner and Yoo argued that "independent" courts would impose rules on states and constrain sovereignty, leading to ineffectiveness. Instead, they believed that tribunals appointed in an ad hoc way to resolve particular disputes will be more effective.

A key part of Posner and Yoo's argument is contrasting international courts with domestic courts, which they believe are subject to mechanisms of political control.[8] Indeed, this distinction between international courts operating in anarchy and domestic courts, backed by the power of the state, is central to much of the writing in the field. Yet the literature on domestic political constraints on courts is now well developed, and a close reading of it suggests that the basic institutional distinctions between international and domestic courts are overstated.[9] Like several other chapters in this handbook, we seek to soften the distinction between the literatures on international and domestic courts.[10] Focusing on political constraints is helpful for developing a unified theory of judicial power that operates at both the domestic and international levels.[11] We draw on ideas developed for the domestic sphere in literature on comparative courts.

Positive theories of domestic courts start with the assumption that judicial decision-making about the law is the product of interactions among various political institutions.[12] Courts issue decisions that comport with some presumed combination of legal requirements and judicial preferences,[13] but whatever their goals,

[6] See, in this handbook, Alter, Ch. 4.

[7] E Posner and J Yoo, "Judicial Independence in International Tribunals" (2005) 93 Cal. L. Rev. 1.

[8] Posner and Yoo, note 7, at 49.

[9] J Staton and W Moore, "Judicial Power in Domestic and International Politics" (2011) 65 Int'l. Org. 553.

[10] See, in this handbook, Huneeus, Ch. 20, and Voeten, Ch. 25.

[11] Voeten, Ch. 25; J Goldsmith and D Levinson, "The Law of States" (2009) 122 Harv. L. Rev. 1791.

[12] L Epstein and J Knight, *The Choices Justices Make* (Washington D.C.: Congressional Quarterly Press 1999); McNollgast, "Politics and the Courts: A Positive Theory of Judicial Doctrine and the Rule of Law" (1995) 68 S. Cal. L. Rev. 1631; McNollgast, "Positive Canons: The Role of Legislative Bargains in Statutory Interpretation" (1992) 80 Geo. L. J. 705.

[13] See also, in this handbook, Voeten, Ch. 25.

judges must pay some attention to the preferences of other actors. For example, in domestic legal systems, a legislature can overrule a judicial interpretation of a particular statute by passing a subsequent statute. This may be easier or more difficult, depending on the institutional structure and array of political preferences at any given time.[14] Legislatures also signal information about their reactions to courts, such that explicit overruling is not always necessary. These factors determine the size and shape of strategic space in which courts operate.

Analogous mechanisms can and do operate at the international level. States can both overrule and discipline tribunals that adopt rules outside the scope of state interests. This suggests that the debate over the merits of "independent" and "dependent" courts is less helpful than a contextual examination of the political constraints under which all international courts operate. Variations in these constraints will go a long way toward explaining the actual behavior of international tribunals, and their ability to effectively constrain the states at which their decisions are directed. We ask, then, not whether international adjudication is purely legal or political; clearly, it is both. Understanding the power and scope of international adjudication requires attention to how courts function as institutions in their political context. This in turn requires elaboration of the sources and modes of political constraint on judicial decision-making.

3 A Synthetic Framework: *Ex Ante* vs. *Ex Post* Institutional Constraints

One way to characterize political constraints is to focus on the points in time at which they are exercised, distinguishing between *ex ante* and *ex post* constraints. *Ex ante* constraints are implemented before decisions are made and include the definition of jurisdiction; formal appointment mechanisms that shape the court; and discursive techniques to get judges to internalize state values. *Ex post* constraints, on the other hand, are exercised after the judges render a decision, and include efforts to ignore, overrule, or reject decisions. An initial point at which political constraints become apparent is institutional design. The instruments that establish and regulate tribunals provide opportunities for states to tinker with institutional design in ways that ensure responsiveness to political interests, both *ex ante* and *ex post*.

[14] RD Cooter and T Ginsburg, "Comparative Judicial Discretion: An Empirical Test of Economic Models" (1996) 16 Int'l Rev. L. & Econ. 295, reprinted in S Voigt (ed.), *Constitutional Political Economy II* (Cheltenham: Edward Elgar 2003) at 160, 161.

3.1 *Ex ante* constraints

Scholars of domestic courts often argue that institutional design can affect political responsiveness, though the evidence for this proposition may be more mixed than is sometimes assumed. Still, in recent years a large body of research in comparative judicial politics has focused on institutional factors as determinants of independence and autonomy in decision-making.[15] Key aspects of institutional design include appointment processes,[16] judicial terms, and jurisdiction. This section examines these arguments, especially as they relate to international tribunals.

When judges can be appointed unilaterally by a state, one might think that the judge will be responsive to state interests. On the other hand, where judicial appointment is by election, judges will in theory be less beholden to any particular state, but arguably more responsive to the collective interests. Even in appointment systems with a single actor, states are constrained from appointing judges who are perceived as *too* partisan. After all, the judge must make credible legal arguments to convince colleagues in rendering decisions. This highlights the fact that international judicial decision-making is typically *collective* in nature. Judicial decisions are, at least in some instances, more than the sum of their parts, and courts are more than fora for preference aggregation. The need to make legal arguments means that states cannot appoint pure agents.

Empirical research has struggled to delineate the influence of appointments on judicial behavior in different courts. Analyzing the International Court of Justice (ICJ), Eric Posner and Miguel de Figuierdo used a multivariate analysis and found that judges rarely vote against their home states, and that they favor states whose wealth level is close to that of their own state.[17] Their research also showed connections, although weaker ones, between judges' voting patterns and the interests of the party that is politically or culturally most similar to that of the judge's home country. Eric Voeten took a similar multivariate approach in his comprehensive analysis of voting patterns on the European Court of Human Rights (ECtHR). He concluded that while judges on the ECtHR do show a slight tendency to favor their own home country when it is a party to a dispute, they do not generally exhibit cultural or geopolitical biases, and the court as a whole can be considered independent.[18] Voeten provided a wealth of additional interesting analysis, showing that career background makes a difference, with former diplomats being more supportive of

[15] See, e.g., G Helmke and J Rios-Figueroa, "Introduction" in G Helmke and J Rios-Figueroa (eds), *Courts in Latin America* (Cambridge University Press 2010) at 1.

[16] For a discussion of judicial appointments and elections, see, in this handbook, Mackenzie, Ch. 34.

[17] E Posner and M de Figuiredo, "Is the International Court of Justice Biased?" (2005) 34 J. Legal Studies 599. Although the authors find no evidence of regional bias, they have little data regarding this last issue because of the lack of participation of two-thirds of the UN membership.

[18] E Voeten, "The Impartiality of International Judges: Evidence from the European Court of Human Rights" (2008) 102 Am. Poli. Sci. Rvw. 417.

national governments.[19] These contrasts could reflect the fact that the membership of the ECtHR, and thus the appointment of its judges, is limited to European countries, which are more homogeneous in their interests and views than is the overall body of UN members. The ICJ, on the other hand, has some features—state consent to jurisdiction and ability to appoint an ad-hoc judge—that make it more akin to an arbitral body than a court,[20] and so there may be some expectation of loyalty on the part of the national judge in a particular case.

Another category of political constraints is discursive. States might promote international law doctrines of fidelity to the constituent instrument, and avoidance of judicial creativity as a kind of *ex ante* constraint to prevent judges from "going rogue." This shows that legal doctrine itself may have a political character, further undermining the law/politics binary that has long dominated certain discussions of international adjudication.

Terms of judges are additional factors that might affect judicial responsiveness to political interests. The crucial factor, it is usually thought, is whether judges can be reappointed or not. When judges can be re-appointed they are incentivized to perform well, but also may be reluctant to challenge powerful state interests. Some international courts allow re-appointment (e.g. the ICJ), while others limit it to a second term only (the WTO Appellate body), and some generally prohibit it (the International Criminal Court, or ICC, and now the ECtHR). Term lengths also vary from the relatively short four years of the WTO Appellate body to nine years at the ICC and ICJ.

Finally, control over the jurisdiction and power of the court, as laid out in its constituent instrument or founding treaty, is an essential tool of *ex ante* control. International adjudicators are only entitled to hear cases properly brought, and the ability of states to define the law is an important source of constraint. Treaty provisions can be laid out with a wide range of detail, either in loose standards or precise rules. As has long been observed, the latter tend to more tightly constrain judicial decision-makers.

Sometimes, of course, states will be unable or unwilling to articulate rules with sufficient precision to constrain judges, but they rarely seem to contemplate broad lawmaking power. Further, states seem to be reluctant to allow judges to decide cases *ex aequo et bono*. The Statute of the International Court of Justice, for example, allows states to permit the court to decide on the basis of such equitable considerations. Historically, however, such permission has not been granted and the court uses equitable considerations very rarely—at least outside the important context of maritime delimitation.[21]

[19] See, in this handbook, Voeten, Ch. 25. See also FJ Bruinsma, "The Room at the Top: Separate Opinions in Grand Chambers of the ECHR (1998-2006)" (2007) 28 Recht der Werkelijkheid 7.

[20] T Ginsburg and R McAdams, "Adjudicating in Anarchy" (2004) 45 Wm. & Mary L. Rev. 1228.

[21] UN Statute of the International Court of Justice (April 18, 1946), Art. 38(2).

In short, defining the terms under which judges will labor, establishing appointment mechanisms and laying out the relevant law and its level of precision all provide sources of constraint through which political considerations can be brought to bear. These techniques tend to be exercised *before* any individual decision is rendered and may have an impact on how judges actually vote.

3.2 *Ex post* constraints

In contrast, *ex post* constraints occur after a judicial decision has been rendered. They are easy to understand using Albert Hirschman's classic framework outlined in "Exit, Voice and Loyalty."[22] A party unhappy with a court decision can comply with the decision that it does not like, remaining loyal to its obligations. Alternatively, it can exit the court's jurisdiction, abandoning the regime. A third possibility is to exercise various forms of voice, remaining loyal to the regime but seeking to modify the ruling it does not like, or to influence future rulings from the tribunal. A fourth possibility is to ignore the ruling or fail to comply with it. This is both a way to avoid certain costs associated with the case at hand and an act of voice that influences future cases.

3.2.1 *Exit*

As an extreme measure, states unhappy with judicial decisions may seek to exit the broader regime of which the court is part. Treaties typically allow for denunciation with notice; the Vienna Convention on the Law of Treaties provides a default provision of 12 months' notice.[23] Decisions by France and the United States to exit the "optional clause" regime of the ICJ after adverse decisions are two high-profile illustrations. The "optional clause" regime, under Art. 36(2) of the ICJ Statute, allows states to file declarations that accept as compulsory the general jurisdiction of the court vis-à-vis any other state that has made a similar declaration. As with international obligations generally, these declarations can be withdrawn, which is exactly what happened after the famous *Nicaragua* case when the court rejected the preliminary objections of the United States.[24] France, too, exited the optional clause after an adverse decision in the *Nuclear Tests* cases.[25] Similarly, the United

[22] AO Hirschman, *Exit Voice and Loyalty: Responses to Decline in Firms, Organizations, and States* (Cambridge, MA: Harvard University Press 1970). See also JHH Weiler, "The Transformation of Europe" (1990) 100 Yale L.J. 2403, 2411.

[23] UN Vienna Convention on the Law of Treaties (adopted May 23, 1969, entered into force January 27, 1980), Art. 56. See E Gaillard and Y Banifatemi, "The Denunciation of the ICSID Convention" (2007) 237 N.Y.L.J. 1; LR Helfer "Exiting Treaties" (2005) 91 Va. L. R. 1579.

[24] United States, "Statement on the U.S. Withdrawal from the Proceedings Initiated by Nicaragua in the International Court of Justice" (1995) 24 ILM 246.

[25] *New Zealand v. France* (*Nuclear Tests* cases) [1974] ICJ 457; *Australia v. France* (*Nuclear Test* cases) [1974] ICJ 253.

States withdrew from the Optional Protocol of the Vienna Convention on Consular Relations after the *Avena* decision in 2004.[26]

Another prominent instance of exit was a decision by several Caribbean states to exit the jurisdiction of the Privy Council in London in response to decisions implementing ECtHR prohibitions against the death penalty.[27] These states established a new Caribbean Court of Justice to replace the appellate jurisdiction of the Privy Council and to interpret the Treaty Establishing the Caribbean Community. Proponents of the new court argued that European judges were imposing their own preferences on Caribbean societies. In addition to these withdrawals, some states withdrew from the American Convention and the Optional Protocol to the International Covenant on Civil and Political Rights. Helfer interpreted these withdrawals as instances of exit in response to human rights adjudicators ignoring the preferences of states.[28]

It should be made clear that the costs of exit are not uniform across states within a given regime. Relatively easy exit from international regimes will allow small numbers of states that are powerful in the issue area to threaten to leave and establish new mechanisms.

3.2.2 *Voice*

When unable or unwilling to exit a regime, states often utilize voice, in the sense of articulating concerns so as to influence others. Joseph Weiler's classic article "The Transformation of Europe" argued that as exit from the European Communities was precluded for legal, economic, and political reasons, state demands for voice increased.[29] This section considers several ways in which states can exercise voice, using mechanisms that operate at the level of individual decisions or mechanisms that operate more generally. In the former category, states can communicate with the court by *ignoring* a particular decision, and hoping that whatever powers the court or other institutions have to enforce the decision will not be effective. Through the latter category, states can also seek to *overrule* the court's interpretation by amending the treaty regime or engaging in formal interpretation when it is provided for. More general mechanisms include the ability to *attack* the court, either explicitly by communicating displeasure or implicitly by trying to limit the court's jurisdiction, composition, or effective power in future cases. States can also seek to limit lawmaking by promoting an attitude of judicial passivity on the part of judges.

[26] *Mexico v. United States of America (Avena and Other Mexican Nationals)* [2004] ICJ 12.

[27] *Pratt and Morgan v. Jamaica* [1994], 2 AC 1, [1993] PC. See generally, J Harrington, "The Challenge to the Mandatory Death Penalty in the Commonwealth Caribbean" (2004) 98 AJIL 126; LR Helfer, "Overlegalizing Human Rights: International Relations Theory and the Commonwealth Caribbean Backlash Against Human Rights Regimes" (2002) 102 Colum. L. Rev. 1832.

[28] Helfer, note 27. [29] Weiler, note 22.

States in some cases can simply ignore the decision of an international court, as Iceland did in the 1970s with the ICJ.[30] Such actions tend to undermine the general application of the rules pronounced in the cases at issue, though this is not always the case. Ignoring a decision is a communicative act expressing displeasure with a court ruling.

In domestic constitutional systems, legislatures can overrule wayward court decisions by passing subsequent legislation. This is the focus of much of the separation of powers literature. In the international arena, the analogous process is formal treaty amendment, but this is usually quite difficult and seldom exercised. There are several reasons for the relative rarity of amendment of treaty provisions to "correct" interpretation of a judicial decision in the international arena. First, to the extent that consent-based treaty regimes require accordance of *all* states to amend the regime, amendment in response to a decision will be difficult. An adverse judicial decision for one party is usually a beneficial decision for another. In bilateral settings, this fact alone makes it unlikely that both parties will agree to overturn a judicial decision. Even if the parties consider the judicial decision Pareto-inferior, they may simply choose to ignore it or conclude a side deal without formally amending the treaty.

In multilateral settings, the analysis is more complicated. Multiple parties typically do not build easy amendment procedures into the treaty design, and the more parties involved the more difficult any amendments will be to conclude. The WTO treaty, for example, involves multi-sectoral trade-offs of commitments by more than 100 countries. For this reason, the treaty is amended only as a package on the basis of multi-year negotiating rounds. The transaction costs of any amendment to multilateral treaties are intentionally high; in order to make the commitments effective, they must be difficult to escape. This makes the potential scope of lawmaking capacity greater in multilateral settings and is a source of concern about courts becoming runaway lawmakers.

Many international courts are embedded in broader international organizations, such as the UN or WTO. The bundling of international courts with broader regimes insulates the tribunals from certain forms of pressure, but also provides a point of leverage to pressure the courts into greater alignment with state preferences. That is, courts can draw on broader institutional resources by resisting pressure, but the institutional structures of larger regimes can also suffer because of adverse decisions. In some cases, the broader organization can act to constrain the jurisdiction of the court in response. One example is the Tribunal of the Southern African Development Community (SADC), which in one of its first cases ruled against the government of Zimbabwe in an eviction case.[31] After Zimbabwe withdrew, the other

[30] *UK v. Iceland* (*Fisheries Jurisdiction* case) [1974] ICJ, LR 3; *Federal Republic of Germany v. Iceland* (*Fisheries Jurisdiction* case) [1974] ICJ, LR 175. See also Shigeru Oda, "The Compulsory Jurisdiction of the International Court of Justice: A Myth?" (2000) 49 Int'l. & Comp L.Q. 251, 260.

[31] *Mike Campbell (Pvt) Ltd. and Others v. Republic of Zimbabwe* [2007] SADCT 2.

member states agreed to limit the jurisdiction of the court to disputes among member states, removing jurisdiction over individual disputes.[32]

Even stand-alone courts such as the ICC are embedded in broader meetings of the states party. Regular meetings of the international organization or states party allow states to signal displeasure in a formal way. To the extent that the entire international organization's reputation is bundled up with that of the dispute resolution mechanism, the secretariat has an incentive to monitor and restrain the court. The embeddedness of certain international courts in broader organizations can thus bundle the legitimacy of the court with the legitimacy of the organization, providing a constraint on the court.

Furthermore, mobilizing public opinion against a court is also possible. The United States' sustained attacks against the ICC before it had even been created illustrate the attraction of this strategy to powerful states. This strategy is distinct from constraints imposed within the meetings of member states.

International tribunals may also be subject to budgetary constraints. States and international organizations can punish courts for negative decisions or reward them for positive ones through monetary resources. For example, the US Congress failed to increase the federal court's budget in the 1960s during a wave of judicial activism by Chief Justice Earl Warren's Court. The United States has from time to time sought to withhold dues from the UN and some of its agencies as a way of signaling displeasure. Pressure from donors to wind down the International Criminal Tribunal for the Former Yugoslavia (ICTY) is another example of such constraints being applied to an international court.[33]

3.2.3 *Facilitating loyalty*

Given the presence of these *ex ante* and *ex post* techniques for political constraints on international courts, what can courts and tribunals do to facilitate the "loyalty" response? The various legal techniques of judicial strategy are well understood in the domestic context. The quality of legal decisions is surely important in this regard. As Walter Murphy suggested a half-century ago, people "are more ready to accept unpleasant decisions which appear to be the ineluctable result of rigorously logical deductions."[34] Some have suggested that this appearance is facilitated by unanimous decisions. Another dimension is selection of cases. Choosing what questions to focus on is as important as the ultimate decisions. Courts have a long history of ducking particularly contentious issues and these techniques are as visible on the international plane as they are on the domestic one.

[32] For a discussion of the SADC Tribunal, see, in this handbook, Romano, Ch. 6.

[33] See, e.g., financing tribunals, in this handbook, Ingadottir, Ch. 27.

[34] W Murphy, *Elements of Judicial Strategy* (University of Chicago Press 1964) 17.

The job of courts is to make decisions that are complied with and, to do this effectively, courts need the support of particular audiences. Sometimes this will be a particular state or set of states powerful enough to insulate the court from attacks and pressure. In other instances, courts might find that it makes sense to appeal to the public.[35] James Cavallaro and Stephanie Brewer, for example, find that the Inter-American Court has frequently appealed to particular interest groups, the media, and the broader public to insulate its decisions from attack.[36]

These hardly exhaust the myriad techniques available to international courts. It is a characteristic of the political context that there is no fail-safe set of strategies. Furthermore, the ability to constrain international courts is differentially distributed in the international system, so that more powerful states are able to exercise greater control over tribunals. This leads to a hypothesis about the political perspective: the strategic decision spaces of international courts will be largely shaped by the power structure of the underlying regimes in which they are embedded. This is a claim subject to potential testing and verification and several studies have examined the issue in the context of particular tribunals.

4 Case Studies

This section provides several case studies of prominent tribunals: the ICJ, the dispute settlement mechanism of the North American Free Trade Agreement (NAFTA), the dispute settlement mechanism of the WTO, the international investment regime under the International Convention for the Settlement of Investment Disputes (ICSID) and the Inter-American Court of Human Rights (IACtHR). These are illustrative only, and we might have looked at any of the more than two dozen other international courts in existence. But the selected tribunals frequently deal with very powerful states and provide a range of illustrations of the dynamics set out in the earlier section.

[35] See G Vanberg, *The Politics of Constitutional Review in Germany* (Cambridge University Press 2005); J Staton, *Judicial Power and Strategic Communication in Mexico* (Cambridge University Press 2010).

[36] JL Cavallaro and SE Brewer, "Reevaluating Regional Human Rights Litigation in the Twenty-First Century: The Case of the Inter-American Court" (2008) 102 AJIL 768.

4.1 ICJ

As the principal judicial organ of the UN, the ICJ plays a central role in the international judicial system.[37] Appointment to the ICJ requires majority votes in both the General Assembly and the Security Council, but the system has evolved in such a way that powerful states have an informal right to nominate judges for a seat on the court. This illustrates how bundling a court with a broader institution can affect the appointment process: states' "true" preferences are constrained by the system of voting blocs in the UN as a whole.

The ICJ is also somewhat constrained by its institutional design. Its jurisdiction is largely consensual, with an advisory jurisdiction to allow certain UN bodies and international organizations to refer legal questions to the ICJ for a declaratory statement of the relevant law. This jurisdiction has been used successfully by international organizations to resolve disputes about their own scope of assignment and powers.[38] This provides the ICJ with at least one audience that can help to insulate the court somewhat from raw political pressure exerted by states.

With regard to the contentious jurisdiction, things are trickier. As mentioned above, powerful states such as the United States and France have exercised the exit option. States have also ignored adverse decisions at times. For example, with regard to an ICJ decision in a case involving a border dispute between Nigeria and Cameroon, Nigeria took the position that it neither accepted nor rejected the pronouncement of the court.[39] Iran ignored the ICJ's decision in the *Case Concerning United States Diplomatic and Consular Staff in Tehran* which called on it to release hostages held in 1980.[40] Still, Conrad Schulte, in a major study of final orders and decisions, has found relatively few instances of non-compliance.[41] Richard McAdams and I, in a parallel study, also found a high level of compliance, but argued that their results reflected an important selection bias.[42] Cases that go all the way to a final resolution are precisely those for which states have an interest in compliance, and generally concern low-stakes matters that do not go to core interests.

37 See, in this handbook, Murphy, Ch. 9.

38 *Reparations for Injuries Suffered in the Service of the United Nations* [1949] ICJ 174.

39 See C Paulson, "Compliance with Final Judgments of the International Court of Justice since 1987" (2004) 98 AJIL 434, 450.

40 *U.S. v. Iran* (*Case Concerning United States Diplomatic and Consular Staff in Tehran*) [1980] ICJ 64.

41 C Schulte, *Compliance with Decisions of the International Court of Justice* (Oxford University Press 2004). See also J Collier and V Lowe, *The Settlement of Disputes in International Law: Institutions and Procedures* (Oxford University Press 2000) at 178 ("All decisions were, sooner or later, complied with."); MK Bulterman and M Kuijer (eds), *Compliance with Judgments of International Courts* (Dordrecht: Kluwer Law International 1996) 35 (most decisions complied with).

42 T Ginsburg and R McAdams, "Adjudicating in Anarchy: An Expressive Theory of International Dispute Resolution" (2004) 45 Wm. & Mary L. R. 1229.

4.2 NAFTA

All treaty regimes have, implicitly, one mechanism analogous to domestic legislation to constrain courts: the possibility of amending the constituent instrument to correct erroneous or misguided interpretations that run foul of the states' preferences. The general rule in international law, however, is that unanimous consent is required to amend treaties. If the treaty regime has only two or three parties, this may not be a difficult threshold to reach. But the larger the number of parties to a multilateral treaty, the more difficult it will be to amend. So, for example, we ought to expect that formal overruling will be more difficult in the WTO, which has 159 states parties at this writing, than it will be in NAFTA, with three. For large multilateral treaties, international courts may have more freedom in which to maneuver than domestic courts, which can be "over-ruled" by majority rule.

NAFTA includes another mechanism for over-ruling decisions: a residual power of the states parties to interpret the international trade agreement.[43] One aspect of this is the power of the non-disputing treaty party to submit views on interpretive issues to the arbitral panel. In addition, NAFTA established a Free Trade Commission, comprised of cabinet-level officials from each of the parties, which is empowered to issue interpretations of the Treaty.[44] The Commission has the power to:

> (a) Supervise the implementation of [the] Agreement; (b) oversee its further elaboration; (c) resolve disputes that may arise regarding its interpretation or application; (d) supervise the work of all committees and working groups established under this Agreement;... and (e) consider any other matter that may affect the operation of this Agreement.[45]

This interpretive function, distinct from the dispute settlement system, serves as a lawmaking constraint on panels without the requirement of formally amending the underlying agreement. Chapter 11 of NAFTA provides that "[a]n interpretation by the [Free Trade] Commission of a provision of this Agreement shall be binding on a Tribunal established under this Section."[46] The states party thus sets up a special body that can both monitor the dispute resolution process and influence it by providing binding interpretations.

This process was used to interpret the standard of expropriation in NAFTA and its relation to general international law. NAFTA Art. 1105 provides that "[e]ach party shall accord to investments of investors of another Party treatment in accordance with international law, including fair and equitable treatment and full protection and security." Some early NAFTA panels had suggested that the standards

[43] See, in this handbook, Baudenbacher and Clifton, Ch. 12.

[44] North American Free Trade Agreement (adopted December 3, 1993, entered into force January 1, 1994), Art. 2001.1, 32 I.L.M. 605, 693.

[45] NAFTA, Art. 2001.2.

[46] NAFTA, Art. 1131.2.

for "fair and equitable treatment" and "full protection and security" were different under NAFTA than under general international law.[47] In an effort to clarify the meaning of Art. 1105, the Free Trade Commission issued an interpretive statement in 2001 that provided: "The concepts of "fair and equitable" and "full protection and security" do not require treatment in addition to or beyond that which is required by the customary standard of treatment of aliens."[48] Following this interpretive statement, the arbitral tribunal in *Loewen v. United States*, an ICSID arbitration brought by a Canadian funeral home operator, declared that " 'fair and equitable treatment' and 'full protection and security' are not free-standing obligations."[49] Rather, they constitute obligations of the host state "only to the extent that they are recognized by customary international law."[50] The *Loewen* tribunal also stated that to the extent earlier NAFTA tribunals in cases such as *Metalclad Corp. v. United Mexican States*, *S.D. Myers v. Government of Canada*, and *Pope & Talbot v. Government of Canada* "may have expressed contrary views, those views must be disregarded."[51]

This pattern shows that states were able to influence a prominent dispute settlement system on a core issue, requiring the panels to apply a relatively clear body of international law rather than create a new potentially conflicting body of law. This "correction" of the judicial panels was somewhat controversial. The late Sir Robert Jennings, former president of the ICJ, criticized this as a quasi-legislative intervention violating "the most elementary rules of due process of justice."[52] But such constraints are inherent in domestic systems of justice as well, and states will be reluctant to delegate *any* authority to resolvers of disputes if judges completely resist political control.

[47] See *Metalclad Corp. v. United Mexican States* (2001) 40 I.L.M. 35, para. 100–1. States were concerned that "fair and equitable" would become a license for arbitrators to award damages in any case where the arbitrators viewed the government action as unfair.

[48] "NAFTA Free Trade Comm'n, Notes of Interpretation of Certain Chapter 11 Provisions" (July 31, 2001), Art. B.2. These notes of interpretation also clarified that other NAFTA treaty norms, which are themselves international law, do not by the terms of Art. 1105 become subject to Ch. 11 dispute resolution. See A Afilalo, "Towards a Common Law of International Investment: How NAFTA Chapter 11 Panels Should Resolve their Legitimacy Crisis" (2004) 17 Geo. Int'l Envt'l L. Rev. 51, 61.

[49] *Loewen Group, Inc. v. United States*, Award [2003] ICSID Case No. ARB (AF)/98/3, 42 I.L.M., para. 128.

[50] *Loewen Group, Inc. v. United States*, Award, note 49, para. 125.

[51] *Loewen Group, Inc. v. United States*, Award, note 49, paras 124–8; Compare *Pope & Talbot, Inc. v. Canada*, Damages, (NAFTA Ch. 11 Arb. Trib. May 31, 2002), 41 I.L.M. para. 47 ("[W]ere the Tribunal required to make a determination whether the Commission's action is an interpretation or an amendment, it would choose the latter.").

[52] See *Methanex Corp. v. United States* [2001] UNCITRAL 1105(1) (second opinion of Robert Y Jennings Q.C.), available at <http://italaw.com/sites/default/files/case-documents/ita0983.pdf> accessed July 27, 2012.

4.3 WTO

Richard Steinberg has analyzed judicial lawmaking at the WTO, and in particular the growth in expansive judicial interpretations that followed the switch from the General Agreement on Trade and Tariffs (GATT) in 1994.[53] This switch famously modified a rule requiring unanimity to adopt panel reports to one requiring unanimity to reject a report. This made it easier to adopt reports, thereby expanding judicial policy space. Steinberg also analyzed *ex ante* constraints, such as appointment processes, and *ex post* processes, such as overruling in the context of the WTO.

Ex ante mechanisms may be more effective than *ex post* ones at the WTO. Members of the Appellate Body are proposed by a special committee and selected by consensus. Major players in the trade arena, however, have informal veto powers, which serve to ensure a certain degree of consent over the composition. Manfred Elsig and Mark Pollack demonstrated that the process is becoming increasingly politicized.[54] Still, overruling the Appellate Body's interpretations is quite difficult because of the large number of parties to the WTO and high voting thresholds. While the WTO's Ministerial Conference and the General Council already have the formal power to adopt binding interpretations of the WTO Agreements by three-fourths majority vote, in practice, the WTO relies on norms of consensus.[55] Even when the formal WTO treaty allows voting, states parties have resisted it. The difficulty of reaching consensus and the need for such consensus to block the adoption of panel reports in turn greatly empowers the dispute resolution system. Some have proposed allowing the Dispute Settlement Body to adopt panel reports in part; others have proposed making legislation and amendment easier in practice. Any successful attempt to make lawmaking easier will lead to a corresponding reduction in the discretion of judicial lawmakers. Indeed, even the proposal may have some effect, as a court might take the threat of modification seriously enough to tone down its decisions. The point is that the states do have some explicit mechanisms for correcting erroneous interpretations of trade agreements, though they may not always choose to exercise them.

4.4 International investment arbitration

Even the international arbitration regime is subject to political influence. Investment law is usually conceived as involving a complex game of cooperation and competition between capital-exporters (home states) and capital-importers (host states).

[53] RH Steinberg, "Judicial lawmaking at the WTO: Discursive, constitutional, and political constraints" (2004) 98 AJIL 264.

[54] M Elsig and M Pollack, "Agents, trustees, and international courts: The politics of judicial appointment at the World Trade Organization" (forthcoming) 18 Eur. J. Int'l Relations.

[55] WTO Dispute Settlement Understanding, Art. IX.2.

For many years, host states criticized the regime of foreign investment centered around the ICSID and the large network of Bilateral Investment Treaties (BITs) providing the primary regulatory regime.[56] Many analysts believed that developing countries could not afford to leave the regime and were forced to submit to rules that were collectively suboptimal.[57]

In 2007, at a presidential summit, President Hugo Chavez announced Venezuela would be leaving several imperialist international organizations, including the ICSID. Shortly thereafter, Bolivia became the first country to withdraw from the ICSID Convention. Two years later, Ecuador followed suit, and, in early 2012, Venezuela became the third Latin American country in five years to exit the convention. This followed an adverse decision handed down by an ICSID arbitration committee against the country for nationalization of an Exxon project.

Beyond exit, host states have exercised voice. Venezuela put out a press release claiming—falsely—that ICSID tribunals "ruled 232 times in favor of transnational interests out of the 234 cases filed throughout its history."[58] The Argentine cases demonstrate another technique: ignoring adverse judgments. During the 1990s, Argentina engaged in an extensive program of liberalization to attract greater foreign investment. It concluded a BIT with the United States in 1991 and pegged its currency to the dollar. In the late 1990s, however, a balance-of-payments problem forced the Argentine government to seek a freeze on US PPI-based inflation adjustments that had been promised. In December 2001, it subsequently enacted an emergency set of capital controls, suspending convertibility of the currency into dollars, and canceling future tariff adjustments. A rash of ICSID claims followed, asserting a variety of claims grounded in international investment law. The claims included indirect expropriation, violation of the obligation to accord fair and equitable treatments, and discrimination. A majority of these decisions were found in favor of Argentina, while others were found against it, often on very similar facts.[59] Of some $40 billion in awards rendered as of this date, less than one percent of it has been collected so far. Argentina has not withdrawn from ICSID, and has instead simply failed to pay the judgments. In 2012, Argentina announced a new expropriation of shares of an oil company called YPF, which is owned by the Spanish firm Repsol.

[56] See, in this handbook, Schreuer, Ch. 14.

[57] A Guzman, "Why LDCs Sign Treaties That Hurt Them: Explaining the Popularity of Bilateral Investment Treaties" (1998) 38 Va. J. Int'l. L. 639.

[58] "Gobierno Bolivariano denuncia convenio con Ciadi" (January 25, 2012) <http://www.mre.gov.ve>. But see S Franck, "Development and Outcomes of Treaty Arbitration" (2009) 50 Harv. Int' l L. J. 435; "Come and get me: Argentina is putting international arbitration to the test" *The Economist* (February 18, 2012) 24 (reporting that 20 percent of cases are found in favor of investors).

[59] *LG&E Energy Corp. v. Argentina*, Award [2007] ICSID Case No. ARB/02/1. But see *CMS Gas Transmission Co. v. Argentina*, Decision on Objections to Jurisdiction [2003] ICSID Case No. ARB/01/8.

4.5 The IACtHR

The IACtHR is often celebrated for its progressive interpretation of human rights law and its creativity regarding remedies.[60] As late as the 1990s, scholars praised the court's ability to generate compliance with its decisions.[61] In the early 2000s, it issued a series of decisions overturning national amnesty laws, thereby allowing the retrospective examination of crimes committed during the region's decades of military rule.

Yet states have been willing to ignore the court and have occasionally even withdrawn. Peru withdrew briefly under the government of Alberto Fujimori but later returned. In recent years, however, there has been renewed challenge to the jurisdiction of the court, emanating this time from the left rather than the right. The so-called Bolivarian Alliance for the Americas, led by Venezuela under Hugo Chavez, has been vociferous in its attacks on the court. The court had criticized the attempts by Chavez to purge the judiciary, but Chavez had ignored its rulings.[62] Similarly, when the commission ruled that Venezuela had to allow an opposition politician, Leopoldo Lopez, to run for office, Chavez ignored it. Not content with ignoring the rulings, the governments began to exercise voice. Venezuela's ambassador to the Organization of American States (OAS) called the court "an instrument of the empire."[63] At the OAS annual meeting in June 2012, President Evo Morales of Bolivia suggested the elimination of the IACtHR and other Bolivarian Alliance countries threatened to withdraw if reforms were not made.

In 2011, the court found itself at odds with the government of Brazil over the large Belo Monte dam in the Amazon, requiring that construction halt for further consultation with local communities. This led the Brazilian government to suspend paying dues to the OAS for a year. The OAS responded with a debate over the IACtHR and agreed to weaken the commission by allowing countries to delay the publication of country-specific reports for a year and allow a right of reply. Further proposals are under discussion for modifying the right of individual petition and reducing the power to order precautionary measures. In a further sign of political backlash in late 2012, Venezuela announced that it was withdrawing from the court in response to adverse rulings, but the court continued to hear cases against it.

[60] *Velasquez-Rodriguez v. Honduras* [1987] Judgment of July 29, 1988, Inter-Am.Ct.H.R. (Ser. C) No. 4 (1988); *I Ximenes Lopez v. Brazil* [2006] Merits, Reparations, and Costs, Inter-Am. Ct. H.R. (ser. C) No. 149, P 8 (July 4, 2006); *Moiwana Village v. Suriname* [2005] I Preliminary Objections, Merits, and Reparations, Judgement, Inter-Am. Ct. H.R. (ser. C) No. 124, (June 15, 2005).

[61] D Cassel, "Peru Withdraws from the Court: Will the Inter-American Human rights System meet the Challenge?" (1999) 20 Hum. Rts. L.J. 167.

[62] Human Rights Watch, "A Decade Under Chávez: Political Intolerance and Lost Opportunities for Advancing Human Rights in Venezuela" (September 18, 2008) available at <http://www.hrw.org/reports/2008/09/18/decade-under-ch-vez>.

[63] "Chipping at the Foundations," *The Economist* (June 9, 2012) 41.

In short, the IACtHR seems to have neglected the need to have a core constituency willing and able to defend it against attacks from governments. By simultaneously challenging what were perceived as core policies of several states at once, including some that had a strong amount of domestic political support, the court seems to have provoked a serious backlash. At this writing, the outcome is uncertain. But the tale illustrates the general phenomenon of political constraints all too clearly.

5 Conclusion

It is useful, though somewhat unfair, to characterize the classical debates in international law as juxtaposing a purely "political" view, that law is simply a reflection of interests, with a "legal" view that sees law as the autonomous product of professional judgment. This parallels studies of the American Supreme Court that sometimes contrast the "attitudinal model," with a "legal model" in which they always vote the law. The domestic literature has increasingly shifted to a more synthetic "strategic" model, in which judicial ability is constrained by the preferences of other actors. Such constraints are always partial and, in every case, there is some zone of judicial autonomy or discretion. Judicial power is neither infinite nor epiphenomenal. In the sophisticated application of this model, the technicalities of the law are important, both in constructing the judicial "preferences" and for legitimation before the broader set of audiences that support judicial power.

This domestic literature has given us a powerful lens through which to examine international courts and tribunals. We now understand that there is a zone of judicial discretion, but that courts operate within political constraints. Indeed, it could hardly be otherwise, for political interests are involved in establishing international courts and providing them with ongoing material and political support.

Research Questions

1. How do institutional design factors, such as appointment processes, influence the behavior of international courts? We have some preliminary empirical work in this regard on Europe, but little on other courts.
2. How has the institutional design of tribunals changed over time? Are states learning new techniques of political control?

3. How do judges respond to states' exiting from jurisdiction after adverse decisions? Are the tendencies toward correcting the source of grievance?
4. To what audiences do states communicate displeasure over adverse decisions?

Suggested Reading

Ginsburg, T, "Bounded Discretion in International Judicial Lawmaking" (2005) 45 Va. J. Int'l L. 631–73.

Helfer, LR, "Exiting Treaties" (2005) 91 Va. L. Rev. 1579–1648.

Staton, J and Moore, W, "Judicial Power in Domestic and International Politics" (2011) 65 Int'l. Org. 553–87.

Steinberg, R, "Judicial lawmaking at the WTO: Discursive, constitutional, and political constraints" (2004) 98 AJIL. 247–75.

CHAPTER 23

THE SPELL OF PRECEDENTS

LAWMAKING BY INTERNATIONAL COURTS AND TRIBUNALS

ARMIN VON BOGDANDY* AND INGO VENZKE**

* Director at the Max Planck Institute for Comparative Public Law and International Law, Heidelberg, Professor at the Goethe-Universität, Frankfurt, and President of the OECD Nuclear Energy Tribunal.
** Senior Research Fellow and Lecturer at the University of Amsterdam.

1 Introduction

This chapter discusses the lawmaking dimension of international adjudication. It starts from the observation that the stark quantitative increase in international adjudication over the past two decades has gone hand in hand with a change in quality. Now more so than before, international courts and tribunals contribute to the making of international law by weaving webs of precedents, imbuing treaties with meaning, and by generally establishing new reference points for legal argument. This is easy to see in some key fields of international law. Whoever wants to make an argument about human rights in Europe can hardly do so without drawing on the rich jurisprudence of the European Court of Human Rights (ECtHR). Reports of the World Trade Organization (WTO) Appellate Body likewise tangibly redistribute argumentative burdens in international trade law. Normative assessments of international judicial lawmaking aside, international adjudication's significant role in "thickening" at least some fields and questions of international law is today beyond dispute.

What remains subject to discussion is how best to understand the contribution of international courts and tribunals to the making of law without overstating—in either theoretical or practical terms—their creativity or constraints. It also merits further effort to elucidate fully the basis and nature of this aspect of judicial authority, to appreciate similarities as well as differences between international courts and tribunals, and to assess better the legitimacy of international judicial lawmaking.[1]

This chapter first revisits theoretical groundwork by discussing how the practice of interpretation generates legal normativity (section 2). Although international law knows no doctrine of *stare decisis* and avows that judgments are only binding *inter partes*, earlier decisions generate new legal normativity because participants in legal discourse are expected—and pushed—to relate their arguments to precedents (section 3). The chapter then turns to showing how lawmaking dynamics unfold in specific fields of international law and in processes of cross-fertilization. This leads to a comparison of judicial institutions and an investigation of different parameters that render international judicial lawmaking more or less likely (section 4). The chapter concludes by taking up questions relating to the legitimacy of international judicial lawmaking (section 5).

[1] We adopt a broad understanding of international courts and tribunals, but we exclude the Court of Justice of the European Union (CJEU). The CJEU is indeed an exceptionally prolific court beyond nation states. But as part of a *supra*national constitutional order it has very little in common with *inter*national judicial institutions.

2 Speaking and Making Law

Few scholars would still advocate a traditional cognitivistic understanding of judicial interpretation. Immanuel Kant argued early on that concrete decisions cannot be deduced from abstract rules, and Hans Kelsen upheld that every act of law *application* is also one of law *making* precisely because abstract rules cannot fully determine their application.[2] The meaning of a norm for any specific case cannot be *discovered*, but only *created*.[3] The linguistic turn has reinforced this thought, emboldening the idea that it is the practice of interpretation that makes international law.[4] Building on semantic pragmatism and its key contention that words do not have meaning other than that attributed to them by their use, Robert Brandom has shown that every decision concerning the use or interpretation of a concept contributes to the shaping of its content.[5] This means that international law is made in the practice of its interpretation.

International legal doctrine strikes a different tone. It points out Article 38 of the Statute of the International Court of Justice (ICJ), which provides that international judicial decisions are "subsidiary means of interpretation." This suggests that decisions are a *Rechtserkenntnisquelle* (a source for recognizing the law) and not in and of themselves a *Rechtsquelle* (a source of law).[6] According to Art. 59 of the ICJ Statute, judicial decisions and concrete legal findings are in any event only binding between the parties.[7]

Tension between this view of legal doctrine, on the one hand, and the creativity of law application, on the other, has led international legal scholarship to speak of adjudication as *developing* the law, thus recognizing judgments' effects beyond the concrete dispute, but stopping short of recognizing their contribution to the *making* of the law. George Abi-Saab, among others, has opined that the role of courts in the development of international law is a truly nebulous subject.[8] The concept of

[2] I Kant, *Critique of Pure Reason* (first published 1781, CUP, Cambridge 1999) A131–48; H Kelsen, *Reine Rechtslehre* (Leipzig: Deuticke 1934) 82–3.

[3] Kelsen, note 2, at 74, 95.

[4] I Venzke, *How Interpretation Makes International Law: On Semantic Change and Normative Twists* (Oxford University Press 2012) 30–1, 55.

[5] RB Brandom, "Some Pragmatist Themes in Hegel's Idealism: Negotiation and Administration in Hegel's Account of the Structure and Content of Conceptual Norms" (1999) 7 European Journal of Philosophy 164, 180.

[6] A Pellet, "Article 38" in A Zimmermann, C Tomuschat, and K Oellers-Frahm (eds), *Statute of the International Court of Justice. A Commentary* (2nd edn, Oxford University Press 2012) 731, paras 304–5.

[7] R Bernhardt, "Article 59" in Zimmermann, Tomuschat, and Oellers-Frahm (n 6) 1416.

[8] See G Abi-Saab, "De la Jurisprudence: Quelques Réflexions sur Son Rôle Dans le Développement du Droit International" in M Pérez González et al., *Hacia un Nuevo Orden Internacional y Europeo* 19 (Madrid: Tecnos 1993) 25.

development has only vague contours, and some scholars notably use *development* interchangeably with *clarification*. For them, "developing" the law means making it visible.[9] Others distinguish the development of international law, a licit activity, from the making of new law, which is not part of the task and function of a court.[10]

It is certainly important for international judges to portray their decisions as firmly based on the law as it stands because this is an important source of their legitimacy. It is in this vein that the ICJ, in an exemplary fashion, stresses that it "cannot legislate.... Rather, its task is to engage in its normal judicial function of ascertaining the existence of legal principles and rules applicable" to the case at hand.[11] This is an unsurprising statement for any international court or tribunal. Some jurists likewise "succumb to their own timorous fiction, that a statement of 'the law' is a statement of fact."[12] But it can hardly be denied that statements of fact are themselves performative statements that contribute to the construction of the world and the making of the law.[13]

That has by now been well recognized. Formulating his account in the context of the New Haven School, Michael Reisman has argued prominently that scholarly teachings and judgments created a myth: that international law could be found by looking at what Art. 38 of the ICJ Statute claims to be the sources of law. In order to find international law, one should rather look at the myriad of legal communications that a plethora of actors utter every day.[14] Other voices from New Haven have developed a theory of transnational legal processes that analyzes the *jurisgenerative* interactions between actors, rather than the formal sources of the law, in trying to understand international lawmaking.[15]

A similar picture emerges in the framework of systems theory, which sees law as a social system that is constituted by communications operating with reference to the binary code of legal and illegal.[16] Only communicative operations can tell what the law is.[17]

[9] See H Lauterpacht, *The Development of International Law by the International Court* (London: Stevens and Sons 1958) 42–3; H Wehberg, *The Problem of an International Court of Justice* (Oxford: Clarendon 1918) 11–12.

[10] See, for example, C Greenwood, "The Development of International Law by the International Criminal Tribunal for the Former Yugoslavia" (1998) 2 Max Plank YB UN L 97, 111.

[11] *Legality of the Threat or Use of Nuclear Weapons*, Advisory Opinion of July 8, 1996 ICJ Reports 226, para 18. See also *Fisheries Jurisdiction* (Gr Brit & N Ir v Ice), Judgment of July 25, 1974 ICJ Reports 3, para 53.

[12] JL Austin, *How to Do Things with Words* (Oxford University Press 1976) 4.

[13] A von Bogdandy and I Venzke, "Beyond Dispute: International Judicial Institutions as Lawmakers" in A von Bogdandy and I Venzke (eds), *International Judicial Lawmaking on Public Authority and Democratic Legitimation in Global Governance* (Heidelberg: Springer 2012) 3.

[14] M Reisman, "International Lawmaking: A Process of Communication" (1981) 75 American Society of International Law Proceedings 101.

[15] HH Koh, "Transnational Legal Process" (1996) 75 Neb L Rev 181.

[16] N Luhmann, *Das Recht der Gesellschaft* (Frankfurt am Main: Suhrkamp 1993) 61.

[17] Luhmann, note 16, at 110.

Views from New Haven and systems theory converge with other contemporary theories on the point that speaking the law contributes to lawmaking.[18] The former school of thought is attuned to the authority of individual interpreters, but developed before the surge of international adjudication of the past two decades. The latter primarily considers domestic settings and places courts at the center of attention. But its take on communicative lawmaking is not well equipped to capture the input of any specific institution, or to evaluate the extent to which they matter. What we need today is a perspective that appreciates the specific contribution of international courts and tribunals to the making of international law. The following section summarizes elements of such a view.

3 Precedents, Expectations, and Authority

In order to appreciate international courts and tribunals as lawmakers, it is necessary to understand well the working of judicial precedents, whose normative force is carried by the expectation of participants in the legal discourse. They underpin international courts' and tribunals' public authority in making international law.

3.1 Precedents

Judicial decisions frequently become influential arguments in later legal discourse.[19] Actors in legal interpretation fight about the meaning of precedents just like they fight about the meaning of instruments that come under the heading of sources. When using precedents strategically, parties push them onto each other and onto the bench. International courts and tribunals are expected to decide consistently; to relate their arguments to earlier, like cases; and, if they deviate from previous jurisprudence, to explain why they do so.[20] As a consequence, interpreters simply cannot escape discussions of case law if they want to make successful arguments. Judicial decisions significantly redistribute argumentative burdens.

[18] JE Alvarez, *International Organizations as Law-Makers* (Oxford University Press 2005) 472.

[19] See M Jacob, 'Precedents: Lawmaking Through International Adjudication' in von Bogdandy and Venzke, note 13, at 35.

[20] AE Boyle and CM Chinkin, *The Making of International Law* (Oxford University Press 2007) 267.

Courts themselves have an interest in arguing from precedent. As Frederick Schauer has argued in his treatment of precedents, courts will place their decisions within a stream of precedents not least because the appearance of consistency will increase their authority and legitimacy.[21] Unsurprisingly, then, international courts have repeatedly stressed the significance of earlier decisions. The Permanent Court of International Justice (PCIJ) found, in its 1927 *Mavrommatis* case, that it had "no reason to depart from a construction which clearly flows from the previous judgments the reasoning of which it still regards as sound."[22] In his thorough analysis of the PCIJ, Ole Spiermann showed that the court displayed an increasing inclination to actively engage in international lawmaking with the help of precedents. Hersch Lauterpacht similarly observed that, "The practice of referring to its previous decisions has become one of the most conspicuous features of the Judgments and Opinions of the Court."[23]

Any judgment lays down the law for the parties to the specific case, *and* it feeds into the general legal discourse. As a matter of fact, it seems that quite a number of judgments candidly aim at influencing the general legal discourse by forcefully establishing abstract and categorical statements as authoritative reference points for later legal practice.[24] Within the later legal discourse, the holding of the judgment, and the reasoning leading to it, become a precedent with which interpreters must grapple in advancing their own legal interests. If the judgment is repeatedly upheld and leads to a *jurisprudence constante*, it is safe to say that it has, in effect, made law.

Categorically marking the lawmaking momentum vested in the justification of legal decisions as an undue expansion of competencies or as a usurpation of power would be plainly short sighted. Justifying a decision is a legal requirement.[25] The alternative, refraining from justifying decisions or from making them public, is not viable. The reasoning that carries legal decisions is critical for the legitimation of judicial authority. It stabilizes normative expectations, which is one of the key functions of law generally.[26] It is precisely by offering a focal point for normative expectations that international courts and tribunals can contribute to the making of international law.

[21] F Schauer, "Precedent" (1987) 39 Stan LR 571, 600.

[22] *Readaptation of the Mavrommatis Jerusalem Concessions* (Jurisdiction), Judgment of October 10, 1927, P.C.I.J Series A No 11, at 18.

[23] O Spiermann, *International Legal Argument in the Permanent Court of International Justice: The Rise of the International Judiciary* (Cambridge University Press 2005) 394; Lauterpacht, note 9, at 9.

[24] Compare O Lepsius, "Die maßstabsetzende Gewalt" in M Jestaedt and others (eds), *Das entgrenzte Gericht* (Berlin: Suhrkamp 2011) 159.

[25] See, eg, ICJ Statute, art 56(1). See also A Ross, *Theorie der Rechtsquellen* (Leipzig: Deuticke 1929) 283; M Kriele, *Theorie der Rechtsgewinnung* (2nd edn, Berlin: Duncker & Humblot 1976) 167–71.

[26] J Habermas, *Between Facts and Norms* (Cambridge, MA: MIT Press 1997) 427; Luhmann, note 16, at 151; TL Stein, "Jurisprudence and Jurists' Prudence: The Iranian-Forum Clause Decisions of the Iran-U.S. Claims Tribunal" (1984) 78 AJIL 1, 48.

3.2 Legitimate expectations

Notwithstanding the absence of a doctrine of *stare decisis*, precedents become powerful as focal points of legal arguments *because* actors expect like cases to be treated alike. We use the example of adjudication in international trade law to illustrate this dynamic. In one of its first cases, the WTO Appellate Body referenced Art. 3.2 of the Dispute Settlement Understanding, noting that, "[T]he dispute settlement system of the WTO is a central element in providing security and predictability to the multilateral trading system." Based on this, the Appellate Body argued that its reports "create legitimate expectations among WTO Members, and, therefore, should be taken into account where they are relevant to any dispute."[27] Although still in the early years of adjudication in the WTO context, Raj Bhala thus identified a system of *de facto stare decisis*.[28] The Appellate Body itself later recalled that WTO members have repeatedly stressed "the importance of consistency and stability" in interpretation. It continued to emphasize that its findings are not limited to each specific case, and critiqued the panel for failing to follow its earlier reports. "We are deeply concerned about the Panel's decision to depart from well-established Appellate Body jurisprudence clarifying the interpretation of the same legal issues," the Appellate Body stated. "The Panel's approach has serious implications for the proper functioning of the WTO dispute settlement system."[29] Disregard for precedents might therefore amount to failure to fulfill a proper judicial function.[30]

The weight that the Appellate Body and other international courts and tribunals attach to their previous decisions almost makes a mockery out of the international law mantra that earlier judicial decisions have no legal effects beyond the parties to the dispute. Relevant actors have come to recognize the systemic impact of adjudication on trade law in general. In the discussion of one of the first Appellate Body reports in the Dispute Settlement Body, the Brazilian representative thus averred:

> It was well-known that in practice any decision of a panel or the Appellate Body with regard to a specific case would go beyond such a specific case. Although no binding precedents had been created, the findings and conclusions of panels and the Appellate Body adopted by the DSB had created expectations concerning future interpretations of the DSU and the WTO Agreement. Therefore, in light of these systemic implications of decisions and

[27] See, *Japan—Taxes on Alcoholic Beverages*, WT/DS8, 10 and 11/AB/R, Appellate Body Report of October 4, 1996, at 15; *United States—Zeroing in Anti-Dumping Measures Involving Products from Korea*, WT/DS402/R, Appellate Body Report of January 18, 2011, para. 7.6.

[28] R Bhala, "The Precedent Setters: De Facto Stare Decisis in WTO Adjudication (Part Two of a Trilogy)" (1999) 9 Journal of Transnational Law and Policy 1.

[29] *United States—Final Anti-Dumping Measures on Stainless Steel from Mexico*, WT/DS344/AB/R, Appellate Body Report of April 30, 2008, para. 162; *United States—Continued Existence and Application of Zeroing Methodology*, WT/DS350/AB/R, Appellate Body Report of February 4, 2009, paras 362–5.

[30] *United States—Continued Existence and Application of Zeroing Methodology* (n 29) para. 362.

recommendations pertaining to a specific case, Brazil wished to state its position with regard to certain findings of the Appellate Body.[31]

It is true that the dynamic of judicial lawmaking with the help of precedents is especially prominent in systems with appellate review. But as section 4 will show, it is certainly not confined to such contexts alone. Nor is it, as the example of the PCIJ already provides, an altogether new phenomenon in international law. It has, however, gained momentum and magnitude together with a rising number of international decisions over the past two decades.[32] Contemporary international courts and tribunals structure the space of legal interpretation with such force that one should categorize their lawmaking practice as an exercise of international public authority.[33]

3.3 International public authority

The notion of international public authority refers to an actor's law-based capacity to legally or factually limit or otherwise affect other actors' use of their liberty.[34] International courts have that capacity also because they enjoy a weighty position in processes of communicative lawmaking. At the same time, sweepingly equating judicial *lawmaking* and *legislation* is hardly convincing. Whether a judicial decision becomes a (powerful) precedent not only depends on *voluntas*, or will, but also on its *ratio*, or reason. If a case is generally understood as having been decided wrongly, this undermines its precedential force and possibly even the authority of the court. If this is so, does it then make sense to understand lawmaking in the practice of adjudication as an exercise of public authority?

In order to amount to an exercise of authority, earlier decisions of international courts and tribunals need to constrain even if they do not persuade. Schauer correctly noted that, "[i]f we are truly arguing from precedent, then the fact that something was decided before gives it present value despite our current belief that the previous decision was erroneous."[35] HLA Hart translated this aspect of authority with the notion of content-independent reasons: reasons, namely, that derive from the status of the person or institution having authority and not from the contents of the command.[36] It is not enough that precedents persuade. The notion

[31] *Minutes of Meeting*, Dispute Settlement Body, November 6, 1998, WT/DSB/M/50.

[32] Many examples in von Bogdandy and Venzke, note 13.

[33] A von Bogdandy and I Venzke, "In Whose Name? An Investigation of International Courts' Public Authority and its Democratic Justification" (2012) 23 EJIL 7.

[34] A von Bogdandy, P Dann, and M Goldmann, "Developing the Publicness of Public International Law: Towards a Legal Framework for Global Governance Activities" (2008) 9 German Law Journal 1375, 1381–2.

[35] Schauer, note 21, at 575. [36] HLA Hart, *Essays on Bentham* (Oxford: Clarendon 1982) 254–5.

of *persuasive* authority, which international courts and scholarship occasionally use, in any event raises the question of how authority could be based upon mere persuasion.[37]

Judicial lawmaking through precedents amounts to an exercise of public authority because it constrains in the absence of agreement in substance. When a party invokes a certain precedent, the reaction of the opponent is usually not to argue that such precedent is not binding. It might argue that it was decided wrongly, but even then it bears the burden of doing so. In addition, since courts have an interest in consistency and only very seldom overrule earlier decisions, parties are well advised to try to give precedents another spin rather than to argue for their reversal. Only rarely does a widespread belief that a case was decided wrongly take root, in which case judicial practice might react accordingly. Typically, then, participants in legal discourse are compelled to relate their arguments to earlier judicial decisions even if they disagree with them.

International courts make law through precedents because they are able to establish their statements about the law as authoritative reference points for later legal discourse. At later stages, other actors, specifically legal counsel, then fight about the meaning of those statements with similar rigor when compared to what may "properly" be qualified as a source of law according to Art. 38 of the ICJ Statute. In Pierre Bourdieu's words, "[T]he judgment represents the quintessential form of authorized, public, official speech… magical acts which succeed because they have the power to make themselves universally recognized. They thus succeed in creating a situation in which no one can refuse or ignore the point of view, the vision, which they impose."[38] The "magic" that underpins international courts' authority, beyond their authorizing statutes, lies in the spell of precedents, in the expectation that like cases are treated alike and in a range of other considerations of social legitimacy that includes the symbolism of judges' robes, the atmosphere of the court room, and the language of the law. A belief in the independence and fairness of international adjudication as well as the appeal of the outcome further add to judicial authority.[39]

[37] For a discussion on the notion of "persuasive authority" in judicial practice see *ADC Affiliate Limited and ADC & ADMC Management Limited v. Republic of Hungary,* ICSID Case No. ARB/03/16, Award of October 2, 2006, para. 293.

[38] P Bourdieu, "The Force of Law: Toward a Sociology of the Juridical Field" (1987) 38 Hastings LJ 814, 838.

[39] For discussons on independence, fairness, and outcome, respectively, see E Benvenisti and G Downs, "Prospects for the Increased Independence of International Tribunals" in von Bogdandy and Venzke, note 13, at 99; T Franck, *The Power of Legitimacy among Nations* (New York: Oxford University Press 1990) 24; Y Shany, "Assessing the Effectiveness of International Courts: A Goal-Based Approach" (2012) 106 AJIL 225.

4 JUDICIAL LAWMAKING IN SPECIFIC FIELDS OF INTERNATIONAL LAW

4.1 International human rights law

When compared to other institutions in the field of human rights, such as the Inter-American Court of Human Rights (IACtHR) or the Court of Justice of the ECOWAS, the ECtHR is the most active institution. It has weaved a tight net of jurisprudence, imbuing the European Convention on Human Rights and Fundamental Freedoms (European Convention) with meaning.[40] The ECtHR has also been recognized as embracing an especially dynamic understanding of legal change and features as a standard reference for methods of "evolutive interpretation."[41] In the seminal 1978 case *Tyler v. United Kingdom*, the court articulated its understanding of the convention as a "living instrument" that must be interpreted in light of present circumstances.[42] This meant that the juvenile court's sentence of birching—a corporal punishment—amounted to degrading treatment in violation of Art. 3 of the European Convention. Article 3 was also later interpreted to prohibit extraditions to countries where the accused would face charges of capital murder, and to require diligence and assurances in extradition cases. The court read a protection against *refoulement* into Art. 3 and thus provided a key anchor for asylum law.[43]

With the notion of "living instrument" and the concomitant ideas of "evolutive" or "dynamic" interpretation, the ECtHR has assumed the competence to follow societal change even where the convention has not been amended to reflect those processes. The court takes such developments on board by referring to a "European consensus"—a common ground among member states that the court typically derives from an overview of members' laws and practice.[44] However, in the same breath with which the ECtHR articulates evolutive or dynamic interpretations, it

[40] For more on the Inter-American Court of Human Rights, see C Binder, "The Prohibition of Amnesties by the Inter-American Court of Human Rights" in von Bogdandy and Venzke, note 13, at 295.

[41] R Bernhardt, "Evolutive Treaty Interpretation, especially of the European Convention on Human Rights" (1999) 42 German Yearbook of International Law 11

[42] *Tyrer v. United Kingdom*, App no 5856/7225, Judgment of April 25, 1978, Series A No 26, para. 31.

[43] *Soering v. United Kingdom*, App no 14038/88, Judgment of July 7, 1989, Series A No 161; *Saadi v. United Kingdom*, App no 13229/03, Judgment of January 29, 2008; *Saadi v. Italy*, App no 37201/06, Judgment of February 28, 2008. Compare A Saccucci, "Diritto d'asilo e Convenzione europea dei diritti dell'uomo" in C Favilli (ed.), *Procedure e garanzie del diritto d'asilo* (Padua: CEDAM 2011) 147.

[44] *Christine Goodwin v. United Kingdom*, App no 28957/95, Judgment of July 11, 2002, paras 84–92; *Hirst v. United Kingdom (No. 2)*, App no 74025/01, Judgment of October 6, 2005, paras 78–82; *Konstantin Markin v. Russia*, App no 30078/06, Judgment of March 22, 2012, paras 99–100 and 126.

habitually reiterates that it cannot create new law or add rights to the convention that it does not already contain.[45]

Still, such assertions do not detract from the fact that the ECtHR has played an active role in shaping the convention. Building on the notion of the European consensus, it has translated prevailing understandings of human rights protection into obligations for all member states. The systemic—that is, lawmaking—effects of its judgments in any specific case are rather evident and clearly seen by the court itself.[46] As early as 1978, the court held that its "judgments in fact serve not only to decide those cases brought before the Court but, more generally, to elucidate, safeguard and develop the rules instituted by the Convention, thereby contributing to the observance by the States of the engagements undertaken by them as Contracting Parties."[47] With direct individual access from the convention's now 47 member states and an average docket of about 1,000 judgments per year, the ECtHR has profoundly shaped human rights in Europe.[48]

4.2 International criminal law

Similarly, international criminal tribunals have significantly developed international criminal law. The International Criminal Tribunal for the Former Yugoslavia (ICTY) found, for instance, that persecution can itself amount to an international crime[49] and that international criminal law also applies in internal armed conflicts.[50] Further, with its sophisticated doctrine of "joint criminal enterprise," the tribunal extended the reach of its personal jurisdiction. The dynamics of appellate review have contributed to the *de facto* precedential force of earlier judgments. The ICTY's Appellate Chamber held that: "The need for coherence is particularly acute [...] where the norms of international humanitarian law and international criminal law are developing."[51] At the same time, the tribunal has ventured far into the field of lawmaking, sometimes justifying its legal claims with downright moral arguments.[52] While legal certainty is especially important in criminal law, reinforced by the principle of *nulla poena sine lege*, the tribunal entered a scene with relatively

[45] Eg, *Johnston v. Ireland*, App no 9697/82, Judgment of December 18, 1986, Series A No 112, para. 53.

[46] For more on empirical baselines, see LR Helfer and E Voeten, "International Courts as Agents of Legal Change: Evidence from LGBT Rights in Europe" 67 Intl Org (forthcoming 2014) 68(2) Int'l Org.

[47] *Ireland v. United Kingdom*, App no 5310/71, Judgment of January 18, 1978, Series A No 25, para. 154.

[48] See also M Fyrnys, "Expanding Competences by Judicial Lawmaking: The Pilot Judgment Procedure of the European Court of Human Rights" in von Bogdandy and Venzke, note 13, at 329.

[49] *Prosecutor v. Mladen Naletilić, Vinko Martinović*, IT-98-34, Judgment of May 3, 2006, para. 574.

[50] *Prosecutor v. Duško Tadić*, IT-94-1-A, Judgment of July 15, 1999, para. 83.

[51] *Prosecutor v. Zlatko Aleksovski*, IT-95-14/1-A, Judgment of May 24, 2000, para. 113.

[52] M Kuhli and K Günther, "Judicial Lawmaking, Discourse Theory, and the ICTY on Belligerent Reprisals" in von Bogdandy and Venzke, note 13, at 365.

little international judicial practice and thus significantly shaped the law through its practice. It has made law, but it has also made law more predictable.

The slightly younger International Criminal Tribunal for Rwanda (ICTR) has also been an active lawmaker, albeit with a lower number of cases. It contributed to the making of international criminal law, among other things, by deciding that hate speech can constitute an international crime and by determining the ways in which crimes of genocide, as well as crimes against humanity, deal with forms of sexual violence.[53] The still younger—but permanent—International Criminal Court (ICC) has only recently rendered its second judgment, and it remains to be seen how it will relate to the case law of the ad hoc tribunals and affect international criminal law. Already it is clear, however, that the formulation of Art. 21 of the ICC Statute on the applicable law is strikingly wider than Art. 38 of the ICJ Statute. Article 21 is crafted specifically so as to fill possible *lacunae* with reference to principles and to national laws.[54]

4.3 International economic law

As explained above, the WTO Appellate Body vested earlier decisions with authority when it argued that they create legitimate expectations.[55] While the dynamics of international judge-made law in the field of trade have intensified with the Appellate Body—established as part of the institutional overhaul leading to the creation of the WTO in 1995—early panel reports under the General Agreement on Tariffs and Trade (GATT) had already contributed palpably to the making of international trade law. Consider, for instance, Art. XXIII GATT, which stipulated that a member could file a complaint if it "consider[s] that any benefit accruing to it directly or indirectly under this Agreement is being nullified or impaired." This previously meant that finding a breach of obligation is neither sufficient nor necessary for a member to file a complaint. The jurisprudence then held that any harm in trade that "could not reasonably have been anticipated" at the time when concessions were negotiated would suffice for bringing a claim.[56] In a landslide shift in the early 1960s, a panel then established that a violation of the GATT would be considered

[53] *Prosecutor v. Ferdinand Nahimana, Jean-Bosco Barayagwiza, Hassan Ngeze*, ICTR-99-52-A, Judgement of November 28, 2007, paras 691–715 and 983–8; *Prosecutor v. Jean-Paul Akayesu*, ICTR-96-4-T, Judgment of September 2, 1998, paras 685–92 and 731–4.

[54] WA Schabas, *The International Criminal Court: A Commentary on the Rome Statute* (Oxford University Press 2010) 381–400; F Jessberger and J Geneuss, "The Many Faces of the International Criminal Court" (2012) 10 J Intl Crim Jus 1081.

[55] See notes 29–33.

[56] Working Party Report, *The Australian Subsidy on Ammonium Sulphate*, GATT/CP.4/39, April 3, 1950, BISD II/188; *Treatment by Germany of Imports of Sardines,* G/26, GATT Panel Report of October 31, 1952, BISD 1S/53.

a "prima facie nullification or impairment" in the sense of Art. XXIII.[57] In practice, this interpretation grew to build up an almost-irrefutable presumption that any violation would also be a nullification or impairment. The GATT Panel in *Oil Fee* later cemented this interpretation by reasoning that a finding of nullification or impairment derives practically *ipso facto* from a violation of the GATT. As John Jackson has observed, the meaning of Art. XXIII was "brought almost full circle by the evolutionary case-by-case process" of adjudication.[58] The interpretative development of Art. XX GATT on general exceptions tells a very similar story, and specifically shows how adjudicators have developed Art. XX into standards for domestic regulatory policy.[59] As of late, a number of key cases has further shaped the open textured Agreement on Technical Barriers to Trade, informed much-disputed questions concerning the Agreement's scope, and continued to form obligations for domestic regulators.[60]

International investment law—with awards from ad hoc arbitral tribunals that are not subject to appellate review and that rest on a web of roughly 3,000 bilateral treaties that do not always speak the same language—*prima facie* provides a difficult setting for lawmaking through adjudication, especially where tribunals are anchored within different institutional frameworks. It is thus not so surprising that some tribunals do not see the need, and maybe not even the possibility, of situating their interpretations within a larger whole of investment law. One tribunal found that "it has not been entrusted, by the Parties or otherwise, with a mission to ensure the coherence or development of arbitral jurisprudence."[61] But an increasing number of tribunals disagrees and instead affirms that there is "a duty to seek to contribute to the harmonious development of investment law and thereby to meet the legitimate expectations of the community of States and investors towards certainty of the rule of law."[62] The field of investment law remains torn, and highlights how lawmaking through precedents also leans quite critically on a shared ethos among its participants. While differences persist between arbitrators and ad hoc tribunals, adjudication has in fact contributed to the making of the law

[57] *Uruguayan Recourse to Article XXIII*, L/1923, GATT Panel Report of November 16, 1962, BISD 11S/95.

[58] JH Jackson, *Sovereignty, the WTO and Changing Fundamentals of International Law* (Cambridge University Press 2006) 143.

[59] I Venzke, "Making General Exceptions: The Spell of Precedents in Developing Art. XX GATT into Standards for Domestic Regulatory Policy" in Bogdandy and Venzke, note 13, at 179.

[60] See *United States—Measures Concerning the Importation, Marketing and Sale of Tuna and Tuna Products*, WT/DS381/AB/R, Appellate Body Report of May 16, 2012.

[61] *Romak S. A. v. Uzbekistan*, PCA Case No. AA 280, UNCITRAL Award of November 26, 2009, para. 171.

[62] *Saipem S.p.A. v. The People's Republic of Bangladesh*, ICSID Case No. ARB/05/7, Award of June 30, 2009, para. 80.

here also, for example, on standards of investment protection, expropriation, and compensation.[63]

4.4 General international law and law of the sea

International judicial lawmaking is above all a phenomenon of younger and revived judicial institutions that often have compulsory jurisdiction, direct access by individuals, or, as is the case with criminal tribunals and the ICC, that can initiate proceedings on their own initiative. These institutions have challenged the ICJ's position as the "World Court" at the center of the legal order. While the ICJ has contributed to legal developments in parts of general international law such as maritime delimitation, its weak jurisdictional basis, its ethos and the relatively low number of disparate cases have prevented it from having a stronger role in the making of international law.[64]

With nuances, such an assessment also holds for the International Tribunal for the Law of the Sea (ITLOS), which came into existence when the United Nations Convention on the Law of the Sea (UNCLOS) entered into force in 1994. Most ITLOS decisions have so far dealt with so-called prompt release cases in which a line of precedents has emerged asserting, among other things, that local remedies need not be exhausted before bringing such cases, and elaborating on what constitutes a "reasonable" bond.[65] Through an Advisory Opinion issued at the request of the International Seabed Authority, the Tribunal's Seabed Disputes Chamber has also contributed to shaping the administrative mechanisms for activities relating to the seabed beyond national jurisdiction, above all by clarifying questions of liability and responsibility.[66] Still, the number of ITLOS cases remains relatively low.

[63] SW Schill, "System-Building in Investment Treaty Arbitration and Lawmaking" in von Bogdandy and Venzke, note 13, at 133.

[64] See N Petersen, "Lawmaking by the International Court of Justice—Factors of Success" in von Bogdandy and Venzke, note 13, at 411; CJ Tams and A Tzanakopoulos, "Barcelona Traction at 40: the ICJ as an Agent of Legal Development" (2010) 23 Leiden Journal of International Law 781.

[65] See, eg, *The "Juno Trader" Case* (Saint Vincent and the Grenadines v Guinea-Bissau), Prompt Release, Judgment of December 18, 2004; S Trevisanut, "The Exercise of Administrative Functions by ITLOS: A Comment on Prompt Release Cases" in N Boschiero and others (eds), *International Courts and the Development of International Law. Essays in Honour of Tullio Treves* (The Hague: T.M.C. Asser Press 2013) 309–21.

[66] *Responsibilities and Obligations of States Sponsoring Persons and Entities with Respect to Activities in the Area*, ITLOS Advisory Opinion of February 1, 2011.

4.5 Fragmentation and cross-fertilization

Some judicial lawmaking unfolds between international courts and tribunals of different regimes.[67] With regard to substantive law, such instances are generally rare and usually confined to exchanges between institutions of specific fields, such as human rights. More often than not, international adjudication projects the functional perspectives of the specific regime in which it is embedded onto the law it applies, thus contributing to processes of fragmentation.[68]

Occasionally, cross-fertilization does transgress regime borders.[69] For instance, ITLOS jurisprudence on prompt release cases and its jurisprudence on what amounts to a reasonable bond against which arrested vessels and crew members may be released was picked up and relied upon by the ECtHR in a complaint by Ioannis Mangouras. Mangouras was captain of the *Prestige*, a ship that spilled oil on Spanish coasts. He brought an unsuccessful complaint against Spain, which held him in custody for 83 days until the ship owner's insurance paid €3 million to release him on bail.[70] The ECtHR relied on ITLOS judgments in finding that the bail was not excessive. Apart from the occasional cross-reference on matters of substance, there is more cross-fertilization when it comes to issues of procedural law.[71] Particularly striking, for instance, is how international courts and tribunals have influenced each other in their decisions on the bindingness of their provisional measures.[72] It seems safe to say that such (procedural) lawmaking by cross-referencing is particularly likely when it increases the powers of the institutions.

4.6 Comparison: design, contexts, and functions

Tom Ginsburg has identified three main factors in the design of international judicial institutions that render them more or less prone to making law.[73] His argument primarily focuses on the constraints that members can place on international institutions. He argues that lawmaking becomes more likely with

[67] H Ruiz Fabri and L Gradoni (eds), *La Circulation des Concepts Juridiques* (Paris: Société de Législation Comparée 2009); RG Teitel and R Howse, "Cross-Judging: Tribunalization in a Fragmented but Interconnected Global Order" (2009) 41 NYU J Intl L & Pol 959.

[68] M Koskenniemi and L Päivi, "Fragmentation of International Law? Postmodern Anxieties" (2002) 15 Leiden Journal of International Law 553–79.

[69] Teitel and Howse, note 67, at 989.

[70] *Mangouras v. Spain*, App no 12050/04, Judgment of September 28, 2010.

[71] C Brown, "The Cross-Fertilization of Principles Relating to Procedure and Remedies in the Jurisprudence of International Courts and Tribunals" (2008) 30 Loy LA Intl & Comp L Rev 219.

[72] K Oellers-Frahm, "Expanding Competence to Issue Provisional Measures—Strengthening the International Judicial Function" (2011) 12 German Law Journal 1279.

[73] T Ginsburg, "Bounded Discretion in International Judicial Lawmaking" (2005) 45 Va J Intl L 631, 639. See also, RH Steinberg, "Judicial Lawmaking at the WTO: Discursive, Constitutional, and Political Constraints" (2004) 98 AJIL 247.

a higher number of parties to any regime, and when it is difficult to amend a treaty. In both cases, judicial interpretations are less likely to be overturned by the political-legislative processes. Judicial lawmaking is also more likely when the costs of exiting a regime are higher, the argument again being that courts are less constrained by the possibility of a member's exit. To these considerations he adds the possibilities of access to the court and the strength of the court's jurisdictional basis.[74] Those design features render it more likely that courts are used in the first place.[75]

Ginsburg's rational choice account of judicial lawmaking may be complemented with a view from functional institutionalism that is specifically attuned to the ways in which international courts and tribunals may interact with domestic actors to build support for their interpretations. Laurence Helfer and Karen Alter have argued that, in the case of the ECJ and ATJ, "International judges are more likely to become expansive lawmakers where they are supported by sub-state interlocutors and compliance constituencies."[76] Further research would be required to determine whether their argument explains the lawmaking behavior of other judicial institutions. Empirical research is only slowly addressing questions of international judicial lawmaking, and is likely to make significant contributions in the future. Theoretical frameworks will develop along the way.[77] It is interesting to note, for instance, that Marc Busch and Krzysztof Pelc found that the adjudicators at the WTO exercise judicial economy—deciding not to pronounce on issues when possible—when third party submissions indicate that there is considerable disagreement.[78] These findings challenge, to some extent, the argument that judicial lawmaking is more likely when constituent members are divided and judges are less likely to be overruled.[79] Judicial economy might, in contrast, be explained by adjudicators' concerns with social legitimacy, as well as the fact that their decisions generally need to persuade to be influential.

An institutions' self-understanding, often influenced by the field of law in which it operates, further impacts the degree to which judicial lawmaking is likely. We have tried to carve out four basic self-understandings of international courts that would impact international judicial lawmaking.[80] First, international courts may understand

[74] Ginsburg, note 73, at 639–42.

[75] B Zangl and others, "Between Law and Politics: Explaining International Dispute Settlement Behavior" (2012) 18 EJIR 369.

[76] KJ Alter and LR Helfer, "Nature or Nurture? Judicial Lawmaking in the European Court of Justice and the Andean Tribunal of Justice" (2010) 64 Intl Org 563.

[77] See JK Staton and WH Moore, "Judicial Power in Domestic and International Politics" (2011) 65 Intl Org 553–87.

[78] ML Busch and KJ Pelc, "The Politics of Judicial Economy at the World Trade Organization" (2010) 64 Intl Org 257–79.

[79] As suggested by Ginsburg, note 73; Benvenisti and Downs, note 39.

[80] A von Bogdandy and I Venzke, "On the Functions of International Courts: An Appraisal in Light of Their Burgeoning Public Authority" (2013) 26 Leiden Journal of International Law 47.

themselves as instruments for the settlement of disputes between the parties—the ICJ is often inspired by this worldview—and would then be less inclined to "contribute to the harmonious development of the law." Second, courts may understand themselves as organs of the international community and may be more disposed to engage in lawmaking if it protects fundamental values of the community; the ECtHR and international criminal tribunals provide cases in point. Third, courts might embrace their roles as institutions of specific legal regimes in an interconnected world order that calls for higher degrees of specific regulation. Such an understanding resonates with adjudicating bodies in international economic law, which stresses the need to stabilize legitimate expectations of government actors and market participants alike. Finally, a fourth basic understanding presents international courts as actors of public authority, which draws primary attention to how their judgments and decisions relate to demands of democratic legitimacy. It reveals judicial lawmaking as part of international courts' mandates, but emphasizes its necessary limits and legitimatory quandaries.

5 Conclusion: The Legitimacy of Judicial Lawmaking

Traditionally, international courts and tribunals have been understood as exercising just one function: settling disputes. In line with this perspective, the legitimacy of international adjudication has rested firmly on the parties' consent: consent to the court's jurisdiction, to the law to be applied, and in some situations even to the judges or arbitrators who are called upon to apply the law. Drawing attention to international courts' lawmaking function challenges this classic narrative of legitimacy.

International adjudicators still try their best to portray their practice as firmly rooted in the consent of the parties, but when this becomes too big a stretch, functional considerations frequently step in to help and complement the consensual basis of legitimacy. Viewed from this angle, international decisions are justified by functional accounts, in the sense that adjudication is taken to promote values, goals, or community interests, and—above all—international peace. The institutional design of some international judicial bodies does support this view, and there are indeed a number of situations in which these sources of legitimacy might carry the justification of international judicial lawmaking quite far. But in light of the growing autonomy of some courts, and in view of the breadth of controversial fields in which international courts are involved, there are now also many constellations in which neither members' consent nor the functional goals can continue to convincingly settle legitimatory concerns with respect to their lawmaking functions.

As important as certain functional goals may be, they cannot offer sufficient bases for concrete decisions that inevitably entail critical normative questions and redistributions of power. Moreover, functional arguments offer no solution to the unavoidable competition between different goals. It may sometimes be true that international adjudication delivers what everyone wants but otherwise fails to achieve.[81] Yet, those instances may be lucky hits. Experience cautions that too much confidence should not be placed even on benevolent and enlightened rulers, not even if they are judges.

Considerations of democratic legitimation remain the gold standard against which any kind of public authority ultimately needs to be assessed, including the authority that international courts and tribunals exercise by way of lawmaking.[82] Under this basic premise, it remains a lasting endeavor to develop strategies that may help legitimize international judicial lawmaking. Such strategies may include elements of the procedural law of international judicial institutions—specifically rules pertaining to transparency, third-party participation, and openness toward *amici curiae*. Procedures for the election of judges may also be reconsidered. Moreover, the type of law that international courts make also matters: do they add substantive content to legal obligations, or do they formulate procedural standards that might even contribute to the legitimation of others' authority?[83] Finally, developments geared toward improving the politico-legislative process, both within the particular regimes in which international courts are embedded and within the international legal order more generally, may further increase the legitimacy of international judicial lawmaking and might break the spell of precedents where necessary.

Research Questions

1. Lawmaking hinges on recognition within communities of interpreters. When a case is generally understood as having been decided wrongly, it has little precedential force, and the authority of the institution might suffer. To what extent does this dynamic

[81] R Howse, "Moving the WTO Forward—One Case at a Time" (2009) 42 Cornell Intl L J 223.

[82] Von Bogdandy and Venzke, note 33, at 29.

[83] M Ioannidis, "A Procedural Approach to the Legitimacy of International Adjudication: Developing Standards of Participation in WTO Law" in von Bogdandy and Venzke, note 13, at 215.

contribute to the legitimacy of international courts' public authority, and does this kind of "discursive control" or "public reasoning" contribute to public authority's democratic justification?

2. What are the attributes that turn cases into leading cases within a community of interpreters? Every regime knows a number of truly seminal cases that are used repeatedly not only in scholarly work but also in pleadings and the justification of judgments. Other cases that on their face may seem no less important fall from view. What are the features of the cases—including their processes, dynamics, key players, and structures—that produce major precedents?
3. It could easily be expected that international judicial lawmaking and increasing judicial authority lead to processes of informal and formal politicization, to greater struggles for influence and control, and possibly to a strengthening of political-legislative procedures. Do we see such reactions, and if so, where? Alternatively, if not, why not?
4. How does international judicial lawmaking affect international law's domestic reception and implementation?

Suggested Reading

Abi-Saab, G, "De la Jurisprudence. Quelques Réflexions Sur Son Rôle Dans le Développement du Droit International" in M Pérez González et al., *Hacia un Nuevo Orden Internacional y Europeo* (Madrid: Tecnos 1993) 19.

Alter, KJ, and Helfer, LR, "Nature or Nurture? Judicial Lawmaking in the European Court of Justice and the Andean Tribunal of Justice" (2010) 64 Intl Org 563.

von Bogdandy, A and Venzke, I (eds), *International Judicial Lawmaking. On Public Authority and Democratic Legitimation in Global Governance* (Heidelberg: Springer 2012).

von Bogdandy, A and Venzke, I, "On the Functions of International Courts: An Appraisal in Light of Their Burgeoning Public Authority" (2013) 26 Leiden Journal of International Law 49.

Dupuy, PM, "Le Juge et la Règle Générale" (1989) 93 Revue Générale de Droit International Public 569.

Ginsburg, T, "Bounded Discretion in International Judicial Lawmaking" (2005) 45 Va J Intl L 631.

Lauterpacht, H, *The Development of International Law by the International Court* (London: Stevens & Sons 1958).

Scobbie, I, "Res Judicata, Precedent, and the International Court: A Preliminary Sketch" (1999) 20 Australian Yearbook of International Law 299.

Shahabuddeen, M, *Precedent in the World Court* (Cambridge University Press 1996).

Steinberg, RH, "Judicial Lawmaking at the WTO: Discursive, Constitutional, and Political Constraints" (2004) 98 AJIL 247.

Treves, T, "Judicial Lawmaking in an Era of 'Proliferation' of International Courts and Tribunals: Development or Fragmentation of International Law?" in R Wolfrum and V Röben (eds), *Developments of International Law in Treaty Making* (Berlin: Springer 2005) 587.

Zarbiyev, F, "Judicial Activism in International Law—A Conceptual Framework for Analysis" (2012) 3 JIDS 247.

CHAPTER 24

CONVERSATIONS AMONG COURTS

DOMESTIC AND INTERNATIONAL ADJUDICATORS

ANDRÉ NOLLKAEMPER*

* André Nollkaemper is Professor of Public International Law and Vice-Dean for Research at the Faculty of Law of the University of Amsterdam.

1 Introduction

National courts hold a peculiar position in the system of international adjudication. Compared to international courts, they are part of a different legal order and are tied to a different community. Their functions, powers, and procedures remain grounded in national, rather than international, law. We therefore do not normally consider adjudicative processes in national courts as "international adjudication." Indeed, the subject is given very limited attention in handbooks on international dispute settlement[1] or chapters on international adjudication in general textbooks on international law.[2]

A full review of international adjudication, however, should cover national courts and their connections with international courts. One reason is the powerful role of national courts in relation to the implementation of international decisions and the eventual settlement of international disputes. This reason is illustrated by the different fates of the judgments of the International Court of Justice (ICJ) in *Avena*,[3] on the one hand, and *Jurisdictional Immunities of the State*, on the other.[4] Whereas the US Supreme Court blocked a speedy implementation of the ICJ judgment in the former case,[5] in the latter case, the Italian Court of Cassation ensured, although somewhat reluctantly, that the ICJ judgment was given effect.[6] National courts are also relevant as they may settle international claims and, thus, substitute for international courts, as well as reinforce interpretations initiated by international courts.

[1] Leading textbooks on international dispute settlement, such as JG Merrills, *International Dispute Settlement* (5th edn, Cambridge University Press 2011) and J Collier and V Lowe, *The Settlement of Disputes in International Law: Institutions and Procedures* (Oxford University Press 2000), do not contain any discussion of the role of national courts in international adjudication.

[2] Chapters on international dispute settlement in leading textbooks on general international law, such as A Cassese, *International Law* (2nd edn, Oxford University Press 2005) 278–95; JG Merrills, "The Means of Dispute Settlement" in MD Evans (ed.), *International Law* (3rd edn, Oxford University Press 2010) and LFL Oppenheim, Sir R Jennings and Sir A Watts (eds), *Oppenheim's International Law: Volume 1, Peace* (9th edn, Oxford University Press 2008), do not discuss the role of national courts.

[3] *Avena and Other Mexican Nationals (Mexico v. United States of America)* (Judgment) [2004] ICJ Rep 12.

[4] *Jurisdictional Immunities of the State (Germany v. Italy: Greece Intervening)* (Judgment) [2012] General List No 143.

[5] *Medellín v. Texas*, 552 U.S. 491, ILDC 947 (US 2008), 30 (B1).

[6] In Italy, the First Criminal Section of the Court of Cassation, in *Criminal Proceedings against Albers and ors*, Final Appeal Judgment (August 9, 2012), ILDC 1921 (IT 2012); the Court of Florence (March 28, 2012), and the Court of Appeals of Turin (see *Federal Republic of Germany v. De Guglielmi* (May 14, 2012), ILDC 1905 (IT 2012)) had given effect to the judgment of the court, albeit on different grounds. See G Cataldi, "The Implementation of the ICJ's Decision in the *Jurisdictional Immunities of the State* case in the Italian Domestic Order: Which balance between Fundamental Human Rights and International Obligations?" [2013] ESIL Reflections 2.

They may also, by a process of contestation, influence future decisions of international courts.

The role of national courts in relation to international adjudication appears to be of increasing relevance. International law deals more often with matters that are also regulated by domestic law.[7] International courts are frequently asked to review matters that have been reviewed by domestic courts. These developments have inspired burgeoning literature on the reception of international judicial decisions in national courts[8] and on communication between national and international courts.[9] However, the qualification "appears" is appropriate. As will be further detailed below, the scope, extent, and relevance of interactions between international and national courts is a matter of some uncertainty. Systematic treatment of the topic is absent, and we lack information to make reliable statements on patterns and trends in practice.

In this chapter, I will explore the interactions between national and international courts in two steps. First, I will discuss the diverse, and partly conflicting, functions that national courts can fulfill in relation to international courts, and explore the (often competing) normative foundations of the exercise of these functions (section 2). Second, I will discuss the mirror image of section 2, and explore what functions international courts can fulfill in relation to national courts. I will also explore what principles apply to the exercise of these functions (section 3). In section 4, I will draw some conclusions and make some observations on areas for research that may improve understanding of the interactions between national and international courts.

The chapter thus proceeds on the basis of a functional analysis. One cannot really speak about "the" relationship between national and international courts. Rather, there is a multitude of legal relationships that, both in their empirical and normative dimensions, are best studied by distinguishing between the different functions that national courts play in relation to international courts and by examining how

[7] JHH Weiler, "The Geology of International Law: Governance, Democracy and Legitimacy" (2004) 64 Zeitschrift für Ausländisches Öffentliches Recht und Völkerrecht, 547, 559–661; A von Bogdandy, "Globalization and Europe: How to Square Democracy, Globalization and International Law" (2004) 15 EJIL 885, 889.

[8] T Barkhuysen, M Van Emmerink and PH Van Kempen (eds), *The Execution of Strasbourg and Geneva Human Rights Decisions in the National Legal Order* (Dordrecht: Martinus Nijhoff Publishers 1999); DA González-Salzberg, "The Implementation of Decisions from the Inter-American Court of Human Rights in Argentina: An Analysis of Jurisprudential Swings of the Supreme Court" (2011) 8 SUR Int'l J Hum Rts 113; C Schulte, *Compliance with Decisions of the International Court of Justice* (Oxford University Press 2004); R Higgins, "National Courts and the International Court of Justice" in M Andenas and D Fairgrieve (eds), *The Transformation of the Law. Liber Amicorum for Lord Bingham* (Oxford University Press 2009) 1013.

[9] See e.g., RB Ahdieh, "Between Dialogue and Decree: International Review of National Courts" (2004) 79 NYU L. Rev. 2029; EA Young, "Institutional Settlement in a Globalizing Judicial System" (2005) 54 Duke LJ 1143.

national and international courts can and should respond to the exercise of these functions by their counterparts.[10]

2 Functions of National Courts in Relation to International Adjudication

We can distinguish between four roles that national courts can perform in relation to international adjudication: substitution, implementation, contestation, and normative development.

2.1 Substitution

In rare conditions, we may consider national courts as a substitute for international courts. That is, they can perform functions that in other situations can be fulfilled by international courts. The legal significance of decisions of national courts on questions of international law may then transcend the domestic legal order.[11] In addition, national courts can arguably compensate for the lack of international courts as a systemic force in the international legal order, in line with Scelle's notion of the *dédoublement fonctionel*.[12]

To frame the role of national courts in this way, we need to make the uncommon step of recognizing that national courts can decide international claims; claims that, in whole or in part, are based on a rule of international law. However, this is not an insurmountable barrier. While the term "international claim" is usually used

[10] A von Bogdandy and I Venzke, "On the Functions of International Courts: an Appraisal in Light of Their Burgeoning Public Authority" (ACIL Research Paper No 2012–10) finalized June 12, 2012, available on SSRN <http://ssrn.com/abstract=2084079> accessed October 12, 2012; KJ Alter, "The Multiple Roles of International Courts and Tribunals: Enforcement, Dispute Settlement, Constitutional and Administrative Review" in JL Dunoff and MA Pollack (eds), *Interdisciplinary Perspectives on International Law and International Relations. The State of the Art* (Cambridge University Press 2013).

[11] RY Jennings, "The Judiciary, International and National, and the Development of International Law" (1996) 45 ICLQ 1, 1–4.

[12] G Scelle, "Règles Générales du Droit de la Paix" (1933) 46 Recueil des Cours 331, 356; A Cassese, "Remarks on Scelle's Theory of 'Role Splitting' (Dédoublement Fonctionnel) in International Law" (1990) 1 EJIL 210; Y Shany, "Dédoublement Fonctionnel and the Mixed Loyalties of National and International Judges" in F Fontanelli, G Martinico and P Carrozza (eds), *Shaping Rule of Law through Dialogue: International and Supranational Experiences* (Groningen: Europa Law Publishing 2010) 27.

in respect of claims brought at the international level,[13] the penetration of international law in the national legal order can extend the use of the term to claims before national courts. What is decisive is the nature of the norm that a claimant invokes. International claims in national courts include claims for compensation for injury resulting from non-performance of an international obligation, claims for annulment or "disapplication" of national laws that contravene international obligations and defensive claims in criminal law against acts that contravene international obligations.

It likewise can be said that, by deciding claims based on international law, national courts help settle international disputes. The term "dispute settlement" need not be confined to procedures at the international level. What makes a dispute an international one is, above all else, the substance of that dispute: a dispute is international when "the rivaling claims are based on international law."[14]

One area where national courts can substitute for international courts is international criminal law. Here the principle of complementarity[15] embodies the notion of substitution. Under the system in the International Criminal Court (ICC) Statute, the presumption is that national courts can perform tasks that otherwise can be assumed by the ICC. Another example is that of cases where exhaustion of local remedies is a precondition for a claim before an international court.[16]

National courts need not be only incidental replacements for international courts where these happen to be unavailable. Rather, they are the primary means for adjudicating claims of private parties. This is embedded in the principle of subsidiarity, which protects the primary role of national courts, and their relative autonomy, by applying international obligations in a specific factual and (national) legal context.[17]

However, the possibility that a national court substitutes for an international court will exist only in rare conditions and is subject to a number of limitations.

[13] Compare the narrower definition of international claims in the context of diplomatic protection: JP Grant and JC Barker, *Encyclopedic Dictionary of International Law* (2nd edn, New York: Oceana Publishing 2004) 83.

[14] A Peters, "International Dispute Settlement: A Network of Cooperational Duties" (2003) 14 EJIL 1, 3.

[15] Rome Statute of the International Criminal Court (July 17, 1998) UN Doc A/Conf.183/9, entered into force July 1, 2002, Article 17; JK Kleffner, *Complementarity in the Rome Statute and National Criminal Jurisdictions* (Oxford University Press 2008); C Stahn and MM El Zeidy, *The International Criminal Court and Complementarity. From Theory to Practice* (Cambridge University Press 2011).

[16] Exhaustion of local remedies is, e.g., required under Art. 35 ECHR and Art. 46 ACHR. In inter-state disputes, the exhaustion of local remedies may be required in claims based on diplomatic protection: see Art. 44 ILC Draft Articles on the Responsibility of States for Internationally Wrongful Acts, With Commentaries (2001) adopted at the 53rd Session, UN Doc A/56/10 (Yearbook of the International Law Commission 2001 Vol II) (ARSIWA) and Art. 14 of the Articles on Diplomatic Protection (ILC Draft Articles on Diplomatic Protection (2006) adopted at the 58th Session UN Doc A/61/10 (ADP)).

[17] PG Carozza, "Subsidiarity as a Structural Principle of International Human Rights Law" (2003) 97 AJIL 38, 67.

First, this construction seems only proper when a national court applies a law that in substance is identical to the law that would apply at the international level. The extent to which this is the case obviously varies widely between states.[18] Even though, in many states, a claim may itself be based on international law, that (incorporated or transformed) international law will, and arguably should, be colored by national law.[19] Moreover, the procedure under which the claim will be adjudicated invariably will be based on national law.[20] In this regard, there is an essential difference between national and international courts. It is also this condition that defines the outer limits of the autonomy protected by the principle of subsidiarity: the principle does not accord unlimited leeway, but is circumscribed by international law itself.

Second, the possibility that national courts can substitute for international courts is dependent on the question of whether national courts are empowered to adjudicate international claims. In many states, this task is entrusted to the political branches.[21] Doctrines limiting the power of national courts to adjudicate international claims include non-justiciability,[22] the separation of powers,[23] the doctrine that the state should speak with one voice (that is, the voice of government),[24] the political question doctrine,[25] and the doctrine of direct effect, which often curtails the judicial application of international law to protect the political branches.[26]

A third condition is that the substitution perspective, strictly speaking, only applies when the actors between whom an international dispute exists appear as parties before a national court. This essentially limits the possibility of a national court substituting for an international court to disputes between private persons and states, notably in human rights cases. For individuals who have a legal stake

[18] D Sloss (ed), *The Role of Domestic Courts in Treaty Enforcement. A Comparative Study* (Cambridge University Press 2009); D Shelton (ed), *International Law and Domestic Legal Systems: Incorporation, Transformation and Persuasion* (Oxford University Press 2011).

[19] K Knop, "Here and There: International Law in Domestic Courts" (2000) 32 NYU J Int'l L & Pol'y 501, 527.

[20] *Breard v. Netherlands*, 949 F. Supp. 1255 (ED Va 1996) (U.S.).

[21] See generally, TM Franck, *Political Questions Judicial Answers* (Princeton University Press 1992); D Haljan, *Separating Powers: International Law before National Courts* (The Hague: TMC Asser Press 2013).

[22] E.g., *R v. Secretary of State for Foreign and Commonwealth Affairs, ex p Pirbhai*, 129 SJ 756, (1985) 107 ILR 475, 479 (Sir John Donaldson MR). See for Ireland, High Court, *Edward Horgan v. An Taoiseach*, ILDC 486 (IE 2003) [114]–[115].

[23] *R (Abbasi) v. Secretary of State for Foreign and Commonwealth Affairs and Secretary of State for the Home Department* [2002] EWCA Civ 1598, ILDC 246 (UK 2002).

[24] R Steinhardt, "Human Rights Litigation and the "One Voice" Orthodoxy in Foreign Affairs" in M Gibney (ed.), *World Justice? US Courts and International Human Rights* (Boulder, CO: Westview Press 1991) 23.

[25] Franck, note 21; B Conforti (rapporteur), *The Activities of National Judges and the International Relations of Their State: Preliminary Report by Rapporteur Benedetto Conforti* (Institute of International Law 1993) 331–3.

[26] J Klabbers, "International Law in Community Law: The Law and Politics of Direct Effect" (2002) 21 YEL 263.

in the performance of such treaties, national courts will be the first and the "natural forum" in which to present their claims.[27] In certain cases, investment disputes might be construed as such.[28] In contrast, only a few cases have been reported where one state has litigated against a foreign state in a court of that state.[29] Indeed, the almost complete absence of inter-state claims in domestic courts casts doubt on the degree to which the major actors in the international legal order see national domestic courts as institutions that substitute for international courts.[30]

To the extent that national courts cannot be considered as true substitutes for international courts, it still may be possible that national courts, by settling *aspects* of a dispute (usually between states, but potentially also involving other subjects of international law), can disaggregate and diffuse an inter-state dispute and facilitate its settlement.[31]

The extent to which national courts may do so will partially depend, first, on overlap between the parties and, second, overlap in the object of the claim. As to the first condition, for inter-state disputes obviously there never will be a full identity of parties in national courts. For instance, claims concerning the Dutch contribution to NATO operations in regard to Kosovo were made both in the ICJ and in a Dutch court. The domestic proceedings were between different parties (involving a claim by Serbian nationals against the Netherlands) than the dispute as it was litigated in the ICJ, that involved an inter-state claim.[32] In the *Breard* and the *LaGrand* cases,[33] the match was closer, as the international proceedings were (partly) based on diplomatic protection and related to the same individuals who litigated domestically.[34]

Also, identity in terms of the object of the claim will be relevant to the contribution of a national proceeding to the settlement of an international dispute. In theory, the claims may be close to identical. If, in the *Breard* case, Breard had sought

[27] A Tzanakopoulos, "Domestic Courts as the 'Natural Judge' of International Law: A Change in Physiognomy" (2010) 3 Select Proceedings of the Eur. Soc'y Int'l L. 155.

[28] TBJ Oliveira, "The Authority of Domestic Courts in Adjudicating International Investment Disputes: Beyond the Distinction between Treaty and Contract Claims" (2013) 4 J. Int'l Disp. Settlement (forthcoming).

[29] See e.g., *Paraguay v. Allen*, 949 F. Supp. 1269 (ED Va. 1996) (U.S.); *Paraguay v. Allen*, US Court of Appeals, 134 F.3d 622 (4th Cir. 1998); Italy, Court of Cassation, *Criminal Proceedings Against Milde* (January 13, 2009), ILDC 1224 (IT 2009).

[30] J Paulsson, *Denial of Justice in International Law* (Cambridge University Press 2005) 4; W Friedmann, *The Changing Structure of International Law* (London: Stevens & Sons 1964) 146–7; B Cheng, *General Principles of Law as Applied by International Courts and Tribunals* (London: Stevens & Sons 1953) 279–89, 357.

[31] See generally on the contribution of national courts to larger processes of (public interest) litigation HH Koh, "Transnational Public Litigation" (1991) 100 Yale L.J. 2347.

[32] *Legality of Use of Force (Serbia and Montenegro v. Netherlands)* (Preliminary Objections, Judgment) [2004] ICJ Rep 1011. The claim was brought by nine individuals from Serbia.

[33] *Breard v. Greene* (April 14, 1998) 523 US 371, ILDC 684 (US 1998); *LaGrand Case (Germany v. United States of America)* (Judgment) [1999] General List no 104.

[34] *LaGrand*, note 33; *Case Concerning the Vienna Convention on Consular Relations (Paraguay v. United States of America)* (Order) [1998] ICJ Rep 248.

annulment of the death sentence and such annulment also would have been the only remedy sought by Paraguay, there would have been an identity of claims between the two cases, and settlement in one case may have had consequences for the other. Similarly, if the plaintiffs in the Dutch Kosovo cases[35] had been granted the remedy of cessation of the bombings by the Netherlands, this would have corresponded to the main objective of the litigation between Yugoslavia and the Netherlands. However, no such identity was actually achieved, limiting the contribution that domestic adjudication could have made to the settlement of the inter-state dispute.

The question as to under what conditions, and with what effects, national courts can function as substitutes for international courts has only been studied in a more or less systematic way in relation to international criminal courts[36] and human rights law.[37] Some narrower studies have been undertaken in relation to investment law[38] and WTO law.[39] For the many other international courts,[40] such studies do not appear to have been conducted. Also the more theoretical question as to under what conditions other actors (states, but also international courts) should accept judgments of national courts as authoritative decisions of international claims, on an equal footing as if they had been rendered by an international court, has hardly been subject to analysis. The same holds for the question of how national courts can, by adjudicating aspects that are components of a potentially broader inter-state dispute, contribute to the diffusion, disaggregation, or prevention of such disputes, is under studied.[41]

2.2 Implementation

Whether national courts can fulfill a function by helping implement decisions of international courts at the domestic level will primarily depend, first of all, on what was ordered by the international court. Not all parts of international decisions need to be implemented, even though they may become legally relevant.[42] We should

[35] *Dedovic and Others v. The Netherlands*, Court of Appeal of Amsterdam, July 6, 2000, NJCM Bulletin (2001) 208.

[36] Kleffner, note 15; MM El Zeidy, *The Principle of Complementarity in International Criminal Law: Origin, Development, and Practice* (Dordrecht: Martinus Nijhoff Publishers 2008); Stahn and El Zeidy, note 15.

[37] H Keller and A Stone Sweet, *A Europe of Rights: The Impact of the ECHR on National Legal Systems* (Oxford University Press 2008).

[38] TBJ Oliveira, note 28.

[39] M Yilmaz (ed.), *Domestic Judicial Review of Trade Remedies: Experiences of the Most Active WTO Members* (Cambridge University Press 2013).

[40] CPR Romano, "A Taxamony of International Rule of Law Institutions" 2 J. Int'l Disp. Settlement (2011) 241, 241–77.

[41] An interesting study in this context is Yilmaz, note 39.

[42] A Gattini, "Domestic Judicial Compliance with International Judicial Decisions: Some Paradoxes" in U Fastenrath et al (eds), *From Bilateralism to Community Interest: Essays in Honour of Bruno Simma* (Oxford University Press 2011).

also distinguish between those parts of an international decision that lend themselves to application by a national court, and those parts that do not. For instance, an international decision that a particular statute is in violation of international law and that that wrong needs to be removed normally could not be implemented by a national court, but rather would be a task for political branches. On the other hand, a national court could play a role in securing compensation for violation of a human right where that has been determined by an international court.[43]

From the perspective of international law, it normally is not relevant whether a decision is implemented by a court or another organ. International law respects the right of states to determine for themselves whether or not they should allow their courts to give effect to an international obligation stemming from a decision of an international court.[44] Whether it is the courts or some other organ that would implement an international decision depends on national law,[45] subject to the requirement that the state implements judgments within a reasonable time.[46]

Occasionally international courts have chosen a more direct approach, and address national courts directly regarding who should follow up the decision.[47] There is no need to object to this practice, as there is no dispute that national courts are the organs of that state. But whether a national court is able to give effect to an international decision remains governed by the limitation of the powers of that court vis-à-vis the political branches.

The fact that a decision of an international court in principle lends itself to implementation by domestic courts, even though it may not be addressed to such courts, obviously does not mean that such courts are, as a matter of domestic law, empowered to do so. National law dictates whether it is for the courts or for other organs to provide a particular remedy that would implement an international decision. Here, we encounter major differences between states. The situation in Europe is exceptional, featuring, despite some resistance, a general trend towards empowerment of national courts to secure effective implementation of judgments of the European Court of Human Rights

[43] E.g., the implementation of the ECtHR's judgment in *Lorse and Others v. the Netherlands* (App no 52750/99), ECHR February 4, 2003 in the Netherlands, Supreme Court, *State of the Netherlands v. L* (October 1, 2003), LJN AI0351; C03/103; NJ 2005/196.

[44] A Gattini, note 42, at 1172–3.

[45] United Kingdom, House of Lords, *R v. Lyons and Others* (November 11, 2002) UKHL 44, ILDC 247 (UK 2002) [105].

[46] *Request for Interpretation of the Judgment of March 31, 2004 in the Case concerning Avena and Other Mexican Nationals (Mexico v. United States of America)* (Judgment) [2009] ICJ Rep 3, [47].

[47] E.g., *Difference Relating to Immunity From Legal Process of a Special Rapporteur of the Commission on Human Rights* (Advisory Opinion) [1999] ICJ Rep 62 [2(d)]; ICSID, *The Loewen Group, Inc and Haymond L Loewen v. United States of America* (2003) ARB(AF)/98/3, 42 ILM 811 [123]. See generally R Higgins, "The Concept of 'the State': Variable Geometry and Dualist Perceptions" in V Gowlland-Debbas (ed.), *The International Legal System In Quest Of Equity And Universality, Liber Amicorum Georges Abi-Saab* (London: Kluwer Law 2001).

(ECtHR).[48] For instance, in Italy, the Court of Cassation held that a national final judgment must be declared unenforceable "where the European Court…has ascertained that the conviction has been pronounced in the presence of a violation of the rules on fair trial provided for in Article 6 of the European Convention."[49] Also, within Latin America, there are many examples of courts that are empowered to give effect to decisions of international courts, notably the Inter-American Court of Human Rights (IACtHR).[50] But, here, the differences in reported practice are significant.[51] Within Africa, willingness and ability to apply international law norms is generally very uneven, with few reported cases where courts of Francophone countries have followed findings of the African Commission on Human Rights.[52] Practice in Asia on giving judicial effect to international law generally, and to international courts in particular, is very scarce.[53]

Abstracting from regional differences, a few points can be made pertaining to the ability and practice of national courts to implement decisions of international courts. First, the distinction between "monist" and "dualist" states is not of much relevance here. In monist states, the status of decisions of international courts is high.[54] However, the fact that a treaty is automatically part of the national legal order does not necessarily, and certainly not in all states, mean that a judgment of a court set up by that treaty is enforceable as if it were a rule of national law. Many states distinguish between treaties, on the one hand, and judgments of international courts, on the other. For instance, in Bulgaria, while treaties are automatically part of the domestic legal order and have constitutional status, no such status is afforded to judgments of international courts, which need to be incorporated separately by

[48] A von Staden, "Rational Choice within Normative Constraints: Compliance by Liberal Democracies with the Judgments of the European Court of Human Rights" (February 6, 2012). Available at SSRN <http://ssrn.com/abstract=2000024> accessed September 24, 2013. One factor that may explain the impact of the ECtHR on domestic judges is the interplay with EU law: see G Martinicio, "Is the European Convention Going to Be "Supreme"? A Comparative-Constitutional Overview of ECHR and EU Law before National Courts" (2012) 23 EJIL 401, 423.

[49] In Italy, Court of Cassation, *Dorigo* (January 25, 2007) Case No 2800/2007, 90 Rivista di Diritto Internazionale 601, ILDC 1096 (IT 2007).

[50] Argentina, *Simón and Others v. Office of the Public Prosecutor* (June 14, 2005) Appeal judgment, ILDC 579 (AR 2005); Brazil, Supreme Federal Court, *Re Ramos Costa* (December 3, 2008), ILDC 1375 (BR 2008); Colombia, Constitutional Court, *Gutiérrez Soler v. Colombia* (May 20, 2005), ILDC 1014 (CO 2005).

[51] See, e.g., Venezuela, Supreme Tribunal of Justice, *Solicitor General of the Republic v. Venezuela* (December 18, 2008), ILDC 1279 (VE 2008).

[52] M Killander and H Adjolohoun, "International Law and Domestic Human Rights Litigation in Africa: An Introduction" in M Killander (ed.), *International Law and Domestic Human Rights Litigation in Africa* (Pretoria University Law Press 2010) 8.

[53] One example of rejection is Sri Lanka, Supreme Court, *Singarasa v. Attorney General* (September 15, 2006), ILDC 518 (LK 2006). The lack of practice is confirmed by the absence of any such case law in the International Law in Domestic Courts database and in the report "International Human Rights Law and Practice" of the International Law Association (Berlin Conference 2004).

[54] *Lorse and Others v. the Netherlands* (App no 52750/99) ECHR February 4, 2003.

legislation.[55] The situation is comparable to that in the United States; in *Medellín*, the US Supreme Court distinguished between the legal status and effect of a treaty and the legal effect of a judgment of the ICJ interpreting such a treaty.[56] Conversely, the fact that courts in "dualistic" states may well be able to give effect to judgments of international courts based on a statute[57] does not matter for the result.

Second, in states where national courts in principle can give effect to a decision of an international court, the possibility to do so will be frequently hampered by the fact that before the dispute in question was submitted to the international court, a national court (and, often, the highest) has made a final decision on the matter. There then may be a clash between the obligation to implement a decision of an international court, on the one hand, and the principle of *res judicata* of national decisions, on the other. This conflict will generally only be solvable by the legislature, which has to allow for a possibility of revisions of national judicial decisions in the light of a later decision by an international court.[58]

Third, and also more generally (apart from this question of revision of final judgments), the ability of national courts to give effect to a decision of an international court cannot be presumed. While in some states national courts have a role in the effectuation of decisions of international courts,[59] that role is often entrusted to the political branches rather than to the courts.[60]

From a normative perspective, the implementation of international decisions, and the limits thereto, eventually rests on an affirmation or rejection of the principle of the primacy of international law in the national legal order. In an era where pluralist approaches are highly popular, this may seem like a non-starter. Yet this principle is not without influence on judicial practice. It helps to appreciate the practice of courts on revision of judgments following decisions of human rights courts.[61] It also helps to assess, for instance, the implementation of the judgment of the ICJ in *Jurisdictional Immunities of a State*[62] and the judgment of the US Supreme Court regarding the state of Nevada in *Gutierrez v. State of Nevada*, giving effect to *Avena*.[63]

However, the practice of courts that are willing to implement international decisions can, at best, be based on supremacy only to a limited extent. That principle

[55] T Lozanova, Analysis, *Prosecutor General v. VS* (July 24, 2007), ILDC 1139 (BG 2007), A3.

[56] *Medellín v. Texas*, note 5, [1a]. [57] Human Rights Act 1998 s 2(1)(a).

[58] See e.g., Cataldi, note 6; T Barkhuysen et al., note 8.

[59] See Bulgaria, Supreme Court of Cassation, *Prosecutor General v. VS*, ILDC 1139 (BG 2007).

[60] See generally, Franck, note 21.

[61] Barkhuysen et al., note 8; P Popelier and C van de Heyning, *Human Rights Protection in the European Legal Order: the Interaction between the European and the National Courts* (Antwerp: Intersentia 2011); HJ Papier, "Execution and Effects of the Judgments of the European Court of Human Rights from the Perspective of German National Courts" (2006) 27 Hum. Rts. L.J. 1.

[62] *Jurisdictional Immunities of the State*, note 4.

[63] United States, Supreme Court of the State of Nevada, *Gutierrez v. State of Nevada*, Case No. 53506 (September 19, 2012).

does not help, for instance, to explain cases where national courts give effect to interpretations of international courts that lack binding effect as such, such as Advisory Opinions of the ICJ[64] and views of the United Nations Human Rights Committee.[65]

An alternative and broader foundation may be discernible in the principle of comity. Applying the principle to the implementation of international decisions is based on a loose analogy with the principle as it applies to inter-state relations.[66] It captures the idea of bridging opposing spheres, such as public/private, national/foreign and indeed national/international.[67] Mutual respect, deference, accommodation, and, where appropriate, recognition will allow for a "smooth interaction" of the relations between national and international courts.[68] Such deference is supported by the recognition of relative institutional competence of international and national courts.[69]

Comity may justifiably expect national courts to pay due deference to decisions of international courts. Thus, while US courts treat WTO Appellate Body decisions as non-binding,[70] courts have recognized that such decisions can be an influential factor in determining whether executive agency actions were in accordance with the United States' international obligations.[71]

While the principle of comity has the virtue of going beyond a purely formal analysis of bindingness and primacy, however, it is of little help in understanding, explaining, or predicting national judicial practice. It does not offer much guidance for distinguishing those cases where deference was due from cases where courts did not allow deference.

All in all, in empirical terms much remains unknown about the effect that national courts have given to decisions of international courts. Some studies have been made on interactions of the ECtHR,[72] the IACtHR,[73] and the ICJ[74] with national courts,

[64] Netherlands, Supreme Court, *Vereniging van Juristen voor de Vrede (Association of Lawyers for Peace) en Stichting Miljoenen Zijn Tegen (Foundation Millions Are Against) v. The State of the Netherlands* (December 21, 2001) Judgment on Appeal in Cassation, ILDC 1758 (NL 2001); South Africa, Constitutional Court, *South Africa v. Basson* (September 9, 2005), ILDC 494 (ZA 2005); United Kingdom, Court of Appeal (Civil Division), *Marchiori v. Environment Agency and Others* (January 25, 2002) Appeal judgment, (2002) EWCA Civ 03, ILDC 241 (UK 2002); Italy, Court of Cassation, *United States v. Tissino and Others, Preliminary Order on Jurisdiction* (February 25, 2009), ILDC 1262 (IT 2009).

[65] R van Alebeek and PA Nollkaemper, "The Legal Status of Decisions by Human Rights Treaty Bodies in National Law" in H Keller (ed.), *UN Human Rights Treaty Bodies. Law and Legitimacy* (Studies on Human Rights Conventions Series, Cambridge University Press 2012).

[66] See generally JR Paul, "Comity in International Law" (1991) 32 Harv. Int'l L.J. 1, 6.

[67] Paul, note 66. [68] Shany, note 12, at 166.

[69] JS Martinez, "Towards an International Judicial System" (2003) 56 Stan. L. Rev. 429.

[70] See *Timken Co v. United States*, Appeal Judgment, 354 F.3d 1334 (Fed. Cir. 2004), January 16, 2004 [23].

[71] See e.g., *Allegheny Ludlum Corp v. United States* (May 13, 2004) Appeal Judgment, 367 F.3d 1339 (Fed. Cir. 2004). Compare also the notion of respectful consideration in *Breard v. Greene* (April 14, 1998) 523 US 371, 118 S Ct 1352, 140 L ed 2d 529 (1998), ILDC 684 (US 1998).

[72] See e.g., Barkhuysen et al., note 8. [73] See e.g., González-Salzberg, note 8.

[74] C Schulte, note 8.

but for most international courts this is *terra incognita*. From the perspective of national courts, studies exist for some states,[75] but for most states the practice of national courts has not been examined from this angle. This has also affected the normative dimensions of this function of national courts. If supremacy does not provide an explanation, we need an alternative concept of the legitimacy or authority of international courts that can justify why and when national courts do or do not implement decisions of international courts. This set of questions needs to be considered in conjunction with the practice of contestation, to which we now turn.

2.3 Contestation

A third function of national courts in relation to international courts is the opposite of "implementation": national courts may contest international interpretations or decisions; that is, reject an international decision and opt for an outcome that is irreconcilable with that decision. While contestation may have a negative connotation, it serves both critical functions in relation to national law (by protecting the national rule of law) and in relation to international law.

Contestation may be based on the different reading of the facts or the law by a national court that in effect reviews the merits of a judgment of an international court. An example is the judgment of the US Supreme Court in *Sanchez-Llamas*.[76] Also, the practice of application of judgments of the ECtHR at the national level shows examples where national courts have arrived at different conclusions than their international counterpart.[77] Contestation may also be based on the ground that a decision of an international court would have violated fundamental (constitutional) principles or rights of the forum state.[78] Contestation may also lead to differing interpretations of international obligations by international and national courts, as was the case in *Avena/Medellin*[79] and in *Al-Khawaja/Horncastle*.[80]

[75] Barkhuysen et al., note 8; JS Martinez, "Enforcing the Decisions of International Tribunals in the US Legal System" (2005) 45 Santa Clara L. Rev. 877.

[76] *Sanchez-Llamas (Moises) v. Oregon* 548 US 331, 126 S Ct 2669 (2006), ILDC 697 (US 2006).

[77] I Jones, "A Political Judgment? Reconciling Hearsay and the Right to Challenge" (2010) 14 Int'l J. Evidence & Proof 232.

[78] See e.g., *Sanchez-Llamas (Moises) v. Oregon* 548 US 331, 126 S Ct 2669 (2006), ILDC 697 (US 2006); Venezuela, Supreme Tribunal of Justice, *Solicitor General of the Republic v. Venezuela* (December 18, 2008), ILDC 1279 (VE 2008); Croatia, Constitutional Court, *Bobetko Report* (November 12, 2002), ILDC 383 (HR 2002); G Martinico, "Is the European Convention Going to Be 'Supreme'? A Comparative-Constitutional Overview of ECHR and EU Law before National Courts" (2012) 23 EJIL 401, 419.

[79] *Avena*, note 3; *Medellín v. Texas*, 552 U.S. 491, ILDC 947 (2008).

[80] *Al-Khawaja and Tahery v. UK* (App nos 26766/05 and 22228/06) ECHR December 15, 2011; *R v. Horncastle and others* [2009] UKSC 14.

Contestation reflects the dualism (or pluralism) between legal orders, in which national courts do not accept the ultimate authority of international courts.[81] National courts may be willing to give effect to decisions of international courts, but only if such norms and decisions are consistent with the standards set by the "receiving" state.[82]

From a normative perspective, this practice is supported by the legitimacy concerns that largely outstrip the legitimating power of formal legality—concerns that are directly relevant to international courts.[83] Such concerns may justify non-compliance with international obligations where international law cannot accommodate such concerns.[84]

A further distinction needs to be made between the internal and external dimensions of contestation. The internal dimension is when a national court that declines to give effect to a decision of an international court in case it conflicts with an obligation under national law can hardly expect, and would not intend to communicate, that the international court should follow the national law in question.

But contestation is more than a simple refusal to give effect to a particular decision because it conflicts with national law. It can have an external dimension, in that a national court can ground a decision on a norm that should have been followed by the international court in question. Its indication of the limits of the ability and willingness of such courts to implement decisions by an international court may lead to feedback that influences future decisions of international courts. An example is the 1982 decision of the Supreme Court of Cyprus refusing to follow the ECtHR *Dungeon* decision[85] on decriminalizing homosexuality by invoking the perception of public morals in Cyprus,[86] with later change triggered by the case law of the ECtHR.[87] Another example is the dialogue between the UK Supreme Court's *Horncastle* judgment[88] and the ECtHR in *Al-Khawaja and Tahery v. United Kingdom*.[89]

[81] N Krisch, *Beyond Constitutionalism: The Pluralist Structure of Postnational Law* (Oxford University Press 2011) 103. Compare D Halberstam, "Constitutional Heterarchy: The Centrality of Conflict in the European Union and the United States" in JL Dunoff and JP Trachtman (eds), *Ruling the World? Constitutionalism, International Law, and Global Governance* (Cambridge University Press 2009) 326–55; B Tamanaha, "Understanding Legal Pluralism: Past to Present, Local to Global" (2008) 30 Sidney L. Rev. 375.

[82] Martinez, note 69, at 446.

[83] See e.g., A von Bogdandy and I Venzke, "In Whose Name? International Courts' Public Authority and its Democratic Justification" (2012) 23 EJIL 7; K Dzehtsiarou and A Greene, "Legitimacy and the Future of the European Court of Human Rights: Critical Perspectives from Academia and Practitioners" (2011) 12 German L.J. 1707.

[84] M Kumm, "Democratic Constitutionalism Encounters International Law: Terms of Engagement" in S Choudhry (ed.), *Migration of Constitutional Ideas* (Cambridge University Press 2007) 263.

[85] *Dudgeon v. UK* (App no 7525/76) (1981) Series A no 45.

[86] *Yiannakis Panayiotou Costa v. The Republic of Cyprus*, Supreme Court of Cyprus, June 8, 1982.

[87] *Modinos v. Cyprus* (App no 15070/89) (1993) Series A no 259.

[88] *R v. Horncastle and others*, note 80.

[89] *Al-Khawaja and Tahery v. UK*, note 80.

This external dimension of contestation, and the resulting interaction with international courts, may be based on national law—for even when contestation is based on purely national law, international courts may be forced to take into account the limits of the ability of national courts to implement particular decisions. However, the feedback loop seems essentially to depend on a common normative sphere. Of particular relevance in this context is human rights law, where a substantive overlap exists between national and international law.[90] The commonality may lead to dialogue, which in turn might lead to mutual accommodation.

In addition to recognizing the value of pluralism, diversity, and autonomy of national legal and political orders, contestation derives its normative justification in part from its facilitation of a process of change in a situation where the political processes around international courts are undeveloped.[91] The rejection processes of decisions of international courts provide a political context for international courts that lack organized political structures. For instance, the lack of a proper political context of the ECtHR (given the rather limited role of the Committee of Ministers) is supplemented and corrected by decisions of national organs, including courts.[92]

While the practice of contestation interface serves important functions, it has a darker side. Once we accept that a claim based on domestic principles can override a claim for performance of a decision of an international court, the question is whether there are any limits to the principles that can be invoked, and how this can be reconciled with the interests of a stable international legal order. It may be argued that this risk is modest when contestation is based on human rights values.[93] But beyond the core of internationally recognized rights, convergence will be quickly lost.

In a pluralist paradigm this is not problematic: indeed, this is its asset. The core of the pluralist understanding is precisely when actors at different levels of governance do *not* share a common, overarching point of reference.[94] Pluralism is a normative (and political) project that, as such, is invulnerable to a critique based on its effects on another legal system from which it necessarily has to be autonomous.

Yet, the questions of what the implications of the pluralistic position are for the supremacy of international law and the interests of international adjudication cannot be circumvented.[95] Supremacy of international law, including the interests

[90] See e.g., Uganda, Constitutional Court, *Kim and Mao v. Attorney General* (March 7, 2008), ILDC 1136 (UG 2008) [4]; Dominican Republic, Supreme Court of Justice, *Juventud Nacional Comprometida, Inc (JUNCO) v. Dominican Republic* (February 9, 2005), ILDC 1095 (DO 2005); Brazil, Superior Tribunal of Justice, *Re Ramos Costa* (December 3, 2008), ILDC 1375 (BR 2008).

[91] Krisch, note 81, at 79, 81; PS Berman "Global Legal Pluralism" (2007) 80 S. Cal. L. Rev. 1155.

[92] Krisch, note 81, pp. 85–9; see also E Benvenisti, "Reclaiming Democracy: The Strategic Uses of Foreign and International Law by National Courts" (2008) 102 AJIL 241.

[93] E.g., M Kumm, "The Legitimacy of International Law: A Constitutionalist Framework of Analysis" (2004) 15 EJIL 907.

[94] Krisch, note 81, at 81.

[95] Krisch also recognizes the problem of stability. Note 81, at 234–5, 240.

served by international adjudication, cannot really be sustained if international law might not be supported at the domestic level. Here lies a major set of questions for future research on the interactions between international and national courts. How do we distinguish between those cases that undermine and hamper the stability and effective implementation of international judgments, and those that, in the long run, help adjust and improve international courts? What are the normative foundations, perhaps beyond a narrow set of principles from human rights law, which can initiate a positive feedback loop? And how can the values of pluralism be balanced with those of an effective system of international adjudication?

2.4 Normative development

A fourth function of national courts in relation to international courts is that they can support the contribution that international courts make to the interpretation and development of international law, and thereby to the stabilization of normative expectations.[96] The fate of pronouncements by international courts will depend in large part on their acceptance and recognition by other actors, and it is here that national courts may play a (modest) role.[97]

National courts have recognized that international decisions, even though they may not be addressed to and strictly binding on "their" state, are legally relevant for determining the contents of the law.[98] That is obviously true for determinations by international courts of the state of customary law. For instance, in the United Kingdom, courts have referred to the ICJ judgment in *Arrest Warrant* to support conclusions drawn on the basis of legislation, or to fill gaps in national law.[99] It may also apply to treaties. As noted by Justice Breyer, even though interpretations by the ICJ do not bind states beyond the scope of Article 59 of the Statute, national courts should interpret treaties to achieve uniformity. The ICJ's position as an international court charged with a duty to interpret international treaties then "provides a natural point of reference for national courts seeking that uniformity."[100] In states party to the European Convention on Human Rights (ECHR), it is routine practice

[96] Von Bogdandy and Venzke, note 83, at 7.

[97] See generally, M Bedjaoui, "The Reception by National Courts of Decisions of International Tribunals" (1995–1996) 28 NYU J. Int'l L. & Pol'y 45; CH Schreuer, "The Authority of International Judicial Practice in Domestic Courts" (1974) 23 Int'l & Comp. L.Q. 681; TM Franck and GH Fox (eds), *International Law Decisions in National Courts* (New York: Transnational Publishers 1996).

[98] Schreuer, note 97, at 687–9.

[99] See United Kingdom, House of Lords, *Jones v. Ministry of the Interior of Saudi Arabia and Aziz* (June 14, 2006) Appeal judgment [2006] UKHL 26, ILDC 521 (UK 2006); *Re Mofaz* (February 12, 2004) First instance, unreported (Bow Street Magistrates' Court), ILDC 97 (UK 2004).

[100] See *Sanchez-Llamas (Moises) v. Oregon* 548 US 331, 126 S Ct 2669 (2006), ILDC 697 (US 2006) (dissenting opinion of Justice Breyer).

that courts consider the jurisprudence of the ECtHR in respect of the article of the Convention on which the claim is based.[101] The same appears to hold for at least some state parties to the American Convention on Human Rights (ACHR).[102]

Such practices may have a strategic aspect: the court will assume that if it does not follow a particular interpretation adopted by an international court and there is a reasonable chance of triggering a case before that very same international court, that international court will then hold against the state. Of course, such a reasonable chance only exists for very few international courts, notably the ECtHR. They may also be strategic in the sense that national courts can thereby strengthen their power vis-à-vis the political branches.[103] But they also have a normative aspect: courts may recognize the interpretation of an international court as an authoritative formulation of an international norm.

This construction is far from a mechanical exercise. First, courts will need to consider decisions as part of a wider process involving other evidence on the state of the law that may point in different directions.[104] International decisions are not among the traditional principles of treaty interpretation, and their weight and impact thus have to be considered in the broader context of the more traditional principles. This relates to the role of consent and intent of states as a legitimizing factor in the development of international law, compared to the degree in which international bodies are accepted as legitimate actors in the interpretation and development of international law.

Second, distinctions may need to be drawn depending on whether states have accepted the jurisdiction of an international court to interpret the treaty. Here we may need to distinguish between relatively integrated treaty regimes with a strong and relatively authoritative international court, as in the case of the ECHR; situations where a state has accepted the jurisdiction of an international court to settle disputes over a treaty, but where that treaty regime lacks the integrative nature that characterizes the ECHR (e.g., the Vienna Convention on Consular Relations for states that have accepted the jurisdiction of the ICJ);[105] and situations where a state

[101] Ireland, *O'Donnell v. South Dublin County Council* (May 22, 2007), ILDC 1067 (IE 2007); Russian Federation, Constitutional Court, *Constitutional Review of Certain Provisions of the Code of Civil Procedure of the Russian Federation*, ILDC 1317 (RU 2009); Cyprus, Supreme Court sitting as Court of Appeals, *Scattergood v. Attorney General* (January 21, 2005), ILDC 921 (CY 2005); Portugal, Supreme Administrative Court, *A and B v. Portuguese State* (November 28, 2007), ILDC 1441 (PT 2007).

[102] E.g., Peru, Constitutional Court, *Callao Bar Association v. Congress of the Republic* (June 19, 2007) Constitutional Review, ILDC 961 (PE 2007); Argentina, Supreme Court of Justice, *Chile v. Arancibia Clavel* (August 24, 2004), ILDC 1082 (AR 2004) [36]; see also Argentina, Supreme Court of Justice, *Simón y Otros s/Privación Ilegítima de la Libertad* (June 14, 2005), ILDC 579 (AR 2005), H6–H7; *Mazzeo and ors*, ILDC 1084 (AR 2007), July 13, 2007.

[103] Compare Benvenisti, note 92. [104] Schreuer, note 97, at 705.

[105] Optional Protocol to the Vienna Convention on Consular Relations Concerning the Compulsory Settlement of Disputes (adopted April 24, 1963) 596 UNTS 487.

has not given an international court an interpretative role in regard to the treaty in question. Again, the (relative) role of initial consent to a process of normative development will be a key factor here.

In this context, it is noteworthy that several courts have referred to decisions of international courts set up by treaties to which they are not a party.[106] The Botswana Court of Appeal, in the *Good* case in 2005, relied on a decision of the ECtHR when deciding whether a deportation of a legal alien amounted to an unlawful expulsion of aliens under Article 13 of the International Convention on Civil and Political Rights.[107] Such decisions recognize, on the basis of a decision of an international court, a particular interpretation of a rule of international law. They illustrate that consent is only one factor and does not determine whether national courts follow or accept interpretations by international courts.

For some international courts, further distinctions may need to be drawn. In the context of the ECtHR, we need to differentiate between single-judge formations, committees, Chambers, and the Grand Chamber, as provided for under Article 26.[108] In regard to such variations, there is something to be said for the flexibility preserved by the UK Human Rights Act, which only requires courts determining issues connected with a convention right to "take account" of judgments of the ECtHR.[109]

The contribution of national courts to the interpretation and development of international law through the reception of interpretations of international courts has been minimally studied.[110] Now that more and more national cases are being reported, this is a fruitful area for more study. Further research might also shed light on the circumstances and conditions under which weight is or is not given to pronouncements of international courts. This question leads directly to the question of legitimacy and authority of international courts, and its effect on the role of such courts in the development of international law.

[106] See generally AM Slaughter, *A New World Order* (Princeton University Press 2004) 80–1.

[107] Botswana, Court of Appeal, *Good v. Attorney-General* (July 27, 2005), ILDC 8 (BW 2005). Other examples are Barbados, Judicial Committee of the Privy Council, *Boyce v. Queen* (July 7, 2004) Privy Council Appeal No 99 of 2002, [2004] UKPC 32, 134 ILR 439; Nepal, Supreme Court, *Dhakal v. Nepal* (June 1, 2007), ILDC 756 (NP 2007); South Africa, Constitutional Court, *South Africa v. Williams and Others* (June 9, 1995), ILDC 654 (ZA 1995).

[108] Protocol No 14 to the Convention for the Protection of Human Rights and Fundamental Freedoms, amending the control system of the Convention (adopted May 13, 2004, entered into force June 1, 2010) CETS 194 (2004).

[109] Human Rights Act 1998, s 2(1)(a); see also C McGrudden, "A Common Law of Human Rights? Transnational Judicial Conversations on Constitutional Rights" (2000) 20 Oxford J. Legal Stud. 499, 503–4.

[110] See Bedjaoui, note 97; and Schreuer, note 97.

3 Functions of International Courts in Relation to National Adjudication

Similar to the need to differentiate with regard to the functions of national courts in relation to international courts, it is important to distinguish between the multiple functions that international courts exercise in relation to national courts. Each function raises different questions and implications for research. This section identifies three such functions, which roughly correspond to the functions of national courts: substitution, review, and normative development.

3.1 Substitution

The possibility that an international court substitutes for a national court, in the sense that it performs a function that otherwise could be performed by a national court, is less realistic than the (already limited) prospect of national courts substituting for international courts. The possibility is essentially limited to the situation where, first, national courts should adjudicate claims that at least in substance are based on international law and where that international law dimension is central to the overall claim, and, second, the national court is unable or unwilling to do so. The complementary relationship between the International Criminal Court (ICC) and national courts[111] is the situation that best approximates these rare conditions.

It should be noted also that while the construction of substitution may be a conceptual stretch, international courts can fulfill a critical function in relation to national legal systems. In those cases where international courts have a role in reviewing and assessing national law and national decision-making, for instance by investment arbitration and international human rights courts, they may promote the rule of law at the national level—both in individual cases and at a more structural level.[112]

The prospect that international courts might actually substitute for national courts is restricted by their limited possibility to determine the facts as these would be considered in national adjudication, by the fact that national adjudication is embedded in a system of national law that cannot possibility be replicated at the international level, and by the fact that international courts may fail to connect to the audiences that national courts may address—a limitation that has hampered the

[111] Kleffner, note 15; and Stahn and Zeidy, note 15.

[112] On the promotion of the rule of law at national level by international institutions, see generally, G Nolte and HP Aust, "International Law and the Rule of Law at the National Level" in M Zürn, A Nollkaemper and R Peerenboom (eds), *Rule of Law Dynamics* (Cambridge University Press 2012) 48.

attempts of international criminal courts to do what national courts might have done.[113] It is for all these reasons that the task of international courts is a subsidiary one.[114]

In principle, then, the task of international courts is not so much to substitute for a national court, but to review decisions of national courts against international law.[115] They act if and to the extent that domestic courts have failed to apply (the substance of) international law properly.[116] The rejection by the ECtHR of the construction that it would be a fourth instance court[117] likewise indicates that the court cannot be seen as a substitution for what a national court should have done.

The proposition that the ECtHR, and perhaps other international courts, cannot be considered as fourth instance courts may, however, be overly formal, and perhaps overly sensitive to sovereignty concerns. If a plaintiff litigates domestically without success, for example, for a breach of the right to freedom of expression, and subsequently wins a case in an international court that orders the state to pay compensation, it is difficult to see that international decision as anything other than a decision that did what the national court should have done. The key requirement for making this perspective a viable one, then, is that the international obligation that is the basis for international judicial review was at the heart of the claim.

3.2 Review

Second, international courts may be called upon to review decisions of national courts. Human rights courts have an obvious role here. Also, the ICC has a function in this regard in admissibility proceedings.[118] In more rare situations, the ICJ will also exercise this function. This will, for instance, be the case if an international dispute involves the exercise of diplomatic protection.[119] Also, in cases of direct injury

[113] See e.g., T Kelsall, *Culture under Cross-Examination: International Justice and the Special Court for Sierra Leone* (Cambridge University Press 2012).

[114] AM Slaughter and W Burke-White, "The Future of International Law is Domestic (or, The European Way of Law)" in J Nijman and A Nollkaemper (eds), *New Perspectives on the Divide Between International Law and National Law* (Cambridge University Press 2007) 110.

[115] *Avena*, note 3, [28]; *LaGrand*, note 33, [52]; *Nottebohm Case (Liechtenstein v. Guatemala)* (n 39) (Dissenting Opinion of Judge Ad Hoc M Guggenheim) 52 [4].

[116] *LaGrand*, note 33.

[117] See, with references to the case law, Council of Europe, "Interlaken Follow-Up. Principle of Subsidiarity" (July 8, 2010) 9–12. See also LR Helfer, "Redesigning the European Court of Human Rights: Embeddedness as a Deep Structural Principle of the European Human Rights Regime" (2008) 19 EJIL 125, 142–3.

[118] Article 17, ICC Statute, note 15; see also Kleffner, note 15.

[119] *Elettronica Sicula S.p.A (ELSI) (United States of America v. Italy)*, (Judgment) [1989] ICJ Rep 15 [52].

to the state, national courts may have ruled on the subject matter of the international dispute.[120]

While all decisions of national courts are commonly treated as facts, not law, from the perspective of the reviewing international court, a distinction may have to be drawn between cases where domestic courts have adjudicated questions of facts or domestic law, and cases where questions of international law were at issue. In the former case, an international court will typically defer to that domestic decision as it is not well positioned to consider such matters of domestic law.[121]

When international courts review decisions of national courts that have applied a rule of international law, the situation may be different, but they will still accord them substantial deference. The principle of subsidiarity suggests that the system should "rely primarily on the most local body capable of giving meaning and effect to human rights."[122] The principle translates into the margin of appreciation,[123] which calls for restraint and deference on the part of international courts in their review of national decisions.[124]

It is true that the role of the principle is more limited in making assessments of the contents and interpretation of international law as such,[125] since it can hardly be maintained that national courts are better positioned for that task. Nonetheless, the principle justifies international courts respecting a freedom of choice of national courts in interpreting and applying international obligations.[126] The ECtHR held in the *Von Hannover* case that where the balancing exercise has been undertaken by the national authorities in conformity with the criteria laid down in the court's case law, the court would require strong reasons to substitute its view for that of the domestic courts.[127]

[120] Examples are: *Questions Relating to the Obligation to Prosecute or Extradite (Belgium v. Senegal)* (Request for the Indication of Provisional Measures: Order) [2009] ICJ Rep 139, [26]; *Jurisdictional Immunities of the State (Germany v. Italy)*, note 4 [13].

[121] *Payment in Gold of Brazilian Federal Loans Contracted in France (France v. Brazil)* (Merits) PCIJ Rep Series A No 21, 124; Y Shany, *Regulating Jurisdictional Relations Between National and International Courts* (Oxford University Press 2007) 183–4; *Nottebohm Case*, note 115 (Dissenting Opinion of Judge Ad Hoc M Guggenheim) 52 [4]; *Certain Questions of Mutual Assistance in Criminal Matters (Djibouti v. France)* (Judgment) General List No 136 [2008] ICJ 1, [146].

[122] Carozza, note 17, at 67.

[123] See on the link with subsidiarity Carozza, note 17; G Letsas, *A Theory of Interpretation of the European Convention on Human Rights* (Oxford University Press 2007) 81.

[124] LR Helfer and AM Slaughter, "Toward a Theory of Effective Supranational Adjudication" (1997) 107 Yale L.J. 273, 316; Letsas, note 123; WW Burke-White and A von Staden, "Investment Protection in Extraordinary Times: The Interpretation and Application of Non-Precluded Measures Provisions in Bilateral Investment Treaties" (2007) 48 Virginia J. Int'l L. 307, 372.

[125] Y Shany, "Toward a General Margin of Appreciation Doctrine in International Law?" (2005) 16 EJIL 907, 936–9.

[126] Shany, note 121.

[127] *Von Hannover v. Germany (Merits and Just Satisfaction)* (App nos 40660/08 and 60641/08) ECHR February 7, 2012 [107].

The support for the principle is not necessarily universal. Though mainly developed in and applied with respect to the ECtHR,[128] it can also be applied to human rights more generally[129] and to other fields such as investment law,[130] the WTO,[131] international criminal courts,[132] and the ICJ.[133] Nevertheless, the fact that the principle has been articulated best and applied most frequently by the ECtHR suggests that the degree to which international courts can rely on and trust national courts to make the proper balances is regime- and region-specific.[134]

In all cases, deference finds its limits in the leeway left by the contents of international obligations. Where decisions of national courts transgress such limits, international courts will contest such decisions. Given their status as "organs of the international legal order," and given that they are embedded in an international legal order that claims primacy over national laws and national courts,[135] international courts will eventually rely on primacy as a principle to structure their relationship with national courts.[136] Where national decisions do not conform to the requirements of international law, international courts will contest them, just as national courts may do in the reverse relationship.

This has, however, proven to be a risky undertaking. International courts will have to be mindful of their relatively modest (or rather weak) position in terms of power and legitimacy. Contestation by international courts risks

[128] R St J MacDonald, "The Margin of Appreciation" in R St J MacDonald et al. (eds), *The European System for the Protection of Human Rights* (1st edn, Berlin: Springer 1993) 83, 123; Helfer and Slaughter, note 124, at 316.

[129] A Legg, *The Margin of Appreciation in International Human Rights Law: Deference and Proportionality* (Oxford University Press 2012).

[130] Burke-White and von Staden, note 124, at 372; WW Burke-White and A von Staden, "Private Litigation in a Public Law Sphere: The Standard of Review in Investor-State Arbitrations" (2010) 35 Yale J. Int'l L.J. 283.

[131] R Becroft, *The Standard of Review in WTO Dispute Settlement: Critique and Development* (Cheltenham: Edward Elgar Publishing 2012); RP Alford, "Reflections on US-Zeroing: A Study in Judicial Overreaching by the WTO Appellate Body" (2007) 45 Columbia J. Transnat'l L. 196, 202; AK Bjorklund, "Reconciling State Sovereignty and Investor Protection in Denial of Justice Claims" (2005) 45 Virginia J. Int'l L. 809, 867–8; CD Ehlermann and N Lockhart, "Standard of Review in WTO Law" (2004) 7 J. Int'l Econ. L. 491, 502.

[132] JI Turner, "Transnational Networks and International Criminal Justice" (2007) 105(5) Mich. L. Rev. 985, 1024; WW Burke-White, "Proactive Complementarity: The International Criminal Court and National Courts in the Rome System of International Justice" (2008) 49 Harvard Int'l L.J. 53, 74.

[133] Shany, note 125, at 936–9.

[134] ML Movsesian, "Judging International Judgments" (2007) 48 Virginia J. Int'l L. 65, 111–13.

[135] G Fitzmaurice, "The General Principles of International law Considered from the Standpoint of the Rule of Law" (1957) 92 Recueil des Cours 85.

[136] E.g. *Treatment of Polish Nationals and Other Persons of Polish Origin or Speech in the Danzig Territory* (Advisory Opinion) PCIJ Rep Series A/B No 44, 4; *Free Zones of Upper Savoy and the District of Gex (France v. Switzerland) (second phase)* (Order) PCIJ Series A No 24, 12; *Castillo Petruzzi et al* (Compliance with Judgment: Order) Inter-American Court of Human Rights, Series C no 59 (November 11, 1999) [5]; WTO, *Brazil-Export Financing Programme for Aircraft* (August 28, 2000) WT/DS46/ARB [3.65].

triggering counter-contestation by national courts, as evidenced in cases such as *Sanchez-Llamas,*[137] *Singarasa,*[138] *and Horncastle.*[139]

Counter-contestation is critical when international decisions depend for their effectiveness on subsequent decisions of national courts. When national courts do not accept and implement them, international courts will quickly have reached the limits of their ability to secure performance of international obligations. In the *Avena Interpretation* judgment, the ICJ made clear that it did not see a particular role for itself in supervising (non)implementation of its judgments by national courts. It framed the initial obligation in such a manner that the proper role of the national court was a matter for domestic law.[140] Regarding the ECtHR, the states parties prefer to maintain the primary role of the Committee of Ministers in this respect, rather than construing this as a role of the court itself.[141]

Rather than opting for a full contestation of national decisions, international courts thus may be inclined to lower their standards of review and opt for a process of dialogue and accommodation that may soften their stand, perhaps in the hope that domestic courts likewise will accommodate them. The sequence of events in *Al-Khawaja/Horncastle* is an example.[142]

The processes of contestation, dialogue, and accommodation by international courts, in connection with the standard of review, are a major area for future research. A key question is what qualities a national decision should display in order to justify broad deference by the ECtHR and, possibly, other international courts. How do international courts justify broad deference in some cases and less deference in other cases, and what interests and values are served by such distinctions? How do international courts soften their standards of review in the light of the envisaged reaction, i.e., counter-contestation, at the national level?

3.3 Normative development

Thirdly, international courts can strengthen the contribution of national courts to normative development. Though the role of national courts here is modest, it is a safe proposition that decisions of national courts may have an effect on the interpretation and development of rules of international law.[143] The question then is whether and how international courts accept prior interpretations by national

[137] *Sanchez-Llamas (Moises) v. Oregon*, note 76.

[138] *Singarasa v. Attorney General*, note 53.

[139] *Al-Khawaja and Tahery v. UK*, note 80; *R v. Horncastle and others*, note 80.

[140] *Avena and Other Mexican Nationals (Mexico v. United States of America)*, note 3.

[141] Gattini, note 42.

[142] *Al-Khawaja and Tahery v. UK*, note 80; *R v. Horncastle and others*, note 80.

[143] See generally MA Waters, "Mediating Norms and Identity: The Role of Transnational Judicial Dialogue in Creating and Enforcing International Law" (2004) 93 Geo. L.J. 487.

courts in the process of interpretation and development of international law. Such uses of decisions of national courts can be considered part of a wider process of judicial dialogue.[144]

The primary contribution of domestic courts to the development of international law is in their role as acts of states that are relevant in the formation of customary international law.[145] There is some evidence that international courts indeed have recognized decisions of national courts as relevant data in the determination of a role of customary law.[146]

A second way to construe the relevance of national case law for the determination and development of international law is in the interpretation of particular provisions of treaties. There is some evidence that international courts see here a useful role for decisions of national courts. The ECtHR makes considerable use of domestic case law in the interpretation and development of the convention through a comparative method.[147] In the *Jelisic* case, the ICTY noted that decisions of national courts should be considered in the interpretation of the Genocide Convention.[148]

Finally, international courts may attribute weight to the identification and determination of general principles of law. For instance, the PCIJ referred to the "principle generally accepted in the jurisprudence in international arbitration as well as by national courts" to the effect that a party is estopped from relying on its own non-fulfillment of an international obligation.[149]

Nonetheless, the process of considering national decisions in the development of international law is fraught with difficulties. One difficulty is that many national

[144] AM Slaughter, "A Global Community of Courts" (2003) 44 Harvard Int'l L.J. 191, 204.

[145] H Lauterpacht, "Decisions of Municipal Courts as a Source of International Law" (1929) 10 BYIL 65, 80; Oppenheim, Jennings and Watts, note 2, at 41; International Law Association, "Final Report of the Committee on Formation of Customary (General) International Law, Statement of Principles Applicable to the Formation of General Customary International Law," Principle 9, reproduced in *The International Law Association: Report of the Sixty-Ninth Conference* (ILA 2000).

[146] *SS "Lotus"* case (*France v. Turkey)* [1927] PCIJ Rep Series A No 10, 23, 26, 28–9; *Case Concerning the Arrest Warrant of April 11, 2000 (Democratic Republic of the Congo v. Belgium)* February 14, 2002, General List no. 121 24 [58]. See also the Separate Opinion of Judges Higgins, Kooijmans and Buergenthal [22]–[24] (considering case-law as part of state practice concerning universal jurisdiction). *Jurisdictional Immunities of the State (Germany v. Italy)*, note 4, [64, 68, 72]; *Prosecutor v. Erdemovic*, Judgment. Case No. IT-96-22-A (ICTY, Appeals Chamber, October 7, 1997) [55] (Joint and Separate Opinion of Judge McDonald and Judge Vohran).

[147] P Mahoney, "The Comparative Method in Judgments of the European Court of Human Rights: Reference Back to National Law" in G Canivet et al. (eds), *Comparative Law before the Courts* (London: BIICL 2004) 135.

[148] *Prosecutor v. Jelisic* (Judgment) ICTY-95-10-T (December 14, 1999) [61].

[149] *Jurisdiction of the Courts of Danzig* (Advisory Opinion), PCIJ Rep Series B No 15 (1928) 27; H Lauterpacht, *The Development of International Law by the International Court* (reprinted by Cambridge University Press 1996) 168. See also *Oil Platforms (Iran v. U.S.)*, Judgment, 2003 I.C.J. 161, 1 (Nov. 6) (Separate Opinion of Judge Simma); see on the ICTY, A Cassese, "The Contribution of the International Criminal Tribunal for the Former Yugoslavia to the Ascertainment of General Principles of Law Recognized by the Community of Nations" in S Yee and W Tieya (eds), *International Law in the Post-Cold War World—Essays in Memory of Li Haopei* (London: Routledge 2001) 43.

decisions that touch on international law are embedded in and complicated by national law, and it may not be easy for an international court to properly appreciate the complexity of such decisions. There is also the inevitable problem of arbitrariness, in that international courts pick some national judicial decisions and not others.[150] The question of what drives the choice of national cases as building blocks in interpretation and development, and what this means in terms of the relative influence of these courts and their legal systems for the development of international law, is yet to be studied.

4 Concluding Observations

The survey conducted in this chapter is necessarily based on a relatively limited set of materials from judicial practice. Notwithstanding the multiplication of international courts and tribunals, as well as the increased reporting of national case law, instances where international and national courts actually interact remain fairly limited. Within the practice that does exist, the diversity is enormous, mainly driven by different functions and powers of national and international courts.

The interactions between international and national courts, like the interactions between international and national legal orders generally, may straddle a continuum ranging from cooperative dialogue and willingness toward recognition and accommodation, on the one hand, to outright competition on the other.

There is little in terms of positive law that is able to provide structure to these patterns. The normative spectrum is essentially dictated by the neutrality of international law, and diversity in national law, complemented by a set of principles that have some degree of recognition in accommodating the needs and interests of international and national courts, such as subsidiarity and comity.

All this suggests that this is an area with major research implications. In part, these are of an empirical nature. On what grounds do national courts follow or contest decisions of international courts? Do the grounds on which national courts accept or contest decisions of international courts differ between states and, if so, why? And how do international courts respond to such contestation—do they recognise this as legitimate checks and balances and do they allow it to influence future judicial decision-making, or do they insist on their hierarchal position, thereby consolidating the opposition between the international and the national normative sphere?

[150] Cassese, note 149, at 45.

These empirical questions raise, in turn, fundamental normative questions. In particular, under what conditions should national courts accept decisions of international courts as authoritative? What are the attributes of international courts or their procedures that should foster and induce acceptance at the national level? And, conversely, under what conditions should international courts accept as authoritative decisions of national courts on matters of international law?

As is evident from the present chapter, all such questions will need to differentiate between the particularities, functions, and powers of international courts in their particular political setting, as well as the particularities, functions, and powers of national courts in their domestic context. The possibility of generalizing empirical and normative findings is likely to remain limited.

Research Questions

1. Under what conditions do, and should, international courts defer to and accept judgments of national courts as authoritative decisions in regard to international claims?
2. What explains differences between national courts in terms of implementation and acceptance of decisions of international courts? What are the driving domestic factors, and what role is played by the legitimacy (or lack thereof) of international courts?
3. How do we distinguish between those forms of judicial contestation that undermine and hamper stability and effective implementation of international judgments, and those that, in the long run, help adjust and improve international courts? What are the normative foundations, beyond a narrow set of principles from human rights law, that can initiate a positive feedback loop?
4. What drives international courts in choosing some national cases as building blocks in interpretation and development of international law (and not others), and what does this mean in terms of the relative influence of these courts (and their legal systems) for the development of international law?

Suggested Reading

von Bogdandy, A, "Pluralism, Direct Effect, and the Ultimate Say: on the Relationship between International and Domestic Constitutional Law" (2008) 6 Int'l J. Constitutional L. 397.

Carozza, PG, "Subsidiarity as a Structural Principle of International Human Rights Law" (2003) 97 AJIL 38.

Franck, TM and Fox, GH (eds), *International Law Decisions in National Courts* (New York: Transnational Publishers 1996).

Keller, H and Stone Sweet, A (eds), *A Europe of Rights: The Impact of the ECHR on National Legal Systems* (Oxford University Press 2008).

Krisch, N, *Beyond Constitutionalism: The Pluralist Structure of Postnational Law* (Oxford University Press 2011).

Legg, A, *The Margin of Appreciation in International Human Rights Law: Deference and Proportionality* (Oxford University Press 2012).

Martinez, JS, "Towards an International Judicial System" (2003) 56 Stanford L. Rev. 429.

Movsesian, ML, "Judging International Judgments" (2007) 48 Virginia J. Int'l L. 65.

Nollkaemper, A, *National Courts and the International Rule of Law* (Oxford University Press 2011).

Schreuer, CH, "The Implementation of International Judicial Decisions by Domestic Courts" (1975) 24 Int'l & Comp. L.Q. 153.

Schulte, C, *Compliance with Decisions of the International Court of Justice* (Oxford University Press 2004).

Shany, Y, *Regulating Jurisdictional Relations Between National and International Courts* (Oxford University Press 2007).

CHAPTER 25

INTERNATIONAL JUDICIAL BEHAVIOR

ERIK VOETEN*

1 Introduction

The field of judicial behavior studies *why* judges make the choices that they do. The most obvious answer is that the law determines judicial decision-making. This answer is not so much wrong as it is incomplete. What the law means and how it should be applied to concrete instances is not always obvious. Judges have discretion in how they interpret the law. The study of judicial behavior examines the factors

* Erik Voeten is the Peter F. Krogh Associate Professor of Geopolitics and Justice in World Affairs at Georgetown University's Walsh School of Foreign Service and the Government Department. I thank Yuval Shany, Cesare Romano, and Karen Alter for helpful comments and suggestions.

that determine how judges use that discretion. This question has mostly focused on identifying extra-legal influences on judicial behavior, including political leanings, career motivations, education, race, gender, culture, socialization, public opinion, panel composition, and appetite.[1]

There are two main strands of research in the study of international judicial behavior. The first, inspired by international relations theory, asks to what extent governments shape judicial behavior. International adjudication promises an arena that is distinct from traditional inter-state diplomacy. But how removed from political considerations are international court judgments? Realists expect government interests to prevail regardless of what the law says. This is not just because powerful governments can and do refuse to implement judgments they dislike, but also because the ability of the powerful to undermine courts will make judges reluctant to rule against them in the first place. Others, however, have more optimistic theories about the ability of international courts to influence government behavior and of judges to act independently of government demands.

The second strand of research is inspired by sociological theories. This research asks how judges are influenced by communication, appropriate norms of behavior (culture), and their past roles and identities. Like the political science literature, the sociological literature focuses on extra-legal factors although it does not share an emphasis on governments.

This chapter evaluates first the political and then the sociological influences on judicial behavior. I define judicial behavior broadly, such that it includes the direction of rulings but also legal reasoning and case management. Nevertheless, most of the literature has focused on judicial decisions, and so will this chapter. I understand the study of international judicial behavior to be the study of *why* international judges behave the way they do, with an emphasis on the extra-legal sources of judicial behavior. This brackets the main motivating question as a positive social science question, the answer to which includes quantitative and qualitative studies by lawyers, sociologists, and political scientists. Still, I leave descriptive and normative discussions of legal doctrine for other chapters. Moreover, while I highlight some normative implications of empirical studies, I limit discussions of judicial ethics. This is not because I find these topics uninteresting or unimportant, but because others in this volume are better equipped to address them.

[1] For a recent volume that provides an overview of perspectives, see C Geyh (ed.), *What's Law Got to Do With It?: What Judges Do, Why They Do It, and What's at Stake* (Palo Alto, CA: Stanford University Press 2011). For the appetite study, see S Danziger, J Levav, and L Avnaim-Pesso, "Extraneous factors in judicial decisions" (2011) 108(17) Proceedings of the National Academy of Science 6889–92.

2 Political Influences

Scholars who emphasize that judges are highly independent from the influence of state governments often refer to judges as "trustees."[2] International judges and governments have a fiduciary relationship in which the latter entrust the former to exercise their expertise when interpreting international law. A different group of scholars analyze the relationship between judges and governments with a principal-agent (P-A) model. The governments, who are the principals, conditionally grant judges the authority to resolve disputes and interpret treaties.[3] Yet governments retain control over a range of mechanisms through which they can influence judges, including the appointment process, budgetary constraints, compliance with decisions, and so on. In the realist version of this argument, international judges simply cater to the wishes of governments. A more modest claim is that the influence of governments on judicial decision-making depends on the effectiveness of these control mechanisms. Governments sometimes design control mechanisms to be ineffective in an effort to boost the credibility of the commitment they make to international law. If this is so, then the trustee model can be derived from the P-A model.[4] Legal scholars have also debated the normative question, "Is a court that is more independent from governments likely to be more or less effective?"[5]

Much of the earlier literature tackled the question of government influence by identifying key cases in which "the law" allegedly pointed courts in a different direction than powerful governments. This led some scholars to conclude that governments still ran the show,[6] while others found that international courts had considerable agency to make governments act against their proclaimed interests[7]—sometimes based on the

[2] See, e.g., K Alter, "Agents or Trustees? International Courts in their Political Context" (2008) 14 EJIR 33; G Majone, "Two Logics of Delegation: Agency and Fiduciary Relations in EU Governance" (2001) 2 E.U. Pol. 103.

[3] See, e.g., G Garrett, "The Politics of Legal Integration in the European Union" (1995) 49 Int'l Org. 171; M Pollack, "Delegation, Agency, and Agenda Setting in the European Community" (1997) 51 Int'l Org. 99.

[4] A Stone Sweet, "Constitutional Courts and Parliamentary Democracy" (2002) 25 West Eur. Pol. 77.

[5] LR Helfer and A-M Slaughter, "Toward a Theory of Effective Supranational Adjudication" (1997) 107 Yale L.J. 273; E Posner and J Yoo, "Judicial Independence in International Tribunals" (2005) 93 Calif. L.R. 1; LR Helfer and A-M Slaughter, "Why States Create International Tribunals: A Response to Professors Posner and Yoo" (2005) 93 Calif. L.R. 889.

[6] Garrett, note 3; G Garrett, RD Kelemen, and H Schulz, "The European Court of Justice, National Governments, and Legal Integration in the European Union" (1998) 52 Int'l Org. 149; G Garrett and BR Weingast, "Ideas, Interests and Institutions: Constructing the European Community's Internal Market" in J Goldstein and RO Keohane (eds), *Ideas and Foreign Policy: Beliefs, Institutions, and Political Change* (Ithica, NY: Cornell University Press 1993) 173–206.

[7] A-M Burley and W Mattli, "Europe before the Court: A Political Theory of Legal Integration" (1993) 47 Int'l. Org. 41; W Mattli and A-M Slaughter, "Revisiting the European Court of Justice" (1998) 52 Int'l. Org. 177; KJ Alter and S Meunier-Aitsahalia, "Judicial Politics in the European Community European Integration and the Pathbreaking Cassis de Dijon Decision" (1994) 26 Comp. Pol. Stud. 535.

same European Court of Justice (ECJ) cases. More recent literature has started to take advantage of the increasing caseload of international courts to examine the question in more disaggregated ways. As a result, the study of international judicial behavior is starting to look more like the study of domestic judicial behavior, although the volume of work in the international arena is still quite limited.

The provisionary evidence for and against governmental influence is mixed and disputed. Below, I break down the evidence in terms of three different charges of judicial bias resulting from government influence.

2.1 Home-state bias

The most straightforward claim is that judges are more lenient toward their home states than to others. Evidence for this proposition can only come from courts where judges both frequently assess their own government's behavior and where the positions of individual judges can be observed because dissents are allowed. The earliest evidence for this proposition comes from the International Court of Justice (ICJ),[8] where judges were found to have voted in favor of their home state about 85 to 90 percent of the time.[9] Similar percentages are found in the European Court of Human Rights (ECTHR), where evidence is available from over 10,000 cases.[10] In both courts, the incidence of judges voting in favor of their home states is statistically significantly different from non-home-state voting behavior.

While judges indisputably display national bias in their rulings, the reasons for this result are open to interpretation. The principal-agent explanation is that governments retain control over the appointment and reappointment of judges. Judges who care about their career prospects should thus be sensitive to government interests. By contrast, one could claim that home-state bias results from cultural or sociological processes. It may be that judges identify more with the claims made by their governments not because they fear losing their jobs, but for reasons similar to why people root for their national teams in soccer tournaments. Or, it could be that judges have a deeper understanding of the legal system of their home states, and are thus more receptive to arguments for why a national legal system seemingly departs from international standards.

This debate cannot be settled conclusively. Some evidence does suggest that career motivations are relevant. Judges of the European Court of Human Rights

[8] I Ro Suh, "Voting Behavior of National Judges in International Courts" (1969) 63 AJIL 224; TR Hensley, "National Bias and the International Court of Justice" (1968) 12 Midwest J. Pol. Sci. 568.

[9] E Posner and M de Figuerido, "Is the International Court of Justice Biased?" (2005) 34 J. Legal Stud. 599.

[10] E Voeten, "The Impartiality of International Judges: Evidence from the European Court of Human Rights" (2008) 102 Am. Pol. Sci. Rev. 417, 417–33.

(ECtHR), who will reach the mandatory retirement age by the end of their terms, show significantly less national bias than judges who face reappointment pressures (controlling for time served on a court).[11] Ad hoc judges, who are appointed on a case-by-case basis, have much stronger national bias than regular judges. Moreover, judges from poorer countries, for whom the salary of an international judge is presumably more attractive relative to their prospects in private practice, display more national bias than judges from richer countries.[12] There is little direct evidence for cultural arguments. For example, national bias does not increase or decrease in specific legal cultures, or at different levels of domestic judicial independence.[13] Yet culture may matter in ways that are more difficult to observe directly.

While careerist motivations are unseemly to some, they have relatively straightforward institutional solutions. For example, longer, non-renewable terms, as the ECtHR recently implemented, should help reduce national bias if career motivations are to blame, but would be of little use if culture is primarily responsible. The literature also finds that judges who had previous careers as diplomats exhibit more national bias than other judges.[14] Thus, implementing longer, nonrenewable terms and reforming selection procedures so as to minimize the presence of former diplomats may be the most effective ways to reduce home-state bias.

While national bias is relatively easy to demonstrate, it ultimately might not matter much for international justice. Judicial decisions are made by panels where the national judge is at most one of seven (regular ECtHR Chambers) or one of nine (ICJ) judges, so they are unlikely to be pivotal. I estimated that out of the ECtHR's first 10,000 judgments, national bias led to about a dozen rulings in which the ECtHR did not find a violation against a state, but would have ruled differently had all judges been non-nationals.[15] However, this result may understate the true problem because this study did not look at admissibility decisions, for which national judges often have a bigger say. Moreover, it may be that effective nationals can sway their colleagues through persuasion or strategic coalition formation. Still, the home-state bias is manageable and may be outweighed by the benefits of expertise and language abilities such judges bring to the table. How this trade-off works out depends on the institutional insulation of judges and the context of each court.

[11] Voeten, note 10, at 417–33. [12] Voeten, note 10, at 417–33.

[13] Voeten, note 10, at 417–33.

[14] Voeten, note 10, at 417–33; FJ Bruinsma, "Judicial Identities in the European Court of Human Rights" in A van Hoek et al., (eds), *Multilevel Governance in Enforcement and Adjudication* (Cambridge: Intersentia 1996) 203–40.

[15] Bruinsma, note 14.

2.2 Geopolitical biases

A second and potentially farther-reaching concern is that judges may more broadly represent the geopolitical interests of their national governments on international courts. If this is so, then judges really are just "diplomats in robes." These concerns are greatest on tribunals that resolve high-stakes inter-state disputes, such as the WTO and the ICJ.[16]

The most influential article that examines this claim is Eric Posner and Miguel de Figueiredo's study of bias at the ICJ.[17] In a quantitative study of all ICJ decisions, they found that judges favor governments with wealth levels and political systems that are similar to their own. However, they found no evidence that judges are influenced by regional or military alliances. Posner and Figueiredo do not take this as direct evidence for strategic bias as it may be possible that judges simply vote in ways that reflect their own psychological or philosophical preferences. There is considerable room for further exploration of this question.[18] For example, scholars could look at the correspondence between the UN General Assembly voting records of countries and ICJ judges.

Evidence from the WTO is more difficult to come by given that heterogeneity among judges is not so easily observable there. We do know that the United States and the European Union go through great pains to ensure that judicial appointees to the Appellate Body (AB) have judicial philosophies that meet their preferences.[19] Moreover, empirical research strongly suggests that third party submissions by governments influence decision-making and judicial reasoning.[20] Yet, governments do not have clear mechanisms to hold individual AB members accountable, and we have no information about how individual panel decisions were reached. This limits our ability to speculate on judicial motivations.

For most international courts, governments have been quite willing to step away from control mechanisms that allow them to directly influence judges to represent their political interests. This makes sense as courts are supposed to increase the credibility of states' commitments to promoting free trade, not expropriating

16 Indeed, there is little evidence for this claim on the ECtHR. See Voeten, note 10.

17 See Posner and de Figuerido, note 9; see also E Posner, "The Decline of the International Court of Justice" in S Voigt, M Albert, and D Schmidtchen (eds), *International Conflict Resolution* (Tübingen: Mohr Siebeck 2006) 111–42.

18 Quite surprisingly given the level of controversy this article invoked, I have not found a follow-up study that looks at this data.

19 R Steinberg, "Judicial Lawmaking at the WTO: Discursive, Constitutional, and Political Constraints" (2004) 98 AJIL 247; M Elsig and MA Pollack, "Agents, Trustees, and International Courts: Nomination and Appointment of Judicial Candidates in the WTO Appellate Body," (2011) paper prepared for presentation at the 4th Annual Conference on the Political Economy of International Organizations (Zurich).

20 M Busch and K Pelc, "The Politics of Judicial Economy at the World Trade Organization" (2010) 64 Int'l. Org. 257; M Busch and E Reinhardt, "Three's a Crowd: Third Parties and WTO Dispute Settlement" (2006) 58 World Pol. 446.

investments, respecting human rights, and so on. If international judges were simply diplomats in robes, then courts would not serve the purposes that states intended when they created these courts. This does not mean that judges cannot be swayed by governments, but neither theory nor evidence lead us to equate international courts with political intergovernmental organizations.

2.3 Policy and institutional motivations

The most important extra-legal motivations ascribed to judges concern their desire for judgments to be implemented, to influence policy and law, and to increase the legitimacy and authority of their respective court or tribunal.[21] These goals are not identical, but they are related. The first goal, of compliance, is the narrowest. Still, judges may care not just that a decision is narrowly implemented (e.g., compensation for a victim), but also that the underlying policies and practices are altered. Moreover, they may believe compliance is important not just because of the immediate legal or policy implications of their judgments, but also because they might believe that if their judgments are not complied with, their court will ultimately lose legitimacy and authority.

Thus, there is a clear link between the desires for compliance and the goal of institutional legitimacy. Yet there can also be tensions between these goals. A court that simply maximizes compliance would take "easy" decisions that require few if any meaningful adjustments from governments. This gives rise to the criticism that good news about compliance may not necessarily be good news for law-based cooperation.[22] Clearly, a court's institutional legitimacy depends not just on compliance but also on the degree to which a court issues consistent, high-quality rulings that are motivated by the law. Thus, courts that want to enhance their legitimacy will sometimes have to adopt rulings that go against the wishes of the powerful.

This tension between legal and political pressures leads judges and courts to act strategically; i.e., they anticipate how their audiences will respond to their rulings and adjust rulings accordingly.[23] For example, Daniel Kelemen described decision-making by the ECJ and the WTO on disputes that involve trade and environmental claims as a strategic trade-off between pressures for legal consistency and

[21] See, e.g., L Baum, "What Judges Want: Judges' Goals and Judicial Behavior" (1994) 47 Political Research Quarterly 749.

[22] G Downs, DM Rocke, and PN Barsoom, "Is the Good News About Compliance Good News About Cooperation?" (1996) 50 Int'l. Org. 379.

[23] For information on strategic judicial behavior, see: L Epstein and J Knight, "Toward a Strategic Revolution in Judicial Politics: A Look Back, A Look Ahead" (2000) 53 Political Research Quarterly 625. An application to international courts is discussed in: RD Kelemen, "The Limits of Judicial Power: Trade-Environment Disputes in the GATT/WTO and the EU" (2001) 34 Comp. Pol. Stud. 622.

appeasing powerful audiences.[24] Debates between principal-agent theorists and proponents of the trustee perspective have concentrated on the strength of these political pressures. Advocates of the trustee perspective maintain that most courts are well insulated from political pressures; non-compliance is often a non-issue; and is difficult. Thus, the need for strategic behavior that balances legal and political pressures is minimal. By contrast, advocates of the principal-agent perspective emphasize the political pressures on courts.

A heated debate in the *American Political Science Review* about alleged political constraints on ECJ decision-making illustrates the controversy. Clifford Carrubba, Matthew Gabel, and Charles Hankla found that the ECJ was significantly more likely to find in favor of a plaintiff if a governmental third-party had submitted an observation to the court that favored the plaintiff.[25] The researchers interpreted this as evidence that the threat of legislative override affects ECJ behavior. Moreover, they found an additional effect of third-party observations when a government was the litigant. The authors argue that the ECJ depends on third-party enforcement of its decisions. Government litigation supported by many other governments (as evidenced by third party observations) makes such third-party enforcement more credible. This suggests that the ECJ takes the likelihood of compliance into account when ruling against a plaintiff.

In a response article, Alec Stone Sweet and Thomas Brunell have reanalyzed Carrubba, Gabel, and Hankla's data and concluded that, "Neofunctionalism wins in a landslide."[26] They find that legislative override was not a credible threat, and that there were no qualitative examples of legislative override in their data. Moreover, there were no cases in which government observations approached unanimity among EU member states, the threshold for legislative override in virtually all the cases in the data. Stone Sweet and Brunell also observe that, on average, member state observations tend to favor the European Commission as frequently as the plaintiff (i.e., governments frequently file in favor of more active enforcement).

Stone Sweet and Brunell make a strong case against override as a credible threat. Moreover, they make an important point that government observations are often in favor of more active enforcement rather than constraining the court.[27] Indeed, there are many governments whose interests are served very well by active ECJ enforcement against member state infringements.[28] Still, this does not settle the issue of

[24] Kelemen, note 23.

[25] CJ Carrubba, M Gabel, and C Hankla, "Judicial Behavior under Political Constraints: Evidence from the European Court of Justice" (2008) 102 Am. Pol. Sci. Rev. 435.

[26] A Stone Sweet and T Brunell, "The European Court of Justice, State Non-Compliance, and the Politics of Override: Reply to Carrubba, Gabel, and Hankla" (2012) 106 Am. Pol. Sci. Rev. 204.

[27] Stone Sweet and Brunell, note 26.

[28] The finding that some governments willingly appoint activist ECtHR judges is also consistent with this more general point. See Voeten, "The Politics of International Judicial Appointments: Evidence from the European Court of Human Rights" (2007) 61 Int'l. Org. 669. On the ECJ, see also M Malecki,

political influence. Non-compliance remains an issue in the European Union.[29] Moreover, Stone Sweet and Brunell did not offer a strong explanation for why member state observations and ECJ rulings are so strongly correlated. This correlation is not likely to be a purely legal story. For example, the correlation remains robust when controlling for the advocate-general's opinion. Stone Sweet and Brunell interpreted the correlation between member state observations and ECJ rulings as evidence that the court exercises "majoritarian activism." This refers to the tendency of the ECJ to rule against a plaintiff when its policies are out of sync with those in a majority of the other EU states.[30] Under this conceptualization, the ECJ acts as an agent of the majority of EU states when the majority cannot pass its preferred policies and regulations through the regular channels. There is no obvious legal imperative to act this way, except if judges maintain a "living instrument" judicial philosophy in which developing practices and norms help guide interpretation of EU law. Yet it is not clear that this guiding principle for judicial behavior can be so easily distinguished from one where judges care about state practices because they are concerned about implementation.[31] Both suggest strong links between judicial behavior and member state preferences.

The issue of how and to what extent threats of non-compliance and legislative override matter for judicial decision-making is hardly settled. The issue has barely been addressed systematically for courts other than the ECJ, and analyses of the ECJ data can still be improved upon. It is also worth repeating that a finding that political constraints "significantly" influence judicial decision-making does not necessarily undermine the promise of international law. Studies of domestic judicial behavior, including in the United States, frequently report evidence that judges, especially those on constitutional review courts, look to the political branches or public opinion when making important decisions.[32] This does not mean that legal concerns are unimportant. For example, Michael Bailey and Forrest Maltzman carefully unpack legal and political factors, and find that both are important to

"The Politics of Constitutional Review: Evidence from the European Court of Justice," (2009) paper presented at the Annual Meeting of the American Political Science Association.

[29] T Börzel, T Hofmann, and D Panke, "Opinions, Referrals, and Judgments: Analyzing Longitudinal Patterns of Non-compliance" (2009) Berlin Working Paper on European Integration No. 13 (Freie Universität Berlin, Berlin Centre for European Integration).

[30] MP Maduro, *We the Court: The European Court of Justice and the European Economic Constitution* (Oxford: Hart Publishing 1998).

[31] For a more detailed treatment of majoritarian activism, see A Stone Sweet and TL Brunell, "Trustee Courts and the Judicialization of International Regimes: The Politics of Majoritarian Activism in the ECtHR, the EU, and the WTO" J. Law & Courts, forthcoming.

[32] A few examples from the US context are: W Mishler and RS Sheehan, "The Supreme Court as a Countermajoritarian Institution? The Impact of Public Opinion on Supreme Court Decisions" (1993) 87 Am. Pol. Sci. Rev. 87; G Caldeira and J Wright, "Organized Interests and Agenda Setting in the U.S. Supreme Court" (1998) 82 Am. Pol. Sci. Rev. 1109.

a different degree for different cases and justices.[33] The study they undertook required extensive coding of precedent and statements by politicians. Datasets on international court judgments do not have this degree of detail—yet. The bigger point, though, is that debates about political influence are hardly unique to international courts.

Another parallel with domestic judicial behavior is the role of judicial philosophies in both appointments and decision-making. Just as Democratic US presidents are more likely to appoint judges that express liberal leaning philosophies on the bench, more pro-European governments are more likely to appoint more "activist" ECtHR judges.[34] Activism in this context refers to the extent to which judges reject claims that governments should have a wide margin of appreciation in implementing the obligations from the European Convention on Human Rights. Similar anecdotal evidence that partisan politics matters exists for the European Court of Justice.[35] This finding suggests that governments may influence judicial decision-making even if they cannot directly sanction judges for non-performance.

The downside of this is that international judges may not be selected only for their competence. As an independent evaluation of the ECtHR appointment process concluded: "Even in the most established democracies, nomination often rewards political loyalty more than merit."[36] Yet there is also a silver lining to this finding: it suggests that some accountability is operative in the sense that the ideological views of the winners of elections get greater representation on the courts than those of the losers. This can provide some counterweight to charges that international courts enhance the democratic deficit of international institutions by creating positions of authority for unaccountable judges.

Numerous other theories by political scientists and legal scholars are built around the assumption that international judges act strategically to make their judgments more effective. Tom Ginsburg and Richard McAdams, for example, argue that the ICJ's lack of enforcement power means that it is more effective when it constructs rulings that create focal points to resolve coordination dilemmas than when its judgments simply impose solutions.[37] Marc Busch and Krzysztof Pelc argue that WTO panels often invoke judicial economy when the broader WTO membership is ambivalent about the precedential consequences of a ruling.[38] These types of

[33] M Bailey and F Maltzman, "Does Legal Doctrine Matter? Unpacking Law and Policy Preferences on the U.S. Supreme Court" (2008) 102 Am. Pol. Sci. Rev. 369.

[34] Voeten, note 28.

[35] KJ Alter, "Who Are the 'Masters of the Treaty'? European Governments and the European Court of Justice" (1998) 52 Int'l Org. 121.

[36] J Limbach et al., *Judicial Independence: Law and Practice of Appointments to the European Court of Human Rights* (London: International Centre for the Legal Protection of Human Rights 2003).

[37] T Ginsburg and R McAdams, "Adjudicating in Anarchy: An Expressive Theory of International Dispute Resolution" (2004) 45 Wm. & Mary L. Rev. 1229–39.

[38] Busch and Pelc, note 20, at 257.

strategic theories of judicial—and court—behavior are likely to become increasingly prolific.

2.4 Summary

It is difficult to maintain that international judges are "trustees" according to the purest meaning of the word, that is, individuals who are selected entirely for their expertise and who are left alone by governments to do what they do best: reach quality judgments based solely on legal considerations. Yet there is also no evidence that international judges are simply "diplomats in robes." Judges don't simply do what national or powerful governments tell them to do. Indeed, governments have explicitly and deliberately designed most international courts to reduce this possibility.

As is so often the case, the messy truth lies somewhere in the middle. There is a fair degree of agreement that this is so. Even staunch advocates of the trustee perspective do not argue that judges operate in splendid isolation.[39] The debates are and should be about the extent to which specific control mechanisms do or do not influence judicial decision-making in specific contexts. Indeed, it is somewhat silly to have only one model for the "international judge," not just because they vary in the degree to which they are insulated, but also because the political pressures they experience vary considerably.[40]

Aside from the influence of home-state bias, which is fairly particular to international courts, there are important similarities between domestic and international judges.[41] Like international judges, domestic judicial appointments are often affected by partisan politics. Like international judges, domestic judges are concerned with the policy and institutional implications of their judgments. Moreover, domestic judges vary considerably in their institutional protections. This suggests opportunities for cross-fertilization between the studies of domestic and international judicial behavior where the study of domestic judicial behavior includes countries other than the United States.[42]

[39] See, Alter, note 2.

[40] A useful impression of these varying pressures can be gleaned from interviews with judges on different courts. See especially, D Terris, CPR Romano, and L Swigart, *The International Judge: An Introduction to the Men and Women Who Decide the World's Cases* (Boston, MA: Brandeis University Press 2007).

[41] JK. Staton and WH Moore, "Judicial Power in Domestic and International Politics" (2011) 65 Int'l. Org. 553; Voeten, note 10.

[42] For a terrific overview of the study of comparative judicial politics, see N Tate, "The Literature of Comparative Judicial Politics: A 118 Year Survey" (2006) prepared for presentation at the 20th World Congress of the International Political Science Association (Fukuoka, Japan).

3 Socio-Legal Influences

As international courts have matured, an increasing number of scholars have begun to look beyond interactions between states and international courts. These scholars are interested in the broader social environment in which international courts operate, and indeed in the social environment created by the court itself. Most of these scholars are inspired by sociological rather than political science theories. Sociologically inspired, or Constructivist, theories of international law have focused less on judicial behavior and more on the effects of international law and court judgments.[43] Still, there are at least three tenets of sociologically inspired research on judicial behavior. First, I examine the communication between judges on various international and national courts. Second, I discuss cultural determinants of judicial behavior. Third, I briefly highlight the literature that examines the role of personal characteristics and professional backgrounds. There is somewhat of a geographic disparity in the research here. While the political science literature is heavily concentrated in the United States, the sociological approach has been more influential in continental Europe, with the exception of the transjudicial communication literature. Since I focus on English language literature, this limits the scope of the review somewhat to transjudicial communication.

3.1 Transjudicial communication

National and international judges increasingly communicate with each other both directly or via their judgments, potentially influencing each other's interpretations of legal issues.[44] According to Anne-Marie Slaughter, such "transjudicial communication" has become an integral part of a "new world order,"[45] leading to an emerging "global jurisprudence" created by a "global community of courts."[46] Harold Koh identified three functions for transjudicial communication: informing the interpretation of parallel rules, shedding empirical light on legal issues, and illustrating how

[43] See, e.g., J Brunnee and SJ Toope, "International Law and Constructivism: Elements of an Interactional Theory of International Law" (2000) 39 Colum. J. Transnat'l L. 19; R Goodman and D Jinks, "How to Influence States: Socialization and International Human Rights Law" (2004) 54 Duke L.J. 621.

[44] See, e.g., A Lester, "The Overseas Trade in the American Bill of Rights" (1998) 88 Colum. L Rev. 537; A-M Slaughter, "A Typology of Transjudicial Communication" (1994) 29 U. Rich. L. Rev. 99; see also, in this handbook, Nollkaemper, Ch. 24, for a more detailed discussion of this literature.

[45] A-M Slaughter, *A New World Order* (Princeton University Press 2005).

[46] A-M Slaughter, "A Global Community of Courts" (2003) 44 Harv. Int'l. L. J. 191.

common standards should be applied.[47] Steven Calabresi and Stephanie Zimdahl add "logical reinforcement" as a fourth function.[48]

Most of the literature on this issue is motivated by the influence of international and foreign courts on US courts. Yet the basic logic applies equally to the influence of domestic and international jurisprudence on international courts.[49] The behavioral assumption underlying transjudicial communication theories is generally that judges want their opinions to have influence. Judges who are unwilling to participate in the transjudicial dialogue undermine their ability to influence other courts. As Slaughter put it:

> This *awareness* of constitutional cross-fertilization on a global scale—an awareness of who is citing whom among judges themselves and a concomitant pride in a cosmopolitan judicial outlook—creates an incentive to be both lender and borrower.[50]

The weakness in this literature is that it mostly relies on selective cases that cite external decisions without providing any indication of how common reliance on external decisions is, what may explain variation in this practice, and how influential these citations are.[51] In the context of international courts, many are concerned about the dynamic opposite to the one Slaughter has described: that international law is getting too fragmented[52] as each institution "[h]as a tendency to go its own separate way."[53] Consistent with this sentiment, some argue that the World Trade Organization's (WTO) Dispute Settlement Body and Appellate Body (DSB and AB, respectively) should be more willing to rely on public international law and engage sources other than their founding treaties.[54] By contrast, the Inter-American

[47] HH Koh, "Transnational Legal Process" (1996) 75 Nb. L. Rev. 181; HH Koh, "International Law As Part Of Our Law" (2004) 98 AJIL 43, 43–57.

[48] SG Calabresi and SD Zimdahl, "The Supreme Court and Foreign Sources of Law: Two Hundred Years of Practice and the Juvenile Death Penalty Decision" (2005) 47 Wm. & Mary L. Rev. 743.

[49] A-M Slaughter and D Zaring, "Networking Goes International" (2006) 2 Ann. Rev. L. & Soc. Sci. 211.

[50] Slaughter, note 45, at 74–5.

[51] For this criticism, see RC Black and L Epstein, "(Re-)Setting the Scholarly Agenda on Transjudicial Communication" (2007) 32 Law & Soc. Inquiry 789.

[52] International Law Commission, "Fragmentation of International Law: Difficulties Arising from the Diversification and Expansion of International Law" (2006) Report of the Study Group of the International Law Commission, Finalized by Martti Koskenniemi. U.N. Doc A/CN.4/L.682.

[53] G Guillaume, "The Proliferation of International Judicial Bodies: The Outlook for the International Legal Order" (October 27, 2000), Speech by His Excellency Judge Gilbert Guillaume, President of the International Court of Justice, to the Sixth Committee of the General Assembly of the United Nations, available at <http://www.icj-cij.org/court/index.php?pr=85&pt=3&p1=1&p2=3&p3=1> accessed July 28, 2013. ICJ Presidents focused on the fragmentation of international law due to the proliferation of international tribunals in three consecutive annual speeches to the UN General Assembly. M Koskenniemi and P Leino, "Fragmentation of International Law? Postmodern Anxieties" (2002) 15 Leiden J. Int'l L. 553.

[54] J Pauwelyn, "The Role of Public International Law in the WTO: How Far Can We Go?" (2001) 95 AJIL 535.

Court of Human Rights (IACtHR) has been accused for being too creative in its use of external judicial decisions, thus undermining regional support for the court.[55] Similarly, the International Criminal Tribunal for the Former Yugoslavia (ICTY) has relied heavily on external court decisions and international customary law to motivate an expansive reading of its mandate.[56]

Why then do some international courts and judges extensively cite decisions from other courts, whereas others do not? The initial evidence suggests that there are large asymmetries in the extent to which international courts rely on one another's jurisprudence, thus contradicting the argument that transjudicial communication is driven by reciprocity principles.[57] Moreover, ECtHR judges sometimes refrain from external citations for strategic reasons. They are more likely to cite external decisions in separate, rather than majority, opinions, and some of the more "activist" judges do so more regularly than others. This suggests that, as in the United States, judicial ideology matters.[58] Yet much more research is needed to answer this question. Citations are a poor proxy for influence given that they are not necessarily decisive influences on the ultimate decisions. Relying on citations as evidence of transnational influence may also cause us to *underestimate* that influence if courts have reasons to conceal such influences. For example, Slaughter suggests that the UN Human Rights Committee has copied its reasoning from the ECtHR without making this explicit.[59]

Moreover, there is a disconnect between the transjudicial communication literature and the literature that highlights the strategic interdependencies between international and domestic courts.[60] If international and domestic courts can build strategic alliances, as this latter literature suggests, then this should be reflected in judgments. However, the transjudicial communications literature has mostly ignored strategic imperatives for borrowing and non-borrowing.

The promise of the transjudicial communication literature is that it conceives of international courts as part of a broader network that includes not only governments but also domestic courts, NGOs, IGOs, and others. This literature, however, has not yet adequately charted how precisely all these actors influence international judicial actors. For example, particularly in criminal and human rights tribunals,

[55] GL Neuman, "Import, Export, and Regional Consent in the Inter-American Court of Human Rights" (2008) 19 EJIL 101.

[56] AM Danner, "When Courts Make Law: How the International Criminal Tribunals Recast the Laws of War" (2006) 59 Vand. L. Rev. 1.

[57] E Voeten, "Borrowing and Nonborrowing among International Courts" (2010) 39 J. Legal Stud. 547.

[58] Voeten, note 57, at 547. [59] Slaughter, note 44, at 106.

[60] One classic and one recent example are discussed in JHH Weiler, "The Transformation of Europe" (1991) 100 Yale L.J. 2403; and KJ Alter and LR Helfer, "Nature or Nurture? Judicial Lawmaking in the European Court of Justice and the Andean Tribunal of Justice" (2010) 64 Int'l. Org. 563–92. See also, in this handbook, Huneeus, Ch. 20 for more details on this vast literature.

NGOs play a significant role in the legal process. To what extent do the briefs and other prepared submissions by NGOs influence legal reasoning? Or, indeed, to what extent do legal documents prepared by other international actors, such as international legal bureaucrats who work for IGOs, matter for legal reasoning? Nevertheless, the network approach and the increasingly sophisticated methods that come with it are highly promising.

3.2 Culture

Cultural influences on judicial behavior can be manifold. First, and most obvious, scholars have pondered how judges from different legal cultures come together to create collective judgments and justifications. Some scholars argue that legal reasoning crucially depends on cultural context. For example, Mitchell Lasser argues that legal justification "shapes (and is shaped by) the judicial system that addresses it, thereby conceptually creating and recreating that system's particular argumentative, conceptual, and institutional universe."[61] Sara Mitchell and Emilia Powell have shown that domestic legal culture powerfully shapes the propensity of governments to accept the compulsory jurisdiction of international courts and the design of those courts.[62] A logical corollary, then, is that domestic legal culture also shapes international judicial behavior. Nevertheless, to the extent that this evidence exists, quantitative[63] and qualitative assessments[64] of judgments, and citation patterns and reasoning, find little evidence for this hypothesis.

A second possibility is that courts develop their own sets of values, norms, and practices that influence how individual judges behave. This research has been shaped by Pierre Bourdieu's work on "legal fields."[65] Bourdieu criticizes both formalists, who view the law as a self-contained system that is autonomous from its social and political environment, and instrumentalists, who conceive of the law as a mere tool in the hands of the powerful. Formalists fail to appropriately acknowledge the influence of those who exercise power outside the legal domain, while instrumentalists do not account for the unique qualities that separate legal practice from

[61] M Lasser, *Judicial Deliberations. A Comparative Analysis of Judicial Transparency and Legitimacy* (Oxford University Press 2004) 298.

[62] S Mitchell and E Powell, *Domestic Law Goes Global: Legal Traditions and International Courts* (Cambridge University Press 2011).

[63] Voeten, note 10; Y Lupu and E Voeten, "Precedent on International Courts: A Network Analysis of Case Citations by the European Court of Human Rights" (2011) 42 Brit. J. Pol. Sci. 413.

[64] N-L Arold, "The European Court of Human Rights as an Example of Convergence" (2007) 76 Nordic J. Int'l L. 305, 320; T Dannenbaum, "Nationality and the International Judge: The Nationalist Presumption Governing the International Judiciary and Why it Must Be Reversed" (2012) 45 Cornell Int'l L. J. 77.

[65] P Bourdieu, "The Force of Law: Toward a Sociology of the Juridical Field" (1986) 38 Hastings L. J. 805.

other social activities. These practices often develop as a consequence of conflict and interaction with those outside the legal field.

In an influential study, Yves Dezalay and Bryant Garth applied this framework to the field of international arbitration and found that Americans from elite law firms acquired a central role, which helped transform the practice of international arbitration into one that resembled the American model more than the continental European one.[66] Others have applied similar frameworks to the spread of American legal values,[67] and have examined the legal practices in human rights, international criminal law, and the construction of Europe.[68] These practices shape how judges and courts perform their daily roles—even if they do not yield precise predictions on how judges will rule on individual cases.

A third way in which culture can affect judicial behavior is through collegial norms. A swath of literature on American judicial behavior suggests that the partisan and/or gender composition of judicial panels affects judges' decisions.[69] Groups of people that deliberately make different decisions than individuals who are left to their own devices. There is no reason this would not be so on international courts. But as far as I can tell, propositions of this type have yet to be investigated in the context of international courts. This is unfortunate as the gender and professional composition of international courts is an issue of considerable institutional importance.

3.3 Roles and backgrounds

Another strand of research examines whether the professional and personal backgrounds of judges shape their behavior on courts. Scholars have observed that international judges come from a wide variety of professional backgrounds, ranging from former diplomats, career judges, academics, and private practitioners, to

[66] Y Dezaley and BG Garth, *Dealing in Virtue: International Commercial Arbitration and the Construction of a Transnational Legal Order* (University of Chicago Press 1996).

[67] B Brake and P Katzenstein, "The Transnational Spread of American Law: Legalization as Soft Power," Working Paper (June 2010), <http://www.iilj.org/courses/documents/HC2010Oct22.Katzenstein.pdf> accessed August 28, 2013.

[68] J Hagan, R Levi, and G Ferrales, "Swaying the Hand of Justice: The Internal and External Dynamics of Regime Change at the International Criminal Tribunal for the Former Yugoslavia" (2006) 31 Law & Soc. Inquiry 585; Y Dezalay and B Garth, "From the Cold War to Kosovo: The Rise and Renewal of the Field of International Human Rights" (2006) 2 Ann. Rev. Law & Soc. Sci. 231; A Cohen and A Vauchez, "The Social Construction of Law: The European Court of Justice and Its Legal Revolution Revisited" (2011) 7 Ann. Rev. Law & Soc. Sci. 417; MR Madsen, "From Cold War Instrument to Supreme European Court: The European Court of Human Rights at the Crossroads of International and National Law and Politics" (2007) 32 Law & Soc. Inquiry. 137. See also, in this handbook, Madsen, Ch. 18 and Vauchez, Ch. 30 for more on this literature.

[69] See, e.g., CR Sunstein, "Deliberative Trouble? Why Groups Go to Extremes" (2000) 110 Yale L.J. 71.

politicians with barely any legal experience. Judges tend to carry their prior identities, expertise, and practices into their new roles as international judges.[70]

Both quantitative and qualitative research provide evidence of this. For example, former diplomats were much more likely to accept the *raison d'état* and thus a higher margin of appreciation for ECtHR member states.[71] Interviews with judges suggest that judges find professional backgrounds "almost more important" than national backgrounds for their work, with judges from different backgrounds preoccupied with different aspects of judicial reasoning, problem solving, and case management.[72] There has been institutional recognition of this too, especially in the context of the International Criminal Court, where judges are now elected from two lists in order to ensure that judicial panels have both knowledge of international criminal law and experience of running criminal trials.[73]

While the role of professional backgrounds has attracted scholarly efforts, relatively little attention has been devoted to personal backgrounds. Perhaps the most obvious personal characteristic of interest is gender, which has attracted a great deal of attention in the domestic literature[74] and is of institutional interest.

3.4 Summary

These three strands of socio-legal research are complementary in their reliance on sociological rather than political science theories as their main sources of theoretical inspiration. Yet they also sometimes have contradictory implications. For example, the literature on professional backgrounds points to important sources of heterogeneity among judges that stems from prior roles, whereas the "field" literature emphasizes the formation of a new, relatively homogenous culture (or fields of international law practice). Moreover, the transjudicial communication literature highlights the common enterprise judges of various stripes engage in, whereas the field literature can be interpreted as leading to potential competition between different fields of judicial practice. These and other sources of tensions between sociological theories should be addressed more explicitly in future literature.

[70] For a discussion of this argument in the domestic context, see L Baum, *Judges and Their Audiences: A Perspective on Judicial Behavior* (Princeton University Press 2006). For an example in the international context, see, Bruinsma, note 14.

[71] Voeten, note 10. [72] Terris et al., note 40, at 64.

[73] The non-permanent international criminal tribunals lacked especially the latter, leading to charges of inefficiency. See M Langer, "The Rise of Managerial Judging in International Criminal Law" (2005) 53 Am. J. Comp. L. 835.

[74] See, e.g., CL Boyd, L Epstein, and AD Martin, "Untangling the Causal Effects of Sex on Judging" (2011) 54 Am. J. Pol. Sci. 389.

4 Conclusions

The study of international judicial behavior is still very much in its infancy. The knowledge reflected in this chapter comes from a relatively small but growing body of research based on relatively few international courts. As international courts continue to issue more decisions, the number of studies will surely expand—as should, hopefully, our understanding of judicial behavior. Within the political science literature, I expect to see an expansion of strategic theories of judicial behavior that take seriously the notion that judges care both about legal consistency and the effectiveness of their rulings. Within the sociological literature, I expect to see more sophisticated analyses of the network of courts and judges, and how they interact and affect each other—albeit not always harmoniously. I also expect more Bourdieu-inspired studies of fields of practice.

The sociological literature has largely developed parallel to the political science literature with few cross-citations. This is unfortunate as there are numerous areas for cross-fertilization. The extent to which governments can and cannot influence judges cannot be seen as an entirely separate question from other sociological influences that lead judges to form separate sets of practices. There is some hope that this might change as some of the sociological approaches are becoming more mainstream in political science.[75] Additional tension exists between the legal field and the social sciences. The history of the study of judicial behavior in the United States provides little encouragement that this tension will be fully resolved.

Research Questions

1. Which mechanisms are the most and least effective ways for governments to influence judicial behavior?
2. Do changes or cross-court variation in the selection procedures of international judges correlate with changes in international judicial behavior?
3. Does judicial reasoning affect the effectiveness of international court judgments?
4. How do personal characteristics, such as gender, influence international judicial behavior?
5. How do network relationships influence international court rulings?

[75] See, e.g., E Adler and V Pouliot (eds), *International Practices* (Cambridge University Press 2011).

Suggested Reading

Alter, KJ, "Agents or Trustees? International Courts in their Political Context" (2008) 14 Eur. J. Int'l Rel. 33.

Baum, L, *Judges and Their Audiences: A Perspective on Judicial Behavior* (Princeton University Press 2006).

Carrubba, CJ, Gabel, M, and Hankla, C, "Judicial Behavior under Political Constraints: Evidence from the European Court of Justice" (2008) 102 Am. Pol. Sci. Rev. 435.

Dezaley, Y and Garth, BG, *Dealing in Virtue: International Commercial Arbitration and the Construction of a Transnational Legal Order* (University of Chicago Press 1996).

Epstein, L and Knight, J, *The Choices Justices Make* (Washington D.C.: CQ Press 1998).

Hafner-Burton, EM, Victor, DG, and Lupu, Y, "Political Science Research on International Law: The State of the Field" (2011) 106 AJIL 47.

Shaffer, G and Ginsburg, T, "The Empirical Turn in International Legal Scholarship" (2012) 106(1) AJIL 1.

Slaughter, AM, "A Global Community of Courts" (2003) Harv. Int'l. L. J. 191.

Staton, JK and Moore, WH, "Judicial Power in Domestic and International Politics" (2011) 65 Int'l Org. 553.

Stone Sweet, A, and Brunell, T, "The European Court of Justice, State Non-Compliance, and the Politics of Override: Reply to Carrubba, Gabel, and Hankla" (1998)" (2012) 106(1) Am. Pol. Sci. Rev. 204–13.

Terris, D, Romano, CPR, and Swigart, L, *The International Judge: An Introduction to the Men and Women Who Decide the World's Cases* (Boston, MA: Brandeis University Press 2007).

Voeten, E, "The Impartiality of International Judges: Evidence from the European Court of Human Rights" (2008) 102 Am. Pol. Sci. Rev. 417.

CHAPTER 26

WHO LITIGATES AND WHY

NATALIE KLEIN*

1 Introduction

Determining who litigates and why are fascinating questions. Which states or non-state entities use international courts to achieve their goals? There are many ways to respond to this question. The answer may be sought from empirical research. Data could be sought from each known international court or tribunal to indicate what states have appeared or which nationals have been participants in international

* Dean, Macquarie Law School, Macquarie University, Sydney, Australia. The author acknowledges the assistance of Shaun Star, Hiruni Alwishewa, and Tejas Thete in gathering data for this chapter.

proceedings. The current landscape of international courts and tribunals indicates that such an exercise would be an immense task. While this chapter inevitably considers some numbers, the purpose is for impression rather than detailed statistical accuracy. In answering "who litigates," we need to think about the legal parameters involved and consider how we can explain who is, or is not, involved in litigation before international courts and tribunals. Numbers will explain part of the story, but other explanatory variables—such as the relative power of the participants, their internal government structures, the economic differences between the parties, the relative importance of the issues in dispute, and the social and political goals—will be important to consider as well.

The jurisdictional parameters of any international court or tribunal are one point at which to begin questioning who litigates. There is much to consider leading into the creation of jurisdiction in any given context, and whether that jurisdiction is ultimately exercised. In examining who litigates and why, the chapter proceeds as follows. Section 2 considers that while the existence of jurisdiction is essentially a question of law, there are different ways to explain why jurisdiction may or may not be available, and then why any particular international actor may select, or be compelled, to participate in a particular court or tribunal. Some explanatory paradigms are briefly described in this part. Section 3 examines in more detail which states have resorted to international litigation and what circumstances allowed for recourse to this mode of dispute settlement. Section 4 addresses the access of non-state actors to international courts and tribunals. It is noted in this regard that the judicial engagement of non-state actors largely depends on the willingness of states to create these avenues. Recurrent themes in this regard relate to distribution of power and national interest, as well as the perceived effectiveness of litigation.

We will see that there are many different ways that states and non-state actors gain access to international courts and tribunals to resolve their disputes, but availability of these mechanisms does not necessarily guarantee their use. As such, a more interesting question is why states refrain from relying on international courts or tribunals when the option exists. Related questions are why states would refuse to become parties to regimes that allow for the resolution of disputes by international litigation, or why states would not agree to the inclusion of litigation for dispute resolution when constructing new legal regimes. It is perhaps then the use of ad hoc courts or tribunals—which involve post hoc consent to jurisdiction—that may provide more fruitful ground for explaining who litigates. The answers to these questions may ultimately be quite speculative, or highly individualistic in relation to a particular state or dispute. The aim of this chapter is to provide some revelations of who is litigating, and suggest how these practices may be explained. Is it possible to find common ground relating to international litigation—or international relations more generally—to explain why states are more or less inclined to litigate? This chapter concludes by laying out the fertile ground for future research from a variety of perspectives.

2 Explanatory Paradigms—An Overview

It is difficult to discern why a particular state might agree to litigate a dispute, or why a state might agree to create a mechanism for non-state actors to pursue litigation either against it or against other states. State decision-making necessarily involves a variety of actors among politicians, bureaucrats, lobbyists, and the media, and it must take into account a tremendous number of factors beyond the legal questions at issue. These considerations include inter alia economic dimensions, social significance, cultural considerations, and political interests. To explain why states decide to litigate, recourse may be sought among some of the key international legal and international relations theories. A selection of these theories is briefly surveyed below to provide a context for the subsequent discussion on the actual practice of states.

2.1 Liberal

The sheer growth in the number of international courts and tribunals, and the increase in compulsory jurisdiction for some of these courts and tribunals, suggest that there is an increasing legalization of international disputes.[1] The growing trend toward litigation can be attributed to greater adherence to the rule of law as a fundamental principle of the international legal order. Consistent with the key tenets of the UN Charter, disputes are to be resolved through peaceful means, including the use of international courts and tribunals, rather than the use of force or coercive tactics stopping short of the use of force.

A liberal perspective prompts inquiry beyond the abstract entity of states to the governments that are the critical decision-makers in those states.[2] Anne-Marie Slaughter has suggested that treaties exclusively between parties whose governments respect human rights, the market, and periodic elections are more likely to be characterized by "deep" cooperation, which then facilitates enforcement via binding dispute settlement.[3] Characterizing governments as "liberal" or "non-liberal" may make it possible to predict with greater certainty whether those states will comply and enforce their international legal obligations. The increasing number of

[1] See RO Keohane, A Moravcsik, and A-M Slaughter, "Legalized Dispute Resolution: Interstate and Transnational" (2000) 54 Int'l. Org. 457.

[2] See Keohane, Moravcsik, and Slaughter, note 1, at 537. See also A-M Slaughter, "The Real New World Order" (1997) 76 Foreign Affairs 183.

[3] See e.g., A-M Slaughter, "International Law in a World of Liberal States" (1995) 6 EJIL 503.

democratic states may align with the growth in reliance on law and legal structures for resolving disputes.

This perspective suggests that liberal states will be those most inclined to turn to international courts or tribunals to resolve their disputes where jurisdiction exists. It may well be that the combination of democratic institutions, economic interests, and cultural value attached to the rule of law make liberal states more inclined to view international litigation in their national interest when choosing or creating modes of dispute settlement.

2.2 Realism

According to a realist perspective, an analysis of which states and non-state actors pursue international litigation must take into account the self-interests being promoted, and how the use of litigation will assert the power of the entity initiating litigation vis-à-vis the other party. For states, a decision on whether to litigate or not will be intensely political because assessments will be driven by both the national interests at stake and the relative gains that may be achieved from litigation. These are factors that might be intimately connected with the legal questions at issue or might stand distinctly from them, depending on the circumstances of each case. For non-state actors, their relative power against a defendant state can depend on their nationality and the support they receive both diplomatically and in the legal proceedings from their state of nationality.[4] A realist perspective demands that priority be accorded to the political interests and power dynamics involved in any decision to litigate.

A realist paradigm can help explain compliance, or lack thereof, in relation to international litigation. If a state fails to comply with a decision of an international court, it is easy to say that the state in question did not consider it in its interest to accept the ruling. Its relative power position in relation to the litigant, or perhaps in relation to international or regional pressure, would also be great enough to withstand censure for failure to comply. An initial assessment as to whether one state will opt to litigate against another may take into account whether compliance will be, or will need to be, forthcoming. The likelihood of compliance then reflects on the perceived effectiveness of international adjudication for resolving international disputes.

[4] This dynamic is more readily identifiable in relation to investor-state arbitrations or claims commissions, rather than situations in which an individual is bringing a claim against his or her own state for human rights violations.

2.3 Knowledge-based theories

In contrast to the rationalist perspective of international law and relations—which is inherent to liberal and realist approaches—an alternative way of understanding state action focuses on knowledge and ideas. Scholars adhering to this perspective consider from where knowledge and ideas are drawn and how they influence interaction between international actors. Within these schools of thought, "constructivism" has highlighted the importance of identity, or how an actor's self-conception and conception of other actors and their respective goals influence their interaction.[5] This process of evaluation has been used to assess compliance and effectiveness of international law.

Within the dispute settlement context, constructivists argue that states that interact on a regular basis may be more inclined to entrust disputes to international litigation. However, they are hesitant to opt for this form of dispute settlement with states with which they have fewer connections. This suggests that where a state has a greater knowledge of the other state, their cooperation is more likely in resolving disputes, and improved understanding of the structures of the international system and the actors involved will enhance relationships over time.[6] Effectiveness of international adjudication will be enhanced in this regard. Where the states in dispute have an intense relationship, there is greater potential for leveraging and linkage of issues for each state to use in seeking to persuade the other state to agree on a particular outcome for the dispute itself, or on the procedures to be used in resolving the dispute.

2.4 Developing country perspectives

The ability to institute international litigation may be considered by developing countries as a useful tool to counter-balance coercive behavior by developed states in a negotiating setting. By turning to an international court or tribunal, a developing country is able to call on a third party—often one that represents many different states—and change the bilateral dynamic at play. In this regard, international litigation may be viewed as an opportunity to allow a focus on law as the means to resolve a dispute rather than permitting economic or power interests to prevail.

However, a concern exists that developing states are not necessarily well-served by international litigation. The expense of running international legal proceedings may prove prohibitive, and there may be financial and political costs that accrue

[5] See e.g., A Wendt, "Collective Identity Formation and the International State" (1994) 88 American Political Science Review 384, 385–6.

[6] See A Hasenclever, P Mayer, and V Rittberger, *Theories of International Regimes* (Cambridge University Press 1997) 188–90.

outside the actual litigation. For example, a developed country may restrict aid or other services provided to the developing country while another aspect of their bilateral relationship is litigated. In this situation, international litigation does not provide an effective means to resolve disputes for these states; they may be less inclined to resort to international courts and tribunals as a result.

A developing country perspective leads us to question whether international courts and tribunals are sufficiently open to taking into account the particular circumstances and experiences of developing countries in the interpretation and application of international law. The substantive body of international law as applied by international courts and tribunals may be criticized as too Western in its focus, and more likely to favor the developed states that were most influential in the creation and evolution of that law. Even where developing countries' specific interests are recognized, as may be seen in the Dispute Settlement Understanding (DSU) of the World Trade Organization (WTO), the application of these principles has been criticized as responding poorly to developing countries' needs.[7] Concerns about the likely interpretation and application of international law may therefore influence the prospective engagement of developing states in international litigation.

2.5 New stream or new approaches to international law

Building on critical legal studies scholarship, theorists have challenged positivist perspectives of international law by showing indeterminacy and contradiction in legal rules, as well as by questioning fictional presentations of international law and its operation. One particular dimension of this enterprise has been to look beyond states as the sole actors in the international system so as to explain the enhanced role for non-state actors in international litigation. The engagement of individuals in resolving disputes that would have previously been resolved in inter-state settings may be explained through a reduced emphasis on state sovereignty and greater recognition of individuals and organizations as rights bearers and subjects of international law.

Beyond those engaged in international litigation proper, the growth and influence of epistemic communities may also explain why international litigation is pursued as a means of dispute settlement. The substantive political values engaged in this regard may then be recognized. Well-organized and well-resourced non-governmental organizations have been able to rally attention to particular

[7] See e.g., G Bercero and P Garzotti, "DSU Reform: What are the Understanding Issues?" in D Georgiev and K Borght (eds), *Reform and Development of the WTO Dispute Settlement System* (London: Cameron May 2006) 123, 145–6; A Alavi, "On the (Non-) Effectiveness of the WTO Special and Differential Treatments in the Dispute Settlement Process" (2007) 41 Journal of World Trade Law 319.

causes and, in democratic societies, influence politicians and government officials who decide whether a dispute should be resolved through an international court or tribunal. These communities are increasingly seeking avenues to participate in international litigation, though their participation is still predominantly indirect through the submission of *amicus* briefs. The criticism of the influence of these communities is that there could be a particular set of values being pursued that are not aligned with other participants in the dispute settlement process. Confidence in the use of international litigation to achieve a state's goals may be undermined in this situation.

Each of these theories highlights particular characteristics of the actors that are likely to be engaged in international litigation: their democratic structure, political power, economic strength, and national values and interests. These traits also influence why states have, or have not, created or accepted jurisdiction from the outset. From our understanding of what might explain why an actor establishes or resorts to international litigation, the next two sections of this chapter seek to examine when particular states and non-state entities are turning to international courts or tribunals to resolve disputes or otherwise promote their international or national agenda. This analysis takes into account how well any of these explanatory paradigms may assist our understanding of who litigates, and furthers our investigation of whether there are common explanations as to who litigates in the international system.

3 Which States Litigate and Why

This section considers the different permanent courts and in what circumstances states can access them for the resolution of their disputes. It further analyzes what sort of cases are referred to these courts, which states bring these cases, and which prefer not to utilize international adjudication or arbitration for the resolution of their disputes. In this regard, we examine participation in mandatory and pseudo-mandatory regimes, as well as participation in ad hoc and *ex post* arbitration or adjudication. As foreshadowed above, the explanatory paradigms are brought to bear in order to assist an understanding of who litigates.

3.1 International Court of Justice

There are two obvious measures that can be used to analyze who litigates at the ICJ. First, which states have accepted the compulsory jurisdiction of the court under

Art. 36(2) of the court's Statute? Second, which states have actually instituted proceedings, either on the basis of the optional clause or by other means?[8] In relation to the first point, 67 states have accepted in advance the court's jurisdiction,[9] which reflects less than a third of the UN membership. Moreover, many of these acceptances are subject to a variety of reservations.

An alternative means of triggering the court's jurisdiction is under a compromissory clause in a treaty or an optional protocol on dispute settlement attached to a treaty. While it may be supposed that the risks associated with allowing a third party to issue a binding decision may prompt states to avoid litigation for highly charged political issues, this assumption is not supported by the widespread use of compromissory clauses consenting to the jurisdiction of the ICJ. In a 2009 publication, Christian Tams noted that there were almost 300 treaties that included compromissory clauses.[10] In reviewing the subject matter of the treaties containing such clauses, Tams concluded:

> [M]any treaties governing important aspects of international relations envisage recourse to the ICJ at the instigation of one party. The potential for ICJ litigation over controversial and highly divisive questions of international relations thus is much bigger than is usually assumed.[11]

The necessary question that then arises is the extent that states have relied on such clauses in instituting proceedings, particularly for the "controversial and highly divisive questions of international relations." Tams observed in this regard that 51 of 114 contentious cases (as of 2007) were "based on compromissory clauses (either exclusively or in relation with other bases of jurisdiction); [this] clearly exceeds that of joint applications and equals that of optional clause proceedings."[12] Yet there has been a trend away from including compromissory clauses in treaties in recent decades.[13]

The other principal way for states to accept the court's jurisdiction is through an *ex post* agreement. The use of special agreements is notable because it reflects instances in which states have taken a decisive step to select adjudication as the means to resolve their dispute. Sixteen cases have been referred to the ICJ on the basis of special agreement.[14] The countries involved span nearly all geographic regions of the

[8] See ICJ Statute, Art. 36(1).

[9] For a full list, see ICJ, Declarations Recognizing the Jurisdiction of the Court as Compulsory <www.icj-cij.org/jurisdiction/index.php?p1=5&p2=1&p3=3> accessed April 22, 2013.

[10] CJ Tams, "The Continued Relevance of Compromissory Clauses as a Source of ICJ Jurisdiction" (June 3, 2009) <http://dx.doi.org/10.2139/ssrn.1413722> accessed September 24, 2013. Tams further notes that there were between 400 and 500 treaties establishing the jurisdiction of the Permanent Court of International Justice, to which the ICJ could refer cases by virtue of Art. 36(5) of its Statute.

[11] Tams, note 10. [12] Tams, note 10. [13] Tams, note 10.

[14] The following 16 cases were submitted to the court by means of special agreements (by date of their addition to the General List): *Asylum (Colombia/Peru)* [1950] ICJ Rep 266; *Minquiers and Ecrehos (France/United Kingdom)* [1953] ICJ Rep 47; *Sovereignty over Certain Frontier Land*

world. Supporting a liberal paradigm, many of the litigants are democracies. Both developed and developing states have been engaged in *ex post* agreements to adjudicate, although not typically in a developed versus developing state framework.

The cases before the ICJ, based on special agreement, have primarily concerned territorial and border disputes. From a realist perspective, we may wonder why two states would agree to adjudication once a dispute has arisen and one state has the advantage of being in physical occupation of the territory in question.[15] Why would the occupying state potentially agree to vacate the land in dispute if the court finds against its claims? Potential hypotheses to consider here include potential side benefits in other aspects of the bilateral relationship, the influence of a third state interposing itself in the dispute, the subjective value of the territory to the states concerned and/or values attached to a "win" in the case, and the political cover provided to a state in its internal politics by a decision of an international court.[16]

In maritime boundary disputes, there is a clearer need to resolve the disagreement because the resources in the disputed area cannot readily be exploited until title is settled.[17] Yet a realist frame would still be unhelpful in this situation, as the more powerful state may prefer to remain in a negotiating setting where it can bring superior economic or political power to bear.[18]

A careful assessment should be made not only of the legal merits of a case, but also the political, economic, and social interests involved for any state deciding whether adjudication at the ICJ will provide an effective means for resolving (parts of) a dispute.[19] There are no clear commonalities between litigating states that could

(Belgium/Netherlands [1959] ICJ Rep 209); *North Sea Continental Shelf (Federal Republic of Germany/Denmark)*; *Federal Republic of Germany/Netherlands* [1969] ICJ Rep 3); *Continental Shelf (Tunisia/Libyan Arab Jamahiriya)* [1982] ICJ Rep 18; *Delimitation of the Maritime Boundary in the Gulf of Maine Area (Canada/United States of America)* [1984] ICJ Rep 246 (case referred to a Chamber); *Continental Shelf (Libyan Arab Jamahiriya/Malta)* [1985] ICJ Rep 13; *Frontier Dispute (Burkina Faso/Republic of Mali)* [1986] ICJ Rep 554 (case referred to a Chamber); *Land, Island and Maritime Frontier Dispute (El Salvador/Honduras)* [1992] ICJ Rep 350 (case referred to a Chamber); *Territorial Dispute (Libyan Arab Jamahiriya/Chad)* [1994] ICJ Rep 6; *Gabcíkovo-Nagymaros Project (Hungary/Slovakia)* [1997] ICJ Rep 7; *Kasikili/Sedudu Island (Botswana/Namibia)* [1999] ICJ Rep 1045; *Sovereignty over Pulau Ligitan and Pulau Sipadan (Indonesia/Malaysia)* [2002] ICJ Rep 625; *Frontier Dispute (Benin/Niger)* [2005] ICJ Rep 90 (referred to a Chamber); and *Sovereignty over Pedra Branca/Pulau Batu Puteh, Middle Rocks and South Ledge (Malaysia/Singapore)* [2008] ICJ Rep 12.

[15] See L Brilmayer and A Faure, "Initiating Territorial Adjudication: The Who, How, When and Why of Litigating Contested Sovereignty" in N Klein (ed.), *Litigating International Law Disputes: Weighing the Options* (Cambridge University Press, forthcoming).

[16] Brilmayer and Faure, note 15.

[17] L Brilmayer and N Klein, "Land and Sea: Two Sovereignty Regimes in Search of a Common Denominator" (2000–2001) 33 NYU J. Int'l. L. & Pol. 703.

[18] See e.g., Treaty on Certain Maritime Arrangements in the Timor Sea (Australia–Timor Leste) (January 12, 2006) [2007] ATS 12.

[19] See e.g., DD Fischer, "Decisions to Use the International Court of Justice: Four Recent Cases" (1982) 26 International Studies Quarterly 251.

reveal which are most likely to litigate at the ICJ, except for highlighting the ever relevant dimension of national interest for the states concerned.

3.2 Participation in mandatory dispute settlement regimes

Whether a state is likely to use a particular international court or tribunal might well depend on the substantive regime that governs the dispute, and whether adjudication or arbitration is a key mode of dispute settlement in that regime. While the ICJ represents an example of a court having compulsory jurisdiction for those states that choose in advance to accept it, other multilateral and regional regimes essentially create mandatory jurisdiction for arbitration or adjudication.

These "regime courts" are different from stand-alone courts, as the former are an integral dimension to the broader legal arrangement and facilitate the enforcement of the legal norms enshrined in those arrangements. In these regimes, states can often choose whether they will become party to the regime or a member of the relevant organization, but there are considerable incentives to participate in the regime so states may take advantage of the substantive rights afforded. The availability of mandatory jurisdiction may be a factor in deciding whether or not to participate,[20] but for those states that do decide to join the treaty or organization, they become future litigants. The further question is then whether or which states are likely to avail themselves of this option for the resolution of disputes that arise in relation to the substantive regime. This practice is examined immediately below.

The inclusion of mandatory jurisdiction was considered pivotal in the drafting of the UN Convention on the Law of the Sea (UNCLOS).[21] Given the large number of compromises that were made during the negotiations of UNCLOS, the inclusion of a dispute settlement system was considered vital to balancing the many interests addressed within the text of the document.[22] Part XV of UNCLOS includes compulsory procedures entailing binding decisions, as well as acknowledging the potential priority that should be accorded to other dispute settlement procedures existing outside the UNCLOS framework[23] and excluding disputes relating to certain issues from the compulsory procedures.[24]

[20] The debates surrounding the United States' ratification of UNCLOS have included concerns about the United States becoming subject to the compulsory dispute settlement procedures and how exceptions to compulsory jurisdiction should be interpreted in line with US interests.

[21] United Nations Convention on the Law of the Sea (adopted December 10, 1982, entered into force November 16, 1994) 1833 UNTS 3 (UNCLOS).

[22] See e.g., "Statement by the President of the Third Conference of 6 December 1982" in *Third United Nations Conference on the Law of the Sea: Official Records* (United Nations 1984) vol. 17, p. 13, para. 48.

[23] UNCLOS, Arts 281–2. [24] UNCLOS, Arts 297–8.

While the dispute settlement procedure in UNCLOS is not comprehensive, the very fact of its creation is significant. Rights and duties associated with ocean use and ocean space are of fundamental political, economic, and social concern for states. As such, the willingness to create a regime that includes mandatory dispute settlement procedures could be an indication that adjudication or arbitration will be a vital component in protecting rights, as well as for interpreting and amplifying the meaning of the provisions of the treaty to facilitate the regulation of state conduct under the terms of UNCLOS.

More than 20 cases have been instituted under UNCLOS since its entry into force, with the vast majority of them including proceedings before the International Tribunal for the Law of the Sea (ITLOS).[25] The states that have utilized the regime can largely be classified in two main ways: neighboring states seeking to resolve points of contention across or relating to borders (i.e., *Mox Plant*,[26] *Johor Straits*,[27] and the maritime boundary cases[28]); and flag states challenging the actions of coastal states (particularly fisheries disputes and cases seeking prompt release of arrested fishing vessels).

For a regime that has been in operation for nearly 20 years—and with 164 states parties—it is noteworthy that states have not often resorted to the available procedures. Indeed, the most active use of the dispute settlement system has been in relation to cases demanding the prompt release of fishing vessels upon payment of a reasonable bond.[29] As the prompt release procedure was included in UNCLOS to counter-balance the enforcement powers of the coastal state,[30] this use demonstrates that states most concerned about enforcing flag state protections under UNCLOS are the ones that resort to adjudication. From a new stream perspective, these cases also illustrate that private interests, namely those of shipping companies or ship owners, could determine which states resort to adjudication.[31]

Comparable to UNCLOS in terms of another constitutive instrument in which states have a considerable interest in being parties to the regime is the WTO Agreement, which also includes a DSU as a fundamental dimension to the overall international

[25] Even if the ITLOS is not the forum under Art. 282, it may still order provisional measures pending the establishment of an ad hoc arbitral tribunal. UNCLOS, Art.290.5.

[26] *MOX Plant Case (Ireland v. United Kingdom)* (Provisional Measures Order of December 3, 2001) [2002] 41 ILM 405.

[27] *Land Reclamation by Singapore in and around the Straits of Johor (Malaysia v. Singapore)* (Provisional Measures) ITLOS Reports 2003, 10.

[28] See e.g., *Guyana v. Suriname* (Award of the Arbitral Tribunal of September 17, 2007) <http://www.pca-cpa.org/showpage.asp?pag_id=1147> accessed May 7, 2012; ITLOS, *Delimitation of the Maritime Boundary between Bangladesh and Myanmar in the Bay of Bengal (Bangladesh/Myanmar)* (Judgment of March 14, 2012) <http://www.itlos.org/fileadmin/itlos/documents/cases/case_no_16/1-C16_Judgment_14_02_2012.pdf> accessed April 22, 2013.

[29] UNCLOS, note 21, Art. 292.

[30] *The Monte Confurco (Seychelles v. France)*, Prompt Release, 125 ILR 203, para. 70.

[31] This point was highlighted by Judge Shearer in the *Volga* case. See *The Volga (Russia v. Australia)* (Prompt Release Order of December 23, 2002) [2002] 126 ILR 433, para. 19 (Judge ad hoc Shearer).

trade regime.[32] Disputes are configured differently under the WTO system in that states are primarily concerned with the nullification and impairment of their benefits arising under the WTO agreements, rather than the more typical dispute concerning the interpretation and application of a relevant treaty and findings of state responsibility. While interpretation and application of the WTO agreements may be a necessary task for resolving a dispute between states, the configuration of the dispute does not adhere to the typical context of state responsibility and reparations characteristic of other inter-state courts and tribunals. The absence of those legal doctrines, with their damaging reputational consequences, may facilitate engagement and acculturation in the WTO proceedings, according to the constructivist paradigm.

The use of the DSU, which was adopted in 1994, far surpasses utilization of UNCLOS in terms of the quantity of cases instituted and resolved, and the number of states involved in the dispute settlement procedures. States may be applicants or respondents, and may also join proceedings as third parties. The third party avenue has broadened participation in WTO litigation. It provides states a low-cost option (economically and politically) that allows them to assert their rights or interests vis-à-vis another state's decisions around trade restrictions, all while maintaining a voice in the resolution of the dispute.

Of the 451 cases decided under the WTO framework to date,[33] 13 states have only been engaged as applicants,[34] whereas 19 states have only been engaged as respondents.[35] The applicant states are extremely diverse, whereas the respondent states are predominantly European. A variety of states have been actively engaged both as applicant and respondent: the United States (103 applicant/119 respondent);[36] the European Union (87 applicant/72 respondent);[37] Argentina (18 applicant/21 respondent); Australia (7 applicant/13 respondent); Brazil (26 applicant/14 respondent); Canada (33 applicant/17 respondent); Chile (10 applicant/13 respondent); China (10 applicant/29 respondent); India (21 applicant/21 respondent); Japan (15 applicant/16 respondent);[38] Republic of Korea (15 applicant/14 respondent); Mexico (23 applicant/14 respondent).

[32] Understanding on Rules and Procedures Governing the Settlement of Disputes, Marrakesh Agreement Establishing the World Trade Organization (opened for signature April 15, 1994, entered into force January 1, 1995) 1867 UNTS 3, Annex 2.

[33] For a full chronological list of cases disputed before the WTO, see WTO, Chronological List of Disputes Cases (updated April 2013) <www.wto.org/english/tratop_e/dispu_e/dispu_status_e.htm> accessed April 22, 2013.

[34] The applicant states are: Antigua and Barbuda (1); Bangladesh (1); Costa Rica (5); El Salvador (1); Honduras (8); Hong Kong, China (1); New Zealand (7); Norway (4); Singapore (1); Sri Lanka (1); Switzerland (4); Chinese Taipei (3); Vietnam (2).

[35] The respondent states are: Armenia (1); Belgium (3); Croatia (1); Denmark (1); Dominican Republic (7); Egypt (4); France (4); Germany (2); Greece (2); Ireland (3); Netherlands (3); Portugal (1); Romania (2); Slovak Republic (3); South Africa (4); Spain (3); Sweden (1); Trinidad and Tobago (2); United Kingdom (3).

[36] The United States has also been a third party on 97 occasions.

[37] The EU has also been a third party on 124 occasions.

[38] Japan has also been a third party on 127 occasions.

The majority of states appearing on both sides of disputes have been applicant and respondent in roughly equal numbers. Noteworthy exceptions are Canada, which has brought almost twice as many claims as applicant compared to the number filed against it as respondent, and conversely Australia and China, which have had far more disputes filed against them compared to the number of times they have been applicants. It is also interesting to note that 36 states have only been engaged in the WTO dispute resolution process as third parties. Of these states, Cuba and Paraguay have been third parties to disputes 15 times.[39] This highlights that many smaller, developing states have the opportunity to be involved in the WTO dispute resolution process without potentially having to bear the brunt of legal costs of bringing or defending an action before the WTO.

In terms of which states litigate under the WTO dispute settlement regime, one noticeable trend is that developed countries use the system significantly more often than developing countries. Scholars who have examined the involvement of developing countries before the WTO have highlighted a range of disincentives for developing countries, including the costs of running the case, the potential for retaliation by economically more powerful members and an inability to secure an effective remedy should a Panel or the Appellate Body ultimately rule in favor of the developing state.[40] In these circumstances, it is not surprising that developing states have been applicants in WTO proceedings half as frequently as developed states,[41] and even then, some developing countries have been more frequent participants than others.[42]

Beyond the global constitutive agreements for which states must accept the possibility of adjudication or arbitration for the resolution of disputes to be participants in the legal regime, regional arrangements also provide a strong role for adjudication or arbitration in the event of disagreement over action taken within the

[39] The 36 states are: Kingdom of Bahrain; Barbados; Belize; Benin; Plurinational State of Bolivia; Cameroon; Chad; Côte d'Ivoire; Cuba; Fiji; Ghana; Grenada; Guyana; Iceland; Israel; Jamaica; Kenya; the State of Kuwait; Madagascar; Malawi; Mauritius; Namibia; Nigeria; Oman; Paraguay; Russian Federation; Saint Kitts and Nevis; Saint Lucia; Saint Vincent and the Grenadines; Kingdom of Saudi Arabia; Senegal; Suriname; Swaziland; Tanzania; Zambia; Zimbabwe.

[40] See e.g., M Busch and E Reinhardt, "Developing Countries and General Agreement on Tariffs and Trade/World Trade Organization Dispute Settlement" (2003) 37 Journal of World Trade 719; C Davis and S Blodgett Bermeo, "Who Files? Developing Country Participation in GATT/WTO Adjudication" (2009) 71 The Journal of Politics 1033.

[41] See A Qureshi, "Participation of Developing Countries in the WTO" (2003) 47 Journal of African Law 174, 176 (discussing the consultation process). In 2009, Hunter Nottage noted that "127 of the 335 consultations requests made during that period were from developing countries, 40 of the 96 panel proceedings completed involved developing-country complainants, and 33 of the 56 appearances before the Appellate Body in 2007 were from developing countries." H Nottage, "Developing Countries in the WTO Dispute Settlement System" (2009) <www.globaleconomicgovernance.org/wp-content/uploads/nottage-working-paper-final1.pdf> accessed April 22, 2013.

[42] See Qureshi, note 41, at 179 (providing Korea, Brazil, Argentina as examples). It should be noted that there is no strict definition of "developing country," and self-selection is often relied upon in this regard.

organization or by member states. The European Court of Justice (ECJ) performs a key role in this regard, addressing, inter alia, claims from member states against institutions within the organization and vice versa.

Other examples of regional agreements include the African Court of Justice and Human Rights, which is intended to serve the African Union, and smaller regional groupings, such as the Common Market for Eastern and Southern Africa, which also have courts to resolve disputes between states. In the African context, the use of these tribunals has been minimal, partially because the institutions have received insufficient funds for full operation. Hence, while there has been some recognition of the important role adjudication could play in regulating state behavior and in dispute management, many African states have not typically availed themselves of these procedures or generally supported their use.

The reasons for this are of course speculative. We must note that countries in Africa have turned to adjudication or arbitration to resolve some disputes.[43] While this practice might suggest that parties prefer to turn to fora outside the region when adjudication is ultimately selected as the preferred dispute settlement mechanism, the regional courts are of sufficiently recent genesis that it is too soon to gauge whether they will become significant dimensions in resolving disputes among relevant African states. Another factor to consider is that states may prefer mechanisms or institutions with which they have more familiarity, thereby enabling them to better predict the outcome.

Another example of a regional regime that requires states to accept the jurisdiction of a relevant dispute settlement body is the North American Free Trade Agreement (NAFTA), a tripartite agreement between Canada, Mexico, and the United States that establishes a dispute settlement mechanism for investment disputes under Chapter Eleven of that agreement. Of the cases filed under the NAFTA framework, 17 have been filed against the United States,[44] 13 have been filed against Canada,[45] and 13 against Mexico.[46] Based on an examination of only these numbers, one could assume that all NAFTA members have been equally engaged in litigation under Chapter Eleven of the Agreement. This practice might align with a liberal paradigm that acknowledges the use of litigation by democratic states with market economies that generally support the rule of law. The constructivist model also

[43] Examples in this regard include *Frontier Dispute (Burkina Faso/Mali)* [1986] ICJ Rep 554; *Land and Maritime Boundary between Cameroon and Nigeria (Cameroon v. Nigeria; Equatorial Guinea intervening)* (Merits) [2002] ICJ Rep 303; *Continental Shelf (Tunisia/Libyan Arab Jamahiriya)* (Merits) [1982] ICJ Rep 18 at the ICJ, as well as claims commissions, such as the Eritrea–Ethiopia Claims Commission, and arbitration panels, such as the Abiyei Arbitration.

[44] US Department of State, "Cases Filed against the United States of America" <http://www.state.gov/s/l/c3741.htm> accessed April 22, 2013.

[45] US Department of State, "Cases Filed against the Government of Canada" <http://www.state.gov/s/l/c3740.htm> accessed April 22, 2013.

[46] US Department of State, "Cases Filed against the United Mexican States" <http://www.state.gov/s/l/c3742.htm> accessed April 22, 2013.

underlines the effectiveness of international adjudication in this context because of the multifaceted linkages between these neighboring states.

A final form of mandatory arbitration or adjudication arises when the UN Security Council orders the establishment of a court or tribunal for the resolution of a dispute. The UN Security Council has a wide range of powers under Chapter VII of the UN Charter, and may impose such mandatory measures on all member states. The key examples here are the International Criminal Tribunal for the Former Yugoslavia (ICTY), the International Criminal Tribunal for Rwanda (ICTR), and the United Nations Claims Commission (UNCC).

For the ICTY and the ICTR, states were not compelled to directly engage with these tribunals because their jurisdiction concerned the criminal prosecution of individuals who were alleged to have committed war crimes, crimes against humanity, and genocide. In any event, Rwanda agreed to the establishment of the ICTR. However, states were called upon to arrest and transfer all indicted persons to the ICTY, which included the states of the former Yugoslavia, such as Serbia and Croatia. For those states, the ICTY and its attendant obligation to cooperate in the arrest and transfer of indictees could be used as a bargaining tool in accession discussions to the European Union. This example demonstrates that which states become involved in litigation—even if only indirectly—can be determined by broader processes at stake. Engagement in litigation can be a pay-off for concessions or agreements on other issues.

3.3 Participants in ad hoc litigation

When a state is not compelled to be involved in adjudication or arbitration because it has not accepted in advance the jurisdiction of a court or tribunal, either by virtue of the optional clause of the ICJ or through participation in a particular treaty or organization, then decisions are made on an ad hoc basis as to whether to refer a matter to a court or tribunal. The ad hoc use of a court or tribunal occurs after a dispute has arisen; it is a deliberate decision to utilize adjudication or arbitration as the preferred method of dispute settlement.

The *ex post* referral of a dispute to adjudication or arbitration raises the question of which states resort to this mode of dispute settlement, and under what circumstances. We noted above that 16 states have relied on special agreements to submit cases to the ICJ. The states doing so the most were Libya,[47] Burkina

[47] See *Continental Shelf (Libyan Arab Jamahiriya/Malta)* (Merits) [1985] ICJ Rep 13, *Continental Shelf (Tunisia/Libyan Arab Jamahiriya)* (Merits) [1982] ICJ Rep 18, *Application for Revision and Interpretation of the Judgment of February 24, 1982 in the Case concerning the Continental Shelf (Tunisia/Libyan Arab Jamahiriya) (Tunisia v. Libyan Arab Jamahiriya)* (Judgment) [1985] ICJ Rep 192.

Faso,[48] Germany,[49] and Malaysia.[50] These cases all concerned border or territory disputes.

A total of 41 ad hoc arbitrations have been concluded under the auspices of the Permanent Court of Arbitration (PCA).[51] The reasons why states may opt for arbitration as opposed to concluding a special agreement for adjudication before the ICJ represent well-trodden ground.[52] Suffice it to note here that the factors for consideration in favoring arbitration over adjudication include the perception of faster proceedings, greater party control in selection of the arbitrators and in questions of procedure, and the possibility of ensuring confidentiality of the pleadings. The ICJ might be preferred because of the financial assistance available to developing states, the costs associated with establishing an ad hoc institution, the greater prestige of the ICJ, and greater potential to secure enforcement of the judgment because of the status of the court.

By way of examples of ad hoc arrangements for arbitration or adjudication, the history of claims commissions reflects reliance by states on judicial or arbitral proceedings to redress claims most commonly arising from natural or juridical persons. Claims commissions have been used following both internal and international armed conflicts, and after revolutions or large-scale civil unrest that have resulted in significant damage or harm to the nationals of another state. Approximately 80 international claims commissions operated during the 1800s, with another 30 or so in place in the first half of the 1900s.[53]

One example of an *ex post* creation of an arbitral tribunal is the Iran–US Claims Tribunal, which was established as part of a broader settlement enshrined within the Algiers Declarations. These Declarations secured the release of US hostages held in Iran and unblocked Iranian assets frozen by a number of countries.[54] The tribunal was established to resolve outstanding claims by US nationals against Iran and vice versa; claims *ex contractu* between the United States and Iran; and property disputes concerning the deposed Shah of Iran.[55] The extent of claims underlined that a formal

[48] See *Frontier Dispute (Burkina Faso/Mali)* [1986] ICJ Rep 554; *Frontier Dispute (Burkina Faso/Niger)*, ICJ, General List No 149, September 14, 2010 <http://www.icj-cij.org/docket/index.php?p1=3&p2=1&case=149> accessed April 22, 2014.

[49] See *North Sea Continental Shelf (Federal Republic of Germany/Denmark; Federal Republic of Germany/Netherlands)* (Judgment) [1969] ICJ Rep 3.

[50] See *Sovereignty over Pedra Branca/Pulau Batu Puteh, Middle Rocks and South Ledge (Malaysia/Singapore)* [2008] ICJ Rep 12; *Sovereignty over Pulau Ligitan and Pulau Sipadan (Indonesia/Malaysia)* [2002] ICJ Rep 625.

[51] This figure does not include pending cases. For a full list of past and pending cases, see Permanent Court of Arbitration, "Cases" <www.pca-cpa.org/showpage.asp?pag_id=1029> accessed April 22, 2013.

[52] See, e.g., C Gray and B Kingsbury, "Developments in Dispute Settlement: Inter-State Arbitration Since 1945" (1992) 63 British Ybk. Intl. L. 97.

[53] J Crook, "Thoughts on Mass Claims Processes" (2005) 99 American Society of International Law Proceedings 80.

[54] See the General Declarations and Claims Settlement Declaration (1981) 20 ILM 224.

[55] See, General Declarations and Claims Settlement Declaration, note 54, Art. II.

mechanism would facilitate the resolution of these cases. Moreover, the composition of the tribunal—which allowed for equal representation of nationals from the United States and Iran, as well as the involvement of neutral arbitrators[56]—and the jurisdictional limitations imposed on the tribunal, placing, for example, the hostage crisis itself outside the subject matter jurisdiction of the tribunal,[57] gave each side sufficient confidence about how the tribunal would operate. Given the ongoing tensions between the United States and Iran, the long-term operation of the tribunal indicates that adjudication or arbitration might be useful to states where it allows them to sequester a particular aspect of their relationship—perhaps one that does not have high political value—and resolve those differences independently of the other facets of their relationship.

States may be keen to resort to adjudication or arbitration when there is a restorative justice element to the process. This arguably was a consideration in the creation of the Special Court for Sierra Leone, the Special Tribunal for Lebanon, and the Extraordinary Chambers of the Cambodian Courts. It potentially reflects a liberal perspective in preferring legalization for dispute resolution and supporting the development of the rule of law in a community emerging from a time of conflict or political strife. While some states may prefer to rely on truth and reconciliation commissions to deal with damaging historical periods, and to recognize and resolve community claims and sentiment, the legal dimensions of a special court proceeding may also be preferred.

The reasons for states to select *ex post* arbitration or adjudication are highly varied. In relation to disputes over territory, Lea Brilmayer and Adele Faure have written that states are more likely to resort to *ex post* arbitration or adjudication to resolve competing territorial claims. They further argued that while a state in occupation of land territory might be less likely to consent to adjudication (as it would potentially have more to lose), an examination of the cases does not support this hypothesis.[58]

A particular state might resort to litigation for several reasons, including responding to domestic political pressure, seeking to level the playing field among the states in dispute, delaying resolution (given the length of time involved in litigation), and acting as a catalyst for the resolution of related disputes.[59] These reasons do not necessarily all align so as to identify any one state or group of states. Just as the factual scenario of any particular dispute varies, so will the decisions of the state and

[56] The Tribunal agreement called for three arbitrators appointed by the United States, three by Iran, and three neutral arbiters, with one of each serving on each tribunal. General Declarations and Claims Settlement Declaration, note 54, Art. III.

[57] See General Declarations and Claims Settlement Declaration, note 54, Art. II.

[58] Brilmayer and Faure, note 15.

[59] S Scott, "Litigation Versus Dispute Resolution Through Political Processes" in Klein, note 15.

its proclivities for resorting to international courts or tribunals to achieve its goals. In this regard, our quest for establishing common traits as to who litigates seems unattainable.

4 Which Non-State Actors Litigate and Why

Though states are frequently seen as the key actors in international dispute settlement, the reality is that many non-state actors are now actively engaged in international courts and tribunals in a range of capacities. Individuals (natural and juridical persons) may be entitled to present claims in their own right, but only if states consent to such an arrangement. States have also agreed that international courts may exercise jurisdiction over the perpetrators of international law violations, primarily in relation to international criminal law. Perhaps more significant has been the increasing influence of non-state actors in international proceedings, irrespective of any decision by states. The acceptance of *amicus curiae* briefs stands out in this regard. This part of the chapter considers these different ways in which non-state actors participate in international litigation. In considering the engagement of non-state actors in international litigation, we can again have recourse to our explanatory paradigms to determine why some actors are more inclined to engage in litigation.

4.1 Victims of international law violations

International law has progressed since the days when non-state actors played a marginalized role before international courts and tribunals. One primary way this has occurred is through the vehicle of diplomatic protection. Under the Vattelian fiction, states could take up the claims of their nationals and assert those claims as if the injuries suffered by the individuals were injuries sustained by the state itself. Diplomatic protection remains a basis for the resolution of inter-state disputes, as demonstrated by recent ICJ cases such as *Avena and Other Mexican Nationals*[60] and *Diallo*.[61] Yet in considering "who litigates," it is clear that the authority for raising

[60] *Avena and other Mexican Nationals (Mexico v. US)* [2004] ICJ Rep 12.

[61] *Ahmadou Sadio Diallo (Republic of Guinea v. Democratic Republic of the Congo)* (Preliminary Objections) [2007] ICJ Rep 582; *Ahmadou Sadio Diallo (Republic of Guinea v. Democratic Republic of the Congo)* (Merits) [2010] ICJ Rep 639.

claims against states for injuries suffered by natural or juridical persons is being transferred to the victims themselves. An examination of this phenomenon is presented below, taking into account the willingness of states to accept this bestowal of authority on non-state actors. How can we best explain this transfer of authority, and when has this transfer occurred? Are some actors more inclined, or more empowered, to do so than others?

4.1.1 *Human rights courts and committees*

As petitioners before human rights courts and committees, individuals play a key role in adversarial proceedings against states when seeking to redress claims of international human rights law violations. Individuals are able to appear, in their own right, before international committees through the various avenues provided for in different human rights treaties.[62] Still, an individual's ability to engage in this international setting is mostly dependent on states accepting the possibility of claims being filed against it. Some exceptions can be drawn in relation to the ECtHR, which is comparable to the courts and tribunals identified above in which a state must accept the jurisdiction of a permanent court for the sake of being part of a regional regime. In this regard, any state that wishes to become a member of the Council of Europe must make a political commitment to ratify the European Convention on Human Rights, which includes mandatory jurisdiction for the ECtHR. By contrast, the same does not hold true in relation to the IACtHR, which is not part of a political regime. Instead, states simply consent to the possibility of claims being brought against them through the Inter-American Commission of Human Rights.

Beyond the potential role of individuals as applicants before different international courts or commissions, there is further potential for victims of human rights violations to have their voices heard in the context of international criminal prosecutions. Victims may appear as witnesses before the ICC, ICTY, and ICTR, and they are offered special services and protections as necessary. Victims are not otherwise able to participate in the ICTY or the ICTR, nor are they entitled to receive compensation from these tribunals. By contrast, the ICC does allow victims a right of participation to express views and concerns through their legal representatives. This procedure has created considerable difficulties thus far.[63]

4.1.2 *Claims commissions and investment disputes*

States may opt to resolve disputes through claims commissions, thereby allowing the state to empower individuals to pursue claims against a respondent state. In this respect, the claimant states remove themselves, to varying extents, from the dispute

[62] These quasi-judicial bodies, however, are outside the scope of this chapter.

[63] See e.g., C Chung, "Victims' Participation at the International Criminal Court: Are Concessions of the Court Clouding the Promise?" (2008) 6 Northwestern Journal of International Human Rights 459.

resolution proceedings. In reviewing the past practice of international claims settlements, David Bederman has observed:

> Aggrieved states seeking compensation for their nationals in the aftermath of hostilities or revolutionary events typically have constituted these claims institutions. With a few notable exceptions, stronger nations have imposed them upon weaker ones. Although the terms of many of the treaties establishing the claims settlements were nominally reciprocal (that is, nationals of both parties could bring claims), in practice, this was rarely the case.[64]

In this context, a state remains engaged as the respondent, even if compelled to do so because the claimants' state of nationality has superior economic, political, or military power.

The claims prompting early examples of claims commissions often involved damage to property or other harm to foreign investments. These claims are most commonly addressed now through procedures available under bilateral investment treaties, or through particular free trade agreements that include investment chapters. There has been considerable growth in bilateral investment treaty arbitrations since the 1980s. Some of the arbitrations occur on the basis of ad hoc arrangements, frequently with reference to the United Nations Commission on International Trade Law (UNCITRAL) Arbitration Rules, whereas others are resolved through the International Centre for the Settlement of Investment Disputes (ICSID).[65]

The typical paradigm of investor-state arbitration is a foreign investor from a developed country instituting proceedings against a developing country for alleged violation of protections afforded under a bilateral treaty.[66] Bilateral investment treaties are commonly intended to promote foreign investment in developing countries by providing guarantees regarding the standard of treatment of investments in the host state, and a procedure by which investors can pursue claims against the state if those standards are breached. Thus, states do not have to take up the claims of their nationals; investors are empowered to act on their own accord. This procedure allows the country of nationality of the investor to remain one step removed from any dispute, potentially (or at least ideally) insulating the inter-state relationship from the dispute. The investors most likely to be involved in this litigation are multinational corporations, which have the economic means to pursue international litigation.

Developing states therefore become the primary litigant states in investment disputes as they seek to defend national decision-making aimed at protecting their own national economies. Although developing states must defend their decisions

[64] DJ Bederman, "The United Nations Compensation Commission and the Tradition of International Claims Settlement" (1994–1995) 27 NYU J. Int'l. L. 1, 3.

[65] Convention on the Settlement of Investment Disputes between States and Nationals of other States (adopted March 18, 1965, entered into force October 14, 1966) 575 UNTS 159.

[66] This is not the only paradigm, however. See e.g., *Philip Morris Asia Limited v. The Commonwealth of Australia*, UNCITRAL, PCA Case No. 2012–12.

against investors, they recognize that the availability of this dispute settlement procedure is good for their national economies in that it promotes foreign investment. States that have found themselves too often engaged in investor-state litigation have been reassessing the relative weight accorded to promoting foreign investment through the availability of investor-state arbitration on the one hand, and protecting other national economic interests on the other.[67]

4.1.3 *Other avenues of involvement:* amicus *briefs*

Non-state actors occasionally have a role before international courts and tribunals of providing an additional voice to inter-state proceedings. This role is manifest in the submission of *amicus* briefs. The use of *amicus* briefs has been particularly scrutinized in the work of the WTO. One of the controversial dimensions of non-state actor involvement in WTO proceedings has been that the interventions have involved non-profit organizations from developed countries. Developing states are again concerned that their voices are silenced in the trade domain in favor of the powerful financial interests of developed states. A further concern is that *amicus* briefs reflect the interests of organizations that are not aligned to the experience of individuals and organizations based in developing states.

The engagement of individuals and non-governmental organizations in international court or tribunal proceedings may reflect an increasing democratization of international judicial proceedings. As such, there might be a greater alignment with the liberal paradigm—one that flies in the face of state-focused constructs. However, *amicus* involvement does not currently appear to be a powerful trend. The resistance by some states to the introduction of *amicus* briefs reflects states' ongoing desire to control access to international courts and tribunals in order to ensure that their interests are promoted to the exclusion of third-party concerns.

4.2 Perpetrators of international law violations

Beyond the transfer of authority to natural or juridical persons to engage directly in different forms of international adjudication, states favor identifying individuals as perpetrators of particular crimes. A distinction may be drawn here between those states that are willing to have their nationals exposed in this way and states that resist involvement in international criminal tribunals. An additional question is the configuration of international courts or tribunals where states can bring claims against non-state actors. These aspects of "who litigates" are considered immediately below.

[67] See e.g., S Franck, "The Legitimacy Crisis in Investment Treaty Arbitration: Privatising Public International Law through Inconsistent Decisions" (2005) 73 Fordham L. Rev. 1521; M Waibel et al. (eds), *The Backlash Against Investment Arbitration* (The Netherlands: Kluwer Law 2010).

4.2.1 *International criminal courts*

The primary avenue for individuals to be held accountable for violations of international law before international courts or tribunals is in relation to international criminal law. Since the Nuremburg Tribunal's famous statement that, "[C]rimes against international law are committed by men, not by abstract entities," there has been general acceptance that states are not necessarily to be held judicially accountable for particular atrocities, but that the involved individuals should be punished. Despite early recognition of individual responsibility and subsequent calls for the establishment of an international criminal court, the creation of such a court was not endorsed for many decades.

The situation changed in the 1990s, following the end of the Cold War and the renaissance of the UN Security Council. Responding to the atrocities committed in the territory of the former Yugoslavia and the genocidal acts committed in Rwanda, the Security Council created the ICTY and the ICTR, taking action on behalf of the international community. This response condemned the human rights abuses that were occurring and, arguably, allowed other, developed states to refrain from military action in the conflict zones.

Following the experience of the ad hoc criminal tribunals, states worked to create a statute for a permanent international criminal court having jurisdiction over alleged perpetrators of the most serious international crimes. The Rome Statute was adopted in 1998 and entered into force in 2002. There are 122 states party to the Rome Statute. Notably absent are the United States, India, China, Russia, and Israel.

During its short lifetime, the ICC has issued indictments against more than 30 individuals, all in connection with crimes committed in Africa. A consequent criticism is that the ICC could be viewed as tantamount to a neocolonial institution, unreasonably targeting African—and, hence, predominantly developing—states. Yet, the cases addressed by the ICC were specifically referred by the states concerned or by the Security Council in relation to Darfur. The other perspective is thus that African states are quickly recognizing the useful role that the ICC could play in bringing the continent's perpetrators of serious crimes to justice.

4.2.2 *National courts*

An important doctrine applying to states and individuals engaged in the ICC's jurisprudence is the principle of complementarity. By virtue of Art. 17 of the ICC Statute, proceedings may only continue before the ICC if a state with jurisdiction is unwilling or genuinely unable to carry out the investigation or prosecution. The operation of this provision is dependent on states party to the ICC Statute implementing it properly into their national laws, thereby allowing national courts to perform this prosecutorial role instead of the ICC.

National courts continue to play an important role in international disputes. When considering who litigates, it is important to note that if states have claims against natural or juridical persons, those claims can most likely be resolved in national courts. Conversely, states and state entities are typically immune from prosecution or enforcement when suits are brought against them before national courts. The power rests with states to waive this immunity if they wish to pursue claims at the national level. As such, it is unusual for states to be presenting claims against individuals rather than vice versa at the international level given the availability of national courts for this purpose. This dynamic arises in certain claims commission proceedings, notably the Iran–US Claims Tribunal, where each state has had an agent operating at the tribunal, but has rarely occurred in the context of investment disputes. States clearly have more tools at their disposal—including their regulatory and enforcement powers—to refrain from litigating before international courts or tribunals in relation to the actions of non-state actors. National courts only become a viable alternative with the agreement of the state.

5 Conclusion

Of course there is no definitive answer as to who litigates and why. A systematic study of each court and tribunal in existence would be necessary to determine which states have engaged most frequently in international litigation as a matter of statistics. If this study were done over a long time frame, it would have to consider changes in the governmental regime of a particular state—such as whether Eastern European states have become more engaged in inter-state litigation with the fall of communist regimes and the establishment of democratic governance—as well as newly independent states.

To truly test developing country perspectives, there would need to be an agreed definition of a developing state and an analysis of how certain variables differ among existing regimes. For example, how many are parties to the WTO DSU compared to a human rights regime or to UNCLOS? For realists, can we undertake a comparative study of a series of cases and assess the relative power of each state involved? Then we would study how that relative power influenced the states' decisions to litigate, along with other decisions that arise during the adjudicative or arbitral process, including compliance. How many such studies would need to be done to be able to draw broad conclusions?

Our explanatory paradigms do provide us with a starting point for analysis. But overcoming the counter-examples and rationalizing the variables is a significant, and perhaps insurmountable, challenge. The most common explanation that has arisen in this chapter relates to the preeminent place of national interest. States that litigate may do so to protect their reputation, economic concerns, and the political decisions of national institutions. These aspects may all feature in assessing incentives, and disincentives, to make use of available jurisdiction for any given dispute.

Ultimately, how much can be posited by a researcher about state decision-making on international litigation when that researcher is not privy to the discussions of those making important strategic and legal decisions? Some legal advice will always be protected by confidentiality obligations; other decisions will be revealed when historic archives are opened or when documents are released unofficially. In the absence of this disclosure, the most fruitful studies about which states engage in international litigation and why are those that can canvas in depth the wide range of factors that may influence state decision-making. In the face of an increasing array of detailed case studies, there may be some potential to start drawing informed conclusions on why and how states and non-state entities use international courts to achieve their goals.

Research Questions

1. In an individual assessment of any particular international court or tribunal, what are the characteristics of the states most involved in litigating cases before that court or tribunal? What states are least involved, notwithstanding the potential existence of jurisdiction?
2. For a particular case decided by an international court or tribunal, what other factors beyond the legal merits of the case influence the institution of proceedings, the proceedings themselves, and compliance with the outcome of the court or tribunal's decision? Relevant sources would need to include the government documentation produced at the time; contemporaneous media reports; activities (such as meetings, reports, and resolutions) of intergovernmental or non-governmental organizations that related to the dispute; and actions of other interested states, even if not directly involved in the case.
3. Could one of the explanatory paradigms be rigorously tested against the proceedings before any particular court or tribunal? This exercise would test the validity of the relevant theory and help determine when international adjudication may be most effective.

Suggested Reading

Allee, TL and Huth, PK, "Legitimizing Dispute Settlement: International Legal Rulings as Domestic Political Cover" (2006) 100 American Political Science Review 219.

Alvarez, JE, "The New Dispute Settlers: (Half) Truths and Consequences" (2003) 38 Tex. Int'l. L. J. 405.

Born, GB, "A New Generation of International Adjudication" (2011) <http://works.bepress.com/gary_born/2> accessed April 22, 2013.

Fischer, DD, "Decisions to Use the International Court of Justice: Four Recent Cases" (1982) 26 International Studies Quarterly 251.

Johns, L, "Courts as Coordinators: Endogenous Enforcement and Jurisdiction in International Adjudication" (2012) 56 Journal of Conflict Resolution 257.

Keohane, RO, Moravcsik, A, and Slaughter, AM, "Legalized Dispute Resolution: Interstate and Transnational" (2000) 54 Int'l. Org. 457.

Klein, N (ed.), *Litigating International Law Disputes: Weighing the Options* (Cambridge University Press, forthcoming).

Koh, T, "International Law and the Peaceful Resolution of Disputes: Asian Perspectives, Contributions, and Challenges" (2011) 1 Asian Journal of International Law 57.

Paulus, AL, "From Neglect to Defiance? The United States and International Adjudication" (2004) 15 EJIL 783.

CHAPTER 27

THE FINANCING OF INTERNATIONAL ADJUDICATION

THORDIS INGADOTTIR*

The multiplication of international courts and their rising profile on the international scene have inevitably given rise to the question of how these international bodies should be funded. Initially a minor aspect of international adjudication, financing has become a major issue, and, at times, a contested one. First, the considerable amount of resources that international courts require is testing states' commitment to international adjudication. Second, and arguably, never before has states' delegation of power to international institutions reached such a high degree

* Associate Professor at Reykjavik University.

of surrender of control as with some international courts.[1] In many instances financing has become the only remaining control mechanism for states, raising complex issues of judicial independence and process integrity.

This chapter does not aim to provide a comprehensive treatment of the complex subject of financing of international adjudicative bodies.[2] It has a more modest aim, more suitable for the purposes of this handbook. It will first provide a general idea of how cost considerations affect courts' design. Then it will consider how much international adjudicative bodies cost to operate, in other words their price. It will then explain where the funds to pay for those courts come from, and how budgets of international adjudicative bodies are drafted and approved. Finally, in the conclusion I will offer some thoughts about the price and value of international adjudicative bodies, and whether their funding reveals any risk to their independence and operation.

1 Cost Considerations Affect Courts' Design

How much a court will cost once it starts operating, and where funds will come from, is a major consideration for states when planning and establishing new international adjudicative bodies. Funding has been an issue since the first permanent international adjudicative institutions, and many of the decisions taken during these formative years of the international judiciary still have effects to this day.

In arbitration, the principle is that each party pays its own costs and both parties split the costs of the tribunal. This was indeed the arrangement provided for under the Hague Conventions of 1899 and 1907.[3] At the Central American Court of Justice, each member state paid for the salary of its own national judge.[4] However, when the Permanent Court of International Justice (PCIJ) was established, it was decided that while the parties would still bear their own litigation costs, the whole membership of the League of Nations should bear the general expenses of the court, as decided

[1] RW Stone, *Controlling Institutions: International Organization and the Global Economy* (Cambridge University Press 2011) 81.

[2] See Suggested Reading section at the end of this chapter.

[3] 1899 Convention for the Pacific Settlement of International Disputes, Art. 57; 1907 Convention for the Pacific Settlement of International Disputes, Art. 85.

[4] On the Central American Court of Justice, see, in this handbook, O'Connell and VanderZee, Ch. 3, and Romano, Ch. 6.

by the Assembly upon the proposal of the Council.[5] This is remarkable because the court was not an organ of the League and membership of the court was optional to the League's members. This departure from earlier practice was meant to relieve the new court of burdensome collection efforts and to assure its financial stability.[6]

One of the most contested issues when establishing the PCIJ was whether states outside the League of Nations could use the court. It was considered unfair that non-member states could use the court free of any cost. At the same time, as Lord Phillimore eloquently put it:

> The practical end of the establishment of the Court is the prevention of War; to achieve this end it is desirable to give access to the Court to the largest possible number of States. There was only one objection to this: the question of expenses which the establishment of the Court involves, but this question is of too little importance to be considered.[7]

In the end, it was settled that non-member states of the League of Nations would contribute to the cost of the tribunal should they appear before it.[8] Looking back in the light of the pending financial concerns today, it is interesting how funding issues were completely absent from the key deliberations of the statute's drafters, the Advisory Committee of Jurists, which included the committee's intense debate on the number of judges of the court, whether individuals should have access to the court, and whether the Permanent Court of International Arbitration (PCIA) should exist beside or merge into the new tribunal.

The International Court of Justice (ICJ), a new court, fully integrated into the United Nations, followed the same financial arrangements as the PCIJ. Unless otherwise decided by the court, each party bore its own costs and the court's own expenses were borne by the whole membership of the United Nations.[9] However, unlike the PCIJ, the ICJ was established as a principal organ of the United Nations, thus making all members of the organization *ipso facto* members of the court, responsible for its expenses.[10] The San Francisco Conference opted for this arrangement without discussion, rejecting a proposal by the Inter-Allied Committee that the financing of the court should be separate from the budget of the United Nations.[11]

[5] Statute of the PCIJ, Art. 33. There was a consensus that all members of the League should bear the cost of the new court and all written proposals submitted to the Advisory Committee of Jurists proposed such an arrangement (see proposals by the Five Neutral Powers, and Denmark, Norway, Sweden and Netherlands), PCIJ, Advisory Committee of Jurists. Procès-Verbaux of the Proceedings of the Committee, June 16–July 24, 1920 with annexes, 97. The Covenant was amended in 1924, providing that the expenses of the League should be borne by the members of the League, as decided by the Assembly.

[6] MO Hudson, *International Tribunals, Past and Future* (Carnegie Endowment for International Peace and Brooking Institution 1944) 62–3.

[7] PCIJ, Advisory Committee of Jurists. Procès-Verbaux of the Proceedings of the Committee, note 5, at 222.

[8] Statute of the PCIJ, Art. 35.3. [9] Statute of the ICJ, Arts 33 and 64.

[10] Charter of the United Nations, Art. 93.1.

[11] G Marston, "The London Committee and the Statute of the International Court of Justice" in V Love and M Fitzmaurice (eds), *Fifty Years of the International Court of Justice: Essays in honour of Sir*

When the creation of the International Tribunal of the Law of the Sea (ITLOS) was negotiated, costs and duplication of functions with the ICJ were considered.[12] Eventually, the tribunal was established, although not as an organ of the United Nations. As in the case of the ICJ, the expenses of the tribunal are borne by the states parties and by the International Seabed Authority on such terms and in such manner as is decided at meetings of the states parties.[13] Although the number of judges at ITLOS is considerably higher than that at the ICJ (21 judges instead of 15), the judges at ITLOS do not sit full time and are not remunerated a fixed amount, like their colleagues at the ICJ, but rather only for the time they actually serve.

A few years later, a slightly different approach was followed at the World Trade Organization (WTO).[14] Like the ICJ and ITLOS, the Appellate Body is funded through assessed contributions of states parties.[15] However, the Appellate Body is composed of seven persons only, and the system of ad hoc judges (applied at both ICJ and ITLOS) was done away with.[16] Financial concerns primarily motivated the departure from century-old concerns of representation on the bench.[17]

The regional human rights courts in Europe and America have recently undergone major procedural changes, partly due to their high case load and limited resources.[18] At the same time, no consensus was reached on improved financing.[19] The jurisdiction of the European Court of Human Rights (ECtHR) might even expand in the near future, dependent on ongoing negotiations on a new protocol allowing the highest national courts to request advisory opinions from the court.[20]

Although just established, the third regional human rights court, the African Court of Human and Peoples' Rights (ACtHPR), is already on a rollercoaster of structural

Robert T Jennings (Cambridge University Press 1996) 49 and 51; S Rosenne, *The Law and Practice of the International Court, 1920–2005, vol. I* (Leiden/Boston, MA: Martinus Nijhoff Publishers 2006) 439.

[12] C-A Fleischhauer, "The Relationship Between the International Court of Justice and the Newly Created International Tribunal for the Law of the Sea in Hamburg" in A von Bogdandy and R Wolfrum (eds), *Max Planck Yearbook of United Nations Law*, Vol. 1 (1997) 328.

[13] ITLOS Statute, Art. 19.

[14] P Van den Bossche, *The Law and Policy of the World Trade Organization* (2nd edn, Cambridge University Press 2008) 171.

[15] Marrakesh Agreement Establishing the World Trade Organization, Art. VII; Understanding on Rules and Procedures Governing the Settlement of Disputes (Annex 2), Art. 17(8).

[16] At the same time it must be broadly representative of membership in the WTO; Dispute Settlement Understanding (DSU), Art. 17.3. Art. 17.1 of the DSU requires that cases be assigned to three-person divisions of the Appellate Body, not to all seven members.

[17] Also, in the context of the DSU reform negotiations, the EC proposed providing the DSB with the power to modify the number of Appellate Body members when necessary to deal with the workload, see Van den Bossche, note 14, at fn 431.

[18] See European Convention on Human Rights, Protocol 14; Inter-American Commission on Human Rights, Resolution 1/2013, Reform of the Rules of Procedure, Policies and Practices.

[19] As for the Organization of American States, see Permanent Council, "Financially Strengthening the Inter-American Human Rights System," presented by the Secretary General of the Organization of American States, OEA/Ser.G, CP/INF.6585/12 (November 15, 2012).

[20] See European Court of Human Rights, Reflection paper on the proposal to extend the Court's advisory jurisdiction, #3853038.

changes—some reflecting pure financial reasons. Due to financial concerns, in 2004, the African Union decided to merge the ACtHPR with the African Court of Justice (the protocol establishing the latter court entered into force on February 11, 2009), and become the African Court of Justice and Human Rights. The merger was adopted in 2008 but has so far failed to receive political backing.[21] Another protocol is currently under consideration by the African Union. At its session in July 2012, the Assembly of the African Union considered a draft protocol proposed by the African Union Executive Council, enlarging the jurisdiction of the future merged court to encompass also individual criminal responsibility.[22] Financial matters will be one of the key considerations in the future handling of this proposal.[23]

Financial considerations had a significant impact on the development of international criminal courts. In the 1937 Convention for the establishment of an International Criminal Court, no consensus could be reached on how to fund the court.[24] However, the financing of the International Military Tribunals in Nuremberg and the Far East, created following World War II, did not seem to be a significant issue.[25]

When the United Nations established the International Criminal Tribunal for the former Yugoslavia (ICTY), it grossly underestimated how expensive it would ultimately be. The tribunal's first budget, in 1994, was a mere US$10 million. In 2011, it was US$163 million, bringing the total cost over the tribunal's lifetime to US$1.8 billion. Likewise, the International Criminal Tribunal for Rwanda (ICTR) was established without much concern for financing. Both ad hoc tribunals' budgets were to be considered expenditures of the United Nations, and as such, borne by the whole membership. However, it was decided that half of the budget of both tribunals would be assessed on the scale of assessment of the peace-keeping budget, rather than the regular scale of assessment, recognizing the UN Security Council members' special responsibilities, and their duty to pay a larger share, in the maintenance of international peace and security. To save money, the two ad hoc tribunals would share the appeal chamber and the prosecutor.[26]

[21] Protocol on the Statute of the African Court of Justice and Human Rights (adopted on July 1, 2008). As of August 14, 2012 only five states out of a necessary 15 have ratified the protocol. See also Frans Viljoen, "AU Assembly should consider human rights implications before adopting the Amending Merged African Court Protocol" (2012) AfricLaw <www.africlaw.com> accessed January 11, 2013.

[22] Decision on the Protocol on Amendments to the Protocol on the Statute of the African Court of Justice and Human Rights—Doc. Assembly/AU/13(XIX)a, para. 2. If all protocols materialize the current operational ACHR will have three sections instead of one: general affairs (primarily economic affairs), human rights, and individual criminal responsibility.

[23] At its last session the Assembly requested the Commission, in collaboration with the ACHR, to submit a study on the "financial and structural implications resulting from the expansion of the jurisdiction."

[24] Hudson, note 6, at 65–6.

[25] See MH Arsanjani, "Financing" in Cassese, Gaeta, and Jones (eds), *The Rome Statute of the International Criminal Court: A Commentary* (Oxford University Press 2002) 316.

[26] Having a shared prosecutor was changed in 2003, giving each tribunal its own prosecutor.

During the early stages of the negotiations leading to the creation of the International Criminal Court (ICC), many states wished the new court to be funded from the regular budget of the United Nations, like the ICJ.[27] Others preferred funding by states parties only, as in the case of ITLOS, arguing that it would enhance the independence of the court.[28] Eventually, the latter approach prevailed, although with the possibility of additional funding from the United Nations, subject to the approval of the General Assembly, particularly in relation to the expenses incurred due to referrals by the Security Council.[29] Several new features of the ICC, not found in previous international criminal courts, had significant financial implications: victims' participation in the court's proceedings, submission of reparations claims from victims, and a Trust Fund for Victims.[30]

The rise of hybrid international criminal courts has been caused, in part, by the mushrooming budgets of the ICTY and ICTR. Rising costs led to a loss of political will to fund additional international criminal courts; the mantra became small and cheap. Although the operations of the hybrid tribunals in Kosovo and East Timor were to be paid from the budget of the United Nations, they were much cheaper than the ad hoc tribunals.

Funders-fatigue led eventually to the creation of the first international criminal court entirely funded on voluntary contributions: the Special Court for Sierra Leone. The Security Council simply refused to support the establishment of that court, unless it was detached from the budget of the United Nations and funded through voluntary contribution, despite the view of the Secretary General that the only realistic solution was for the court to be financed from assessed contributions.[31]

2 The Price of International Adjudication

As illustrated by Table 27.1, the total cost of international courts differs considerably. Their share of the total budget of the relevant organization also varies significantly.

[27] On the issue of financing in the negotiations process, see S Rama Rao, "Financing of the Court, Assembly of States Parties and the Preparatory Commission" in RS Lee (ed.), *The International Criminal Court: The making of the Rome Statute* (The Hague/London/Boston, MA: Kluwer Law International 1999).

[28] Rama Rao, note 27, at 402–4. [29] Rome Statute of the International Criminal Court, Art. 115.

[30] Rome Statute of the International Criminal Court, Arts 68, 75, and 79.

[31] United Nations, General Assembly, Request for a subvention to the Special Court for Sierra Leone UN (November 17, 2011) A/66/563, para 5.

Table 27.1 Budget of selected international adjudicative bodies and percentage of the budget of the organization to which it is attached*

Court	Year	Budget	Percentage of organization's total budget
ICJ	2011	US$23,287,450	0.66
ICTY	2011	US$163,736,150	4.7
ICTR	2011	US$128,540,750	3.6
ICC	2013	€115.6 million (US$150.3 million)	N/A
ITLOS	2012	€10,199,300 (US$13,259,090)	N/A
ECtHR	2012	€67 million (US$87 million)	28
IACtHR and Commission	2012	US$6.8 million (US$2.1 and 4.7 million respectively)	8
CJEU	2011	€334 million (US$434 million)	0.26
WTO	2010	CHF5.5 million (US$5.88 million)	2

* The budget of many adjudicative bodies is set over two years. In those instances their budget was divided by half. The total budget of the United Nations includes its regular budget, its peacekeeping budget, and the budget of ICTY and ICTR. The exchange rate used was 1 CHF= 1.07US$, and 1 € = 1.3 US$.

3 The Sources of Funding

It is perhaps surprising how little the funding of international organizations has changed over time. The method adopted with the establishment of the League of Nations—assessed contributions by member states—is still the primary source of funding of international organizations and courts. Innovative ideas of new funding resources, such as global taxes, continue to be raised, but without gaining much support. The reason is simple; states will hold on to the power of their purse, both as an organization's ultimate budget authority, and as its principal providers.[32] Withholding of sources continues to be a common control mechanism used by states.[33] The only new funding mechanism that has taken root is voluntary contributions. However, when such funding has been relied on for the operation of international courts, it has failed.

[32] T Ingadottir, "Financing International Organizations" in J Klabbers and A Wallendahl (eds), *Research Handbook on the Law of International Organizations* (Cheltenham: Edward Elgar 2011) 108, 125.

[33] CA Bradley and JG Kelley, "The Concept of International Delegation" (2008) 71 Law & Contemp. Probs. 24.

3.1 Funding with assessed contributions of member states

Most international courts are funded with assessed contributions of member states. While parties to cases pay their own costs, it is the member states of relevant organizations that pay the expenses of the court. According to Art. 17 of the Charter of the United Nations, the expenses of the organization shall be borne by the members as apportioned by the General Assembly. Since the budget of most international courts is incorporated into the budget of the larger organization, the cost is paid by all members of that organization. Thus, contributing states are not necessarily parties to the statute of the relevant court, nor have accepted its jurisdiction, nor have even ever used it (or even intend to use it). For instance, all member states of the Organization of American States are assessed with the costs of the Inter-American Court of Human Rights (IACtHR), despite the fact that they may not have ratified the American Convention on Human Rights (for instance, the United States). And even while all members of the United Nations are *ipso facto* members of the ICJ, only 69 have accepted its compulsory jurisdiction. At the same time, paying the expenses of the ICJ has not been considered equivalent to membership to its statute.[34] Still, membership of a few organizations does entail acceptance of the compulsory jurisdiction of relevant courts, such as at the Council of Europe, European Union, and the WTO, and all paying members are therefore within the jurisdiction of the relevant courts.

Funding by member states is a double-edged sword. On the positive side, the court, funded by all members of a mother organization, is indifferent to how many states have accepted its jurisdiction. Even more importantly, this arrangement leaves no room for threats of funding withdrawals. For instance, when states withdraw their consent to its jurisdiction, such states will continue to contribute to the court via the regular budget of the parent organization. Withdrawal of the United States from the compulsory jurisdiction of the ICJ in 1986 is a case in point. Despite its withdrawal, the US had to continue to pay for the expenses of the court. This gives courts some cushioning from direct state control or "revenge." Also, by funding the costs of an organization, member states have invested in the court, enhancing their interest and responsibility in the undertaking.

The negative side of this arrangement is that funding may be caught in political affairs of the larger organization, where the withholding of funds remains an important means of control for member states. So any such withholding, for reasons unrelated to the court, will have an impact on the court's funding. Furthermore, some may argue that the arrangement of having parties only paying their own costs, and not of the court, may cause some unnecessary litigation. This concern may underlie

[34] This happened with respect to Serbia. During its contested membership period at the United Nations, it had been assessed and it paid for the budget of the United Nations, and hence of the court.

recent proposals presented at the Council of Europe to have complainants to the ECtHR pay fees. Finally, the system also gives national parliaments a certain role in the process, since national parliaments are involved in processing the assessment in the national budget. This has had a great impact on the funding of the ICC, as the Security Council's refusal to pay for its referrals to the court is partly traced to US national legislation preventing any funding of the court.[35]

3.2 Scale of assessment

When the primary funding source of an international organization consists of assessed contributions from member states, the ultimate question is how member states can fairly share the burden of financing. The answer is left to the political will of member states as few constitutions of international organization set out any guidance on this. From the establishment of the United Nations, the General Assembly has regularly adopted an assessment scale based on the so-called "capacity to pay" principle. The methodology behind the principle has largely remained the same. The "capacity to pay" of a member state is measured mainly by estimates of gross national product (GNP), adjusted by factors such as external debt, per capita income adjustment and population. However, the principle has never been applied fully. Since the first assessment scale was adopted, it has been subject to arbitrary maximum and later minimum levels, a subject of fierce debate. Currently, no state bears more than 22 percent or less than 0.001 percent of the budget. Furthermore, there is a maximum assessment rate for the least developed countries of 0.01 percent. In 2012, only the United States was benefitting from the upper ceiling of 22 percent. Only 16 states contribute more than one percent of the budget, with the top six states contributing in total 55 percent: France, China, Germany, Japan, the United Kingdom, and the United States.

The importance of the United Nations's scale of assessment is heightened because many other international organizations base their scale of assessment on it. Other organizations funded by assessed contributions by member states have opted to copy the United Nations scale *mutatis mutandis* (including floors and ceilings), adjusted to its membership, whether it be organizations of the United Nations' family, such as the United Nations Conference on the Law of the Sea (UNCLOS), or those outside the UN, such as the ICC.[36] Different assessment scales do exist, however, such as that for the WTO.[37]

[35] The 2000–1 Foreign Relations Authorization Act prohibits the United States from funding the ICC.

[36] Before Japan ratified the Rome Statute of the ICC, it called on ICC Assembly of States Parties to apply the UN ceiling, see Statement by HE Kyoji Komachi Ambassador of Japan to the Netherlands at the Assembly of States Parties to the Rome Statute of the International Criminal Court, November 23, 2006.

[37] On different types of assessment scales, see HG Schermers and NM Blokker, *International Institutional Law* (4th edn, Leiden/Boston, MA: Martinus Nijhoff Publishers 2003) 624–41.

Undeniably, due to their position, stronger states have had a major impact on international courts. For instance, strong states have had a major influence on the drafting of the statutes of international courts. Even states that have not become parties to an international court, such as the United States with respect to the ITLOS and ICC, have affected the drafting of their statutes. The unwritten rule that the permanent members of the Security Council always have a judge at the ICJ is also an example of the advantaged position of strong states at international courts. But does a major financial contribution by a state give it certain influence or status? Does it matter that the United States is paying 22 percent of the cost of the ICJ, Japan is paying 22 percent of the cost of the ICC, and Norway is paying 89 percent of the cost of the EFTA Court? In his harsh critique of international justice, *Mirages of International Justice*, Matthew Parish argues:

> Add to this the iron economic law that stronger states will contribute more to the Court's budget than weaker ones, and thus the functioning of the Court will be more adversely affected by the withdrawal of the former. Thus a court in respect of which jurisdiction is optional to its litigants has a structural incentive to decide cases in favour of strong states and against weak ones, lest it condemn itself to irrelevance and penury through strong states' rejection and criticism of it, and withdrawal of funding from it.[38]

For reasons discussed above, this criticism is not fully justified as even though a state can withdraw from a jurisdiction of a court, it might still need to pay for the cost of the court. And minor financial contributors do prevail at times over major ones at international courts.[39] It is possible to point to isolated events regarding the organization of courts where the question of a state's financial weight can be raised, but whether they prove that a strong position is attached to major financial contribution is difficult to ascertain.[40] However, the larger financial contributors have been given a major voice in the adoption of the budget, holding *de facto* a veto right.[41]

On the other hand, the absence of financially strong states at an international court will inevitably limit its resources. When the ICC was established, some worried that the court would not survive financially without a US membership. Today, some consider that the ICC's current dependency on financial support from EU member states thwarts its universal aspirations.[42]

[38] M Parish, *Mirages of International Justice: the Elusive Pursuit of a Transnational Legal Order* (Cheltenham: Edward Elgar 2011), at 69.

[39] See for instance *Antigua and Barbuda v. US* at the Appellate Body of the World Trade Organization and *Djibouti v. France* at the ICJ.

[40] For instance, following the accession of Japan to the ICC, making it the largest contributor to its budget, a Japanese judge was elected at the following session. Since Norway became the far largest contributor to the budget of the EFTA Court in 1996, the Registrar of the Court has been a Norwegian with one exception.

[41] See section 4.1 of this chapter.

[42] CPR Romano, "The United States and International Courts: Getting the Cost-Benefit Analysis Right" in *The Sword and the Scales: The United States and International Courts and Tribunals* (Cambridge University Press 2009) 419, at 444.

Inevitably, being a major financial contributor to an organization will always carry a heavy political weight, irrespective of any black letter of equal voting rights and international ownership of the organization. To remedy this reality, unsuccessful efforts have been made at the United Nations (including by the secretariat and Sweden) to have the maximum assessment level lowered to 10 percent.[43] Other organizations have succeeded in adopting relatively lower ceilings. For example, the African Union has set its maximum assessment level at 15 percent.

3.3 Funding by voluntary contributions

Most, if not all, international tribunals have benefitted from voluntary contributions. The Peace Palace itself, hosting the PCIA, PCIJ, and, later, the ICJ, was a gift from Andrew Carnegie. The ad hoc criminal tribunals have also benefitted from voluntary contributions. Still, such contributions were only a fraction of the regular budget of the tribunals and primarily covered their extra-budgetary activities. Various tribunals have also established trust funds to financially assist states to bring cases to the tribunals. However, these trust funds have been meager and few states have benefitted from them. And due to the poor status of the funds, the awards have in no way reflected the real litigation cost.[44] The Rome Statute of the ICC gives a strong statutory framework for voluntary contributions, both to the court, under Art. 116, and to the Trust Fund for Victims, under Art. 79.

Few courts are heavily dependent on voluntary contributions for their regular budget. The IACtHR is one of them and in 2012 voluntary contributions covered 41.6 percent of the court's activities.[45] The Special Court for Sierra Leone became the first international court intended to be fully funded by voluntary contributions. Frequently the host state of international tribunals contributes to the housing of the tribunals: the

[43] FK Lister, *Fairness and Accountability in U.N. Financial Decision-Making* (New York: United Nations Association of the United States of America 1987) 42–3.

[44] A Trust Fund to Assist States in the Settlement of Disputes through the International Court of Justice was established in 1989 under the Financial Regulations and Rules of the United Nations. Since its creation, only seven states have benefitted from the Trust Fund's financial assistance. The Permanent Court of Arbitration has since 1994 had a Financial Assistance Fund, which aims at helping developing countries meet part of the costs involved in international arbitration or other means of dispute settlement offered by the court, see Permanent Court of Arbitration Financial Assistance Fund for Settlement of International Disputes, Terms of Reference and Guidelines (as approved by the Administrative Council on December 11, 1995), available at <http://www.pca-cpa.org/> accessed July 29, 2013 As of the end of 2011, grants of assistance have been made to two Asian states. In 2001 the General Assembly of the United Nations requested the Secretary General of the UN to establish a Trust Fund to assist states parties to settle disputes through the ITLOS. See UN Doc. A/RES/55/7 (February 27, 2001), Annex I, para 2. The Trust Fund has never been used.

[45] IACtHR, Annual Report 2012, at 86. The biggest contributors were the Spanish International Cooperation Agency for Development (AECID) and the Norwegian Ministry of Foreign Affairs.

Netherlands does so with respect to current housing of the ICC, Germany with respect to the ITLOS, and Costa Rica with respect to the IACtHR.[46]

While voluntary contributions have generally been regarded as desirable, the view in most cases is that they should only be additional and accessory to courts' budgets. Fear for the independence of courts has been one of the main reasons for this position. During the negotiation of the Rome Statute of the ICC, states were weary of the arrangement. Although they allowed it, they adopted further criteria as conditions for the acceptance of voluntary contributions.[47] Similarly, issues of the "international nature" of tribunals have also arisen. For instance, during the first years of the ad hoc criminal tribunals gratis personnel were gratefully accepted by the tribunals. However, due to criticism that this obscured the international nature of the court, the practice was reduced. This was certainly not an issue in some later tribunals, such as the Special Court for Sierra Leone. The court was established by an agreement between Sierra Leone and the United Nations, but primarily funded by four states, the United States being the largest contributor (40 percent of the court's budget). The large role of contributing states in the operation of the court did not seem to cause major controversy.

Voluntary contributions have proved to be volatile and unreliable. And it is highly questionable whether the operation of a court should be solely dependent on them. As noted regarding voluntary contributions in the Annual Report of the IACtHR:

> Without them, the Inter-American Court would have to reduce drastically its jurisdictional activities, making the protection of human rights in Americas ineffective. Thus, it is matter of some concern that a high percentage of the Court's regular expenses is covered by voluntary contributions rather than by regular resources of the OAS.[48]

At the same time, while the Organization of American States is not willing to increase funding of the court via its regular fund, any restrictions set by member states on voluntary contributions to the court would be devastating to its operation.[49]

Securing voluntary contributions is a major undertaking. For instance, in 2012 alone, the Special Court for Sierra Leone conducted 96 fundraising meetings. Even if an organization manages to secure sufficient pledges, donors have no legal duty to honor the commitment. Often an organization is not even able to secure enough pledges, let alone have them fulfilled. This was a major difficulty with respect to the Special Court for Sierra Leone. The court started its operations without sufficient pledges and had from the outset major difficulties in securing funding, jeopardizing its whole operation. In the end, it was rescued and some of its cost incorporated into

[46] For instance, the Netherlands recently made a commitment of paying 50 percent of the rent of the interim premises of the ICC, an amount of up to €3 million per year from 2013 to 2015. Since the inception of the ITLOS, Germany has contributed €55 million to the court (in addition to its assessed contributions).

[47] Rome Statute of the International Criminal Court, Art. 116 and Financial Regulation 7.3.

[48] IACtHR, Annual Report 2012, at 86.

[49] This was an intense debate at the Forty-Fourth Special Session of the General Assembly of the OAS, Washington D.C., March 22, 2013.

the regular budget of the United Nations. The sad funding saga of the Special Court for Sierra Leone should serve as an important lesson for all other international courts, or in the words of United Nations Advisory Committee on Administrative and Budgetary Questions (ACABQ):

> ... the Committee notes the problems of sustaining voluntary contributions to finance judicial proceedings. The Committee therefore recommends that the lessons learned from this experience be taken into considerations for future international tribunals and courts.[50]

Last but not least, states can have major control over international courts via voluntary contributions. To some extent, it can be considered a positive side of voluntary contribution—financial support is linked to political support. However, the donor base for voluntary contributions is narrow in all organizations, making the funding extremely vulnerable in case of sudden reductions of funding or withdrawal. And as discussed above, this is a powerful tool in the hands of states. Furthermore, even if pledges materialize and are successfully collected, they tend to be earmarked. In this environment, the wishes of individual donors can truly determine the *de facto* agenda of an organization relying on voluntary funding, irrespective of its set priorities.[51]

3.4 Other sources

A few international courts are funded via different sources, such as the United Nations Compensations Commission (UNCC), which is funded with a percentage of Iraqi oil sales. The arrangement was set by the Security Council in the establishment of the UNCC, and has not been copied by later tribunals of the United Nations. To enhance its independence, the Caribbean Court of Justice is funded by a trust fund established in the sum of US$100 million, so as to enable the recurrent expenditure of the court to be financed by income from the fund.[52]

Courts of arbitration, such as the Permanent Court of Arbitration (PCA) and the International Centre for Settlement of Investment Disputes (ICSID), are funded by the parties in each case. For instance, in arbitration at ICSID, the tribunal will, unless the parties agree otherwise, assess the expenses of the tribunal members, and

[50] UNGA Request for a subvention to the Special Court for Sierra Leone, Report of the Advisory Committee on Administrative and Budgetary Questions (December 14, 2012) UN Doc A/67/648 para. 6.

[51] See discussion on voluntary contributions and independence of the Special Court for Sierra Leone in M Wierda and A Triolo, "Resources" in L Reydams et al. (eds), *International Prosecutors* (Oxford University Press 2012), at 158–9.

[52] For a detailed account of the establishment of the Caribbean Court of Justice, see K Malleson, "Promoting Judicial Independence in the International Courts: Lessons from the Caribbean" (2009) I.C.L.Q. 671.

the expenses of the Centre, and decide how and by whom those expenditures shall be paid. This decision forms part of the award.[53]

Some international courts contemplate additional sources, in addition to assessed contributions and voluntary contributions. The ITLOS is set to be financed both from assessed contributions from states parties and the International Seabed Authority, cf. Art. 19 of the Statute of the Tribunal. It was hoped that an increase in deep seabed mining would provide the authority with a source of independent revenue, enabling it to pay its share of the expenses of the tribunal without the need for states parties' contributions.

The ICC contemplates fines and forfeiture of proceeds, property, and assets derived directly or indirectly from the adjudged crime, cf. Art. 109 of the Rome Statute, to go the court and its Trust Fund for Victims. Furthermore, according to Art. 115 of the Rome Statute, the ICC is to be financed from assessed contributions from states parties, and from funds provided by the United Nations, subject to the approval of the General Assembly, in particular in relation to the expenses incurred due to referrals by the Security Council. Article 115 was a compromise between those that favored that the cost of the ICC should be entirely borne by the United Nations, as the court would act on behalf of the entire international community, and those who favored funding outside the United Nations budget.[54] The understanding of sharing the cost in the case of referrals by the Security Council is reflected in the Relationship Agreement between the ICC and the United Nations.[55] In case of referrals by the Security Council, funds provided from the United Nations have been considered justifiable in light of the services rendered by the ICC to the United Nations.[56]

At the time of writing, the Security Council has referred two situations to the ICC—the situation in Darfur and Libya. However, when the Security Council referred the situations, it made clear it was not going to take on any cost:

> [The Security Council r]ecognizes that none of the expenses incurred in connection with the referral, including expenses related to investigations or prosecutions in connection with that referral, shall be borne by the United Nations and that such costs shall be borne by the parties to the Rome Statute and those States that wish to contribute voluntarily.[57]

[53] R Mackenzie et al. (eds), *Manual on international courts and tribunals* (2nd edn, Oxford University Press 2010) 149.

[54] See M Halff and D Tolbert, "Article 115" in O Triffterer (ed.), *Commentary on the Rome Statute of the International Criminal Court* (2nd edn, Munich: C.H. Beck, Hart, Nomos 2008) 1705, at 1712.

[55] Negotiated Relationship Agreement between the International Criminal Court and the United Nations (ICC-ASP/3/Res.1), Art. 13(1).

[56] Halff and Tolbert, note 54, at 712.

[57] UN Security Council, Resolution 1593 (2005) S/RES/1593 (2005) para. 7; UN Security Council, Resolution 1970 (2011) S/RES/1970 (2011) para. 8. See also detailed discussion in J O'Donohue, "Financing the International Criminal Court" (2013) 12(1) ICLR 269, at 294.

This position by the Security Council has caused considerable debate within the Assembly of States Parties of the ICC, as well as the General Assembly of the United Nations. States are caught between the position that the United Nations should pay for rendered services from the ICC, while realizing that such funding might hinder a referral from the Security Council at all. While Art. 115 is not binding on the United Nations, the relationship agreement between the two organizations truly reflects the understanding that the United Nations would fund referrals by the Security Council. Only a few years ago, the refusal by the United Nations to contribute to the cost of referrals was thought unlikely by commentators, including high level staff members of the United Nations.[58]

4 The Budget of International Courts

Because international adjudication bodies are funded by states, states can use funding to exercise a large degree of control over courts. The key questions are who prepares the budget and who adopts it.

4.1 Budgetary authority

The budget of all international courts is adopted by those who ultimately pay: member states of the organization to which the court is attached or states parties to the court's statute. For example, the budget of the ICJ, ICTY, and ICTR is adopted by the General Assembly of the United Nations. The budget of the ECtHR is adopted by the Committee of Ministers of the Council of Europe. In some instances, states not subject to the jurisdiction of a given court may have budgetary authority over it and contribute to its expenditure, such as the United States with respect to the IACtHR, or many members of the General Assembly with respect to the ICJ. A few courts are international organizations in their own right and thus have budgetary independence from larger organizations.An example is the ICC, whose budget is adopted and paid for by the Assembly of States Parties.

While the constitutive instruments of most international courts stipulate who has authority to ultimately adopt the budget, they tend to be silent as to how the budget is prepared. This is usually detailed in a separate set of legal instruments called

[58] See Arsanjani, note 25, at 325.

"financial regulations." During the drafting of the Charter of the United Nations, the question was raised whether it should be stipulated further how the General Assembly was to adopt the budget of the ICJ, but in the end the issue was left out.[59] Few courts play a major role in the preparation of their own budget. For instance, the IACtHR draws up its own budget and submits it for approval by the General Assembly of the Organization of American States, through the General Secretariat. However, the latter may not introduce any changes to it.[60] The Financial Rules of the United Nations ensure the draft budget from the ICJ a similar treatment. Although the Secretary General can attach recommendations and modifications to the budget, it cannot be changed.[61]

In most cases, budgets drafted by courts go through scrutinizing procedures and amendments before their submission to assemblies of states parties. At the United Nations, the ACABQ serves a key role in this regard. The committee is composed of 16 independent experts elected by the General Assembly. Its authority is considerable. On one occasion, a decision on the establishment of a new international court was aborted due to financial concerns raised by the committee.[62] At the ICC, the Committee on Budget of Finance of the ICC, made up of 12 experts of recognized standing in financial matters, also plays a considerable role. The committee reviews the budget proposed by the court and makes recommendations to the Assembly, almost exclusively for cuts. The committee's recommendations have been criticized for questioning strategic decisions of senior officials of the court. Furthermore, the committee's recommendation that requested sources for a new investigation team should be deferred has been criticized as undermining the independence of the court's prosecutor.[63]

The final decision on a court's budget is taken by the relevant assembly of states parties. Adoption of the budget is an important decision, requiring enhanced majority, in most cases on the basis of equal voting rights. However, in practice, some states have more budgetary power than others. At the United Nations, with respect to budgetary decisions, for the past 20 years there has been an informal understanding that the biggest contributors have a greater say in the discussion and adoption of the budget, and at times a *de facto* veto right. Member states of other international organizations have also been willing to adhere to similar informal understandings.[64]

[59] R Schmidt and W Koschorreck, "Article 17" in B Simma (ed.), *The Charter of the United Nations* (2nd edn, Oxford University Press 2002) 295; See also Rosenne, note 11, at 439.

[60] Statute of the IACtHR, (adopted by the General Assembly of the OAS at its Ninth Regular Session, October 1979) (Resolution No. 448), Art. 26.

[61] Financial Regulations and Rules of the United Nations (ST/SGB/2003/7), regulation 2.14.

[62] The establishment of an international criminal court in Kosovo was cancelled, following views from the ACABQ, see T Ingadottir, "The Financing of Internationalized Criminal Courts and Tribunals" in CPR Romano et al. (eds), *Internationalized Criminal Courts* (Oxford University Press 2004) 271.

[63] O'Donohue, note 57, at 276.

[64] For instance, during the tenth meeting of UNCLOS, an unsuccessful proposal was made that provided for the inclusion of an additional paragraph of rule 53 to the effect that decisions on budgetary

4.2 Budget cuts and budget ceilings

The threat of an actual use of budget cuts can be a powerful mechanism available to states to control international organizations and international courts.[65] This tool can be used for different reasons. It has been used to react to unpopular decisions. When the ICJ declined to exercise jurisdiction in the South West Africa (second phase) case, incurring the wrath of newly independent African states, as well as several developed states, the General Assembly's Fifth Committee refused to adopt supplementary estimates to the court.[66] Following precautionary measures granted by the Inter-American Commission of Human Rights, directed at Brazil regarding its Belo Monte dam, Brazil suspended its annual contribution and withdrew its ambassador from the Organization of American States. Budget cuts can also play a role in institutional balance within an international organization, such as at the UN with respect to the Security Council and the General Assembly. The General Assembly can use its power of the purse to control the Security Council, as happened with the first budgets of the ICTY.[67]

In particular, budgetary cuts are powerful control instruments over international criminal courts, as the budget covers both the costs of the work of judges and also that of the office of the prosecutor, which carries out investigations. There is already a debate at the ICC on the propriety of some of the budget cuts. But the same can be said for many other international courts. This is particularly relevant for courts where states have few other avenues of control, such as courts with compulsory jurisdiction and where *locus standi/ratione personae* is beyond the control of states. Indeed, some high officials at the regional human rights courts are of the opinion that budget cuts are deliberately directed at the operation of the courts.[68] The budget

and financial matters should be taken by a three-fourths majority of states parties present and voting, provided that such majority included states parties contributing at least three fourths of the expenses of the tribunal. One of the main arguments raised against the proposal was that so far member states had approved the budgets of the tribunal by consensus and there was no need to change the rules since the current system worked well.

[65] Bradley and Kelley, note 33, at 24. Karen Alter considers that with the exception of international criminal courts, cutting budgets of international courts is not an effective control tool. K Alter, "Agents of trustees? International courts in their political context" (University of Bremen, Collaborative Research Center 597, 2004). See also K Alter, "Delegating to International Courts: Self-Binding vs. Other-Binding Delegation" 71 Law & Contemp. Probs. (2008) 37, at 55.

[66] See discussion by Rosenne, note 11, at 445 and 493.

[67] J Klabbers, "Checks and Balances in the Law of International Organizations" in M Sellers (ed.), *Autonomy and the Law* (Dordrecht: Springer 2007) 141, at 147. On the small first budgets of the ICTY, see GJ Bass, *Stay the Hand of Vengeance: the Politics of War Crimes Tribunals* (Princeton University Press 2000) 221–2, and RJ Goldstone, *For Humanity: Reflections of a War Crimes Investigator* (New Haven, CT: Yale University Press 2000) 77–85.

[68] A judge at the European Court of Human Rights goes as far as saying that states are taking advantage of the immense backlog the court is facing while lacking sources to handle it, and in that way diverting the court from its principal purpose of checking the human rights abuses of governments. See Terris et al. (eds), *The International Judge: An Introduction to the Men and Women Who Decide*

of the ITLOS for the years 2013–2014 is four percent lower than proposed by the tribunal, causing intense discussion.[69] The development of the budget situation of the ICJ in the last decade, frequent budget cuts while the court is facing an increased workload, has prompted some calls for a review of whether the current financial arrangement between the court and the UN "has impaired the judicial standing of the Court and its ability to undertake the functions which the Charter requires of it."[70]

Cutting budgets of international courts without limiting the number of cases that can reach them is a recipe for delays in justice, a growing backlog of cases and eventual paralysis. This is why when states want to reduce expenditure, they need to not only reduce budgets but in parallel narrow the jurisdiction of international courts or otherwise change their structure. For instance, it can be argued that the creation of hybrid courts had more to do with financial concerns, rather than with the admirable ambition of bringing justice closer to victims.[71] Such financial concerns may also explain why some tribunals were given direct guidance to keep the number of cases low. For instance, the Special Court of Sierra Leone was instructed to prosecute only "the most responsible ones," and the mandate of the ICC was limited in a way that the court should determine that a case is inadmissible if the case is not of sufficient gravity to justify further action by the court. The ad hoc tribunals, ICTY and ICTR, had to face serious limitations to their work following the Security Council completion strategy.[72] As mentioned earlier, in order to reduce cost, major structural changes have been made to the regional courts in Africa. As for Europe, Protocol 14 to the European Convention of Human Rights reduced the number of judges that have to sit in each case and added a new inadmissibility ground. Further changes are also being discussed. For instance, the Council of Europe is seriously considering adopting fees for complainants to the ECtHR.[73]

Even within the current framework, court officials are making major decisions affecting the judicial process in order to reduce costs. The less ambitious role taken on by criminal courts is evident in the case numbers. The striking numbers are 161 indictments at the ICTY, 75 at the ICTR, 12 at the Special Court for Sierra Leone, and finally only 18 indictments at the ICC in eight situations. The judges at the ECthHR adopted their own measures to deal with the immense case load and lack

the World Cases (Oxford University Press 2007), at 163. In an interview with the author, one of the Commissioners of the IACtHR stated that the recent attempts to block voluntary contributions to the commission and the court were deliberately made to prevent the organs from doing their work.

[69] UNCLOS, Meeting of State Parties, Report of the twenty-second Meeting of States Parties (July 11, 2012), SPLOS/251, paras 46–51.

[70] Rosenne, note 11, at 495.

[71] See Ingadottir, note 62, at 271.

[72] This raised some serious questions regarding their independence, see Wierda and Triolo, note 51, at 157.

[73] See Council of Europe, Terms of reference for the Committee of Experts on the Reform of the Court (DH-GDR), valid from January 1, 2012 until December 31, 2013.

of resources by introducing the "pilot procedure" which has no statutory base.[74] Interestingly, in light of states' close eye on any judicial activism on behalf of international courts, this practice seems to have been widely accepted. In its processing of petitions, the Inter-American Commission of Human Rights has recently prioritized some situations over others.[75]

Albeit not as blunt as an outright cut, imposing a ceiling on the budget is another way to exert control over a court. These days, most budgets of international organizations are based on "zero real growth," irrespective of their tasks and inflation. This recent policy has led to fierce discussions. Indeed, in theory international organizations operate in a closed budgetary system: that is to say first the relevant organs decide what activities the organization will carry out and then resources are allocated consequently, not the other way around.[76] However, the common practice of budget ceilings operates against this assumption.

In recent years, the use of budget ceilings has had a major effect on the budget of international courts. Zero real growth policy is currently applied for instance to the budget of the United Nations, Council of Europe, UNCLOS, the WTO, and has been applied, at times, at the ICC.[77] The restriction is extremely harsh for international courts as most do not control how many cases they will receive, and theirs workload are generally on the rise. So while their work increases, in some cases dramatically, their budget stays behind. The restriction has also larger effect. In her pleas to the Assembly of States Parties, the Registrar of the International Criminal Court had this to say on zero-growth policies:

> The level of the budget must correspond to the level of the Court's activities; increasing when required by a higher workload and decreasing if activities go down. Nevertheless, "zero-growth" communicates to persons being investigated and to those involved in conflicts that the Court is not to be feared, that its hands are tied, its threats empty, and that it cannot take on more cases despite its mandate of ending impunity. As I said at the opening, the Court must be able to grow; to grow its expertise, its productivity, its impact and its influence.[78]

[74] See Rule 61 of the Rules of the Court. See also European Court of Human Rights, Factsheet—Pilot judgments, January 2013, available at <http://www.echr.coe.int/NR/rdonlyres/61CA1D79-DB68-4EF3-A8F8-FF6F5D3B3BB0/0/FICHES_Arrets_pilotes_EN.pdf> accessed February 12, 2013.

[75] Rules of Procedure of the Inter-American Commission on Human Rights, Art. 29, as amended by Resolution 1/2013.

[76] Schermers and Blokker, note 37, at 925.

[77] The policy has been questioned at the UNCLOS meeting of states parties. See for instance the debate during the tenth meeting of states parties.

[78] International Criminal Court, Eleventh Session of Assembly of States Parties, Statement of Ms. Silvana Arbia, the Registrar on budget, November 16, 2012.

5 Conclusion

As figures make clear, international courts command a considerable amount of resources, attracting attention for various reasons. First, the enhanced role and authority of international courts invites criticism of those opposed to these institutions. Their cost is in particular an easy target for criticism. Second, as we saw, the budget of most international courts is part of a larger budget of a founding organization and, therefore, is intertwined with other developments. Many member states have been demanding administrative reform, such as at the United Nations, which has required extensive scrutiny of organization's costs, including of their courts. Third, the introduction of budget ceilings at some of these organizations has made the issue of financing all the more relevant, as some courts now find themselves competing with costs of other activities or bodies of the organization. Fourth, the recent world fiscal crisis is adding additional pressure of austerity measures as many states are reducing their budget deficits with heavy cuts in expenditure. Finally, and not least, the high budget of international criminal courts has truly changed the landscape. This new generation of courts is truly testing whether states are willing to put their money where their mouth is when it comes to international justice.

What does all this money in the end buy? The legal literature discussing the effectiveness of international courts includes costs as one of the parameters in evaluating such effectiveness (along with factors such as usage, compliance, and impact). Yuval Shany argues for a comprehensive approach to assessing international courts' effectiveness, a goal-based approach, and that such an analysis must include cost-effectiveness.[79] He describes cost-effectiveness as the relationship between inputs and outputs. One of the inputs is resources as determined by budgets. As for outputs, Shany argues that when measuring effectiveness one must differentiate between outputs and outcomes. Outputs alone, such as the number of decisions issued by a court, are only one part of the picture and do not capture the outcomes of the court, which have a larger impact on legal norms and state behavior.[80] This impact is rather difficult to capture with nickels and dimes.

Who are the beneficiaries—the parties, the international community or even mankind? Furthermore, if this cost was lower or not there, would it simply move from one pocket to another and surface in a different budget? And any comparison of numbers is subject to the eye of the beholder. The cost of the ICC in the year 2011 was €103 million, while the world military expenditure the same year is estimated

[79] Y Shany, "Assessing the Effectiveness of International Courts: A Goal-Based Approach" (2012) 106 AJIL 225, at 237–8.

[80] Shany, note 79, at 249.

to have been US$1,738 billion, making the cost of the ICC only 0.008 percent of that amount.[81] If we were to adopt a different perspective, however, the cost of some of the international courts can easily be targeted. While the ICTR spent US$1.7 billion for the trials of just 100 individuals, the Rwandan government had only a fraction of that amount to conduct trials of over one million individuals. An additional variant in this exercise could be the cost of other states handling the prosecution. For example, the costs related to the single trial of Francois Bazaramba in Finland is estimated at US$2 million.

Numbers may shed some light on whether states are following words with deeds, i.e., whether courts are given the budget to carry out their given mandates. That inquiry is timely as, in recent years, most international courts have faced cuts to proposed budgets. And the numbers indicate that courts are becoming resource driven, rather than mandate driven. For instance, at the ECtHR, over the last three years the number of incoming applications has risen by 47 percent with no increase in staff.[82] The Registrar at the ICC complains that the court's budget has only increased by 10 percent in the last five years, while its case load has more than doubled.[83]

In addition, while states keep budgets of international courts frozen, they are in many cases not willing to enter into statutory amendments to meet courts' constantly increasing case load. The IACtHR has for years demanded to be altered from a part-time institution to a full-time one, with no avail. At the ECtHR, rather than increase the number of judges, Protocol 14 opted for more limited rescue measures involving procedural amendments. Due to rising case load, in 2011 the European Court of Justice proposed that the number of judges of the General Court would be increased by 12, from 27 to 39. This proposal was quickly removed from the negotiated reform package.[84]

At the same time that courts are dealing with mounting case loads and non-adjusted budgets, their mandates keep expanding. Membership to most international courts has risen, some significantly. Additional protocols and amendments are constantly in the making, further expanding the jurisdiction of adjudicative bodies. Evidently, states do have a major belief in the role of international adjudicative bodies in international dispute settlement. At the same time states are increasingly putting their work and independence at risk. In some cases the reason is simple donor fatigue, in others the reason is of much more concern—states' attempts to hinder a court's work through its budget and funding.

[81] See Stockholm International Peace Research Institute, *SIPRI Yearbook 2012: Armaments, Disarmament and International Security* (Oxford University Press 2012), at 150.

[82] Council of Europe, Programme and Budget 2012–2013, CM(2012)1E, 626.

[83] International Criminal Court, Eleventh session of the State Parties, Statement of Ms. Silvana Arbia, the Registrar, November 14, 2012.

[84] See Draft Amendments to the Statute of the Court of Justice of the European Union and to Annex I thereto, Luxembourg, March 28, 2011.

Research Questions

1. To what extent are states able to control international courts via financing?
2. Does financing affect independence of international courts?
3. Are some international courts severely underfunded?
4. How can international courts be funded differently?

Suggested Reading

Alter, KJ, "Agents of trustees? International courts in their political context" (TranState working papers, No. 8 (2004) <http://hdl.handle.net/10419/28258> accessed July 29, 2013.

Bradley, CA and Kelley, JG, "The Concept of International Delegation" (2008) 71 Law & Contemp. Probs 1–36.

Esposito Massicci, C, "Article 33" in A. Zimmermann et al. (eds), *Statute of the International Court of Justice: A commentary* (Oxford University Press 2006) 525.

Ingadottir, T, "Financing International Organizations" in J Klabbers and A Wallendahl (eds), *Research Handbook on the Law of International Organizations* (Cheltenham: Edward Elgar 2011) 108.

O'Donohue, J, "Financing the International Criminal Court" (2013) 12(1) ICLR 269.

Romano, CPR, "The Price of International Justice" (2005) 4 The Law and Practice of International Courts and Tribunals 281–328.

Rosenne, S, *The Law and Practice of the International Court 1920–2005* (Leiden/Boston, MA: Martinus Nijhoff Publishers 2006) Vol. I, Ch. 8.

Schermers, HG and Blokker, NM, *International Institutional Law* (4th revision, Leiden/Boston, MA: Martinus Nijhoff Publishers 2003).

Shany, Y, "Assessing the Effectiveness of International Courts: A Goal-Based Approach" (2012) 106(225) AJIL 225, 237–8.

Tortora, G, "Financing of the Special Tribunals for Sierra Leone, Cambodia and Lebanon" (2013) 12(1) ICLR 93.

Wierda, M and Triolo, A, "Resources" in L Reydams et al. (eds), *International Prosecutors* (Oxford University Press 2012).

Wippman, D, "The Costs of International Justice" (2006) 4 AJIL 861.

PART V

KEY ACTORS

CHAPTER 28

WHO ARE INTERNATIONAL JUDGES?

LEIGH SWIGART* AND DANIEL TERRIS**

1 Introduction

International adjudication is not a mechanical system. It is a network of human actors of whom the key figures are judges and arbitrators. Their work is inevitably shaped by their backgrounds and experiences, and the quality of

* Leigh Swigart is Director of Programs in International Justice and Society at the International Center for Ethics, Justice, and Public Life at Brandeis University.

** Daniel Terris is Director of the International Center for Ethics, Justice, and Public Life at Brandeis University. The authors wish to thank Kate Alexander and Shelby Magid for their research assistance.

international justice rests in large part on their collective knowledge, wisdom, and effectiveness.

A generation ago, the idea emerged that international adjudicators belonged to an "invisible college" of international lawyers, a professional community bound together not only by their legal expertise but through identification with a cause.[1] This informal but nevertheless influential network consisted largely of men who circulated among elite academic and professional institutions, and who therefore brought a relatively consistent cosmopolitan outlook to their work in international law.

The passage of time, changes in values, and the dramatic expansion of the world of international adjudication—especially the growing number of courts and tribunals—have wrought many changes, including the transformation of "the exclusive invisible college... beyond all recognition."[2] At the same time, international courts have come under intense scrutiny by states, the media, and the broader public. New questions are being raised about the backgrounds, independence, and competence of the men and women who serve on the international bench. A broad examination of the demographics of international judges and the main trends that illustrate their current collective profile can help to address such concerns involving these critical actors.

We have stated above that the backgrounds of individual judges "inevitably" affect their work. In one sense, this is a truism, since no person is a blank slate. But this claim engages an extensive scholarly debate over how much individual backgrounds matter in the behavior of judges at both the domestic and the international levels. Some have argued that factors beyond individual background are more important; for example, the collective culture of a court might tend to outweigh personal experience.[3] Indeed, some judges themselves espouse this point of view, arguing that they tend to put aside personal experience and preferences in favor of the judicial role and expectations of their particular institution.[4]

Few observers, however, would be willing to claim that demographics and backgrounds make no difference at all. It is counterintuitive to think that the work of international courts would be the same if there were no judges at all from Africa, or no women, or if the international bench were comprised exclusively of women and men whose entire previous careers had been spent as law professors. The challenge, then, is to identify exactly what difference individual backgrounds do make—a

[1] O Schachter, "The Invisible College of International Lawyers" (1977) 2 Northwestern University Law Review 72.

[2] JE Alvarez, "The Democratization of the Invisible College" (IL. Post, November 8, 2007) <http://www.asil.org/ilpost/president/pres071108.html> accessed December 14, 2012.

[3] See E Voeten, in this handbook, Ch. 25 at section 3.3.

[4] D Terris, CPR Romano and L Swigart, *The International Judge: an Introduction to the Men and Women Who Decide the World's Cases* (University Press of New England and Oxford University Press 2007) 131–40.

research endeavor that is, as Eric Voeten describes it, "in its infancy." The relevant studies focus on how backgrounds might influence judicial behavior regarding the specific and vital work of legal reasoning and decision-making. But a consideration of demographics also points us toward broader questions about the work of judges and their institutions. After all, individual backgrounds and experiences may affect such matters as judicial interaction with colleagues; dependence on or from political pressures; management of the courtroom; and judicial ethics and conduct. We also need to understand more about whether and how the composition of courts affects their legitimacy in the broader geopolitical context.

This chapter focuses on the fundamentals—a snapshot of the international judiciary at a particular point in time. These basic data (with judges and arbitrators considered separately) can serve as a starting point for further consideration of the broader questions.

2 International Judges: A Collective Profile

Any answer to the question, "Who are international judges?" must begin with a look at the individuals who currently occupy those positions. In December 2012, 304 judges were serving on 21 of the most significant international judicial bodies, with various geographic and subject matter jurisdictions.[5]

The modal profile of an international judge in December 2012 featured the following characteristics: citizenship in a European state; male; between 58 and 67 years old; and significant past work experience in the public sector as a judge, civil servant, and/or member of one or more national or international bodies. Such a profile should not, however, lead the observer to make assumptions about the homogeneity of the international bench. While the characteristics identified above occur most frequently in the data set, the diversity of those who fall outside the mode contribute a considerable degree of heterogeneity to the collective profile of the men and women who serve as judges on international courts and tribunals today.

[5] These bodies were selected because they are either prominent on the global or a regional stage, active in terms of the number of cases they handle, or both. The benches of the following institutions were included in the analysis: ACtHPR, ATJ, BCJ, CCJ, CACJ, EACJ, ECJ, ECOWAS CJ, EFTA C, ECtHR, ECCC, IACtHR, ICC, ICJ, ICTY, ICTR, ITLOS, MPTR, SCSL, STL, and WTO AB. Information about judges was gathered through the biographies provided on court and tribunal websites, with additional information sought when needed. Complete information was not available for all international judges in the analyzed group.

2.1 Nationality

International organizations tend to be focused on the nationalities of their employees, believing that a balanced distribution of citizenship among its staff will ensure that all voices, traditions, and viewpoints are fairly represented. While the label of nationality is generally understood, it may also serve as a stand-in for other attributes, such as race, religion, culture, and even language. International courts and tribunals are no exception, reflecting in part the historical relation of these courts to arbitration. Most have rules that determine how many judges will come from a particular state or region, with the aim of achieving geopolitical balance while remaining silent about many other possible descriptors for the individuals who serve on their benches.[6]

The 304 international judges identified in December 2012 came from a broad sweep of the world's sovereign states, with 111 different nationalities represented within the group. While this figure suggests a generally wide geographical diversity on the international bench, a closer analysis reveals an uneven distribution across the globe, largely due to the uneven distribution of the courts themselves.[7] Because they are guaranteed seats on the Court of Justice of the European Community (ECJ) and the European Court of Human Rights (ECtHR), small European countries such as Cyprus and Malta, which are members of both bodies, have at least two international judges at any given time.[8] Luxembourg has even more because of its participation in the Benelux Court of Justice (BCJ). But in Asia and the Pacific, where no comparable regional courts exist, there are dozens of smaller and island nations whose nationals only serve as international judges on the rare occasion that they are chosen for such courts as the International Court of Justice (ICJ) or the International Tribunal for the Law of the Sea (ITLOS).

When sorted according to the UN regional classification system, half of international judges in December 2012 came from Europe.[9] By contrast, Asia was dramatically underrepresented; its international judges comprised just 13 percent of the total group, even though the region's population accounts for 58 percent of the world's total. If the 13 Cambodian judges of the Extraordinary Chambers in the Courts of Cambodia (ECCC) are excluded from the calculation, Asia's representation drops to just 26 international judges—less than nine percent of the total group.

[6] For a full discussion of how the nationality and other attributes of international judges play out in the context of international courts and tribunals, see L Swigart, "The 'National Judge': Some Reflections on Diversity in International Courts and Tribunals" (2010) 42 McGeorge L. Rev. 223.

[7] See K Alter, in this handbook, Ch. 4.

[8] Malta had four international judges in December 2012, with Maltese nationals serving on the benches of the ICTY and ITLOS as well.

[9] This includes judges from both the "Eastern Europe" and "Western Europe and other" categories, the latter including North America, Australia, and New Zealand.

One noticeable trend in recent years has been an increase in the presence of African judges on the international bench: currently 60 members out of the total group of 304. The establishment of the African Court on Human and Peoples' Rights (ACtHPR) in 2006 automatically added 11 to the continent's total. But even without this boost, Africa's share had been climbing. Among the 13 courts on which a similar analysis was performed in 2006, African representation has increased from 20 judges in 2006 to 30 on the same courts in 2012.[10]

Nationality also largely determines the legal system in which an international judge has been trained and which shapes his or her thinking and practice. The majority of judges (193, or 63 percent) came from countries whose legal systems were based on the civil law tradition, again reflecting the cast of continental Europe.[11] Just 32 judges (11 percent) hailed from purely common law countries, largely from the UK, North America, and the Caribbean. The remaining 79 judges (26 percent) came from mixed legal systems, either civil and common law—as found in South Africa and the Philippines—or a civil- or common-law system mixed with customary and/or religious law, as found in most countries in Africa and South Asia. Judges from such systems are presumably well prepared for—or at least less bothered by—the mixture of civil and common law practices that characterizes the procedures of many international courts.

The existing evidence suggests that nationality matters in international courts to the extent that judges are more likely to side with their own countries in contested decisions.[12] This phenomenon troubles some observers, but it provides reassurance to others, who reason that states will have more confidence in bodies where they feel that their views are represented. In most international courts, in any case, this possible bias on the part of judges is mitigated by the size and composition of the panels and the benches.

Nationality may well be more important in other ways, especially regarding the legitimacy of international judicial bodies. This can cut both ways. Smaller countries and developing nations may feel more confidence in courts with greater global representation, but more powerful countries have shown a tendency to back away from legal fora where they feel their own influence is diminished.

[10] In order to determine trends and changes in the international judiciary over time, this group of 304 has been compared to a similar snapshot collected in 2006 as part of the research for a monograph devoted to the international judiciary. See Terris, Swigart and Romano, note 4. Since the original snapshot was based on 215 judges from a smaller group of 13 courts and tribunals, comparisons have been adjusted so that the same group of institutions has been analyzed. The 13 courts analyzed in 2006 were: ATJ, CCJ, ECJ, ECtHR, EFTA C, IACtHR, ICC, ICJ, ICTR, ICTY, ITLOS, SCSL, and the WTO AB. As of December 2012, there were a total of 205 judges sitting on these courts.

[11] Our classification follows that found at Juriglobe: <http://www.juriglobe.ca/eng/syst-onu/index-alpha.php> accessed December 14, 2012. The distribution of legal training for international judges roughly follows the distribution of legal systems throughout the world.

[12] See E Voeten, in this handbook, Ch. 25, at section 2.

2.2 Gender

The international bench has historically been a preserve of men, but the most recent trend is distinctly toward including women. Of 304 judges on 21 courts in December 2012, 80 (26 percent) were women.

The overall figures are again distorted by uneven distribution. Of the 80 female international judges, 31 of them were serving on two courts: the International Criminal Court (ICC) and the ECtHR. The ICC is one of the few courts that requires the "fair representation of women" among its judges, and its selection process has a complicated formula for ensuring balanced gender representation.[13] The ICC had the distinction of becoming the first female-majority international bench in 2009.

The ECtHR has adopted a number of resolutions and guidelines in recent years that also aim to bring about more balanced gender representation on its bench, particularly through ensuring that judicial candidates of both sexes are put forward by Council of Europe member states.[14] This strategy seems to be working. In December 2012, 18 of 47 sitting ECtHR judges were women, giving that court the highest number of female judges in absolute terms, although they still represented only 38 percent of the bench.

Excluding the ICC and ECtHR, just 49 women (16 percent) sat on the benches of the remaining 19 courts. A slow but steady movement towards gender equality is palpable, however. In 2012, the ICJ could boast only three women on its bench of 15; nevertheless, this figure was triple its total of a single female judge in 2006. The 80 women serving as international judges in December 2012 hailed from 56 countries, suggesting a widespread willingness among states to put forward strong female candidates.

What difference does the movement toward gender equality on the bench make? Broadly, there is little scholarly evidence to support the idea that more women judges make a substantial difference in how international courts conduct their work. Even at the domestic level, it appears that women judges behave differently only in a small subset of cases in important areas such as sex discrimination.[15] The evidence suggests that it will be difficult to detect much difference between the work of men and women on interstate courts such as the ICJ or the World Trade Organization Appellate Body (WTO AB), but in criminal courts and human rights courts, where many cases touch on gender-sensitive issues, there is ample opportunity for exploration. Certainly, women judges themselves are quick to identify why gender matters

[13] R Mackenzie et al., *Selecting International Judges: Principle, Process, and Politics* (Oxford University Press 2010).

[14] Guidelines of the Committee of Ministers on the selection of candidates for the post of judge at the European Court of Human Rights, II.8, adopted by the Committee of Ministers on March 28, 2012 at the 1138th meeting of the Ministers' Deputies.

[15] CL Boyd, L Epstein, AD Martin, "Untangling the Causal Effects of Sex on Judging" (2010) 54 American Journal of Political Science 389.

on the bench of these courts. One frequently cited example is the treatment of rape as a war crime in the jurisprudence of the International Criminal Tribunal for the former Yugoslavia (ICTY) and the International Criminal Tribunal for Rwanda (ICTR).[16] Furthermore, as with nationality, legitimacy questions remain important; clearly this was an important factor in the decision of the Assembly of States Parties to establish a system of gender balance in the selection process for judges at the ICC.

2.3 Age

It will come as no surprise that most international judges are in their fifties or sixties, in the later stages of their careers. Of the 215 judges for whom birthdates were available in December 2012, 159 (74 percent) were between 50 and 70. Thirty-six judges (17 percent) were more than 70 years old. Older judges tended to cluster in particular courts, such as ITLOS, where a number of judges have been re-elected multiple times since the court's establishment, and the ICTY, where the completion strategy has prompted some judges to stay longer in order to help bring the court's work to its conclusion.

There is a modest trend toward appointing or electing younger judges in recent years, particularly in Europe. In some cases, this may reflect the circumstances of countries where political changes and/or a relatively small pool of experienced judges have encouraged the nomination of younger candidates.[17]

Diversity of age in the international judiciary may be an asset for some courts, like other forms of diversity. Younger judges can bring fresh perspectives and a different sensibility regarding key issues. But youth on the international bench may also create some hidden problems, such as a threat or a perceived threat to judicial independence. For older judges, service on an international bench is often a final permanent post before retirement, or before returning to an academic position. But a younger judge is likely to be in a different situation altogether. A man or woman appointed to the ECtHR bench at the age of 38, for example, will complete his or her non-renewable nine-year term of service in Strasbourg at age 47, with two decades or more of professional life ahead. As the date of return home approaches, this young judge may well have to think about the prospect of future employment within his or her government. Even for the strongest judge, concerns about judicial independence may well emerge in the later years of the term.[18]

16 Terris, Swigart and Romano, note 4, at 39–48.

17 In December 2012, for example, the ECtHR bench had four judges under age 40: Julia Laffranque of Estonia, Kristina Pardalos of San Marino, Nona Tsotsoria of Georgia, and Ganna Yudkivska of Ukraine.

18 N Vajic, "Some Remarks Linked to the Independence of International Judges and the Observance of Ethics Rules in the European Court of Human Rights" in C Hohmann-Dennhardt, P Masuch, and

2.4 Professional background

2.4.1 *Legal training*

A large majority of international judges received their first degrees in law in their countries of origin. The exceptions tend to be men and women from smaller nations whose home countries either do not have a recognized law school, or for which there is a strong connection to a former colonial power—such as many countries of the Commonwealth of Nations.[19] International exposure for these exceptions, then, begins in many cases with the acquisition of a second or third degree overseas. Approximately two-thirds of the international judges in 2012 earned one or more degrees outside their countries of origin. This was most often an LL.M. degree—usually in continental Europe, the United Kingdom, or the United States. A number of judges also earned degrees outside the strict confines of a legal education, studying in such areas as public administration, economics, political science, and philosophy.

2.4.2 *Professional tracks*

Four distinct professional tracks may lead to a position on the bench of an international court or tribunal: service as a career national judge; affiliation with an academic institution; civil service (either in a domestic or international capacity); and the private practice of law. Most judges, however, have experience in more than one of these tracks, and some have careers in which their commitments are so varied that they cannot be neatly classified. Of the 268 judges for whom information regarding professional backgrounds was available in December 2012, 71 (26 percent) had worked primarily as judges, 52 (19 percent) were associated with the professoriate, 55 (21 percent) had spent most of their careers in civil service, 28 (11 percent) had worked in private practice or in another legal capacity (e.g. as a prosecutor or arbitrator), and 62 (23 percent) had worked substantially in two or more of the above-mentioned career tracks.

National judges

International judges who have been career judges at home more often come from countries with pure or mixed civil-law traditions, where lawyers generally enter the judiciary at a much earlier stage in their professional lives. Nonetheless, the judicial systems of common-law countries also produce many international judges. For the majority, appointments to the international bench have followed service on their nation's highest court. Examples include ECtHR judge Alvina Gyulumyan, who sat

M Villiger (eds), *Grundrechte und Solidarität: Festschrift für Renate Jaeger* (Kehl am Rhein: N.P. Engel ed. 2011) 179.

[19] For example, ITLOS Judge Jose Luis Jesus of Cape Verde studied law at the University of Lisbon, SCSL Judge Richard Lussick of Samoa studied at the University of Sydney, and CCJ Judge and President Sir Charles Michael Dennis Byron of St. Kitts and Nevis studied at Cambridge University.

on Armenia's Constitutional Court before moving to Strasbourg, and Caribbean Court of Justice (CCJ) judge Desiree Bernard, who previously served as a high court judge of the Supreme Court of Guyana, a Justice of Appeal, and finally Chief Justice of Guyana. Incidentally, Bernard was the first woman to hold any of those positions.

Academics

Those who have principally worked within an academy were appointed to the international bench after many years of holding a full professorship, generally in their country of origin. Despite being full-time professors, these academics usually have had extensive commitments outside their university service, especially on national and international commissions where they applied and acquired expertise in such fields as human rights, international trade, and humanitarian law. Fausto Pocar of Italy—a judge and former president of the ICTY—followed this path to the international judiciary.

Civil servants

The category of "civil service" covers a broad range of positions within government. It includes domestic positions, such as a post within a ministry of justice, a legal adviser within the executive branch, or a state prosecutor. ICJ judge Joan Donoghue of the United States illustrates this path to the international bench, having previously served for many years as an adviser on international law to the US government. So too does ICC judge René Blattmann of Bolivia, who served as Minister of Justice and Human Rights in his home country. Some civil servants, on the other hand, have spent considerable time overseas as diplomats and/or representatives of their countries in a legal capacity in an intergovernmental organization.

Another type of civil service is performed primarily in the *international* sphere. There are international judges whose prior professional activities have been carried out largely in organizations such as the UN, or in regional bodies in the Americas or Africa. ITLOS judge L Dolliver M Nelson of Grenada, for example, spent many years working at the Division for Ocean Affairs in the United Nations Office of Legal Affairs, and played an important role in establishing the International Seabed Authority as well as the tribunal to which he was later elected.

Practicing lawyers

A relatively small number of international judges have spent the bulk of their careers before their judicial service as practicing lawyers. Many practiced in the broad area of human rights law—including fields such as labor law—and are now serving on one of the human rights bodies in Europe, Africa, or the Americas. This professional path has been followed by IACtHR judge Margarette Macaulay of Jamaica, who has largely spent her legal career as an advocate for the rights of women and children. Sophia AB Akuffo of the ACtHPR (Ghana) took a more unusual path; she worked as a lawyer for Ghana Airways and Mobil Oil in West Africa before opening her own firm, being appointed to the Supreme Court of Ghana, and finally being elected to the regional human rights court.

Mixed career tracks

Those individuals who are impossible to categorize have had more than one substantial professional commitment. For example, some began their careers as academics, working for 15 years or more in the professoriate before being appointed to a domestic judgeship, where they might have served for a decade before being appointed or elected to the international bench. Others served as domestic judges after working for many years in private practice or civil service, and then transitioned into a position on an international bench. Experience in international organizations or representation of one's government at an intergovernmental body, or in a case before an international court, might also appear on the judges' curricula vitae. One example is the career of ICJ judge Kenneth Keith of New Zealand, whose previous experience included work as a barrister, a law professor and dean, an active practicing international lawyer, and a judge of the Supreme Court of his home country.

2.4.3 *International experience*

International experience also counts a great deal in the path towards an international judgeship, even for those individuals whose careers have largely been spent within their home countries. The experience of ICC judge Sanji Mmasenono Monageng offers a variation on this theme. After serving as a magistrate in her native Botswana and acting as the founding chief executive officer of the Law Society of Botswana, she was elected to the African Commission of Human and Peoples' Rights, eventually serving as its chair. During this time, Monageng also served in the High Courts of The Gambia and Swaziland as part of the Commonwealth Programme, thus gaining national experience outside Botswana. This combination of national and international experience, along with her expertise in human rights law, led to her nomination and election to the ICC in 2009.

One noticeable trend that is accelerating as the international justice community grows and strengthens is the tendency for judges to move from one international court to another. Among the 2012 group, at least 35 (13 percent) had served on another international bench prior to their current positions. This phenomenon is significant because it in many ways demonstrates recognition that there is a defined profession of international judge and that prior experience in another international institution can be beneficial.

Sometimes serving on a second international court is a matter of moving from one regional body to another. ECJ Judges Egils Levits of Latvia and Uno Lõhmus of Estonia, for example, both previously served at the ECtHR. Similarly, Tanzanian Augustino Ramadhani of the ACtHPR was once a judge at the East African Court of Justice (EACJ). In the case of criminal courts, tenure on a second international bench can be a matter of applying expertise in a different setting. Christine Van den Wyngaert of Belgium and Elizabeth Odio Benito of Costa Rica both served at the ICTY before being elected to the ICC—a logical move since the ad hoc tribunals are closing down while the newer court is permanent.

Other individuals have transitioned from one type of international court to another. CCJ President Sir Charles Michael Dennis Byron of St. Kitts and Nevis finished his time as judge and president of the ICTR and then became president of the CCJ, a regional court of the Caribbean. His colleague Erik Møse of Norway, also once ICTR judge and president, became a judge at the ECtHR after an intermediary stint as judge of the Supreme Court in his home country. Antônio Augusto Cançado Trindade of Brazil served for many years on the bench of the IACtHR until elected to the ICJ—the same exact path followed earlier by his colleague Thomas Buergenthal of the United States.

Another minor but distinct phenomenon is the tendency for judges to be appointed to the bench of a court with which they have had a previous association. At least 22 of the 2012 group had played a different formal professional role in their courts, including Howard Morrison of the United Kingdom, who was a defense counsel at the ICTY and ICTR before being elected as an ICTY judge; IACtHR Judge Manuel Ventura Robles (from Costa Rica) who was previously secretary/registrar of his court; and Ganna Yudkivska (from the Ukraine) of the ECtHR, who was formerly a lawyer in the registry of that court. While working in a court is no clear guarantee of a direct path to a judgeship, familiarity with a court's rules, habits, and functions is clearly considered an asset as states put forward names of potential candidates. There is also a pattern among criminal court judges in particular of individuals having served in the office of the prosecutor in a different institution. While movement between courts can contribute positively to the cross-pollination of ideas and practices, it also has the potential downside of insularity and the closure of opportunities to newcomers bringing fresh ideas to international judicial bodies.

In contrast to gender, some initial scholarly research and consensus suggests that professional background helps to define and shape a judge's work. Diplomats, for example, are more likely to give greater latitude to the arguments of states.[20] But again, further research is needed beyond the strict questions of legal reasoning and decision-making. For example, some observers criticized the early benches of the ICTY and the ICTR for poor management of their courtrooms, especially regarding the slow pace of trials. Judges with more courtroom experience, it was suggested, might have conducted the proceedings more efficiently.[21] Again, we will need to understand whether professional background is an influence that fades with time,

[20] See E Voeten, in this handbook, Ch. 25, at section 3.3.

[21] PM Wald, "Reflections on Judging: At Home and Abroad" (2004) 7 U. Pa. J. Const. L. 219, 226.

as academics get more used to the practical elements of judging or as diplomats begin to lose the habit of repressing their own opinions in favor of those of their governments. In any case, study in this area will be challenging for the very reason we have stressed above: the professional backgrounds of most international judges fall into more than one category, making specific influences more difficult to trace.

3 Changes over Time

The characteristics of the international bench have changed significantly as the arena of international justice has widened. This trend emerges from a comparison of the composition of the benches of three key courts at intervals of 20 years: the ICJ benches of 1972, 1992, and 2012; the ECtHR benches for the same years; and the ICTY bench of 1993 (its first bench) and that of 2012 (as its end date nears).

3.1 The ICJ in 1972, 1992, and 2012

The composition of the ICJ shows more stability over time than any other international court, a function of its age and the rules and traditions governing its role as the "principal judicial organ of the United Nations." The size of its bench—15 permanent judges—was identical in 2012 to its size in 1992 and 1972, and the geographical spread of the bench was quite similar. By tradition, the five permanent members of the Security Council each have a "slot" on the ICJ, and Germany, Italy, and Japan are frequently represented on the bench as well. The nationalities of almost half of the members are therefore consistent over time. The remaining eight judges represent the rest of the "principal legal systems of the world"; at all three time periods, these eight positions were more or less evenly divided among Europe, Africa, Asia, and Latin America.

The trend towards younger judges is discernible at the ICJ, but only barely. The average age of its bench dropped from 68 in 1972 to 67 in 1992, with a somewhat greater drop to 64 by 2012. As noted earlier, the ICJ did have three women on its bench in 2012; no woman had been elected to the ICJ as of either 1972 or 1992. The first woman to be elected to the ICJ as a permanent judge was Dame Rosalyn Higgins in 1995. Compared to other courts, the ICJ leans more toward judges with backgrounds in the civil service, a reflection of a larger-than-usual number of diplomats nominated by their home countries. This stability makes the ICJ *sui generis* in a world where expansion and growth have brought significant changes to international adjudication.

However, the ICJ has also been marked by the recirculation of international judicial expertise that increasingly characterizes the international judiciary. In 2012, three of its fifteen judges had had prior experience on another international court or tribunal: Mohamed Bennouna of Morocco at the ICTY; Antônio Augusto Cançado Trindade of Brazil at the IACtHR; and Julia Sebutinde of Uganda at the SCSL. Many of them had also previously served as judges ad hoc at the ICJ and/or served as counsel for their governments in cases before the ICJ—and in the case of Ronny Abraham of France, before the ECtHR and ECJ.

3.2 The ECtHR in 1972, 1992, and 2012

The most dramatic changes that have occurred at the ECtHR over the past 40 years are a result of the expansion of the membership of the court itself. In 1972, the court had only 17 judges—principally from the countries of Western Europe that constituted the bulk of the parties to the European Convention on Human Rights at that time. By 1992, as the Cold War ended and the number of countries in the Council of Europe increased, the ECtHR had grown to 28. In 2012, after the full embrace of the convention by the newly independent nations of the former Soviet Union, the number of judges on its bench had increased to 47.

It is not surprising, perhaps, that a court focused on issues of human rights should have taken significant strides toward gender equality since the early 1970s. The 1972 bench of the court included only one woman, and even by 1992 there were only two women among 27 judges. There was dramatic change over the next two decades, however; in 2012, 18 of the ECtHR's 47 judges were women.

The period between 1992 and 2012 also witnessed a dramatic drop in the average age of ECtHR judges, as mentioned above. On both the 1972 and the 1992 benches, the average age was almost exactly 65. But by 2012, this had dropped by 10 years to an average age of 55, including several judges under 40. One driver for this change was the appointment of several very young judges from Eastern Europe, as states preferred to put forward candidates who had received their education in the years after the break-up of the Soviet Union. But this was only one factor. In fact, the average age of the judges from the same 27 countries represented on the ECtHR in 1992 had also dropped in 2012—from 65 to 56—suggesting that the trend toward nominating much younger judges was a wider phenomenon.

In terms of professional background, the ECtHR, like the ICJ, has been relatively consistent in its balance. The majority of judges on the ECtHR in 2012 came from backgrounds as national judges, as academics, or as a mixture of both. Compared to the ICJ and some other international courts, the number of judges with backgrounds primarily as civil servants is relatively small. This balance has changed little since 1972.

3.3 The ICTY in 1993 and 2012

The first judges of the ICTY took their seats in November 1993, so this court provides a window into how a criminal court evolves from its founding to its old age, since the court was winding down its business by 2012. The original ICTY bench consisted of 11 judges: seven at the trial level and four on appeals. Its nine men and two women, with an average age of 64, had principally been either distinguished academics or national judges on a supreme court or other high-ranking court in their home countries. The task of the first judges of the ICTY was to construct the rules of procedure and the legal infrastructure for the first international criminal court since Nuremberg. With uncertainty over how quickly the actual trials would begin, knowledge of international law was privileged over practical experience on the bench in the first ICTY cadre.

By 2012, the ICTY bench had expanded to 26, including nine *ad litem* judges brought on to speed up the pace of the court as it implemented its "completion strategy."[22] The 26 included seven women, following a trend towards more gender equality. The ICTY was, however, an anomaly in one respect: the average age of its judges actually increased, from 64 to 67, between 1993 and 2012. The court's clearest trend in professional terms was toward appointment of men and women with significant experience as national judges. More than half the 2012 bench had principally worked as judges before their appointment to the ICTY, and others had had some judicial experience alongside stints in legal positions in the executive branch. Direct experience in presiding over criminal cases was thus more prevalent among the 2012 bench, though by no means universal.

4 Trends

Three key trends involving international judges emerge from this overview: increasing diversity, new paths to the international bench, and active movement among a wide range of international courts and tribunals.

[22] F Pocar, "Completion or Continuation Strategy?: Appraising Problems and Possible Developments in Building the Legacy of the ICTY" (2008) 6 J. Int'l Crim. Just. 655.

4.1 Diversity

The increasing diversity of the international judiciary, taken as a whole, is striking and palpable. The mix of countries represented, gender, age, professional background, and international experience is significantly greater than it was 20 years ago. Of course, the main driver for this increasing diversity is the expansion of the international judiciary itself. The establishment of newer courts in Africa and the expansion of existing courts in Europe are the main factors. While it is true that the most established courts—such as the ICJ—have changed relatively little in the demographics of their composition, the changing face of the international judiciary means more opportunities for "buy-in" among various constituencies. More than half the nations of the world—58 percent—can boast of having at least one of their nationals serving on an international court. Despite the continued domination of men on certain international benches, women around the world can witness the strong contributions of female judges across the board.

4.2 New career tracks

The broader overall diversity of the international judiciary has created new routes to the international bench. Civil service—with its attendant political connections within the government bodies that nominate judges to the international bench—continues to confer certain advantages. The international bench is also still populated by a significant number of men and women whose background is primarily as scholars of the law. But there is a distinct shift away from those whose experience has been purely civil service or the professoriate, and more towards those who have also been players in the broader legal arena. An increasing number of judges are earning their stripes in private practice, including as labor or human rights lawyers who have sometimes built their careers by initiating legal challenges against their own governments.

Above all, what characterizes the professional backgrounds of international adjudicators is the eclectic nature of their experience: law professors who have served on multiple national and international bodies, judges who have been in and out of academia, lawyers who have additional degrees in fields such as public policy. In part, the diversity of routes to the international bench is driven by the variability of their nomination processes. Different processes exist among the various international courts, and even for the same court, states can sometimes have widely varying nomination procedures.[23]

[23] See R Mackenzie, in this handbook, Ch. 34.

4.3 Movement between international courts

Meanwhile, more courts, more judges, and more circulation in international circles mean that more judges are moving between international courts and tribunals. Many courts now have more than one judge with previous international judicial experience, ensuring that benches have access to the practices and jurisprudence of other bodies.[24] Furthermore, the movement is not simply between courts with similar jurisdictions, such as the transition from the ICTY or the ICTR to the ICC, but also encompasses movement between very different types of court. Such movement might serve to enhance the transmission of legal thinking across traditional jurisdictional lines.

5 International Arbitrators

Judges on international courts and tribunals are only one "class" of international adjudicators. The other class, international arbitrators, are both more numerous and more difficult to describe collectively. Judges, after all, are appointed to permanent benches for fixed terms; their positions and qualifications are defined more or less clearly by the founding statutes of their institutions. Arbitrators, on the other hand, are generally chosen by the parties themselves on a case-by-case basis from a global pool of international lawyers. Some individuals are enormously active as arbitrators, serving at any one time on multiple panels; such men and women can be consistent and influential players as international adjudicators. But other individuals may serve on only a single panel as a unique event in their careers, or may simply be on a list of those available to serve as arbitrators. Given the fluidity and variability among the class of international arbitrators, one cannot construct a snapshot in time that is comparable to a collective portrait of international judges.

There are at least 11 active international intergovernmental organizations that have established pools of international adjudicators.[25] Some are established for general dispute settlement; others assemble rosters of international legal experts in specific fields, ranging from commercial disputes to highly specialized areas such as sports or the environment.

[24] Report of the Brandeis Institute for International Judges 2012, available at <http://www.brandeis.edu/ethics/internationaljustice/biij/index.html> accessed December 14, 2012.

[25] CPR Romano, "A Taxonomy of International Law Institutions" (2011) 2 JIDS 241, 263.

One way to create a collective profile is to focus on the membership of one of these bodies of international arbitrators at a moment in time. The Permanent Court of Arbitration (PCA) is the oldest and best known of these bodies; it was founded in The Hague in 1899 and has the broadest scope in terms of disputes that its members settle. The PCA is famously not a court, nor do its members sit in any "permanent" fashion. Its membership represents an influential cross-section of individuals engaged in international arbitration at the highest levels.

In June 2011, the PCA had 346 members. By the rules of the organization, each member country may name up to four members of the PCA. This means that national origin is more or less evenly distributed.[26] In formal terms, therefore, geographical diversity is a given among PCA membership. In one way, this reflects the geographical diversity among the international judiciary, which is also skewed to encompass the broadest possible swath of nations. The difference, however, is that PCA membership does not ensure opportunities for active participation in arbitration since the arbitral panels are constructed only by mutual consent of the parties.

The professional backgrounds of PCA members mirror closely those in the international judiciary. The four basic professional categories—civil servants, national judges, academics, and private lawyers—are consistent between both groups of adjudicators. Relatively more arbitrators have backgrounds in civil service and private practice than among the group of judges. The tilt toward civil servants probably reflects the primacy of political figures in the executive branch in naming members of the PCA; the tilt toward private lawyers could reflect the expectation that arbitrators as a group may adjudicate more commercial and business cases than judges on the full range of international courts and tribunals. The counterweight is that there are significantly fewer PCA members with recent experience as national judges: 13 percent in the PCA, as opposed to 23 percent among international judges in 2012. Presumably arbitrators as a class have less need for specific experience on the bench than their judicial counterparts. As with the international judges, many PCA members have experience in multiple career tracks, making them difficult to categorize.

At the same time, PCA membership more closely resembles an "old boys club" than the international judiciary as a whole. Nearly 90 percent of PCA members are men. The public and sometimes unseemly regional and global politics that govern the selection process for international judges has its drawbacks, but it has produced pressure—and sometimes specific requirements—to add more women to the bench. No such pressure is applied in the selection process for the PCA, making it easy for states to overlook gender balance in their nominations.

[26] Naturally, this means that some larger and more active states are significantly under-represented on the PCA list. There are many more than four active and influential international arbitrators from the United States, the United Kingdom, France, and Japan, for example, but each has a maximum of four members of the PCA.

The interlocking circles of international adjudicators can be detected in the number of PCA members with direct experience on the international bench. More than 10 percent of the members of the PCA are current or former judges (permanent, ad hoc, or *ad litem*) on international courts. Many other PCA members have appeared in international courts as counsel. This reflects the same kind of circulation among international institutions that is increasingly common among international judges.

When it comes to international arbitrators, however, a fuller study of the group as a whole will have to examine not only the potential pool of arbitrators but also the degree to which they are active. Because they are selected on an ad hoc basis, arbitrators depend even more than judges on what one study has described as "symbolic capital": evidence of public stature in domestic and international legal circles.[27] This can make the jump to *success* in the field a considerable hurdle, though it is clear that a "diversified portfolio" of professional achievements is a critical asset.[28]

6 Conclusion

As early as 1977, Oscar Schachter observed in his article about the invisible college of international lawyers that international judgments will be more credible and authoritative when made by a broadly representative group than by an exclusive and like-minded one. "This leads to the conclusion that the professional community of international lawyers should aim at a wide international participation embracing persons from various parts of the world and from diverse political and cultural groupings," he wrote.[29] After examining the collective profile of today's international adjudicators and documenting its steady move toward inclusivity over the past several decades, it would seem that the international legal community has in some ways met this lofty goal.

The impact of these changes has yet to be fully assessed not only in terms of decision-making, but also in how judges operate within a court and a system as colleagues, managers, and political actors, among other roles. Another question that this chapter raises is the extent to which international adjudicators can and

[27] Y Dezalay and BG Garth, *Dealing in Virtue: International Commercial Arbitration and the Construction of a Transnational Legal Order* (University of Chicago Press 1996) Ch. 2.

[28] Dezalay and Garth, note 27, at 19.

[29] Schachter, note 1, at 222.

should be studied as a group. Much of the current scholarship focuses on one or two relatively homogenous courts. Measuring the influence of demographics across the full range of international judges and arbitrators will be more difficult. Even though the number of individuals is relatively small, the varied circumstances of the composition of the courts and arbitral bodies, their selection processes and their political situation makes comparison across institutions challenging, in addition to complicating efforts to identify precisely the changing nature of the "invisible college."

The evidence suggests that this invisible college still exists, however, insofar as there is a group of individuals bound together by the common cause of international justice. The college, however, has taken on a significantly modified form. The voices of women and young professionals are now prominent, as are voices from disparate parts of the world. As the number of individuals and institutions involved has expanded in recent decades, the circulation of ideas and people within this sphere has become a looser and less insular process—which in turn enhances the sharing of knowledge and the development of international law. This more "visible" college has the potential to bring new reserves of legitimacy and public confidence to the work of international courts and tribunals.

Research Questions

1. The authors of this chapter argue that the "invisible college" of international judges persists in a modified and more "visible" form. Does the persistence of this network mean that international judges share certain definable and distinctive characteristics in their outlook and ideas about international law when they take their positions on the bench? Over time, does their experience on the bench have a fundamental impact on their outlook?
2. The number of female international judges is still disproportionately low, but it is growing. What barriers to the advancement of women still exist in the nomination and selection procedures? Is the movement toward gender equality on the bench making a fundamental difference in the work of international courts?
3. Which specific academic and international institutions have had the most substantial and demonstrable impact on the training and preparation of international judges? Are there particular ideas or practices in international courts and tribunals that can be traced to these influential organizations?
4. Does the increased movement of judges from one international judicial institution to another affect the sharing of knowledge and best practices in the international legal sphere? To what extent can the effects of various forms of judicial dialogue be detected in the work of international courts and tribunals?

Suggested Reading

Alvarez, JE, "The Democratization of the Invisible College" (IL. Post, November 8, 2007) <http://www.asil.org/ilpost/president/pres071108.html> accessed December 14, 2012.

International Center for Ethics, Justice, and Public life, Reports of the Brandeis Institute for International Judges (2002, 2003, 2004, 2006, 2007, 2009, 2010, and 2012) <http://www.brandeis.edu/ethics/internationaljustice/biij/index.html> accessed December 14, 2012.

Mackenzie, R et al., *Selecting International Judges: Principle, Process, and Politics* (Oxford University Press 2010).

Mundis, DA, "The Election of Ad Litem Judges and Other Recent Developments at the International criminal Tribunals" (2001) 14 LJIL 367.

Russell, PH and Malleson, K (eds), *Appointing Judges in an Age of Judicial Power: Critical Perspectives from around the World* (University of Toronto Press 2006).

Schachter, O, "The Invisible College of International Lawyers" (1977) 2 Northwestern University Law Review 72.

Swigart, L, "The 'National Judge': Some Reflections on Diversity in International Courts and Tribunals" (2010) 42 McGeorge L. Rev. 223.

Terris, D, Romano, CPR, and Swigart, L, *The International Judge: An Introduction to the Men and Women Who Decide the World's Cases* (Oxford University Press 2007).

Wald, PM, "Reflections on Judging: At Home and Abroad" (2004) 7 University of Pennsylvania Journal of Constitutional Law 219.

CHAPTER 29

THE INTERNATIONAL BAR

ERAN STHOEGER* AND

MICHAEL WOOD**

"The lack of a specialized bar before the [Law of the Sea] Tribunal, of a minimum level of qualification in international law, of rules of professional conduct and of an organization entrusted with the task of enforcing them, may…pose a problem."[1]

* Research Analyst, Security Council Report, and member of legal teams in several interstate disputes.

** Barrister, 20 Essex Street, Member of the International Law Commission.

[1] Judge ad hoc Cot, "*Grand Prince*" *(Belize v. France)* (Prompt Release, Judgment of April 20, 2001) ITLOS Reports 2001, 17, para. 13. In the original French: "L'absence d'un barreau spécialisé devant le Tribunal, d'un niveau de qualification minimum en droit international, de règles de déontologie et d'un organisme chargé le cas échéant d'un rappel à l'ordre peuvent néanmoins poser problème."

1 Introduction

Judge Cot's gently expressed concerns remain valid. Others have been more forthright.[2] The question addressed in this chapter is whether there are structural problems with the "international bar" that may underlie such concerns.

There is no single unified international bar, or even distinct bars in different subject-matter areas or regions. The term "international bar" has no clear meaning, and the international bar has no formal structure. It is used here simply to refer to those lawyers who act as counsel in cases before international courts and tribunals.[3]

We concentrate in this chapter on counsel before the International Court of Justice (ICJ), the International Tribunal for the Law of the Sea (ITLOS), and inter-state arbitrations (such as those under Annex VII of the United Nations Convention on the Law of the Sea); but we refer to other courts and tribunals where there are particular points worth noting. We do not address the position of lawyers appearing before international criminal courts and tribunals, to which special considerations apply.[4]

A central issue is whether there are any general principles that apply to the qualification and conduct of members of the international bar. Is there a "common law of international courts and tribunals"[5] in this regard? It seems clear that there is not, at least not yet. Scholars and practitioners have sought to identify a minimum set of ethical standards that, in their eyes, would contribute to the integrity and fairness of international litigation. So an initial question is whether there could or should be a common set of standards, and here some skepticism seems in order. While individual courts and tribunals might seek to prescribe rules, it is doubtful that they have the power to do so. Also, the states that established the courts and tribunals may themselves be unwilling to do so. In any event, it seems unlikely that general rules could be established across the range of international courts and tribunals.

In addition to a lack of professional standards, members of the international bar need not possess any formal qualifications, rendering the international bar generally unregulated. These two related issues are surveyed in section 2. However, while

[2] See, e.g., Judge Oda's reference, to which Judge Cot drew attention, to "ambitious private lawyers" in his Declaration in *Armed Activities on the Territory of the Congo (Democratic Republic of the Congo v. Uganda)* (Provisional Measures) [2000] ICJ Rep 111, 131–3.

[3] We do not cover those who act as agents, as they raise distinct issues (Oda, note 2), unless they also act as counsel. Sir Franklin Berman, "Article 42" in A Zimmermann et al., (eds), *The Statute of the International Court of Justice: A Commentary* (2nd edn, Oxford University Press 2012) 1083. Nor do we cover those lawyers who appear before international courts and tribunals as advisers or experts or in any capacity other than that of counsel.

[4] For more on those appearing before international criminal courts and tribunals, see, in this handbook, Heller, Ch. 31 and Gibson, Ch. 32.

[5] C Brown, *A Common Law of International Adjudication* (Oxford University Press 2007).

the international bar is in theory open to all, section 3 shows that in practice it consists of a restricted number of litigators with similar characteristics, implicitly excluding others. While the current situation may have proven generally efficient, the chapter concludes with thoughts on how the international bar could and should develop in the future.

2 The Regulation of Legal Representation and Professional Standards

The practice in inter-state disputes is that states are normally represented by agents.[6] These agents are most often officials of the state which they represent, but that is not necessarily the case.[7] Is there a duty also to be represented by lawyers? The texts governing both the ICJ and the ITLOS suggest not. Article 42 of the ICJ Statute requires states to be represented by an agent, yet leaves the assistance of counsel or advocates to the discretion of the state.[8] The Rules of the ITLOS similarly provide that states shall be represented by agents before the tribunal, with the use of counsel or advocates at their discretion.[9]

In national settings, qualifications are meant to ensure a certain level of (continuing) substantive knowledge and professionalism. They attest to the competence of those acquiring them. Nevertheless, only in rare cases have rules been laid down concerning who may appear before an international court, or regulating the conduct of such persons. One such example is the Statute of the Court of Justice of the European Union (EU). Article 19 lays down the qualifications necessary for those representing parties before the EU courts, differentiating between representatives of states and EU institutions, and representatives of other parties (such as individuals). Whereas the former shall be represented by agents (and may be assisted by advisers or lawyers if they so choose), other parties must be represented by lawyers. Only a lawyer authorized to practice in a national jurisdiction may represent or assist a

[6] S Rosenne, *The Law and Practice of the International Court of Justice 1920–2005* (4th edn, Leiden, Boston, MA: Martinus Nijhoff 2006) 1119, 1132–7.

[7] Berman, note 3, at 1082.

[8] Statute of the International Court of Justice (adopted June 26, 1945, entered into force on October 24, 1945) 33 UNTS 993, Art. 42.2. (Hereafter ICJ Statute.)

[9] ITLOS Rules of the Tribunal (ITLOS/8) (as amended on March 17, 2009), Art. 53. <http://www.itlos.org/fileadmin/itlos/documents/basic_texts/Itlos_8_E_17_03_09.pdf> accessed July 31, 2012.

party. University professors may also appear, provided they are nationals of a member state that entitles them to practice law in domestic jurisdictions. Thus, while lawyers appearing before the EU courts must be qualified to practice in a national jurisdiction, states are not required to be represented by accredited lawyers.

On the other hand, neither the Statute nor the Rules of the ICJ or ITLOS say anything about who is qualified to act as counsel and, therefore, appear and plead. For this reason, writers discussing the qualifications of those appearing as counsel before the ICJ tend to write about the qualifications they believe the court expects counsel to possess, rather than their actual qualifications.[10] And while expectations, rather than set rules, are discussed, the literature—with few exceptions—has not thoroughly examined whether these expectations have been met.[11] The matter does not seem to be regulated in inter-state arbitration either. Though qualifications of counsel could be covered in ad hoc arbitration agreements, this does not seem to be done. This may be attributed to notions of sovereignty and the right of a state to choose its representatives as it pleases. The only exception seems to be the ICJ's Practice Directions VII and VIII of February 7, 2002, which touch upon specific issues regarding the nomination of judges ad hoc and agents and counsel.[12] Practice Direction VII states that in the interest of the sound administration of justice, parties should "refrain from designating as agent, counsel or advocate in a case before the Court a person who is sitting as a judge *ad hoc* in another case before the Court." And Practice Direction VIII stipulates that "parties should refrain from designating as agent, counsel or advocate in a case before the Court a person who in the three years preceding the date of the designation was a Member of the Court, judge *ad hoc*, Registrar, Deputy-Registrar or higher official of the Court."

The issue addressed in these Practice Directions may well arise in other contexts. For example, in international investment arbitrations it is common for the same person to act as counsel in one case and arbitrator in another—including where similar issues may arise. This practice has become a matter of controversy, and some practitioners have decided it is inappropriate.

The expectation may be that states will appoint as counsel those possessing the proper qualifications to address the judges or arbitrators, in particular those qualified to appear before the higher courts of their own country or academics from recognized institutions of higher education.[13] Though this is normally the case, the survey conducted in section 3 shows that this is not always so.

[10] Berman, note 3, at 1084.

[11] Several examples of judges expressing their dissatisfaction with the level of advocacy are given in A Sarvarian, *Professional Ethics at the International Bar* (Oxford University Press 2013) Chs IV and V. See Judge Cot, separate opinion, *M/V "Louisa" Case (Saint Vincent and the Grenadines v. Spain)* (Judgment of May 28, 2013), ITLOS Reports 2013.

[12] The Practice Directions, which supplement the Rules of the Court, are available at <http://www.icj-cij.org/documents/index.php?p1=4&p2=4&p3=0> accessed July 29, 2012.

[13] Berman, note 3, at 1084.

It seems unlikely that specific ethical standards apply widely to members of the international bar. International standards, such as those adopted by the International Bar Association,[14] are addressed to lawyers practicing in national systems. In any event, whether national standards apply to members of a national legal profession, when appearing before an international court or tribunal, would depend upon their precise terms. Whether or not they formally apply, professionally qualified lawyers are likely to be guided by national ethical codes.

In the absence of regulation, international courts and tribunals presumably rely on the informal application of national standards. As one author has written, in the context of the ICJ, "The Court has been able to rely on the assumption that those carrying the legal argument before it... will regard themselves as bound by similar ethical rules and professional obligations as when appearing before their own national courts."[15]

That may be true, but the absence of regulation and agreed standards of conduct may bring about different practices amongst counsel from different legal traditions on various issues of substance, and the recurring need for the bench to be aware and take account of differences in counsel conduct in order to ensure that procedures are fair and equality is guaranteed.[16] For example, divergences may arise regarding preparation of witnesses or *ex-parte* communication with arbitrators.[17]

Without agreed standards, diverging conduct by opposing counsel may create practical difficulties and an inherent unfairness in the proceedings, with differing practices providing one side an advantage over another.[18] These differing practices may become more prevalent as more and more actors resort to international adjudication on an increasing number of issues.[19] In addition to the practical difficulties, the lack of clarity as to which ethical rules apply as a result of the absence of standards regulating the conduct of counsel may eventually jeopardize the legitimacy of

[14] International Bar Association, "IBA International Principles on Conduct for the Legal Profession," adopted on May 28, 2011 by the International Bar Association, <www.ibanet.org/Document/Default.aspx?DocumentUid=1730FC33-6D70-4469-9B9D-8A12C319468C> accessed July 31, 2012. It does not appear that the authors of this document had in mind the position of counsel before international courts and tribunals. Nevertheless, some of its principles may offer useful guidance, such as Principle 2 (Honesty, integrity, and fairness).

[15] Berman, note 3, at 1084.

[16] J Paulsson, "Cultural Differences in Advocacy in International Arbitration" in D Bishop and EG Kehoe (eds), *The Art of Advocacy in International Arbitration* (2nd edn, New York: Juris 2010) 15–21; CA Rogers, "The Ethics of Advocacy" in Bishop and Kehoe (eds), *The Art of Advocacy* 52–6.

[17] Rogers, note 16, at 52–4.

[18] Rogers, note 16, at 55; see also DF Vagts, "The International Legal Profession: A Need for More Governance?" (1996) 90 AJIL 250–61; D Bishop, "Ethics in International Arbitration" (Keynote Address at the XXth International Council for Commercial Arbitration Congress, May 26, 2010) <www.arbitration-icca.org/media/0/12763302233510/icca_rio_keynote_speech.pdf> accessed July 31, 2012.

[19] G Born, "A Code of Conduct for Counsel in International Arbitration" (November 16, 2010) Kluwer Arbitration Blog <http://kluwerarbitrationblog.com/blog/2010/11/16/a-code-of-conduct-for-counsel-in-international-arbitration> accessed July 31, 2012; Sarvarian, note 11, at Ch. II.

the legal system and confidence in international adjudication, in an era of increased public scrutiny.[20]

While ethical standards vary, there are undoubtedly some central principles that ought to apply to all appearing before an international court or tribunal (even those not members of a national bar). One example is the uncontroversial principle at issue in the recent controversy in the pages of the *American Journal of International Law* between Judge Stephen Schwebel and Paul Reichler over Nicaragua's handling of evidence in the *Armed Activities* case: Reichler is surely right to say that "[a]s officers of the Court, we have an ethical obligation not to submit, or to allow a client to submit, false evidence."[21] Another such principle is the importance of not contravening the confidentiality of lawyer-client communications, including when they are obtained accidentally (as may happen if counsel are staying at the same hotel and using the same business center).

Another matter of general standards of counsel and ethics has arisen regarding the distinction between counsel and witnesses. In one case, at the request of one party, the President of an ICJ Chamber decided that a counsel for the other party was to be treated as a witness after attesting to certain points of fact in his pleadings.[22] The counsel then waived any relevant privileges and was cross-examined as any other witness.[23]

A similar issue arose in the *Pulp Mills* case.[24] In its judgment, the court voiced criticism of the conduct of both parties in having individuals attesting to facts also plead as counsel during the proceedings:

> The Court indeed considers that those persons who provide evidence before the Court based on their scientific or technical knowledge and on their personal experience should testify before the Court as experts, witnesses or in some cases in both capacities, rather than counsel, so that they may be submitted to questioning by the other party as well as by the Court.[25]

The court then hinted at the implications such conduct may have on its treatment of such evidence and its assessment of its impartiality.[26]

In his separate opinion, Judge Greenwood emphasized that such a dual role as expert and counsel blurs the distinction between evidence and advocacy, which is fundamental to the proper conduct of litigation before all courts. To have people

[20] Rogers, note 16, at 63–4; Bishop, note 18, at para. 10–11; Sarvarian, note 11, at Ch. II.

[21] PS Reichler, "The *Nicaragua* Case: A Response to Judge Schwebel" (2012) 106(2) AJIL 316. But see WM Reisman on the "Shawcross dilemma" in WM Reisman, "The Quest for World Order and Human Dignity in the Twenty-first Century: Constitutive Process and Individual Commitment" (2012) Hague Recueil, Vol. 351, Ch. XV (International law as a profession: dilemmas of identity and commitment).

[22] *Elettronica Sicula S.p.A. (ELSI) (U.S. v. Italy)* (Judgment) [1989] ICJ Rep 15, at 19.

[23] *Elettronica Sicula S.p.A. (ELSI)*, note 22, at 19; Berman, note 3 at 1087, fn. 62; Rosenne, note 6, at 1134–5.

[24] *Pulp Mills on the River Uruguay (Argentina v. Uruguay)* (Judgment) [2010] ICJ Rep 14.

[25] *Pulp Mills*, note 24, at 72, para. 167. [26] *Pulp Mills*, note 24, at 72–3, para. 168.

involved in the preparation of evidence submitted pleading "as counsel, rather than giving evidence as witnesses or experts, was both unhelpful to the Court and unfair to the other Party."[27]

Challenges to counsel (as opposed to challenges to members of the bench) are understandably rare. Two challenges to counsel were decided upon by arbitral tribunals constituted under the International Centre for Settlement of Investment Disputes (ICSID). In *Hrvatska v. Slovenia*, the claimant challenged a counsel appointed by the respondent who was a barrister at the same chambers as the president of the tribunal.[28] The claimant was notified of the participation of the barrister only shortly before the oral phase. The arbitral tribunal found that the tribunal lacked the explicit power to exclude counsel, and that the parties may seek representation as they see fit, as a fundamental principle.[29] Yet it found an overriding exception to that principle in the principle "of the immutability of properly constituted tribunals" which allows for the disqualification of counsel when a party alters its legal representation in a way that is found to imperil the tribunal's perceived legitimacy.[30] Accordingly, the barrister was excluded from the proceedings.

Two years later, another arbitral tribunal established under the ICSID faced a similar challenge to counsel.[31] In *Rompetrol v. Romania*, the respondent sought to challenge counsel for the claimant on the grounds that he was once employed by the same law firm as the president of the tribunal. The tribunal explicitly refrained from adopting the approach taken in *Hrvatska v. Slovenia*, and questioned whether the powers necessary for a tribunal to preserve the integrity and effectiveness of its proceedings should extend to the exclusion of counsel, where such powers were not explicitly granted to the tribunal.[32]

Without passing judgment on the substance of standards applicable to counsel, the tribunal differentiated between the obligations of an impartial and independent arbitrator, to that of counsel, partial to his or her party, "so long as he does so with diligence and with honesty, and in due compliance with the applicable rules of professional conduct and ethics."[33] The tribunal then commented that it is not uncommon, in disputes involving states, that counsel had professional dealings with arbitrators in other cases; and that any other decision might infringe on the

[27] *Pulp Mills*, note 24, at 72–3, para. 168; Greenwood Sep. Op., at 231, para. 27.

[28] *Hrvatska Elektroprivreda d.d. v. Republic of Slovenia* (ICSID Case No. ARB/05/24) (Order Concerning the Participation of a Counsel of May 6, 2008), <http://icsid.worldbank.org/ICSID/FrontServlet?requestType=CasesRH&actionVal=showDoc&docId=DC950_En&caseId=C69> accessed July 29, 2012.

[29] *Hrvatska Elektroprivreda d.d. v. Republic of Slovenia*, note 28, at 10, paras 24–5.

[30] *Hrvatska Elektroprivreda d.d. v. Republic of Slovenia*, note 28, at 10, para. 26.

[31] *The Rompetrol Group N.V. v. Romania* (ICSID Case No. ARB/06/3) (Decision on the Participation of a Counsel of January 14, 2010), <http://icsid.worldbank.org/ICSID/FrontServlet?requestType=CasesRH&actionVal=showDoc&docId=DC1370_En&caseId=C72> accessed July 29, 2012.

[32] *The Rompetrol Group N.V. v. Romania*, note 31, pp. 9–10, paras 22–3.

[33] *The Rompetrol Group N.V. v. Romania*, note 31, pp. 7–8, para. 19.

inherent right of the party to choose its own counsel.[34] Finally, the tribunal concluded that regardless of what the correct answers may be to these questions of principle, tribunals should only disqualify counsel rarely, when an undeniable need to safeguard the integrity of the arbitral process exists.[35] The authors submit that this is the correct approach, and that the earlier decision in *Hrvatska v. Slovenia* should be confined to its own particular facts.

One other challenge to counsel took place in an unpublished annulment proceeding under ICSID, of which Doak Bishop spoke in May 2010.[36] According to Bishop, the claimant's counsel was challenged on the grounds that he had represented the respondent some five years earlier in a related proceeding. While the annulment committee stressed that it had no say on the question of the counsel's ethical responsibilities whatever they may be, it took the view that the duty to treat the parties fairly and equally necessarily included the power to ensure that generally recognized principles of conflict of interest and the protection of confidential information were complied with.[37] Recognizing that neither the codes of conduct binding counsel before national jurisdictions nor the Council of Bars and Law Societies of Europe (CCBE) code of conduct were applicable, the committee found that counsel was not in breach of any general principle.[38] Thus, this decision seems in line with the view mentioned above, that some general principles inevitably control counsel's conduct before international courts and tribunals.

In view of this not entirely satisfactory situation, it is not surprising that efforts have been made to devise general ethical standards that could apply to counsel appearing before international courts and tribunals, most notably the International Law Association's "Hague Principles on Ethical Standards for Counsel Appearing Before International Courts and Tribunals."[39] These have been private initiatives, and so far seem to have had little impact. But one may hope that there is at least a growing awareness of the issues, both in arbitration and before permanent courts and tribunals.

Within the wider context of international litigation, developing ethical standards may address the concerns regarding an unlevel playing field amongst counsel and the integrity of the profession and the system. Reliance on qualifications in national jurisdictions on the other hand, even if adopted in all international forums,

[34] *The Rompetrol Group N.V. v. Romania*, note 31, pp. 9–10, para. 22.

[35] *The Rompetrol Group N.V. v. Romania*, note 31, pp. 6, para. 16.

[36] Bishop, note 18, paras 10–11. [37] Bishop, note 18, paras 10–11.

[38] Bishop, note 18, paras 10–11.

[39] P Sands, "The ILA Hague Principles on Ethical Standards for Counsel Appearing Before International Courts and Tribunals" (2011) 10 L. & Prac. Int'l Cts. & Tribunals 1, 1–5; P Sands, "Interaction between Counsel and International Courts and Arbitral Tribunals: Ethical Standards for Counsel" in R Wolfrum and I Gätzschmann (eds), *International Dispute Settlement: Room for Innovation?* (Heidelberg, New York, Dordrecht, London: Springer 2012) 127–58.

cannot fully address these concerns. Moreover, if one focuses on the interstate context, given that among the already limited number of counsel that appear before courts and tribunals (see section 3) not all are necessarily qualified to appear before national jurisdictions, it may indeed be wise to focus more on standards than qualifications which would further limit the ability of newcomers to enter this field of practice.

On the other hand, any move in this direction would have to be reconciled with existing national standards applicable to counsel when acting before national jurisdictions, in one way or another, or else issues of lawyers simultaneously bound by differing ethical standards may be exacerbated.

Lacking regulation, one would expect a variety of people from different backgrounds to be members of the international bar. Section 3 surveys, to the extent possible, who have been acting as international litigators in the past 15 years.

3 Who Acts as Counsel before International Courts and Tribunals?

Who makes up what Alain Pellet refers to as the *barreau invisible* or *barreau occulte*—the "invisible bar" or "hidden bar"—of international counsel? Very little has been written on this question. In an article from the late 1990s focused mainly on the preparation of a case before the ICJ, Pellet himself briefly discussed the identity of those appearing before the Court in the 12 preceding years (1986–1997), giving some "not particularly scientific statistics." He found that there was a small ICJ "mafia" that are trusted by states to represent them before the court as counsel. He identified six British and four French nationals within this core group, and noted the predominance of law professors and of men as opposed to women. Pellet acknowledged that the international bar—insofar as it relates to the ICJ—was a quasi-monopoly that was hard to join.[40]

This section will try to present a contemporary profile of "members of the international bar" over a 16-year period, from 1997–2012. At a panel held during the American Society of International Law annual meeting in 2012, one participant said:

[40] A Pellet, "The Role of the International Lawyer in International Litigaton" in C Wickremasinghe (ed.), *The International Lawyer as Practitioner* (London: British Institute of International and Comparative Law 2000) 147–50.

The problem is this: the universe of lawyers who get to argue on behalf of states before the ICJ or ITLOS, or in inter-state arbitrations, is relatively small, and almost all are older white men from Europe and North America.[41]

Based on a survey of contentious cases and advisory opinions before the ICJ and ITLOS, and inter-state cases administered by the Permanent Court of Arbitration (PCA), over the last 16 years, we examined whether such impressions, shared by many participants and observers, are correct. The aim was to see who appeared as counsel in contemporary inter-state litigation, and what characteristics they shared. When analyzing representation in advisory procedures, oftentimes the precise role of those representing a state or international organization is not specified in the official records. Therefore only those presenting substantive arguments have been included. For example, the survey only included agents who addressed points of substance in their oral presentations.

Relying on publicly available information (mainly the information provided by states and then appearing in the verbatim records and judgments) the sex, nationality, occupation, and qualifications of those appearing were compiled, to the extent possible. The results and conclusions do not purport to provide a precise statistical analysis but rather reflect general trends.

During the period examined (1997–2012), agents and counsel were listed in 33 contentious cases and three advisory opinions before the ICJ. Fifteen contentious cases were heard by ITLOS and one advisory opinion. Also during that period, a list of agents and counsel were provided in eight inter-state arbitrations under the auspices of the PCA (including those which have yet to reach the oral phase). In total, 60 cases were examined. It was found that 601 people were listed as agents or counsel in these cases, with 375 of them making oral presentations.

A closer look at the list of counsel is telling. Most were nationals of the party for whom they were acting—or of the state they represented in advisory proceedings—and appeared as counsel only when their own state engaged them. Such persons may well be taken on for particular reasons and not for their expertise as members of the international bar.[42] In fact a much smaller group of individuals was engaged by a state to act as counsel—and occasionally as agents—when they were not nationals of that state. One author has referred to this group as those who:

[41] P Reichler in "Preparation of Cases before International Courts and Tribunals" (2012) 106 Am. Soc. Int'l L. Proc. 158.

[42] D Bowett, "The Conduct of International Litigation" in D Bowett et al. (eds), *The International Court of Justice: Process, Practice and Procedure* (London: British Institute of International and Comparative Law 1997) 1–20; Pellet, note 40, at 148, also excludes counsel pleading on behalf of their state of nationality from his statistics.

... represent a variety of foreign states other than their own governments, who are well-known to the Judges and Registrar of the Court, who know how things work out in practice, and who understand by experience the difficulties, pitfalls and tricks of the trade.[43]

In the cases surveyed, 129 counsel, or just under 20 percent, were persons representing a state other than that of their nationality.

Within this core group few appear repeatedly as counsel, suggesting that this field of law remains a limited group of people, and breaking into the field—as well as staying in it—continues to be difficult. Of the ten counsel with most appearances, eight were academics (though most of these were also practitioners), six pleaded exclusively in English and one in both English and French. The woman who appeared most had appeared only four times and was also acting as agent in those instances. A look at the most recent cases heard before the ICJ shows that the vast majority of counsel engaged by the parties had previously pleaded before the court, some several times.

Are there any characteristics shared by this core group of counsel? The overwhelming majority are from what could be labeled the "West" (Western Europe, the United States, Australia, Canada, New Zealand), practitioners and academics alike. Non-national counsel from other countries who have appeared in the cases surveyed are few: the authors have counted only seven such counsel, of whom only five pleaded in the cases surveyed. Within this small number of individuals, at least three have links to academic institutions in Western countries.

These findings tend to confirm the impression that the world of inter-state litigation is dominated by a small group of people. While international litigation had been a scarce and mainly Eurocentric occurrence in the past, it has become a more regular and global phenomenon, involving states from all regions. This trend has yet to be fully reflected in the characteristics of the international bar. As can be inferred from Pellet's personal account, this may have to do with the fact that those that join this circle, while knowledgeable in their own right, are often personally acquainted with those already practicing in inter-state litigation.[44] Under the circumstances, it is not easy for newcomers to join the international bar. This difficulty of "admission" is not only unfair to potential litigators—first and foremost those that do not share the characteristics of this group—but possibly denies states representation by those most competent to act as counsel. However, the limited access is probably in large measure explained by the reluctance of states to include less well-established figures among their counsel.[45]

[43] K Highet, "A Personal Memoir of Eduardo Jiménez de Aréchaga" (1994) 88 Am. Soc. Int'l L. Proc. 577, at 579.

[44] Pellet, note 40, at 150–1.

[45] Pellet, note 40, at 148.

3.1 Gender

One thing that stands out is the predominant number of males amongst counsel. Of the 601 counsel and agents, only 67 were female. Of the 375 making oral presentations, 41 were women. Thirteen of the 120 agents were women. That is, in each case, just over 10 percent. A slightly higher percentage of women took part in advisory proceedings. Thirteen of 84 individuals representing the state (or an international organization) in these procedures were women, about 15 percent.

3.2 Language

Another aspect examined was the language used by counsel. It should be noted that while pleaders before the ICJ and ITLOS may normally plead in either of the two official languages, English or French, ad hoc arbitrations may specify one language in which all proceedings will take place.[46] In the cases examined, 235 counsel addressed the courts or tribunals in English whereas 121 addressed them in French, a 2:1 ratio. Nineteen made oral pleadings in both languages, half of them agents of the states. English was the only language used in all of the PCA inter-state cases with publicly available records of oral pleadings. When looking solely at ICJ cases, the differential between the use of English and French is slightly lower, with 184 speakers addressing the Court in English and 105 in French, a 1.75:1 ratio.

Language differences may also relate to differences in style between pleaders. This element, along with others such as a common law or civil law approach to pleading, contributes to differences in style, emphasis, and terminology.[47] There may be a conscious effort to include in legal teams both civil and common lawyers, and both English and French speakers, particularly before the ICJ.[48]

[46] See e.g., Arbitration Agreement between the Government of the Republic of Slovenia and the Government of the Republic of Croatia, November 4, 2009 ITLOS, Rules of the Tribunal, note 9, Art. 43; ICJ Statute, note 8, Art. 39. Article 39 allows the parties to agree to the conduct of proceedings in only one of the court's official languages. Even when such agreements were reached, in practice this did not preclude counsel from pleading in the other language during the oral phase. See MG Kohen, "Art. 39" in A Zimmermann et al. (eds), *The Statute of the International Court of Justice: A Commentary* (2nd edn, Oxford University Press 2012) 917 fn. 46.

[47] For more on this see J Crawford and A Pellet, "Anglo-Saxon and Continental Approaches to Pleading Before the ICJ; Aspects des modes continentaux et Anglo-Saxons de plaidoiries devant la C.I.J." in I Buffard et al. (eds), *International Law between Universalism and Fragmentation, Festschrift in Honour of Gerhard Hafner* (Leiden, Boston, MA: Martinus Nijhoff 2008) 831–69, in particular at 867.

[48] Pellet, note 40, at 151–3.

3.3 Academics and practitioners

Whereas in national forums only qualified members of the profession can appear before local courts, those appearing before international courts and tribunals may be professionally qualified, but this is by no means always the case, especially among academics. And, within the academic circles, some who have pleaded are not yet professors, but are still pursuing academic titles (such as doctoral students). Historically, the participation of academics in international adjudication may stem from the days when such adjudication was a rare event, which allowed full-time professors to appear occasionally as counsel. Indeed, it may be that in those days international law was largely an academic field of law, not one for professional litigators.[49] Nowadays, the lack of a qualification requirement in the forums examined leads to an interesting split in the professional background and qualifications of counsel. According to the available information concerning 271 counsel, there is essentially an equal split between academics and practitioners. Though some academics were listed as members of a country's bar or as qualified counsel on a national level, many were not listed as possessing such credentials.[50] In any case, while in most national legal systems the split between practicing lawyers and academics is visible, the line dividing academics and practitioners within the international bar is blurred, if it exists at all.

3.4 Fragmentation and specialization

Although many ICJ cases in recent years have dealt with maritime delimitation, the establishment of ITLOS as a specialized venue for the law of the sea has opened somewhat the international bar in inter-state disputes to new members. For example, of the counsel appearing in the eight ITLOS cases concerning the prompt release of vessels, only three also participated in the other cases surveyed. Thus, the establishment of a new specialized forum may open the international bar to newcomers, to a certain extent. At the same time, some negative reactions surfaced when certain counsel were viewed as unfamiliar with the practices and procedures of the forum before which they were appearing.[51]

[49] Pellet, note 40, at 150.

[50] Of course, this does not necessarily entail that they do not in fact possess such qualifications.

[51] Cot, note 1.

3.5 Newcomers

The number of counsel engaged by states is limited, and those within that group tend to share the characteristics mentioned above. Nevertheless, there seem to be a few ways in which a newcomer can enter the group and develop a career as counsel before international courts and tribunals. First, a characteristic of many counsel mentioned above is that they are academics as well as practitioners, perhaps reflecting the rather academic nature of public international law. This avenue of joining a class of litigators through the academic world seems uncommon in the national context. Second, much like other fields of law, some counsel are partners or associates in law firms or members of chambers and *cabinets* which specialize, at least to some degree, in international litigation before courts and tribunals. Third, some counsel first appeared in inter-state disputes as agents or representatives of their state of nationality, later building on that experience and pleading on behalf of other states. And fourth, some started as assistants to counsel.[52] Governments need to appreciate the advantages of having a team that mixes "experienced Counsel who can avoid worrying slips and have solid know-how and other able international lawyers who can bring 'new blood' and new ideas."[53]

4 Conclusions

As Judge Cot said in the *"Grand Prince"* Case, "[l]awyers play an irreplaceable role before international tribunals in aiding the administration of justice."[54] On the whole, international justice has been well served by the lawyers that appear in the various courts and tribunals. They are dedicated to their profession, to presenting each case to the best of their ability on behalf of their client, while feeling at least to some degree that they owe allegiance also to the court and more broadly to the international legal system. At the same time, the current situation is not without its problems. We have highlighted two in this brief overview, the lack of common ethical standards, and the narrow pool from which counsel are chosen. However, neither problem should be exaggerated. The pool is inevitably widening with the growth in litigation. And there seems to be a growing awareness of the issues, which itself should lead to improvements. As one author has written:

> more attention will certainly have to be devoted to the question whether the "Bar"—the loose collectivity of persons engaged by States to advance their legal and factual argument in

[52] Pellet, note 40, at 158–9.
[53] Pellet, note 40, at 149.
[54] Cot, note 1, at para. 9.

cases before the Court (including in advisory proceedings)—requires some greater degree of organization and regulation, on the basis that this has shown itself in all legal cultures to be a necessary element of a mature judicial system.[55]

Research Questions

1. Should the "international bar" be regulated? Should international courts rely on national qualifications and standards, or should specialized rules and standards be conceived?
2. In the absence of applicable standards, do international courts and tribunals have an inherent power to exclude a state-appointed counsel, and under what conditions should they do so? What standards should these bodies apply?
3. How would regulating the international bar affect its composition?
4. Would the international judicial system benefit from expanding the international bar? Should and could steps be taken to open the field to under-represented groups?

Suggested Reading

Berman, F, Sir, "Article 42" in A Zimmermann et al. (eds), *The Statute of the International Court of Justice: A Commentary* (2nd edn, Oxford University Press 2012) 1078–87.

Cot, J-P, "Appearing 'for' or 'on behalf of' a State: The Role of Private Counsel before International Tribunals" in N Ando, E McWhinney and R Wolfrum, (eds), *Liber Amicorum Judge Shiguru Oda* (The Hague, London, New York: Kluwer Law International 2002) 835–47.

Cot, J-P, "The Bar" in K Bannelier, T Christakis, and S Heathcote (eds), *The ICJ and the Evolution of International law: The enduring impact of the Corfu Channel case* (Abingdon: Routledge 2012) 21–38.

Crawford, J, "Advocacy before International Tribunals in State-to-State Cases" in D Bishop and EG Kehoe (eds), *The Art of Advocacy in International Arbitration* (2nd edn, New York: Juris 2010) 303–30.

Crawford, J and Pellet, A, "Anglo-Saxon and Continental Approaches to Pleading Before the ICJ; Aspects des modes continentaux et Anglo-Saxons de plaidoiries devant la C.I.J." in I Buffard et al. (eds), *International Law between Universalism and Fragmentation, Festschrift in Honour of Gerhard Hafner* (Leiden, Boston, MA: Martinus Nijhoff 2008) 831–69.

Kazazi, M, "Commentary on the Hague Principles on Ethical Standards for Counsel Appearing before International Courts and Tribunals" (2011) 10 L. & Prac. Int'l Cts. & Tribunals 17–23.

[55] Berman, note 3, at 1087.

Paulsson, J, "Cultural Differences in Advocacy in International Arbitration" in D Bishop and EG Kehoe (eds), *The Art of Advocacy in International Arbitration* (2nd edn, New York: Juris 2010) 15–21.

Pellet, A, "The Role of the International Lawyer in International Litigaton" in C Wickremasinghe (ed.), *The International Lawyer as Practitioner* (London: British Institute of International and Comparative Law 2000) 147–62.

Pellet, A, United Nations Audiovisual Library of International Law Lecture Series, Counsel before the International Court of Justice, An interview with Mr. Alain Pellet <http://untreaty.un.org/cod/avl/ls/Pellet_CT_video_2.html> accessed April 11, 2013.

Reisman, WM, "The Quest for World Order and Human Dignity in the Twenty-first Century: Constitutive Process and Individual Commitment" (2012) Hague Recueil, Vol. 351, Ch XV (International law as a profession: dilemmas of identity and commitment).

Rogers, CA, "The Ethics of Advocacy" in D Bishop and EG Kehoe (eds), *The Art of Advocacy in International Arbitration* (2nd edn, New York: Juris 2010) 49–66.

Rosenne, S, *The Law and Practice of the International Court of Justice 1920–2005* (4th edn, Leiden, Boston, MA: Martinus Nijhoff 2006) 1132–7.

Sands, P, "The ILA Hague Principles on Ethical Standards for Counsel Appearing Before International Courts and Tribunals" (2011) 10 L. & Prac. Int'l Cts. & Tribunals 1, 1–5.

Sands, P, "Interaction between Counsel and International Courts and Arbitral Tribunals: Ethical Standards for Counsel" in R Wolfrum and I Gätzschmann (eds), *International Dispute Settlement: Room for Innovation?* (Heidelberg, New York, Dordrecht, London: Springer 2012) 127–58.

Sarvarian, A, *Professional Ethics at the International Bar* (Oxford University Press 2013).

Shashank, KC Rose, "A Study of Lawyers Appearing before the International Court of Justice 1999–2012," Working Paper (forthcoming).

Vagts, DF, "The International Legal Profession: A Need for More Governance?" (1996) 90 AJIL 250–61.

Valencia-Ospina, E, "International Courts and Tribunals, Agents, Counsel, and Advocates" in R Wolfrum (ed.), *Max Planck Encyclopedia of Public International Law* (Oxford University Press 2012), Vol. V, 515–18.

Wood, M, Reichler, P, Pratt, M, Kinnear, M, and Berman, F, "Preparation of Cases before International Courts and Tribunals" (2012) 106 Am. Soc. Int'l L. Proc. 153–65.

Working Session of the Study Group on the Practice and Procedure of International Tribunals, "The Hague Principles on Ethical Standards for Counsel Appearing Before International Courts and Tribunals" (including some initial reactions to the Hague Principles) in International Law Association Report of the Seventy-Fourth Conference (The Hague 2010) (London: International Law Association 2010) 952–60.

CHAPTER 30

COMMUNITIES OF INTERNATIONAL LITIGATORS

ANTOINE VAUCHEZ*

1 Introduction

As a remainder of the traditional legal representation where judging is a solitary and independent act, international courts have long been considered reified

* Research Professor, Centre européen de sociologie et de science politique (CNRS), Université Paris 1-Sorbonne.

collectives forming separate and self-standing *units* of analysis. Such representations implicitly assume the existence of a sharp divide between an "inside" and an "outside" of a court. Likewise, international courts' case law has often been regarded as essentially "reactive" to *external* challenges brought to them by equally separate and self-standing entities: the "parties" to the trials (states, NGOs, companies, etc.). Despite regular calls for a shift in the scholarship,[1] what lies in between "the court" and "the parties" has not raised much interest: the literature has remained strikingly oblivious of litigation's specific experts, be they legal agents, clerks, litigants, etc. This contrasts with the generalized agreement that litigation opportunities have been central to the emergence of international courts.[2]

In the field of legal scholarship, this relates to a general underestimation of the role of agency in legal change. It is quite striking to note that out of a total of 8,150 contributions to international law *Festschriften* that have been authored between 1930 and 2000, only eight deal with legal professionals (judges, litigants, and so on).[3] In the neo-functionalist literature, arguably the dominant political science literature on international courts so far, the lack of interest originates in a rather restrictive understanding of "the (international or regional bodies of) law" as a transparent instrument strategically seized by self-interested social groups to circumvent the obstacles of national modes of regulation.[4] For different reasons, it converges with legal scholarship in maintaining lawyers in a blind spot, as invisible defenders of the different "heavy" interests (companies, states, international organizations, interest groups, associations, etc.) that confront each other before the various international courts.

In light of the Weberian tradition of sociology of law, one should adopt a deeper view of the social dynamics underpinning law and take the relative autonomy of the legal realm more seriously. Law actually exists as a specific and relatively autonomous social world with specific professional conceptions of worth and wealth, commonsensical ideas about the political and social importance of law, and even, under certain circumstances, a specific agenda. This is easily evidenced at the international or regional level.[5] Historically, the development of international courts has coincided with the formation of specific communities of lawyers who master the

[1] See in particular H Schepel and R Wesseling, "The Legal Community: Judges, Lawyers, Officials and Clerks in the Writing of Europe" (1997) 3(2) Eur. L.J. 165–88.

[2] K Alter and L Helfer, "Nature or Nurture: Judicial Lawmaking in the European Court of Justice and the Andean Tribunal of Justice" (2010) 64 Int'l Org. 4.

[3] Compare P Macalister-Smith and J Schwietzke (eds), *Public International Law: Concordance of the Festschriften* (Berliner Wissenschafts-Verlag 2006).

[4] For a review, see A Stone Sweet, "The European Court of Justice and the Judicialization of EU Governance" (2010) 5 Living Rev. Euro. Gov. 2, <http://www.livingreviews.org/lreg-2010-2> accessed on March 27, 2013.

[5] G Sacriste and A Vauchez, "The Force of International Law: Lawyers' Diplomacy on the International Scene in the 1920s" (2007) 32(1) Law & Soc. Inquiry 83–108.

particular judicial style of the court. Just like there is no "artist" without a "network of cooperation" that makes up the "art world," famously studied by Howard Becker, there is no "court" without a (more or less stable) world of professionals. Professionals include those that are directly employed by the court itself (judges but also law clerks, administrative support, legal translators, etc.) to a variety of groups professionally connected to the court (from lawyers to legal scholars, to in-house jurists).[6]

To put it differently, international courts' lawyers are not random individuals thrown into international litigation by the sole virtue of their clientele's demand. Rather, they tend to polarize around small groups of recognized legal experts where it is assumed that "clients" should turn to if they want to put all chances on their side. As numbered by French international lawyer Alain Pellet, "the same 14 advocates pleaded 3 cases or more each in the 20 cases decided by the International Court of Justice" between 1986 and 1997, thereby forming the "invisible bar" of the court.[7] As they master the court's inner rules, official languages and practical know-how, these lawyers are in the most privileged position to identify long-term legal issues and short-term opportunities. Alongside the legal services of international organizations, these core lawyers are the true "repeat players" who can pursue long-term interests and rule-change strategies,[8] and channel the clients' demands as needed. As Martin Shapiro put it, "the lawyers created the clients as often as the clients [created] the lawyers."[9] More generally, as they fill in the gap between "the court" and "the parties," these lawyers act as "middlemen" or brokers, operating in between the demand of "the parties" and the supply side ("the court"). They collectively frame both the input, from social interests to "legal strategies," and the output, from raw decisions to consolidated "jurisprudence." As lawyers, they act as "filters," narrowing down social claims into the most relevant set of legal alternatives and categories of one given court. While they act as *de facto* gatekeepers to the court, they are simultaneously the most natural "translators" of its judicial decisions in terms of political and social implications and opportunities.

Thereby, legal professionals are not merely agents, as hypothesized in the principals/agents model, nor are they mere transmission belts for the different groups who use their service, such as companies, states, international organizations, interest groups, not-for-profit organizations etc. They have agency and may pursue agendas: this is why it is of critical interest to study how these legal practitioners are

[6] H Becker, *Art Worlds* (Berkeley University Press 1984).

[7] Quoted in D Terris, CPR Romano and L Swigart, *The International Judge. An Introduction to the Men and Women Who Decide the World's Cases* (Oxford University Press 2007) 84.

[8] M Galanter, "Why the 'Haves' Come Out Ahead: Speculations on the Limits of Legal Change" (1974) Law & Soc'y Rev., 95–160. In the case of the ECJ, see the quantitative analysis presented in C Marchand and A Vauchez, "Lawyers as Europe's Middlemen: A sociology of Litigants Pleading Before the European Court of Justice" in M Mangenot and J Rowell (eds), *A Political Sociology of the European Union. Reassessing Constructivism* (Manchester University Press 2010) 68–87.

[9] M Shapiro, "Juridicalization of Politics in the United States" (1994) 15(2) Int'l Pol. Sci. Rev. 109.

structured in communities and what is their role. While it is "so deeply embedded in the routine of the legal system that it is hardly noticeable,"[10] the relationship between legal communities[11] and courts is explored in this chapter. Section 2 examines how international courts and transnational legal communities of lawyers are mutually dependent, particularly during the formative period of worldwide or regional jurisdictions. Section 3 considers in more detail what the underlying social dynamics of these transnational communities are. Section 4 provides an analytical discussion of the historical functions of these specialized legal communities.

2 Courts and Legal Communities: A Mutual Dependence

Any analysis of the symbiotic relationship between "international courts" and their "legal communities" should start from the simple yet instrumental fact that international courts are particularly precarious institutions, especially when compared to their national counterparts.[12] Not only do they lack the backing of the state, but they cannot count on the existence of a supranational judicial profession because there is no such thing as a supranational body competent for setting common educational requirements, nor is there an identified breeding ground from which international courts could select and recruit their members.[13] Equally important in the precariousness of international courts is the fact that from the moment of their creation, they are confronted with a vast array of competitors both in the field of law (national supreme courts, other international courts) and in that of international affairs (national diplomats or intergovernmental organizations). In other words, newly-built international courts do not mechanically succeed in claiming a "natural" domain of jurisdiction of their own by the mere force of the black letter of the treaties. More often than not, their existence as an "authentic" jurisdiction capable of producing an authoritative body of case law is initially questioned by a variety of groups and professions (such as national

[10] M Shapiro and A Stone Sweet, *On Law, Politics and Judicialization* (Oxford University Press 2002) 175.

[11] The term of "community" is not used here in its classic sociological meaning, but rather along the lines of legal parlance, that is, without any specific assumption concerning the more or less cohesive structure of these networks.

[12] A Vauchez, "Keeping the Dream Alive: The Transnational Fabric of Integrationist Jurisprudence" (2012) 5(1) Eur. Pol. Sci. Rev. 51–71.

[13] Ever since the creation of the Permanent Court of International Justice, many have advocated the creation of corporations of international lawyers or of a supranational judiciary or bar, without ever finding substantial political support.

scholarships, national supreme courts, and diplomats) who essentially oppose their development, if not entirely ignore their very existence.

The early days of the European Court of Justice (ECJ) are quite emblematic in this regard. The ECJ initially struggled to affirm an authentically legal authority for the interpretation of the Rome Treaties due to the dynamics of international politics and constrained by the essentially economic mission of the European Communities. Some international jurists of the time were disdainful toward the ECJ because they thought the court might as well evolve into a mere chamber of the International Court of Justice (ICJ) or merge with the European Court of Human Rights (ECtHR). There is no need to discuss such extreme positions to observe that the ECJ was initially kept at a distance from the disputes of legal and political interpretation of the new treaties that emerged soon after they were signed. While national jurisdictions were reluctant to recognize the court as a genuine "interlocutor" in this area,[14] an important share of the disputes brought to the ECJ in the first decade of its existence were actually settled out of court.[15]

In other words, it takes a lot of proactive efforts and interventions for international courts to secure institutional and legal space for themselves in a busy and competitive playing field. They need to unsettle ideationally and professionally entrenched paradigms of law. Without the formal homologation of their claims as truly "legal" ones (i.e., without them appearing competent to speak in the name of the law), their very existence as "courts" is at risk of being, to put it in the words of a former ECJ president, no more than "a variation on the old story of Baron Münchhausen who dragged himself out of the mud by pulling on his own hair."[16]

Thus, many elements converge in establishing the precarious grounds on which international courts are built. On that basis, it is quite safe to hypothesize their strong dependence on the existence of a "support structure."[17] In the absence of a state apparatus responsible for instilling respect and ensuring enforcement of international courts' decisions, their fiduciary value is highly dependent upon the court's capacity to generate continuous support from a variety of lawyers who will authenticate its legal accomplishments, act as vigilant custodians, and defend its authority against a variety of external criticisms. In the absence of a feed court from which to recruit new members, these legal networks are also key in providing a transnational breeding ground of judges (often former students, research assistants, law clerks, or

[14] K Alter, *Establishing the Supremacy of European Law* (Oxford University Press 2001); J Weiler, "A Quiet Revolution. The European Court of Justice and its Interlocutors" (1994) 26(4) Comp. Pol. Stud. 510–34.

[15] S Scheingold, *The Rule of Law in European Integration* (Montreal: McGill University Press 1965) 269.

[16] A Donner, "Les rapports entre la compétence de la Cour de justice des communautés européennes et les tribunaux internes" (1965) 115 Recueil des Cours de l'Académie de Droit International 61.

[17] C Epp, *The Rights Revolution. Lawyers, Activists and Supreme Courts in Comparative Perspective* (Chicago University Press 1998); More recently, S Teles, *The Rise of the Conservative Legal Movement: The Battle for Control of the Law* (Princeton University Press 2008).

interns) already socialized to the court's core beliefs and therefore willing to perpetuate its legacy.

This strategic role played by the courts' "support structure" makes it all the more important that international judges themselves, although they could be the natural promoters of the courts' importance, can hardly engage in open promotion strategies. Such course of action would appear to be undue activism and would jeopardize the courts' legitimacy. Therefore, it is not surprising that the emergence of such legal communities is most often promoted by a series of "intermediate" actors, who are simultaneously "insiders" and "outsiders" to the courts. Such figures include advocate-generals,[18] law clerks,[19] members of the registry and of the courts' administration;[20] it may also include litigants with lasting interests (and practice) in the courts' case law, such as, for example, intergovernmental organizations' legal services or segments of legal scholarship.[21] These intermediate actors have a larger margin for maneuver than the judges themselves. In addition, they can claim a more intimate knowledge of the court's case law than the broad legal public because they have direct access to the court's legal material. As a consequence, they are in a privileged situation when it comes to speaking authoritatively about the court's "authentic" intentions, detailing the scope of a decision and foreseeing the future of its case law.

Just like the other courts' professionals (judges, clerks, jurists, etc...), legal practitioners "have an enormous self-interest in defending...courts, most basically in proclaiming their courtness."[22] As such, they are the natural paladins of the court, alerting a variety of national audiences about the legal, political, and academic relevance of the new court. One example is when Stéphanie Hennette-Vauchez identified the role of the "Convention people" in Strasbourg. The "Convention people" were key entrepreneurs who engaged in an instrumental and multifaceted promotion of the European Convention on Human Rights after its signature in 1950. These "Convention people" included academics, members of the Registry, administrators (civil servants and jurists) of the Council of Europe's Human Rights directorate. They included figures such as Michele de Salvia, Karel Vasak, Marc-André Eissen, and others, who were extremely active in commenting on decisions by the European Commission and Court of Human Rights in law journals, installing European Court law chronicles, writing monographs on the European Convention of Human Rights, sitting on the scientific

[18] N Burrows and R Greaves (eds), *The Advocate General and EC Law* (Oxford University Press 2007).

[19] S Kenney, "Beyond principals and agents: seeing courts as organizations by comparing référendaires at the ECJ and law clerks at the US Supreme Court" (1999) 33(5) Comp. Pol. Stud. 593–625, at 622.

[20] S Hennette-Vauchez, "The European Convention on Human Rights and the Birth of (European) Human Rights Law as an Academic Discipline" in A Vauchez and B de Witte (eds), *Lawyering Europe: European Law as a Transnational Social Field* (Oxford: Hart Publishing 2013).

[21] J Bailleux, "Comment l'Europe vint au droit" (2010) 60(2) Revue française de science politique 295–318.

[22] Shapiro and Stone Sweet, note 10, at 175.

boards of research institutes specialized in European human rights law (such as, for instance, the *Institut international des droits de l'homme*), editing *Festschriften* and biannual volumes on the court's jurisprudence and, later on, launching ad hoc law journals (*Rivista italiana di diritti umani, Revue des droits de l'homme*) or opening specialized chairs in universities.[23]

3 Transnational Litigation Communities

As they are integral to designing the various positions opened up by the very existence of international courts (as treaty drafters as well as academic entrepreneurs), these first communities of legal practitioners tend to monopolize those positions. This is the case of the first generation of EU lawyers who were engaged in a game of role switching: they worked successively as law clerks or judges at the European Court of Justice, legal agents representing their governments, lawyers defending their clients (states or firms), members of the European Commission's Legal service, and law professors committed to the establishment of EU law as a new academic discipline.[24] These forerunners often move across the private–public, national–European, legal–political, practice–academic borders. This continuous movement across sectors and across "principals" allowed for an early concentration of legal authority around a small group of "repeat players." This was done to the extent that one could characterize the movement as a form of "cartelization" of the emerging European legal market around a limited number of multi-positioned lawyers able to play all parts in the new legal field.

The formation of transnational legal networks is, however, also embedded in and benefits from broader social and political support to the parent body. In the absence of a sustained and financially relevant case law that would allow for the specialization of groups of litigants,[25] the existence of a lasting legal interest in international

[23] For extra-European examples, see the case of legal professionals and the Organization for Harmonization in Africa of Business Laws as presented by C Dickerson, "Harmonizing Business Laws in Africa: OHADA Calls the Tune" (2005) 44(1) Columbia J.Transnat'l L. 17.

[24] A Vauchez, *L'Union par le droit. L'invention d'un programme institutionnel pour l'Europe* (Paris: Presses de Sciences Po 2013).

[25] The ECJ is probably an exception as the growing importance of the case law favored the emergence of a structured space of European litigation specialists with corresponding law firms in Brussels and antenna of the Council of European bars.

courts depends on support from: international organizations, philanthropic foundations such as Carnegie, Rockefeller or Ford Foundations; and civil society organized interests such as pan-European movements, business networks, and NGO. All these groups are instrumental to securing around international courts a dense web of learned societies, research institutes, book series, *Festschriften*, journals, and conferences, free from the criticism of nationally-anchored elites, be they legal professoriate, supreme court judges or diplomats.

It comes as no surprise that the first transnational venues for international lawyers emerged thanks to the continuous financial and logistic support of the Carnegie Foundation, which famously sponsored the annual meetings of the *Institut de droit international*, the schooling of newcomers through the creation of the Academy of International Law of The Hague, as well as the building of the Peace Palace (1907) in which, from the beginning, it was expected that the much-hoped for World Court would be hosted.[26]

Equally important was, in the case of the Court of Justice of the European Union (CJEU), the role of the European Commission, whose Legal Service strategically designed and partially subsidized a new learned society with a view to building—in the very terms of its first president—"the private army of the Communities."[27] The *Fédération internationale pour le droit européen* (FIDE) united pan-European jurists devoted to the political advancement of the communities and EC in-house lawyers who were empirically making the emerging European legal order (CJEU judges, law clerks, the European Commission's legal advisers, and so on). All of them shared a genuine interest in building new legal rationales that would exemplify and support EC law's radical novelty in the realm of international law.[28] The role of specific NGOs, civic networks and transnational advocacy coalitions, particularly in the field of human rights[29] or in those of environment and trade, is equally important in activating or maintaining forms of cause lawyers before the ECtHR or the World Trade Organization (WTO).

One should not, however, adopt an irenic vision of these legal "communities." They are equally sites of contention where a number of lawyers engage in battles over the definition of the nature and future of the court, discuss the meaning of its case law and frame the future priorities (e.g., organizational reforms or new legal

[26] M Koskenniemi, *The Gentle Civilizer of Nations: The Rise and Fall of International Law (1870–1960)* (Cambridge University Press 2001).

[27] Quoted in Vauchez, note 24.

[28] K Alter, "Jurist Advocacy Movements in Europe" in Alter (ed.), *The European Court's Political Power: Essays on the Influence of the European Court of Justice on European Politics* (Oxford University Press 2009) 63–91; A Vauchez, "The Transnational Politics of Jurisprudence: Van Gend en Loos and the Making of EU Polity" (2010) 16(1) Eur. L.J. 1–28.

[29] M Madsen (ed.), *The European Court of Human Rights* (Oxford University Press 2011) 50; on transnational human rights' activism, see M Keck and K Sikkink, *Activists Beyond Borders: Advocacy Networks in International Politics* (Ithaca, NY: Cornell University Press 1998).

challenges) and urgencies that it faces. These arenas are often crossroads for legal professionals coming from a great variety of national education and professional training patterns. As a result, actors engage in more or less overt competition over the most relevant types of know-how and credentials to persuasively perform international lawyering and judging. As in the case of international commercial arbitration, "there is a continuing competition for business and for legitimacy between civil law and common law, 'grand old men' and 'technocrats,' academics and practitioners."[30] Moreover, as the case law increases, the initially stable and rather cohesive milieu of specialized legal professionals progressively loses its community-like atmosphere. In the case of the ECJ, the stability and homogeneity of the early group of a few dozen lawyers gave way to a more heterogeneous and shifting constellation of specialized professionals and organizations composed of several thousand people. In turn, the correlated risk of undermining the court's case law opened the way for a variety of maintenance strategies through which a select group of centrally placed judges attempted to maintain a sense of community across roles and poles. Not only eulogies, commemorative rituals, *Festschriften*, but also conferences and congresses, counted among the tools they utilized in order to revive a community by codifying its core beliefs and legal principles at a time when diversity, heterogeneity, and the potential accompanying conflicts seemed to prevail.[31] The "family" and the "community" became recurrent metaphors for these cohorts of EU lawyers, who relied on them for their capacity to reactivate transversal solidarity across the variegated sub-groups of the court's professionals.

Yet, these various actors retain common interests beyond the fragmented and competitive structure of transnational "legal communities." For a start, they all share a common interest, if not devotion, to the court. For example, state legal agents from the *Conseil d'Etat* or the *Avvocatura dello Stato* pleading in Strasbourg or Luxembourg on behalf of their national governments, on the one hand, and competition lawyers trained in American LL.M.s now working for Anglo-American law firms in Brussels, on the other hand. These two figures of European legal practice certainly have little in common in terms of their training, career paths, amounts of international experience, and, last but not least, conceptions of European law (a tool for diplomacies or a critical device for market operations?). Indeed, they embody almost radically antagonistic versions of what it is to be a European lawyer: its functions in EU polity, the specific criteria of its legal excellence, its most valued legal credentials, its most estimated skills, degrees, and professions, etc. Yet, even though they may plead against each other before national and European courts, both the *conseillers d'Etat* and the business lawyers share the common assumptions

[30] Y Dezalay and B Garth, "Merchants of Law as Moral Entrepreneurs: Constructing International Justice from the Competition for Transnational Business Disputes" (1995) 29 Law and Soc'y Rev. 1, 27.

[31] A Vauchez, "Keeping the Dream Alive: The Transnational Fabric of Integrationist Jurisprudence" (2012) 5(1) Eur. Pol. Sci. Rev. 51–71.

that an essential part of Europe's future takes place in these judicial arenas and that all governments and market actors should act accordingly. As they contribute to building competing rationales and techniques for European integration, they are similarly engaged in elevating the general status of Euro-law in both public and private European affairs, turning it into one fundamental prerequisite for the access and ascent to private corporations or public bureaucracies. As such, they are best coined as "associated rivals."

4 The Co-Production of Jurisprudence and Judicial Identities

Transnational legal communities have historically performed a certain number of functions. In particular, they have allowed forms of strategic litigation, thereby opening new possible legal avenues for courts. As they are key in continuously reactivating a common sense of mission, they are a privileged arena for repeat players who are "pursuing long-term goals (the change in the state of law) with diffuse pay-offs." They enable an uninterrupted flow of test cases. Suffice it to consider the CJEU. Most of the lawyers who successfully changed the course of its case law in the 1960s and 1970s were deeply embedded in the FIDE, the pan-European legal networks established with the support of the European Commission. LFD Ter Kuile and Gert Meier, both active FIDE members, were respectively the litigants of *Van Gend en Loos* and *Rewe Zentral AG*, which were two cases that made the history of the CJEU.[32] In particular, Ter Kuile had been a member of a study group of the Dutch section of the FIDE devoted to identifying the direct effect of the various parts of Rome treaties. Eliane Vogel-Polsky is another interesting example because she promoted a series of landmark decisions on non-discrimination and gender equality under EC law (the Defrenne cases I, II, III, respectively in 1971, 1976, and 1978). Vogel-Polsky was a labor law professor at the Université libre de Bruxelles at the time the university housed a strong pan-European legal scholarship. She identified the legal potential of Art. 119 of the Treaty of Rome as early as 1967 and attributed its direct effect along the lines of *Van Gend en Loos* jurisprudence.[33] Hence,

[32] Vauchez, note 28; K Alter and S Meunier-Aitshalia, "Judicial politics in the European Community: European Integration and the Pathbreaking Cassis de Dijon Decision" (1999) 26 Comp. Pol. Stud. 535–61.

[33] E Vogel Polski, "L'article 119 du traité de Rome peut-il être considéré comme self-executing?" (1967) 82 Journal des tribunaux 283–7; For a complete account of the Defrenne saga see F Hagner,

these legal networks provide international courts with incentives and rationales to extend the scope or to reorientate the path of case law. They offer new opportunities to consolidate and widen courts' agendas. On the whole, communities of international litigants, such as the FIDE, are typically "neo-functionalist interest groups" as they favor pushing legal doctrines to their breaking points and as they provide legal rationales for new spill-overs beyond the black letter of international treaties.

These networks are simultaneously interpretative communities. As they are strategically positioned in a situation of preempting most of the hermeneutic space available, they are playing an active role in co-defining and co-producing consolidated legal interpretations. In particular, they are integral to the production of "jurisprudence." "Jurisprudence" is not the natural outcome of the flow of case law, but rather the product of mobilizations around the definition and maintenance of its meaning and direction over time. This is most conspicuous with respect to the *Van Gend en Loos* jurisprudence, whose status as the CJEU milestone and landmark case is the product of an uninterrupted flow of legal writing in academic journals, debates in congresses, and further ECJ cases, more often than not produced by jurists that had been directly or indirectly involved in the case. In many respects, scholarship looked like an in-house product and the court a ventriloquial institution capable of speaking in one voice both through the decisions it issued and the commentary it generated. Such an intimate relationship can even be semi-officially acknowledged, as was sometimes the case during the annual congress of the FIDE. Indeed, these congresses were, and still are, organized during court intersession periods, to allow for its academic and judicial parts to actually meet and exchange. Beyond the case law, such co-production also extends to the building and maintenance of courts' judicial identities (the common conception of the role of justice, standards of judges' excellency, rules of legal standing, preferred judicial procedure, etc.). The fate of the preliminary ruling of Art. 177 was the critical lever for the progressive empowerment of the CJEU. Such a "success story" can hardly be understood without accounting for the role of the FIDE in recognizing such an instrument as the best avenue for those who intended to engage in strategic litigation. More broadly, these networks capture legal and professional imagination and provide teleological narratives for the future (foreseeable and desirable) developments of the court's jurisprudence as well as role models for future generations.[34]

As these communities of litigants often cut across international courts, they can also be essential levers for inter-institutional and cross-organizational interaction in the field of international justice. Academic conferences; transnational expert bodies; advocacy coalitions; university-based research institutes, such as the Brandeis

Les particuliers et l'ordre communautaire. L'égalité de traitement entre les hommes et les femmes (Geneva: Institut européen de l'Université de Genève 2003).

[34] D Kennedy, "The Politics of the Invisible College: International Governance and the Politics of Expertise" (2001) 5(3) Eur. Hum. Rts. L. Rev. 463–598.

Institute for International Judges; inter-personal networks, such as the Yale network of global judges; or think tanks, such as the Project on International Courts and Tribunals, all foster a sort of judicial diplomacy as much as a circulation of experts and expertise. In a context of increased fragmentation of transnational legal orders, these interlocking networks and overlapping memberships offer critical opportunities for mainstreaming international judicial practices. If the ECtHR and the CJEU appear today to be relatively tightly "entangled courts," this is in large part the result of transnational mobilizations across both courts. After many years of traditional communication with one another throughout their respective case law, both these courts engaged in regular bilateral meetings and conferences during which they debated the evolution of their respective case law and ways of avoiding the risk of contradictions. Laurent Scheeck states, "[t]he mutually reinforcing relationship results from the mobilization of some leaders of both courts who opted in favor of a high-profile, diplomatic socialization."[35] While this is a very singular example, it sheds light on bilateral and multilateral relationships, a form of judicial diplomacy, that occur across international courts and yet remain rather ignored. In fact, although it generally attracts less attention, the ECtHR has also established close relationships with its Inter-American counterpart. Thomas Buergenthal, a famous international lawyer from the United States who was chosen by Costa Rica to join the newly established Inter-American Court of Human Rights and who later served at the ICJ, testifies that ever since 1979 "an informal agreement between the Inter-American Court and the European Court, providing for periodic meetings between judges of the two courts, alternating between Strasbourg and San José" was in place, which was viewed as bringing "international support outside our region."[36]

5 Conclusion

This chapter has exemplified what could be gained from considering the social and professional embeddedness of international courts and replacing judges into a *continuum* of social and professional ties. Drawing from recent works in the field of political science, legal scholarship, sociology, and history, we have first shown how, in a context of international courts' structural precariousness, the symbiotic

[35] L Scheeck, "Constitutional Activism and Fundamental Rights in Europe: Common Interests Through Transnational Socialization" in M Mangenot and J Rowell, note 8, 109–27.

[36] T Buergenthal, "Remembering the Early Years of the Inter-American Court of Human Rights" (2005) Center for Human Rights and Global Justice Working Paper, New York University 1, 14.

relationship between a given international court and its corresponding "legal community" is a key element of its social authority. The role of these communities in collectively maintaining the symbolic power of international courts helps us understand the care with which a transnational *esprit de corps* is being activated and maintained over time. We have also argued that such a focus on the legal communities provides a more realistic account of the transnational politics of legal change (advocacy coalitions, case-law reversals, landmark decisions), and of the dynamics of institutionalization of international courts (establishing and codifying the court's judicial style, legitimacy building and maintenance, etc.).

This leading role in bringing about social and political change through law has led some scholars to speculate about their crucial "democratic" role as they open new avenues for social change, in particular in areas such as minority rights, non-discrimination, or environmental protection.[37] This optimistic vision of the contribution of international lawyers to democratic empowerment, closely linking litigation and democratization, should be tempered. Some have pointed to the fact that such "emancipatory functionalism" discourse was a professional ideology of lawyers and judges who claim to "take power in the hands of national politicians and bureaucrats."[38] Others, in a more sociological vein, have questioned whether the role of international litigators in opening decision-making processes to new actors (transnational interest groups, NGOs) was going along with a simultaneous closure of the public policy debates at the international level to actors endowed with high levels of legal credentials and legal competence.[39]

Research Questions

1. To what extent is international litigation practice polarized around a set of repeat players specialized in each specific type of international court?
2. To what extent do these established communities of lawyers act as filters or control levers for the "social demands" of justice?
3. In what measure do transnational legal communities constitute a breeding ground and manage to have an impact on the recruitment of future international judges?
4. How organized and structured are the academic and professional networks and fora that cut across international and regional courts?

[37] R Cichowski, *The European Court and Civil Society. Litigation, Mobilization and Governance* (Oxford University Press 2007).

[38] H Schepel, "Law and European Integration: Socio-Legal Perspectives" (2004) 4 EUSA Review 1–4.

[39] A Vauchez, "Democratic Empowerment through Euro-Law?" (2008) 7 Eur. Pol. Sci. Rev. 444–52.

Suggested Reading

Alter, K, *Establishing the Supremacy of European Law* (Oxford University Press 2001).

Alter, K, "The Evolving International Judiciary" (2011) 7 Annual Review of Law and Social Sciences, 387–415.

Cichowski, R, *The European Court and Civil Society. Litigation, Mobilization and Governance* (Oxford University Press 2007).

Dezalay, Y and Garth, B, *Dealing in Virtue. International Commercial Arbitration and the Construction of a Transnational Legal Order* (Chicago University Press 1996).

Kennedy, D, "The Politics of the Invisible College: International Governance and the Politics of Expertise" (2001) 5 European Human Rights Law Review 3, 463–598.

Koskenniemi, M, *The Gentle Civilizer of Nations. The Rise and Fall of International Law (1870–1960)* (Cambridge University Press 2001).

Madsen, M (ed.), *The European Court of Human Rights at 50* (Oxford University Press 2011).

Shapiro, M and Stone Sweet, A, *On Law, Politics and Judicialization* (Oxford University Press 2002).

Terris, D et al., *The International Judge. An Introduction to the Men and Women Who Decide the World's Cases* (Oxford University Press 2007).

Vauchez, A, "The Transnational Politics of Jurisprudence. Van Gend en Loos and the Making of EU Polity" (2010) 16 European Law Journal 1, 1–28.

Vauchez, A and de Witte, B (eds), *Lawyering Europe. European Law as a Transnational Social Field* (Oxford: Hart Publishing 2013).

Weiler, J, "A Quiet Revolution. The European Court of Justice and Its Interlocutors" (1994) 26 Comparative Political Studies 4, 510–34.

CHAPTER 31

THE ROLE OF THE INTERNATIONAL PROSECUTOR

KEVIN JON HELLER*

1 Introduction

The role of the international prosecutor is uniquely challenging. Unlike domestic prosecutors, who at least in theory have the ability to prosecute all of the serious crimes over which they have jurisdiction, international prosecutors are never

* Associate Professor and Reader, Melbourne Law School. Thanks to Martin Clark for his superb research assistance.

able to prosecute more than a small fraction of the suspects who have committed an international crime.[1] International prosecutors thus enjoy much greater discretion than their domestic counterparts.[2] At the same time, international prosecutors operate in much more normatively complicated situations than domestic prosecutors; most domestic crimes are perceived as deviant and unacceptable, whereas international crimes—particularly those that are prosecuted by international adjudicative bodies[3]—are nearly always committed for ideological reasons that make their prosecution profoundly controversial.[4] International prosecutors thus also tend to face far more intense political pressures—from states, the United Nations, non-governmental organizations, etc.—than their domestic counterparts.

Because international prosecution is both highly discretionary and politically charged, the legitimacy of international criminal justice depends, in large part, on the ability of tribunals to strike an appropriate balance between independence and accountability. As Frédéric Mégret has noted:

> At one extreme, a Prosecutor who was "absolutely accountable" would be a Prosecutor who would have to account for every one of his acts. This would be the same thing as saying that the Prosecutor was not independent. Indeed, at a certain level it would mean that he or she was not the Prosecutor, but merely someone carrying out prosecutions whose principles and modalities had been decided elsewhere. At the other extreme, a Prosecutor who is absolutely independent is a Prosecutor who ceases to be meaningfully accountable or, which amounts to the same thing, is accountable only to him or herself.[5]

This chapter explores the tension between independence and accountability that is the defining characteristic of the international prosecutor's role. Section 2 addresses the structural independence of the prosecutor and the Office of the Prosecutor (OTP) from both external political actors and other organs of the tribunal. Section 3 examines the prosecutor's functional independence—his or her practical ability to exercise their discretion free from undue limitation.

[1] L Côté, "Independence and Impartiality" in L Reydams et al. (eds), *International Prosecutors* (Oxford University Press 2012) 352.

[2] WA Schabas, "Prosecutorial Discretion v. Judicial Activism at the International Criminal Court" (2008) 6 J Int'l Crim Justice 731, 734–5.

[3] In keeping with traditional terminology, this chapter refers to international adjudicative bodies as "tribunals."

[4] Côté, note 1, at 321.

[5] F Mégret, "Accountability and Ethics" in Reydams et al., note 1, at 418.

2 Structural Independence

Structural independence is formal; it refers to the specific provisions in a tribunal's enabling statute that guarantee prosecutorial independence. Adequate structural guarantees are not a sufficient condition of prosecutorial independence—even formally independent prosecutors can willingly or unwillingly cede their independence—but they are clearly a necessary condition. Structural independence has two aspects: the institutional independence of the OTP as a collective entity, and the individual independence of the prosecutor himself or herself.

2.1 Institutional independence

Institutional independence is normally guaranteed by provisions in a tribunal's statute that establish the OTP as "a separate organ" of the tribunal and prohibit the prosecutor from "seek[ing] or receiv[ing] instructions from any Government or from any other source."[6] Institutional independence thus has two aspects: the OTP's formal independence from external political actors, such as states and international organizations such as the UN, and the OTP's formal independence from the other organs of the tribunal of which it is a part.

2.1.1 *Independence from external political actors*

The enabling statutes of most international tribunals[7] contain language that prohibits the prosecutor from being instructed by external political actors. The provision quoted above appears verbatim or nearly verbatim in the statutes of the International Criminal Court (ICC), the International Criminal Tribunal for the Former Yugoslavia (ICTY), the International Criminal Tribunal for Rwanda (ICTR), the Special Court for Sierra Leone (SCSL), and the Special Tribunal for Lebanon (STL).[8] It also appears, in forms adapted to the particular structure of the tribunal in question, in the statutes of the Extraordinary Chambers in the Courts of Cambodia (ECCC)[9] and the Special Panels

[6] ICTR Statute, Art. 15.2.

[7] For the sake of readability, this chapter uses "international" to describe any adjudicative body that was either created by the UN or has a significant international component. Some scholars distinguish between tribunals that operate outside a national judiciary and tribunals that are part of a national judiciary, referring to the former as "international" and the latter as "internationalized." See, e.g., in this handbook, William Schabas, Ch. 10. Relevant structural differences between "international" and "internationalized" tribunals will be noted in the text.

[8] See Côté, note 1, at 337.

[9] The ECCC Statute refers to "the Co-Prosecutors" because the OTP consists of an international prosecutor and a Cambodian co-prosecutor. ECCC Statute, Art. 19.

for Serious Crimes (SPSC).[10] It does not appear, by contrast, in the statutes of either the War Crimes Chamber of the Court of Bosnia & Herzegovina (B&H WCC) or the Regulation 64 Panels (R64) in Kosovo.

The importance of a statutory provision guaranteeing the OTP's institutional independence from external political actors is illustrated by the experience of tribunals that lack such a provision. The statutes of the first two international criminal tribunals, the International Military Tribunal at Nuremberg (Nuremberg Tribunal) and the International Military Tribunal for the Far East (Tokyo Tribunal), were silent on institutional independence. As a result, the Soviet Union was able to order its prosecutor at the Nuremberg Tribunal to argue (falsely) that the Nazis were responsible for the Katyn Massacre,[11] while the United States was also able to insist that the OTP at the Tokyo Tribunal grant immunity to the notorious Unit 731, the unit of the Imperial Japanese Army responsible for widespread medical atrocities during the war.[12] Similarly, the United Nations Interim Administration Mission in Kosovo (UNMIK) consistently micromanages prosecutorial strategy at the R64, including ordering the OTP to avoid indicting a number of powerful political figures.[13]

To be sure, a statutory provision guaranteeing prosecutorial independence does not necessarily protect an OTP from political interference. Most obviously, the Security Council remains free to amend the statutes of the tribunals it has created (the ICTY, ICTR, and STL), to limit their funding, and even to shut them down. Similarly, the Assembly of States Parties (ASP) controls the ICC's budget, has the power to remove the prosecutor for misconduct, and can always amend the Rome Statute.[14]

Whether those powers represent an illegitimate infringement upon prosecutorial independence is a difficult issue—one for which there is no categorical answer. On the one hand, there is no question that decisions by the Security Council and the ASP concerning statutory provisions, budget, and personnel can have a profound impact on how a prosecutor exercises discretion. On the other hand, Luc Côté's observation regarding completion strategies is generally applicable:

> [W]e can draw an analogy between the power of the executive branch, such as a Ministry of Justice, to exercise general control or issue guidelines to prosecutors in a domestic legal system, and the power of the Security Council to ask the prosecutor to take means to close down the operation of the courts. In such a case, the Security Council directives would not be construed as an infringement of the prosecutor's independence but rather as the exercise

[10] Because the SPSC was part of the UN transitional administration, section 4 of the SPSC Statute provided that the prosecutor "shall act... without improper influence, direct and indirect, from any source, whether within or outside the civil administration of East Timor."

[11] RE Conot, *Justice at Nuremberg* (New York: Harper & Row 1983) 452–4.

[12] See A Cassese (ed.), *The Oxford Companion to International Criminal Justice* (Oxford University Press 2009) 375.

[13] Côté, note 1, at 397.

[14] Rome Statute of the International Criminal Court, July 17, 1998, UN Doc. A/CONF.183/9, Art. 112.2.

by a non-prosecutorial authority of a power to give general instructions that are consistent with their lawful authority.[15]

That said, it is possible to imagine the Security Council or ASP using its "lawful authority" in an illegitimate manner. The critical factor would appear to be whether the use in question was motivated by general administrative concerns or was specifically designed to affect prosecutorial strategy. Uses in the latter category are obviously more problematic than uses in the former, although even changes motivated by administrative concerns—such as the need for a tribunal to wind down operations—can undermine prosecutorial independence. Specific examples of both kinds of changes are discussed in more detail below.

2.1.2 *Independence from other organs of the tribunal*

Most enabling statutes also establish the OTP as a separate organ of the tribunal. Such is the case at the ICC, ICTY, ICTR, SCSL, and the STL.[16] The ECCC's Internal Rules recognize the Office of the Co-Prosecutors as an "independent office within the ECCC,"[17] while the B&H WCC Statute considers the OTP a "separate organ of Bosnia and Herzegovina," reflecting the fact that the Chamber functions as part of the national criminal justice system. By contrast, the SPSC and R64 statutes treat the OTP as part of their respective UN transitional administrations—part of the executive branch, not separate organs of the tribunals.

Status as a separate organ of the tribunal is critical to prosecutorial independence, because it means that the other organs—the Registry and the judiciary—do not have the formal authority to issue binding directives to the OTP concerning prosecutorial strategy.[18] Once again, however, practice has proven messier than theory. Various Registries, particularly those at the UN-created tribunals, have often used their general administrative authority over budgeting and personnel in ways that are inconsistent with the OTP's independence—and all too often the OTP has done too little to resist the encroachment.[19] The first deputy prosecutor at the ICTR, for example, was "strongly encouraged" to resign after an internal investigation concluded that he believed that only the Registry could rectify serious operational shortcomings in the OTP, a position that "effectively abolished the independence of the Prosecutor's Office and reduced it to yet another section of the Registry."[20]

Fortunately, "[t]he time when the UN Secretariat would instruct the Registry to suspend all official travel by the OTP due to budget squeezes or would criticize the Chief Prosecutor for taking too many trips abroad, among others to Washington, seems to have slowly given way to a better account and respect of the independence of the OTP and the neutrality of the Registry."[21] The B&H WCC statute provides the

[15] Côté, note 1, at 397. [16] See Côté, note 1, at 327.
[17] ECCC Internal Rules, Rule 13.1. [18] Côté, note 1, at 328.
[19] See Mégret, note 5, at 436; Côté, note 1, at 334. [20] See Mégret, note 5, at 436.
[21] Côté, note 1, at 336.

OTP with its own administration[22] and control over its own budget.[23] Similarly, the Rome Statute specifically guarantees that "[t]he Prosecutor shall have full authority over 'the management and administration of the Office, including the staff, facilities and other resources thereof.'"[24]

The relationship between the OTP and the judiciary is more complicated. Although judges cannot dictate prosecutorial strategy, they clearly have the authority to ensure that the prosecution "handles its case in a manner which is both fair and expeditious and does not prejudice the rights of the accused."[25] That authority generally takes two different forms. First, it permits the judges to review OTP decisions and issue binding orders to the OTP concerning a wide variety of pre-trial and trial issues. Examples include ordering the OTP to disclose particular kinds of evidence to the defense and confirming that charges brought by the OTP are supported by the requisite quantum of supporting evidence. This kind of supervision is generally consistent with prosecutorial independence, particularly when the judicial review in question is mandated by the tribunal's enabling statute or procedural rules.[26]

Second, judicial authority to protect the fairness of a trial also permits the judges to discipline individual members of the OTP for engaging in prosecutorial misconduct. Discipline can include—in increasing order of seriousness—oral admonishment, the imposition of sanctions and holding the prosecutor in contempt. Such remedies do not threaten prosecutorial independence as long as the judges, "as part of their general power of supervision, are only interested as such in whether the statute and rules are respected, rather than specifically upholding codes of ethics."[27] Indeed, judges have specifically recognized that they have "no express powers of discipline over members of the Prosecution" for ethical violations.[28]

A number of tribunals have experienced serious conflict between the OTP and the judiciary regarding alleged prosecutorial misconduct. At the ICTY, for example, the OTP's failure to disclose evidence that could have undermined the credibility of one of its key prosecution witnesses in the *Furundžija* case led the Trial Chamber to issue a "formal complaint"—one arguably not authorized by the tribunal's rules of procedure—about the OTP's "serious misconduct."[29] Similarly, in the *Barayagwiza* case at the ICTR, the OTP's repeated and flagrant violation of the defendant's rights—which included allowing him to remain in detention for nearly a year without being informed of the charges against him—led the Appeals Chamber to initially order the defendant's release and then, following a questionable reversal

[22] B&H WCC Statute, Art. 15.3. [23] B&H WCC Statute, Art. 9.

[24] Rome Statute, Art. 42.2.

[25] *Prosecutor v. Furundžija*, The Trial Chamber's Formal Complaint to the Prosecutor Concerning the Conduct of the Prosecution, IT-95-17/1-PT, June 5, 1998, para. 5.

[26] Mégret, note 5, at 469. [27] Mégret, note 5, at 470–2.

[28] *Furundžija*, Formal Complaint, note 25, at para. 12. [29] Mégret, note 5, at 452–3.

discussed in more detail in section 3.1.2 of this chapter, to order the Trial Chamber to give the defendant a significant discount at sentencing.[30]

The most dramatic and revealing showdown, however, took place during the *Lubanga* case at the ICC. During trial, and with the full agreement of the Victims and Witnesses Unit, the Trial Chamber ordered the OTP to reveal the identity of a prosecution intermediary whom the defense alleged had pressured witnesses into giving false testimony. The prosecutor refused, claiming the following:

> The Prosecution is sensitive to its obligation to comply with the Chamber's instructions. However, it also has an independent statutory obligation to protect persons put at risk on account of the Prosecution's actions. It should not comply, or be asked to comply, with an Order that may require it to violate its separate statutory obligation by subjecting the person to foreseeable risk. The Prosecutor accordingly has made a determination that the Prosecution would rather face adverse consequences in its litigation than expose a person to risk on account of prior interaction with this Office. This is not a challenge to the authority of the Chamber, it is instead a reflection of the Prosecution's own legal duty under the Statute.[31]

Not surprisingly, the Trial Chamber did not agree with the prosecutor's characterization of his position. On the contrary, the judges described it as "a profound, unacceptable and unjustified intrusion into the role of the judiciary"[32] and immediately stayed the proceedings "as an abuse of the process of the Court because of the material non-compliance with the Chamber's orders."[33] The Appeals Chamber ultimately lifted the stay, but it also emphasized—correctly—that the prosecutor had no authority to refuse to comply with a binding order of the Trial Chamber.[34]

2.2 Individual independence

Institutional independence protects the OTP as a collective entity. Individual independence, by contrast, protects prosecutors themselves—as well as their members of staff—by guaranteeing "an environment free from fear of personal reprisals of any kind in the exercise of [their] professional duties."[35] Individual independence thus requires an international tribunal to have adequate procedures regarding appointment, tenure, discipline, and removal. In general, international prosecutors enjoy greater individual independence than their domestic

[30] *Prosecutor v. Barayagwiza*, Judgment and Sentence, ICTR-99-52-T, December 3, 2003, para. 1106. Because of the misconduct, the Trial Chamber sentenced the defendant to 35 years instead of life imprisonment.

[31] *Prosecutor v. Lubanga*, Redacted Decision on the Prosecution's Urgent Request for Variation of the Time-Limit to Disclose the Identity of Intermediary 143, ICC-01/04-01/06, July 8, 2010, para. 14.

[32] *Prosecutor v. Lubanga*, note 31, at para. 27.

[33] *Prosecutor v. Lubanga*, note 31, at para. 31.

[34] Mégret, note 5, at 434.

[35] Côté, note 1, at 323.

counterparts, who are normally subject to the demands of the executive branch of their government.[36]

2.2.1 *Appointment*

International prosecutors have always been chosen by actors external to the tribunals themselves. The Allied powers selected the Nuremberg and Tokyo Tribunal prosecutors; the Security Council selected the ICTY and ICTR prosecutors; the UN Secretary-General selected the SCSL, ECCC, and STL prosecutors; and the Special Representative of the Secretary-General selected the SPSC and R64 prosecutors. The role of external actors in the appointment process does not necessarily undermine prosecutorial independence. As Côté notes, "It is not the political nature of the body appointing the prosecutor that really matters, but the process by which it is done. The recruitment process preceding the appointment needs to be fair, impartial, and based on objective and transparent criteria such as professional qualifications and experience."[37]

In practice, however, the appointment process has proven to be anything but "objective and transparent." The appointment of the first ICTY prosecutor, for example, has been described as a "protracted" and "politicized" failure.[38] The UN Secretary-General's first formal nominee, M Cherif Bassiouni, was effectively vetoed by the United Kingdom. The second nominee, Ramon Escovar-Salom, was appointed by the Security Council but resigned before taking up the post. Finally, Antonio Cassese, the President of the Tribunal, asked Richard Goldstone whether he would accept a Security Council appointment—an "unusual move" given the procedures that were in place.[39]

The appointment of the SCSL's first prosecutor, David Crane, was equally politicized. Crane was appointed largely because he was "backed aggressively by the United States, the SCSL's main funder"; he had not been the UN's first choice.[40] Crane's politicized appointment nevertheless provided a dramatic illustration of the importance of structural prosecutorial independence. Crane not only immediately promised to investigate all of the parties to the conflict in Sierra Leone, he ultimately brought charges against Charles Taylor, the President of Liberia, despite the fact that Taylor's indictment was stridently opposed by the US government.[41]

[36] Côté, note 1, at 323.
[37] Côté, note 1, at 342.

[38] GJ Bass, *Stay the Hand of Vengeance—The Politics of War Crimes Tribunals* (Princeton University Press 2000) 217.

[39] Côté, note 1, at 343.

[40] M Wierda and T Perriello, "The Special Court for Sierra Leone under Scrutiny," International Center for Transitional Justice, March 2006, at 21, available at <http://ictj.org/sites/default/files/ICTJ-SierraLeone-Special-Court-2006-English.pdf> accessed July 29, 2013.

[41] International Crisis Group, "The Special Court for Sierra Leone: Promises and Pitfalls of a New Model," August 4, 2003, at 16.

Fortunately, the appointment process has improved over time. Perhaps stung by the Crane experience, the UN Secretary-General now selects the SCSL, ECCC, and STL prosecutors on the basis of recommendations made by selection panels that consist of international judges and a representative of the Secretary-General.[42] The ICC's appointment process, in which a candidate must be "elected by secret ballot by an absolute majority of the members of the Assembly of States Parties,"[43] is even more democratic, though not particularly transparent. Moreover, when it came time to elect the court's second prosecutor, the Bureau of the ASP created a Search Committee to vet potential candidates through an extensive interview process. The committee ultimately forwarded four finalists to the ASP, which then selected the Gambia's Fatou Bensouda, who had previously served as the ICC's deputy prosecutor.

2.2.2 *Tenure*

Prosecutors cannot be considered independent if they can be removed from office at will by the external political actor that appointed them. For that reason, enabling statutes nearly always contain a provision regarding the prosecutor's tenure and possible reappointment. The prosecutor at the ICTY and ICTR is appointed for four years; the prosecutor at the SCSL and STL is appointed for three. Prosecutors at these tribunals are all also eligible for reappointment. By contrast, the drafters of the Rome Statute believed that a short tenure combined with potential reappointment would give the ASP too much power to undermine prosecutorial independence. Article 42.4 of the Rome Statute thus provides that the prosecutor shall serve a nine-year term and cannot be re-elected. The ICC's approach is likely the better one: the short tenure of the ICTY and ICTR prosecutors made it possible for the Security Council to refuse to re-appoint Carla Del Ponte as the ICTR prosecutor as punishment for her stated desire to prosecute members of Rwanda's ruling party, the Rwandan Patriotic Front.[44]

Even limited tenure provisions, however, are better than nothing. R64 prosecutors are not only appointed by the SRSG through a process completely devoid of transparency, they are given only three- or six-month contracts.[45] Their resulting lack of job security, combined with the fact the OTP is structurally part of UNMIK, has made prosecutorial independence effectively non-existent at the R64.[46]

2.2.3 *Discipline*

As discussed earlier, the judiciary has the ability to discipline prosecutors for violations of rules contained in a tribunal's statute and rules of procedure. Prosecutors can

[42] Côté, note 1, at 344. [43] Rome Statute, Art. 42.

[44] See Côté, note 1, at 383–4; Mégret, note 5, at 482.

[45] J Cerone and C Baldwin, "Explaining and Evaluating the UNMIK Court System" in C Romano et al. (eds), *Internationalized Criminal Courts and Tribunals* (Oxford University Press 2004) 54.

[46] Côté, note 1, at 395–6.

also be disciplined administratively. Mégret has noted that "the possibility of some sort of disciplinary proceedings has increasingly become part of what is expected to ensure…accountability," particularly "in cases where behaviour is not quite captured by the categories of prosecutorial misconduct inscribed in statutes, rules, or codes."[47] Depending on the fairness of the actor responsible for resolving disputes, such administrative discipline can obviously threaten prosecutorial independence. For that reason, some tribunals have wisely adopted procedures designed to ensure the legitimacy of the disciplinary process. For example, because of the Cambodian government's repeated attempts to undermine the independence of the Office of the Co-Prosecutors, the ECCC Statute provides that international prosecutors can be disciplined only by the UN.[48] Even better, the ICC's Rules of Procedure specifically define the various forms of "serious misconduct," "serious breach of duty," and "misconduct of a less serious nature";[49] provide a judicial screening mechanism for unfounded complaints;[50] and guarantee the affected prosecutor the right to contest the complaint with the help of counsel.[51]

2.2.4 *Removal*

Removal presents the most serious challenge to prosecutorial independence. On the one hand, prosecutorial misconduct—professional or personal—may be so serious that removal is warranted, perhaps even necessary. On the other hand, the threat of removal, particularly for actions taken in a professional capacity, can have a profoundly chilling effect on prosecutorial discretion. It is thus surprising that only two enabling statutes contain specific provisions concerning removal. The R64 Statute provides that a prosecutor can be removed from office for "serious misconduct" or "failure in the due execution of office."[52] Similarly, the Rome Statute permits the removal of a prosecutor for either "serious misconduct" or "serious breach of duties";[53] the latter is defined as being "grossly negligent in the performance of his or her duties" or knowingly acting in contravention of those duties.[54]

3 Functional Independence

Functional independence concerns what is commonly called "prosecutorial discretion," the freedom of the prosecutor to decide which situations to investigate, what suspects to indict, what charges to bring, and how to present the case against

[47] Mégret, note 5, at 477.
[48] ECCC Internal Rules, Rule 6.4.
[49] ICC Rules of Procedure, Rules 24 and 25.
[50] ICC Rules of Procedure, Rule 26.
[51] ICC Rules of Procedure, Rule 27.
[52] UNMIK/REG/2000/6 (R64 Statute), s. 4.1.
[53] Rome Statute, Art. 46.
[54] ICC Rules of Procedure, Rule 24.

the defendant at trial. Such independence thus "puts in practice the objective of institutional and individual independence: ensuring that the prosecutor will be able to function independently."[55] Indeed, the contours of functional independence are determined by structural independence; the enabling statute and procedural rules of a tribunal serve as the *ex ante* ground rules that the prosecutor is obliged—ethically and legally—to follow.

In general, statutory and procedural features of a tribunal limiting discretion cannot be considered inconsistent with prosecutorial independence; such limits are simply emanations of the "lawful authority" of the political actor that created the tribunal. That understanding of functional independence, however, is subject to three qualifications. First, it is possible to imagine "lawful" institutional design that limits prosecutorial discretion so radically that it could be considered inconsistent with any defensible understanding of functional independence. Second, other organs of the tribunal, particularly the judiciary, may interpret the structural limitations in a manner that unfairly limits prosecutorial discretion. Third, as noted earlier, the external political actor that created a tribunal may amend the statute or procedural rules in a way that unjustifiably interferes with the right of the prosecutor to determine prosecutorial strategy. The first situation, fortunately, has proven rare—although the R64's structure, which places the OTP within the executive and provides prosecutors with virtually no individual independence, might qualify. The second and third situations, by contrast, have been regrettably common. Particularly egregious examples are discussed in section 3.1.2.

3.1 Pre-trial

3.1.1 *Powers*

Prosecutorial discretion is at its apex during the pre-trial stage of a case.[56] All international tribunals entrust the prosecutor with the primary, if not exclusive, authority to conduct investigations and make charging decisions. The SCSL Statute, for example, provides that "the Prosecutor shall be responsible for the investigation and prosecution of persons who bear the greatest responsibility for serious violations of international humanitarian law and crimes under Sierra Leonean law committed in the territory of Sierra Leone since 30 November 1996."[57] Similar language, adapted to the jurisdiction of the tribunal in question, appears in the statutes of the ICTY, ICTR, STL, B&H WCC, SPSC, and R64.[58] Pre-trial, the judiciary's role is generally limited to applying and enforcing restrictions on prosecutorial discretion that appear in the tribunal's enabling statute and rules of procedure,[59] such as holding a

[55] Côté, note 1, at 350. [56] S Vasiliev, "Trial" in Reydams et al., note 1, at 702.
[57] SCSL Statute, Art. 15.1. [58] See Côté, note 1, at 351. [59] Mégret, note 5, at 469.

confirmation hearing to ensure that the charges against a suspect are supported by the requisite quantum of evidence.

Two exceptions to this general structure are worth noting. To begin with, although the ECCC co-prosecutors have the exclusive authority to decide which suspects to investigate and what charges to bring, the co-investigating judges actually conduct the investigation[60] and decide whether the charges are warranted.[61] The co-investigating judges may also charge new individuals with the crimes identified by the co-prosecutors in their formal submission.[62] Such power-sharing clearly minimizes the discretion of the co-prosecutors, but it cannot be considered inherently inconsistent with prosecutorial independence; the arrangement simply reflects the ECCC's civil-law origins.[63] That said, it is possible for the co-investigating judges to use their authority in a manner that does unjustifiably undermine prosecutorial discretion. An important example of such use is discussed in section 3.1.2.

The ICC also represents a deviation from the international norm—although in a manner that maximizes instead of minimizes the prosecutor's functional independence. Unlike the other international tribunals, all of which have been "ad hoc" in the sense that they were created to address a specific atrocity, the ICC has potentially global jurisdiction. The drafters of the Rome Statute thus had to carefully consider how the jurisdiction of the court would be triggered. One mechanism they chose was to give the prosecutor the *proprio motu* power to investigate any situation within the jurisdiction of the court if he or she concludes "that there is a reasonable basis to proceed with an investigation."[64] That "radical and unprecedented"[65] authority has always been controversial; many states believe that it gives the prosecutor too much—and too unconstrained—discretion.[66]

Regardless of the merits of the ICC debate, there is no question that international prosecutors enjoy a great deal of discretion within their spheres of competence. Not only do all OTPs face atrocity situations in which the number of guilty suspects far exceeds the number of perpetrators who can be prosecuted, the statutory standards for making investigative and prosecutorial decisions are notoriously amorphous. The Rome Statute's emphasis on "gravity" and the "interests of justice," for example, leaves "enormous space for highly discretionary determinations."[67] As William Schabas has noted, it is nearly impossible to use "gravity" to explain the ICC prosecutor's decision to charge Thomas Lubanga Dyilo solely with the war crime of conscripting and using child soldiers. When the OTP took control of the case, Lubanga was facing much more serious domestic charges—genocide and crimes against humanity—in the Democratic Republic of Congo.[68]

[60] ECCC Statute, Art. 23. [61] ECCC Internal Rules, Rule 55.4.

[62] ECCC Internal Rules, Rule 55.4. [63] Côté, note 1, at 351. [64] Rome Statute, Art. 15.3.

[65] WA Schabas, *An Introduction to the International Criminal Court* (Cambridge University Press 2007) 354.

[66] Schabas, note 2, at 734. [67] Schabas, note 2, at 735. [68] Schabas, note 2, at 741.

That said, the ICC's OTP at least deserves credit for issuing a series of papers that attempt to explain how the office makes investigative and prosecutorial decisions.[69] No other international tribunal—past or present—has exhibited a comparable level of transparency. The ICC's practice is superior, even if the criteria identified by the OTP are not binding. As Côté notes, "in addition to enhancing the quality of their decision-making, [transparent] guidelines will protect the independence of prosecutors, shielding them from accusations of bias, or of initiating politically motivated prosecutions."[70]

3.1.2 *Limitations*

Although at its apex during the pre-trial phase, the prosecutor's functional independence is not absolute. Formal and informal limitations on that independence exist at each stage of the pre-trial process. Some of those limitations are justifiable, while others are more problematic—although it can be difficult to articulate a clear principle that distinguishes between justifiable and unjustifiable limitations.

Duty of impartiality

All international prosecutors are obligated to exercise their discretion in an impartial manner. Perhaps surprisingly, the duty of impartiality is rarely imposed by a tribunal's enabling statute. The exceptions are the SPSC, which requires prosecutors to "perform their functions as established in the present regulation impartially... without bias and prejudice, and in accordance with their impartial assessment of the facts,"[71] and the Rome Statute, which provides that neither the prosecutor nor the deputy prosecutor "shall participate in any matter in which their impartiality might reasonably be doubted on any ground."[72] The duty of impartiality is more often imposed as an ethical obligation via a code of professional conduct. The ICTY and ICTR Standards of Professional Conduct, for example, require prosecutors "to be, and appear to be, consistent, objective and independent, and avoid all conflicts of interest."[73] The Code of Prosecutorial Ethics at the B&H WCC is even more detailed, not only requiring prosecutors to perform their functions "without favour, bias, or prejudice," but also providing that the duty of impartiality applies "not only to the prosecutorial decisions but also to the process by which the decisions are made."[74]

The general duty of impartiality is obviously a justified limitation on prosecutorial independence. More interesting is the very specific duty imposed by Art. 54.1 of the Rome Statute, which provides that the prosecutor shall, "in order to establish the truth, extend the investigation to cover all facts and evidence relevant to an assessment of whether there is criminal responsibility under this Statute, and, in doing

[69] See, e.g., Office of the Prosecutor, Report on Prosecutorial Strategy, September 2006.

[70] Côté, note 1, at 356.

[71] UNTAET/REG/2000/16 (SPSC Statute), Arts 4.1, 4.2.

[72] Rome Statute, Art. 42.7.

[73] Standards of Professional Conduct, Art. 2.c.

[74] Code of Prosecutorial Ethics, Prosecutor's Office of Bosnia and Herzegovina, Art. 2.

so, investigate incriminating and exonerating circumstances equally." This is an unprecedented requirement; the statutes of previous tribunals simply required the prosecutor to disclose whatever exculpatory evidence came into his or her possession.[75] Indeed, Art. 54.1 effectively transforms the prosecutor from "partisan advocate" into a "minister of justice" whose fundamental obligation is to ascertain the truth, not obtain convictions.[76]

Opening investigations

The prosecutor's discretion to determine investigative strategy is limited in a number of ways. At the ICC, three formal limitations are particularly notable. The first concerns the prosecutor's ability to investigate a situation *proprio motu*. Such an investigation can proceed only if the Pre-Trial Chamber is convinced, based on the OTP's formal submissions, that "there is a reasonable basis to proceed with an investigation."[77] That limitation is obviously inconsistent with the traditional understanding of prosecutorial discretion, but the *proprio motu* power itself would not have been included in the Rome Statute without it.[78] It is thus difficult to argue that the restriction is illegitimate.

The second limitation concerns the relationship between the ICC and the Security Council. Article 13.b of the Rome Statute permits the Security Council to refer situations to the court for investigation.[79] The referral power clearly limits "the prosecutor's independence and his capacity to exercise a kind of global prosecutorial discretion."[80] That said, it remains an open question whether the OTP is obligated to investigate a situation referred to the court by the Security Council. Article 53.1 provides that "the Prosecutor shall, having evaluated the information made available to him or her, initiate an investigation unless he or she determines that there is no reasonable basis to proceed under this Statute." Read literally, that provision would permit the prosecutor to decline to investigate a referred situation if she believed that the crimes committed therein were not adequately grave or that an investigation would not serve the interests of justice—two considerations that Art. 53.1 deems relevant to the "reasonable basis" inquiry.

[75] See, e.g., ICTR Rules of Procedure, Rule 68. [76] Vasiliev, note 56, at 704.

[77] Rome Statute, Art. 15.4.

[78] J Wouters et al., "The International Criminal Court's Office of the Prosecutor: Navigating Between Independence and Accountability?" (2008) 8 Int'l Criminal L Rev 273, 279–80.

[79] It is worth noting that the Security Council believes it has the authority to exempt certain categories of potential perpetrators from the court's jurisdiction when it refers a situation. Both the Darfur and Libya referrals purport to deprive the court of jurisdiction over nationals of states that have not ratified the Rome Statute. See, e.g., SC Res. 1953 (2005), para. 36 (Darfur). Such exclusions are obviously fundamentally at odds with prosecutorial discretion, and it is an open question whether they are legitimate. Nothing in the Rome Statute supports them; Art. 13.b, for example, simply permits the Security Council to refer a "situation" writ large.

[80] JD Ohlin, "Peace, Security, and Prosecutorial Discretion" in C Stahn and G Sluiter (eds), *The Emerging Practice of the International Criminal Court* (Leiden: Brill 2008) 192.

The third limitation on the ICC prosecutor's investigative discretion is the principle of complementarity. Article 17.1.a of the Rome Statute prohibits the prosecutor from pursuing any case that "is being investigated or prosecuted by a State which has jurisdiction over it, unless the State is unwilling or unable genuinely to carry out the investigation or prosecution." The principle of complementarity thus significantly limits the prosecutor's freedom to determine which suspects to investigate and prosecute. Nevertheless, because the limitation was a condition of the court's existence,[81] it should be considered a legitimate restriction imposed on the OTP by the states that created the court.

Those three limitations are formal. All OTPs, including at the ICC, also face informal limitations on their ability to determine investigative strategy. One is funding: the failure of the international community to adequately fund a tribunal can prevent the prosecutor from investigating suspects he or she believes are responsible for serious crimes. That was the case at the SPSC and R64[82] —and insiders report that it is currently the case at the ICC, whose lack of funding threatens to prevent the OTP from investigating new situations and pursuing more cases in the situations it is already investigating. OTPs at tribunals that are financed through voluntary contributions are particularly vulnerable to funding-based interference. An early UN planning mission to the SCSL, for example, emphasized that the voluntary funding of the tribunal meant that the "structure and staffing requirements" of the OTP needed to reflect "an exceptionally clear and well-defined prosecutorial strategy"—a statement that, in Mégret's view, "came close to charting the way it thought the Prosecutor should conduct at least the initial stages of investigation."[83]

An equally important informal limitation is the OTP's dependence on states for cooperation. It is a truism of international criminal justice that tribunals do not have their own police force; for an OTP to carry out its prosecutorial strategy effectively, states must be willing to conduct searches, locate witnesses, arrest suspects, and so on. Unfortunately, such cooperation has often been lacking—with devastating results for prosecutorial independence.

Consider, for example, Louise Arbour's failure at the ICTY to investigate NATO's bombing campaign during the war in Kosovo. After dramatically asserting her prosecutorial independence by convening a commission of experts to study possible NATO violations of international humanitarian law during the campaign, Arbour followed the commission's recommendation and decided not to open a formal investigation. Arbour's commission cited two rationales for not investigating: lack of legal clarity, and the fact that an investigation would be "unlikely to result in the acquisition of sufficient evidence to substantiate charges against high

[81] WA Schabas, "First Prosecutions at the International Criminal Court" (2007) 27 Human Rights L J 25, 28.

[82] Côté, note 1, at 394. [83] Mégret, note 5, at 464.

level accused or against lower level accused for particularly heinous offences."[84] Few scholars accepted the first rationale,[85] and the second rationale was viewed as a tacit admission by Arbour that NATO's refusal to cooperate—specifically noted in the commission's report[86]—made it impossible for her office to effectively investigate its actions. Arbour's unwillingness to pursue an investigation did not sit well with critics; Côté speaks for many when he says that "it seems as though the Prosecutor gave up before having a real fight, not quite what is expected from an impartial and independent prosecutor."[87]

Two incidents at the ICTR further illustrate the difficult relationship between state cooperation and prosecutorial independence. The first involved the situation discussed earlier in section 2.1.2: the Appeals Chamber's decision to order the release of Jean-Bosco Barayagwiza as a remedy for the OTP's flagrant denial of his rights under the ICTR Statute. In protest of the decision, Rwanda suspended all cooperation with the tribunal and refused to issue a visa to its prosecutor, Carla Del Ponte. Del Ponte immediately asked the Appeals Chamber to "reconsider" its decision, openly admitting that "her ability to continue with prosecutions and investigations depend[ed] on the government of Rwanda." That statement—to say nothing of the Appeals Chamber's subsequent decision to backtrack on its original order—was fundamentally inconsistent with the OTP's independence. As Judge Nieto-Navia pointed out, "[t]he proposition put forward by the Prosecutor that political considerations can play a role in the Appeals Chamber's decision making and actions is not acceptable."[88]

The second ICTR incident concerned Del Ponte's inability to follow through on her promise to prosecute members of Rwanda's ruling party, the RPF, for committing serious—and very well documented—crimes during the 1994 genocide. Once again, Del Ponte openly acknowledged that Rwanda's outraged refusal to cooperate explained her actions. Indeed, she wrote in her memoirs that Paul Kagame had told her that "you are destroying Rwanda, you will disrupt the reconstruction of the nation, stop the investigation… we will not allow you to do this."[89] No RPF official was ever indicted, either by Del Ponte or by her successor.

Closing investigations

In some situations, external political actors or other organs of a tribunal are able to close an investigation opened by the OTP. The most striking example is the Security Council's right, pursuant to Art. 16 of the Rome Statute, to defer any investigation

[84] Final Report to the Prosecutor by the Committee Established to Review the NATO Bombing Campaign Against the Federal Republic of Yugoslavia, para. 90.

[85] See Côté, note 1, at 378 (noting the critical response).

[86] Final Report to the Prosecutor, note 84, at para. 90.

[87] Côté, note 1, at 378.

[88] *Prosecutor v. Barayagwiza*, Decision on Prosecutor's Request for Review or Reconsideration, ICTR-97-19-AR72, March 31, 2000, Declaration of Judge Rafael Nieto-Navia, para. 7.

[89] C Del Ponte, *Madame Prosecutor: A Memoir* (New York: Other Press 2008) 225.

or prosecution for one year, renewable indefinitely. That right obviously limits the OTP's discretion, but once again the provision in question was a necessary condition of the OTP's structural independence, making the limit justifiable.

The unusual structure of the ECCC, in which investigations are conducted by the co-investigating judges, also permits investigations to be closed against the will of the co-prosecutors. Despite the opposition of the Cambodian government and the Cambodian co-prosecutor, the international co-prosecutor decided to investigate two individuals associated with the notorious Tuol Sleng prison (Case 003). Nearly two years later, the co-investigating judges announced that they were terminating the investigation. Critics rightly denounced the decision as politically motivated and inconsistent with the independence of the co-prosecutors; the co-investigating judges had not interviewed the suspects or questioned the witnesses.[90]

Finally, open investigations can be terminated as a result of a tribunal's completion strategy. The ICTR, for example, will close with three indicted suspects still at large. Even more dramatically, when the Security Council decided in 2004 to terminate the SPSC, it gave the tribunal only one year to complete its operations. As a result, the OTP was forced to leave 469 murders uninvestigated and 186 murders investigated but not prosecuted.[91]

Decisions to prosecute

Some prosecutors also face judicial limitations on the individuals they can prosecute. The most dramatic example of such a limitation is Rule 28.A of the ICTY Rules of Procedure, judicially adopted in 2004, which gives a group of judges, the Bureau, the right to reject an OTP indictment on the ground that it fails to concentrate on "one or more of the most senior leaders suspected of being most responsible for crimes within the jurisdiction of the Tribunal." Carla Del Ponte was incensed by the judges' adoption of the rule, which was requested by the Security Council as part of the tribunal's completion strategy, insisting—to no avail—that it was "contrary to the Statute and unnecessary in light of the independence given to me under the Statute of the Tribunal."[92] The judges of the ICTR, by contrast, agreed with her assessment; they categorically refused to adopt a similar rule.[93]

Decisions not to prosecute

The ICC is unique in that the Rome Statute permits the Pre-Trial Chamber, in limited circumstances, to review the prosecutor's decision not to investigate a situation or prosecute a particular suspect. Article 53.3.a provides that, in general, the Pre-Trial

[90] Open Society Justice Initiative, "Recent Developments at the ECCC," June 2011 Update, at 31–6.

[91] KJ Heller, "Completion" in Reydams et al., note 1, at 898.

[92] Quoted in D Mundis, "The Judicial Effects of the Completion Strategies on the Ad Hoc International Criminal Tribunals" (2005) 99 American J Int'l L 142, 148.

[93] Heller, note 91, at 908.

Chamber may ask the prosecutor to reconsider his or her decision at the request of the Security Council or the state that referred the situation in question to the court.[94] More dramatically, Art. 53.3.b authorizes the Pre-Trial Chamber to review *proprio motu* a decision not to investigate or prosecute that is based specifically on "the interests of justice." The provision provides that, "in such a case, the decision of the Prosecutor shall be effective only if confirmed by the Pre-Trial Chamber." If the Pre-Trial Chamber does not confirm the prosecutor's decision, Rule 110 of the ICC's Rules of Procedure requires the prosecutor to "proceed with the investigation or prosecution." That is a very significant limitation on prosecutorial discretion—one that seems more difficult to justify than the Pre-Trial Chamber's right to review a positive decision to investigate or prosecute.

Removing charges

Finally, the ICTY alone permits the judiciary to remove charges against the OTP's will. The provision in question is Rule 73*bis* of the Rules of Procedure, which provides that, following a hearing, the Trial Chamber "may direct the Prosecutor to select the counts in the indictment on which to proceed." Carla Del Ponte objected to the judiciary's adoption of Rule 73*bis*, which was also motivated by the tribunal's completion strategy, on the same grounds that she had earlier objected to Rule 28.A. She claimed that the rule violated the ICTY's system "of checks and balances" and insisted that "only the Security Council has the power to modify the ICTY Statute, which guarantees the independence of the Prosecutor and assigns to her the responsibility of determining which charges to bring a prosecution."[95] Del Ponte's objections seem valid, especially as no other tribunal has gone beyond giving the Trial Chamber the right to request the prosecutor to trim an indictment.[96]

From the standpoint of prosecutorial discretion, the ICTY Appeals Chamber's actions in the *Jelisić* case are equally problematic. After trial, the defendant was acquitted of genocide.[97] The prosecution appealed, and the Appeals Chamber agreed that the acquittal was erroneous. The Appeals Chamber nevertheless refused—without hearing from the prosecutor—to permit Jelisić to be retried for genocide, justifying its decision by citing the "uncertain longevity" of the ICTY and the fact that the tribunal's resources were "limited in terms of manpower."[98] The Appeals Chamber's decision elicited a blistering dissent from Judge Patricia Wald, who rightly pointed out that it does not fall "within the judicial function to veto a retrial on 'practical' or 'policy' grounds. Any such decision based on 'judicial economy' inevitably reflects judges' views as to which cases are 'worthy' and which

[94] Rome Statute, Art. 53.3.

[95] Statement by the Tribunal's Prosecutor Carla Del Ponte to the Security Council, June 7, 2006, LM/MOW/1084e.

[96] See, Côté, note 1, at 332.

[97] He had earlier pleaded guilty to war crimes and crimes against humanity.

[98] *Prosecutor v. Jelisić*, Appeal Judgment, IT-95-10-A, July 5, 2001, para. 75.

are not. That, however, is the job of the Prosecutor who must calibrate legal and policy considerations in making her choices on how to utilize limited resources."[99]

3.2 Trial

At trial, "broad prosecutorial discretion gives way to judicial dominion."[100] As the ICTY Appeals Chamber noted in *Milošević*, "Once the indictment has been confirmed by a judge, and once the indictment has been filed, the Prosecutor becomes a party before the Tribunal, and thus subject to the power of a Chamber to manage the proceedings, in the same way as any other party before the Tribunal."[101]

3.2.1 *Powers*

The prosecution's primary power at trial is to control the presentation of its case: which witnesses to call, what questions to ask them, which documents to introduce into evidence, how to conduct cross-examination, etc.[102] The contours of that power, however, depend on the particular institutional structure of the tribunal. Sergey Vasiliev has identified three different kinds of structure. The first is the "distinct case model," which is the most adversarial. This model provides the prosecution with two opportunities to present its evidence: during its case-in-chief and to rebut the defense's case-in-chief. It also generally gives the prosecution the primary right to determine how the evidence should be introduced during those stages of the trial. Most international tribunals have fallen into the distinct-case category, including the Nuremberg and Tokyo Tribunals, the ICTY, the ICTR, the SCSL, the STL, and the B&H WCC.[103]

At the opposite end of the spectrum is the "thematic organization model." This model, which represents the inquisitorial tradition, is characterized by the lack of a distinct prosecution case. The co-prosecutors and other parties "participate in the development of evidence by consecutively questioning the accused as well as witnesses and experts called to testify on predetermined topics of trial agenda set by the Court."[104] Only the ECCC has adopted the thematic organization model.

The third and final institutional structure is the "variable model." This model is characterized by what Vasiliev calls "constructive uncertainty": there is no predetermined organization for every trial. Instead, the judiciary has the authority to adopt—on a case-by-case basis—the distinct-case model, the thematic-organization model or even a hybrid of the two. The variable model, which has been adopted

[99] *Prosecutor v. Jelisić*, note 98, Partial Dissenting Opinion of Judge Wald, at para. 14.
[100] Vasiliev, note 56, at 713.
[101] *Prosecutor v. Milošević*, Reasons for Refusal of Leave to Appeal from Decision to Impose Time Limit, IT-02-54-AR73, May 16, 2002, para. 13.
[102] Vasiliev, note 56, at 714.
[103] Vasiliev, note 56, at 753–7.
[104] Vasiliev, note 56, at 751.

by the ICC, renders the contours of the prosecutor's powers extremely uncertain; their ability to determine how the prosecution's evidence should be presented will depend on the trial structure that the Trial Chamber adopts in a particular case.[105]

3.2.2 *Judicial limitations*

Even at tribunals that follow the distinct-case model, prosecutorial discretion is still subject to important—and sometimes questionable—limitations. Rule 73*bis* at the ICTY, for example, permits the Trial Chamber to determine "the time available to the Prosecutor for presenting evidence."[106] Rule 73*bis* at the ICTR and Rule 127 at the STL are similar. The ICTY judges have often availed themselves of that power, limiting the prosecution's time by 25 percent in *Prlić*[107] and imposing a 14-month maximum on the prosecution's case-in-chief in *Milošević*.[108] The prosecutor protested in both cases (with the support of the defense in *Prlić*) that the limit in question was inconsistent with the OTP's independence, but was unsuccessful each time.

ICTY Rule 73*bis*—like many of its counterparts at other tribunals—also permits the Trial Chamber to limit the number of witnesses the prosecution can call at trial and to impose restrictions on how long the prosecution can examine its own witnesses.[109] Those rules do not appear to have been challenged by prosecutors, but the co-international prosecutors did protest a decision by the ECCC Trial Chamber in *Duch*—Case 001—that limited prosecutors to 30 minutes of examination, with extensions being granted "only with some reluctance and after debate."[110] That limitation was arguably inconsistent with the co-prosecutor's independence, even given the inquisitorial thematic-organization model followed by the ECCC. After all, the co-prosecutors still bear the formal burden of proving the defendant's guilt beyond reasonable doubt.[111]

3.2.3 *Victim participation*

Victim participation can also limit prosecutorial independence at trial—particularly at the ICC, ECCC, and STL, all of which permit victims to formally participate in trial proceedings. At the ECCC, for example, victims are civil parties who are entitled to call and examine witnesses, question the defendant, and make closing statements at the end of trial.[112] Similarly, legal representatives of victims at the ICC

[105] Vasiliev, note 56, at 760–3. [106] ICTY Rules of Procedure, Rule 73*bis*.c.ii.

[107] P Murphy, "Discussion" (2008) 6 J Int'l Criminal Justice 681, 686.

[108] *Milošević*, Time Limit Decision, note 101, at para. 3.

[109] ICTY Rules of Procedure, Rule 73*bis*.c.ii; see also STL Rules of Procedure, Rule 127; SCSL Rules of Procedure, Rule 73*bis*.d.

[110] Vasiliev, note 56, at 759. [111] ECCC Internal Rules, Rule 87.1.

[112] ECCC Internal Rules, Rules 79–94.

can attend hearings, make submissions, question witnesses, and even introduce evidence of the defendant's guilt.[113]

The *Lubanga* trial provides a striking example of the potential conflict between prosecutorial independence and the interests of victims. As noted earlier, the prosecutor charged the defendant only with (multiple counts of) the war crime of conscripting and using child soldiers. Nearly four months into the trial, the lawyers for the victims participating in the case formally requested that the Trial Chamber re-characterize the facts in the prosecution's charging document so as to add the crime against humanity of sexual slavery and the war crimes of sexual slavery and cruel treatment. The prosecutor objected to the proposed "re-characterization," insisting that the Rome Statute gave him the exclusive right to amend the charges against a defendant.[114] The Appeals Chamber ultimately agreed with the prosecutor, but not until after the Trial Chamber indicated its willingness to grant the victims' request.[115]

4 Conclusion

The role of the international prosecutor is defined by the tension between independence and accountability. No tribunal can be legitimate if it permits the prosecutor to be controlled by external political actors or by other organs of the court. At the same time, making prosecutors accountable to no one but themselves is a recipe for misconduct, which has been all too common. The question, then, is how to design a tribunal in a manner that maximizes the discretion of the prosecutor while still ensuring that there are procedures in place capable of preventing discretion's worst excesses. If past and present tribunals are any indication, it is far easier to design a tribunal that errs in the direction of either excessive freedom or excessive control than it is to design a tribunal that strikes an appropriate balance between the two.

[113] ICC Rules of Procedure, Rule 91.

[114] *Prosecutor v. Lubanga*, Judgment on the Appeals of Mr. Lubanga Dyilo and the Prosecutor Against the Decision of Trial Chamber I of July 14, 2009 Entitled "Decision Giving Notice to the Parties and Participants that the Legal Characterisation of the Facts May Be Subject to Change in Accordance with Regulation 55(2) of the Regulations of the Court," ICC-01/04-01/06, December 8, 2009, para. 55.

[115] See *Prosecutor v. Lubanga*, note 114, at para. 94.

Research Questions

1. Are all *ex ante* restrictions in a tribunal's enabling statute legitimate, or can a tribunal be designed in a manner that is inconsistent with prosecutorial independence?
2. To what extent has prosecutorial misconduct been a problem at international tribunals—and could that misconduct have been prevented by better institutional design?
3. Which tribunal's institutional structure best reconciles independence and accountability?
4. Should victims be given the right to formally participate in trial proceedings, given the threat that their participation poses to prosecutorial independence?

Suggested Reading

Bass, GJ, *Stay the Hand of Vengeance—The Politics of War Crimes Tribunals* (Princeton University Press 2000).

Côté, L, "Independence and Impartiality" in L Reydams et al. (eds), *International Prosecutors* (Oxford University Press 2012).

Danner, AM, "Enhancing the Legitimacy and Accountability of Prosecutorial Discretion at the International Court" (2003) 97 AJIL 510.

Greenawalt, A, "Justice Without Politics? Prosecutorial Discretion at the International Criminal Court" (2007) 39 NYU J Int'l L & Pol. 583.

Jallow, H, "Prosecutorial and International Criminal Justice" (2005) 3 J Int'l Criminal Justice 145.

Mégret, F, "Accountability and Ethics" in L Reydams et al. (eds), *International Prosecutors* (Oxford University Press 2012).

Ohlin, J, "Peace, Security, and Prosecutorial Discretion" in C Stahn and G Sluiter (eds), *The Emerging Practice of the International Criminal Court* (Leiden: Brill 2008).

Del Ponte, C, *Madame Prosecutor: A Memoir* (New York: Other Press 2008).

Schabas, W, "Prosecutorial Discretion v. Judicial Activism at the International Criminal Court" (2008) 6 J Int'l Crim Justice 731.

Vasiliev, S, "Trial" in L Reydams et al. (eds), *International Prosecutors* (Oxford University Press 2012).

Wouters, J et al., "The International Criminal Court's Office of the Prosecutor: Navigating Between Independence and Accountability?" (2008) 8 Int'l Criminal L Rev 273.

CHAPTER 32

DEFENSE COUNSEL IN INTERNATIONAL CRIMINAL TRIALS

KATE GIBSON*

* Defense Counsel at the International Criminal Tribunal for Rwanda and Special Court for Sierra Leone. With thanks to the dedicated defense lawyers and investigators alongside whom I have been lucky enough to work, and to Christopher M Rassi, the most defense-friendly international prosecutor of them all.

1 Introduction

"There is hardly a more unpopular job than defending a person accused of genocide."[1]

Despite defense lawyers being an indispensible fixture in criminal trials, public opinion still ascribes a moral complicity to lawyers representing "genocidaires" or "war criminals." A Judge of the International Criminal Tribunal for the Former Yugoslavia (ICTY) observed that witnesses "see defense counsel allied with their nemeses in the docks."[2] This is an uncomfortable stigma for lawyers who are familiar with being afforded the same measure of respect, regardless of the role they play in the judicial process. Nor can this stigma be reconciled with the position that "the very premise of our adversary system of criminal justice is that partisan advocacy on both sides of a case will best promote the ultimate objective that the guilty be convicted and the innocent go free."[3]

Progress has been made from a time when ICTY defense counsel were not permitted to enter the tribunal's cafeteria without a security escort[4] and when the International Criminal Tribunal for Rwanda (ICTR) openly measured its success by the number of convictions secured by prosecutors. Despite this progress, and despite a recent focus on international defense counsel following some high-profile arrests,[5] the existing literature discussing the work of defense counsel in international criminal trials remains limited, particularly when viewed against the wealth of academic commentary on domestic defense practitioners.[6]

Much of the early literature took the form of critiques of defense counsel performance,[7] and was written by non-practitioners. Perhaps as a consequence, there

[1] T Cruvellier, *Court of Remorse: Inside the International Criminal Tribunal for Rwanda* (The University of Wisconsin Press 2006) 35.

[2] PM Wald "The [ICTY] Comes of Age: Some Observations on Day-to-Day Dilemmas of an International Court" (2001) 5 Wash. U.J.L. & Pol'y 87, 104.

[3] *Herring v. New York*, 422 U.S. 853, 862 (1975).

[4] JA McMorrow "Creating Norms of Attorney Conduct in International Tribunals: A Case Study of the ICTY" (2007) 30 B. C. Int'l. & Comp. L. Rev. 139, 152.

[5] See, e.g., the arrests of four ICC staff members as detailed in *Prosecutor v. Saif Al-Islam Gaddafi and Abdullah Al-Senussi*, Public Redacted Version of the Corrigendum to the "Defence Response to the Application on behalf of the Government of Libya pursuant to Article 19 of the ICC Statute" (July 31, 2012) ICC-01/11-01/11-190-Corr-Red, para. 15. See also the arrest of a defense investigator in *Prosecutor v. Gotovina* (Decision on Gotovina Defence Appeal against March 12, 2010 Decision on Requests for Permanent Restraining Orders Directed to the Republic of Croatia) (February 14, 2011) IT-06-90-AR73.5, para. 5.

[6] Perhaps the first comprehensive analysis is JT Tuinstra, *Defence Counsel in International Criminal Law* (The Hague: TMC Asser Press 2009). See also JI Turner, "Legal Ethics in International Criminal Defense" (2010) 10 Chi. J. Int'l. L. 685.

[7] See, e.g., MS Ellis, "The Evolution of Defence Counsel appearing before the International Criminal Tribunal for the Former Yugoslavia" (2003) 37 New Eng. L. Rev. 949; Wald, note 2.

has been little written about the practical ethical questions to which international criminal defense counsel are regularly exposed, particularly when conflicts arise between national professional obligations and the obligations before the international courts. Nor has attention been focused on the impact of interference in defense investigations by states adverse to the accused, or the practical impact of the inequality of resources allocated to the defense.

This chapter raises these points below, not with the hope of providing exhaustive study, but rather as a basis for further exploration. It will also outline the role of defense lawyers, their professional conduct and relationship with the international courts, and the main challenges which differentiate domestic and international criminal practice.

2 The Role of Defense Counsel in International Criminal Trials

Evidently, the overarching task of defense counsel in international criminal trials is to test the prosecution evidence and present exculpatory evidence, while ensuring that the rights of defendants are observed. Although this description could equally apply to domestic criminal practice, in an international criminal context the task is considerably more complex.

First, defense counsel before international criminal courts must become familiar with a complex international conflict, review a lengthy indictment and supporting materials,[8] become accustomed to the substantive principles of international criminal and international humanitarian law, learn how to negotiate the inner administrative workings of an unfamiliar Registry and court management system, assemble a team of lawyers and investigators willing to relocate to Tanzania, Sierra Leone, Cambodia, or The Netherlands for an unknown period of time, build a relationship with a defendant who may or may not share a common language and conduct investigations in the field. Responsibility for investigations is particularly novel to civil lawyers, where this task falls firmly within the purview of the investigative judge.

[8] The prosecution at the Special Tribunal for Lebanon (STL) disclosed 20,000 pages of supporting materials in its first case of *Prosecutor v. Salim Jamil Ayyash* et al. See STL Press Release "Prosecutor Bellemare welcomes tribunal's order to unseal the indictment" (August 17, 2011) <http://www.stl-tsl.org/en/media/press-releases/> accessed March 4, 2013.

International criminal trials are also infamous for the colossal volume of disclosure through which defense teams must wade. It is not uncommon, particularly at the ICTY, for the number of pages of disclosure to run into the millions.[9] The relative infancy of this field also gives rise to preliminary motions challenging the legality and jurisdiction of the courts,[10] while at the International Criminal Court (ICC) cases will generally also involve complex challenges to the admissibility of the case.[11]

Defense counsel also contribute to the establishing of the truth of the events in question. The underlying subject matter litigated in international criminal trials is invariably complex. While it is often beneficial for prosecutors to present a version of events at its simplest, defendants often benefit from the shades of grey in a conflict or story. As a result, defense counsel often delve into these complexities, which can result in uncovering and presenting a more nuanced version of events that is closer to their historical truth. As a corollary, defense lawyers have also been credited with taking the lead in uncovering evidence.[12] At the ICTR, it was defense teams who presented documents from the UN archives[13] and who introduced a wealth of relevant material from the traditional Rwandan Gacaca courts.[14] At the ICC, despite the critical relevance of Aveba village to the prosecution case in *Katanga*, the prosecution never conducted investigations on site.[15] The defense lawyers were the first to visit the area in March 2008, with the prosecution first appearing during the judicial site visit after the close of the evidence in 2012.[16] Defense counsel accordingly play a significant role in both defending the interests of the accused, and contributing to the legitimacy of the field as a whole.

[9] *Prosecutor v. Karadžić* (Decision on Request for Review of Decision on Defence Team Funding) (January 31, 2012) IT-95-5/18-T, at 15, 33.

[10] See, e.g., *Prosecutor v. Salim Jamil Ayyash et al.*, (Motion on behalf of Salim Jamil Ayyash Challenging the Legality of the Special Tribunal for Lebanon) (May 4, 2012) STL-11-OI/PT/TC.

[11] See, e.g., *Prosecutor v. Muthaura et al.* ("Judgment on the Appeal of the Republic of Kenya Against the Decision of Pre-Trial Chamber II of May 30, 2011 entitled 'Decision on the Application by the Government of Kenya Challenging the Admissibility of the Case'") (August 30, 2011) ICC-01/09-02/11-274.

[12] See, e.g., the Musema Defence team's presentation of the records from the Gisovu Tea Factory, as explained in Cruvellier, note 1, at 97, 98.

[13] See, e.g., *Prosecutor v. Bagosora et al.* (Decision on Request to Admit United Nations Documents into Evidence Under Rule 89(C)) (May 25, 2006) ICTR-98-41-T.

[14] *Prosecutor v. Setako* (Judgment) [2010] ICTR-04-81-T, at 20–23.

[15] *Prosecutor v. Katanga & Ngudjolo* (Transcript) (November 25, 2009) ICC-01/04-01/07-T-81-Red-ENG WT, at 65, 66.

[16] *Prosecutor v. Katanga & Ngudjolo* (Transcript) (May 21, 2012) ICC-01/04-01/07-T-338.

3 Who are Defense Counsel?

3.1 How defense counsel are chosen

Any attempt to describe the typical defense counsel is futile. Some generalizations are possible. We know that at one point, 66 percent of ICTY counsel were from the former Yugoslavia,[17] and that most counsel at the ICTR are francophone, with many coming from Cameroon and Canada,[18] and that all defendants before the Extraordinary Chambers in the Courts of Cambodia (ECCC) are presently represented by at least one Cambodian counsel.[19]

Any impression that these figures are a direct result of the preference of the defendants is not strictly accurate. The right of a defendant to choose his counsel is a component of a fair trial,[20] but is not an unfettered right. It is afforded only to "those defendants who can financially bear the costs" of representation.[21] Given that nearly every defendant indicted by the international courts has been declared indigent, they are assigned counsel by the Registry.[22]

Before an individual can be assigned to represent a defendant, he or she must be admitted to the list of eligible counsel.[23] Initially, the criteria for admission were less than onerous, with the ICTY having no minimum requirement of relevant experience. Following criticism,[24] the ICTY now requires seven years of relevant experience in criminal proceedings[25] and established competence in relevant areas of law.[26] The ICTR has since followed suit,[27] while the ICC requires more than ten years of "the necessary relevant experience" practicing criminal law.[28] Additionally, defense counsel must be proficient in one of the "working languages" of the court,[29] although this requirement is arguably less relevant when the defendant speaks

[17] Ellis, note 7, at 955.

[18] UN Doc. A/54/634 (November 1999) para. 204.

[19] "Defence Teams of the Extraordinary Chambers of the Courts of Cambodia" (February 2012) <http://www.eccc.gov.kh/en/dss/defence-teams> accessed March 4, 2012.

[20] ICCPR, Art. 14.3.d; ECHR, Art. 6.3.c.

[21] *Prosecutor v. Akayesu*, (Judgment) [2001] ICTR-96-4-A, para. 60.

[22] See, e.g., UN Doc. A/54/634 (1999), noting that approximately 90 percent of defendants before the ICTY had been declared indigent.

[23] ICTY Rules, Rule 45; ICTR Rules, Rule 44*bis*; ICC Rules, Rule 21.

[24] "Report of the Expert Group to Conduct a Review of the Effective Operation and Functioning of the [ICTY and ICTR]" (November 1999) UN Doc. A/54/634, at 210.

[25] ICTY Rules, Rule 45.B.iii; ICTY Directive on the Assignment of Defence Counsel ("ICTY Directive") (July 11, 2006) Art. 14.A.iv.

[26] ICTY Rules, Rule 45.B.ii and ICTY Directive, Art. 14.A.iii.

[27] ICTR Rules, Rule 45.A; ICTR Directive on the Assignment of Defence Counsel (June 15, 2007) Art. 13i.

[28] ICC Rules, Rule 22; ICC Regulations, Reg. 67.

[29] ICTY Rules, Rule 44.A.ii; ICTR Rules, Rule 45.A; ICC Rules, Rule 22.1.

Kinyarwanda, Lingala, or Zaghawa—a rare Saharan language—as in the *Banda* case before the ICC.[30]

These lists of eligible defense counsel reveal why defendants do not (or cannot) necessarily select lawyers from their national system. While 40 out of the 107 lawyers on the ICTY's list of eligible counsel come from the former Yugoslavia,[31] only 4 Rwandans feature on the ICTR's list of 139 eligible lawyers.[32] This is certainly reflective of the political realities in Rwanda, rather than a dearth of qualified lawyers. Given that the Rwandan Prosecutor-General has publicly accused "defense lawyers for genocide suspects" of engaging in genocide denial, a crime punishable by life imprisonment in Rwanda,[33] it is not difficult to understand the reluctance of national lawyers to work for the ICTR defense. At the ICC, only 53 of the 411 eligible lawyers come from the states whose nationals are being tried.[34] For example, although the ICC has indicted both the former president and first lady of Cote d'Ivoire, at the time of writing the ICC's list of eligible counsel had no lawyers from Cote d'Ivoire.

Even if a defendant's chosen counsel is on the list, at the ICTY and ICTR, the decision ultimately rests with the registrar.[35] The ICTY registrar has refused to assign counsel because of an inability to speak the court's working languages,[36] prior judicial impropriety or contempt,[37] and potential conflicts of interest.[38] Interestingly, the ICTR Guidelines provide that appointment "should reflect the need to form a team with experience in the tradition of both common and civil law and knowledge of the two working languages of the Tribunal."[39] The Chamber in *Butare* held that when appointing counsel for the six co-defendants, the registrar must consider "geographical distribution, [and] a balance of the principal legal systems of the world."[40] This was apparently in response to an over-representation of Canadian

[30] *Prosecutor v. Abdallah Banda Abakaer Nourain & Saleh Mohammed Jerbo James* (Order to the Registry to commence training of Zaghawa interpreters) (July 1, 2011) ICC-02/05-03/09.

[31] List of Defence Counsel Available for Assignment to Indigent Suspects and Accused (copy on file with author).

[32] List of Defence Counsel (copy on file with author).

[33] "Democracy and Genocide Denial Politics in Rwanda," address by Mr. Martin Ngoga to the Atlantic Counsel, Washington DC, Transcript (July 20, 2010).

[34] List of Counsel (September 22, 2011), <http://icc-cpi.int/iccdocs/PIDS/other/WebListOfCounsel 11122012Eng.pdf> accessed August 30, 2013.

[35] *Prosecutor v. Ntakirutimana* (Decision on the Motions of the Accused for Replacement of Assigned Counsel) (June 11, 1997) ICTR-96-10-T.

[36] *Prosecutor v. Šljivančanin* (Decision on the Assignment of Defence Counsel) (August 20, 2003) IT-95-13/1-PT.

[37] *Prosecutor v. Kunarac* et al. (Decision on the Request of the Accused Radomir Kovać to Allow Mr. Milan Vujin to Appear as Co-Counsel Acting Pro Bono) (March 14, 2000) IT-96-23&23/1.

[38] *Prosecutor v. Martić* (Decision on Appeal against Decision of the Registry) IT-95-11-PT (August 2, 2002).

[39] "Guidelines for the Remuneration of Counsel Appearing before the ICTR" (September 1, 2008), para 1.5.1

[40] *Prosecutor v. Nyiramasuhuko & Ntahobali* (Decision on a Preliminary Motion by the Defence for the Assignment of a Co-Counsel to Pauline Nyiramasuhuko) (March 13, 1998) ICTR-97-21-T.

lawyers,[41] despite their significant advantage of being able to work in both English and French, and familiarity with both common and civil law systems. Arguably the promotion of mutual confidence between a defendant and his counsel is a greater contributing factor to a fair trial and expeditious proceedings than promoting diversity in nationalities of those who appear.[42]

3.2 Relative experience

In the early days of the ICTY, commentators called into question the ability of lawyers from non-adversarial systems to provide adequate representation. In 2001, an ICTY Judge noted that: "[t]he bulk of defence counsel are Balkan-trained lawyers and typically not experienced at cross-examination. Some are quick learners but others are painfully awkward and unfocused."[43] The head of the International Bar Association stated that "[o]ften the local Yugoslav attorneys who appear in front of the ICTY lack the skills necessary to undertake a massive international war crimes case."[44] Similar criticisms were made of Timorese lawyers appearing in front of the East Timor Special Panels.[45]

None of these critiques questioned the appropriateness of imposing a predominantly adversarial system on defendants from civil law traditions. This debate aside, the criticism being directed at defense counsel certainly had the ability to collectively discredit defense teams, but also had wider implications. If the accused were not receiving adequate representation, then the legitimacy of the international courts was at stake.

Perhaps in response to these concerns, there was a push for the appointment of common-law trained counsel, or counsel not from the former Yugoslavia. The head of the International Bar Association suggested that the "paradigm for international war crimes tribunals" was the *Tadić* defense team, consisting of two Dutch lawyers and an English barrister responsible for cross-examination.[46] This approach, however, ignores that mutual trust and confidence between a defendant and his counsel is often grounded in their shared background. It also disregards the significant

[41] M Greaves, "The Right to Counsel before the ICTY and ICTR for Indigent Suspects: An Unfettered Right?" in Sir Richard May et al. (eds), *Essays on ICTY Procedure and Evidence in Honour of Gabrielle Kirk McDonald* (Leiden: Kluwer 2001) 177–85.

[42] See *Prosecutor v. Ntakirutimana* (Dissenting Opinion of Judge Yakov Ostrovsky on the Request of the Accused for Change of Assigned Counsel) (June 11, 1997) ICTR-96-10-T.

[43] Wald, note 2, at 104.

[44] Ellis, note 7, at 957. See also D Tolbert, "The ICTY and Defense Counsel: A Troubled Relationship" (2003) 37 New Eng. L. Rev. 975, 979.

[45] "Summary of the report to the Secretary-General of the Commission of Experts to Review the Prosecution of Serious Violations of Human Rights in Timor-Leste (then East Timor) in 1999" (July 15, 2005) UN Doc. S/2005/458.

[46] Ellis, note 7, at 959.

advantage of local knowledge. Congolese lawyers representing Congolese defendants at the ICC have an undeniable head start. They understand the background to the conflict, know how to hurdle investigative obstacles in the Democratic Republic of Congo and often have direct access to witnesses. They understand government and military structures, the geographical layout of the relevant areas, local terminology and customs, and know which sources of information are likely to be credible. They can communicate with witnesses in their native language, a significant benefit in terms of putting witnesses at ease and eliciting relevant evidence. The dramatic events at the close of the *Duch* trial at the ECCC also contradict the suggestion that a local and international pairing is necessarily the ideal. On the final day of trial, Duch abandoned a two-year defense strategy of accepting responsibility for crimes committed, deciding instead to side with his Cambodian counsel and seek an acquittal. This directly contradicted the closing pleadings given by his French counsel, led to confusion on the part of the bench as to the defense strategy, and exposed Duch to arguably valid criticism from the prosecution as to the genuine nature of his previous testimony accepting responsibility for the crimes in issue.[47]

In reality, each case, each court, and each defendant is different. Each merits a case-by-case assessment of which lawyers can ensure the most effective representation for the particular client in question. Sweeping generalizations concerning the ability of counsel from particular regions are outdated, as are rigid views regarding the ideal composition of defense teams.

3.3 Collective traits

An anecdotal survey of defense counsel across the different international criminal courts produces a diverse array of philosophical and ideological leanings, reflective of the different legal cultures and backgrounds from which the group is drawn.

One commonly identified collective trait, however, is a commitment to fair trials in the face of monumental institutional and political obstacles. Also shared is a willingness to commit to a particular client for several years (often at the expense of a national practice), and to conduct investigations in post-conflict states. Many are drawn to a working life which favors freedom over stability, choosing to commit to cases rather than institutions, and are generally less likely be guided by mantras such as "the end of impunity" or "no peace without justice," which are viewed as difficult to reconcile with the selective nature of international criminal prosecutions.

A significant number of defense counsel also expressed concern that their participation in international criminal trials risks legitimizing a flawed system that fails

[47] See, for an overview, T Cruvellier, "Duch trial ends with a twist" 95 International Justice Tribunal (December 9, 2009), at 2. See also Bernard Mangiante's film, *The Khmer Rouge and the man of non-violence* (2011).

to encompass sufficient fair trial guarantees, and fails to offer reasonable prospects of acquittal due to the political realities at play. For example, the ICTR has held defendants in pre-trial detention—with no prospect of provisional release—for up to seven years before the commencement of trial,[48] and defendants regularly wait for more than a decade before judgment. By continuing to participate in a system which fails to meet international standards of expeditious trials, there is a risk that defense counsel are condoning (or appear to condone) these failings. On a practical level, many defense counsel have experienced the frustration of being unable to present exculpatory testimony because witnesses refuse to be associated with the defense out of fears for their security.[49] When this occurs, there is a legitimate concern that defense counsel are contributing to a judgment which does not reflect the truth of the events, and are acting as fig leaves to the defective international justice machinery.[50] Although these apprehensions arguably emphasize the need for a strong and coherent body of defense lawyers to counterbalance and challenge those within the courts who openly prioritize convictions above all else, they remain legitimate concerns that are widely shared by practicing defense counsel.

4 Professional Conduct

4.1 Is there a need for regulation of professional conduct?

Requirements for admission to practise differ between national jurisdictions, but generally include a substantive legal component, demonstrated good character, and ongoing compliance with ethical obligations. This calls into question whether the conduct of defense counsel before international criminal courts should be regulated by additional, uniform "international" codes of conduct.

Serious professional breaches by international defense counsel are rare, but have occurred. Few within the field are unfamiliar with Krajišnik's counsel, who was dismissed prior to the commencement of the trial at the ICTY for failing to disclose that he had been suspended from practice in the United States. Despite having

[48] See, e.g., *Prosecutor v. Gatete* (Judgment) [2011] ICTR-2000-61-T, para. 58.

[49] As early as 1997, the ICTR reported to the Security Council that two witnesses in its first cases of *Akayesu* and *Rutaganda* had been killed following their testimony. "Second Annual Report of the ICTR" (December 2, 1997) UN doc. A/52/582, para. 51.

[50] With thanks to defense counsel for sharing their views, and particular thanks to Sareta Ashraph, Wayne Jordash, and Peter Robinson.

billed significant fees in the pre-trial phase, he informed the presiding judge that his preparation was "locked in his brain," leaving his replacement counsel with "a vast amount of material in a barely organized state."[51] Nor has it been easy for defense counsel to shake off early allegations of "fee-splitting," where some counsel were accused of sharing their fees with their clients' families.[52] These and other concerns prompted a separate regulatory code for defense counsel appearing before international courts.

4.2 The regulation of conduct

As a result of these concerns, the ICTY judges drafted a "Code of Professional Conduct for Defense Counsel" two years after the start of the ICTY trials.[53] An ICTR version followed in 1998.[54] The ICC Code was differentiated by consultation with defense lawyers' organizations and bar associations,[55] and was formalized in 2005.[56] The codes regulate the duties of confidentiality, honesty, independent representation, diligence, loyalty to clients, and avoiding conflicts of interest.

There are obvious difficulties in constructing a code that appropriately reflects the diversity of legal traditions. Ethical conduct prohibited in certain jurisdictions is perfectly acceptable in others. For example, while it may be appropriate for civil lawyers to discuss a case informally with judges, this is prohibited in adversarial systems.[57] British counsel are prohibited from meeting witnesses in advance of trial,[58] whereas it would be considered inappropriate in the United States for defense counsel not to interview a witness if there were an opportunity to do so.[59]

As such, defense counsel have found themselves caught between domestic ethical obligations and their duties to the international courts.[60] The international ethics

[51] *Prosecutor v. Krajišnik* (Judgment) [2009] IT-00-39-A, paras 45–6.

[52] "Report of the Office of Internal Oversight Services on the Investigation into Possible Fee-splitting Arrangements Between Defence Counsel and Indigent Detainees at the International Criminal Tribunal for Rwanda and the International Tribunal for the Former Yugoslavia" (February 1, 2001) UN Doc A/55/759.

[53] Code of Professional Conduct for Defence Counsel Appearing before the International Tribunal (ICTY Code) (June 12, 1997) IT/125.

[54] Code of Professional Conduct for Defence Counsel (ICTR Code) (March 14, 2008).

[55] MS Ellis, "Defense Counsel Appearing Before International Tribunals: Past Experiences and Future Challenges" (2005) 4 J. Hum. Rts. 491, 505.

[56] ICC Code of Professional Conduct for Counsel (ICC Code) (December 2, 2005) UN. Doc. ICC-ASP/4/Res.1.

[57] McMorrow, note 4, at 141.

[58] "Rules of Conduct for Counsel and Judges: A Panel Discussion on English and American Practices" (1994) 7 Geo. J. Legal Ethics 865, 868–73.

[59] McMorrow, note 4, at 142.

[60] See, e.g., *Prosecutor v. Barayagwiza* (Decision on Defence Counsel Motion to Withdraw) (November 2, 2000) ICTR-97-19-T.

codes purport to take precedence over any national obligations.[61] This is unhelpful, however, when the codes are devoid of the detail needed to provide practical guidance in the complex ethical dilemmas that can arise. The ICC Code remains inconclusive or silent on a number of important questions, such as self-representation, division of authority between client and lawyer, and the impeachment of truthful witnesses.[62] Moreover, many ethical questions are unique to international criminal trials. For example, in the *Media* case before the ICTR, the Appeals Chamber ordered a stay of proceedings and release of the accused Barayagwiza on the basis of a violation of his rights.[63] When this decision was later reversed,[64] the accused instructed his counsel not to represent him. After continued non-cooperation, Barayagwiza's counsel argued it was unethical for them to continue to attend court in contravention of their client's instructions, and referred to the professional codes of their respective national bars in Canada and the United States prohibiting them from acting against a client's instructions.[65] Rejecting their request, the chamber declined to find "most exceptional circumstances" warranting withdrawal, on the grounds that the Barayagwiza's failure to give instructions was simply "an attempt to obstruct judicial proceedings." In such a situation the Appeals Chamber reasoned it could not be reasonably argued that counsel was under an obligation to follow his instructions.[66] This put the defense counsel in difficult territory given their obligations to their national bar.

In another example, an ICTR defense counsel received disclosure of confidential material that was subject to witness protective measures in one trial, but was highly exculpatory for a previous ICTR client.[67] He was bound by the witness protective measures in place, but under an ongoing duty to act in the interest of his previous client. Nothing in the ICTR Code of Conduct provided guidance for this situation. In such uncharted territory, the instinct to default to national ethical obligations is understandable, despite the asserted precedence of the codes of the international courts. However, asserting compliance with national standards is not an ideal position for counsel should the chamber take a different view of the impugned conduct.

Judges are also drawn from varied national traditions, and will invariably hold defense counsel to different ethical standards. One counsel appearing before both the ICTR and ICTY noted "I would get sanctioned frequently in the tribunal in

[61] ICTY Code, Art. 19; ICTR Code, Art. 19; ICC Code, Art. 4.

[62] Turner, note 6, at 685.

[63] *Barayagwiza v. The Prosecutor* (Decision) ICTR-97-19-AR72 (November 3, 1999).

[64] *Barayagwiza v. Prosecutor* (Decision Prosecutor's Request for Review or Reconsideration) ICTR-97-19-AR72 (March 31, 2000).

[65] *Prosecutor v. Barayagwiza* (Decision on Defence Counsel Motion to Withdraw) ICTR-97-19-T (November 2, 2000), para. 19.

[66] *Prosecutor v. Barayagwiza* (Decision on Defence Counsel Motion to Withdraw) ICTR-97-19-T (November 2, 2000), paras 24–5. See also *Prosecutor v. Blagojević* (Judgment) T-02-60-A (May 9, 2007), Partly Dissenting Opinion of Judge Shahabuddeen, para. 2.

[67] *Prosecutor v. Casimir Bizimungu et al.* (Judgment) [2011] ICTR-99-50-T, at 119–32.

Rwanda for doing the same things I was doing in the tribunal for Yugoslavia, where it would be appreciated by the Judges."[68]

4.3 The consequences of breaches

Defense counsel who fall (or step) outside the bounds of propriety face a complex and multi-tiered regime of enforcement before the international courts. The ICTY's menu of sanctions for disciplinary complaints includes a warning or public reprimand, a maximum fine of €50,000, a suspension of two years and/or expulsion.[69] The sanctions administered by the ICC are similar and the court's decisions are automatically sent to the counsel's national bar.[70] If the conduct in question obstructs the proceedings, the chamber can impose sanctions for misconduct.[71] Misconduct has been found when counsel refused to withdraw despite a conflict of interest;[72] refused to commence a case and exhibited allegedly inappropriate courtroom comportment;[73] or refused to appear.[74] Conduct that interferes with the proper administration of justice may warrant a conviction for contempt of court.[75] Contempt sanctions at the ICTY and ICTR include up to seven years' imprisonment and fines of up to €100,000.[76] At the ICC, the fine is linked to the assets of the defense counsel, with a prison sentence of up to five years.[77] Findings of contempt have been entered against defense counsel found guilty of influencing witnesses (where a fine of 15,000 Dutch guilders was imposed),[78] and of stating the name of a protected witness in public session (which resulted in a fine of 4,000 Dutch guilders).[79]

This disciplinary structure raises some concerns. First, the overarching problem with this multi-layered system of enforcement is that "[u]nhappily, the *ad hoc* Tribunals do not apparently consider it a problem that misconduct, disciplinary

[68] P Robinson, Counsel for Joseph Nzirorera (ICTR) and Dr. Radovan Karadžić (ICTY), in the forthcoming documentary "Defense and International Justice."

[69] ICTY Code, Art. 47.C. [70] ICC Code, Arts 41–2.

[71] ICTY Rules, Rule 46; ICTR Rules, Rule 46; ICC Statute, Art. 70.

[72] *Prosecutor v. Gotovina* (Decision on a Finding of Misconduct of Attorney Miroslav Šeparović) (March 6, 2007) IT-06-90, at 4.

[73] *Prosecutor v. Nshogoza* (Further Decision to Sanction Defence Counsel for Misconduct) (March 17, 2009) ICTR-07-91-T.

[74] *Ntabakuze v. The Prosecutor* (Order Imposing Sanctions on Ntabakuze's Lead Counsel) (April 21, 2011) ICTR-98-41-A-A.

[75] ICTY Rules, Rule 77; ICTR Rules, Rule 77; ICC Statute. Art. 70.

[76] ICTY Rules, Rule 77.G; ICTR Rules, Rule 77.G.

[77] ICC Statute, Art. 70.3; ICC Rules, Rule 166.3.

[78] *Prosecutor v. Tadić* (Judgment on Allegations of Contempt against Prior Counsel Milan Vujin) (January 31, 2000) IT-94-1-A-R77.

[79] *Prosecutor v. Aleksovski* (Judgment on Appeal by Anto Nobio against Finding of Contempt) (May 30, 2001) IT-95-14/1.

proceedings and contempt proceedings may be instituted simultaneously."[80] This raises questions of proportionality. Second, defense counsel are officers of the court. As former ICTY President Judge Robinson, noted, "[u]nless there is evidence of *mala fides*, counsel should be given the benefit of the doubt,"[81] particularly given that defense counsel "may or even should push the limits of what is legally permissible to conduct a vigorous defence on their client's behalf."[82] It is questionable whether the regularity with which defense counsel are warned, particularly for conduct such as being late to court,[83] can be reconciled with these principles.

Moreover, reporting warnings to national disciplinary authorities[84] can impact counsel's standing and ability to obtain further employment. This is particularly problematic if defense counsel have received warnings for acts that would not breach their own national ethical standards. Accusations of unprofessional conduct "are easily formed and hard to dismiss."[85] There are regrettably several examples of allegations being carelessly leveled at defense counsel that ultimately were found to have no basis.[86]

5 Institutionalization vs. Independence

5.1 Status of defense counsel

Unlike prosecutors, who are staff members of the international courts, defense counsel operate outside the institutional structure. The Registry remunerates counsel who represent indigent defendants, but this does not give rise to a relationship of employment.

80 Tuinstra, note 6, at 235.

81 *Prosecutor v. Aleksovski* (Separate Opinion of Judge Patrick Robinson) [2001] IT-95-14/1, para. 4.

82 Tuinstra, note 6, at 230.

83 *Prosecutor v. Akayesu* (Issuance of a Warning against Defence Counsels) (March 19, 1998) ICTR-96-4-T.

84 See, e.g., *Prosecutor v. Musema* (Warning and Notice to Counsel in terms of Rule 46(A)) (October 31, 1997) ICTR-96-13-I.

85 L Arbour, "Legal Professionalism and International Criminal Proceedings" (2006) 4 J. Int'l Crim. J. 674, 684.

86 See, e.g., *Prosecutor v Simić et al.* (Scheduling Order in the Matter of Allegations Against Accused Milan Simić and his Counsel) (June 20, 2000) IT-95-9-R77, para. 99; *Prosecutor v. Nyiramasuhuko et al.* (Decision on the Prosecutor's Allegations of Contempt, the Harmonisation of the Witness Protection Measures and Warning to the Prosecution Counsel) (July 10, 2001) ICTR-97-21-T, para. 9.

5.2 The importance of independence

Former ICTY Deputy Prosecutor David Tolbert noted that in the early layout of the ICTY, "[w]ith the Prosecutor and Court located cheek by jowl and defense counsel situated generally off site, there is perhaps a metaphor for where the defense fits into the scheme of things."[87] Today at the ICC, the defense offices are still located away from the main building housing the courtrooms, chambers, and the prosecution. Defense lawyers must return to the off-site building during court breaks in order to access documents, files, and even photocopiers.

Despite the logistical pitfalls of this "arms-length" approach to defense teams, this separation reflects their independence from the court. It is this independence that facilitates frank and open communication with defendants, promoting the efficacy and legitimacy of proceedings. If defense counsel were employed as staff members, loyalties could be divided between the defendant and the institution, which are unlikely to share the same interests. Their independent status also liberates defense counsel from the political constraints under which the courts themselves operate.

5.3 The shortcomings of independence

Independence, however, comes at a price. In order to locate and access relevant evidence, state cooperation is often needed. Prosecution requests for cooperation carry the weight of the UN or the ICC behind them. Defense requests for access to military or government archives are often met with a resounding silence.[88] Although the prosecution has an obligation to disclose exculpatory material, exceptions exist if the material was provided on a confidential basis.[89] While subpoenas can force cooperation in certain limited circumstances, the ICTY and ICTR take the position that the principle of equality of arms does not apply to "conditions outside the control of a court,"[90] often leaving defendants without a remedy.

A litany of practical disadvantages also stem from defense counsel's independent status at the ICTY and ICTR. These include lack of access to legal research databases shared only between chambers and the prosecution, and a prohibition on holding UN drivers' licenses, which restricts independent investigations as defense counsel must always be transported by UN drivers and as such their movements

[87] Tolbert, note 44, at 976.

[88] See, e.g., *Prosecutor v. Hadžihasanović & Kubura* (Decision on Defence Access to EUMM Archives) (September 12, 2003) IT-01-47.

[89] ICTY Rules, Rule 70.B; ICTR Rules, Rule 70.B; ICC Rules, Rule 77; STL Rules, Rules 117–18.

[90] *Prosecutor v. Kayishema & Ruzindana* (Judgment) [2001] ICTR-95-1-A, para. 73, citing *Prosecutor v. Tadić* (Appeals Chamber Judgment) [1999] IT-94-1-A, para. 49. The ICC has recognized this disparity in access to evidence. If a state refuses disclosure to protect national security information, the court can draw appropriate inferences. ICC Statute, Art. 72.7.

are always recorded. Defense counsel also fall outside the health care and security regimes in place. This may seem like a petty complaint, but in practice this restriction prevented ICTR defense team members in Tanzania from seeking assistance from UN doctors or security, even in emergencies.

6 Main Challenges to Effective Representation at the International Level

Extensive domestic criminal practice does not necessarily facilitate an easy transition to international criminal trial advocacy. The differences between domestic and international criminal practice are significant, and can directly impact counsel's ability to effectively defend the accused. While the challenges are many, three of the most significant obstacles are discussed below.

6.1 Presenting the evidence of victims and witnesses of international crimes

Providing a forum for victims and witnesses to tell their stories has been heralded as a significant accomplishment of international criminal trials. In reality, participating as a witness in international criminal proceedings is often frustrating at best, and traumatic and distressing at worst.[91]

Many witnesses who appear before international criminal courts have had no formal education. Many have considerable difficulty providing the date or duration of events, or estimating distances or numbers of people. Some do not know their age, nor can they sketch locations or sites, read documents, or even easily recognize familiar objects in photographs.[92] As such, defense counsel familiar with rapid, concise, and complex exchanges with witnesses in domestic trials must quickly adjust to a different reality. Moreover, witnesses have often left their homes for the first time to travel to the seat of the court and are required to testify in public for hours

[91] MB Dembour and E Haslam, "Silencing Hearings? Victim-witnesses at War Crimes Trials" (2004) 15 EJIL 151.

[92] See generally, N Combs, *Fact Finding Without Facts: The uncertain evidentiary foundations of international criminal convictions* (Cambridge University Press 2010) 21–105.

on end about unimaginable horror. It is not surprising in these circumstances that testimony which seemed coherent in the field seemingly differs when presented in the courtroom environment.

The need for translation further complicates the process. Translation is carried out, for example, from Lingala, to French, to English (and back), or Kinyarwanda, to French, to English (and back), often resulting in testimony being distorted, regardless of the experience or best efforts of the interpreters. Leading evidence through translation requires extraordinary concentration, as counsel must be alive to potential misunderstandings or mistranslations, and must pace examinations accordingly. As such, even the most experienced counsel will often be unable to fall back on domestic experience to surmount these daily challenges.

6.2 Political obstacles

Access to witnesses, documentary material, and relevant sites is essential to the preparation of a defense case. Investigative work becomes impossible, however, when the post-conflict regime is hostile to the defendant or his defense.

In the first ICTY case, defense counsel explained that, "[i]n preparing the defence, we have struggled with the hostility and suspicion with which the Tribunal is viewed in the Serb Republic... there have been active attempts to prevent us from obtaining evidence."[93]

Sixteen years later, these same political obstacles continue to hamstring defense investigations in both the Former Yugoslavia and Africa. In the *Bemba* case before the ICC,[94] it is impossible for the defence to access witnesses or archives in the Central African Republic, which is led by the defendant's former adversary, given the risks to those who are perceived to be cooperating with the investigation. Even in situations where the state in question is ostensibly cooperating, such as in Rwanda, political realities mean that many witnesses who are in possession of relevant exculpatory information are too concerned for their security to risk testifying on behalf of a defendant.

Defense investigations are also not without risk. In theory, defense team members enjoy "functional immunity" for acts that fall within their official functions.[95] In practice, ICTR defense counsel Peter Erlinder was arrested in Rwanda and held for three weeks,[96] an investigator from the Gotovina defense team at the ICTY was

[93] *Prosecutor v. Tadić* (Michail Wladimiroff, Opening Remarks) (May 17, 1996) IT-94-1-T, at 69.

[94] *Prosecutor v. Jean-Pierre Bemba*, ICC-01/05-01/08.

[95] *Prosecutor v. Gotovina* (Decision on Gotovina Defence Appeal against March 12, 2010 Decision on Requests for Permanent Restraining Orders Directed to the Republic of Croatia) (February 14, 2011) IT-06-90-AR73.5, para. 33. See also "Agreement on the Privileges and immunities of the International Criminal Court" (2002) ICC Statute, Arts 18, 48.

[96] K Gibson, "The Arrest of ICTR Defense Counsel Peter Erlinder in Rwanda" (2010) 14 (25) Am. Soc. Int'l L. Insights 1.

indicted in Croatia for alleged concealment of material,[97] and four ICC staff members were detained in Libya for 26 days, including Melinda Taylor, who had been appointed by the ICC to act as defense counsel for Saif al-Islam Gaddafi.[98] This utter disregard for the rights of defense counsel is of particular concern for counsel representing ICC defendants, where witnesses are often located in states that are not party to the ICC Statute, and who do not recognize—or choose not to respect—the immunity afforded to defense teams. The impact on the rights of defendants is plain; interference with defense teams' ability to investigate and prepare to challenge the case against the accused undermines the fairness of the proceedings as a whole, and accordingly the legitimacy of the process.

Of course, in certain cases before the ICTY, the prosecution has also faced political obstacles,[99] while the ICC's prosecution has struggled against the well-documented non-cooperation of Sudan.[100] However, under the more familiar model of the vanquished regime being prosecuted with the assistance of the victor, defense teams will continue to face hurdles to accessing evidence, which demonstrably infringes on their ability to present a full defense.

6.3 Inequality of arms

Although prosecution and defense in domestic cases do not enjoy a parity of resources under most national systems, these domestic gaps pale in comparison to the gaps that exist in international criminal courts.

The ICTY Appeals Chamber has held that the principle of "equality of arms" requires only the same access to the powers of the court and the same rights of both parties to present their cases, rather than the allocation of equal resources to the parties.[101] The prosecution bears the burden of proving its case beyond reasonable doubt and must comply with more onerous disclosure obligations, while defendants are under no obligation to mount a defense or even to present evidence.

Even with these considerations in mind, it is still astonishing that the ICC prosecution budget in 2013 was €28.27 million, while the total budget allocated to defense teams was €2.6 million, more than ten times less. This €2.6 million also includes the

[97] *Prosecutor v. Gotovina*, note 95, para. 5.

[98] *Prosecutor v. Saif Al-Islam Gaddafi and Abdullah Al-Senussi*, Public Redacted Version of the Corrigendum to the "Defence Response to the 'Application on behalf of the Government of Libya pursuant to Article 19 of the ICC Statute'" (July 31, 2012) ICC-01/11-01/11-190-Corr-Red, para. 15.

[99] C del Ponte and C Sudetic, *Madame Prosecutor: Confrontations with Humanity's Worst Criminals and the Culture of Impunity* (New York: Other Press 2008) 53, 56–7.

[100] *Prosecutor v. Ahmand Muhammad Harun and Ali Muhammad Ali Abd-al-Rahman* (Decision informing the United Nations Security Council about the lack of cooperation by the Republic of the Sudan) (May 25, 2010) ICC-02/05-01/07.

[101] *Prosecutor v. Tadić* (Appeals Chamber Judgment) (July 15, 1999) IT-94-1-A, paras 29–56.

cost of duty counsel for suspects and witnesses, and almost a third is allocated to the "Counsel Support Section" who administer the legal aid system, and not to defense teams or defense investigations.[102] Practically, this means defense teams at the ICC are comprised of four of five members, while prosecution teams are staffed by large numbers of trial attorneys, investigators, analysts, legal and language assistants, and interns. Any attempt by the defense to engage more that two unpaid interns at a time is inexplicably prohibited by the "Counsel Support Section." As such, the prosecution has more manpower to conduct investigations, review evidence and raise or challenge procedural anomalies during the trial, placing the prosecution at an undeniable advantage.

These same concerns have been long-standing at the Yugoslavia and Rwanda tribunals, where the prosecution can call on teams of permanent investigators and analysts and can rely on evidence archives built up over years of investigations. Defense teams—appointed sometimes only months prior to the start of a given trial—have been required to start from scratch. The ICTR Appeals Chamber recently found no violation of Kalimanzera's rights despite the prosecution employing a team of 35 investigators between 1999 and 2008, compared to the defense's ability to employ two investigators for a 2.5-month period in 2008.[103] Suggestions that "defense counsel could attempt to get sponsorship from NGOs"[104] to supplement funding is difficult to reconcile with both the political realities of defense work and defense teams' professional obligation of independence.

These three challenges are not the only that exist. Some counsel confront the added obstacle of representing hostile defendants.[105] Counsel at the Special Tribunal for Lebanon (STL) represent defendants *in absentia*, which requires presenting a defense case with no client instructions.[106] Also difficult is the widespread use of witness protective measures, which prohibit disclosure of witness identities and often prevent protection witness allegations from being thoroughly investigated.[107]

[102] International Criminal Court Assembly of States Parties, "Approved Programme Budget for 2013 of the International Criminal Court" (March 1, 2013) (copy on file with the author).

[103] *Kalimanzira v. Prosecutor* (Appeals Chamber Judgment) (October 20, 2010) ICTR-05-88-A, paras 36–7.

[104] MS Ellis "Defense Counsel Appearing Before International Tribunals: Past Experiences and Future Challenges" (2005) 4 J. Hum. Rts. 491, 495.

[105] *Prosecutor v. Barayagwiza* (Decision on Defence Counsel Motion to Withdraw) (November 2, 2000), ICTR-97-19-T, para. 19; *Prosecutor v. Milošević*, (Appeal Against the Trial Chamber's Decision on Assignment of Defence Counsel) (September 29, 2004) IT-02-54-A, para. 66.

[106] *Prosecutor v. Ayyash* et al. (Decision to Hold Trials *In Absentia*) (February 1, 2012) STL-11-01/I/TC, para. 111.

[107] 85 to 90 percent of witnesses at the ICTY and ICTR testified using pseudonyms. A Dieng, "International Criminal Justice: From Paper to Practice—A Contribution from the International Criminal Tribunal for Rwanda to the Establishment of the International Criminal Court" (2002) 25 Fordham Int'l. L. J. 701. At the ICC, the majority of witnesses have been granted protective measures. Of the 28 prosecution witnesses called in *Prosecutor v. Lubanga*, 22 were heard either partly or completely in private session. International Bar Association, "The ICC Trials: An Examination of Key Judicial Developments at the International Criminal Court" (May 2010) 17.

These challenges can give the impression to counsel coming from national practice that the international system is weighted against the accused. Unflinching and vigorous efforts, novel strategies and flawless teamwork are required to confront these various challenges and achieve effective representation of accused before international courts.

7 Conclusion

One former ICTY judge wrote that, '[a] vigorous, unintimidated, knowledgeable defense is the *sine qua non* of a fair trial.'[108] The interests of justice require a strong and properly resourced defense, regardless of the charges leveled by the prosecution. Despite a positive shift in the recognition of defense lawyers within the machinery of international justice, many challenges remain. This is particularly true as the ICC slowly attempts to assert a leading role, despite institutional hostility to defense teams that is still far greater than that found at the Yugoslavia and Rwanda tribunals.[109] A forceful commitment to meaningful equality of arms—and an active regard to the interests of both defense counsel and the defendants they represent—will undoubtedly contribute to the fairness of international criminal trials, and the ultimate legacy of the international criminal courts.

Research Questions

1. Are there other examples of conduct permissible in civil or common law systems, yet prohibited by the codes governing defense counsel at the international criminal courts?
2. In what ways could judges of international criminal courts be more active in ensuring functional equality of arms as between the prosecution and defense teams?
3. How could the ICC do more to ensure the ability of defense counsel to investigate without interference by non-state parties?
4. Is the frequent use of the rhetoric of "ending impunity" at the ICC—also contained in the preamble to the Rome Statute—problematic when viewed in light of the right of an accused to be presumed innocent?

[108] Wald, note 2, at 102.

[109] According to discussions with defense counsel who have appeared before both the ICC and either the ICTY and ICTR.

Suggested Reading

Combs, N, *Fact-Finding Without Facts: The Uncertain Evidentiary Foundations of International Criminal Convictions* (Cambridge University Press 2010).

Cruvellier, T, *Court of Remorse: Inside the International Criminal Tribunal for Rwanda* (The University of Wisconsin Press 2006).

Tuinstra, JT, *Defence Counsel in International Criminal Law* (The Hague: TMC Asser Press 2009).

Turner, JI, "Legal Ethics in International Criminal Defense" (2010) 10 Chi. J. Int'l. L. 685.

CHAPTER 33

THE ROLE OF REGISTRIES AND LEGAL SECRETARIATS IN INTERNATIONAL JUDICIAL INSTITUTIONS

STÉPHANIE CARTIER* AND CRISTINA HOSS**

* Legal Officer with the United Nations Office of Legal Affairs (OLA) and former Adjunct Professor at Fordham University.

** Legal Officer with the International Court of Justice (ICJ) and Visiting Lecturer at Leiden University. Formerly Research Fellow at the Max-Planck-Institute for Comparative Public Law and Public International Law in Heidelberg.

The views expressed in this chapter are personal to the authors and do not necessarily reflect those of the United Nations, the International Court of Justice, or of any other particular organization.

1 Introduction

Justice cannot be rendered without trust in judicial institutions. Yet trust is not easily established or maintained in adversarial and, at times, inflammatory judicial proceedings. All judicial institutions, in particular those at the international level, strive to inspire trust by ensuring that their findings are both fair and in accordance with the law. In such context, all Registries and Legal Secretariats (RLS), as organs of the judicial institutions, play an indispensable role in inspiring trust in their institution by interacting with the parties in a fair and effective manner, in the midst of conflicting views and interests. Parties are more likely to accept adverse findings if they believe that their case was handled with utmost care, not only by individual judges, but also by those with whom they are in regular contact at RLS. This is true in any international judicial institution, such as inter-state courts, international criminal courts, and human rights courts. A fair, strictly neutral, and discrete RLS greatly contributes to generating trust in any judicial institution.

Although all RLS of international judicial institutions aim to inspire and preserve trust, irrespective of the nature of their jurisdiction, divergent practices arise to respond to the specific needs of each institution. To name just one example, the registrars of international criminal jurisdictions are in charge of the administration of detention centres and have the mandate to take decisions regarding the rights of the accused. That role is rather different from the role of RLS in inter-state disputes or in regional human rights courts.

To describe what is or should be the role of RLS in international courts and tribunals is thus not an easy task. Even when some international judicial institutions appear to have a similar codified role, the degree of leadership exercised by RLS in practice may depend on the degree of activism exercised by judges in the daily operations of the institutions. Although RLS engage in communications with parties and the public, they are counterintuitively far less visible to the general public than the judges. Moreover, some of the work performed by RLS is sometimes protected by stringent confidentiality rules.

To complicate matters even more, very few scholarly publications have thus far shed light on this relatively new function in the international legal system. The work of RLS is thus in large part shrouded in mystery. Such mystery generates much speculation about the exact nature and extent of their influence in certain judicial operations, such as deliberations, judicial decision-making, and the drafting of judgments.

With all these factors and caveats in mind, the analysis hereafter presents trends in the role and responsibilities of RLS based on the governing instruments of international judicial institutions, the legal literature, and the authors' experience. It does not reflect any possible incident that might have occurred in different proceedings and it cannot be in any way exhaustive.

In order to assess the essential trust-building role of RLS in international judicial institutions, it is necessary to examine their specific responsibilities as well as the selection process and terms of office of registrars. Section 2 provides a brief overview of the workforce employed by RLS across the broad range of international courts and tribunals. Focus is next turned in section 3 to the statutory and non-statutory role and responsibilities of RLS of international judicial institutions. Lastly, section 4 scrutinizes how registrars are selected and their terms of office across a broad range of international judicial institutions.

2 Overview of the Workforce in Current RLS

As international courts and tribunals have multiplied, so have RLS as organs of such institutions, employing a registrar as the administrative head of the institution as well as several legal officers and support staff to assist their institution. As of April 2013, there are approximately 2,228 staff members working with RLS of the broad spectrum of international courts and tribunals. It is estimated that approximately 429 lawyers work for the registries of international courts and tribunals.[1]

RLS are principally concentrated in Europe like their parent international judicial institution. The number of staff members working for the RLS of inter-state dispute courts ranges from 14 at the World Trade Organization Appellate Body (WTO AB) to 120 at the International Court of Justice (ICJ).[2] The registries of

[1] This figure includes the lawyers who assist the chambers of international courts and tribunals. The numerical information contained in this section was found in the most recent annual reports of international judicial institutions and/or communicated to the authors by several registries of international courts and tribunals in April or September 2013.

[2] As for inter-state dispute courts, the Registry of the ICJ is the largest, with 120 staff members in total, including 24 lawyers. The Registry of the PCA employs 41 staff members in total, including

international criminal courts and tribunals are generally the largest of international judicial institutions, employing several hundred individuals (430 staff members at the International Criminal Court (ICC) Registry, 180 at the International Criminal Tribunal for Former Yugoslavia (ICTY) Registry, 241 at the Special Tribunal for Lebanon (STL) Registry, 190 at the International Criminal Tribunal for Rwanda (ICTR) Registry, 123 at the Special Court for Sierra Leone (SCSL) Registry).[3] The size of registries supporting international criminal courts and tribunals necessarily reflects heftier administrative functions performed by the RLS of such institutions, and a correspondingly larger budget. The size of most international criminal courts and tribunals is rivalled by the European Court of Human Rights (ECtHR), which has a total of 672 staff members.[4]

Accordingly, the differences in staffing of international courts and tribunals may reveal significant differences in the nature of and extent of the functions of RLS. The common and different responsibilities of RLS in international courts and tribunals are examined further below.

25 lawyers. The Registry of ITLOS has 35 staff members in total, including 4 lawyers. The WTO AB is the smallest inter-state dispute court, with 14 staff members in total, including 10 lawyers. (Figures as of April 2013.)

[3] With regard to international criminal courts and tribunals, the registry is usually an organ of the court that is separate from the chambers. International criminal courts and tribunals employ a large number of staff members as compared with inter-state dispute courts, because of the diversity and complexity of their responsibilities. The largest international criminal tribunal is currently the ICTY, with 787 staff members in total. The second largest international criminal court is the ICC with 700 staff members in total; 430 individuals work for the registry of the ICC and 48 staff members work for chambers, including 32 lawyers and 16 support staff (according to the Proposed Programme Budget for 2013, ICC-ASP/11/10 of the ICC, August 16, 2012). The STL is the third largest international criminal tribunal with 393 staff members in total; 241 staff members work for the Registry of the STL, including 9 lawyers, and 12 lawyers assist the chambers. At the ICTR, there are 190 staff members working for the registry, including 4 lawyers assisting the chambers. At the SCSL, the 123 staff members work for the Registry in Freetown and in The Hague; one lawyer works for the Registry and 7 lawyers work for the chambers. The Registry of the MICT, which is currently expanding, has 32 staff members, including 9 lawyers (across the two branches for the ICTY and ICTR). (Figures as of April 2013.)

[4] The ECtHR is by far the largest human rights court, and the international judicial institution that employs the largest number of lawyers. There is a total 672 staff members at the ECtHR, 274 of whom are permanent lawyers. (Figures as of September 2013.) By contrast, the other regional human rights courts seem modest. There are 60 staff members working at the Registry of the IACtHR, including 18 lawyers. At the ACtHPR, there is a total of 90 posts, 44 filled and 46 vacant. (Figures as of April 2013.)

3 The Main Roles and Responsibilities of RLS of International Judicial Institutions

It is reported that, when asked about the secrets of good court administration, the late Registrar of the Special Court of Sierra Leone and of the Special Tribunal for Lebanon answered:

> "A registrar should be like the referee at the football match which ends with the crowd asking 'where's the ref?' "[5]

It is hard to tell whether this holds true for all international judicial and arbitral institutions but Mr. Vincent candidly describes the functions of a registrar. The main functions are generally described in very broad and non-exhaustive terms in the respective statutes of courts and tribunals.

The registrars of international criminal jurisdictions have a different role from that of the role of the registrars in other mechanisms for the settlement of inter-state disputes. This is the case regarding functions of the registry concerning all non-judicial units combined within the registry, such as the detention unit, the defence counsel unit, the victims' representative unit, the public information and outreach unit, as well as different kinds of administrative units.[6]

One should also bear in mind another difference that arises between international criminal courts and tribunals and other international judicial institutions with regard to the responsibility of the registrar in administering the court or tribunal. While the registrar of the ICJ is considered to be the head of administration, he exercises this authority under the supervision and control of the president and the court.[7]

By contrast, the registrars of international criminal courts or tribunals are ultimately responsible for the administration of their court or tribunal, subject to an oversight by the international organization or the member states that established it. The registrar of the ICC administers the court under the authority of the Assembly of States Parties. The registrars of the ICTY and ICTR fulfill their functions under the Secretary-General's authority who will have delegated administrative and financial authority to the registrar of the institution, not to the president or judges.

[5] G Robertson, Robin Vincent obituary "Legal pioneer who brought justice to war-torn Sierra Leone" (*The Guardian*, June 22, 2011) <http://www.guardian.co.uk/law/2011/jun/22/robin-vincent-obituary> accessed November 28, 2012.

[6] See, e.g., ICTY and ICTR, SCSL, STL, and the ICC.

[7] In particular, Art. 26, para. 3, Rules of Court: "In discharge of his functions, the Registrar shall be responsible to the Court."

The registrars of the SCSL and STL, who are the only UN staff members in these institutions, are accountable to the secretary-general and are subject to the general oversight of their respective management committees. Such a situation may be explained by the administrative complexity of international criminal courts and tribunals, which is illustrated by the plurality of units serviced by the registrars and the large number of staff members employed in such institutions, as explained above. It should be noted, however, that the presidents do exercise a supervisory role over the registrars in some respects, in a general sense of oversight rather than direct authority or responsibility. Further, in a spirit of cooperation the registrars consult with the judges on matters that concern staff members who work directly with them.

All RLS of international judicial institutions share the same objective of ensuring the smooth and orderly conduct of judicial proceedings involving conflicting interests in the international legal system, irrespective of the nature of the dispute or the identity of the parties. The functions of the registrars and RLS that enable them to achieve this objective are examined further below.

3.1 Administrative functions

Registrars are generally perceived as the principal administrators of courts. As such, it is often incumbent upon them to administer the court's budget,[8] which may be a source of tension between the registry and the bench or between the registry and other organs of a court (the Office of the Prosecutor, for instance, in international criminal courts).[9]

The administrative functions and statutory obligations of the registrar at the ICJ have been extensively described elsewhere.[10] They are set out in Art. 26 of the Rules of Court. Similar provisions govern the attributions of the registrar of the International Tribunal of the Law of the Sea (ITLOS). Registrars of international criminal courts and tribunals have, however, a much broader field of action. Notably, in addition to traditional administrative functions, registrars are responsible for victims and witnesses, for the detention unit, for the management of the defence counsel, and for legal assistance.[11]

[8] Rules of Court (ICJ), Art. 26(1)(j); Rules of the Tribunal (ITLOS), Art. 36(1)(l).

[9] United Nations General Assembly "Report of the Expert Group to Conduct a Review of the Effective Operation and Functioning of the International Tribunal for the Former Yugoslavia and the International Criminal Tribunal for Rwanda" UN Doc A/54/634 (1999), para. 245.

[10] See P Couvreur, "The Registrar of the International Court of Justice: Status and functions" in CJ Piernas (ed.), *The Legal Practice in International Law and European Community law, A Spanish Perspective* (Leiden: Brill 2007) 7–61.

[11] ITLOS, Art. 36 of the Rules; ICTY, Rule 33; ICC, Rule 13.

As far as the ICJ is concerned, the main administrative decisions are taken by members of the court, the judges, upon recommendation of its administrative and budgetary committee and implemented by the registrar.[12] Arguably, this is a quite unusual course of functioning for an international court that should focus on its judicial work, but it can be observed that some other courts and tribunals appear to be equally reluctant to leave the management and operation of the institution entirely to their registrar. Since ultimate responsibility for the court lies with the president of the ICJ, the judges' involvement in the organization and functioning is rather natural and it would be abnormal for a registry to operate without consulting with the bench. When the PCIJ was operational, the role of the registrar might have been somewhat different. Since judges were present only when the court was in session, the registrar, together with the president, would have to take more decisions as to the conduct of the proceedings. For instance, Ole Spiermann suggests that Hammarskjöld, the registrar of the PCIJ from 1921 to 1936 (the year of his election as a judge), had exercised more influence on the work of the PCIJ than most of its members.[13] Some registrars have been elected judges of "their" jurisdictions; and even though it is in no way to be considered a common career path to follow, it can be constructive to elect a member on the bench who is familiar with all the aspects of an institution.[14]

Nowadays, certain permanent courts and tribunals are better organized. For instance, the ICJ has its own Rules Committee,[15] Library Committee,[16] and Administrative and Budgetary Committee[17] that make decisions normally carried out by the registrar of the court.

The registrar of the ICJ also prepares a preliminary draft budget and represents the court when the competent authorities of the United Nations consider the court's budget.[18] This preliminary draft is submitted to the Budgetary and Administrative Committee of the court and then submitted for approval to the full court.

In arbitral tribunals, constituted ad hoc, the secretariat has full responsibility for the administration and is responsible to the states parties that instituted

[12] The ICTY has a "Bureau" composed of the President and the Vice President and the Presiding Judges of Trial Chambers. See ICTY Rules of Procedure, Rule 23.

[13] O Spiermann, "Historical Introduction" in Zimmermann, Tomuschat, Oellers-Frahm (eds), *The Statute of the International Court of Justice-A Commentary* (Oxford University Press 2006) 59. Regrettably, the author does not provide details to substantiate this proposition.

[14] See section 4.1 of this chapter.

[15] The Rules Committee was formally founded in 1979. Its task is to advise the court on procedural issues and working methods. Before 1979, the ICJ plenary would discuss such matters at their regular meetings.

[16] The Library Committee was established in 1970 and supervises the acquisitions for the library of the court and the modernization of its services.

[17] The administrative and budgetary committee is composed of the president (chair), the vice-president, both ex officio, and four to five judges elected every three years, at the same time as the election of the president and the vice president takes place.

[18] Revised Instructions for the Registry, Arts 24 to 28.

the secretariat. For instance, the PCA Secretary General[19] reports annually to the Administrative Council of the states parties, responsible for conducting the functioning of the International Bureau of the PCA, but the involvement of the council in the daily work of the International Bureau will be naturally less significant than in other courts and tribunals.

3.2 The "channel of communication" with the parties and the host state

Across the broad spectrum of international judicial institutions, RLS are the usual channel of communication between the parties and the courts and tribunals.[20] Thus, registries are the courts' spokesperson or main interlocutor with the parties, even though parties to proceedings might wish to consult among themselves in order to address issues relating to the general coordination of procedures. Registries not only receive every communication from the parties in judicial matters, they also issue communications that the court or tribunal wishes to transmit to the parties. The parties' direct and indispensable interactions with the registry thereby shape their perception of the judicial institution itself.

Registrars are also entrusted with the task of ensuring that the parties' communications or pleadings conform with the formal requirements set out in the relevant governing instruments. In that sense, the registry plays a pivotal role in giving guidance to the parties in the course of the proceedings.

When exercising these duties, the registrar must ensure the strict equality of the parties in the proceedings at all times. Any real or perceived inequality of the parties may deeply disturb proceedings and challenge the credibility and authority of any court or tribunal. Registries also assist parties in the procedural preparation of their cases; they will normally have prepared "practice directions" for parties in which parties or potential parties to cases will find indications as to the operating mechanism of a judicial institution. On the parties' request, the registries may provide practical information to the parties on the procedures before the court, without giving advice on the substance of the dispute, or commenting on the parties' judicial strategy, which would be considered inappropriate. Some states might need more assistance than others. Some states are better equipped in terms of infrastructure

[19] Rules of Procedure of the Administrative Council of the Permanent Court of Arbitration, Art. VIII.

The International Bureau, subject to the control and direction of the council, is established as a permanent institution. It is to serve as intermediary to the powers and as registry for the court, under the conditions provided by the convention, and to facilitate the business of the council. The secretary-general at its head shall be appointed by the council for a five-year term of office.

Under Art. IX, the secretary-general shall receive his instructions from the president on behalf of the Administrative Council. He shall be responsible for the archives and in charge of the staff.

[20] See in particular, the Rules of Court for the ICJ, Art. 26, para. 1(a).

but also in terms of their access to information and legal expertise in international dispute settlement. Making the information available to those states and providing them with the basic documents, with earlier jurisprudence of the institutions but also being personally at their disposal to discuss the different procedures available to states can be a decisive factor for a state to engage in judicial proceedings.

This assistance by the registry is of utmost importance in international criminal mechanisms since the defendants and their legal representatives may not be familiar with all the aspects and specific procedures developed over the years; the same holds for victims who wish to participate in proceedings, a possibility which is open to them before the ICC. Those individuals are entitled to obtain assistance from the registry legal staff.

In many institutions, the registry may engage in communications with the host states to address the courts' and the judges' privileges and immunities. Regarding UN judicial institutions, with the exception of the ICJ, the registry is required to consult with the UN Office of Legal Affairs on questions of privileges and immunities, since the Secretary-General has the prerogative to decide such questions. It is of utmost importance for the proper functioning of any international organization, but even more so for judicial or arbitral institutions, that the host country, and any other state that is directly or indirectly involved in a dispute, guarantee the judges' immunities in conformity with the relevant agreement on privileges and immunities and the host country's agreement. Indeed, international judges, like national judges, need to be able to exercise their judicial duties free from threats of lawsuits in domestic jurisdictions.

Registries are also generally in charge of informing the general public on activities of the courts or tribunals. Judges generally abstain from commenting on cases or decisions, with very few exceptions.[21] The rationale behind this policy is mainly that any judicial decision should be self-explanatory. Members of any judicial organ should, under normal circumstances, express themselves in the decision itself and in their separate opinions if applicable. However, it is rather common for the registries to prepare a press release on decisions of a court or tribunal. Depending on the structure and size of the institution, there may be an information or press department,[22] or even an outreach office charged with giving information to the press and

[21] For instance, the president of the court made a declaration to the press on the occasion of the delivery of a decision of the court. It was the case of a judgment on the merits in the case concerning the *Application of the Convention on the Prevention and Punishment of the Crime of Genocide (Bosnia and Herzegovina v. Serbia and Montenegro)*, February 26, 2007, when President Rosalyn Higgins made a short declaration to the Press after the pronouncement of the Judgment. In the case concerning *Pulp Mills on the River Uruguay (Argentina v. Uruguay)*, President Higgins made a declaration on July 13, 2006, after the reading of the order on Argentina's request for the indication of provisional measures denying that the situation was such that it required the court to indicate any such measures. Another meeting with the press was organized by President Gilbert Guillaume, one week after his election to the presidency of the court.

[22] As is the case with the ICJ, where the registry has an information department, currently staffed with four persons, including the administrative assistant and the head of department.

public. The registry thus has an important role to play in communicating decisions and judgments as to be understood by the general public.

3.3 Legal support and assistance in legal drafting

The registrar and registry lawyers are generally called upon to provide general legal support, not necessarily directly related to the conduct of a specific case. For instance, this support is often provided to the "Rules Committee" of courts which is composed of judges and is in charge of assessing and reviewing the rules of procedure of courts. For instance, the ICC established an Advisory Committee on Legal Texts, pursuant to Regulation 4 (1) of the Regulations of the Court, which is composed of three judges, one representative from the office of the prosecutor, one representative from the registry and one representative of counsel included in the list of counsel. Where such committees exist, they are assisted by the legal secretariats that provide the committees with necessary preparatory documents and background papers.[23]

The most delicate and controversial question is whether registries may or may not intervene in the drafting of decisions or judgments. While such question is rarely addressed in legal literature,[24] speculation abounds among parties, academia, and the general public.[25]

Professor Hugh Thirlway, long-time Principal Legal Officer of the International Court of Justice, opined that different views might exist in different legal traditions, or according to personal convictions as to whether the judge should only make a decision and say what the law is, or whether the judge should always draft the text of the decision in whole or in part. For Hugh Thirlway, the distinction to be drawn is between "the decision on the issues in a case, and the expression of that decision in the best words possible. The first task is for the judges alone; but the Registry staff can and do help in the performance of the second."[26] There is a very thin line, however, that separates the two. As rightly noted by many authors, including Hugh Thirlway, "law is a matter of words; and it may be said that the choice of words to convey a legal point is in itself the decision of, or a decision on, that point."[27]

[23] R Jennings, "General Introduction" in Zimmermann, Tomuschat, Oellers-Frahm (eds), *The Statute of the International Court of Justice—A Commentary* (Oxford University Press 2006) 34.

[24] The most notable exception being H Thirlway, "The Drafting of ICJ Decisions, Some personal recollections and observations" (2006) 5(1) Chinese Journal of International Law 15–28.

[25] See, for instance, A Alvarez-Jimenez, "The WTO AB's Decision-Making Process: A Perfect Model For International Adjudication?" (2009) 12(2) Journal of International Economic Law 289–331; see also D Terris, CPR Romano and L Swigart, *The International Judge: An Introduction to the Men and Women Who Decide the World's Cases* (Lebanon, NH: Brandeis University Press 2007) 57–8.

[26] Thirlway, note 24, at 15–28. [27] Thirlway, note 24, at 21.

However, at the ICJ, the internal practice governing the drafting procedure ensures that judges draft the decisions of the court in a collegial effort. The court does not entrust the drafting to a single judge, the "juge rapporteur," but requires each and every member of the court to participate in the drafting process. The drafting is initially only entrusted to a three-member drafting committee and later all members of the court are invited to submit written amendments. After two readings of the decision, it is finally adopted after the completion of the second reading. This drafting procedure, set out in the Resolution concerning the Internal Judicial Practice of the Court of July 5, 1968, gives decisions of the World Court a particularly high level of authority. However, the procedure is rather time-consuming (all the more so since it is simultaneously performed in the two official languages of the court) and it can take up to nine months between the closing of hearings and the announcement of the judgment by the court, depending on the factual complexity of the case, and cannot be followed by most other courts and tribunals.

Depending on the number of cases and the number of available resources, allowing for greater involvement of the secretariats in the drafting of decisions can be necessary. While it is not unusual for registries to summarize the factual part and the arguments of the parties, every court and tribunal has its own internal practice as to whether the registry might also be involved in drafting of the decisions themselves.

However, if registries had a more important statutory role to play in judicial decision-making and in the drafting of the decisions and judgments, a legitimacy problem could arise.[28] While judges are elected or appointed to adjudicate cases, law clerks or other legal staff members should not assume or appear to assume judicial authority, and judges should not abdicate their judicial responsibility by leaving judgment-drafting and other judicial tasks to law clerks. At all times it remains incumbent upon the judges, as elected or appointed judicial officials, to ensure that their judicial authority and legitimacy is maintained.

3.4 The custodians of the "institutional memory" of international judicial institutions

In many judicial bodies, the RLS will be the only permanent institution of that particular body. They will also be the guardians of the archives of the court or

[28] A particularly strong stance against the involvement of RLS has been taken by Professor Jan Hendrik Dalhuisen, in his additional opinion attached to *Compañía de Aguas del Aconquija S.A. and Viventi Universal S.A. v. Argentine Republic* (ICSID case no. ARB/97/3) (Annulment proceedings). To quote just a few statements made in that opinion: " 2. It is clear that the Secretariat wants to obtain for

tribunal. Registrars, as heads of RLS, also play an important part in preserving the institutional memory of international judicial institutions. Registrars are thus critical actors in preserving the institutional and jurisprudential memory of international judicial institutions. While most tribunals exist for a long time, including the ad hoc tribunals of Yugoslavia and Rwanda, the judges' terms of office end after four, six, nine, or maybe twelve years: no international judge is appointed or elected for life and only very few judges go further than two mandates in the same institution.[29]

The most striking example in this respect might be the Permanent Court of Arbitration (PCA) where the only permanent institution is the International Bureau, with the composition of the arbitral tribunal changing with every case. The practical consequence (though not a statutory result) flowing from this situation is that the RLS will, in general, have deep knowledge of procedural precedents. The changing composition of courts and tribunals is risky in the sense that little continuity, and therefore little coherence, in decision-making could potentially occur. At the same time, a permanent bench with lifetime terms of office would probably be less inclined to adapt to contemporaneous legal developments and be more aware of continuity than one might deem appropriate. It appears that the staggered renewal of the bench is the most appropriate procedure to ensure continuity without impeding new developments.

In case the decision-makers face a new procedural situation, they will be able to revert to the registry in order to examine precedents in earlier cases, not necessarily to follow the same conduct, but in order to make a well-informed decision.

Generally speaking, a more important role might be attributed to RLS of non-permanent institutions, such as the PCA. The day-to-day administration of cases, the main budgetary decisions as well as the conducting of proceedings is in the hands of the Secretary General of the PCA, together with an ever-increasing number of legal secretaries and legal counsel.

itself a greater role in the conduct of ICSID cases and in the process also wants to involve itself in the drafting of the decision.... I believe this in general to be outside the Secretariat's remit and undesirable.... 3. ... It is clear that the Secretariat has no original powers in the dispute resolution and decision taking process.... 5. ... Moreover, getting some presentable text out of the Secretariat... delayed the final result considerably... 9. In this case, the ICSID Secretariat even took the view that on its own initiative it could intervene to 'streamline' the texts earlier agreed by the present ad hoc Committee and senior Secretariat members approached individual Committee Members informally with a view to amending the text. This naturally caused great stress in the Committee, raising many fundamental issues of propriety, independence, open and direct communication between Committee Members, and confidentiality."

[29] Judge Oda from the ICJ being the most notable example. He was elected for the first time in 1976 and retired from the bench in 2003, after two re-elections.

4 Selecting Registrars

The constitutive instruments of many courts provide rules on the selection of registrars, while some courts have sparse written rules or guidelines on this subject.[30] Given the importance of the role of registrars in international courts for their fair, smooth, and orderly functioning and for the overall credibility and legitimacy of international justice institutions, it would seem highly desirable to develop detailed rules and guidelines on this matter for all international judicial institutions. The following sections examine the required qualifications of registrars, as well as the election or appointment process of registrars across the broad spectrum of international judicial institutions.

4.1 Required qualifications of registrars

Few governing instruments of international judicial institutions provide detailed rules on the qualifications that are required of registrars, but generally there are also few details about the required qualifications of international judges. When these instruments provide guidelines, a legal background does not always appear necessary. However, in most courts, the practice has been to appoint a lawyer as registrar,[31] except in some international criminal jurisdictions, like the Special Court for Sierra Leone and the Special Tribunal for Lebanon, which both appointed Mr. Robin Vincent as registrar, who had experience as a court administrator. Mr. Vincent claimed that his function as the Registrar of the Special Court for Sierra Leone was "95 percent administrative."[32]

In some courts, legal background is specifically indicated as one of the areas of expertise that registrars should demonstrate. At the ICJ, the judges, in their Rules of Court, have given some general information on what should be the general qualifications for the registrar of that court in their view. Article 22(3) of the Rules of

[30] See the governing instruments of the WTO AB, the WTO DSU, and WTO AB Working Procedures on Appellate Review, in which no mention is made of the role to be performed by the director of the WTO AB Secretariat.

[31] Since the creation of the WTO AB in 1995, only lawyers have been appointed to the position of "director" of the Appellate Body Secretariat. The same holds true for ICJ and ITLOS Registrars, as well as ICTY and ICC Registrars.

[32] In an interview with the ICTJ on the handbook he had authored: R Vincent, *An Administrative Practices Manual for Internationally Assisted Criminal Justice Institutions* (New York: International Center for Transitional Justice 2007). The interview was available at <http://www.ictj.org/en/news/features/1742.html> in July 2007.

Court adopted by the court in 1978 with little changes made to the relevant article as it stood in 1922 (Art. 17) provides:

> Nominations shall indicate the relevant information concerning the candidate, and in particular information as to his age, nationality, and present occupation, university qualifications, knowledge of languages, and any previous experience in law, diplomacy or the work of international organizations.[33]

At ITLOS, the judges have adopted a very similar provision in the rules of that tribunal, emphasizing experience in the field of the law of the sea:

> Nominations shall be accompanied by the relevant information concerning the candidates, in particular information as to age, nationality, present occupation, academic and other qualifications, knowledge of languages and any previous experience in law, especially the law of the sea, diplomacy or the work of international organizations.[34]

By contrast, the Rome Statute of the ICC does not specify whether or not legal background or administrative competencies are necessary for the registrar. It provides:

> The Registrar and the Deputy Registrar shall be persons of high moral character, be highly competent and have an excellent knowledge of and be fluent in at least one of the working languages of the Court.[35]

However, the Rome Statute of the ICC emphasizes the administrative nature of the role that states parties have given to the registrar as "the principal administrative officer of the Court,"[36] who shall exercise his or her functions "under the authority of the President of the Court," and who should be "responsible for the non-judicial aspects of the administration and servicing of the Court, without prejudice to the functions and powers of the Prosecutor in accordance with [A]rticle 42."[37] Still, since 2003, two lawyers, who had previously acted as judges in their respective national state, have been successively appointed to this post.

Although there may be little guidance in the governing instruments on the qualifications required for registrars, the nature of the tasks assigned to registrars should serve as a guide for judges or other appointing authorities in determining the extent to which legal background is necessary for their registrar. For instance, if the registrar were likely to provide legal advice and to exercise quasi-judicial powers, especially when it comes to the provision of legal aid and detention issues in international criminal jurisdictions, or if the registrar may be called upon to participate in the deliberations and drafting of judgments, legal background would be essential.

[33] Rules of Court of the ICJ, Art. 22(3).

[34] ITLOS Rules of the Tribunal, Art. 32(3).

[35] Rome Statute of the ICC, Art. 43(3). See also, for instance, the Rules of Court of the ECtHR, which are somewhat succinct and stipulate: "The candidates shall be of high moral character and must possess the legal, managerial and linguistic knowledge and experience necessary to carry out the functions attaching to the post;" Rules of Court of the ECtHR, Rule 15(1).

[36] Rome Statute of the ICC, Art. 43(2).

[37] Rome Statute of the ICC, Art. 43(1) and (2).

It also seems critical for applicants to demonstrate experience in court administration. For a registrar heading a large court administration with a large number of legal staff, it might be less imperative to have a legal background as the registrar can rely on the work of the legal staff. Nevertheless, any registrar will need thorough knowledge and understanding of procedural aspects of the work of any court or tribunal. Non-lawyers will have acquired this knowledge in years of practical experience, but will need legal staff to assist and support them in carrying out the legal and judicial tasks incumbent upon the post holder. When legal background is necessary, knowledge of public international law is critical for registrars working in judicial institutions that emanate from the international legal system, irrespective of the nature of their jurisdiction.

Furthermore, as noted above, some registrars have later become judges of their own court. Åke Hammarskjöld was appointed by the secretary-general of the League of Nations as the first Registrar of the Permanent Court of International Justice and was later elected to serve on the same court as judge. Paul Mahoney had spent approximately 30 years as an administrator with the ECtHR, including as registrar, when he was elected as judge. Manuel Ventura-Robles[38] and Peter Van den Bossche also had professional experience as registrars before they were elected to serve as judges of their respective court, the IACtHR and the WTO AB. Accordingly, professional experience with a court as registrar has sometimes been considered to be valuable for candidates who aspire to become judges of the same court.

Lastly, it should be emphasized that in any international judicial institution, there can be no fairness without effectiveness, and there can be no effectiveness without fairness. Accordingly, judges or other appointing authorities must select registrars who are not only knowledgeable about the law, most particularly public international law, and experienced in court administration, but they must also be fair and effective in carrying out their daily operations. Such considerations must prevail at all times during any selection process of registrars.

4.2 Selection of registrars

There are different practices and trends with regard to the selection of registrars in: (i) international courts and tribunals created by a multilateral treaty between states, and (ii) international courts created as subsidiary organs of an international organization, by a bilateral treaty between a state and an international

[38] The Vice-President Ventura-Robles, Judge since 2012, was the Registrar of the IACtHR from 1990 to 2003; Judge Mahoney, elected as a Judge in 2012, was the Registrar of the ECtHR from 2001 to 2005. Former Registrar of the ICJ (1980–1986), Santiago Torres Bernárdez, is frequently designated by states to sit as a judge ad hoc in cases before the court.

organization or by a resolution by an international organization. Such differences will be examined below.

4.2.1 *International courts and tribunals created by a multilateral treaty between states*

In most international courts or tribunals created by a multilateral treaty between states, judges themselves control the selection process of registrars. Since registrars act as principal administrators of such courts, it seems legitimate for judges to select them. Judges elect their registrar at the ICJ, ITLOS, the ICC, and the ECtHR.[39]

Whether registrars should be elected or appointed by the judges, however, is another matter.[40] Elections at regular intervals, as opposed to appointments, presuppose some form of campaigning on the part of the registrar and other contestants. Elections at regular intervals needlessly politicize such a position.

Even when judges control the selection process of registrars in courts created by a multilateral treaty, states parties may remain interested in the nomination process of registrars. At ITLOS, for example, when the first registrar tendered his resignation, some UNCLOS states parties emphasized the "need to have the next Registrar elected from a broad range of candidates" and the "need for transparency in the election process."[41]

At the ICC, states parties play a more direct role in the selection process of the registrar. Although ICC judges elect the registrar by an absolute majority through a secret ballot, they are also required to "tak[e] into account any recommendation by the Assembly of States Parties."[42] It is noteworthy that during the preparatory process leading to the adoption of the Rome Statute, some proposed that the registrar, like the prosecutor, be elected by the Assembly of States Parties.[43] An author recalls:

> A majority of delegations felt that the Registrar's position could not be equated with that of the Prosecutor. The Registrar is essentially the chief administrative officer of the Court. The proper functioning of the Court would be seriously compromised if the Presidency, for example, could not exercise administrative authority and oversight over the Registrar. Direct

[39] See Rules of Court of the ICJ, Art. 22(1) and (2); Rules of the Tribunal of ITLOS, Art. 31(1); Rome Statute of the ICC, Art. 43(4); European Convention on Human Rights, Art. 25(e); see also the Rules of Court of the ECtHR, Rule 15(1) and (3).

[40] See, for instance, D Tolbert, "Reflections on the ICTY Registry" (2004) 2 Journal of International Criminal Justice 480, 481–2, which contrasts the appointment of the registrar at the ICTY and the election of the registrar at the ICC.

[41] United Nations Convention on the Law of the Sea, "Report of the Eleventh Meeting of States Parties" (June 14, 2001) SPLOS/73, para. 29.

[42] Rome Statute of the ICC, Art. 43(4); Rules of Procedure and Evidence of the ICC, Rule 12(3).

[43] PrepCom Draft Statute, Art. 44(2); see also MR Rwelamira, "Chapter Five: Composition and Administration of the Court" in RS Lee (ed.), *The International Criminal Court: The Making of the Rome Statute—Issues, Negotiations, Results* (The Hague: Kluwer 1999) 170.

oversight is essential for the smooth running of the Court. Consequently there was general agreement that the Registrar should be under the direct supervision of the Presidency.[44]

In sum, in most international courts and tribunals created by a multilateral treaty between states, the judges' authority to select the registrar appears legitimate. Member states, as negotiators of the treaty, have also manifested their interest in such process, but to a lesser extent. A more active involvement in such a decision on the part of member states may give rise to concerns, since member states may sometimes play the role of parties before such international judicial institutions. In any event, registrars should be appointed by the judges, not elected, in order to avoid an unnecessary politicization of that position.

4.2.2 *International courts and tribunals established as subsidiary organs of an international organization*

In international courts and tribunals established as subsidiary organs of an international organization, by a bilateral treaty between a state and an international organization or by a resolution of an international organization, the principal organs of the international organization concerned may also have a valid claim to participating in the important administrative decision of the appointment of the registrar. In such courts, the international organization and the judges are sometimes statutorily required to consult with one another on the selection of the registrar. In these circumstances, however, it can be unclear whether the registrars are accountable to the international organization concerned, or to the judges. The reporting line, or line-management, of registrars may become blurred, and such a situation may detrimentally affect the overall fairness and effectiveness of RLS.

In the ICTY, ICTR, and SCSL, the secretary-general of the United Nations is tasked by statute with the appointment of the registrar, after consultation with the president of the court, who is, in turn, required by the Rules of Procedure and Evidence to "seek the opinion of the Permanent Judges" on this matter before consulting with the Secretary-General.[45] While the secretary-general of the United Nations is primarily responsible for selecting the registrar pursuant to this rule, the registrar's function is nonetheless to "administer and service" the court or tribunal. In the context of the ICTY and ICTR, this situation has sometimes been perceived as a general accountability problem of the tribunals, including their registries, and has fuelled criticism by some commentators.[46]

[44] Rwelamira, note 43, at 170.

[45] Updated Statute of the ICTY, Art. 17(3); Statute of the ICTR, Art. 16(3); Statute of the Special Court for Sierra Leone, Art. 16(3) and Rule 30 of of the courts' Rules of Procedure and Evidence.

[46] R Zacklin, "The failings of ad hoc international tribunals" (2004) 2 Journal of international Criminal Justice 541–5; see also 2009 Report of the Brandeis Institute for International Judges, Brandeis University, available at <http://www.brandeis.edu/ethics/pdfs/internationaljustice/biij/BIIJ2009.pdf> p. 39, accessed July 30, 2013.

Robin Vincent, for instance, claimed that the registrar of internationally assisted criminal justice institutions "should be—and should be seen to be, entirely independent of the line management arrangements of any other appointee(s) in the institution, including and especially the judiciary."[47] In his view, it should not be incumbent upon the judges to appoint or renew the appointment of the registrar, since such an arrangement "is likely, from time to time, to put a Registrar in an extremely difficult position in the course of his interaction and relationship with the president and other judges." While acknowledging that a registrar has "both a duty and a responsibility to provide effective support to the president and other judges at all times," he argued that when the secretary-general makes an appointment, "the appointee is ultimately responsible to the Secretary-General or his/her representative within the UN system."[48]

The governing instruments of the STL and of the UN International Residual Mechanism for Criminal Tribunals (MICT) reflect the aforementioned position. Neither the Statute of the STL nor its Rules of Procedure and Evidence grant formal authority to the president of that tribunal, or to any other judges, to appoint or re-appoint the registrar. Likewise, none of the governing instruments of the MICT grants any authority to the president, or to any other judges, in appointing or re-appointing the registrar.[49] This situation represents a departure from the practice that had previously been established by the governing instruments of many other international criminal jurisdictions, namely, the Statute of the SCSL, the Statute of the ICTY, the Statute of the ICTR, which all provide that the registrar is to be appointed by the secretary-general "after consultation with the President," as explained above.[50]

At the same time, it should be noted that while the registrar of the STL is to be appointed by the secretary-general, the registry of the STL is "responsible for the administration and servicing of the Tribunal… [u]nder the authority of the President of the Special Tribunal," pursuant to its Statute.[51] Similarly, the Rules of Procedure and Evidence of the MICT provide that the registrar is responsible for the administration and servicing of the MICT "[u]nder the authority of the President."[52] In practice, such provisions may generate an expectation that the president of the MICT is to be consulted on the selection of the registrar.

A similar situation may be found in the WTO AB, an inter-state dispute tribunal. Much like the statutes of the STL and the MICT, the governing instruments of the

[47] R Vincent, *An Administrative Practices Manual for Internationally Assisted Criminal Justice Institutions* (International Center for Transitional Justice 2007) 11.

[48] Vincent, note 47, at 11–12.

[49] See Statute of the STL, Art. 12, and Statute of the MICT, Art. 15.

[50] Statute of the SCSL, Art. 16(3); Updated Statute of the ICTY, Art. 17(3); Statute of the ICTR, Art. 16(3).

[51] Statute of the STL, Art. 12.

[52] Rules of Procedure and Evidence of the MICT, Art. 31(A).

WTO AB do not give its judges (who are referred to as "Appellate Body Members") a formal role in the recruitment and selection of the registrar (who is referred to as the "Director" of the WTO AB Secretariat). According to recommendations made by the Preparatory Committee of the WTO, which were approved by the WTO Dispute Settlement Body (DSB) in February 1995, it is incumbent upon the "Director-General of the WTO, in consultation with the Chairman of the DSB," to select the "support staff," which presumably include the registrar, the legal officers, and administrative assistants. However, such "support staff" are to be independent from the WTO Secretariat and "answerable to the Appellate Body."[53] In practice, the requirement of accountability of the registrar to the WTO AB may also raise an expectation that the judges are to be consulted in the selection process.

Information pertaining to whether or not WTO AB Members are involved in the selection process of its registrar is not accessible to the general public. It would be highly desirable for the Director-General of the WTO and the Chair of the DSB to consult with WTO AB members on the selection of the Director of the WTO AB since they are in charge of servicing them and are "answerable" to them. Again, one can only notice the inherent contradiction and the possible risk of an accountability problem akin to the one found in certain international criminal jurisdictions.

In sum, there appears to be a disagreement and different practices relating to the questions of who should participate in the selection of registrars and what the appropriate reporting line or line-management of registrars should be across different international judicial institutions. Whether by the judges or by another appointing authority, registrars should be appointed to their post to avoid the difficulties associated with an election process.

While some distance from the bench may facilitate the effective performance of the registrar's function, careful thought should be given to the potential consequences of a reporting line that would completely exclude judges. The judicial independence of international courts and tribunals could be, or reasonably appear to be, threatened if judges are deprived of any capacity to influence important administrative decisions affecting their judicial work, such as the selection of the registrar. As explained above, registrars play a significant role in rendering justice alongside judges by ensuring fairness and building trust among parties. At the same time, it is legitimate for the principal organs of international organizations establishing the court or tribunal as well as for member states to be involved in such an important administrative decision, as creators and funders of judicial institutions who are also interested in their overall effectiveness.

[53] Recommendations by the Preparatory Committee to the WTO, PC/IPL/13, Sub-Committee on Institutional, Procedural and Legal Matters, "Establishment of the Appellate Body," approved December 6, 1994, and agreed to by the DSB in WT/DSB/M/1, Minutes of Meeting Held in the Centre William Rappard on February 10, 1995, circulated February 28, 1995, para. 17.

4.3 Tenure of registrars

The practices of international courts vary on the registrar's terms of office. Some registrars are appointed for limited terms of office renewable only once, while others are appointed for limited but renewable terms of office, and still others can be granted the status of "permanent" staff.

The rationale behind limited terms of office might derive from the idea that, like judges, registrars should serve on the basis of a rotation to ensure that a greater number of experts with different legal, cultural, and linguistic backgrounds have access to the post. Some could argue that it may also prevent registrars from gaining undue influence over the judicial proceedings and improperly arrogating judicial authority. Ultimately, however, the continuity of judicial institutions militates in favor for, and not against, the long service of registrars.

The terms of office of registrars, which are usually decided by judges themselves in the rules of their court, are generally shorter than the terms of office of judges,[54] except for most international criminal jurisdictions in which the terms of office of registrars are the same as the judges' and subject to reappointment.[55] The shorter term of office of registrars, when decided by judges, may reveal an unseemly power struggle between the judges and the registrars. It should be noted, however, that registrars of international courts usually serve on a full-time basis,[56] as opposed to judges on some international courts.[57] In judicial institutions where most judges sit on their bench on a part-time basis, registrars are more likely than judges to become the unofficial guardians of the institutional and jurisprudential memory of such judicial institutions.

When terms of office for registrars are limited, they range from five to seven years. They are not always renewable. At the ICJ, the registrar's tenure is a seven-year renewable term.[58] The registrar of the ECJ is appointed for a renewable term of office

[54] In the ICC, the term of office of registrars is five years and the registrar is eligible for re-election only once (judges are appointed for a single nine-year term). In the ICJ, registrars are elected for seven-year terms and may be re-elected (judges serve a renewable term of nine years). At ITLOS, registrars are elected for a term of five years and may be re-elected (judges serve a renewable term of nine years).

[55] See Updated Statute of the ICTY, Art. 17(3); Statute of the ICTR, Art. 16(3); Statute of the SCSL, Art. 16(3); and Statute of the STL, Art. 12(3).

[56] See, for instance, Rome Statute of the ICC, Art. 43(5).

[57] For instance, the judges of ITLOS and of the MICT (with the exception of their respective presidents) and all seven members (judges) of the WTO AB serve their judicial institution on a part-time basis.

[58] A reduction of the term of office from seven to three years, as suggested by the UN Joint Inspection Unit (UN Doc. A 55/834, para. 46), was not endorsed by the court on the grounds that it was already difficult enough to find suitable candidates for a duration of seven years and that it would be even more difficult to find a candidate for a three-year period. The court also considered that the length of the term of office was justified historically by the need to guarantee the independence of the incumbent, which was why equivalent terms of office were traditional for registrars of other international courts. See Couvreur, note 10, at 7–61.

for six years, which is the same duration as the term of office for judges themselves.[59] At ITLOS, judges had originally adopted a renewable seven-year term of office for the registrar in the Rules of the Tribunal, but they reduced that period of time to five years in an amendment adopted in 2001.[60] The ECtHR registrar similarly serves a renewable five-year term. The ICC has the same five-year approach, with the marked difference that it is renewable only once.[61]

Short terms of office for registrars are not reconcilable with their role and responsibilities as guardians of international judicial institutions. History has shown that trust in judicial institutions can only be built incrementally over long periods of time. In courts where judges are appointed for short terms of office or on a part-time basis, it is advisable to ensure stability, effectiveness, and continued fairness in court administration via longer terms of office for registrars. For these reasons, geographical representation and rotation should not be a primary consideration in the selection of registrars. The necessity of institutional stability, effectiveness, and continued fairness should outweigh other representational requirements for the position of registrars in order to allow them to participate meaningfully in building the greatest degree of trust in their respective international judicial institution.

5 Conclusion

In sum, RLS play a critical role in maintaining the stability and preserving the institutional memory of courts. The most reputable RLS are not only effective, but they inspire trust and confidence among parties. They also act in a manner that is unnoticeable and remains unnoticed by the public and at the same time ensure that the court's or tribunal's administration runs smoothly, without incidents of a procedural or diplomatic nature, notably by ensuring that parties obtain the necessary secretarial assistance, that all preparatory documents are ready when needed (possibly including translations), and that the records of proceedings are properly

[59] Rules of Procedure of the ECJ, Art. 12(4) and Treaty on the Functioning of the EU, Art. 253(1).

[60] Amendment to the Rules of the International Tribunal for the Law of the Sea, as adopted by ITLOS on September 21, 2001, available at <http://www.itlos.org/fileadmin/itlos/documents/basic_texts/Rules.amend.21.09.01.E.pdf> accessed September 8, 2013. See also UNCLOS, "Annual report of the International Tribunal for the Law of the Sea for 2001, Presented by the Registrar," (March 19, 2002) SPLOS/74, para. 66. The aforementioned annual report of ITLOS, presented by the registrar himself to its parent body, explains that such a decision had been based "on a study of the conditions of service of Registrars in international courts."

[61] Rules of Court of the ECtHR, Rule 15(2): "2. The Registrar shall be elected for a term of five years and may be re-elected." See also Rome Statute of the ICC, Art. 43(3).

maintained. Legal assistance in drafting rules of courts or judgments is another helpful tool used by members of a court or tribunal insofar as judges or arbitrators are not unduly set aside or put under any pressure.

In light of the nature of the tasks performed by registrars as heads of RLS, the decision as to how to select them is of crucial importance for any international judicial institution, in which judges, states parties and the principal organs of the international organization establishing them may wish to play a part to varying degrees. Registrars of international judicial institutions should preferably all have a solid legal background in public international law, experience with court administration, and a reputation for fairness and effectiveness. They should be appointed, not elected, to their post, since elections unnecessarily politicize such a position. Long terms of office should be favored in order to ensure the greatest possible degree of continuity and predictability within international judicial institutions.

From this very brief and admittedly sometimes eclectic overview, it can be seen that the quality, discretion, and experience of RLS can be of pivotal importance to the success of a mechanism for dispute resolution. Reputable RLS can greatly contribute to the success of an international judicial institution. Conversely, a poor performance by RLS can cause significant and enduring damage to an institution if they fail to carry out their various functions effectively, and, most importantly, if they fail to inspire and maintain trust in their institution. In any event, the multiplication and specialization of RLS in recent years are to be commended, since they have contributed to transforming significantly the international legal order toward a greater legalization or judicialization of international relations. Indeed, more and more international courts and tribunals settle disputes, or try individuals, by providing objective and fair determinations of international law, and more and more international lawyers assist them in this important task, as registrars or as staff members of RLS.

Research Questions

1. To what extent can the institutional legal culture and the influence of the RLS in decision-making be assessed through scientific methods? What is the role of the RLS in coining the institutional legal culture and how can judges, individually or collectively, change the legal culture of an institution?
2. To what extent is the role of RLS and registrars comparable to that of RLS and registrars in domestic judicial systems? Are the differences warranted, taking into account the realities of the international legal system, or should we find more inspiration in domestic judicial systems? Does the common law/civil law divide translate into particular functions of RSL?

3. Should registrars in international criminal jurisdictions be granted more representational responsibilities in order to alleviate the burden of presidents?
4. What are or should be the ethical rules applicable to staff members of RLS and registrars? Should all staff members of RLS and registrars in international judicial institutions be subject to the same ethical rules?

Suggested Reading

Couvreur, P, "The Registrar of the International Court of Justice: Status and functions" in CJ Piernas (ed.), *The Legal Practice in International Law and European Community law, A Spanish Perspective* (Leiden: Brill 2007) 7–61.

Dalhuisen, JH, Additional opinion attached to *Compania de Aguas del Aconquija S.A. and Viventi Universal S.A. v. Argentine Republic* (ICSID case no. ARB/97/3) (Annulment proceedings).

Rwelamira, MR, "Chapter Five: Composition and Administration of the Court" in RS Lee (ed.), *The International Criminal Court: The Making of the Rome Statute—Issues, Negotiations, Results* (The Hague: Kluwer 1999).

Terris, D, Romano, C, and Swigart, L, *The International Judge: An Introduction to the Men and Women Who Decide the World's Cases* (Lebanon, NH: Brandeis University Press 2007).

Thirlway, H, "The Drafting of ICJ Decisions, Some personal recollections and observations" (2006) 5(1) Chinese Journal of International Law 15–28.

Tolbert, D, "Reflections on the ICTY Registry" (2004) 2 Journal of International Criminal Justice 480–5.

Vincent, R, *An Administrative Practices Manual for Internationally Assisted Criminal Justice Institutions* (New York: International Center for Transitional Justice 2007).

Zacklin, R, "The failings of ad hoc international tribunals" (2004) 2 Journal of International Criminal Justice 541–5.

PART VI

SELECTED LEGAL AND PROCEDURAL ISSUES OF INTERNATIONAL ADJUDICATION

CHAPTER 34

THE SELECTION OF INTERNATIONAL JUDGES

RUTH MACKENZIE*

1 Introduction

As the decisions rendered by international courts impact upon states, industry, communities, and individuals, scrutiny falls upon the judges who render those decisions. Questions are raised about their national and professional backgrounds; the way in which they are appointed and the way in which they conduct themselves while in

* Senior Lecturer in International Law, University of Westminster.

office; and the extent to which they are fulfilling or exceeding their judicial mandates. The questions of the composition of the bench and the judicial appointment process arise as soon as states begin to consider the establishment of a new standing international court, and may frustrate attempts to establish such bodies.[1] Once a tribunal is established, the way that judicial selection procedures are designed and operate in practice has implications for the functioning and effectiveness of the tribunal. It will also influence perceptions of the legitimacy of the tribunal, as users and observers of the tribunal assess the way in which its work reflects their interest and values, and make their own judgments about its members. Rules and practices on judicial selection and tenure are also closely linked to the issue of the independence of individual judges, and of the tribunal as a whole, and regard must be had to the extent to which they might allow, or be perceived to allow, for interference in judicial activity.

There is no single model of judicial selection across international courts and tribunals and generalizations cannot easily be made.[2] As this handbook demonstrates,[3] a wide array of tribunals have been established, and much depends on the function of the court in question, the mode of its establishment, and whether it is international, regional, or subregional in nature. However, international courts are established by states, often within the context of wider multilateral or regional cooperation arrangements and organizations. Almost invariably, states are the principal, and very often the only, decision-makers in the judicial appointment process. The most typical form of judicial selection procedure in international courts involves the nomination of candidates by a state, and the election of judges from among those candidates by an intergovernmental body. In this sense, the judicial selection process is inherently political,[4] and raises concerns that candidates may be selected not solely, or even principally, on the basis of merit, but rather on the basis of extraneous political considerations or bargains.

In 2011, the Institut de Droit International addressed the issue of the position of the international judge, noting that "the quality of international courts and tribunals depends first of all on the intellectual and moral character of the judges,"[5]

[1] See, e.g., D Caron, "War and International Adjudication: Reflections on the 1899 Peace Conference" (2000) 4 AJIL 21–2, on debates over the establishment of a permanent international court at the 1899 and 1907 Hague Peace Conferences.

[2] D Terris, CPR Romano and L Swigart, *The International Judge: An Introduction to the Men and Women who Decide the World's Cases* (Oxford University Press 2007) 15.

[3] See C Romano in this handbook, Ch. 5.

[4] G Abi-Saab, "Ensuring the Best Bench: Ways of Selecting Judges" in C Peck and RS Lee (eds), *Increasing the Effectiveness of the International Court of Justice: proceedings of the ICJ/UNITAR Colloquium to Celebrate the 50th Anniversary of the Court* (The Hague: Martinus Nijhoff 1997) 176. For an empirical study of the judicial selection process in the International Court of Justice (ICJ) and International Criminal Court (ICC), see R Mackenzie et al., *Selecting International Judges: Principle, Process and Politics* (Oxford: Oxford University Press 2010).

[5] Institut de Droit International, Resolution on the Position of the International Judge, 6 RES EN FINAL, September 9, 2011, Art. 1, <http://www.idi-iil.org/idiE/resolutionsE/2011_rhodes_06_en.pdf> accessed September 3, 2013.

and adopted guidelines suggesting improvements in international judicial appointment procedures. In the same year, the Human Rights Institute of the International Bar Association adopted a resolution on values pertaining to such appointments.[6] A Study Group of the International Law Association has also addressed the nomination, election, and appointment of international judges, in the context of principles on the independence of the international judiciary.[7] In relation to specific tribunals, non-governmental organizations have been particularly active in monitoring and seeking to reform judicial selection procedures in regional human rights courts and in the International Criminal Court (ICC). As the developments discussed below testify, in relation to some tribunals, states have responded to, and in some instances initiated, calls for reform, and the last several years have seen a host of developments and a degree of innovation both in recently established tribunals and in some courts of longer standing. Proposals to reform judicial selection procedures for international courts, and recent reforms put in place for some of them, do not generally seek to remove states from the appointment process, but instead to put in place mechanisms to ensure that only properly qualified candidates are put forward for election or appointment and to enhance the transparency of the selection process.

Section 2 of this chapter briefly considers some of the wider considerations to be taken into account in relation to the election and appointment of judges in international courts. Section 3 seeks to give an overview of key elements of the judicial selection process in international courts. Finally, section 4 offers some concluding observations.[8]

2 Judicial Selection in the Intergovernmental Context

Principles and practices of judicial selection and tenure are intertwined with broader considerations of the effectiveness, legitimacy, and the independence of international courts. Such bodies will only operate effectively, and fairly, if they are staffed by

[6] International Bar Association's Human Rights Institute Resolution on the Values pertaining to Judicial Appointment to International Courts and Tribunals, adopted October 31, 2011, <http://www.ibanet.org/Article/Detail.aspx?ArticleUid=CA79763C-39CC-4B54-8174-DD247A894150> accessed June 1, 2013.

[7] See P Sands, C McLachlan, and R Mackenzie, "The Burgh House Principles on the International Judiciary" (2005) 4 Law and Practice of International Courts and Tribunals 247.

[8] This chapter focuses on the issue of selection of judges of permanent international courts and does not address the appointment of arbitrators.

appropriately qualified and experienced individuals who are capable of properly managing and disposing of the cases that come before them and who adhere to the highest professional ethical standards. Judicial appointments processes must therefore be grounded first and foremost in considerations of the merit of the candidates. However, in the political context within which international courts are established and operate, other considerations inevitably play an important role in achieving and maintaining acceptance of a tribunal by the states that created it. In relation to the International Court of Justice (ICJ), Abi-Saab has observed that "what counts is not to eliminate politics from the elections, which is a contradiction in terms, but to improve and widen the range of nominations so that political choice can be exercised from among a sufficient number of highly qualified candidates."[9] Thus, while the intergovernmental context means that there is always a political dimension to the judicial appointments process, the "choice is between a process in which the politics is open, acknowledged, and possesses some degree of balance, or a system in which political power and influence is masked, unacknowledged, and unilateral."[10]

Where state discretion in the selection procedure leaves room for appointments on the basis of political patronage, or for possible interference in or influence upon the work of sitting judges, there will be a negative impact on the perceived independence of the tribunal.[11] Such concerns are particularly prominent in relation to accounts of national nomination procedures,[12] as well as provisions and practices on re-election and re-appointment.[13] Alter has observed that since international judicial appointments are generally not controlled by any *one* state, international judges may be "institutionally less subject to appointment politics than their domestic counterparts."[14] However, as the review in section 3 of this chapter indicates, in some contexts, single states may well exercise a decisive (or veto) role in the appointments process, in such a way that formal multilateral "checks" built into the process, such as selection by vote, have little or no real effect.[15] While political control over the judicial appointments process may contribute to ensuring accountability of courts,

[9] Abi-Saab, note 4, at 184.

[10] PH Russell, "Conclusion" in K Malleson and PH Russell (eds), *Appointing Judges in an Age of Judicial Power: Critical Perspectives from around the World* (Toronto, London: University of Toronto Press 2006) 420

[11] RO Keohane, A Moravcsik and A-M Slaughter, "Legalized Dispute Resolution: Inter-State and Transnational" in JL Goldstein et al. (eds), *Legalization and World Politics* (Cambridge, MA, London: MIT Press 2001) 76.

[12] See section 3.3 of this chapter. See, e.g., R Mackenzie et al., *Selecting International Judges: Principle, Process and Politics* (Oxford University Press 2010) 63–99.

[13] See section 3. 5 of this chapter. See also, e.g., G Ulfstein, "The International Judiciary" in J Klabbers, A Peters and G Ulfstein (eds), *The Constitutionalization of International Law* (Oxford University Press 2009) 131: "The independence of the judges would, however, increase if they were elected for an extended period of time, or were not eligible for re-election."

[14] KJ Alter, "Agents or Trustees? International Courts in their Political Context" (2008) 14 EJIR 33, at 46.

[15] On the role of the United States and EU in appointments to the WTO Appellate Body, see M Elsig and MA Pollack, "Agents, Trustees and International Courts: The Politics of Judicial Appointments at

it gives rise to justified concerns about the impact on the independence of international tribunals.[16] These concerns have manifested themselves recently in relation to the Southern African Development Community (SADC) Tribunal, which was effectively suspended when the SADC member states failed to reappoint or replace judges after the tribunal handed down a decision against a member state.[17] This has been followed by agreement among the SADC member states to review and restrict the mandate of the tribunal.[18]

The response of SADC states is a stark example of *ex post* political intervention in the functioning of a court. Complaints are by no means uncommon that judges in other tribunals have exceeded the proper scope of their function by engaging in inappropriate judicial activism or lawmaking.[19] A number of commentators have examined how states' decisions about international judicial appointments may be determined by their expectations of the role of international courts and of judicial behavior.[20] Analysis of the politics of judicial selection drawing upon principal-agent approaches suggests that while states establish formally independent courts, they will seek to influence them *ex ante* by seeking to nominate and appoint as judges individuals who they deem likely to promote state interests, as well as those who may share the state's views on the appropriate scope of the court's

the WTO," EJIR, September 5, 2012, DOI:10.1177/1354066112448201, published online at <http://ejt.sagepub.com/content/early/2012/09/05/1354066112448201.full.pdf+html> accessed June 4, 2013; and RH Steinberg, "Judicial Lawmaking at the WTO: Discursive, Constitutional and Political Constraints" (2004) 98 AJIL 247, at 264.

16 P Mahoney, "The International Judiciary: Independence and Accountability" (2008) 7 Law and Practice of International Courts and Tribunals 313; G Ulfstein, note 13, at 147 on the balance between independence and democratic control.

17 Communique of the Extraordinary Summit Heads of State and Government of the Southern African Development Community, Windhoek, Namibia, May 20, 2011, para. 7. See F Cowell, "The Death of the Southern African Development Community Tribunal's Human Rights Jurisdiction" (2013) 13 Human Rights Law Review 153.

18 Final Communique of the 32nd Summit of SADC Heads of State and Government, Maputo, Mozambique, August 18, 2012, para. 24. The action taken by SADC member states in relation to the tribunal has been challenged before the African Commission on Human and Peoples' Rights, see Communication 409/12, African Union, EX.CL/782(XXII) Rev.2, Combined 32nd and 33rd Activity Report of the African Commission on Human and Peoples' Rights, para. 21, Table 2. It has also prompted a request for an advisory opinion from the African Court on Human and Peoples' Rights (ACtHPR), Request 002/2012 by the Pan African Lawyers' Union (PALU) and the Southern African Litigation Centre, see <http://www.african-court.org/en/index.php/2012-03-04-06-06-00/advisory-opinion> accessed September 25, 2013.

19 At such times, the identity and qualifications of the judges, as well as the mandate of the tribunal as a whole might be called into question. One striking example appeared in a UK newspaper in 2011: "Named and Shamed: the European human rights judges wrecking British law," an article denouncing certain judgments of the ECtHR and accompanied by photographs and "profiles" of some of the judges, challenging their experience and qualifications, *Daily Mail*, February 5, 2011.

20 See, e.g., E Voeten, "The Politics of International Judicial Appointments" (2008–2009) 9 Chicago Journal of International Law 387; Elsig and Pollack, note 15; Alter, note 14; and in this handbook, Voeten, Ch. 25.

functions.[21] Alternative approaches have employed notions of trusteeship, highlighting the significance of personal reputation and expertise of the judges, and professional norms, in enhancing the independent authority and legitimacy of international courts.[22]

The requirement of judicial independence, in terms of freedom of the court and the judges from external interference, finds support in the provisions of the governing instruments of most, if not all, international courts and tribunals, as well as in relevant declarations of principles.[23] Another aspect of the nexus between judicial independence and judicial selection relates to the composition of international tribunals and the fact that in most instances, the "requirement of independence … must, however, be balanced with the need for representativeness of the tribunals' composition."[24] In most international courts, there are fewer seats on the court than there are states parties to the court's constitutive instrument. In such instances, there is bound to be competition between states, as well as between candidates, for seats on the bench, and the governing instrument of each court almost invariably contains rules that relate to their allocation. Requirements for equitable geographic representation,[25] and other representation requirements, on the bench of most international (and regional) tribunals seem at odds with the notion of the appointment of independent judges based on merit.[26] But assessments of the legitimacy of many tribunals seem to depend, inter alia, both upon appraisals of the judges that compose it and upon perceptions of its representativeness. Such considerations affect the willingness of states to entrust adjudication to permanent international courts, as opposed to arbitral tribunals or other forms of dispute settlement. That representativeness requirements remain central to states' recognition of the legitimacy of international courts poses the challenge of constructing judicial selection procedures that ensure that standards of competence and independence are met, while, at the same time, achieving the representational mix of judges that maintains state confidence and acceptance of the tribunal.

The considerations briefly surveyed in this section make international judicial selection procedures complex, challenging, and dynamic processes. Different considerations may influence the balancing exercise in different international, regional and subregional contexts, as well as in different substantive contexts. While there is no single model that seems likely to be acceptable across the board, there are some common elements to the process and these are addressed in the next section.

[21] See, e.g., Elsig and Pollack, note 15. [22] For example, Alter, note 14.

[23] For example, see those cited at notes 5, 6, and 7. [24] Ulfstein, note 13, at 130.

[25] On this and other "representation" requirements in the composition of international courts, see section 3.1 of this chapter.

[26] G Abi-Saab has noted in relation to the ICJ that a "certain amount of dynamic tension, not to say contradiction, makes itself felt if we compare what the Statute requires in the judges individually (Article 2), with what it requires in the Bench as a whole." Abi-Saab, note 4, at 168.

3 Rules, Practice, and Innovation in International Judicial Selection

3.1 Composition of international courts

The process for selecting judges for international courts has been a matter of concern for states since the beginnings of the establishment of a permanent international judiciary. Disagreement about the means for allocating seats on a new permanent court of justice was one of the reasons for the failure to establish such a court at the Hague Peace Conferences in 1899 and 1907.[27]

In a few regional tribunals, each state to the court's constitutive instrument is entitled to have a judge on the court.[28] In such circumstances, each state will generally nominate a candidate for appointment by common agreement,[29] or will be required to provide a list of candidates for election.[30]

In most cases, however, and in all the global courts, there are fewer seats on the court than there are states parties to the court's constitutive instrument. In these cases, as discussed in section 2, "representativeness" is likely to be a key concern of states, reflected in rules and conventions applicable to the tribunal in question. Most commonly, there are requirements that on the bench as a whole there is representation of different legal systems and/or fair or equitable geographic distribution of seats.[31]

3.1.1 *Legal systems*

Representation of the "principal legal systems of the world" is required to be taken into account in judicial elections to most of the global international courts,[32] and such considerations may also play a role in regional tribunals established in regions with different linguistic communities and diverse legal traditions.[33] In relation to the ICJ

[27] See Caron, note 1.

[28] For example, the ECtHR, the ECJ, and the Andean Community Tribunal of Justice.

[29] For example, the ECJ, but see now the Article 255 panel discussed in section 3.4 of this chapter.

[30] For example, ECtHR.

[31] For example, ICJ Statute, Art. 9, which also refers to the "representation of the main forms of civilization"; ITLOS Statute, Art. 2; ICC Statute, Art. 36.8; WTO DSU, Art. 17.3; and in regional tribunals, see for example, Protocol on the establishment of the ACtHPR, Art. 14.2 (providing in relation to the election of judges, that the Assembly of the African Union shall "ensure that in the Court as a whole there is representation of the main regions of Africa and of their principal legal traditions.") Many international courts and tribunals also include a provision that no two judges on the court shall be nationals of the same state, see for example ICJ Statute, Art. 3.1; IACtHR Statute, Art. 4.2.

[32] ICJ Statute, Art. 9; ITLOS Statute, Art. 2.2 (where such representation is to be "assured"); ICC Statute, Art. 36.8.a.i.

[33] ACtHPR Protocol, Art. 14.2.

Statute, Fassbender has observed that this requirement in the Statute of the Permanent Court of International Justice "was not envisaged as an end in itself. Its purpose was to ensure that the Court would be equipped with the legal expertise necessary for the performance of its functions." Through such representation, the international court would be "inspired by ideas and concepts developed in the various domestic legal orders of the individual members of the community of States."[34] The legal systems to be represented are not enumerated in the texts, and in practice, such considerations seem to be given effect through rules and conventions on regional representation.

3.1.2 *Geographic distribution*

The global courts typically refer in some way to regional representation on the court. The United Nations Convention on the Law of the Sea (UNCLOS) provides for "equitable geographical distribution"[35] of seats on the International Tribunal for the Law of the Sea (ITLOS), and the ICC Statute refers to "equitable geographic representation."[36] The WTO Appellate Body should be "broadly representative of membership in the WTO."[37] Such provisions tend to be implemented through conventional or other arrangements for regional representation "quotas" which are closely guarded by regional groups. For example, in the ICJ, the conventional "allocation" of seats among the regional groups of the United Nations reflects the regional composition of the Security Council. Such arrangements can result in dissatisfaction and calls for reallocation of seats, to better reflect the membership profile of the tribunal in question.[38] In the global courts, provisions relating to the composition of the bench, that are in practice implemented through regional representation arrangements, place a good deal of power in the hands of the UN regional groups when it comes to the nomination and election of judicial candidates. Thus some regional groups may agree to rotate seats among subregions, and/or may endorse a single regional candidate, reducing competition and the role of the other states in choosing among qualified candidates.[39]

3.1.3 *Power and judicial representation on international courts*

The governing instruments of international and regional courts do not explicitly reserve seats on the bench for particular states. Nonetheless, it is clear that in

[34] B Fassbender, "Article 9" in A Zimmermann et al., *The Statute of the International Court of Justice: A Commentary* (2nd edn, Oxford University Press 2012) 292–317, at 307.

[35] ITLOS Statute, Art. 2.2.

[36] ICC Statute, Art. 36.8.a.ii.

[37] WTO Dispute Settlement Understanding, Art. 17.3.

[38] For example, in relation to ITLOS, see Report of the Nineteenth Meeting of States Parties, United Nations Convention on the Law of the Sea, Doc SPLOS/203, July 24, 2009, paras 96–102.

[39] For a fuller discussion of this issue in relation to the ICJ and ICC, see Mackenzie et al., note 4, at 24–43 and 105–10; and see sections 3.3 and 3.4 of this chapter.

practice certain states are virtually guaranteed a place on some courts should they put forward candidates. These practices are not written into the legal provisions of a court's governing instrument, but tend to be established or evolve as a result of power politics and tacit conventions. The most obvious example of the relation between power and judicial representation is the convention that the five permanent members of the Security Council (P5) have a seat on the ICJ. While there is no formal legal basis for this tradition (and indeed Art. 2 of the ICJ Statute provides that judges should be elected "regardless of their nationality"[40]), in practice it has not been seriously challenged in ICJ judicial elections to date, albeit that it clearly vexes many other UN member states. In the WTO, the United States and the European Union have been represented on the Appellate Body since its establishment, and it appears that this practice of constant, or regular, representation may now have been extended to other significant trading powers. Danner and Voeten have also found that in the ICTY, powerful states were overrepresented on the tribunal, with major NATO states "de facto guaranteed judgeships if they desired them" and judges from the Security Council P5 members usually elected.[41] In other courts, while there may not be "reserved" places as such, certain states appear to have a notable record of success in getting their judicial candidates elected. It is reasonable to question whether such successes might sometimes be attributable, at least in part, to factors other than the personal and professional qualities of the candidate: for example, the regional power of the state in question, its contribution to the budget of the court, and/or the weight the nominating state attaches to the importance of the appointment and its experience and effort in campaigning for international judicial elections.[42]

3.1.4 *Gender representation*

A more recent development in provisions on the composition of some international courts is the requirement that there be fair representation of male and female judges on the bench. In most international courts, the number of female judges has traditionally been, and remains, disproportionately low.[43] A number of arguments have been put forward in favor of measures to support fair representation of female judges on the bench of international courts. These include the suggestion that female judges may offer particular, and different, perspectives and experience, especially in relation to certain issues that may arise in criminal and human rights proceedings, as well as the more straightforward point that women should be better

[40] See Fassbender, note 34, at 297–8.

[41] A Danner and E Voeten, "Who is Running the International Criminal Justice System" in DD Avant, M Finnemore, and SK Sell (eds), *Who Governs the Globe* (Cambridge University Press 2010) 35–71, at 48–9.

[42] In relation to the ICJ and ICC, see Mackenzie et al., note 4, at 105–36.

[43] See Swigart and Terris in this handbook, Ch. 28.

represented on international courts so that such bodies better reflect the population subject to their authority.[44]

The statutes of the ICC[45] and ACtHPR[46] contain statutory provisions calling for fair or adequate gender representation to be taken into account in nominating and/or selecting candidates. In relation to the ICC, the Assembly of States Parties adopted voting procedures for judicial elections designed to ensure that these representation provisions were fulfilled.[47] Some other, longer-established, courts contain no such statutory provision, but the relevant intergovernmental or other electoral body has adopted further guidelines or requirements designed to achieve a more gender-balanced bench. The clearest example here is the ECtHR.[48] The implementation of gender representation requirements has not been without controversy. Some objections to such provisions and practices relate to their potential impact on state discretion in the nomination process, while others have questioned whether gender-based selection requirements might compromise merit-based appointments.[49] However, considerations of legitimacy would seem to support approaches designed to achieve more balanced gender representation across international courts, including those such as the ICJ and ITLOS.[50]

3.1.5 *Range of expertise*

As well as specifying, in more or less detail, the qualifications required of individual judges,[51] a court's governing instrument may make explicit the range of expertise which should be represented on the court as a whole. Such requirements are geared toward the competence and effectiveness of the court: they are designed to enable it to fulfill its mandate. At the global level, for example, the ICC Statute provides that states parties should take into account the need for judges with legal expertise on specific issues, including, but not limited to, violence against women or children,[52] and requires a mix of judges with expertise in criminal law and procedure and relevant areas of international law. Perceptions of what constitutes the right balance of

[44] N Grossman, "Sex on the Bench: Do Women Judges Matter to the Legitimacy of International Courts" (2012) 12 Chicago Journal of International Law 647, at 668 and 673 (Simply put, "[p]erhaps the strongest argument for sex representation on international courts is that women make up almost half of the world's population.")

[45] See ICC Statute, Art. 36.8.a.iii. [46] ACtHPR Protocol, Art. 12.2.

[47] See ICC-ASP/3/Res.6, paras 15–25.

[48] See further section 3.3.1 of this chapter. See also A Mowbray, "The Consideration of Gender in the Process of Appointing Judges to the European Court of Human Rights" (2008) 8 Human Rights Law Review 549.

[49] See, for example, the discussion in Mackenzie et al., note 4, at 47–9.

[50] See N Grossman, note 44. [51] See section 3.2 of this chapter.

[52] ICC Statute, Art. 36.8.b. As noted above, provisions on the nomination of candidates for ICC judicial posts require individuals to have expertise in criminal law and procedure or in relevant areas of international law. Procedures adopted for the ICC elections have been designed to ensure that the composition of the ICC reflects an appropriate balance between the various areas of expertise.

expertise may evolve over the life of a tribunal: in relation to the ICC, it has generally been acknowledged that as the court began to conduct criminal trials, more judges with expertise in criminal law and procedure were required.[53]

Getting the right mix of expertise is of particular importance where the mandate of the court incorporates distinct substantive areas of law. Thus, the Protocol establishing the Caribbean Court of Justice (CCJ) requires that at least three of the judges of that court have expertise in international law, including international trade law.[54] Similarly, the initiative to create an African Court of Justice and Human Rights[55] would create a body requiring judicial expertise in human rights and international law. The same combination appears to be required in regional and subregional courts established as part of economic integration arrangements which have subsequently assumed a mandate to address certain human rights issues.[56]

3.2 Qualifications of individual judges

Individuals appointed as judges to international courts must clearly have the appropriate personal qualities and professional qualifications and experience. These are addressed in the governing instruments of all international courts with varying specificity. Recent innovations and reform of international judicial selection procedures have principally focused on ensuring that candidates for judicial office fulfil the minimum criteria for office set out in the statute and other governing instruments of the court in question. As we discuss later, these may include requirements concerning the information to be made available about the qualification of candidates and the way in which candidates were identified, as well as "screening" mechanisms to review the qualifications of candidates before they are put forward for election.

Almost all court statutes refer in some way to the requirement of high moral character or integrity,[57] a requirement which, although rather general in nature, is clearly

[53] See Swigart and Terris in this handbook, Ch. 28.

[54] Agreement establishing the CCJ, Art. IV.1. On the jurisdiction of the CCJ, see Agreement establishing the CCJ, Parts II (Original Jurisdiction) and III (Appellate Jurisdiction).

[55] Merging the African Court of Justice and the African Court of Human and Peoples' Rights. See Statute of the African Court of Justice and Human Rights, Annex to the Protocol on the Statute of the African Court of Justice and Human Rights (Sharm El-Sheikh, July 1, 2008, not in force). Article 3 of the Statute provides that there will be 16 judges on the court, and Art. 6 provides that eight of these will be elected from a list of candidates with recognized competence and experience in international law, and eight from a list with recognized competence and experience in human rights law.

[56] Such as the CJEU, and the Court of Justice of the Economic Community of West African States (ECOWAS). On the latter, see KJ Alter, LR Helfer, and JR McAllister, "A New International Human Rights Court for West Africa: The ECOWAS Court of Justice" (2013) 107 AJIL (4) [forthcoming].

[57] ICJ Statute, Art. 2; ICC Statute, Art. 36.3.a; IACtHR Statute, Art. 4; CCJ Agreement, Art. IV.11.

of utmost importance in relation to the issue of adherence to applicable standards of judicial ethics. In its 2011 resolution, the International Bar Association Human Rights Institute elaborated upon the personal qualities that holders of international judicial office should display, following the approach of the Bangalore Principles of Judicial Conduct.[58]

As regards the specific qualifications and/or professional experience required, there are quite significant differences in the level of detail imposed by the governing instruments of the various courts and tribunals. As might be expected, the statutes of courts with specialized subject-matter jurisdiction tend to be more explicit in terms of specific experience required. The statute of the CCJ provides an example of more detailed requirements, specifying minimum qualifications in terms of years of experience as a judge, legal practitioner, or teacher of law.[59] The ICC Statute requires that judges have "established competence" in criminal law and procedure and "the necessary relevant experience" in criminal proceedings, or established competence in relevant areas of international law and "extensive experience in a professional legal capacity which is of relevance to the judicial work of the Court."[60] Several international courts follow the general prescription of the ICJ Statute that judges should "possess the qualifications required in their respective countries for appointment to the highest judicial offices," and/or be jurisconsults of recognized competence.[61]

Given that international courts invariably have specified working languages, the ability of judges to work in one or more of those languages is important to the efficient functioning of the court. Still, it remains unusual to see this issue addressed explicitly in the statutes of the various courts,[62] although in some instances it has been addressed in guidance or supplementary requirements.[63]

[58] The eight qualities referred to are: independence; impartiality; integrity; propriety; ability to dispense equal treatment; competence; diligence; and empathy. IBA-HRI Resolution, note 6, and the Bangalore Principles of Judicial Conduct, 2002, <http://www.unodc.org/pdf/crime/corruption/judicial_group/Bangalore_principles.pdf> accessed June 1, 2013.

[59] CCJ Agreement, Art. IV.10.

[60] ICC Statute, Art. 36.3.b.ii.

[61] ICJ Statute, Art. 2; and see, e.g.: ECtHR, Art 21.1; IACtHR Statute, Art. 4; ATJ Treaty, Art. 6; ICTY Statute, Art. 13; TFEU, Art. 253; Protocol on the Statute of the African Court of Justice and Human Rights, Art. 4.

[62] ICC Statute, Art. 36.3.c. For a discussion on the issue and challenges of language in the functioning of international courts, see Brandeis Institute for International Judges, *International Justice: Past, Present and Future* (2009) 19–25, <http://www.brandeis.edu/ethics/pdfs/internationaljustice/biij/BIIJ2009.pdf> accessed June 1, 2013.

[63] For example, in relation to the ECtHR, the Council of Europe Parliamentary Assembly has required that "candidates should possess an active knowledge of one official language of the Council of Europe and a passive knowledge of the other." Recommendation 1646 (2009), *Nomination of candidates and election of judges to the European Court of Human Rights*, para. 4.4.

3.3 Identification of candidates for judicial appointment

3.3.1 *Nomination by states or by a national body*

In almost all international courts and tribunals, the power to nominate candidates for appointment as a judge rests with states. The governing instruments of most courts give little or no guidance as to how the nomination process should be conducted, although it is evident that states should be guided by the provisions discussed earlier concerning the characteristics, qualifications, and experience of judges. Nonetheless, states generally have very wide discretion in putting forward individuals for appointment.

As is well-known, in the ICJ, the nomination is formally made not by states, but by the Permanent Court of Arbitration national group.[64] However, in many cases, governments still seem to play a prominent or decisive role in the nomination of ICJ candidates.[65] The ICJ Statute encourages the national group to consult in the nomination process with its highest courts of justice, law faculties, and national academies devoted to the study of law.[66] It is unclear how and to what extent such consultation takes place in practice, and few formal procedures seem to be in place.[67] It is widely acknowledged that in many states the nomination process for international judicial appointments is highly politicized and lacks transparency. Nonetheless, a few states have sought to formalize nomination processes for international courts, sometimes drawing upon national judicial appointment procedures. Some states have opened up national nomination procedures to open competition in relation to some courts, if not all. A number of Council of Europe (CoE) states now advertise vacancies for nominees to the ECtHR. The United Kingdom, among others, also applies this practice in relation to other international judicial vacancies for which it is entitled to nominate a candidate, including the ECJ, ICTY, and the ICC.[68]

While guidance on the nomination process may not be contained in the statute of a court, relevant intergovernmental or other electoral bodies have sometimes sought to provide guidance.[69] The most prominent examples here have been the

[64] ICJ Statute, Art. 4. This method was intended, inter alia, to reduce the role of political considerations in the nomination of candidates; see P Georget, V Golitsyn and R Zacklin, "Article 4" in Zimmermann et al., note 34, 254–271, at 261.

[65] See P Sands, "Global Governance and the International Judiciary: Choosing our Judges" (2003) 56 Current Legal Problems 481; Mackenzie et al., note 4, at 63–99.

[66] ICJ Statute, Art. 6.

[67] See, however, LF Damrosch, "Ensuring the Best Bench: Ways of Selecting Judges: Commentary by Professor Lori Fisler Damrosch" in C Peck and RS Lee (eds), *Increasing the Effectiveness of the International Court of Justice: proceedings of the ICJ/UNITAR Colloquium to Celebrate the 50th Anniversary of the Court* (The Hague: Martinus Nijhoff 1997) 188.

[68] M Wood, "The Selection of Candidates for International Judicial Office: Recent Practice" in TM Ndiaye and R Wolfrum (eds), *Law of the Sea, Environmental Law, and Settlement of Disputes, Liber Amicorum Judge Thomas A. Mensah* (Leiden: Martinus Nijhoff 2007) 357, 366–8.

[69] See, e.g., African Union, *Note Verbale*, BC/OLC/66.5/8/Vol.V, April 5, 2004, concerning the first nomination and election of judges to the ACtHPR.

Parliamentary Assembly, and more recently the Committee of Ministers, of the CoE in respect of nominations to the ECtHR.[70] Over several years, the Parliamentary Assembly, which is responsible for electing judges from among slates of three candidates put forward by each state party, has provided significant additional direction on the listing of candidates, information to be provided (in the form of a model curriculum vitae), and the process by which candidates should be identified and selected at the national level. The Assembly has called for open and transparent national processes, including public advertisement of vacancies.[71] The guidance is designed to ensure that the nomination process is both more transparent, and that it yields a national slate of well-qualified candidates. It responds in part to the practice of some states that appear to have sought to steer the appointment of the national judge by putting forward one strong candidate alongside two others who lack the requisite qualifications and experience—thus giving the Assembly little real choice in the selection process.[72] The Assembly has also sought to redress gender imbalance on the ECtHR, by requiring states to include both male and female nominees on their lists and rejecting lists that do not meet this requirement. However, some tension arises where the Assembly is perceived to be adding additional substantive qualifications or criteria for election to the bench, beyond those that have been agreed by states in the convention itself.[73] National nomination procedures have also been addressed by the CoE Committee of Ministers, which in 2010 established an advisory panel of experts to advise states parties whether their candidates meet the criteria for appointment set out in the ECHR, even *before* the list of candidates is transmitted to the Assembly for consideration and election.[74] In 2012, the Committee of Ministers adopted guidelines on the selection of candidates for the post of judge at the ECtHR.[75] These highlight, inter alia, that the procedure for eliciting applications should be made public and should be stable and established in advance through codification or by settled administrative practice.

3.3.2 *Direct applications*

A rather recent innovation in a limited number of international tribunals allows prospective candidates for judicial office to apply *directly* for appointment. These

[70] The process of judicial appointments to the ECtHR has perhaps been subject to more scrutiny than that of any other international or regional court: by institutions of the CoE, by member states and by non-governmental organizations. See for example, J Limbach et al., *Judicial Independence: Law and Practice of Appointments to the European Court of Human Rights* (London: Interights 2003).

[71] CoE, Assembly Resolution 1646 (2009).

[72] See Limbach et al., note 70, at 19.

[73] Advisory Opinion on certain legal questions concerning the lists of candidates submitted with a view to the election of judges to the European Court of Human Rights, February 12, 2008.

[74] CoE, Resolution CM/Res (2010) 26 on the establishment of an Advisory Panel of Experts on Candidates for Election as Judges to the European Court of Human Rights.

[75] CM (2012) 40finalE/29 March 2012.

include the European Union Civil Service Tribunal,[76] and the United Nations Disputes Tribunal.[77] Both of these tribunals are established to deal with staff claims within an intergovernmental organization. However, the CCJ also provides for direct application for judicial posts. In this instance, judicial appointments are taken out of the hands of states and entrusted to a Regional Judicial and Legal Services Commission, in a process designed to alleviate concerns about the independence of the court from political interference.[78] There are few signs such approaches are likely to be more widely adopted in the near or medium term in other standing regional or international tribunals. Where procedures for direct application are put in place, the identity and composition of the appointing entity requires consideration and agreement. In the case of the CCJ, judges are appointed by the Regional Judicial and Legal Services Commission; in the UN Disputes Tribunal and EU Civil Service Tribunal, the appointment of judges remains in the hands of an intergovernmental entity acting after consultation with, or recommendation from, an advisory body.

3.4 Election and appointment

The most common process for appointing international judges remains election by an intergovernmental body. So while nomination is typically a national procedure, the electoral process is international. Thus, for the ICJ, there are elections in the General Assembly and Security Council; for ITLOS, among the states parties to the Law of the Sea Convention; for the ICTY and ICTR, in the UN General Assembly; and in the ICC, in the Assembly of States Parties to the Rome Statute of the ICC. The electors are states and the process is inevitably political, particularly where elections take place within the wider context of an intergovernmental organization such as the United Nations. The election may be more or less competitive depending in part on the degree of regional and bilateral bargaining that has taken place beforehand. In relation to international courts, regional groups may make agreements within regions and subregions about the nomination of and support for regional candidates, limiting any real choice among candidates for the wider electorate. It is widely acknowledged that elections to international courts such as the ICJ and

[76] Council Decision (EC) 2004/752 of November 2, 2004 establishing the European Union Civil Service Tribunal [2004] OJ L333/7; see H Cameron, "The Establishment of the European Union Civil Service Tribunal" (2006) 5 Law and Practice of International Courts and Tribunals 273.

[77] United Nations General Assembly Resolution 62/228, A/RES/62/228, February 6, 2008; United Nations General Assembly, Report of the Internal Justice Council, UN Doc. A/63/489, October 16, 2008, see especially para. 6 ("The Council considered that the process to identify suitable candidates should ensure the independence, professionalism and accountability of the judges. To that end, the Council decided that a full public process should be instituted to identify suitable candidates.")

[78] CCJ Agreement, Art. IV.7 and Art. V.3. For a detailed discussion, see K Malleson, "Promoting Judicial Independence in the International Courts: Lessons from the Caribbean" (2009) 58 International and Comparative Law Quarterly 671.

ICC have been characterized by vote trading arrangements between states. In this sense, despite occasional political exhortations to the contrary, elections to international judicial bodies tend to be treated in a similar manner to those for other political positions in intergovernmental organizations.[79] That this is the case further increases the need to ensure that the national nomination process identifies the most well-qualified candidates.

A number of new mechanisms have been established or proposed in some tribunals to seek to ensure that only suitably qualified candidates go through to the election or appointment process. The existence of such mechanisms seems implicitly to acknowledge that states sometimes nominate candidates who do not fulfill the minimum requirements. The emerging trend is for the establishment of some form of advisory "screening" procedure prior to the election or appointment of candidates, to review the qualifications and experience of nominees in order to ensure they meet the criteria established in the governing instrument of the court in question. In 2011, the Assembly of States Parties to the ICC agreed to establish an advisory committee on nominations, as enabled by Art. 36.4.c of the ICC Statute,[80] to facilitate that the highest-qualified individuals are appointed as ICC judges. This development followed an interesting non-governmental initiative to set up an Independent Panel on ICC Judicial Elections, in the wake of concerns about the qualifications of certain candidates and the failure of states to establish an advisory committee for the early ICC judicial elections.[81]

A screening process has existed for some time in the ECtHR, whereby a sub-committee of the Parliamentary Assembly reviews and interviews candidates put forward by states prior to the election of judges.[82] In the Court of Justice of the European Union (CJEU), since 2010, a panel has been established to "give an opinion on candidates' suitability to perform the duties of Judge and Advocate-General of the Court of Justice and General Court before the governments of Member States make the appointments."[83] This panel is composed of seven persons from among former members of the CJEU, members of national supreme courts and lawyers of recognized competence. This development may be particularly important in the context of the EU courts, where each member state is entitled to one judge on each of the ECJ and General Court,[84] and judges are appointed by "common accord,"

[79] "International Courts and Tribunals Interest Group: Judicial Selection," Remarks by Patrick Lipton Robinson (2011) 105 ASIL Procs. 67, at 69.

[80] ASP Res ICC-ASP/10/Res.5, para. 19.

[81] See Independent Panel on ICC Judicial Elections, <http://iccindependentpanel.org/> accessed June 1, 2013.

[82] The adequacy of this process was reviewed in Limbach et al., note 70.

[83] TFEU, Art. 255. On the establishment and functioning of the panel, see Lord Mance, "The Composition of the European Court of Justice," text of a talk given to the United Kingdom Association for European Law, October 19, 2011, <http://www.supremecourt.gov.uk/docs/speech_111019.pdf> accessed June 1, 2013.

[84] Under the TFEU, it is possible that the number of judges on the General Court may be increased, but discussions about such an increase initiated in 2011 have encountered difficulty on the question of how additional seats on the General Court might be allocated.

effectively giving each member state a power of appointment if there is no screening mechanism in place. In its work to date, the Article 255 panel has given unfavorable opinions concerning a small number of candidatures.[85] Another subregional model exists in the context of the ECOWAS Community Court of Justice, where in 2006 the Community Judicial Council was designated to enhance the role of chief justices of ECOWAS member states in the process of selecting judges for the ECOWAS Court.[86]

While there are now more of these types of mechanism, experience is still quite limited. It remains to be seen if they will assuage concerns about the nature and outcomes of some national nomination procedures and about the political nature of the election and appointment process and, if so, whether they might be more widely adopted for other international tribunals.

3.5 Tenure and re-election

The terms of office, and the possibility of re-election, of international judges vary across international courts. Relatively short terms of office, coupled with the possibility of re-election, give rise to concerns about judicial independence. There is anecdotal evidence that states may sanction judges who have not been seen as supportive of national interests by failing to nominate them for reappointment.[87] Such measures may depend to some degree on the extent to which any individual judge's behavior on the court can be monitored, for example through voting records, and/or separate and dissenting opinions.[88] In addition, where there is a change of government in the nominating state, judges who might otherwise be eligible for re-election may find that they are not put forward.[89] Given the political nature of the judicial selection process, there is at least a risk that the independence of judges nearing the end of their term and up for re-election could be called into question.

For these reasons, single non-renewable terms of office may be preferred. Where terms of office are non-renewable, there is a strong argument that judges should

[85] Second Activity Report of the panel provided for under Article 255 of the Treaty on the Functioning of the European Union, 5091/13, December 26, 2012. The report notes that since the beginning of its work, in 2011, the panel had delivered 43 opinions (on candidatures for the office of Judge or Advocate-General), of which 5 were unfavorable, p.6.

[86] See Alter et al., note 56.

[87] For example, Brandeis Institute for International Judges, note 62, at 37. The role of the nationality of judges in influencing their approach to and decisions in cases before them has been considered extensively in relation, in particular, to ad hoc judges, but also in relation to national judges in the ICJ. See, for example, AM Smith, "'Judicial Nationalism' in International Law: National Identity and Judicial Autonomy at the ICJ" (2005) 40 Texas Int'l Law J. 197.

[88] Voeten, note 20, at 403.

[89] For example, in relation to the 2001 elections to the ECtHR, see J Hedigan "The Election of Judges to the European Court of Human Rights' Rights" in M Kohen (ed.), *Promoting Justice, Human Rights and Conflict Resolution through International Law, Liber Amicorum Lucius Caflisch* (The Hague: Martinus Nijhoff 2007) 235–53, at 245.

be appointed for a relatively long term.[90] This would seem to promote efficiency in the court to enable judges to develop their "on-the-job" expertise and make a real contribution to the work of the court. One perceived drawback of a longer term may be the impact on the rotation of seats among states and implementation of equitable geographic distribution requirements. Furthermore, while shorter renewable terms might be seen to enhance accountability of judges at the expense of independence,[91] longer terms of office might be perceived to limit the accountability of international judges.[92] The challenges of balancing considerations of accountability and independence are not easily resolved and are being addressed in different ways in different tribunals. To the extent that a trend is discernible, it appears now to be in favor of longer, non-renewable terms of office,[93] but this approach is by no means universal. Appointment of judges for life tenure or until a fixed retirement age does not seem to be a popular option.[94]

4 Conclusions

Judicial selection processes in international courts are subject to growing public and state scrutiny. The overall picture is characterized by diversity, evolution, and innovation, but it is also still largely characterized by intergovernmental control and state interest. Politics continues to play an integral, and often decisive, role in the composition of international courts and in the appointment of individual judges. States have a strong interest in retaining influence over judicial appointments where international judges exercise decision-making power across a growing range of

[90] For example, the Institut de Droit International suggests that "In order to strengthen the independence of judges, it would be desirable that they should be appointed for long terms of office, ranging from nine to twelve years. Such terms of office should not be renewable." Institut de Droit International, Resolution on the Position of the International Judge, note 5, at Art. 2.1. The ECtHR has recently moved from six-year terms of office with the possibility of re-election, to a single nine-year term, ECHR, Art. 23.1.

[91] L Epstein, J Knight and O Shvetsova, "Comparing Judicial Selection Systems" (2001–2002) 10(7) Wm. & Mary Bill Rts. J. 7, at 33, in relation to domestic judicial selection.

[92] Since, during their terms of office, judges may be removed from office only in accordance with the relevant statutory provisions of the court in question and, in most international courts, by a resolution of the other judges on the court. See, for example, ICJ Statute, Art. 18; ECHR, Art. 23.4; ACtHPR, Art. 19.

[93] For example, ICC Statute, Art. 36.9.a; ECHR, Art. 23.1 (as amended by Protocol No. 14, in force June 1, 2010).

[94] However, see CCJ Agreement, Art. IX.3, providing that a judge of the CCJ shall hold office until the age of 72 years, subject to other provisions of the Agreement on tenure.

issues affecting state interests. In this context, principles and mechanisms for ensuring the independence of the international courts and of international judges, once appointed, are of great importance.

Reforms to judicial selection procedures in some tribunals, such as the adoption of guidelines for nominations and the introduction of mechanisms to screen the qualifications of candidates, promise to promote merit-based appointments without challenging the overarching political context in which the courts are established and appointed. Review and analysis of experience with such guidelines and mechanisms will be a useful tool in informing further improvement and innovation in the future. More radical reforms, such as the creation of judicial appointment commissions without formal governmental representation, have not made much headway at the international level. Moreover some international courts seem to remain impervious as yet even to the soft developments and reforms that have taken place elsewhere.

Research Questions

1. What impact does the introduction of mechanisms to screen nominations for judicial appointments in certain international courts have on national nomination processes and on judicial elections?
2. Do longer, non-renewable terms of office for international judges enhance the independence of the international judiciary?
3. Is there a role for judicial appointments commissions for international and regional courts, along the lines of the model adopted for the CCJ?
4. How can demands for "representativeness" be met without compromising merit-based judicial appointments? Is there still a place for representation requirements in independent international courts?

Suggested Reading

Abi-Saab, G, "Ensuring the Best Bench: Ways of Selecting Judges" in C Peck and RS Lee (eds), *Increasing the Effectiveness of the International Court of Justice: proceedings of the ICJ/UNITAR Colloquium to Celebrate the 50th Anniversary of the Court* (The Hague: Martinus Nijhoff/UNITAR 1997) 166–87.

Alter, KJ, "Agents or Trustees? International Courts in their Political Context" (2008) 14 EJIR 33.

Elsig, M and Pollack, MA, "Agents, Trustees and International Courts: The Politics of Judicial Appointments at the WTO" EJIR September 5, 2012, DOI:10.1177/1354066112448201, published online at <http://ejt.sagepub.com/content/early/2012/09/05/1354066112448201.full.pdf+html> accessed June 4, 2013.

Hedigan, J, "The Election of Judges to the European Court of Human Rights" in M Kohen (ed.), *Promoting Justice, Human Rights and Conflict Resolution through International Law, Liber Amicorum Lucius Caflisch* (Leiden, Boston, MA: Martinus Nijhoff 2007) 235–53.

Mackenzie, R et al., *Selecting International Judges: Principle, Process, and Politics* (Oxford University Press 2010).

Mahoney, P, "The International Judiciary: Independence and Accountability" (2008) 7 Law and Practice of International Courts and Tribunals 313.

Malleson, K, "Promoting Judicial Independence in the International Courts: Lessons from the Caribbean" (2009) 58 International and Comparative Law Quarterly 671.

Sands, P, "Global Governance and the International Judiciary: Choosing our Judges" (2003) 56 Current Legal Problems 481.

Terris, D, Romano, CPR, and Swigart, L, *The International Judge: An Introduction to the Men and Women Who Decide the World's Cases* (Oxford University Press 2007).

Voeten, E, "The Politics of International Judicial Appointments" (2008–2009) 9 Chicago Journal of International Law 387.

Wood, M, "The Selection of Candidates for International Judicial Office: Recent Practice" in TM Ndiaye and R Wolfrum (eds), *Law of the Sea, Environmental Law, and Settlement of Disputes, Liber Amicorum Judge Thomas A. Mensah* (Leiden: Martinus Nijhoff 2007) 357–68.

CHAPTER 35

INTERNATIONAL JUDICIAL ETHICS

ANJA SEIBERT-FOHR*

1 Conceptualizing Judicial Ethics in International Adjudication

Judicial ethics—or the rules that seek to ensure the personal independence, impartiality, and diligence of adjudicators by guiding their judicial and extra-judicial

* Professor of Law, Georg-August-University of Göttingen, Germany. The author wishes to express her sincere gratitude to Jannika Jahn for her very dedicated research assistance and to Katharina Stock for her efficient editing assistance.

conduct—in international adjudication is a relatively young and still evolving field.[1] While standards of judicial ethics at the national and transnational levels are old and well established, their applicability at the international level is not automatic because of fundamental differences in context. Although it may be tempting to draw from domestic rules on judicial conduct in order to fill this gap,[2] there are structural differences between domestic and international adjudication to consider. The standards developed for the domestic sphere can hardly be transferred lock, stock, and barrel to international adjudication, which is different in nature, composition and function.[3] Thus, international courts and tribunals are confronted with the challenge of developing their own judicial culture. This culture must satisfy universal expectations of fairness and propriety.[4]

International judges are a broad array of different—and not exclusively legal—professionals, such as academics, legal advisers, diplomats, judges, counsels, civil servants, and others,[5] who, unlike most of their domestic counterparts, have only a limited term of office that either ends on or has to be renewed after expiry. This makes it more difficult to establish a common culture of independence among judges.[6] For most, being a member of an international court is a parenthesis in a different career.[7] Previous and subsequent professional activities may affect the individual's appearance of independence.[8] Many might have expressed opinions on controversial issues before they were appointed judges.[9] The fact that the pool of qualified candidates for judicial office is rather limited further aggravates the problem.[10]

[1] For a discussion of the evolving ethical standards for counsel in international adjudication, see, in this handbook, Sthoeger and Wood, Ch. 29, at section 2.

[2] Brandeis University, "Toward an International Rule of Law" (2001) 24 Pac McGeorge Gl Bus & Dev LJ 201, 241–2; J Terhechte, "Judicial Ethics for a Global Judiciary—How Judicial Networks Create their own Codes of Conduct" (2012) 10 Ger LJ 501.

[3] The need to modify principles applicable to national tribunals for use in international courts was stressed as early as during the drafting of the Statute of the Permanent Court of Justice. A Fachiri, *The Permanent Court of International Justice* (2nd edn, Oxford University Press 1932) 56, cited by C Brown, "The Evolution and Application of Rules concerning Independence of the International Judiciary" (2003) 2 LPICT 63, 82.

[4] T Meron, "Judicial Independence and Impartiality in International Criminal Tribunals" (2005) 99 AJIL 359, 360.

[5] See, in this handbook, Swigart and Terris, Ch. 28, at section 2.4.

[6] D Terris, "Tests of Character" in D Terris, C Romano, and L Swigart (eds), *The International Judge* (Oxford University Press 2007) 191, 192.

[7] Some international judges are even appointed only part-time, ad hoc, or *ad litem*. For more on this issue, see R Mackenzie and P Sands, "International Courts and Tribunals and the Independence of the International Judge" (2003) 44 Harv. Int'l. L. J. 271, 283.

[8] For a discussion of the impact of professional backgrounds on judicial behavior see, in this handbook, Voeten, Ch. 25, at section 3.3.

[9] F Mégret, "International Judges and Experts' Impartiality and the Problem of Past Declarations" (2011) 10 LPICT 31, 32.

[10] J Brubaker, "The Judge Who Knew Too Much" (2008) 26 Berkeley J. Int'l. L. 111, 143; Mackenzie and Sands, note 7, at 280; C Romano, "Staffing Internationalized Judicial Bodies" in C Romano, A Nollkaemper, and J Kleffner (eds), *Internationalized Criminal Courts and Tribunals: Sierra Leone, East Timor, Kosovo and Cambodia* (Oxford University Press 2004) 235–70.

Another difference from domestic courts is that in international adjudication, sovereign states retain control over the establishment and the scope of jurisdiction of international courts and judicial selection.[11] In a legal system in which judges are selected by those same states that might later become parties to a dispute, independence and impartiality might have a different meaning.[12] This is even more so with respect to ad hoc judges.[13]

Not only is it difficult to develop a common standard for judges from various jurisdictions with different legal training and diverse cultural and professional understandings and habits,[14] it is all the more difficult to articulate standards that are globally acceptable. Can ethical standards be developed for the entire range of international courts and tribunals?[15] Is it possible to articulate uniform rules that are valid for inter-state litigation, international criminal prosecution, human rights litigation, trade disputes, and inter-state and mixed arbitration?

This chapter gives an overview of the relevant legal rules that have been developed over time in various fields of international adjudication. The analysis will focus on the three key values that must guide judicial conduct: independence, impartiality, and diligence.

2 Normative Standards: An Overview

Early rules of judicial ethics date back to the origins of international adjudication.[16] The 1907 Convention on the Pacific Settlement of International Disputes provided that members of the Permanent Court of Arbitration (PCA) were prevented from acting as agents, counsel, or advocates except on behalf of the power

[11] Mégret, note 9, at 32; See, in this handbook, Ginsburg, Ch. 22, at section 3.

[12] This issue is particularly relevant in international arbitration. It has repeatedly arisen before the Iran–US Claims Tribunal. Brown, note 3, at 93.

[13] See ICJ, Practice Direction VII (2009); N Valticos, "Pratique et Étique d'un Juge 'ad hoc' à la Court International de Justice" in N Ando, E Mc Whinney, and R Wolfrum (eds), *Liber Amicorum Judge Shigeru Oda* (The Hague: Kluwer Law International 2002) 107.

[14] For a discussion of the different national and cultural backgrounds of international judges and their impact on perceptions of impartiality and independence, see L Swigart, "The 'National Judge': Some Reflections on Diversity in International Courts and Tribunals" (2011–2012) 42 McGeorge L. Rev. 223; Terris, note 6, at 192. According to Detlev Vagts, the more countries and cultures that are involved, the more disputes about standards of behavior arise. D Vagts, "The International Legal Profession" (1996) 90 AJIL 250.

[15] Y Shany, "Squaring the Circle? Independence and Impartiality of Party-Appointed Adjudicators in International Legal Proceedings" (2008) 30 LoyLA Int'l & Comp. L. Rev. 473.

[16] For more on the historical developments since 1899, see Brown, note 3, at 66–86.

which appointed them.[17] Twelve years later, the Statute of the Permanent Court of International Justice (PCIJ) stipulated that the court was to be composed of independent judges.[18] These judges had to make solemn declarations in open court that they would exercise their powers "impartially and conscientiously."[19] However, what was specifically required of them was largely left undefined. Only provisions on dismissal, recusal, and the prohibition of incompatible functions were articulated.[20]

These scant provisions were cut and pasted into the Statute of the ICJ,[21] which was later complemented by the Rules of Court.[22] The provisions of the PCIJ and ICJ were eventually ported to the relevant conventions, statutes, and rules of procedure of other international courts, including the ITLOS,[23] the dispute settlement system of the World Trade Organization (WTO),[24] ICSID tribunals,[25] Iran–US Claims Tribunal,[26] European Court of Human Rights (ECtHR),[27] Inter-American Court of Human Rights (IACtHR),[28] and Court of Justice of the European Union (CJEU).[29]

As Dinah Shelton noted in her study on legal norms on the independence of international tribunals, in recent decades there has been an increasing trend to further specify the rules governing judicial ethics in international adjudication.[30] Some institutions, such as the International Criminal Court (ICC), ECtHR, European Court of Justice (ECJ), Caribbean Court of Justice (CCJ), and WTO, have complemented their founding documents by adopting codes of ethics.[31] The codes seek to specify the obligations inherent in judicial office, improve transparency, and promote public confidence in adjudication,[32] thus reducing the need for outside

[17] Convention on the Pacific Settlement of International Dispute of 1907, Art. 62.

[18] PCIJ Statute, Art. 2.

[19] PCIJ Statute, Art. 20.

[20] PCIJ Statute, Arts 16, 17, 18, 24. For a discussion of the interpretation of these provisions by the PCIJ, see Brown, note 3, at 78–81.

[21] ICJ Statute, Arts 16.1, 17.1/2, 18.1.

[22] ICJ Rules of Court, Art. 24; ICJ Practice Direction VII; compare to, for after office conduct, ICJ Practice Direction VIII (for ad hoc judges only). See also Brown, note 3, at 83–4.

[23] ITLOS Statute, Arts 2.1, 5.1, 7, 8.1, 9, 11, 27 (Annex VI UNCLOS); ITLOS Rules of Court, Art. 5.1.

[24] WTO Dispute Settlement Understanding, Art. 8.2, 17–18; WTO DSU Preamble Rules of Conduct; WTO DSU Rules of Conduct, II.1, VII.1/2, VIII; Working Procedures for Appellate Review (2010), Arts 2.2, 8–11, 13, 19; Rules of conduct for the understanding on rules and procedures governing the settlement of disputes, Governing Principle II.

[25] Washington Convention, Arts 14.1, 40, 57, 63.a.

[26] Iran–US Claims Tribunal Rules of Procedure (1983), Arts 9–10, 15.

[27] ECHR, Arts 21.3, 23.4, 40.1/2, ECtHR Rules of Court, Rules 3.1, 7, 28.2.d/e, 33.1–5, 63.1–3; ECtHR Resolution on Judicial Ethics (June 23, 2008) Principles I, III–VI.

[28] American Convention on Human Rights (ACHR), Arts 52, 71; IACtHR Statute, Arts 4, 11, 18, 19; IACtHR Rules of Procedure, Art. 21.

[29] TFEU, Art. 254; ECJ Statute, Arts 2, 4, 5.1–3, 31 (Protocol 3); ECJ Rules of Procedure, Arts 3, 56.1; ECJ Code of Conduct (2007/C 223/01), Arts 1.3, 2, 6.1–2.

[30] D Shelton, "Legal Norms to Promote the Independence and Accountability of International Tribunals" (2003) 2 LPICT 27, 29.

[31] ICC Code of Judicial Ethics, ICC-BD/02-01-05; ECJ Code of Conduct, ECtHR Resolution on Judicial Ethics; CCJ Code of Judicial Conduct; WTO Rules of Conduct (1996).

[32] N Vajic, "Some Remarks Linked to the Independence of International Judges and the Observance of Ethical Rules in the European Court of Human Rights" in C Hohmann-Dennhardt, P Masuch,

control that might be detrimental to judicial independence. On the other hand, ethical guidelines have been criticized as vague and leaving enforcement largely to the judges themselves.[33] Most ethics rules are not binding but are mere guidelines. Certain areas are still left largely unregulated.[34] Be that as it may, ultimately codification can only go so far. Ethics transcend normative rules and codes.[35] They are a matter of judicial culture and character, which is equally significant for the purpose of nurturing integrity and fairness.[36] As Judge Buergenthal of the ICJ put it:

> Judicial ethics are not matters strictly for hard and fast rules—I doubt that they can ever be exhaustively defined—they are matters of perception and of sensibility to appearances that courts must continuously keep in mind to preserve their legitimacy.[37]

3 Basic Values of Judicial Ethics and their Design

Judicial ethics are concerned with various aspects of judicial behavior, the most salient of which are independence, impartiality, and diligence.

3.1 Independence

Judicial independence does not mandate absolute neutrality. Judges' personal backgrounds cannot be ignored.[38] All that is asked from judges is that they maintain an

and M Villinger (eds), *Grundrechte und Solidarität, Durchsetzung und Verfahren, Festschrift für Renate Jaeger* (Kehl am Rhein: N. P. Engel Verlag 2011) 183.

[33] Terris, note 6. According to Terris, international judges are reluctant to codify behavioral standards in order to avoid the empowerment of outside actors threatening judicial independence. In this vein, see also Brandeis University, "Authority and Autonomy: Defining the Role of International and Regional Courts, Ethical Topic: Toward the Development of Ethics Guidelines for International Courts" (2003) at 20, <http://www.brandeis.edu/ethics/pdfs/internationaljustice/biij/BIIJ2003.pdf> accessed October 8, 2012.

[34] Among the open issues is for example the conduct of judges vis-à-vis counsel. Terris, note 6, at 194.

[35] Terris, note 6, at 207.

[36] D Terris, CPR Romano, and L Swigart, "Toward a Community of International Judges" (2008) 30 LoyLA Intl & Comp L Rev 419, 467.

[37] Legal Consequences of the Construction of a Wall in the Occupied Palestinian Territory (Dissenting Opinion of Judge Buergenthal) [2004] ICJ Rep. 3, at 9.

[38] K Llewellyn, "A Realistic Jurisprudence—The Next Step" (1930) 30 Colum. L. Rev. 431. For more on the question of to what degree international judges are and may be influenced by their own perceptions, see, Terris, note 6 at 207.

open mind and exercise a certain degree of detachment.[39] This applies to individual judges and to the court as a whole.

Almost all founding documents of international courts either require judges to be independent or demand that judges perform their duties independently.[40] Judges are requested not to engage in activities incompatible with their independence.[41] The CCJ Code is most elaborate in defining the meaning of independence. It specifies that judges "shall exercise the judicial function independently on the basis of the judge's assessment of the facts and in accordance with a conscientious understanding of the law, free of any extraneous influences, inducements, pressures, threats or interference, direct or indirect, from any quarter or for any reason."[42] For this purpose judges shall also be independent of their colleagues[43] and preserve the institutional and operational independence of the court.[44]

The question of whether and to what extent international adjudicators may engage in extra-judicial activities has been a thorny issue, especially in the case of those international courts where judges serve only part-time.[45] On the one hand, it is necessary to recruit judges who are part of and have a solid understanding of society and the international community.[46] On the other hand, their involvement in extra-judicial activities should limit neither their working capacity nor their independence and impartiality.

Usually rules of conduct distinguish between outside occupation and other extra-judicial activities that may or may not be remunerated. Some statutes provide that members of the court may not exercise any political or administrative function, or engage in any other occupation of a professional nature.[47] Yet, outside activities that are not permanent in nature tend to be less regulated. For example, whether or

39 Terris, note 6, at 211.

40 Washington Convention, Art. 14.1 and Rule 6.2; ICSID Additional Facility Rules, Schedule C, Arts 8, 13.2b; UNCITRAL Rules, Art. 6.7; International Chamber of Commerce Rules, Arts 3.1, 11.1 and Appendix II; SCC Rules, Art. 14.1; LCIA Rules, Arts 5.2, 11; Rome Statute, Art. 40.1; ICTY Statute, Art. 12.1; ICJ Statute, Art. 2; ITLOS Statute, Art. 2.1; ECHR, Art. 21.3; ECtHR Rules of Court, Rule 3.1; ECtHR Resolution on Judicial Ethics Principle I; TFEU, Art. 254; WTO DSU Rules of Procedure, Art. 8.2; WTO DSU Rules of Conduct II.1; ICC Code of Judicial Ethics, Art. 3.1; CCJ Code of Conduct, Principle II.

41 ECHR, Art. 21.3, ECtHR Rules of Court, Rules 4.1, 21.2.c, ECtHR Resolution on Judicial Ethics Principle I, VII; ACHR, Art. 71, IACtHR Statute, Art. 18.

42 CCJ Code of Conduct Principle II.2.1.

43 CCJ Code of Conduct Principle II.2.3.

44 CCJ Code of Conduct Principle II.2.4.

45 For the IACtHR see IACtHR Statute, Art. 16.1.

46 For the importance of judges maintaining engagement in society, see S Shetreet, "Standards of Conduct of International Judges: Outside Activities" (2003) 2 LPICT 127, 161; L Caflisch, "Independence and Impartiality of Judges: The European Court of Human Rights" (2003) 2 LPICT 169, 173.

47 See e.g., ICJ Statute, Art. 16.1. For more on the practice and interpretation of this provision, see P Couvreur, "Article 16 Statute of the International Court of Justice" in A Zimmermann et al. (eds), *The Statute of the International Court of Justice: A Commentary* (2nd edn, Oxford University Press 2012) 357, 365–71; UN Doc. A/C, 5/50/18, para. 29–33; Shelton, note 30, at 54. See also Protocol 3 of the ECJ Statute Title I, Art. 4. For a discussion of the incompatibility of any political function with judicial office, see also Burg House Principles, Principle 8.2. For example, Judge Odio Benito's election as Vice-President of Costa Rica was found not to disqualify her before the ICTY. The Tribunal considered her independence not to be compromised by the mere fact that she was to some extent subject to executive

not judges of the ICJ should be able to serve as arbitrators has been discussed for some time now, without reaching a firm consensus.[48] It is not a moot discussion. Not only has the case load of the ICJ increased in recent years so that additional activities outside the court may have a detrimental effect on the court's ability to deal with cases within a reasonable time, but the party appointing a judge as an arbitrator might someday become a party to a dispute before the court.[49]

The question of to what extent extra-judicial activities might affect international judges is more complex in the case of international criminal courts and human rights litigation. There, pressure comes not only from states but also from a range of other actors. Therefore, the incompatibility provision of the Rome Statute of the ICC is more comprehensive than those of courts hearing inter-state disputes. It prohibits any activity—not just occupation—that is likely to interfere with the judicial functions or to affect confidence in the judges' independence.[50] This includes the exercise of political functions. Likewise, IACtHR judges are not allowed to take other positions if those activities would affect their independence or impartiality.[51] Judicial office is incompatible with executive office and office in international organizations.[52] ECtHR judges may not engage "in any activity which is incompatible with their independence, impartiality or with the demands of a full-time office."[53] Moreover, they shall refrain from "any activity or membership of an association, and avoid any situation, that may affect confidence in their independence." Arguably this comprises political and administrative functions that are explicitly ruled out for judges of the ICJ and the ITLOS.

The concrete scope of incompatibility for extra-judicial activities varies among international adjudicative bodies, reflecting the different composition of the courts. While some courts are composed of full-time judges, others are not. For example, while judges of the ICJ and full-time judges of the ICC shall not engage during their terms of office in any other occupations,[54] ITLOS judges, who are only occupied part-time, may continue any professorships. The ECtHR, whose judges are full-time, also does not entirely rule out other professional activities. The judges

supervision. Judge Odio Benito had declined to assume any functions as a vice president until completing her duties on the trial panel in the *Celibici* Case. *Prosecutor v. Delalic* (Judgment) ICTY-96-21-A (February 20, 2001) para. 683–4. At ITLOS, judges may not be associated with or financially interested in an enterprise concerned with the commercial use of exploitation of the resources of the sea or seabed. ITLOS Statute, Art. 7. This provision derives from the court's jurisdiction with respect to deep seabed mining and other resources of the sea, and thus reflects the specific function of the court as regards these subjects. For a more general discussion of extra-judicial activities, see, Shetreet, note 46.

[48] Terris, note 6, at 201; Couvreur, note 47, at 368–9.

[49] Mackenzie and Sands, note 7, at 282–3.

[50] Rome Statute, Art. 40.2. See also ICC Code of Judicial Ethics, Art. 3.2. The ICC's provision has been criticized as too vague, leaving room for errors. Shetreet, note 46, at 160.

[51] ACHR, Art. 71; IACtHR Statute, Art. 18.

[52] IACtHR Statute, Art. 18.1.

[53] ECtHR, Art. 21.3. For a discussion of the court's practice see Caflisch, note 46, at 172.

[54] ICJ Statute, Art. 16.1; Rome Statute, Art. 40.3.

are merely prevented from extra-judicial activities that are incompatible with the demands of their judicial duties.[55]

Members of the ECJ may also undertake activities that are not considered detrimental to their independence, such as academic work, teaching activities, conferences, seminars, or symposia.[56] But the remuneration for these activities may not be out of the ordinary.[57] Moreover such external activities may not interfere with the judges' obligation to devote themselves fully to the performance of their judicial duties.[58] They may also be authorized to engage in non-profit-making associations in cultural, artistic, social, sporting, or charitable fields—unless they compromise their independence.[59]

In most courts, the court itself decides on the compatibility of its judges' extra-judicial activities and judicial functions.[60] The "Burgh House Principles On The Independence Of The International Judiciary," which were articulated by the Study Group of the International Law Association (ILA) on the Practice and Procedure of International Courts and Tribunals in association with the Project on International Courts and Tribunals, call for each court to establish an appropriate mechanism to guide judges on the issue of extra-judicial activities.[61] Outright prohibitions on specific extra-judicial activities are exceptional. Most courts set independence, impartiality, and diligence as the relevant general standards, and leave the application of these standards to the particular situation at hand. Though such a case-by-case approach may be detrimental to legal certainty, it is ultimately preferable to sweeping limitations that insulate judges from public life and are thus not in the interest of meaningful international adjudication.[62]

Finally, in order to avoid later commitments affecting judges during their term of office, there has been a trend to provide also for post-service limitations.[63] These provisions are aimed at preventing serving judges from being influenced by their former peers. Special knowledge regarding pending cases could give former judges an unwarranted benefit if they become counsel after the expiration of their terms of

[55] ECHR, Art. 31.3. For the rule governing ad hoc judges, see Rules of the Court, Rule 28.2.c.

[56] ECJ Code of Conduct, Art. 5.2, 5.3. See also CCJ Code of Conduct, Principle I.

[57] ECJ Code of Conduct, Art. 5.2.

[58] ECJ Code of Conduct, Art. 5.1. See also S Rozes, "Independence of Judges of the Court of Justice of the European Communities" in S Shetreet and J Deschênes (eds), *Judicial Independence: The Contemporary Debate* (Dordrecht: Nijhoff 1985) 501.

[59] ECJ Code of Conduct, Art. 5.3.

[60] See e.g., ICJ Statute, Art. 16.2; ITLOS Statute, Art. 7.3; ECHR, Art. 21.3. The main exception is the ECJ, where extra-judicial occupation, whether gainful or not, is impermissible for ECJ judges unless exemption is exceptionally granted by the European Council, acting by a simple majority. Statute of the ECJ, Protocol 3 TFEU, Art. 4. For observations on the lack of practice concerning this provision, see, Brown, note 3, at 88.

[61] Burgh House Principles on The Independence of The International Judiciary, Principle 8.3.

[62] Brubaker, note 10, at 145–6.

[63] See also Terris, note 6, at 202.

office. Practice Direction VIII of the ICJ asks parties to refrain from designating as agent, counsel, or advocate a person who in the preceding three years was a judge of the court, including an ad hoc judge.[64] Though the direction is not addressed to the judges but to parties to a dispute, it is nevertheless relevant for judicial ethics. In a similar vein, the ECJ's Code provides that judges cannot act as representatives of parties before the European courts for a period of three years after the end of their terms of office.[65] In the case of the ECtHR, the cooling-off period for judges is only two years.[66]

These provisions are the outcome of a balancing approach that weighs judicial independence against judges' legitimate interest in continuing their professional lives after the end of their judicial tenures. The Burgh House Principles, which were intended to set out a minimum standard generally applicable to international judges, go even further in establishing post-office limitations. They also regulate other forms of involvement with prior parties to a dispute. While in office, judges are called upon not to seek or accept any future employment or benefit from any of the parties to a case on which they sit,[67] and to exercise appropriate caution when accepting employment, appointment, or benefit after the end of their judicial terms.[68]

3.2 Impartiality

Judicial independence and impartiality are closely related and cannot easily be distinguished. They are often mentioned in the same breath.[69] Most provisions requiring international judges to be independent also provide for their impartiality.[70] This is also true of arbitral tribunals.[71] However, there is a crucial difference between the two standards. Independence addresses external forms of influence on adjudication, including inducements, pressures, threats, and direct or indirect interference with the decision-making process.[72] Impartiality concerns the internal predispositions of the adjudicator, with respect to the matter in dispute, the adjudicator's relationship to the parties, and the parties' positions.

[64] See also Burgh House Principles, Principle 13.3.

[65] ECJ Code of Conduct, Art. 6.2. See also ECJ Statute, Art. 4; ECJ Rules of Procedure, Art. 3.2.

[66] Rules of the Court, Rule 4.2. [67] Burgh House Principles, Principle 13.1.

[68] Burgh House Principles, Principle 13.4.

[69] See e.g., ICTY, Art. 13; ECHR, Art. 21.3; WTO DSU Rules of Conduct II.1; CCJ Code of Conduct, Principle II.2.2.

[70] ICTY, Art. 13; ECHR, Art. 21.3; WTO DSU Rules of Conduct II.1; CCJ Code of Conduct, Principle II.2.2.

[71] International Chamber of Commerce Rules, Art. 22.4, UNCITRAL Rules, Art. 6.7; SCC Rules, § 19.2, LCIA Rules, § 5.2.

[72] See e.g., CCJ Code of Conduct, Principle II.2.1; The Burgh House Principles, Principle 1.1.

Impartiality forbids any bias, personal prejudice, and lopsidedness.[73] Typically, *ex parte* communications are impermissible.[74] Pursuant to Principle 12.1 of the Burgh House Principles, judges must exercise appropriate caution in their personal contacts with parties and all other persons associated with a pending case in order to avoid jeopardizing their impartiality. The WTO Dispute Settlement Understanding Rules and Procedures Art. 18.1 restricts *ex parte* communications to other bodies and forbids such communications between a panel and the Appellate Body.

Most international courts and tribunals require their judges to avoid conflicts of interest.[75] If conflicts arise, judges are expected to recuse themselves. Not only conflicts of interest should be avoided, but also the mere perception of a conflict of interest.[76] At the ECtHR, a judge may not take part in the consideration of a case if his or her independence or impartiality may *legitimately* be called into doubt.[77]

In an effort to specify situations giving rise to a conflict of interest, or perception of conflict, most courts provide, for example, that judges may not act as agent, counsel, or advocate in any case.[78] Nor may they participate in the decision of a case in which they have previously taken part.[79] The ICC Rules of Procedure and Evidence go to greater lengths.[80] So does the CCJ.[81]

The problem is approached in rather general terms in arbitration. The IBA Guidelines specify situations giving rise to justifiable doubts regarding an arbitrator's impartiality, including financial or personal interests in the matter at stake.[82] They also take into consideration prior relations between an arbitrator and a party to a dispute beyond the particular case at issue. However, it is controversial whether these guidelines are applicable only in commercial arbitration or also in inter-state arbitration. Their applicability in disputes between states was denied by

[73] Mégret, note 9, at 44. [74] WTO DSU Rules of Conduct VII.2.

[75] ICC Code of Judicial Ethics, Art. 4.2; ECJ Code of Conduct, Art. 3, Resolution on Judicial Ethics ECtHR II; WTO DSU Rules of Conduct II.1; CCJ Code of Conduct, Principles I.1.10, IV.4.6.3, IV.4.7.

[76] For example, the ICC Code provides in Art. 4.2 that judges shall avoid any conflict of interest or being placed in a situation that might "reasonably be perceived as giving rise to a conflict of interest."

[77] ECtHR, Rule 28.2 (emphasis added by the author); pursuant to ECtHR Resolution on Judicial Ethics Principle II, judges shall ensure the "appearance of impartiality."

[78] ICJ Statute, Art. 17.1; ITLOS Statute, Art. 7.1; Rome Statute, Art. 40.1/2; ECJ Statute, Art. 4.

[79] ICJ Statute, Art. 17.2; ITLOS Statute, Art. 8.1, CCJ Code of Conduct Principle IV.4.6.2; Statute IACtHR, Art. 19; Rome Statute, Art. 41.1/2.a; ECJ Code of Conduct, Art. 6.1/2; ECtHR Rules of Court, Rule 4.1.

[80] The ICC does not permit a personal interest in the case, such as a spousal, parental or other close family; personal or professional relationship, or a subordinate relationship, with any of the parties (Rule 34.1.a); involvement in the case in a private capacity (34.1.b); performance of functions prior to judicial office (34.1.c); and expression of opinions (34.1.d).

[81] CCJ Code of Conduct, Principle IV.4.6.3. Principle 4.6.1 provides that judges should disqualify themselves if they have actual bias or prejudice concerning a party, or personal knowledge of disputed evidentiary facts concerning the proceedings. Furthermore, judges shall disqualify themselves if they or members of their family have an economic interest in the outcome of the proceedings.

[82] IBA Guidelines General Standard (2), Conflict of Interests.

the UNCLOS Arbitral Tribunal in *Mauritius v. UK*.[83] In that case, the court considered the prior engagement of one of the arbitrators as counsel for one of the parties to the dispute. It eventually found that this prior engagement did not undermine the arbitrator's perceived or actual impartiality.[84]

Whenever a conflict of interest and/or perceived bias exists, judges are called upon to seek advice from their peers and from the president of the court in order to smooth out differences among national standards on impartiality.[85] External advice from the bar may also be beneficial. While several decisions by international courts on disqualification have further elaborated the meaning of impartiality,[86] in the end a need remains for generally framed statutory provisions that are open for non-standard situations. Their meaning should be specified and regularly updated in the code of ethics.[87]

Impartiality might also be impinged whenever judges hold or express opinions. But this raises the question of to what extent judges should be limited in the exercise of the fundamental human right to freedom of speech and association.[88] The ECJ's Code of Conduct, Art. 1.3 provides that judges shall generally refrain from making statements outside the court that might harm the reputation of the court, or that might be interpreted as "the adoption of a position by the Court on issues falling outside its institutional role." The Resolution on Judicial Ethics of the ECtHR (Art. VI) asks judges to exercise their freedom of expression "in a manner compatible with the dignity of their office." Judges are to refrain from making public statements or remarks undermining the authority of the court or giving reasonable doubt as to their impartiality.[89] Similar wording can be found in the Code of Judicial Ethics of the ICC and in the Burgh House Principles.[90]

Most standards distinguish between comments on pending cases, which are generally impermissible,[91] and participation in general public debate. The latter

[83] *Mauritius v. UK*, Reasoned Decision on Challenge (November 30, 2011), <http://www.pca-cpa.org/showpage.asp?pag_id=1429> accessed October 12, 2012, paras 45, 67, 165, 167.

[84] *Mauritius v. UK*, note 83, at para. 173. But see Burgh House Principles, Principle 10.

[85] This form of communication has been described as a general practice of international judges. Brandeis University, "International Justice: Past, Present, and Future" (2009) at 30 <http://www.brandeis.edu/ethics/pdfs/internationaljustice/biij/BIIJ2009.pdf> accessed October 9, 2012.

[86] See section 3.2 of this chapter, *Legal Consequences of the Construction of a Wall in the Occupied Palestinian Territory*, Order of January 30, 2004, ICJ Rep. 2004, Rep. 3; *Mauritius v. UK*, note 83.

[87] Brubaker advocates a case-by-case determination of a conflict of interest instead of framing general rules on outside activities. Brubaker, note 10, at 145.

[88] Brandeis University, International Justice: Past, Present, and Future (2009), at 30 <http://www.brandeis.edu/ethics/pdfs/internationaljustice/biij/BIIJ2009.pdf> accessed October 9, 2012, pp. 29–30; Brandeis University, Complementarity and Cooperation: The Challenges of International Justice (2004), pp. 22–5 <http://www.brandeis.edu/ethics/pdfs/internationaljustice/biij/BIIJ2004.pdf> accessed October 9, 2012.

[89] Brandeis University, note 88.

[90] ICC Code of Judicial Ethics, Art. 9.1; Burgh House Principles, Principle 7.1.

[91] ICC Code of Judicial Ethics, Art. 9.2; CCJ Code of Conduct, Principle IV.4.4. For a more general rule on extrajudicial comments on judgments and subjects likely to come before the court, see Burgh House Principles, Principle 7.3.

is permissible in principle because it often does not jeopardize the impartiality of the court. Thus, a judge is disqualified if an expression of opinion could objectively, adversely affect that judge's impartiality.[92] To determine the appearance of bias, the standard is the perspective of a reasonable, fair-minded, and informed person.[93] While public speech on non-legal issues and engagement in historical, educational, cultural, sporting, or similar social and recreational activities are usually not thought to affect judicial impartiality, the situation is different with respect to political issues.[94] Most courts prohibit judges from exercising political functions. The Caribbean Code even asks judges to refrain from membership in political parties, attendance at political gatherings, and contributions to political campaigns.[95] Judges are generally prevented from engaging in political activity.[96]

With respect to judges' freedom of association, the most far-reaching limitation might be at the ECtHR, where judges are barred from "any activity or membership of an association."[97] It is not clear whether this also includes associations representing the interests of judges in promoting judicial independence. At the CCJ, an exception is made for professional organizations.[98] The court only asks judges to refrain from such membership if confidence in the judge's impartiality is actually jeopardized.[99]

Somewhat related is the issue of judges' public visibility. Observers disagree whether judges should seek to attract public attention to their work and how they should interact with the media.[100] Some judges have argued that they should speak only through judgments, while others recognize a judicial role in educating the public.[101] Public visibility, however, may give rise to public pressure, which can be detrimental to the independence and impartiality of international courts.[102] Daniel Terris, Cesare Romano, and Leigh Swigart have argued that international judges, unlike their national counterparts, should seek more public attention and explain the principles of international justice in order to enhance transparency and attain public confidence in—and recognition for—international adjudication.[103] International judges, they say, carry a responsibility to the long-term success of their courts and thus should cautiously promote their institutions.[104] How this can be done without jeopardizing the independence and impartiality of the court, as well as its ability to

[92] ICC Rules of Procedure and Evidence, Rule 34.1.d. Similar terminology is used by the ECtHR Rules of Court, see Rule 28.2.d.

[93] See CCJ Code of Conduct, Principles I.1.6, I.1.7.

[94] See e.g., CCJ Code of Conduct, Principle I.1.13.

[95] CCJ Code of Conduct, Principle I.1.8. [96] CCJ Code of Conduct, Principle I.1.7.

[97] ECtHR's Resolution on Judicial Ethics, Principle I.

[98] CCJ Code of Conduct, Principle I.1.20.

[99] CCJ Code of Conduct, Principle I.1.6. [100] Brandeis University, note 2, at 245.

[101] Brandeis University, note 88, at 22–3; Brandeis University, note 2, at 241. See also Terris, note 6, at 200; Terris, Romano, and Swigart, note 36, at 459–61.

[102] Terris, Romano, and Swigart, note 36, at 457. [103] Terris, note 6, at 210.

[104] Terris, note 6, at 210; see also Shetreet, note 46, at 132.

cope with its case load is still an unsettled matter that will require further attention in the future.[105]

All in all, the standards for impartial behavior are rather broad in scope and affect judges not only in their professional but also in their private lives. While judges are called upon to recuse themselves from a case if impartiality is at issue, it is debatable whether perception of lack of impartiality should necessarily give rise to a judge's disqualification—especially if he or she refuses to resign.[106]

The requirements for disqualification vary among international courts, as evidenced by Joseph R. Brubaker's study on issue conflicts.[107] The ICJ has been reluctant to disqualify judges on the basis of prior activities and general statements. An exception occurs when a judge has previously taken part as counsel, judge, or in any other capacity in the case. The court has given a narrow reading to this provision, requiring involvement in the particular legal dispute for disqualification.[108] For example, in its Advisory Opinion on *Legal Consequences for States of the Continued Presence of South Africa in Namibia*, the court considered the former capacity of three judges as representatives of their government in UN organs. They had been generally dealing with matters concerning South West Africa. The court held that this involvement did not amount to a participation in the case at issue and therefore did not accede to the objections raised by South Africa.[109]

A similar decision was taken by the majority of the court in 2004 when Israel challenged Judge Elaraby's participation in the advisory opinion on the *Legal Consequences of the Construction of a Wall in the Occupied Palestinian Territory*. Neither his earlier capacity as a diplomatic representative of his country, nor a controversial newspaper interview about his views on Israel, was considered a sufficient basis for excluding him from participating in the case.[110] According to the court's interpretation, former counsels are disqualified only if their service relates to the case in dispute. Judge Elaraby's statements in the interview were considered general in nature as opposed to directly related to the specific question posed in the Wall opinion.[111] Judge Buergenthal dissented and criticized the narrow approach of the court.[112] He pleaded for a broader basis for disqualification, arguing that all courts, including the ICJ, must be guided by the goal of avoiding the impression

[105] Brandeis University, note 2, at 245.

[106] Compare the majority opinion in *Legal Consequences of the Construction of a Wall in the Occupied Palestinian Territory*, note 86, with the dissenting opinion by Judge Buergenthal, at 9 *et seq.*

[107] Brubaker, note 10.

[108] Couvreur, note 47, at 385.

[109] *Legal Consequences for States of the Continued Presence of South Africa in Namibia* (South West Africa) (Advisory Opinion) [1971] ICJ Rep 16, 18–19.

[110] *Legal Consequences of the Construction of a Wall*, note 86, at para. 5.

[111] *Legal Consequences of the Construction of a Wall*, note 86, at para. 5.

[112] *Legal Consequences of the Construction of a Wall*, note 86, at para. 9. See also, Brubaker, note 10, at 146–7; Y Shany and S Horovitz, "Judicial Independence in The Hague and Freetown: A Tale of Two Cities" (2008) 21 LJIL 113, 125–7.

that a judge will not be able to consider a case in a fair and impartial manner. In his view, Judge Elaraby's interview had created an "appearance of bias" that required the court to preclude his participation in the proceedings.[113] Regrettably, the majority did not agree with him. A few years later, the UNCLOS Arbitral Tribunal concurred with the ICJ majority's narrow construction of the grounds of disqualification.[114]

International human rights courts and international criminal courts have adopted a stricter approach.[115] Article 41.2 of the Rome Statute provides that a judge of the ICC shall not participate in any case in which his or her impartiality might reasonably be doubted on any ground. One of the grounds specified is if a judge has previously been involved in the case before the court. However, there may also be other instances that lack impartiality and therefore preclude a judge from participating in a case.[116] For example, a judge may not take part in the consideration of a case if he or she has publicly expressed opinions that are "objectively capable of adversely affecting his or her impartiality."[117]

The ICTY elaborated on the standards of impartiality in international criminal proceedings in *Prosecutor v. Furundzija*. The Tribunal's Rules of Procedure and Evidence provide for disqualification if a judge has a personal interest in the case, or if he or she has or has had any association that might affect his or her impartiality.[118] The Appeals Chamber interpreted this provision as covering actual bias and "unacceptable appearance of bias."[119] A judge would be disqualified if he or she was a party to the case or had a financial interest in the outcome of a case, or if the decision would lead to "the promotion of a cause in which he or she is involved, together with one of the parties" or "the circumstances would lead a reasonable observer, properly informed, to reasonably apprehend bias."[120] A reasonable observer, according to the Appeals Chamber, is "an informed person with knowledge of all the relevant circumstances, including the traditions of integrity and impartiality that form a part of the background and apprised also of the fact that impartiality is one of the duties that Judges swear to uphold."[121]

The Special Court for Sierra Leone (SCSL) adopted a similar standard in *Prosecutor v. Sesay*. The court considered the impartiality of Judge Robertson, who, in a book published before he was appointed to the court, had described the atrocities committed by one of the rebel groups in Sierra Leone as "crimes against humanity" and had called for the prosecution of its leaders.[122] The court concluded that he

[113] *Legal Consequences of the Construction of a Wall*, note 86, at 9–10.

[114] *Mauritius v. UK*, note 83, at para. 166.

[115] ECtHR's Rules of Court, Rule 28.2.e, provides that a judge is disqualified if his or her impartiality may legitimately be questioned.

[116] See ICC Rules of Procedure and Evidence, Rule 34.1.

[117] ECtHR Rules of Court, Rule 28.2.

[118] ECtHR Rules of Court, Rule 15.1.

[119] *Prosecutor v. Furundzija* (Judgment) ICTY-95-17/1-A (July 21, 2000) para. 189.

[120] *Prosecutor v. Furundzija*, note 119.

[121] *Prosecutor v. Furundzija*, note 119, at para. 190.

[122] G Robertson, *Crimes against Humanity: The Struggle for Global Justice* (2nd edn, New York: New Press 2002) 496.

was disqualified in any case involving members of that group, since a reasonable person reading these statements would have a "legitimate reason to fear that Justice Robertson lacks impartiality."[123]

In sum, it is apparent that the standard governing impartiality is different in inter-state adjudication compared to other forms of international adjudication. But it is a difference that is hard to explain or justify. The same standard should apply in inter-state, human rights, and international criminal adjudication.[124] It is difficult to see why disqualification should be limited to prior participation in a case and not apply to other kinds of involvement that carry an equal risk of jeopardizing the impartiality of a judge. That being said, whether an earlier comment or engagement compromises impartiality needs to be determined on the basis of each individual case.[125] According to Joseph Brubaker, it is important to consider the proximity, depth, and timing of the adjudicator's statements or commitments in order to determine whether there is an actual conflict of interest requiring disqualification.[126]

3.3 Diligence

Apart from being independent and impartial, adjudicators are required to act with reasonable diligence.[127] When swearing in, judges take an oath to exercise their powers conscientiously.[128] Whereas some codes of ethics distinguish between integrity, confidentiality, propriety, equality, competence, and diligence,[129] the term "diligence" is used in this chapter as an overall concept of the faithful fulfillment of duties in general.[130]

[123] *Prosecutor v. Sesay* (Decision on Defence Motion seeking the Disqualification of Justice Robertson from the Appeals Chamber) SCSL-2004-15-AR15 (March 13, 2004) para. 15.

[124] Shany and Horovitz, note 112, at 128–9.

[125] Brandeis University, note 2, at 244. For relevant decisions by the WTO dispute settlement, see, Brubaker, note 10, at 124–6. For the relevant standards of the Iran–US Claims Tribunal, see, Brown, note 3, at 90–3. For the issue of whether statements made in an official capacity are less likely to prompt impartiality, see *Prosecutor v. Furundzija*, note 119, at para. 199.

[126] Brubaker, note 10, at 123. For further criteria, namely the specificity of the comment, the strength of opinion, the mode of expression, see Mégret, note 9, at 49–63. According to Mégret, legal writing is insufficient to challenge a judge's impartiality, note 9, at 56–7. Statements made in an official capacity and expert opinions are treated differently from private and activist opinions. The latter are more likely to give rise to bias. Note 9, at 58–62.

[127] ICC Code of Judicial Ethics, Art. 6; ECtHR Resolution on Judicial Ethics, Principle IV; CCJ Code of Conduct, Principle VI; LCIA Rules, Art. 10.2. The Rules of the ICJ, ITLOS, and the ICC specify that judges solemnly undertake to perform their duties "honourably, faithfully, impartially and conscientiously." ICJ Statute, Art. 20; Rome Statute, Art. 45; ITLOS Statute, Art. 11.

[128] Rules of the ICJ, Art. 4.1; Rules of Procedure and Evidence, Rule 5.1.a; ITLOS Rules, Art. 5.1. See also ICTY Rules of Procedure and Evidence, Rule 14.A.

[129] ICC Code of Judicial Ethics, CCJ Code of Conduct; Rules of conduct for the understanding on rules and procedures governing the settlement of disputes; ECtHR Resolution on Judicial Ethics.

[130] See e.g., the oath provided for in Appendix I to the Agreement establishing the CCJ.

Diligence, above all, requires attendance and attention.[131] At the ICC, judges are required to devote their professional activities to their judicial duties. The CCJ Code requires that judicial duties must take precedence over all other activities.[132] Judicial decision-making may not be delegated to court staff. Diligence also requires judges to be prepared in each individual case. Furthermore, as a matter of efficiency, the case load must be completed with "reasonable promptness,"[133] without undue delay[134] or unwarranted expense.[135] The Rome Statute expects trials at the ICC to be expeditious so that the rights of defendants are guaranteed.[136]

Most statutory provisions require the selection of persons of high moral character and integrity for judicial office.[137] Accordingly, judicial conduct must be consistent with this high moral character.[138] Once appointed, judges are required to behave with integrity.[139] This is particularly relevant for courtroom behavior. Not only are judges obliged to act with fairness,[140] requiring equal treatment and sensitivity to different arguments, they must also maintain order and decorum in the course of proceedings.[141] Propriety requires respectful conduct vis-à-vis the parties, witnesses, attorneys, prosecutors, and others involved in the proceedings. At the ICC, judges are required to maintain order, act in accordance with commonly accepted decorum, and remain patient and courteous towards all participants and members of the public present in judicial proceedings.[142] Judges of the court must be vigilant in controlling the manner of questioning of witnesses or victims, and must give special attention to equal protection of the law.[143] Propriety also calls for honesty and punctuality.

Even off the bench, judges are obliged to act consistently with the dignity of judicial office[144] and not to engage in conduct incompatible with the diligent discharge of judicial duties.[145] Apart from the obvious prohibition against corruption, judges must ensure that their conduct is above reproach.[146] Again, the relevant standard is the view of a reasonable, fair-minded, and informed person. Judges must accept restrictions that might seem burdensome to ordinary citizens. The obligation to

[131] For this issue and other cases in which diligence has been challenged, see Brown, note 3, at 92–3.

[132] Principle 6.1–2.

[133] CCJ Code of Conduct, Principle VI.6.5.

[134] ICC Code of Judicial Ethics, Art. 7.4.

[135] ICC Rules of Procedure and Evidence, Rule 24.2.b; LCIA Rules, Art. 10.2.

[136] Rome Statute, Art. 64.2; ICC Code of Judicial Ethics, Art. 7.3. See also ICTY Statute, Art. 20.1.

[137] ITLOS Statute, Art. 2.1; Rome Statute, Art.36.a; ICTY Statute, Art. 13; ECHR, Art. 21.1; Agreement establishing the CCJ, Art. 4.11.

[138] ECtHR Resolution on Judicial Ethics, Principle III.

[139] ICC Code of Judicial Ethics, Art. 5.1; ECJ Statute Title I, Art. 4; Agreement establishing the CCJ, Art. 4.11; CCJ Code of Conduct, Principle III.

[140] LCIA Rules, Art. 10.2. For the duty to act in a fair manner, see also, Rome Statute, Art. 64.2; ICTY Statute, Art. 20.1; CCJ Code of Conduct, Principle VI.6.5.

[141] CCJ Code of Conduct, Principle VI.6.6.

[142] ICC Code of Judicial Ethics, Art. 8.1.

[143] ICC Code of Judicial Ethics, Art. 8.2.

[144] CCJ Code of Conduct, Principle I.1.2.

[145] CCJ Code of Conduct, Principle VI.6.7.

[146] CCJ Code of Conduct, Principle III.

behave with integrity[147] continues even after the end of judicial office.[148] Judges cannot directly or indirectly accept any gift, advantage, privilege, or reward that can be reasonably perceived as intended to influence the performance of their duties.[149]

Almost all judicial ethics instruments provide for confidentiality. Adjudicators are asked to maintain the secrecy of their deliberations, and not to disclose information accessed during the course of their judicial work.[150] They also cannot make any statements about pending proceedings,[151] or use confidential information for financial or other purposes unrelated to the judicial function of a judge.[152] Even after the completion of their judicial office, former judges are required to behave with discretion.[153]

Finally, the obligation to uphold judicial competence is another dimension of diligence. This involves the maintenance and, if need be, the development of professional skills by means of continuing education. For example, judges of the ICC are asked to take reasonable steps to maintain and improve their knowledge, skills, and personal qualities necessary for judicial office.[154] Judges of the ECtHR are called upon to continue to develop their professional skills in order to maintain a high level of competence.[155]

4 Universality of Judicial Ethics?

4.1 Unity in diversity

This survey of judicial ethics shows that there is a broad range of regulations.[156] Yet, despite variations between different international jurisdictions, there are overarching principles that are applicable to all forms of international adjudication.[157]

[147] ICC Code of Judicial Ethics, Art. 5.1; ECJ Statute, Title I, Art. 4; Agreement establishing the CCJ, Art. 4.11; CCJ Code of Conduct, Principle III.

[148] Statute of the ECJ, Art. 4.

[149] Pursuant to the ICC Code of Judicial Ethics, Art. 5.1. and 5.2, CCJ Code of Conduct, Principle III.3.2; ECtHR Resolution on Judicial Ethics, Principle III.

[150] Rome Statute, Art. 64.4.c; ICC Rules for Procedure and Evidence, Rule 5.1.a; ICC Code of Judicial Ethics, Art. 6; ECtHR Resolution on Judicial Ethics, Principle V; WTO DSU Rules of Conduct VII.1; ECJ Statute, Title I, Art. 2; CCJ Code of Conduct, Principle I.1.17. See also Burgh House Principles 1.4 and 7.2.

[151] WTO DSU Rules of Conduct VII.2; Burgh House Principles, Principle 7.2.

[152] CCJ Code of Conduct, Principle I.

[153] ECJ Statute, Title I, Art. 4. See also, the declaration pursuant to Rules of Procedure ECJ, Art. 3.2.

[154] In the ICC Code of Judicial Ethics, Art. 7.2.

[155] ECtHR Resolution on Judicial Ethics, Principle VI.

[156] To observe the lack of homogeneity among international courts and tribunals, see Brandeis University, note 33, at 19–21.

[157] See also Mackenzie and Sands, note 7; Brown, note 3, at 66, 96. Terhechte has identified values that are common to different international codes of conduct. Terhechte, note 2. According to Vagts,

In the Burgh House Principles, the ILA Study group attempted to distil a core set of guiding principles.[158] However, the implementation of such general standards requires that the specifics of each tribunal be taken into account.[159] For example, at international criminal tribunals, the due process rights of the accused require special consideration.[160] Other courts are confronted with different threats to judicial independence and impartiality. In investment disputes, for example, judges might have financial interests that give rise to conflicts of interest. Another factor is the particular composition of a court, that is, whether judges serve on a full- or part-time basis, ad hoc or *ad litem*.[161] A different set of interests might be involved, including functional considerations, which seek to preserve the existence, functioning, and integrity of the relevant courts.[162] After all, judicial independence is not an absolute value. It needs to be weighed against other, sometimes competing principles.

Arbitration might be one of those areas of international adjudication that requires adjusted standards,[163] particularly in regard to impartiality. Yuval Shany, for example, has pointed out that the Burgh House Principles apply to party-appointed adjudicators only insofar as they are appropriate.[164] He argued for differentiating between party-appointed and ad hoc judges in international courts and other international judges because the increased party control in arbitration requires a lesser degree of judicial independence and impartiality.[165] This "functional approach," which Catherine Rogers has also subscribed to,[166] seeks to differentiate between different adjudicative functions, and to tailor specific ethical standards to party-appointed

allowance should be made for differences, and international tribunals and arbitral institutions should be able to adapt the universal standards for their use. Vagts, note 14.

158 P Sands, C McLachlan, and R Mackenzie, "The Burgh House Principles on the Independence of the International Judiciary" (2005) 4 LPICT 247.

159 Vajic, note 32, at 182. 160 Shany and Horovitz, note 112.

161 Sands, McLachlan, and Mackenzie, note 158.

162 A Seibert-Fohr, "Judicial Independence—The Normativity of an Evolving Transnational Principle" in A Seibert-Fohr (ed.), *Judicial Independence in Transition* (Heidelberg: Springer 2012) 1279.

163 The question is also relevant in inter-state adjudication with respect to judges appointed ad hoc by a party to a case. Brubaker, note 10, at 145; AF Lowenfeld, "The Party-Appointed Arbitrator in International Controversies: Some Reflections" (1995) 30 Tex. Int'l. L. J. 59, 60. Separate Opinion of Judge Lauterpacht, *Application of the Genocide Convention on the Prevention and Punishment of the Crime of Genocide* (*Bosnia and Herzegovina v. Serbia and Montenegro*) [1993] ICJ Rep 407, 408–9.

164 According to Shany, the provisions on security of tenure, extra-judicial activity, past links to a party, and post-service limitations are inappropriate for party-appointed adjudicators. Shany, note 15, at 485–6. See also Burgh House Principles, Preamble, para. 5. For recognition that there is a difference between the standards of independence of permanent courts and international arbitration, see also Shelton, note 30, at 58.

165 Shany, note 15, at 474, 487–90.

166 Catherine Rogers, however, does not advocate a lower standard of impartiality, but one that is genuine to the specific role of each arbitrator. She calls for an understanding of the term "impartiality" that is defined specifically for the international arbitration context. C Rogers, "Regulating International Arbitrators: A Functional Approach to Developing Standards of Conduct" (2005) 41 Stan. J. Int'l L. 53, 57, 106.

adjudicators.[167] She favors, in the interests of more flexibility, a lower "manifest lack of independence" standard for party-appointed adjudicators. This standard tolerates, for instance, past relations as well as peripheral or indirect ongoing relations with the appointing party.[168]

As we mentioned above, the UNCLOS Arbitral Tribunal concluded that the standard of independence and impartiality for inter-state disputes was different from the one for international commercial arbitration and investment arbitration.[169] However, the tribunal also suggested that there is a uniform standard for all inter-state disputes under the UN Law of the Sea Convention, regardless of whether a dispute is submitted to a court (ITLOS or ICJ) or to an arbitral tribunal pursuant to Annex VII.[170] Since all three institutions may decide similar issues, they should conform to a similar standard of impartiality, according to the Arbitral Tribunal.

The decision in *Mauritius v. UK* reflects the general growing convergence among the different modes of adjudication in public international law. Though arbitral tribunals have traditionally been considered different from international courts in that they are more closely related to the parties, the significance of their decisions goes far beyond the *inter-partes* relationship. Like their judicial counterparts, they do not just settle disputes between the parties. Their decisions have important effects *erga omnes* by stating and advancing international law more generally.[171] Accordingly, it is not only in the interest of the parties involved in the dispute, but in the interest of all entities subject to international law, that the independence, impartiality, and diligence of arbitral tribunals should be ensured.

Arguably, this is the reason for the growing demand for judicial independence and impartiality in international arbitration as well. Several rules regulating international commercial arbitration provide that arbitrators may be challenged if there are "justifiable doubts to their impartiality or independence."[172] A similar rule has been adopted for the Iran–US Claims Tribunal.[173] These and similar provisions have led Joseph Brubaker to discern a trend of subjecting all adjudicators to the same standard of impartiality.[174] The expectations for the independence and impartiality of arbitrators seem to be changing. Some arbitrators no longer act as counsel to

[167] Shany, note 15, at 485 (referencing *Amco Asia Corp. v. Indonesia*, ICSID Case, ARB/81/1, Decision on the Proposal to Disqualify an Arbitrator, June 24, 1982, at 7. Reprinted in WM Tupman, "Challenge and Disqualification of Arbitrators in International Commercial Arbitration" (1989) 38 ICLQ 26, 44–45).

[168] Shany, note 15, at 487.

[169] *Mauritius v. UK*, note 83.

[170] *Mauritius v. UK*, note 83, at para. 168.

[171] See e.g., A von Bogdandy and I Venzke (eds), *International Judicial Lawmaking* (Heidelberg: Springer 2012); C Giorgetti (ed.), *The Rules, Practice, and Jurisprudence of International Courts and Tribunals* (Leiden: Nijhoff 2012).

[172] UNCITRAL Rules, Art. 12.1, SCC Rules, Art. 15.1, LCIA Rules, Art. 19.3.

[173] Tribunal Rules of Procedure (May 3, 1983), Art. 10. For the interpretation of this rule see Brown, note 3, at 91–3.

[174] Brubaker, note 10, at 145.

avoid conflicts of interest.[175] This may even serve as a model for the future of international adjudication more generally.

5 Conclusion

In 1967, Thomas Franck called for a community of international judges "with its own norms, roles, symbols and administrative practices working to generate a loyalty with precedence over all others." He advocated for the development of an international judicial ethos in order to foster judicial impartiality despite ideological and cultural differences in the world, and for a generally recognized code of conduct.[176] Almost half a century later, there are indications that such a common ethos has emerged.[177] In their study on the international judge, Terris, Romano, and Swigart hailed the beginning of a shared judicial culture, interactions, and common legal thinking among international judges.[178] This is also reflected in the growing regulation of judicial ethics. Nevertheless, ensuring independent, impartial, and diligent international adjudication is no less important today than it was 50 years ago, and the multiplication of international adjudicative fora has only intensified the problem.

Judicial independence, impartiality, and diligence are the core values of judicial ethics. In their very essence, these values are transnational principles that apply to all forms of adjudication, be they domestic, transnational, or international dispute settlement mechanisms.[179] Transnational rules have been a point of departure for spelling out analogous standards for international courts. However, transplant is useful only as far as core standards are concerned. Beyond them, on more concrete issues, the specific nature of international adjudication calls for some idiosyncrasy. The specific structure of international governance has to be considered when specifying the particular exigencies of judicial ethics in international adjudication. Within the broad range of international dispute settlement, the specific implementation of independence, impartiality, and diligence may vary according to the function, composition, and structure of each body.

175 See also Burgh House Principles, Principle 10. See, in this handbook, Swigart and Terris, Ch. 28, at section 5.

176 T Franck, "Some Psychological Factors in International Third-Party Decision-Making" (1967) 19 Stan. L. Rev. 1217, 1236–47. For more recent analysis in this vein, see also, Swigart, note 14.

177 Terris, Romano, and Swigart, note 36, at 432. 178 Terris, note 6.

179 For a detailed comparative analysis of judicial independence in national courts and the transnationality of this principle, see, Seibert-Fohr, note 162.

Nevertheless, common denominators exist. There is a growing consensus among international judges on the necessary standards of behavior both on and off the bench. Empirical research attributes this, among other factors, to common legal education.[180] Judges who have trained at the same universities tend to share similar perceptions, and they are more likely to develop a common professional ethos.[181] Although such a shared understanding is an important foundation for independence, impartiality, and diligence, there is a growing demand for codifying and specifying international judicial ethics.[182] This is reflected in the rising number of documents regulating judicial conduct.

Judicial ethics is still an evolving area of international adjudication—one with flaws and shortcomings. While disqualification has attracted considerable attention, other areas of judicial behavior remain somewhat neglected. There is little guidance, for instance, on such matters as courtroom and off-bench behavior.[183] Some issues are dealt with on an ad hoc basis, sometimes lacking the necessary transparency[184] and formal procedure.[185] Though judicial ethics can never be regulated exhaustively, it seems advisable to further specify existing standards to prevent misbehavior—and enhance transparency and predictability—thereby improving the overall legitimacy of international adjudication. While most norm-setting in recent years has been done by international judges themselves, it is essential to advance a broader dialogue among all international legal professions to avoid allegations of judicial corporatism and to increase transparency and legitimacy.[186] This will also help make the standards for judicial ethics in international adjudication truly universal.

Research Questions

1. Is there a shared universal understanding of judicial ethics? How can it be identified?
2. Should the elaboration of judicial ethics rules be left to international courts themselves? To what extent should they be legally binding?
3. What is the proper role for court presidents in international judicial ethics?

180 Shany, note 15.

181 For a discussion of the training of international judges, see, in this handbook, Swigart and Terris, Ch. 28, at section 2.4.1.

182 Vagts, note 14, at 260.

183 Vagts, note 14, at 260. See also Brandeis University, note 33, at 21–3.

184 Mackenzie and Sands, note 7, at 285.

185 Vagts criticized that disqualification at the ICJ is difficult to rationalize in the absence of reasoned decisions. Vagts, note 14, at 255–6. For more on the informality of current procedures, see also, Terris, note 6.

186 Shelton suggested the formation of a professional association of international judges. Shelton, note 30, at 62.

4. Is there a need to increase the accountability of the international judiciary? What means of accountability can be reconciled with the imperatives of judicial independence? Which additional actors could be involved in judicial oversight?

Suggested Reading

Brown, C, "The Evolution and Application of Rules concerning Independence of the International Judiciary" (2003) 2 LPICT 63.

Brubaker, JF, "The Judge Who Knew Too Much: Issue Conflicts in International Adjudication" (2008) 26 Berkley J. Int'l L. 111.

Mégret, F, "International Judges and Experts' Impartiality and the Problem of Past Declarations" (2011) 10 LPICT 31.

Rogers, CA, "Regulating International Arbitrators: A Functional Approach to Developing Standards of Conduct" (2005) 41 Stan. J. Int'l. L. 53.

Sands, P, McLachlan, C, and Mackenzie, R, "The Burgh House Principles on the Independence of the International Judiciary" (2005) 4 LPICT 247.

Shany, Y, "Squaring the Circle? Independence and Impartiality of Party-Appointed Adjudicators in International Legal Proceedings" (2008) 30 Loy. L.A. Int'l & Comp. L. Rev. 473.

Shelton, D, "Legal Norms to Promote the Independence and Accountability of International Tribunals" (2003) 2 LPICT 27.

Shetreet, S, "Standards of Conduct of International Judges: Outside Activities" (2003) 2 Law & Prac. Int'l Cts. & Tribunals 127.

Terris, D, "Tests of Character" in D Terris, C Romano, and L Swigart (eds), *The International Judge* (Lebanon, NH: Brandeis University Press 2007).

Vagts, D, "The International Legal Profession: A Need for More Governance?" (1996) 90 AJIL 250.

Valticos, N, "Pratique et Étique d'un Juge 'ad hoc' à la Court International de Justice" in N Ando, E McWhinney, and R Wolfrum (eds), *Liber Amicorum Judge Shigeru Oda* (The Hague: Kluwer Law International 2002).

CHAPTER 36

JURISDICTION AND ADMISSIBILITY

YUVAL SHANY*

THE role of international courts and tribunals in international life is decisively influenced by their jurisdictional powers and the rules on admissibility to which they are subject. This is because the ability of international courts to fulfill their various functions—dispute resolution, law enforcement, norm-interpretation, information production, expressing the values of the international community, etc.—depends on the level of actual and potential business that they can expect to attract or generate. Still, judicial business stems from the jurisdictional provisions found in the relevant courts' constitutive instruments, since such provisions dictate who can

* The author thanks his co-editors, as well as the members of the research group on Exploring Conditions for Effective International Adjudication (Ms. Sivan Shlomo, Dr. Victor Peskin, Mr. Thorbjörn Björnsson, Ms. Sigall Horovitz, Dr. Shai Dotan, Dr. Maria Varaki, and Mr. Simon Hentrei) for their useful comments to an earlier draft. Thanks are also due to Ms. Galit Farkash Heller who assisted in researching the chapter. The writing of the chapter was made possible through the support of the European Research Council's Frontier Research Program.

access the courts, what issues may be litigated, what legal claims may be raised in the course of litigation and, at times, what remedies can be sought. Put differently, the legal powers of international courts, and the political influence that emanates therefrom on international relations, are determined by the courts' jurisdictional provisions. Any study of the role and impact of international adjudicative bodies must therefore consider the configuration of their jurisdictional powers.

Rules on admissibility are also important for the study of international courts and tribunals, since they represent potential limits on jurisdictional powers—that is, they define the circumstances under which courts can or should decline to exercise jurisdiction over cases brought before them. What's more, unlike jurisdictional provisions which are pre-determined by the court's "mandate providers" (the states and/or intergovernmental organizations (IGOs) that established the court and drafted its key constitutive instruments) and/or by the actual parties to litigation, rules of admissibility typically allow courts to engage in some degree of case selection in response to their internal policy preferences and external expectations. Thus, rules on admissibility provide international courts with important policy tools that mediate between their legal powers, their institutional interests and concerns, and the prevailing environmental conditions.

Despite their centrality to understanding the legal powers of international courts (which underlies their political influence) and the proclivity of judges on international courts to utilize such powers (through which judicial policies may be advanced), much of the international adjudication literature and some of the case law fail to define jurisdiction and admissibility in a manner which is theoretically sound, and which captures their role in the life of international courts. This chapter offers a conceptual framework for studying jurisdiction and admissibility, and illustrates research questions, involving specific courts and court cases, which such a study may include.

The chapter will proceed as follows. Section 1 will discuss the main taxonomies used in the case law and in the literature about international courts and tribunals. Key distinctions will be offered in this regard between jurisdiction and admissibility and between jurisdiction and the merits of the case. Section 2 will map out the main jurisdictional dimensions and conditions existing in international adjudication and introduce the principal rules on admissibility found in the constitutive instruments of international courts and in judicial practice. Section 3 will briefly analyze some actual decisions on jurisdiction and admissibility issued by a variety of international courts. Through these few examples, I will comment on the actual role that jurisdictional and admissibility rules play in the life of international courts and tribunals, and discuss the policy options they represent and facilitate.

For reasons of space, the chapter will focus on some international courts only—attempting to be reflective, however, of the jurisdictional diversity of the universe of international courts (global v. regional; general v. specific; criminal v. non-criminal). Other courts will be mentioned, if at all, more succinctly. Furthermore, I will discuss in this chapter jurisdiction and admissibility only as relating to the power to hear or decline to adjudicate a case brought before international adjudicative bodies. Other uses of these terms in the international law literature—for instance, specific exercises of judicial powers (such as jurisdiction to issue provisional measures or to grant specific remedies) or specific determinations relating to conduct of litigation (such as the admissibility of evidence)—are covered in other chapters of the handbook.[1]

1 Jurisdiction: Terminology

1.1 The traditional taxonomy

Traditionally, the legal literature describes four principal categories of jurisdiction of international adjudicative bodies: Jurisdiction *ratione personae* (personal jurisdiction), jurisdiction *ratione materiae* (subject-matter jurisdiction), jurisdiction *ratione temporis* (temporal jurisdiction), and jurisdiction *ratione loci* (spatial or territorial jurisdiction).[2] These four categories, discussed below, offer useful analytical categories. In plain terms, they answer some basic questions such as: Who are the parties to the case? What are the issues that can be discussed? When did the dispute arise? And where did the events in question occur? Yet, reliance on these four distinctive dimensions should not divert our attention from other questions, equally important, from a practical point of view, relating to the conditions required for adjudication to take place, such as were local remedies exhausted or were any circumstances precluding jurisdiction present?[3]

International courts may adjudicate cases only if all the applicable jurisdictional requirements are satisfied—that is, if all of the dimensions of the case brought before them fall within the legal mandate conferred upon them and if all other jurisdictional conditions are met. It is therefore useful, when studying the legal powers of international courts, to move away from a typology centered on the four-dimensional treatment of jurisdiction to another typology, which also reflects the applicable jurisdictional conditions and considers in all cases the source of the

[1] See e.g., in this handbook, Brown Ch. 38, Riddell Ch. 39, and Gray Ch. 40.

[2] See e.g., CF Amerasinghe, *Jurisdiction of International Courts* (Leiden: Brill 2003) 53.

[3] Rome Statute on the International Criminal Court (July 17, 1998) 2187 UNTS 90 (ICC Statute), Art 16, limiting exercise of ICC jurisdiction in cases where the Security Council ordered a twelve-month deferment of the proceedings.

court's legal authority (an aspect of jurisdiction, which, as the next sub-section shows, has important legal and political implications).

1.2 Foundational jurisdiction v. specific jurisdiction

The jurisdiction of international courts—i.e., their legal authority to adjudicate cases—is based upon notions of delegation and consent. In a world legal order which is still premised, by and large, on state sovereignty, international courts—like other IGOs—derive their legal powers from member states that empower international courts by way of delegation (alternatively, international courts derive legal powers from IGOs, who, in turn, derive delegated authority from their own member states).[4] Still, delegation of power to IGOs under international law is often partial and conditional, and in many cases, IGOs can only exercise power subject to the additional consent of the involved states. For example, the UN General Assembly (UNGA) is authorized to recommend the adoption of texts of new international treaties;[5] but the entry into force of any given treaty for any specific UN member state depends on the latter's consent. Thus, what had been actually delegated to the UNGA by the UN member states was the power to propose a new norm of international law.

In the same vein, international courts may be invested with only limited delegated power. The International Court of Justice (ICJ), for instance, may adjudicate cases only if the parties to litigation have expressed an additional consent to its exercise of jurisdiction.[6] As a result, the delegation of power to the court under the UN Charter and the ICJ Statute has been limited by the principle of state consent to adjudication. Only when the two sets of authorizations overlap (that is, when the parties to the statute have delegated to the ICJ the potential power to hear a case and the parties to a particular dispute have conferred on it the actual power to hear the case) can the ICJ exercise jurisdiction.

One useful way to understand the jurisdiction of international courts, which incorporates both notions of delegation and consent, is to view the provisions found in their constitutive instruments as a source of foundational jurisdiction, and to view the specific authorization granted by the parties to the case as a source of specific jurisdiction. Foundational jurisdiction thus comprises a delegation of power from the member states (or sponsoring IGO) to the court, operating from

[4] J Klabbers, *Introduction to International Institutional Law* (2nd edn, Cambridge University Press 2009) 55–6.

[5] UN Charter, Art. 13.

[6] Statute of the International Court of Justice, Annex to the Charter of the Untied Nations (June 26, 1945) (ICJ Statute), Art. 36.

the moment of its establishment onwards,[7] and specific jurisdiction represents the parties' consent to the adjudication of any particular case.

The foundational jurisdiction of international courts not only delineates the four principal dimensions of jurisdictional powers (power over persons and issues, and over events in time and space), it also introduces conditions precedent to the exercise of jurisdiction—including, in some cases, prior party consent. Consequently, the breadth of the foundational jurisdiction of any given international court may determine its capacity to act, as well as the room left for its further empowerment through specific jurisdiction (e.g., the room left for party consent). It also delineates, by negative implication, the legal powers still residing with the member states (and their own national courts). The legal powers transferred and those remaining with states (and other relevant actors, such as national courts and IGOs) may vary significantly across different judicial institutions.

For older courts, such as the ICJ, the foundational grant of authority has been modest. States have only authorized the ICJ to exercise some ancillary powers—e.g., the issuance of provisional measures if *prima facie* jurisdiction exists, the power of *kompetenz-kompetenz* (or *la compétence de la compétence*, that is to say, the power to decide on its own competence), and the power to issue advisory opinions.[8] Most importantly, they did not authorize the court to adjudicate cases without the consent of all parties. The modest level of power delegated to the court might be reflective of the limited interest of states in surrendering control over the resolution of the disputes to which they are party. It is also perhaps indicative of their limited belief in the court's across-the-board usefulness.

The upshot of this jurisdictional configuration is that the main contours of the ICJ's legal powers to adjudicate are found in the realm of specific jurisdiction—that is, in the specific grant of jurisdiction to the ICJ by the parties to any given case, who have consented to its exercise of judicial authority. Such consent may also be regarded as a form of delegation—a transfer of power from states to the court to identify the legal norms governing a particular set of circumstances and to apply them to the facts of the case.[9] Although the ICJ Statute does control the contours of the exercise of specific jurisdiction, namely by regulating the manner in which state consent

[7] Note, however, that these foundational powers are not fixed in time: with the accession of new states to the court's constitutive instruments, its foundational jurisdiction may be extended to establish its legal power over these new states. Furthermore, the constitutive instruments and the foundational jurisdiction they confer upon international courts may be amended from time to time. See e.g., Protocol 11 to the European Convention on Human Rights and Fundamental Freedoms restructuring the control machinery established thereby (May 11, 1994) ETS 155.

[8] UN Charter, Art. 96; ICJ Statute, Arts 36(6), 41.

[9] Put differently, the parties delegate to the court their power to engage in self-interpretation of the law. On the self-interpretation power, see e.g., P Weil, "The Court Cannot Conclude Definitively... 'Non Liquet Revisited'" (1998) 36 Columbia Journal of Transnational Law 109, 119; B Pastore, "International Law in a Changing World: Towards a Judge Made Law?" in G Zaccaria (ed.), *International Justice and Interpretation* (Berlin: LIT Verlag 2002) 151, 167.

to adjudication can be expressed (including who can grant consent and in what form consent can be expressed),[10] the actual dimensions and conditions of ICJ jurisdiction are found mostly in the documents establishing specific consent to its jurisdiction. Consequently, the jurisdiction of the ICJ is, by and large, consensual in nature.

For newer courts, however, such as the WTO dispute settlement system (WTO DSS) or the post-Protocol 11 European Court of Human Rights (ECtHR), the jurisdictional "center of gravity" is found in the realm of foundational jurisdictional. This is because, when ratifying the relevant constitutive instruments, the member states have accepted the jurisdiction of an international court over future cases brought against them, without requiring any additional consent before the exercise of jurisdiction.[11] The role of specific jurisdiction in proceedings brought to a court endowed with "compulsory" foundational jurisdiction is merely to define, in concrete terms, the actual factual and legal controversy that the court ought to adjudicate upon (that is, to refer a specific case to the court). In compulsory jurisdiction courts, this framing is typically undertaken unilaterally by the applicant in the proceedings at the time the court is seized ("act of seisin"). The respondent may contribute to defining the scope of the case, by choosing not to contest certain factual or legal allegations raised by the applicants, or by bringing counter-claims when possible.

The distinction between foundational jurisdiction and specific jurisdiction is relevant not only for understanding the power relations between any given international court and the potential parties to cases before it (i.e., whether jurisdiction is compulsory or optional in nature), but is also important for delineating the precise scope of the court's jurisdictional power and reconciling between different jurisdictional provisions emanating from different sources of authorization.

For example, the parties to a dispute cannot, by way of consent, authorize the ICJ to exercise jurisdiction if one or more of the disputing states fails to meet the statute's criteria for access to the court.[12] This is because the parties to a case do not have the legal authority, even when acting jointly, to expand the jurisdiction of the court beyond the scope of the foundational jurisdiction that was determined by its mandate providers. For the same reasons, the parties cannot bring to the ECtHR, by way of agreement, cases not involving human rights issues, and they cannot circumvent

[10] ICJ Statute, Art. 36.

[11] See e.g., Understanding on Rules and Procedures governing the Settlement of Disputes (Annex 2 of the WTO Agreement) (April 15, 1994) 33 ILM 1226 (DSU), Art. 6; European Convention on Human Rights and Fundamental Freedoms (November 4, 1950) ETS 5 (ECHR), Arts 33–4 (as amended by Protocols 11 and 14).

[12] ICJ Statute, Art. 35; see e.g., *Legality of Use of Force (Serbia and Montenegro v. Belgium)* [2004] ICJ Rep 279, 299 ("[T]he question whether Serbia and Montenegro was or was not a party to the Statute of the Court at the time of the institution of the present proceedings is fundamental... The Court can exercise its judicial function only in respect of those States which have access to it under Article 35 of the Statute. And only those States which have access to the Court can confer jurisdiction upon it").

strict jurisdictional conditions introduced in the constitutive instruments (e.g., the six-month rule, which prevents the untimely lodging of complaints).[13] A different rule would have allowed the parties to any given case to "hijack" the court's agenda, and to steer it in directions to which it is ill equipped to turn. Such a development may not only be ineffective, it might also be viewed as illegitimate, as it might run contrary to the reasonable expectations of third parties, who are parties to the court's constitutive instruments and fund its operations, directly or indirectly.

Still, when the constitutive instruments permit so, explicitly or implicitly,[14] the parties to the case may extend or limit the court's jurisdiction through specific jurisdictional authorizations or conditions. For example, the ECtHR is authorized to receive cases alleging a violation of the European Convention on Human Rights (ECHR) only if the case is ripe for international adjudication and all local remedies were exhausted.[15] However, the respondent party may stipulate upon the court's jurisdiction by waiving its right to insist upon the exhaustion of local remedies.[16] Under the Convention establishing the International Centre for the Settlement of Investment Disputes (ICSID), the situation is quite the opposite. Although the convention disposes with the need to exhaust local remedies, parties ratifying the convention may insist on the reintroduction of such a requirement (limiting the jurisdiction of the center accordingly).[17] Critically, however, it is the instrument laying down the court's foundational jurisdiction that determines whether the parties may or may not confer upon the court additional legal powers or detract from any existing powers.

Note that most of the literature on jurisdiction and admissibility treats temporal conditions, such as the aforementioned rules on exhaustion of local remedy or the six-month rule,[18] as matters of admissibility, not jurisdiction.[19] By contrast, I propose, for the reasons provided below, to regard them as jurisdictional conditions. They delineate the scope of power delegated to the court by the parties and

[13] See e.g., *X v. France*, App no 9587/81, 29 D&R 228, 240 (ECHR, December 13, 1982); *K v. Ireland*, App no 10416/83, 38 D&R 158, 160 (ECHR, May 17, 1984).

[14] See e.g., UNCLOS Annex VI: Statute of the International Tribunal for the Law of the Sea, Art. 22 (authorizing ITLOS to hear with the agreement of the parties disputes under other law of the sea treaties); Convention on the Settlement of Investment Disputes between States and Nationals of Other States (March 18, 1965) 575 UNTS 159 (ICSID Convention), Art. 25(2)(b) (allowing states to expand investor rights of judicial recourse to foreign-controlled local investors).

[15] ECHR, Art. 35(1).

[16] See e.g., *De Wilde v. Belgium* (1971) Eur. Ct HR Series A No 12, at para. 55.

[17] ICSID Convention, Art. 25.

[18] Another example of a temporal condition precedent is the duty to negotiate a dispute prior to its adjudication; See e.g., DSU, Art. 4(7). See also *Application of the International Convention on the Elimination of All Forms of Racial Discrimination (Georgia v. Russia)* (ICJ Judgment of April 1, 2011), at paras 148–84.

[19] See e.g., J Collier and V Lowe, *The Settlement of Disputes in International Law: Institutions and Procedures* (Oxford University Press 1999) 191; JG Merrills, *International Dispute Settlement* (5th edn, Cambridge University Press 2011) 171.

prescribe that it may review cases brought only at a certain time in their "life." The scope of jurisdiction conferred upon international courts thus consists of the intersection between the different jurisdictional dimensions (often phrased in positive terms) and the jurisdictional conditions (often phrased in negative terms) found in the relevant jurisdiction-creating instruments.[20]

According to the construction offered here, the principle of consent to adjudication (found, for instance, in Art. 36 of the ICJ Statute) constitutes a jurisdictional condition similar in its effect to a temporal condition such as the exhaustion of local remedies. Both conditions must be satisfied for a court to have legal authority to exercise jurisdiction over cases referred to it.

1.3 Jurisdiction v. admissibility

Another taxonomical question surrounded with even greater confusion and controversy pertains to the distinction between jurisdiction and admissibility. This is not a mere technical issue. The distinction goes to the question of what legal powers international courts have, and how much discretion they can exercise in selecting the cases before them. Put differently, qualifying an issue as jurisdictional may imply control over the business of the court by the member states or sponsoring IGO, whereas qualifying it as one of admissibility may suggest increased control by the court over its docket.

In some of the literature, legal standards qualifying as jurisdictional conditions are deemed more fundamental in nature and less amenable to party stipulation or waiver than issues of admissibility. For example, Amerasinghe suggests that conditions for the exercise of jurisdiction that may be waived by the parties should be classified as admissibility (or irreceivability) conditions.[21] Another attempt to offer a distinction between jurisdiction and admissibility (also involving a notion of curability, but focusing on temporality, not on waiver by the parties) can be found in the recent investment arbitration case *Abaclat v. Argentina*, where the majority on the panel opined that "While a lack of jurisdiction *stricto sensu* means that the

[20] For support, see *Abaclat and Others v. Argentina* (Dissenting Opinion of Georges Abi-Saab) October 28, 2011, at para. 126 <http://italaw.com/cases/35> accessed July 31, 2013 ("[J]urisdiction is first and foremost a power, the legal power to exercise the judicial or arbitral function. Any limits to this power, whether inherent or consensual, i.e. stipulated in the jurisdictional title (consent within certain limits, or subject to reservations or conditions relating to the powers of the organ) are jurisdictional by essence").

[21] Amerasinghe, note 2, at 192. Amerasinghe's position appears, however, to exclude most, if not all manifestations of specific jurisdiction from the definition of jurisdiction (or competence). Since almost all of consent-based jurisdictional powers can be stipulated upon by the parties (by way of agreement of waiver of objections), adopting Amerasinghe's proposed definition might leave us with very few specific jurisdictional conditions.

claim cannot at all be brought in front of the body called upon, a lack of admissibility means that the claim was neither fit nor mature for judicial treatment."[22] At the other extreme, Thirlway proposes that all conditions emanating from the consent of the parties—expressed in the jurisdiction-conferring instruments (i.e., both foundational and specific jurisdictional bases) should be viewed as jurisdictional in nature, although he too accepts the practical utility of sequencing certain objections.[23]

The analytical distinction I propose here is somewhat different than that used in most of the existing literature. To my mind, questions of jurisdiction (foundational and specific) appertain to questions of power—i.e., whether or not an international court has been authorized to adjudicate a case (or category of cases). Thus, if precedent conditions, such as the failure to pursue alternative remedies or regulate the court's power to adjudicate, have not been satisfied, the court does not have the legal authority to adjudicate. They are therefore jurisdictional conditions (albeit of a possible transient nature). Note also that if a court has been granted with jurisdiction over a specific case and all jurisdictional conditions have been met, then it has no choice but to adjudicate the case (unless the case is inadmissible, as explained below). Put differently, jurisdiction entails not only a legal power to adjudicate, but also a non-discretionary legal obligation to do so.

Unlike questions of jurisdiction that pertain to whether legal power exists or not, questions of admissibility pertain to whether or not the court may decline to exercise the power to adjudicate.[24] For example, some treaty norms or legal doctrines allow international courts to exercise discretion in deciding whether or not to adjudicate cases on the basis of open-ended standards such as "the interests of justice" or "abuse of process."[25] Their application implies that although the court in question has the legal power to exercise jurisdiction, it may decline to do so for certain reasons. Put differently, admissibility denotes a right, not a duty to adjudicate.[26]

The distinction between jurisdiction and admissibility based on their relationship to delegated power is analytically sound and functionally useful. Understanding admissibility as an exception to jurisdiction may support dealing with jurisdiction

[22] *Abaclat*, note 20, at para. 247 (decision of August 4, 2011). See also *Abaclat* dissent, at para. 18 ("Generically, the admissibility conditions relate to the claim, and whether it is ripe and capable of being examined judicially, as well as to the claimant, and whether he or she is legally empowered to bring the claim to court").

[23] H Thirlway, "The Law and Procedure of the International Court of Justice: 1960–1989, Part Two" (1990) 61 British Yearbook of International Law 1, 114–15.

[24] For a somewhat similar view, see G Fitzmaurice, "The Law and Procedure of the International Court of Justice: General Principles and Substantive Law" (1950) 27 British Yearbook of International Law 1, 13.

[25] See e.g., ICC Statute, Art. 53; ECHR, Art. 35(3)(a).

[26] For the distinction between legal rights entailing duties and legal powers entailing privileges, see WN Hohfeld, "Some Fundamental Legal Conceptions as Applied in Judicial Reasoning" (1913) 23 Yale Law Journal 16.

before admissibility[27] and, more significantly, allocating the burden of proof as follows. The applicant would typically establish the court's jurisdiction over the claim,[28] whereas the respondent would typically incur the burden of establishing that good reasons exist for the court to decline to exercise its legal powers.[29] This does not exclude the power of some courts to raise at times, at their own initiative, issues of jurisdiction and admissibility.

The distinction offered here also implies that international courts have more limited discretion in applying jurisdictional provisions than admissibility rules. This is because the question of whether or not the court has legal power to act has a binary answer. Either legal power was validly delegated to the court or not. By contrast, the question whether or not the court should decline to exercise jurisdiction is more open-ended and may invite the consideration of multiple policy considerations as well as the interests of justice. For example, the ECtHR court must reject for lack of jurisdiction a case not pertaining to human rights issues or a case submitted in violation of the six-month rule. At the same time, the ECtHR has broad discretion to engage in case selection when it considers, whether, on balance, respect for human rights requires examination of a human rights case in which the victim suffered no significant disadvantage.[30]

1.4 Questions of merits of an antecedent character

Another category, which may help us in understanding the legal options available to international courts when confronting cases they do not wish to adjudicate, involves questions of merits of an antecedent character. Certain international courts may preliminarily reject cases not only for lack of jurisdiction and inadmissibility, but also if the applications brought to them clearly lack merit. Some international courts have been explicitly authorized to summarily dismiss cases that are manifestly unfounded,[31] whereas other courts have developed legal doctrines leading to a similar outcome. For example, in the 1966 *South West Africa* case, the ICJ upheld the right to dismiss a case on the basis of a question of merit having an "antecedent

[27] See also Thirlway, note 23, at 115.

[28] *Factory at Chorzow (Germany v. Poland)* [1927] PCIJ Rep Series A No. 9, at 32 ("It is true that the Court's jurisdiction is always a limited one, existing only in so far as States have accepted it; consequently, the Court will, in the event of an objection—or when it has automatically to consider the question—only affirm its jurisdiction provided that the force of the arguments militating in favour of it is preponderant").

[29] See e.g., WTO, *US—US—Measure Affecting Imports of Woven Wool Shirts and Blouses from India-Appellate Body Report* (May 23, 1997) WT/DS33/AB/R, 14 ("it is a generally-accepted canon of evidence in civil law, common law and, in fact, most jurisdictions, that the burden of proof rests upon the party, whether complaining or defending, who asserts the affirmative of a particular claim or defence").

[30] ECHR, Art. 35(3)(b).

[31] See e.g., ECHR, Art 35(3)(a).

character," which is the question of standing vis-à-vis the subject matter of the claim.[32] The fact that the two applicants (Ethiopia and Liberia) based their substantive claims against South Africa on a legal instrument (the mandate for South West Africa, deriving from the League of Nations Covenant), which they had no legal power to invoke because they were not parties to it, was reason enough to reject the case without examining the other claims that they raised.[33] One may regard the discretion exercised by the court in the *South West Africa* case as comparable to the discretion often exercised with respect to questions of admissibility. Similar to some admissibility cases, the court took the position that a weighty reason (the hopelessness of the case) justified its decision to decline to adjudicate the remainder of the claim.

In practice, international courts have not always clarified whether their preliminary decisions not to hear a case appertain to questions of jurisdiction and/or admissibility, or to the merits of the case at hand. For example, in its 2001 decision to dismiss the application in the *Bankovic* case (a case brought against a number of NATO member states, alleging their responsibility for an attack on the TV station in Belgrade on April 23, 1999), the ECtHR held that the application was inadmissible because of the lack of a jurisdictional link between the victims and the respondent states.[34] This really constitutes, despite language suggesting otherwise, a preliminary decision on the lack of merit of the case. It held, in effect, that the applicants do not come with the geographical scope of protection provided by the ECHR. As a result, there was no need to review other aspects of the case.

2 Mapping of Jurisdictional and Admissibility Claims

After proposing a conceptual framework for understanding the jurisdiction of international courts as delegated power and of admissibility as the power to decline to exercise judicial power, I will briefly discuss in this section the main jurisdictional dimensions and conditions that define the powers of existing international

[32] *South West Africa (Ethiopia v. SA)* [1966] ICJ Rep 6, 18.

[33] *South West Africa (Ethiopia v. SA)*, note 32, ("a distinction has to be made between, on the one hand, the right to activate a court and the right of the court to examine the merits of the claim, and, on the other, the plaintiff party's legal right in respect of the subject-matter of that which it claims, which would have to be established to the satisfaction of the Court").

[34] *Bankovic v. Belgium*, 2001-XII Eur. Ct. H.R. 333, at para. 82.

courts. I will then discuss the main admissibility questions confronting international courts in practice.

2.1 Jurisdictional dimensions

As noted before, the literature on international adjudication traditionally categorizes the jurisdiction of international courts as consisting of four dimensions, responding to four questions: Who can adjudicate? What substantive issues can be adjudicated? When and where have the adjudicated events occurred? (Or when and where did the legal claims arise?). The point I have made is that such a treatment of jurisdiction is hardly exhaustive, and not fully satisfactory. First, besides jurisdictional dimensions, one should review jurisdictional conditions, which tend to limit the legal powers delegated to courts. Second, it is important to discuss jurisdictional dimensions and conditions against the context of another, no less important distinction between foundational and specific jurisdiction. The following segments will therefore discuss the powers delegated to international courts, as well as the limits placed upon them, and will distinguish, where relevant, between the foundational and specific origins of these jurisdictional powers. Understanding the legal configuration underlying a court's power structure allows us to investigate its legal power, its potential for adjudication, and its actual and potential political impact.

2.1.1 *Personal jurisdiction*

Under jurisdiction *ratione personae* (personal jurisdiction), international courts are competent to hear cases only when brought by certain parties against certain other parties, provided that a number of relevant conditions have been met. This combination of foundational and specific jurisdictional powers and limits on such powers defines the geographical reach of the court and the legal nature of the parties over which the court may exercise its authority (e.g., states, IGOs, private individuals).[35]

For example, the ICJ—a universal court—can only adjudicate contentious cases involving states when (1) the states in question are parties to its statute (or have accepted the statute for the purpose of the case and complied with several attendant requirements)[36] and (2) the adjudicating states have accepted the court's jurisdiction over the specific case.[37] The International Criminal Court (ICC), another potentially universal court, can only hear cases brought by the prosecutor against natural persons, provided that authorization to adjudicate was received from the relevant state of that person's nationality, or state where the events took place, or from the Security

[35] See in this handbook, Romano, Chapter 5, at section 2. [36] ICJ Statute, Art. 35.
[37] ICJ Statute, Art. 36.

Council.[38] At the same time, a regional court such as the Court of Justice of the European Union (CJEU) only exercises authority over states, IGOs, and individuals situated inside a certain geographical region (the European Union). Its personal jurisdiction over legal and natural persons changes for different heads of jurisdiction. Enforcement claims are brought against states by an IGO (the Commission) or other states,[39] administrative claims are brought against IGOs by states, other IGOs, or private persons[40] and preliminary rulings are brought, in effect, by parties to domestic litigation (typically private persons and local government entities) via national courts.[41]

2.1.2 *Subject-matter jurisdiction*

Under jurisdiction *ratione materiae* (subject-matter jurisdiction), international courts may only adjudicate cases that raise those factual and legal questions which the constitutive instruments have defined and/or that one or more of the parties have agreed to refer to adjudication. This dimension of jurisdiction defines the substantive reach of international courts, a reach described by Cesare Romano in this handbook as uneven in its spread.[42] There is only one permanent court with virtually unlimited subject-matter foundational jurisdiction—the ICJ.[43] Still, the latter court's specific jurisdiction—i.e., the jurisdictional powers actually conferred upon the court by the parties to the dispute, tends to relate to a certain substantive category of disputes (e.g., disputes over land and maritime boundary delimitation or the treatment of aliens) and to omit other areas of international interaction from its scope.[44]

Other courts are invested with more limited foundational subject-matter jurisdiction, covering either an entire field of law or just a specific instrument within such a field. For example, the ICSID may adjudicate any investment dispute,[45] and human rights courts, such as the ECtHR or the Inter-American Court of Human Rights (IACtHR), can only address, when exercising their contentious jurisdiction, cases raising allegations of violation of specific human rights instruments which they have been authorized to apply (e.g., the ECHR and the American Convention on Human Rights (ACHR)).[46]

[38] ICC Statute, Arts 12–13. States may authorize the ICC generally or specifically—either through joining the statute or depositing an ad hoc declaration under Art. 12(3) of the ICC Statute.

[39] Treaty of the Functioning of the European Union (March 30, 2010) OJ C83/47, Arts 258–9.

[40] TFEU, Art. 263. [41] TFEU, Art. 267.

[42] See in this handbook, Romano, Ch. 5, at section 3.

[43] ICJ Statute, Art. 36. Disputes referred to the court must be legal in nature, and raise international law questions. See e.g., *Applicability of the Obligation to Arbitrate under Section 21 of the United Nations Headquarters Agreement of June 26, 1947* [1988] ICJ Rep 12, 27.

[44] See also Y Shany, "No Longer A Weak Department Of Power? Reflections On The Emergence Of A New International Judiciary" (2009) 20 EJIL 73, 83–4.

[45] ICSID Convention, Art. 25.

[46] ECHR, Art. 31(1); American Convention on Human Rights (November 22, 1969) 1144 UNTS 123, Art. 62(3).

2.1.3 *Temporal jurisdiction*

Under jurisdiction *ratione temporis* (temporal jurisdiction), international courts may, at times, only have the power to review cases involving facts that have occurred or legal claims that have been consolidated before and/or after certain dates. Such limits on the power delegated to a court allow states to reduce some of the uncertainties associated with international adjudication and to exclude past events (or future development) from the court's docket.

For example, the International Criminal Tribunal for Rwanda (ICTR) may only review cases involving crimes that allegedly occurred in 1994,[47] and the International Criminal Tribunal for the Former Yugoslavia (ICTY) reviews cases involving crimes that have allegedly occurred after 1991.[48] In both cases, temporal restrictions were primarily designed to focus the tribunals' attention on a specific armed conflict in which crimes of exceptional magnitude have occurred. By contrast, the ICC has been authorized to address crimes which have occurred after July 1, 2002 (the date of the ICC Statute's entry into force), or any later date in which jurisdiction over the crime was established (e.g., the date of entry into force of the statute for new ratifying states).[49] Such a temporal restriction was designed to prevent the utilization of the court for settling past political accounts by way of criminal adjudication;[50] it may also have served to direct the power of the court to ongoing or recent conflicts, where its intervention may be most useful.

Note that even courts that have unlimited temporal foundational jurisdiction may experience such limitations through instruments conferring upon them specific jurisdiction. Thus, for instance, although the ICJ Statute contains no temporal limits on the power of the court to adjudicate cases, such limits are often imposed in the instrument defining the scope of the parties' consent to jurisdiction.[51]

2.1.4 *Spatial or territorial jurisdiction*

Jurisdiction *ratione loci* (spatial or territorial jurisdiction) ties the jurisdictional powers of an international court to events occurring in a particular geographical area. Such a limit may derive implicitly from the regional nature of the membership in the treaty establishing the court (e.g., the CJEU or the African Court on Human and Peoples' Rights (ACtHPR)) and/or the language of the legal instrument that

[47] Statute of the International Criminal Tribunal for Rwanda (November 8, 1994) U.N. Doc. S/RES/955, Art. 1.

[48] Statute of the International Criminal Tribunal for the Former Yugoslavia (May 25, 1993) U.N. Doc. S/RES/827, Art. 1.

[49] ICC Statute, Art. 11.

[50] See e.g., S Bourgon, "Jurisdiction *ratione temporis*" in A Cassese et al. (eds), *The Rome Statute of the International Criminal Court: A Commentary* (Oxford University Press 2002) 543, 551.

[51] See e.g., European Convention for the Peaceful Settlement of Disputes, June 29, 1957, ETS 23, Art. 27. This provision served as the basis for the decision of the ICJ to dismiss a case for lack of jurisdiction in *Certain Property (Liechtenstein v. Germany)* [2005] ICJ Rep 6.

the court applies (e.g., the ECHR applies only to areas controlled by Council of Europe member states). Geographical limits may be explicitly stipulated in the constitutive instrument establishing the court's jurisdiction. For example, the ICTY and ICTR's jurisdiction was geographically limited to Rwanda and neighboring states and to the Former Yugoslavia, respectively.[52] This limit underscores, for better or worse, the selective nature of the exercise of criminal jurisdiction by these tribunals.

Finally, it may be noted that consent to the jurisdiction of the ICJ (a court with unlimited *ratione loci* foundational jurisdiction) often defines the case to be referred to the court in specific geographical terms.[53]

2.2 Jurisdictional conditions

Besides the four dimensions of international jurisdiction, the power of international courts to adjudicate specific cases is controlled by a series of jurisdictional conditions (which can be foundational or specific in origin). It is the combination of grants of authority in the four aforementioned jurisdictional dimensions and the attendant conditions that define any given court's jurisdiction. Although some of the conditions are habitually referred to, in practice and in the literature, as conditions of admissibility, they should be properly qualified and studied as jurisdictional in nature. Although they are more circumstance-dependent than the four dimensions of authorization, like them they operate to determine the scope of judicial power.

The three main "families" of jurisdictional conditions are consent-related conditions, conditions pertaining to alternative venues, and time limits. As was already noted, some constitutive instruments stipulate that the exercise of jurisdiction by an international court depends on obtaining the prior consent of the parties, or on some other form of prior authorization. Such conditions suggest that the empowerment of international courts by the state parties has been partial and tentative, and that member states and IGOs were reluctant to surrender control over their past and future disputes. As a result, courts operating under consent conditions would have to continually nurture the confidence and support of potential parties to adjudication in order to attract new cases.

The most conspicuous member of the family of consent-based courts, the ICJ, can only exercise contentious jurisdiction with the consent of both parties (expressed by way of a *compromis*, a compromissory clause, optional clause jurisdiction or *forum*

[52] ICTR Statute, Art. 7; ICTY Statute, Art. 8.

[53] See e.g., Declaration on behalf of the government of Canada, May 10, 1994, sec. 2(a) <http://www.icj-cij.org/jurisdiction/index.php?p1=5&p2=1&p3=3&code=CA> accessed July 31, 2013 ("disputes arising out of or concerning conservation and management measures taken by Canada with respect to vessels fishing in the NAFO Regulatory Area, as defined in the Convention on Future Multilateral Co-operation in the Northwest Atlantic Fisheries, 1978, and the enforcement of such measures"); the provision has been applied in *Fisheries Jurisdiction (Spain v. Belgium)* [1998] ICJ Rep 432.

prorogatum).[54] The expression of state consent in such cases is needed not only for the conduct of adjudication per se, but also for the specific dimensions of the jurisdiction to be exercised (personal, subject-matter, temporal, and spatial jurisdiction). Still, expressions of consent often come with additional conditions and limitations.

Another example of a prior-consent jurisdictional condition can be found in the 1965 ICSID Convention, which stipulates that two sets of agreements are needed for an ICSID arbitration to take place. The host state and the state of nationality of the investor must be parties to the 1965 Convention[55] and the host state and the investor must agree to refer a specific investment dispute to arbitration (by way of a *compromis*, a contractual arbitration clause or reliance on a unilateral invitation to arbitrate extended by the host state—what is sometimes referred to as arbitration without privity).[56] Consent to jurisdiction, or to some heads of jurisdiction, is also a condition under the constitutive instruments of other courts, such as the IACtHR,[57] ACtHPR,[58] ITLOS,[59] the Caribbean Court of Justice (CCJ),[60] and the Central American Court of Justice (CACJ).[61]

Another set of jurisdictional conditions provides that international adjudication should be activated only in the absence of alternative dispute resolution venues. At times, parties are instructed to actively pursue other venues before seizing the relevant international court; at other times, it may be sufficient just to show that other venues are inadequate. Underlying such jurisdictional conditions may be the notion that some venues are better suited than international adjudication to settle disputes or to enforce legal norms. For example, national courts may have closer familiarity with the contested facts than their international counterparts or have greater access to private litigants, stronger social legitimacy and stronger enforcement mechanisms.[62] Similarly, negotiations may be a more effective and less costly way than international

[54] ICJ Statute, Art. 36; S Rosenne, *The Law and Practice of the International Court of Justice 1920–2005* (4th edn, Leiden: Martinus Nijhoff 2006) Ch. 9 *in passim*.

[55] ICSID Convention, Art 25(1), 25(4). The contracting states may exclude certain categories of disputes from the scope of the jurisdiction of ICSID.

[56] ICSID Convention, Art. 25(1); C Schreuer, *The ICSID Convention: A Commentary* (Cambridge University Press 2001) 294.

[57] American Convention on Human Rights (November 22, 1969) 1144 UNTS 123, Art. 62.

[58] Protocol to the African Charter on Human and Peoples' Rights on the Establishment of an African Court on Human and Peoples' Rights (June 9, 1998) Art. 34(6) <http://www.au.int/en/sites/default/files/PROTOCOL_AFRICAN_CHARTER_HUMAN_PEOPLES_RIGHTS_ESTABLISHMENT_AFRICAN_COURT_HUMAN_PEOPLES_RIGHTS_1.pdf > accessed September 2, 2013.

[59] United Nations Convention on the Law of the Sea (December 10, 1982) 1833 UNTS 3, Art. 287.

[60] Agreement establishing the Caribbean Court of Justice (February 14, 2001), Art. XXV <http://www.caribbeancourtofjustice.org/wp-content/uploads/2011/09/ccj_agreement.pdf> accessed July 31, 2013.

[61] Estatuto de la Corte Centroamericana de Justicia (December 11, 1992) competencia at para. 3 <http://portal.ccj.org.ni/Ccj2/LinkClick.aspx?fileticket=As1kDvgOEh4=&tabid=67> accessed July 31, 2013.

[62] See e.g., Y Shany, "Capacities and Inadequacies: A Look at the Two Separation Barrier Cases" (2005) 38 Isr. L. Rev. 230, 240–2.

adjudication to amicably solve complicated problems.[63] Finally, some international courts may have a greater expertise in some areas of law than others, or there may be better suited procedures or legal facilities to address certain disputes.[64]

Another possible explanation for jurisdictional conditions providing for adjudication as a last resort only may be, again, that certain states are reluctant to empower international courts in a manner that leads to the surrender of control over their legal disputes. By according a right of way to other dispute settlement venues over which they retain some influence (such as national courts or negotiations), states may be able to minimize the loss of control over the dispute associated with international adjudication.[65]

One prominent example of an alternative venue jurisdictional condition may be found in the ICC Statute's complementarity regime, which limits the court's jurisdiction to cases that national courts are unwilling or unable to adjudicate.[66] Other examples are found in compromissory clauses containing conditions precedent providing for a duty to negotiate the dispute prior to adjudication,[67] *electa una via* (or fork in the road) provisions, which deprive the UNCLOS dispute settlement proceedings of jurisdiction over cases the parties agreed to refer elsewhere,[68] and exhaustion of local remedies provisions, found in some international instruments conferring foundational jurisdiction on international courts.[69]

Finally, one may find jurisdictional conditions appertaining to the timeliness of the claim. By insisting on conditions precedent that prescribe waiting periods, such as the 60 days of consultation under the WTO DSS,[70] states limit their exposure to rash adjudication and facilitate the operation of alternative remedies. In fact, one can regard some of the aforementioned residual jurisdiction provisions also as timeliness jurisdictional conditions, intended to ensure that judicial resources are efficiently employed only on those cases ripe for adjudication, where resort to adjudication is clearly necessary.[71]

[63] See e.g., G Biehler, *Procedures in International Law* (Berlin: Springer 2008) 298.

[64] See e.g., Y Shany, *The Competing Jurisdictions of International Courts and Tribunals* (Oxford University Press 2003) 259–60.

[65] See *Application of CERD*, note 18, at para. 154.

[66] ICC Statute, Art. 17. One should note that the statute itself considers this provision "issues of admissibility."

[67] See e.g., International Convention on the Elimination of All Forms of Racial Discrimination (December 21, 1965) 660 UNTS 195, Art. 22. This provision has been the subject of a recent ICJ case—*Application of CERD*, note 18, at para. 141.

[68] See e.g., *Southern Bluefin Tuna (Australia v. Japan)* (Decision) August 4, 2000, available through <www.worldbank.org/icsid> accessed July 31, 2013. See also Declaration by the United Kingdom of Great Britain and Northern Ireland of July 5, 2004, <http://www.icj-cij.org/jurisdiction/index.php?p1=5&p2=1&p3=3&code=GB> accessed July 31, 2013 (accepting the compulsory jurisdiction of the ICJ except "any dispute which the United Kingdom has agreed with the other Party or Parties thereto to settle by some other method of peaceful settlement").

[69] See e.g., ECHR, Art. 35(1); UNCLOS, Art. 295.

[70] DSU, Art. 7(4).

[71] See e.g., *Application of CERD*, note 18, at para. 131.

Another subset of timeliness conditions involves outdated claims, whose period of limitation has passed. The most famous example in this regard is found in the above-mentioned six-month rule under the ECHR.[72] Other examples of such cut-off provisions can be found, especially in mass claim procedures.[73] Here, the principal motivations of the relevant states appear to be the preservation of legal certainty and the easing of the burden associated with defending long-dormant claims.[74] Such conditions, whose effect is to limit the potential for judicial business, may also suggest some ambivalence toward exposure to international adjudication.

2.3 Admissibility rules

When the contours of a case submitted to adjudication exceed the relevant court's jurisdictional dimensions or if any jurisdictional condition has not been met, the court must reject jurisdiction, as it does not have the legal power to adjudicate the case in question. Rules of admissibility are different, however, in the sense that they do not assume a lack of power to adjudicate, but rather the power to decline to adjudicate, notwithstanding having the legal authority to do so.

A useful formulation of the distinction between jurisdiction and admissibility is found in the ICJ's advisory opinion process, where the court has repeatedly held that it may refuse to render an opinion on cases validly referred to it (a possibility never seized upon by the ICJ, however):

> The fact that the Court has jurisdiction does not mean, however, that it is obliged to exercise it: "The Court has recalled many times in the past that Article 65, paragraph 1, of its Statute, which provides that 'The Court may give an advisory opinion…' [emphasis added], should be interpreted to mean that the Court has a discretionary power to decline to give an advisory opinion even if the conditions of jurisdiction are met [cite omitted]."[75]

There are three principal legal bases on which international courts may rely to decline to exercise jurisdiction that has been lawfully vested in them: an explicit or implicit authorization to exercise a discretionary power to decline jurisdiction; an inherent power to decline jurisdiction in suitable cases; and declining jurisdiction on the basis of an "external" rule of international law. These distinctions are significant not only from a purely legal perspective; they also reflect variations in the levels at which international courts have been empowered, or need to be empowered, in order to exercise control over their docket. In addition, they reflect differences in

72 ECHR, Art. 35(1).

73 See e.g., Declaration of the Government of the Democratic and Popular Republic of Algeria (Algiers Accords) (January 19, 1981) 20 ILM 223, Art. III(4).

74 See *X v. France*, note 13.

75 See e.g., *Accordance with international law of the unilateral declaration of independence in respect of Kosovo* [2010] ICJ Rep 403, 415–16.

the ways international courts view their operations as either self-contained in nature and tied to a specific legal regime, or part of a broader international law system.

The first basis for declining jurisdiction involves a general authorization to exercise discretion with respect to the propriety or effectiveness of adjudicating any specific case such as that found in Art. 65 of the ICJ Statute (dealing with advisory proceedings). More typically, however, the grant of authority is somewhat more limited, pointing to specific considerations such as the "interests of justice,"[76] the requirements of "respect for human rights,"[77] or prevention of "abuse of process."[78] Some courts have also been authorized to reject manifestly ill-founded claims[79]—an authorization which amounts to a discretionary power to summarily dismiss what appear to be meritless cases (see section 3.2).

A more controversial set of admissibility decisions rests on the theory of inherent powers. According to that theory, international courts may resort to certain non-enumerated powers in order to protect fundamental interests, such as their judicial function, judicial economy, and respect for the rule of law in international affairs.[80] The classic example in this category is the *Northern Cameroons* case, in which the ICJ refused to hear a moot case, comprising of legal questions that did not have any practical implications. According to the court:

> The Court has, however, already indicated that even if, when seized of an Application, the Court finds that it has jurisdiction, it is not obliged to exercise it in all cases. If the Court is satisfied, whatever the nature of the relief claimed, that to adjudicate on the merits of an Application would be inconsistent with its judicial function, it should refuse to do so.[81]

In other cases, international courts have declined, arguably relying on inherent powers, to adjudicate manifestly ill-founded applications[82] or to facilitate patently abusive proceedings.[83]

Finally, some international courts have upheld their right to decline jurisdiction where the exercise of jurisdiction would have run contrary to a general international law principle, which binds the parties to the dispute or binds the court itself. For instance, the PCIJ opined in the *Minority Schools* case that it would have to decline jurisdiction in the face of an exclusive jurisdiction clause directing the dispute elsewhere.[84] Another example can be found in the ICJ's *Monetary Gold* case,

[76] ICC Statute, Art. 53. [77] ECHR, Art. 35(3)(b).

[78] UNCLOS, Art 294(1); ECHR, Art. 35(3)(a).

[79] See e.g., ECHR, Art. 35(3)(a); ICC Statute, Art. 61(7).

[80] C Brown, *A Common Law of International Adjudication* (Oxford University Press 2009) 55–7; C Brown, in this handbook, Ch. 38.

[81] *Northern Cameroons (Cameroon v. UK)* [1963] ICJ Rep 15, 37.

[82] See e.g., *Legality of Use of Force (Yugoslavia v. Belgium)* [1999] ICJ Rep 124, 138.

[83] *Phoenix Action Ltd. v. Czech Republic*, ICSID Award of April 15, 2009, at para. 144.

[84] See *Minority Schools in Upper Silesia (Minority Schools) (Germany v. Poland)* [1928] PCIJ Rep Series A No 15, at 23 ("This principle [of competence to hear a case referred by the parties] only becomes inoperative in those exceptional cases in which the dispute which States may desire to refer to the Court would fall within the exclusive jurisdiction reserved to some other authority").

where the court held that an application strongly implicating the rights of third states (whose legal interests "would form the very subject-matter of the decision") is inadmissible.[85] Adjudicating a case under these terms would arguably violate the principle that states cannot be made subject to adjudication without their consent—an important principle of international law. Thus, although the court was properly invested with jurisdiction, it took the view that jurisdiction should be declined in order to protect an important international law principle. Arguably, such an approach shows a belief on the part of the court in the need to sustain the welfare of the international legal system as a whole.

3 Application of Jurisdictional and Admissibility Rules

3.1 Discretion in the exercise of jurisdiction

The conferral of jurisdiction upon an international court implies an act of empowerment. It simultaneously entails an act of disempowerment—the exclusion of certain parties, issues and events (in time and space) from the court's scope of authority, with or without conditions. When determining their jurisdiction, international courts give effect to this category-based distinction between included and excluded disputes, which is relevant not only for the case at hand but for future cases as well. This is why states parties to adjudication, as well as third states, may invest considerable efforts in trying to influence the court's jurisprudence on jurisdictional matters.

In all events, international courts enjoy some interpretative discretion in construing the scope of the relevant jurisdictional dimensions and conditions, and in applying them to a concrete set of facts. This is especially the case in situations where the language of the jurisdictional authorizations or conditions is open-ended.[86] Inevitably, such law-interpretation and law-application exercises have been influenced by policy considerations. Courts hungry for cases or eager to advance a certain normative agenda may read their jurisdictional powers in an expansive manner, while conservative courts whose approach to state sovereignty is

[85] *Monetary Gold Removed from Rome in 1943 (Italy v. France)* [1954] ICJ Rep 19, 32.

[86] Fitzmaurice had remarked that all cases where jurisdictional challenges are raised reveal less than full consent to the court's jurisdiction. Fitzmaurice, note 24, at 10–11. In such cases, courts arguably have some discretion in determining whether the facts reveal that genuine and specific consent was granted.

deferential or those facing a heavy case load may construe their jurisdiction rather narrowly.

Thus, for example, the ICJ refused in the *Fisheries Jurisdiction* case to embrace a canon of interpretation calling for the treating of jurisdictional conditions as exceptions to the rule, warranting a narrow construction. When dealing with a reservation appended by Canada to its optional clause declaration, excluding from the court's jurisdiction certain disputes over fishing, it held that:

Conditions or reservations thus do not by their terms derogate from a wider acceptance already given. Rather, they operate to define the parameters of the State's acceptance of the compulsory jurisdiction of the Court. There is thus no reason to interpret them restrictively.[87]

Such an outcome may not only be indicative of some degree of judicial conservatism and respect for state consent as the basis of ICJ jurisdiction, it may also reflect a long-term policy calculus: reluctance by the court to give optional clause reservations the effect intended by the reserving states may deter states from submitting clause declarations to begin with. So, paradoxically, respect for the wish of a state to invest the court with only restricted jurisdiction may mean more cases in the long run.

An example of a more activist approach to construing a jurisdictional provision can be found in the decision of the SADC Tribunal in *Campbell v. Zimbabwe*, which, in effect, transformed an economic integration court into a human rights court.[88] By reading specific normative contents into Art. 4 of the SADC Treaty, which lists the general principles of the SADC Community, the tribunal considerably expanded the categories of cases subject to its jurisdiction—illustrating thereby the relationship between the breadth of subject-matter jurisdiction and the applicable law. The backlash felt against this decision—which resulted in the suspension of the SADC Tribunal's operations—puts in question the wisdom of the tribunal's pursuit of an expansive interpretation of its legal authority and confirms that under certain political conditions more (jurisdiction) may mean less (cases).

Finally, one may mention the ICC's narrow construction of the complementarity principle—a central jurisdictional condition. This legal strategy has resulted in an increase of the court's legal powers. For example, in *Prosecutor v. Katanga*, the Pre-Trial Chamber held that the principle of complementarity does not apply in cases of complete inaction by the state court, citing policy reasons in support of this view. According to the Pre-Trial Chamber, unless the court adopts such an interpretation:

The Court would be unable to exercise its jurisdiction over a case as long as the State is theoretically willing and able to investigate and to prosecute the case, even though that State has

[87] *Fisheries Jurisdiction (Spain v. Canada)* [1998] ICJ Rep 432, 453.

[88] *Campbell v. Zimbabwe*, SADC case 2/2007, 24–5, <http://www.saflii.org/sa/cases/SADCT/2008/2.html> accessed September 2, 2013. For more discussion of this case, see in this handbook, Romano, Ch. 6, at section 2.1 and Ginsburg, Ch. 22, at section 3.2.2.

no intention of doing so. Thus, a potentially large number of cases would not be prosecuted by domestic jurisdictions or by the International Criminal Court.[89]

The normative agenda of ending impunity was the apparent reason for adopting a narrow interpretation of the conditions for deferring to national courts, which excluded cases of inaction. By limiting complementarity to situations of active investigation or prosecution before national courts, the court increased its legal powers and decreased the risk that some cases would fall between the cracks—that is, outside the power of the court and the actual handling of national courts. It also created a strong incentive for parties interested in invoking the complementarity exception to jurisdiction to take active steps against potential suspects.

Whether an international court embraces a broad or narrow construction of some or all of its jurisdictional provisions, what it should not do is engage in ad hoc case selection when construing general jurisdictional standards. The interpretation and application of jurisdictional provisions and conditions delineate the general powers of the court, thereby reflecting or facilitating a category-based choice of cases. There is no room under such a construction for treating differently similar cases that raise essentially identical jurisdictional problems.

When viewed from this perspective, the ICJ's series of cases on Yugoslavia appears to deserve criticism. Holding in one case that Yugoslavia did not have access to the court when it submitted a case against NATO members because of its non-membership in the statute, but that in another case it could participate as a respondent in two suits brought against it by Bosnia-Herzegovina and Croatia during the same period of time, smacks of improper case-by-case selection in jurisdictional matters. While it may have been politically convenient for the court to dismiss the cases against the NATO member states (whose acts in the Balkans were connected to a humanitarian intervention) and to retain the cases against Yugoslavia in which genocide was alleged, the differences in the application of jurisdictional standards to the same set of facts undermine the court's credibility in applying its own jurisdiction in a consistent manner.[90]

3.2 Exercise of discretion in admissibility decisions

Whereas jurisdiction serves as a category-based filter, rules of admissibility typically allow courts greater latitude to engage in case-by-case selection. The greater flexibility attendant on rules of admissibility is in fact one of the purposes of allowing courts to decline jurisdiction that was properly invested in it. For example, the ICC Prosecutor

[89] *Prosecutor v. Katanga*, ICC Appeals Chamber Judgment of September 25, 2009 (Admissibility), at para. 79.

[90] For a general discussion of the relationship between coherence and legitimacy, see TM Franck, *The Power of Legitimacy Among Nations* (Oxford University Press 1990) 150 *et seq.*

issued in 2007 a policy paper with the following criteria for deciding whether to dismiss cases in the "interests of justice": the gravity of the crime, the interests of victims, the particular circumstances of the accused, and other potential considerations, such as other justice mechanisms and peace processes.[91]

Arguably, the combination of open-ended standards (interests of justice) with a discretionary evaluation of facts offers the Office of the Prosecutor almost unlimited powers of discretion in selecting cases. It stands to reason that the Pre-Trial Chamber, when supervising the "interest of justice" decisions of the Office of the Prosecutor—engaging thereby in review of the admissibility of the cases before the court—would consider similar open-ended factors. For researchers, a key question would be to identify and critically evaluate the actual policy considerations underlying discretionary case selection, as applied in the various courts or families of courts.

One set of policies, which appears to be advanced by discretionary admissibility decisions, pertains to judicial propriety—i.e., the need to conduct judicial business in ways conducive to the preservation of judicial legitimacy. This is sometimes referred to in ICJ case law as protection of the judicial function.

International courts derive much of their legitimacy from the perceived separation between law and politics, and from certain judicial myths, such as complete judicial independence and impartiality and the even-handedness of the legal process. Courts also benefit from their reputation as guardians of the rule of law. However, once a court is faced with a case threatening this set of images and perceptions, then, arguably, it should have the legal power to defend itself from being dragged down a harmful procedural road in response to the parties' abusive tactics. Thus, for example, in its *dicta* in *Free Zones* (1929) the PCIJ opined that the court would be required to preserve its judicial function, even in the face of an agreement to the contrary by the parties seeking to limit its power to pronounce upon the law and subject its judgment to their approval, or requiring it to judge a legal case on the basis of non-legal interests.[92] In another PCIJ case, *Eastern Carelia*,[93] the court refused to provide an advisory opinion, citing inter alia the difficulties associated with adjudicating a dispute (even in the form of advisory proceedings) without the cooperation of one of the parties. Arguably, concerns about the fairness and effectiveness of a one-sided process led the court to resist jurisdiction in that case.[94]

[91] *Policy Paper on the Interests of Justice* (*ICC Office of the Prosecutor*, September 2007) <http://www.icc-cpi.int/NR/rdonlyres/772C95C9-F54D-4321-BF09-73422BB23528/143640/ICCOTPInterestsOfJustice.pdf> accessed July 31, 2013.

[92] *Free Zones of Upper Savoy and the District of Gex (France v. Switzerland)* [1932] (PCIJ Rep Series A/B) No 46, at 161–2.

[93] *Status of Eastern Carelia* [1923] PCIJ Rep Series B No 5.

[94] The case was not followed in subsequent ICJ cases, even those involving serious problems of procedural fairness. Compare *Judgment No. 2867 of the Administrative Tribunal of the International Labour Organization upon a Complaint Filed against the International Fund for Agricultural Development*, Advisory Opinion of February 1, 2012, at para. 44.

Considerations of legality can also affect judicial propriety concerns. This includes, for example, instances where the exercise of jurisdiction by an international court would run against an important international law principle, such as consent to adjudication.[95] It could reflect poorly on the court as a guardian of the rule of law if it were to allow its utilization in a manner that infringes basic international law principles. Still, international courts may have different views on whether or not "rule of law" concerns support a generous application of rules of admissibility, resulting in a decline of jurisdiction. Thus, for example, the ECtHR refused in *Soering v. UK* (1989) a case dealing with extradition of a suspected murderer to the United States to accept an objection to the admissibility claim alleging that adjudication of the conditions on death row in the United States would intrude on the legal rights and interests of the United States, a non-member state.[96] One may argue that the court viewed in the circumstances of the case the harm caused to the principle of consent to adjudication, as applied to third states, outweighed by an even stronger "rule of law" interest—the need to ensure effective protection for the rights of individuals (especially in distasteful death penalty cases).

Admissibility objections may also serve to enhance the ability of international courts to attain their policy goals, such as enhancing their effectiveness.[97] Thus, for example, by declining jurisdiction over manifestly ill-founded applications the ECtHR has been able to focus on the relatively few cases that may contribute to the protection of human rights in Europe. Indeed, Greer notes that the vast majority of cases submitted to the court are rejected as inadmissible, ill-foundedness being the most popular category for case dismissal.[98] A recent case, involving an application of the post-Protocol 14 "insignificant disadvantage" v. "respect for human rights" admissibility balancing test,[99] exemplifies this. In the case, the ECtHR held:

> The Court further observes that the problem of non-enforcement in Romania has been addressed on numerous occasions in its judgments... The examination of this application on the merits would not introduce any new element in this regard (see *Gaftoniuc*, cited above). The Court therefore concludes that respect for human rights as defined in the Convention and its Protocols does not require an examination of the application on the merits.[100]

In other words, effectiveness considerations militate against regarding a hopeless minor case as admissible. Such exercise of judicial power would not, in the circumstances of the case, promote the court's normative aims and should therefore be resisted.

95 See e.g., *Monetary Gold Removed from Rome in 1943 (Italy v. France)* [1954] ICJ Rep 19, 32.

96 *Soering v. UK* (1989) 161 EHRR Series A.

97 See generally, Y Shany, "Assessing the Effectiveness of International Courts: A Goal-Based Approach" (2012) 106 AJIL 225; on effectiveness, see in general in this handbook, Helfer, Ch. 21.

98 S Greer, *The European Convention on Human Rights: Achievements, Problems and Prospects* (Cambridge University Press 2007) 174.

99 ECHR, Art. 35(3)(b).

100 *Savu v. Romania*, ECtHR Decision of November 10, 2011, at paras 29–30.

A similar set of considerations may underlie the resistance employed by some international courts against what appeared to them to be attempts to force upon them fruitless tasks, or tasks fundamentally different from what they were intended to perform.[101] For instance, in the famous *Northern Cameroons* case (1963) the ICJ held:

> The function of the Court is to state the law, but it may pronounce judgment only in connection with concrete cases where there exists at the time of the adjudication an actual controversy involving a conflict of legal interests between the parties. The Court's judgment must have some practical consequence in the sense that it can affect existing legal rights or obligations of the parties, thus removing uncertainty from their legal relations. No judgment on the merits in this case could satisfy these essentials of the judicial function.[102]

Admittedly, it is hard to see why in light of the near empty docket of the court in the 1960s, the court was so concerned about judicial economy. It is therefore possible that other policy considerations were at play. Perhaps, one may speculate, the court wished to avoid the controversies associated with the decolonization process—a concern similar to the one that may have led it three years later to decline jurisdiction in *South West Africa* (invoking lack of merit as a matter of an antecedent character).

Finally, the application of rules of admissibility may also function as a jurisdiction-regulating mechanism, informed by the availability of other dispute settlement or problem-solving forums.[103] For example, in both the *MOX*[104] and *SGS v. Philippines* cases,[105] the existence of legal obligations found in other treaties and contractual provisions directing the disputes to other fora have led the tribunals to stay proceedings (but not to decline jurisdiction—a more drastic measure). Still, international courts tend to retain cases even in the face of jurisdictional competition, where they have a strong institutional interest in doing so. This may be the

[101] See e.g., *Foglia v. Novello* (1981) ECR 3045, at para. 18 ("The duty assigned to the court by Art. 177 [TFEU, Art. 267] is not that of delivering advisory opinions on general or hypothetical questions but of assisting in the administration of justice in the member states. It accordingly does not have jurisdiction to reply to questions of interpretation which are submitted to it within the framework of procedural devices arranged by the parties in order to induce the court to give its views on certain problems of community law which do not correspond to an objective requirement inherent in the resolution of a dispute. A declaration by the court that it has no jurisdiction in such circumstances does not in any way trespass upon the prerogatives of the national court but makes it possible to prevent the application of the procedure under article 177 for purposes other than those appropriate for it").

[102] *Northern Cameroons*, note 81, at 32–3. One might question the staying power of this reasoning, as a number of advisory proceedings that took place before the ICJ can be seen as exercises rather devoid of practical significance. See e.g., *Accordance with international law of the unilateral declaration of independence in respect of Kosovo* [2010] ICJ Rep 403.

[103] See *Minority Schools*, note 84.

[104] *MOX Plant (Ireland v. UK)* (Procedural Order No. 3) June 24, 2003, <http://www.pca-cpa.org/showpage.asp?pag_id=1148> accessed July 31, 2013 (UNCLOS arbitral tribunal).

[105] *SGS v. Philippines*, Decision of January 29, 2004, <http://italaw.com/cases/documents/1019> accessed July 31, 2013 (ICSID arbitral tribunal).

case either because they feel that their exercise of judicial powers is needed for the purpose of protecting the systemic welfare of their regime (the WTO dispute settlement bodies seem to have taken this approach when confronted with calls to decline jurisdiction in favor of regional dispute settlement mechanisms),[106] or because they are keen on preserving their own relevance and judicial business.

4 Conclusion

Lawyers and political scientists seeking to understand the role, function, and potential of international courts must treat jurisdictional questions as an important starting point for studying international adjudication. This is because jurisdictional rules serve as focal points for the expectations of three important constituencies—the mandate providers, the parties to the dispute, and the court itself. Through shaping the jurisdiction of a court, by way of lawmaking, jurisdiction-invocation, and interpretation and application of jurisdictional provisions, these constituencies define the power of international courts and channel the application of judicial power.

Whereas jurisdictional rules define the potential power of the court, rules on admissibility, which I propose to regard as rules authorizing courts to decline to exercise judicial power, allow the translation of general judicial policies, relating to justice, fairness, legality, legitimacy, and effectiveness to specific cases. They therefore offer another rich field for studying the actual policy choice of different international courts.

Research Questions

1. What are the legal-political dynamics explaining the configuration of foundational and specific jurisdiction? What are the legal policies underlying the interpretation of jurisdiction provisions by different international courts?
2. How do differences in judicial goals and policy preferences manifest themselves in judicial decisions on jurisdiction and admissibility?
3. Can any correlations be identified between the scope of jurisdiction, usage rates, and compliance? What are possible explanations for such correlations?

[106] See WTO, *Mexico—Tax Measures on Soft Drinks and Other Beverages—Appellate Body Report* (March 6, 2006) WTO Doc. WT/DS308/AB/R, at para. 46; WTO, *Argentina—Definitive Anti-Dumping Duties on Poultry from Brazil—Panel Report* (April 22, 2003) WTO Doc. WT/DS241/R, at para. 7.42.

4. Do categories matter? Can it be established that the categorization of preliminary objections as jurisdictional objections or admissibility objections of questions of merits having an antecedent nature affect judicial outcomes?

Suggested Reading

Amerasinghe, CF, *Jurisdiction of International Courts* (Brill 2003).

Capps, P et al. (eds), *Asserting Jurisdiction: International and European Legal Perspectives* (Oxford: Hart 2003).

Collier, J and Lowe, V, *The Settlement of Disputes in International Law: Institutions and Procedures* (Oxford University Press 1999).

Fitzmaurice, G, "The Law and Procedure of the International Court of Justice: General Principles and Substantive Law" (1950) 27 British Yearbook of International Law 1.

Merrills, JG, *International Dispute Settlement* (5th edn, Cambridge University Press 2011).

Rosenne, S, *The Law and Practice of the International Court of Justice 1920–2005* (The Hague: Martinus Nijhoff 2006).

Shany, Y, *The Competing Jurisdictions of International Courts and Tribunals* (Oxford University Press 2003).

Shany, Y, "No Longer a Weak Department of Power? Reflections on the Emergence of a New International Judiciary" (2009) 20 EJIL 73.

Thirlway, H, "The Law and Procedure of the International Court of Justice: 1960–1989, Part One" (1989) 27 British Yearbook of International Law 1.

CHAPTER 37

THIRD PARTIES

YAËL RONEN AND

YAEL NAGGAN*

* Dr. Yaël Ronen is Senior Lecturer at Sha'arei Mishpat College in Hod Hasharon, Israel. Yael Naggan is a law graduate of the Hebrew University in Jerusalem.

1 Introduction

The participation of third parties in the proceedings of international court and tribunals serves numerous functions. Primarily, it informs the court of various interests—legal, political, economic, or moral[1]—not presented by the parties. It thus offers a more comprehensive factual and legal picture relating to the dispute, enabling the court to deliver a more harmonious judgment.[2] Third-party participation also alleviates judicial workload by averting the need for multiple litigations and the risk of contradictory judgments. At the same time, it changes the nature of litigation, weakening its adversarial and party-driven character. Parties may find themselves addressing issues which they did not expect to litigate and facing unanticipated adversaries. Third-party participation therefore brings to the fore the tension between two views of the international legal process: as a means for comprehensive conflict prevention[3] and development of international law, and a party-driven mechanism for dispute resolution.

Existing literature on third parties is limited. Christine Chinkin's 1993 *Third Parties in International Law* examined the theory and practice of the main courts active at the time. Chinkin concluded that third-party claims had been infrequently made—and even less frequently upheld—in the ICJ and international arbitration bodies, whereas in regional human rights courts they were a more common phenomenon.[4] This analysis was exceptional in that it considered third-party participation in adjudication in the broader context of third parties in international law. Other literature tends to focus on particular institutions or actors, especially non-state actors. Although Chinkin's study also touched on the evolution of the international legal system into a multi-party one, it dealt little with the reformulation of the adversarial process, which is the focus of this study. Cross-cutting issues have received little attention, as have the commonalities and differences among types of courts or tribunals.

This chapter examines third-party participation in contentious cases in international courts and tribunals. Section 2 discusses third-party participation serving a personal interest in the outcome of the case or in the law that emerges from the case. Section 3 examines a discrete category of interveners, namely victims of human rights violations and international crimes, in international criminal or other proceedings. Section 4 concerns third-party participation in pursuit of a public interest, commonly referred to as *amicus curiae* participation.

[1] CM Chinkin, *Third Parties in International Law* (Oxford: Clarendon Press 1993) 18.

[2] *Sovereignty over Pulau Ligitan and Pulau Sipadan (Indonesia/Malaysia)* (Separate Opinion of Judge ad hoc Weeramantry) [2001] ICJ Rep 630, para. 20.

[3] *Sovereignty over Pulau Ligitan and Pulau Sipadan*, note 2, at para. 21.

[4] Chinkin, note 1, at 275–88.

2 Third Party Intervention Serving a Personal Interest Which May be Affected by the Result of the Particular Case

2.1 The interest served by intervention

Intervention is generally regarded as necessary to protect third-party interests from prejudice by the judgment or the process. Formally, the legal interests of third parties cannot be prejudiced by a process in which they did not participate, because international law does not recognize binding precedent as a source of law. Judicial decisions operate only between the parties and only with respect to the particular case. However, the reality is that the decisions of reputable judicial and arbitral bodies carry weight beyond the confines of particular cases, and serve as guidance both to other judicial bodies and to decision makers.[5] The phenomenon of third-party participation is therefore an acknowledgment of the power of reality over formality.

Some courts accommodate interveners to protect only a legal interest[6] or right,[7] while others also allow intervention to protect other interests—economic, political, social, etc. The focus on legal interests has been criticized for preserving the *status quo ante*, whereas taking into account other interests facilitates cooperative adjustment and development.[8] The interest motivating the intervention must be substantial and closely linked to the case.[9] Moral interests are not generally regarded as sufficient grounds for intervention.[10] In the International Court of Justice (ICJ), a general interest in the development of international law would not

[5] CM Chinkin, "Article 63" in A Zimmermann et al. (eds), *The Statute of the International Court of Justice* (Oxford University Press 2006) 1370–1, 1390–1.

[6] ICJ Statute, Art. 62; ITLOS Statute, Art. 63; ATJ Statute, Art. 72.1; CCJ Agreement, Art. XVIII.1. ACHPR Protocol, Art. 5 refers to "an interest" in general, but ACHPR Rules of Court, Rule 53, requires a "legal interest."

[7] See e.g., UNAT Statute, Art. 6; World Bank AT, Rules of Tribunal, Rule 21.1; OASAT Rules of Procedure, Art. 44; IMF AT, Rule XIV.1.

[8] Chinkin, note 1, at 21.

[9] WTO AB Working Procedures, Art. 24.1; WTO, *EC: Tariff Preferences—Panel Report* (December 1, 2003) WT/DS246/R paras 5.11, 5.46; EGC Rules of Procedure, Art. 115.1.f; EFTA Rules of Procedure, Art. 89.1.e; EACJ Rules of Procedure, Rule 26.2.e; ECOWAS Rules of Court, Art. 89.1.e; ATJ Statute Art. 72.1; CCJ Rules 14.2; CCJA Rules of Procedure, Art. 45.2.f; ASEAN Protocol (2010), Art. 13.1; ICSID Arbitration Rules, Rule 37.2, NAAEC Art. 24.2; CoEAT Statute Art. 10.

[10] See e.g., *Mrs P v. The Commission* (Order of October 4, 1979) [1979] ECR 3299.

ordinarily justify intervention,[11] but other courts are more accommodating. For example, the mandate of the European Court of Human Rights (ECtHR) allows particularly broad intervention (including any person "concerned"),[12] stating that parties to the ECtHR may intervene when the issue under consideration addresses a point of general public international law[13] or may have implications for their legal systems.[14]

In practice, the requirement of a close link to the case is often foregone. In the European Court of Justice (ECJ) the distinction between an interest "in the result of the case," namely in the operative part of the final judgment, and an interest in the success of the arguments, has become blurred. Thus, where a case establishes a principle of general application, a third party affected by the operation may be permitted to intervene.[15] For similar reasons, any World Trade Organization (WTO) member state claiming to have an interest in the outcome of the dispute may take part in the proceedings.[16]

An exceptional right to intervene due to an interest in the development of the law not linked directly to a case is allowed at the ICJ, International Tribunal for the Law of the Sea (ITLOS), Caribbean Court of Justice (CCJ), and Permanent Court of Arbitration (PCA). These courts not only allow intervention but actively solicit it, whenever at issue is the construction of a treaty to which states or organizations[17] other than those concerned in the case are parties.[18] The exclusivity of intervention in treaty interpretation but not in questions of general international law can hardly be justified on normative grounds.[19] It might be justified on practical grounds, namely limiting the number of potential interveners and potential issues, to ensure that intervention does not become unmanageable.

[11] *Continental Shelf (Tunisia/Libyan Arab Jamahiriya)* (Application to Intervene) Judgment, [1981] ICJ Rep 3, para. 33.

[12] ECHR, Art. 36.2.

[13] See e.g., the intervention of Denmark, Estonia, Poland, Portugal, and UK in *Behrami v. France* App No 71412/01 and *Saramati v. France, Germany and Norway*, App No 78166/01 [GC] (Admissibility) (May 2, 2007).

[14] See e.g., Germany's intervention in *Üner v. The Netherlands*, ECHR 2006-IX; D Harris et al., *Law of the European Convention on Human Rights* (Oxford University Press 2009) 854.

[15] KPE Lasok, *The European Court of Justice: Practice and Procedure* (London: Butterworths 1994) 158 (discussing case law).

[16] G Sacerdoti, "The Dispute Settlement System of the WTO: Structure and Function in the Perspective of the First 10 Years" (2006) 5 The Law and Practice of International Courts and Tribunals 49, 60–1.

[17] Intervention by right, under ITLOS Statute, Art. 32.2 and CCJ Agreement, Art. XVIII.3, and by leave under the ICJ Rules of Court, Rule 43.2, 43.3.

[18] ICJ Statute, Art. 63; ITLOS Statute, Art. 32.3; CCJ Agreement, Art. XVIII.3; 1899 Hague Convention Art. 56; 1907 Hague Convention, Art. 84. The ICJ's practice indicates that the right is not absolute. Chinkin, note 1, at 1373. ITLOS Rules of Tribunal, Art. 102 also suggests that the right is not absolute, given that the tribunal can entertain objections to a declaration of intervention.

[19] Chinkin, note 1, at 184–5.

2.2 Who may intervene

If the purpose of intervention is primarily to protect the interests of non-parties, access to the court should be available to anyone reasonably under risk of being directly, substantially, and adversely affected by the proceedings. On the other hand, parties to the litigation should not become excessively burdened by accountability to third parties.[20] Also, third parties should not benefit from intervention to achieve, by indirect means, litigious goals that they cannot achieve directly. Indeed, in most courts, intervention is reserved for those actors who may institute original proceedings.[21]

Intervention by legal and natural persons is often subject to special regulation.[22] Thus, in ITLOS, natural and legal persons may be party to proceedings under Section XI of the Convention on the Law of the Sea, but they may not intervene. In the ECJ and EFTA (European Free Trade Association) Court, individuals may not intervene in cases to which only states or EU organs are parties.[23] On the other hand, in the CCJ and the International Centre for Settlement of Investment Disputes (ICSID), any person may intervene, even though only nationals of contracting states may institute original proceedings.[24] In the African Court on Human and Peoples' Rights (ACtHPR), the Commission, NGOs, and individuals may institute proceedings (the latter two by leave of the court), but may not intervene.[25]

The protection of interests takes exceptional precedence in the ICJ, where states may intervene regardless of whether they have a jurisdictional link to the court.[26] Admittedly, the provision on intervention was originally drafted on the assumption that jurisdiction would be universal and compulsory, but it was deliberately retained in its existing form even when that assumption had proven overly optimistic, making it impossible to argue that its implication is inadvertent.[27] The ICJ and ITLOS also allow intergovernmental organizations to participate in proceedings concerning the construction of their constituent instruments, or of international conventions adopted thereunder.[28]

[20] NAFTA, *Methanex Corporation v. U.S.*, Decision on the Tribunal on Petitions from Third Persons to Intervene as "Amici Curiae," UNCITRAL (January 15, 2001), para. 36.

[21] ITLOS Statute, Arts 20, 31; WTO AB Working Procedures, Art. 10; ECHR, Arts 33, 34, 36.2; ASEAN 2010 Protocol, Arts 1.b, 13; NAFTA Art. 2013; CAS Procedural Rules, Rule 41.4; UNAT Statute, Art. 6.2.d; CoEAT Statute, Art. 10; World Bank AT, Rules 21, 22.

[22] Treaty for the Establishment of the East African Community (adopted November 30, 1999, entered into force, July 7, 2000, amended December 14, 2006 and August 20, 2007) 2144 UNTS 255 (EACJ Treaty), Arts 28–31, 40; ECOWAS Statute, Arts 9.2, 21.

[23] CJEU Statute, Art. 40.

[24] CCJ Agreement, Arts XII, XIII.1; ICSID Convention, Art. 36.1 and Arbitration Rules, Rule 37.2. See also CCJA Rules, Art. 45.1; ATJ Statute, Arts 39, 72.

[25] ACHPR Protocol, Arts 5, 5.2.

[26] *Land, Island and Maritime Frontier Case (El Salvador/Honduras, Nicaragua intervening)* (Application for Intervention) [1990] ICJ Rep 92, paras 100–1.

[27] *Pulau Ligitan*, Separate Opinion, note 2, at para 10.

[28] ICJ Statute, Art. 34.3; ITLOS Rules, Art. 84.3.

In the international criminal tribunals, a state directly affected by an interlocutory decision may request a review of the decision.[29] Provisions on participation of states are relatively numerous in the International Criminal Court (ICC) Statute because the principle of complementarity invites a greater scope of potential involvement of states, especially on issues of jurisdiction and admissibility.[30]

2.3 Object of intervention

Third-party intervention is incidental to the main proceedings; it must not introduce an entirely new dispute, so as not to usurp the original parties' control. At the same time, it is difficult to see why the ability of an interested party to alert the court to what it believes to be its rights[31] should be contingent upon the existing parties' formulation of their own claims.[32] This is especially pertinent in the context of proprietary rights. Distinguishing an intervention in an existing dispute from the introduction of a new case may therefore be difficult, for example, if an intervener claims an interest on grounds unrelated to those asserted by the parties.

Protection of the intervener would be served by allowing a wide range of interventions, including on issues that are peripheral to the main proceedings.[33] An inclusive approach would also advance a more harmonious development of international law. Again, party control and other factors, such as court expertise, militate against over-inclusiveness. In some courts, particularly courts of regional integration,[34] interveners must join interests with a party and submit arguments in support of an already existing claim. This ensures that the parties do not need to face numerous, possibly mutually exclusive, fronts.

Opinions vary on whether the incidental character of third-party participation precludes intervention in preliminary stages.[35] In the ECtHR, intervention formally only follows the declaration of an application admissible,[36] but practice varies.[37] In courts where the intervener must accept the case as it is at the time of intervention, the intervener can only argue against admissibility if the respondent does.[38]

[29] ICTY Rules of Procedure and Evidence 108bis, STL Rules of Procedure and Evidence 178. See also ICTY Rule 105 and SCSL Rule 65.B.

[30] ICC Statute, Arts 18, 19.2. See also Art. 72.4 (addressing national security).

[31] Chinkin, note 1, at 168.

[32] Similarly, see ICJ, *Pulau Ligitan*, Separate Opinion, note 2, at para. 21.

[33] Chinkin, note 1, at 170.

[34] CJEU Statute, Art. 40; EFTA Statute, Art. 36; ATJ Statute, Art. 52.1; ECOWAS Rules, Art. 89.1.e; CCJA, Rule 45.1; EACJ Treaty, Art. 40; but see also CoEAT Statute, Art. 10.2.

[35] S Rosenne (with the assistance of Y Ronen), *The Law and Practice of the International Court, 1920–2005* (4th edn, vol III, Leiden: Brill 2006) 1476; Chinkin, note 1, at 179.

[36] Compare ECHR, Art. 36 with ECHR, Arts 27–8; but see ECHR Art. 29.

[37] *TI v. UK* (Decision), March 7, 2000, ECHR 2000-III.

[38] EACJ, *Prof Peter Anyang' Nyongo and Others v. Attorney General of Kenya and Others*, Reference No 1 of 2006 (March 30, 2007) 13.

Therefore, the intervener cannot remove the dispute from the stage set by the parties.[39]

2.4 Intervention by right or leave

The original parties' control over the ability of a third party to participate finds expression in rules on whether participation is by right or by leave of the court, and on whether these parties can influence the decision of the court. A party's right to respond to the request for intervention secures its substantive interest, without allowing it to deprive a third party of the opportunity to protect its own interests, not even by collusion.

In the ECtHR, both states exercising diplomatic protection and the Commissioner of Human Rights intervene by right. Even in intervention requests by other states or legal and natural persons the parties have no right to respond to the request for intervention.[40] In the WTO, North American Free Trade Agreement (NAFTA), and North American Commission on Environmental Conservation (NACEC), intervention is also by right.[41] At the other end of the spectrum, in the Court of Arbitration for Sport (CAS), intervention is only possible by consent of the parties.[42]

More common, however, is intervention by leave of the court after the parties have had an opportunity to present their view on the request for intervention.[43] A right to respond is also prevalent in courts where interveners must support one of the parties, demonstrating that the extent of party control is not necessarily related to the potential scope of intervention.

In the administrative tribunals, individuals must apply to intervene. However, the tribunals' discretion seems to be limited to determining whether requests are admissible. It appears that the parties do not have a right to react to requests and, therefore, intervention is effectively by right. Intervention of the administration of the international organization in question, where available, characteristically exists

[39] See e.g., ECJ, *CIRFS and Others v. Commission* Case C-313/90 (March 24, 1993), paras 19–22; EFTA, Rules 89.4; 89.5.a; ATJ Statute, Art. 72.3; ECOWAS Rules, Arts 89.4, 89.5.a; CCJA Rules, Art. 45.4; EACJ Rules of Procedure, Rule 36.5.

[40] ECtHR Rules of Court, Rule 44.

[41] WTO Dispute Settlement Understanding, Art. 10.2; NAFTA, Art. 2013; NAAEC, Art. 29. For more on various aspects of third-party participation in the WTO, see L Bartels, "Procedural Aspects of Shared Responsibility in the WTO Dispute Settlement System" (November 27, 2012) University of Cambridge Faculty of Law Research Paper, <http://ssrn.com/abstract=2181526> accessed April 23, 2013.

[42] CAS Procedural Rules, Rule 41.4.

[43] See ICJ Rules, Art. 83.1; ITLOS Rules, Art. 101.1; EGC Rules, Art. 116.1; EFTA Rules, Art. 89.2; EACJ Treaty, Art. 40; ECOWAS Rules, Art. 89.2; CCJA Rules, Art. 45.1.f.1; EACJ, Rule 36.3; ICSID Arbitration Rules 37.2. In the CCJ, the prospective intervener may respond to the parties' responses to the application. CCJ Rules 14.3.1, 14.3.3.

by right.[44] An exception is the International Monetary Fund (IMF) Administrative Tribunal, where the parties are entitled to present their views on the request for intervention, and the tribunal seems to have discretion whether to grant the request. Notably, a successful intervener in this tribunal participates as a party.[45]

2.5 Rights of interveners

The rights of interveners are more limited than those of parties, reflecting the interveners' non-party status and the incidental character of their participation. Interveners are often entitled to receive copies of the parties' pleadings and documents, but such receipt may be partial if documents are confidential.[46] Interveners are also entitled to submit written, and sometimes oral, observations on the subject matter of the intervention.[47] They may not usually rebut the arguments of the parties, present questions, or call witnesses, although in individual cases courts have been willing to go beyond the minimum procedural rights.[48] Some courts determine participatory rights on an entirely case-by-case basis.[49]

To ensure that the parties are not prejudiced by such participation, they are usually entitled to respond to interventions.[50] Some courts have discretion whether to allow responses.[51] In international criminal tribunals, the party upon whose motion the court issued the impugned decision has a right to respond, while the other party may respond if the court deems that the interests of justice so require.[52]

[44] UNAT Rules, Art. 19; CoEAT Statute, Art. 10; World Bank AT Rules 21.1, 21.4, 22.1; OASAT Rules, Arts 44, 46, 48.

[45] IMF AT Rules XIV.3, XIV.4.

[46] ICJ, *Land, Island and Maritime Frontier Case*, note 26, at para. 102; ICJ Rules, Art. 85.1; ITLOS Rules, Art.103.1; WTO Dispute Settlement Understanding, Art. 10.3; EGC Rules, Art. 116.2; EFTA Rules, Art. 89.3; CCJ Rule 14.4.1; CCJA Rules, Art. 45.4; EACJ Rule 36.4; ECOWAS Rules, Art. 89.3; ASEAN 2010 Protocol, Art. 13.2; NAFTA Art. 2013; NAAEC Art. 29; UNAT Rules, Art. 20.2 (allowing intervention by the administration). In some instances, the transmission of documents is subject to the tribunal's discretion. See e.g., UNAT Rules, Art. 19.3; World Bank AT Rule 21.3; OASAT Rules, Art. 47.2.

[47] ICJ Rules, Arts 85.1, 85.3; ITLOS Rules, Arts 103.1, 103.3; WTO DSU, Art. 10.2, 17.4; WTO AB Working Procedure, Art. 24.1; EGC Rules, Arts 116.3, 116.6; EFTA Rules, Arts 89.1, 89.5; CCJ Rule 14.4.2; CCJA Rules, Art. 45.6; EACJ Rule 36.4; ECOWAS Rules, Arts 89.5, 89.7; ASEAN 2010 Protocol, Art. 13.2; NAFTA Art. 2013, NAAEC Art. 29; ECtHR Rule 44.3.a; ACHPR Rules 53.5, 53.6; UNAT Rules Art. 20.2 (with respect to intervention by the administration).

[48] WTO, *EC: Sugar Subsidies (Thailand)—Panel Report* (October 15, 2004) WT/DS283/R, para. 2; WTO, *EC: Bananas (Mexico)—Panel Report* (May 22, 1997) WT/DS27/R/MEX paras 7.6–7.9; ECtHR, *T v. UK*, App no 24724/94 (December 16, 1999), para. 4.

[49] CoEAT Rules of Procedure, Rule 39.2.

[50] ICJ Rules, Art. 85.1; ITLOS Rules, Art. 103.1; CCJ Rule 14.4.3; CCJA Rules, Art. 45.6; EACJ, *Anyang' Nyong'o*, note 38, at 9, 13; ICSID Arbitration Rules 37.2; ECtHR Rule 44.6; ACHPR Rule 53.5.

[51] EGC Rules, Art. 116.5; EFTA Rules, Art. 89.6; ECOWAS Rules, Art. 89.6.

[52] ICTY Rule 108bis; STL Rule 178.

2.6 Binding nature of decision

With very few exceptions, the constitutive instruments and rules of procedure of the various courts are silent on the consequences of intervention. In ITLOS, the East African Court of Justice (EACJ),[53] and the ECJ,[54] the intervener would be bound by the court's decision insofar as the decision relates to the subject matter of the intervention. The statute of the Andean Tribunal of Justice (ATJ) is exceptionally explicit in stating that the intervener would not be bound by the decision.[55] Under ICJ jurisprudence, "the right to be heard…does not carry with it the obligation of being bound by the decision."[56] On the other hand, states intervening in the interpretation or the application of a treaty are bound by the judgment "equally with the parties to the proceedings,"[57] although only "in respect of that particular case."[58]

The practical consequences of the two rules are not, however, dissimilar. Interveners are not parties, and the court does not adjudicate on their own interests directly. The court's decision is therefore unlikely to be operatively directed at them, rendering the question of its binding nature with respect to the particular case moot. Since a decision is only binding with respect to the particular case, the intervener, like the parties, cannot be bound beyond it. However, if third parties are given the opportunity to influence the progression and possibly the outcome of a case, even against the opposition of the parties, it would seem unfair that they benefit from intervention without bearing some corresponding commitment. Hence, it has been suggested that they should lose all claims that conflict with the rights of parties that the judgment may recognize.[59]

2.7 Practice

The ICJ has received half a dozen requests for intervention, and has consented to only three. Two of those concerned boundary disputes.[60] In the third, the ICJ noted,

[53] ITLOS Statute, Art. 31.3; EACJ Rule 36.6. [54] Lasok, note 15, at 153.

[55] ATJ Statute, 72.1.

[56] *Land, Island and Maritime Frontier Case (El Salvador v. Honduras, Nicaragua intervening)* (Merits) [1992] ICJ Rep 351, para. 423.

[57] ICJ Statute, Art. 63.2; ITLOS Statute, Art. 232.3; CCJ Agreement, Art. XVIII.3.

[58] See e.g., ICJ Statute, Art. 59.

[59] *Continental Shelf*, note 11, Separate Opinion of Judge Oda, para. 9; S Rosenne, "The International Tribunal for the Law of the Sea and the International Court of Justice: Some Points of Difference" in R Platzöder and PA Verlaan (eds), *The Baltic Sea: New Developments in National Policies and International Cooperation* (The Hague: Martinus Nijhoff 1996) 211.

[60] *Land, Island and Maritime Frontier Case*, note 26; *Land and Maritime Boundary between Cameroon and Nigeria, Equatorial Guinea Intervening* (Application to Intervene) [1999] ICJ Rep 1029; *Jurisdictional Immunities of the State (Germany v. Italy, Greece intervening)* (Order on Application by the Hellenic Republic for Permission to Intervene) [2011] General List No 143.

inter alia, that neither party objected to the request for intervention.[61] International organizations have accepted invitations to intervene a handful of times, but have never initiated an intervention.[62] Declarations of intervention in the context of treaty interpretation have only been made three times before the ICJ, and only once successfully (in part).[63] There have not been such interventions on the basis of the Hague Conventions under the PCA.[64] In ITLOS there has not yet been any intervention of third parties.

In the WTO DSB, state parties have intervened in more than 200 of the 450 or so cases.[65] Intervention is also a common phenomenon in the practice of the ECJ,[66] with a significant effect on rulings.[67] It has also occurred in the ATJ, CCJ, and EACJ.[68] The ECtHR often allows intervention by states.[69] In the IACtHR, only the Commission and states may institute proceedings, rendering the need for intervention more limited. In the ACtHPR there had been no intervention as of late 2012.

On a number of occasions, states have requested a review of interlocutory decisions in the International Criminal Tribunal for the former Yugoslavia (ICTY), regarding orders to provide documents,[70] and to arrest and surrender.[71] The International Criminal Tribunal for Rwanda (ICTR) has allowed Rwanda to

[61] *Jurisdictional Immunities of the State*, note 60, at para. 6.

[62] P-M Dupuy, "Article 34" in Zimmermann, note 5, at 553–4.

[63] *Haya de la Torre Case* [1951] ICJ Rep 71, 77.

[64] Chinkin, note 1, at 265.

[65] H Horn, L Johannesson, and PC Mavroidis, "The WTO Dispute Settlement System 1995–2010: Some Descriptive Statistics" (2011) IFN Working Paper 891 (Research Institute of Industrial Economics), Table 5; The WTO Dispute Settlement Dataset, updated June 11, 2011 available at: <http://go.worldbank.org/X5EZPHXJYo> accessed August 23, 2013.

[66] Lasok, note 15, at Ch. 5.

[67] CJ Carrubba, M Gabel and C Hankla, "Judicial Behavior under Political Constraints: Evidence from the European Court of Justice" (2008) 102 American Political Science Rev. 435, 449–50.

[68] CCJ, *Trinidad Cement Limited v. The Caribbean Community*, Application No OA 2 of 2009, August 10, 2009 [2009] CCJ 4 (OJ); CCJ, *Trinidad Cement Limited and Another v. The State of the Co-operative Republic of Guyana*, Application No OA 2 of 2009 [2010] CCJ 1 (OJ), March 29, 2010; EACJ, *Anyang' Nyong'o*, note 38; EACJ, *Mtikila v. Attorney General of the United Republic of Tanzania and Others*, Reference No 2 of 2007 (April 25, 2007) <http://www.eacj.org/judgments.php> accessed April 23, 2013. There has been no intervention in the CCJA, <http://www.ohada.org/jurisprudence.html> accessed April 23, 2013. There is no information available regarding ECOWAS. The ASEAN dispute mechanism has never been used. See NUS Centre for International Law, "Dispute Settlement in ASEAN" <http://cil.nus.edu.sg/dispute-settlement-in-asean/> accessed April 23, 2013.

[69] See e.g., The Russian Federation's intervention in *Slivenko v. Latvia* (2004) 39 EHRR 24; Republic of Cyprus in *Djavit An v. Turkey* ECHR 2003-III.

[70] See e.g., ICTY, *Prosecutor v. Milutinović* (Decision on Request of the USA for Review) IT-05-87-AR108Bis.2 (May 12, 2006).

[71] ICTY, *Prosecutor v. Bobetko* (Decision on Challenge by Croatia to Decision and Orders of Confirming Judge) IT-02-62-AR54*bis* & IT-02-62-AR108*bis* (November 29, 2002).

intervene in the proceedings concerning a case referral by the tribunal.[72] In the ICC, both Kenya and Libya have challenged the admissibility of cases.[73]

3 Victims of International Crimes and Violations of International Human Rights Law

3.1 The interests served

Victim participation in international criminal proceedings is a new phenomenon, introduced in the work of the ICC, Extraordinary Chambers in the Courts of Cambodia (ECCC), and the Special Tribunal for Lebanon (STL). This development reflects a shift in international criminal law, emphasizing restorative and not only retributive justice.[74] Enabling victims to articulate their views and concerns is perceived as a necessary mechanism to implement the right to justice.[75] An appreciation of the right of victims to justice has also guided the ECtHR and IACtHR, where it has long been recognized[76] that even when alleged victims were barred from instituting proceedings, they were the true complainants. Where alleged victims do not

[72] The ICTR relied on ICTR Rules of Procedure and Evidence 74, "*amicus curiae*," although it acknowledged Rwanda's "practical interest." *Prosecutor v. Kanyarukiga* (Decision on the Request of the Republic of Rwanda for Leave to Appear as *Amicus Curiae*) ICTR-2002-78-I (November 9, 2007) paras 2, 5.

[73] *Prosecutor v. Gaddafi and Al-Senussi* (Application on Behalf of the Government of Libya Pursuant to Article 19 of the ICC Statute) ICC-01/11-01/11-130-Red (May 1, 2012); *Prosecutor v. Ruto and Others* (Application on Behalf of the Government of the Republic of Kenya Pursuant to Article 19 of the ICC Statute) ICC-01/09-01/11-19 (March 31, 2011).

[74] AAC Trindade, *The Access of Individuals to International Justice* (Oxford University Press 2011) 201–2; ICC, Report of the Court on the Strategy in Relation to Victims, ICC-ASP/8/45 (November 10, 2009) ("ICC Strategy") paras 2–4; K Ambos, "The Structure of International Criminal Procedure: 'Adversarial,' 'Inquisitorial' or Mixed?" in M Bohlander (ed.), *International Criminal Justice: A Critical Analysis of Institutions and Procedures* (London: Cameron May 2007) 446–7.

[75] ICC, *Prosecutor v. Katanga and Chui* (Decision on the Set of Procedural Rights Attached to Procedural Status of Victim at the Pre-Trial Stage of the Case) ICC-01/04-01/07-474 (May 13, 2008), paras 31–2, 38.

[76] JE Méndez, "The Inter-American System of Protection: Its Contributions to the International Law of Human Rights" in S Power and G Allison (eds), *Realizing Human Rights: Moving from Inspiration to Impact* (New York: St. Martin's Press 2000) 133–4.

benefit from specific arrangements for participation, they can access the court on the same terms as other interveners.[77]

Victims participate in the international criminal tribunals by right, provided that certain factual conditions are fulfilled.[78] In practice, the tribunals enjoy a wide measure of discretion, with the ICC determining the stages of participation that are "appropriate" and the STL considering whether such participation would "be in the interest of justice."[79]

While victims align with the prosecution in seeking the conviction of the defendant, their interests might not entirely coincide with those of the prosecution. For example, in *Lubanga*, the victims and ICC Prosecutor were in dispute over the characterization of the conflict. The court accepted the victims' arguments, and subsequently the charges were amended to include war crimes committed during an international armed conflict.[80] Victims thus redefined the contours of the dispute between the parties. At the same time, the obligations of the prosecutor or the court to respond to victims' views have yet to be elucidated.[81]

3.2 Who may participate as a victim

Victims are defined, for procedural purposes, as natural persons who have suffered harm—be it physical, mental, emotional, or material—as a direct result of the commission of the crimes charged in the case.[82] The ICC, and subsequently the STL, also recognize as participating victims natural persons who

[77] See, e.g. *T v. UK*, note 48. Victims failed to intervene in the ECOWAS *Habré* proceedings—probably because under ECOWAS Protocol, only states may intervene. Ruling: *Hissein Habré v. République du Sénégal*, Role General No ECW/CCJ/APP/07/08, Arrêt No ECW/CCJ/JUD/06/10 (November 18, 2010), paras 3–4.

[78] ICC Statute 68.3; ICC Strategy, note 74, para 45; ECCC Internal Rules, Rule 23.2; STL, *Prosecutor v. Ayyash and Others* (Decision on Victims' Participation in the Proceedings) STL-11-01/PT/PTJ (May 8, 2012), paras 91, 98, 101.

[79] ICC Statute, Art. 68.3; STL Rule 86.B.x.

[80] ICC, *Prosecutor v. Lubanga* (Decision on the Confirmation of Charges), ICC-01/04-01106-803 (January 29, 2007).

[81] S Zappalà, "The Rights of Victims v. the Rights of the Accused" (2010) 8 Journal of International Criminal Justice 137, 142.

[82] *Prosecutor v. Lubanga* (Redacted version of "Decision on indirect victims") ICC-01/04-01/06-1813 (April 8, 2009), para. 52; *Prosecutor v. Abu Garda* (Decision on the 34 Applications for Participation at the Pre-Trial Stage of the Case) ICC-02/05-02/09-121 (September 25, 2009), paras 12–13; ECCC Rule 23bis.1.b; STL Rule 2. For a critique of the reference to harm in the context of participatory rights, see Zappalà, note 81, at 154–7. The ICC also recognizes as victims organizations that have sustained direct harm to non-commercial property. See ICC Rules of Procedure and Evidence, Rule 85.b; *Prosecutor v. Lubanga* (Judgment Pursuant to Article 74 of the Statute) ICC-01/04-01/06-2842 (March 14, 2012), para. 17 (recognizing a school as a victim).

have suffered indirect harm.[83] This expansion has been lauded as correct in light of the impact of international crimes on third persons,[84] notwithstanding the fact that it significantly broadens the possible number of participants. Notably, in the ICC and STL victims may only participate if their personal interests are potentially affected by the proceedings.[85] The meaning of "personal interests" has not been clarified, and in fact may shift during the process.[86] Under the IACtHR, a victim is a person whose rights under the American Convention on Human Rights, or another treaty of the Inter-American System, have allegedly been violated.[87]

3.3 Rights of participating victims

Victim participation presents two main challenges to securing the right of the accused to a fair trial.[88] Substantively, it implies that certain crimes were committed in given circumstances, and that certain people were the victims, thereby undermining the presumption of innocence.[89] Practically, the participation of numerous alleged victims is likely to place a heavy burden on the tribunal, both in terms of financial and human resources.[90] This tension is reflected in the statutes of all the relevant tribunals, which emphasize that victim participation shall be permitted "in a manner which is not prejudicial to or inconsistent with the rights of the accused and a fair and impartial trial."[91] In the ICC and ECCC, as well as in the IACtHR, alleged victims may participate (in that capacity) at all stages of the proceedings. In the STL, victim participation follows the confirmation of an indictment.[92]

[83] ICC Rule 85; STL Rule 2; STL, *Ayyash*, note 78, paras 23, 39–45, 49–50, 59; but see ICC, *Prosecutor v. Lubanga* (Decision on Victims' Participation), ICC-01/04-01/06-1119 (January 18, 2008) Dissenting Opinion of Judge Pikis, para. 3.

[84] K Ambos, "The First Judgment of the International Criminal Court (Prosecutor v. Lubanga): A Comprehensive Analysis of the Legal Issues" (2012) 12 Intl. Crim. L. Rev. 115, 117.

[85] ICC Statute, Art. 68.3; ICC, *Lubanga*, Victims' Participation, note 83, para. 86; STL Statute, Art. 17.

[86] R Cryer et al., *An Introduction to International Criminal Law and Procedure* (Cambridge University Press 2010) 481.

[87] IACtHR Rules, Art. 2.33. [88] Ambos, note 84, at 116. [89] Zappalà, note 81, at 146–7.

[90] Ambos, note 84, at 116.

[91] ICC Statute, Art. 68.3; STL Statute, Art. 17; and similar wording in Law on the Establishment of the Extraordinary Chambers in the Courts of Cambodia for the Prosecution of Crimes Committed during the Period of Democratic Kampuchea, Art. 33.

[92] ICC Statute, Arts 68.3, 15.3, 19.3; *Prosecutor v. Lubanga* (Judgment on the appeal of Mr. Thomas Lubanga Dyilo against the decision of Pre-Trial Chamber I entitled "Décision sur la demande de mise en liberté provisoire de Thomas Lubanga Dyilo") ICC-01/04-01/06-824 (February 13, 2007) paras 38, 45; ECCC Rule 23; IACtHR Rules, Art. 25.1; STL Rule 86.A.

Legal representation is an important tool in maintaining the balance between the victims' right to effective participation[93] and the rights of the accused.[94] In the ICC, participating victims are entitled to legal representation.[95] In the ECCC and STL, legal representation is obligatory,[96] as is the case for multiple alleged victims in the IACtHR.[97] In all four institutions, the court may arrange for common representation where it is necessary to ensure the effectiveness of the proceedings while maintaining the distinct interests of the victims.[98]

Particular attention has been given to the relationship between victim and witness status, to ensure that victim participation does not adversely affect the rights of the defense.[99] Since victims receive privileged information, the genuineness of their testimony as witnesses may be undermined.[100] The ECCC prohibits concurrent victim and witness status altogether,[101] and the STL discourages it.[102] The ICC has clarified that participating victims who testify as witnesses do not accrue rights beyond those of persons who are solely victims or witnesses.[103] To safeguard the rights of the accused, the defense may cross-examine them.[104]

The criminal tribunals allow victims to receive notifications[105] and documents,[106] and to make written and oral submissions.[107] The ICC and ECCC also allow participation in hearings, including closed ones.[108] Victims may invite and question experts.[109] The ECCC allows victims to appeal various decisions.[110] The STL allows victims to file motions and participate actively in the appeal.[111] Beyond that, the rights of participating victims have been decided largely on a case-by-case basis. Thus, the ICC has allowed

[93] ICC, *Prosecutor v. Lubanga* (Decision on the Request by Victims a/0225/06, a/0229/06 and a/0270/07 to Express their Views and Concerns in Person and to Present Evidence during the Trial) ICC- 01/04-01/06-2032-Anx (June 26, 2009), para. 26.

[94] STL, *Ayyash*, note 78, at para. 102.iii; see also, ICC, *Lubanga*, Judgment, note 82, at para. 14.ix.

[95] ICC Rule 90; ICC, *Lubanga*, Judgment, note 82, at para. 14.ix.

[96] ECCC Rule 23ter.1; STL Rule 86.C.ii. The STL pre-trial judge may authorize otherwise.

[97] IACtHR Rules, Art. 25.2.

[98] ICC Rule 90.1, 90.2; ECCC Rule 23ter, 23quater; STL Rule 87.C.ii, 87.D; IACtHR Rules, Art. 25.2.

[99] ICC, *Lubanga*, Victims' Participation, note 83, at para. 134.

[100] Zappalà, note 81, at 142, 146–7, 151–2.

[101] ECCC Rule 23.4.

[102] STL Rule 86.B.v, 150.D provides an exception when a Chamber decides that the interests of justice require that a victim give evidence. See STL, *Ayyash*, note 78, at para. 102.i.

[103] In *Lubanga*, three individual victims and a school were authorized to testify. Judgment, note 82, at paras 19, 21.

[104] ICC, *Prosecutor v. Katanga and Chui* (Decision on the Modalities of Victim Participation at Trial) ICC-01/04-01/07-1788 (January 22, 2010), paras 86–7.

[105] ICC Rule 91, ECCC Rule 67.5.

[106] STL Rule 87.A.

[107] ICC Rule 91, ECCC Rule 12ter.6.

[108] ICC, *Lubanga*, Victims' Participation, note 83, at para. 113; ECCC Rules 91.2, 94.1, 94.2.

[109] ICC Rule 91; ECCC Rule 31.10; STL Rule 87.B.

[110] ECCC Rule 74.4.

[111] STL Rules 87.B, 87.C.

victims to receive confidential documents,[112] to call and question witnesses, to tender evidence,[113] and to participate anonymously, albeit in a limited manner.[114]

On the one hand, the ICC has expressed a preference for a systematic approach to ensure that victim participation is not prejudicial to or inconsistent with the rights of the accused,[115] such as equality before the law. On the other hand, the court has noted that in order to ensure a fair and impartial trial, it must consider applications "on their individual merits, balancing a wide variety of factors that will include the requirements and circumstances of the trial as a whole."[116] This prevarication is not surprising, given that the terms of participation are strongly linked to the object of participation, which has not yet received comprehensive analysis.[117]

3.4 Practice

By the end of 2010, some 860 out of more than 2,300 applications for victim participation had been approved in the ICC.[118] In *Lubanga*, 129 individual victims were authorized to participate in the pre-trial and trial proceedings.[119] In the ECCC, fewer than 100 victims participated in *Duch*, the court's first trial, while more than 3,000 victims have been authorized to participate in the second trial.[120] The STL has thus far approved 58 out of 73 applications submitted.[121]

[112] See e.g., *Prosecutor v. Abu Garda* (Decision on Victims' Modalities of Participation at the Pre-Trial Stage of the Case) ICC-02/05-02/09-136 (October 6, 2009), paras 13–15; *Lubanga*, Victims' Participation, note 83, at para. 106.

[113] *Prosecutor v. Lubanga* (Judgment on the Appeals of the Prosecutor and the Defence against Trial Chamber I's Decision on Victims' Participation of January 18, 2008) ICC-01/04-01/06-1432 (July 11, 2008), paras 86–105; but see the partly dissenting opinions by Judge Pikis, at paras 7–9, 14–15 and Judge Kirsch, at paras 6–15, 24, 30. See also ECCC Rule 80.2; STL Rules 87.A, 87.B.

[114] *Lubanga*, Victims' Participation, note 83, at paras 130–1; *Katanga*, Decision on Procedural Rights, note 75, at paras 182–3; *Katanga*, Victim Participation, note 104, at paras 92–3.

[115] *Katanga*, Decision on Procedural Rights, note 75, at paras 49–50.

[116] *Lubanga*, Decision on the Request by Victims, note 93, at para. 27.

[117] Cryer et al., note 86, at 485.

[118] Registry and Trust Fund for Victims Fact Sheet, RC/ST/V/INF.3 (June 1, 2010); *Prosecutor v. Nourain and Jamus* (Decision on Victims' Participation at the Hearing on the Confirmation of the Charges) ICC-02/05-03/09-89 (October 29, 2010).

[119] ICC, *Lubanga*, Judgment, note 82, at para. 15.

[120] S Horovitz, "Victim Participation in International Criminal Tribunals" in F Pocar and L Carter (eds), *International Criminal Procedure: The Interface of Civil Law and Common Law Legal Systems* (Massachusetts: Edward Elgar 2013) 166.

[121] STL, *Ayyash*, note 78.

4 Third Party Intervention Serving a Public Interest—*Amicus Curiae*

4.1 The interest served

Broadly defined, *amici curiae* are natural or legal persons who, without being parties to the case, submit their views to the court on matters of fact and law, in the pursuit of a public interest related to the subject matter of the case, such as human rights and environmental protection.[122] *Amicus curiae* participation is usually granted to bodies that have particular expertise that might contribute to the court's deliberations.[123] More often than not they are NGOs. Thus, *amici curiae* are not disinterested actors. Their goal, however, is to introduce public interest considerations into the decision—and indirectly, to impact the development of international law—rather than to affect the outcome of the specific case. The interests represented by *amicus curiae* briefs may differ from those of the parties.[124]

Amicus curiae participation presents particular challenges in international commercial arbitration, where, together with consensualism, confidentiality and privacy of proceedings have traditionally been the main attractions.[125] International investment arbitration, however, has undergone a notable transformation. Citing the hybrid public-private nature of this arbitration, NAFTA and ICSID, in 2001 and 2005, respectively, declared their willingness to receive *amicus curiae* briefs. In a sharp departure from former stances, they have welcomed the transparency that *amicus curiae* participation entails.[126]

Amicus curiae participation is formally regulated in most courts and tribunals,[127] while others have accepted *amicus curiae* briefs on the basis of their residual

[122] O De Schutter, "Sur l'émergence de la société civile en droit international: le rôle des associations devant la Cour européenne des droits de l'homme," (1996) 7 EJIL 72; KF Gomez, "Rethinking the Role of Amicus Curiae in International Investment Arbitration: How to Draw the Line Favorably for the Public Interest" (2012) 35 Fordham Intl. L. J. 510, 543–4.

[123] ICSID, *Aguas Argentinas, S.A. et al v. The Argentine Republic*, Case No ARB/03/19, Order in Response to a Petition for Transparency and Participation as *Amicus Curiae* (May 19, 2005), para. 24.

[124] ICSID, *Biwater Gauff (Tanz.) Ltd. v. United Republic of Tanzania*, Case No ARB/05/22, Award, PP 1–3 (July 24, 2008), para. 359.

[125] Gomez, note 122, at 526.

[126] Respondent in NAFTA, *Methanex*, note 20, at paras 17, 19; ICSID, *Aguas Argentinas*, note 123, at paras 19–21. See also UNCITRAL, Settlement of Commercial Disputes: Preparation of a Legal Standard on Transparency in Treaty-Based Investor-State Arbitration, Note by the Secretariat, UN Doc A/CN.9/WG.II/WP/166, July 29, 2011.

[127] ICJ Statute, Art. 34.2 (limited to intergovernmental organizations); ITLOS Statute, Arts 84.1, 84.2; WTO DSU Art. 13; ICSID Arbitration Rule 37.2.a; CAS Procedural Rules 41.4; Iran–US Claims Tribunal Rules of Procedure, Rule 15 note 5; ECHR Art. 36.2; IACtHR Rules, Arts 2.3, 44; ACHPR Rule 45.1; ICC Rules 103, 149; ICTY Rule 74; ICTR Rule 74; SCSL Rule 74; STL Rule 131; ECCC Rule 33; UNAT Rules, Art. 23.1, 23.2; World Bank AT Rule 25.2; IMF AT Rule XV.

powers.[128] *Amicus curiae* participation, more than intervention in the pursuit of personal interests, demonstrates the transformation of the judicial process from a bilateral to a public one.

4.2 Rights of *amici curiae*

Amicus curiae participation is always subject to the discretion of the court. Practice differs on whether it extends to preliminary stages. The EACJ has allowed an *amicus curiae* to argue no cause of action,[129] while the NAFTA tribunal stated that participation at the preliminary stage was inappropriate.[130] The PCA has also refused to accept *amicus curiae* briefs concerning its jurisdiction.[131]

In WTO panels, ECtHR and IACtHR, ICSID and NAFTA, *amicus curiae* briefs may refer to questions of both fact and law,[132] while in the ACtHPR they may only address facts.[133] In the ICTY and WTO Appellate Body, they may only refer to questions of law.[134] In the ECtHR and international criminal tribunals, *amicus curiae* briefs may only address issues specified by the court.[135] Participation is primarily in writing, although oral participation is not excluded.[136] In ICSID and NAFTA, requests for access to hearings have generally been denied,[137] so as to protect the confidentiality of the proceeding. Since *amicus curiae* participation is intended to provide useful information to the court, but not to obtain information from the parties,[138] *amici curiae* are not routinely served with papers or other relevant documents,[139] and cannot examine or cross-examine witnesses.[140]

[128] As demonstrated by the practice of the WTO, ICSID, and NAFTA, see section 4.2 of this chapter.

[129] EACJ, *Anyang' Nyong'o*, note 38, at 13.

[130] NAFTA, *United Parcel Service of America Inc and Government of Canada*, Decision of the Tribunal on Petitions for Intervention and Participation as *Amici Curiae* (October 17, 2001) para. 71.

[131] PCA, *Chevron Corporation (USA) and The Republic of Ecuador*, Case No 2009-23 Procedural Order No 8 (April 18, 2011) para. 20.

[132] D Zagorac, "International Courts and Compliance Bodies: The Experience of Amnesty International" in T Treves et al. (eds), *Civil Society, International Courts and Compliance Bodies* (The Hague: TMC Asser 2005), 25; IACtHR Rules, Art. 2.3.

[133] ACHPR Rule 45.1.

[134] ICTY, "Information concerning the Submission of *Amicus Curiae* Briefs," IT/122 (March 27, 1997) para. 5.b; WTO AB Working Procedures, Art. 17.6.

[135] D Shelton, "The Participation of Nongovernmental Organizations in International Judicial Proceedings" (1994) 88 AJIL 611, 634–5; ICTY Rule 74; ICTR Rule 74; ICC Rule 103; SCSL Rule 74.

[136] ECtHR Rule 44.3.a; IACtHR Rules, Art. 2.3; ICTY "*Amicus Curiae*," note 134, para. 5.a; ICC Rule 103.1; STL Rule 131.A; Iran–US Claims Tribunal Rule 15, note 5.

[137] Gomez, note 122, at 553.

[138] Letter from ICSID Secretary of the Tribunal entitled "Piero Foresti, Laura de Carli and others v. Republic of South Africa (ICSID Case No ARB(AF)/07/1)" (October 5, 2009).

[139] But see IMF AT Rule XV, exceptionally allowing *amici curiae* to receive the parties' pleadings.

[140] Shelton, note 135, at 612.

Despite the importance of ensuring due process, not all courts and tribunals allow the parties to respond to *amicus curiae* briefs. Such an opportunity exists in some international criminal tribunals[141] and in arbitral tribunals.[142] These tribunals emphasize that the guiding principle in determining the terms of participation of *amici curiae* is the need to ensure "that the parties are treated with equality and that at an appropriate stage of the proceedings each party is given a reasonable opportunity of presenting its case,"[143] and to minimize the additional burden on both the parties and the tribunal while giving the tribunal the benefit of the views of suitable *amici curiae* in appropriate circumstances.[144] In the IACtHR, *amicus curiae* briefs are provided to the parties "for their information."[145]

4.3 Practice

There has been practically no *amicus curiae* participation in the ICJ,[146] which, as a matter of general policy, is reluctant to expand the dispute beyond the limits proscribed by the parties. There has also not been any *amicus curiae* participation in ITLOS. In its 2004 session, the tribunal discussed the matter of *amicus curiae* but decided that it was premature to develop guidelines on the matter.[147] In 2010, the tribunal received an *amicus curiae* statement from two NGOs requesting to participate in advisory proceedings, but decided not to consider the statement part of the documentation in the case.[148]

WTO instruments explicitly empower only the panels to solicit *amicus curiae* briefs. However, in 1998 in *US-Shrimp*, the WTO Appellate Body concluded that the panels, as well as the Appellate Body, may accept unsolicited *amicus curiae* briefs.[149] This ruling was severely criticized, particularly by developing states,[150] but with time has become less controversial. By 2012, the WTO Appellate Body had accepted 21 of

[141] ICTY *"Amicus Curiae,"* note 134, paras 5.c, 5.e; ICC Rule 103.2; STL Rule 131.B; ECCC Rule 33.2. See also World Bank AT Rule 25.2.

[142] NAFTA, Statement of the Free Trade Commission on Non-disputing Party Participation, para. 5. These tribunals generally reserve the discretion to decide on the terms of participation upon consultation with the parties. NAFTA, *United Parcel Service*, note 130, para. 72.

[143] UNCITRAL Arbitration Rules (as revised in 2010) Art. 17.1.

[144] ICSID, *Aguas Argentinas*, note 123, para. 15. [145] IACtHR Rules, Art. 44.3.

[146] Chinkin, note 1, at 227; Dupuy, note 62, at 551.

[147] ITLOS, Annual report of the International Tribunal for the Law of the Sea for 2004, SPLOS/122 (March 30, 2005), para. 41.

[148] ITLOS, Annual Report of the International Tribunal for the law of the Sea for 2010, Doc SPLOS/222 (April 4, 2011), para. 34.

[149] *US—Import Prohibition of Certain Shrimp and Shrimp Products—AB Report* (October 12, 1998) WT/DS58/AB/R.

[150] Their concern was that since such briefs entail additional expenditure, they would give an unfair advantage to developed states; and that they would strengthen the position of NGOs, commonly perceived as unsympathetic to the policies of developing states.

39 briefs submitted to it in 15 proceedings, although it has not expressly stated that it had relied upon any of these submissions for its findings.[151] The EACJ, in contrast, has explicitly expressed agreement with the *amici curiae*,[152] and has even highlighted that they "very ably and conscientiously assisted the Court without any attempt to side with any other party in the reference. The Court, as a friend of the *amicus curiae*, was guided accordingly."[153] *Amicus curiae* briefs have been accepted in ICSID from both states and NGOs.[154] The pertinent provision on *amicus curiae* briefs has also been invoked in the Iran–US Claims Tribunal by both Iran and the United States as the non-arbitrating parties, as well as by non-state actors, albeit infrequently.[155] The PCA has also received requests for *amicus curiae* participation.[156]

The ECtHR is liberal in permitting *amicus curiae* participation, mostly of human rights organizations.[157] *Amicus curiae* briefs are submitted in relatively few cases,[158] but they are often mentioned in judgments.[159] The data tentatively suggest a correlation between *amicus curiae* participation and a finding by the court that violations of human rights had occurred.[160] The IACtHR accepted *amicus curiae* briefs as early as its first contentious case,[161] and has never refused an *amicus curiae* request.[162] Briefs have been submitted in about one-third of its cases,[163] but the impact of these briefs is uncertain as the IACtHR rarely refers to them explicitly in its reasoning.

The ICTY and ICTR have accepted and sought *amicus curiae* on legal issues[164] —a practice that began as early as the jurisdiction phase of the first case to be heard by the

[151] G Marceau and M Hurley, "Transparency and Public Participation: A Report Card on WTO Transparency Mechanisms" (2012) IV Trade, Law and Development 19, 29–31.

[152] EACJ, *Attorney General of Kenya v. Independent Medical Legal Unit*, Appeal No 1 of 2011 (March 15, 2012), 12.

[153] EACJ, *Calist Mwatela and Others v. East African Community*, Application No 1 of 2005 (October 2006), 24.

[154] See e.g., Costa Rica and Nicaragua in *Commerce Group Corp and San Sebastian Gold Mines, Inc. and The Republic of El Salvador*, Case No ARB/09/17 (February 21, 2011), paras 39–40.

[155] NAFTA, *Methanex*, note 20, para. 32. For practice, see Chinkin, note 1, at 265 fn 63.

[156] PCA, *Chevron Corporation (USA)*, note 131.

[157] See also *Pretty v. UK* 35 EHRR 1, where the Catholic Bishops' Conference of England was permitted to make written submissions on the moral issues underlying euthanasia.

[158] LH Mayer, "NGO Standing and Influence in Regional Human Rights Courts and Commissions" (2010) 36 Brook. J. of Int'l. L. 911, 924.

[159] Shelton, note 135, at 635.

[160] Shelton, note 135, at 637. For a discussion of the impact of Amnesty International in particular, see Zagorac, note 132, at 21–6.

[161] *Velásquez Rodríguez Case*, Judgment, Inter-American Court of Human Rights Series C No 4 (July 29, 1988), para. 34.

[162] Shelton, note 135, at 638. [163] Mayer, note 158, at 930.

[164] D Mundis, "Amicus Curiae" in A Cassese (ed.), *The Oxford Companion to International Criminal Justice* (Oxford University Press 2009) 243.

ICTY.[165] Some of these briefs have been particularly influential,[166] especially in *Akayesu*, where an *amicus curiae* brief by 45 organizations had a role in the prosecutor's decision to amend the charges to include rape and sexual violence.[167] The ICC has both allowed the submission of *amicus curiae* briefs[168] and solicited them.[169]

5 Conclusion

In the *Pulau Ligitan* case, Judge ad hoc Weeramantry predicted, with respect to third-party participation in international adjudication, that "[t]he closely interknit global society of tomorrow will see a more immediate impact upon all States of relations or transactions between any of them, thus enhancing the practical importance of this branch of procedural law."[170] Yet reality is much more humble. Third-party intervention, of any kind, has not become a prominent phenomenon, and certainly not one which threatens the functioning of courts and tribunals.

Reluctance to allow third-party participation is particularly apparent in inter-state courts dealing with political issues. In the WTO and courts of economic integration and cooperation, third-party participation is more prevalent. On a regional level, third party participation is particularly common in Europe, where judicial activity of all kinds is much more robust than in other regions. While some formal provisions on third-party participation have remained dead letters, certain courts

[165] *Prosecutor v. Tadić* (Appeals Chamber Decision on the Defence Motion for Interlocutory Appeal on Jurisdiction) IT-94-1 (October 2, 1995), paras 7, 50. For appointment of *amicus curiae* to replace the prosecutor in cases of conflict of interests, see ICTY Rule 77; STL Rule 134.c.ii; SCSL Rule 77.c.iii.

[166] H Woolaver and S Williams, "The Role of the Amicus Curiae Before International Criminal Tribunals" (2006) 6 International Criminal Law Review 151.

[167] J Razzaque, "Changing role of friends of the court in the International Courts and Tribunals" (2001) 1 Non-State Actors and International Law 169, 188–90. For an exceptional use of *amicus curiae* in a case involving self-representation by the accused, see *Prosecutor v. Krajišnik* (Decision on Krajišnik's Request to Self-Represent, on Counsel's Motions in relation to Appointment of *Amicus Curiae*, and on the Prosecution Motion of February 16, 2007) IT-00-39-A (May 11, 2007).

[168] See e.g., *Prosecutor v. Bemba Gombo* (Decision on Request for Leave to Submit *Amicus Curiae* Observations Pursuant to Rule 103 of the Rules of Procedure and Evidence) ICC-01/05-01/08-451 (July 17, 2009); *Prosecutor v. Gaddafi and al-Senussi* (Lawyers for Justice in Libya and Redress Trust's Observations Pursuant to Rule 103 of the Rules of Procedure and Evidence) ICC-01/11-1/11-172 (June 8, 2012).

[169] Situation in Darfur, ICC-02/05, Decision Inviting Observations in Application of Rule 103 of the Rules of Procedure and Evidence (July 24, 2006).

[170] ICJ, *Pulau Ligitan*, note 2, at para. 1.

and tribunals, such as the WTO, NAFTA, ICSID, and the IACtHR, have developed procedures for third-party participation through jurisprudence, especially for *amicus curiae*.

The intensification of third-party participation reflects the broadening of issues regulated by international law, which leads to overlaps and intersection among legal relationships. It also reflects the expanding range of non-state participants, in particular NGOs and individuals. It constitutes an element in the gradual but perceptible evolution of international law from a system of multiple sets of *inter partes* arrangements to a comprehensive, multi-layered legal order.

Nonetheless, the significance of third party participation is critically understudied. There have been a few studies on the impact of third-party participation in the courts of the European Union and the WTO from a political science perspective.[171] Data on the matter is sparse, but more crucially, the substantive impact of third-party participation remains to be explored at depth.

Research Questions

1. What is the substantive impact of third-party participation on the decisions of courts and tribunals? Does it direct the argumentation or reasoning of decisions in any particular way? Should this question be asked by reference to particular types of courts, parties, or issues?
2. The statutes of courts and tribunals are at best laconic as to the effects of decisions on intervening third parties. Are third parties legally bound by decisions and should they be? Is their future conduct prejudiced by their participation? Should it be?
3. The significance of victim participation in international criminal proceedings has not been elucidated. What does the obligation of prosecutors and courts to take them into account consist of? What are, and should be, the consequences for not doing so?
4. Courts have expressed different opinions as to the implications of third-party participation being ancillary to the proceedings, for such participation to address preliminary issues and take place in preliminary stages. This issue merits unpacking and clarification.

[171] Carrubba, Gabel, and Hankla, note 67, and sources cited there; ML Busch and E Reinhardt, "Three's a Crowd: Third Parties and WTO Dispute Settlement" (2006) 58 World Politics 446.

Suggested Reading

Bonafé, BI, "Interests of a Legal Nature Justifying Intervention before the ICJ" (2012) 25 LJIL 739.

Brabandere, de, E, "NGOs and the Public Interest: The Legality and Rationale of Amicus Curiae Interventions in International Economic and Investment Disputes" (2011) 12 Chicago Journal of International Law 85.

Chinkin, CM, *Third Parties in International Law* (Oxford: Clarendon Press 1993).

Schutter, de, O, "Sur l'émergence de la société civile en droit international: le rôle des associations devant la Cour européenne des droits de l'homme" (1996) 7 EJIL 372.

Lasok, KPE, *The European Court of Justice: practice and procedure* (London: Butterworths 1994).

McGonigle Leyh, B, *Procedural Justice?—Victim Participation in International Criminal Proceedings* (Antwerp: Intersentia 2011).

Mayer, LH, "NGO Standing and Influence in Regional Human Rights Courts and Commissions" (2010) 36 Brooklyn Journal of International Law 911.

Rosenne, S, *Intervention in the International Court of Justice* (Dordrecht: Martinus Nijhoff Publishers 1993).

Woolaver, H and Williams, S, "The Role of the Amicus curiae before International Criminal Tribunals" (2006) 6 International Criminal Law Review 151.

Zappalà, S, "The Rights of Victims v. the Rights of the Accused" (2010) 8 Journal of International Criminal Justice 137.

CHAPTER 38

INHERENT POWERS IN INTERNATIONAL ADJUDICATION

CHESTER BROWN*

* Professor of International Law and International Arbitration, Faculty of Law, University of Sydney. The views expressed in this chapter are strictly personal and do not necessarily reflect the views of any organizations or institutions with which the author is presently or has in the past been affiliated.

1 Introduction

The existence of "inherent powers" is a controversial issue in international adjudication. A number of international courts and tribunals have asserted the existence of and exercised such powers, and the existence of inherent powers also has doctrinal support.[1] However, other international courts and tribunals, parties to international proceedings and writers variously contend that they do not exist, or that they are extremely limited, and may be exercised only in "compelling circumstances."[2] In addition, Professor Thirlway invokes concerns relating to the legitimacy of international courts and tribunals asserting inherent powers—and overreaching their proper function—when he argues:

> When jurisdiction is referred to, it must always be asked, "jurisdiction to do what?" Jurisdiction or competence is not, in the sense in which those terms are used in relation to a dispute, a general property vested in the court or tribunal contemplated: it is the power, conferred by the consent of the parties, to make a determination on specified disputed issues which will be binding on the parties because that is what they have consented to.[3]

Such concerns, which are related to criticisms of judicial lawmaking by international courts and tribunals,[4] would appear to be heightened by the fact that when international courts have asserted inherent powers, they have rarely sought to provide any justification for their authority to do so, or indicated the limits (if any) on the exercise of such powers.

[1] See, e.g, M Paparinskis, "Inherent Powers of ICSID Tribunals: Broad and Rightly So" in T Weiler and I Laird (eds), *Investment Treaty Arbitration and International Law* (New York: JurisNet 2012) 11; C Brown, *A Common Law of International Adjudication* (Oxford University Press 2007) 55–82; C Brown, "The Inherent Powers of International Courts and Tribunals" (2005) 76 British Yearbook of International Law 195, 197 (and in particular the sources cited in fn 11); P Gaeta, "The Inherent Powers of International Courts and Tribunals" in LC Vohrar et al. (eds), *Man's Inhumanity to Man: Essays on International Law in Honour of Antonio Cassese* (Alphen aan den Rijn: Kluwer Law International 2003) 353.

[2] See, e.g., *Lehigh Valley Railroad Company (US v. Germany)* (Sabotage Claims) (1933) 8 RIAA 160, 170 (international tribunals do not have inherent powers); *Hrvatska Elektroprivreda v. Slovenia*, ICSID Case No ARB/05/24, Ruling of May 6, 2008, para. 14 (Slovenia's contention that international courts do not have authority to grant the requested relief); *Rompetrol Group NV v. Romania*, ICSID Case No ARB/06/3, Decision of the Tribunal on the Participation of a Counsel (January 14, 2010), para. 16 (the asserted inherent power can only be exercised in "compelling circumstances"); see also *LaGrand (Germany v. United States)*, Counter-Memorial of the United States, paras 138–65 available at <www.icj-cij.org> accessed July 31, 2013 (the United States' submissions on the International Court of Justice's lack of power to order binding provisional measures.)

[3] H Thirlway, "The Law and Procedure of the International Court of Justice 1960–1989: Part Nine" (1998) 69 British Yearbook of International Law 1, 6, 21; see also, in this handbook, Besson, Ch. 19, at section 4.

[4] See also, in this handbook, von Bogdandy and Venzke, Ch. 23; and Alvarez, Ch. 8, at section 4.

In light of this controversy, the purpose of this chapter is to consider the existence and source of inherent powers, and from this, to identify their scope of application and any limitations on their use. It commences with a general introduction to the sources of law relevant to international procedure (section 2). It then turns to a consideration of inherent powers as they are exercised by domestic courts and tribunals, and examines the validity of some objections to the extension of this doctrine to international adjudication proceedings (section 3). It then provides several illustrative examples of the exercise of inherent powers by international courts (section 4). In determining the scope of inherent powers, it is important to identify their source; four possible sources are considered, before the conclusion is reached that the proper source of inherent powers lies in the necessity for international courts and tribunals to fulfil their functions (section 5). These functions are then examined, and it is argued that the functions of international courts and tribunals that most frequently justify the exercise of inherent powers are the settlement of international disputes and the proper administration of international justice. It is noted that the limitations of these functions likewise restrict the assertion of inherent powers (section 6). The significance of this chapter is the establishment of a sound juridical basis for the exercise of inherent powers, which can be used by international courts faced with procedural issues for which their constitutive instruments and rules make no provision.

2 Sources of Procedural Law in International Adjudication

As inherent powers are usually asserted in the context of the procedural law applicable before international courts, it is appropriate to begin with a general inquiry into the sources of those norms. In the past, writers have expressed uncertainty about those sources,[5] but it is convenient to begin with Art. 38 of the Statute of the International Court of Justice (ICJ), which is widely regarded as having general application to international courts and tribunals.[6] This of course provides in part

[5] H Thirlway, "Procedural Law and the International Court of Justice" in V Lowe and M Fitzmaurice (eds), *Fifty Years of the International Court of Justice* (1996) 389; see also H Thirlway, "Procedure of International Courts and Tribunals" in R Bernhardt (ed.), *Encyclopedia of Public International Law vol III* (Heidelberg: Max Planck Institute for Comparative Public Law and International Law 1992) 1128.

[6] E.g., I Brownlie, *Principles of Public International Law* (7th edn, Oxford University Press 2008) 4–5; M Virally, "The Sources of International Law" in M Sørensen (ed.), *Manual of Public International Law*

that the ICJ shall apply "international conventions," international custom "as evidence of a general practice accepted as law," general principles of law and as subsidiary means for determining the rules of law, "judicial decisions and the teachings of the most highly qualified publicists of the various nations."[7]

Of these sources of law, it is apparent that some are more important than others. The constitutive instruments of most international courts and tribunals are "international conventions," so it is appropriate to begin with such instruments, which are the product of state consent. These instruments usually provide for certain procedural rules, and also confer certain powers on international courts. A well-known power is, for example, the competence of each international court to determine the extent of its own jurisdiction, or the *compétence de la compétence*.[8] Other powers that are often expressly conferred by constitutive instruments include the power to grant provisional measures,[9] the power to permit the intervention of third parties,[10] the power to give an interpretation of judgments and awards,[11] and the power to revise judgments and awards.[12]

While the constitutive instruments set out the framework of the procedure applicable before each international court and tribunal, they do not always make detailed provisions for the procedural powers of the international court they establish. In drafting the Statute of the Permanent Court of International Justice ("PCIJ") in 1920,[13] for instance, the Advisory Committee of Jurists did not make any concerted effort to establish the procedure to be applied by the PCIJ. Instead the Committee decided that most questions of procedure should be left to the PCIJ itself,[14] and included Art. 30 in the PCIJ Statute, which conferred on the PCIJ the power to frame rules of procedure.[15] The ICJ has retained this power in Art. 30 of

(London: Macmillan 1968) 116, 121–2; JL Brierly, *The Law of Nations* (6th edn, Oxford: Clarendon Press 1963) 56.

7 Statute of the International Court of Justice (ICJ Statute), Art. 38(1).

8 E.g., ICJ Statute, Art. 36(6); Convention for the Settlement of Investment Disputes between States and Nationals of Other States (ICSID Convention), Art. 41(1); Convention for the Protection of Human Rights and Fundamental Freedoms (European Convention), Art. 32(2).

9 E.g., ICJ Statute, Art. 41; ICSID Convention, Art. 47; American Convention on Human Rights (American Convention), Art. 63(2).

10 E.g., ICJ Statute, Arts 62–3; ECtHR, Art. 36; Understanding on Rules and Procedures Governing the Settlement of Disputes (DSU), Art. 10(2). See, in this handbook, Ronen and Naggan, Ch. 37, at section 1.

11 E.g., ICJ Statute, Art. 60; ICSID Convention, Art. 50; American Convention, Art. 67.

12 E.g., ICJ Statute, Art. 61; ICSID Convention, Art. 51.

13 Statute of the Permanent Court of International Justice (PCIJ Statute). PCIJ Ser D, (No 1), 7 (1926).

14 PCIJ/Advisory Committee of Jurists, *Procès-Verbaux of the Proceedings of the Advisory Committee of Jurists, July 16th–July 24th 1920* (1920) 247–8.

15 PCIJ Statute, Art. 30.

the ICJ Statute, and other international courts also have this power.[16] In addition, most international courts have an express power to make procedural orders for the conduct of the proceedings.[17]

The constitutive instruments and the rules of procedure of international courts thus provide the usual point of departure for a discussion of the powers of international courts. Yet, such instruments do not necessarily make exhaustive provision for the procedural law or the procedural powers of such courts and may contain gaps, or *lacunae*. First, *lacunae* may be found where an issue has deliberately not been addressed by the drafters of the instrument.[18] Second, even if the negotiators of the constitutive instruments of international courts seek to establish a comprehensive set of procedural rules and manage to reach complete agreement on the powers accorded to the court, such drafters can never completely envisage the circumstances that might arise in the future.[19] Third, constitutive instruments may simply contain ambiguities. These might be inadvertent, or ambiguous language may be intentionally included as an alternative to omitting any reference to a matter on which the negotiating parties have not been able to reach agreement.[20] Faced with *lacunae* in their constitutive instruments over procedure and remedies, a review of international jurisprudence demonstrates that international courts have resorted to other sources of law, such as customary international law, general principles of law, and judicial decisions, so long as these do not contradict their constitutive instrument.[21] And in addition to these sources of procedural norms, international courts have also relied on a more controversial source of law relating to procedure; that is, the exercise of powers that are not conferred on them by their constitutive instruments. It is to a consideration of these powers—known as "inherent powers"—that this chapter now turns.

3 Inherent Powers Generally

The adjective "inherent" is used to describe something which "exist[s] in something as a permanent attribute or quality; forming an element, esp. a characteristic or essential element of something; belonging to the intrinsic nature of that which is

[16] ICJ Statute, Art. 30; see also Statute of the International Tribunal for the Law of the Sea (ITLOS), Art. 16; European Convention, Art. 26(d); American Convention, Art. 60; and DSU, Art. 17(9).

[17] See, e.g., ICJ Statute, Art. 48; ITLOS Statute, Art. 27; DSU, App 3, para. 11; ICSID Convention, Art. 44.

[18] See, e.g., E Gordon, "The World Court and the Interpretation of Constitutive Treaties" (1965) 59 AJIL 94, 804–5; H Lauterpacht, "Restrictive Interpretation and the Principle of Effectiveness in the Interpretation of Treaties" (1949) 26 British Yearbook of International Law 48, 53.

[19] Gordon, note 18, at 803.

[20] Gordon, note 18, at 810–13.

[21] See especially Brown, "Inherent Powers," note 1, at 199–205.

spoken of."[22] An "inherent power" might thus be said to be one that derives from an office, position, or status.[23] An inherent power of a court might, then, derive "from its nature as a court of law."[24] As a source of judicial power, "inherent powers" appear to have their origin in the practice of English courts, which have invoked their inherent jurisdiction to exercise certain procedural powers and to protect their process from being abused "from early times."[25] The exercise of inherent powers has, however, not been limited to English courts, with the courts of other common law countries claiming "inherent powers" in a myriad of instances. These courts have, for instance, variously invoked inherent powers to make rules of court and practice directions,[26] to prevent abuse of the court's process,[27] to stay proceedings[28] and to exercise control over persons before them, including persons who are in contempt of court.[29] While the use of inherent powers is certainly more prevalent in common law countries, the exercise by courts of jurisdictional powers not expressly provided for in legislation or statutory rules is not unknown in civil law countries.[30]

Despite the widespread exercise of inherent powers by domestic courts, there appears to be no consensus on the source of these powers.[31] Two views can be discerned in the literature and case law. On one view, only "superior" courts—which owe their existence not to any statute, but to the exercise of the sovereign's prerogative—can exercise inherent powers.[32] According to another view, however, all courts endowed with a particular jurisdiction have those powers, which are necessary to enable them to act effectively.[33] It is unnecessary to resolve this dispute, which remains contested, but it is suggested that the latter view appears more accurately to reflect the reality.[34]

[22] *Oxford English Dictionary* (1933 edn) vol. V, 293.

[23] *Black's Law Dictionary* (abridged 7th edn, 2000) 953.

[24] IH Jacob, "The Inherent Jurisdiction of the Court" (1970) 23 Current Legal Problems 23, 24; on the inherent powers of domestic courts generally, see also JA Jolowicz, "Practice Directions and the Civil Procedure Rules" (2000) 59 Cambridge Law Journal 53; and MS Dockray, "The Inherent Jurisdiction to Regulate Civil Proceedings" (1997) 113 Law Quarterly Review 120.

[25] *Metropolitan Bank v. Pooley* (1885) 10 App Cas 210, 220–1 (Lord Blackburn); see also Jacob, note 24, at 25–27; and *Connelly v. DPP* [1964] AC 1254, 1301.

[26] Jolowicz, note 24; Jacob, note 24, at 33–7; e.g., *Thomas v. Arn*, 474 US 140, 146–7 (1985); *Connelly v. DPP* [1964] AC 1254, 1347; *Practice Direction (Trials in Middlesex)* [1958] 1 WLR 1291.

[27] *Connelly v. DPP* [1964] AC 1254, 1301; *R v. Forbes; ex parte Bevan* (1972) 127 CLR 1, 7–8; *Taylor v. Taylor* (1979) 143 CLR 1, 6; *Re Regina and Unnamed Person* (1985) 20 CRR 188, 190–1; *Emilia Shipping Inc v. State Enterprise for Pulp and Paper Industries* [1991] 2 MLJ 379.

[28] *R v. Duval* [1995] 3 NZLR 202, 205; *Spiliada Maritime Corporation v. Cansulex* [1987] AC 460, 476.

[29] *Connelly v. DPP* [1964] AC 1254, 1301; *R v. Forbes; ex parte Bevan* (1972) 127 CLR 1, 7; *Young v. United States*, 481 US 787, 793 (1987); *Re Regina and Unnamed Person* (1985) 20 CRR 188, 190–1.

[30] Brown, "Inherent Powers," note 1, at 206, fn 71; and Jacob, note 24, at 23; compare Gaeta, note 1, at 365.

[31] Dockray, note 24, at 120.

[32] See, e.g., Jacob, note 24, at 27–8.

[33] See, e.g., *Connelly v. DPP* [1964] AC 1254, 1301 (Lord Morris of Borth-y-Gest).

[34] Brown, "Inherent Powers," note 1, at 207.

Before turning to the practice of international courts, it should be observed that certain theoretical objections have been made to the exercise of inherent powers by international adjudicative bodies, in addition (and, indeed, related) to the expressions of concern regarding "legitimacy" which have been noted above. Such objections are based on the fundamental differences that exist between the functions of national courts and international courts.[35] The first objection is that, in contrast to national courts, international tribunals do not have unlimited compulsory jurisdiction, and the second (related) objection is that the international instruments that establish international courts are constitutive of their powers; accordingly, such courts can only exercise those powers which are expressly conferred, and for them to do otherwise lacks legitimacy.[36] But in response to the first objection, arguably, the method of creation of a particular jurisdiction does not necessarily explain the legal effects of that jurisdiction.[37] As for the second objection, it can be said that just because the constitutive instrument of one international court contains an express power where another does not, this "should not be used to justify, *a contrario*, a failure to develop necessary or desirable rules of general international law."[38] In any event, these theoretical objections are simply not borne out by substantial judicial and arbitral practice.

4 Inherent Powers in International Adjudication

Inherent powers have been asserted in the practice of many international courts. The ICJ discussed the nature of its inherent powers most extensively in its judgment in the *Nuclear Tests* case of 1974, where it held that:

[T]he Court possesses an inherent jurisdiction enabling it to take such action as may be required, on the one hand, to ensure that the exercise of its jurisdiction over the merits, if

[35] See, e.g., H Lauterpacht, *Private Law Sources and Analogies of International Law* (London: Longmans, Green & Co 1927) 84–5; Thirlway, note 3, at 21; see also S Rosenne, *The Law and Practice of the International Court 1920–1996* (Alphen aan den Rijn: Kluwer 1997) 528–9.

[36] See, e.g., Thirlway, note 3, at 6.

[37] A Orakhelashvili, "The Concept of International Judicial Jurisdiction: A Reappraisal" (2003) 3 Law and Practice of International Courts and Tribunals 501, 505.

[38] J Crawford, "International Law as an Open System" in J Crawford (ed.), *International Law as an Open System: Selected Essays* (London: Cameron May 2002) 17, 35.

and when established, shall not be frustrated, and on the other, to provide for the orderly settlement of all matters in dispute.[39]

Other international courts and tribunals have also exercised inherent powers. So, the ICSID Tribunal in *Hrvatska Elektroprivreda v. Slovenia* held in 2008:

[A]s a judicial formation governed by public international law, the Tribunal has an inherent power to take measures to preserve the integrity of the proceedings.[40]

The Appeals Chamber of the Special Tribunal for Lebanon (STL) has also acknowledged that it has inherent powers, and explained the concept in 2010 as:

[T]he power...to determine incidental legal issues which arise as a direct consequence of the procedures of which the Tribunal is seized by reason of the matter falling under its primary jurisdiction. This inherent jurisdiction arises as from the moment the matter over which the Tribunal has primary jurisdiction is brought before an organ of the Tribunal.... The inherent jurisdiction is thus ancillary or incidental to the primary jurisdiction and is rendered necessary to ensure a good and fair administration of justice.[41]

And the Iran–United States Claims Tribunal held in 2011:

[T]he Tribunal accepts that an international arbitral tribunal, such as the present one, possesses certain inherent powers. Inherent powers "are those powers that are not explicitly granted to the tribunal but must be seen as a necessary consequence of the parties' fundamental intent to create an institution with a judicial nature." It has been suggested that "the source of the inherent powers of international courts and tribunals is their need to ensure the fulfilment of their functions."[42]

In pursuance of their inherent powers, international courts have on many occasions exercised powers not expressly conferred on them. In addition, international courts have exercised powers which are contained in their constitutive instruments, but have noted that in doing so, they are exercising inherent powers, lending weight to the suggestion that such provisions really do no more than declare the existence of powers which international courts already possess.[43]

Perhaps the most well-known example of an inherent power is the *compétence de la compétence*, the power of the court to determine the extent of its own jurisdiction. International tribunals have from the earliest days of modern international arbitration

[39] *Nuclear Tests (Australia v. France)* [1974] ICJ Rep 253, 259–260 (references omitted); see also *Nuclear Tests (New Zealand v. France)* [1974] ICJ Rep 457, 463 (references omitted).

[40] *Hrvatska Elektroprivreda v. Slovenia*, ICSID Case No ARB/05/24, Ruling (May 6, 2008) para. 33.

[41] Decision on Appeal of Pre-Trial Judge's Order Regarding Jurisdiction and Standing of November 10, 2010 (CH/AC/2010/2, Special Tribunal for Lebanon, Appeals Chamber), para. 45.

[42] *Iran v. United States* (Iran–US Claims Tribunal, Decision Ruling on Request for Revision by Iran of July 1, 2011, Decision No DEC 134-A3/A8/A9/A14/B61-FT), para. 59 (footnotes omitted), citing D Caron, L Caplan, and M Pellonpää, *The UNCITRAL Arbitration Rules: A Commentary* (Oxford University Press 2006) 915; and Brown, "Inherent Powers," note 1, at 228.

[43] See, e.g., G Fitzmaurice, *The Law and Procedure of the International Court of Justice* (Cambridge: Grotius Publications 1986) 451–7.

found that they have this power. For instance, the two American-appointed commissioners in the *Betsey* case, an arbitration under Article VII of the *Jay Treaty* of 1794,[44] filed separate opinions in which they defended the power of the right of the majority of the Commission to determine its jurisdiction, even though that power was not expressly provided for in the *Jay Treaty*.[45] In 1872, the *Alabama Arbitrations*, conducted under the Treaty of Washington,[46] also provided some support for the existence of this power,[47] and subsequent arbitral and judicial decisions have provided clearer authority.[48] And in 1953, the ICJ confirmed the inherent nature of the power in *Nottebohm*, where it stated that "[a]n international tribunal has the right to decide as to its own jurisdiction and has the power to interpret for this purpose the instruments which govern that jurisdiction."[49] The ICJ added that although the ICJ Statute provided in Art. 36(6) for this power, it possessed the power as an inherent power; this was because Art. 36(6) of the ICJ Statute merely adopted "a rule consistently accepted by general international law in the matter of international arbitration."[50] The *compétence de la compétence* has been recognized in the jurisprudence of many other international courts.[51]

International courts have also exercised many other procedural powers as inherent powers, including the powers to frame rules of procedure, make procedural orders, and devise procedures for matters not contemplated in their constitutive instruments.[52] Specific examples include the power to rule on counterclaims,[53] the power to make site visits,[54] the power to order the preparation of an independent expert report,[55] the power

[44] Treaty of Amity, Commerce and Navigation (Jay Treaty) (signed November 19, 1794, entered into force October 28, 1795) 12 Bevans 13.

[45] See, eg, the account in JB Moore, *History and Digest of the International Arbitrations to which the United States has been a Party* (Vol III, Washington D.C.: US Government Printing Office 1898) (hereinafter referred to as "Moore"), 2277–91 (Opinion of Commissioner Gore), 2291–2303 (Opinion of Commissioner Pinkney).

[46] Treaty of Washington, signed May 8, 1871, (GB–US), 61 British Foreign and State Papers 40, 12 Bevans 170 (entered into force June 17, 1871).

[47] Moore, note 45, at 624–46; compare the observations of I Shihata, *The Power of the International Court to Determine Its Own Jurisdiction* (The Hague: Nijhoff 1965) 18–19.

[48] E.g., *Rio Grande Irrigation and Land Company (UK v. US)* (1923) 6 RIAA 131, 135–6; *Interpretation of the Greco-Turkish Agreement*, PCIJ Rep, Ser B, (No 16), 20 (1928).

[49] *Nottebohm (Liechtenstein v. Guatemala)* [1953] ICJ Rep 111, 119–120; on this point, see also *Norwegian Loans (France v. Norway)* [1957] ICJ Rep 9, 34, 44 (Sep Op Sir Hersch Lauterpacht).

[50] *Nottebohm (Liechteinstein v. Guatemala)* [1953] ICJ Rep 111, 119.

[51] E.g., WTO, *US—Anti-Dumping Act of 1916—Report of the Appellate Body* (August 28, 2000) WT/DS136/AB/R, para. 54, fn 30; see also WTO, *Mexico—Corn Syrup (Article 21(5))—Report of the Appellate Body* (October 22, 2001) WT/DS132/ABR/RW, paras 35–7; WTO, *Mexico—Taxes on Soft Drinks—Report of the Appellate Body* (March 6, 2006) WT/DS308/AB/R, para. 45; *Ivcher Bronstein v. Peru*, IACtHR Series C No 54, paras 31–3 (September 24, 1999); *Marks & Umann v. Iran* (1985) 8 Iran-USCTR 290, 296–7; *Klöckner v. Cameroon* (Annulment) (1985) 114 243, 251–2; *Prosecutor v. Dusko Tadic* (1996) 35 ILM 32, 40.

[52] Brown, "Inherent Powers," note 1, at 211–22.

[53] E.g., ICJ Rules, Art. 80.

[54] E.g., *Diversion of Water from the Meuse* (1937) PCIJ Rep Series A/B No 70, at 9.

[55] See, e.g., *Lighthouses Arbitration* (1956) 12 RIAA 155, 228–9, 245, 256–7.

to issue practice directions,[56] and the power to hear preliminary objections regarding the court's jurisdiction and admissibility separately from the merits.[57] The PCIJ's dictum in *Mavrommatis Palestine Concessions* on this last question aptly describes the powers of international courts to make decisions over procedural issues that are not expressly provided for:

> Neither the Statute nor the Rules of Court contain any rule regarding the procedure to be followed in the event of an objection being taken *in limine litis* to the Court's jurisdiction. The Court therefore is at liberty to adopt the principle which it considers best calculated to ensure the administration of justice, most suited to procedure before an international tribunal and most in conformity with the fundamental principles of international law.[58]

Other procedural powers exercised by international courts in the course of judicial proceedings have been asserted to be inherent, such as the power to grant provisional measures. In *E-Systems, Inc v. Iran*, the Iran–US Claims Tribunal held that it had "an inherent power . . . to conserve the respective rights of the parties and to ensure that this Tribunal's jurisdiction and authority are made fully effective";[59] the Inter-American Court of Human Rights made a similar finding in *Velásquez Rodríguez*.[60] International courts and tribunals have also recognized that they possess inherent powers which relate to the post-adjudication phase, such as the powers of rectification, interpretation, and revision.[61]

The foregoing section is not an exhaustive review of the exercise of inherent powers in international adjudication.[62] Rather, it has merely sought to illustrate their existence in several notable situations. In light of this practice, and in order to ascertain when international courts can exercise such powers and what the limitations are on their exercise, there is a need to arrive at a proper understanding of their source.

[56] See, e.g., ICJ Practice Directions of October 31, 2001, April 4, 2002, July 30, 2004, December 13, 2006, and January 30, 2009, at <www.icj-cij.org> accessed November 11, 2012.

[57] *Mavrommatis Palestine Concessions (Greece v. UK)* (1924) PCIJ Rep Series A No 2, 1, at 16.

[58] *Mavrommatis Palestine Concessions*, note 57.

[59] *E-Systems, Inc. v. Iran* (1983) 2 Iran-USCTR 51, 57; see also *Rockwell International Systems, Inc v. Iran* (1985) 2 Iran-USCTR 310, 311; *Ford Aerospace and Communications Corporation v. Air Force of Iran* (1984) 6 Iran-USCTR 104, 108–9.

[60] *Velásquez Rodríguez* (1989) 28 ILM 291, 302. For earlier examples, see *Veerman v. Germany* (1957) 25 ILR 522, 523; and *Scheidt v. Germany* (1957) 25 ILR 555; *Trail Smelter (US v. Canada)* (1938) 3 RIAA 1911, 1934–7; *Gramophone Co Ltd v. Deutsche Grammophon AG*, 1 TAM 857, 859 (Ang-Ger MAT, 1922); *Honduras/Nicaragua (Treaty of Corinto signed January 20, 1902)* [1902] *US Foreign Relations* 881.

[61] See, e.g., *Continental Shelf (Revision and Interpretation)* [1985] ICJ Rep 192, 198 (power of rectification); *Ringeisen (Interpretation)* (1972) ECtHR Series A No 16, 8 (power of interpretation); and *Effect of Awards of Compensation* [1954] ICJ Rep 47, 55 (power of revision).

[62] For further examples, see Brown, "Inherent Powers," note 1; Paparinskis, note 1.

5 Source of Inherent Powers

Despite the rich practice of international courts and tribunals in asserting inherent powers, such bodies have typically failed to articulate clearly what they consider to be the source of those powers.[63] In its dictum in *Nuclear Tests*, the ICJ arguably indicated three different sources of its "inherent jurisdiction":

Such inherent jurisdiction, on the basis of which the Court is fully empowered to make whatever findings may be necessary for the purposes just indicated, derives from the mere existence of the Court as a judicial organ established by the consent of states, and is conferred upon it in order that its basic judicial functions may be safeguarded.[64]

The ICJ first states that its inherent jurisdiction derives from "the mere existence of the Court as a judicial organ." This suggests any judicial organ possesses inherent powers. The ICJ then appears immediately to contradict this assertion with the statement that the inherent jurisdiction is "conferred upon it," which does not sit comfortably with the idea of an "inherent power." If a power is "inherent," then there should be no need for any conferral. And the ICJ then goes on to state that the inherent jurisdiction exists in order to safeguard "its basic judicial functions." This suggests the inherent jurisdiction derives from the existence of expressly conferred functions and powers, and that the inherent powers exist in order to ensure that the expressly conferred powers can be performed. In addition to these sources noted by the ICJ, a fourth possible source of inherent powers is the concept of "general principles of law."

There is a degree of overlap between these sources and some of the distinctions between them may seem artificial. Nevertheless, it is important to distinguish these possible sources in order to identify the most appropriate justification for the exercise of inherent powers in international adjudication. This is because it is the source of inherent powers that provides guidance on any limitations that might exist to restrict the exercise of such powers.

5.1 General principles of law

In a few cases, international tribunals have explained the inherent character of a power by pointing to the existence of a "general principle of law" specifically providing for such a power.[65] For instance, in *Genie Lacayo (Judicial Review)*, the

[63] See, e.g., Gaeta, note 1, at 354–5, 358–61; E Lauterpacht, "'Partial' Judgments and the Inherent Jurisdiction of the International Court of Justice" in V Lowe and M Fitzmaurice (eds), *Fifty Years of the International Court of Justice* (Cambridge: Grotius Publications 1996) 465, 477, 483.

[64] *Nuclear Tests (Australia v. France)* [1974] ICJ Rep 253, 259–60.

[65] See also Gaeta, note 1, at 359.

IACtHR held that it had an inherent power to revise its judgments, noting that this finding accorded with "the general principles of both domestic and international procedural law."[66] In another example, the PCIJ held, in the context of its power to indicate provisional measures, that there was a general principle of law that parties must abstain from actions which would prejudice the rights that are the subject of proceedings.[67] Some writers have adopted this approach in an effort to explain the source of some inherent powers, such as the *compétence de la compétence*,[68] as lying in general principles of law.

This basis for the existence of inherent powers is attractive, and does provide a sound explanation for the exercise of some inherent powers by international courts. But general principles of law are unlikely to provide a basis for all cases where international courts seek to exercise an inherent power. This is because there are relatively few general principles that are widely applicable in domestic legal orders and do not always relate to the existence of procedural powers. Moreover, when international courts invoke procedural powers that are not expressly conferred on them, they have only rarely done so by reference to a general principle of law.

5.2 Implied powers

Another possible basis for the exercise of inherent powers can be found in the doctrine of implied powers. This doctrine essentially rests on the canon of treaty interpretation known as *effet utile*, according to which the terms of treaties, including the powers of international institutions, are to be interpreted so as to make them effective rather than ineffective.[69] This principle has been applied on numerous occasions by international courts, typically in the context of the powers of international organizations,[70] but also, on occasion, in order to ensure the effective exercise of their own functions. One such example can be found in the judgment of the ICJ in the *LaGrand* case, where the court applied the principle of effectiveness in determining that its provisional measures had binding force.[71]

The doctrine of implied powers certainly has some appeal as a justification for the exercise of inherent powers. Yet to regard inherent powers as being identical with

[66] *Genie Lacayo (Judicial Review)*, IACtHR Series C No 45, para. 9 (September 13, 1997).

[67] *Electricity Company of Sofia and Bulgaria* (1938) PCIJ Rep Series A/B No 79, 194, 199.

[68] E.g., B Cheng, *General Principles of Law as Applied by International Courts and Tribunals* (first published 1953, Cambridge: Grotius Publications 1987 edn) 275–8.

[69] E.g., R Gardiner, *Treaty Interpretation* (Oxford University Press 2008) 159–61; H Lauterpacht, *The Development of International Law by the International Court* (Cambridge: Grotius Publications 1958) 227–8.

[70] E.g., *Reparation for Injuries* [1949] ICJ Rep 174, 182; see also *Certain Expenses* [1962] ICJ Rep 151, 168; *Effect of Awards of Compensation* [1954] ICJ Rep 47, 56–8; *Legality of the Use by a State of Nuclear Weapons (WHO Request)* [1996] ICJ Rep 66, 78–9.

[71] E.g., *LaGrand* (2001) 40 ILM 1069, 1093.

implied powers is not entirely accurate, for the doctrine of implied powers is really no more than a manifestation of the principle of effectiveness in treaty interpretation.[72] Martins Paparinskis explains the distinction between inherent powers and implied powers as follows:

> [T]he former concept relates to the nature of the powers, while the latter explains the manner of their exposition in the particular instrument. Inherent powers may be either implied or expressly set out. For example, rules on competence-competence, interim protection, preliminary objections and intervention are inherent and expressly set out in the Statute of the ICJ. Similarly, implied powers may be inherent judicial powers. However, they can also relate to any other interpretative exercise applying the principle of effectiveness to identify powers not expressly set out.[73]

It follows that the doctrine of implied powers is not the best explanation of the source of inherent powers in international adjudication.

5.3 Nature of international courts as judicial bodies

In some cases, international courts have found they have inherent powers simply because the relevant powers are usually attributed to "judicial bodies," and this view has also attracted the support of writers.[74] The ICJ certainly included this basis in its dictum in *Nuclear Tests*, where it said, inter alia, that its inherent jurisdiction "derive[d] from the mere existence of the Court as a judicial organ established by the consent of states."[75] And in *Effect of Awards of Compensation*, in considering whether judgments issued by the United Nations Administrative Tribunal were final, the ICJ described that body, by reference to its statute, in the following terms:

> [T]hese provisions and the terminology used are evidence of the judicial nature of the Tribunal. Such terms as "tribunal," "judgment," competence to "pass judgment on applications," are generally used with respect to judicial bodies.[76]

The ICJ also observed that such provisions "are of an essentially judicial character and conform with rules generally laid down in statutes or laws issued from courts of justice."[77]

However, the judicial character of international courts and tribunals is also less than satisfactory as a source of their inherent powers. In particular, it is a circular argument to maintain that courts and tribunals can exercise certain powers, simply

72 Paparinskis, note 1, at 14. 73 Paparinskis, note 1, at 14–15.

74 E.g., H Thirlway, "Dilemma or Chimera? Admissibility of Illegally Obtained Evidence in International Adjudication" (1984) 78 AJIL 622, 626.

75 *Nuclear Tests (Australia v. France)* [1974] ICJ Rep 253, 259–60.

76 *Effect of Awards of Compensation* [1954] ICJ Rep 47, 52.

77 *Effect of Awards of Compensation*, note 76.

because such powers are the type of powers that "courts" or "tribunals" usually have. Moreover, to say that a power is inherent "in a court" is unhelpful when one does not take account of the nature or function of the court or legal system in question.[78]

5.4 Functional justification

A fourth (and, it is argued, more satisfactory) source of the inherent powers of international courts is their need to ensure the fulfillment of their functions. The instances reviewed above where international courts have exercised inherent powers can be justified on this basis. Significantly, it is consistent with the dicta of a range of international courts and tribunals on the basis of inherent powers, including the ICJ, which held that it had such powers, inter alia, "in order that its basic judicial functions may be safeguarded."[79] Other international tribunals that have relied on their functions as the source of inherent powers include the ICTY Appeals Chamber,[80] the WTO Appellate Body,[81] the Iran–United States Claims Tribunal,[82] the Special Tribunal for Lebanon,[83] and a number of ICSID tribunals.[84]

In addition, this "functional justification" for the existence of inherent powers has found support in doctrinal writings;[85] even Professor Thirlway, who takes a restrictive view of the inherent powers of international courts, agrees that:

> The true justification for an inherent jurisdiction must be, as stated by Fitzmaurice, that "the power to exercise it…is a necessary condition of…any court of law…being able to function at all."[86]

[78] Compare Paparinskis, note 1, at 15–16. [79] *Nuclear Tests* [1974] ICJ Rep 253, 259–60.

[80] *Prosecutor v. Blaskic* (1997) 110 ILR 688, 704.

[81] WTO, *Mexico—Taxes on Soft Drinks—Appellate Body Report* (March 6, 2006) WT/DS308/AB/R, para. 45.

[82] *Iran v. United States* (Decision Ruling on Request for Revision by Iran of July 1, 2011, Decision No DEC 134-A3/A8/A9/A14/B61-FT), para. 59.

[83] Decision on Appeal of Pre-Trial Judge's Order Regarding Jurisdiction and Standing of November 10, 2010 (CH/AC/2010/2, Special Tribunal for Lebanon, Appeals Chamber), para. 45.

[84] *Hrvatska Elektroprivreda v. Republic of Slovenia* (ICSID Case No ARB/05/24, Ruling of May 6, 2008), para. 33, where the tribunal agreed that there was an "inherent power of an international court to deal with any issues necessary for the conduct of matters falling within its jurisdiction," and that such a power existed "independently of any statutory reference," citing *Prosecutor v. Beqa Beqaj* (Case No IT-03-66-T-R77, Judgment on Contempt Allegations (May 27, 2005)), paras 9–10. See also *RSM Production Corporation v. Grenada* (ICSID Case No ARB/05/14, Decision on RSM Production Corporation's Application for a Preliminary Ruling of December 7, 2009), para. 20. Compare the narrower approach in *Rompetrol Group NV v. Romania* (ICSID Case No ARB/06/3, Decision of the Tribunal on the Participation of a Counsel of January 14, 2010), paras 14–16.

[85] Brown, "Inherent Powers," note 1, at 222–9; Paparinskis, note 1, at 15–17; Gaeta, note 1, at 364–8; E Lauterpacht, note 63, at 480.

[86] Thirlway, note 3, 41, citing *Northern Cameroons* [1963] ICJ Rep 15, 97, 103 (Sep Op Fitzmaurice).

The conclusion that the source of inherent powers is found in the necessity of international courts to fulfill their functions raises the question of the extent of those functions. This is because the functions of international courts define which powers international courts may exercise as inherent powers, and where any limitations lie.

6 Functions of International Adjudication

There is an active debate about the functions of international adjudication,[87] and two main schools of thought can be distinguished. In one view, the function of international courts is a private function; that is, that international courts are created in order to settle disputes referred to them. In other words, their task is "to do justice" between the litigant states, and to render a judgment or award which takes account of all relevant facts,[88] which is limited to the *petitum* of the dispute, and which is made with final and binding force. This function can be discerned from the constitutive instruments and the jurisprudence of many international courts. For instance, arbitration under the auspices of the PCA has as its object the settlement of disputes between states by judges of their own choice, and on the basis of respect for law.[89] This private function is also reflected in Art. 42(1) of the ICSID Convention, which stipulates that the function of arbitral tribunals established under that convention is to "decide a dispute in accordance with such rules of law as may be agreed by the parties."[90] Article 38(1) of the ICJ Statute also states the function of that body as being "to decide in accordance with international law such disputes as are submitted to it."[91]

In another view, however, international adjudication also has a public function, which goes beyond the settlement of the dispute. According to this view, the goal of mere settlement is too focused on the private aspect of disputes and is not conducive to the positive creation of norms which can generate obedience among

[87] See especially Alvarez, in this handbook, Ch. 8; Besson, in this handbook, Ch. 19, at section 2; see also R Jennings, "The Role of the International Court of Justice" (1997) 68 British Yearbook of International Law 1, 1–9; AS Muller, D Raic and JM Thuransky (eds), *The International Court of Justice: Its Future Role after Fifty Years* (The Hague: Nijhoff 1997); Rosenne, note 35, at 162–78.

[88] On the "fact-finding" function of international courts and tribunals, see also Alvarez, in this handbook, Ch. 8, at section 2.

[89] 1899 Convention, Art. 15; 1907 Convention, Art. 37.

[90] ICSID Convention, Art. 42(1). [91] ICJ Statute, Art. 38(1).

members of the community being regulated by that system of norms.[92] This public function encompasses several considerations, each of which may be equally important. One of these functions is ensuring the proper administration of international justice. This is distinct from the function of settling disputes, in that it emphasizes the need for effectiveness and efficiency in judicial decision-making, and it is well established in the jurisprudence of international courts, as well as in the literature.[93] Several inherent powers have been justified on the basis of the need to ensure the proper administration of international justice, such as the power to dismiss proceedings summarily,[94] the power to suspend proceedings,[95] and the power to prevent any "abuse of process," such as the commencement of vexatious parallel proceedings.[96] The STL articulated this aspect of the judicial function as comprising the following considerations:

> (i) to ensure the fair administration of justice; (ii) to control the process and the proper conduct of proceedings; and (iii) to safeguard and ensure the discharge by the court of its judicial functions.[97]

Another manifestation of the public function of international adjudication is the role that international courts play in the clarification and the progressive development of international law.[98] Sir Hersch Lauterpacht also saw a broader role for the ICJ than the mere settlement of disputes; he argued that "the development of international law by international tribunals is, in the long run, one of the important conditions of their continued successful functioning and of their jurisdiction."[99] The case for this function is arguably strengthened if the international court in question is established within the context of a particular regime.[100] It might be said, for instance, that the ICJ, as "the principal judicial organ" of the UN, fulfills a public or constitutional role in the UN system.[101] The European Court of Human Rights

[92] E.g., O Fiss, "Against Settlement" (1983–1984) 93 Yale Law Journal 1073, 1085–6, 1089–90.

[93] See, e.g., *Mavrommatis Palestine Concessions* (1924) PCIJ Rep Series A No 2, 16; *Legality of Use of Force (Yugoslavia v. Spain)* [1999] ICJ Rep 761, 773–4; *Legality of Use of Force (Yugoslavia v. United States)* [1999] ICJ Rep 916, 925–6; see also JB Moore, *International Adjudications: Ancient and Modern—History and Documents* (New York: Oxford University Press 1929) vol I, xxii, lviii–lix, and the references cited therein.

[94] *Legality of Use of Force (Yugoslavia v. Spain)* [1999] ICJ Rep 761, 773–4; *Legality of Use of Force (Yugoslavia v. US)* [1999] ICJ Rep 916, 925–6.

[95] *SPP v. Egypt*, 3 ICSID Case No Rep 112, 129–30 (1985); *MOX Plant* (Procedural Order No 3) (2003) 42 ILM 1187, 1191; *SGS v. Philippines* (Jurisdiction), ICSID Case No ARB/02/6, (January 29, 2004) para. 175.

[96] See, e.g., *Waste Management v. United Mexican States* (2002) 41 ILM 1315, 1324–5.

[97] Decision on Appeal of Pre-Trial Judge's Order Regarding Jurisdiction and Standing of November 10, 2010 (CH/AC/2010/2, Special Tribunal for Lebanon, Appeals Chamber), para. 48.

[98] H Lauterpacht, note 69, at 5–7.

[99] H Lauterpacht, note 69, at 6–7; see also C de Visscher, *Theory and Reality in Public International Law* (Princeton University Press 1968) 390.

[100] See, e.g., Alvarez, in this handbook, Ch. 8, at section 5, who refers to a "governance function" of international courts and tribunals.

[101] *UN Charter*, Art. 92; Jennings, note 87, at 1–9.

(ECtHR) has also held that its functions were "not only to decide those cases brought before it, but more generally, to elucidate, safeguard and develop the rules instituted by the Convention."[102] The WTO dispute settlement system also arguably fulfills a constitutional role in overseeing the implementation of the WTO Agreement and its covered agreements.[103] Under Art. 3(2) of the Dispute Settlement Understanding (DSU), an explicit goal of the dispute settlement system is to provide jurisprudence to help ensure the predictability and stability of the world trading system.[104]

A further element of the public function of international adjudication is the consideration of interests other than those of the parties to the dispute. A number of international courts have taken account of broader community interests, which is evidenced in part by the practice of certain international courts in accepting the submission of *amicus curiae* briefs, frequently in the absence of an express power to do so.[105]

These aspects of the broader public function—the proper administration of international justice, the development of the law, and the consideration of public interests—are important functions of international courts, as is the private function of settling disputes, and the fulfillment of other functions that may be specific to individual regimes.

Each of these functions may, in certain circumstances, provide the justification for the exercise of certain inherent powers, if the international court deems such powers necessary for the fulfillment of its functions. This may arise in a variety of situations, and in this sense, it is not possible to compile an exhaustive list of the inherent powers of international courts. Yet the justification for the existence of inherent powers will most often be found in the functions of settling disputes and ensuring the proper administration of international justice. This is because inherent powers are mainly connected with the procedure applicable before international courts, and the fulfillment of the more immediate functions of these bodies.

It should be observed, however, that these functions have limitations that also apply to the assertion by international courts and tribunals of inherent powers. As the source of inherent powers lies in the need for international courts to fulfill their functions, the extent of the functions of each international court (including functions that may be particular to that court or tribunal) will necessarily determine

[102] E.g., *Ireland v. United Kingdom* (1978) ECtHR Series A No 25, 62; J Collier and V Lowe, *The Settlement of Disputes in International Law: Institutions and Procedures* (Oxford: Oxford University Press 1999) 13.

[103] E.g., J Jackson, "The Varied Policies of International Juridical Bodies: Reflections on Theory and Practice" (2004) 25 MJIL 869, 869–70, 878.

[104] DSU, Art. 3(2).

[105] E.g., *Methanex Corporation v. United States* (NAFTA, Order of January 15, 2001), paras 31, 47; *United Parcel Services of America, Inc v. Canada* (NAFTA, Order of October 17, 2001), para. 73; and *Aguas Argentinas, SA, Suez, Sociedad General de Aguas de Barcelona, SA, and Vivendi Universal, SA v. Argentina*, ICSID Case No ASRB/03/19, Decision (May 19, 2005), paras 9–16.

the scope of these powers.[106] Different international courts, such as, say, the ICTY and the ITLOS, may have differing specific functions in addition to the common general functions of settling disputes and ensuring the proper administration of international justice. So, an international criminal tribunal arguably has an inherent power to punish an individual for contempt of the tribunal, but this power would not necessarily be inherent in the functions of a tribunal which decides inter-State disputes.[107]

A further limiting factor may be found in the constitutive instrument of international courts and tribunals; there may be a *clause contraire* in the statute or rules of procedure of the international court or tribunal, or the exercise of an inherent power may more generally be inconsistent with the terms of the relevant statute or rules of procedure.[108] The first of these limitations was recognized by the ICJ in the *Nottebohm* case, where it held that an international tribunal had an inherent power to determine the extent of its own jurisdiction "in the absence of agreement to the contrary."[109] Sir Hersch Lauterpacht also recognized this in his separate opinion in *Norwegian Loans*, where he held that "[c]learly the Court cannot act otherwise than in accordance with its Statute."[110] As to the second of these limitations, it may be that the constitutive instrument in question does not expressly exclude the exercise of a certain procedural power, but the exercise of that power may nonetheless be inconsistent with the procedures actually provided for.[111] The Iran–United States Claims Tribunal accurately encapsulated the scope of inherent powers, and the limitations on their exercise by international courts and tribunals, as follows:

> In the Tribunal's view, in order to determine which powers international courts and tribunals may exercise as inherent powers one must take into account the particular features of each specific court or tribunal, including the circumstances surrounding its establishment, the object and purpose of its constitutive instrument, and the consent of the parties as expressed in that and related instruments.[112]

[106] Brown, "Inherent Powers," note 1, at 237–8; Paparinskis, note 1, at 17–18.

[107] Gaeta, note 1, at 370–1; Brown, "Inherent Powers," note 1, at 238.

[108] Brown, "Inherent Powers," note 1; Paparinskis, note 1, at 17–18.

[109] *Nottebohm (Liechtenstein v Guatemala)* [1953] ICJ Rep 111, 119.

[110] *Norwegian Loans* [1957] ICJ Rep 9, 34, 45 (Sep Op Sir Hersch Lauterpacht).

[111] For an example of this type of limitation, see *Heathrow Airport User Charges (United States-United Kingdom)* (1993) 102 ILR 564; and Brown, "Inherent Powers," note 1, at 240–1.

[112] *Iran v. United States* (Decision Ruling on Request for Revision by Iran of July 1, 2011, Decision No DEC 134-A3/A8/A9/A14/B61-FT), para. 61.

7 Conclusion

This chapter has examined international courts' exercise of inherent powers relating to questions of international procedure. The assertion of such powers by international courts and tribunals has in the past proved controversial. But there is now a significant body of practice which demonstrates that international courts are not restricted to exercising the procedural powers which are conferred by their constitutive instruments—whether express or implied—but can also exercise inherent powers, so long as applicable restrictions on their use are respected. Concerns relating to the "legitimacy" of international adjudicative bodies resorting to such extra-statutory powers are occasionally raised, but it is not apparent that such concerns are reflected in the record of compliance with the judgments and awards of such bodies.[113] This may be due to the fact that the exercise of such powers usually relates to procedural issues, rather than the endgame of international proceedings; but all litigators are aware that issues of procedure can be (and often are) as important as issues of substance.[114]

The consideration of the nature, source, and scope of inherent powers in international adjudication provided in this chapter, together with the proposition that international courts should operate as "normal" courts,[115] can serve to assist international tribunals faced with novel procedural issues. International courts have the ability to devise new procedures and adopt those employed by other international tribunals in similar circumstances. It is suggested that international courts might, through the careful exercise of such powers, better manage the complex challenges being posed to the administration of international justice.

Research Questions

1. To what extent have the differing functions of various international adjudicative bodies been invoked to justify the expansion of the judicial powers of those bodies?
2. Are inherent powers more far-reaching than what international courts and tribunals can achieve by resorting to notions of judicial or arbitral "discretion" in deciding procedural issues?

[113] On such issues, see especially in this handbook, Huneeus, Ch. 20, at section 2.1.8; and C Schulte, *Compliance with Decisions of the International Court of Justice* (Oxford University Press 2004).

[114] E.g., E Lauterpacht, "Principles of Procedure in International Litigation" (2011) 345 Recueil des cours 391, 406–9.

[115] R Higgins, "Respecting Sovereign States and Running a Tight Courtroom" (2001) 50 International and Comparative Law Quarterly 121, 131–2.

3. Does the relationship between the parties and the international court or tribunal in question impact on the likelihood of that international court exercising powers that are not expressly conferred on it? (Compare, e.g., sovereign states appearing before the ICJ, with a private party and government ministry, acting in a non-governmental commercial capacity before an ICSID arbitral tribunal.)
4. Is there a discernible reduced level of compliance in the case of decisions and judgments of international courts and tribunals where the adjudicative body concerned has exercised an inherent power that was contested by one of the litigants in the course of the proceedings?

Suggested Reading

Brown, C, "The Inherent Powers of International Courts and Tribunals" (2005) 76 British Yearbook of International Law 195.

Brown, C, *A Common Law of International Adjudication* (Oxford University Press 2007).

Fitzmaurice, Sir G, *The Law and Procedure of the International Court of Justice*, 2 vols (Cambridge: Grotius Publications 1986).

Gaeta, P, "The Inherent Powers of International Courts and Tribunals" in LC Vohrar et al. (eds), *Man's Inhumanity to Man: Essays on International Law in Honour of Antonio Cassese* (Alphen aan den Rijn: Kluwer Law International 2003) 353.

Lauterpacht, Sir H, *The Development of International Law by the International Court* (Cambridge: Grotius Publications 1958).

Orakhelashvili, A, "The Concept of International Judicial Jurisdiction: A Reappraisal" (2003) 3 Law and Practice of International Courts and Tribunals 501.

Paparinskis, M, "Inherent Powers of ICSID Tribunals: Broad and Rightly So" in T Weiler and I Laird (eds), *Investment Treaty Arbitration and International Law* (New York: JurisNet 2012) 11.

Thirlway, H, "The Law and Procedure of the International Court of Justice 1960–1989: Part Nine" (1998) 69 British Yearbook of International Law 1.

CHAPTER 39

EVIDENCE, FACT-FINDING, AND EXPERTS

ANNA RIDDELL*

1 Introduction

The capacity of any adjudicative body to deliver a comprehensive and durable resolution to a case relies not only on that body's ability to know and understand the

* Publications Editor, British Institute of International and Comparative Law; Ph.D. student at the European University Institute, Florence.

relevant principles of law, but also on its capacity to ground the application of those principles on a reasonable and reliable account of the factual situation giving rise to the case.

Different legal systems adopt different approaches to fulfill this essential aspect of the judicial function. For instance, the two main legal families—the common law and the civil law—differ as to how they approach evidence. The common law presumes the truth to lie somewhere between the opposing positions of the two parties; it is the task of the court to referee the competition between them, fought by means of adducing evidence to support their case. To this end, there are various rules to exclude certain forms of evidence, and prioritize or change the use of others, all designed to ensure the regularity and fairness of the litigation, but few powers for a judge to request evidence. Conversely, in civil law, the search for truth relies as much on the intervention and expertise of the judiciary as it does on the involvement of the parties. Judges actively engage in establishing the case facts, for example, by conducting investigations, seeking additional evidence and even examining witnesses. Thus, civil law tends to have fewer technical rules on evidence.[1]

At the international level, adjudicative bodies have traditionally been afforded a very significant degree of freedom to ascertain the facts underlying their decisions. The international law of evidence comprises only a basic set of broad principles and eschews more technical rules regulating the admission, exclusion, and evaluation of evidence. Indeed, according to Sandifer, author of one comprehensive study on the subject, "no rule of evidence thus finds more frequent statement in the cases than the one that international tribunals are not bound to adhere to strict rules of evidence."[2]

This chapter aims to clarify the peculiarities of fact-finding in the international context and to examine the manner in which the various forms of evidence are adduced, handled, and assessed by the various international adjudicative bodies.

2 Evidence and Fact-Finding in the International Context

The importance of fact-finding and proper management and appreciation of evidence cannot be overstated. If adjudicative bodies cannot be trusted to render

[1] D Sandifer, *Evidence before International Tribunals* (Rev edn, University Press of Virginia 1975) 2–4.

[2] Sandifer, note 1, at 9.

judgment based on a proper application of the law to the facts of the case, their legitimacy will be fundamentally undermined. As Alford has observed: "the legal guidance which [a] court gives, or the judgment which it renders will be a useless abstraction unless it is based on actual events, formulated in the light of existing events, and designed to influence the shape of future events,"[3] and a tribunal can only learn of these events through evidence. Whilst there are virtues of flexible rules in evidentiary practice, a lack of certainty as to how a tribunal arrives at its judgment could be seen to undermine the legitimacy of that judgment. Further, if it is unclear to the parties that the judgment is based on a full appreciation of the facts, it may be that they will be reluctant to comply with the judgment, impacting the effectiveness of the tribunal. It is therefore crucial that even if flexibility is closely guarded, adjudicative bodies must do their best to demonstrate that they have fully understood and utilized all the material before them, in order to protect their legitimacy and efficacy.

The multiplication of international judicial bodies means that there are a variety of different motivating factors and different approaches to evidence and fact-finding, which must be acknowledged in a chapter seeking to examine the topic as a whole. At the apex there is the International Court of Justice (ICJ)—the only active international adjudicative body with general jurisdiction. There are the permanent tribunals, whose jurisdiction is tied to particular types of legal dispute or certain areas of international law, e.g. International Tribunal for the Law of the Sea (ITLOS), the International Criminal Court (ICC), and the human rights courts. There are the quasi-judicial and dispute settlement bodies, such as the international administrative tribunals, the claims and compensation tribunals, the permanent arbitral tribunals, and the ad hoc tribunals created specifically and temporarily to address the consequences of certain localized incidents. The latter includes those established solely under the United Nations (UN), such as the International Criminal Tribunals for Former Yugoslavia and Rwanda (ICTY, ICTR) and the "internationalized" or hybrid tribunals created by a state jointly or with the help of the UN, e.g. the Special Court for Sierra Leone (SCSL), or the Extraordinary Chambers in the courts of Cambodia.[4] The differing functions, parties, and procedures of these tribunals renders a general analysis of evidentiary practice difficult, though attempts have been made to do so where possible, and attention has been drawn to the adjudicative bodies which are exceptions to a particular rule.

For the international adjudicative bodies who deal with states, one possible explanation for the flexible rules is the desire of these bodies to respect the sovereignty of

[3] NH Alford, "Fact-Finding by the World Court" (1958) 4 Villanova Law Review 38.

[4] See the Project for International Courts and Tribunals "Synoptic Chart" <http://www.pict-pcti.org/publications/synoptic_chart.html> accessed April 29, 2013; see also discussion by C Romano, "The Proliferation of International Judicial Bodies: The Pieces of the Puzzle" (1999) 31 N.Y.U. J. Int'l L. & Pol. 709 and "A Taxonomy of International Rule of Law Institutions" (2011) 2 JIDS 1, 241.

litigating states by accommodating each state's own notion of the most appropriate way of presenting and substantiating its version of events. However, this justification does not exist for those tribunals not dealing with states, such as the international criminal tribunals, and indeed, sometimes states might actually prefer more precise rules. For example, in the human rights courts, the beneficiaries of vague and flexible evidentiary rules are more likely to be the plaintiffs, and not states.

Another potential explanation could be that often the great importance, sensitivity, and complexity of the interests at stake in international litigation demand that an international judicial body pursue the truth in the most thorough and comprehensive manner possible, which can be facilitated by flexibility in proceedings. Failure or mistake in the determination of the facts can have wide-ranging and long-lasting consequences, affecting not just the parties but also the very ideals and interests of international justice. Flexible rules of evidence decrease the likelihood that procedural technicalities might become an obstacle to the settlement of the dispute. As the Permanent Court of International Justice (PCIJ) said in its judgment in the case of the *Free Zones of Upper Savoy and the District of Gex*: "the decision of an international dispute of the present order should not depend mainly on a point of procedure."[5] Similarly, Hersch Lauterpacht argued that in international proceedings, "the importance of the interests at stake precludes excessive or decisive reliance upon formal and technical rules."[6] Ultimately, the imperative of finding a sound basis for a judicial decision, and of avoiding procedural difficulties, is sharpened by the fact that the decisions of most international adjudicative bodies are final and may not be reviewed or overruled by a higher judicial authority.

Less exacting rules of evidence might be necessary in the light of the fact that obtaining evidence in international claims might be more difficult and expensive than in municipal litigation. There are numerous factors that make managing evidence more challenging for international bodies: there is often a significant lapse between the occurrence of the events of the dispute and the proceedings; events may have taken place far from the seat of the tribunal; evidence may be situated within the territory of a state which is not a party to the proceedings or does not cooperate with the tribunal; and the written evidence may be in poor condition or impossible to locate. The greatest difference to national courts is that powers to coerce the production of evidence do not exist or are very limited in most international adjudicative bodies. For these reasons, international adjudicative bodies have long been reluctant to adopt restrictive evidentiary rules and have continually espoused the necessity of freedom in matters of fact-finding. Indeed, as Sandifer has remarked, in international litigation, "technicalities are taboo."[7]

[5] Case of the *Free Zones of Upper Savoy and the District of Gex (Switzerland v. France)* PCIJ Rep Series A/B No 46, at 155–6.

[6] H Lauterpacht, *The Development of International Law by the International Court* (New York: Frederick A Prager 1958) 366; see also Sandifer, note 1, at 4–5.

[7] Sandifer, note 1, at 5.

Another possible explanation is perhaps that tribunals themselves are keen to retain the possibility of flexibility in their approach, to avoid having their ability to decide cases as they deem proper being curtailed by strict evidentiary rules. Perhaps the fact that judges often come from different legal traditions with different ideas of the role of a judge and different approaches to fact-finding means codifying rules would be problematic and unduly restrictive. The justification for not adopting a strict approach in the ICC seems to represent a compromise between the common (adversarial) and civil (inquisitorial) approaches to criminal law.[8]

Yet, flexibility and informality come at a price. Many international adjudicative bodies have come under fire for lack of rigor in managing fact-finding. Their lack of a principled and consistent approach, such as would be found in a national tribunal, causes commentators to wonder whether this undermines the adjudication process.[9] For example, as Schofield and Carleton note, the ICJ failing to use experts to clarify matters outside the knowledge of the bench resulted in a judgment in the *Cameroon v. Nigeria* case that has been impossible to apply.[10] Even the judges of the ICJ themselves have recently lamented the court's casual approach to the crucial issue of how evidence is examined.[11]

[8] D Scheffer and A Cox, "The Constitutionality of the Rome Statute of the International Criminal Court" (2008) 98(3) The Journal of Criminal Law and Criminology 992.

[9] A Riddell and B Plant, *Evidence Before the International Court of Justice* (London: British Institute of International and Comparative Law 2009); A Watts, "Enhancing the Effectiveness of Procedures of International Dispute Settlement" in JA Frowein and R Wolfrum (eds), *Max Planck Yearbook of United Nations Law* (Vol. 5, The Hague: Kluwer Law International 2001) 29–30; C M Schofield and C H Carleton, "Technical Considerations in Law of the Sea Dispute Resolution" in AG Oude Elferink and DR Rothwell (eds), *Oceans Management in the 21st Century* (The Hague: Martinus Nijhoff 2004); R Pietrowski, "Evidence In International Arbitration" (2006) 22(3) Arbitration International 373; CN Brower, "Evidence Before International Tribunals: The Need for Some Standard Rules" (1994) 28 International Lawyer 47.

[10] *Land and Maritime Boundary Between Cameroon and Nigeria (Cameroon v. Nigeria, Equatorial Guinea intervening)* [2002] ICJ Rep 303. Errors in the court's appreciation of the technical evidence presented resulted in the boundary being wrongly drawn and impossible to demarcate on the ground. Ten years after the Judgment was given, a commission is still working on the task of trying to interpret the ICJ's decision according to a UN OWA Press Release of August 29, 2012. For a full discussion of the errors made, see Riddell and Plant, note 9, 9.VI.C, at 348 *et seq.*, and Schofield and Carleton, note 9.

[11] *Case concerning Pulp Mills on the River Uruguay (Argentina v. Uruguay)* (Dissenting Opinion Judges Al-Khasawneh and Simma) [2010] ICJ Rep 108–20. Judges Al Khasawneh and Simma noted the growing dissatisfaction in the academic literature with the level of attention being paid to the issue of fact-finding at para. 3, and called upon the court to adopt a more rigorous approach in paras 7–17; *Pulp Mills* (Dissenting Opinion Judge ad hoc Vinuesa) [2010] ICJ Rep 281, para. 95. Judge ad hoc Vinuesa was particularly critical, stating: "The Court does itself a disservice by not ensuring that its ruling is based on factual certainty."

3 Powers of International Tribunals with Regard to Evidence

Despite the general flexibility, international adjudicative bodies do have rules on evidence and fact-finding. The majority of them are found either in the constitutive documents of the courts themselves, or in their rules of procedure.[12] Where express provisions do not exist, international judges often resort to general principles of law, or to the rules applied by other international tribunals.[13] Examples of general principles that have made their way into the lexicon of international rules of evidence are *audi alteram partem*, or the principle that each party has the right to be heard, and *iura novit curia*, or the principle that the judge can be presumed to know the law.

In general, the powers of international adjudicative bodies to manage the production of evidence can be divided into the following: the power to require the parties to produce evidence; the power to make its own investigations; and the power to engage experts.

3.1 Power to request the production of evidence

It is uncontested that international adjudicative bodies have the power to request the production of evidence. This power is often spelled out in the judicial body's legal instrument. The ICJ's powers are laid down in Arts 34(2) and 49 of the ICJ Statute, with further provision in Art. 62(1) of the Rules. The arbitration rules of the United Nations Commission on International Trade Law (UNCITRAL) also give an arbitral body the power to "require the parties to produce documents, exhibits or other evidence within such a period of time as the arbitral tribunal shall determine."[14] The ITLOS Rules,[15] the International Centre for the Settlement of Investment Disputes (ICSID) Convention,[16] the European Court of Justice (ECJ)

[12] Such rules are often created or amended by the tribunal themselves, by an express power in their constitutive instruments. For example, the Statute of the ICJ gives the court the power to amend its Rules of Procedure in Art. 30, which it has done several times, including issuing a completely revised set of rules in 1978. In the absence of express provision, it is sometimes considered that international courts also have an inherent power to manage the gathering of evidence.

[13] B Cheng, *General Principles of Law as Applied by International Courts and Tribunals* (Rev edn, Cambridge University Press 1987) 257–386.

[14] United Nations Commission on International Trade Law Arbitration Rules (UNCITRAL Arbitration Rules), UN Doc. A/RES/65/22 (2011) available at <http://www.uncitral.org/pdf/english/texts/arbitration/arb-rules-revised/arb-rules-revised-2010-e.pdf> accessed April 29, 2013.

[15] ITLOS/8 Rules of the Tribunal, Art. 77.

[16] Article 43(a) of the Convention for the Settlement of Investment Disputes between States and Nationals of Other States, 575 UNTS 159 (entered into force October 14, 1966) (ICSID Convention).

Statute,[17] the ICC Statute,[18] and the Rules of the European Court of Human Rights (ECtHR)[19] and Inter-American Court of Human Rights (IACtHR),[20] among others, all contain such provisions.

Logically, the parties have a corresponding obligation to disclose material, especially where explicitly requested to do so. Legally, this obligation derives from various sources. In the ICJ, it has been suggested that it emanates from states' obligations to comply with the UN Charter, of which the ICJ Statute is a part.[21] An ICSID Tribunal held in *Biwater Gauff* that the obligation to produce documents upon request was "an international legal obligation arising from the State's consent by way of the BIT to ICSID arbitration."[22] In the ICTY and the ICTR, the power also ultimately stems from the UN Charter. The ad hoc tribunals have been established by the Security Council acting under Chapter VII of the UN Charter, which gives the council mandatory powers.[23]

However, it is not clear what the effects of a party's non-compliance with a request to disclose would be, given that these adjudicative bodies do not have coercive powers of their own. An exception might be that under the World Trade Organization (WTO) Dispute Settlement Understanding (DSU) rules, Art. 13 provides that panels have broad authority to seek information from the parties themselves and elsewhere, which has been judicially interpreted as a corresponding duty of disclosure on the parties.[24] However, even where the legal instruments spell out a specific power to compel the production of evidence or witnesses,[25] they are silent as to the consequences of a failure to do so. All the ICJ Statute says is that the court may take "formal note" of any failure to fulfill a request for evidence.[26]

Can an international adjudicative body infer from the refusal to produce evidence that the evidence in question would in fact be prejudicial to the position of the party refusing to produce it? Sandifer notes that "international tribunals necessarily must proceed with greater caution." In dealing with sovereign states rather than with individuals, it cannot lightly be presumed that one of the parties

[17] Protocol on the Statute of the Court of Justice, Consolidated Version of the EEC Treaty, Art. 21.

[18] Rules of Procedure and Evidence of the International Criminal Court, Arts 64(6)(d) and 69(3).

[19] European Court of Human Rights Rules of Court, Art. 42(1).

[20] Inter-American Court of Human Rights, Rules of Procedure, Art. 44(2).

[21] C Brown, *A Common Law of International Adjudication* (Oxford University Press 2012) 105.

[22] *Biwater Gauff (Tanzania) Ltd v. Tanzania*, ICSID Case No ARB/05/22, Procedural Order No 2 (May 24, 2006) 8–9.

[23] *Prosecutor v. Blaskic (Subpoenae duces tecum)* (Trial Chamber Decision 1997) 110 ILR 607, at 699.

[24] WTO, *Canada—Measures Affecting the Export of Civilian Aircraft–Appellate Body Report*, DSR 1999-III, 1377, at 1427. The Appellate Body held that members are "under a duty and an obligation to 'respond promptly and fully' to requests made by panels for information." See also J Pauwelyn, "The Use of Experts in WTO Dispute Settlement" (2002) 51(2) International and Comparative Law Quarterly 329.

[25] E.g. ICC Rules of Procedure and Evidence, Art. 69(3), note 18; Iran–US Claims Tribunal Rules of Procedure, Art. 24(3), 1 Iran-USCTR 57.

[26] ICJ Statute, Art. 49.

to the litigation is guilty of negligence or of *mala fides* in the prosecution of a case before an international tribunal.[27] However, in the *Barcelona Traction* case in the ICJ, Judge Jessup made the important point that if there is a genuine reason for a state wishing to conceal evidence which, if released, might prejudice their national interests, they can plead national security as was done in the *Corfu Channel* case and in 2007, in the *Genocide Convention* case. Therefore, it can be presumed that, in the absence of a "justification" of this kind, the party simply does not want to adduce an item of evidence which might be contrary to their case, and the tribunal may therefore draw an adverse inference.[28] The WTO has agreed with this analysis, concluding in the *Canada—Aircraft* case that "the Panel had the legal authority and the discretion to draw inferences from the facts before it—including the fact that Canada had refused to provide information sought by the Panel."[29]

3.2 Power to make investigations *proprio motu*

Often, international adjudicative bodies have considerable authority to obtain evidence on their own initiative. The ICJ, for example, possesses wide powers to make whatever arrangements it considers necessary to collect additional evidence.[30] It may, for example, call witnesses or experts to give evidence, though it cannot compel them.[31]

One very specific investigative power, common in international tribunals, is the ability to arrange visits by members of the tribunal to sites connected with the dispute. Although the ICJ possesses this power, it has made very little use of it. It made a site visit on only one occasion, in the *Gabčíkovo-Nagymaros* case.[32] In the *El Salvador/Honduras* case, it actually refused El Salvador's request to make a visit to the land frontier with Honduras.[33] It is possible that this reluctance is related to the rather antiquated view that the ICJ primarily decides disputes on the law, not disputes based on complex facts. As President Schwebel stated in his Report in

[27] Sandifer, note 1, at 170.

[28] *Case Concerning the Barcelona Traction Light and Power Company Limited (Belgium v. Spain)* (Separate Opinion Judge Jessup) [1970] 3 ICJ Rep 215, para. 97

[29] *Canada—Aircraft*, note 24, at 1433.

[30] ICJ Instrument, Art. 48.

[31] Rules of the ICJ, Art. 62(2).

[32] From April 1 to 4, 1997, between the two opening rounds of pleading, the court visited a number of sites along the Danube river, and took note of the technical explanations given by the representatives who had been designated for the purpose by the parties. See further P Tomka and S Wordsworth, "The First Site Visit of the International Court of Justice in Fulfillment of its Judicial Function" (1998) 92 AJIL 133–40.

[33] *Land, Island and Maritime Frontier Dispute (El Salvador/Honduras: Nicaragua intervening)* [1992] ICJ Rep 361–2, para. 22.

1997: "clearly, issues of the law can usually be decided without such an exercise."[34] It might be the potential high cost of such visits or the difficulty of making them in contentious cases where the situation on the ground may not be safe, that has deterred the ICJ and other bodies from making more use of this power. ICSID tribunals also have the power to "visit any place connected with the dispute or conduct enquiries there,"[35] and the European Commission of Human Rights has exercised this power on several occasions, for example in *B v. UK*.[36] ITLOS and the ECtHR have both given themselves the power to conduct site visits in developing their own rules of procedure.[37]

Even when the power is not spelled out in the constitutive instrument, it can be considered inherent of the international judicial function. Several arbitral tribunals have conducted site visits despite lacking an express power to do so.[38]

3.3 Power to engage experts

Frequently international adjudicative bodies have the power to appoint experts to conduct enquiries or give opinions on certain facts within their professional expertise.

Many adjudicative bodies explicitly possess the power to appoint experts whenever needed. The United Nations Convention on the Law of the Sea (UNCLOS) provides in Art. 289 that, in scientific or technical disputes, experts may be appointed to sit with the tribunal.[39] The UNCITRAL Arbitration Rules provide that an arbitral tribunal may appoint one or more independent experts "after consultation with the parties."[40] WTO panels have the power to "seek information and technical advice from any individual or body which it deems appropriate" in Art. 13(1) of the DSU.[41]

[34] Statement by Judge Stephen M. Schwebel, President of the International Court of Justice to the fifty-second session of the General Assembly in connection with the annual report of the International Court of Justice, (October 27, 1997), available at: <http://www.icj-cij.org/presscom/index.php?pr=89&p1=6&p2=1&search=%22a%E9rien%22&PHPSESSID=13e30913f2119335bab74996731e8328> accessed August 1, 2013.

[35] ICSID Convention, Art. 43(b).

[36] *B v. UK* (1981) 32 Dec & Rep 5, at 8.

[37] ITLOS, Art. 81; ECtHR, Rule 42(2).

[38] e.g. in *Maritime Boundary Arbitration Between Guyana and Suriname*, the tribunal hydrographer made a site visit in order to establish the precise location of markers which were in contention, see "Report of the Site Visit, David Gray, 30 July 2007," <http://www.pca-cpa.org/showpage.asp?pag_id=1147> accessed August 1, 2013.

[39] Article 289 of United Nations Convention on the Law of the Sea (December 10, 1982) <https://www.un.org/depts/los/convention_agreements/texts/unclos/UNCLOS-TOC.htm> accessed August 1, 2013.

[40] UNCITRAL Arbitration Rules, Art. 29.

[41] Article 31(1) Understanding on the Rules and Procedures Governing the Settlement of Disputes, Annex 2 of the WTO Agreement, 1994 <http://www.wto.org/english/tratop_e/dispu_e/dsu_e.htm> accessed August 1, 2013.

The ECJ also has this power in Art. 22 of the ECJ Statute.[42] The ICJ is empowered in Art. 50 to commission an expert opinion or enquiry, in whatever form it requires, be it an investigation, a written report, or oral testimony. The specific wording of these provisions varies, from simply appointing experts to give evidence, to inviting experts to sit on the tribunal, for example as "assessors,"[43] to commissioning an expert investigation.

However, while certain international adjudicative bodies make frequent use of experts, others do it seldom. The ICJ has appointed experts only in the *Corfu Channel* and *Gulf of Maine* cases, and, in the latter, it was required to do so by the terms of the Special Agreement between the parties bringing the case before the court.[44] The court has often been requested to appoint independent experts by the parties, but has always declined to do so. This fact has attracted criticism in the literature and also from its own judges.[45] In the *Pulp Mills* case, several judges actually criticized the court's refusal to do so and called for a greater focus on fact-finding.[46]

One possible explanation why international adjudicative bodies rarely appoint their own experts, even where they are accustomed to hearing those of the parties, is that they do not wish to be seen to delegate their judicial function to an expert, in case this undermines the perceived legitimacy of the final decision or of the tribunal itself. Further, the expense of using independent experts will fall on the adjudicative body where it makes the appointment, and, therefore, this task is often left to the parties.[47]

[42] CJEU Statute, Art. 22, OJ L 228, 23.8.2012, p. 1, <http://curia.europa.eu/jcms/upload/docs/application/pdf/2012-10/staut_cons_en.pdf> accessed August 1, 2013.

[43] This power is contained in Art. 30(2) of the ICJ Rules, though arguably the court has never openly made use of it. See Riddell and Plant, note 9, at 9.III.A for a discussion on the use of assessors in the ICJ.

[44] *Delimitation of the Maritime Boundary in the Gulf of Maine Area (Canada/United States of America)* (Appointment of Expert, Order of March 30, 1984) [1984] ICJ Reports 165; see also *Maritime Delimitation* (Judgment at 256) paras 8 and 18.

[45] See e.g., *Temple of Preah Vihear (Cambodia v. Thailand)* (Dissenting Opinion of Judge Wellington Koo) [1962] ICJ Rep 100; *Case Concerning Kasikili/Sedudu Island (Botswana/Namibia)* (Separate Opinion of Judge Oda) [1999] ICJ Rep 1118–19, at para. 6; *Military and Paramilitary Activities in and against Nicaragua (Nicaragua v. United States of America)* (Dissenting Opinion of Judge Schwebel) [1984] ICJ Rep 323, at para. 134.

[46] *Case concerning Pulp Mills on the River Uruguay*, note 11, at para. 95. Judge ad hoc Vinuesa's dissenting opinion suggests that the court may have decided not to appoint its own expert to evaluate the scientific and technical evidence because of the delay that would have caused.

[47] There is evidence that the ICJ does have recourse to its own experts, but privately and without informing the parties, which would solve the problem of legitimacy questions, and likely be a smaller expense. As Jennings observes: "the Court has not infrequently employed cartographers, hydrographers, geographers, linguists, and even very specialised legal experts to assist in the understanding of the issues in a case before it; and has not on the whole felt any need to make this public knowledge or even to apprise the parties." R Jennings, "International Lawyers and the Progressive Development of International Law" in J Makarczyk (ed.), *Theory of International Law at the Threshold of the 21st Century: Essays in Honour of Krzystof Skubiszewski* (The Hague: Martinus Nijhoff 1996) at 416.

The tribunals that frequently use experts generally have more rules pertaining to their employment, for example, concerning their qualifications or the manner in which they give evidence. However, that is not always the case. For example, the United Nations Compensation Commission (UNCC) made extensive use of experts to assist the review of more than 2.6 million claims for losses resulting from Iraq's invasion and occupation of Kuwait, but the UNCC Rules provided merely that the commissioners could: "request additional information from any other source, including expert advice, as necessary."[48]

4 Questions of Proof

When it comes to proof, the two key issues are: who bears the burden (i.e. which party must furnish the court with evidence on a certain matter); and the required standard of proof.

4.1 Burden of proof

Since Roman times, courts of law have relied on the maxim *actori incumbit onus probandi*[49] or "the claimant carries the burden of proof."

As Amerasinghe has explained, the ability to determine who bears the burden of proof "is an inherent power which is essential for the proper functioning of international tribunals."[50] Despite a variety of approaches and differences of opinions as to the degree of applicability of the rule, various international adjudicative bodies, including several arbitral tribunals,[51] the PCIJ,[52] the ICJ,[53] and human rights

[48] UN Compensation Commission, Governing Council Decision Approving Provisional Rules for Claims Procedure, Art. 36 (b), UN Doc S/AC.26/1992/10 (June 26, 1992).

[49] Dig. XXXI 22 in fine; Cod Just IV 19, 15 (a.293); IV, 30, 10 (a.293).

[50] C Amerasinghe, *Evidence in International Litigation* (The Hague: Martinus Nijhoff 2005) 75.

[51] E.g., ICSID and NAFTA tribunals, WTO Panels and the WTO Appellate Body. See *Plama Consortium Ltd v. Bulgaria*, ICSID Case No ARB/03/24, Decision on jurisdiction (February 8, 2005) paras 118–20, 167; *Canfor Corporation v. US* (Order of the Consolidation Tribunal of September 7, 2005), para. 93; and WTO, *EC–Tariff Preferences–Report of the Appellate Body* WT/DS246/AB/R, paras 87–8.

[52] For discussion, see cases: *Legal Status of Eastern Greenland*, PCIJ Series A/B No 53, 1933, at 49, paras 100–1; *The Case of the SS Lotus*, PCIJ Series A No 9, 1927, at 18; *The Mavrommatis Jerusalem Concessions*, PCIJ Series A No 5, 1925, at 6.

[53] In the *Nicaragua* case the ICJ stated: "Ultimately, however, it is the litigant seeking to establish a fact who bears the burden of proving it; and in cases where evidence may not be forthcoming, a submission may in the judgment be rejected as unproved, but is not to be ruled out as inadmissible in limine on the basis of an anticipated lack of proof." *Military and Paramilitary Activities in and against*

bodies,[54] have consistently applied the *actori incumbit probatio* rule. The Iran–US Claims Tribunal has even included the principle in Art. 24(1) of its Rules: "Each party shall have the burden of proving the facts relied on to support his claim or his defence."[55] However, the application of the rule in the international context is not devoid of problems. It is not always possible to discern which party is the applicant and respondent in international proceedings. This is particularly evident when a case is brought jointly by two states by special agreement. Further, in the case of requests for advisory opinions, there are technically no parties, so there can be no legal burden.[56]

In international human rights tribunals, the burden of proof functions somewhat differently, perhaps to mitigate the potential inequality between an individual applicant and a state respondent. There exists a *prima facie* obligation on the applicant to adduce enough evidence of a violation to bring the case before the court, but once it is accepted, the burden of proof falls on the respondent state to prove that it did not commit a violation of human rights, or that its actions were justified under one of the legitimate limitations (e.g., contained in the second paragraph of Arts 8–11 of the European Convention on Human Rights).

In practice, most international tribunals approach the question of who bears the burden of proof pragmatically, rather than dogmatically. For example, the ICJ has been careful to examine which party is seeking to rely on certain facts, rather than adhering to the traditional applicant/respondent dichotomy.[57] In the *Temple of Preah Vihear* case, it stated:

As concerns the burden of proof, it must be pointed out that though, from the formal standpoint, Cambodia is the plaintiff, having instituted the proceedings, Thailand is also a claimant because of the claim which was presented by her … which relates to the sovereignty over the same piece of territory. Both Cambodia and Thailand base their respective claims on a series of facts and contentions which are asserted or put forward by one party or the other. The burden of proof in respect of these will of course lie on the Party asserting them or putting them forward.[58]

Nicaragua (Nicaragua v. United States of America) (Judgment on Jurisdiction and Admissibility) [1984] ICJ Rep 436, para. 101.

[54] Such as the UN Human Rights Committee and the Inter American Court of Human Rights. See e.g. respectively *Bordes and Temeharo* (1996) HRC Decision No 645/1995 para. 5.5 and *Velasquez Rodriguez* (1989) 28 ILM 291, at 315.

[55] Iran–US Claims Tribunal Rules, Art. 24(1).

[56] R Wolfrum, "Evidence in International Courts and Tribunals" (2006) X *The Max Planck Encyclopedia of Public International Law* 565, para. 72.

[57] Sandifer, note 1, at 369–70; G White, *The Use of Experts by International Tribunals* (Syracuse University Press 1965) 8; A Riddell, "Report on the Oral Proceedings in the Application of the Convention on the Prevention and Punishment of the Crime of Genocide (*Bosnia and Herzegovina v. Serbia and Montenegro*): Selected Procedural Aspects" (2007) 2 LJIL 414.

[58] *Temple of Preah Vihear*, note 45, at 15.

4.2 Standard of proof

The standard of proof is the measure against which "the value of each piece of evidence as well as the overall value of the evidence in a given case should be weighed and determined."[59]

If the burden of proof seems complicated in international litigation, the standard of proof is even more so. The difficulties stem from the different approaches of the common law and civil law legal traditions.

At what point will the strength of the evidence amount to proof? It must be noted here that the issue of the standard of proof is largely connected with the weight ascribed to evidence. A certain standard will not be reached merely by adducing large volumes of evidence; the individual items of evidence offered need to be accorded sufficient weight for them to constitute an element of proof.

In common law, there are two main standards that are applied. Generally, the standard adopted in civil cases is that of the "preponderance of evidence," also known as the "balance of probabilities." However, in criminal cases, because of the presumption of innocence and the potential deprivation of liberty, the standard of proof is much higher; criminal cases must be established beyond reasonable doubt.

In the civil legal tradition, the standard of proof is approached differently. It is not a question of probability, as in the common law, but is a matter for the personal appreciation of the judge, or "*l'intime conviction du juge*." If the judge considers himself to have been persuaded by the argument on a certain matter, then the standard of proof has been met. The former President of the Iran–United States Claims Tribunal succinctly stated: "the burden of proof is that you have to convince me."[60] A civil law judge generally sees less need for a specific standard which must be met, as the question of whether the party bearing the burden of proof has established their case is essentially a subjective one, which can be answered with reference to the "inner, deep-seated, personal conviction of the Judge."[61]

Thus, not only do the two predominant legal traditions have different rules on the standard of proof, but their entire conceptual basis is different. "[T]he concept of an identifiable or quantifiable standard of proof emanates from the common law system,"[62] and does not exist in the civil legal tradition. However, on closer examination, it is not clear that this difference is as marked as one might think. The objective standards of the common law allow a degree of subjectivity in the weighing

[59] M Kazazi, *Burden of Proof and Related Issues—A Study on Evidence Before International Tribunals* (The Hague: Kluwer Law International 1996) 323.

[60] GM Von Mehren and CT Salomon, "Submitting Evidence in an International Arbitration: The Common Lawyer's Guide" (2003) 20 JIA 290.

[61] KM Clermont and E Sherwin, "A Comparative View of Standards of Proof" (2002) 50 Am J of Comparative L 246.

[62] E Valencia-Ospina, "Evidence before the International Court of Justice" (1999) 1(x) Intl L FORUM du droit International 203–7.

up of two cases when deciding on the balance of probabilities. Nevertheless, it is likely that this conceptual division is the source of the uncertainty that seems to exist as to the applicable standard of proof in international adjudicative bodies.

In international adjudication, it would seem that there are more than two standards of proof that are applied. The most exacting standard is of course "beyond reasonable doubt." This standard has not featured particularly heavily in the international context, given the difficulty of parties adducing evidence to establish any fact to this extent. However, it naturally has a place in the international criminal tribunals, where it is appropriate in light of the potential consequences of a guilty verdict. The Rome Statute of the ICC requires that the accused be found guilty beyond reasonable doubt,[63] and the other criminal tribunals have similar provisions in their constitutive documents. The human rights bodies too have on occasion seen fit to apply this standard,[64] and the ICJ has also appeared to apply it, for example in the *Corfu Channel* case, when faced with a "charge of exceptional gravity against a State."[65]

The other common law standard of the "preponderance of evidence" has also made an appearance in international litigation. Judge Lauterpacht in the ICJ *Norwegian Loans* case recognized this standard, considering that "the degree of burden of proof... to be adduced ought not to be so stringent as to render the proof unduly exacting."[66] It is perhaps the standard most appropriately applied in cases where one party has particular difficulty in producing evidence, for example, where it is in the hands of the other party, and the tribunal cannot compel its production. However, it is perhaps only appropriate for such circumstances, given that matters before international tribunals are often of great importance not only to the parties but also internationally, and deciding them simply on a balance of evidence could produce some rather controversial results.

Moving away from the traditional common law standards, the lower standard of "sufficiency of evidence" has also been used. In the ICJ, it was mentioned in the *Corfu Channel* case,[67] the *Nicaragua* case,[68] the *Oil Platforms* case,[69] and on numerous occasions in the *Armed Activities on the Territory of the Congo* case.[70] The ITLOS has applied this standard in *M/V "Saiga."*[71] The ICJ has also referred to being "convinced" when speaking of the standard relevant to a breach of treaty

[63] ICC Rules of Procedure and Evidence, Art. 66.

[64] See e.g., in the ECtHR *Aydin v. Turkey* [1997] 6 ECHR Rep No 50 1867, at 1889.

[65] *Corfu Channel (United Kingdom of Great Britain and Northern Ireland v. Albania)* [1949] ICJ Rep, at 18.

[66] *Certain Norwegian Loans* (Separate Opinion Judge Lauterpacht) [1957] ICJ Rep 9 at 39–40.

[67] *Corfu Channel*, note 65, at16.

[68] *Nicaragua*, note 45, at para. 110.

[69] *Case Concerning Oil Platforms (Islamic Republic of Iran v. United States of America)* [2003] ICJ Rep 189, paras 57, 61, and 76.

[70] *Armed Activities on the Territory of the Congo (Democratic Republic of the Congo v. Uganda)* [2005] ICJ Rep 168, 59 para. 173, 67 para. 208, 77 para. 246, 90 para. 298, 98 para. 334, 100 para. 342.

[71] *M/V "Saiga,"* 110 ILR 736, 750.

provisions;[72] this standard was also famously applied in the *Velasquez Rodriguez* case by the IACtHR, which said the truth of allegations had to be established "in a convincing manner."[73] This standard has also been mentioned in the ITLOS by Vice-President Wolfrum in his Separate Opinion in the *M/V "Saiga" (No 2)* case.[74]

"Sufficiency of evidence" can be an irritatingly vague concept for someone trained in the common law legal tradition. For example, Judge Buergenthal in the *Oil Platforms* case expressed discontent with the vague approach to the standard of proof:

> What is meant by 'insufficient' evidence? Does the evidence have to be 'convincing,' 'preponderant,' 'overwhelming' or 'beyond a reasonable doubt' to be sufficient? The Court never spells out what the here relevant standard of proof is.[75]

However, those with a civil law background do not consider that there is anything amiss with the way international tribunals approach the question of the standard of proof at present, being accustomed to the matter being "internal" to the individual judge, and not something that needs to be publicly articulated, considering it unnecessary to adopt a rigid standard. In addition, there may be those amongst the common lawyers who believe that a concrete standard is inappropriate in international adjudication because it may deny tribunals some of their usual flexibility of approach, which is important to retain given the wide range of cases which come before them. In the end, as Foster has observed: "Standards of proof are not a focus of attention in international tribunals... In effect the standard of proof usually used in international tribunals usually comes down to whether a tribunal considers that the evidence supports one proposition better than it does another."[76] It seems that in practice international adjudicative bodies follow the civil law by not enunciating a particular standard, and therefore are able to adjust the level of proof required for a particular fact with ease.[77]

4.3 Judicial Notice

"Judicial notice" is "a court's acceptance, for purposes of convenience and without requiring a party's proof, of a well-known and indisputable fact."[78] According to Cross

72 *Application of the Convention on the Prevention and Punishment of the Crime of Genocide (Bosnia and Herzeovina v. Serbia and Montenegro)* [2007] ICJ Rep 76, para. 209.

73 *Velasquez Rodriguez*, note 54, 285.

74 *M/V "Saiga" (No 2)* (Separate Opinion Judge Wolfrum) 120 ILR 143, 220–3.

75 *Oil Platforms* (Separate Opinion Judge Buergenthal), note 69, at 286.

76 C Foster, "The Adjudication of International Disputes Involving Scientific Uncertainty" (Ph.D. Thesis, Cambridge University 2003) 87.

77 Brower, note 9, at 48–9.

78 See BA Garner (ed.), *Black's Law Dictionary* (8th edn, Eagan, MN: West Group 2004).

and Tapper, "judicial notice refers to facts which a judge can be called upon to receive and to act upon either from his general knowledge of them, or from inquiries to be made by himself for his own information from sources to which it is proper for him to refer."[79] Thus, certain allegations of the parties which are within the knowledge of the court need no evidence in support of them, so proof may be dispensed regarding facts of common knowledge or public notoriety, or which are self-evident in the case circumstances, in order to expedite the hearing of cases.

Since the Nuremberg Trials, judicial notice has been incorporated in the rules of evidence of international adjudicative bodies.[80] Indeed, judicial notice is particularly useful when an international adjudicative body is called to decide on the guilt or innocence of several defendants in several trials who have participated in the same acts and events. Thus, to save valuable time and resources, in 2006, the UN Security Council encouraged the ICTY and ICTR to make greater use of judicial notice.[81] Another benefit is that it encourages uniformity in judicial decisions concerning a particular set of events, and thus uniformity in creating a historical record. The ICTY and ICTR Rules of Procedure and Evidence provide for the taking of judicial notice in Rule 94, which dictates there are three categories of facts which may be the subject of judicial notice: facts of common knowledge, adjudicated facts, and documentary evidence. The approach differs depending on whether the fact is of common knowledge or not. When the fact is of common knowledge, judicial notice is mandatory[82] and the only room for discretion lies in the definition of such fact and the assessment of whether it is of common knowledge.[83] Judicial notice of adjudicated

[79] R Cross, *Cross and Tapper on Evidence* (8th edn, London: Butterworth 1995) at 69.

[80] Article 21 of the Charter of the International Military Tribunal states: "The Tribunal shall not require proof of facts of common knowledge but shall take judicial notice thereof. It shall also take judicial notice of official governmental documents and reports of the United Nations, including the acts and documents of the committees set up in the various allied countries for the investigation of war crimes, and of records and finding of military or other Tribunals of any of the United Nations." Charter of the International Military Tribunal of August 8, 1945.

[81] Report on the International Tribunal for the Prosecution of Persons Responsible for Serious Violations of International Humanitarian Law Committed in the Territory of the Former Yugoslavia since 1991 (UN General Assembly Security Council of August 21, 2006) 8, available at <http://www.securitycouncilreport.org/atf/cf/%7B65BFCF9B-6D27-4E9C-8CD3-CF6E4FF96FF9%7D/ICTY%20S2006%20666.pdf> accessed August 27, 2013.

[82] The ICTR Appeals Chamber in *Prosecutor v. Karemera, Ngirumpatse, Nzirorera* ICTR-98-44-AR73(C) emphasized the fact that Rule 94(A) is *not* discretionary: "The Trial Chamber was obliged to take judicial notice of them, since judicial notice under Rule 94(A) is not discretionary."

[83] In the ICTR, a Chamber defined facts of common knowledge as: "facts of such notoriety, so well known and acknowledged that no reasonable individual with relevant concern can possibly dispute them. The notion was interpreted in the *Semanza* Decision to be "those facts which are not subject to reasonable dispute including, common or universally known facts, such as general facts of history, generally known geographical facts and the law of nature," *Prosecutor v. Casimir Bizimungu* et al (Decision of Prosecution's Motion for Judicial Notice Pursuant to Rules 73, 89, and 94) ICTR-99-50-I (December 2, 2003) para. 23.

facts and documentary evidence is discretionary, however. Rule 94(B) creates a presumption for the truth of the fact, but one that may still be challenged.[84]

Outside the international criminal law sphere, despite few explicit rules or case law on the matter, the doctrine appears to be generally accepted, and Brown suggests that: "all international courts may exercise the power to take judicial notice of 'notorious facts' in order to supplement evidence adduced by the parties."[85] For example, the ECtHR has stated it has taken judicial notice of facts in several cases.[86] In the ICJ, in the *Genocide Convention* case, Professor Franck, in his pleadings, noted that the fact that the court "will take notice of 'the notoriety of the facts' was recognized in 1951, in the *Fisheries* case and, again, in the *Nuclear Tests* cases."[87] He therefore asked the court "to consider some facts as 'notorious' because of the frequency and regularity with which they have entered the public domain: mostly through reports of reliable observers."[88]

Whilst it is uncontroversial that an adjudicative body may take judicial notice of a fact decided by another branch or differently constituted chamber of that same body, the question arose in the *Genocide Convention* case before the ICJ as to whether a different body may also take judicial notice of such adjudicated facts. The court was asked to establish whether genocidal acts had occurred in Bosnian territory during the war in the region, and to decide whether Serbia and Montenegro were responsible for the commission of these internationally wrongful acts. To answer these questions, the court was required to verify certain factual allegations that had previously been the subject of various proceedings in the ICTY. The court was careful to distinguish its proceedings from those conducted in the ICTY, given that the ICJ litigation was civil in character, and concerned the issue of state responsibility, whereas the ITCY proceedings dealt with individual accountability for criminal conduct. It further decided that the majority of decisions made by the latter tribunal would not meet their rigorous standards of proof. However, judgments of the Trial Chamber following a full hearing were deemed to satisfy the standards of proof; the court said it "should in principle accept as highly persuasive relevant findings of fact made by the Tribunal at trial,"[89] thus taking "cross-court judicial notice" of

[84] See *Prosecutor v. Slobodan Milošević* (Decision on the Prosecution's Interlocutory Appeal Against the Trial Chamber's Apr 10, 2003 Decision on Prosecution Motion for Judicial Notice of Adjudicated Facts), IT-02-54-AR73.5 International Criminal Tribunal for the Former Yugoslavia (ICTY), October 28, 2003, in Considerations.

[85] Brown, note 21, at 104.

[86] E.g. in *Jabari v. Turkey* Appl. No 40035/98 Council of Europe: European Court of Human Rights, July 11, 2000, the court said: "It has taken judicial notice of recent surveys of the current situation in Iran and notes that punishment of adultery by stoning still remains on the statute book," para. 41.

[87] *Application of the Convention on the Prevention and Punishment of the Crime of Genocide* (Oral Proceedings) [(CR 2006/3)] ICJ Rep 24, para. 12 (Professor Franck).

[88] *Application of the Convention on the Prevention and Punishment of the Crime of Genocide*, note 87, at para. 14.

[89] *Application of the Convention on the Prevention and Punishment of the Crime of Genocide (Bosnia and Herzeovina v. Serbia and Montenegro)* [2007] ICJ Rep 80, para. 223.

adjudicated facts. The desirability of this concept is questionable, given the different nature of the tribunals and the fact that parties before the tribunal in question may not have accepted the jurisdiction of the tribunal whose decision is being judicially noted. However, it is unlikely that an adjudicative body would accept the decisions reached by another international tribunal uncritically, simply by reason of its status as another international judicial body; the potential to resort to decisions of other tribunals certainly has the potential to fulfill the efficiency and uniformity goals of the judicial notice doctrine.

5 Evaluation of Evidence

5.1 Admissibility of evidence

International tribunals are generally unencumbered by the need to develop rules governing the admissibility of evidence in the same manner that their national cousins are, and, as a result, they tend to admit everything that is submitted to them. In 1925, in connection with the amendment of the rules of the PCIJ, Judge Huber noted that: "The Parties may present any proof that they judge useful and the Court is entirely free to take the evidence into account to the extent that it deems it pertinent."[90] President Higgins of the ICJ also noted the freedom of the parties to present the court with all the evidence they see fit in her speech to the General Assembly of the United Nations in 2007, and further stated: "The parties are entitled to expect that we will examine every single thing they put before us, and we do."[91] This is a necessary corollary of the sovereignty of the parties before the court, as Brower notes: "For obvious diplomatic reasons international tribunals are reluctant to spurn anything proffered by a sovereign."[92] The ICC too has a provision that gives the court the authority to freely assess all evidence before it.[93]

However, some exceptions are to be found. Overall, commentators have pointed to good judicial order as the most important policy limitation on a liberal evidentiary standard,[94] and, thus, there are some types of evidence that may not readily

[90] *Acts and Documents Concerning the Organization of the Court* (Judgment) (Addendum to No 2 *Revision of the Rules of Court*) [1926] PCIJ Rep Series D No X, 250.

[91] Speech by HE Judge R Higgins, President of the International Court of Justice to the General Assembly of the United Nations, November 1, 2007, available at <http://www.icj-cij.org/presscom/files/3/14113.pdf> accessed April 29, 2013.

[92] Brower, note 9, at 148. [93] ICC Rules of Evidence and Procedure, Art. 63(2).

[94] WM Reisman and E Freedman, "The Plaintiff's Dilemma: Illegally Obtained Evidence and Admissibility in International Adjudication" (1982) 76 AJIL 739, at 740–1.

be admitted. For instance, evidence that may be held to be inadmissible in international tribunals is evidence that has been obtained in violation of international law,[95] time-barred[96] or late-filed evidence,[97] evidence of uncertain authenticity,[98] and irrelevant evidence.[99] The ICJ has occasionally exercised its discretionary authority to refuse evidence offered.[100] For example, evidence resulting from prior settlement negotiations between the parties was held inadmissible in the *Burkina Faso/Mali* case. The reason for this was that in order to reach a settlement, the parties may have compromised on a well-founded case, and would not want evidence of these earlier negotiations to prejudice their case before the court.[101] The chamber agreed[102] that it should apply the *Chorzow Factory* rule that: "The Court cannot take into account declarations, admissions or proposals which the Parties may have made during direct negotiations between themselves, when such negotiations have not led to a complete agreement."[103]

5.2 Evaluation of evidentiary weight

The almost complete lack of rules dictating what evidence is admissible before international adjudicative bodies gives the weighing of evidence great importance.

[95] C Amerasinghe, *Evidence in International Litigation* (The Hague: Martinus Nijhoff 2005) at 179. Amerasinghe notes an "absence of clear precedents on the inadmissibility of evidence obtained through illicit acts." Indeed, few cases have expressly dealt with the question, the main one being the *Corfu Channel* case in the ICJ, note 65, in which the court neither relied on the evidence obtained through a violation of international law nor indicated whether it was admissible or not. For further discussion on this, see Reisman and Freedman, note 94.

[96] This can relate to either evidence of the facts occurring after the close of proceedings, or evidence occurring subsequent to the acts that are the cause of the dispute. An example of the latter is the *Island of Palmas* case in which an exchange of notes which occurred after the critical date of the dispute was held to be inadmissible, *Island of Palmas (Netherlands v. USA)* PCIJ (1928) Award of April 4, 1928, at 482.

[97] For example, in the ICJ, Art. 56 (1) of the Rules of Court provides that: "After the closure of the written proceedings, no further documents may be submitted to the Court by either party except with the consent of the other party or as provided in paragraph 2 of this Article." The ITLOS too has also held that late-filed documents will be inadmissible without the consent of the other party: *The "Grand Prince" case (No. 8) (Belize v. France)* Prompt Release, Judgment, ITLOS Reports 2001, paras 28–9.

[98] Generally it is assumed that documents are authentic unless questioned, and thus there are no provisions concerning this in international tribunals. The matter arose in the *Qatar v. Bahrain* case in the ICJ, in which Bahrain challenged the authenticity of 82 documents annexed to the Memorial of Qatar. Efforts were made by the court and the parties to quarantine the documents in question, but they were not declared inadmissible. Despite Qatar's denial of forgery, most observers have drawn that conclusion, leading to accompanying negative inferences. See e.g. M Mendelson, "The Curious Case of Qatar v Bahrain in the International Court of Justice" (2001) 72 BYIL 183, at 200.

[99] Whilst no specific rule exists barring the submission of irrelevant evidence in the majority of tribunals, it can be considered likely that a tribunal will do so where necessary.

[100] Sandifer, note 1, at 184–5. [101] Kazazi, note 59; Pietrowski, note 9, at 402.

[102] *Frontier Dispute (Burkina Faso/Republic of Mali)* [2005] ICJ Rep 632, para. 147.

[103] *Factory at Chorzow* (Merits) PCIJ Series A No 17, at 51.

By considering the procedural and substantive dimensions of the evidence brought before it, tribunals afford themselves the flexibility necessary to evaluate the great variety of evidentiary forms the parties employ during the proceedings. The task is a difficult one, as was nicely described by Judge Franck in the *Pulau Ligitan and Pulau Sipadan* case in the ICJ:

> To weigh, on the one hand, occasional administration of turtle egg harvesting and of a bird sanctuary—neither of these, apparently, in situ—together with the establishment of a few navigational lights against, on the other hand, naval and air patrolling and piracy-control appears to me like trying to weigh precisely a handful of feathers against a handful of grass: it can be done, but not very convincingly.[104]

An examination of the case law of the various international adjudicative bodies reveals several broad themes which shed light on the factors taken into consideration when evaluating a piece of evidence. These are generally considered in no specific order, and indeed, may not even be discussed in relation to many pieces of evidence since judges are free to make their own evaluation. However, this examination may come to the fore when it appears there could be some flaw or bias or other problem with the evidence, resulting in a discussion on the weight it should be ascribed.

One such consideration is the source of the evidence; whether it is partisan or independent, whether the source has any interest in the case, and whether the evidence is corroborated by other evidence. Another is the procedure that was followed to bring the evidence to the attention of the tribunal: how the information was initially collected, how it was presented to the tribunal, and whether it was submitted in accordance with the procedural requirements of that tribunal. The relationship of the evidence to events will also be considered: whether the information is direct observation or hearsay, the timing of the preparation of the document, and the purpose for the document, i.e. whether it was prepared specifically for litigation. Finally, the question of verification arises, whether it has been tested by cross-examination, or whether it is corroborated by other sources.

The evaluation of the weight attached to evidence is a subjective task, even in domestic courts. However in domestic courts there is generally more guidance to be found on what a court may find persuasive or not and more discussion of the weighing task. In international adjudicative bodies, it may be a necessary caution that there is little to be found in judgments on how certain pieces of evidence have been evaluated. An exception, however, could be the international criminal tribunals, whose task it is to determine an individual's guilt or innocence based on the most reliable and relevant evidence that can be obtained. In a critique of fact-finding particularly in the ICTR,[105] Combs calls for the basis of the acceptance of evidence

[104] *Sovereignty over Pulau Ligitan and Pulau Sipadan (Indonesia/Malaysia)* (Dissenting Opinion Judge Franck) [2002] ICJ Rep 625, at 4.

[105] NA Combs, *Fact-Finding Without Facts: The Uncertain Evidentiary Foundations of International Criminal Convictions* (Cambridge University Press 2010).

to be explained in the judgment, in order to remedy the perceived deficiency of relying on unreliable or insufficient evidence to support a decision.

6 Conclusion

Whilst it is not yet possible to discern a coherent body of law called the "international law of evidence," many international adjudicative bodies approach the subject in similar ways. However, there are obvious differences between the various types of international adjudicative bodies, which affect their appreciation of evidence. An international criminal tribunal, an arbitral tribunal, or a human rights court, given their different nature, parties, purpose, and procedure, approach the same problem in different ways. One will have developed rules on witness testimony, another on documentary evidence, another on the use of experts. Each tribunal has adapted the rules and practice from domestic litigation into the international sphere in a way that is appropriate to the subject matter of the tribunal. However, despite these specificities, it can be observed that the proceedings in all adjudicative bodies tend to be characterized by flexibility and the freedom of the parties. The degree of deference shown by the given body to the parties ultimately depends very much on its nature—a greater degree of deference will be shown by those bodies dealing with cases where the parties are sovereign states, while those hearing, for instance, international commercial disputes, will apply more stringent and less flexible rules.

Certain issues appear more prominent in international adjudication than in domestic jurisdictions. The question of proof, for example, is usually well understood in national courts, based on either the common or civil tradition, but once transplanted to the international context, often suffers from uncertainty as to the relevant standard to be applied, or the operation of the burden of proof. Here tribunals are faced with two competing ideals: flexibility in adjudication and certainty for the parties. If one standard is adopted the flexibility of the tribunal is lost, but the parties have some concrete guidance. If, in order to retain some flexibility, the tribunal adopts variable or varying standards, then certainty for the parties is lost, and there may be a detrimental impact upon the perceived legitimacy of the tribunal and its judgments. However, in international litigation, it is clear that flexibility is prevailing; it would appear that international adjudicative bodies are well-equipped to determine the burden and standard of proof to be applied, even if they do not necessarily make this explicit.

The use of experts is another aspect much discussed in the international context, particularly given the increasing frequency of disputes of a technical or scientific nature. The difficulties over the burden and standard of proof emanate from the deeply held beliefs about the judicial function stemming from national procedures which are not necessarily warranted in international adjudication. Practice regarding experts, however, does not suffer from the same issue, and could very easily be significantly improved by tribunals making use of powers already available to them, and perhaps supplemented by some further "rules." The benefits of properly employing experts when dealing with highly complex matters clearly outside the knowledge of the judges are as obvious as the detriment to cases where expert evidence has not been made use of or has been misunderstood, for example, in the *Cameroon v. Nigeria* case in the ICJ, discussed above. It is critical that international tribunals accept that they cannot themselves be expert in all fields, and employ those who are, in order to reach a sound judgment based on the objective facts before them, rather than making a decision that avoids those facts because they are not well understood.

The main criticism of the way international adjudicative bodies handle evidence is essentially their apparent insufficient focus on the appreciation of facts, particularly when they are of a complex scientific or technical nature, a perception which stems from a lack of developed rules and procedures, and the little discussion on the virtue of "flexibility." The potential to criticize international tribunals for these apparent errors in approach appears strong, and indeed, it has become popular in recent academic literature to do so, given the huge importance of basing decisions with a potentially fundamental impact on litigants on a proper appreciation of the evidence. However, it should be recalled that international tribunals have generally conducted their difficult task in an impressive manner, particularly given the many pressures upon them that are entirely absent in their domestic counterparts, such as international politics. As Crook has noted:

> Despite their importance, the processes by which courts and tribunals determine facts generally operate without explanation and out of sight. Good English-language literature on fact-finding in international adjudication is sparse. This dearth is in no small part because fact-finding rests on the unique facts of individual cases. Understanding decision-makers' choices in a case requires close understanding of the underlying factual record, something which few outside observers have time or inclination (or, with closed proceedings, the ability) to pursue.[106]

However, given the growing focus on the issue of evidence, it would be inadvisable for international adjudicative bodies to completely ignore calls to examine their practices and procedure regarding evidence and fact-finding. From the recent *Pulp Mills* judgment, it is clear that the ICJ is beginning to feel the weight of criticism in this regard and some judges are calling for improvements, or at least, consideration

[106] JR Crook, "Review of 'Evidence Before the International Court of Justice' by A Riddell and B Plant" (2013) 107(1) AJIL 259.

of the issues. This is certainly to be encouraged, and it is hoped that this discussion, and others like it, will be of assistance to these tribunals when considering their evidentiary practices.

Research Questions

1. Could the development of an "international law of evidence" have any benefits for international courts and tribunals and the parties before them?
2. Would it be beneficial for individual tribunals to develop more comprehensive "rules" on evidence and fact-finding, even if such "rules" were predominantly granting the tribunal flexibility in their approach?
3. What methods can international tribunals employ to facilitate and improve their use of experts?
4. How can international tribunals best deal with large volumes of complex evidence in the increasing numbers of technical and scientific disputes before them?

Suggested Reading

Brower, CN, "Evidence Before International Tribunals: The Need for Some Standard Rules" (1994) 28 International Lawyer 47.

Brown, C, *A Common Law of International Adjudication* (Oxford University Press 2012).

Cheng, B, *General Principles of Law as Applied by International Courts and Tribunals* (Rev. edn, Cambridge University Press 1987).

Clermont, KM and Sherwin, E, "A Comparative View of Standards of Proof" (2002) 50 Am J of Comparative L 246.

Kazazi, M, *Burden of Proof and Related Issues—A Study on Evidence Before International Tribunals* (The Hague: Kluwer Law International 1996).

Pietrowski, R, "Evidence In International Arbitration" (2006) 22 Arbitration International 3.

Reisman, WM and Freedman, E, "The Plaintiff's Dilemma: Illegally Obtained Evidence and Admissibility in International Adjudication" (1982) 76 AJIL 739.

Riddell, A and Plant, B, *Evidence Before the International Court of Justice* (British Institute of International and Comparative Law 2009).

Rosenne, S, *The Law and Practice of the International Court 1920-2005* (4th edn, The Hague: Martinus Nijhoff 2006).

Sandifer, D, *Evidence before International Tribunals* (Rev edn, University Press of Virginia 1975).

Wolfrum, R, "Evidence in International Courts and Tribunals" in R Wolfrum (ed.), *The Max Planck Encyclopedia of Public International Law* (Oxford University Press 2008), online edition <www.mpepil.com> accessed July 31, 2013.

CHAPTER 40

REMEDIES

CHRISTINE GRAY*

1 Introduction

In 1985, I raised the question of whether there was an international law of remedies and concluded that the mass of arbitral and judicial practice had fallen short of producing a coherent set of universally applicable rules.[1] At that time, there were only four permanent international courts of any significance: the International Court of Justice (ICJ), the European Court of Justice (ECJ), the European Court of Human Rights (ECtHR), and the Inter-American Court of Human Rights (IACtHR). However, it should also be noted that there had been 200 years of arbitral practice.

* Professor of International Law, University of Cambridge.

[1] C Gray, "Is there an international law of remedies?" (1985) 56 BYIL 25.

There have been two main changes affecting the international law on remedies since then: proliferation of tribunals and the Articles on State Responsibility from the International Law Commission (ILC).

Today there are far more permanent international tribunals than in the 1980s.[2] The focus in this chapter will be on the ICJ, inter-state arbitration tribunals, the International Tribunal on the Law of the Sea (ITLOS), the World Trade Organization Appellate Body (WTO AB), the ECJ (now part of the Court of Justice of the EU), the European and Inter-American human rights courts, and the United Nations Compensation Commission (UNCC). The aim here is to consider the practice of a representative sample of the different types of tribunal.[3]

As this handbook makes evident, tribunals can be classified in different ways. They can be divided according to parties or subject matter; whether they are regional or universal, permanent or ad hoc; or according to whether they have compulsory jurisdiction. The question is whether this diversity means that the tribunals award different types of remedies or have taken different approaches to remedies. Is there any consistency to be found? Has the growth in importance of international adjudication brought a more conscious consideration of remedies by the many tribunals? The expanding literature on tribunals has given little general consideration to remedies,[4] though there are now several studies of remedies in specific bodies.

The second main development in international law was the completion of the ILC's Articles on State Responsibility in 2001.[5] Part II of these Articles deals with the content of the international responsibility of a state. It first sets out the legal consequences arising from a wrongful act, including the obligation on a wrongdoing state to stop its wrongful act (cessation) and to offer assurances and guarantees of non-repetition.[6] It then makes provision for reparation. Article 31 sets out the general principle requiring full reparation for the injury caused by an internationally wrongful act. Articles 34 through 39 on reparation give more specific content to this principle. Article 34 provides for three remedies to be awarded singly or in combination: restitution, compensation, and satisfaction. This chapter will concentrate on these three remedies. ILC Articles 35 through 37 on the individual remedies are brief, but the Commentaries provide more discussion, if not more precise guidance.[7] The ICJ has made occasional reference to the general provisions of the ILC

[2] See, in this handbook, Dupuy and Viñuales, Ch. 7.

[3] It will not cover international criminal tribunals. On these see, in this handbook, Schabas, Ch. 10.

[4] The main recent works are C Brown, *A Common Law of International Adjudication* (Oxford University Press 2007) and D Shelton, *Remedies in International Human Rights Law* (2nd edn, Oxford University Press 2005).

[5] Report of the 53rd session, ILC (2001), GAOR 56th session, Supp.10.

[6] Report of the 53rd session, ILC, note 5, at Art. 30.

[7] J Crawford, *The ILC's Articles on State Responsibility: Introduction, Text and Commentaries* (Cambridge University Press 2002).

Articles on remedies, and so has ITLOS.[8] However, it is clear that the ILC's Articles have not brought uniformity between all the various tribunals with regard to remedies.

These two developments, the proliferation of tribunals and the completion of the ILC Articles, make it timely to revisit the question of remedies. An examination of the jurisprudence of the different tribunals quickly makes clear that there is still little evidence of any consistent decision-making on remedies. There is little cross-reference between the tribunals, except to the decision of the PCIJ in the *Chorzow Factory* case.[9] This is regularly referred to by the ICJ itself and by other tribunals such as human rights courts, ITLOS in *M/V Saiga*,[10] and the Ethiopia–Eritrea Claims Commission (EECC).[11] In contrast, it is not referred to by the CJEU or WTO tribunals. The principle set out in *Chorzow Factory*, a case on the illegal expropriation of a factory, is that reparation must, as far as possible, wipe out the consequences of the illegal act and re-establish the situation which would in all probability have existed if that act had not been committed. The ideal remedy is restitution in kind, or if this is not possible, payment of a sum corresponding to the value which restitution in kind would bear.

In fact, actual restitution is still unusual in inter-state cases, even in the practice of the ICJ itself. In human rights tribunals, in cases brought by individuals, it has grown in importance in recent years. But where other tribunals have quoted the *Chorzow* principle, they have generally done so simply in support of the principle of full reparation. The international tribunals under consideration make little if any reference to each other's jurisprudence on remedies. It seems that there may be many special regimes on remedies, rather than one universal regime. Chester Brown recently considered whether there is a "common law" of remedies and found very little sign of this.[12]

1.1 The power to award remedies

Almost all the tribunals under consideration in this chapter have been given express powers to decide on reparation. Some constituent instruments specify which remedies may be awarded; some do not. Some provide only for the award of compensation; others are more wide-ranging. Where there is no express provision, as most notably with the ICJ (apart from that in Art. 36.2 of the Statute of the Court[13]) and

[8] *M/V Saiga (St Vincent and the Grenadines v. Guinea)* (1997) 120 ILR 143.
[9] *Case Concerning the Factory at Chorzow Factory (Germany v. Poland)* PCIJ Rep Series A No 13.
[10] *M/V Saiga*, note 8, at para. 170.
[11] EECC, *Ethiopia's Ius ad Bellum Claims* 1–8, (2006) 45 ILM 430 [24].
[12] Brown, note 4, at 224.
[13] The relevant part of Art. 36(2) provides that state parties may accept the jurisdiction of the court in all legal disputes concerning "The nature and extent of the reparation to be made for the breach of an international obligation."

ITLOS (apart from the provision for prompt release in Art. 292 UNCLOS), it is no longer controversial that jurisdiction to decide a case includes jurisdiction to determine remedies in that case.[14] This was first established in the *Chorzow Factory* case where the PCIJ held that the power to decide the case included the power to award compensation. This remedial power was extended in *LaGrand* to include assurances of non-repetition,[15] and in *Avena* to the power to order restitution.[16] ITLOS also accepted this principle. There is nothing specific on remedies in UNCLOS Part XV on the Settlement of Disputes, apart from the provision for prompt release, but in *M/V Saiga* ITLOS assumed that it had the power to award the remedies listed in the ILC Articles.[17] It is striking that the ECJ and the WTO AB have not gone so far.[18] That is, the tribunals with the strongest provisions for compulsory jurisdiction do not necessarily assert the most far-reaching jurisdiction with regard to remedies.

1.2 Special regimes

Different tribunals have taken different approaches to remedies. Permanent tribunals with compulsory jurisdiction in specialized areas decide on remedies according to the specific provisions in the relevant treaties. Thus, there are express provisions on remedies in the WTO, UNCC, IACtHR, and ITLOS (on prompt release). The particular nature of the legal regimes in these cases requires provision for appropriate remedies.

There are also special regimes when it is necessary to handle large numbers of claims; in such cases the tribunal may adopt a special approach to remedies.[19] There was express provision for this approach with regard to the UNCC, which had to deal with the enormous number of claims arising out of the Iraqi invasion of Kuwait. Similarly, the EECC developed its own approach to the mass of claims arising out of the large-scale conflict between Ethiopia and Eritrea.

In some cases, the remedy may depend on the primary obligation breached. Thus, the subject matter of the case determines the remedy. The ILC made provision for this type of special regime in Art. 55.[20] The question of whether there was a special regime for violations of the *Vienna Convention on Consular Relations* was considered by the ICJ in *Tehran Hostages*.[21] Perhaps most controversially, this question also arises with regard to the remedies for unlawful expropriation.[22]

[14] Brown, note 4, at 54, 66, 75.

[15] *LaGrand (Germany v. USA)* [2001] ICJ Rep 466 at paras 46–8, 117–27.

[16] *Mexico v. USA* [2004] ICJ Rep 12 at paras 115–21.

[17] *M/V Saiga*, note 8.

[18] See section 3.2 of this chapter.

[19] See in this handbook, Caron, Ch. 13.

[20] Crawford, note 7, at 306.

[21] *US Diplomatic and Consular Staff in Tehran (USA v. Iran)* [1980] ICJ Rep 3 at para. 86.

[22] C Gray, *Judicial Remedies in International Law* (Oxford University Press 1987) 188; C Gray, "Restitution" in J Crawford, A Pellet, and S Olleson (eds), *The Law of State Responsibility* (Oxford University Press 2010) 595.

2 Overview of Remedies by the ICJ

It is generally acknowledged that the ICJ has a special role among international tribunals because of its universal jurisdiction in terms of subject matter and of states parties and because of its role as the principal judicial organ of the UN.[23] But it cannot be claimed that it sees its role as the development or clarification of the law rather than the settlement of particular disputes; different judges take very different approaches to this question. In particular, the ICJ's discussion of remedies has been limited. There are some signs that it is bolder in its approach today than it was 30 years ago, though it is still cautious in its orders to states parties. The consent-based nature of its jurisdiction necessarily limits its role. Also, the ICJ is called on to make decisions on remedies only in state responsibility cases; it decides on remedies in only a small proportion of its judgments on the merits. This chapter considers whether there has been any more express discussion of remedies since the completion of the ILC Articles, and what impact, if any, the ICJ has had on other tribunals.

2.1 The *Bosnia-Herzegovina Genocide* case

The *Bosnia-Herzegovina Genocide* case (2007) gives a good overview of remedies in its separate section on reparation, and is unusual in its relatively extensive discussion of this question, although it does not go into underlying policy considerations.[24] In this case, Serbia was accused of being responsible for genocide during the civil war in Bosnia. As its starting point, the ICJ referred to the *Chorzow Factory* principle that a state is entitled to compensation insofar as restitution is not possible, and to its reliance on this principle in its own pronouncements in the *Danube Dam* case[25] and the *Wall* Advisory Opinion.[26] The court also referred to ILC Art. 31 on the general principle of full reparation and to Art. 36 on compensation. The applicant state had recognized that restitution was not appropriate. Nor could compensation be awarded because there was no causal link between the breach of international law—the failure to prevent genocide—and the harm. This is typically the crucial problem with establishing a claim to financial compensation before international tribunals.

[23] See in this handbook, Murphy, Ch. 9.

[24] *Application of the Convention on the Prevention and Punishment of the Crime of Genocide (Bosnia and Herzegovina v. Serbia and Montenegro)* (Merits) [2007] ICJ Rep 43 at para. 459.

[25] *Gabcikovo-Nagymaros Project (Hungary/Slovakia)* [1997] ICJ Rep 7 at para. 152.

[26] *Legal Consequences of the Construction of a Wall in the Occupied Palestinian Territory* [2004] ICJ Rep 136.

The court accordingly held that Bosnia was entitled to reparation in the form of satisfaction. The court determined that the most appropriate form of satisfaction, as Bosnia itself had suggested, was a declaration that Serbia had failed to comply with the *Genocide Convention* when it failed to prevent and punish the genocide.[27] Bosnia also asked for guarantees and assurances of non-repetition. The court held that there was nothing to justify this. It made no reference to the ILC Articles on this point.[28] Finally, Bosnia asked for symbolic compensation for Serbia's failure to comply with the court's 1993 Orders for Provisional Measures. The court held that this non-compliance merged with the breaches of the substantive obligations of prevention and punishment. Therefore, it was not appropriate to order symbolic compensation, but only to make a declaration as satisfaction.[29] The court has also avoided the question whether there are any special rules governing the remedies for violations of orders of provisional measures in other cases.[30]

2.2 The declaratory judgment

It is clear from *Bosnia-Herzegovina Genocide* that the declaratory judgment plays a central role as a remedy for violation of international law in the jurisprudence of the ICJ. The case most often referred to in this regard is *Corfu Channel* (1949), where the ICJ first held that a declaratory judgment that there had been a breach of international law could provide adequate satisfaction for harm to a state.[31] This is still the remedy most often awarded by the ICJ, as can be seen in recent cases.[32] A declaratory judgment leaves it to the discretion of the wrongdoing state to take appropriate measures to comply with international law. ITLOS took the same approach in *M/V Saiga*. There, Saint Vincent had claimed it was entitled to compensation for violation of its rights with respect to ships flying its flag. ITLOS declared that Guinea had acted wrongfully and violated the rights of Saint Vincent in arresting the *M/V Saiga* and in using excessive force. The tribunal considered that these declarations constituted adequate reparation.[33]

However, declaratory judgments do not play the same role in the rare inter-state cases before the ECtHR.[34] In these cases, the court's declaratory judgment that there has been a breach of the convention is not given as satisfaction for an injury to the

[27] *Bosnia-Herzegovina Genocide* case, note 24.

[28] *Bosnia-Herzegovina Genocide* case, note 24, at para. 466.

[29] *Bosnia-Herzegovina Genocide* case, note 24, at paras 467–9.

[30] *LaGrand* case, note 15.

[31] *UK v. Albania* (Merits) [1949] ICJ Rep 4, 35, 36.

[32] *Certain Questions of Mutual Assistance in Criminal Matters (Djibouti v. France)* [2008] ICJ Rep 177; *Application of the Interim Accord of September 13, 1995 (Macedonia v. Greece)* [2011] ICJ Rep; *Jurisdictional Immunities of the State (Germany v. Italy)* [2012] ICJ Rep.

[33] *M/V Saiga*, note 8, at para. 176.

[34] Art. 33 ECHR provides for inter-state cases; only a few of these have been decided by the court.

claimant state. The aim of inter-state proceedings is not to compensate states for harm to their nationals, but to secure compliance with the treaty regime. In contrast, the ECtHR does expressly award declarations as satisfaction in cases brought by injured individuals.[35] Similarly, the declaratory judgment given by the ECJ in enforcement cases against member states is not given as satisfaction for the state or the EU Commission bringing the case. The focus is not on reparation of injury to member states or EU institutions; the aim of these proceedings is to secure compliance with community obligations.[36]

2.3 Restitution and other orders

The situation in *Bosnia-Herzegovina Genocide*—that restitution was not an appropriate remedy in the circumstances and had not been requested by Bosnia—is typical in international judicial practice.[37] ILC, Art. 35 sets out the limits on restitution: it cannot be awarded where it would be materially impossible or disproportionate. States have often made claims for restitution, and the ICJ has made statements in principle that it may award this far-reaching type of judgment. However, actual awards of restitution or other orders have been rare—and handed down cautiously. The ICJ has not discussed the primacy or availability of restitution since *Chorzow Factory*, but the question is one that has provoked controversy among commentators. In some of its judgments, the ICJ has made statements that there is an obligation on a state party to act in a certain way. Thus, in *Temple of Preah Vihear* (1962), it held that there was an obligation on Thailand to withdraw any military or police forces and to restore any sculptures and other objects taken from the temple.[38] Some commentators have interpreted this and similar statements as amounting to an order for restitution, but there is room for doubt as to whether this is really so. Kerbrat argues that this was simply a statement of legal obligation—of the consequences of a breach—rather than a direct order.[39] Similarly, in early arbitration cases, there were few actual awards of restitution. Commonly cited examples of this remedy may not actually have involved an award of restitution.[40]

The ICJ seems to have gone further in its more recent judgments. However, it is still cautious—perhaps too cautious, in that sometimes its judgments are not specific enough to make clear what action should be taken to bring the dispute to an end. For example, in *Danube Dam* (1997) the court held that the 1977 Treaty on

[35] Section 5.1 of this chapter. [36] Section 3.2 of this chapter.

[37] Gray, "Restitution," note 22, at 595.

[38] *US Diplomatic and Consular Staff in Tehran (USA v. Iran)* [1980] ICJ Rep 3; *Land and Maritime Boundary between Cameroon and Nigeria (Cameroon v. Nigeria)* [2002] ICJ Rep 303.

[39] Y Kerbrat, "Interaction between the forms of reparation" in Crawford, Pellet, and Olleson, note 22, at 573, 583–5.

[40] Kerbrat in Crawford, Pellet, and Olleson, note 22, at 573, 583–5.

the regime for the Danube remained in force; the parties were therefore under an obligation to consider in what way the multiple objectives of the treaty could best be served. The court went on to consider the legal consequences of the internationally wrongful acts committed by the parties. It held that under the *Chorzow* principle, the parties had to resume cooperation in the utilization of the shared water resources of the Danube and implement the multi-purpose program in an equitable and reasonable manner. However, the parties were unable to agree on the implementation of the court's judgment. Slovakia later made a request for an additional judgment.[41] The initial judgment clearly had not been specific enough to bring an end to the dispute.

In *Avena and other Mexican nationals*, Mexico sued the United States for breaching the Consular Convention in its treatment of foreign nationals.[42] The problems that arose from leaving the choice of means of implementation of the court's judgment to the respondent state were again apparent in this case. At the provisional measures stage, the ICJ rejected the United States' claim that it could not order restitution because this would interfere with the US criminal judicial system; in principle restitution was available.[43] Mexico had requested restitution in the form of the annulment of the convictions and sentences of its nationals, but the court said that the violation of the Consular Convention did not require retrial.[44] Restitution required the United States only to provide, by means of its own choosing, review and reconsideration of the convictions and sentences. The court did stipulate that the review and reconsideration should be effective.[45]

This cautious judgment proved problematic.[46] The US federal government tried to postpone the executions of Mexican nationals in compliance with the ICJ's judgment, but the US judiciary and state bodies did not cooperate, and the executions went ahead.[47] Mexico made an unsuccessful "Request for Interpretation" of the *Avena* judgment.[48] However, the ICJ was not willing to address the real difficulties in securing the implementation of the ICJ's judgment in the United States. The United States subsequently terminated its acceptance of the ICJ's jurisdiction in disputes concerning the Consular Convention.

Most recently, in *Jurisdictional Immunities of the State*, the ICJ held that Italy had violated Germany's sovereign immunity by allowing actions in its national courts against Germany for war crimes committed during World War II.[49] Italy had a duty to re-establish the situation which existed before the wrongful act was committed,

[41] ICJ Press Release 1998/28.

[42] *Avena and other Mexican nationals* [2004] ICJ Rep12; See A Orakhelashvili, "Judicial Competence and Judicial Remedies in the *Avena* Case" (2005) 18 LJIL 31.

[43] *Avena*, note 42, at paras 31–4.

[44] *Avena*, note 42, at paras 117, 121–4.

[45] *Avena*, note 42, at para. 138.

[46] Judge Sepulveda in his Dissenting Opinion was critical of the court's terminology and said that the court should be more specific.

[47] (2008) 47 ILM 281.

[48] [2009] ICJ Rep 3.

[49] *Germany v. Italy* [2012] ICJ Rep.

provided that this was not materially impossible and did not involve a disproportionate burden. The ICJ referred to ILC Art. 35 on restitution. The fact that some violations were committed by judicial organs and that some of the legal decisions had become final in Italian domestic law did not relieve Italy of its obligation to provide restitution. The ICJ accordingly found that "Italy must, by enacting appropriate legislation or by resorting to other means of its choosing, ensure that the decisions of its courts and those of other judicial authorities infringing the immunity which the Federal Republic of Germany enjoys under international law cease to have effect." This is more specific than the court's judgments in earlier cases, but Italy still has the right to choose the means it considers best suited to achieving this result.

It is interesting that other tribunals—the CJEU, WTO, and large-scale claims commissions—do not have express powers under their constituent instruments to order restitution, nor have they have asserted the right to do so. They have referred to the *Chorzow* principle only as a basis for an order of full compensation, and not in order to assert a right to order restitution. In contrast, human rights tribunals have used the discretion available to them under their constituent treaties to make elaborate orders designed to secure the protection of human rights.

2.4 Cessation and assurances of non-repetition

In its Articles on State Responsibility, the ILC draws a distinction between reparation—the three remedies—and other consequences of a wrongful act, such as the obligation of cessation and guarantees of non-repetition.[50] The Commentary on the ILC Articles attempts to justify this distinction on the basis that cessation and guarantees of non-repetition are forward-looking, designed to secure future performance of violated obligations. In practice this distinction is not always clear. In recent years, claimant states have often asked the ICJ for orders of cessation and non-repetition as a form of reparation. Cessation overlaps with restitution—the re-establishment of the situation that existed before the unlawful act. However, cessation is available only when there is a continuing breach, and there is no express requirement in the Articles that cessation be proportionate. In theory, it is not necessary for a tribunal to order cessation; the obligation to cease unlawful conduct derives from the operation of the law.[51] Some ICJ judgments that have been said to order restitution could, in fact, be interpreted as statements of the obligation of cessation.[52]

[50] O Corten, "The Obligation of Cessation" in Crawford, Pellet, and Olleson, note 22, at 545; S Barbier, "Assurances and Guarantees of Non-repetition" in Crawford, Pellet, and Olleson, note 22, at 551.

[51] *Dispute Regarding Navigational and Related Rights (Costa Rica v. Nicaragua)* [2009] ICJ Rep 213 at para. 148.

[52] *Germany v. Italy* [2012] ICJ Rep. See also *Rainbow Warrior (New Zealand v. France)* [1990] 82 ILR 499.

Since the ILC started its work on this topic, states have increasingly requested assurances or guarantees of non-repetition of wrongful acts. The ICJ has apparently treated this as a remedy by including it in its discussion of reparation.[53] It has not, however, referred to the work of the ILC on this question. Some have argued that Art. 30 is a progressive development rather than codification of the existing law.[54] The ICJ has not yet actually ordered assurances or guarantees of non-repetition, but it does refer to commitments by states as to their future behavior as satisfying such requests. Similarly, the ECtHR and the IACtHR have not specifically ordered guarantees of non-repetition, but they have given remedies designed to secure implementation of the obligations of states parties. The remedies of the WTO system are also forward looking, although the WTO AB does not require express guarantees of non-repetition.

The leading ICJ case on non-repetition of wrongful acts is *LaGrand* (2001), another case concerning the United States' violations of its obligations under the Consular Convention.[55] There, restitution was no longer possible because the United States had already executed the German nationals whose rights had been violated before the judgment. Therefore, Germany sought two different types of guarantees of non-repetition. First, Germany requested a straightforward general assurance of non-repetition. The ICJ held that, because the United States had said that it was taking substantial measures to prevent recurrence of breach, this commitment must be regarded as meeting Germany's request for a general assurance of non-repetition.[56] Second, Germany sought other assurances that in future cases against German nationals the United States would ensure the effective exercise of the rights under the Consular Convention. The court did not order these assurances. It had not found that US law was inherently inconsistent with the Consular Convention. It noted that the United States had apologized to Germany for its breach of the convention. However, it said that in future an apology would not suffice if the United States failed in its obligations and the foreign nationals were subject to prolonged detention or convicted and sentenced to severe penalties. In such cases, review and reconsideration of the conviction and sentence would be necessary. The choice of means must be left to the United States.

LaGrand set the tone for later cases. The ICJ has said that, as a general rule, there is no reason to suppose that a state whose act has been declared wrongful by the court would repeat that act in the future; its good faith must be presumed. While the court may order a state to offer assurances of non-repetition or to take specific measures to ensure that the wrongful act is not repeated, it may only do so when

[53] As in the *LaGrand*, *Bosnia-Herzegovina Genocide*, and *Dispute Regarding Navigational and Related Rights* cases.

[54] Barbier, note 50, at 553–5.

[55] *LaGrand*, note 15.

[56] *LaGrand*, note 15, at paras 120–1.

there are special circumstances.[57] This may help to explain why the ECJ also does not go beyond declaratory judgments to make such orders.

2.5 Damages

Numerous early arbitral decisions awarded damages, but these decisions have not produced clear rules on the assessment of damages. Commentators have tended to pick and choose between the cases in an attempt to extract generally applicable rules. The actual award of damages has been rare in the jurisprudence of the World Court, although financial compensation has been requested in many cases. The PCIJ awarded damages only in the *SS Wimbledon* case for the refusal of passage through the Kiel canal.[58] In that case, it did not give much reasoned explanation of the assessment of damages in international law; it did not provide any discussion of general theoretical issues; or refer back to earlier arbitral practice.[59] In *Chorzow Factory*, the PCIJ did identify the general principles of reparation set out above and it also asserted the principle of damages for lost profits. However, the parties eventually came to a settlement on the question of damages for Poland's expropriation of the factory. It is therefore difficult to extract any specific rules from these two cases. Before 2012, the ICJ made only one other award of damages, in *Corfu Channel*, for harm to British warships blown up by mines. This was based on the opinion of court-appointed experts who concluded that the claim submitted by the United Kingdom was a fair and accurate assessment of the damage sustained; the court itself did not discuss relevant rules of assessment.

ILC Art. 36 says nothing specific on the assessment of compensation except that, "[T]he compensation shall cover any financially assessable damage including loss of profits insofar as it is established." The ILC Commentaries select certain cases for attention, but the basis on which they do so is not clear. These cases help to illustrate the heads of damage (that is, the types of damage) which have been compensated in the past, but show great diversity on the methods of assessment.[60] Most commentators conclude that arbitral and judicial decisions have established what types of damage may be compensated, but that there is little consistency in the actual methods of assessment.[61]

[57] *Avena*, note 42; *Cameroon v. Nigeria*, note 38; *Armed Activities on the Territory of the* Congo (*DRC v. Uganda)* [2005] ICJ Rep 168; *Costa Rica v. Nicaragua*, note 51; *Pulp Mills on the River Uruguay (Argentina v. Uruguay)* [2010] ICJ Rep 14; *Macedonia v. Greece*, note 32; *Germany v. Italy*, note 49.

[58] *UK, France, Italy and Japan v. Germany* (1923) PCIJ Rep Series A No 1.

[59] See Gray, *Judicial Remedies*, note 22, at 78.

[60] Crawford, Commentaries, note 7.

[61] Brown, note 4; Shelton, note 4. Barker takes a contrary view, but even he admits that the methods of assessing compensation for property damage and harm to businesses are very diverse. J Barker, "Compensation" in Crawford, Pellet, and Olleson, note 22, at 599. On the award of interest, see P Nevill, "Awards of Interest by International Courts and Tribunals" (2007) 78 BYIL 255.

In 2012, the ICJ gave its second judgment on compensation in *Diallo*.[62] It found that the Democratic Republic of Congo (DRC) had violated its human rights obligations in its treatment of Diallo, a national of Guinea. The court said that it had taken into account the practice of other international adjudicative bodies (such as ITLOS, ECtHR, IACtHR, EECC, and the UNCC) that had applied general principles governing compensation when fixing the amount due.[63] In *Diallo*—unusually—the ICJ did cite many relevant cases of other tribunals, in particular human rights cases. It seems that it was concerned with finding the appropriate guidance on compensation for violations of human rights. The ICJ referred to several human rights cases on the general principle that a state may claim compensation for non-material damage to injured individuals, but not to establish any specific method of assessment. Like the human rights tribunals, the ICJ did not require any specific evidence of non-material damage suffered by Diallo as a result of his detention and expulsion. The court awarded $85,000 based on equitable considerations, but it arrived at this figure without explanation. Guinea had requested $250,000 for non-material harm, while the DRC had argued that $35,000 would be enough. In regards to Guinea's significant claims for Diallo's loss of earnings and material injury, the court held that Guinea had failed to bring adequate evidence. Nevertheless, without explanation, it awarded $10,000 under this head.[64] The judgment provides little general guidance on the actual assessment of the amount of compensation.

The same type of impressionistic approach can also be seen in an award of damages by ITLOS for the unlawful arrest and detention of a ship in *M/V Saiga*.[65] ITLOS referred to the *Chorzow* principle that reparation should wipe out all the consequences of an illegal act. It also referred to the ILC Articles when considering the available remedies. It then held that Saint Vincent was entitled to reparation for damage suffered directly by it, and for damage or other loss suffered by the *M/V Saiga*, including all persons involved or interested in its operation. This should cover injury to persons, unlawful arrest, detention or other forms of ill-treatment, damage to or seizure of property, and other economic losses, including loss of profit. But the tribunal offered no explanation of its assessment of reparation. It noted that Saint Vincent had submitted substantial documentation, and that Guinea had challenged the validity of some claims and the reasonableness of the amounts, and had questioned the evidence submitted in respect of some of the claims. In explanation of its award, the tribunal said only, "After a careful scrutiny of invoices and other documents submitted," it was awarding more than $2 million to Saint Vincent.

[62] *Ahmadou Sadio Diallo (Compensation) (Guinea v. DRC)* [2012] ICJ Rep.
[63] *Diallo*, note 62, at para. 13. [64] *Diallo*, note 62, at para. 55.
[65] *M/V Saiga*, note 8, at paras 167–77.

It is the EECC that has given the most detailed consideration to the assessment of damages in recent years, though it did so in an unusual context: that of compensation for the unlawful use of force. It struggled to identify general rules on damages on the basis of past adjudicative practice. It is noteworthy that the commission said that it could derive no real help from either the ICJ or the UNCC in this regard.

Finally, as we will see in the next section, there is a striking contrast with regard to financial compensation between the ICJ and inter-state arbitration on the one hand, and the special regimes of the WTO and the EU on the other. There is no treaty provision for the CJEU to award damages in inter-state cases, and it has not asserted a right to do so. The award of compensation in the WTO system is a last resort, designed not to compensate for past loss, but to secure performance of WTO obligations in the future.

3 Special Regimes: International Organizations

The ICJ Statute makes no detailed provision on remedies. In contrast, the treaties establishing some specialized tribunals with mandatory jurisdiction have created special regimes designed to further the particular aims of the organizations involved. These do not necessarily give the tribunal more power with regard to remedies. It remains an open question whether these more elaborate provisions necessarily provide a more effective system than that of the ICJ. They certainly do not provide a universally applicable model for remedies.

3.1 WTO AB

The WTO DSU establishes its own unique procedures to deal with inter-state disputes; it makes detailed provision for the remedies available from its ad hoc panels and standing Appellate Body.[66] The legal framework is set out in the General Provisions of the DSU, Art. 3.7, which states:

The first objective of the dispute settlement mechanism is usually to secure the withdrawal of the measures concerned if these are found to be inconsistent with the provisions of any

[66] See WTO website <http://www.wto.org/> accessed August 27, 2013; K Bagwell, "Remedies in the WTO: an Economic Perspective" in M Janow, V Donaldson, and A Yanovich (eds), *The WTO: Governance, Dispute Settlement and Developing Countries* (New York: Juris Publishing 2008) 733.

of the covered agreements. The provision of compensation should be resorted to only if the immediate withdrawal of the measure is impracticable[,] and as a temporary measure pending the withdrawal of the measure which is inconsistent with a covered agreement. The last resort which this Understanding provides to the Member invoking the dispute settlement procedures is the possibility of suspending the application of concessions or other obligations under the covered agreements on a discriminatory basis vis-à-vis the other Member, subject to authorization by the Dispute Settlement Body (DSB) of such measures.

The first remedy available to a claimant state is set out in Art. 19 DSU:

Where a panel or the Appellate Body (AB) concludes that a measure is inconsistent with a covered agreement, it shall recommend the Member concerned to bring the measure into conformity with the agreement. In addition to its recommendations, the panel or AB may suggest ways in which the Member concerned could implement the recommendation.

This is prospective; there is no remedy for harm done by past breaches. The aim is to secure performance of WTO obligations in the future. Sometimes the WTO AB makes specific recommendations when it thinks there is only one possible course of action. Sometimes it suggests various alternative courses of action; sometimes it leaves the choice of action to the state. This is a matter for the discretion of the WTO AB.

Second, if these recommendations are not implemented within a reasonable period of time, Art. 22 DSU provides for "compensation." This type of compensation is very different from that awarded by other tribunals. It is prospective because the compensation is only for future harm. It does not date back to the time of the illegal act. It is temporary, in that it is only payable until implementation of the Panel/WTO AB recommendation. It is also voluntary, in that it is for the parties rather than the Panels or the WTO AB to agree on the amount and form of compensation.[67]

Finally, if no satisfactory agreement is reached, Art. 22 provides that the claimant state may request permission from the Panels/WTO AB to invoke the third remedy available under the DSU: the suspension of certain of its obligations to the defendant state under the WTO agreements—that is, retaliation. There are different views on whether this provision aims to induce compliance with WTO obligations by the wrongdoing state, or to punish the wrongdoing state, or to rebalance the relationship between the states parties. The DSU itself is silent on the matter. There is an ongoing debate as to whether this system is fair to developing states, which may not in practice be able to take measures against developed states.[68] Some commentators

[67] There is some debate as to whether the Appellate Body could go further and award compensation for past losses caused by violation of the WTO agreements, but the better view seems to be that this is possible only where specific treaties allow for it, See B Mercurio, "Why Compensation Cannot Replace Trade Retaliation in the WTO DSU" (2009) 8 World Trade Review 315.

[68] See e.g., M Bronckers and N van den Broek, "Financial compensation in the WTO" (2003) 8 Journal of International Economic Law 101; A Davies, "Reviewing Dispute Settlement at the WTO" (2006) 5 World Trade Law Review 31.

suggest that compensation would be a better remedy. More fundamentally, many commentators have expressed concern that the compliance mechanisms of the current DSU system actually undermine the system by allowing the claimant state to abandon its WTO obligations in response to a breach by the defendant state; they argue that this does not further trade liberalization.[69] The EU system does not allow such measures.

3.2 CJEU

The jurisdiction of the CJEU is more extensive than that of the WTO AB and the ICJ. It is the most extensive of any international tribunal in regards to the types of action, the eligible parties, and the types of decision available to it.[70] Also, the CJEU has the widest range of procedures to secure remedies: inter-state cases under Art. 259 of the Treaty on the Functioning of the European Union (TFEU), actions by the EU Commission against Member States under Art. 258 TFEU, individual actions against EU institutions for review of the legality and annulment of community measures (Arts 263, 264 TFEU), and for the failure to act of EU institutions (Arts 265, 266 TFEU), individual actions for damages against EU institutions (Arts 268 and 340.2 TFEU), and preliminary rulings under Art. 267 TFEU. The CJEU has developed these remedies without express reference to international law or to national law.

Here the focus will be on actions against member states, which are the most similar to traditional inter-state claims in international law. Inter-state cases under Art. 259 are very rare, as are inter-state cases before the ECtHR.[71] Such claims are seen as hostile actions. Further, given that the aim of the judicial procedure is to ensure compliance with human rights law or EU law rather than to secure a remedy for an injured state, it is not surprising that they remain exceptional. In contrast, the number of enforcement cases brought by the EU Commission against member states under Art. 258 is rising, and the system is under strain.[72] These proceedings are intended to ensure general and uniform observance of EU law. Their role is not to remedy harm to other states or to the EU, but to bring an end to violations in order to secure the objectives of the EU. This explains why the ECJ allows enforcement actions to proceed even when a respondent state has remedied its breach before the case reaches the court; there is no need for a continuing dispute to be in existence. In contrast, the position taken by the ICJ in cases such as *Nuclear Tests*[73] and *Northern Cameroons*,[74] where it insisted that there should be a continuing dispute

[69] Mercurio, note 67. [70] See in this handbook, Baudenbacher and Clifton, Ch. 12.
[71] See section 5.1 of this chapter.
[72] P Craig and G de Búrca, *EU Law* (5th edn, Oxford University Press 2008) 409.
[73] *Australia v. France* [1974] ICJ Rep 253.
[74] *Cameroon v. UK* [1961] ICJ Rep 15.

for a case to be admissible, indicates that it saw its role in these cases as primarily to settle disputes between states.[75]

In EU enforcement actions against member states, whether by the commission or by another state, the remedy is a declaratory judgment that the state has violated EU law. The ECJ has not ordered the adoption of any specific measures, nor has it ordered the annulment of national acts, awarded damages, or declared that there is an obligation on a state to take certain measures. It seems paradoxical that the ECJ exercises a less extensive jurisdiction over member states than does the ICJ. The court of the more integrated community apparently has a narrower jurisdiction in this regard. However, rather than advocate a more extensive jurisdiction for the ECJ, it might be wiser to recognize the peculiar suitability for international relations of the narrow type of declaratory judgment used by the ECJ.[76] When there are problems with compliance with an ECJ judgment, the commission can bring an additional action before the court. Initially, this was just to obtain a second declaratory judgment, but there is now provision for the court to impose a fine or a penalty payment.[77] The commission is increasingly using this mechanism, although not many cases have actually reached the court.[78]

4 Special Regimes: Mass Claims

4.1 UNCC

The UNCC has developed its own special system to address the multitude of claims facing it, partly on the basis of its constituent instrument and partly through its own jurisprudence.[79] The UNCC was created in 1991 and operated until 2005 as a subsidiary organ of the UN Security Council.[80] It was a unique body made up of a Governing Council, Panels of Commissioners, and a Secretariat. Unlike earlier claims

[75] See, in this handbook, Alvarez, Ch 8.

[76] E.g. Craig and de Búrca say this is a weakness of the system, note 72, at 431.

[77] TFEU, Art. 260.

[78] I Kilbey, "The Interpretation of Art. 260 TFEU" (2010) 35 EL Rev 370.

[79] T Mensah, "UN Compensation Commission" in R Wolfrum (ed.), *The Max Planck Encyclopedia of International Law* (Oxford University Press 2008) online at <http://opil.ouplaw.com/home/EPIL> accessed August 1, 2013; L Boisson de Chazournes and D Campanelli, "The UNCC: Time for an Assessment" in A Fischer-Lescano (ed.), *Frieden in Freiheit: Festschrift für Michael Bothe* (Baden Baden: Nomos 2008) 3.

[80] The UNCC was set up in accordance with the cease-fire SC Res 687 (1991) and under SC Res 692 (1991).

commissions, the UNCC was not an adjudicative body before which parties appeared. It was a political organ that performed an essentially fact-finding mission of verifying claims and evaluating losses. Its mandate was to process claims and pay compensation for losses and damage suffered as a direct result of Iraq's unlawful invasion and occupation of Kuwait in accordance with a series of Security Council resolutions. The UNCC's function was to process the largest number of claims ever before a tribunal in a reasonable time. It received more than 2.6 million claims for nearly $370 billion. It did so by adopting special procedures. It concluded the processing of claims in 2005.

The UNCC Governing Council established criteria for the payment of claims; Panels of Commissioners verified and evaluated claims from individuals, corporations, and states. They were mandated to apply Security Council Resolution 687, which asserted Iraq's liability for "direct loss, damage, including environmental damage and depletion of natural resources…as a result of Iraq's unlawful invasion and occupation of Kuwait." The UNCC was also required to apply other relevant Security Council resolutions, as well as criteria established by the Governing Council for the various categories of claims. According to Rule 31 of the UNCC Rules, "In addition, where necessary, Commissioners shall apply other relevant rules of international law." The Governing Council accordingly established six categories of claims: four by individuals, one by corporations, and one by governments and international organizations. With regard to the claims by individuals, the Governing Council established a fixed sum for Category A claims by those forced to leave Iraq or Kuwait following the invasion (US$2,500 for individuals; US$5,000 for families), and for Category B claims by individuals who suffered serious personal injury or death (US$2,500 for individuals; US$10,000 for families). Other tribunals have not taken this fixed sum approach. The IACtHR and the EECC considered and rejected this possibility. The ECtHR has developed other procedures to deal with large numbers of claims.

Larger claims by individuals, corporations, and states had to be calculated by the Commission on the basis of the available evidence. These were divided into Category C and Category D claims by individuals for claims including loss of property and harm to businesses up to and over $100,000, respectively; Category E claims by corporations; and Category F claims by states and international organizations. All the awards were for financial compensation, except for those by Panel F4 in cases of environmental damage. This panel made recommendations on details of projects to be undertaken with the compensation. A follow-up program was established to monitor the implementation of the projects.

4.2 EECC

The EECC was established under the 2000 Algiers Agreement to decide claims arising out of the 1998–2000 conflict between Eritrea and Ethiopia. Its awards on damages on the basis of the "relevant rules of international law" were affected by three special considerations.[81] First, the commission determined that the parties' economic positions were relevant. The parties were among the poorest on earth, and the amounts sought were huge. Thus, awards of such magnitude would impose crippling burdens.[82] The commission interpreted the *Chorzow Factory* principle as saying that compensation should be remedial—not punitive.[83] Compensation should also take account of the limits set by human rights law, which would prevent an award which harmed the social and economic rights of the nationals of the respondent state. The commission rejected Ethiopia's claims for billions of dollars for the moral damage suffered by nationals from physical pain and mental anguish. It also rejected Ethiopia's claims for harm to its territorial integrity, security, and international standing.[84] The amounts were wholly disproportionate to Eritrea's limited economic capacity.

Second, the Algiers Agreement imposed a deadline on the commission. Accordingly, it adopted simplified procedures.[85] Third, the evidence was often uncertain. The commission would make the best estimates possible.[86] However, it took account of the importance of the interests at stake; it granted claims even if there was limited proof in respect of claims where there was serious loss or special humanitarian circumstances.[87] It also accepted the trade-off that has become fundamental to recent international efforts to address injuries affecting large numbers of victims, that is adopting less rigorous standards of proof but also reduced compensation levels.[88] Overall, the commission said that its awards would be much less than the parties claimed.[89]

The commission discussed the standard of legal causation at length.[90] It showed that it was impossible to identify any clear, generally applicable international law rules on this central question. The commission rejected the "reasonableness" test suggested by Ethiopia as subjective. It could not be seen as a general principle of law. Given the varying approaches to causation adopted by differing international tribunals, the concept had not attained the status of a rule of customary international law. The UNCC's adoption of the "direct injury" test was of questionable relevance because its Governing Council was a political organ. The best test was that of

[81] 49 ILM 101 (2010). See M Matheson, "Eritrea-Ethiopia Claims Commission: Damage Awards" (2009), 13(13) ASIL Insight 1, September 4, 2009.

[82] *Final Award, Ethiopia's Damages Claim* (2010) 49 ILM 101 at paras 18–23.

[83] *Final Award, Ethiopia's Damages Claim*, note 82, at para. 26.

[84] *Final Award, Ethiopia's Damages Claim*, note 82, at paras 54–65.

[85] *Final Award, Ethiopia's Damages Claim*, note 82, at paras 8–17.

[86] *Final Award, Ethiopia's Damages Claim*, note 82, at paras 35, 36, 37.

[87] *Final Award, Ethiopia's Damages Claim*, note 82, at para. 311.

[88] *Final Award, Ethiopia's Damages Claim*, note 82, at para. 38.

[89] *Final Award, Ethiopia's Damages Claim*, note 82, at para. 2.

[90] *Decision Number 7: Guidance regarding* Ius ad Bellum *Liability*, July 13, 2007, <www.pca-cpa.org/upload/files/EECC_Decision_No_7.pdf> accessed August 1, 2013.

"proximate cause," put forward by Eritrea, even though it was not a general principle of law or customary international law.

The commission applied this test in its Final Award on Ethiopia's *Ius ad bellum* claims.[91] It held that Eritrea had violated Art. 2.4 of the UN Charter on May 12, 1998 in occupying Badme and other territory, but that it was not liable for all the damage done throughout the entire war. The questions posed were what injury was proximately caused by Eritrea's breach, and what was the scope of Eritrea's liability. The commission found that the ICJ and other tribunals had not given any concrete guidance.[92] The assessment of the causal connection between Eritrea's acts in May 1998 and ensuing events was complicated and uncertain. The question was whether particular consequences were or should have been foreseen by Eritrea's leaders in the exercise of reasonable judgment at the time of the breach in May 1998.[93]

In determining the amount of *ius ad bellum* compensation, the commission said that it faced difficult and unsettled questions about the principles to be applied. It noted: "Past judicial decisions and state practice offer limited guidance. While decisions provide some assistance in identifying types of damage that may be compensable in cases concerning the use of force, they rarely examine questions relating to quantification."[94] The ICJ had only determined compensation once, in *Corfu Channel*, and the claims were different in that case. Given the limited guidance available from past decisions, the commission weighed several factors. A threshold question was whether an award of damages should be designed to serve the exceptional purpose of helping deter future violations of Art. 2.4, or designed for the more conventional purpose of providing appropriate compensation. The commission asserted the latter purpose; it doubted that possible awards of compensation would be likely to deter a state contemplating action in breach of *ius ad bellum*.

The commission also considered whether compensation should reflect a precise quantification of the damage or a more general assessment of the character of the injury. These claims often involved damage that was uncertain in extent and effect, and that occurred in remote locations. Clear proof of specific injury was often lacking, and requiring rigorous proof would have defeated the objective of providing compensation and exceeded the capacities of the parties and the commission. The commission would make its best assessment, though this would frequently involve rough approximations. In total, the commission awarded $161 million to Eritrea and $2 million to individual Eritreans: Eritrea had claimed $6 billion. It awarded $174 million to Ethiopia, which had claimed $14.3 billion.

The commission took an unusual step in discussing both the aims of compensation and the decisions of other tribunals in its attempts to identify international

[91] *Final Award, Ethiopia's Damages Claim*, note 82, at para. 271.
[92] *Final Award, Ethiopia's Damages Claim*, note 82, at para. 288.
[93] *Final Award, Ethiopia's Damages Claim*, note 82, at para. 290.
[94] *Final Award, Ethiopia's Damages Claim*, note 82, at paras 306–17.

law rules on compensation. It could not derive any specific guidance from the decisions of the ICJ. From the UNCC and other claims commissions, it extracted the principle that there could be a trade-off between adequate evidence and the level of compensation.

5 Special Regimes: Human Rights Courts

5.1 ECtHR

The ECtHR also has to deal with a large number of claims. It faces a backlog of over 150,000 cases. In its early days, its main remedy was the declaratory judgment, which it held was a sufficient remedy for individuals in many cases. Subsequently, it became more willing to award financial compensation for harm done by violations, and even to determine that there was an obligation to make restitution in exceptional cases. In recent years, states parties have accepted radical new procedures to deal with the challenges posed by the court's enormous case load. These have involved it in a more far-reaching specification of the human rights obligations of states parties in order to secure compliance in the future as well as compensation for past injuries.

Article 41 of the European Convention on Human Rights (ECHR) provides the treaty framework for the court's award of remedies: "If the Court finds that there has been a violation of the Convention or the Protocols thereto, and if the internal law of the High Contracting Party concerned allows only partial reparation to be made, the Court shall, if necessary, afford just satisfaction to the injured party." The term "just satisfaction" in Art. 41 is familiar from the jurisprudence of the ICJ and the ILC's Articles, but the term is used in a special way in the ECHR. It does not refer to satisfaction as a remedy for states, but rather for injured individuals. The choice of the term "satisfaction" has been interpreted by the ECtHR as giving it the discretion to develop its own system of remedies. The Practice Direction of March 28, 2007 spells out the proper approach for the court to take in just satisfaction claims, on the basis of its 40-year jurisprudence on remedies: "The award of just satisfaction is not an automatic consequence of a finding by the European Court of Human Rights that there has been a violation of a right." Under Art. 41, the court may order just satisfaction only if domestic law does not allow complete reparation, and only if just satisfaction is "necessary."

In the early days of the ECtHR, it was the declaratory judgment which played a central role as the primary remedy in individual cases, and it remains the only remedy in the rare inter-state cases decided under Art. 33 of the ECHR. According to the Practice Direction, the court may find that for some heads of alleged prejudice the finding of violation, in itself, constitutes just satisfaction without the need to afford financial compensation. When it does award financial compensation as just satisfaction, the court adopts a flexible approach and awards the satisfaction it regards as just in the particular case. Its guiding principle is equity, which involves a consideration of what is fair, just, and reasonable in all the circumstances of the case, including not only the position of the applicant but also the overall context in which the breach occurred.[95] It does not refer to the decisions of other tribunals in its awards, though it does refer to its own case law on compensation for pecuniary harm in complex cases.

The ECtHR's Practice Direction notes that the court may find reasons of equity to award less than the value of the actual damage sustained, or even not to make any award at all if the situation complained of, or the amount of damage sustained, is due to the applicant's own fault. The court may also consider the respective positions of the party injured by a violation and the state which is responsible for the public interest. Finally, the court will normally take into account the local economic circumstances. It may take guidance from domestic standards, but it is never bound by them. It makes clear that the purpose of the award is to compensate the applicant, not to punish the state responsible. Claims for punitive damages are not acceptable. These important guidelines make it clear that special considerations apply in the calculation of damages for violations of human rights.

In many cases, the court is willing to assume that the violation has caused non-pecuniary damage, such as mental or physical suffering. In some of these cases, it has been willing to award financial compensation for this. Such awards for non-pecuniary damage are often not fully reasoned.[96] There is often a striking contrast between the amount claimed and the actual award.[97] The court tends to stress the equitable nature of assessment, and the Practice Direction acknowledges that the nature of the damage does not lend itself to precise calculation. It is not surprising that awards for this type of subjective harm are unpredictable. Shelton argues that the court is influenced by the nature of the victim and the degree of sympathy it feels.[98]

In contrast, a stricter approach seems to apply in claims for pecuniary loss. These claims are often unsuccessful because applicants fail to establish a causal link

[95] See e.g., *Al-Skeini v. UK*, Application No 55721/07, 7.7.11 (GC).

[96] See e.g., *Varnava v. Turkey*, Application No 160604/90, 18.9.2009 (GC); *Ilascu v. Moldova and Russia*, Application No 4878799, 8.7.2004 (GC).

[97] See e.g., *Guérin v. France*, Application No 25201/94, 29.7.98 (GC); *Al Skeini v. UK*, note 95.

[98] Shelton, note 4, at 345–8.

between the violation and the alleged harm. The Practice Direction says that the principle with regard to pecuniary damage is that it should place the applicant in the position in which she would have been had the violation not taken place, ie *restitutio in integrum* as the measure of compensation. Normally, the court's award will reflect the full amount of the damage, but if this cannot be calculated the court will make an estimate.

More recently the court has taken a more far-reaching approach. It does not actually make orders of restitution under Art. 41, but it increasingly spells out the reparation required as a consequence of the violation. The Committee of Ministers has the power to supervise compliance with the court's judgments under Art. 46 on the binding force and execution of judgments, and to refer cases of non-compliance back to the court. The court has interpreted this provision as allowing it to enter into the question of the appropriate consequences of its finding of a violation. The 2007 Practice Direction spells out this position clearly. The court's awards will normally be in the form of a sum of money to be paid to the victim. Only in extremely rare cases can the court consider a consequential order aimed at putting an end to or remedying the violation in question. The court may, however, decide at its discretion to offer guidance for the execution of its judgments under Art. 46.

For example, in *Papamichalopoulos v. Greece*, the military dictatorship in Greece had expropriated land as a holiday resort for army officers and their families. The court did not itself order restitution, but spelled out Greece's obligations under international law "to put an end to the breach and make reparation for its consequences in such a way as to restore... the situation existing before the breach." It was for the state to effect *restitutio in integrum*, "the Court having neither the power nor the practical possibility of doing so itself." If there was no restitution within six months, then compensation was to be paid. It is striking that the court's approach to restitution is less strict than that of *Chorzow Factory* and the ILC Articles. Although it makes restitution the primary remedy, it allows for compensation instead after six months and does not require that restitution be impossible.[99]

Assanidze v. Georgia, a wrongful detention case, set out what has become the consistent approach of the court:[100]

The Court reiterates that in the context of the execution of judgments in accordance with Art. 46 of the Convention, a judgment in which it finds a breach imposes on the respondent state a legal obligation under that provision to put an end to the breach and to make reparation for its consequences in such a way as to restore as far as possible the situation existing before the breach. If, on the other hand, national law does not allow... reparation

[99] LG Loucaides, "Reparations for violation of human rights under the European Convention and *Restitutio in Integrum*" (2008) EHRLR 182.

[100] Application No 71503/01, April 8, 2004, at paras 198–202.

to be made for the consequences of the breach, Art. 41 empowers the Court to afford the injured party such satisfaction as appears to it to be appropriate.

A judgment in which the court finds a violation imposes on the respondent state a legal obligation not just to pay sums awarded by way of just satisfaction, but also to choose, subject to supervision by the Committee of Ministers, the measures to be adopted in its domestic legal order to put an end to the violation and make all feasible reparation so as to restore as far as possible the situation existing before the breach. With regard to the measures that Georgia must take, the court reiterated that its judgments were essentially declaratory in nature and that, in general, it was for the state to choose the means to be used in its domestic legal order to discharge its obligations under Art. 46. Discretion as to the manner of execution of a judgment reflects the freedom of choice of states. "However, by its very nature, the violation found in the instant case does not leave any real choice as to the measures required to remedy it." The state must secure the applicant's release from detention at the earliest possible date.

Since 2004, the court has taken a more active role through the so-called "Pilot Judgment" procedure. This is designed to deal with large groups of identical cases deriving from the same underlying problem. The court calls on the government concerned to bring its domestic legislation into line with the convention, and indicates the general measures to be taken. This allows the court to play a more prescriptive role. It determines whether there has been a violation of the convention; identifies the dysfunction at the root of the violation; gives clear indications to the government as to how it can eliminate this dysfunction; and bring about the creation of a domestic remedy capable of dealing with similar cases. The central idea behind the Pilot Judgment procedure is that applicants will obtain redress more quickly if an effective remedy is established at the national level than if their cases are processed on an individual basis at the ECtHR in Strasbourg.

The Pilot Judgment procedure was finally included in Rule 61 of the court in 2011. It provides, "The Court shall in its pilot judgment identify... the type of remedial measures which the Contracting Party concerned is required to take at the domestic level by virtue of the operative provisions of the judgment." When adopting a Pilot Judgment, the court may reserve the question of just satisfaction pending the adoption by the respondent state of the measures specified in the Pilot Judgment. This makes it clear that the court in its Pilot Judgment is merely spelling out the consequences of the violation, and that this is separate from its award of just satisfaction under Art. 41. An award of just satisfaction will only be necessary if the state fails to comply with the Pilot Judgment. The position today is therefore that the ECtHR will give precise recommendations in only two types of cases: first, in Pilot Judgment cases, and second, in exceptional cases where the nature of the violation is such as to leave no real choice as to the measure to remedy it. Otherwise the court's remedies are declaratory judgments and financial compensation.

5.2 IACtHR

The IACtHR does not face the same overwhelming number of claims as the ECtHR, though there has been a significant increase in the number of group claims which has had an impact on the court's approach to remedies. Article 63.1 of the Inter-American Convention on Human Rights governs its jurisdiction to grant remedies: "If the Court finds that there has been a violation of a right or freedom protected by this Convention, the Court shall rule that the injured party be ensured the enjoyment of his right or freedom that was violated. It shall also rule, if appropriate, that the consequences of the measure or situation that constituted the breach of such right or freedom be remedied and that fair compensation be paid to the injured party." This gives the court very wide powers—wider than those of the ECtHR and of most other international tribunals.[101] The IACtHR's decisions on reparation are one of the most striking features of its jurisprudence. After a cautious start,[102] the court has interpreted Art. 63 creatively. It has often ordered the respondent state to take specific measures, giving detailed and complex instructions.[103] It makes orders under Art. 63, but may also refer to the requirements of substantive articles to support rulings that there is an obligation on wrongdoing states to act in a certain way. For instance, in the case of disappearances, a finding by the Court of a duty to investigate, to prevent, and to punish forms part of the judgment on the merits, as it concerns the state's duty to ensure rights under Art. 1 of the Convention.

The court's view is that customary international law requires restitution,[104] but where this is not possible, it must order the adoption of measures to ensure that respect for the violated rights is guaranteed. Accordingly, it has ordered a series of often far-reaching measures to ensure respect for the rights harmed and to redress the consequences of the violations. Typically it has held that a declaratory judgment does constitute reparation, but that it is not, in itself, sufficient reparation for an injured individual, in contrast to the ECtHR. And in general, the IACtHR holds that financial compensation is by its nature not an adequate remedy because human rights injuries cannot be quantified. Nevertheless, it has made many awards for financial compensation. As with the ECtHR, claims for material harm often fail because the claimant cannot show a causal link between the breach and the harm. However, claims for moral injury are common, and are often compensated on the basis of discretion and equity. It is difficult to find any

[101] The ECtHR has taken a more active role in its Pilot Judgment procedure. Article 27 of the *Protocol to the African Charter on Human and Peoples' Rights* (entered into force January 25, 2004) also gives the African Court considerable discretion; it provides that the African Court shall make "appropriate orders to remedy the violation, including the payment of fair compensation or reparation."

[102] See *Velasquez Rodriguez v. Honduras*, IACtHR Series C No 7 (1989).

[103] T Antkowiak, "Remedial Approaches to Human Rights Violations" (2008) 46 ColJTransL 351.

[104] See e.g., *Moiwana v. Suriname* IACtHR Series C No 124 [170] (2005).

consistency between these awards, and the court is often vague as to how it calculates the sums awarded.

One of the first landmark cases which shows the court's radical approach to remedies was *Aloeboetoe v. Suriname* (1993).[105] As reparation for the unlawful killings of villagers, the court ordered Suriname to reopen the village school and provide it with staff, to establish a medical clinic and to set up a Trust Fund. In many cases where the state has been involved in disappearances, the court has ordered the government concerned to find and return the remains of the disappeared as reparation for the victims' families.[106] In cases of unlawful detention, the court has ordered not only the release of the victim, but also the provision of a new job, benefits, and a pension.[107]

In recent cases, the court has required not only that the state accept its responsibility, but also that it make a public apology. In some cases it has given detailed instructions as to the manner of the apology. It has required the creation of monuments to preserve the victim's memory and prevent the recurrence of the violations. In cases where indigenous peoples have been massacred, the court has also ordered restoration of community infrastructure, or has required the state to set up a fund for health, housing, and education. In some of these cases, the court has called for participation by the affected community. In appropriate cases, it has ordered the state to change its institutions, provide human rights training for state officials, amend its laws, or ratify human rights treaties.[108]

The IACtHR has taken full advantage of the discretion given to it by Art. 63. It has been concerned to develop more effective remedies in order to uphold the human rights regime. A state should not be able to pay for the right to continue to violate human rights; financial compensation may not be adequate and may indeed be too burdensome for the state. Thomas Antkowiak argues that other tribunals should follow the IACtHR's approach of ruling that money is not enough to compensate human rights victims. In particular, he argues that the ICC should take account of jurisprudence of IACtHR in its provision of reparation for victims.[109] However, this raises the question as to whether those remedies, which place greater demands on defendant states, are less likely to be complied with.[110]

[105] IACtHR Series C No 11 (1993).

[106] See e.g., *Moiwana v. Suriname*, IACtHR Series C No 124 (2005).

[107] See e.g., *Loayza-Tamayo v. Peru*, IACtHR Series C No 42 (1998).

[108] See *Castillo-Petruzzi v. Peru*, IACtHR Series C No 52 (1999).

[109] Antkowiak, note 103, at 414. Article 75 of the Rome Statute provides that, "The Court shall establish principles relating to reparations to, or in respect of, victims, including restitution, compensation and rehabilitation." The ICC has recently made its first *Decision establishing principles and procedures to be applied to reparations* in the *Lubanga* case (2012), ICC-01/04-01/06-2904.

[110] See, in this handbook, Huneeus, Ch. 20.

6 Conclusion

The diversity of tribunals is clearly reflected in the diversity of their practice on remedies. Even the fundamental general principle in *Chorzow Factory*—that restitution in kind is the primary remedy or, if this is not possible, then payment of full compensation—is not universally followed, and is readily abandoned where it is impractical. Thus, restitution is not available in the CJEU or in the WTO AB; these tribunals that exercise compulsory jurisdiction in furtherance of the goals of their organization do not necessarily exercise the most far-reaching power to award remedies in inter-state claims. Restitution is clearly not possible in mass claims, such as those addressed by the UNCC and the EECC. In contrast, the ICJ has gradually become more assertive in spelling out the obligations of states parties, although it still displays some caution in respecting the discretion of states. It is human rights tribunals that seem most concerned to re-establish the rule of law after violations, and to secure compliance with human rights obligations; they are able to do so because of their wide powers under their constituent treaties. Even so, the ECtHR does not often order restitution; it is the IACtHR that has ordered the most far-reaching measures.

As for full compensation, this was clearly not awarded by the UNCC or the EECC. The large number of claims required an approach based on equity and compromise. Again, the tribunals often held up as models by their supporters, the ECJ and the WTO AB, do not provide full financial compensation for harm. Their focus is on future compliance rather than compensation. The human rights tribunals do aim at full compensation, but this is difficult to assess in cases of moral harm, and may be overridden by public interest concerns.

The most striking feature of the jurisprudence of the ICJ on compensation is the varied subject matter. In *Diallo*, the ICJ turned to human rights tribunals for assistance; it seemed that the subject matter played an important role with regards to the remedy. The particular nature of each of the ICJ's cases meant that ITLOS and the EECC were not able to derive specific guidance from its decisions on compensation. Similarly, the ILC's Article on compensation does not offer detailed guidance, though it seems possible that the cases singled out by the ILC will, in the future, attract more attention than others, at least in the pleadings of states.

Research Questions

1. How does the approach of international tribunals to remedies compare to that of national courts in cases against the organs of their national governments?

2. Is restitution really the ideal remedy in international law? How far do the limits on this form of reparation in the ILC Articles on State Responsibility undermine its primacy?
3. Is there any evidence that tribunals' decisions on remedies have an impact on states' decisions as to whether to comply with their legal obligations? Do they affect decisions as to whether to initiate litigation? If not, does it matter that tribunals' decisions are inconsistent?
4. Why do the WTO AB and the CJEU take a narrow view of their powers to issue orders to states parties?

Suggested Reading

Antkowiak, T, "Remedial Approaches to Human Rights Violations" (2006) 46 ColJTransL 351.

Brown, C, *A Common Law of International Adjudication* (Oxford University Press 2007).

Crawford, J, Pellet, A, and Olleson, S (eds), *The Law of State Responsibility* (Oxford University Press 2010) 545–638.

Dashwood, A et al., *Wyatt and Dashwood's EU Law* (6th edn, Oxford: Hart 2011).

Gray, C, *Judicial Remedies in International Law* (Oxford University Press 1987).

Greiff, de, P, *The Handbook of Reparation* (Oxford University Press 2006).

Matheson, M, "Eritrea–Ethiopia Claims Commission: Damage Awards" (2009) 13(13) ASIL Insight 1.

Mensah, T, "UN Compensation Commission" in R Wolfrum (ed.) *Max Planck Encyclopedia of Public International Law* online at <http://opil.ouplaw.com/home/EPIL> accessed August 1, 2013.

Shelton, D, *Remedies in International Human Rights Law* (2nd edn, Oxford University Press 2005).

Tanzi, A, "Restitution" in R Wolfrum (ed.), *Max Planck Encyclopedia of Public International Law* online at <http://opil.ouplaw.com/home/EPIL> accessed August 1, 2013.

Wittich, S, "Compensation" in R Wolfrum (ed.), *Max Planck Encyclopedia of Public International Law* online at <http://opil.ouplaw.com/home/EPIL> accessed August 1, 2013.

Annex 1

INTERNATIONAL JUDICIAL BODIES: RECAPITULATION

Name	Abbreviation	Type	Sub-type	Status	Substatus	Geographic scope	Operational since	Year of creation (if never operational)	Number of states subject to compulsory jurisdiction	Average number of judgments on the merits (2006–2011)	Seat
Court of the Eurasian Economic Community	CEEC	Regional Court		**Operative**		Europe/ Asia	2012		5	–	Minsk
Special Tribunal for Lebanon	STL	International Criminal Courts	Hybrids	**Operative**		Arab Countries	2009		1	0.33	The Hague

(Continued)

Name	Abbreviation	Type	Sub-type	Status	Substatus	Geographic scope	Operational since	Year of creation (if never operational)	Number of states subject to compulsory jurisdiction	Average number of judgments on the merits (2006–2011)	Seat
Extraordinary Chambers in the Courts of Cambodia	ECCC	International Criminal Courts	Hybrids	**Operative**		Asia	2006		1	0.17	Phnom Phen
Court of Bosnia & Herzegovina (Section I—War Crimes Chamber)	B&H WCC	International Criminal Courts	Hybrids	**Operative**		Europe	2005		1	27.67	Sarajevo
ASEAN Appellate Body	ASEAN AB	Regional Court		Inoperative	Dormant	Asia	2005		10	–	Jakarta
International Criminal Court	ICC	International Criminal Courts	Permanent	**Operative**		Universal	2004		122	2.17	The Hague
African Court on Human and Peoples' Rights	ACtHPR	Human Rights Courts		**Operative**		Africa	2004		26	1.33	Arusha
Permanent Review Tribunal of the Mercosur	MPTR	Regional Court		**Operative**		Americas	2004		6	1.33	Asuncion
Arab Investment Court	AIC	Regional Court		**Operative**		Arab Countries	2003		19	1.50	Cairo

Court of Justice of the African Union	CJAU	Regional Court		Inoperative	Foresaken	Africa	2003		–	–	–
Special Court for Sierra Leone	SCSL	International Criminal Courts	Hybrids	**Operative**		Africa	2002		1	0.67	Freetown
Regulation 64 Panels in the Courts of Kosovo	R64	International Criminal Courts	Hybrids	Inoperative	Terminated	Europe	2001		1	–	Pristina
Caribbean Court of Justice	CCJ	Regional Court		**Operative**		Americas	2001		12	9.33	Port of Spain
Court of Justice of the Economic Community of West African States	ECOWAS CJ	Regional Court/HR Court		**Operative**		Africa	2001		15	7.83	Abuja
East African Community Court of Justice	EACJ	Regional Court		**Operative**		Africa	2001		5	4.50	Arusha
Serious Crimes Panels in the District Court of Dili, East Timor	SPSC	International Criminal Courts	Hybrids	Inoperative	Terminated	Asia	2000		1	–	Dili
Court of Justice of the Central African Monetary Community	CEMAC CJ	Regional Court		**Operative**		Africa	2000		6	N/A	N'Djamena

(Continued)

Name	Abbreviation	Type	Sub-type	Status	Substatus	Geographic scope	Operational since	Year of creation (if never operational)	Number of states subject to compulsory jurisdiction	Average number of judgments on the merits (2006–2011)	Seat
Southern Africa Development Community Tribunal	SADC T	Regional Court		**Operative**		Africa	2000		15	4.00	Windhoek
Court of the Union State between the Russian Federation and the Republic of Belarus	RBUS CJ	Regional Court		Inoperative	Foresaken	Europe		1999	2	–	–
Court of Justice of the Common Market for Eastern and Southern Africa	COMESA CJ	Regional Court		**Operative**		Africa	1998		1	N/A	Khartoum
Common Court of Justice and Arbitration of the Organization for the Harmonization of Corporate Law in Africa	OHADA CCJ	Regional Court		**Operative**		Africa	1997		15	63.17	Abidijan

International Tribunal for the Law of the Sea	ITLOS	State-Only Courts	Universal	**Operative**		Universal	1996		33	1.00	Hamburg
Court of Justice of the West African Economic and Monetary Union	WAEMU CJ	Regional Court		**Operative**		Africa	1996		9	0.83	Ouagadougou
World Trade Organization Appellate Body	WTO AB	State-Only Courts	Universal	**Operative**		Universal	1995		159	4.33	Geneva
International Criminal Tribunal for Rwanda	ICTR	International Criminal Courts	Ad-Hoc	**Operative**		Africa	1995		1	6.17	Arusha
European Free Trade Association Court	EFTA C	Regional Court		**Operative**		Europe	1994		3	14.33	Luxemburg
Central American Court of Justice (Corte Centroamericana de Justicia)	CACJ (Managua)	Regional Court		**Operative**		Americas	1994		5**	9.33	Managua
International Criminal Tribunal for the Former Yugoslavia	ICTY	International Criminal Courts	Ad-Hoc	**Operative**		Europe	1993		7	5.33	The Hague

(Continued)

Name	Abbreviation	Type	Sub-type	Status	Substatus	Geographic scope	Operational since	Year of creation (if never operational)	Number of states subject to compulsory jurisdiction	Average number of judgments on the merits (2006–2011)	Seat
Economic Court of the Commonwealth of Independent States	ECCIS	Regional Court		**Operative**		Europe/ Asia	1993		9	5.50	Minsk
Court of Justice of the African Economic Community	AEC CJ	Regional Court		Inoperative	Foresaken	Africa	1991		–	–	–
Court of Justice of the Arab Maghreb Union	AMU CJ	Regional Court		Inoperative	Dormant	Arab Countries	1989		5	–	Nuakchott
International Islamic Court of Justice	IICJ	State-Only Courts	Regional	Inoperative	Foresaken	Arab Countries/ Asia		1987	–	–	Kuwait
Andean Tribunal of Justice	ATJ	Regional Court		**Operative**		Americas	1984		4	171.50	Quito
Court of Justice of the Economic Community of Central African States	ECCAS CJ	Regional Court		Inoperative	Foresaken	Africa	1983		–	–	–

Judicial Board of the Organization of Arab Petroleum Exporting Countries	JB OAPEC	Regional Court		Inoperative	Dormant	Americas	1980		10	–	Kuwait
Inter-American Court of Human Rights	IACtHR	Human Rights Courts		**Operative**		Americas	1979		20	16.83	San Jose
Benelux Economic Union Court of Justice	BCJ	Regional Court		**Operative**		Europe	1974		3	3.67	Brussels
European Tribunal on State Immunity	ETSI	Regional Court		Inoperative	Dormant	Europe	1972		6	–	Strasburg
European Court of Human Rights	ECtHR	Human Rights Courts		**Operative**		Europe	1959		47	1481.17	Strasburg
Western European Union Tribunal	WEUT	Regional Court		Inoperative	Foresaken	Europe		1957	–	–	Luxemburg
European Nuclear Energy Tribunal	ENET	Regional Court		Inoperative	Dormant	Europe		1957	16	–	Paris
European Court of Justice/Court of Justice of the European Union (since 2010)	CJEU (ECJ)	Regional Court/HR Court		**Operative**		Europe	1952		28	1087.00	Luxemburg
International Court of Justice	ICJ	State-Only Courts	Universal	**Operative**		Universal	1946		69	1.83	The Hague

(*Continued*)

Name	Abbreviation	Type	Sub-type	Status	Substatus	Geographic scope	Operational since	Year of creation (if never operational)	Number of states subject to compulsory jurisdiction	Average number of judgments on the merits (2006–2011)	Seat
International Military Tribunal for the Far-East	IMTFE	International Criminal Courts	Military	Inoperative	Terminated	Asia	1946		1	–	Tokyo
International Military Tribunal at Nuremberg	IMT	International Criminal Courts	Military	Inoperative	Terminated	Europe	1945		1	–	Nuremberg
Arab Court of Justice	ACJ	State-Only Courts	Regional	Inoperative	Foresaken	Arab Countries		1945	–	–	–
Inter-American Court of International Justice	IACIJ	State-Only Courts	Regional	Inoperative	Foresaken	Americas		1938	–	–	–
International Central American Tribunal	ICAT	State-Only Courts	Regional	Inoperative	Foresaken	Americas		1923	–	–	–

Permanent Court of International Justice	PCIJ	State-Only Courts	Universal	Inoperative	Terminated	Universal	1922		45*	–	The Hague
Central American Court of Justice (Corte de Justicia Centroamericana)	CACJ (Cartago)	State-Only Courts	Regional	Inoperative	Terminated	Americas	1908		5	–	Cartago, Costa Rica
International Prize Court	IPC	State-Only Courts	Universal	Inoperative	Foresaken	Universal		1907	–	–	The Hague

N/A = Data not available; — = Data not applicable or relevant (e.g. because the seat of the body was never selected or because it operated outside the 2006–2011 period).

"Between 1921 and 1940, effective declarations were made by forty-five States. Nine States made the declarations without limiting the time of their duration and eight States recognized the jurisdiction for periods of years and thereafter until notice of termination; but in most cases, the declarations were made for a definite period of years, and on the expiration of the period some of them were not renewed. At certain times, declarations were in force for as many as forty-one States; on July 1, 1944, the declarations of twenty-eight States were still in force." M Hudson, International Tribunals: Past and Future (Carnegie Endowment for International Peace and Brookings Institution 1944) at 76.

** The Central American Court of Justice has held that that by virtue of having ratified the Protocol of Tegucigalpa and becoming member of SICA, Costa Rica is *ipso facto* subject to the jurisdiction of the Court, with no need for separate ratification of the Court's Statute. Central American Court of Justice, Judgment No. 12-06-12-2011, June 21, 2012 <http://vianica.com/downloads/docs/1.pdf> accessed February 1, 2013. However, Costa Rica has refused to participate in proceedings and rejected the decision.

Annex 2

STATES SUBJECT TO COMPULSORY JURISDICTION (AS AT JULY 1, 2013)

	Global				Europe						Europe/ Asia		Asia		Arab World			Arab/ Africa		Africa									Latin America & Caribbean					
	State			Crim	HR	Criminal		Reg. Integ.					Crim	Reg. Integ.	Criminal	Reg. Integ.			HR	Criminal		Reg. Integ.							HR	Reg. Integ.				
	ICJ	ITLOS	WTO	ICC	ECHR	B&H WCC	ICTY	CJEU	EFTA CJ	BCJ	CEEC	ECCIS	ECCC	ASEAN AB	STL	AIC	JB OAPEC	AMU CJ	ACHPR	SCSL	ICTR	ECOWAS CJ	WAEMU CJ	CEMAC CJ	OHADA CCJ	COMESA CJ	SADC T	EAC CJ	IACHR	Mercosur TPR	CCJ	ATJ	CACJ	TOTAL
Afghanistan				1																														1
Albania			1	1	1																													3
Algeria																	1	1	1															3
Andorra				1	1																													2

Angola		1	1																								1							3
Antigua and Barbuda			1	1																											1			3
Argentina		1	1	1																									1	1				5
Armenia			1		1							1																						3
Australia	1	1	1	1																														4
Austria	1	1	1	1	1			1																										6
Azerbaijan					1							1																						2
Bahamas																																		0
Bahrain			1													1	1																	3
Bangladesh		1	1	1																														3
Barbados	1		1	1																									1		1			5
Belarus											1	1																						2
Belgium	1	1	1	1	1			1		1																								7
Belize			1	1																											1			3
Benin			1	1																		1	1		1									5
Bhutan																																		0
Bolivia			1	1																									1	1		1		5
Bosnia and Herzegovina				1	1	1	1																											4
Botswana	1		1	1																							1							4
Brazil			1	1																									1	1				4
Brunei Darussalam			1											1																				2

(Continued)

	Global				Europe						Europe/Asia		Asia		Arab World			Arab/Africa		Africa									Latin America & Caribbean					
	State			Crim	HR	Criminal		Reg. Integ.					Crim	Reg. Integ.	Criminal	Reg. Integ.			HR	Criminal		Reg. Integ.							HR	Reg. Integ.				
	ICJ	ITLOS	WTO	ICC	ECHR	B&H WCC	ICTY	CJEU	EFTA CJ	BCJ	CEEC	ECCIS	ECCC	ASEAN AB	STL	AIC	JB OAPEC	AMU CJ	ACHPR	SCSL	ICTR	ECOWAS CJ	WAEMU CJ	CEMAC CJ	OHADA CCJ	COMESA CJ	SADC T	EAC CJ	IACHR	Mercosur TPR	CCJ	ATJ	CACJ	TOTAL
Bulgaria	1		1	1	1			1																										5
Burkina Faso			1	1															1			1	1		1									6
Burundi			1	1															1							1		1						5
Cambodia	1		1	1									1	1																				5
Cameroon	1		1																					1	1									4
Canada	1	1	1	1																														4
Cape Verde		1	1	1																		1												4
Central African Republic			1	1																				1	1									4
Chad			1	1																				1	1									4
Chile		1	1	1																									1					4
China			1																															1
Colombia			1	1																									1			1		4
Comoros				1															1						1	1								4

Congo (Republic of the)			1	1															1					1	1									5
Cook Islands				1																														1
Costa Rica	1		1	1																									1				1*	4
Côte d'Ivoire	1		1	1															1			1	1		1									7
Croatia		1	1	1	1		1	1																										6
Cuba			1																															1
Cyprus	1		1	1	1			1																										5
Czech Republic			1	1	1			1																										4
Democratic People's Republic of Korea																																		0
Democratic Republic of the Congo	1		1	1																						1	1							5
Denmark	1		1	1	1			1																										5
Djibouti	1		1	1												1										1								5
Dominica	1		1	1																											1			4
Dominican Republic	1		1	1																									1					4
Ecuador		1	1	1																									1			1		5
Egypt	1		1													1	1									1								5
El Salvador			1																										1				1	3
Equatorial Guinea																								1	1									2
Eritrea																										1								1

(*Continued*)

	Global				Europe						Europe/ Asia		Asia		Arab World			Arab/ Africa		Africa										Latin America & Caribbean					
	State			Crim	HR	Criminal		Reg. Integ.					Crim	Reg. Integ.	Criminal	Reg. Integ.			HR	Criminal		Reg. Integ.							HR	Reg. Integ.				
	ICJ	ITLOS	WTO	ICC	ECHR	B&H WCC	ICTY	CJEU	EFTA CJ	BCJ	CEEC	ECCIS	ECCC	ASEAN AB	STL	AIC	JB OAPEC	AMU CJ	ACHPR	SCSL	ICTR	ECOWAS CJ	WAEMU CJ	CEMAC CJ	OHADA CCJ	COMESA CJ	SADC T	EAC CJ	IACHR	Mercosur TPR	CCJ	ATJ	CACJ	TOTAL
Estonia	1	1	1	1	1			1																										6
Ethiopia																										1								1
European Union			1																															1
Fiji		1	1	1																														3
Finland	1	1	1	1	1			1																										6
France			1	1	1			1																										4
Gabon			1	1															1					1	1									5
Gambia	1		1	1															1			1												5
Georgia	1		1	1	1																													4
Germany	1	1	1	1	1			1																										6
Ghana			1	1															1			1												4
Greece	1	1	1	1	1			1																										6
Grenada			1	1																											1			3

Guatemala			1	1																									1				1	4
Guinea	1		1	1																		1	1		1									6
Guinea-Bissau	1		1																			1	1		1									5
Guyana			1	1																											1			3
Haiti	1		1																										1					3
Holy See																																		0
Honduras	1		1	1																									1				1	5
Hong Kong			1																															1
Hungary	1	1	1	1	1			1																										6
Iceland			1	1	1				1																									4
India	1		1																															2
Indonesia			1											1																				2
Iran																																		0
Iraq																1	1																	2
Ireland	1		1	1	1			1																										5
Israel			1																															1
Italy		1	1	1	1			1																										5
Jamaica			1																												1			2
Japan	1		1	1																														3
Jordan			1	1												1																		3
Kazakhstan											1	1																						2
Kenya	1		1	1															1							1		1						6
Kiribati																																		0

(*Continued*)

	Global				Europe						Europe/Asia		Asia		Arab World			Arab/Africa		Africa										Latin America & Caribbean					
	State			Crim	HR	Criminal		Reg. Integ.					Crim	Reg. Integ.	Criminal	Reg. Integ.			HR	Criminal		Reg. Integ.							HR	Reg. Integ.				
	ICJ	ITLOS	WTO	ICC	ECHR	B&H WCC	ICTY	CJEU	EFTA CJ	BCJ	CEEC	ECCIS	ECCC	ASEAN AB	STL	AIC	JB OAPEC	AMU CJ	ACHPR	SCSL	ICTR	ECOWAS CJ	WAEMU CJ	CEMAC CJ	OHADA CCJ	COMESA CJ	SADC T	EAC CJ	IACHR	Mercosur TPR	CCJ	ATJ	CACJ	TOTAL
Kosovo							1																											1
Kuwait			1													1	1																	3
Kyrgyzstan			1								1	1																						3
Lao People's Democratic Rep			1											1																				2
Latvia		1	1	1	1			1																										5
Lebanon															1	1																		2
Lesotho	1		1	1															1								1							5
Liberia	1			1																		1												3
Libya																1	1	1	1							1								5
Liechtenstein	1		1	1	1				1																									5
Lithuania	1	1	1	1	1			1																										6
Luxembourg	1		1	1	1			1		1																								6

Macao			1																															1
Madagascar	1	1	1	1																						1	1							6
Malawi	1		1	1															1							1	1							6
Malaysia			1											1																				2
Maldives			1	1																														2
Mali			1	1															1			1	1		1									6
Malta	1		1	1	1			1																										5
Marshall Islands				1																														1
Mauritania			1													1		1	1															4
Mauritius	1		1	1															1							1	1							6
Mexico	1	1	1	1																									1					5
Micronesia (Federated States of)																																		0
Monaco					1																													1
Mongolia			1	1																														2
Montenegro		1	1	1	1		1																											5
Morocco			1															1																2
Mozambique			1																1								1							3
Myanmar			1											1																				2
Namibia			1	1																							1							3
Nauru				1																														1
Nepal			1																															1
Netherlands	1		1	1	1			1		1																								6
New Zealand	1		1	1																														3

(*Continued*)

	Global				Europe						Europe/ Asia		Asia		Arab World			Arab/ Africa		Africa									Latin America & Caribbean					
	State			Crim	HR	Criminal		Reg. Integ.					Crim	Reg. Integ.	Criminal	Reg. Integ.			HR	Criminal		Reg. Integ.							HR	Reg. Integ.			
	ICJ	ITLOS	WTO	ICC	ECHR	B&H WCC	ICTY	CJEU	EFTA CJ	BCJ	CEEC	ECCIS	ECCC	ASEAN AB	STL	AIC	JB OAPEC	AMU CJ	ACHPR	SCSL	ICTR	ECOWAS CJ	WAEMU CJ	CEMAC CJ	OHADA CCJ	COMESA CJ	SADC T	EAC CJ	IACHR	Mercosur TPR	CCJ	ATJ	CACJ	TOTAL
Nicaragua	1		1																										1				1	4
Niger			1	1															1			1	1		1									6
Nigeria	1		1	1															1			1												5
Norway	1		1	1	1				1																									5
Oman		1	1													1																		3
Pakistan	1		1																															2
Palau																																		0
Palestine																1																		1
Panama	1		1	1																									1					4
Papua New Guinea			1																															1
Paraguay	1		1	1																									1	1				5
Peru	1		1	1																									1			1		5

Philippines	1		1	1									1																				4
Poland	1		1	1	1			1																									5
Portugal	1	1	1	1	1			1																									6
Qatar			1													1	1																3
Republic of Korea			1	1																													2
Republic of Moldova			1	1	1							1																					4
Romania			1	1	1			1																									4
Russian Federation			1		1						1	1																					4
Rwanda			1																1		1					1		1					5
Sahrawi Arab Democratic Republic																																	0
Saint Kitts and Nevis			1	1																											1		3
Saint Lucia			1	1																											1		3
Saint Vincent and the Grenadines		1	1	1																											1		4
Samoa			1	1																													2
San Marino				1	1																												2
Sao Tome and Principe																																	0
Saudi Arabia			1													1	1																3
Senegal	1		1	1															1			1	1		1								7

(*Continued*)

	Global				Europe						Europe/Asia		Asia		Arab World			Arab/Africa		Africa									Latin America & Caribbean					
	State			Crim	HR	Criminal		Reg. Integ.					Crim	Reg. Integ.	Criminal	Reg. Integ.			HR	Criminal		Reg. Integ.							HR	Reg. Integ.				
	ICJ	ITLOS	WTO	ICC	ECHR	B&H WCC	ICTY	CJEU	EFTA CJ	BCJ	CEEC	ECCIS	ECCC	ASEAN AB	STL	AIC	JB OAPEC	AMU CJ	ACHPR	SCSL	ICTR	ECOWAS CJ	WAEMU CJ	CEMAC CJ	OHADA CCJ	COMESA CJ	SADC T	EAC CJ	IACHR	Mercosur TPR	CCJ	ATJ	CACJ	TOTAL
Serbia				1	1		1																											3
Seychelles				1																						1	1							3
Sierra Leone			1	1																1		1												4
Singapore			1											1																				2
Slovakia	1		1	1	1			1																										5
Slovenia	1		1	1	1		1	1																										6
Solomon Islands			1																															1
Somalia																1																		1
South Africa			1	1															1								1							4
South Sudan																																		0
Spain	1	1	1	1	1			1																										6
Sri Lanka			1																															1
Sudan	1															1										1								3

Suriname	1		1	1																								1		1			5
Swaziland	1		1																							1	1						4
Switzerland	1	1	1	1	1																												5
Sweden	1		1	1	1			1																									5
Syria																1	1																2
Taiwan (Chinese Taipei)			1																														1
Tajikistan			1	1							1	1																					4
Thailand			1											1																			2
The former Yugoslav Republic of Macedonia			1	1	1		1																										4
Timor-Leste	1	1		1																													3
Togo	1		1																1			1	1		1								6
Tonga			1																														1
Trinidad and Tobago		1	1	1																										1			4
Tunisia		1	1	1												1		1	1														6
Turkey			1		1																												2
Turkmenistan																																	0
Tuvalu																																	0
Uganda	1		1	1															1							1		1					6
Ukraine			1		1																												2

(*Continued*)

	Global				Europe						Europe/Asia		Asia		Arab World			Arab/Africa		Africa									Latin America & Caribbean					
	State			Crim	HR	Criminal		Reg. Integ.					Crim	Reg. Integ.	Criminal	Reg. Integ.			HR	Criminal		Reg. Integ.							HR	Reg. Integ.				
	ICJ	ITLOS	WTO	ICC	ECHR	B&H WCC	ICTY	CJEU	EFTA CJ	BCJ	CEEC	ECCIS	ECCC	ASEAN AB	STL	AIC	JB OAPEC	AMU CJ	ACHPR	SCSL	ICTR	ECOWAS CJ	WAEMU CJ	CEMAC CJ	OHADA CCJ	COMESA CJ	SADC T	EAC CJ	IACHR	Mercosur TPR	CCJ	ATJ	CACJ	TOTAL
United Arab Emirates			1													1	1																	3
United Kingdom	1		1	1	1			1																										5
United of Republic of Tanzania		1	1	1															1								1	1						6

United States			1																															1
Uruguay	1	1	1	1																									1	1				6
Uzbekistan												1																						1
Vanuatu			1	1																														2
Venezuela			1	1																										1				3
Viet Nam			1											1																				2
Yemen																1																		1
Zambia			1	1																						1	1							4
Zimbabwe			1																							1	1							3
TOTAL	**69**	**33**	**159**	**122**	**47**	**1**	**7**	**28**	**3**	**3**	**5**	**9**	**1**	**10**	**1**	**19**	**10**	**5**	**26**	**1**	**1**	**15**	**9**	**6**	**16**	**19**	**15**	**5**	**20**	**6**	**12**	**4**	**4**	

* The Central American Court of Justice has held that that by virtue of having ratified the Protocol of Tegucigalpa and becoming member of SICA, Costa Rica is *ipso facto* subject to the jurisdiction of the Court, with no need for separate ratification of the Court's Statute. Central American Court of Justice, Judgment No. 12-06-12-2011, June 21, 2012 <http://vianica.com/downloads/docs/1.pdf> accessed February 1, 2013. However, Costa Rica has refused to participate in proceedings and rejected the decision.

Index

ICs = international courts
see page xxiii for court abbreviations